Auditing & Assurance Services

Auditing & Assurance Services

Timothy J. Louwers, PhD, CPA, CISA, CIA, CFF
Jackson E. Ramsey Centennial Chair in Business
James Madison University

Robert J. Ramsay, PhD, CPA
Arthur Andersen Alumni Professor of Accounting
The University of Kentucky

David H. Sinason, PhD, CPA, CIA, CFE, CFSA
PwC Professor of Accountancy
Northern Illinois University

Jerry R. Strawser, PhD, CPA
KPMG Chair of Accounting
Texas A&M University

Jay C. Thibodeau, PhD, CPA
Professor of Accountancy
Bentley University

AUDITING & ASSURANCE SERVICES
International Edition 2013

Exclusive rights by McGraw-Hill Education (Asia), for manufacture and export. This book cannot be re-exported from the country to which it is sold by McGraw-Hill. This International Edition is not to be sold or purchased in North America and contains content that is different from its North American version.

Published by McGraw-Hill/Irwin, a business unit of The McGraw-Hill Companies, Inc., 1221 Avenue of the Americas, New York, NY 10020. Copyright © 2013, 2011, 2008, 2007, 2005 by The McGraw-Hill Companies, Inc. All rights reserved. No part of this publication may be reproduced or distributed in any form or by any means, or stored in a database or retrieval system, without the prior written consent of The McGraw-Hill Companies, Inc., including, but not limited to, in any network or other electronic storage or transmission, or broadcast for distance learning.
Some ancillaries, including electronic and print components, may not be available to customers outside the United States.

10 09 08 07 06 05 04 03 02 01
20 15 14 13 12
CTP   MPM

When ordering this title, use ISBN 978-1-259-07120-1 or MHID 1-259-07120-0

Printed in Singapore

www.mhhe.com

Some people come into our lives and quickly go. Some stay awhile and leave footprints on our hearts and we are never quite the same.

Anonymous

We dedicate this book to the following educators whose footprints we try to follow:

Professor Homer Bates
(University of North Florida)

Professor Stanley Biggs
(University of Connecticut)

Professor Lewis C. Buller
(Indiana State University)

Professor Patrick Delaney
(Northern Illinois University)

Professor William Hillison
(Florida State University)

Professor John Ivancevich
(University of Houston)

Professor Richard Kochanek
(University of Connecticut)

Professor Jack Robertson
(University of Texas at Austin)

Professor Robert Strawser
(Texas A&M University)

Professor Sally Webber
(Northern Illinois University)

Professor "IBM Jim" Whitney
(The Citadel)

Meet the Authors

Timothy J. Louwers teaches advanced auditing and fraud auditing at James Madison University, where he holds the Jackson E. Ramsey Centennial Chair in Business.

Professor Louwers received his undergraduate and master's degrees from The Citadel and his Ph.D. from Florida State University. Prior to beginning his academic career, he worked in public accounting with KPMG, specializing in financial, governmental, and information systems auditing. He is a certified public accountant (South Carolina and Virginia), a certified internal auditor, and a certified information systems auditor. He is also certified in financial forensics and is the incoming president of the Forensic and Investigative Accounting Section of the American Accounting Association.

Professor Louwers's research interests include auditors' reporting decisions and ethical issues in the accounting profession. He has authored or coauthored 10 books and more than 40 articles on a wide range of accounting, auditing, and technology-related topics, including publications in the *Journal of Accounting Research, Accounting Horizons,* the *Journal of Business Ethics, Behavioral Research in Accounting, Decision Sciences,* the *Journal of Forensic Accounting, Issues in Accounting Education,* the *Journal of Accountancy,* the *CPA Journal,* and *Today's CPA*. Some of his published work has been reprinted in Russian and Chinese. He is a respected lecturer on auditing and technology-related issues and has received teaching excellence awards from the University of Houston and Louisiana State University. He has appeared on both local and national television news broadcasts, including MSNBC and CNN news programs.

Robert J. Ramsay is the Arthur Andersen Alumni Professor of Accounting in The Von Allmen School of Accountancy at The University of Kentucky.

Professor Ramsay completed his Ph.D. at Indiana University in 1991. He teaches auditing and advanced auditing. He has previously taught information systems, advanced managerial accounting, and a seminar on research in judgment and decision making. His research interests relate to auditor judgment and decision making. Professor Ramsay was a recipient of the 2008 American Accounting Association Wildman Medal given annually to authors of the publication that has the greatest likelihood of making the most significant impact on the practice of public accounting, including audit, tax, and management services.

Professor Ramsay has been active in the American Accounting Association, serving on the professionalism and ethics committee, the notable contributions to accounting literature award screening committee, and the annual meeting committee as Auditing section chair. He is also active in the AAA Auditing section where he served on the auditing standards committee, the nominations committee, and as chairman of the 2003 Mid-Year Meeting. Professor Ramsay worked nine years for Arthur Young & Company serving clients in the restaurant, mining, electronics, and manufacturing sectors. He also worked four years as vice president, controller, for Chi-Chi's, Inc., a publicly held restaurant company. He currently serves on the audit committee of a large nonprofit agency.

David H. Sinason is the PwC Professor of Accountancy at Northern Illinois University (NIU) and director of the NIU Internal Audit program.

Professor Sinason received a B.S. in engineering from the University of Illinois, a B.B.A. and M.Acc. in accounting from the University of North Florida, and a Ph.D. in accounting from Florida State University. He has certifications as a certified public accountant, a certified internal auditor, a certified financial services auditor, and a certified fraud examiner. Professor Sinason has written more than 40 articles, mostly in the areas of assurance services, fraud prevention and detection, and auditor liability.

Professor Sinason has taught in the areas of accounting information systems, auditing and assurance services, and financial accounting. He has received teaching awards at each of the universities where he has taught including the 2002–2003 Department of Accountancy and Northern Illinois University Awards for Excellence in Undergraduate Teaching.

Jerry R. Strawser   is Dean of Mays Business School at Texas A&M University and holds the KPMG Chair in Accounting.

Prior to his current appointment, Professor Strawser served as interim executive vice president and provost at Texas A&M University, interim dean of the C. T. Bauer College of Business at the University of Houston and Arthur Andersen & Co. Alumni Professor of Accounting.

Professor Strawser has coauthored three textbooks and more than 60 journal articles. In addition to his academic experience, Professor Strawser had prior public accounting experience at two Big Five accounting firms. He has also developed and delivered numerous executive development programs to organizations such as AT&T, Centerpoint Energy, Continental Airlines, ConocoPhillips, Halliburton, KBR, KPMG, Minute Maid, PricewaterhouseCoopers, McDermott International, Shell, Southwest Bank of Texas, and the Texas Society of Certified Public Accountants. Professor Strawser is a certified public accountant in the state of Texas and earned his BBA and Ph.D. in Accounting from Texas A&M University.

Jay C. Thibodeau   is a Professor of Accountancy at Bentley University.

Professor Thibodeau received his B.S. degree from the University of Connecticut in 1987 and his Ph.D. from the University of Connecticut in 1996. He joined the accountancy faculty at Bentley in 1996 and has worked there ever since. In addition to his academic experience, Professor Thibodeau currently consults with the Audit Learning and Development group at KPMG. He previously worked as an auditor at Deloitte and has consulted with PricewaterhouseCoopers' Learning & Education group. At Bentley University, he serves as the coordinator for all audit and assurance curriculum matters.

Professor Thibodeau has coauthored two textbooks and more than 30 journal articles. He currently serves as the chair of the Strategic Data and Research Fulfillment Initiative for the American Accounting Association's Auditing Section. He also serves on the editorial boards of *Current Issues in Auditing* and *Advances in Accounting Education*. He has received national recognition for his work three times: first, for his doctoral dissertation, winning the Outstanding Doctoral Dissertation Award presented by the American Accounting Association's ABO Section; second, for curriculum innovation, winning the Joint AICPA/AAA Collaboration Award; and third, also for curricular innovation, winning the Auditing Section's Innovation in Assurance Education Award.

Brief Contents

PART ONE
The Contemporary Auditing Environment

1. Auditing and Assurance Services   1
2. Professional Standards   35

PART TWO
The Financial Statement Audit

3. Engagement Planning   76
4. Management Fraud and Audit Risk   116
5. Risk Assessment: Internal Control Evaluation   168
6. Employee Fraud and the Audit of Cash   220
7. Revenue and Collection Cycle   268
8. Acquisition and Expenditure Cycle   317
9. Production Cycle   367
10. Finance and Investment Cycle   409
11. Completing the Audit   453
12. Reports on Audited Financial Statements   493

PART THREE
Stand-Alone Modules

Please refer to page xix-xx of the Front Matter for guidance on when to best integrate these modules.

A. Other Public Accounting Services   546
B. Professional Ethics   587
C. Legal Liability   633
D. Internal, Governmental, and Fraud Audits   677
E. Overview of Sampling   714
F. Attributes Sampling   751
G. Variables Sampling   794
H. Auditing in a Computerized Environment   838

CASES   C1
INDEX   I1

Contents

PART ONE
THE CONTEMPORARY AUDITING ENVIRONMENT

Chapter 1
Auditing and Assurance Services 1

User Demand for Reliable Information 2
   Information and Information Risk 2
Auditing, Attestation, and Assurance Services 4
   Definition of Financial Statement Auditing 4
   Attestation Engagements 6
   Assurance Services 7
   Examples of Assurance Services 8
Management's Financial Statement Assertions 10
   Existence or Occurrence (Existence, Occurrence) 12
   Rights and Obligations 12
   Completeness (Completeness, Cutoff) 12
   Valuation and Allocation (Accuracy or Valuation) 13
   Presentation and Disclosure (Classification, Understandability) 13
   Importance of Assertions 14
Professional Skepticism 15
Public Accounting 18
   Assurance Services 18
   Tax Services 20
   Consulting and Advisory Services 20
Other Kinds of Engagements and Information Professionals 21
   Internal Auditing 21
   Governmental Auditing 22
   Regulatory Auditors 23
Become a Professional and Get Certified! 23
   Education 24
   Examination 24
   Experience 25
   State Certificate and License 25
   Skill Sets and Your Education 27
Summary 27
Key Terms 28
Multiple-Choice Questions for Practice and Review 28
Exercises and Problems 32

Chapter 2
Professional Standards 35

Introduction 36
Generally Accepted Auditing Standards (GAAS) 37
Fundamental Principle: Responsibilities 42
Fundamental Principle: Performance 46
Fundamental Principle: Reporting *(AU 700, AU 705, AS 1, AS 5)* 53
Evaluating the Quality of Public Accounting Firms' Practices 55
   System of Quality Control 56
   Peer Review 58
   PCAOB Inspection of Firms 59
Summary 61
Key Terms 62
Multiple-Choice Questions for Practice and Review 63
Exercises and Problems 67
Appendix 2A 74
Attestation Standards 74

PART TWO
THE FINANCIAL STATEMENT AUDIT

Chapter 3
Engagement Planning 76

Introduction 77
Pre-Engagement Activities *(AU/ISA 300, AS 10)* 77
   Client Acceptance or Continuance 78
   Compliance with Independence and Ethical Requirements 80
   Engagement Letters 81
Audit Plan *(AU/ISA 300, AS 10)* 81
   Staffing the Audit Engagement 84
   Considering the Work of Internal Auditors (AU/ISA 610) 84
   Use of Specialists (AU/ISA 620) 85
   Use of Information Technology (IT) Auditors 85
   Time Budget 86
Materiality *(AU/ISA 320, AS 11)* 87
   Materiality Calculation 88
Audit Procedures for Obtaining Audit Evidence *(AU/ISA 500, AS 15)* 90
   1. Inspection of Records and Documents 93
   2. Inspection of Tangible Assets 95
   3. Observation 95
   4. Inquiry 95
   5. Confirmation 96
   6. Recalculation 97
   7. Reperformance 97
   8. Analytical Procedures 97

Planning in a Computerized Environment 99
   Effect of Client's Computerized Processing on Audit Planning 100
Audit Documentation (*AU/ISA 230, AS 3*) 104
   Permanent Files 104
   Current Files 105
   Audit Documentation Arrangement and Indexing 106
Summary 108
Key Terms 109
Multiple-Choice Questions for Practice and Review 110
Exercises and Problems 112

Chapter 4
Management Fraud and Audit Risk 116

Introduction 117
Management's Responsibility For Managing Risk 118
   Enterprise Risk Management 119
Auditor's Risk Assessment (*AU 315, AS 12*) 121
   Fraud (AU 240, AU 316) 122
   Types of Fraud 123
   Other Definitions Related to Fraud 126
The Audit Risk Model (*AU 320, AS 8*) 127
   Audit Risk 127
   Inherent Risk 127
   Control Risk 128
   Detection Risk 128
   Risk Model—A Summary 128
Assessing Inherent Risk—"What Could Go Wrong?"(*AU 315, AS 12*) 131
   Understanding the Client's Business and Its Environment 133
   Industry, Regulatory, and Other External Factors 133
   The Nature of the Company 134
   Selection and Application of Accounting Principles, Including Related Disclosures 135
   Company Objectives, Strategies, and Related Business Risks 136
   Company Performance Measures 136
Gathering Information, Assessing and Responding to Risks 137
   General Business Sources 137
   Company Sources 137
   Information from Client Acceptance or Continuance Evaluation, Audit Planning, Past Audits, and Other Engagements 137
   Preliminary Analytical Procedures (AU 520, AU 329) 138
   Audit Team Discussions (Brainstorming) 143
   Inquiry of Audit Committee, Management, and Others within the Company 143
   Assessing Risk Factors 144
   Respond to Significant Risks (AU 330, AS 15) 144
   Evaluate Accumulated Results of Audit Procedures 145
   Communicate Fraud Risks 145
   Document Risk Assessment 146

Auditors' Responsibilities for Noncompliance with Laws and Regulations (*AU 350, AS 17*) 146
Audit Strategy Memorandum 148
Summary 149
Key Terms 149
Multiple-Choice Questions for Practice and Review 151
Exercises and Problems 154
Appendix 4A 164
Selected Financial Ratios 164

Appendix 4B 165
Sample Abridged Audit Plan 165

Chapter 5
Risk Assessment: Internal Control Evaluation 168

Introduction 169
Internal Control Defined 170
Management versus Auditors' Responsibility for Internal Control 172
   Auditors' Internal Control Responsibilities 172
Components of Internal Control 175
   Control Environment 176
   Risk Assessment 178
   Control Activities 178
   Information and Communication 183
   Monitoring 184
Internal Control Evaluation 185
   Phase 1: Understand and Document the Client's Internal Control 185
   Phase 2: Assess the Control Risk (Preliminary) 191
   Phase 3: Identify Controls to Test and Perform Tests of Controls 193
Responsibilities in Public Company Audits Required by PCAOB *Auditing Standard No. 5* 196
   Requirements 197
Auditor Reports on Internal Control over Financial Reporting 200
Modifications to the Auditors' Standard Report on Internal Control over Financial Reporting 202
   Material Weaknesses in the Entity's Internal Control over Financial Reporting 202
   Effect of an Adverse Opinion on Internal Control on the Auditor's Opinion on the Financial Statements 204
   Restriction on the Scope of the Engagement 204
   Other Report Modifications 205
Internal Control Communications 206
Summary 207
Key Terms 208
Multiple-Choice Questions for Practice and Review 209
Exercises and Problems 213
Appendix 5A 219
Audit Plan 219

Chapter 6
Employee Fraud and the Audit of Cash 220

Employee Fraud Overview 221
   Employee Fraud Red Flags 222
   Characteristics of Fraudsters 223
The Fraud Triangle (*AU/ISA 315, AS 12*) 225
   Motivation 225
   Opportunity 226
   Rationalization 227
Fraud Prevention 227
   Managing People Pressures in the Workplace 228
   Internal Control Activities and Employee Monitoring 228
   Integrity by Example and Enforcement 230
Cash Internal Control Considerations 231
   Control Activities for Cash Receipts 232
   Tests of Controls over Cash Receipts 234
   Control Considerations for Cash Disbursements 235
   Tests of Controls over Cash Disbursements 235
   Risk of Material Misstatement at the Relevant Assertion Level 236
Audit Evidence Used to Test Cash 236
   Cash Receipts Journal 236
   Cash Disbursements Journal 237
   Bank Reconciliations 237
   Canceled Checks 237
   Bank Statements 239
The Audit of Cash 240
   Bank Reconciliation 240
   Schedule of Interbank Transfers 244
   Proof of Cash 245
Audit Cases: More Schemes and Ways to Detect Them 246
"Extended Procedures" to Detect Fraud 248
Summary 251
Key Terms 251
Multiple-Choice Questions for Practice and Review 252
Exercises and Problems 255
Appendix 6A 265
Internal Control Questionnaires 265

Appendix 6B 267
Audit Plans 267

Chapter 7
Revenue and Collection Cycle 268

Introduction 269
Overall Audit Approach for the Revenue and Collection Cycle 269
Inherent Risks in the Revenue and Collection Cycle 271
   Revenue Recognition 271
   Collectability of Accounts Receivable 273
   Customer Returns and Allowances 273
Revenue and Collection Cycle: Typical Activities 274
   Entity-Level Controls 275
   Receiving and Processing Customer Orders, Including Credit Granting 275
   Delivering Goods and Services to Customers 276
   Billing Customers and Accounting for Accounts Receivable 276
   Audit Evidence in Management Reports and Data Files 277
Control Risk Assessment 279
   Control Considerations 279
   Tests of Controls 280
   Summary: Control Risk Assessment 282
Substantive Procedures in the Revenue and Collection Cycle 283
   Analytical Procedures 284
   Confirmation of Accounts and Notes Receivable 285
   Alternative Procedures 289
   Review for Collectability 289
   Cutoff and Sales Returns 290
   Rights and Obligations 290
   Presentation and Disclosure 291
Audit Risk Model Summary 292
Fraud Cases: Extended Audit Procedures (AU 240) 292
   Dual-Purpose Nature of Accounts Receivable Confirmations 292
Summary 300
Key Terms 300
Multiple-Choice Questions for Practice and Review 301
Exercises and Problems 304
Appendix 7A 313
Internal Control Questionnaires 313

Appendix 7B 315
Audit Plan 315

Chapter 8
Acquisition and Expenditure Cycle 317

Introduction 318
Inherent Risks in the Acquisition and Expenditure Cycle 319
Acquisition and Expenditure Cycle: Typical Activities 320
   Purchasing Goods and Services 321
   Receiving the Goods or Services 322
   Recording the Asset or Expense and Related Liability 323

Audit Evidence in Management Reports
and Data Files 323
   Open Purchase Orders 323
   Unmatched Receiving Reports 323
   Unmatched Vendor Invoices 323
   Accounts (Vouchers) Payable Trial Balance 324
   Purchases Journal 324
   Fixed Asset Reports 324
Control Risk Assessment 325
   Entity-Level Controls 325
   Control Considerations 325
   Custody 325
   Periodic Reconciliation 326
   Tests of Controls 326
   Summary: Control Risk Assessment 326
Substantive Procedures in the Acquisition
and Expenditure Cycle 328
   The Completeness Assertion 328
   *Auditing Other Accounts in the Acquisition
     and Expenditure Cycle 330*
   Other Expenses 334
   Presentation and Disclosure 334
Audit Risk Model Summary 335
Finding Fraud Signs in Accounts Payable 335
Fraud Cases: Extended Audit Procedures
(ISA/AU 320) 336
Audit Issues in the Expense and Acquisition Cycle 339
Summary 341
Key Terms 341
Multiple-Choice Questions for Practice and Review 342
Exercises and Problems 344

Appendix 8A 351

Internal Control Questionnaires 351

Appendix 8B 354

Audit Plans 354

Appendix 8C 356

The Payroll Cycle 356

Chapter 9

Production Cycle 367

Phar-Mor, Inc. 368
Inherent Risks in the Production Cycle 369
Typical Activities in the Production Cycle 369
   Sales Forecasts 370
   Production Planning 370
   Production 372
   Inventory Control 372
   Cost Accounting 372
Audit Evidence in Management Reports and Files 373
   Sales Forecast 374
   Inventory Reports 374
   Production Plans and Reports 374

Control Risk Assessment 375
   Entity-Level Controls 376
   Control Considerations 376
   Custody 376
   Internal Control Questionnaire 377
   Tests of Controls 377
   Direction of Tests of Controls 379
   Summary: Control Risk Assessment 379
Substantive Procedures in the Production
Cycle 380
   Analytical Procedures 380
   Physical Inventory Observation 381
   Pricing and Compilation 386
   Inventory—A Ripe Field for Fraud 387
   Accounting Firm Tips 388
   Presentation and Disclosure Assertions 388
Audit Risk Model Summary 389
Fraud Case: Extended Audit Procedures *(Standard
240)* 389
Summary 391
Key Terms 393
Multiple-Choice Questions for Practice and
Review 393
Exercises and Problems 396

Appendix 9A 405

Internal Control Questionnaires 405

Appendix 9B 407

Audit Plans 407

Chapter 10

Finance and Investment Cycle 409

Introduction 410
Inherent Risks in the Finance and Investment
Cycle 411
   Lease Accounting 412
   Loan Covenants 413
   Related-Party Transactions 413
   Complex Transactions 414
   Impairments 414
   Presentation and Disclosure 414
Finance and Investment Cycle: Typical
Activities 415
   *Financing the Entity through Debt and Stockholder
     Equity 415*
   Financial Planning 415
   Raising Capital 416
   *Investing Transactions: Investments
     and Intangibles 417*
Control Risk Assessment 421
   Control Considerations 421
   Control over Accounting Estimates 422
   Authorization 423

Record Keeping 423
Custody 423
Summary: Control Risk Assessment 424
Financing Activities: Assertions and Substantive Procedures 425
Long-Term Liabilities and Related Accounts 425
Stockholders' Equity: Substantive Procedures 427
Investing Activities: Assertions and Substantive Procedures 428
Derivative Instruments, Hedging Activities and Investments in Securities (AU 332) 429
Auditing Fair Value Measurements (AU 328) 429
Fraud Cases: Extended Audit Procedures (AU 316) 432
Summary 436
Key Terms 437
Multiple-Choice Questions for Practice and Review 438
Exercises and Problems 442
Appendix 10A 449
Internal Control Questionnaires 449
Appendix 10B 451
Substantive Audit Plans 451

Chapter 11
Completing the Audit 453

Introduction 454
Audit Timeline 456
Procedures Performed During Fieldwork 457
Completing Substantive Procedures 457
Attorney Letters 459
Written Representations 463
Ability to Continue as a Going Concern 465
Adjusting Entries and Financial Statement Disclosure 467
Audit Documentation Review 469
Subsequent Events and Subsequently Disovered Facts 470
Subsequent Events 471
Subsequently Discovered Facts 472
Responsibilities Following the Audit Report Release Date 474
Omitted Procedures 474
Communications with Individuals Charged with Governance (AU 260, AU 265, AS 5) 475
Management Letter 476
Summary of Audit Communications 476
Summary 477
Key Terms 478
Multiple-Choice Questions for Practice and Review 479
Exercises and Problems 482

Chapter 12
Reports on Audited Financial Statements 493

Introduction 494
Reports Accompanying the Entity's Financial Statements 496
Reporting on the Entity's Financial Statements 497
Purpose of the Report 497
The Standard Report 498
Reports Other Than the Standard Report 503
Auditors' Reports on Departures from GAAP 504
Auditors' Reports When Scope Limitations Exist 507
Scope Limitation Reports 507
Lack of Independence 510
Auditors' Reports Referencing Other Matters Encountered During the Audit 511
Consistency (AS 6, AU 708) 512
Reporting on "Going-Concern" Uncertainties (AU 341, AU 570) 513
Justified Departures from GAAP 514
Group Financial Statements (AU 600) 516
Other Modifications 518
Other Reporting Topics 519
Association with Financial Statements 519
Reporting on Comparative Statements 520
Reporting on Summary Financial Statements (AU 810) 521
Other Information Accompanying Audited Financial Statements (AU 720) 522
Required Supplementary Information (AU 730) 523
The Future of Audit Reporting 523
Summary 524
Key Terms 526
Multiple-Choice Questions for Practice and Review 528
Exercises and Problems 530
Appendix 12A 544
Auditing Standards Board Report for Nonpublic Entities (AU 700) 544

PART THREE
STAND-ALONE MODULES

Module A
Other Public Accounting Services 546

Introduction 548
Attestation Engagements 548
Introduction to Attestation Engagements 548
Applying Agreed-Upon Procedures (AT 201) 549
Financial Forecasts and Projections (AT 301) and Pro Forma Financial Information (AT 401) 550

An Examination of an Entity's Internal Control over Financial Reporting that Is Integrated with an Audit of Its Financial Statements (AT 501) 552
Compliance Attestation (AT 601) 553
Management's Discussion and Analysis (AT 701) 554
Service Organizations (AT 801) 554
Unaudited Financial Statements: Reviews and Compilations 558
Review Services 558
Compilation Services 560
Other Review and Compilation Topics 561
Summary of Audits, Reviews, and Compilations 562
Responsibilities Related to Reporting on Interim Financial Information (AU 930) 563
Report on Interim Information in a Company's Annual Report 565
Other Topics: Special and Restricted-Use Reports 565
Specified Elements, Accounts, or Items (AU 805) 565
Special Purpose Frameworks 566
Reports on Application of Requirements of an Appropriate Financial Reporting Framework (AU 915) 568
Assurance Services 570
Why Develop New Assurance Services? 570
Definition: Assurance Services 571
Extensible Business Reporting Language (XBRL) 572
Enhanced Business Reporting 572
Trust Services 572
Sustainability Reporting 574
Summary 576
Key Terms 576
Multiple-Choice Questions for Practice and Review 577
Exercises and Problems 580

Module B

Professional Ethics 587

Introduction 589
General Ethics 589
An Ethical Decision Process 590
Philosophical Principles in Ethics 591
The Imperative Principle 592
The Principle of Utilitarianism 593
The Generalization Argument 593
Ethical Codes of Conduct 594
U.S. Securities and Exchange Commission (SEC) 595
The Public Company Accounting Oversight Board (PCAOB) 595
The International Federation of Accountants (IFAC) 596
The Professional Ethics Executive Committee (PEEC) of the American Institute of CPAs (AICPA) 596

An Emphasis on Independence 598
American Institute of Certified Public Accountants 598
SEC and PCAOB Independence Rules 603
Other Effects of Sarbanes-Oxley on Auditor Independence 605
Governmental Accountability Office (GAO) Independence Requirements 606
AICPA Rules of Conduct: Integrity and Objectivity, Responsibilities to Clients, and Other Responsibilities 607
Rule 102: Integrity and Objectivity 607
Rule 201: General Standards 608
Rule 202: Compliance with Standards 609
Rule 203: Accounting Principles 609
Rule 301: Confidential Client Information 610
Rule 302: Contingent Fees 612
Rule 501: Acts Discreditable 612
Rule 502: Advertising and Other Forms of Solicitation 613
Rule 503: Commissions and Referral Fees 614
Rule 505: Form of Organization and Name 615
The International Ethics Standards Board for Accountants (IESBA) Code 616
Consequences to Violating the Code of Professional Conduct 617
Self-Regulatory Discipline 617
Public Regulation Discipline 618
Summary 619
Key Terms 620
Multiple-Choice Questions for Practice and Review 621
Exercises and Problems 624

Module C

Legal Liability 633

The Legal Environment 635
Liability under Common Law 637
Liability to Clients 637
Liability to Third Parties 638
Liability for Compilation and Review Services 643
Liability under Statutory Law 644
The Securities Act of 1933 (Securities Act) 645
Section 11: Civil Liability 645
Auditors' Defenses under the Securities Act 646
Section 13: Statute of Limitations 647
Section 17: Antifraud 647
Section 24: Criminal Liability 647
The Securities Exchange Act of 1934 (Securities Exchange Act) 648
Section 10 and Rule 10b-5: Antifraud 648
Section 18: Civil Liability 650
Auditors' Defenses under the Securities Exchange Act 650
Section 32: Criminal Liability 651
Foreign Corrupt Practices Act (FCPA) 651
Summary of Auditors' Liability to Clients and Third Parties 652

The Changing Landscape of Auditors' Liability 654
  Sarbanes-Oxley 655
  Racketeer Influenced and Corrupt Organizations Act 656
  Aiding and Abetting 656
  Organization of Accounting Firms as Limited Liability Partnerships 657
  Proportionate Liability 657
  Class Action Suits 658
  Auditors' Liability Caps 659
  Other Recent Developments 660
Summary 661
Key Terms 661
Multiple-Choice Questions for Practice and Review 662
Exercises and Problems 667

Module D

Internal, Governmental, and Fraud Audits 677

Introduction 678
"External," Governmental, and Internal Audits 679
Internal Audits 679
  Independence (IIA Standards 1100 and 1110) 680
  Value-Added Audit 682
  Scope of Service 683
  Internal Audit Standards 685
  Internal Audit Reports 686
Governmental Audits 688
  Types of Audits 689
  Audit Procedures—Economy, Efficiency, and Program Results Audits 690
  GAO Government Auditing Standards 692
  Single Audit Act of 1984 and Amendments of 1986 693
  GAO Audit Reports 694
Fraud Audits 696
  The Art of Fraud Examinations 697
  Fraud Examiner Responsibilities 698
  Building a Fraud Case 700
  Protecting the Evidence 700
  Obtaining Litigation Support 700
Summary 700
Key Terms 702
Multiple-Choice Questions for Practice and Review 702
Exercises and Problems 705

Module E

Overview of Sampling 714

Introduction 715
What Is Sampling? 715
  When Should Sampling Be Used? 716
  Sampling Risk versus Nonsampling Risk 716
  Statistical Sampling versus Nonstatistical Sampling 719

The Basic Steps Involved with Sampling 720
  Planning 720
  Performing 720
  Evaluating the Sample Results 724
  Documenting the Sampling Procedure 725
Use of Sampling in the Audit 726
  Attributes Sampling 726
  Variables Sampling 730
  Summary: Sampling Risks for Audit Sampling 733
An Overview of Audit Sampling 733
  Planning 734
  Performing 734
  Evaluating 736
  Documenting the Sampling Procedure 736
Summary 736
Key Terms 737
Multiple-Choice Questions for Practice and Review 739
Exercises and Problems 742

Module F

Attributes Sampling 751

Introduction 752
Attributes Sampling: Planning 753
  Determining the Objective of Sampling 753
  Defining the Deviation Conditions 753
  Defining the Population 754
Attributes Sampling: Performing 756
  Determining Sample Size: Factors to Consider 756
  Determining Sample Size: Using AICPA Sampling Tables 759
  Selecting the Sample 763
  Measuring Sample Items 764
Attributes Sampling: Evaluating 765
  Calculating the Upper Limit Rate of Deviation 765
  Making the Evaluation Decision 768
  Qualitative Evaluation of Deviations 770
Attributes Sampling: Documenting 771
Sequential Sampling and Discovery Sampling 772
Nonstatistical Attributes Sampling 773
Summary 775
Key Terms 775
Multiple-Choice Questions for Practice and Review 776
Exercises and Problems 779
Appendix F.A 792

Sample Selection Methods 792

Module G

Variables Sampling 794

Introduction 795
Definition of Variables Sampling 795

Sampling in Substantive Procedures: Monetary Unit Sampling (MUS) 796
   MUS: Planning 797
   MUS: Determining Sample Size 798
   MUS: Selecting the Sample 804
   MUS: Measuring Sample Items 805
   MUS: Evaluating Sample Results 806
Classical Variables Sampling 812
   Classical Variables Sampling: Planning 812
   Classical Variables Sampling: Determining Sample Size 813
   Classical Variables Sampling: Selecting the Sample 815
   Classical Variables Sampling: Measuring Sample Items 815
   Classical Variables Sampling: Evaluating Sample Results 815
   Other Approaches to Classical Variables Sampling 817
MUS versus Classical Variables Sampling 817
Nonstatistical Sampling 818
Variables Sampling: Documenting 820
Summary 820
Key Terms 821
Multiple-Choice Questions for Practice and Review 822
Exercises and Problems 825

Module H

Auditing in a Computerized Environment 838

Introduction 839
Computrized Processing Systems 840
Computer Controls 843
   General Controls 843
   Automated Application Controls 849
   Output Controls 853

Assessing Control Risk in a Computerized Environment 855
Testing Controls in a Computerized Environment 857
   Techniques Using Actual Data 858
   Techniques Using Simulated Data 861
   Benchmarking 862
   Summary 863
End-User Computing and Other Environments 864
   End-User Computing Control Considerations 864
   Service Organizations 866
Computer Abuse and Computer Fraud 866
   Preventive, Detective, and Damage-Limiting Controls 868
   Computer Forensics 869
Summary 870
Key Terms 870
Multiple-Choice Questions for Practice and Review 872
Exercises and Problems 874

Cases

Anderson: An Obstruction of Justice? C1
PTL Club—The Harbinger of Things to Come? C5
GM: Running on Empty? C11
Unhealthy Accounting at HealthSouth C14
KPMG: How Many Firms? C17
Something Went Sour at Parmalat C20
GE: How Much Are Auditors Paid? C23
Satyam Computer Services, Ltd.—India's Enron C26

Index I1

As auditors, we are trained to investigate beyond appearances to determine the underlying facts—in other words, to *look beneath the surface.* The recent financial crisis has made this skill even more crucial to the business community. As a result of this recent crisis and of the financial statement accounting scandals that occurred at the turn of the century, understanding the auditor's responsibility related to fraud, maintaining a clear perspective, probing for details, and understanding the big picture are indispensable to effective auditing. The author team of Louwers, Ramsay, Sinason, Strawser, and Thibodeau has dedicated years of experience in the auditing field to this new edition of *Auditing & Assurance Services,* supplying the necessary investigative tools for future auditors.

Cutting-Edge Coverage

The fifth edition of *Auditing & Assurance Services* is the most up-to-date auditing text on the market. All chapters and modules in the fifth edition have been revised to incorporate the eight new standards (*AS 8–AS 15*) adopted by the PCAOB that relate to the auditor's assessment of and response to risk in a financial statement audit and that include guidance related to audit planning, supervision, materiality, and other important considerations. **All chapters and modules have also been revised to incorporate the latest updates from the international standards of auditing (ISAs) and the Auditing Standards Board (ASB).** In fact, each chapter now begins with a list of the AU/ISA sections that are covered from the Codification of Statements on Auditing Standards published by the AICPA. Fraud awareness, a thorough understanding of internal controls, and the ability to use technology effectively are the hallmarks of a successful auditor in the post-Sarbanes-Oxley auditing environment. With *Auditing & Assurance Services,* 5e, students are prepared to take on auditing's latest challenges.

Engage Your Students

An effective accounting textbook integrates real-world scenarios with theoretical discussion. *Auditing & Assurance Services* places the student in the role of decision maker, using situations from companies such as General Motors, General Electric, Time Warner, Disney, Hewlett-Packard, and Walmart to illustrate the application of auditing concepts. Importantly, the author team employs a rigorous monthly process by which they scrutinize leading business and academic publications (e.g., *The Wall Street Journal*) for relevant real-world auditing headlines. The result is that *each* chapter features relevant and recent examples, including infamous accounting scandals that occurred at Satyam, Enron, Siemens, HealthSouth, Adelphia Communications Corporation, and WorldCom. The Louwers author team uses a conversational, yet professional, tone—hailed by reviewers as a key strength of the book.

> *"The tone of the textbook is in a conversational manner that allows for more student-friendly reading material."*
> —Aretha Hill, Florida A&M University

Market-Leading Technology

Auditing in modern business utilizes the latest technology. The author team of *Auditing & Assurance Services* has again included the educational version of **ACL software** in the fifth edition at no extra cost so students can benefit from the kind of cutting-edge software they'll use the first day on the job. Exercises to accompany ACL are included on the book's Web site, **www.mhhe.com/louwers5e**. In addition, the selection of **Kaplan CPA Review audit simulations** allows students to go online and complete simulations similar to those on the CPA exam—seamlessly integrating technology with the textbook.

Fraud Awareness

The fraud coverage in *Auditing & Assurance Services* is the most extensive available and is complemented by real-world examples chosen to engage students. The authors use short **"Auditing Insight" boxes** to provide real-life (and often humorous!) examples of fraud as well as examples of how auditors contributed to solving the case. Extended discussions of fraud cases at Satyam, Parmalat, HealthSouth, KPMG, Andersen, General Motors, and the PTL Club, just to name a few, give students an inside view of fraud detection. Chapters 4 and 6 cover management and employee fraud, respectively, and Module D focuses on the Certified Fraud Examiner Exam. With the **Apollo Shoes Case**, the only stand-alone fraud audit case available on the market (available online), *Auditing & Assurance Services* is truly the leading auditing textbook for fraud coverage.

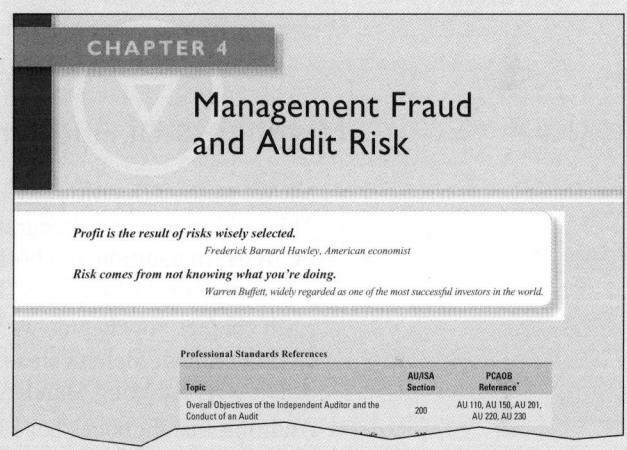

Comprehensive Cases

Eight comprehensive cases are included: Arthur Andersen, PTL Club, General Motors, HealthSouth Corporation, KPMG, Parmalat, General Electric, and Satyam Computer Services, Ltd.

Flexible Organization

Auditing & Assurance Services teaches students auditing concepts by emphasizing real-life contexts when describing the auditing process. The authors use chapters and modules to achieve this goal. Although the chapters follow a logical sequence that we recommend professors consider for their classes, **the modules have been written to be used on a stand-alone basis.** In essence, the modules have been

> *"The format allows you to integrate the modules into the chapter material in any way you would find useful."*
> —Frank J. Beil, University of Minnesota

deliberately prepared for entirely flexible implementation of these topics without excessive reliance on chapter sequencing. We encourage you to integrate these modules into your syllabi in a manner that best suits your approach to the auditing course.

Chapters	Modules
The first 12 chapters cover the auditing process extensively with a multitude of cases designed to give students a better understanding of how a best-practice concept developed from real-world situations.	Modules A–H provide instructors additional material that can be used throughout the course. Topics such as fraud, ethics, sampling, and technology are covered in the modules, which are designed to be taught whenever instructors want to introduce the topic in their course.

Highlights of *Auditing & Assurance Services*, 5e

- **NEW! to the 5th edition:** *Connect® Accounting*! See pages xxvi–xxvii for details.
- This edition has fully integrated the eight new standards (*AS 8–AS 15*) adopted by the PCAOB. In addition, the book has fully integrated the latest updates from the international standards of auditing (ISAs) and the Auditing Standards Board (ASB).
- Each chapter now begins with a list of the AU/ISA Sections that are covered from the Codification of Statements on Auditing Standards published by the AICPA and the list of PCAOB Auditing Standards covered in that chapter.
- Auditing Insight boxes have been added and updated in many chapters.
- Chapter 1 has been revised to incorporate the major changes to the structure and the content of the auditing section of the CPA examination for 2011.
- Chapters 3 and 4 have been reversed in the Table of Contents to better reflect the financial statement audit sequence. In addition, chapters 3 and 4 have been completely rewritten to reflect the content of the PCAOB and international risk standards as well as the AICPA clarified standards.
- Recent pronouncements and the new format for the auditors' report on the financial statements of nonpublic entities (Chapter 12) and written representations (Chapter 11) are incorporated.
- Module H has been revised to more clearly focus on how the use of computerized processing affects the audit team's study and assessment of internal control.
- All chapters and modules have been revised to incorporate professional standards adopted by July 2011, and international standards of auditing (ISAs).

Association to Advance Collegiate Schools of Business (AACSB) Statement

The McGraw-Hill Companies is a proud corporate member of AACSB International. Understanding the importance and value of AACSB accreditation, *Auditing and Assurance Services,* 5e, recognizes the curricula guidelines detailed in the AACSB standards for business accreditation by connecting selected questions in the text and test bank to the six general knowledge and skill guidelines in the AACSB standards. The statements contained in *Auditing and Assurance Services,* 5e, are provided only as a guide for the users of this textbook. The AACSB leaves content coverage and assessment within the purview of individual schools, their mission, and their faculty. While *Auditing and Assurance Services,* 5e, and the teaching package make no claim of any specific AACSB qualification or evaluation, we have within *Auditing and Assurance Services,* 5e, labeled selected questions according to the six general knowledge and skills areas.

Part I: The Contemporary Auditing Environment

CHAPTER 1: Auditing and Assurance Services
- Revised the introduction to help motivate students by emphasizing the importance of acquiring technical knowledge about auditing.
- Added a discussion of the increase in demand for assurance services that relate to sustainability and/or environmental reporting as more and more organizations seek to demonstrate their efforts related to going "green."
- Updated the Hurt Professional Skepticism scale to incorporate the final published paper (Kathy Hurtt, "Development of a Scale to Measure Professional Skepticism," Auditing; A Journal of Practice & Theory, May 2010).
- Updated the financial results for the Big Four accounting firms through 2010.
- Updated the GAO engagement examples.
- Updated each of the certification requirements (e.g., CPA, CISA).

CHAPTER 2: Professional Standards
- Added an introductory vignette discussing the impact of a negative PCAOB inspection report on the accounting firm Beckstead and Watts, which ultimately led to deliberations as to the constitutionality of the PCAOB.
- Expanded discussion of evidence to more fully identify factors that affect the relevance and reliability of audit evidence.
- Included McDonald's 2011 audit report to demonstrate the contents of an actual audit report and how this report reflects the guidance in the reporting principle.
- Provided a summary of findings from PCAOB inspections of audits conducted by Big Four firms from 2007 through 2009.
- Added additional end of chapter materials requiring students to review hypothetical scenarios and identify potential violations of the responsibilities, performance, and reporting principles.

Part II: The Financial Statement Audit

CHAPTER 3: Engagement Planning
- Chapter 3 has been thoroughly revised to incorporate the eight new standards (*AS 8–AS 15*) adopted by the PCAOB.
- Added emphasis about the importance of complying with appropriate ethical requirements for each audit engagement.
- The revised chapter now includes sections on auditing procedures, materiality, and engagement planning, while Chapter 4 includes the material related to understanding the client's business, preliminary analytical procedures and risk assessment.
- Added a brief discussion of the auditing implications related to cloud computing.

CHAPTER 4: Management Fraud and Audit Risk
- Chapter 4 was rewritten to reflect the new PCAOB risk standards as well as changes in international and AICPA standards.
- Added Exhibit 4.1 to illustrate the relationship between business risk and audit risk.
- Added recent fraud statistics from *The Network* and *BDO Consulting*.
- Updated research on effective brainstorming techniques.
- Responsibilities for Illegal Acts is updated for AU 250, *Consideration of Laws and Regulations in an Audit of Financial Statements*.
- Added a Sample Audit Plan as Appendix 4B.

CHAPTER 5: Risk Assessment: Internal Control Evaluation
- Revised the introduction to emphasize the critical importance of understanding internal control in the audit process, which is consistent with the revised auditing standards.
- The chapter now begins with the definition of internal control. The discussion of management's responsibility for the internal control system has also been streamlined and improved.
- Added emphasis about the importance of the risk of material misstatement at the assertion level.

- Removed the detailed discussion of computer information processing controls from the chapter (this material is covered in detail in Module H).
- Added a brief comment about recent academic research that demonstrated the importance of tone at the top to earnings quality.
- Added a point of emphasis about the importance of general information technology controls and the use of password access controls to achieve proper segregation of duties.

CHAPTER 6: Employee Fraud and the Audit of Cash
- Added a paragraph that emphasizes the importance of professional skepticism, illustrated by three very recent fraud stories.
- Added a paragraph emphasizing the importance of a strong control environment and tone at the top towards the prevention of fraud at an entity.
- Added transition language to better connect the section on employee fraud with the audit of cash.
- Added language to improve the discussion of the use of electronic confirmation requests by auditors.

CHAPTER 7: Revenue and Collection Cycle
- The confirmation discussion has been updated for e-mail, fax, and verbal responses.
- Added discussion of required disclosures for the revenue and collection cycle.

CHAPTER 8: Acquisition and Expenditure Cycle
- New *ISAs* and *AS* coverage have been added.
- The risk assessment discussion has been conformed to new standards.
- Added discussion of the bidding process for purchasing.
- Added discussion for auditing the income tax provision.
- Added discussion for the required disclosures for the acquisition and expenditure cycle.

CHAPTER 9: Production Cycle
- New *ISAs* and *AS* coverage have been added.
- Added analysis of presentation and disclosure of inventory in Boeing Corporation's 2010 annual report.
- PCAOB inspections have been updated.

CHAPTER 10: Finance and Investment Cycle
- New *ISAs* and *AS* coverage have been added.
- PCAOB inspections have been updated.

CHAPTER 11: Completing the Audit
- Added a new introductory vignette that discusses Dell Inc.'s delay in filing audited financial statements with the SEC.
- Provided recent examples from PCAOB inspection reports related to issues encountered by Big Four firms in completing the audit.
- Added discussion of analytical procedures performed during the completion stages of the audit.
- Added discussion of evaluating accounting estimates for reasonableness during the completion stages of the audit, along with providing an example of key estimates used by Best Buy in preparing its financial statements.
- Included a summary of Microsoft's contingencies in discussion of attorney letters.
- Revised section on written representations for issuance of AU 580, including the new format for written representations provided by the standard.
- Expanded discussion of the auditors' responsibility to assess going-concern, including recent going-concern issues experienced at Borders Group, Inc.
- Included a summary of academic research that examines the negotiation process between auditors and client personnel with respect to adjustments identified during the audit.
- Updated discussion of subsequent events and subsequently discovered facts to consider new guidance provided by AU 560.
- Included current examples of subsequent events from the annual reports of Citigroup, Dupont, Federal Mogul, Hewlett-Packard, Kellogg Company, Pfizer, and Praxair.
- Updated discussion of omitted procedures to consider guidance provided by AU 585.
- Included discussion of academic research that examines auditors' meetings with audit committees to discuss important matters encountered during the examination.

CHAPTER 12: Reports on Audited Financial Statements
- Added summaries for reporting issues where multiple options exist (departures from GAAP and scope

limitations) to ensure that students are able to understand how the auditors' reports would be affected by these issues immediately following detailed coverage of the reports themselves.
- Incorporated new guidance related to emphasis-of-matter and other-matter paragraphs from AU 706.
- Incorporated new guidance and terminology for the audits of group financial statements from AU 600.
- Updated reporting examples throughout the chapter to provide more current examples of report modifications.
- Included a brief summary of recent report changes that have been identified for consideration by the PCAOB, including the preparation of an auditors' discussion and analysis report, the expansion of auditors' responsibility to provide assurance on information outside the financial statements, and the clarification of various language and concepts used in the auditors' report.
- Added an Appendix to discuss the new wording and format adopted by the AICPA for reports used for the audits of nonpublic entities in AU 700.
- Added additional end-of-chapter material that requires students to identify the type of opinions issued in various reporting scenarios and how the auditors' report would be modified.
- Added additional end-of-chapter material that addresses reporting options for departures from GAAP and scope limitations assuming various scenarios regarding the pervasiveness and materiality of these issues.

Part III: Stand-Alone Modules

MODULE A: Other Public Accounting Services
- The new attestation standard on service organizations *(SSAE 16)* has been added. Service Organization Controls (SOCs), a new category of reports, are discussed.
- The discussion of reviews and compilations has been completely revised for SSARS 16.
- Updated the coverage of assurance services to include reports on sustainability. A recent example of a sustainability report for Starbucks, Inc. is included.

MODULE B: Professional Ethics
- Added a new opening paragraph designed to link this module with the responsibilities principle in Chapter 2. Specifically, this chapter focuses on the third responsibility, complying with relevant ethical requirements.
- Emphasized the special importance of the imperative principle for students of auditing.
- Added a section on the International Federation of Accountants (IFAC), the group responsible for the International Code of Ethics for Professional Accountants (IESBA Code). The most recent edition of the IESBA code was made effective on January 1, 2011.
- Described a recent revision to rule 101 of the AICPA Code of Professional Conduct. It is now prohibited for members of an audit team and their supervisors to have vested retirement benefits with an audit client.
- Added a section on the IESBA Code, which must be followed by auditors whenever an audit engagement is completed for a multinational client.

MODULE C: Legal Liability
- Updated introductory vignette on litigation involving BDO Seidman for its audits of E.S. Bankest to include the ultimate resolution of this litigation.
- Updated summary of major settlements involving Big Four accounting firms to include settlements occurring since 2008.
- Expanded discussion of the Foreign Corrupt Practices act to include reference to recent investigations of Hewlett-Packard and Goldman Sachs for potential violations.
- Expanded discussion of academic research examining auditor litigation to include recent studies that investigated the factors affecting the litigation risk faced by audit firms.
- Added additional end-of-chapter material that requires students to assess potential auditor liability to clients, third parties under common law, and third parties under statutory law.

MODULE D: Internal, Governmental, and Fraud Audits
- Updated coverage of the reliance of Congress on the GAO.

MODULE E: Overview of Sampling
- Added an Auditing Insight illustrating acceptable and unacceptable use of sampling outside of auditing.
- Included new auditing insights from PCAOB inspections.

MODULE F: Attributes Sampling
- Discussed PCAOB inspection findings related to attributes sampling.

MODULE G: Variables Sampling
- Increased emphasis has been given to the latest AICPA Audit Guide on "Audit Sampling," including new tables for determining sample size.
- Discussed PCAOB inspection findings related to variables sampling.

MODULE H: Auditing in a Computerized Environment
- Provided recent examples from PCAOB inspection reports related to issues encountered by audit teams in evaluating computer controls.
- Added a simple example of computerized processing of sales transactions to more clearly illustrate differences and audit issues introduced when clients use computerized processing systems.
- Revised chapter throughout to reinforce how the client's use of computerized processing systems affects the major stages of the audit team's study and evaluation of internal control.
- Included an illustration that compares how audit teams test controls in a manual environment and the implications for testing those same controls in a computerized environment.
- Expanded coverage of tests of controls to illustrate how auditors use inquiry, observation, reperformance, and inspection of documentary evidence to evaluate the operating effectiveness of both general controls and automated application controls.
- Included a section on how audit teams can use a benchmarking approach (under *Auditing Standard 5*) to evaluate the operating effectiveness of automated application controls.
- Provided an illustration of how students encounter input controls when ordering merchandise from online providers.
- Modified section on service organizations to identify possible implications of the emergence of "cloud computing."
- Included recent examples of computer fraud and cyber attacks experienced by Citigroup, Inc, Google, Inc, Lockheed Martin, Michaels Stores, Inc., the Nasdaq Stock Market, Public Broadcasting Services, and Sony Corp.
- Added additional end-of-chapter material that requires students to identify tests of controls that would be used to evaluate the operating effectiveness of general and automated application controls.

McGraw-Hill Connect® Accounting

Less Managing. More Teaching. Greater Learning.
Available for the first time with Louwers *Auditing & Assurance Services,* McGraw-Hill *Connect® Accounting* is an online assignment and assessment solution that connects students with the tools and resources necessary to achieve success through faster learning, more efficient studying, and higher retention of knowledge.

Online Assignments
Connect Accounting helps students learn more efficiently by providing feedback and practice material when and where they need it. *Connect Accounting* grades homework automatically and gives immediate feedback on any questions students may have missed.

Simple assignment management
With *Connect Accounting*, creating assignments is easier than ever, so you can spend more time teaching and less time managing. The assignment management function enables you to:

- **Create and deliver assignments easily with selectable end-of-chapter questions and test bank items.**
- Streamline lesson planning, student progress reporting, and assignment grading to make classroom management more efficient than ever.
- **Go paperless with the eBook** and online submission and grading of student assignments.
- Have assignments scored automatically, giving students **immediate feedback** on their work and comparisons with correct answers.
- Access and review each response; manually change grades or leave comments for students to review.
- Reinforce classroom concepts with **Interactive Applications** such as **drag & drop activities** and **comprehension cases, which ask students to apply their understanding of auditing material in an interactive, fun environment and then answer related critical thinking questions.**

Instructor Library
The *Connect Accounting* Instructor Library is your repository for additional resources to improve student engagement in and out of class. You can select and use any asset that enhances your lecture. The *Connect Accounting* Instructor Library includes:

- *Solutions Manual*
- *Instructor PowerPoints*
- *Test Bank*
- *Solutions to ACL assignments*
- *eBook version of the text*

Student Library
- The *Connect Accounting* Student Library is the place for students to access additional resources, such as lectures, practice materials, an eBook and more.

Student progress tracking
Connect Accounting keeps instructors informed about how each student, section, and class is performing, allowing for more productive use of lecture and office hours. The progress-tracking function enables you to:

- View scored work immediately and track individual or group performance with assignment and grade reports.
- Access an instant view of student or class performance relative to learning objectives.
- Collect data and generate reports required by many accreditation organizations, such as AACSB and AICPA.

McGraw-Hill's *Connect Plus Accounting*
McGraw-Hill reinvents the textbook learning experience for the modern student with *Connect Plus Accounting,* which provides seamless integration of the eBook and *Connect Accounting. Connect Plus Accounting* provides all of the *Connect Accounting* features plus the following:

- An integrated eBook, allowing for anytime, anywhere access to the textbook.
- Dynamic links between the problems or questions you assign to your students and the location in the eBook where that problem or question is covered.
- A powerful search function to pinpoint and connect key concepts in a snap.

In short, *Connect Accounting* offers you and your students powerful tools and features that optimize your time and energies, enabling you to focus on course content, teaching, and student learning. *Connect Accounting* also offers a wealth of content resources for both instructors and students. This state-of-the-art, thoroughly tested system supports you in preparing students for the world that awaits.

For more information about *Connect,* go to **www.mcgrawhillconnect.com**, or contact your local McGraw-Hill sales representative.

Online Course Management

McGraw-Hill Higher Education and Blackboard have teamed up. What does this mean for you?

1. **Your life, simplified.** Now you and your students can access McGraw-Hill's *Connect* and *Create™* right from within your Blackboard course—all with one single sign-on. Say goodbye to the days of logging in to multiple applications.
2. **Deep integration of content and tools.** Not only do you get single sign-on with *Connect* and *Create™,* you also get deep integration of McGraw-Hill content and content engines right in Blackboard. Whether you're choosing a book for your course or building *Connect®* assignments, all the tools you need are right where you want them—inside of Blackboard.
3. **Seamless Gradebooks.** Are you tired of keeping multiple gradebooks and manually synchronizing grades into Blackboard? We thought so. When a student completes an integrated *Connect* assignment, the grade for that assignment automatically (and instantly) feeds your Blackboard grade center.

4. **A solution for everyone.** Whether your institution is already using Blackboard or you just want to try Blackboard on your own, we have a solution for you. McGraw-Hill and Blackboard can now offer you easy access to industry leading technology and content, whether your campus hosts it, or we do. Be sure to ask your local McGraw-Hill representative for details.

In addition to Blackboard integration, course cartridges for whichever online course management system you use (e.g., WebCT or eCollege) are available for Louwers 5e. Our cartridges are specifically designed to make it easy to navigate and access content online. They are easier than ever to install on the latest version of the course management system available today.

Tegrity Campus, a new McGraw-Hill company, provides a service that makes class time available 24/7 by automatically capturing every lecture in a searchable format for students to review when they study and complete assignments. With a simple one-click start-and-stop process, you capture all computer screens and corresponding audio. Students can replay any part of any class with easy-to-use browser-based viewing on a PC, Mac, iPod or iPad, or any other mobile device.

Educators know that the more students can see, hear, and experience class resources, the better they learn. In fact, studies prove it. With Tegrity Campus, students quickly recall key moments by using Tegrity Campus's unique search feature. This search helps students efficiently find what they need, when they need it, across an entire semester of class recordings. Help turn all your students' study time into learning moments immediately supported by your lecture. To learn more about Tegrity, watch a 2-minute Flash demo at **http://tegritycampus.mhhe.com.**

McGraw-Hill Customer Care Contact Information

At McGraw-Hill, we understand that getting the most from new technology can be challenging. That's why our services don't stop after you purchase our products. You can e-mail our Product Specialists 24 hours a day to get product-training online. Or you can search our knowledge bank of Frequently Asked Questions on our support website. For Customer Support, call **800-331-5094** or visit **www.mhhe.com/support.** One of our Technical Support Analysts will be able to assist you in a timely fashion.

For Instructors...

INSTRUCTOR'S RESOURCE CD-ROM (ISBN 0077425839)

This all-in-one resource includes essential course supplements such as the Test Bank, Solutions Manual, and Instructor PowerPoint® presentations. All items are prepared by the text authors.

ONLINE LEARNING CENTER (OLC)
www.mhhe.com/louwers5e

Instructors will find a wealth of material that complements *Auditing & Assurance Services,* including an electronic version of the Solutions Manual, solutions to the Apollo Shoes Case, **monthly updates from the authors,** and sample syllabi in addition to all of the material available on the Instructor's Resource CD-ROM. A monthly update service, **the Updated Auditor,** provides references and brief summaries of accounting and business articles appearing in popular and business media. Publications excerpted include *The Wall Street Journal, Forbes, Fortune, Bloomberg Businessweek, CFO.com,* and various academic journals. Students and instructors also can access the **Kaplan CPA Review simulations** from the Online Learning Center—all of which are fully integrated into the end-of-chapter material in the textbook.

For Students...

STUDY GUIDE (ISBN 0077425855)

The Study Guide reviews the highlights of *Auditing & Assurance Services* and includes an overview of each chapter in the textbook. Following each chapter summary is a self-assessment section that includes multiple-choice questions, as well as exercises, problems, and simulations. Solutions to all items in the self-assessment section are included. Instructors also can assign study guide content within *Connect Accounting*.

ONLINE LEARNING CENTER (OLC)
www.mhhe.com/louwers5e

The OLC for *Auditing & Assurance Services* provides students with the full Apollo Shoes Case, Kaplan CPA Review simulations, text updates, multiple-choice quizzes, student PowerPoint presentations, and chapter summaries.

Acknowledgments

OUR SINCEREST THANKS...

The American Institute of Certified Public Accountants (AICPA) has generously given permission for liberal quotations from official pronouncements and other AICPA publications, all of which lend authoritative sources to the text. In addition, several publishing houses, professional associations, and accounting firms have granted permission to quote and extract from their copyrighted material. Their cooperation is much appreciated because a great amount of significant auditing thought exists in this wide variety of sources.

A special acknowledgment is due to the Association for Certified Fraud Examiners (ACFE). The ACFE has been a generous contributor to the fraud auditing material in this text. The authors also acknowledge the valuable inclusion of the educational version of ACL software in the fifth edition, which significantly enhances the practical application of the book. A special thanks to Michael K. Shaub for his valuable critique of Chapter 5.

Also, the authors are particularly grateful to Jeannie Folk of College of DuPage for her many insightful comments over the past several years. The feedback she contributed while teaching from our text has contributed greatly to the clarity and accuracy of subsequent editions. Thanks to Helen Roybark for her help with the preparation of tagging for *Connect Accounting*.

We are also sincerely grateful to the following individuals for their participation in the fourth edition review process for *Auditing & Assurance Services*:

Michael Akers,
Marquette University

Sylvia Anderson,
University of Maryland University College

Allen Blay,
Florida State University

Marie Blouin,
Penn State—Harrisburg

Alexander K. Buchholz,
Brooklyn College of the City University of New York

Karl Dahlberg,
Rutgers University

Raymond Elson,
Valdosta State University

Patricia Feller,
Nashville State Community College

Andy Garcia,
Bowling Green State University

Richard Hale,
Midway College

Venkataraman Iyer,
The University of North Carolina at Greensboro

Philip Levine,
Berkeley College

Ramesh Narasimhan,
Montclair State University

Byron Pike,
Minnesota State University—Mankato

Sharon Polansky,
Texas A&M University—Corpus Christi

Dwayne Powell,
Arkansas State University

Pamela Roush,
University of Central Florida

Jaysinha Shinde,
Eastern Illinois University

Frank Venezia,
State University at Albany

Barbara Vinciguerra,
Moravian College

Bobby Waldrup,
University of North Florida

Xu Zhaohui,
University of Houston—Clear Lake

Douglas Ziegenfuss,
Old Dominion University

In addition, we would like to recognize our outstanding staff at McGraw-Hill: Publisher, Tim Vertovec; Sponsoring Editor, Donna Dillon; Editorial Coordinator, Jessica Wiley; Marketing Director, Brad Parkins; Project Manager, Harvey Yep; Designer, Mary Sander; Media Project Manager, Daryl Horrocks; and Full-Service Project Manager, Michelle Gardner. For their encouragement, assistance, and guidance in the production of this book, we are grateful.

Few understand the enormous commitment of time and energy that it takes to put together a textbook. As authors, we are constantly scanning *The Wall Street Journal* and other new outlets for real-world examples to illustrate theoretical discussions, rereading and rewriting each other's work to make sure that key concepts are understandable, and double-checking our solutions to end-of-chapter problems. Among the few who do understand the time and energy commitment are our family members (Barbara Louwers; Sue Ramsay; Karen, Matthew, Joshua, and Adam Sinason; Susan and Meghan Strawser; and Ellen, Jenny, Eric, and Jessica Thibodeau) who uncomplainingly endured endless refrains of "I just need a couple more minutes to finish this section." Words cannot express our gratitude to each of them for their patience and unending support.

Tim Louwers
Bob Ramsay
Dave Sinason
Jerry Strawser
Jay Thibodeau

Auditing and Assurance Services

Our system of capital formation relies upon the confidence of millions of savers to invest in companies. The auditor's opinion is critical to that trust.

James R. Doty, Chairman, Public Company Accounting Oversight Board (PCAOB)

Professional Standards References

Topic	AU/ISA Section	PCAOB Reference*
Overall Objectives of the Independent Auditor and the Conduct of an Audit	200	AU 110, AU 150, AU 201, AU 201, AU 220, AU 230
Consideration of Fraud in a Financial Statement Audit	240	AU 316
Audit Evidence	500	AS 15
Attestation Standards	AT 50	AT 50
Compliance Audits of Governmental Entities and Recipients of Governmental Assistance	935	AU 801

*AU and AT references represent standards issued by the ASB prior to April 16, 2003, that have not been superseded or amended by the PCAOB.

LEARNING OBJECTIVES

You are about to embark on a journey of understanding how auditors work to keep the capital markets safe and secure for the investing public. You should know that students demonstrate success in the auditing course quite differently than they do in other accounting courses. For example, when taking financial accounting, students typically demonstrate success by correctly identifying the proper journal entry for a given set of facts and circumstances. In auditing, success is typically demonstrated by completing multiple choice and short answer questions based on the professional standards that regulate the auditing process. Overall, this book provides you with a comprehensive set of materials that will allow you to master these professional auditing standards. Chapter 1 provides an introduction to the auditing and assurance profession.

Your objectives are to be able to:

LO 1-1 Define *information risk* and explain how the financial statement auditing process helps to reduce this risk, thereby reducing the cost of capital for a company.

LO 1-2	Define and contrast *financial statement auditing, attestation,* and *assurance type* services.	LO 1-5	Describe the organization of public accounting firms and identify the various services that they offer.
LO 1-3	Describe and define the assertions that management makes about the recognition, measurement, presentation, and disclosure of the financial statements and explain why auditors use them as the focal point of the audit.	LO 1-6	Describe the audits and auditors in governmental, internal, and operational auditing.
		LO 1-7	List and explain the requirements for becoming a certified information professional.
LO 1-4	Define professional skepticism and explain its key characteristics.		

USER DEMAND FOR RELIABLE INFORMATION

LEARNING OBJECTIVE 1-1
Define *information risk* and explain how the financial statement auditing process helps to reduce this risk, thereby reducing the cost of capital for a company.

Enron, WorldCom, HealthSouth, Bernard Madoff Investments, Parmalat, Satyam, Tyco, Fannie Mae—the list of financial accounting frauds that have been uncovered in recent years has been shocking to the business community. Investor confidence was understandably shaken because investors depend on reliable financial statement information to make their investment decisions about a company. So, where were the auditors? How could they have missed such high-profile frauds? These questions are not easy to answer. Before we attempt to address these, we must first explain the vital role that information assurance providers (such as financial statement auditors) play in supplying key decision makers (management, investors, and creditors) with useful, understandable, and timely information. When you have a better understanding of why auditing has been so critical in establishing America's capital markets as the strongest in the world, we will explore the issues surrounding the financial accounting frauds identified here. Because many of you likely are planning to enter the public accounting profession, we hope that you will equip yourself with this knowledge so that you may help avoid similar problems in the future and play a key role in maintaining public confidence in both the auditing profession and the capital markets.

Information and Information Risk

All businesses make a countless number of decisions each and every day. Decisions to purchase or sell goods or services, lend money, enter into employment agreements, or buy or sell investments depend in large part on the quality of useful information. These decisions affect *business risk,* the chance a company takes that customers will buy from competitors, that product lines will become obsolete, that taxes will increase, that government contracts will be lost, or that employees will go on strike. In other words, **business risk** is *the risk that an entity will fail to meet its objectives.* If the company fails to meet its objectives enough times, the company may ultimately fail. To minimize these risks and take advantage of other opportunities presented in today's competitive business environment, decision makers such as chief executive officers (CEOs) demand *timely, relevant,* and *reliable* information. Similarly, investors and creditors demand high-quality information to make educated financial decisions. Information professionals (such as accountants, auditors, and other information assurance providers) help satisfy this demand.

Four environmental conditions increase user demand for relevant, reliable information:

1. *Complexity.* Events and transactions in today's global business environment are numerous and often very complicated. You may have studied derivative securities and hedging activities in other accounting courses, but investors and other decision makers may not have your level of expertise when dealing with these complex transactions. Furthermore, they are not trained to collect, compile, and summarize the key operating information themselves. They need the services of information professionals to make the information more understandable for their decision processes.

2. *Remoteness.* Decision makers are usually separated from current and potential business partners not only by a lack of expertise but also by distance and time. Investors may not be able to visit distant locations to check up on their investments. They need to employ full-time information professionals to do the work they cannot do for themselves.
3. *Time-sensitivity.* Today's economic environment requires businesses, investors, and other financial information users to make decisions more rapidly than ever before. The ability to promptly obtain high-quality information is essential to businesses that want to remain competitive in our global business environment.
4. *Consequences.* Decisions can involve significant investment of resources. The consequences are so important that reliable information, obtained and verified by information professionals, is an absolute necessity. Enron's aftermath provides a graphic example of how decisions affect individuals' (as well as companies') financial security and well-being. Enron's stock dropped from $90 to $0.90 in little more than a year, leaving employees who had invested their life savings in the company virtually penniless. To put this drop in perspective, an investor's $5 million investment in Enron stock in 2000 (enough for an enjoyable retirement) was worth only $50,000 a year later.

AUDITING INSIGHT — The Consequences of Fraudulent Financial Information

Bernard Madoff, a former chairman of the NASDAQ Stock Market and a respected Wall Street adviser and broker for the past 50 years, was arrested after his sons turned him in for running "a giant Ponzi scheme," bilking investors out of an estimated $50 billion. Many investors, including actors, investment bankers, politicians, and sports personalities, lost their life savings. Some who had already retired, now in their 70s and 80s, were forced to go back to work. Others lost their retirement homes. Charities and pensions that had invested heavily were wiped out.

Although some of the world's most knowledgeable investors fell prey to the scam, numerous red flags were present for all who were wise enough to see them. First, his fund returned 13–16% per year, every year, no matter how the markets performed. Second, his stated strategy of buying stocks and related options to hedge downside risk could not have occurred because the number of options necessary for such a strategy did not exist. Third, although his firm claimed to manage billions of dollars, its auditing firm had only three employees, including a secretary and a 78-year-old accountant who lived in Florida.

Source: "Fund Fraud Hits Big Names," *The Wall Street Journal*, December 13, 2008, pp. A1, A7; "Fees, Even Returns and Auditor All Raised Flags," *The Wall Street Journal*, December 13, 2008, p. A7; "Top Broker Accused of $50 Billion Fraud," *The Wall Street Journal*, December 12, 2008, pp. A1, A14; "Probe Eyes Audit Files, Role of Aide to Madoff," *The Wall Street Journal*, December 23, 2008, A1, A14.

A further complication in effective decision making is the presence of information risk. **Information risk** is *the probability that the information circulated by a company will be false or misleading.* Decision makers usually obtain their information from companies or organizations with which they want to conduct business, to provide loans, or to buy or sell stock. Because the primary source of information is the target company itself, an incentive exists for that company's management to make their business or service appear to be better than it actually may be, to put their best foot forward. As a result, preparers and issuers of financial information (directors, managers, accountants, and other people employed in a business) might benefit by giving false, misleading, or overly optimistic information. This potential *conflict of interest* between information providers and users, along with financial statement frauds such as those of **Enron** and **WorldCom,** leads to a natural skepticism on the part of users. Thus, they depend on information professionals to serve as independent and objective intermediaries who will lend credibility to the information. This *lending of credibility* to information is known as providing **assurance**. When the assurance is provided for specific assertions made by management, we refer to the assurance provided as **attestation**. And, when the assertions are embodied in a company's financial statements, we refer to the attestation as **auditing**.

> ⌕ REVIEW CHECKPOINTS
>
> 1.1 What is business risk?
> 1.2 What conditions increase the demand for reliable information?
> 1.3 What risk creates a demand for independent and objective outsiders to provide assurance to decision makers?

AUDITING, ATTESTATION, AND ASSURANCE SERVICES

LEARNING OBJECTIVE 1-2
Define and contrast *financial statement auditing, attestation,* and *assurance type services.*

Now that you understand why decision makers need independent information professionals to provide assurance on key information, we further define auditing and expand the discussion of attestation and assurance services in this section and explain their roles in today's information economy.

Definition of Financial Statement Auditing

The focus of this book is on the financial statement auditing process, by far and away the most common type of auditing and assurance service provided in today's market. Many years ago, the American Accounting Association (AAA) Committee on Basic Auditing Concepts provided a very useful general definition of *auditing* as follows:

> *Auditing* is a systematic process of objectively obtaining and evaluating evidence regarding assertions about economic actions and events to ascertain the degree of correspondence between the assertions and established criteria and communicating the results to interested users.[1]

A closer look at the definition reveals several ideas that are important to any type of auditing engagement. Auditing is a *systematic process.* It is a purposeful and logical process and is based on the discipline of a structured approach to reaching final decisions. It has a logical starting point, proceeds along established guidelines, and has a logical conclusion. It is not haphazard, unplanned, or unstructured.

The process involves obtaining and evaluating *evidence.* Evidence consists of all types of influences that ultimately guide auditors' decisions and relates to *assertions made by management about economic actions and events.* When beginning a financial statement audit engagement, an independent auditor is provided financial statements and other disclosures by management and thus obtains management's implicit assertions about economic actions and events (that the assets on the balance sheet really exist, that revenue recorded on the income statement really occurred, that the list of liabilities on the balance sheet is complete, etc.) as well as assertions that the financial statement disclosures are fairly presented.

External auditors generally begin work with explicit representations from management, financial statement numbers and information disclosed in footnotes, and then set out to obtain evidence to prove or disprove these representations. Other auditors, however, often are not provided with explicit representations. An internal auditor may be assigned to evaluate the cost effectiveness of the company's policy to lease, rather than to purchase, heavy equipment. A governmental auditor may be assigned to determine whether goals of providing equal educational opportunities have been achieved with federal grant funds. Oftentimes, these latter two types of auditors must develop the explicit performance criteria or benchmarks for themselves.

The purpose of obtaining and evaluating evidence is to ascertain the degree of correspondence between the assertions made by the information provider and established criteria. Auditors will ultimately communicate their findings to interested users. To communicate in an efficient and understandable manner, auditors and users must have

---

[1] American Accounting Association Committee on Basic Auditing Concepts, *A Statement of Basic Auditing Concepts* (Sarasota, FL: American Accounting Association, 1973).

EXHIBIT 1.1
Overview of Financial Statement Auditing

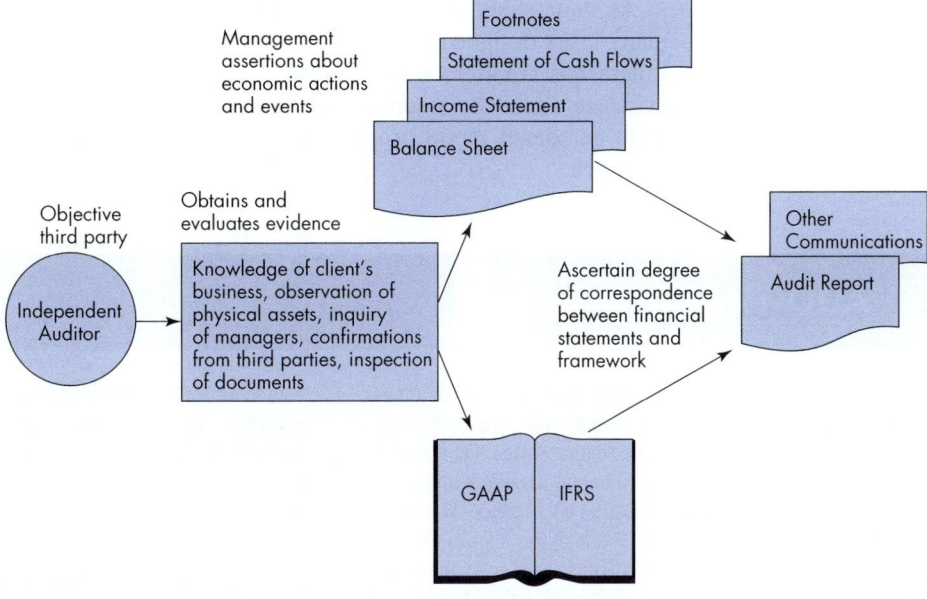

a common basis for measuring and describing financial information. This basis is the established criteria essential for effective communication.

Established criteria may be found in a variety of sources. For independent auditors, the criterion is whatever the applicable financial reporting framework is, whether it is accounting principles generally accepted in the U.S. (GAAP) or international financial reporting standards (IFRS). Internal Revenue Service (IRS) agents rely heavily on criteria specified in the Internal Revenue Code. Governmental auditors may rely on criteria established in legislation or regulatory agency rules. Bank examiners and state insurance board auditors look to definitions, regulations, and rules of law. Internal and governmental auditors rely a great deal on financial and managerial models of efficiency and effectiveness. All auditors rely to some extent on the sometimes elusive criteria of general truth and fairness. Exhibit 1.1 depicts an overview of financial statement auditing.

The American Accounting Association definition is broad and general enough to encompass external, internal, and governmental auditing. The more specific viewpoint of external auditors in public accounting practice is reflected in a statement of the main objective of a financial statement audit by the American Institute of Certified Public Accountants (AICPA), the public accounting community's professional association:

> The purpose of an audit is to enhance the degree of confidence that intended users can place in the financial statements. This is achieved by the expression of an opinion by the auditor on whether the financial statements are prepared, in all material respects, in accordance with an applicable financial reporting framework. In the case of most general purpose frameworks, that opinion is on whether the financial statements are presented fairly, in all material respects, in accordance with the framework. An audit conducted in accordance with generally accepted auditing standards and relevant ethical requirements enables the auditor to form that opinion. (AU 200.11).[2]

---

[2] The *Statements on Auditing Standards (SASs)* and *Statements on Standards for Attestation Engagements (SSAEs)* are authoritative AICPA pronouncements on auditing and attestation theory and practice. *Statements on Auditing Procedure (SAPs)* numbers 1–54 were codified into SAS 1 in 1972. Statements on Auditing Standards are issued periodically by the Auditing Standards Board (ASB). Taken together, the SASs form the basis for U.S. generally accepted auditing standards (GAAS). You can find the number of the most recent *SAS* or *SSAE* by referring to the AICPA website (www.aicpa.org). Throughout this text, *SAS* references are followed by parenthetical section numbers (e.g., AU 200), which refer to the Codification of Statements on Auditing Standards published by the AICPA. *SSAE* references are followed by parenthetical section numbers (e.g., AT 101), which refer to the Attestation Standards published by the AICPA.

As your study of external auditing continues, you will find that auditors perform many tasks designed to reduce the risk of giving an inappropriate opinion on financial statements. Auditors are careful to work for trustworthy clients, to gather and analyze evidence about the assertions in financial statements, and to take steps to ensure that audit personnel report properly on the financial statements when adverse information is known.

AUDITING INSIGHT

Although most of the largest public accounting firms (collectively referred to as the "Big 4") trace their roots to the turn of the 19th century, auditing in the United States has a rich history. When the Pilgrims had a financial dispute with the English investors who financed their trip, an "auditor" was sent to resolve the difference. George Washington sent his financial records to the Comptroller of the Treasury to be audited before he could be reimbursed for expenditures he made during the Revolutionary War. One of the first Congress's actions in 1789 was to set up an auditor to review and certify public accounts. Even the "modern" concept of an audit committee is not so modern; the bylaws of the Potomac Company, formed in 1784 to construct locks on the Potomac River to increase commerce, required that three shareholders annually examine the company's records.

Source: D. Flesher, G. Previts, and W. Samson, "Auditing in the United States: A Historical Perspective," *Abacus* 41 (2005), pp. 21–39.

Attestation Engagements

Many people appreciate the value of auditors' attestations on historical financial statements, and, as a result, they have found other types of information to which certified public accountants (CPAs) can *attest*. The all-inclusive definition of an **attest engagement** is

> An engagement in which a practitioner is engaged to issue a report on subject matter, or an assertion about subject matter that is the responsibility of another party. (AT 101.01)

By comparing the AAA's earlier definition of auditing with the definition of attestation, you can see that the auditing definition is a specific type of attestation engagement. According to the earlier definition, in an audit engagement, an auditor (more specific than a *practitioner*) issues a report on assertions (financial statements) that are the responsibility of management. Other examples of attestation engagements completed by CPAs (discussed more in Module A) appear in the following box.

Examples of Attestation Engagements

- **Agreed Upon Procedures Engagements** (AT 201), such as verifying inventory quantities and locations.
- **Financial Forecasts and Projections** (AT 301), such as analysis of prospective or hypothetical "what-if" financial statements for some time period *in the future*.
- **Reporting on Pro Forma Financial Information** (AT 401), such as retroactively analyzing the effect of a proposed or consummated transaction on the *historical* financial statements "as if" that transaction had already occurred.
- **An Examination of an Entity's Internal Control Over Financial Reporting that Is Integrated with an Audit of Its Financial Statements** (AT 501), focused on the design and operating effectiveness of an entity's internal control over financial reporting.
- **Compliance Attestation** (AT 601), such as ascertaining a client's compliance with debt covenants.
- **Examination of Management's Discussion and Analysis** (AT 701), prepared pursuant to the rules and regulations of the Securities and Exchange Commission (SEC).
- **Reporting on Controls at a Service Organization (AT 801)**, such as organizations that provide outsourced processes that are likely to be relevant to the user entities' internal control over financial reporting.

AUDITING INSIGHT — Fore!

Wilson Sporting Goods Company is using CPAs to prove that amateur golfers can hit Wilson's Ultra golf ball farther than they can hit competitors' golf balls. Wilson says the CPAs certify that Wilson's Ultra outdistances its competitors by an average of 5.7 yards per drive. While Marlene Baddeloo, the engagement manager for the accounting firm that oversees Wilson's golf ball competitions, concedes "anyone could pace off a golf driving range to see how far a ball goes," she says firm staffers have checked that Wilson employees haven't doctored the results at more than 30 driving ranges. "We also make sure the amateurs participating aren't affiliated with Wilson or its competitors and haven't been paid to participate." Providing assurance on golf ball distance is certainly a unique engagement for a CPA firm, but it sure makes the firm's employees happy. "Our personnel love . . . [to] wear shorts and spend the day out in the air," says Ms. Baddeloo. "I get a lot of volunteers."

Source: Lee Berton, "After This, CPAs May Take Over Instant-Replay Duties for Football," *The Wall Street Journal*, July 9, 1991, p. B1.

Assurance Services

While *auditing* refers specifically to expressing an opinion on financial statements and *attestation* refers to expressing an opinion on an expanded set of financial information beyond financial statements or a specified element of financial statement information, *assurance services* include many areas of information, including nonfinancial information. The following Auditing Insight box indicates how the quality of information can assist both buyers and sellers in today's market.

AUDITING INSIGHT

Exhibit 1.2 shows two 1976 **Topps** Mike Schmidt baseball cards. The card on the right was offered on eBay with the seller's representation that the card was in Near Mint/Mint condition. This representation is a standard description and is the equivalent of a grade 8 on a standard 10-point scale used in grading the quality of a trading card. The card was purchased on **eBay** for $11.55.

Within a week, a second 1976 Topps Mike Schmidt baseball card was sold on eBay. Again, this card was offered with the seller's representation that the card was in Near Mint/Mint condition (card on the left). The only difference was that this card had been sent to **Professional Sports Authenticator** (PSA), a company that verifies the authenticity and quality of sports items. Note that it does not buy or sell sports merchandise; it acts only as an independent third party expressing a professional opinion regarding the merchandise in question. This card sold for $22.53.

The only difference between the two transactions was that the buyers of the card on the right had more information concerning the risk inherent in the transaction. Why was the first transaction riskier? What were the buyers' concerns? Were the concerns only from intentional misstatements? How did the grading of the card by PSA reduce these concerns? What are the incentives for PSA to grade the card accurately? How does the business of PSA relate to the profession of auditing?

EXHIBIT 1.2
Professional Sports Authenticators as Third-Party Assurors

Although the primary focus of our earlier discussion of information risk was in the context of economic decisions, information risk is present whenever someone must make a decision without having complete knowledge. The AICPA expanded the profession's traditional focus on accounting information to include all types of information, both financial and nonfinancial. The expanded services are collectively referred to as **assurance services,** which are defined by the AICPA as independent professional services that improve the quality of information, or its context, for decision makers. The major elements, and boundaries, of the definition are

- *Independence.* CPAs want to preserve their attestation and audit reputations and competitive advantages by preserving integrity and objectivity when performing assurance services.[3]
- *Professional services.* Virtually all work performed by CPAs (accounting, auditing, data management, taxation, management, marketing, finance) is defined as a professional service as long as it involves some element of judgment based on education and experience.
- *Improving the quality of information, or its context.* The emphasis is on information, CPAs' traditional stock in trade. CPAs can enhance quality by assuring users about the reliability and relevance of information, and these two features are closely related to the familiar credibility-lending products of attestation and audit services. *Context* is relevance in a different light. For assurance services, improving the context of information refers not to the information itself, but to how the information is used in a decision-making context. An example would be providing key information in a database that could be used by management to make important decisions.
- *For decision makers.* They are the consumers of assurance services, and they personify the consumer focus of new and different professional work. They may or may not be the client that pays the fee, and they may or may not be one of the parties to an assertion or other information. The decision makers are the beneficiaries of the assurance services. Depending upon the assignment, decision makers may be a very small, targeted group (e.g., managers of a database) or a large targeted group (e.g., potential investors interested in a mutual fund manager's performance).

Examples of Assurance Services

While they are subsets of assurance services, attestation and audit services are highly structured and intended to be useful for large groups of decision makers (e.g., investors, lenders). On the other hand, assurance services other than audit and attestation services tend to be more customized for use by smaller, targeted groups of decision makers. In this sense, nonaudit assurance services bear some resemblance to consulting services. For example, as more and more companies and organizations seek to demonstrate their efforts related to corporate social responsibility and/or going "green," demand is increasing for assurance services related to sustainability and/or environmental reporting. We also present a few more examples of assurance services to illustrate the variety of services that fall under the assurance service umbrella. Some will look familiar and others may defy imagination. Be aware, however, that public accounting firms must pick and choose the services that they wish to provide to the market, based on the expertise that lies within the firm. Nobody maintains that all public accounting firms will want or be able to provide all the assurance services.

- XBRL (eXtensible Business Reporting Language) reporting.
- Enterprise risk management assessment.
- Information risk assessment and assurance.
- Third-party reimbursement maximization.

---

[3] A survey commissioned by the AICPA found that CPAs are viewed more positively than any other business professional by both business decision makers and investors. Sixty-nine percent of investors and 74 percent of business decision makers feel that "CPAs have a unique perspective that is valuable when making business and financial decisions, even when those decisions are not directly related to accounting." In terms of attributes ascribed to CPAs, they are most associated with integrity, competence, and objectivity ("Brand Research Shows CPAs Viewed Positively in Marketplace," *AICPA News Update,* October 20, 2008).

- Rental property operations review.
- Customer satisfaction surveys.
- Evaluation of investment management policies.
- Fraud and illegal acts prevention and deterrence.
- Accounts receivable review and cash enhancement.
- Internal audit outsourcing.

Attestation and audit services are special types of assurance services, but consulting services are not. In providing consulting services, CPAs use their professional skills and experiences to provide recommendations to a client for outcomes such as information system design and operation; in assurance services, the focus is entirely on the information that decision makers use. However, like consulting services, assurance services have a "customer focus," and CPAs develop assurance services that add value for customers (decision makers). Exhibit 1.3 depicts the relationships among assurance, attestation, and auditing services.

Although audits are specific types of assurance engagements, and auditors can be described more generally as information assurors, hereafter we will use the term *auditor* instead of *information assuror* because of the specific responsibilities that auditors have under GAAS, as well as under regulatory bodies such as the SEC and the Public Company Accounting Oversight Board (PCAOB). However, many of the procedures that auditors perform as part of an audit engagement are similar to those performed as part of other information assurance engagements. We will point out these shared procedures when appropriate.

AUDITING INSIGHT — The Future of Assurance Services and Financial Reporting

Advances in information technology have allowed for more efficient reporting platforms that better meet the needs of decision makers. In that spirit, the AICPA is currently focused on a number of initiatives to help auditors meet the needs of their clients. Among the initiatives, the need to help companies with XBRL implementations for SEC reporting has taken center stage. XBRL (also referred to by the SEC as interactive data), is an information format designed specifically for business reporting. Through the "tagging" of specific data items (cash, inventory, sales transactions, etc.), XBRL facilitates the collection, summarization, and reporting of financial information in a medium that users can easily transform for their own decision-making purposes. For example, once the XBRL-formatted data is downloaded, users are able to easily compare information across companies, across financial reporting frameworks (such as IFRS and U.S. GAAP), and even across countries using different currency denominations. Information can be tagged early in the data collection process (at point of sale) such that preparers can easily collect and summarize financial information. Combining financial information from multiple accounting information systems in different company divisions is no longer the nightmare that it once was. The SEC now requires the 500 largest U.S. public companies and foreign private issuers listed with the SEC to use XBRL for SEC filings; all other public companies were to begin reporting in XBRL in 2010 or 2011, with all public companies filing in XBRL within the following three years.

Source: "The Shifting Paradigm in Business Reporting and Assurance," AICPA Assurance Services Executive Committee, 2008; and SOP 09-01, "Performing Agreed-Upon Procedures Engagements That Address the Completeness, Accuracy, or Consistency of XBRL-Tagged Data," both available through the AICPA's Website (www.aicpa.org).

EXHIBIT 1.3
The Relationships among Auditing, Attestation, and Assurance Engagements

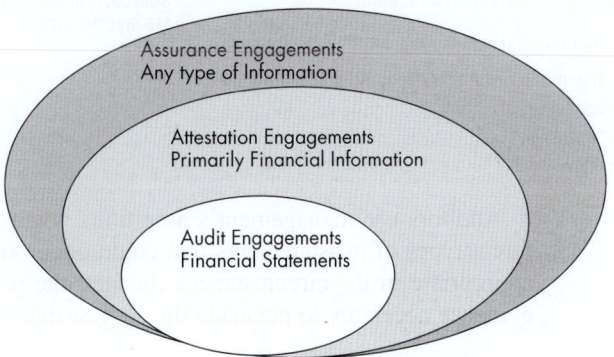

↳ REVIEW CHECKPOINTS

1.4 Define and explain auditing. What would you answer if asked by an anthropology major, "What do auditors do?"
1.5 What is an *attest engagement*?
1.6 What is an *assurance engagement*?
1.7 In what ways are assurance services similar to attestation services (including audits of financial statements)?
1.8 What are the four major elements of the broad definition of assurance services?

MANAGEMENT'S FINANCIAL STATEMENT ASSERTIONS

LEARNING OBJECTIVE 1-3
Describe and define the assertions that management makes about the recognition, measurement, presentation and disclosure of the financial statements and explain why auditors use them as the focal point of the audit.

From your earlier studies, you know that accounting is the process of recording, classifying, and summarizing into financial statements a company's transactions that create assets, liabilities, equities, revenues, expenses, and related disclosures. It is the means of satisfying users' demands for financial information that arise from the forces of complexity, remoteness, time-sensitivity, and consequences.

Auditing does not include the function of financial report production. The function of **financial reporting** is to provide statements of financial position (balance sheets), results of operations (income statements, statements of shareholders' equity, and statements of comprehensive income), changes in cash flows (statements of cash flows), and accompanying disclosures (footnotes) to outside decision makers who do not have access to management's internal sources of information. A company's accountants, under the direction of its management, perform this function. In fact, auditing standards emphasize that the financial statements are the responsibility of a company's management. Thus, the financial statements contain management's assertions about *transactions and events* that occurred during the period being audited (primarily the income statement, statement of shareholders' equity, statement of comprehensive income, and statement of cash flows), assertions about *account balances* at the end of the period (primarily the balance sheet), and assertions about financial statement *presentation and disclosure* (primarily the footnote disclosures).

▽ AUDITING INSIGHT — Sarbanes-Oxley and Management's Responsibility for Financial Reporting

Congress passed the Sarbanes-Oxley Act in 2002 in an attempt to address a number of weaknesses found in corporate financial reporting in the wake of recent accounting scandals. One of its most important provisions (Section 302) states that key company officials must certify the financial statements. Certification means that the company's chief executive officer and chief financial officer must sign a statement indicating

1. They have read the financial statements.
2. They are not aware of any false or misleading statements (or any key omitted disclosures).
3. They believe that the financial statements present an accurate picture of the company's financial condition.

Management must also make assertions regarding the effectiveness of the company's internal controls over financial reporting.

Source: U.S. Congress, *Sarbanes-Oxley Act of 2002*, Pub. L. No. 107-204, 116 Stat. 745 (2002).

Auditors use management's assertions when assessing risks by determining the different types of misstatements that could occur and developing audit procedures that are appropriate in the circumstances. In fact, the procedures are completed to provide the evidence necessary to persuade the auditor that there is no material misstatement related

EXHIBIT 1.4 Management Assertions

(1) PCAOB Assertions	ASB Assertions (2) Assertions about Events and Transactions	ASB Assertions (3) Assertions about Account Balances	ASB Assertions (4) Assertions about Presentation and Footnote Disclosures	(5) Key Questions
Existence or occurrence	Occurrence	Existence	Occurrence	Do the assets listed really exist? Did the recorded sales transactions really occur?
Rights and obligations		Rights and obligations	Rights and obligations	Does the company really own the assets? Are related legal responsibilities identified?
Completeness	Completeness	Completeness	Completeness	Are the financial statements (including footnotes) complete? Were all transactions recorded?
	Cutoff			Are transactions at the beginning or end of a period included in the proper period?
Valuation or allocation	Accuracy	Valuation and allocation	Accuracy	Are the accounts valued correctly?
			Valuation and allocation	Are expenses allocated to the period(s) benefited?
Presentation and disclosure	Classification		Classification	Were all transactions recorded in the correct accounts?
			Understandability	Are the disclosures understandable to users?

to each of the relevant assertions identified for an engagement. Auditors then report to the financial statement users that the assertions are reliable by expressing an opinion that the company's presentation of financial position, results of operations, and cash flows are fairly presented in accordance with generally accepted accounting principles. As you study this section, keep in mind the importance of the management assertions.

Exhibit 1.4 provides a list of all of management's assertions and some of the key questions that the audit team must address. Note that column 1 in Exhibit 1.4 denotes the traditional management assertions, currently used by the PCAOB.[4] The Auditing Standards Board (ASB)[5] provided an additional classification of management assertions (columns 2 through 4 in Exhibit 1.4). You will note that the ASB assertions, while in direct alignment with the PCAOB assertions, do provide greater detail and clarity for students of auditing to conceptualize. As a result, largely all of the firms auditing public companies with international operations feature the ASB assertions to guide in their auditing processes. The key questions (column 5) indicate how each of these assertions, both PCAOB and ASB, are utilized when evaluating specific aspects of management's financial statements and disclosures. Each of the assertions is defined and described in detail in the following sections, organized along the lines of the PCAOB assertions identified in column 1, with the aligned ASB assertion following in parenthesis.

---

[4] The Public Company Accounting Oversight Board (PCAOB) is a nonprofit corporation established by Congress to oversee the audits of public companies. The Securities and Exchange Commission (SEC) has oversight authority, including approval of all standards and rules. The PCAOB is discussed in more detail in Chapter 2.

[5] The (ASB) was established by the profession to issue auditing standards. Standards issued by the ASB apply to audits of all companies. The ASB is discussed in more detail in Chapter 2.

Existence or Occurrence (Existence, Occurrence)

Numbers on financial statements are meaningless unless they *faithfully represent* actual transactions, assets, and liabilities of the company. (*Note*: As a general rule, the *occurrence* transaction relates to events and transactions (as indicated in column 2 of Exhibit 1.4), while the *existence* assertion relates to account balances (as indicated in column 3). Therefore, auditors must view the balance sheet as management's assertions that reported assets, liabilities, and equities actually exist. To test the existence assertion, auditors count cash and inventory, confirm receivables and insurance policies with customers, and perform other procedures to obtain evidence whether management's assertion is in fact correct. Similarly, management asserts that each of the revenue and expense transactions summarized on the income statement or disclosed in the financial statement footnotes really occurred during the period being audited. As an auditor, you must develop audit procedures to ensure that the reported sales transactions really occurred and were not created to fraudulently inflate the company's profits.

AUDITING INSIGHT Q: When Is a Sale of Computer Disk Drives Not a Sale?
A: When They Are Bricks.

Miniscribe was a manufacturer of computer disk drives. When sales did not occur at a sufficient level to support the company's efforts to obtain outside financing, management generated fictitious sales to fraudulently boost the company's net income. After first sending obsolete inventory to customers who never ordered the goods, the company packaged bricks (about the same size and shape as the company's disk drives of that time) in disk drive boxes and shipped them to "customers" that were in fact company-owned warehouses.

Rights and Obligations

The objective related to rights and obligations is to determine that amounts reported as assets of the company represent its property rights and that the amounts reported as liabilities represent its obligations. In simpler terms, the objective is to obtain evidence about *owning* and *owing*. You should be careful about *ownership*, however, because the idea includes assets (rights) for which a company does not actually hold title. For example, an auditor will have a specific objective of obtaining evidence about the amounts capitalized for leased property. Likewise, *owing* includes accounting liabilities a company may not yet be legally obligated to pay. For example, specific objectives would include obtaining evidence about the estimated liability for product warranties. The auditor also has an obligation to ensure that the details of the company's obligations are disclosed in the footnotes to the financial statements.

Completeness (Completeness, Cutoff)

Management asserts that all transactions, events, assets, liabilities, and equities that should have been recorded have been recorded. In addition, management asserts that all disclosures that should have been discussed in the footnotes have been included. Thus, auditors' specific objectives include obtaining evidence to determine whether, for example, all inventory on hand is included, all inventory on consignment is included, all accounts payable are included, all notes payable are included, all expenses are recorded, and so forth. A verbal or written management representation saying that all transactions are included in the accounts is not considered a sufficient basis for deciding whether the completeness assertion is true. Auditors need to obtain persuasive evidence about completeness.

Cutoff is a special aspect of completeness. **Cutoff** refers to accounting for revenue, expense, and other transactions in the *proper period* (neither postponing some recordings to the next period nor accelerating next-period transactions into the current-year accounts). Simple cutoff errors can occur when (1) a company records late December sales invoices for goods not actually shipped until early January; (2) a company records cash receipts through the end of the week (e.g., Friday, January 4) and the last batch for the year should have been processed on December 31; (3) a company fails to record accruals for expenses incurred but not yet paid, thus understating both expenses and liabilities; (4) a company fails to record purchases of materials shipped FOB shipping point but not yet received and, therefore, not included in the ending inventory, thus understating both inventory and accounts payable; and (5) a company fails to accrue unbilled revenue through the fiscal year-end for customers on a cycle billing system, thus understating both revenue and accounts receivable. In auditor's jargon, the **cutoff date** generally refers to the client's year-end balance sheet date.

Valuation and Allocation (Accuracy or Valuation)

Management asserts that the transactions and events have been recorded accurately and that account balances have been valued correctly. The audit objective related to valuation and allocation is to determine whether proper values have been assigned to assets, liabilities, and equities. Accuracy refers to the appropriate recording of the transactions involving these items. Auditors obtain evidence about specific valuations and mathematical accuracy by comparing vendors' invoices to inventory prices, obtaining lower-of-cost-or-market data, evaluating collectability of receivables, recalculating depreciation schedules, and so forth. Many valuation, accuracy, and allocation decisions amount to decisions about the proper application of GAAP (or IFRS).

Presentation and Disclosure (Classification, Understandability)

Management asserts that all transactions and events have been presented correctly and that all relevant information has been disclosed to financial statement users, usually in the footnotes to the financial statements. This assertion embodies several different components. First, disclosures must be relevant (e.g., footnote disclosure of important accounting policies) and reliable.

Second, transactions must be classified in the correct accounts (e.g., proper current and long-term balance sheet classification of liabilities). To test this assertion, auditors perform audit procedures such as analyzing repair and maintenance expenses to ensure that that they should in fact be expensed rather than capitalized. Similarly, auditors will test from the opposite direction, examining additions to buildings and equipment to ensure that transactions that should have been expensed were not in fact capitalized.

AUDITING INSIGHT — Is Your Telephone Bill an Asset?

WorldCom routinely leased telephone lines from local telephone companies (basically the last segment entering subscribers' homes). However, rather than record the cost of these lines as an expense on the income statement, the company capitalized them as assets on the balance sheet, resulting in an estimated $11 *billion* fraudulent overstatement of net income. WorldCom management argued that because the leased lines were not fully used to capacity, the expense should be deferred until the lines started to produce revenue (i.e., the matching concept).

Moreover, because they controlled the telephone lines as a result of the long-term lease agreements, no one else could use the telephone lines and, therefore, the exclusivity rights should be treated as an asset. (This explanation is analogous to your saying that your monthly phone bill expense is really an asset because no one else can use your phone number while you use it.) An internal auditor uncovered the fraud and reported her findings to the company's board of directors.

Third, to be useful to decision makers, information must be understandable. *Statement of Financial Accounting Concepts (SFAC) No. 2*, "Qualitative Characteristics of Accounting Information," defines *understandability* as "the quality of information that enables users to perceive its significance." The responsibility levied on auditors is to make sure that the financial statements are "transparent." In other words, investors should be able to understand how the company is doing by reading a its financial statements and footnotes and not have to rely on additional financial experts or lawyers to help them figure out what the fine print is saying. Another way to regard this assertion is to ask whether the disclosures have been written in *plain English*.

> ### AUDITING INSIGHT Say What?
>
> Financial analysts generally regarded Enron's financial disclosures in its annual report as incomprehensible. In fact, Enron's management took pride in the fact that no one could figure out what they were doing to generate incredibly high revenues. A 2003 Congressional Joint Committee on Taxation concluded that Enron's tax avoidance schemes (including 692 partnerships in the Cayman Islands) were "so complex that the IRS has been unable to understand them" (*The New York Times*, February 13, 2003). Following is an excerpt from *Enron's 2001 Annual Report* describing some of its business activities:
>
> Trading Activities. Enron offers price risk management services to wholesale, commercial and industrial customers through a variety of financial and other instruments including forward contracts involving physical delivery, swap agreements, which require payments to (or receipt of payments from) counter-parties based on the differential between a fixed and variable price for the commodity, options and other contractual arrangements. Interest rate risks and foreign currency risks associated with the fair value of the commodity portfolio are managed using a variety of financial instruments, including financial futures.

Unfortunately, due in large part to the incomprehensibility of its financial disclosures, no one realized the extreme risks that the company was taking until it was too late. The company, which reported the fifth highest revenues in the United States in 2000, filed for bankruptcy in 2001.

Importance of Assertions

The financial statement assertions are important and can be difficult to comprehend. The key questions that must be answered about each assertion become the *focal points* for audit procedures. In other words, audit procedures are the means to answer the key questions posed by management's financial statement assertions. When evidence-gathering audit procedures are specified, you need to be able to relate the evidence produced by each procedure to one or more specific assertions. In essence, the secret to writing and reviewing a list of audit procedures is to ask, "Which assertion(s) does this procedure produce evidence about?" Then ask, "Does the list of procedures (the *audit plan*) cover all the assertions?" Exhibit 1.5 illustrates how the assertions relate to the financial statements.

While standard-setting bodies such as the PCAOB and ASB try to neatly categorize transactions, balances, and disclosures by the different assertions, the *real world* is seldom as orderly. For example, while cutoff procedures provide evidence about completeness, they also provide evidence about valuation and existence. Prematurely recording sales transactions inflates revenue and/or asset values because the transaction did not *occur* by the income statement date. Similarly, if a cutoff test shows a delay in recording a liability, the liability is not only incomplete, but *undervalued* as well. Thus, errors in financial statements may affect multiple management assertions.

> ### ↳ REVIEW CHECKPOINTS
>
> 1.9 What is the difference between financial statement auditing and financial accounting?
>
> 1.10 List and briefly explain each of the Auditing Standards Board's management assertions. List some key questions that auditors must answer with evidence related to each management assertion.
>
> 1.11 Why is the Auditing Standards Board's set of management assertions important to auditors? Do these assertions differ from those included in PCAOB standards? If so, how are they different?

EXHIBIT 1.5 Management Assertions and Their Relationship to the Financial Statements

STATEMENT OF FINANCIAL CONDITION
APOLLO SHOES INC.
in thousands

As of December 31	2012	2011
Assets		
Cash	$3,245	$3,509
Accounts Receivable (Net of Allowances of $1,263 and 210, respectively) (Note 3)	15,148	2,738
Inventory (Note 4)	15,813	13,823
Prepaid Expenses	951	352
Current Assets	$35,157	$20,422
Property, Plant, and Equipment (Note 5)	1,174	300
Less Accumulated Depreciation	(164)	(31)
	$1,010	$269
Investments (Note 6)	613	613
Other Assets	14	0
Total Assets	$36,794	$21,304
Liabilities and Shareholders' Equity		
Accounts Payable and Accrued Expenses	$4,675	$3,556
Short-Term Liabilities (Note 7)	10,000	0
Current Liabilities	$14,675	3,556
Long-Term Debt (Note 7)	0	0
Total Liabilities	$14,675	3,556
Common Stock	8,105	8,105
Additional Paid-in Capital	7,743	7,743
Retained Earnings	6,271	1,900
Total Shareholders' Equity	$22,119	$17,748
Total Liabilities and Shareholders' Equity	$36,794	$21,304

The accompanying notes are an integral part of the consolidated financial statements.

- **Existence**—Does this cash really exist?
- **Rights and Obligations**—Does the company really own this inventory?
- **Valuation and Allocation**—Are these investments properly valued?
- **Occurrence**—Did these sales transactions really take place?
- **Completeness**—Are all the expenses included? Are they recorded in the correct period?

NOTES TO CONSOLIDATED FINANCIAL STATEMENTS
APOLLO SHOES, INC.

1. Summary of Significant Accounting Policies

Business activity The Company develops and markets technologically superior podiatric athletic products under various trademarks, including *SIREN, SPOTLIGHT*, and *SPEAKERSHOE*.

Marketable Securities Investments are valued using the market value method for investments of less than 20%, and by the equity method for investments greater than 20% but less than 50%.

Cash equivalents Cash equivalents are defined as highly liquid investments with original maturities of three months or less at date of purchase.

Inventory valuation Inventories are stated at the lower of First-in, First-out (FIFO) or market.

Property and equipment and depreciation Property and equipment are stated at cost. The Company uses the straight-line method of depreciation for all additions to property, plant and equipment.

Intangibles Intangibles are amortized on the straight-line method over periods benefited.

Net Sales Sales for 2012 and 2011 are presented net of sales returns and allowances of $4.5 million, and $0.9 million, respectively, and net of warranty expenses of $1.1 million, and $0.9 million, respectively.

Income taxes Deferred income taxes are provided for the tax effects of timing differences in reporting the results of operations for financial statements and income tax purposes, and relate principally to valuation reserves for accounts receivable and inventory, accelerated depreciation and unearned compensation.

Net income per common share Net income per common share is computed based on the weighted average number of common and common equivalent shares outstanding for the period.

Reclassification Certain amounts have been reclassified to conform to the 2006 presentation.

2. Significant Customers

Approximately 15%, and 11% of sales are to one customer for years ended December 31, 2012 and 2011, respectively.

STATEMENTS OF INCOME
APOLLO SHOES INC.
in thousands (except per share data)

For year ended December 31,	2012	2011
Net Sales (Note 2)	$240,575	$236,299
Cost of Sales	$141,569	$120,880
Gross Profit	$99,006	$115,419
Selling, General and Administrative Expenses	$71,998	$61,949
Interest Expense (Note 7)	$875	0
Other Expense (Income)	($204)	($1,210)
Earnings from Continuing Operations Before Taxes	$26,337	$54,680
Income Tax Expense (Note 10)	$10,271	$21,634
Earnings from Continuing Operations	$16,066	$33,046
Discontinued Operations, Net of tax benefit		($31,301)
Extraordinary Item, Net of tax benefit (Note 11)	($11,695)	
Net Income	$4,371	$1,745
Earnings Per Common Share		
From Continuing Operations	$1.98	$4.08
Other	($1.44)	($3.86)
Net Income	$0.54	$0.22
Weighted shares of common stock outstanding	8,105	8,105

The accompanying notes are an integral part of the consolidated financial statements.

- **Presentation and Disclosure**—Are these disclosures understandable? Has everything been disclosed that should be?

PROFESSIONAL SKEPTICISM

LEARNING OBJECTIVE 1-4
Define professional skepticism and explain its key characteristics.

Professional skepticism is an auditor's responsibility *not* to accept management assertions without corroboration, a responsibility to ask management to "prove it" (with evidence). The occurrence of errors and fraud in financial reports dictates this basic aspect, which underlies the importance of professional skepticism: *A potential conflict of interests always exists between the auditors and the management of the enterprise under audit.* This potential conflict arises because management wants to present the company in the best possible light, while auditors must ensure that the information about the company's financial condition is "presented fairly."

Having recognized this potential conflict, auditors must be professional in their relationships with management, not adversarial or confrontational. Nevertheless, knowing that a potential conflict of interests always exists causes auditors to perform procedures to search for errors and frauds that could have a material effect on the financial statements. Even though the vast majority of audits do not contain fraud, auditors have responded by performing additional work on all audits because of misdeeds perpetrated by a few people in a few companies.

AUDITING INSIGHT — Why be Skeptical?

When **Lehman Brothers** filed for bankruptcy in September 2008, it was reportedly the largest bankruptcy in U.S. history. How could such a large firm seem to collapse so suddenly? Auditors at **Ernst & Young** (EY) have been identified, along with other investment banks and senior Lehman executives, for having played a role in the firm's demise. In fact, the attorney general of New York filed a civil fraud lawsuit against EY in December 2010 and is claiming that the accounting firm helped to "disguise" the financial condition of Lehman for at least seven years. eg. The lawsuit describes a "cozy" relationship between Lehman and Ernst. The reason? "Two of Lehman's chief financial officers were former EY employees during much of the seven-year period when the transactions occurred" and "Ernst & Young charged Lehman $150 Million in audit fees over a seven-year period of time."

Source: "Ernst Accused of Lehman Whitewash," *The Wall Street Journal,* December 22, 2010, p. C1.

Persuading a skeptical auditor is not impossible, just somewhat more difficult than persuading a normal person in an everyday context. Skepticism is a manifestation of objectivity, holding no special concern for preconceived conclusions on any side of an issue. In fact, the auditor should not care about the impact that an economic transaction has on the "bottom line" of a company, only that the accounting rules were followed, were properly applied, and the financial statements are appropriate for the user's needs. Skepticism is not being cynical, hypercritical, or scornful. The properly skeptical auditor asks these questions: (1) What do I need to know? (2) How well do I know it? (3) Does it make sense? (4) What can go wrong?

Auditors understand that receiving explanations from an entity's management is merely the first step in an engagement process, not the last. Listen to the explanation, and then examine or test it by looking at sufficient competent audit evidence. The familiar phrase "healthy skepticism" should be viewed as a show-me attitude, not a predisposition to accepting unsubstantiated explanations. Auditors must gather the evidence needed, uncover all of the implications from the evidence, and then arrive at the most appropriate and supportable conclusion. Time pressure to complete a financial statement audit engagement is no excuse for failing to exercise professional skepticism. Too many auditors have gotten themselves into trouble by accepting a manager's glib explanation and stopping too early in an investigation without seeking corroborating facts.

Although the SEC places constraints on the common practice of auditors joining public clients that they have previously audited, often close relationships exist between former colleagues now employed by the client and members of the audit team. In these cases, the audit team must guard against being too trusting in accepting representations about the client's financial statements. Of more concern is the fact that former colleagues have inside knowledge of the firm's practices and procedures, knowing where the audit team will probably look (and where they might not look).

To summarize, due care requires an auditor to be professionally skeptical and question all material assertions made by management whether oral or written. While this attitude must be balanced by maintaining constructive client relationships, auditors should not assume management to be perfectly honest. The key lies in auditors' skeptical attitude toward gathering and evaluating the evidence necessary to reach supportable conclusions.

AUDITING INSIGHT — Professional Skepticism

"Doveryai no Proveryai" (Trust, but Verify)
—Ronald Reagan to Soviet Prime Minister Gorbachev during Cold War missile reduction talks

THE HURTT SKEPTICISM SCALE

How skeptical are you? Answer the following 30 questions to find out. As a benchmark, business students typically fall between 90 to 150 points; auditors score much higher.

Questions	Strongly Disagree					Strongly Agree
1. I often accept other people's explanations without further thought.	1	2	3	4	5	6
2. I feel good about myself.	1	2	3	4	5	6
3. I wait to decide on issues until I can get more information.	1	2	3	4	5	6
4. The prospect of learning excites me.	1	2	3	4	5	6
5. I am interested in what causes people to behave the way that they do.	1	2	3	4	5	6
6. I am confident of my abilities.	1	2	3	4	5	6
7. I often reject statements unless I have proof that they are true.	1	2	3	4	5	6
8. Discovering new information is fun.	1	2	3	4	5	6
9. I take my time when making decisions.	1	2	3	4	5	6
10. I tend to immediately accept what other people tell me.	1	2	3	4	5	6
11. Other people's behavior does not interest me.	1	2	3	4	5	6
12. I am self-assured.	1	2	3	4	5	6
13. My friends tell me that I usually question things that I see or hear.	1	2	3	4	5	6
14. I like to understand the reason for other people's behavior.	1	2	3	4	5	6
15. I think that learning is exciting.	1	2	3	4	5	6
16. I usually accept things I see, read, or hear at face value.	1	2	3	4	5	6
17. I do not feel sure of myself.	1	2	3	4	5	6
18. I usually notice inconsistencies in explanations.	1	2	3	4	5	6
19. Most often I agree with what the others in my group think.	1	2	3	4	5	6
20. I dislike having to make decisions quickly.	1	2	3	4	5	6
21. I have confidence in myself.	1	2	3	4	5	6
22. I do not like to decide until I've looked at all of the readily available information.	1	2	3	4	5	6
23. I like searching for knowledge.	1	2	3	4	5	6
24. I frequently question things that I see or hear.	1	2	3	4	5	6
25. It is easy for other people to convince me.	1	2	3	4	5	6
26. I seldom consider why people behave in a certain way.	1	2	3	4	5	6
27. I like to ensure that I've considered most available information before making a decision.	1	2	3	4	5	6
28. I enjoy trying to determine if what I read or hear is true.	1	2	3	4	5	6
29. I relish learning.	1	2	3	4	5	6
30. The actions people take and the reasons for those actions are fascinating.	1	2	3	4	5	6

Source: Kathy Hurtt, "Development of a Scale to Measure Professional Skepticism," *Auditing: A Journal of Practice & Theory 29*, no. 1 (May 2010), pp. 149–171.

18 Part One *The Contemporary Auditing Environment*

> ↪ **REVIEW CHECKPOINT**
>
> 1.12 Why should auditors act as though there is always a potential conflict of interest between the auditor and the management of the enterprise under audit?

PUBLIC ACCOUNTING

LEARNING OBJECTIVE 1-5
Describe the organization of public accounting firms and identify the various services that they offer.

Many people think of public accounting, financial statement auditing, and information assurance services in terms of the largest international accounting firms. Notwithstanding this perception, the practice of public accounting is conducted in thousands of practice units ranging in size from sole proprietorships (individuals who "hang out a shingle" in front of their homes) to the largest international firms with thousands of professionals. Furthermore, many public accounting firms no longer designate themselves as *CPA firms*. Many of them describe their businesses and their organizations as *professional services* firms, or some variation on these terms. Exhibit 1.6 shows an organization for a typical public accounting firm. However, some firms differ in their organization. Some have other departments such as small business advisory and forensic accounting. Other firms may be organized by industry (e.g., entertainment, oil and gas, health care, financial institutions) to take advantage of firmwide expertise. Some firms have other names for their staff and management positions.

Assurance Services

Generally speaking, assurance services involve the lending of credibility to information, whether financial or nonfinancial. CPAs have assured vote counts (Academy Awards), dollar amounts of prizes that sweepstakes have claimed to award, accuracy of advertisements, investment performance statistics, and characteristics claimed for computer software programs. While assurance services (separate and distinct from auditing) currently represent a fairly small part of a normal firm's operating revenues, the AICPA continues to make a considerable effort to sell these additional services to the public and businesses.

AUDITING INSIGHT   Pushing the Envelopes

On Oscar night, Hollywood's Best Kept Secret Award surely goes to the six-member team of hard-working **PwC** accountants. Charged with counting the ballots and keeping them safely padlocked until the big night, the PwC crew puts in ten 12-hour days in the weeks leading up to the Oscars. They even commit the winners to memory in case one of the starry-eyed presenters loses the envelope. Here's the behind-the-scenes peek into Hollywood's most sacrosanct ritual:

- 1,700 "person hours" for PwC to count and verify the ballots by hand.
- 450,000 ballots counted by PwC during its 77 years on the job.
- 2,575 winners' envelopes stuffed by the PwC team since 1941.

Source: PwC.com.

At the present time, assurance services primarily include financial statement audit engagements and attestation engagements. We discuss these services as a component of assurance services that public accounting firms offer.

Audit Services

Most of the large, international accounting (Big 4) firms were founded around the turn of the 20th century (late 1800s/early 1900s) during the Industrial Revolution as European

EXHIBIT 1.6
Public Accounting Firm Organization

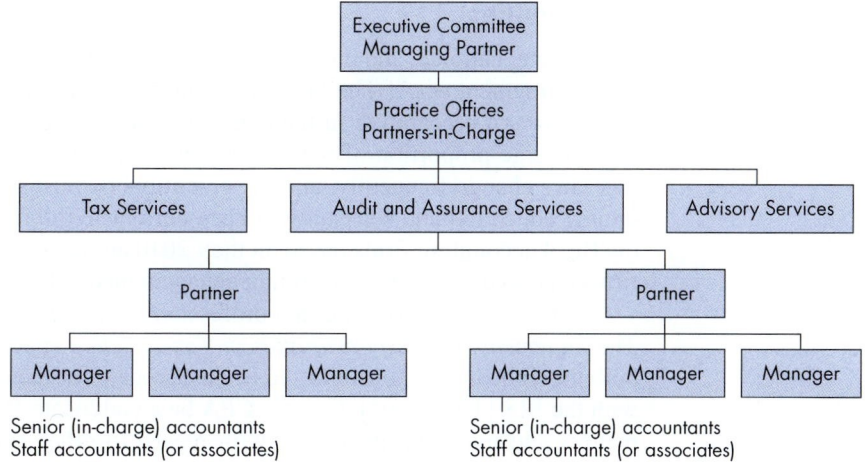

financiers sent representatives (individuals whom we now refer to as *auditors*) to check up on their investments (mostly railroads) in the United States. As such, the primary focus of their practice has been traditional accounting and auditing services. Audits of traditional financial statements remain the most frequent type of assurance engagement that public companies (and most large and medium nonpublic companies) demand. Exhibit 1.7 shows the auditing (and other assurance services) revenues of the Big 4 accounting firms based on their 2010 annual reports. This level of auditing activity dramatically drops as the size of the public accounting firm decreases. In other words, smaller firms usually provide more of the other types of nonaudit attestation engagements.

Nonaudit Attestation Engagements

Basic accounting and review services are "nonaudit" services, performed frequently for medium and small businesses and not-for-profit organizations. Small public accounting firms perform a great deal of this type of nonaudit work. For example, CPAs can perform a *compilation,* which consists of preparing financial statements from a client's books and records, without performing any evidence-gathering work. They can also perform a *review,* in which limited evidence-gathering work is performed but which is narrower in scope than an audit. Although these are the most common attestation engagements, CPAs also can attest to the accuracy of management's discussion and analysis (MD&A) that accompanies the financial statements in an annual report, an entity's internal controls, and hypothetical "what-if" projections relating to mergers or acquisitions.

EXHIBIT 1.7 Revenues for the Big Four CPA Firms

	Deloitte & Touche[1]	Ernst & Young[2]	KPMG[3]	PwC[4]
Total revenues (in billions)	$26.6	$21.3	$20.6	$26.6
Auditing and assurance services revenues (in billions and as a percent of revenue)	$11.7 44%	$10.1 47%	$9.9 48%	$13.3 50%
Tax revenues (in billions and as a percent of revenue)	$5.4 20%	$5.7 27%	$4.1 20%	$7.1 27%
Consulting and advisory services revenues (in billions and as a percent of revenue)	$9.5 36%	$5.5 26%	$6.6 32%	$6.2 23%

[1]Deloitte.com, Annual Review 2010.
[2]Ernst & Young Global Review 2010.
[3]KPMG International Annual Review 2010.
[4]PwC.com, Annual Review 2010.

Tax Services

Local, state, national, and international tax laws are often called "accountant and attorney full-employment acts"! The laws are complex and CPAs perform tax planning services and tax return preparation in the areas of income, gift, estate, property, and other taxation. A large proportion of the practice in small public accounting firms is tax related. Tax laws change frequently, and tax practitioners must spend considerable time in continuing education and self-study to keep current. Exhibit 1.7 shows the tax revenues of the Big 4 accounting firms based on their 2010 annual reports. Smaller public accounting firms tend to do more tax consulting engagements and fewer audit engagements.

The role of tax consulting in a professional services firm has at times faced scrutiny. The *Statements on Responsibilities in Tax Practice* specifically state that "A CPA has both the right and responsibility to be an advocate for the client" in arguing tax positions with the IRS [TX 112.04]. Can the CPA be an advocate for the client with respect to tax matters and maintain objectivity with regard to other audit matters? Recent guidance from the Public Company Accounting Oversight Board (PCAOB) prohibits an accounting firm from providing audit services to a public company if the accounting firm provides tax consulting on aggressive interpretations of tax laws or "listed" transactions (those included on the U.S. Treasury Department's list of questionable tax strategies), if contingent fees (i.e., fees depending on a certain outcome) are involved, or if the public accounting firm provides tax services for key company executives. In all three cases, the PCAOB argues that auditor independence would be impaired. Providing normal corporate tax return preparation and advice is permissible as long as the audit committee discusses with the accounting firm the implications of the tax consulting fees on auditor independence and pre-approves the relationship in writing.

Consulting and Advisory Services

Prior to the turn of this century (the 1990s), the largest public accounting firms handled a great deal of consulting business. Consulting and management advisory services seemed to present a great new revenue opportunity, and the field appeared to be virtually unlimited. Public accounting firms tried to become "one-stop shopping centers" for clients' auditing, taxation, and business advice needs.

The Securities and Exchange Commission (SEC), the governmental agency charged with investor protection, expressed reservations as to whether the performance of nonaudit services (such as consulting) impaired a public accounting firm's ability to conduct an independent audit. The SEC's concern was that the large amount of revenues generated from consulting services might sway the auditor's opinion on the company's financial statements. The public accounting firms, on the other hand, argued that the provision of consulting services allowed them a closer look at the client's operations, providing a synergistic, positive effect on the audit.

In response to the spate of corporate frauds, Congress resolved this difference of opinion, in part, by passing the Sarbanes-Oxley Act of 2002 (hereafter referred to as *Sarbanes-Oxley*), a broad accounting and corporate governance reform measure. Sarbanes-Oxley prohibits public accounting firms from providing any of the following services to a public audit client: (1) bookkeeping and related services; (2) design or implementation of financial information systems; (3) appraisal or valuation services; (4) actuarial services; (5) internal audit outsourcing; (6) management or human resources services; (7) investment or broker/dealer services; and (8) legal and expert services (unrelated to the audit). Public accounting firms may provide general corporate tax return preparation and advice and other nonprohibited services to public audit clients if the company's audit committee has approved them in advance. To briefly summarize these restrictions, Sarbanes-Oxley prohibits public accounting firms from performing any client services in which the auditors may find themselves making managerial decisions or auditing their own firm's work (e.g., auditing financial records, documents, or journal entries that they themselves created).

Although consulting services approached almost 50 percent of a professional service firm's business in the 1990s, firm consulting revenues fell to between 23 and 36 percent of the Big 4 firms' total revenues in 2010 (see Exhibit 1.7). This decrease is due to both the divestiture of many firms' consulting practices (partially in response to Sarbanes-Oxley audit client service restrictions) as well as increases in audit revenues as a result of Sarbanes-Oxley's increased audit requirements. Most of the large firms now provide consulting only for companies that they do not audit.

Small public accounting firms are not required to follow Sarbanes-Oxley guidelines for their non-SEC clients. Often, private businesses regard their public accounting firms as business partners that can provide an array of services and a wealth of business information.

⤷ REVIEW CHECKPOINTS

1.13 What are some examples of assurance services performed on nonfinancial information?

1.14 What are some of the major areas of public accounting services?

OTHER KINDS OF ENGAGEMENTS AND INFORMATION PROFESSIONALS

LEARNING OBJECTIVE 1-6
Describe the audits and auditors in governmental, internal, and operational auditing.

The AAA and the AICPA definitions of auditing clearly apply to the financial audit practice of independent external auditors who practice auditing in public accounting firms. The word *audit*, however, is used in other contexts to describe broader types of work.

The variety of engagements performed by different kinds of information assurors causes some problems with terminology. In this textbook, *independent auditor, external auditor,* and *CPA* will refer to people doing audit work with public accounting firms. In the internal and governmental contexts discussed here, auditors are identified as *operational auditors, internal auditors,* and *governmental auditors*. Although all of these professionals are information assurors (and many are certified public accountants), the term *CPA* in this book will refer to auditors in public practice.

Internal Auditing

The Board of Directors of the Institute of Internal Auditors (IIA) defines **internal auditing** and states its objective as follows:

> Internal auditing is an independent, objective assurance and consulting activity designed to add value and improve an organization's operations. It helps an organization accomplish its objectives by bringing a systematic, disciplined approach to evaluate and improve the effectiveness of risk management, control, and governance processes.[6]

Internal auditors are employed by organizations such as banks, hospitals, city governments, and industrial companies or work for CPA firms that provide internal audit services. Internal auditors often perform *operational audits*. **Operational auditing** refers to the study of business operations for the purpose of making recommendations about the efficient and effective use of resources, effective achievement of business objectives, and compliance with company policies. The goal of operational auditing is to help managers discharge their management responsibilities and improve profitability.

Internal auditors also perform audits of financial reports for internal use or limited external distribution (e.g., reports to regulatory agencies) much like external auditors audit financial statements distributed to outside users. Thus, some internal auditing work is similar to the auditing described elsewhere in this textbook. In addition, the services provided

---

[6] This definition and other information about internal auditing may be found on the Institute of Internal Auditors' website (www.theiia.org).

by internal auditors include (1) reviews of internal control systems to ensure compliance with company policies, plans, and procedures; (2) compliance with laws and regulations; (3) appraisals of the *economy* and *efficiency* of operations; and (4) reviews of effectiveness in achieving program results in comparison to established objectives and goals.

It should be noted that the AICPA defines operational auditing performed by independent CPA firms as a distinct type of management consulting service whose goal is to help a client improve the use of its capabilities and resources to achieve its objectives. So, internal auditors consider operational auditing integral to internal auditing and external auditors define it as a type of assurance service offered by public accounting firms. Providing these types of internal audit services has been a growing business for many large CPA firms. However, both the SEC and the PCAOB prohibit CPA firms from providing these services to their own public audit clients.

Governmental Auditing

The U.S. Government Accountability Office (GAO) is an accounting, auditing, and investigating agency of the U.S. Congress, headed by the U.S. comptroller general. In one sense, GAO auditors are the highest level of internal auditors for the federal government. Many states have audit agencies similar to the GAO. These agencies answer to state legislatures and perform the same types of work described in the following GAO definition. In another sense, GAO and similar state agencies are really external auditors with respect to government agencies they audit because they are organizationally independent.

Many government agencies have their own internal auditors and inspectors general. Well-managed local governments also have internal audit departments. For example, most federal agencies (Department of Defense, Department of Human Resources, Department of the Interior), state agencies (education, welfare, controller), and local governments (cities, counties, tax districts) have internal audit staffs. Governmental and internal auditors have much in common.

The GAO shares with internal auditors the same elements of *expanded-scope* services. The GAO, however, emphasizes the accountability of public officials for the efficient, economical, and effective use of public funds and other resources. The generally accepted government auditing standards (GAGAS) define and describe *expanded-scope* governmental auditing as follows:

> The term "audit" includes both financial and performance audits. . . . Financial related audits include determining whether (1) financial information is presented in accordance with established . . . criteria [e.g. GAAP], (2) the entity has adhered to specific financial compliance requirements [with laws and regulations], and (3) the entity's internal control . . . over financial reporting and/or safeguarding assets is suitably designed and implemented to achieve the control objectives. . . . Performance audits include economy and efficiency audits and program audits.[7]

In this definition, you can see the attest function applied to financial reports and a compliance audit function applied with respect to laws and regulations. All government organizations, programs, activities, and functions are created by law and are surrounded by regulations that govern the things they can and cannot do. For example, a program established to provide school meals to low-income students must comply with regulations about the eligibility of recipients. A compliance audit of such a program involves a study of schools' policies, procedures, and performance in determining eligibility and handing out meal tickets.

Also in this definition, you see *performance audits* referring to a category that includes two types: (1) economy and efficiency audits and (2) program audits. Governments are concerned about accountability for the appropriate use of taxpayers' resources; performance audits are a means of seeking to improve accountability for the efficient and economical use of resources and the achievement of program goals. In addition, the program audit helps determine whether the financial resources being spent are helping

---

[7] The complete Government Auditing Standards can be found on the GAO's website (www.gao.gov).

the government truly achieve its stated objectives. Performance audits, like internal auditors' operational audits, involve studies of the management of government organizations, programs, activities, and functions.

Regulatory Auditors

For the sake of clarity, other kinds of auditors deserve separate mention. The U.S. Internal Revenue Service employs auditors. They take the "economic assertions" of taxable income made by taxpayers in tax returns and determine their correspondence with the standards found in the Internal Revenue Code. They also audit for fraud and tax evasion. Their reports can either clear a taxpayer's return or claim that additional taxes are due.

State and federal bank examiners audit banks, savings and loan associations, and other financial institutions for evidence of solvency and compliance with banking and other related laws and regulations. In the 1980s and early 1990s and even more recently, these examiners made news as a result of the large number of failures of U.S. financial institutions.

Some GAO Engagement Examples

- *Opportunities to Reduce Potential Duplication in Government Programs, Save Tax Dollars, and Enhance Revenue* (GAO-11-318SP).
- *USDA's Oversight of the McGovern-Dole Food Education Program Needs Improvement* (GAO-11-544)
- *Enhanced Guidance on Commercial Real Estate Risks Needed* (GAO-11-489).
- *Information Security: Further Efforts Needed to Address Significant Weaknesses at the Internal Revenue Service* (GAO-07-364).
- *NASA: Issues Surrounding the Transition from the Space Shuttle to the Next Generation of Human Space Flight Systems* (GAO-07-595T).

↳ REVIEW CHECKPOINTS

1.15 What is *operational* auditing? How does the AICPA view operational auditing?
1.16 What are the elements of *expanded-scope* auditing according to the GAO?
1.17 What is *compliance* auditing?
1.18 Name some other types of auditors in addition to external, internal, and governmental auditors.

▽ BECOME A PROFESSIONAL AND GET CERTIFIED!

LEARNING OBJECTIVE 1-7
List and explain the requirements for becoming a certified information professional.

If you plan a career in accounting (which we hope you do given that you are reading this book!), you are on your way to being known as an accounting professional. Congratulations. To do so, it is absolutely essential that you acquire the knowledge required to do your job and certification indicates that you have acquired that knowledge. While being certified as a certified public accountant (CPA) is generally regarded as the highest mark of distinction in the public accounting profession, other certifications may be more applicable to your chosen career aspirations. For example, a certified internal auditor (CIA) certification or certified management accountant (CMA) certification may be equally acceptable for those individuals working with companies to achieve specific goals, both financial and nonfinancial. Other certifications available in the fraud auditing and forensic accounting fields include the certified fraud examiner (CFE) and the certified forensic accountant (CFA) certifications. If you enjoy information systems, key certifications include the certified information systems auditor (CISA), the certified information systems security professional (CISSP), and the certified information technology professional

(CITP). Regardless of your career choice, a certification adds credibility that will assist you throughout your career.

Education

Education requirements vary across certifying organizations. For the CPA certification, state boards of accountancy, the regulatory agencies in each state, set the education requirements for taking the CPA examination and receiving a CPA certificate. Most states presently require 150 semester hours of college education before receiving a CPA certificate, but a few states will allow you to sit for the CPA examination after only 120 semester hours of college education. Other certifications (such as the CIA) allow you to take the exam before you have graduated.

In addition to entry-level education requirements, all certifying organizations have regulations about *continuing professional education* (CPE). At present, the AICPA and most states require 120 contact hours (not semester or quarter college hours) over three-year reporting periods with no less than 20 hours in any one year. Once certified, you can obtain CPE hours in a variety of ways: continuing education courses, in-house training, college courses, and private-provider courses. Many CPAs obtain CPEs by joining a professional accounting organization's local chapter. These types of courses range in length from one hour to two weeks, depending on the subject. Many CPE providers offer courses online.

Examination

The AICPA Board of Examiners administers the Uniform CPA Examination. The 14-hour computer-based examination was significantly revised in 2011. The exam covers Auditing and Attestation (AUD), Financial Accounting and Reporting (FAR), Regulation (REG) and Business Environment and Concepts (BEC). In the AUD section, beyond mastery of U.S. auditing standards, you will now also need to demonstrate an understanding of the International Auditing and Assurance Standards Board (IAASB) and its role in establishing international standards on auditing (ISAs) and the difference between ISAs and the U.S. auditing standards. Candidates are also expected to demonstrate an awareness of the International Ethics Standards Board for Accountants (IESBA) and its role in establishing requirements of the International Federation of Accountants (IFAC) Code of Ethics for Professional Accountants and the independence requirements that apply. The content specific outline (CSO) for the auditing section are (with rough approximations of weights given to each area):

Topic	Weight	M/C Questions (60% of grade)	Task–Based Simulations (40% of grade)
Auditing & Attestation (AUD) (4 hours)	100%	90	7
• Engagement Acceptance and Understanding the Assignment	12–16%		
• Understanding the Entity and its Environment (including Internal Control)	16–20%		
• Performing Audit Procedures and Evaluating Evidence	16–20%		
• Evaluating Audit Findings, Communications, and Reporting	16–20%		
• Accounting and Review Services Engagements	12–16%		
• Professional Responsibilities	16–20%		

Source: www.cpa-exam.org; Content Specific Outlines (CSOs) for REG, FAR, and BEC can also be found at this site.

The Uniform CPA Examination consists of multiple-choice question "testlets" (24–30 questions each) as well as task-based simulations introduced by the Board of Examiners in

2011. These task-based simulations are short case studies in which you will have to apply your accounting and auditing knowledge. A simulation may involve identifying a potential problem, electronically researching the topic using a database of authoritative standards, and reporting your findings. The exam is kept "TOP SECRET" (and revealing any exam secrets can result in our certifications being revoked), but we have provided task-based simulations from Kaplan CPA Review in the end-of-chapter materials in subsequent chapters.

General information about the examination can be obtained from the CPA Candidate Bulletin (available online or to download). This information is also available online (www.cpa-exam.org). Because qualifications for taking the CPA examination vary from state to state, you should contact your state board of accountancy for an application or more information. You can find your state board of accountancy website through the National Association of State Boards of Accountancy (NASBA) website (www.nasba.org). Exhibit 1.8, found on the next page, lists the requirements for the most commonly recognized professional certifications.

Experience

Although not required to *sit* for a professional exam, experience is required to *become certified*. Most states and territories require a person who has attained the education level and passed the CPA examination to have a period of experience working under a practicing CPA before awarding a CPA certificate. Experience requirements vary across states, but most jurisdictions require two to three years of experience. A few states require that the experience be obtained in a public accounting firm, but most of them accept experience in other organizations (GAO, internal audit, management accounting, Internal Revenue Service, and the like) as long as the applicant performs work requiring accounting judgment and is supervised by a competent accountant, preferably a CPA. Other certifying organizations also have experience requirements.

State Certificate and License

The AICPA does not issue CPA certificates or licenses to practice. Rather, all states and territories have state accountancy laws and state licensing boards to administer them. After satisfying state requirements for education and experience, successful candidates receive their CPA *certificate* from their state board of accountancy. At the same time, new CPAs must pay a fee to obtain a state *license* to practice or work for a CPA firm that is licensed to practice in their state. Thereafter, state boards of accountancy regulate the behavior of CPAs under their jurisdiction (enforcing state codes of ethics) and supervise the continuing education requirements.

After becoming a CPA licensed in one state, a person can obtain a CPA certificate and license in another state by filing the proper application with the second state board of accountancy, meeting that state's requirements, and obtaining another CPA certificate. Many CPAs hold certificates and licenses in several states. From a global perspective, individuals must be licensed in each country. Similar to CPAs in the United States, *chartered accountants* (CAs) practice in Australia, Canada, Great Britain, and India.

AUDITING INSIGHT | Auditors Make a Run for the Border

Efforts are currently underway through the AICPA and NASBA to streamline the licensing process so that CPAs can practice across state lines without having to have 50 different licenses. Under the concept of **substantial equivalency**, as long as the licensing (home) state requires (1) 150 hours of education, (2) successful completion of the CPA exam, and (3) one year of experience, a CPA can practice (either in person or electronically) in another substantial equivalency state without having to obtain a license in that state. As of March 2010, 47 states have enacted provisions to allow CPAs licensed in other states to practice without notification (but agreeing to be under the state's automatic jurisdiction). This *uniform mobility* arrangement is temporary, however; a CPA who relocates to another state must seek licensing in that state.

Source: AICPA State Regulation and Legislation Team at www.aicpa.org

EXHIBIT 1.8 Certification Requirements

	Certified Public Accountant (CPA)	Certified Information Systems Auditor (CISA)	Certified Internal Auditor (CIA)	Certified Fraud Examiner (CFE)	Certified Management Accountant (CMA)
Education Level	Varies by state. Check with your state board of accountancy	No specific degree requirement	Bachelor's degree or its educational equivalent	Bachelor's degree or its educational equivalent	Bachelor's degree, or pass the CPA examination, or score in the 50th percentile on the GMAT
Experience	Varies by state. Check with your state board of accountancy	5 years of professional IS auditing, control, or security work experience for certification	2 years of internal auditing experience or its equivalent for certification	2 years of professional experience for certification	2 continuous years of professional experience in management accounting and/or financial management
Exam Coverage	1. Auditing and attestation (AUD) 2. Financial accounting and reporting (FAR) 3. Regulation (REG) 4. Business environment and concepts (BEC)	1. The process of auditing information systems 2. Governance and management of IT 3. Information systems acquisition, development and implementation 4. Information systems operations, maintenance and support 5. Protection of information assets	1. The internal audit activity's role in governance, risk, and control 2. Conducting the internal audit engagement 3. Business analysis and information technology 4. Business management skill	1. Fraud prevention and deterrence 2. Legal elements of fraud 3. Fraud investigation 4. Financial transactions	1. Financial planning, performance and control 2. Financial decision making
Test Length	4 parts, 14 hours	1 part, 4 hours (200 mc questions)	4 parts (100 mc questions each), 11 hours	4 parts (125 mc questions each), 10 hours	2 parts (100 mc questions and two 30-minutes essays, each) 8 hours
Passing Score	75%	450 (on a 800-point scale)	600 (on a 750-point scale)	75%	360 per part (on a 500-point scale)
Test Dates	On demand in 1st two months of each calendar quarter	June, December	On demand	Self-administered	On demand during the months of Jan, Feb, May, Jun, Sep, and Oct
Administering Body	American Institute of Certified Public Accountants	Information Systems Audit and Control Association	Institute of Internal Auditors	Association of Certified Fraud Examiners	Institute of Management Accountants
Website	www.aicpa.org	www.isaca.org	www.theiia.org	www.acfe.com	www.imanet.org

Skill Sets and Your Education

The requirements to become certified are rather strenuous, but they may not be enough! Let us take you on a brief tour of the core competencies listed by the AICPA, the Association of Certified Fraud Examiners (ACFE), the Institute of Internal Auditors (IIA), the Institute of Management Accountants (IMA), the Information Systems Audit and Control Association (ISACA), and other guidance-providing groups: history, international culture, psychology, economics, mathematics (calculus and statistics), national and international political science, art, literature, inductive and deductive reasoning, ethics, group dynamic processes, legal-political-social forces impinging on business, finance, capital markets, managing change, history of accounting, regulation, information systems, taxation, and (oh, yes) accounting and auditing. And administrative capability, analytical skills, business knowledge, communication skills (writing and speaking), efficiency, intellectual capability, marketing and selling, model building, people development, capacity for putting client needs first, and more.

We hope you are suitably impressed by this recitation of virtually all of the world's knowledge. You will be very old when you accomplish a fraction of the skill development and education suggested. Now the good news: (1) not everyone needs to be completely knowledgeable in all of these areas upon graduation from college; (2) learning and skill development evolve over a lifetime; and (3) no one expects you to know everything and operate as a "Lone Ranger." Audit teams composed of members specializing in some areas with other members specializing in others seem to work best in practice. We do, however, stress the need to continue your education even after you leave school. Learning should be a lifelong pursuit, not something that ends when you receive your diploma.

> ↳ **REVIEW CHECKPOINTS**
>
> 1.19 Why is continuing education required to maintain certification?
>
> 1.20 Why do you think experience is required to become certified?
>
> 1.21 What are some of the functions of a state board of public accountancy?
>
> 1.22 What are some of the limitations to practicing public accounting across state and national boundaries?

Summary

Decision makers need more than just information; they need reliable information. Internet buyers rely on website information when purchasing online. Financial analysts and investors depend on financial reports for making stock investment decisions. Suppliers and creditors use financial reports to decide whether to give trade credit and bank loans. Labor organizations use financial reports to help determine a company's ability to pay wages. Government agencies and Congress use financial information in preparing analyses of the economy and in making laws concerning taxes, subsidies, and the like. These various users rely on independent information assurors such as CPAs to reduce information risk. Auditors (and other information assurance providers) assume the role of certifying (or attesting to) published financial information, thereby offering users the valuable service of assurance that information risk is low.

This chapter begins by defining information risk and explains how auditing and assurance services play a role in minimizing this risk. The financial statements are explained in terms of the primary assertions that management makes in them, and these assertions are identified as the focal points of the auditors' procedural evidence-gathering work. Auditing is practiced in numerous forms by various practice units, including public accounting firms, the Internal Revenue Service, the U.S. Government Accountability Office, internal audit departments in companies, and several other types of regulatory auditors. Fraud examiners, many of whom are internal auditors and inspectors, have found a niche in auditing-related activities.

The public accounting profession recognizes that, in today's information economy, information risk exists in areas outside of financial transactions. Assurance services is a broad category of information-enhancement services that build on CPAs' auditing, attestation, accounting, and consulting skills to create products useful to a wide range of decision makers (customers). While reliable information helps make capital markets efficient and helps people know the consequences of a wide variety of economic decisions, CPAs practicing the assurance function are not the only information professionals at work in the economy. Bank examiners, IRS auditors, state regulatory agency auditors (e.g., auditors in a state's insurance department), internal auditors employed by a company, and federal government agency auditors all practice information assurance in one form or another.

Most auditors aspire to become certified public accountants, which involves successfully completing a rigorous examination, obtaining practical experience, and maintaining competence through continuing professional education. Auditors also obtain credentials as certified internal auditors, certified management accountants, certified information systems auditors, and certified fraud examiners. Each of these fields has large professional organizations that govern the professional standards and quality of practice of its members.

Key Terms

assurance: The *lending of credibility* to information, 3
assurance services: The provision of independent professional information, opinion, or report concerning the quality of information or its context for decision makers, 8
attest engagement: The provision of an opinion on subject matter or an assertion about the subject matter that is the responsibility of another party, 6
attestation: The lending of credibility to assertions made by a third party, 3
auditing: The systematic process of objectively obtaining and evaluating evidence regarding assertions about economic actions and events to ascertain the degree of correspondence between the assertions and established criteria and communicating the results to interested users, 3
business risk: The probability an entity will fail to meet its objectives and, ultimately, fail, 2
cutoff (or cutoff date): A date, normally the client's year-end balance sheet date, around which transactions should be recorded in the proper period (year), 12–13
financial reporting: Broad-based process of providing statements of financial position (balance sheets), results of operations (income statements, statements of shareholders' equity, and statements of comprehensive income), changes in cash flows (statements of cash flows), and accompanying disclosure notes (footnotes) to outside decision makers who have no internal source of information, 10
information risk: The probability that the information circulated by a company will be false or misleading, 3
internal auditing: An assurance and consulting activity that provides management information regarding efficient and effective operations; compliance with laws, regulations, policies, and procedures; and other organizational performance issues designed to reduce risk and add value to the organization, 21
operational auditing: The study of business operations for the purpose of making recommendations about the efficient use of resources, effective achievement of business objectives, and compliance with company policies, 21
professional skepticism: An auditor's tendency *not* to believe management's assertions without sufficient corroboration, 15
substantial equivalency: The process through which CPAs licensed in one state can practice in another state, 25

Multiple-Choice Questions for Practice and Review

 All applicable Exercises and Problems are available with McGraw-Hill's *Connect® Accounting*

LO 1-2

1.23 Which of the following would be considered an assurance engagement?
   a. Giving an opinion on a prize promoter's claims about the amount of sweepstakes prizes awarded in the past.
   b. Giving an opinion on the conformity of the financial statements of a university with generally accepted accounting principles.
   c. Giving an opinion on the fair presentation of a newspaper's circulation data.
   d. Giving assurance about the average drive length achieved by golfers with a client's golf balls.
   e. All of the above.

LO 1-4 1.24 It is always a good idea for auditors to begin an audit with the professional skepticism characterized by the assumption that
   a. A potential conflict of interest always exists between the auditor and the management of the enterprise under audit.
   b. In audits of financial statements, the auditor acts exclusively in the capacity of an auditor.
   c. The professional status of the independent auditor imposes commensurate professional obligations.
   d. Financial statements and financial data are verifiable.

LO 1-2 1.25 In an attestation engagement, a CPA practitioner is engaged to
   a. Compile a company's financial forecast based on management's assumptions without expressing any form of assurance.
   b. Prepare a written report containing a conclusion about the reliability of a management assertion.
   c. Prepare a tax return using information the CPA has not audited or reviewed.
   d. Give expert testimony in court on particular facts in a corporate income tax controversy.

LO 1-6 1.26 A determination of cost savings obtained by outsourcing cafeteria services is most likely to be an objective of
   a. Environmental auditing.
   b. Financial auditing.
   c. Compliance auditing.
   d. Operational auditing.

LO 1-6 1.27 The primary difference between operational auditing and financial auditing is that in operational auditing
   a. The operational auditor is not concerned with whether the audited activity is generating information in compliance with financial accounting standards.
   b. The operational auditor is seeking to help management use resources in the most effective manner possible.
   c. The operational auditor starts with the financial statements of an activity being audited and works backward to the basic processes involved in producing them.
   d. The operational auditor can use analytical skills and tools that are not necessary in financial auditing.

LO 1-2 1.28 According to the AICPA, the purpose of an audit of financial statements is to
   a. Enhance the degree of confidence that intended users can place in the financial statements.
   b. Express an opinion on the fairness with which they present financial position, results of operations, and cash flows in conformity with accounting standards promulgated by the Financial Accounting Standards Board.
   c. Express an opinion on the fairness with which they present financial position, result of operations, and cash flows in conformity with accounting standards promulgated by the U.S. Securities and Exchange Commission.
   d. Obtain systematic and objective evidence about financial assertions and report the results to interested users.

LO 1-1 1.29 Bankers who are processing loan applications from companies seeking large loans will probably ask for financial statements audited by an independent CPA because
   a. Financial statements are too complex for the bankers to analyze themselves.
   b. They are too far away from company headquarters to perform accounting and auditing themselves.
   c. The consequences of making a bad loan are very undesirable.
   d. They generally see a potential conflict of interest between company managers who want to get loans and the bank's needs for reliable financial statements.

LO 1-5 1.30 The Sarbanes-Oxley Act of 2002 prohibits public accounting firms from providing which of the following services to an audit client?
   a. Bookkeeping services.
   b. Internal audit services.
   c. Valuation services.
   d. All of the above.

LO 1-1 1.31 Independent auditors of financial statements perform audits that reduce
   a. Business risks faced by investors.
   b. Information risk faced by investors.
   c. Complexity of financial statements.
   d. Timeliness of financial statements.

LO 1-6 1.32 The primary objective of compliance auditing is to
   a. Give an opinion on financial statements.
   b. Develop a basis for a report on internal control.
   c. Perform a study of effective and efficient use of resources.
   d. Determine whether auditee personnel are following laws, rules, regulations, and policies.

LO 1-7 1.33 What requirements are *usually* necessary to become licensed as a certified public accountant?
   a. Successful completion of the Uniform CPA Examination.
   b. Experience in the accounting field.
   c. Education.
   d. All of the above.

LO 1-6 1.34 The organization primarily responsible for ensuring that public officials are using public funds efficiently, economically, and effectively is the
   a. Governmental Internal Audit Agency (GIAA).
   b. Central Internal Auditors (CIA).
   c. Securities and Exchange Commission (SEC).
   d. Government Accountability Office (GAO).

LO 1-6 1.35 Performance audits usually include [two answers]
   a. Financial audits.
   b. Economy and efficiency audits.
   c. Compliance audits.
   d. Program audits.

LO 1-3 1.36 The objective in an auditor's review of credit ratings of a client's customers is to obtain evidence related to management's assertion about
   a. Completeness.
   b. Existence.
   c. Valuation and allocation.
   d. Rights and obligations.
   e. Occurrence.

LO 1-4 1.37 Jones, CPA, is planning the audit of Rhonda's Company. Rhonda verbally asserts to Jones that all expenses for the year have been recorded in the accounts. Rhonda's representation in this regard
   a. Is sufficient evidence for Jones to conclude that the completeness assertion is supported for expenses.
   b. Can enable Jones to minimize the work on the gathering of evidence to support Rhonda's completeness assertion.
   c. Should be disregarded because it is not in writing.
   d. Is not considered a sufficient basis for Jones to conclude that all expenses have been recorded.

LO 1-1 1.38 The risk to investors that a company's financial statements may be materially misleading is called
   a. Client acceptance risk.
   b. Information risk.
   c. Moral hazard.
   d. Business risk.

LO 1-3

1.39 When auditing merchandise inventory at year-end, the auditor performs audit procedures to ensure that all goods purchased before year-end are received before the physical inventory count. This audit procedure provides assurance about which management assertion?
   a. Cutoff.
   b. Existence.
   c. Valuation and allocation.
   d. Rights and obligations.
   e. Occurrence.

LO 1-3

1.40 When auditing merchandise inventory at year-end, the auditor performs audit procedures to obtain evidence that no goods held on consignment are included in the client's ending inventory balance. This audit procedure provides assurance about which management assertion?
   a. Completeness.
   b. Existence.
   c. Valuation and allocation.
   d. Rights and obligations.
   e. Occurrence.

LO 1-3

1.41. When an auditor reviews additions to the equipment (fixed asset) account to make sure that repair and maintenance expenses are not understated, she wants to obtain evidence as to management's assertion regarding
   a. Completeness.
   b. Existence.
   c. Valuation and allocation.
   d. Rights and obligations.
   e. Occurrence.

LO 1-5

1.42 The Sarbanes-Oxley Act of 2002 generally prohibits public accounting firms from
   a. Acting in a managerial decision-making role for an audit client.
   b. Auditing the firm's own work on an audit client.
   c. Providing tax consulting to an audit client without audit committee approval.
   d. All of the above.

LO 1-7

1.43 Substantial equivalency refers to
   a. An auditor's tendency not to believe management's assertions without sufficient corroboration.
   b. Providing consulting work for another firm's audit client in exchange for the other firm's providing consulting services to one of your clients.
   c. The waiving of certification exam parts for an individual holding an equivalent certification from another professional organization.
   d. Permitting a CPA to practice in another state without having to obtain a license in that state.

LO 1-2

1.44 Which of the following best describes the relationship between auditing and attestation engagements?
   a. Auditing is a subset of attestation engagements that focuses on the certification of financial statements.
   b. Attestation is a subset of auditing that provides lower assurance than that provided by an audit engagement.
   c. Auditing is a subset of attestation engagements that focuses on providing clients with advice and decision support.
   d. Attestation is a subset of auditing that improves the quality of information or its context for decision makers.

LO 1-2

1.45 Which of the following *best* describes the focus of the following engagements?

	Auditing Engagement	Attestation Engagement	Assurance Engagement	Consulting Services Engagement
a.	Any information	Financial statements	Advice and decision support	Financial information
b.	Financial information	Advice and decision support	Financial statements	Any information
c.	Advice and decision support	Any information	Financial information	Financial statements
d.	Financial statements	Financial information	Any information	Advice and decision support

LO 1-7

1.46 Which of the following is a reason to obtain professional certification?
   a. Certification provides credibility that an individual is technically competent.
   b. Certification often is a necessary condition for advancement and promotion within a professional services firm.
   c. Obtaining certification is often monetarily rewarded by an individual's employer.
   d. All of the above.

Exercises and Problems

 All applicable Exercises and Problems are available with McGraw-Hill's *Connect®* Accounting

LO 1-2

1.47 **Audit, Attestation, and Assurance Services.** Following is a list of various professional services. Identify each by its apparent characteristics as audit engagement, attestation engagement, or assurance engagement. Because audits are a subset of attestation engagements, which are a subset of assurance engagements, choose the most specific description. In other words, if you believe the engagement is an audit engagement, select only audit engagement rather than checking all three. Similarly, the choice of assurance engagement for an audit, while technically correct, would not be the best choice.

	Audit Engagement	Attestation Engagement	Assurance Engagement
Real estate demand studies			
Ballot for awards show			
Utility rates applications			
Newspaper circulation audits			
Third-party reimbursement maximization			
Annual financial report to stockholders			
Rental property operation review			
Examinations of financial forecasts and projections			
Customer satisfaction surveys			
Compliance with contractual requirements			
Benchmarking/best practices			
Evaluation of investment management policies			
Information systems security reviews			
Productivity statistics			
Internal audit strategic review			
Financial statements submitted to a bank loan officer			

LO 1-4

1.48 **Controller as Auditor.** The chairman of the board of Hughes Corporation proposed that the board hire as controller a CPA who had been the manager of the team that conducted Hughes Corporation's audit engagement. The chairman thought that hiring this person would make the annual audit unnecessary and would consequently result in saving the professional fee paid to the auditors. The chairman proposed to give this new controller a full staff to conduct such investigations of accounting and operating data as necessary. Evaluate this proposal.

LO 1-3

1.49 **Management Assertions.** Complete the following chart indicating the corresponding Auditing Standards Board assertions and whether the assertion relates to transactions, balances, or disclosures.

PCAOB Assertion	Corresponding ASB Assertion	Nature of Assertion
Existence or Occurrence		
Rights and Obligations		
Completeness		
Valuation and Allocation		
Presentation and Disclosure		

LO 1-5, 1-6

1.50 **Operational Auditing.** Bigdeal Corporation manufactures paper and paper products and is trying to decide whether to purchase Smalltek Company. Smalltek has developed a process for manufacturing boxes that can replace containers that use fluorocarbons for expelling a liquid product. The price may be as high as $45 million. Bigdeal prefers to buy Smalltek and integrate its products while leaving the Smalltek management in charge of day-to-day operations. A major consideration is the efficiency and effectiveness of Smalltek's operations. Bigdeal wants to obtain a report on the operational efficiency and effectiveness of the Smalltek sales, production, and research and development departments.

Required:

Who can Bigdeal engage to produce the report resulting from this operational audit? Several possibilities exist. Are there any particular advantages or disadvantages in choosing from among them?

LO 1-1, 1-2

1.51 **Auditor as Guarantor.** Your neighbor Loot Starkin invited you to lunch yesterday. Sure enough, it was no "free lunch" because Loot wanted to discuss the annual report of Dodge Corporation. He owns Dodge stock and just received the annual report. Loot says, "Our auditors prepared the audited financial statements and gave an unqualified opinion, so my investment must be safe."

Required:

What misconceptions does Loot Starkin seem to have about the auditor's role with respect to Dodge Corporation?

34 Part One *The Contemporary Auditing Environment*

LO 1-6

1.52 **Identification of Audits and Auditors.** Audits may be characterized as (a) financial statement audits, (b) compliance audits, (c) economy and efficiency audits, and (d) program results audits. The work can be done by independent (external) auditors, internal auditors, or governmental auditors (including IRS auditors and federal bank examiners). Following is a list of the purposes or products of various audit engagements:

	Type of Audit	Type of Auditor
1. Analyze proprietary schools' spending to train students for low-demand occupations.		
2. Determine whether an advertising agency's financial statements are fairly presented in conformity with GAAP.		
3. Study the effectiveness of the Department of Defense's expendable launch vehicle program.		
4. Compare costs of municipal garbage pickup services to comparable service subcontracted to a private business.		
5. Investigate financing terms of tax shelter partnerships.		
6. Study a private aircraft manufacturer's test pilot performance in reporting on the results of test flights.		
7. Conduct periodic examinations by the U.S. Comptroller of Currency of a national bank for solvency.		
8. Evaluate the promptness of materials inspection in a manufacturer's receiving department.		
9. Report on the need for the states to consider reporting requirements for chemical use data.		
10. Render a public report on the assumptions and compilation of a revenue forecast by a sports stadium/racetrack complex.		

Required:
For each of the engagements listed, indicate (1) the type of audit (financial statement, compliance, economy and efficiency, or program results) and (2) the type of auditors you would expect to be involved.

LO 1-3

1.53 **Financial Assertions and Audit Objectives.** You are engaged to examine the financial statements of Spillane Company for the year ended December 31. Assume that on November 1, Spillane borrowed $500,000 from Second National Bank to finance plant expansion. The long-term note agreement provided for the annual payment of principal and interest over five years. The existing plant was pledged as security for the loan. Due to the unexpected difficulties in acquiring the building site, the plant expansion did not begin on time. To use the borrowed funds, management decided to invest in stocks and bonds and on November 16, invested the $500,000 in publicly traded securities.

Required:
Develop specific assertions (audit objectives) related to securities (assets) based on management's five (PCAOB) general assertions.

LO 1-7

1.54 **Internet Exercise: Professional Certification.** Each state has unique rules for certification concerning education, work experience, and residency. Visit the website for your state board of accountancy and download a list of the requirements for becoming a CPA in your state. Although not all of the state boards of accountancy have websites, you can find those of most states by accessing the National Association of State Boards of Accountancy at its website (http://www.nasba.org).

LO 1-7

1.55 **Internet Exercise: Professional Certification.** Visit the website of the Institute of Internal Auditors (www.theiia.org), the Institute of Management Accountants (www.imanet.org), The Association of Certified Fraud Examiners (www.acfe.com), or the Information Systems Audit and Control Association (www.isaca.org). Review the information regarding the certifications available. Does the organization explain the benefits of having its certification? What topics are covered on the certification exam? What are the minimum requirements to take the exam? What additional experience is required to receive the certification?

LO 1-5

1.56 **Mini-Case: The Market for Audit Services.** Refer to the mini-case "KPMG: How Many Firms?" shown on page C17 and respond to question 4.

Professional Standards

In today's regulatory environment, it's virtually impossible to violate rules.

Bernard Madoff, money manager, approximately one year prior to being arrested for embezzling $50 billion from investors in a Ponzi scheme

Professional Standards References

Topic	AU/ISA Section	PCAOB Reference*
Overall Objectives of the Independent Auditor and the Conduct of an Audit	200	AU 110, AU 150, AU 201, AU 210, AU 220, AU 230
Planning	210, 300	AS 9
Quality Control	220	AU 161
Supervision	220	AS 10
Risks of Material Misstatement	315	AS 12
Materiality	320	AS 11
Audit Evidence	500	AS 15
Written Representations	580	AU 333
Reporting on Financial Statements	700	AS 1, AS 5, AU 530
Modifications to Reports on Financial Statements	705	AU 410, 508
Attestation Standards	AT 50	AT 50
Quality Control	QC 10	QC 20
Peer Reviews	PR 100	N/A

*AU, AT, and QC references represent standards issued by the ASB prior to April 16, 2003, that have not been superseded or amended by the PCAOB.

LEARNING OBJECTIVES

Chapter 1 provides a general introduction to professional accounting practice. Chapter 2 discusses the standards that govern the conduct of audit examinations (generally accepted auditing standards) and how these standards provide the explicit guidance that must be followed during audits. In addition, Chapter 2 identifies important policies and procedures implemented by auditing firms (through a system of quality control) to ensure that the firm's audits comply with appropriate professional standards and can withstand scrutiny by regulatory bodies. Finally, the chapter discusses external monitoring efforts that evaluate the quality of audit firms' work.

Your objectives are to be able to:

LO 2-1 Understand the development and source of generally accepted auditing standards.

LO 2-2 Describe the fundamental principle of *responsibilities* and how this principle relates to the characteristics and qualifications of auditors.

LO 2-3 Describe the fundamental principle of *performance* and identify the major activities performed in an audit.

LO 2-4 Understand the fundamental principle of *reporting* and identify the basic contents of the auditors' report.

LO 2-5 Understand the role of a system of quality control and AICPA and PCAOB monitoring efforts in enabling public accounting firms to meet appropriate levels of professional quality.

LO 2-6 (Appendix) Identify the need for attestation standards and the use of these standards in attestation engagements.

INTRODUCTION

The introductory quote from Bernie Madoff suggests that a strong regulatory environment results in compliance with established rules. Who sets the rules and standards for audits? Until 2002, the accounting profession was *self-regulated;* that is, the standards governing audits were established by members of the profession themselves (through the **American Institute of Certified Public Accountants**, or AICPA). While critics indicated that self-regulation was akin to having university students establish the systems used to determine their grades, this practice continued for more than 60 years and, while some concerns were raised during this time, remained largely unchanged.

Largely as a result of the audit failures related to **Enron** and **WorldCom**, Congress passed the Sarbanes-Oxley Act of 2002 (Sarbanes-Oxley). Among other reforms, this act created the **Public Company Accounting Oversight Board (PCAOB)** to provide external and independent oversight over the audits of public entities (a **public entity** is one who offers registered securities, such as stocks and bonds, for sale to the general public). Among other matters, the PCAOB is responsible for registering public accounting firms, establishing standards for audit engagements, and inspecting the quality of audits conducted by registered public accounting firms.

Despite its relatively short life, the PCAOB has not been without controversy. In addition to criticisms of the increased costs for public companies of complying with the PCAOB's standards related to internal control, the PCAOB's inspection process has come under fire. **Beckstead and Watts, LLP** is a single office firm in Las Vegas, Nevada, with one partner and two professional staff that serves 61 clients. In its September 28, 2005, inspection report, the PCAOB identified deficiencies in 8 of the 16 Beckstead audits it inspected; in two of those cases, the entity's financial statements needed to be restated based on procedures performed by Beckstead in response to the PCAOB's findings.[1] While these findings suggest some deficiencies

---

[1] PCAOB inspection reports are publicly available on the PCAOB's website (http://pcaobus.org/Inspections/Reports/Pages/default.aspx).

in Beckstead's work, the firm's response to the inspection process is anything but favorable. It notes that:

> Our American dream is gone. The PCAOB's relentless tactics and scrutiny is forcing us out of business. . . . During the entire Inspection Process our firm's client based has diminished. Revenues have declined. Profitability has decreased by 60% in 2006 compared to 2005. Our ability to attract new clients has been hindered because of the public posting of the Inspection Report.[2]

In response, Beckstead joined with the **Free Enterprise Fund** in filing a lawsuit challenging the constitutionality of the PCAOB based on both the process through which members of the PCAOB are appointed as well as the powers held by those members. In a case that many critics of the PCAOB and Sarbanes-Oxley hoped would result in significant changes (*Free Enterprise Fund v. Public Company Accounting Oversight Board [PCAOB]*), the U.S. Supreme Court ruled that the inability of the SEC to remove board members for purposes other than "good cause" violates the separation of powers principle of the Constitution. However, rather than an extensive revision of either Sarbanes-Oxley or the nature of the PCAOB, the justices ruled that PCAOB members should be subject to at-will removal by the SEC.[3]

For audits to provide assurance to users in allowing them to make decisions with respect to an entity, it is critical that the work be performed in accordance with appropriate professional standards. The preceding vignette identifies two important issues with respect to this matter. First, according to the PCAOB, Beckstead's audits were not conducted in accordance with professional standards. Second, the PCAOB arrived at this conclusion through a review of the documentation related to audits conducted by Beckstead. The development of professional auditing standards, actions taken by audit firms to ensure that their audits comply with these standards, and monitoring efforts by external bodies (such as the PCAOB) to evaluate the quality of audit firms' work are the focal points of this chapter.

GENERALLY ACCEPTED AUDITING STANDARDS (GAAS)

LEARNING OBJECTIVE 2-1
Understand the development and source of generally accepted auditing standards.

A profession can be defined as a "vocation requiring knowledge of some department or learning or science" or "any vocation or business."[4] Two unique characteristics of a profession are that a body of knowledge is required to participate in the profession and individuals within the profession owe a duty or responsibility to others as they conduct themselves within the profession. Given this definition, auditing certainly qualifies as a profession. As a result, certain standards and guidelines are necessary to identify (1) the characteristics auditors should possess and (2) the types of activities that auditors should and should not engage in while in the practice of the profession of auditing.

Two historical milestones have a significant impact on the development of auditing standards. On December 9, 1938, a scandal of epic proportions broke at **McKesson & Robbins,** a large pharmaceutical company. The company's president, F. Donald Coster, was arrested for embezzling almost $20 million from the company. Coster gained wealth during prohibition by importing alcohol for the production of hair tonic (although most of the alcohol was instead sold to bootleggers). With McKesson & Robbins, he "bought" and "sold" pharmaceuticals from around the world; in reality, the company's operations were little more than a labyrinth of paperwork. Price Waterhouse & Co. (now **PwC**), the company's auditors for more than 10 years, failed to discover that the company had inflated inventory and receivables through the falsification of supporting documents (including one

---
[2] http://www.becksteadwatts.com/OpEds.html (accessed May 9, 2011).
[3] "Supreme Court: A Sarbox Split," *CFO.com*, June 28, 2010; "After Ruling, 'Sarbox' Still Law of Land," *The Wall Street Journal*, June 29, 2010, p. C10.
[4] www.dictionary.com.

phony shipment from the United States to Australia by truck!). Auditors merely accepted management's assertions about inventory and receivables balances without verifying their existence. The case resulted in an SEC investigation that found the following:[5]

1. Auditors failed to employ necessary vigilance, inquisitiveness, and analysis of the evidence available (professional skepticism) as would be expected of an auditing professional.
2. Although auditors are not guarantors and should not be responsible for detecting all fraud, the discovery of gross overstatements in the accounts is a major purpose of an audit.

The accounting profession reacted quite strongly to the scandal. In 1939, the AICPA first developed standards that served as the basis for audits of both public and non-public (private) entities. From 1939 through 2002, the AICPA's Auditing Standards Board issued *Statements on Auditing Procedures* (1939–1972) and *Statements on Auditing Standards (SASs)* (1972–present) to provide guidance for the conduct of audits.[6] As noted in the Introduction to this chapter, following the massive frauds at **Enron** and **WorldCom** (and the inability of those entities' auditors to identify the frauds), Sarbanes-Oxley created the PCAOB and delegated the responsibility for developing standards for the audits of public entities to this body. The PCAOB issues *Auditing Standards,* which are subject to the formal approval of the Securities and Exchange Commission (SEC). The authorization for developing standards for the audits of non-public entities continues to remain with the Auditing Standards Board of the AICPA.

With respect to its responsibility for the audits of public entities, the PCAOB declared that any existing standards that had been issued by the AICPA effective as of April 16, 2003,[7] would serve as *Interim Auditing Standards* and would continue to be amended as considered necessary with the issuance of *Auditing Standards.* As a result, when identifying the appropriate auditing standards for public entities, the appropriate source would be:

- A pronouncement issued by the AICPA prior to April 2003 that has not been amended or superseded by the PCAOB (*Interim Auditing Standard*).
- A pronouncement issued by the PCAOB that has been approved by the SEC *(Auditing Standard).*

Taken together, the relevant pronouncements of the AICPA and PCAOB are collectively referred to as **generally accepted auditing standards (GAAS)**.[8]

GAAS are auditing standards that identify necessary qualifications and characteristics of auditors and guide the conduct of the audit examination. The purpose of GAAS is to meet the objectives of an audit examination, which are (AU 200.11):

- To obtain reasonable assurance about whether the financial statements as a whole are free of material misstatement, whether due to fraud or error, thereby enabling auditors to express an opinion on whether the financial statements are presented fairly, in all material respects, in accordance with an applicable financial reporting framework; and
- To report on the financial statements, and communicate as required by GAAS, in accordance with the auditor's findings.

Generally, auditors that do not follow the guidance provided in GAAS are presumed to have performed deficient audits. Auditing standards may impose *unconditional requirements* on auditors (in which they are expected to fully comply with the provisions of the standards) or *presumptively mandatory requirements* (in which auditors can depart from

---

[5] *Accounting Series Release No. 19* (1940).

[6] *Statements on Auditing Standards (SAS)* are authoritative AICPA pronouncements on auditing theory and practice. *Statements on Auditing Procedure (SAP) Nos. 1–54* were codified into *SAS 1* in 1972. While the original 10 generally accepted auditing standards have been modified for editorial changes over time (most recently by *SAS 113* in 2006), the basic content has not changed significantly.

[7] This date encompasses all pronouncements through *SAS 101*, "Auditing Fair Value Measurements and Disclosures."

[8] The auditing standards for public entities are sometimes referred to as *PCAOB standards,* to distinguish them from the standards for nonpublic entities.

the standards under appropriate circumstances and with appropriate documentation). The auditing standards literature also includes *interpretive publications* (which includes *Interpretations,* exhibits, *AICPA Audit and Accounting Guides,* and *AICA Auditing Statements of Position*). Although officially considered less authoritative and less binding than the guidance in the *SASs* and *Auditing Standards,* auditors still must justify any departures from these publications, which provide guidance on the application of GAAS in specific circumstances, including engagements for entities in certain industries. The relationship among these various pronouncements is summarized in the following graphic.

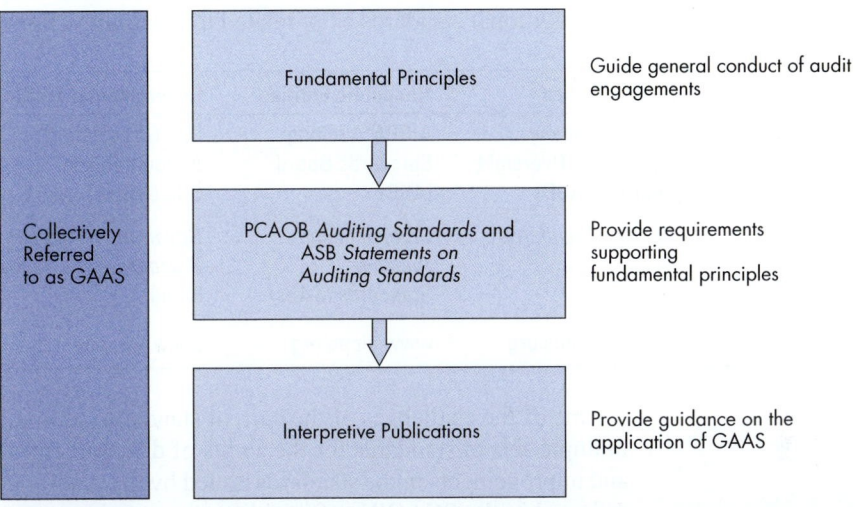

AUDITING INSIGHT Big GAAS/Little GAAS

The delineation of responsibility for setting auditing standards to different bodies for public entities (which are typically larger) and nonpublic entities has created concerns that two markedly different sets of auditing standards will emerge. This issue is known as "Big GAAS/Little GAAS" and raises concerns that the standards of audits for nonpublic entities will result in audits that provide a reduced level of assurance to users of those entities' financial statements. Those favoring separate (more rigorous) standards for public entity audits typically cite the higher risk, complexity, and costs of these audits and the large number of individuals (current and potential stockholders) whose decisions are affected by the entity's financial statements. Opponents of the "Big GAAS/Little GAAS" model have generally called for a single set of principles-based auditing standards scalable to entities of all sizes, since audits are intended to provide a similar level of assurance to all users of financial statements and that users have similar expectations as to the level of assurance provided by the auditors, regardless of the size of the entity.

Source: PricewaterhouseCoopers, "Generally Accepted Auditing Standards for Large and Smaller Entities: Big GAAS, Little GAAS." (http://www.pwc.com.au/assurance/financial/assets/GAAS_Oct07.pdf) (accessed May 9, 2011).

Auditing standards are quite different from *audit procedures*. **Audit procedures** are the particular and specialized actions that auditors take to obtain evidence in a specific audit engagement. **Auditing standards**, on the other hand, are quality guides to the audit that apply to all audits. Procedures may vary, depending on the complexity of an accounting system, on the type of entity, or on other situation-specific factors. For example, loans are liabilities for most entities but are assets for financial institutions. Auditors must use different procedures to audit loans depending on the type of client they are auditing. This difference is the reason auditors' reports refer to an audit "conducted in accordance with *standards* of the Public Company Accounting Oversight Board" (emphasis added) rather than in accordance with audit procedures.

In addition to the standards for U.S. public and nonpublic entities, it is important to note that separate auditing standards have been developed for governmental and foreign entities. A summary of the body charged with establishing standards as well as the standards themselves for various types of audits follows. If an accounting firm audits public and private entities throughout the world, that firm may be subject to multiple (sometimes conflicting) standards issued by the ASB, PCAOB, and IAASB, among others. For this reason, auditors and regulators have a great interest in *convergence*—that is, making the standards coordinated, if not uniform, throughout the world. The *ISAs* are a first step in the development of one consistent set of guidelines that auditors worldwide can follow. While the *ISAs* are similar to U.S. rules, some differences exist. Recently, the ASB has embarked upon a project to redraft existing *SASs* to clarify certain elements of these standards and highlight the convergence of these standards with *ISAs*.[9] While the focus in this text will be on audits of U.S. public and nonpublic entities (and therefore pronouncements of the PCAOB and AICPA), it is important that students be aware that additional standards exist related to the audits of governmental and foreign entities.

	Public Entities	**Nonpublic Entities**	**Governmental Entities**	**Foreign Entities**
Rule-making body	Public Company Accounting Oversight Board (PCAOB)	AICPA Auditing Standards Board (ASB)	U.S. Government Accountability Office (GAO)	IFAC International Auditing and Assurance Standards Board (IAASB)
Standards	*Auditing Standards (ASs)*	*Statements on Auditing Standards (SASs)*	*Government Auditing Standards* (The Yellow Book)	*International Standards on Auditing (ISAs)*
Website	www.pcaobus.org	www.aicpa.org	www.gao.gov	www.ifac.org

One of the challenges of the current standards-setting environment is the existence of multiple sets of standards for the audits of different entities. In addition, recent revisions and improvements in the standards issued by the Auditing Standards Board have not been reflected in the PCAOB's official literature as either an *Auditing Standard* or an *Interim Auditing Standard*. A recent discussion of the PCAOB and its standards-setting process indicates that large firms are integrating newly-issued IAASB and ASB standards into their methodologies if the related topics are not covered by a PCAOB *Auditing Standard*.[10] Clearly, in this environment, it is important that students have an understanding and mastery of ASB, IAASB, and PCAOB standards.

> ### ↳ REVIEW CHECKPOINTS
>
> 2.1 Define *generally accepted auditing standards* (GAAS). Who is responsible for developing standards for the audits of public entities? Who is responsible for developing standards for the audits of nonpublic entities?
>
> 2.2 Identify the role of the following bodies in the auditing standards-setting process: (1) the AICPA; (2) the PCAOB; (3) the SEC.
>
> 2.3 What are the two possible sources of auditing standards for the audits of public entities?

Organization of GAAS

Until recently, the body of GAAS emerged from 10 basic standards that were classified into three broad categories: *general standards, standards of field work,* and *standards of reporting.* An ASB Exposure Draft and resultant pronouncement[11] identified three fundamental principles (similar in nature to the original 10 basic standards) underlying an audit. These fundamental principles (related to responsibilities of the audit team, performance of the audit, and reporting the results of the engagement) are established to meet

---

[9] See the AICPA's "Clarification and Convergence" plan at http://www.aicpa.org/InterestAreas/AccountingAndAuditing/Resources/AudAttest/AudAttestDueProc/DownloadableDocuments/ASB_Convergence_Plan.pdf (accessed May 9, 2011).

[10] S.M. Glover, D.F. Prawitt, and M.H. Taylor, "Audit Standard Setting and Inspection for U.S. Public Companies: A Critical Assessment and Recommendations for Fundamental Change," *Accounting Horizons,* June 2009, pp. 221–237.

[11] "Preface: Principles Underlying an Audit Conducted in Accordance with Generally Accepted Auditing Standards" and "Overall Objectives of the Independent Auditor and the Conduct of an Audit in Accordance with Generally Accepted Auditing Standards" (AU 200).

EXHIBIT 2.1   Comparison of AICPA Generally Accepted Auditing Standards with Fundamental Principles

10 Basic Standards	Fundamental Principles
General Standards	**Responsibilities Principle**
1. The auditor must have adequate technical training and proficiency to perform the audit.	Auditors are responsible for: • Having appropriate competence and capabilities to perform the audit. • Complying with relevant ethical requirements. • Maintaining professional skepticism and exercising professional judgment throughout the planning and performance of the audit.
2. The auditor must maintain independence in mental attitude in all matters relating to the audit.	
3. The auditor must exercise due professional care in the performance of the audit and the preparation of the report.	
Standards of Field Work	**Performance Principle**
1. The auditor must adequately plan the work and must properly supervise any assistants.	To express an opinion, the auditor obtains reasonable assurance about whether the financial statements as a whole are free from material misstatement, whether due to fraud or error. To obtain reasonable assurance, which is a high but not absolute level of assurance, the auditor: • Plans the work and properly supervises any assistants. • Determines and applies appropriate materiality level or levels throughout the audit. • Identifies and assesses risks of material misstatement, whether due to fraud or error, based on an understanding of the entity and its environment, including the entity's internal control. • Obtains sufficient appropriate audit evidence about whether material misstatements exist, through designing and implementing appropriate responses to the assessed risks.
2. The auditor must obtain a sufficient understanding of the entity and its environment, including its internal control, to assess the risk of material misstatement of the financial statements whether due to error or fraud, and to design the nature, timing, and extent of further audit procedures.	
3. The auditor must obtain sufficient appropriate audit evidence by performing audit procedures to afford a reasonable basis for an opinion regarding the financial statements under audit.	
Standards of Reporting	**Reporting Principle**
1. The auditor must state in the auditor's report whether the financial statements are presented in accordance with generally accepted accounting principles (GAAP).	Based on evaluation of the evidence obtained, the auditor expresses in the form of a written report, an opinion in accordance with the auditor's findings, or states that an opinion cannot be expressed. The opinion states whether the financial statements are presented fairly, in all material respects, in accordance with the applicable financial reporting framework.
2. The auditor must identify in the auditor's report those circumstances in which such principles have not been consistently observed in the current period in relation to the preceding period.	
3. When the auditor determines that informative disclosures are not reasonably adequate, the auditor must so state in the auditor's report.	
4. The auditor must either express an opinion regarding the financial statements, taken as a whole, or state that an opinion cannot be expressed, in the auditor's report. When the auditor cannot express an overall opinion, the auditor should state the reasons therefore in the auditor's report. In all cases where an auditor's name is associated with financial statements, the auditor should clearly indicate the character of the auditor's work, if any, and the degree of responsibility the auditor is taking, in the auditor's report.	

the objectives of an audit and are supported by objectives and requirements of specific *SASs*. Exhibit 2.1 compares the traditional 10 basic standards and the fundamental principles established by the ASB.[12] While these principles have been issued by the ASB and are not formally applicable to the audits of public entities, they are consistent with and reflect the requirements of GAAS for audits of public entities.

[12] In the "Explanatory Memorandum" to the *Exposure Draft,* the ASB noted that, while the fundamental principles would supersede the 10 standards, the principles essentially preserve the functions currently served by these 10 standards and provide a structure for the codification of the redrafted *SASs*.

Recall from Chapter 1 the definition of *auditing* as

> . . . a systematic process of objectively obtaining and evaluating evidence regarding assertions about economic actions and events to ascertain the degree of correspondence between the assertions and established criteria and communicating the results to interested users.

Closer examination of the fundamental principles reveals that they closely parallel that definition. For example, the *responsibilities* principle defines objectivity and identifies the important role that objectivity plays in the audit. The *performance* principle requires, among other things, auditors to plan the work (i.e., conduct the audit using a "systematic process") and to "obtain and evaluate evidence" through assessing the risk of material misstatement and gathering sufficient appropriate evidence. Finally, the *reporting* principle provides guidance for "communicating the results" of the audit about whether the financial statements are prepared using "established criteria" (an applicable financial reporting framework, or GAAP).

> ### ↳ REVIEW CHECKPOINT
> 2.4 Identify and briefly describe the three fundamental principles underlying GAAS.

FUNDAMENTAL PRINCIPLE: RESPONSIBILITIES

LEARNING OBJECTIVE 2-2
Describe the fundamental principle of *responsibilities* and how this principle relates to the characteristics and qualifications of auditors.

The fundamental principle of *responsibilities* relates to the personal integrity and professional qualifications of auditors. This principle addresses the following responsibilities of auditors:

Auditors are responsible for:

- *Having appropriate competence and capabilities to perform the audit.*
- *Complying with relevant ethical requirements; and,*
- *Maintaining professional skepticism and exercising professional judgment, throughout the planning and performance of the audit.*

As shown in the following figure, most of the issues related to responsibilities are addressed before a firm accepts a prospective client. However, professional skepticism and professional judgment must be considered and exercised by the auditor throughout the entire engagement.

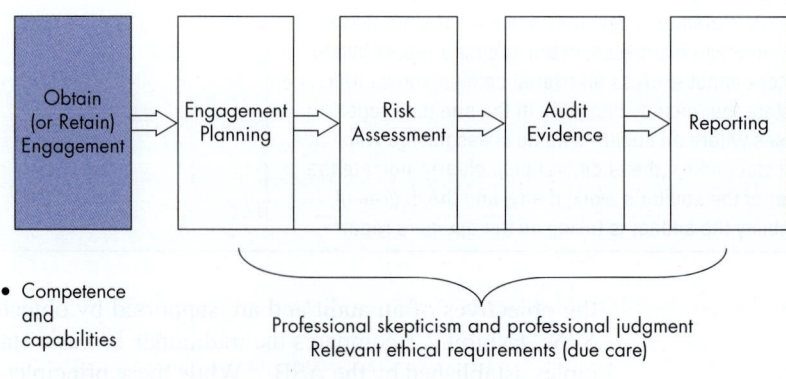

Competence and Capabilities

Competence and *capabilities* begin with *education* in accounting because auditors hold themselves out as experts in accounting standards, financial reporting, and auditing. In addition to university-level education prior to beginning their careers, auditors are also required to participate in *continuing professional education* throughout their careers to ensure that their knowledge keeps pace with changes in the accounting and auditing profession. In fact, one of the important requirements for maintaining a CPA license is sufficient continuing professional education.

Education is only one element of competence and capabilities. Another important dimension is *experience,* which is gained with hands-on practice and on-the-job training. An important component of this experience is the ability to develop and apply professional judgment in real-world audit situations. These situations include various judgments related to gathering evidence related to the fairness of an entity's financial statements and evaluating whether that evidence indicates that the financial statements are prepared according to generally accepted accounting principles. (Recall that professional judgment is also an important component of the performance principle, which will be discussed later).

Independence and Due Care

The responsibilities principle requires auditors to comply with appropriate ethical requirements; two important requirements relate to *independence* and *due care*. Auditors must maintain independence *in mental attitude;* that is, auditors are expected to be unbiased and impartial with respect to the financial statements and other information they audit. This "state of mind" is often referred to as the auditor possessing **independence in fact**. This independence allows auditors to form an opinion on the entity's financial statements without being affected by influences that might compromise that opinion.

It is not only important for auditors to be unbiased; they must also *appear* to be unbiased. **Independence in appearance** relates to others' (particularly financial statement users') perceptions of auditors' independence. For example, while owning a single share of stock in a client would not likely influence auditors' mental attitude (i.e., auditors would be *independent in fact*), it is not likely that third-party users would perceive auditors to be independent (i.e., auditors would not be independent in appearance). The rules relating to independence (as provided by the AICPA Code of Professional Conduct and the SEC) primarily relate to independence in appearance.

Over time, the concept of independence has evolved and various attempts have been made to identify types of activities auditors can and cannot engage in while retaining their independence. In 2001, the SEC issued rules that prohibited auditors from providing financial systems implementation and internal audit services to their clients; interestingly, these types of services were among those provided by **Arthur Andersen** to many of its clients (including **Enron**). Additional restrictions were provided by Sarbanes-Oxley to include other types of services, along with the requirement that *all* nonaudit services were required to be approved by the entity's audit committee. In addition, Sarbanes-Oxley included the following requirements intended to address auditor independence for audits of public entities:

- Limiting the service for the engagement partner and the engagement quality partner on a particular client engagement to a maximum of five years.
- Prohibiting a firm from conducting the audit if a client employee with financial oversight responsibility was a member of the audit engagement team during the year under audit.
- Requiring a one-year "cooling off" period before an auditor is permitted to assume employment for a client in a key management position.

While independence is a complex concept and many different threats to independence exist, two general types of relationships that are believed to jeopardize (or compromise) independence are

1. *Financial relationships,* such as owning shares of stock in a client or having a loan outstanding to or from a client.
2. *Managerial relationships,* such as the ability to act in a decision-making capacity on behalf of a client or to provide advice on systems or information that will subsequently be audited.

Clearly, the relationships just listed would impair perceptions of auditors' independence, but other considerations are necessary. For example, while it seems safe to conclude that an audit team member's spouse should be restricted from the preceding types of relationships for a client for which the team member is providing services, could that spouse have these types of relationships with respect to a client served by a distant office of the team member's firm? Could the audit team member's third cousin have such relationships? A full discussion of AICPA and SEC rules (and various interpretations of those rules) related to independence is provided in Module B of this text. Independence must be zealously guarded because the general public will grant social recognition of professional status to auditors only as long as they are perceived to be independent.

AUDITING INSIGHT — Independent Auditors?

In an investigation of independence violations at **PricewaterhouseCoopers (PwC)**, an independent consultant disclosed that the accounting firm's personnel had committed more than 8,000 independence violations. A detailed review of the violations revealed the following:

- 45.2 percent of the reported violations involved partners who perform services related to audits of financial statements.
- Almost half of the reported violations involved investments in securities, mutual funds, bank accounts, or insurance products associated with a client.
- Almost 32 percent of reported violations involved holdings of a client's stock or stock options.
- Six of 11 partners at the senior management level and each of the 12 regional partners who help administer PwC's independence program reported at least one violation (one reported 38 violations and another reported 34 violations).

The consultant's report, "Report on the Internal Investigation of Independence Issues at PricewaterhouseCoopers, LLP," concluded, "The combined results of the self-reporting and random tests of those reports indicated that approximately 86.5 percent of PwC partners and 10.5 percent of all other PwC professionals had independence violations." In response to the report, then-SEC Chief Accountant Lynn E. Turner stated, "This report is a sobering reminder that accounting professionals need to renew their commitment to auditor independence."

PwC employees noted a number of reasons for the violations, including failure to check their investments against the firm's client list after the merger of PwC's two legacy firms (Price Waterhouse and Coopers & Lybrand). Others suggested that the independence rules were just too complex. Since the disclosure of the violations, PwC has implemented a new proactive monitoring system that requires all partners and managers to report all investments; employees are then notified automatically if there are any independence concerns.

Source: SEC Press Release 2000–4.

A second ethical requirement identified by the responsibilities principle is that of due care. **Due care** reflects a level of performance that would be exercised by reasonable auditors in similar circumstances. This standard is often referred to as that of a prudent auditor; auditors are expected to possess the skills and knowledge of others in their profession but are not expected to be infallible. This aspect relates to the competence and capabilities of the auditor to perform the engagement and issue appropriate reports. One specific element of due care noted by the standards is the need for auditors to plan and perform the audit with an appropriate level of professional skepticism as discussed in the following section.

Professional Skepticism and Professional Judgment

Professional skepticism and professional judgment are necessary responsibilities of auditors throughout the entire audit process. **Professional skepticism** is a state of mind that is characterized by appropriate questioning and a critical assessment of audit evidence. When exhibiting professional skepticism, auditors do not assume that management is dishonest, nor do they assume that management is unquestionably honest. Rather, auditors evaluate and consider:

- Contradictory audit evidence obtained through different procedures.
- The reliability of documentary evidence.
- The reliability of information obtained from management and those charged with governance of the entity (e.g., the audit committee).

Professional judgment is the application of relevant training, knowledge, and experience in making informed decisions about appropriate courses of action during the audit engagement. These judgments relate to the evidence obtained during the audit and the conclusions reached based on this evidence. Auditors are required to demonstrate this characteristic throughout the entire audit process as they do professional skepticism. Professional judgment is required as auditors gather evidence, evaluate evidence, and draw conclusions based on evidence. In addition to demonstrating appropriate levels of professional judgment, auditors are also required to carefully document their professional judgment in such a manner that experienced auditors with no previous relationship with the audit can understand the judgments made in reaching conclusions on significant issues.

AUDITING INSIGHT — Madoff and the Responsibilities Principle

A preliminary investigation of the actions of David Friehling (the individual responsible for the audits of **Bernard L. Madoff Investment Securities LLC**) illustrated the following potential violations of elements of the responsibilities principle:

- Friehling did not verify the existence of assets or securities trades made by Madoff's company, suggesting a lack of professional skepticism and a lack of due care.
- Friehling was the sole auditor at Friehling and Horowitz, raising the question as to whether a "one-man" firm has the capability to effectively audit a company as large as Madoff's.
- Friehling and his family had investment accounts as Madoff's company worth more than $14 million, a "blatant" conflict of interest that raises questions about his independence.

Source: "Accountant Arrested for Sham Audits," *The Wall Street Journal*, March 19, 2009, p. C1.

↳ REVIEW CHECKPOINTS

2.5 Distinguish between independence in fact and independence in appearance. Can auditors be independent in fact yet not be perceived to be independent in appearance?

2.6 What is due care? To what standards are auditors held with respect to due care?

2.7 Define *professional skepticism* and *professional judgment*. During what stages of the audit are auditors required to demonstrate these characteristics?

FUNDAMENTAL PRINCIPLE: PERFORMANCE

LEARNING OBJECTIVE 2-3
Describe the fundamental principle of *performance* and identify the major activities performed in an audit.

The fundamental principle of *performance* sets forth general quality criteria for conducting an audit. As noted in the preceding section, in addition to the elements of this principle, the performance of the audit is also influenced by the need for auditors to exercise *professional skepticism* and *professional judgment* throughout the audit process. The performance principle states that:

> To express an opinion, the auditor obtains reasonable assurance about whether the financial statements as a whole are free from material misstatement, whether due to fraud or error. To obtain reasonable assurance, which is a high but not absolute level of assurance, the auditor:
>
> - plans the work and properly supervises any assistants.
> - determines and applies appropriate materiality level or levels throughout the audit.
> - identifies and assesses risks of material misstatement, whether due to fraud or error, based on an understanding of the entity and its environment, including the entity's internal control.
> - obtains sufficient appropriate audit evidence about whether material misstatements exist, through designing and implementing appropriate responses to the assessed risks.

As the preceding reflects, the performance principle contains five elements: (1) reasonable assurance, (2) planning and supervision, (3) materiality, (4) risk assessment, and (5) audit evidence. These are discussed in the remainder of this section.

Reasonable Assurance

The concept of **reasonable assurance** recognizes that a GAAS audit may not detect all material misstatements and auditors are not "insurers" or "guarantors" regarding the fairness of the entity's financial statements. However, auditors should provide a high level of assurance (or confidence) regarding their work. Auditors provide reasonable assurance through considering various risks relating to the likelihood of material misstatement in the financial statements and performing audit procedures to control the overall risk to an acceptably low level. This is done through the risk assessment process, an additional element of the performance principle (discussed next).

One question that may arise is that, given the importance of an audit, why don't auditors try to achieve absolute assurance? This level of assurance is simply not possible for the following reasons:

- In the course of the engagement, audit teams will make mistakes and misinterpretations. Such mistakes and misinterpretations are consistent with the concept of due care, which recognizes that auditors are not infallible.
- The nature of financial reporting is such that certain aspects of this process are subject to management judgments and estimates (for example, the useful lives used to depreciate property, plant, and equipment may differ from the actual lives of these assets).
- The nature of many audit procedures is such that they cannot always be relied on to detect misstatements (issues related to audit evidence are discussed later in this section).
- In many cases, because of the need to complete an audit within a reasonable period of time and to achieve a balance between benefit and cost, auditors evaluate only a sample of transactions and components.

Because of these limitations, an audit conducted in accordance with GAAS may fail to detect material misstatements. However, these limitations do not provide auditors an "excuse" to fail to gather appropriate evidence. While no guarantee exists that all material misstatements will be identified, the concept of reasonable assurance does require auditors to reduce the risk of failing to detect a material misstatement to an acceptably low level.

Planning and Supervision (AU 210, AU 220, AU 300, AS 9, AS 10)

After obtaining or retaining the engagement, the next major stage of the audit is planning, as in the following figure. The professional standards contain several considerations for planning and supervising an audit. They are concerned with (1) preparing an audit plan and supervising the audit work, (2) obtaining knowledge of the client's business, and (3) dealing with differences of opinion among the accounting firm's own personnel.

STAGES OF AN AUDIT

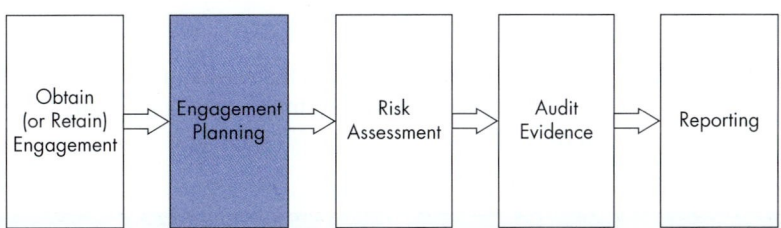

GAAS require the preparation of a written audit plan. An **audit plan** (formerly referred to as an *audit program*) is a list of the audit procedures auditors need to perform to gather sufficient appropriate evidence on which to base their opinion on the financial statements. The procedures in an audit plan should be stated in enough detail to instruct the assistants about the work to be done. (You will see detailed audit plans later in this textbook.)

Auditors are also required to obtain an understanding of the client's business and industry. This knowledge helps auditors identify areas for special attention (the accounts or classes of transactions where frauds or errors might exist), evaluate the reasonableness of accounting estimates made by management, evaluate management's responses to inquiries, and make judgments about the appropriateness of management's choices among accounting principles. Auditors gain this understanding of a business through discussions with management and other client personnel, through experience with other entities in the same industry, and reviewing AICPA accounting and audit guides, industry publications, other entities' financial statements, business periodicals, and textbooks.

Members of an audit team may sometimes disagree among themselves on audit decisions ranging from inclusion or omission of procedures to conclusions about the fair presentation of an account or the entire financial statements. When differences of opinion arise, audit personnel should consult with one another and with experts in the firm to try to resolve the disagreement. If they do not achieve resolution, the firm should have procedures to allow audit team members to document the disagreement and to dissociate themselves from the matter. In this case, the basis for the final audit decision on the matter also should be provided in the audit documentation for later reference.

Just as having advance notice of assignments and examinations makes it easier for you (as a student) to perform better on those assignments, timing is also important for audit planning. To have time to plan an audit, auditors should be engaged before the client's fiscal year-end (also known as the **date of the financial statements**). The more advance notice auditors have, the better they are able to provide enough time for planning. The audit team may be able to perform part of the audit at an *interim date*—a date some weeks or months before year-end—and thereby make the rest of the audit work more efficient. For example, in examining property, plant, and equipment, auditors may evaluate activity in the account balance up to some date during the year (say November 10) and then evaluate activity occurring between that date and the year-end (the roll-forward period), as shown below. Essentially, at December 31, auditors have evaluated the account balance through the interim date (in this case, November 10) and will evaluate the remainder of the activity following year-end. Doing so permits audit work to be "shifted" from after year-end to prior to year-end and allows the audit to be completed on a more timely basis.

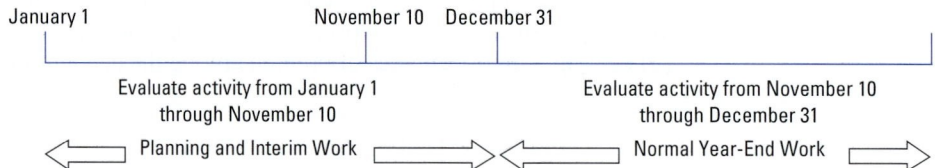

Engagement planning is discussed in greater detail in Chapter 3. In addition, planning activities related to the audit of various accounts and cycles are discussed in Chapters 6 through 10.

AUDITING INSIGHT | Too Late

FastTrak Corporation had a disagreement with its auditors because the partner in charge of the engagement would not agree to let management use operating lease accounting treatment for some heavy equipment whose leases met the criteria for capitalization. FastTrak fired the auditors 10 weeks after the date of the company's financial statements and then started contacting other public accounting firms to perform the audit. However, the deadline for filing the auditors' report with the SEC was within two weeks. Every other firm contacted by FastTrak refused the audit because it could not be planned and performed properly on such short notice with such a tight deadline.

Materiality (AU 320, AS 11)

The concept of **materiality** recognizes that auditors should focus on matters that are important to financial statement users. One common way of viewing materiality is the dollar amount that would influence the lending or investing decisions of financial statement users. Auditors and users do not expect account balances to be accurate to the penny; after all, many entities round their financial statements to the thousands, or even millions, of dollars! For example, **Walmart** reported net income of $16.4 billion in 2011; clearly, a misstatement of $1,000 would not affect users' decisions, but a misstatement of $1 billion might. Materiality is recognized as part of the objective of an audit, which is "to obtain reasonable assurance about whether the financial statements as a whole are free of *material* misstatement" (emphasis added) (AU 200.11).

The audit team considers materiality in planning the audit, performing the audit, and evaluating the effect of misstatements on the entity's financial statements. Auditors are responsible only for providing reasonable assurance that misstatements *material* to the entity's financial statements are identified. Stated another way, auditors are not responsible for detecting misstatements that are not material to the financial statements.

While the concept of materiality appears to be relatively straightforward, implementation of materiality during the audit requires high levels of professional judgment. For example, suppose a small dollar misstatement (in absolute terms) resulted in an entity meeting its earnings expectations or resulted in an entity reporting higher earnings than in the previous year. Certainly, these impacts would likely influence investment decisions, even if the dollar amount is relatively small. Circumstances such as these are referred to as *qualitative materiality* factors and should also be considered by auditors. The role of materiality in the planning stages of the audit is discussed in more detail in Chapter 3.

Risk Assessment (AU 315, AS 12)

An important part of the performance principle is for auditors to identify important concerns (or risks) they face in the audit. This process is referred to as *risk assessment* and follows engagement planning, as follows:

STAGES OF AN AUDIT

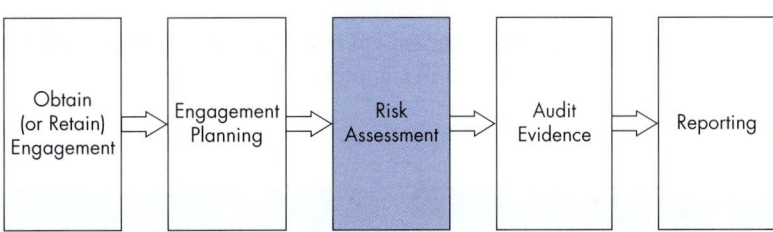

The risk assessment process requires an understanding of the client, its operating environment, and its industry. This includes internal controls operating within the client's accounting information systems that ultimately produce the client's financial statements. **Internal control** may be defined as the policies and procedures implemented by an entity to prevent or detect material accounting frauds or errors and provide for their correction on a timely basis. Satisfactory internal control reduces the probability of frauds or errors in the accounts. This understanding provides the foundation for the work auditors do in assessing the **risk of material misstatement**, a combination of **inherent risk** (the probability that a material misstatement, either an error or fraud, will occur) and **control risk** (the probability that a material misstatement, either an error or fraud, will not be prevented or detected on a timely basis by the entity's internal controls). One way to think of the risk of material misstatement is the likelihood that an error or fraud will exist in the financial statements prior to considering the auditors' work.

The primary purpose of assessing the risk of material misstatement is to help auditors determine the *nature, timing, and extent of audit procedures* necessary for gathering evidence about the fairness of the entity's financial statements. The process of risk assessment presumes two necessary relationships:

1. Effective internal control reduces the control risk, and auditors thus have a reasonable basis for reducing the necessary effectiveness of further audit procedures.
2. Ineffective internal control increases control risk, and auditors must increase the necessary effectiveness of further audit procedures.

Because these audit procedures are used to obtain evidence with respect to the fairness of the account balance (i.e., to "substantiate" the account balance), they are referred to as **substantive procedures**. A depiction of this relationship follows:

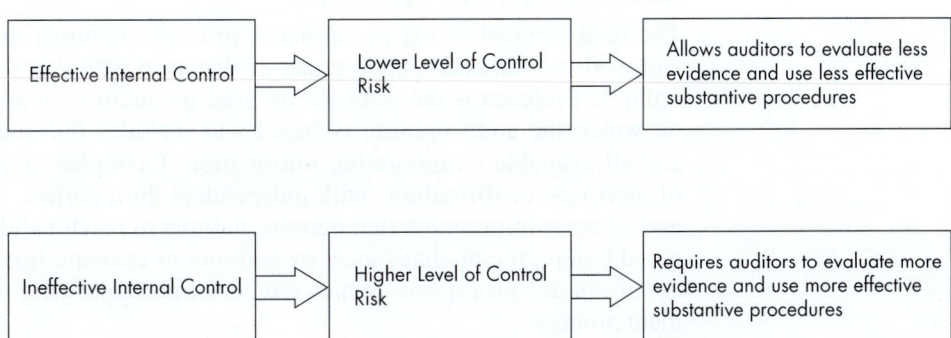

The importance of internal control in the audit examination is evidenced by an increase in auditors' responsibility for internal control in the audit of public entities through the issuance of *Auditing Standard No. 5 (AS 5)* by the PCAOB. Under this standard, auditors are required to evaluate (through testing the operating effectiveness of specific controls) and report on the effectiveness of the entity's internal control over financial reporting for public entities; this is one example where the auditors' responsibility in the audit of a public entity exceeds that for the audit of a nonpublic entity. Internal control (and the related reports on internal control) is discussed in more detail in Chapter 5; in addition, important elements of internal control related to the audit of various accounts and cycles are discussed in Chapters 6 through 10.

AUDITING INSIGHT | Control Lapse Contributes to Duplicate Payments

Allstate Trucking processed insurance claims on damages to shipments in transit on its trucks, paying them from a self-insurance payment reserve. After payment, the claims documents were not marked "paid." Later, the same documents were processed again for duplicate payments to customers who kicked back 50 percent to a dishonest Allstate employee. Auditors learned that the documents were not marked "paid," concluded that the specific control risk of duplicate payments was high, extended their procedures to include a search for duplicate payments in the damage expense account, found them, and traced the problem to the dishonest employee. Embezzlements of $35,000 per year were stopped.

How could this fraud have been prevented? If the claims documents were marked "paid" after the first payment, this fact would have been noted by Allstate's personnel, who would not have permitted the documents to be processed a second time.

REVIEW CHECKPOINTS

2.8 Define *reasonable assurance*. Why must auditors provide reasonable (rather than absolute) assurance?

2.9 What three elements of planning and supervision are considered essential in audit practice?

2.10 Why is the timing of the auditors' appointment an important matter in the conduct of a financial statement audit?

2.11 What is *materiality*? During what stages of the audit do auditors consider materiality?

2.12 For what reasons do auditors obtain an understanding of a client's internal control?

2.13 What is the basic relationship between the effectiveness of the client's internal control and the necessary effectiveness of substantive procedures?

Audit Evidence (AU 500, AS 15)

The final element of the performance principle requires that the audit team collect and evaluate sufficient appropriate evidence to afford a reasonable basis for their opinion. **Evidence** is the information used by auditors in arriving at the conclusions on which the audit opinion is based and includes the underlying accounting data and all available corroborating information. Examples of evidence include minutes of meetings, confirmations with independent third parties, invoices, analyst reports, and all other information that permits auditors to reach valid, logical conclusions. As noted before, the methods used by auditors to evaluate this evidence are referred to as *substantive procedures*, which are performed following the auditors' risks assessment process.

STAGES OF AN AUDIT

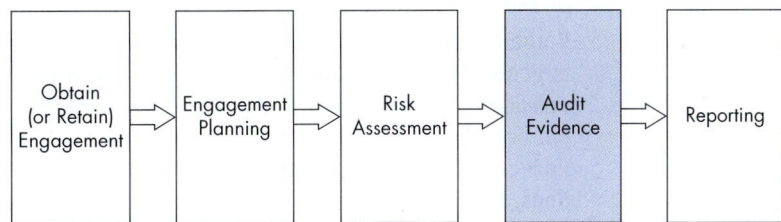

The performance principle requires auditors to gather "sufficient appropriate" evidence; another term that is used to refer to sufficient appropriate evidence is **persuasiveness**. Evidence is said to be persuasive when it provides support for the auditors' opinion. The concept of persuasiveness reflects the reality that auditors will not gather absolute, or convincing evidence; to do so would require auditors to examine every transaction or component of an account balance or class of transactions. Rather, auditors will gather evidence that provides reasonable assurance. Because the persuasiveness of evidence relies on both its "sufficiency" and its "appropriateness," we will discuss briefly discuss both of these dimensions next.

To be considered **appropriate**, evidence must be **relevant** and **reliable**. *Relevance* refers to the nature of information provided by the audit evidence; for example, when auditors confirm accounts receivable with customers, this provides evidence that the account is legitimate (i.e., the sale actually took place) but does not provide evidence that the account will ultimately be collectible. The nature of information provided by evidence is operationalized through the *management assertions* identified and discussed in Chapter 1.

Reliability refers to the extent of trust that auditors can place in evidence; evidence that is reliable can be thought of as being of *high quality*. Professional standards note that evidence is more reliable when (1) it is obtained directly by auditors (rather than indirectly from other sources), (2) it is obtained from sources outside the entity rather than internal to the entity, (3) the entity's internal controls are more effective rather than less effective, and (4) it is represented by original source documents rather than photocopies, facsimiles, or documents that have been converted into electronic form.

In gathering evidence, one factor that auditors may influence is the source of the evidence. In evaluating potential sources, auditors consider the following hierarchy of *audit evidence quality* (the hierarchy starts with the strongest form of evidence and proceeds to the weakest).

1. Auditors' *direct, personal knowledge,* obtained through *physical observation* and auditors' own *mathematical computations,* is generally considered the most reliable evidence.
2. Documentary evidence obtained directly from external sources (**external evidence**) is generally considered reliable. There may be factors, however, that might affect the reliability of evidence received from external sources, including the knowledge and objectivity of the source.
3. Documentary evidence that has originated outside the client's information processing system but that has been received and processed by the client (**external-internal evidence**) is generally considered reliable when internal control is strong although less reliable than *external evidence.* To reduce the likelihood for fraud, original documents are preferred to photocopies.
4. **Internal evidence** consisting of documents that are produced, circulated, and finally stored within the client's information system is generally considered low in reliability. However, internal evidence is used extensively when it is produced under satisfactory conditions of internal control. Sometimes internal evidence is the only type available. As the following Auditing Insight related to **HealthSouth** reveals,

auditors must be alert for the possibility that internal documents are fraudulently prepared by the client.

5. **Verbal evidence** provided by the client's officers, directors, owners, and employees is generally considered the least reliable form of evidence. While verbal evidence is considered to be a weak form of evidence, GAAS require that auditors obtain written corroboration from the client to emphasize management's responsibility for the fairness of the financial statements. This corroboration (known as **written representations**, or management representations) addresses the fairness of the entity's financial statements, availability of all financial records and related data, internal control over financial reporting, and other specific representations about the financial statements and accounts.

AUDITING INSIGHT — Whom Can You Trust?

"The level of fraud and financial deception that took place at **HealthSouth** is a blatant violation of investor trust, and **Ernst & Young** is as outraged as the investing public." In a public statement, the accounting firm asserted that HealthSouth, one of its largest clients, tried to deceive the firm's audit team by creating false documents to support fraudulent journal entries. To support the firm's claim, the statement cited a court hearing in which a former HealthSouth employee testified that "he knew of at least three occasions where company executives prepared false documents specifically to conceal fraud from Ernst."

Source: "Did HealthSouth Auditor Ernst Miss Key Clues to Fraud Risks?" *The Wall Street Journal,* April 10, 2003, pp. C1, C3.

In sum, to be appropriate, evidence must be both relevant and reliable. Substantive procedures provide more persuasive evidence when they are designed and performed to obtain evidence that is more relevant and reliable.

While *appropriateness* relates to evidence *quality,* **sufficiency** relates to evidence *quantity.* Auditors are required to gather enough evidence to support an opinion on the financial statements, but how much evidence is enough? The auditing profession has no official standard, leaving the matter of sufficiency to auditors' *professional judgment.* Note that the standard refers to "sufficient" rather than "absolute" evidence. For large entities, auditors do not audit all of the transactions and components but examine a sample of these items in drawing their conclusions. Although auditors can use statistical sampling to determine sufficiency in a numerical sense (e.g., confidence levels), from a practical standpoint, *sufficient evidence* can be defined as enough evidence to stand the scrutiny of other auditors (supervisors and reviewers) and outsiders (such as critics, judges, and jurors). The real test of sufficiency is whether auditors can persuade others that their evidence is strong enough to reach the same conclusions they have reached.

The sufficiency and appropriateness of evidence is reflected in the necessary level of detection risk. **Detection risk** represents the risk that the audit team's substantive procedures will fail to detect a material misstatement. As auditors require higher quality evidence (lower detection risk), they must gather more relevant and reliable evidence (appropriateness) and evaluate a larger number of transactions or components (sufficiency). Evidence-gathering procedures are discussed in more detail in Chapter 3. In addition, specific approaches to gathering evidence in the examination of various accounts and cycles are discussed in Chapters 6 through 10.

Exhibit 2.2 summarizes the key characteristics of evidence just discussed. Note that detection risk is affected by both the sufficiency and the appropriateness of audit evidence. Also note that the appropriateness is affected by both the relevance of the evidence as well as its reliability.

EXHIBIT 2.2
Key Characteristics of Audit Evidence

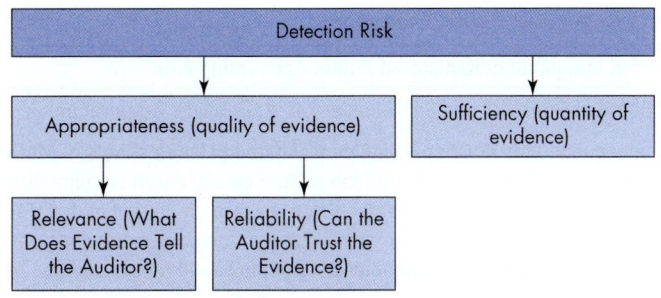

> ### ⌕ REVIEW CHECKPOINTS
>
> 2.14 Define *audit evidence*.
> 2.15 Define *external, external-internal,* and *internal documentary evidence*.
> 2.16 Distinguish between relevance and reliability as these concepts relate to audit evidence. How are relevance and reliability associated with the appropriateness of audit evidence?
> 2.17 How does the source of evidence affect its reliability?
> 2.18 How are the sufficiency and appropriateness of evidence related to detection risk?

▽ FUNDAMENTAL PRINCIPLE: REPORTING (AU 700, AU 705, AS 1, AS 5)

LEARNING OBJECTIVE 2-4
Understand the fundamental principle of *reporting* and identify the basic contents of the auditors' report.

The ultimate objective of the audit—the report on the audit—is guided by the fundamental principle of reporting, which states:

> *Based on evaluation of the evidence obtained, the auditor expresses in the form of a written report, an opinion in accordance with the auditor's findings, or states that an opinion cannot be expressed. The opinion states whether the financial statements are presented fairly, in all material respects, in accordance with the applicable financial reporting framework.*

As the following graphic shows, reporting is the final stage of an audit and occurs following the gathering of audit evidence.

STAGES OF AN AUDIT

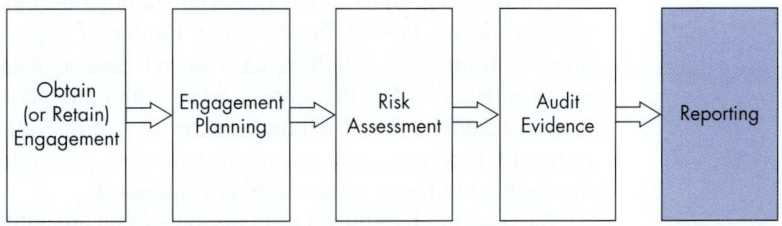

An example of an auditors' report is shown in Exhibit 2.3, and you should review it in relation to the following discussion.

The report in Exhibit 2.3 is the report form used for public entities; while differences in wording exist, the report for nonpublic entities conveys essentially the same information. You should understand the term *financial statements* to include not only the traditional financial statements but also all footnote disclosures and additional information (e.g., earnings per share calculations) that are integral elements of the basic financial presentation required by GAAP.

EXHIBIT 2.3 Example Auditor's Report for Public Company

Report Title	**Report of Independent Registered Public Accounting Firm**
Addressee	The Board of Directors and Shareholders of McDonald's Corporation
Introductory Paragraph	We have audited the accompanying consolidated balance sheets of McDonald's Corporation as of December 31, 2010 and 2009, and the related consolidated statements of income, shareholders' equity, and cash flows for each of the three years in the period ended December 31, 2010. These financial statements are the responsibility of the Company's management. Our responsibility is to express an opinion on these financial statements based on our audits.
Scope Paragraph	We conducted our audits in accordance with the standards of the Public Company Accounting Oversight Board (United States). Those standards require that we plan and perform the audit to obtain reasonable assurance about whether the financial statements are free of material misstatement. An audit includes examining, on a test basis, evidence supporting the amounts and disclosures in the financial statements. An audit also includes assessing the accounting principles used and significant estimates made by management, as well as evaluating the overall financial statement presentation. We believe that our audits provide a reasonable basis for our opinion.
Opinion Paragraph	In our opinion, the financial statements referred to above present fairly, in all material respects, the consolidated financial position of McDonald's Corporation at December 31, 2010 and 2009, and the consolidated results of its operations and its cash flows for each of the three years in the period ended December 31, 2010, in conformity with U.S. generally accepted accounting principles.
Internal Control Paragraph	We also have audited, in accordance with the standards of the Public Company Accounting Oversight Board (United States), McDonald's Corporation's internal control over financial reporting as of December 31, 2010, based on criteria established in *Internal Control–Integrated Framework* issued by the Committee of Sponsoring Organizations of the Treadway Commission and our report dated February 25, 2011 expressed an unqualified opinion thereon.
	Ernst & Young LLP (signed) Chicago, Illinois February 25, 2011

The reporting principle requires the auditor to express an opinion on the entity's financial statements (or indicate that an opinion cannot be expressed). With respect to this requirement, the opinion paragraph of **Ernst & Young's** report begins with the phrase "In our opinion," which represents the expression of an opinion.

In expressing this opinion, the auditor is required to assess the financial statements against an applicable financial reporting framework. A **financial reporting framework** is a set of criteria used to determine the measurement, recognition, presentation, and disclosure of material items in the financial statements; three examples of financial reporting frameworks are GAAP, *International Financial Reporting Standards (IFRS),* or a special purpose framework (such as cash or tax bases). Again, referring to Ernst & Young's report in Exhibit 2.3, the opinion paragraph concludes that **McDonald's** financial statements present its financial condition, results of operations, and cash flows ". . . in conformity with U.S. generally accepted accounting principles" (GAAP). In this case, GAAP is the applicable financial accounting framework.

The report in Exhibit 2.3 is an example of an **unqualified opinion**, which indicates that the entity's (in this case, McDonald's) financial statements present its financial condition, results of operations, and cash flows in conformity with GAAP. "Unqualified" means "good" in the sense that auditors are not calling attention to anything wrong with the financial statements. In other cases, the entity's financial statements (or elements within those financial statements) are materially misstated and do not present the entity's financial condition, results of operations, and cash flows in conformity with GAAP; collectively, these situations are known as **departures from GAAP**. In such cases, report modifications are necessary.

- An **adverse opinion** is the opposite of an unqualified opinion and concludes that the entity's financial statements are not presented in conformity with GAAP (or other financial reporting framework such as International Financial Reporting Standards, or IFRS).

- A **qualified opinion** concludes that *except for* a relatively isolated (usually limited) departure, the entity's financial statements are presented in conformity with GAAP (or other financial reporting framework, such as IFRS). Qualified opinions can also be issued for auditors' inability to conduct a GAAS audit (a **scope limitation**).
- In some cases (for example, if a scope limitation is highly significant or the auditor lacks independence), auditors may choose not to express an opinion on the entity's financial statements. This type of report is referred to as a **disclaimer of opinion**. (A disclaimer of opinion is an indication that an opinion cannot be expressed.)

When these situations are encountered, auditors will add an explanatory paragraph to their report and modify some of the paragraphs of the report shown in Exhibit 2.3. These and other report modifications are discussed further in Chapter 12.

One important phrase in the opinion paragraph is "... in all material respects. ..." The concept of materiality has been discussed previously as part of the *performance* principle; used in a reporting context, it communicates that the audit team is unaware of any material misstatements in the financial statements. The choice of report (unqualified, qualified, or adverse) depends on the nature and materiality (significance) of the effect of the GAAP departure.

The report shown in Exhibit 2.3 expresses the auditors' conclusion on the fairness of McDonald's financial statements. The last paragraph of this report references a report on McDonald's internal control over financial reporting. This report will also be presented along with McDonald's financial statements and expresses the auditors' conclusion regarding the effectiveness of McDonald's internal control over financial reporting. This report and the process through which auditors evaluate the effectiveness of internal control are discussed in Chapter 5.

Exhibit 2.3 provides the reporting language for audits of public entities; some changes to this report which have recently been proposed by the PCAOB are discussed in more detail in Chapter 12. AU 700 prescribes the wording and form of an audit report for nonpublic entities; while the message and contents are similar, some differences do exist. It is important to note that auditors are required to report on internal control only for public entities. As a result, the auditors' report on a nonpublic entity will not contain this paragraph.

> ↳ **REVIEW CHECKPOINT**
>
> 2.19 What is a *financial reporting framework*? How is the financial reporting framework related to the auditors' reporting responsibilities?
>
> 2.20 What are the four types of audit opinions? What is the conclusion of each one?

▽ EVALUATING THE QUALITY OF PUBLIC ACCOUNTING FIRMS' PRACTICES

LEARNING OBJECTIVE 2-5
Understand the role of a system of quality control and AICPA and PCAOB monitoring efforts in enabling public accounting firms to meet appropriate levels of professional quality.

To this point in the chapter, we have discussed the professional standards related to audit engagements. Many organizations are interested in ensuring that public accounting firms meet these engagement standards and maintain high levels of quality in their practices. For example, the SEC provides general oversight of the accounting and auditing professions, investigates audit failures (situations in which auditors fail to detect material financial statement misstatements), and levies fines against firms that have been found negligent in conducting audits. In addition, the PCAOB (for audits of public entities) and AICPA Center for Public Company Audit Firms (CPCAF) (for audits of nonpublic entities) review the work of member firms to ensure that their audits comply with professional standards.

However, one important issue that has not been addressed is the nature of actions that are routinely taken by firms themselves to ensure that their work is of high quality and meets the professional standards discussed in this chapter. For example, how do firms ensure that the personnel assigned to engagements are independent with respect to the client and have the appropriate level of competence to handle the assignment? What process do firms use when deciding to either accept or continue an audit engagement? The answers to these and other questions are reflected in policies and procedures implemented by firms as part of a system of quality control, which is the focus of this section.

System of Quality Control

Statement on Quality Control Standards No. 8 (*SQCS 8*), "A Firm's System of Quality Control" notes that the purpose of a **system of quality control** is to provide the firm reasonable assurance that the firm and its personnel:

- Comply with professional standards and applicable regulatory and legal requirements.
- Issue reports that are appropriate in the circumstances.

Simply stated, a system of quality control is implemented by firms to ensure that their work is of high quality and meets the expectations of professional standards. Section 103 of Sarbanes-Oxley established broad areas of quality control standards that were required of registered public accounting firms. These areas serve as the basis for the following six elements of a system of quality control identified by *SQCS 8*:

1. **Leadership responsibilities for quality within the firm ("tone at the top").** Undoubtedly, you have heard the phrase "leadership by example." In order for quality control standards to be effective, it is important that the firm's management take a lead role in clearly and consistently demonstrating its own commitment to quality control and high-quality work. Doing so will make it clear to all personnel that high-quality work is valued and will be rewarded. Some examples of how this can be done include:
   - Assigning management responsibilities in such a manner that commercial considerations do not override the quality of work performed.
   - Basing performance evaluation, compensation, and promotion opportunities for personnel on the quality of work performed.
   - Devoting sufficient resources for developing, communicating, and supporting the firm's quality control policies and procedures.

   It may seem unusual to specify that personnel decisions should be based on the quality of work performed. After all, what other basis should be used? Both the **Enron** and **WorldCom** cases provided anecdotal evidence that suggested the fear of losing a key client (and the impact of that loss on individual auditors' performance evaluations and opportunities within the firm) contributed to the audit failures in those cases. Although the ability to generate revenues (through providing expanded services to existing clients, retaining existing clients, or acquiring new clients) is certainly an important attribute, it should not come at the expense of a quality audit engagement. Thus, formal and public support from the firm's management team for audit quality will reduce the likelihood of decisions being influenced by financial considerations at the potential sacrifice of audit quality.

2. **Relevant ethical requirements.** Earlier in this chapter, we discussed independence and the importance of independence to the auditing profession. Firms should take various actions to ensure that personnel assigned to engagements are both independent in fact and independent in appearance with respect to the firm's clients, such as:
   - Communicating independence requirements to personnel.
   - Identifying circumstances and relationships that create threats to independence and taking appropriate action to eliminate those threats or reduce them to an acceptable level.
   - Obtaining written confirmation from all firm personnel with respect to their compliance with appropriate independence requirements.

3. **Acceptance and continuance of client relationships and specific engagements.** As discussed in Chapter 3, one of the most important decisions facing an audit firm is that of accepting an engagement (for a new client) or continuing to perform an engagement (for an existing client). Even in the most long-standing auditor-client relationships, it is important that firms develop formal policies and procedures to consider relevant factors and document their acceptance and continuance decisions. When deciding whether to accept a new client or continue an engagement with an existing client, firms should focus on three important issues:
    1. The integrity and business reputation of the client.
    2. The firm's ability to adequately perform the engagement with an appropriate level of professional competence.
    3. The firm's ability to comply with legal and ethical requirements related to the engagement.

    The purpose of this process is to avoid association with a client whose management lacks integrity and to ensure that the firm can perform the engagement at an appropriate level.

    If firms decide to withdraw from an engagement after considering the preceding matters, *SQCS 8* notes that the firm should document significant issues, consultations, conclusions, and the basis for any conclusions related to its decision to withdraw.

4. **Human resources.** The quality of any professional services organization (such as an audit firm) is based on the quality of its people. Effective quality control policies and procedures should be implemented to ensure that firms hire quality personnel, assign these personnel to engagements for which they have the appropriate capabilities, provide professional development opportunities to those individuals, and effectively evaluate, compensate, and promote them. These practices will increase the likelihood that a high-quality audit is conducted by ensuring that the firm has high-quality personnel and that these individuals have the ability to assume the responsibilities assigned to them.

5. **Engagement performance.** The performance principle (discussed earlier in this chapter) discussed a number of significant issues related to the conduct of an audit engagement. Integral components of this principle include ensuring that work is appropriately planned, assistants are properly supervised, the work is appropriately performed in compliance with GAAS, and that the work is reviewed and any deficiencies are addressed. Firms frequently use manuals and other standardized forms of documentation to meet the preceding objectives.

    In addition to the matters relating to the conduct of an individual engagement, firms should also develop processes for ensuring that:
    - Engagement documentation is retained for an appropriate period of time and firm personnel maintain the confidentiality of this information.
    - Consultation with other offices of the firm or other auditors is sought when dealing with complex, unusual, difficult, or contentious issues.
    - Policies and procedures for resolving differences of opinion within the engagement team are established and followed, when such differences occur.
    - Firms conduct **engagement quality control reviews** for engagements meeting specified criteria identified by the firm (for example, engagements in a highly volatile industry or engagements that meet certain risk criteria). An engagement quality control review includes an internal evaluation of the significant judgments made by the audit team and the conclusions reached in formulating its report.

6. **Monitoring.** The purpose of monitoring is to provide the firm with reasonable assurance that policies and procedures comprising the system of quality control are operating effectively and complied with in practice. Essentially, monitoring involves actions taken within the firm to evaluate the quality of its practices in the five other dimensions of quality control. Examples of procedures used to monitor quality control include:
    - Reviews of selected administrative and personnel records.
    - Reviews of engagement documentation, reports, and the client's financial statements.

- Discussions with firm personnel.
- Assessments of the (1) appropriateness of the firm's guidance materials and professional aids, (2) compliance with policies and procedures on independence, (3) effectiveness of continuing professional education, and (4) decisions regarding the acceptance and continuance of client relationships and specific engagements. Firms may accomplish the above monitoring activities through either an ongoing post-issuance review of engagement documentation or targeted inspection procedures for a sample of engagements conducted by the firm.

The accompanying Auditing Insight "Quality Control Deficiencies" identifies some deficiencies related to the human resources and engagement performance dimensions of quality control.

Peer Review

In the 1970s, because of concerns regarding audit quality, the accounting profession implemented a self-regulatory process for monitoring firm quality. Under this process (known as **peer review**), public accounting firms engaged other firms to study and report on quality control policies and procedures and whether the quality of the firm's audit practice was consistent with its system of quality control. Firms that audited public entities were required to join the AICPA SEC Practice Section and subject their practices to peer review once every three years.

AUDITING INSIGHT — Quality Control Deficiencies

While PCAOB inspections of firms' systems of quality control are not publicly available, a recent summary of inspections of the eight largest public accounting firms in the first four years of the review program identified two common deficiencies in the firms' systems of quality control:

1. Partners' performance evaluations and compensation were not affected by the quality of their work.
2. Auditors were not held accountable for significant deficiencies in audits that were later revealed by PCAOB inspections or internal monitoring efforts.

Source: "PCAOB to Auditors: Turn Up the Skepticism," *CFO.com*, December 8, 2008.

While requiring peer review was an important signal regarding audit quality, a frequent criticism is that firms could select their own reviewers, resulting in a small number of firms actually receiving unfavorable opinions. The Public Oversight Board (which oversees the AICPA's SEC Practice Section and should not be confused with the PCAOB) noted that "peer review has come under considerable criticism from members of Congress, the media, and others. 'You scratch my back, I'll scratch yours' is the prevailing cynical view of peer review raised by many."[13] For example, Lennox and Pittman's[14] study of 1,982 peer review reports from 1997 to 2007 revealed that 1,918 (approximately 97 percent) were unmodified opinions that concluded firms were maintaining effective systems of quality control; 1,706 of these reviews disclosed two or fewer weaknesses in the firm's systems. In the small number of instances when modified opinions were received, reviewed firms frequently elected to change reviewers. Because of these concerns, as well as highly publicized failures in the audits of **Enron** and **WorldCom**, Sarbanes-Oxley requires that firms auditing public entities undergo an independent

---

[13] Public Oversight Board, *The Road to Reform: A White Paper from the Public Oversight Board on Legislation to Create a New Private Sector Regulatory Structure for the Accounting Profession*, 2002, pp. 22–23.

[14] C. Lennox and J. Pittman, "Auditing the Auditors: Evidence on the Recent Reforms to the External Monitoring of Audit Firms," *Journal of Accounting and Economics*, February 2010, pp. 84–103.

review (referred to as an *inspection*) conducted by the PCAOB. These inspections are discussed in the following section.

Today, peer reviews for firms auditing nonpublic entities are still conducted through the AICPA's Center for Public Company Audit Firms Peer Review Program. While firms subject to the PCAOB inspection requirements can still choose to have peer reviews in addition to the PCAOB inspection, most have chosen not to do so. Most of the peer reviews conducted following the creation of the PCAOB's monitoring requirement are related to engagements performed by firms who audit only nonpublic entities and are therefore not subject to the PCAOB inspection requirements.

PCAOB Inspection of Firms

Earlier in this chapter, we addressed the role of the PCAOB in establishing auditing standards. In addition to this role, the PCAOB is also charged with *monitoring* the quality of work performed by firms auditing public entities and bringing appropriate action against those firms if substandard work is identified. This monitoring (referred to as an **inspection**) replaces the peer review requirements of the AICPA for firms auditing public entities.

Under Sarbanes-Oxley, firms auditing public entities are required to register with the PCAOB and undergo an inspection of their practice, as follows:

- For firms performing audits of more than 100 public entities, inspections are conducted on an annual basis.
- For firms performing audits of 100 or fewer public entities, inspections are conducted every three years.

As of May 2010, based on information from the PCAOB's website, a total of 2,457 auditing firms are registered with the PCAOB; of these, 850 issued audit reports during 2009. Of the 850 firms issuing audit reports in 2009, 9 were required to have annual inspections because they conducted audits for more than 100 companies.

PCAOB inspections are conducted by individuals chosen by the PCAOB who are not current employees of public accounting firms; the selection of inspectors by an outside body (the PCAOB), not the reviewed firm itself, overcomes an important criticism of the peer review process. These inspections consist of a review of a sample of audit engagements conducted by the firm as well as an overall evaluation of the firm's *system of quality control*. Copies of the PCAOB's inspection reports can be found (on a firm-by-firm basis) on the PCAOB's website. These reports detail the deficiencies identified by the PCAOB on the sample of audit engagements (the name of the client is not identified); information regarding deficiencies in the firm's quality control are not publicly disclosed and will be disclosed only if the firm fails to address those deficiencies within a year following the inspection. A study by Church and Shefchik[15] on the inspection reports of large accounting firms (those auditing more than 100 issuers) from 2005–2010 concluded that:

- The most frequent deficiencies cited by the PCAOB were related to the failure to gather or document sufficient audit support (53.3 percent of deficiencies) followed by the failure of the firm to adequately evaluate an accounting issue (28.0 percent of deficiencies).
- 11.4 percent of all identified deficiencies resulted in accounting misstatements.
- The number of deficiencies has significantly declined over the six-year inspection period from 2005–2010.[16]

A summary of reported deficiencies for audits conducted by Big Four firms is provided in the Auditing Insight "Grading the Firms." In its first monetary action against one

---

[15] B. Church and L. Shefchik, "PCAOB Inspections and Large Accounting Firms," Unpublished working paper, Georgia Tech University, 2011.

[16] For a summary of inspection reports issued to smaller accounting firms (those with 100 or fewer issuer clients), see D.R. Hermanson, R.W. Houston, and J.C. Rice, "PCAOB Inspections of Smaller CPA Firms: Initial Evidence from Inspection Reports," *Accounting Horizons*, June 2007, pp. 137–152. In addition, B. Daugherty and W. Tervo, "PCAOB Inspections of Smaller CPA Firms: The Perspective of Inspected Firms," *Accounting Horizons* (June 2010), pp. 189–219 provide an interesting summary of the perceptions of smaller CPA firms to the PCAOB's inspection process.

of the Big Four firms, the PCAOB fined **Deloitte & Touche** (now **Deloitte**) $1 million for failing to exercise due professional care and obtain sufficient evidence in its audit of **Ligand Pharmaceuticals**.[17]

AUDITING INSIGHT — Grading the Firms

The following table summarizes PCAOB inspection activity for the Big Four firms (**Deloitte, Ernst & Young, KPMG,** and **PwC**) for each of the last three years. It is important to note that the number of audits inspected was not disclosed in inspection reports until 2010 and that some audits had more than one deficiency:

Audits Inspected	Number of Audits Inspected	Audits in Which Deficiencies Were Identified	Number of Deficiencies Identified	Audits in Which Departure from GAAP not Identified by Firms
2010 Reports (2009 Audits)	267	37	54	1
2009 Reports (2008 Audits)	Not available	30	38	3
2008 Reports (2007 Audits)	Not available	29	44	2

In 2010, the most common deficiencies were related to audit procedures involved with (1) determining the fair value of securities, derivatives, and financial instruments (13 audits), (2) evaluating the allowance for loan losses (four audits), and (3) testing impairment of goodwill and other intangible assets (seven audits).

What were the firms' responses? For the departures from GAAP, the client restated its financial statements and reissued them. In other cases, firms performed additional procedures related to the deficiencies or increased their level of documentation for work that had been performed but not included in the original audit documentation.

Source: PCAOB website, http://pcaobus.org/Inspections/Reports/Pages/default.aspx.

The very public nature of the PCAOB inspection process raises the question as to whether clients react to negative inspection reports by choosing to dismiss the current (incumbent) auditors. (Recall **Beckstead's** accusation from the opening vignette in this chapter that having its inspection report posted harmed the firm's ability to attract new clients.) The findings of Abbott et al.[18] indicate that when a non-Big 4 or non-national firm receives a negative report from the PCAOB, entities having stronger audit committees (those with all outside directors and at least one director classified as a financial "expert") are likely to initiate an auditor change. This finding provides preliminary evidence that PCAOB reports are an important signal of audit quality.

AUDITING INSIGHT — PCAOB Sanctions Two Auditors

The PCAOB alleged that an **Ernst & Young** partner and the senior manager on the audit of a client that was selected for inspection had created, backdated, and filed audit documentation related to the valuation of that client's investments following the audit. In addition, it was alleged that these individuals authorized other members of the audit team to alter documentation contained in the files that the PCAOB inspection team reviewed. Although the two auditors did not admit or deny the PCAOB's findings, they accepted bans of three years (for the partner) and two years (for the senior manager) for participating in the audit of public entities. The three-year ban was the longest ever imposed by the PCAOB on a partner of a Big Four firm.

Source: "Auditors Banned from Some Work," *The Wall Street Journal,* August 2, 2011, p. C3.

---

[17] "Deloitte Receives $1 Million Fine," *The Wall Street Journal,* December 11, 2007, p. C8.
[18] L.J. Abbott, K. Gunny, and T. Zhang, "When the PCAOB Talks, Who Listens? Evidence from Client Firm Reaction to Adverse, GAAP-Deficient PCAOB Inspection Reports," Unpublished working paper, University of Wisconsin–Milwaukee, 2011.

⌕ REVIEW CHECKPOINTS

2.21 What is a *system of quality control*? Identify the six elements of a system of quality control.

2.22 What factors should auditors consider in deciding whether to accept or continue the engagement with a particular client? What should firms do if they decide to withdraw from an engagement?

2.23 What type of firms generally have peer reviews conducted by the AICPA's Center for Public Company Audit Firms Peer Review Program?

2.24 What role does the PCAOB play in connection with the monitoring and regulation of public accounting firms?

2.25 How frequently are firms required to have PCAOB inspections?

Summary

This chapter discussed the professional standards that apply to audit engagements and identified important mechanisms that enable public accounting firms to provide professional services to meet those standards. From an auditing standpoint, generally accepted auditing standards form the basis for professional engagements and the necessary qualifications and characteristics of auditors. These standards are based on three basic principles, which reflect the overall conduct of the audit examination:

1. Responsibilities, which require that auditors possess competence and capabilities, comply with relevant ethical requirements, maintain professional skepticism, and exercise professional judgment.
2. Performance, which involves planning the work and supervising assistants, determining and applying appropriate materiality levels, identifying and assessing the risk of material misstatement, and obtaining sufficient appropriate audit evidence.
3. Reporting, which requires that auditors express an opinion about the fairness of the entity's financial statements.

To provide reasonable assurance of compliance with these standards, firms develop systems of quality control that prescribe policies and procedures related to (1) the responsibilities of firm leadership for quality, (2) ethical requirements, (3) acceptance and continuance of client relationships and specific engagements, (4) human resources, (5) engagement performance, and (6) monitoring the effectiveness of the system of quality control. Under Sarbanes-Oxley, firms conducting audits of public entities are required to have inspections of selected engagements and their systems of quality control by the PCAOB. The purpose of these inspections is to identify deficiencies in engagements conducted by the firms and provide suggestions for improvements in their systems of quality control.

This chapter discussed professional standards and monitoring requirements related to the audits of public and nonpublic entities. Following is a summary of the professional standards and monitoring activities for these audits.

	Professional Standards	Monitoring Requirements
Public entity	• *Auditing Standards* issued by the PCAOB • *Interim Auditing Standards* (*Statements on Auditing Standards* issued prior to April 2003 that have not been amended or superseded by the PCAOB)	Annual or triennial inspections conducted by the PCAOB (frequency depends upon number of audits performed by the firm)
Nonpublic entity	*Statements on Auditing Standards* issued by the ASB of the AICPA	Triennial peer reviews conducted through the AICPA Center for Public Company Audit Firms Peer Review Program

Key Terms

adverse opinion: A report stating that the financial statements are not presented in conformity with GAAP; the opposite of an unqualified opinion, 54

American Institute of Certified Public Accountants (AICPA): As related to professional auditing standards, the body charged with establishing auditing standards for the audits of nonpublic entities through *Statements on Auditing Standards (SASs)* issued by the Auditing Standards Board. Some existing *SASs* that have not been amended or superseded by the PCAOB serve as *Interim Auditing Standards* for the audits of public entities. 36

appropriate (audit evidence): Characteristics related to the quality (relevance and reliability) of audit evidence, 51

attestation standards: (Appendix) A general set of standards intended to guide attestation work in areas other than audits of financial statements, 74

audit procedures: The specialized actions auditors take to obtain evidence in an engagement, 39

audit plan: A list of the audit procedures auditors need to perform to gather sufficient appropriate evidence on which to base their opinion on the financial statements, 47

auditing standards: The audit quality guides that apply to all audits, 39

control risk: The probability that a material misstatement (error or fraud) will not be prevented or detected on a timely basis by the entity's internal controls, 49

date of the financial statements: The date of the end of the latest period covered by the financial statements, 47

departure from GAAP: A situation in which the entity's financial statements (or elements within those financial statements) are materially misstated and do not present the entity's financial condition, results of operations, and cash flows in conformity with GAAP, 54

detection risk: The risk that the audit team's substantive procedures will fail to detect a material misstatement, 52

disclaimer of opinion: The explicit statement by auditors that they express no opinion and no assurance on the fair presentation of the financial statements in accordance with GAAP, 55

due care: A level of performance that would be exercised by reasonable auditors in similar circumstances; auditors are expected to possess the skills and knowledge of others in their profession and are not expected to be infallible, 44

engagement quality control review: An internal evaluation of the significant judgments made by the audit team and the conclusions reached in formulating its report, 57

evidence: The information used by auditors in arriving at the conclusion on which the audit opinion is based, which includes the underlying accounting data and all available corroborating information, 50

external evidence: The documentary evidence obtained directly from independent external sources, 51

external-internal evidence: Documentary evidence that has originated outside the client's information processing system but that has been received and processed by the client, 51

financial reporting framework: A set of criteria used to determine the measurement, recognition, presentation, and disclosure of material items in the financial statements, 54

generally accepted auditing standards (GAAS): Standards that identify necessary qualifications and characteristics of auditors and guide the conduct of the audit examination, 38

independence (in appearance): The extent to which others (particularly financial statement users) perceive auditors to be independent, 43

independence (in fact): An auditor's mental attitude and impartiality with respect to the client, 43

inherent risk: The probability that a material misstatement (error or fraud) will occur, 49

inspection: An evaluation of an accounting firm's audit engagements and system of quality control conducted by the PCAOB and required for any firms providing auditing services to public entities, 59

internal control: The policies and procedures implemented by an entity to prevent or detect material accounting errors or frauds and provide for their correction on a timely basis, 49

internal evidence: Documentary evidence that is produced, circulated, and maintained within the client's information system, 51

materiality: As it relates to financial reporting, the dollar amount that would influence the lending or investing decisions of financial statement users, 48

persuasiveness: An overall measure of the ability of evidence to support the auditors' opinion. Persuasive audit evidence reflects evidence that is both sufficient and appropriate. 51

peer review: A study of a firm's quality control policies and procedures followed by a report on the quality of the firm's audit practice in accordance with its system of quality control. Peer reviews are conducted through the AICPA's Center for Public Company Audit Firms Peer Review Program and are generally performed for firms that do not audit public entities. 58

professional judgment: The application of relevant training, knowledge, and experience in making informed decisions about appropriate courses of action during the audit engagement, 45
professional skepticism: A state of mind that is characterized by appropriate questioning and a critical assessment of audit evidence, 45
Public Company Accounting Oversight Board (PCAOB): As related to professional auditing standards, the body charged with establishing auditing standards for the audits of public entities through the issuance of *Auditing Standards.* These standards are subject to approval by the SEC. Some existing standards issued by the AICPA that have not been amended or superseded by the PCAOB serve as *Interim Auditing Standards* for the audits of public entities. The PCAOB is also responsible for the inspection of firms that perform audits of public entities. 36
public entity: An entity that offers registered securities, such as stock and bonds, for sale to the general public, 36
qualified opinion: An auditors' report issued when the financial statements contain departures from GAAP or a scope limitation was encountered in the audit examination, 55
reasonable assurance: Concept that a GAAS audit may not detect all material misstatements and auditors are not "insurers" or "guarantors" regarding the fairness of the entity's financial statements, 46
relevant: The characteristic of audit evidence related to the nature of the evidence and the information it provides to the auditors, 51
reliable: The characteristic of audit evidence related to the level of trust that can be placed with respect to evidence, 51
risk of material misstatement: The combined probability that a material misstatement (error or fraud) will occur and not be prevented or detected on a timely basis by the entity's internal controls, 49
substantive procedures: Procedures used by auditors to obtain assurance as to the fairness of the entity's financial statements, 49
sufficiency (audit evidence): The measure of the quantity of audit evidence (the number of transactions or components evaluated), 52
system of quality control: The policies and procedures implemented by firms to provide a firm with reasonable assurance that the firm and its personnel (1) comply with professional standards and applicable regulatory and legal requirements and (2) issue reports that are appropriate in the circumstances, 56
unqualified opinion: A "clean" opinion that makes no mention of accounting or auditing deficiencies. The conclusion of an unqualified opinion is that the financial statements present the financial condition, results of operations, and cash flows in accordance with GAAP. 54
verbal evidence: Responses to audit inquiries provided by the client's officers, directors, owners, and employees, 52
written representations: Written assertions provided by management to auditors on matters such as the fairness of the entity's financial statements, availability of all financial records and related data, internal control over financial reporting, and other specific representations about the financial statements, 52

Multiple-Choice Questions for Practice and Review

 All applicable Exercises and Problems are available with McGraw-Hill's *Connect® Accounting*

LO 2-3

2.26 Which of the following categories of principles is most closely related to gathering audit evidence?
  a. Performance.
  b. Reasonable assurance.
  c. Reporting.
  d. Responsibilities.

LO 2-2

2.27 To exercise due care, an accountant should
  a. Take continuing professional education classes.
  b. Report whether the financial statements are in accordance with GAAP.
  c. Gather enough audit evidence to have complete assurance that there is enough support for the opinion on the financial statements.
  d. Conduct the engagement in accordance with GAAS and ensure that the engagement is completed on a timely basis.

LO 2-5 2.28 One of an accounting firm's basic objectives is to provide professional services that conform to professional standards. Reasonable assurance of achieving this objective can be obtained by following
   a. Generally accepted auditing standards.
   b. Standards within a system of quality control.
   c. Generally accepted accounting practices.
   d. International auditing standards.

LO 2-2 2.29 Which of the following best demonstrates the concept of professional skepticism?
   a. Relying more extensively on external evidence rather than internal evidence.
   b. Focusing on items that have a more significant quantitative effect on the entity's financial statements.
   c. Critically assessing verbal evidence received from the entity's management.
   d. Evaluating potential financial interests held by auditors in the client.

LO 2-3 2.30 The primary purpose for obtaining an understanding of the entity's environment (including its internal control) in a financial statement audit is
   a. To determine the nature, timing, and extent of substantive procedures to be performed.
   b. To make consulting suggestions to the entity's management.
   c. To obtain direct sufficient appropriate audit evidence to afford a reasonable basis for an opinion on the financial statements.
   d. To determine whether the entity has changed any accounting principles.

LO 2-3 2.31 Ordinarily, what source of evidence should least affect audit conclusions?
   a. External documentary evidence.
   b. Inquiry of management.
   c. Documentation prepared by the audit team.
   d. Inquiry of entity legal counsel.

LO 2-3 2.32 The most persuasive evidence regarding the existence of newly-acquired computer equipment is
   a. Inquiry of management.
   b. Documentation prepared externally.
   c. Observation of auditee's procedures.
   d. Physical observation.

LO 2-3 2.33 Which of the following procedures would provide the most reliable audit evidence?
   a. Inquiries of the client's internal audit staff.
   b. Inspection of prenumbered client purchase orders filed in the vouchers payable department.
   c. Inspection of vendor sales invoices received from client personnel.
   d. Inspection of bank statements obtained directly from the client's financial institution.

LO 2-3 2.34 Breaux & Co., CPAs require that all audit documentation indicate the identity of the preparer and the reviewer. This procedure provides evidence relating to which of the following?
   a. Independence.
   b. Adequate competence and capabilities.
   c. Adequate planning and supervision.
   d. Gathering sufficient appropriate evidence.

LO 2-2 2.35 Which of the following concepts is *least* related to the standard of due care?
   a. Independence in fact.
   b. Professional skepticism.
   c. Prudent auditor.
   d. Reasonable assurance.

LO 2-3   2.36 The evidence considered most appropriate by auditors is best described as
a. Internal documents such as sales invoice copies produced under conditions of strong internal control.
b. Written representations made by the president of the entity.
c. Documentary evidence obtained directly from independent external sources.
d. Direct personal knowledge obtained through physical observation and mathematical recalculation.

LO 2-3   2.37 Auditors' understanding of the internal control in an entity contributes information for
a. Determining whether members of the audit team have the required competence and capabilities to perform the audit.
b. Ascertaining the independence in mental attitude of members of the audit team.
c. Planning the professional development courses the audit staff needs to keep up to date with new auditing standards.
d. Planning the nature, timing, and extent of substantive procedures on an audit.

LO 2-5   2.38 Which of the following elements of a system of quality control is related to firms receiving independence confirmations from its professionals with respect to clients?
a. Acceptance and continuance of client relationships and specific engagements.
b. Engagement performance.
c. Monitoring.
d. Relevant ethical requirements.

LO 2-2   2.39 Which of the following is most closely related to the responsibilities principle?
a. The auditors' responsibility to issue a report as a result of their examination.
b. The requirement that auditors gather sufficient, appropriate evidence upon which to base an opinion on the financial statements.
c. The auditors' compliance with relevant ethical requirements of independence and due care.
d. The auditors' responsibility to plan the audit and properly supervise assistants.

LO 2-2   2.40 Kramer, CPA, consulted an independent appraiser regarding the valuation of fine art for a not-for-profit museum. Consultation with a specialist in this case would
a. Be considered as exercising proper due care.
b. Be considered a failure to follow GAAS because Kramer should have known how to value fine art before accepting the engagement.
c. Not be considered a violation of GAAS because GAAS does not apply to not-for-profit entities.
d. None of the above.

LO 2-4   2.41 Which of the following topics is *not* addressed in the auditors' report for a public entity?
a. Responsibilities of the auditor and management in the financial reporting process.
b. Absolute assurance regarding the fairness of the entity's financial statements in accordance with GAAP.
c. A description of an audit engagement.
d. A summary of the auditors' opinion on the effectiveness of the entity's internal control over financial reporting.

LO 2-3   2.42 Which of the following recognizes that an audit conducted under generally accepted auditing standards may not detect all material misstatements?
a. Absolute assurance.
b. Professional judgment.
c. Persuasiveness of audit evidence.
d. Reasonable assurance.

LO 2-3 2.43 Which of the following combinations would provide the auditor the most persuasive evidence?

	Source of Evidence	Effectiveness of Internal control
a.	Internal	More effective
b.	Internal	Less effective
c.	External	More effective
d.	External	Less effective

LO 2-3 2.44 Which of the following is most closely related to the relevance of audit evidence?

a. Auditors decide to physically inspect investment securities held by a custodian instead of obtaining confirmations from the custodian.

b. In addition to confirmations of accounts receivable, auditors perform an analysis of the aging of accounts receivable to evaluate the collectability of accounts receivable.

c. In response to less effective internal control, auditors increase the number of customer accounts receivable confirmations mailed compared to that in the prior year.

d. Because of a large number of transactions occurring near year-end, auditors decide to confirm a larger number of receivables following year-end instead of during the interim period.

LO 2-3 2.45 Which of the following statements is *not* true with respect to the performance principle?

a. Auditors are required to prepare a written audit plan during the planning stages of initial audits but are not required to do so in continuing audits.

b. Audit teams consider materiality in planning the audit, performing the audit, and evaluating the effect of misstatements on the entity's financial statements.

c. In assessing the risk of material misstatements, the audit team considers the effectiveness of the entity's internal controls in preventing and detecting misstatements.

d. Auditors are required to consider both the relevance and reliability of evidence in evaluating whether the evidence they have gathered is appropriate.

LO 2-5 2.46 Which of the following is true with respect to PCAOB inspections of accounting firms?

a. All firms performing audits of public companies are required to have annual inspections conducted by the PCAOB.

b. PCAOB inspections review a sample of audits conducted by firms as well as the firm's systems of quality control.

c. All results of PCAOB inspections are made available to the public following the inspection.

d. Firms performing audits of 100 or fewer public entities may elect to have a peer review conducted through the AICPA in lieu of a PCAOB inspection.

LO 2-6 2.47 (Appendix) Which of the following is a conceptual difference between attestation standards and generally accepted auditing standards?

a. The attestation standards provide a framework for the attest function beyond historical financial statements.

b. The requirement that the practitioner be independent is not required under attestation standards.

c. The attestation standards do not permit an attestation engagement to examine prospective "what-if" financial statements.

d. Requirements related to evidence are not included in the attestation standards.

LO 2-6 2.48 (Appendix) The attestation standards do *not* contain a requirement that auditors obtain

a. Adequate knowledge in the subject matter of the assertions being examined.

b. An understanding of the client's internal controls.

c. Sufficient evidence for the conclusions expressed in an attestation report.

d. Independence in mental attitude.

LO 2-4

2.49 Which of the following best describes the general contents of the introductory paragraph of the auditors' report?

a. A description of an audit examination, including the fact that the audit was conducted under standards established by the PCAOB.

b. The auditors' conclusion with respect to the fairness of the entity's financial statements.

c. Statements identifying the responsibility of auditors and management in the financial reporting process.

d. The auditors' conclusion with respect to the effectiveness of the entity's internal control over financial reporting.

LO 2-4

2.50 Which of the following opinions would be issued if auditors believed that the entity's financial statements were *not* presented in conformity with GAAP?

a. Adverse opinion.

b. Disclaimer of opinion.

c. Qualified opinion.

d. Unqualified opinion.

LO 2-4

2.51 Which of the following principles is most closely associated with the auditors' conclusion as to the fair presentation of the entity's financial statements?

a. Communication principle.

b. Performance principle.

c. Reporting principle.

d. Responsibilities principle.

Exercises and Problems

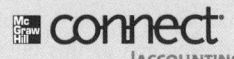 All applicable Exercises and Problems are available with McGraw-Hill's *Connect® Accounting*

LOs 2-1, 2-5

2.52 **AICPA and PCAOB Responsibilities.** The creation of the PCAOB by the Sarbanes-Oxley Act has impacted both the standards-setting process and the periodic review of the quality of an audit firm's work.

Required:

a. Identify the responsibilities of the AICPA, PCAOB, and SEC in the auditing standards-setting process.

b. Which standard(s) provide guidance for the audits of public entities? Which standard(s) provide guidance for the audits of nonpublic entities?

c. What role do the AICPA and PCAOB play in the periodic review of the quality of audit firms' work?

LO 2-2

2.53 **Independence.** You are meeting with executives of Cooper Cosmetics Corporation to arrange your firm's engagement to audit the corporation's financial statements for the year ending December 31. One executive suggests the audit work be divided among three staff members. One person would examine asset accounts, a second would examine liability accounts, and the third would examine income and expense accounts to minimize audit time, avoid duplication of staff effort, and curtail interference with entity operations.

Advertising is the corporation's largest expense and the advertising manager suggests that a staff member of your firm whose uncle owns the advertising agency that handles the corporation's advertising be assigned to examine the Advertising Expense account because the staff member has a thorough knowledge of the complex contact between Cooper Cosmetics and the advertising agency.

Required:

a. To what extent should auditors follow the client's suggestions for the conduct of an audit? Discuss.

b. List and discuss the reasons that audit work should not be assigned solely according to asset, liability, and income and expense categories.

c. Should the staff member of your accounting firm whose uncle owns the advertising agency be assigned to examine advertising costs? Discuss.

LO 2-2

2.54 **Independence.** Generally accepted auditing standards require auditors to be independent. Included within this standard are the concepts of independence in fact and independence in appearance.

Required:

a. Define independence in fact and independence in appearance.

b. What two general types of relationships would normally compromise auditors' independence?

c. For each of the following separate situations, discuss whether you believe the auditors' independence has been compromised.

1. The auditors' firm provides extensive consulting services to the client; these services provide revenues to the firm that exceed revenues received from the audit engagement.

2. The spouse of the partner in charge of the audit engagement occupies an executive-level position within the client.

3. A distant relative of a partner within the firm occupies an entry-level position within a client of the firm (the audit is conducted by another office of the firm with which the partner has infrequent contact).

4. A staff member within the firm owns shares of stock of one of that firm's clients (she is not a member of the engagement team serving that client).

LO 2-2

2.55 **Responsibilities Principle.** Martin is considering submitting a proposal to conduct the audit examination of Phillip, Inc., a manufacturer and distributor of automotive parts to the large automobile manufacturers. Martin learned of this client opportunity through one of its staff accountants, who is a cousin of Phillip's chief financial officer. In evaluating this opportunity, Martin first inquired with Phillip as to the reason for a change in auditors and was assured that the former auditors decided not to continue auditing Phillip, Inc. because it no longer possessed the necessary expertise to audit clients in the automotive parts industry. A conversation with Phillip's former auditors confirmed this explanation, so Martin is currently evaluating this opportunity.

Phillip is a particularly attractive engagement for Martin because it would allow the firm to enter into the manufacturing market. Most of Martin's clients are in the services industry and are much smaller than Phillip. Martin is concerned about the numerous locations of Phillip's warehouses and the ability to conduct an appropriate observation of Phillip's year-end inventory balances; however, Martin's staff accountant noted that the firm could engage other auditors to assist with this aspect of the audit engagement. As a manufacturing entity, inventory (and the related cost of goods sold) is highly material to Phillip's financial statements. Alternatively, Phillip indicated that its previous auditors would observe physical inventory at the different warehouses on different days, reducing the need for them to rely on the work of others. To ensure that inventory was not transferred from one location to another and "double counted," the auditors obtained a written statement from Phillip indicating that no such transfers occurred.

After considering these factors, Martin has decided to submit a proposal for the audit of Phillip. If accepted, Martin will take appropriate actions to ensure that the appropriate firm personnel are independent in fact and in appearance with respect to Phillip.

Required:

Identify issues related to the responsibilities principle that Martin should consider in its decision to submit a proposal to conduct the audit of Phillip.

LO 2-3

2.56 **Performance Principle: Planning.** Your public accounting practice is located in a city of 15,000 people. The majority of your work, conducted by you and two assistants, consists of compiling clients' monthly statements and preparing income tax returns for individuals from cash data and partnership returns from books and records. You have a small number of audit clients; given the current size of your practice, you generally consider it a challenge to accept new audit clients.

One of your corporate clients is a retail hardware store. Your work for this client has been limited to preparing the corporation income tax return from a trial balance submitted by the bookkeeper.

On December 26, you receive from the president of the corporation a letter containing the following request:

> We have made arrangements with First National Bank to borrow $500,000 to finance the purchase of a complete line of appliances. The bank has asked us to furnish our auditors' certified statement as of December 31, which is the closing date of our accounting year. The trial balance of the general ledger should be ready by January 10, which should allow ample time to prepare your report for submission to the bank by January 20. In view of the importance of this certified report to our financing program, we trust you will arrange to comply with the preceding schedule.

Required:
From a theoretical viewpoint, discuss the difficulties that are caused by such a short notice audit request.

(AICPA adapted)

LO 2-3

2.57 **Performance Principle: Evidence.** Generally accepted auditing standards (the performance principle) require auditors to gather *sufficient appropriate* evidence on which to base an opinion.

Required:
a. Briefly define the characteristics "sufficient" and "appropriate" as they relate to audit evidence.
b. What are relevance and reliability (as they relate to audit evidence)? How do these concepts relate to the auditors' requirement to gather sufficient appropriate evidence?
c. List the five basic sources of audit evidence based on the reliability (from most reliable to least reliable) and provide one example of each type of evidence.
d. How does the effectiveness of the entity's internal control affect the sufficiency and appropriateness of evidence gathered by auditors?

LO 2-3

2.58 **Performance Principle: Relative Appropriateness of Evidence.** In considering what constitutes sufficient appropriate audit evidence, a distinction should be made between underlying accounting data and all corroborating information available to auditors.

Required:
What presumptions can be made about
a. The relative reliability of evidence obtained from external and internal sources?
b. The role of internal control with respect to internal evidence produced by a client's information processing system?
c. The relative persuasiveness of auditors' observation and recalculation evidence compared to external, external-internal, and internal documentary evidence?

LO 2-3

2.59 **Performance Principle.** You have accepted the engagement of auditing the financial statements of the C. Reis Company, a small manufacturing firm that has been your client for several years. Because you were busy writing the report for another engagement, you sent a staff accountant to begin the audit with the suggestion that she start with accounts receivable. Using the prior-year's audit documentation as a guide, she prepared a trial balance of the accounts, aged them, prepared and mailed positive confirmation requests, examined underlying support for charges and credits, and performed other work she considered necessary to obtain evidence about the validity and collectability of the receivables. At the conclusion of her work, you reviewed the audit documentation she prepared and found she had carefully followed the prior year's audit documentation.

Required:
The opinion rendered by auditors states that the audit was made in accordance with generally accepted auditing standards. Identify the important components of the performance principle and relate them to the audit of C. Reis Company by indicating how they were fulfilled or, if appropriate, how they were not fulfilled.

(AICPA adapted)

LO 2-3

2.60 **Performance Principle.** Identify how each of the following statements relates to the performance principle by considering which element(s) of the principle are related to that statement. (A statement may be related to more than one element). Use the following elements in providing your response:
- Reasonable assurance
- Planning and supervision
- Materiality
- Risk assessment
- Audit evidence

a. Evaluating the effectiveness of the client's internal control in preventing or detecting misstatements.
b. Obtaining an understanding of the client's business and industry.
c. Acknowledging that the risk of failing to detect a material misstatement cannot be reduced to zero.
d. Obtaining confirmations from the client's customers as to the ending balances in accounts receivable.
e. Preparing a written audit plan.
f. Designing audit procedures to identify misstatements that would have a significant effect on financial statement users' decisions.
g. Considering the likelihood that the account balance contains a material misstatement.
h. Failing to detect material misstatements because of audit team mistakes and misinterpretations in evaluating evidence.

LOs 2-2, 2-3

2.61 **Responsibilities and Performance Principles.** Respond to each of the following comments that you heard related to the audit of Swan Company, a public entity.

a. "We don't need to consider the risk of material misstatement in our work because we really can't do anything to reduce that risk."
b. "Because the client has not implemented effective internal controls, we need to gather more persuasive evidence. This means we need to test a greater number of transactions and obtain more reliable forms of evidence."
c. "We will really need to spend a lot of time and effort on this audit. Because this client has just filed for a bond offering, we can't allow for any misstatements in the financial statements. We need to guarantee the accuracy of the client's financial statements."
d. "Because this company has $140 million in revenues, we really shouldn't be concerned about smaller accounts because they are not likely to have a major impact on the financial statements."
e. "I know it will be more time consuming and expensive, but we are required to physically inspect the stock certificates held by the client rather than obtain confirmation from the custodian. After all, our own direct observation is more reliable than receiving a confirmation."

LO 2-4

2.62 **Reporting Principle.** The reporting principle requires auditors to express their opinion through the issuance of a written report.

Required:
a. What is the purpose of the auditors' opinion and report?
b. What are the major paragraph(s) in the auditor's report on the examination of a public entity? What are the major contents of each of these paragraphs?
c. What are the four types of opinions that auditors can issue? What circumstances would result in the issuance of each type of opinion?
d. How does the concept of materiality influence the auditors' report?

LOs 2-2, 2-3, 2-4

2.63 **Comprehensive Principles Case Study.** Ray, the owner of a small entity, asked Holmes, CPA, to conduct an audit of the entity's records. Ray told Holmes that the audit was to be completed in time to submit audited financial statements to a bank as part of a loan application. Holmes immediately accepted the engagement and agreed to provide an auditors' report within three weeks. Ray agreed to pay Holmes a fixed fee plus a bonus if the loan was granted.

Holmes hired two accounting students to conduct the audit and spent several hours telling them exactly what to do. Holmes told the students not to spend time reviewing the controls but instead to concentrate on proving the mathematical accuracy of the ledger accounts and on summarizing the data in the accounting records that support Ray's financial statements. The students followed Holmes' instructions and, after two weeks, gave Holmes the financial statements, which did not include footnotes. Holmes studied the statements and prepared an unqualified auditors' report. The report, however, did not refer to generally accepted accounting principles or to the fact that Ray had changed to the accounting standard for capitalizing interest.

Required:
Briefly describe each of the principles and indicate how the action(s) of Holmes resulted in a failure to comply with these principles.

(AICPA adapted)

LOs 2-2, 2-3, 2-4

2.64 **Fundamental Principles (Comprehensive).** In each of the following scenarios, identify which of the elements of the fundamental principles is most applicable. In addition, discuss what action(s) (if any) you believe auditors should take with respect to these issues.

a. An entity has contacted you about performing its audit engagement. You have not previously served a client in the entity's industry, which has many industry-specific accounting issues that are both technical and complex.

b. An entity has entered into a number of lease agreements. Based on the requirements of GAAP, you believe that these obligations meet the criteria for being classified as capital leases; however, the entity has elected to treat these leases as operating leases, providing full and complete disclosure of this treatment in the footnotes to the financial statements.

c. Because of a disagreement with its current auditors, an entity has contacted you about conducting its current-year audit. However, because the previous auditors have just recently resigned the engagement, you have some questions as to whether an audit can be completed in time to meet the entity's deadlines for providing audited financial statements to a lender.

d. Based on the effectiveness of the entity's internal control, you have assessed control risk at low levels and decided that a smaller number of customer accounts need to be confirmed.

e. An entity has contacted you about performing their audit engagement. This entity became aware of your firm because the husband of one of your partners is currently serving as the entity's chief financial officer.

f. One of your clients is currently a potential defendant in several cases because of the damage caused by one of its products. Because this entity does not believe that it is likely to receive an unfavorable outcome from this litigation, it did not disclose the potential litigation in the footnotes accompanying their financial statements.

g. You are performing tests of the client's controls over the processing of revenue transactions to determine whether these controls are operating effectively and can be relied upon to prevent or detect misstatements.

h. One of your supervisors has requested a number of clarifications based on her review of your work on an audit engagement. A subsequent meeting with her has resolved these clarifications, and you both have concluded that your work supports the opinion on the client's financial statements.

LOs 2-2, 2-3, 2-4

2.65 **Fundamental Principles (Comprehensive).** Identify which of the major fundamental principles (responsibilities, performance, or reporting) is most closely related to each of the following:

a. The need for auditors to consider their financial relationships with prospective clients.

b. An auditor has raised some questions with respect to management's response to various inquiries concerning pending litigation facing the client.

c. The auditors' consideration of the effectiveness of the entity's internal control on the nature, timing, and extent of substantive procedures.

d. The auditors' evaluation of the magnitude of a misstatement that would impact perceptions of the entity's profitability.

e. The auditors' issuance of a disclaimer of opinion because of a significant scope limitation.

f. Relevant education and experience requirements for CPA licensure.

g. The inability of an audit examination to provide absolute assurance with respect to detecting all material misstatements.

h. The requirement that auditors possess the skills and knowledge of others in their profession.

i. The preparation of a written audit plan that guides the conduct of the audit engagement.

j. The auditors' issuance of a qualified opinion because of a departure from GAAP.

LOs 2-2, 2-3, 2-4   2.66   **Fundamental Principles (Comprehensive).** Comment upon each of the following statements you heard in a conversation between two newly hired staff auditors.

a. "Of course, I'm qualified to be assigned to this engagement. I have an accounting degree from a top university and was an honors graduate. I know some of the accounting rules have changed since I graduated, but I'll be able to figure that out as we go through the audit."

b. "It doesn't really matter what others think. . . . I'm completely independent of Acme Industries and should be a member of the audit team. While I own some stock, it's a small amount and I'm holding it for the long term, anyway."

c. "You really have to question everything the client tells you. That's what professional skepticism is all about. It's a shame you can't believe a word they say."

d. "While the evidence is lower in quality, we typically use internal evidence when we audit property, plant, and equipment. It just takes too much time and costs too much to get more reliable evidence."

e. "On that last job, we really planned the audit well. We were able to finish everything by November 1 and didn't need to do any work after year-end."

f. "We're not too worried about internal control. We always do the same substantive procedures anyway, so why take the time to look at the client's controls?"

g. "Because the client isn't accounting for its leases properly, we need to issue either a qualified opinion or a disclaimer of opinion. Just how large a dollar impact does this have on the financial statements?"

h. "When we evaluate items for materiality, the only thing we need to worry about is the absolute dollar amount. There really isn't anything else we need to consider."

LO 2-5   2.67   **System of Quality Control.** Each of the following quality control policies and procedures is typical of ones that can be found in public accounting firms' systems of quality control. Identify each of them with one of the six elements of quality control identified by *SQCS 8*.

a. Assign management responsibilities in such a manner that commercial considerations do not override the quality of work performed.

b. Establish policies and procedures for resolving differences of opinion among firm personnel that arise during professional engagements.

c. Develop policies and procedures to ensure that professionals are provided appropriate professional development opportunities.

d. Review engagement documentation, reports, and the client's financial statements.

e. Develop effective performance evaluation, compensation, and advancement procedures.

f. Identify circumstances and relationships that create threats to independence and take appropriate action to eliminate those threats or reduce them to an acceptable level.

g. Identify whether the firm possesses the competency, capability, and resources to appropriately serve a specific client.

h. Devote sufficient resources to develop, communicate, and support the firm's quality control procedures.

i. Retain engagement documentation for a sufficient period of time to satisfy the needs of the firm, professional standards, laws, and regulations.

LO 2-5   2.68   **Evaluating Quality Control.** Two types of processes available to public accounting firms for evaluating the quality of their work are peer reviews and PCAOB inspections.

Required:

a. What are the major characteristics of peer reviews and PCAOB inspections?
b. What types of firms typically have peer reviews and PCAOB inspections? How frequently are these evaluations conducted?
c. What were some of the criticisms of the peer review process that led to the creation of the PCAOB inspection process?

LO 2-5

2.69 **Internet Exercise: Public Company Accounting Oversight Board Inspection Reports.** Refer to the website of the Public Company Accounting Oversight Board (PCAOB) (www.pcaobus.org) and review the information under "Inspections" and select the most current inspection report for one of the Big Four firms (Deloitte, Ernst & Young, KPMG, and PwC).

Required:

a. What information is contained in the "public" version of the PCAOB's inspection reports? Is there any additional information that you would like to see?
b. What categories of practices, policies, and procedures are evaluated in the PCAOB's inspection of the firm's quality control system?
c. For the firm you selected, how many practice offices had audits inspected by the PCAOB?
d. For the firm you selected, for how many audits (issuers) did the PCAOB find deficiencies?
e. Identify five deficiencies that were cited in the PCAOB's inspection report. For each deficiency, to which of the elements of the principles does it most closely relate? (If the firm had fewer than five deficiencies, evaluate all of the deficiencies identified in the report.)
f. Briefly summarize the firm's response (if any) to the PCAOB's inspection report.

LO 2-6

2.70 (Appendix) **Investment Performance Attestation.** Nancy Drew is the president of Mystery Capital Management, Inc. Mystery manages $1.2 billion in two mutual funds, one a stock fund and the other a bond fund. Competition for investors' money is fierce, and hundreds of money management companies compete by advertising their funds' performance statistics. The U.S. Securities and Exchange Commission has criticized the advertisements for misrepresenting the returns investors can actually earn. In addition to the investment performance statistics, money management firms also advertise the amounts of their fees, usually representing no-load or low-fee arrangements, but they often do not advertise the Rule 12(b) expenses allowed under SEC rules.

Ms. Drew has retained your accounting firm to give an opinion on the fair presentation of Mystery Capital Management's investment performance statistics and expense ratios used in its advertisements. The plan is to present your report in the entity's advertisements.

Required:

For each of the attestation standards, state its applicability in relation to the engagement.

Appendix 2A

Attestation Standards

LEARNING OBJECTIVE 2-6
Identify the need for attestation standards and the use of these standards in attestation engagements.

An audit is a form of attestation; however, some engagements do not call for the relatively extensive scope and conclusions that result from an audit. **Attestation standards** represent a general set of standards intended to guide attestation work in areas other than audits of financial statements. Because assurance services are constantly evolving, there are currently no specific assurance standards. However, because of their similarity to attestation engagements, accountants often rely on attestation standards for guidance in the conduct of other types of assurance engagements. The attestation standards were issued after GAAS and, as in Exhibit 2.A1, the ideas are consistent with the fundamental principles discussed in this chapter. (The information in Exhibit 2.A1 is sequenced to correspond to the ordering of the attestation standards, which differs slightly from that of the principles.)

While Exhibit 2.A1 reveals many similarities between attestation standards and the principles, some differences can be seen. With respect to practitioner competence, the responsibilities principle presumes knowledge of accounting and requires competence and capabilities as auditors (meaning auditors of financial statements because that was the only type of attestation being performed using GAAS). On the other hand, the attestation standards are more general, requiring training and proficiency (which is similar in nature to competence and capabilities) in the "attest function" and knowledge of the "subject matter." The *attest function* refers to the ability to recognize the information being asserted, to determine the evidence relevant to the assertions, and to make decisions about the correspondence of the information asserted with suitable criteria. The "knowledge of the subject matter" is not confined to accounting and financial assertions because attestations may cover a wide variety of information (e.g., environmental standards).

The attestation standards, unlike the performance principle, have no specific requirements for determining materiality levels or obtaining an understanding of the entity and its environment to assess the risk of material misstatement. Again, these differences reflect the fact that attestation engagements may cover a wide variety of information that is not confined to accounting and financial assertions; determining materiality levels or assessing the risk of material misstatement may not be appropriate for all attest engagements.

Reporting is different under the attestation standards and the reporting principle because attestations on nonfinancial information do not depend on generally accepted accounting principles. Accounting principles are the only criteria for financial statement audits. The attestation standards speak of "criteria against which the subject matter was evaluated" and provide flexibility for attestations on a wide variety of informational assertions. In addition, the principles do not specifically address two reporting issues (stating significant reservations about the engagement and indicating that the report is intended only for specified parties) identified in the attestation standards. The reason that attestation standards limit distribution of the report is to prevent any misunderstandings about the services the accountant is providing (e.g., a user believing that an audit was conducted when an attestation engagement of lesser scope was performed).

EXHIBIT 2.A1 **Comparison of Attestation Standards and Principles**

Attestation Standards	Principles
General Standards	
1. The *practitioner* must have adequate technical training and proficiency to perform the *attest engagement*.	Auditors are responsible for having appropriate competence and capabilities to perform the audit.
2. The *practitioner* must have adequate knowledge of the subject matter.	
3. The *practitioner* must have reason to believe that the subject matter is capable of evaluation against criteria that are suitable and available to users.	
4. The *practitioner* must maintain independence in mental attitude in all matters relating to the engagement.	Auditors are responsible for complying with appropriate ethical requirements.
5. The *practitioner* must exercise due professional care in the planning and performance of the engagement and the preparation of the report.	Auditors are responsible for maintaining professional skepticism and exercising professional judgment throughout the planning and performance of the audit.
Standards of Field Work	
1. The *practitioner* must adequately plan the work and must properly supervise any assistants.	To obtain reasonable assurance . . . the auditor plans the work and properly supervises any assistants.
[Depending upon the subject matter, determination of materiality may not be required for an attestation engagement.]	To obtain reasonable assurance . . . the auditor determines and applies appropriate materiality level or levels throughout the audit.
[Depending upon the subject matter, assessment of the risk of material misstatement may not be required for an attestation engagement.]	To obtain reasonable assurance . . . the auditor identifies and assesses risks of material misstatement, whether due to fraud or error, based on an understanding of the entity and its environment, including the entity's internal control.
2. The *practitioner* must obtain sufficient evidence to provide a reasonable basis for *the conclusion that is expressed in the report*.	To obtain reasonable assurance . . . the auditor obtains sufficient appropriate evidence about whether material misstatements exist, through designing and implementing appropriate responses to the assessed risks.
Standards of Reporting	
1. The *practitioner* must identify the subject matter or the assertion being reported on and state the character of the engagement in the report.	Based on evaluation of the evidence obtained, the auditor expresses in the form of a written report, an opinion in accordance with the auditor's findings, or states that an opinion cannot be expressed. The opinion states whether the financial statements are presented fairly, in all material respects, in accordance with the applicable financial reporting framework.
2. The *practitioner* must state the *practitioner's* conclusion about the *subject matter or the assertion* in relation to *criteria against which the subject matter was evaluated* in the report.	
3. The *practitioner* must state all of the *practitioner's significant reservations about the engagement*, the *subject matter*, and if applicable, the *assertion* related thereto in the report.	
4. The *practitioner* must state in the report that the report is intended solely for the information and use of the *specified parties* under the following circumstances [detail omitted].	

Engagement Planning

Vision without action is a daydream.
Action without vision is a nightmare.
Japanese proverb

Professional Standards References

Topic	AU/ISA Section	PCAOB Reference*
Overall Objectives of the Independent Auditor	200	AU 110, AU 150, AU 201, AU 201, AU 220, AU 230
Terms of Engagement	210	AU 310
Quality Control for an Audit Engagement	220	AS 7
Supervision of the Audit Engagement	220, 300	AS 11
Audit Documentation	230	AS 3
Consideration of Fraud in a Financial Statement Audit	240	AU 316
Consideration of Laws and Regulations	250	AU 317
Audit Planning	300	AS 10
Consideration of Internal Control in an Integrated Audit		AS 5
Identifying and Assessing the Risks of Material Misstatement	315	AS 12
Materiality	320	AS 11
Auditors' Responses to Risks of Material Misstatement	330	AS 13
Audit Considerations Relating to an Entity Using a Service Organization	402	AS 5
Audit Evidence	500	AS 15
External Confirmations	505	AU 330
Analytical Procedures	520	AU 329
Related Parties	550	AU 334
Consideration of the Internal Audit Function in a Financial Statement Audit	610	AU 341
Using the Work of an Audit Specialist	620	AU 336

* AU and AT references represent standards issued by the ASB prior to April 16, 2003, that have not been superseded or amended by the PCAOB.

LEARNING OBJECTIVES

In August 2010, the PCAOB adopted eight new standards (AS 8–AS 15) related to the auditor's assessment of, and response to, risk in a financial statement audit. Collectively, the standards also include guidance related to audit planning, supervision, materiality, and other related topics. In this chapter, we cover engagement planning, beginning with pre-engagement activities, supervision, materiality, and the effects of computer processing. Next, we cover the types of audit procedures that can be completed, including computer-assisted auditing techniques (CAATs). In Chapter 4, we provide comprehensive coverage of an auditor's assessment of risk.

Your objectives are to be able to:

LO 3-1 List and describe the required pre-engagement activities that auditors undertake before beginning an audit engagement.

LO 3-2 Understand the importance of planning the audit engagement so that it is conducted in accordance with professional standards.

LO 3-3 Define *materiality* and explain its importance in the audit planning process.

LO 3-4 List and describe the eight general types of audit procedures for gathering evidence.

LO 3-5 List and discuss matters of planning that auditors should consider related to the client's computer environment and describe how CAATs can be used to improve the efficiency of the audit process.

LO 3-6 Define what is meant by the proper form and content of audit documentation.

INTRODUCTION

In a planning memo dated February 6, 2001, the **Arthur Andersen** audit team assigned to the **Enron** engagement discussed whether Andersen should remain as Enron's auditor. Specifically, the engagement planning team had identified some questionable investment practices and expressed concern that Enron was engaging in "intelligent gambling." Despite these reservations, the Andersen engagement planning team concluded that the firm had the "appropriate people and processes in place to serve Enron and manage our engagement risks." Less than a year later, Enron was in bankruptcy and Andersen was in the midst of a federal investigation that would lead to its ultimate dissolution. What went wrong in Andersen's planning process? It is an important question because no current auditing firm wants to suffer the same consequences as Arthur Andersen. This chapter is devoted to audit planning with close attention to auditors' early identification of the risks of material misstatement that exist at both the overall financial statement level and at the management assertion level. In fact, the primary reason for engagement planning is to first identify the risks of material misstatement at the financial statement and the assertion level and second to execute auditing procedures (both substantive and control tests) that are designed to mitigate these risks to an acceptable level, which then allows the auditor to issue an opinion (hopefully unqualified) on the fairness of the financial statements. However, before beginning to work on the audit plan, the auditor must complete a number of required pre-engagement activities that help to determine whether to accept a new client or agree to work with an existing client for another year.

PRE-ENGAGEMENT ACTIVITIES (AU/ISA 300, AS 10)

LEARNING OBJECTIVE 3-1
List and describe the required pre-engagement activities that auditors undertake before beginning an audit engagement.

Public accounting firms try to reduce their own business risks by carefully managing their audit engagements. To do so, public accounting firms undertake several activities before beginning any audit engagement. In general, these activities can be called *risk management activities*. Risk in an audit engagement generally refers to the probability that the firm could "blow" the audit opinion. That is, issue a clean, unqualified audit opinion when in fact a material misstatement *does* exist in the financial statements. Because of the importance of these activities, the new professional standards for public companies state the auditor should perform the following activities: (1) perform procedures regarding the acceptance or continuance of the audit client relationship, (2) determine compliance with independence and ethics requirements, and (3) reach a contractual understanding with the client for the terms and conditions of the audit engagement. Each of these areas is now discussed.

Client Acceptance or Continuance

An important element of a public accounting firm's quality control policies and procedures is a system for deciding whether to accept a new client and, on a continuing basis, deciding whether to continue providing services to existing clients. Public accounting firms are not obligated to accept undesirable clients, nor are they obligated to continue to serve clients when relationships deteriorate or when the management comes under a cloud of suspicion. The process activities are clearly focused on understanding and managing risk to the audit firm. In fact, to mitigate their business risk, public accounting firms devote substantial time to make sure that the audit clients that they serve do not become the next Enron, **WorldCom, Waste Management**, or even Bernie Madoff.

STAGES OF AN AUDIT

Obtain (or Retain) Engagement → Engagement Planning → Risk Assessment → Substantive Procedures → Reporting

AUDITING INSIGHT — Public Accounting Firms Will Dump Risky Clients

In recent years, the most prestigious public accounting firms have become more aggressive in dumping audit clients that they deem to be high risk. For example, **PricewaterhouseCoopers** "parted ways" with about 50 or 60 public companies in 2003; **Ernst & Young** says it walked away from 200 public and private audit engagements; **Deloitte**, another 70. To ferret out potential lemons, public accounting firms have increased their scrutiny of information that prospective clients submit about everything from finance to management changes. Accountants are grilling former auditors about management integrity.

Performing audits of public companies involves significant reputation and litigation risks to the public accounting firms because they are lending their credibility to the client's financial statements filed with the SEC. As a result, each of the largest firms takes dramatic steps to protect its reputation and avoid working with risky clients.

Sources: "Accounting Firms Aim to Dispel Cloud of Corporate Fraud," *The Wall Street Journal*, May 27, 2003, p. C1; "In-Depth Guide to Public Company Auditing: The Financial Statement Audit," *Center for Audit Quality*, May, 2011 (available at www.thecaq.org).

Auditing a client that has integrity generally results in a problem-free engagement. Conversely, despite conducting an audit in accordance with generally accepted auditing standards, it is difficult for a public accounting firm to avoid appearing "guilty by association" with a client that lacks integrity. The public accounting firm that has been terminated or has voluntarily withdrawn from the engagement (whether the audit has been completed or not) is known as the **predecessor auditor**. To reduce the risk of accepting a problem client, auditing standards require a prospective auditor to initiate contact with and *attempt* to obtain basic information directly from the predecessor regarding issues that reflect directly on the *integrity of management*. The audit client must grant its approval before the communication can occur between the prospective auditor and the predecessor auditor. In addition, client acceptance and continuance policies and procedures generally include:

- Obtaining and reviewing financial information about the prospective client: annual reports, interim statements, registration statements, Form 10-Ks, and reports to regulatory agencies.
- Detailed criminal background checks of senior managers.
- Inquiring of the prospective client's bankers, legal counsel, underwriters, analysts, or other persons who do business with the entity for information about the entity and its management.
- Considering whether the engagement would require special attention or involve unusual risks to the public accounting firm.
- Evaluating the public accounting firm's independence with regard to the prospective client.
- Considering the need for individuals possessing special skills or knowledge to complete the audit (e.g., IT auditor, valuation specialist, industry specialist).

The firms also search for news articles, lawsuits, and bankruptcy court outcomes naming the entity, the chairman of the board, the CEO, the CFO, and other high-ranking officers. In fact, the firms often engage private investigators to conduct additional searches for information when the prospective clients are financial institutions, companies accused of fraud, companies under SEC or other regulatory investigation, companies that have changed auditors frequently, and companies showing recent losses. These characteristics are red flags of potential problems, and public accounting firms want to know as much as they can about the companies and their officers before entering into a relationship with them. Without a doubt, management integrity (or lack thereof) is the primary reason for accepting (or not accepting) an audit engagement.

Client continuance decisions are similar to acceptance decisions except that the firm will have more firsthand experience with the entity. Retention reviews may be done annually or on occurrence of major events such as changes in management, directors, ownership, legal counsel, financial condition, litigation status, nature of the client's business, or scope of the audit engagement. In general, conditions that would have caused a public accounting firm to reject a prospective client can develop and lead to a decision to discontinue the engagement. For example, a client company could expand and diversify on an international scale so that a small public accounting firm might not have the competence to continue the audit. In addition, it would not be unusual to see newspaper stories about public accounting firms dropping clients after directors or officers admit to falsification of financial statements or to theft and misuse of corporate assets.

AUDITING INSIGHT — Deloitte & Touche Refuses to Go All In

Deloitte (formerly **Deloitte & Touche**) recently withdrew as auditor for **WPT Enterprises, Inc.**, the creator of the **World Poker Tour**, just as the company was starting its new online poker enterprise. The Big Four firm cited additional "audit risks" associated with the new gaming venture that would consume too many resources to adequately audit this client. Not noted in its resignation letter are concerns about the legality of online gaming. It is illegal in the United States, and part of the audit team's responsibilities would have included investigating whether any online gambling customers were residing in the United States. Additionally, online gambling requires complex software that involves a general lack of transparency.

Source: "For Audit Firms, All Bets Are Off," *The Wall Street Journal*, July 21, 2005, p. C3.

As stated previously, for a new audit engagement, public accounting firms are required to attempt to communicate with the predecessor auditor, if any, for information on management's integrity; on disagreements with management about accounting principles, audit procedures, or similar matters; and the reasons for a change of auditors. Companies are free to, and often do, change auditors periodically, sometimes as a result of corporate policy to rotate auditors, sometimes because of fee considerations, and sometimes because of arguments about the scope of the audit or the acceptability of accounting principles. It is possible that a change in auditors occurred for the purpose of procuring new auditors who will agree with management's treatment of questionable accounting treatments. Not surprisingly, these types of disagreements between auditors and management would be of interest to investors.

As a result, whenever a public company changes auditors, the company must file a *Form 8-K* report with the SEC and disclose that the board of directors approved the change. **Form 8-K**, the "special events report," is required whenever certain significant events occur such as changes in control and legal proceedings. Public companies also must report any disagreements with the former auditors concerning matters of accounting principles, financial statement disclosure, or auditing procedure. At the same time, the former auditor must submit a letter stating whether the auditors agree with the explanation and, if not, provide particulars. These documents are available to the public through the SEC's Electronic Data Gathering, Analysis, and Retrieval (EDGAR) system, available on the SEC's website (www.sec.gov). The purpose of these public disclosures is to make information available about client–auditor conflicts that have occurred.

AUDITING INSIGHT — Former Client Failed to Disclose Dispute in 8-K

The public accounting firm told the SEC (in the required accountant's letter) that a former client incorrectly reported no disagreements preceding the firm's dismissal as the company's auditor. A disagreement *had* occurred involving the company's wish to capitalize the cost of moving an acquired company's headquarters to another city in accounting for the acquisition. The public accounting firm believed the costs were expenses of the period and were not related to the acquisition.

Note: Another public accounting firm, however, agreed with the company's preferred accounting treatment. The company dismissed the former firm and hired the public accounting firm that agreed with its position.

Source: *Accounting Today.*

If you read closely, professional standards require only that the auditors *attempt* to communicate with the predecessor auditors. The AICPA Code of Professional Conduct does not permit the predecessor to provide information obtained during the terminated engagement without the explicit consent of the client. Confidentiality remains even when the auditor–client relationship ends. Therefore, auditing standards require the prospective public accounting firm to ask that the consent be given to permit the predecessor auditor to speak. If this consent is refused, the refusal should be regarded as a *red flag* and the prospective auditor should be cautious about accepting the engagement.

Compliance with Independence and Ethical Requirements

If you recall from Chapter 2, the *responsibilities principle* requires auditors to comply with appropriate ethical requirements for each audit engagement; two important requirements relate to *independence* and *due care*. Auditors must maintain independence *in mental attitude;* that is, auditors are expected to be unbiased and impartial with respect to the financial statements and other information they audit. This "state of mind" is often referred to as the auditor possessing **independence in fact**. This independence allows auditors to form an opinion on the entity's financial statements without being affected by influences that might compromise that opinion. It is not only important for auditors to be unbiased but also they must also *appear* to be unbiased. **Independence in appearance** relates to others' (particularly financial statement users') perceptions of auditors' independence.

In fact, if the auditor is not independent, the financial statements are considered unaudited for all practical purposes. A lack of independence can result in disciplinary action by regulators and/or professional organizations and litigation by those who relied on the financial statements (e.g., clients and investors). The profession, as a whole, depends on the value of independence in that the auditor's opinion on the financial statements loses its value if the auditor is not considered to be independent from the management of the firm. As a result of the importance placed on independence, public accounting firms must have a process in place to ensure that they are independent of the company being audited.

Engagement Letters

Professional standards require auditors to reach a mutual understanding with clients concerning engagement requirements and expectations and to document this understanding, usually in the form of a written letter. When a new client is accepted or when an audit engagement continues from year to year, an **engagement letter** should be prepared. This letter sets forth the understanding with the client, including in particular: (1) the objectives of the engagement, (2) management's responsibilities, (3) the auditors' responsibilities, and (4) any limitations of the engagement. Other matters of understanding such as the ones shown in Exhibit 3.1 also may be included in the letter. For example, the additional internal control considerations required by the Public Company Accounting Oversight Board (PCAOB) in *Auditing Standard 5* are mentioned in the example engagement letter.

In effect, the engagement letter acts as a contract. Thus, it serves as a means for reducing the risk of misunderstandings with the client and as a means of avoiding legal liability for claims that the auditors did not perform the work promised.

Many public accounting firms also have policies about sending a **termination letter** to former clients. Such a letter is a good idea because it provides an opportunity to deal with the subject of future services, in particular: (1) access to audit documentation by successor auditors, (2) reissuance of the auditors' report when required for SEC reporting or comparative financial reporting, and (3) fee arrangements for such future services. The termination letter also may include a report of the auditors' understanding of the circumstances of termination (e.g., disagreements about accounting principles and audit procedures, fees, or other conflicts). These matters can be of great interest to prospective auditors who know to ask for a copy of the termination letter.

> ### ↳ REVIEW CHECKPOINTS
>
> 3.1 What sources of information can auditors use in connection with deciding whether to accept a new client?
>
> 3.2 Why do predecessor auditors need to obtain the client's consent to give information to prospective auditors? What information should prospective auditors try to obtain from predecessor auditors?
>
> 3.3 What benefits are obtained by having an *engagement letter*? What is a *termination letter*?

AUDIT PLAN (AU/ISA 300, AS 10)

LEARNING OBJECTIVE 3-2
Understand the importance of planning the audit engagement so that it is conducted in accordance with professional standards.

An **audit plan** is a comprehensive list of the specific audit procedures that the audit team needs to perform to gather sufficient appropriate evidence on which to base their opinion on the financial statements. The professional standards require that the auditor plan each audit engagement, including the establishment of an overall strategy for each audit engagement. Specifically, when planning the engagement, the auditor needs to develop and document a plan that describes the nature, timing, and extent of the procedures to be performed to assess the risk of material misstatement at the financial statement and the assertion level. Next, the auditor must carefully plan the nature, timing, and extent of control tests and substantive tests that are designed to mitigate these risks to an acceptable level. This planning process is required to be led by the assigned engagement partner.

EXHIBIT 3.1 Engagement Letter

October 15, 2012

Dear Mr. Lancaster:

This letter will confirm our understanding of the arrangement for our audit of the financial statements of Dunder-Mifflin, Inc. for the year ending December 31, 2012.

We will audit the Company's balance sheet at December 31, 2012, and the related statements of income, comprehensive income, stockholders' equity, and cash flows for the year then ended, for the purpose of expressing an opinion on them. We will also audit whether Dunder-Mifflin, Inc. maintained effective internal control over financial reporting as of December 31, 2012, based on criteria established in Internal Control—Integrated Framework issued by the Committee of Sponsoring Organizations of the Treadway Commission (COSO criteria). Dunder-Mifflin, Inc.'s management is responsible for these financial statements and for maintaining effective internal control over financial reporting. Management is also responsible for making financial records and related information available for audit and for identifying and ensuring that the company complies with the laws and regulations that apply to its activities. Lastly, management is responsible for adjusting the financial statements to correct material misstatements and for affirming to us in the representation letter that the effects of any uncorrected misstatements aggregated by us during the current engagement and pertaining to the latest period presented are immaterial, both individually and in the aggregate, to the financial statements taken as a whole. Our responsibility is to express an opinion on these financial statements and an opinion on the effectiveness of the company's internal control over financial reporting based on our audits. If, for any reason, we are unable to complete the audit or are unable to form or have not formed an opinion, we may decline to express an opinion or decline to issue a report as a result of the engagement.

We will conduct our audits in accordance with the standards of the Public Company Accounting Oversight Board (United States). Those standards require that we plan and perform the audit to obtain reasonable assurance about whether the financial statements are free of material misstatement and whether effective internal control over financial reporting was maintained in all material respects. Our audit of the financial statements includes examining, on a test basis, evidence supporting the amounts and disclosures in the financial statements, assessing the accounting principles used and significant estimates made by management, and evaluating the overall financial statement presentation. Our audit of internal control over financial reporting includes obtaining an understanding of internal control over financial reporting, testing and evaluating the design and operating effectiveness of internal control, and performing such other procedures as we considered necessary in the circumstances. We believe that our audits provide a reasonable basis for our opinions.

A company's internal control over financial reporting is a process designed to provide reasonable assurance regarding the reliability of financial reporting and the preparation of financial statements for external purposes in accordance with generally accepted accounting principles. A company's internal control over financial reporting includes those policies and procedures that (1) pertain to the maintenance of records that, in reasonable detail, accurately and fairly reflect the transactions and dispositions of the assets of the company; (2) provide reasonable assurance that transactions are recorded as necessary to permit preparation of financial statements in accordance with generally accepted accounting principles, and that receipts and expenditures of the company are being made only in accordance with authorizations of management and directors of the company; and (3) provide reasonable assurance regarding prevention or timely detection of unauthorized acquisition, use, or disposition of the company's assets that could have a material effect on the financial statements.

Because of its inherent limitations, internal control over financial reporting may not prevent or detect misstatements. Also, projections of any evaluation of effectiveness to future periods are subject to the risk that controls may become inadequate because of changes in conditions, or that the degree of compliance with the policies or procedures may deteriorate.

Our fee for these services will be at our regular per diem rates, plus travel and other out-of-pocket costs. Invoices will be rendered on a monthly basis and are payable on presentation.

If this letter correctly expresses your understanding, please sign the enclosed copy where indicated and return it to us.

Very truly yours,

Smith & Smith, CPAs

DUNDER-MIFFLIN, Inc.

By _____

Date _____

STAGES OF AN AUDIT

Obtain (or Retain) Engagement → **Engagement Planning** → Risk Assessment → Substantive Procedures → Reporting

The professional standards are absolutely clear that "the nature and extent of planning activities that are necessary" for each audit engagement, "depend on the size and complexity of the company, the auditor's previous experience with the company, and changes in circumstances that occur during the audit."[1] As a result, audit firms spend a considerable amount of time on risk assessment at both the financial statement level and the financial statement assertion level for the client being audited.

Importantly, this process begins with a detailed understanding of the client's business, industry, and strategy to achieve competitive advantage in their marketplace. During this process, the auditor should obtain an understanding of important events that have affected the client, its operations, the financial statements, and ultimately the management assertions. It is this understanding that provides the base of knowledge necessary to assess audit risk, providing the underlying basis to construct the audit plan.

For example, the evaluation of inherent risk is likely to vary for different financial statement accounts and may even vary for different classes of transactions related to the same financial statement account. Ultimately, the audit plan will need to identify the relevant financial statement assertions (i.e., *existence, occurrence, completeness, cutoff, rights and obligations, valuation and allocation, accuracy, classification,* and *understandability*) for the significant financial statement accounts and disclosures of an audit client. Because of the importance of risk assessment to the financial statement audit process, we devote exclusive attention to this subject in Chapter 4.

The risk assessment process provides the basis to determine the nature, timing, and extent of internal control tests and substantive tests of account balances and disclosures at an audit client. That is, for each relevant assertion, the auditor must determine the combination of control and substantive tests that will be necessary to gather enough evidence to persuade the auditor that no material misstatement exists for the relevant assertion being audited. When the tests are complete, audit team members will often indicate the date that the procedure was performed and where the evidence is documented in the audit plan. Thus, audit plans are used not only for quality control and supervision but also as documentation to show that the audit engagement was planned and supervised in accordance with professional standards.

Although risk assessment is absolutely critical in the audit planning process, there are many other aspects of audit planning. The remainder of this chapter will focus on all other aspects of the audit plan. So, one must remember that the professional standards require that "planning the audit includes establishing the overall audit strategy for the engagement and developing an audit plan, which includes, in particular, planned risk assessment procedures and planned responses to the risks of material misstatement."[2] Although mitigating these risks is ultimately the primary reason for engagement planning, this overriding objective is essentially contained in the three additional goals of audit planning:

- To make sure that the firm has the requisite staff to conduct the audit in accordance with professional standards in a timely and profitable manner;
- To determine materiality; and

---

[1] PCAOB *Auditing Standard No. 9,* "Audit Planning," August, 2010.
[2] Ibid.

- To outline the specific audit procedures, including control tests and substantive tests that need to be executed properly in order to be in compliance with professional standards.

Staffing the Audit Engagement

When a new client is obtained, most public accounting firms assign a full-service team to the engagement. For a typical audit engagement, this team usually consists of the audit engagement partner (the person with final responsibility for the audit and usually an industry specialist), an audit manager, an IT audit specialist, a tax partner, a **quality assurance partner**, and audit staff. The assignment of staff depends on the riskiness of the engagement. For new clients, companies with complex transactions and public companies, more experienced staff members are typically assigned. No matter the type of engagement, planning meetings should include all team members and focus on the financial statement accounts that represent the highest risk of material misstatement.

These planning meetings help to ensure that the engagement is properly planned and that the audit team (especially new) members are properly supervised. The meetings also are intended to be brainstorming sessions to (1) ensure that all audit team members are informed about potential risks in the engagement and (2) increase team members' awareness for potential fraud. This required brainstorming session is discussed in more detail in Chapter 4.

Considering the Work of Internal Auditors (*AU/ISA 610*)

External auditors must obtain an understanding of a client's internal audit department and its work as part of the understanding of the client's internal control. Internal auditors were discussed briefly in Chapter 1 and will be discussed in more detail in Module D, but here we talk about the working relationship between internal and external auditors. Audit efficiency can be realized when the two groups work together. However, prior to using the work of internal auditors, external auditors should consider internal auditors' *objectivity* and *competence*:

- *Objectivity.* Internal auditors can never be considered *independent* in the same sense as external auditors because internal auditors are employed and compensated by the client; however, they can (and should) be *objective*.[3] Internal auditors' objectivity is investigated by learning about their organizational status and lines of communication in the company. The theory is that objectivity is enhanced when the internal auditors report directly to the audit committee of the board of directors. Objectivity is questioned when the internal auditors report to divisional management, line managers, or other persons with a stake in the outcome of their findings. Objectivity is especially questioned when managers have some power over the pay or job tenure of the internal auditors. Similarly, objectivity is questioned when individual internal auditors have relatives in audit-sensitive areas or are scheduled to be promoted to positions in the activities under internal audit review.
- *Competence.* Internal auditors' competence is investigated by obtaining evidence about their educational and experience qualifications, their certifications (CPA, CIA, CISA, etc.) and continuing education status, the department's policies and procedures for work quality and for making personnel assignments, the supervision and review activities, and the quality of reports and audit documentation. This evidence enables the external auditors to evaluate internal auditors' performance.

Favorable conclusions about competence and objectivity enable external auditors to accept the internal auditors' documentation and work on review, assessment, and monitoring of a company's internal control procedures. Internal auditors also can assist (under the supervision of the independent audit team) with performing other parts of the audit, reducing the external auditors' work, and avoiding duplication of effort. For example,

---

[3] Internal auditors refer to their level of objectivity as *independence*. This concept is discussed further in Module D.

internal auditors often confirm accounts receivable and conduct observations and make test counts during physical inventory counts. By relying in part on this work, external auditors may be able to reduce the nature, timing, or extent of their own procedures in the same areas. Be careful to note, however, that this utilization of internal auditors' work cannot be a complete substitute for the external auditors' own procedures and evidence related to accounting judgments and material financial statement balances.

The external auditors cannot share responsibility for audit decisions with the internal auditors and must supervise, review, evaluate, and test the work they performed. This requirement applies to both the work of obtaining an understanding of the internal control and the work of using internal auditors' evidence about account balances. In other words, internal auditors should never be delegated tasks that require the external auditors' *professional judgment*. Thus, although internal auditors may investigate accounts receivable confirmation exceptions, they normally would not be involved in assessing the reasonableness of the company's allowance for doubtful accounts. Following is an illustration of how one Big Four firm addresses the use of internal auditors on its engagements. Note that internal auditors' work can be utilized more extensively without reperformance when the account balance involves low judgment and risk, and internal auditors are considered to be more competent and objective.

Reliance on Internal Auditors

	Objectivity and Competence	
	Low	High
High Judgment/Risk	Auditor should not rely on internal auditors' work	
Low Judgment/Risk	Reperform 50 percent of internal auditor's work	Reperform 30 percent of internal auditor's work

Use of Specialists (*AU/ISA 620*)

The understanding of the business can lead to information that indicates the need to employ *specialists* on the audit. **Specialists** are persons skilled in fields other than accounting and auditing—actuaries, appraisers, attorneys, engineers, and geologists—who are not members of the audit team. Auditors are not expected to be experts in all fields of knowledge that can contribute information to the financial statements. When a specialist is engaged, auditors must know about his or her professional qualifications, experience, and reputation. A specialist should be unrelated to the company under audit if possible. Auditors must obtain an understanding of a specialist's methods and assumptions. Provided some additional auditing work is done on the data used by the specialist, auditors may rely on the specialist's work in connection with audit decisions. Normally, specialists are not referred to in the auditor's report unless the specialist's findings (e.g., a difference in an estimate from that of management) cause the auditors' report to be modified (e.g., because of a GAAP departure). In these cases, references to specialists' findings may facilitate understanding the nature of the GAAP departure.

Use of Information Technology (IT) Auditors

When planning the engagement, the engagement partner or manager might find that certain specialized skills are needed to evaluate the effect of computerized processing on the audit, to understand the flow of transactions, or to design and perform audit procedures. These IT auditors are members of the audit team and are called on when the need for their skills arises, just as statistical sampling specialists or SEC specialists are available when their expertise is needed. For example, the audit team could need specialized skills relating to various methods of data processing, programming languages, software packages, or computer-assisted audit techniques. Audit managers and partners should possess sufficient computer knowledge to know when to call on specialists and to understand and supervise their work.

Time Budget

The timing of the work and the number of hours that each segment of the engagement is expected to take are detailed in a preliminary time budget. *Time budgets* are used to maintain control of the audit by identifying problem areas early in the engagement, thereby ensuring that the engagement is completed on a timely basis. Time budgets are usually based on the prior year's performance for continuing clients while taking changes in the client's business into account. In a first-time audit, the budget may be based on a predecessor auditor's experience or on general experience with similar companies. Extra time also may be assigned to those accounts containing the highest amount of audit risk. A simple time budget for an audit engagement follows.

	Audit Time Budget (hours)	
	Interim	Year-End (Final)
Knowledge of the business	15	
Internal audit familiarization	10	
Internal control evaluation	30	10
Audit plan preparation	25	
Related-parties investigation	5	15
Client conferences	10	18
Cash	10	15
Accounts receivable	15	5
Inventory	35	20
Accounts payable	5	35
Representation letters		20
Financial statement review		25
Report preparation		12

This time budget is illustrative—actual time budgets are much more detailed. Most budgets specify the expected time by level of staff people on the team (partner, manager, in-charge accountant, staff assistant, IT specialist). The illustration shows time at *interim* and at *year-end*. **Interim audit work** refers to procedures performed several weeks or months before the balance sheet date. (Account balances audited during interim are later *rolled forward* at year-end.) **Year-end audit work** refers to procedures performed shortly before and after the balance sheet date. Public accounting firms typically spread the workload out during the year by scheduling interim audit work so they will have enough time and people available when several audits have year-ends on the same date (December 31 is common). For many public accounting firms, the auditing "busy season" runs from September through March of the following year. The interim work typically consists of risk assessment work, internal control testing, and substantive testing of balances as they exist at the early date.

Everyone who works on the audit engagement is typically required to report the time taken to perform procedures for each phase of the audit. These time reports are recorded by budget categories for the purposes of (1) evaluating the efficiency of the audit team members, (2) compiling a record for billing the client, and (3) compiling a record for planning the next audit. Although the purposes of a time budget are straightforward, time budgets create job pressures. Staff members are under pressure to meet the budget, and beginning auditors often experience frustration over learning how to do audit work efficiently.

> ### ↳ REVIEW CHECKPOINTS
>
> 3.4 What is the purpose of a planning memorandum?
>
> 3.5 List some items normally documented in a planning memorandum.
>
> 3.6 What must external auditors do to use the work of internal auditors in the audit of an entity's financial statements?
>
> 3.7 What must external auditors do to use the work of specialists in the audit of an entity's financial statements?
>
> 3.8 For a typical audit engagement, describe the persons and skills that are normally assigned to a full-service audit team?

▽ MATERIALITY (AU/ISA 320, AS 11)

LEARNING OBJECTIVE 3-3
Define *materiality* and explain its importance in the audit planning process.

As you already know, financial statement measurements and information in some footnote disclosures are not flawlessly accurate. As recognized in the scope paragraph of the auditor's standard report, the financial statements are a function of the "accounting principles used and significant estimates made by management." The choices of depreciation method (straight line versus accelerated), inventory valuation method (e.g., FIFO, LIFO, weighted average cost), or classification of marketable securities (available for sale, trading, or held to maturity) all affect final financial statement numbers. Furthermore, many financial measurements are based on estimates such as the estimated depreciable lives of fixed assets or the estimated amount of uncollectible accounts receivable. Thus, you must think of net income not as the one "true" figure but as one possible measure in a range of potential net income figures allowable under the relevant reporting framework (e.g., GAAP or IFRS).

Because of the range permitted, some amount of inaccuracy is permitted in financial statements because (1) unimportant inaccuracies do not affect users' decisions and hence are not material, (2) the cost of finding and correcting small misstatements is too high, and (3) the time taken to find them would delay issuance of financial statements. Although accounting numbers are not absolutely accurate, accountants and auditors want to maintain that financial reports are materially accurate and do not contain material misstatements.

As a result, in order to plan the nature, timing and extent of audit procedures to be performed, an auditor "should establish a **materiality** level for the financial statements as a whole that is appropriate in light of the particular circumstances. This includes consideration of the company's earnings and other relevant factors." The professional standards also now require that the "materiality level for the financial statements as a whole needs to be expressed as a specified amount."[4]

You cannot really think usefully about how to mitigate the risk of material misstatement at the financial statement and assertion level without also thinking about the size of the misstatement that would be considered material in the marketplace for the audit client. Information is material if it is likely to influence financial statement users' decisions. Thus, *material information* is a synonym for *important information*. The emphasis is on the financial statement users' point of view, not on the auditors' or managers' points of view. Although financial statement users are expected to have a basic knowledge of business and financial statements as well as an understanding of the limitations of the audit process, auditors remain conservative when setting the materiality level.

As referenced in PCAOB *AS 11*: In interpreting the federal securities laws, the Supreme Court of the United States has held that a fact is material if there is "a substantial likelihood that the . . . fact would have been viewed by the reasonable investor as having significantly altered the 'total mix' of information made available." As the Supreme Court has noted, determinations

---

[4] PCAOB *Auditing Standard No. 11*, "Consideration of Materiality in Planning and Performing an Audit," August 2010.

of materiality require "delicate assessments of the inferences a 'reasonable shareholder' would draw from a given set of facts and the significance of those inferences to him."[5]

As a result, the engagement partner needs to think carefully about the appropriate level of materiality during the planning process. By doing so, the auditor helps to avoid unnecessary surprises on the audit engagement. Suppose that near the end of an audit, the partner decided that all misstatements of more than $50,000 should be considered material but then realized that the nature, timing, and extent of substantive procedures had been completed assuming a materiality level of $250,000! Clearly, more work should have been done to increase the precision of the audit, but this should have been planned for at the beginning.

The professional standards also require that the "auditor should evaluate whether, in light of the particular circumstances, there are certain accounts or disclosures for which there is a substantial likelihood that misstatements of lesser amounts than the materiality level established for the financial statements as a whole would influence the judgment of a reasonable investor." If so, "the auditor should determine the amount or amounts of tolerable misstatement for purposes of assessing risks of material misstatement and planning and performing audit procedures at the account or disclosure level."[6]

Therefore, auditors use *performance materiality* (an amount less than materiality for the financial statements as a whole) to make sure that the aggregate of uncorrected and undetected immaterial misstatements does not exceed materiality for the financial statements as a whole. For example, auditors may use different amounts (smaller than overall financial statement materiality) when auditing particular classes of transactions, account balances, or disclosures. The audit team cannot look at every transaction, so the concept of performance materiality takes this risk into account. When auditors use sampling, performance materiality is referred to as *tolerable misstatement*.

The extent to which performance materiality is based on the overall materiality is a matter of professional judgment and, as a result, the amount may vary from auditor to auditor, so you should not be surprised that there are different methods for assigning performance materiality to accounts. The auditing standards do not even require that the overall materiality amount be assigned to individual accounts in dollar amounts. You will find many different thought processes and methods used in practice. However, most start with a top-down approach: judging an overall material amount for the financial statements (e.g., $200,000 would materially misstate an entity's balance sheet) and then determining performance materiality to particular accounts (e.g., receivables, inventory) to help determine the amount of work to be done in each area. Such a top-down approach is considered theoretically preferable because this method requires the audit team to think first about the financial statements taken as a whole.

Materiality Calculation

Although some accountants wish that definitive, quantitative materiality guidelines could be issued by standard setters, many fear the rigidity that such guidelines would impose. Therefore, in the end, materiality is a matter of professional judgment that must be decided upon by the engagement partner on each audit engagement. However, on each audit engagement, the planning process begins with a calculation of a preliminary materiality amount that is based on a relevant benchmark and a rule of thumb percentage applied to that benchmark.

The choice of appropriate benchmark relates directly back to the financial statement users. When making an initial determination of materiality, the auditor should consider what is most important to users. For example, for an asset management company or a hedge fund, it is likely that total net assets would be the most appropriate benchmark. However, for a company in the manufacturing industry, profit before tax (PBT) is likely to be most appropriate. If PBT fluctuates widely, a normalized, or average, PBT over recent years may be substituted for the current-year PBT, or the relation may be to the trend change of PBT. For a high-technology start-up, perhaps total revenue would be best. The benchmark

[5] Ibid.
[6] Ibid

for nonprofit entities may be gross revenue, or total contributions, or a figure important in the statement of cash flows. Although many different benchmarks may be used, auditors most commonly use PBT, total net assets or total revenues as the benchmark for their initial determination of materiality. Of course, in the end, it is a matter of professional judgment.

The best rule of thumb seems to be that anything less than 5 percent is probably not material and anything more than 10 percent probably is material. Once again, the rule of thumb varies depending on the facts and circumstances of the audit engagement. The SEC, however, cautions auditors about overreliance on certain quantitative benchmarks to assess materiality, noting that "misstatements are not immaterial simply because they fall beneath a numerical threshold."[7] Thus, auditors must examine both quantitative and qualitative factors when assessing materiality. Some of the more common qualitative factors that auditors use in making materiality judgments are the nature of the item or issue, engagement circumstances, and possible cumulative effects—all discussed in the following paragraphs.

Nature of the Item or Issue

An important qualitative factor is the descriptive nature of the item or issue. An illegal payment is important primarily because of its nature as well as because of its absolute or relative amount. In addition, the auditor would consider any type of fraud committed by a member of management material regardless of the amount. In addition, generally speaking, potential errors in the more liquid assets (cash, receivables, and inventory) are considered more important than potential errors in other accounts (such as fixed assets and deferred charges).

Engagement Circumstances

An auditors' legal liability is a relevant consideration. That is, auditors generally place extra emphasis on detection of misstatement in financial statements that will be widely used (publicly held companies) or used by important outsiders (bank loan officers). Troublesome political events in foreign countries also can cause auditors to try to be more accurate with measurements and disclosures. Other circumstances that affect materiality involve amounts that could turn a net loss into a profit or allow a company to meet earnings expectations. In these circumstances, when management can exercise discretion over an accounting treatment, auditors tend to exercise more care and use a more stringent materiality criterion. Finally, matters surrounded by uncertainty about the outcome of future events usually come under more stringent materiality considerations.

Possible Cumulative Effects

At the end of each audit engagement, auditors must also evaluate the aggregate sum of known or potential misstatements. For example, consider an audit for which overall materiality is set at $50,000. If the audit test work revealed five individual $15,000 misstatements, they would each, on their own, be considered immaterial. However, what if all five misstatements each had the effect of increasing net income? In that situation, the auditor must factor in the probability that the aggregate of uncorrected and undetected misstatements could exceed overall materiality for the financial statements.

AUDITING INSIGHT — Things Add Up at HealthSouth

HealthSouth was able to conceal its $1.4 billion accounting fraud from its auditors Ernst & Young LLP, in part because it broke it up into smaller pieces. Knowing that the auditors were examining all expenses over $5,000, HealthSouth capitalized approximately $1 billion in expenses with transaction amounts ranging between $500 and $4,999. By capitalizing the transactions (and then depreciating them over a long period of time) rather than expensing them in the current year, HealthSouth was able to report significantly higher net income for the current year.

Source: "Ex-Employee Took His Case to Auditors, Then Internet—but Convinced No One," *The Wall Street Journal*, May 20, 2003, pp. A1, A13.

---

[7] SEC *Staff Accounting Bulletin No. 99*, "Materiality," August 12, 1999.

Although we have presented a number of different factors affecting overall materiality, decisions about materiality ultimately remain a function of auditors' professional judgment. Many experienced auditors will state that these judgments are among the most difficult they make. And materiality is one of the most important audit concepts you will learn about because of its pervasive effect on the audit engagement. To summarize, on an audit engagement, the audit team uses materiality three ways:

- As a guide to *planning substantive testing procedures*—directing attention and audit work to those items or accounts that are important, uncertain, or susceptible to material misstatements.
- Auditors use *performance materiality* to make sure that the aggregate of uncorrected and undetected immaterial misstatements does not exceed materiality for the financial statements as a whole. For example, auditors may use an amount smaller than overall financial statement materiality when auditing particular classes of transactions, account balances, or disclosures.
- As a guide for making *decisions about the audit report.* An account such as inventory can be material in an audit context because of its size or its place in the financial statements.

↳ REVIEW CHECKPOINTS

3.9 What is meant by material information in accounting and auditing?

3.10 How does an audit team use materiality on an audit engagement?

AUDIT PROCEDURES FOR OBTAINING AUDIT EVIDENCE (AU/ISA 500, AS 15)

LEARNING OBJECTIVE 3-4
List and describe eight general types of audit procedures for gathering evidence.

Auditors use audit procedures for three purposes. First, they use audit procedures to gain an understanding of the client and the risks associated with the client (*risk assessment procedures*). These procedures are covered in detail in Chapter 4. Second, auditors use audit procedures to test the operating effectiveness of client internal control activities (*tests of controls*) discussed in Chapter 5. Finally, auditors use audit procedures to produce evidence about management's assertions (i.e., relating to *existence, occurrence, completeness, cutoff, rights and obligations, valuation and allocation, accuracy, classification,* and *understandability*) related to the amounts and disclosures in a client's financial statements (*substantive procedures*). Exhibit 3.2 shows the relationship among the assertions, the types of evidence available to the auditor, and the procedures most closely related to each.

Once the risk assessment procedures have been completed and the relevant financial statement assertions have been identified, an auditor then considers whether specific control activities are in place to prevent or detect a misstatement related to each of the relevant financial statement assertions. Ultimately, the audit plan needs to specify a list of procedures that must be completed to gather sufficient and appropriate evidence directed toward achieving particular audit objectives. For example, an internal control audit plan would contain the specific procedures that are needed to obtain an understanding of the client's internal control system related to the relevant financial statement assertions. If the auditor decides to rely on specific internal control activities, the plan would also identify the specific types of internal control tests that would need to be completed in order to validate the operating effectiveness of the internal control activities.

EXHIBIT 3.2 Assertions, Evidence, and Audit Procedures

PCAOB Assertions	ASB Assertions	Key Questions	Examples of Evidence Available	Representative Audit Procedures
Existence or occurrence	Existence	Do the assets recorded really exist?	The physical presence of the assets	Inspection of tangible assets
	Occurrence	Did the recorded sales transactions really occur?	Client shipping documents	Inspection of records or documents (vouching)
Completeness	Completeness	Are the financial statements (including footnotes) complete?	Documents prepared by the client	Inspection of records or documents (tracing)
	Cutoff	Were all transactions recorded in the proper period?	Client receiving, shipping reports	Inspection of records or documents (tracing or vouching)
Rights and obligations	Rights and obligations	Does the entity really own the assets? Are related legal responsibilities identified?	Statements by independent parties	Confirmation
Valuation and allocation	Valuation or allocation	Are the accounts valued correctly?	Client-prepared accounts receivable aging schedule	Reperformance
	Accuracy	Were transactions recorded accurately?	Vendor invoices	Inspection of records or documents (tracing or vouching)
Presentation and disclosure	Classification	Were all transactions recorded in the proper accounts?	Comparisons of current-year amounts with those from the prior year	Analytical procedures
	Understandability	Are the presentations and disclosures understandable to users?	Management-prepared financial statements and footnotes	Inquiry

A **substantive audit plan** would contain a list of audit procedures for gathering evidence related to the relevant assertions identified for the significant financial statement accounts and disclosures at an audit client. The substantive audit plan (i.e., the *nature, timing, and extent* of procedures) depends almost exclusively upon the assessment of risk at an audit client. As an example, consider the nature of procedures. There are two ways to conduct substantive tests: (1) substantive analytical procedures and (2) tests of details.

When completing an analytical review to gather evidence, the auditor must develop an independent expectation of what he or she thinks the account balance should be. Once this is developed, the expectation is compared to the recorded amount. Any significant differences must be investigated and then corroborated with evidence. When applying substantive test of details, the auditor must seek to understand the account balance and/or economic transaction to ensure, based on valid and reliable evidence, that the amount was recorded in accordance with the applicable financial reporting framework. In general, analytical procedures are considered more efficient while a test of details is considered more effective. Thus, an auditor must take great care in determining the nature of the testing procedure (i.e., substantive analytical procedure or test of detail) to specify in the audit plan.

EXHIBIT 3.3A Dunder-Mifflin Trial Balance, December 31, 2012

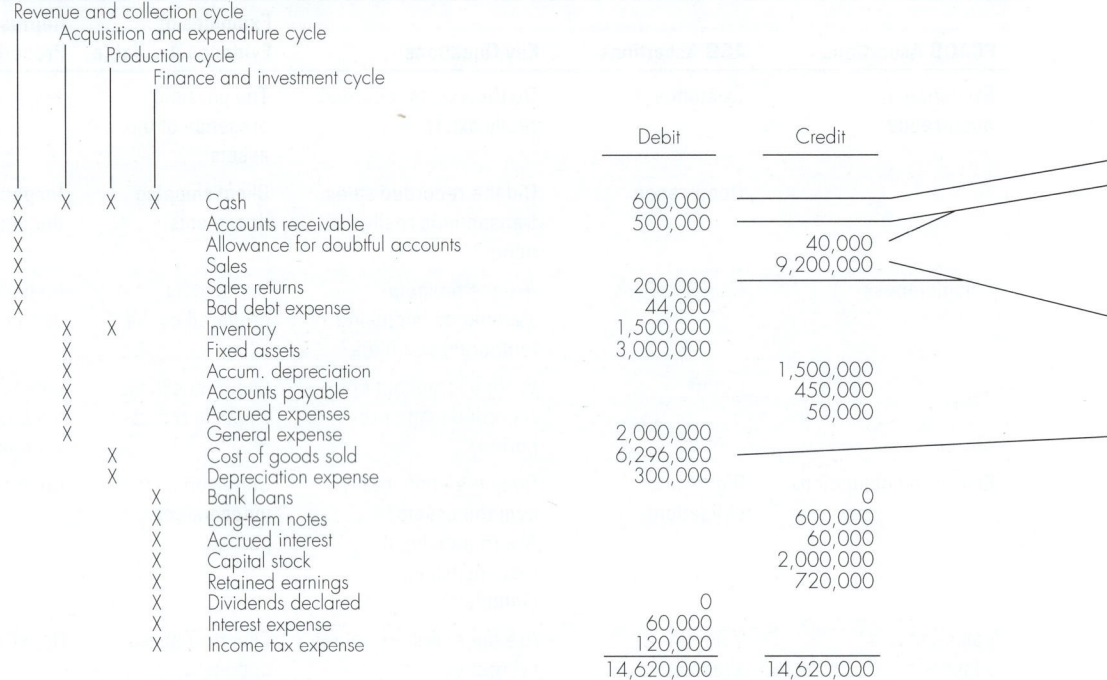

					Debit	Credit
X	X	X	X	Cash	600,000	
X				Accounts receivable	500,000	
X				Allowance for doubtful accounts		40,000
X				Sales		9,200,000
X				Sales returns	200,000	
X				Bad debt expense	44,000	
	X	X		Inventory	1,500,000	
	X			Fixed assets	3,000,000	
	X			Accum. depreciation		1,500,000
	X			Accounts payable		450,000
	X			Accrued expenses		50,000
	X			General expense	2,000,000	
		X		Cost of goods sold	6,296,000	
		X		Depreciation expense	300,000	
			X	Bank loans		0
			X	Long-term notes		600,000
			X	Accrued interest		60,000
			X	Capital stock		2,000,000
			X	Retained earnings		720,000
			X	Dividends declared	0	
			X	Interest expense	60,000	
			X	Income tax expense	120,000	
					14,620,000	14,620,000

To simplify the audit plan, auditors typically group the accounts into *cycles* (see Exhibit 3.3A). A *cycle* is a set of accounts that go together in an accounting system. Most audit firms recognize four cycles and each of these cycles is featured in a chapter of this book: (1) the revenue and collection cycle (Chapter 7), (2) the acquisition and expenditure cycle (Chapter 8), (3) the production cycle (Chapter 9), and (4) the finance and investment cycle (Chapter 10). Using the revenue and collection cycle as an example, the idea of the cycle organization is to group together accounts (sales, accounts receivable, cash) related to one another by the transactions that normally affect them all. This cycle starts with a sale to a customer along with recording an account receivable, which is later collected in cash or provided for in an allowance for doubtful accounts.

REVIEW CHECKPOINTS

3.11 There are two primary ways to conduct substantive tests. What are they? Explain how the tests are different?

3.12 Identify the four cycles in an accounting system that are covered in this book. Identify the accounts that can be identified within each of the cycles identified.

In general, auditors use eight general audit procedures to gather evidence: (1) inspection of records and documents (*vouching, tracing, scanning*), (2) inspection of tangible assets, (3) observation, (4) inquiry, (5) confirmation, (6) recalculation, (7) reperformance, and (8) analytical procedures. One or more of these procedures may be used no matter what account balance, control procedure, class of transactions, or other information is under audit. In the following sections, we discuss these audit procedures in more detail.

EXHIBIT 3.3B Dunder-Mifflin Unaudited Financial Statements

FINANCIAL POSITION			
Cash	$ 600,000	Accounts payable	$ 450,000
Accounts receivable	460,000	Accrued expenses	110,000
Inventory	1,500,000	Current debt	200,000
Current Assets	$2,560,000	Current Liabilities	$ 760,000
Fixed assets (net)	$3,000,000	Long-term debt	$ 400,000
Accum. depreciation	(1,500,000)	Capital stock	2,000,000
Fixed Assets (net)	$1,500,000	Retained earnings	900,000
Total Assets	$4,060,000	Total Liabilities and Stockholder Equity	$4,060,000

RESULTS OF OPERATIONS	
Sales (net)	$9,000,000
Cost of goods sold	6,296,000
Gross Profit	$2,704,000
General expenses	$2,044,000
Depreciation expense	300,000
Interest expense	60,000
Operating Income before Taxes	$ 300,000
Income tax expense	120,000
Net Income	$ 180,000

CASH FLOWS	
Operations:	
Net income	$ 180,000
Depreciation	300,000
Increase in accounts receivable	(141,500)
Decrease in inventory	50,000
Decrease in accounts payable	(25,000)
Decrease in accrued expenses	(15,000)
Decrease in accrued interest	(20,500)
Cash Flow from Operations	$328,500
Investing Activities:	
Purchase Fixed Assets	$ 0
Financing Activities:	
Repay bank loan	$(275,000)
Repay notes payable	(200,000)
Financing Activities	$(475,000)
Increase (decrease) in cash	$(146,500)
Beginning balance	746,500
Ending Balance	$ 600,000

NOTES TO FINANCIAL STATEMENTS
1. Accounting Policies
2. Inventories
3. Plant and Equipment
4. Long-term Debt
5. Stock Options
6. Income Taxes
7. Contingencies
Etc.

1. Inspection of Records and Documents

Much auditing work involves gathering evidence by examining authoritative documents prepared by independent parties and by the client. Such documents can provide "evidence of varying degrees of reliability, depending on their nature and source," regarding many of management's assertions.

Documents Prepared by Independent Outside Parties

A great deal of documentary evidence is external-internal (i.e., documents initially prepared by an external party but received by the client). The signatures, seals, engraving, or other distinctive artistic attributes of formal authoritative documents make such sources more reliable (less susceptible to alteration) than ordinary documents prepared by outsiders. Some examples of both types of documents are listed here:

Formal Authoritative Documents	Ordinary Documents
1. Bank statements	1. Vendors' invoices
2. Title papers (e.g., automobiles)	2. Customers' purchase orders
3. Insurance policies	3. Loan applications
4. Notes receivable (on unique forms)	4. Notes receivable (on standard bank forms)
5. Securities certificates	5. Insurance policy applications
6. Indenture agreements	6. Simple contracts
7. Elaborate contracts	7. Correspondence

Documents Prepared and Processed by the Client

Documentation of this type is internal evidence. Some of these documents may be quite informal and not very authoritative or reliable. As a general proposition, the reliability of these documents depends on the quality of internal control under which they were produced and processed. Some of the most common of these documents are:

Internal Documents

1. Sales invoice copies
2. Sales summary reports
3. Cost distribution reports
4. Loan approval memos
5. Budgets and performance reports
6. Documentation of transactions with subsidiary or affiliated companies
7. Shipping documents
8. Receiving reports
9. Requisition slips
10. Purchase orders
11. Credit memoranda
12. Transaction logs
13. Batch control logs (computerized)

Vouching—Examination of Documents

The important point about *vouching* in the examination of documents is the *direction* of the search for audit evidence. In **vouching**, an auditor selects an item of financial information, usually from a journal or ledger, and follows its path back through the processing steps to its origin (i.e., the *source documentation* that supports the item selected). The auditor finds the journal entry or data input list, the sales summary, the sales invoice copy, and the shipping documents, and, finally, the customer's purchase order. Vouching of documents can help auditors decide whether all recorded data are adequately supported (the *existence* and *occurrence* assertions), but vouching does not provide evidence to show whether all events were recorded (the *completeness* assertion). (If the auditors verify amounts, evidence regarding *valuation and allocation* also may be obtained.)

Tracing—Examination of Documents

Tracing in the examination of documents takes the *opposite* direction from vouching. When an auditor performs **tracing**, the auditor selects a basic source document and follows its processing path *forward* to find its final recording in a summary journal or ledger. For example, samples of payroll payments are traced to cost and expense accounts, sales invoices to the sales accounts, cash receipts to the accounts receivable subsidiary accounts, and cash disbursements to the accounts payable subsidiary accounts.

Using tracing, an auditor can decide whether all events were recorded (the *completeness* assertion) and complement the evidence obtained by vouching. (Similar to vouching, if auditors evaluate dollar amounts, tracing also can provide some evidence with respect to *valuation and allocation*.) However, you must be alert to events that were not captured in the source documents and not entered into the accounting system. For example, the search for unrecorded liabilities for raw materials purchases must include examination of invoices received in the period following the fiscal year-end and examination of receiving reports dated near the year-end. In practice, the terms *vouch* and *trace* are often used interchangeably. The important concept is the *direction* of the test.

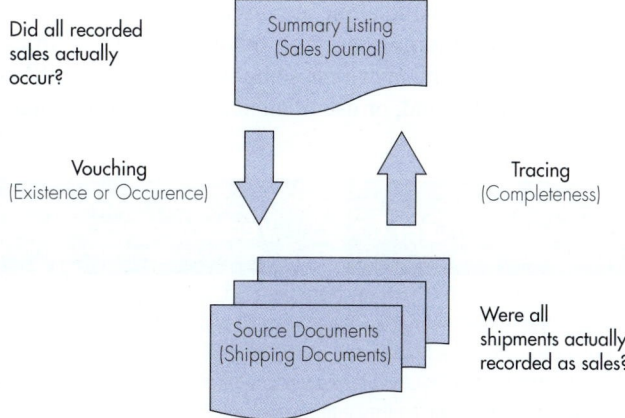

Scanning—Examination of Documents

Scanning is the way auditors exercise their general alertness to unusual items and events in clients' documentation. A typical scanning directive in an audit plan is: "Scan the expense accounts for credit entries; vouch any to source documents."

In general, scanning is an "eyes-open" approach of looking for anything unusual. The scanning procedure usually does not produce direct evidence itself, but it can raise questions for which other evidence must be obtained. Scanning can be accomplished on digital records using computerized audit software to select records to be printed out for further audit investigation. Typical items discovered by the scanning effort include debits in revenue accounts, credits in expense accounts, unusually large accounts receivable write-offs, unusually large paychecks, unusually small sales volume in the month following the year-end, and large cash deposits just prior to year-end. Scanning can contribute some evidence related to the existence of assets and the completeness of accounting records, including the proper cutoff of material transactions.

2. Inspection of Tangible Assets

Inspection of tangible assets includes examining property, plant, and equipment, inventory, and securities certificates. Physical inspection of tangible assets provides compelling evidence of *existence* and may provide tentative evidence of *valuation*. For example, audit team members can verify the existence of specific pieces of equipment listed on the client's fixed-asset register by locating them and noting their condition (*valuation*). However, inspection does not necessarily provide evidence that the entity owns the assets (*rights*). For example, fixed assets on the client's premises may be leased under operating lease agreements and inventory inspected by auditors may be held on consignment.

3. Observation

Although inventory observation often refers to the physical inspection of inventory (i.e., tangible assets), auditors use *observation* when they view the client's physical facilities and personnel on an inspection tour, when they watch personnel carry out accounting and control activities (such as observing client inventory counts), and when they participate in a surprise payroll distribution. Observation also can produce a general awareness of events in the client's offices. In this sense, observation is commonly used as a test of controls.

4. Inquiry

Inquiry is a procedure that generally involves the collection of oral (but sometimes written) evidence from independent parties and management (commonly referred to as *management representations*). Important inquiries and responses should be documented in writing. Auditors typically use inquiry procedures during the early planning stages of the engagement. Evidence gathered by formal and informal inquiry generally cannot stand alone as convincing, and auditors must corroborate responses with independent findings based on other procedures. An exception to this general rule is a negative statement in which someone volunteers adverse information such as an admission of theft, fraud, or use of an accounting policy that is misleading.

AUDITING INSIGHT | Verbal Inquiry = Interview

Auditors conduct interviews almost every day. Sometimes these seem more like casual conversations than "interviews." Nevertheless, the following guides for the inquiry/interview procedure can help you obtain good information and maintain good relations with client personnel.

1. *Prepare.* Think about the information you want to obtain, the questions to ask, and the best person to interview.
2. *Make an appointment.* Call in advance for a time or at least ask permission to interrupt: "Do you have time to talk with me about [subject]?" Introduce yourself and make enough conversation to warm up the person without wasting time.
3. *Don't ask the questions.* Try to get the person to describe the accounting, the controls, or whatever the subject in his or her own words. You will get more information. Just firing off questions makes the meeting an interrogation. Most auditors find it difficult to think of all of the right questions ahead of time anyway. Do not exhibit a questionnaire or checklist; doing so makes the interview too mechanical. You can take informal notes to remember the substance of the interview.
4. *Ask questions.* Fill in the gaps in the person's description or explanation by asking prompting questions to elicit additional descriptions and explanations. Start with broad, open-ended questions and use specific questions to obtain more detail.
5. *Listen carefully.* Repeat items you don't completely understand.
6. *Be noncommittal.* Refrain from expressing your own value judgments or criticisms while you talk with the client personnel. Don't reveal any audit-sensitive information.
7. *Close gracefully.* Thank the person for the time and information. Ask permission to return later for "anything I forgot."
8. *Document the interview.* Write a memorandum for the audit documentation. Now you can get out the questionnaire or checklist, complete it, and see whether you overlooked anything important.

5. Confirmation

Confirmation by direct correspondence with independent parties is a procedure widely used in auditing. It can produce evidence of *existence* and *ownership* and sometimes of *valuation* and *cutoff*. Auditors typically limit their use of confirmation to major transactions and balances about which outside parties could be expected to provide information. A selection of confirmation applications includes the following:

- Banks—cash and loan balances.
- Customers—receivables balances.
- Borrowers—note terms and balances.
- Agents—inventory on consignment or in warehouses.
- Lenders—note terms and balances.
- Policyholders—life insurance contracts.
- Vendors—accounts payable balances.
- Registrar—number of shares of stock outstanding.
- Attorneys—litigation in progress.
- Trustees—securities held, terms of agreements.
- Lessors—lease terms.

Several important points about confirmations are important to remember. First, confirmation letters are typically printed on the client's letterhead and signed by a client officer; third parties usually do not release information without client permission. Second, confirmation requests should seek information the recipient can supply such as the amount of a balance or the amounts of specified invoices or notes. Third, the audit firm should control confirmations rather than giving them to client personnel for mailing. The audit team should be very careful that the recipient's address is reliable and not subject to alteration by the client in such a way as to misdirect the confirmation. Lastly, responses should be returned directly to the audit firm, not to the client.

6. Recalculation

Auditor recalculation of calculations previously performed by client personnel produces compelling mathematical evidence. A client calculation is either right or wrong. Client calculations performed by computer programs can be recalculated using computer-assisted audit techniques (CAATs) with differences printed out for further audit investigation. Mathematical evidence can serve the objectives of *existence* and *valuation* for financial statement amounts that exist principally as calculations, for example, depreciation, interest expense, pension liabilities, actuarial reserves, bad debt reserves, and product guarantee liabilities. Recalculation, in combination with other procedures, is also used to provide evidence of *valuation* for all other financial data.

7. Reperformance

Although similar to recalculation, reperformance is broader in approach. Reperformance can involve any client control procedure such as matching vendor invoices with supporting purchase orders and receiving reports. Reperformance may be done either manually or with the assistance of CAATs. An auditor, for example, can verify that an accounts receivable aging schedule was prepared properly by sorting accounts receivable by due date.

8. Analytical Procedures

Auditors can evaluate financial statement accounts by studying and comparing relationships among financial and nonfinancial data. The methods of study and comparison are known as **analytical procedures**. Auditors are required to use them when planning the audit and when performing the final review of the financial statements before the audit report is issued. In addition, auditors use analytical procedures to provide evidence about management's financial statement assertions during the testing phase of the audit.

Analytical procedures take the following five general forms. Auditors need to be careful to use independent, reliable information for analyses. The sources of information shown for the analytical procedures are very important.

Analytical Procedures	Sources of Information
1. Comparison of current-year account balances to balances of one or more comparable periods	Financial account information for comparable period(s) *Example: Current year's cost of goods sold compared to last year's balance*
2. Comparison of the current-year account balances to anticipated results found in the company's budgets and forecasts	Company budgets and forecasts *Example: Current year's cost of goods sold compared to the company's budgeted amount*
3. Evaluation of the relationships of current-year account balances to other current-year balances for conformity with predictable patterns based on the company's experience	Financial relationships among accounts in the current period *Example: Days' sales in inventory*
4. Comparison of current-year account balances and financial relationships (e.g., ratios) with similar information for the industry in which the company operates	Industry statistics *Example: Days' sales in inventory compared to industry averages*
5. Study of the relationships of current-year account balances with relevant nonfinancial information (e.g., physical production statistics)	Nonfinancial information such as physical production statistics *Example: Days' sales in inventory compared to unfilled orders*

Because analytical procedures can only direct attention to unusual relationships, many auditors consider the evidence they produce to be "soft." Instead, many auditors feel more comfortable with recalculation, observation, confirmation, and inspection of documents that are perceived to produce "hard" evidence. However, you should resist this distinction. Analytical procedures have been shown to be quite effective if executed properly. Indeed, Hylas and Ashton collected evidence on procedures used to detect misstatements requiring financial statement adjustment in a large number of audits.[8] They found that auditors ultimately credited analytical procedures for discovery of 27 percent of all misstatements. Because of their effectiveness in directing attention to high-risk areas, professional standards require that analytic procedures be used during *planning* and during *final evaluation* stages of the audit. Although not required to be used during other stages of the engagement, auditors must consider the value of analytical procedures, especially because they are usually less costly than more detailed, document-oriented procedures. Consequently, analytical procedures often take a prominent place in the *audit plan*.

AUDITING INSIGHT — Potholes in the Audit Procedures Road

Performing specified audit procedures might not be enough. The following true stories highlight the need for caution in the conduct of audit procedures.

RECALCULATION
An auditor calculated inventory valuations (quantities × price) thinking the measuring unit was the actual number of items counted, when the client had actually recorded counts in dozens (12 units for each item listed), thus causing the inventory valuation to be 12 times the actual measure.

INSPECTION OF TANGIBLE ASSETS
Although observing the fertilizer tank assets in ranch country, the auditor was fooled when the manager was able to move them to other locations and place new identification numbers on them. The auditor "observed" the same tanks many times.

OBSERVATION
A team visited a building restoration client's job site to verify that the company was actually performing the restoration services. Unbeknownst to the team, the client (**ZZZ Best**) had rented the vacant building for the day, put up its "building restoration" signs, and had its employees in hard hats milling around for the audit team's benefit.

CONFIRMATION
Executives at an Italian grocery company (**Parmalat**) faxed a forged bank confirmation to auditors in order to conceal a $5 billion fraud. The auditors never questioned why they received a fax from the bank rather than a mailed confirmation.

INQUIRY
Seeking evidence of the collectability of accounts receivable, the auditors "audited by conversation" and took the credit manager's word about the collection probabilities on the over-90-day past due accounts. They sought no other evidence.

INSPECTION OF RECORDS AND DOCUMENTS (VOUCHING)
In the HealthSouth audit, auditors requested supporting documentation for an asset purchased for one of the company's Kansas locations. The problem was that it was a fraudulent transaction recorded as an asset to avoid treating the transaction properly as an expense. To conceal the fraud from the auditors, a vice president in the accounting department found a similar purchase invoice for an asset purchased for another location, scanned it into her computer, and then electronically changed the shipping information to match the invoice requested by the auditors.

INSPECTION OF RECORDS AND DOCUMENTS (SCANNING)
The auditors extracted a list of all of the bank's loans for more than $1,000. They neglected to perform a similar scan for loans with negative balances, a condition that should not occur. The bank had information processing problems that caused many loan balances to be negative, although the trial balance balanced!

↳ REVIEW CHECKPOINTS

3.13 What is meant by (a) *vouching*, (b) *tracing*, and (c) *scanning*? What is the difference between vouching and tracing?

3.14 List eight basic audit procedures.

3.15 What are the five types of general analytical procedures? List five sources of information for analytical procedures.

3.16 When are analytical procedures required during an audit engagement?

---

[8] R. E. Hylas and R. H. Ashton, "Audit Detection of Financial Statement Errors," *Accounting Review,* October 1982, pp. 751–65.

PLANNING IN A COMPUTERIZED ENVIRONMENT

LEARNING OBJECTIVE 3-5
List and discuss matters of planning that auditors should consider related to the client's computer environment and describe how CAATs can be used to improve the efficiency of the audit process.

The technology application (e.g., SAP, Peachtree) used to process accounting transactions will affect an entity's financial reporting process and will influence the procedures and techniques used to accomplish the organization's financial reporting goals and objectives. The following are characteristics that an auditor needs to consider when evaluating a client's computerized environment:

- *Possibility of temporary transaction trails.* An **audit trail** is a chain of evidence provided through coding, cross-references, and documentation connecting account balances and other summary results with the original transaction source documents. Some computerized systems are designed so that a complete transaction trail useful for audit purposes could exist only for a short time or only in computer-readable form. Often the loss of hard-copy documents and reports and the temporary nature of the audit trail require external auditors to alter both the timing and nature of audit procedures.

- *Uniform processing of transactions.* Computerized processing subjects similar transactions to the same processing instructions. Consequently, computerized processing virtually eliminates the occurrence of random errors normally associated with manual processing; as a result, programming errors (or other similar systematic errors in either the computer hardware or software) will result in all similar transactions being processed incorrectly when those transactions are processed under the same conditions.

- *Potential for errors and frauds.* The potential for individuals to gain unauthorized access to or alter data without visible evidence as well as to gain access (direct or indirect) to assets can be greater in computerized information systems than in manual systems. Employees have more access to information through numerous terminals hooked together in a common computer network. Less human involvement in handling transactions processed by computers can reduce the potential for observing errors and frauds. Errors or fraud made in designing or changing application programs can remain undetected for long periods.

- *Potential for increased management supervision.* Computerized information systems offer management a wide variety of analytical tools to review and supervise the company's operations. The availability of these additional controls can enhance the entire system of internal control and, therefore, reduce control risk. For example, traditional comparisons of actual operating ratios with those budgeted as well as reconciliation of accounts frequently are available for management review on a timelier basis when such information is computerized.

- *Initiation or subsequent execution of transactions by computer.* With automatic transaction initiation, certain transactions can be initiated or executed automatically by a computerized system without human review. Computer-initiated transactions include the generation of invoices, checks, shipping orders, and purchase orders. Without a human-readable document indicating the transaction event, the correctness of automatic transactions is difficult to judge. The authorization of these transactions cannot be documented in the same way as those in a manual accounting system, and management's authorization of these transactions can be implicit in its acceptance of the design of the system. For example, authorization of transactions occurs when certain flags are installed in programs or records (e.g., inventory quantity falling below reorder point). Therefore, authorization is more difficult to trace to the proper person. Control procedures must be designed into the system to ensure the genuineness and reasonableness of automatic transactions and to prevent or detect erroneous transactions.

- *Use of cloud computing applications.* With cloud computing, an audit client may be accessing certain software applications and data contained in the "cloud" via the Internet with its laptop, tablet, smartphone, or other computing device. By accessing software applications and data in this manner, a client may save substantial computing costs because it need not purchase its own software site licenses and/or data storage hardware. However, this decision is not without risk because data security, service interruptions, and data migration issues can occur. Control procedures must be designed to ensure the completeness and accuracy of the informational flows to and from the "cloud" and that data security within the "cloud" is ensured.

Effect of Client's Computerized Processing on Audit Planning

Almost all organizations use computers in data processing to some extent. Client automation raises some difficulties (e.g., temporary transaction trails, potential for fraud) that are perhaps less likely in manual transaction processing. On the positive side, auditors can use the speed and accuracy of their own laptops to increase audit efficiency and effectiveness. Accordingly, when evaluating the effect of a client's computerized processing on an audit of financial statements, auditors should consider matters such as the following:

- The extent to which the computer is used in each significant accounting application (e.g., sales and billing, payroll).
- The complexity of the computer operations used by the entity (e.g., batch processing, online processing, outside service centers).
- The organizational structure of the computerized processing activities.
- The availability of data required by the auditor.
- The computer-assisted audit techniques (CAATs) available to increase the efficiency of audit procedures.
- The need for specialized skills.

Extent to Which Computers Are Used

When the client uses computers to process significant accounting applications, the audit team could need computer-related skills to understand the flow of these transactions. The extent of computer use also can affect the nature, timing, and extent of audit procedures.

Complexity of Computerized Operations

When assessing the complexity of computerized information processing, the audit team members should consider their training and experience relative to the methods of information processing. A review of the client's computer hardware could show the extent of complexity involved. If the client *outsources* significant accounting applications (e.g., payroll), the audit team could need to coordinate audit procedures with service auditors at the processing center.

Organizational Structure of Computerized Processing

Clients can exhibit great differences in the way their computerized processing activities are organized. The degree of centralization inherent in the organizational structure can vary. A highly centralized organizational structure generally has all significant computerized processing controlled and supervised at a central location. The control environment, the computer hardware, and the computerized systems can be uniform throughout the company. Auditors can obtain most of the necessary computerized processing information by visiting the central location. At the other extreme, a highly decentralized organizational structure generally allows various departments, divisions, subsidiaries, or geographical locations to develop, control, and supervise computerized processing in an autonomous fashion. In this situation, the computer hardware and the computer systems usually are not uniform throughout the company. Thus, auditors could need to visit many locations to obtain the necessary audit information.

Availability of Data

Computerized systems provide an ability to store, retrieve, and analyze large quantities of data. Input data, certain computer files, and other data the audit team needs might exist for only short periods or only in computer-readable form. In some computerized information systems, hard copy input documents may not exist at all because information is entered directly. For example, electronic signatures have replaced manual signatures on electronic purchase orders sent directly to vendors via electronic data interchange with the consequence that the auditors are not able to examine a hard-copy signature. The client's data retention policies may require auditors to arrange for some information to be retained for review. Alternatively, auditors might need to plan to perform audit procedures at a time when the information is still available.

In addition, certain information generated by the computerized system for management's internal purposes can be useful in performing analytical procedures. For example, because storage is easy, the client can save larger amounts of operating information (*data warehousing*) such as sales information by month, by product, and by salesperson. Such information can be accessed (*data mining*) for use in analytical procedures to determine whether the revenue amounts are reasonable. Auditors also can drill down to examine individual transactions that compose a general ledger account balance.

The Need for Specialized Skills

CPA firms generally have auditors who are specially trained to evaluate computerized controls and processes. Often they may be called on to write specialized computer programs to retrieve and analyze data. See Module H for even more discussion of how to audit computerized controls and processes.

> **⌕ REVIEW CHECKPOINTS**
>
> 3.17 What additional planning matters should be considered about a client's computerized processing environment?
>
> 3.18 What are the general characteristics of transactions that are typically computerized?
>
> 3.19 Define *audit trail*. How could a computerized system's transaction audit trail in an advanced system differ from one in a simple system or a manual system?

Use of Computer-Assisted Audit Techniques (CAATs)

In general, computer-assisted audit techniques (CAATs) allow the auditor to complete a number of tasks with their own laptop computer. CAATs allow the auditor to directly access the complete set of a client's dataset for the year under audit. In addition, in today's environment, auditors use their laptop regularly to perform such clerical steps as preparing the working trial balance, posting adjusting entries, grouping accounts that represent one line item on the financial statement into lead schedules, computing comparative financial statements and common ratios for analytical procedures, preparing supporting audit documentation schedules, and producing draft financial statements. Many auditors also use computers to assess control risk, perform sophisticated analytical functions on individual accounts, access public and firm databases for analysis of unusual accounting and auditing problems, and utilize decision support software to make complex evaluations. See Exhibit 3.4 for an illustration of the phases of using the computer as an audit tool that a typical public accounting firm has moved through over the past several years.

You need to know about CAATs because they are used on most audits in which the client's accounting records are stored in computer files or in a database. Most CAATs software packages consist of a set of preprogrammed editing, operating, and output subroutines so that original programming is not required and the same software can be used

EXHIBIT 3.4 Using the Computer as an Audit Tool

Applications	Goals and Objectives	Software Available
Phase 1: Automating the Audit Process		
Trial balance and audit documentation	Overall audit efficiency	Electronic workpapers developed by public accounting firms and vendors
Adjusting and updating financial data	Automation of time-consuming activities	Firm developed or vendor supplied
Time and budget data	Improved control	Firm developed or vendor supplied
Audit plan, memorandum, and report generation	Efficiency and increased readability	Word processing
Preparation and consolidation of financial statements preparation	Efficient automation	Firm developed or vendor supplied
Tax return preparation and analysis	Efficient automation	Firm developed or vendor supplied
Phase 2: Basic Auditing Function		
Spreadsheet analysis audit documentation	Efficiency in common audit documentation	Vendor supplied, firm-developed uses
Analytical procedures evaluation	Improved overall analysis of ratios, fluctuations	Part of automated audit documentation packages
Sampling planning, selection, and evaluation	Evidence collection and evaluation efficiency	Statistical, firm developed
Text retrieval	Search GAAP and GAAS pronouncements	Public resources (e.g., Compact Disclosure, Lexis-Nexis, FARS, ReSOURCE) or firm developed
Phase 3: Advanced Auditing Functions		
Analytical procedures for specific accounts	Improved auditor analysis	Firm developed
Access to client files on larger computers	Ability to download directly into automated audit documentation software	Vendor supplied or firm developed
Access to firm and public databases	Provide auditor with reference information	Personal computer as a terminal, Internet
Modeling and decision support systems	Improved auditor decisions	Firm-developed decision support systems
Continuous monitoring	Improved audit effectiveness	Firm developed or vendor supplied

on different clients' computerized systems. For the most part, the widely used CAATs packages (such *ACL* and *IDEA*) are very similar. Most have been developed from standard spreadsheet and database applications, so if you understand spreadsheet software, you can use most of the audit-specific functions. The applications, however, have been modified so that auditors can perform common audit tasks at the touch of a button by accessing predeveloped macros. In our experience, about one week of intensive training is sufficient to learn how to fully use a CAATs package's capabilities on the financial statement audit.

Computerized accounting applications capture and generate voluminous amounts of data that usually are available only on machine-readable records. CAATs can be used to access the data and organize it into a format useful to the audit team. Audit software can be used to accomplish many different audit procedures:

- *Recalculation.* Of course, the computer can verify calculations with more speed and accuracy than can be done by hand. The audit software can be used to test the accuracy of client computations and to perform analytical procedures to evaluate the reasonableness of account balances. Examples of this use are to (1) recalculate depreciation expense, (2) recalculate extensions on inventory items, (3) compute file totals, and (4) compare budgeted, standard, and prior year data with current-year data.

- *Confirmation.* Auditors can program statistical or judgmental criteria for selecting customers' accounts receivable, loans, and other receivables for confirmation. The CAATs can be used to print the confirmations and get them ready for mailing. It can do everything except carry them to the post office!

- *Document examination* (limited). CAATs can compare audit evidence from other sources to company records efficiently. The audit evidence must be converted to machine-readable form and then can be compared to company records on computer files. Examples are (1) comparing inventory test counts with perpetual records, (2) comparing adjusted audit balances on confirmed accounts receivable to the audit file of the recorded balances, and (3) comparing vendor statement amounts to the company's record of accounts payable.

- *Scanning.* Auditors can use CAATs to examine records to determine quality, completeness, consistency, and correctness. This is the computerized version of scanning the records for exceptions to the auditors' criteria. For example, scan (1) accounts receivable balances for amounts over the credit limit, (2) inventory quantities for negative balances or unreasonably large balances, (3) payroll files for terminated employees, or (4) loan files for loans with negative balances.

- *Analytical procedures.* CAATs functions can match data in separate files to determine whether comparable information is in agreement. Differences can be printed out for investigation and reconciliation. Examples are comparing (1) payroll details with personnel records, (2) current and prior inventory to details of purchases and sales, (3) paid vouchers to check disbursements, and (4) current- and prior year fixed asset records to identify dispositions. CAATS also can summarize and sort data in a variety of ways. Examples are (1) preparing general ledger trial balances, (2) sorting inventory items by location to facilitate observations, and (3) summarizing inventory turnover statistics for obsolescence analysis.

- *Fraud investigation.* CAATs can be used in a variety of ways to search for fraudulent activities. For example, lists of vendor addresses can be compared to employee address files to see whether employees are paying invoices to companies that they own or operate. Duplicate payments can be found by sorting payments by invoice number and amount paid. Telephone records can be quickly sorted and scanned to ensure that employees are not misusing company telephones.

Notwithstanding the powers of the computer, several general audit procedures are outside its reach. The computer cannot observe and count physical things (inventory, for example), but it can compare auditor-made counts to the computer records. The computer cannot examine external and internal documentation; thus, it cannot vouch accounting output to sources of basic evidence. (An exception would exist in a computerized system that stores the basic source documents on magnetic media.) However, when manual vouching is involved, computer-assisted selection of sample items is quick and easy. Finally, CAATs can never take the place of the auditor's professional judgment (determining the reasonableness of the allowance for doubtful accounts, for example).

↳ REVIEW CHECKPOINTS

3.20 What are computer-assisted audit techniques (CAATs)?

3.21 What are some audit procedures that can be performed using CAATs?

3.22 What advantages are derived from using CAATs to (a) perform recalculations and (b) select samples and print confirmations?

AUDIT DOCUMENTATION (AU/ISA 230, AS 3)

LEARNING OBJECTIVE 3-6
Define what is meant by the proper form and content of audit documentation.

An engagement is not complete without preparation of proper documentation. PCAOB *Auditing Standard 3* defines **audit documentation** as:

> the written record of the basis for the auditor's conclusions that provides the support for the auditor's representations, whether those representations are contained in the auditor's report or otherwise.

In other words, audit documentation provides the auditors' record of compliance with generally accepted auditing standards. The documentation (usually in the form of either electronic files or hard copy *workpapers*) should contain support for the decisions regarding planning and performing the audit, procedures performed, evidence obtained, and conclusions reached. Even though the auditors legally own the audit documentation, professional ethics require that the files not be transferred without consent of the client because of the confidential information recorded in them.

Auditors often use the term *workpapers,* but it is becoming unfashionable. Public accounting firms rarely use *paper* to document their findings anymore; more commonly, firms are using electronic documents. Today, automated audit software allows auditors to create, share, edit, review, correct, approve, and finalize audit documentation without the "paper," thereby reducing the storage space requirements of hard copy workpapers. In addition to reduced storage costs, auditors' use of electronic documentation can result in improved efficiency because the electronic documents can be easily updated and modified from year to year. Finally, automated audit software reduces the time spent on numbering, referencing, initialing, dating, and reviewing ("ticking and tying") by automating these tasks through the use of macro programs. In the past, these largely clerical tasks consumed large quantities of audit effort that is now directed more productively to more critical aspects of the audit. Most automated audit engagement management programs utilize commonly used word processor and spreadsheet applications to prepare audit documentation, audit plans, and audit memos. For example, auditors prepare memos using word processing software, and financial schedules (such as bank reconciliations and depreciation schedules) using spreadsheet software.

Audit documentation can be classified in two categories: (1) *permanent files* (which contain information that is relevant to ongoing client relationships) and (2) *current files* (which relate to just one year of the client relationship). The following sections describe the information contained in each file in more detail.

Permanent Files

The **permanent files** (or **continuing audit files**) contain information of *continuing audit significance* over many years' audits of the same client. The audit team may use this file year after year, but each year's current audit documentation is stored after the files have served their purpose. Documents of permanent interest and applicability include:

1. Copies or excerpts of the corporate or association charter, bylaws, or partnership agreement.
2. Copies or excerpts of continuing contracts such as leases, bond indentures, and royalty agreements.
3. A history of the company, its products, markets, and background.
4. Copies or excerpts of minutes of meetings of stockholders and/or directors on matters of lasting interest.
5. Continuing schedules of accounts whose balances are carried forward for several years, such as owners' equity, retained earnings, partnership capital, and the like.
6. Copies of prior years' financial statements and audit reports.
7. Client organization chart.

Copies of financial statements and auditors' reports from prior years also may be included. Public accounting firms collect articles and other information regarding a client and key personnel throughout the year. This information is often placed in the permanent file to facilitate a review of the client prior to continuing the relationship. Because of the importance of the documents contained and summarized in this one place, the permanent file is a ready source of information for familiarization with the client by new personnel on the engagement.

Current Files

The current files include all client acceptance or continuance documentation along with planning documentation for the year under audit. They usually include the engagement letter, staff assignment notes, conclusions related to understanding the client's business, results of preliminary analytical procedures, assessments of audit risks, and the assessment of audit materiality. Many public accounting firms follow the practice of summarizing these data in a **planning memorandum** with specific directions about the effect on the audit.

Basically, the planning memo summarizes all important overall planning information and documents that the audit team is following generally accepted auditing standards. All planning becomes a basis for preparing the **audit plan**, which is a list of the audit procedures to be performed by the audit team to gather sufficient appropriate evidence on which to base their opinion on the financial statements. Auditing standards require a *written* audit plan for each relevant assertion on the audit.

The planning documentation includes a listing of each relevant financial statement assertion to be investigated during the audit, the record of the procedures performed, the evidence obtained, and the decisions made in the course of the audit. Audit documentation should be prepared in sufficient detail to provide a clear understanding of its purpose, source, and the conclusions reached. The audit documentation communicates the quality of the audit, so it must be clear, concise, complete, neat, well indexed, and informative. Each workpaper must be complete in the sense that it can be removed from the audit documentation file and considered on its own with proper cross-references available to show how the document coordinates with other audit documentation. In other words, the documentation must be sufficient to enable an experienced auditor, having no previous connection with the engagement, to understand (1) the nature, timing, extent, and results of procedures, (2) the conclusions reached with respect to the area covered by the audit documentation, and (3) the audit team member performing the work, the date of work, the audit team member reviewing the work, and the date of review. The audit documentation should also be sufficient to allow another auditor to reperform the work if necessary.

The most important facet of the current audit evidence documentation files is the requirement that they show the auditors' conclusions. The documentation must record the management assertions that were audited (book values or qualitative disclosures), the evidence gathered about them, and final conclusions. Professional audit standards require the audit documentation show that (1) the client's accounting records agree or reconcile with the financial statements, (2) the work was adequately planned and supervised, (3) a sufficient understanding of the client's internal control was obtained, and (4) sufficient appropriate audit evidence was obtained as a reasonable basis for an audit opinion. Common sense also dictates that the audit documentation be sufficient to show that the financial statements conform to the relevant accounting framework and that the disclosures are adequate. The audit documentation also should explain how exceptions, unusual accounting questions, and findings contradictory to the audit team's final conclusions were resolved or treated. In addition, the resolution of any differences among audit team members must be documented. Taken altogether, these features should demonstrate that all auditing standards were observed and executed.

EXHIBIT 3.5 Current Audit Documentation File

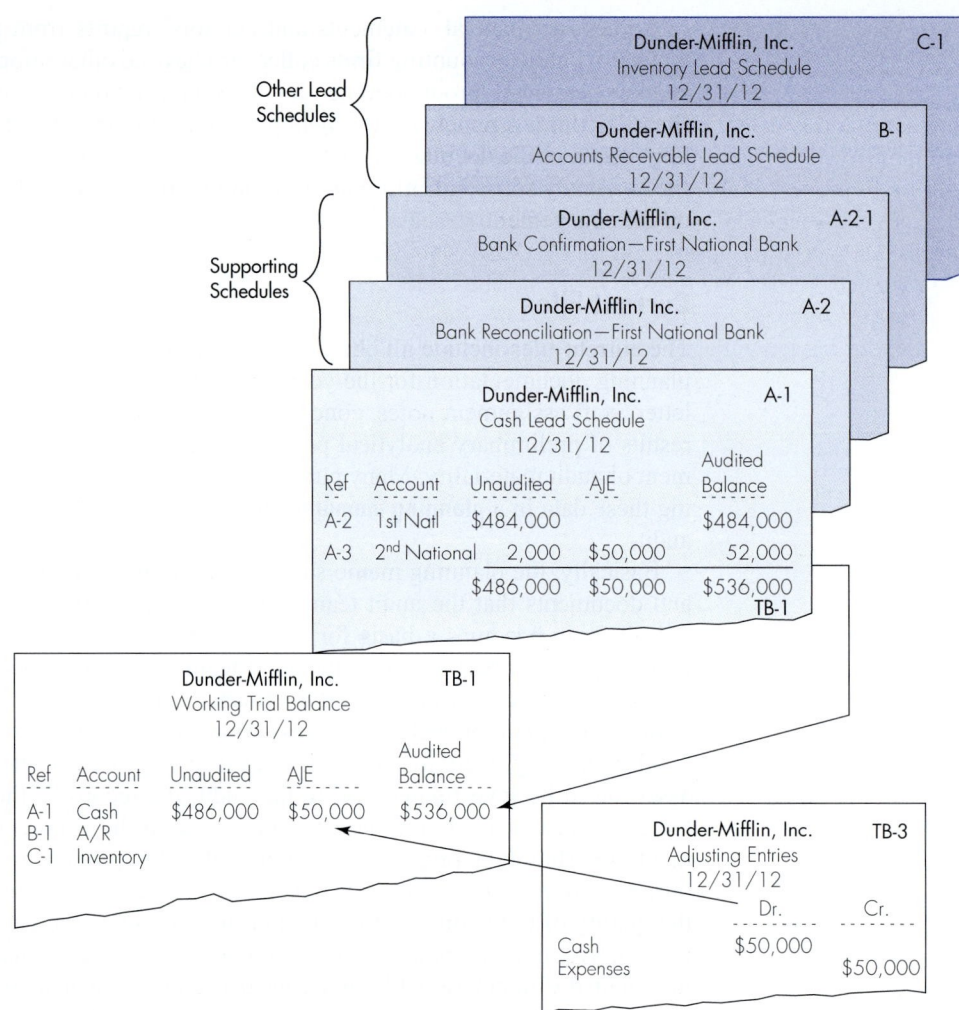

Audit Documentation Arrangement and Indexing

Each public accounting firm has a different method of arranging and indexing audit documentation files. In general, however, the documentation is grouped (or electronically hyperlinked) in order behind the trial balance according to balance-sheet and income-statement captions. Usually, the current assets appear first, followed by fixed assets, other assets, liabilities, equities, income, and expense accounts. A **lead schedule** is a summary of the accounts or components in an account group. For cash, the lead schedule includes all of the company's cash accounts. For inventory, the lead schedule may include inventory amounts by product line, cost of goods sold, and reserves for obsolescence. The amounts on the lead schedule should agree with prior year numbers, the current-year general ledger amounts, and, after any adjustments, the audited financial statements. The typical arrangement is shown in Exhibit 3.5.

Several audit documentation preparation techniques are quite important for the quality of the finished product. The points explained here are illustrated in Exhibit 3.6.

- *Indexing.* Each document (whether electronic or paper) is given an index number, like a book page number, so it can be found, removed, and replaced without loss.
- *Cross-referencing.* Numbers or memoranda related to other documents carry the index of the other documents so the connections can be followed.
- *Heading.* Each document is titled with the name of the company, the balance-sheet date, and a descriptive title of the contents of the document.

EXHIBIT 3.6 Illustrative Audit Documentation

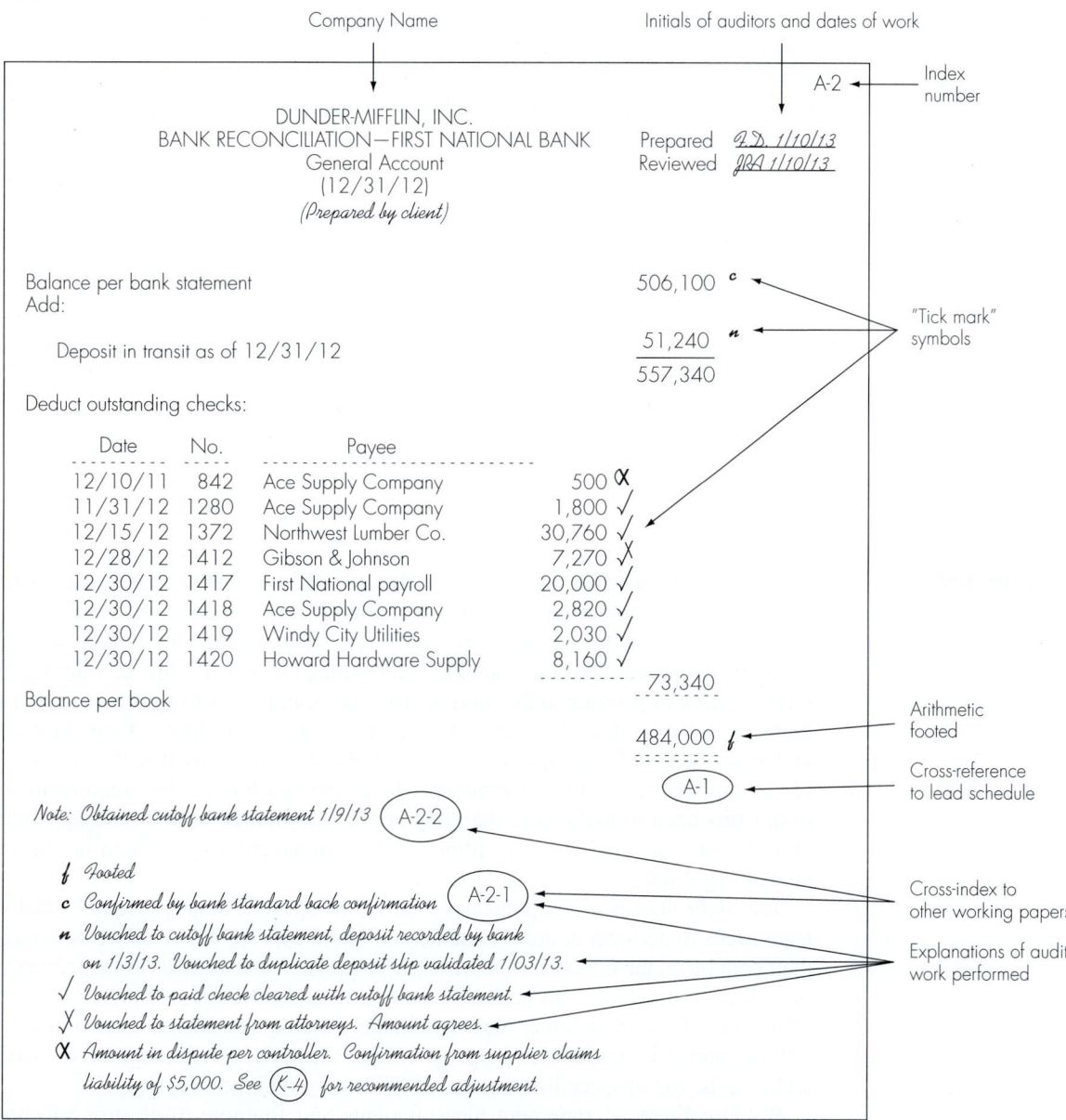

- *Signatures and initials.* The auditor who performs the work and the supervisor who reviews it must sign the audit documentation so personnel can be identified.
- *Dates of audit work.* The dates of performance and review are recorded on the documents so reviewers of the documentation can tell when the work was performed.
- *Audit marks and explanations.* Audit marks (or "tick marks") are the auditor's shorthand for abbreviating comments about work performed. Audit marks always must be accompanied by a full explanation of the auditing work. (Notice in Exhibit 3.6 the auditor's confirmation of the disputed account payable liability.) On electronic documents, comments can be hyperlinked so that reviewers can find additional explanations of audit procedures performed.

AS 3 requires that audit documentation, including workpapers and other documents that form the basis of the engagement, be retained for seven years following the conclusion of the engagement (usually the audit report release date). *AS 3* also stresses that audit documentation to be retained include those documenting discussion and subsequent resolution of differences in professional judgment among the audit team members. PCAOB regulations also require that all documentation must be finalized within 45 days of the audit report's release date. With sufficient (documented) justification, auditors may subsequently add, but may not remove, documentation after the 45-day period. Although the *AS 3* requirements are only for public companies, most public accounting firms use the same requirements for their nonpublic clients.

> ### ↳ REVIEW CHECKPOINTS
>
> 3.23 What information would you expect to find in a permanent audit file?
> 3.24 What information would you expect to find in a current audit file?
> 3.25 What is considered the most important content of the auditor's current audit documentation files?
> 3.26 What are the documentation retention requirements of AS 3?

Summary

This chapter contains a description of the specific set of planning activities that auditors undertake when completing an engagement. *Pre-engagement activities* start with the work of deciding whether to accept a new client and, on an annual basis, deciding whether to continue the engagement for existing clients. Public accounting firms are not obligated to provide audit services to every company or organization that requests them, and they regularly exercise discretion when deciding which they choose to undertake. For audit engagements, the investigation may involve the cooperative task of communicating with the former (predecessor) auditors of the organization. In addition, firms need to make sure that they are in compliance with both independence and ethical requirements before deciding whether to accept a new client or continue with an existing client.

The *audit plan* is a comprehensive list of the specific audit procedures that the audit team needs to perform in order to gather sufficient appropriate evidence on which to base their opinion on the financial statements. Although risk assessment (discussed in Chapter 4) provides the basis to determine the nature, timing, and extent of procedures to be performed at an audit client, many other aspects of audit planning are also discussed in this chapter. Other planning issues include properly staffing the audit, considering the work of internal auditors, the use of specialists, the use of IT auditors and the time budget.

Because financial statement measurements and footnote disclosure information are not flawlessly accurate, auditors need to ultimately ensure that the financial statements are materially accurate and do not contain material misstatements. Information is material if it is likely to influence financial statement users' decisions. As a result, the engagement team needs to think carefully about the appropriate level of materiality during the planning process. The auditor will then use this materiality as a guide to (1) plan and execute substantive testing procedures, (2) evaluate audit evidence, and (3) make final decisions about the auditor's report.

Auditors use a variety of procedures to gather evidence about management's assertions related to the amounts and disclosures in a client's financial statements. In general, auditors use eight general audit procedures to gather evidence: (1) inspection of records and documents (*vouching, tracing, scanning*), (2) inspection of tangible assets, (3) observation, (4) inquiry, (5) confirmation, (6) recalculation, (7) reperformance, and (8) analytical procedures. One or more of these procedures may be used no matter what account balance, control procedure, class of transactions, or other information is under audit. Auditors must consider a number of factors when planning based on the audit client's computing environment. And of course, the selection of procedures to be completed must always be tailored to the exacting nuances of the client's computing environment. Finally, computer-assisted audit techniques (CAATs) can improve both engagement effectiveness and efficiency and should be considered by auditors on each engagement.

The closing topic is a brief preview of audit documentation with some basic pointers about their form, content, and purpose. At this point, we have accepted (or retained) the client, gained an understanding of the client and its business, and assessed inherent risk in the financial statement accounts. The next step in the audit process is the auditors' risk assessment, which serves as the focus of the next chapter.

Key Terms

analytical procedures: The reasonableness tests used to gain an understanding of financial statement accounts and relationships, 97

audit documentation: The written basis for the auditor's conclusions, 104

audit plan: A list of the audit procedures the auditors need to perform to gather sufficient appropriate evidence on which to base their opinion on the financial statements, 81

audit trail: The chain of evidence provided through coding, cross-references, and documentation connecting account balances and other summary results with the original transaction source documents, 99

continuing audit files (or permanent files): The audit documentation containing information of *continuing audit significance* for current and past audits of the same client, 104

engagement letter: A letter from the public accounting firm to the management of an engagement client setting forth the terms of the engagement, 81

Form 8-K: The "special events report" filed with the SEC whenever certain significant corporate events occur such as changes in control, legal proceedings, and changes of auditor, 80

independence in appearance: The extent to which others (particularly financial statement users) perceive auditors to be independent, 80

independence in fact: Auditors' mental attitude and impartiality with respect to the client, 80

interim audit work: The procedures performed several weeks or months before the balance-sheet date, 86

lead schedule: A summary of the accounts in or components of an account group, 106

materiality: An amount or event that is likely to influence financial statement users' decisions, 87

permanent files (or continuing audit files): The audit documentation containing information of *continuing audit significance* for current and past audits of the same client, 104

planning memorandum: The document summarizing the preliminary analytical procedures and the materiality assessment with specific directions about the effect on the audit, 105

predecessor auditor: The public accounting firm that has been terminated or has voluntarily withdrawn from an audit engagement (whether the audit has been completed or not), 78

quality assurance partner: The second audit partner on the audit team as required for audits of financial statements filed with the SEC and who reviews the audit team's work in critical audit areas (those areas with the highest potential audit risk), 84

specialists: The persons skilled in fields other than accounting and auditing—actuaries, appraisers, attorneys, engineers, and geologists—who are not members of the public accounting firm, 85

substantive audit plan: The specification of substantive procedures for gathering direct evidence on management's assertions, 91

termination letter: The documentation provided to former clients dealing with the subject of future services, in particular (1) access to audit documentation by new auditors, (2) reissuance of the auditors' report when required for SEC reporting or comparative financial reporting, and (3) fee arrangements for such future services. The termination letter also can contain a report of the auditor's understanding of the circumstances of termination (e.g., disagreements about accounting principles and audit procedures, fees, or other conflicts), 81

tracing: An audit procedure in which the auditor selects a basic source document and follows its processing path *forward* to find its final recording in a summary journal or ledger. In practice, however, the term *tracing* may be used to describe following the path in either direction, 94

vouching: An audit procedure in which an auditor selects an item of financial information, usually from a journal or ledger, and follows its path back through the processing steps to its origin (i.e., the *source documentation* that supports the item selected), 94

year-end audit work: The procedures performed shortly before and after the balance-sheet date, 86

Multiple-Choice Questions for Practice and Review

All applicable Exercises and Problems are available with McGraw-Hill's Connect® Accounting

LO 3-1

3.27 When initiating communications with predecessor auditors, prospective auditors should expect
   a. To take responsibility for obtaining the client's consent for the predecessor to give information about prior audits.
   b. To conduct interviews with the partner and manager in charge of the predecessor public accounting firm's engagement.
   c. To obtain copies of some or all of the predecessor auditors' audit documentation.
   d. All of the above.

LO 3-2

3.28 Generally accepted auditing standards require that auditors always prepare and use
   a. A written planning memorandum explaining the auditors' understanding of the client's business.
   b. A written client consent to discuss audit matters with prospective auditors.
   c. A written audit plan.
   d. The written time budgets and schedules for performing each audit.

LO 3-2

3.29 When planning an audit, which of the following is *not* a factor that affects auditors' decisions about the quantity, type, and content of audit documentation?
   a. The auditors' need to document compliance with generally accepted auditing standards.
   b. The existence of new sales contracts important for the client's business.
   c. The auditors' judgment about their independence with regard to the client.
   d. The auditors' judgments about materiality.

LO 3-6

3.30 Audit documentation that shows the detailed evidence and procedures regarding the balance in the accumulated depreciation account for the year under audit will be found in the
   a. Current file audit documentation.
   b. Permanent file audit documentation.
   c. Administrative audit documentation in the current file.
   d. Planning memorandum in the current file.

LO 3-6

3.31 An auditor's permanent file audit documentation most likely will contain
   a. Internal control analysis for the current year.
   b. The most recent engagement letter.
   c. Memoranda of conference with management.
   d. Excerpts of the corporate charter and bylaws.

LO 3-3

3.32 Which of the following is *not* a benefit claimed for the practice of determining materiality in the initial planning stage of an audit?
   a. Being able to fine-tune the audit work for effectiveness and efficiency.
   b. Avoiding the problem of doing more work than necessary (overauditing).
   c. Being able to decide early what type of audit opinion to issue.
   d. Avoiding the problem of doing too little work (underauditing).

LO 3-5

3.33 Spreadsheet software would be most useful for which of the following audit activities?
   a. Testing internal controls over computerized accounting applications.
   b. Preparing an audit plan.
   c. Preparing a comparison of current-year expenses with those from the previous year.
   d. Drafting a planning memorandum.

LO 3-5   3.34 Which of the following is an advantage of computer-assisted audit techniques (CAATs)?
a. The CAATs programs are all written in one computer language.
b. The software can be used for audits of clients that use differing computer equipment and file formats.
c. The use of CAATs has reduced the need for the auditor to study input controls for computer-related procedures.
d. The use of CAATs can be substituted for a relatively large part of the required testing.

LO 3-5   3.35 A primary advantage of using CAATs in the audit of an advanced computerized system is that it enables the auditor to
a. Substantiate the accuracy of data through self-checking digits and hash totals.
b. Utilize the speed and accuracy of the computer.
c. Verify the performance of machine operations that leave visible evidence of occurrence.
d. Gather and store large quantities of supportive audit evidence in machine-readable form.

LO 3-2   3.36 An audit engagement letter should normally include which of the following matters of agreement between the auditor and the client?
a. Schedules and analyses to be prepared by the client's employees.
b. Methods of statistical sampling the auditor will use.
c. Specification of litigation in progress against the client.
d. Client representations about availability of all minutes of meetings of the board of directors.

LO 3-2   3.37 When auditing Vandalay Jewelry, Costanza, CPA was not familiar with the quality and cut of the company's precious jewel inventory. To address this shortcoming, Costanza hired Benes, an expert in jewel valuation, to assist in the inventory valuation. Should Costanza refer to Benes's work in the audit report?
a. Yes, the auditors' report should mention the fact that a specialist was used.
b. The auditors' report should mention the use of the specialist only when the specialist's findings affect the auditors' conclusions.
c. The use of a specialist need not be mentioned if the auditors decide not to take responsibility for the specialist's findings.
d. The auditors' report should mention the specialist only if Vandalay agrees with the specialist's findings.

LO 3-2   3.38 Which of the following engagement planning procedures would most likely assist the auditor in identifying related-party transactions before the balance-sheet date?
a. Interviewing internal auditors about their reporting responsibilities.
b. Reviewing accounting records for recurring transactions occurring near year-end.
c. Inspecting communications with the client's legal counsel regarding recorded contingent liabilities.
d. Scanning the minutes for significant transactions with members of the board of directors.

LO 3-2   3.39 Which of the following communications is most likely to be written before the balance-sheet date?
a. A report to the audit committee on the results of testing of internal control over cash receipts.
b. Confirmation letters to vendors confirming the amounts they owe to the client.
c. An attorney's letter regarding contingent liabilities.
d. An engagement letter.

LO 3-2   3.40 Which of the following procedures would most likely be performed during planning?
a. Surprise counts of the client's petty cash fund.
b. Reporting internal control deficiencies to the audit committee.
c. Performing a search for unrecorded liabilities.
d. Identifying related parties.

LO 3-1   3.41 Prior to accepting a new audit engagement, a public accounting firm should
   a. Attempt to contact the predecessor auditors.
   b. Evaluate the integrity of management.
   c. Assess the firm's resources to ensure that they are sufficient to permit them to accept the engagement.
   d. All of the above.

LO 3-4   3.42 An audit plan contains
   a. Specifications of audit standards relevant to the financial statements being audited.
   b. Specifications of procedures the auditors believe appropriate for the financial statements under audit.
   c. Documentation of the assertions under audit, the evidence obtained, and the conclusions reached.
   d. Reconciliation of the account balances in the financial statements with the account balances in the client's general ledger.

LO 3-4   3.43 The revenue cycle of a company generally includes which accounts?
   a. Inventory, accounts payable, and general expenses.
   b. Inventory, general expenses, and payroll.
   c. Cash, accounts receivable, and sales.
   d. Cash, notes payable, and capital stock.

LO 3-4   3.44 When auditing the existence assertion for an asset, auditors proceed from the
   a. Financial statement amounts back to the potentially unrecorded items.
   b. Potentially unrecorded items forward to the financial statement amounts.
   c. General ledger back to the supporting original transaction documents.
   d. Supporting original transaction documents to the general ledger.

LO 3-4   3.45 Confirmations of accounts receivable provide evidence primarily about which two assertions?
   a. Completeness and valuation.
   b. Valuation and rights and obligations.
   c. Existence and rights and obligations.
   d. Existence and completeness.

LO 3-3   3.46 With respect to the concept of materiality, which one of the following statements is correct?
   a. Materiality depends only on the dollar amount of an item relative to other items in the financial statements.
   b. Materiality depends on the nature of a transaction rather than the dollar amount of the transaction.
   c. Materiality is determined by reference to AICPA guidelines.
   d. Materiality is a matter of professional judgment.

LO 3-4   3.47 When evaluating whether accounting estimates made by management are reasonable, the audit team would be most interested in which of the following?
   a. Key factors that are consistent with prior periods.
   b. Assumptions that are similar to industry guidelines.
   c. Measurements that are objective and not susceptible to bias.
   d. Evidence of a conservative systematic bias.

Exercises and Problems

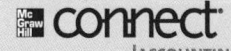 All applicable Exercises and Problems are available with McGraw-Hill's *Connect® Accounting*

LO 3-4   3.48 **General Audit Procedures and Financial Statement Assertions.** The eight general audit procedures produce evidence about the principal management assertions in financial statements. However, some procedures are useful for producing evidence about certain assertions while other procedures are useful for producing evidence about other assertions. The assertion being audited can influence the auditors' choice of procedures.

Required:
Opposite each general audit procedure, write the management assertions most usefully audited by using each procedure.

Audit Procedures	PCAOB Assertions	ASB Assertions
a. Inspection of records or documents (vouching)		
b. Inspection of records or documents (tracing)		
c. Inspection of records or documents (scanning)		
d. Inspection of tangible assets		
e. Observation		
f. Confirmation		
g. Inquiry		
h. Recalculation		
i. Reperformance		
j. Analytical procedures		

LO 3-4

3.49 **Audit Procedures.** Auditors frequently refer to the terms *principles* and *procedures*.

Required:
a. What is the difference between auditing principles and auditing procedures?
b. List eight different types of procedures auditors can use during an audit of financial statements and give an example of each.

LO 3-4

3.50 **Confirmation Procedure.** A CPA accumulates various types of evidence on which to base the opinion on financial statements. Among this evidence are confirmations from third parties.

Required:
a. What is an audit confirmation?
b. What characteristics of the confirmation process and the recipient are important if a CPA is to consider the confirmation evidence appropriate?

LO 3-4

3.51 **Potential Audit Procedure Failures.** For each of the general audit procedures of (1) recalculation, (b) observation, (c) confirmation (accounts receivable, securities, or other assets), (d) inquiry, (e) inspection of internal documents, (f) recalculation, (g) reperformance, and (h) analytical procedures, discuss one way the procedure could be misapplied or the auditors could be misled in such a way as to render the work (audit evidence) misleading or irrelevant. Give examples that are different from the examples in Chapter 3.

LO 3-6

3.52 **Audit Documentation.** The preparation of audit documentation is an integral part of an auditor's examination of financial statements. On a recurring engagement, auditors review the audit plans and audit documentation from the prior audit while planning the current audit to determine their usefulness for the current-year work.

Required:
a. (1) What are the purposes or functions of audit documentation?
  (2) What records may be included in audit documentation?
b. What factors affect the auditors' judgment of the type and content of the audit documentation for a particular engagement?

c. What should be included in audit documentation to support auditors' compliance with generally accepted auditing standards?

d. How can auditors make the most effective use of the prior year's audit plans in a recurring audit?

(AICPA adapted)

LO 3-1

3.53 **Communications between Predecessor and Prospective Auditors.** Assume that Smith & Smith, CPAs, audited Apollo Shoes, Inc., last year. Now CEO Larry Lancaster wishes to engage Anderson, Olds, and Watershed, CPAs (AOW) to audit its annual financial statements. Lancaster is generally pleased with the services provided by Smith & Smith, but he thinks the audit work was too detailed and interfered excessively with normal office routines. AOW has asked Lancaster to inform Smith & Smith of the decision to change auditors, but he does not wish to do so.

Required:

List and discuss the steps AOW should follow with regard to dealing with a predecessor auditor and a new client before accepting the engagement.

LO 3-1

3.54 **Predecessor and Prospective Auditors.** The president of Allpurpose Loan Company had a genuine dislike for external auditors. Almost any conflict generated a towering rage. Consequently, the company changed auditors often.

The firm of Wells & Ratley, CPAs, was recently hired to audit the 2012 financial statements. W&R succeeded the firm of Canby & Company, which had obtained the audit after Albrecht & Hubbard had been fired. A&H audited the 2011 financial statements and rendered a report that contained an additional paragraph explaining an uncertainty about Allpurpose Loan Company's loan loss reserve. Goodbye A&H! The president then hired Canby & Company to audit the 2012 financial statements, and Chris Canby started the work, but before the audit could be completed, Canby was fired and W&R was hired to complete the audit. Canby & Company did not issue an audit report because the audit was not finished.

Required:

Does the Wells & Ratley firm need to initiate communications with Canby & Company? With Albrecht & Hubbard? With both? Explain your response in terms of the purposes of communications between predecessor and successor auditors.

LO 3-1

3.55 **Client Selection.** You are a CPA in a regional public accounting firm that has 10 offices in three states. Mr. Shine has approached you with a request for an audit. He is president of Hitech Software and Games, Inc., a five-year-old company that has recently grown to $500 million in sales and $200 million in total assets. Shine is thinking about going public with a $25 million issue of common stock, of which $10 million would be a secondary issue of shares he holds. You are very happy about this opportunity because you know Shine is the new president of the Symphony Society board and has made quite a civic impression since he came to your medium-size city seven years ago. Hitech is one of the growing employers in the city.

Required:

a. Discuss the sources of information and the types of inquiries that you and the firm's partners may make in connection with accepting Hitech as a new client.

b. Do professional audit standards require any investigation of prospective clients?

c. Suppose Shine also told you that 10 years ago his closely held hamburger franchise business went bankrupt, and on investigation, you learn from its former auditors (your own firm in another city) that Shine played fast and loose with franchise-fee income recognition rules and presented such difficulties that your firm resigned from the audit (before the bankruptcy). Do you think the partner in charge of the audit practice should accept Hitech as a new client?

LO 3-2

3.56 **Using the Work of Internal Auditors.** North, CPA, is planning an independent audit of the financial statements of General Company. In determining the nature, timing, and extent of the audit procedures, North is considering General's internal audit function, which is staffed by Tyler.

Required:

a. In what ways can the internal auditor's work be relevant to North, the independent auditor?

b. What factors should North consider and what inquiries should North make in deciding whether to use Tyler's internal audit work?

(AICPA adapted)

LO 3-5

3.57 **Using the Computer to Discover Intentional Financial Misstatements in Transactions and Account Balances.** AMI International is a large office products company. Headquarters management imposed pressure on operating division managers to meet profit forecasts. The division managers met these profit goals using several accounting manipulations involving the record-keeping system that maintained all transactions and account balances on computer files. Employees who operated the computer accounting system were aware of the modifications of policy the managers ordered to accomplish the financial statement manipulations. The management and employees carried out these activities:

1. Deferred inventory write-downs for obsolete and damaged goods.
2. Kept open the sales entry system after the quarterly and annual cutoff dates, recording sales of goods shipped after the cutoff dates.
3. Recorded as sales transactions that had been coded as leases of office equipment.
4. Recorded shipments to branch offices as sales.
5. Postponed recording vendors' invoices for parts and services until later, but the actual invoice date was faithfully entered according to accounting policy.

Required:

Describe one or more procedures that could be performed with CAATs to detect signs of each of these transaction manipulations. Limit your answer to the actual work accomplished by the computer software.

LO 3-2

3.58 **Internet Exercise: Audit Plans on the Internet.** Auditnet (www.auditnet.org) is a website that provides support for practicing internal and external auditors. One of the resources that is offered is a library of audit plans for a number of different audit areas. If you need an audit plan, you can simply visit the site, download a plan, and modify it to meet the needs of your client's engagement.

Required:

Access the Auditnet website, browse through the plans, and download an audit plan that interests you. There is a free 30-day basic level subscription that is available when you register. For the steps listed on the selected audit plan, identify which of the general categories of audit procedures (recalculation, observation, confirmation, etc.) is represented by that step.

LO 3-5

3.59 **ACL Case.** ACL is one of the most widely used computer assisted audit techniques (CAATs) used by internal and external auditors today. We are providing you with an opportunity to master this software package before you even begin your professional accounting career. While a demonstration version of the software is included with your textbook, an ACL tutorial and exercises can be found on the textbook website (www.mhhe.com/louwers5e). Go to the ACL link at www.mhhe.com/louwers5e and complete the tutorial.

Management Fraud and Audit Risk

Profit is the result of risks wisely selected.
        Frederick Barnard Hawley, American economist

Risk comes from not knowing what you're doing.
        Warren Buffett, widely regarded as one of the most successful investors in the world.

Professional Standards References

Topic	AU/ISA Section	PCAOB Reference[*]
Overall Objectives of the Independent Auditor and the Conduct of an Audit	200	AU 110, AU 150, AU 201, AU 220, AU 230
Consideration of Fraud in a Financial Statement Audit	240	AU 316
Consideration of Laws and Regulations	250	AU 317
Communications with Those Charged with Governance	260	AU 380
Planning	300	AS 10
Risks of Material Misstatement	315	AS 12
Materiality	320	AS 11
Responses to Risks of Material Misstatement	330	AS 13
Audit Evidence	500	AS 15
Analytical Procedures	520	AU 329
Accounting Estimates	540	AU 342
Related Parties	550	AU 334

[*] AU, AT, and QC references represent standards issued by the ASB prior to April 16, 2003, that have not been superseded or amended by the PCAOB.

LEARNING OBJECTIVES

Your objectives are to be able to:

LO 4-1 Define *business risk* and understand how management addresses business risk with the enterprise risk management model.

LO 4-2 Explain auditors' responsibility for risk assessment, and define and explain the differences among several types of fraud and errors that might occur in an organization.

LO 4-3 Describe the audit risk model and explain the meaning and importance of its components in terms of professional judgment and audit planning.

LO 4-4 Understand sources of inherent risk factors including the client's business and environment.

LO 4-5 Understand sources of information for assessing risks including analytical procedures, brainstorming, and inquiries. Explain how auditors respond to assessed risks.

LO 4-6 Explain auditors' responsibilities with respect to a client's failure to comply with laws or regulations.

LO 4-7 Describe the content and purpose of an audit strategy.

INTRODUCTION

Take a step back in time to March 2001. **Enron**, one of the world's largest energy companies, reported revenues that ranked it among the top 10 U.S. companies. The company had doubled its revenues from 1999 to 2000, and company management predicted that it would do so again for the 2001 fiscal year. Arthur Andersen, then one of the world's five largest public accounting firms, provided auditing and consulting services to Enron, earning Andersen a million dollars a week in fees. While the auditors expressed concerns with respect to some of Enron's aggressive accounting practices, the future appeared strong for both companies. Andersen's planning team projected both increased growth for Enron and increased fees for Andersen.

Fast-forward nine months. By December 2001, Enron was a shell of its former self. The company had terminated almost its entire workforce, leaving its Houston skyline-dominating complex of buildings dark and empty. Enron's share price had plummeted from $90 in August 2000 to less than a dollar by December 2001, leaving many of its employees who had invested their life savings in the high-flying energy company out of work and virtually penniless. Enron's failure struck an irreparable blow to Andersen's reputation; one by one, Andersen's other clients decided to find other auditors rather than be associated with a firm that was now labeled by media as "low quality." Beset with shareholder lawsuits and government-led investigations of its audit practices and allegations of obstruction of justice, the firm struggled to maintain its very existence. After providing auditing services for almost a century to some of America's largest companies, Andersen decided to leave the practice of auditing public companies by August 31, 2002. Most of the firm's personnel also left the failing firm, attempting to find positions with other firms that had picked up Andersen's departing clientele. The firm's partnership equity, depleted by litigation and shareholder settlements, had been reduced to almost nothing, leaving new partners with nothing to show for the hundreds of thousands of dollars they paid to buy into the firm's partnership. Accounting students with prestigious (and lucrative) offers from Enron and Andersen found themselves scrambling for jobs when their offers were rescinded late in the recruiting season.

How could one of the largest and fastest-growing companies (Enron) implode within a matter of months? How could one of the oldest and most venerable auditing firms (Arthur Andersen) miss the abuses going on at one of its largest clients, resulting in the firm's ultimate dissolution? The answers to both of these questions lie in the risks that each company chose to undertake and the failure of both to adequately monitor and control those risks. In this chapter, we will discuss the risks that businesses face and how managers and auditors try to control the risks that they face.

MANAGEMENT'S RESPONSIBILITY FOR MANAGING RISK

LEARNING OBJECTIVE 4-1
Define *business risk* and understand how management addresses business risk with the enterprise risk management model.

Risks are unavoidable. We take risks every day, and if we didn't, we couldn't accomplish anything. As noted by the quote above from economist Frederick Barnard Hawley, taking risks is necessary to achieve goals and earn profits, so management must wisely manage the risks that they take. Risks that could adversely affect companies' ability to achieve *objectives* and execute *strategies* are called **business risks**. Business risks might result from setting inappropriate objectives and strategies, or from changes or complexity in the company's operations or management. A company's objectives are the overall plans established by management or the board of directors, and strategies are the approaches by which management intends to achieve its objectives.

If you think about the financial statements as a window into the operations and results of a business, you can imagine peering through them to see activities of thousands of employees, suppliers, and customers working to achieve their goals. You should also be able to see the effects of the environment, including economic and political events, weather occurrences, technological advances, and social and demographic patterns. Given this view of financial statements, it's easier to understand why auditors need to be aware of their clients' business risks.

Exhibit 4.1 illustrates the risks faced by entities and their auditors. After setting objectives and strategies for obtaining them, companies engage in various business processes to accomplish the objectives. Uncertainties from the business's environment, including the economy, competitors, regulators, customers, suppliers, investors, and so on create business risks that managers try to mitigate with control activities. Of course, risks can arise within the business through employee and management failures as well. The results of the events and transactions are recorded through information processing where errors and frauds can occur resulting in misstated financial statements (*inherent risk*), which can lead users to incorrect decisions (*information risk*). Managers build in controls to prevent this from happening, but they may not function as intended (*control risk*). The investors rely on auditors to reduce information risk, but there is also a risk that the auditors will give an incorrect opinion (*audit risk*).

EXHIBIT 4.1 Sources of Risk

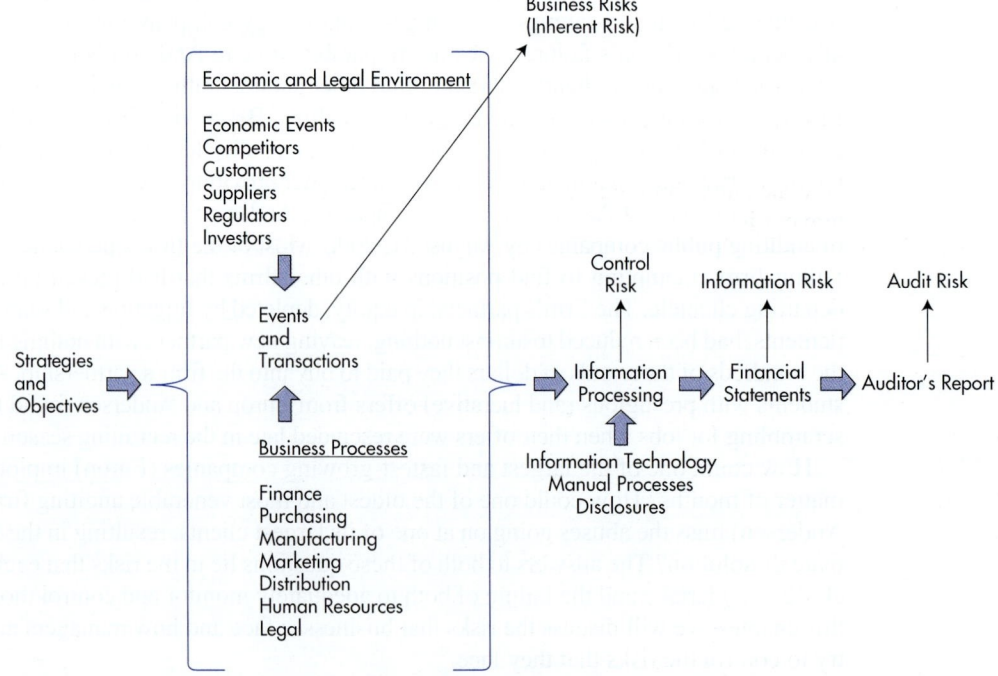

EXHIBIT 4.2
Enterprise Risk Management (ERM) Framework

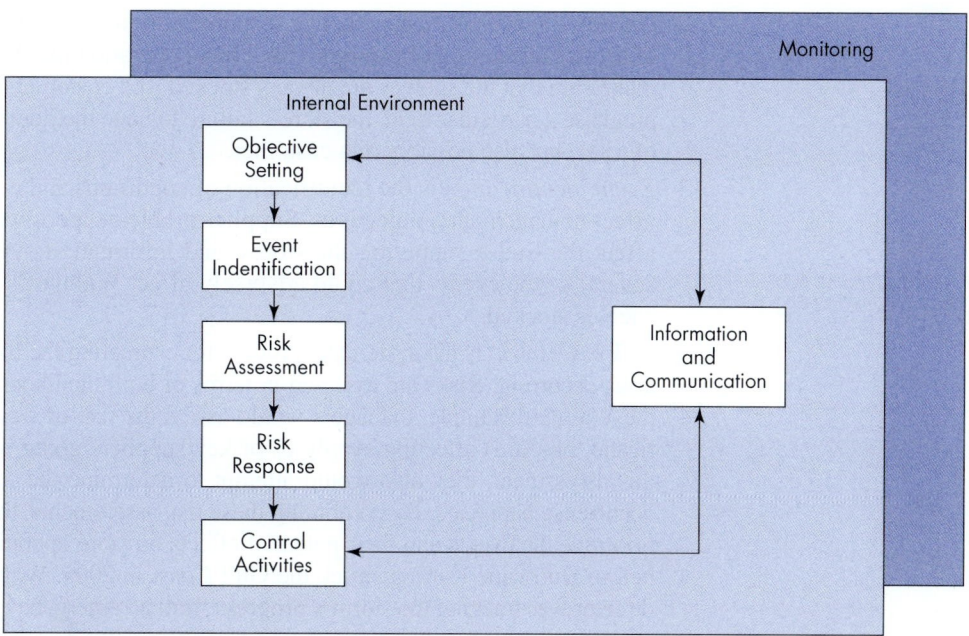

The Paradox of Risk
The paradox of risk is that it results from the future being different from the past, while traditional risk management relies upon the future being similar to the past.
 Frank Knight (as quoted in "Managing Risk from the Mailroom to the Boardroom," *Tone at the Top,* June 2003).

Enterprise Risk Management

Given the rapidly changing environment in which today's businesses operate, management, internal auditors, and external auditors must focus on the risks to the entity's operations (each from a different perspective) and ensure that controls are in place to eliminate, mitigate, or compensate for those risks. One way for managers to address these concerns is to employ an **enterprise risk management (ERM)** framework such as the one developed by the Committee of Sponsoring Organizations (COSO)[2] to facilitate assessing and mitigating business risk. COSO defines ERM as "a process, effected by an entity's board of directors, management and other personnel, applied in strategy setting and across the enterprise, designed to identify potential events that may affect the entity, and manage risks to be within its risk appetite, to provide reasonable assurance regarding the achievement of entity objectives." In other words, management, boards, and employees have to be constantly thinking about what could go wrong with the business and how they can prevent it.

The ERM framework (Exhibit 4.2) is composed of eight elements: (1) internal environment, (2) objective setting, (3) event identification, (4) risk assessment, (5) risk response, (6) control activities, (7) information and communication, and (8) monitoring.

1. *Internal environment* is the "risk consciousness" of the organization and includes the organization's risk management philosophy and "risk appetite," its integrity and ethical values, and the environment in which it operates.

---

[2] The Committee of Sponsoring Organizations of the Treadway Commission (COSO) is a private sector initiative established in 1985 composed of five financial professional associations: the Institute of Internal Auditors, the American Institute of Certified Public Accountants, the American Accounting Association, the Institute of Management Accountants, and the Financial Executives Institute. COSO's stated goal is "to improve the quality of financial reporting through a focus on corporate governance, ethical practices, and internal control" (www.coso.org).

2. *Objective setting* is management's responsibility to determine the goals and objectives of the organization. For example, for a retail operation like **Walmart,** an objective is to make sure that the shelves are always stocked. If a customer goes to a Walmart store to purchase a particular item, the store's failure to have the item results in the loss not only of a sale but also possibly of a customer.

3. *Event identification* is the identification of conditions and events that could adversely affect management's objectives. Supplier problems, poor weather conditions that can affect the trucks supplying the stores, and information system breakdowns are just several of the events that could adversely affect Walmart's ability to keep its stores' shelves stocked.

4. *Risk assessment* is the systematic process for estimating the likelihood of adverse conditions occurring. Risks are assessed in terms of both likelihood and impact. Again using the Walmart example, managers would assess the risk of weather conditions (e.g., hurricane, blizzard) affecting supply or of key suppliers going out of business. As part of this assessment, they also would attempt to determine the financial impact if such an occurrence happened. By combining these risk assessments, they would be able to better prioritize the events and their potential effects on store operations. For example, a week before Hurricane Katrina struck the Gulf Coast in 2005, Walmart's business continuity director was tracking the storm's progress from an emergency command center.

5. *Risk response* addresses how the organization will prevent or respond to the adverse conditions if they actually occur. The responses include management policies and procedures to eliminate, mitigate, or compensate for the risks identified. In Walmart's case, the company has established an excellent logistic system. When items are purchased at each Walmart location, the cash registers, which are electronically linked with the corporate headquarters, track sales and remaining inventory. When inventory levels become low, goods are shipped from centrally located warehouses to prevent shortages from occurring. To control for supplier shortages, Walmart uses suppliers with proven reputations. Other responses include having adequate insurance levels to protect against losses from theft, fire, or natural disaster. Derivative securities could be used to hedge against changes in interest rates or changes in the prices of raw materials.

6. *Control activities* are policies and procedures to ensure that risk responses are appropriate given the circumstances and environment in which the organization operates. Responding to Hurricane Katrina's progress, Walmart had prepositioned supply truck convoys just outside of the hurricane's path, ready to roll into the affected areas once roads had been cleared. Because of Walmart's preparations, the company was able to supply victims generators, dry ice, and drinking water within days of the storm. Contrast this response with that of the Federal Emergency Management Agency (FEMA), the government agency charged with aiding victims after natural disasters, which struggled to get supplies to victims even weeks after the storm.

7. *Information and communication* link all components of the ERM. In Walmart's case, its information system is instrumental in providing management with key information so that risks could be minimized or eliminated.

8. *Monitoring* includes regular management and supervisory activities over risk management activities to make sure they remain in place and operate effectively. Many companies, including Walmart, have large internal audit groups to monitor their ERM process.

↳ REVIEW CHECKPOINTS

4.1 What is business risk?

4.2 How can the enterprise risk management framework help managers address business risk?

AUDITOR'S RISK ASSESSMENT (AU 315, AS 12)

LEARNING OBJECTIVE 4-2
Explain auditors' responsibility for risk assessment, and define and explain the differences among several types of fraud and errors that might occur in an organization.

Audit standard setters have paralleled the development of ERM, which is the responsibility of the company, by developing risk assessment standards to guide auditors in assessing and dealing with a client's business risks and other risks that might affect the financial statements. The risk assessment approach employs a top-down evaluation of the client's risk that goes far beyond looking at just the accounting process and preparation of the financial statements. The standards recognize that most business risks are eventually reflected in the financial statements. So audit teams now devote a significant amount of their engagement planning to their clients' business risks. Firms believe they must learn more about their clients' business strategies and processes to understand whether the financial statements are fairly presented.

Gaining an understanding of strategies and processes involves gathering evidence in areas not previously addressed by auditors. Auditors might ask production personnel about labor problems or marketing personnel about product quality or competition. The process has been criticized by some as being more consulting than auditing, but it is essential in order to assess the risk of material misstatements. It addresses factors that audit team members could miss by getting lost in the details of a traditional "bottom-up" approach. That approach begins with a focus on individual accounts and disclosures that compose the financial statements but often misses the big picture. Business risk assessment also makes auditors much more knowledgeable about their client's business and its environment. We should note that, even when taking such a top-down approach, the audit team ultimately still has to tie procedures to key accounts and assertions.

Under this approach, auditors view all activities in a client's organization first in terms of risks that threaten the attainment of strategies and objectives and then in terms of management's plans and processes to mitigate the identified risks (for example, by using ERM). The auditors obtain an understanding of the client's objectives. Then risks are identified and the auditors determine how *management* plans to mitigate these risks. The three basic ways that management can mitigate a risk are (1) avoid it, (2) control it, and (3) share it. Alternatively, management can choose to accept the risk.

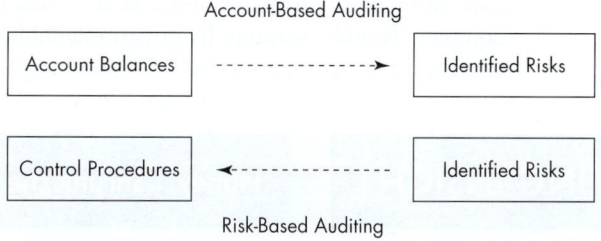

One key question you might be asking is this: "How can I gain the skills to study and evaluate management risk mitigation?" Answer: "It is not easy!" You need to rely on knowledge of marketing, management, production, finance, statistics, business law, economics, taxation, operations research, and even other nonbusiness subjects. Such studies are important because they serve as a foundation for organizing your practical experiences and the development of your critical thinking skills and common sense business management. You can expect very little to be routine in assessing a client's business risk. Understanding such broad issues in an entity makes audit assignments exciting (yes, exciting) challenges. This is the reason that the CPA exam includes a *Business Environment and Concepts (BEC)* section that covers knowledge of the general business environment and business concepts that CPAs need to know in order to understand the underlying business reasons for and accounting implications of business transactions as well as the skills needed to apply that knowledge.

In addition to *business risks* just discussed, auditors must assess the risk of providing incorrect information to financial statement users. **Information risk** is the probability that the information distributed by an entity will be *materially* false and misleading. Auditors' evidence-gathering and reporting reduce this risk to financial statement users, but the team itself faces the risk of issuing an incorrect opinion on the financial statements—giving an unqualified audit opinion when unknown material misstatements (whether due to errors, frauds, or noncompliance with laws or regulations that directly affect the financial statements) actually exist in the statements. This overall risk is known as *audit risk*. Auditing standards require auditors to design audits to provide *reasonable assurance* of detecting material errors and frauds to minimize audit risk.

Fraud (*AU 240, AU 316*)

Fraud is the act of knowingly making material misrepresentations of fact with the intent of inducing someone to believe the falsehood and act on it and, thus, suffer a loss or damage. Through both fraud and aggressive financial reporting, some companies have caused financial statements to be misstated, usually by (1) overstating revenues and assets, (2) understating expenses and liabilities, and (3) giving disclosures that are misstated or that omit important information.[3] Fraud that affects financial (or other) information and causes financial statements to be materially misstated often arises from the perceived need to get through a difficult period. The difficult period may be characterized by cash shortage, increased competition, cost overruns, and similar events that cause financial difficulty. Managers usually view these conditions as temporary, believing that getting a new loan, selling stock, or otherwise buying time to recover can overcome them. In the meantime, falsified financial statements are used to benefit the company. Generally, fraudulent financial statements show financial performance and ratios that are more favorable than current industry experience or than the company's own history. Sometimes the performance meets exactly the earnings targets announced by management months earlier. Exhibit 4.3 illustrates three areas of factors that might indicate increased risk of fraudulent financial reporting.

On the other hand, there are times when management finds it beneficial to understate assets and revenues and overstate expenses and liabilities. This can be in times when profits are low anyway and management wants to put reserves in a "cookie jar"[4] to be used to increase profits in future years. Understating profits also can be desirable if the company is under scrutiny by governmental bodies, taxing authorities, labor, or competitors (or, in one case, a spouse's divorce lawyer).

⊙ AUDITING INSIGHT　　Honey, I Shrunk the Company

Beazer Homes USA Inc. recently settled charges by the Securities and Exchange Commission that it intentionally *understated* its income (through the use of "cookie jar" reserves) between 2000 and 2005 in order to smooth over losses when the housing boom ended. The SEC also alleged that the homebuilder "cut side deals with investors in the builder's model homes in order to evade auditors and book additional profit." The SEC filed a civil complaint against the company's former chief accounting officer.

Source: "Beazer Settles Charges over Its Accounting," *The Wall Street Journal*, September 25, 2008, p. B2, http://www.sec.gov/news/press/2009/2009-146.htm.

---

[3] An academic study (see M. Nelson, J. Elliott, and R. Tarpley, "How Are Earnings Managed? Examples from Auditors," *Accounting Horizons*, November 2002) examined more than 500 attempts to manage earnings that were detected by auditors. The majority (more than 50 percent) of the attempts involved improper expense reductions, approximately 20 percent involved improper revenue increases, and the remainder involved business combinations and other accounting artifices.

[4] *Cookie jar* reserves are overaccruals created by a company (credit accrual, debit expense). In times when the company struggles, it reverses the overaccrual (debit accrual, credit expense) to pump up profits. Auditors are in a fix because they can't object to the company correcting the overaccrual.

EXHIBIT 4.3   Fraud Risk Factors

Management's Characteristics and Influence	Industry Conditions	Operating Characteristics and Financial Stability
• Management has a motivation (bonus compensation, stock options, etc.) to engage in fraudulent reporting. • Management decisions are dominated by an individual or a small group. • Management fails to display an appropriate attitude about internal control and financial reporting. • Managers' attitudes are very aggressive toward financial reporting. • Managers place too much emphasis on earnings projections. • Nonfinancial management participates excessively in the selection of accounting principles or the determination of estimates. • The company has a high turnover of senior management. • The company has a known history of violations. • Managers and employees tend to be evasive when responding to auditors' inquiries. • Managers engage in frequent disputes with auditors.	• Company profits lag those of its industry. • New requirements are passed that could impair stability or profitability. • The company's market is saturated due to fierce competition. • The company's industry is declining. • The company's industry is changing rapidly.	• A weak internal control environment prevails. • The company is not able to generate sufficient cash flows to ensure that it is a going concern. • There is pressure to obtain capital. • The company operates in a tax haven jurisdiction. • The company has many difficult accounting measurement and presentation issues. • The company has significant transactions or balances that are difficult to audit. • The company has significant and unusual related-party transactions. • Company accounting personnel are lax or inexperienced in their duties.

Auditors need to know about the *red flags*, those telltale signs and indications that have accompanied many frauds. Because of the double-entry bookkeeping system, fraudulent accounting entries always affect at least two accounts and two places in financial statements. Because many frauds involve improper recognition of assets, there is a theory of the "dangling debit," which is an asset amount that can be investigated and found to be false or questionable. Frauds may involve the omission of liabilities, but the matter of finding and investigating the dangling credit is normally very difficult. It "dangles" off the books. Misstated disclosures also present difficulty, mainly because they involve words and messages instead of numbers. Omissions may be difficult to notice, and misleading inferences may be very subtle. Exhibit 4.3 presents some other conditions and circumstances (fraud risk factors) that have characterized situations in which frauds occurred; these items are the red flags that were discussed earlier.

Types of Fraud

Financial statements may be materially misstated as a result of *errors* or *fraud*. While accounting errors are usually unintentional, fraud consists of knowingly making material misrepresentations of fact with the *intent* of inducing someone to believe the falsehood and act on it and, thus, suffer a loss or damage. This definition encompasses all means by which people can lie, cheat, steal, and dupe other people. **Management fraud** is deliberate fraud committed by management that injures investors and creditors through materially misstated information. Because management fraud usually takes the form of deceptive financial statements, management fraud is sometimes referred to as **fraudulent financial reporting.** *AU 240* defines fraudulent financial reporting as "intentional misstatements, including omissions of amounts or disclosures in financial statements to deceive financial statement users. It can be caused by the efforts of management to manage earnings in order to deceive financial statement users by influencing their perceptions about the entity's performance and profitability."

AUDITING INSIGHT — When CEOs Go Bad

Perpetrator (age at trial)	Company	Verdict	Punishment
Conrad Black (62)	Hollinger International Inc.	Found guilty of three counts of mail fraud and one count of obstruction of justice related to the looting his company of millions of dollars without proper board approval or disclosure.	Currently serving 6½ years in federal prison.
Kim Woo Choong (69)	Daewoo	Found guilty of fraud and embezzlement charges by a South Korean court.	Currently serving a 10-year sentence in Korea; forfeited $22 billion in assets.
Bernie Ebbers (63)	WorldCom	Found guilty on fraud and conspiracy charges related to an $11 billion accounting scandal.	Currently serving a 25-year sentence in federal prison.
Ronald E. Ferguson (66)	General Re	Found guilty of colluding with others to create sham transactions to make a customer (AIG) appear financially stronger than it actually was; the fraud cost AIG shareholders more than $500 million.	Sentenced to 2 years in prison.
Walter Forbes (64)	Cendant	Found guilty of conspiracy to commit securities fraud and two counts of making false statements.	Currently serving more than 12 years in prison; ordered to pay $3.3 billion in restitution.
Dennis Kozlowski (59)	Tyco International	Found guilty of stealing $600 million from the company.	Currently serving an 8-year sentence in New York state prison.
Sanjay Kumar (44)	Computer Associates 28 International, Inc. (CA)	Pleaded guilty to obstruction of justice and securities fraud charges related to CA's $3.3 billion accounting scandal.	Fined $8 million and sentenced to 12 years in prison.
Ken Lay (64)	Enron	Found guilty of securities fraud and related charges.	Suffered a massive coronary and passed away while awaiting sentencing.
Bernie Madoff (71)	Madoff Investment Securities	Pleaded guilty to securities fraud, money laundering, filing false statements with the SEC, wire fraud, mail fraud, and several other charges.	Sentenced to 150 years in prison.
Angelo R. Mozilo (72)	Countrywide Financial	On Friday, October 15, 2010, Mozilo reached a settlement with the SEC over securities fraud and insider trading charges.	Mozilo agreed to pay $67.5 million in fines and accepted a lifetime ban from serving as an officer or director of any public company; it is the largest settlement by an individual or executive connected to the 2008 housing collapse.
Chung Mong-koo (68)	Hyundai	Found guilty of embezzlement and breach of fiduciary duty.	Appellate court reduced his 3-year prison sentence to community service and a $1 billion contribution to charity.
John Rigas (80)	Adelphia Communications, Inc.	Found guilty on 18 felony counts of fraud and conspiracy.	Currently serving a 12-year sentence in federal prison.
Richard Scrushy (52)	HealthSouth	Although 15 other executives were found guilty related to the fraud, Scrushy was acquitted of 36 criminal conspiracy charges related to the fraud; he was later found guilty of other bribery, conspiracy, and mail fraud charges.	Scrushy settled civil charges with the SEC for $81 million, On June 18, 2009, Judge Allwin E. Horn ruled that Scrushy was responsible for HealthSouth's fraud, and ordered him to pay $2.87 billion.
Jeffrey Skilling (52)	Enron	Found guilty of securities fraud and related charges.	Currently serving a 16-year sentence in prison. On June 24, 2010, the Supreme Court vacated part of Skilling's conviction and sent the case back to the lower court for further proceedings.
Calisto Tanzi (70)	Parmalat	Found guilty of securities laws violations related to his company's 2003 collapse amidst a giant financial fraud.	Sentenced to 10 years in prison.
Henry Yuen (53)	Gemstar-TV Guide International	Lost a civil trial for his role in fraudulently inflating revenues between 2000 and 2002.	Ordered to pay civil fines of $22.3 million, Mr. Yuen is currently "at large."

Sources: "Ebbers Is Sentenced to 25 Years for $11 Billion WorldCom Fraud," *The Wall Street Journal*, July 14, 2005, p. A1; "Daewoo Founder Gets Prison Term," The Wall Street Journal, May 31, 2006, p. B9; "Scrushy Is Convicted in Bribery Case," *The Wall Street Journal*, June 30, 2006, p. A3; "Ahold's Ex-CEO, Finance Chief Are Found Guilty in Fraud Case," *The Wall Street Journal*, May 23, 2006, p. B9; "Ex-CEO of Cendant Is Found Guilty in Third Trial," *The Wall Street Journal*, November 1, 2006, p. C3; "Skilling Gets 24 Years in Prison," *The Wall Street Journal*, October 24, 2006, p. C1; "Gemstar's Yuen Said He Destroyed Evidence; Judge: 'A No-Brainer,'" *The Wall Street Journal*, April 25, 2006, p. A1; "Yao Guilty in Fraud Case," *The Wall Street Journal*, March 15, 2007, p. C5; "Press Baron Black Guilty in Fraud Case," *The Wall Street Journal*, July 14, 2007, p. A3; "Former Sentinel Executives Agree to Settle Fraud Suit," *The Wall Street Journal*, May 20, 2008, p. C7; "Ex-CEO Agrees to Give Back $620 Million," *The Wall Street Journal*, December 7, 2007, p. A1; "Authorities Rule Out Samuel Israel Suicide," *The Wall Street Journal*, June 17, 2008, p. C7; "Trial Ends for Samsung Ex-Chairman," *The Wall Street Journal*, July 11, 2008, p. B5; "Former Samsung Chairman Found Guilty," *The Wall Street Journal*, July 17, 2008, p. B6; "Scandal-Plagued Samsung Chairman Quits," *BusinessWeek*, April 22, 2008, http://www.businessweek.com/globalbiz/content/apr2008/gb20080422_646584.htm (referenced August 10, 2010); "Parmalat Founder Gets Prison Term," *The Wall Street Journal*, December 19, 2008, p. B2; "Ex-General Re CEO Gets 2 Years," *The Wall Street Journal*, December 16, 2008; p. C7, Laurence Viele Davidson,, "HealthSouth's Scrushy Liable in $2.88 Billion Fraud (Update 3)," *Bloomberg*, June 18, 2009; http://www.bloomberg.com/apps/news?pid=new sarchive&sid=a89tFKR4OevM (referenced August 10, 2011); Adam Liptak"Justices Limit Law Used for Corruption Cases"" *The New York Times*, June 25, 2010, p1; Gretchen Morgenson, "Angleo Mozilo of Countrywide Settles Fraud Case for $67.5 Million," *The New York Times*, October 16, 2010, p.1.

AUDITING INSIGHT | Wayward CFOs Often Coerced by CEOs, Study Says

When CFOs are caught fudging the numbers, it's more likely they were pressured by upper management than looking for some immediate financial benefit. At least that's the way The Conference Board sees it after analyzing more than 20 years of accounting and auditing enforcement actions by the Securities and Exchange Commission. The study found that CFOs have an inherently higher risk of litigation in accounting manipulation cases, yet they often do not get the personal financial benefits of cooking the books. However, when CEOs apply enough pressure, CFOs may acquiesce and set aside their role as watchdog of financial reporting quality.

Source: Tammy Whitehouse, *Compliance Week,* May 20, 2011.

Exhibit 4.4 shows some acts and devices that are often involved in financial frauds. Notice that these actions may be perpetrated *by* the organization or may be perpetrated *upon* the organization. Collectively, these are known as **white-collar crimes**—the misdeeds of people who wear ties to work and steal with a pencil or a computer terminal. White-collar crime produces ink stains instead of bloodstains.

It is important to note that audit teams are concerned with fraud *only as it affects the financial statements.* That is, audit teams are not responsible to detect all fraud but are responsible to detect cases where fraudulent activity results in *materially* misstated financial statements. For example, if a warehouse employee is misappropriating inventory but that embezzlement does not result in materially misstated financial statements, auditors do not have responsibility for detecting this fraud. However, if management is intentionally misstating revenues in order to meet earnings expectations, auditors *are* responsible for detecting this misstatement. That is not to say that auditors would ignore immaterial fraud (they would typically report immaterial fraud to the next higher level above where the fraud occurred) but only that auditors' primary responsibility is to design procedures to provide *reasonable assurance* that *material* frauds that might misstate the financial statements are detected.

**EXHIBIT 4.4
Overview of Types of Frauds**

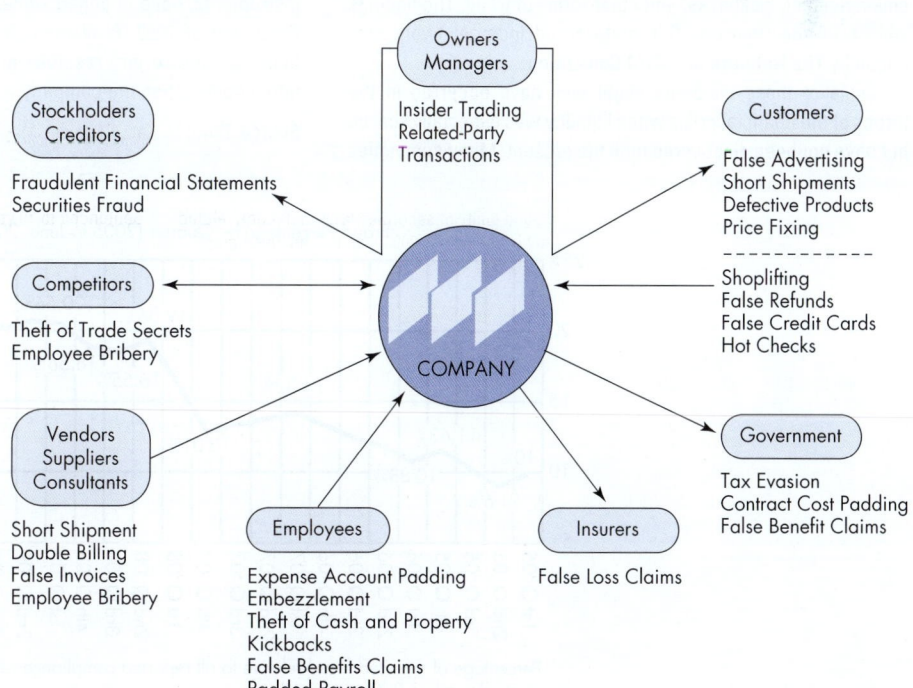

Other Definitions Related to Fraud

Employee fraud is the use of fraudulent means to misappropriate funds or other property from an employer. It usually involves falsifications of some kind: using false documents, lying, exceeding authority, or violating an employer's policies. It consists of three phases: (1) the fraudulent act, (2) the conversion of the funds or property to the fraudster's use, and (3) the cover-up. Employee fraud can be classified as either embezzlement or larceny. This type of fraud is discussed in detail in Chapter 6

Embezzlement is a type of fraud involving employees or nonemployees wrongfully misappropriating funds or property entrusted to their care, custody, and control, often accompanied by false accounting entries and other forms of deception and cover-up.

Larceny is simple theft; for example, an employee misappropriates an employer's funds or property that has not been entrusted to the custody of the employee.

Defalcation is another name for employee fraud, embezzlement, and larceny. Auditing standards also call it *misappropriation of assets.*

Errors are unintentional misstatements or omissions of amounts or disclosures in financial statements.

Auditing standards require that auditors specifically assess the risk of material misstatement due to fraud for each engagement. Fraud risk factors relate to both misstatements arising from fraudulent financial reporting and misstatements arising from *misappropriations of assets* (usually as a result of employee theft and the resultant attempt to conceal this theft through erroneous journal entries). Furthermore, auditors should consider these risk factors when determining what audit procedures to perform.

AUDITING INSIGHT   Fraud on the Rise?

After a dip through the third quarter of 2010, reported frauds rose to near all-time highs in the first quarter of 2011. The percentage of reported corporate frauds compared with all other reported incidents increased in the first quarter of 2011. Of the 30,000 ethics-and-compliance-related reports in the first quarter, more than 6,100 concerned accounting or auditing irregularities, embezzlement, kickbacks, and other forms of fraud. The findings stem from the Quarterly Corporate Fraud Index Network produced by **The Network** and **BDO Consulting**.

Some of those incidents might well have occurred in the throes of the financial crisis when liquidity was especially scarce but have not been discovered until the present. Many companies found themselves holding assets for which there were only sluggish or inactive markets. That made those assets hard to value, offering the temptation to artificially inflate their worth.

Over the entire course of the 2000s, accounting fraudsters increasingly used estimates. Still, the current forms of such fraud, which have tended to focus on the valuation of financial instruments, have changed since the era before the Sarbanes-Oxley Act of 2002. Previously, frauds involved such things as booking "cookie jar" reserves and "then reversing them back into income when the company wasn't doing well.

Source: David M. Katz, CFO.com, May 24, 2011.

Percentage of reported fraud relative to all reported compliance-related incidents at approximately 1,000 organizations.
Source: The Network, Inc., "Quarterly Corporate Fraud Index."

> ## ⌕ REVIEW CHECKPOINTS
>
> 4.3 Why do auditors need to be aware of their clients' business risks?
>
> 4.4 What are the defining characteristics of (a) white-collar crime, (b) employee fraud, (c) embezzlement, (d) larceny, (e) defalcation, (f) management fraud, and (g) errors?
>
> 4.5 What types of conditions provide opportunities for financial statement fraud?

▽ THE AUDIT RISK MODEL (AU 320, AS 8)

Audit Risk

LEARNING OBJECTIVE 4-3
Describe the audit risk model and explain the meaning and importance of its components in terms of professional judgment and audit planning.

Audit risk is the probability that an audit team will express an inappropriate audit opinion when the financial statements are materially misstated (i.e., give an unqualified opinion on financial statements that are misleading because of material misstatements that the auditors failed to discover). Such a risk always exists, even when audits are well planned and carefully performed. Of course, the risk is much higher in poorly planned and carelessly performed audits. The auditing profession has no official standard for an acceptable level of overall audit risk except that it should be "appropriately" low. In practice, audit risk is evaluated for both the financial statements as a whole and for each *relevant assertion* for *significant accounts and disclosures*. A **significant account or disclosure** is an account or disclosure that has a reasonable possibility of containing a material misstatement regardless of the effect of controls. **Relevant assertions** are management assertions that have a reasonable possibility of containing material misstatements without regard to the effect of controls

Audit risk (see Exhibit 4.5) can be broken down into the risks that (1) a material misstatement occurs (*inherent risk*), (2) is not prevented or detected by client internal controls (*control risk*), and (3) is not detected by the auditor's procedures (*detection risk*). Inherent risk and control risk are combined into **risk of material misstatement (RMM)**, which is the risk a material misstatement exists in the financial statements before auditors apply their procedures. Each of these components is now discussed.

Inherent Risk

Inherent risk is the probability that, in the absence of internal controls, material errors or frauds could enter the accounting system used to develop financial statements. You can think of inherent risk as the *susceptibility* of the account to misstatement. In other words "what could go wrong?"—inherent risk is a function of the nature of the client's business, the major types of transactions, and the effectiveness and integrity of its managers and accountants. It is important to understand that for different accounts, different *assertions* are riskier than others. For example for cash, *existence* is riskier than *valuation*;

EXHIBIT 4.5 Inherent, Control, and Detection Risk

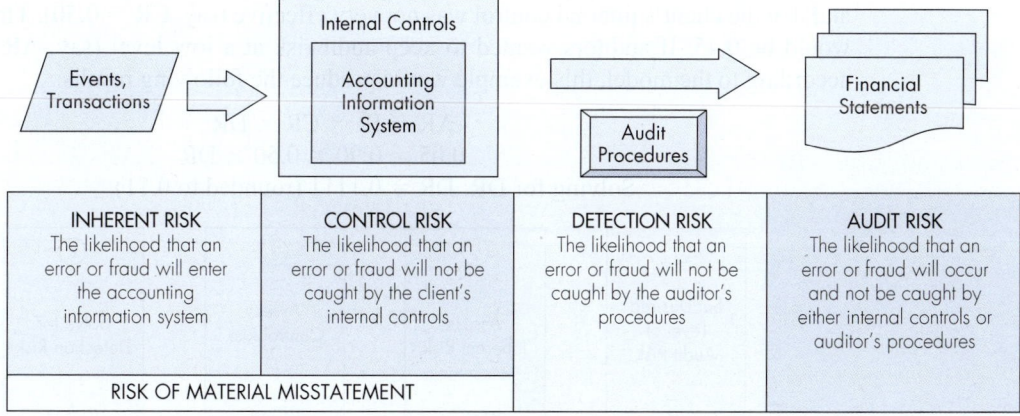

for receivables, *valuation* is riskier than *completeness*; and for liabilities, *completeness* is riskier than *existence*. Thus, auditors focus their attention on *relevant assertions*. Auditors do not create or control inherent risk. They can only try to assess its magnitude. This will be discussed in more detail later in the chapter.

Control Risk

Control risk is the probability that the client's internal control activities will *fail* to prevent or detect material misstatements provided that they enter or would have entered the accounting system in the first place. So, for the things that could "go wrong" as discussed, "What is the client doing about them?" Recall from our discussion of auditing standards in Chapter 2 that one of the major purposes of internal control is to ensure appropriate processing and recording of transactions to help ensure the production of reliable financial statements. Auditors do not create or manage control risk. They can only evaluate an entity's control system and assess the probability of its failure to prevent or detect material misstatements.

External auditors' task of control risk assessment starts with learning about an entity's controls designed to prevent, detect, and correct the inherent risks discovered. The auditors then observe and test the control activities if necessary to determine whether they are operating effectively. This process is discussed in detail in Chapter 5.

Detection Risk

Detection risk is the probability that audit procedures will *fail* to detect material misstatements provided that any have entered the accounting system in the first place and have not been prevented or detected and corrected by the client's internal controls. In contrast to inherent risk and control risk, auditors are responsible for performing the evidence-gathering procedures that manage and establish detection risk. These audit procedures represent the auditors' opportunity to detect material misstatements in financial statements. In other words, unlike inherent risk and control risk, auditors can and do influence the level of detection risk.

In Chapter 3, you studied substantive procedures, the procedures used to detect material misstatements in dollar amounts and disclosures presented in the financial statements and footnotes. The two categories of *substantive procedures* are (1) tests of detail of transactions and balances and (2) substantive analytical procedures, which study plausible relationships among financial and nonfinancial data. Detection risk is produced when procedures in these two categories fail to detect material misstatements.

Risk Model—A Summary

The foregoing components of audit risk can be expressed in a model that assumes that each of the elements is *independent*. Thus, the risks are *multiplied* as follows:

Audit risk (AR) = Inherent risk (IR) × Control risk (CR) × Detection risk (DR)

Auditors want to perform an audit of a particular assertion or disclosure well enough to hold the AR to a relatively low level (e.g., 0.05, which means that, on average, 5 percent of audit opinions would be wrong). For example, suppose that an audit team thought *valuation* of a particular inventory balance was subject to great inherent risk (say, IR = 0.90) and that the client's internal control was not very effective (say, CR = 0.50). Thus, RMM would be 0.45. If auditors wanted to keep audit risk at a low level (say, AR = 0.05), according to the model, this example would produce the following results:

$$AR = IR \times CR \times DR$$
$$0.05 = 0.90 \times 0.50 \times DR$$
Solving for DR: DR = 0.1111 (rounded to 0.11)

① Set Desired Level of Audit Risk [0.05]

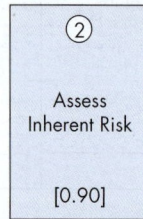
② Assess Inherent Risk [0.90]

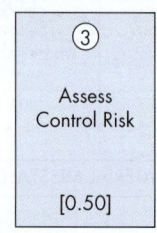
③ Assess Control Risk [0.50]

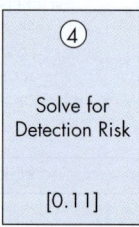
④ Solve for Detection Risk [0.11]

EXHIBIT 4.6
Audit Risk Process

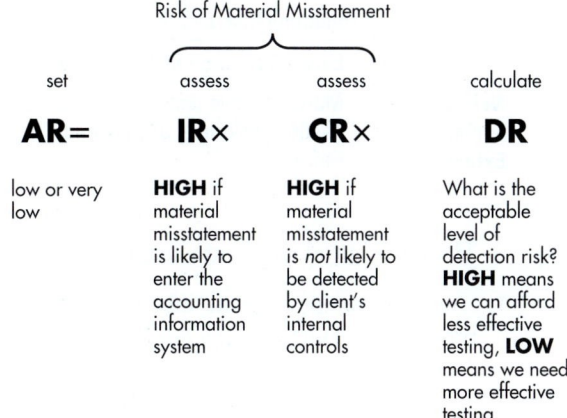

You should notice that planned detection risk (DR) depends on the other risks. DR is derived from the others by solving the risk model equation. It is not an independent judgment. Hence,

$$DR = AR/(IR \times CR)$$
$$DR = 0.11 = 0.05/(0.90 \times 0.50)$$

While *detection risk* is defined as the risk that the auditors' procedures *fail* to detect material misstatements, it is important that you understand that the *application* of DR is different. The 11 percent represents *the amount of risk the auditors can allow* and still maintain overall audit risk at 0.05. Then the auditors design procedures so DR will not exceed 0.11 (approximately). Exhibit 4.6 provides a visual display of the steps in the audit risk process.

Based on the allowable detection risk, auditors modify the *nature,* the *timing,* and the *extent* of their audit procedures. The *nature* of the procedures refers to the overall *effectiveness* of audit procedures in detecting misstatements. While inquiry of management as to whether accounts receivable listed on the balance sheet really exist is an audit procedure, it certainly is not an *effective* one. A much more effective procedure would be to confirm accounts receivable directly with the client's customers. *Timing* refers to when the audit procedures take place. While confirmation of accounts receivable may be performed at an interim period, auditors are expressing an opinion on year-end balances. The closer the procedures are performed to year-end (the date of the financial statements), the more effective they are because there is less chance of a material misstatement occurring between the interim confirmation date and year-end. Finally, *extent* refers to the number of tests performed. Clearly, the more accounts receivable confirmations that are mailed to customers, the greater the chance of finding errors and fraud.

Note that there is an inverse relationship between RMM and detection risk. In other words, the greater the risk of material misstatement, the lower the detection risk that auditors could allow in order to maintain the level of audit risk with which they feel comfortable. This makes sense. If the relevant assertion is risky or the related controls are poor, auditors would want to reduce detection risk by modifying the nature, timing, and extent of their procedures to increase their effectiveness. On the other hand, if the account is not risky and controls are strong, the auditor could employ less effective (and presumably lest costly) substantive audit procedures.

The practical problem here is knowing whether the audit has been planned and performed well enough to limit the detection risk as low as 0.11. The risk model is only a conceptual tool. Auditors cannot calculate the *exact* DR (or, for that matter, IR or CR), so the model represents more of a way to think about audit risks than a way to calculate them. However, the AICPA *Audit Sampling* Guide uses this model to calculate risks and the related sample sizes.

	Detection Risk and the Nature, Timing, and Extent of Audit Procedures	
	Lower Detection Risk Allowed	**Hisher Detection Risk Allowed**
Nature	More effective tests	Less effective tests
Timing	Testing performed at year-end	Testing can be performed at interim
Extent	More tests	Fewer tests

The model produces some insights, including these:

1. Auditors cannot estimate inherent risk to be zero and omit other evidence-gathering procedures. Thus, you *cannot* have the condition

$$AR = IR\ (= 0) \times CR \times DR = 0$$

2. Auditors cannot place complete reliance on internal controls to the exclusion of other audit procedures. Thus, you cannot have the condition

$$AR = IR \times CR\ (= 0) \times DR = 0$$

3. Auditors would not seem to exhibit due professional care if the level of audit risk was too high, for example:

$$AR = IR\ (= 0.80) \times CR\ (= 0.80) \times DR\ (= 0.50) = 0.32$$

4. Although permissible, audit teams rarely choose to rely exclusively on evidence produced by substantive procedures. Even if they think that control risk is high, auditors often perform some tests of controls to make sure the controls are in place. The concern is that if the controls are so weak (or nonexistent) as to fail to detect material misstatements, an audit team would probably not feel comfortable relying solely on substantive procedures. For example, this combination would generally not be considered wise:

$$AR = IR\ (= 1.00) \times CR\ (= 1.00) \times DR\ (= 0.05) = 0.05$$

To this point, the components of the audit risk model have been expressed *quantitatively* (as a number). In practice, most firms use *qualitative* measures of audit risk such as "low," "moderate," and "high." Whether expressed quantitatively or qualitatively, audit theory places control risk on a probability continuum, and the qualitative control risk categories are points with underlying control risk probabilities (Exhibit 4.7).

When risk is measured qualitatively, how do firms multiply words? Rather than multiplying, firms use a matrix approach similar to the one in Exhibit 4.8. Auditors find the appropriate detection risk by reading the cell at the intersection of the assessed levels of inherent risk and control risk.

EXHIBIT 4.7
Qualitative and Quantitative Control Risk

Control Risk Categories (qualitative)	Representative Control Risk Probabilities (quantitative)
Low control risk	0.10–0.45
Moderate control risk	0.40–0.70
Control risk slightly below the maximum	0.60–0.95
Maximum control risk	1.00

EXHIBIT 4.8
Matrix Approach to Detection Risk Determination

		CONTROL RISK		
		Low	Moderate	High
INHERENT RISK	Low	High Detection Risk	Moderate to High Detection Risk	Moderate Detection Risk
	Moderate	Moderate to High Detection Risk	Moderate Detection Risk	Low to Moderate Detection Risk
	High	Moderate Detection Risk	Low to Moderate Detection Risk	Low Detection Risk

REVIEW CHECKPOINTS

4.6 Define *audit risk*.
4.7 What are the components of the risk of material misstatement (RMM)? Audit risk?
4.8. How is the Audit Risk Model used to plan the audit?
4.9 What is meant by the terms *nature, timing*, and *extent* of audit procedures?

ASSESSING INHERENT RISK—"WHAT COULD GO WRONG?" (AU 315, AS 12)

LEARNING OBJECTIVE 4-4
Understand sources of inherent risk factors including the client's business and environment.

Recall that **inherent risk** is the probability that, in the absence of internal controls, material errors or frauds could enter the accounting system used to develop financial statements. Auditors' basis for assessing a client's inherent risk is found in their familiarity with the types of misstatements that could occur for each assertion in any account balance or class of transactions. Clearly, hundreds of innocent errors and not-so-innocent fraud schemes are possible. Instead of trying to learn hundreds of possible errors and frauds, it is better to start with seven general categories of errors and fraud. In a sense, these seven categories answer the audit question: "What can go wrong?" Exhibit 4.9 shows the seven categories with some examples.

Assessment of inherent risk can be based on a variety of information. The risk assessment process is summarized in Exhibit 4.10.

The best indicator of current misstatement is material misstatements that were discovered during the previous audit. Also, changes in transactions, technology, personnel, or accounting principles may increase the risk of misstatement. The nature of the client's business can produce complicated transactions and calculations that are subject to information processing and accounting treatment error. For example, real estate, franchising, and oil and gas transactions are frequently complicated and subject to accounting error. Some types of inventories are more difficult than others to count, value, and

EXHIBIT 4.9 General Categories of Misstatements

	Error Examples	Fraud Examples
1. Invalid transactions are recorded.	A computer malfunction causes a sales transaction to be recorded twice.	Fictitious sales are recorded and charged to nonexistent customers.
2. Valid transactions or disclosures are omitted from the financial statements.	Shipments to customers are never recorded because of problems in the company's information processing system.	Shipments are made to an employee's friend and purposely never recorded.
3. Transaction or disclosure amounts are inaccurate.	An employee calculates depreciation incorrectly.	A company "short ships" a shipment to a customer and bills the customer for the full amount ordered.
4. Transactions are classified in the wrong accounts.	Sales to a subsidiary company are recorded as sales to outsiders instead of intercompany sales, or the amount is charged to the wrong customer account receivable record.	A loan to the company's CEO (not permitted under Sarbanes-Oxley) is classified as an account receivable to conceal the transaction.
5. Transaction accounting and posting are incorrect.	Sales are posted in total to the accounts receivable control account, but some are not posted to individual customer account records.	Capital leases are accounted for as operating leases in order to keep related liabilities off the balance sheet.
6. Transactions are recorded in the wrong period	The company fails to record a shipment that was sent by a supplier FOB shipping point in December, but the shipment was not received (or recorded) until January.	Shipments made in January (of the next fiscal year) are backdated and recorded as sales in December.
7. Disclosures are incomplete or misleading.	Inaccurate calculations in the tax footnote.	Failure to disclose litigation against the company.

EXHIBIT 4.10 The Risk Assessment Process

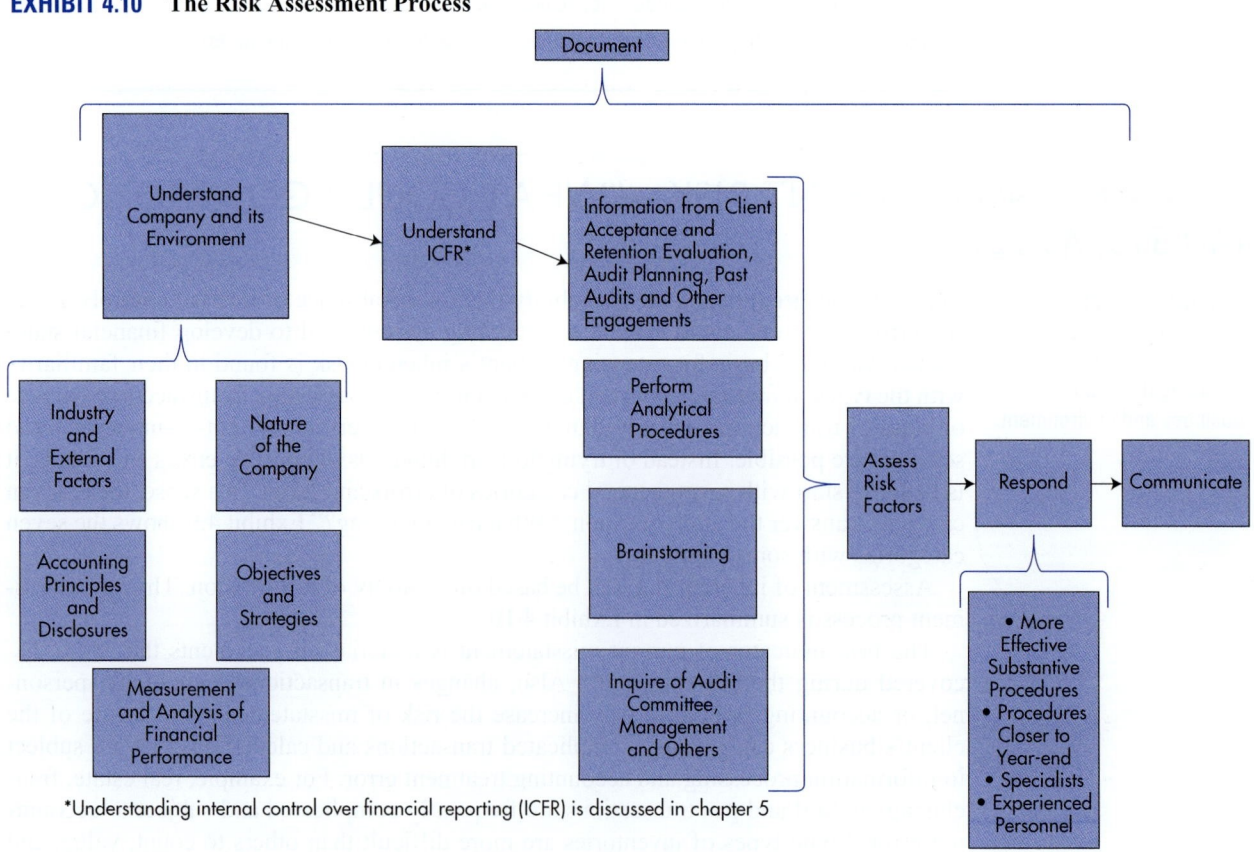

*Understanding internal control over financial reporting (ICFR) is discussed in chapter 5

keep accurately in perpetual records. The following factors have been suggested as being related to the susceptibility of accounts to misstatement or fraud:

- *Dollar size of the account.* The higher the account balance, the greater the chance of having errors or fraud in the account.
- *Liquidity.* The greater the account's liquidity (ability to be easily converted to cash), the more susceptible the account is to fraud. For example, cash is more susceptible to theft than, say, a building.
- *Volume of transactions.* The higher the volume of transactions, the higher the chance of error or fraud occurring in the transactions.
- *Complexity of the transactions.* Very complex transactions (e.g., those involving derivative securities or hedging transactions) tend to have a higher percentage of errors than simple transactions.
- *Subjective estimates.* Subjective measurements (e.g., estimating the allowance for doubtful accounts) tend to have more errors and fraud than objective measurements (e.g., counting petty cash).

Understanding the Client's Business and Its Environment

Knowledge and understanding of the client's business in the context of the client's industry is essential in an audit. Auditing standards require auditors to obtain a thorough understanding of the business to plan and perform the audit work. Obtaining an understanding of the company includes understanding:

- Relevant industry, regulatory, and other external factors.
- The nature of the company and related parties.
- The effect of client computerized processing (discussed in Chapter 3).
- The company's selection and application of accounting principles, including related disclosures.
- The company's objectives and strategies and those related business risks that might reasonably be expected to result in risks of material misstatement.
- The company's measurement and analysis of its financial performance.

Industry, Regulatory, and Other External Factors

Obtaining an understanding of relevant industry, regulatory, and other external factors encompasses the competitive environment and technological developments; the regulatory environment, including the applicable financial reporting framework (e.g., U.S. GAAP or IFRS) and the legal and political environment; and external factors, including general economic conditions. Auditors must understand the broad economic environment in which the client operates, including such things as the effects of national economic policies (e.g., price regulations and import/export restrictions), the geographic location and its economy (e.g., northeastern states versus sunbelt states), and developments in taxation and regulatory areas (e.g., industry regulation, approval processes for products in the drug and chemical industries).

Industry characteristics are also important. There is a great deal of difference in the production and marketing activities of banks, insurance companies, mutual funds, supermarkets, hotels, oil and gas industries, agriculture organizations, manufacturers, and so forth. Industry expertise also involves knowledge of the competition and an understanding of the client's market. Few auditors are experts in all of these areas. Public accounting firms typically have people who are expert in one or two industries and rely on them to supervise audits in those industries. Indeed, some public accounting firms have reputations for having many audit clients in a particular industry while others have a larger presence in other industries.

In addition, auditors should be aware of the effects that economic distress and slow recovery can have on their clients. PCAOB inspectors recently identified instances where auditors sometimes failed to comply with PCAOB auditing standards in connection with the economic crisis, such as fair value measurements, impairment of goodwill, indefinite-lived intangible assets, and other long-lived assets, allowance for loan losses, off-balance sheet structures, revenue recognition, inventory, and income taxes.[5]

The Nature of the Company

Obtaining an understanding of the nature of the company includes understanding:

- *The company's organizational structure and management personnel.* Is the client centralized or decentralized? Who makes the decisions? Are senior managers familiar with accounting and reporting requirements? Do they value the importance of good controls? Are any officers, employees, or shareholders involved in related-party transactions?
- *The sources of funding of the company's operations and investment activities.* Is the company funded by debt or equity? Are there restrictions placed by lenders that management must meet? Does it have the financing in place to meet future cash requirements? Are any lenders or shareholders involved in related-party transactions?
- *The company's significant investments.* Is the company invested in other companies for strategic purposes? Do investments provide a significant source of income? What is the company's investment policy? Do overseas investments present a risk of nationalization? Are any subsidiaries involved in related-party transactions?
- *The company's operating characteristics, including its size and complexity.* Does the company operate internationally? Do subsidiaries operate in diverse industries?
- *The sources of the company's earnings, including the relative profitability of key products and services, and key supplier and customer relationships.* Are there any threats to loss of revenue from losing suppliers or customers? Could key products be overtaken by competitors' products? Could advances in technology make the client's products obsolete? Are any customers or suppliers *related parties?*

Identification of Related Parties

Related parties include those individuals or organizations that can influence or be influenced by decisions of the company, possibly through family ties or investment relationships. Because one of the basic assumptions of historical cost accounting is that transactions are valued at prices agreed on by two *independent* parties (i.e., "arm's-length transactions"), *valuation* of related-party transactions is particularly troublesome. For example, auditors must remember that the economic substance of a particular transaction (and its effect on the financial condition of the entity) could be significantly different from its legal form (e.g., capitalized leases versus operating leases). Auditors strive to identify related-party relationships and transactions during planning to be able to obtain evidence that the financial accounting and disclosure for them are proper. Some methods include reviewing the board of directors' meeting minutes, making inquiries of key executives, and reviewing stock ownership records (5 percent ownership in the company is usually used as a good cutoff).

Auditors also should question the persuasiveness of the evidence obtained from related parties because the source of the evidence may be biased. Hence, auditors should obtain evidence of the purpose, nature, and extent of related-party transactions and their effect on financial statements, and the evidence should extend beyond inquiry of management.

---

[5] Report on Observations of PCAOB Inspectors Related to Audit Risk Areas Affected by the Economic Crisis, September 29, 2010.

AUDITING INSIGHT The Perils of Related-Party Transactions

Although related-party transactions are approved by some company boards, various critics charge that such transactions do not pass the "smell test" and should be avoided, especially given the spate of recent accounting scandals. A recent study noted that 40 percent of the S&P 500 companies has business relationships with other companies that are somehow related.

Enron CFO Andrew Fastow made millions by managing investment partnerships that had significant dealings with Enron. By "selling" appreciated assets to Fastow's LJM partnerships, Enron was able to record profits before the company would normally earn them. The financing vehicles were also instrumental in keeping significant debt off Enron's balance sheet. The problem was that Fastow's millions came at Enron's expense. Although there were safeguards in place to prevent such conflicts of interest, Enron's board of directors waived the rules preventing such transactions. Board members later stated that they had not realized how much Fastow was making from the deals (approximately $45 million). Arthur Andersen expressed concern about the related-party transactions but withdrew its reservations when the board signed off on the relationship. The risky partnerships, based on overvalued assets and collateralized with Enron stock, represented one of the primary reasons for Enron's ultimate collapse.

XINHUA FINANCE LTD.
Loretta Fredy Bush, who became well known in Asia as the U.S. chief executive of Xinhua Finance Ltd., was indicted on U.S. fraud charges along with two associates. The Office of the U.S. Attorney in Washington, D.C., is seeking forfeiture of $50 million generated in an alleged fraud by Ms. Bush and two of the company's other former directors, cofounder Dennis L. Pelino, 63, and California investment banker Shelly S. Singhal, 43. The charges filed in U.S. District Court for the District of Columbia, set forth in a grand-jury indictment, allege "conspiracy to defraud the U.S. Securities and Exchange Commission, investors and others and to enrich themselves through a series of undisclosed and disguised related-party transactions and insider trading." In one series of transactions over a number of years, prosecutors allege Ms. Bush and Mr. Pelino sold Xinhua Finance stock valued at more than $25 million and concealed the fact from investors with the help of Mr. Singhal, who made it appear the shares were pledged as loan collateral. Finance shares dropped to ¥1,390 each in Tokyo, down from more than ¥75,000 in March 2007.

Sources: "'Related-Party' Deals Abound at Companies," *The Wall Street Journal*, December 3, 2004, p. C3; "Visionary's Dream Led to Risky Business; Opaque Deals, Accounting Sleight of Hand Built an Energy Giant and Ensured Its Demise," *The Washington Post*, July 28, 2002, p. A1.; "Global Finance: Xinhua Finance Founders Charged" James T, Areddy. *The Wall Street Journal*, May 12, 2011, p. C.3

Selection and Application of Accounting Principles, Including Related Disclosures

Auditors should evaluate whether the company's selection and application of accounting principles are appropriate for its business and consistent with the applicable financial reporting framework and accounting principles used in the relevant industry. Auditors should pay attention to significant changes in the company's accounting principles, financial reporting policies, or disclosures and the reasons for such changes; significant accounting principles in controversial or emerging areas; and the methods the company uses to account for significant and unusual transactions.

Accounting estimates are a concern because numerous fraud cases have involved the deliberate manipulation of estimates to increase net income. **Accounting estimates** are approximations of financial statement numbers and are often included in financial statements. Examples include valuation of investment securities, net realizable value of accounts receivable, market (lower than cost) value of inventory, depreciation expense, insurance loss reserves, percentage-of-completion contract revenues, pension expense, warranty liabilities, fair value, and many more. Management is responsible for making accounting estimates. Auditors are responsible for determining that all appropriate estimates have been made, that they are reasonable, and that they are presented in conformity with GAAP and adequately disclosed.

With respect to auditing accounting estimates, auditors are supposed to (1) monitor the differences between management's estimates and the closest reasonable estimates supported by the audit evidence and (2) evaluate the differences taken altogether for indications of a systematic bias. For example, management may estimate an allowance for doubtful accounts to be $50,000, and the auditors may estimate that the allowance could be $40,000 to $55,000. In this case, management's estimate is within the auditors' range of reasonableness. However, the auditors should note that the management estimate leans toward the conservative side (more than the auditors' $40,000 lower estimate but not much less than the auditors' higher $55,000 estimate). If other estimates exhibit the same conservatism and the effect is material, the auditors will need to evaluate the overall reasonableness of the effect of all estimates taken together.

Company Objectives, Strategies, and Related Business Risks

The purpose of obtaining an understanding of the company's objectives, strategies, and related business risks is to identify business risks that could reasonably be expected to result in material misstatement of the financial statements. Of course the best starting point is with management whose job it is to be knowledgeable about the company's risks, possibly by using the ERM model discussed earlier in this chapter. The following are examples of situations in which business risks might result in material misstatement of the financial statements:

- *Industry developments,* for example, a potential related business risk might be that the company does not have the personnel or expertise to deal with the changes in the industry.
- *New products and services,* for example, a potential related business risk might be that the new product or service will not be successful.
- *Expansion of the business,* for example, a potential related business risk might be that the demand for the company's products or services has not been accurately estimated.
- *The effects of implementing a strategy,* particularly any effects that will lead to new accounting requirements.
- *Financing requirements,* for example, a potential related business risk might be the loss of financing due to the company's inability to meet financing requirements.

Company Performance Measures

The purpose of obtaining an understanding of the company's performance measures is to determine what information management and others deem to be key indicators of company performance. They also reveal what items management or financial statement users might be sensitive to. For example, measures used to determine management compensation or analysts' ratings might place pressure on management to manipulate results. Also, auditors might gain a better understanding of their clients by reviewing measures management uses to monitor operations, such as budget variances or trend analysis. Finally, those measures might be indicators of qualitative materiality factors.

> ### ↳ REVIEW CHECKPOINTS
>
> 4.10 What is meant by the nature of the company?
> 4.11 Why should auditors understand their clients' performance measures?
> 4.12 What is the major concern with evidence obtained from related parties?

GATHERING INFORMATION, ASSESSING AND RESPONDING TO RISKS

LEARNING OBJECTIVE 4-5
Understand sources of information for assessing risks including analytical procedures, brainstorming, and inquiries. Explain how auditors respond to assessed risk.

Auditors have to keep up with developments in their clients' industries and in the overall economy. Only a few of the hundreds of sources are described briefly here. The AICPA industry accounting and auditing guides are a good place to start. These guides explain the typical transactions and accounts used by various types of businesses and not-for-profit organizations. Many databases and information sources are available on the Internet (e.g. The Library of Congress E-Resources Online Catalog, http://eresources.loc.gov/). Auditors should read public information about the company such as company-issued press releases, company-prepared presentation materials for analysts or investor groups, and analyst reports, observing or reading transcripts of earnings calls, and, to the extent publicly available, other meetings with investors or rating agencies. Auditors also need to obtain an understanding of compensation arrangements with senior management, including incentive compensation arrangements, changes or adjustments to those arrangements, and special bonuses by reviewing the documents and discussing the arrangements with management. Board of directors compensation committee minutes often contain useful discussions about the intent of such arrangements.

General Business Sources

Most industries have specialized trade magazines and journals. You may not choose to read *Grocer's Spotlight* for pleasure, but magazines of this special type are very valuable for learning and maintaining an industry expertise. In addition, specific information about public companies can be found in registration statements and 10-K reports filed with the SEC. General business magazines and newspapers often contribute insights about an industry, an entity, and individual corporate officers. Many are available, including such leaders as *Bloomberg Businessweek, Forbes, Fortune, Harvard Business Review, Barron's,* and *The Wall Street Journal*. Auditors typically read several of these regularly. Additionally, many companies present "company story" information on their websites. A visit to them can provide a wealth of information about products, markets, and strategies. For public companies, auditors should also monitor the client's daily stock price for any unusual trading activity that might indicate new information that might affect the company's business risk.

Company Sources

Other early information-gathering activities include (1) reviewing the corporate charter and bylaws or partnership agreement, (2) reviewing contracts, agreements, and legal proceedings, and (3) reading the minutes of the meetings of directors and committees of the board of directors. The minutes provide a history of the company, critical events and transactions, and future company intentions. A company's failure to provide minutes is a significant scope limitation that could result in the public accounting firm's disclaiming an opinion on the company's financial statements.

Information from Client Acceptance or Continuance Evaluation, Audit Planning, Past Audits, and Other Engagements

A great deal of information about the client is gathered in the pre-engagement planning process discussed in Chapter 3. Auditors evaluate the competence and integrity of management and the riskiness of the business before taking or continuing a client. As noted, the best indicator of the risk of a material misstatement is the presence of misstatements in previous audits that required adjusting entries. For example, for nonpublic clients, public accounting firms often develop client income tax provisions once the audit is complete; thus, the income tax adjusting entry would show up as

What's in the Minutes of Meetings?

Boards of directors are responsible for monitoring their company's business. The minutes of their meetings and the meetings of their committees (e.g., executive committee, finance committee, compensation committee, and audit committee) frequently contain information of vital interest to the independent auditors. Some information examples follow:

- Amount of dividends declared.
- Elections of officers and authorization of officers' salaries.
- Authorization of stock options and other incentive compensation arrangements.
- Acceptance of contracts, agreements, and lawsuit settlements.
- Approval of major purchases of property and investments.
- Discussions of possible mergers and divestitures.
- Authorization of financing by stock issuance, long-term debt issuance, and leases.
- Approval to pledge assets as security for debts.
- Discussion of negotiations on bank loans and payment waivers.
- Approval of accounting policies and accounting for estimates and unusual transactions.
- Authorizations of individuals to sign bank checks.

Auditors take notes or make copies of important parts of these minutes and compare them to information in the accounts and disclosures (e.g., compare the amount of dividends declared to the amount paid, compare officers' authorized salaries to amounts paid, compare agreements to pledge assets to proper disclosure in the notes to financial statements).

---

an adjustment every year. Finally, auditors who have industry expertise often have more than one client in that industry, so they can transfer general knowledge of risks encountered in other clients while maintaining confidentiality standards required by the profession.

Preliminary Analytical Procedures (AU 520, AU 329)

The auditors' own analyses of the client's financial statements can contribute a significant understanding of the business and how it has operated for the period covered by the financial statements. **Analytical procedures** are *reasonableness tests;* auditors compare their estimates of account balances with those recorded by management. According to auditing standards, *analytical procedures* must be applied in the planning stages of each audit. During this critical point of the engagement, auditors use analytical procedures to identify potential problem areas so that subsequent audit work can be designed to reduce the risk of missing something important. Analytical procedures during planning also provide an organized approach—a standard starting place—for becoming familiar with the client's business. Auditors need to remember that preliminary analytical procedures are based on unaudited data, so they should consider the effectiveness of controls over their reliability when deciding how much weight to place on the results.

Auditors should perform five steps when completing analytical procedures:

1. *Develop an expectation.* A variety of sources can provide evidence for auditors' expectations of the balance in a particular account:
   - Comparison of current-year account balances to balances for one or more comparable periods (e.g., vertical and horizontal analyses).
   - Comparison of the current-year account balances to anticipated results found in the company's budgets and forecasts.
   - Evaluation of the relationships (ratios) of current-year account balances to other current-year balances for conformity with predictable patterns based on the company's experience.
   - Comparison of current-year account balances and financial relationships (e.g., ratios) with similar information for the industry in which the company operates.
   - Study of the relationships of current-year account balances with relevant nonfinancial information (e.g., physical production statistics).

2. *Define a significant difference.* Basically, the question is, "What percentage (or dollar) difference from your expectation can still be considered reasonable?" It is important that this decision be made *before* making the comparison to prevent auditors from rationalizing differences and failing to follow up.
3. *Compare expectation with the recorded amount.* Many auditors start with comparative financial statements and calculate year-to-year changes in balance-sheet and income-statement accounts (**horizontal analysis**). They next calculate common-size statements (**vertical analysis**) in which financial statement amounts are expressed as percentages of a base, such as sales for the income-statement accounts or total assets for the balance-sheet accounts. These initial calculations (see Exhibit 4.11) provide a basis for describing the financial activities for the current year under audit. Although vertical and horizontal analyses are basic beginning analytical procedures; other analytical procedures; including mathematical time series and regression calculations, complicated comparisons of multiyear data, and trend and ratio analyses can be more complex.
4. *Investigate significant differences.* Auditors typically look for relationships that do not make sense as indicators of problems in the accounts, and they use such indicators to plan additional audit work. In the planning stage, analytical procedures are used to identify potential problem areas so that subsequent audit work can be designed

EXHIBIT 4.11 Dunder-Mifflin, Inc.—Preliminary Analytical Procedures Data

	Prior Year		Current Year		Change	
	Balance	Common Size	Balance	Common Size	Amount	Percent Change
Income						
Sales (net)	$9,000,000	100.00%	$9,900,000	100.00%	$ 900,000	10.00%
Cost of goods sold	6,750,000	75.00	7,200,000	72.73	450,000	6.67
Gross margin	2,250,000	25.00	2,700,000	27.27	450,000	20.00
General expense	1,590,000	17.67	1,734,000	17.52	144,000	9.06
Depreciation	300,000	3.33	300,000	3.03	0	0.00
Operating income	360,000	4.00	666,000	6.46	306,000	85.00
Interest expense	60,000	0.67	40,000	0.40	(20,000)	−33.33
Income taxes (40%)	120,000	1.33	256,000	2.59	136,000	113.33
Net income	$ 180,000	2.00%	$ 370,000	3.74%	$ 190,000	105.56%
Assets						
Cash	$ 600,000	14.78%	$ 200,000	4.12%	($400,000)	−66.67%
Accounts receivable	500,000	12.32	900,000	18.56	400,000	80.00
Allowance for doubtful accounts	(40,000)	−0.99	(50,000)	−1.03	(10,000)	25.00
Inventory	1,500,000	36.95	1,600,000	32.99	100,000	6.67
Total current assets	2,560,000	63.05	2,650,000	54.63	90,000	3.52
Equipment	3,000,000	73.89	4,000,000	82.47	1,000,000	33.33
Accumulated depreciation	(1,500,000)	−36.95	(1,800,000)	−37.11	(300,000)	20.00
Total assets	$4,060,000	100.00%	$4,850,000	100.00%	$ 790,000	19.46%
Liabilities and Equity						
Accounts payable	$ 500,000	12.32%	$ 400,000	8.25%	($100,000)	−20.00%
Bank loans, 11%	0	0.00	750,000	15.46	750,000	
Accrued interest	60,000	1.48	40,000	0.82	(20,000)	−33.33
Total current liabilities	560,000	13.79	1,190,000	24.53	630,000	112.50
Long−term debt, 10%	600,000	14.78	400,000	8.25	(200,000)	−33.33
Total liabilities	1,160,000	28.57	1,590,000	32.78	430,000	37.07
Capital stock	2,000,000	49.26	2,000,000	41.24	0	0.00
Retained earnings	900,000	22.17	1,260,000	25.98	360,000	40.00
Total liabilities and equity	$4,060,000	100.00%	$4,850,000	100.00%	$ 790,000	19.46%

to reduce the risk of missing something important. The application demonstrated here can be described as *attention directing:* pointing out accounts that could contain errors and frauds. The insights derived from *preliminary* analytical procedures do not provide direct evidence about the numbers in the financial statements. Although the insights derived from preliminary analytical procedures provide only limited evidence about the numbers in the financial statements, they do help auditors identify risks as an aid in preparing the audit plan.

5. *Document each of the preceding steps.*

For companies that have not undergone any significant changes in operations, current-year recorded amounts should be fairly similar to those of the prior year (step 1). Because changes are not expected, auditors can identify any changes over 10 percent and $100,000 as deserving additional attention (step 2). Note that the threshold is *both* 10 percent *and* $100,000 instead of just one trigger or the other. A change in an account balance from $100 to $200 is a 100 percent change, but the change is clearly immaterial. Similarly, an increase in sales from $9.9 million to $10 million meets the $100,000 threshold but does not appear unreasonable in percentage terms. In Step 3, auditors compare expectations with the recorded balances. Exhibit 4.11 contains financial balances for the prior year (consider them audited) and the current year (consider them unaudited at this stage). Common-size statements (vertical analysis) are shown in parallel columns, and the dollar amount and percentage change (horizontal analysis) are shown in the last two columns.

The investigation of significant differences (step 4) is probably the most critical step in the analytical procedures process. After generating basic financial data and relationships, the next step is to determine whether the financial changes and relationships actually describe what is going on within the company. According to the current-year unaudited financial statements in Exhibit 4.11, the company increased net income by increasing sales 10 percent, reducing cost of goods sold as a proportion of sales, and controlling other expenses. At least some of the sales growth appears to have been prompted by easier credit (accounts receivable increased by 80 percent) and more service (more equipment in use). The company also appears to have used much of its cash and borrowed more to purchase the equipment, to make its payment on the long-term debt, and to pay dividends. Inventory and cost of goods sold, on the other hand, remained fairly constant compared to the previous year with both accounts increasing by only 6.7 percent.

The next step is to ask, "What could be wrong?" and "What errors and frauds, as well as legitimate explanations, could account for these financial results?" For these explanations, we limit our attention to the Accounts Receivable and Inventory accounts. At this point, some other ratios can help support the analysis. Exhibit 4.12 contains several familiar ratios (Appendix 4A at the end of this chapter contains these ratios and their formulas).

- *Question:* Are the accounts receivable collectible? (*Alternative:* Is the allowance for doubtful accounts large enough?) Easier credit can lead to more bad debts. The company has a much larger amount of receivables, the days' sales in receivables has increased significantly, the receivables turnover has decreased, and the allowance for doubtful accounts is smaller in proportion to the receivables. If the prior year's allowance for bad debts at 8 percent of receivables was appropriate and conditions have not become worse, it could be that the allowance should be closer to $72,000 than $50,000. The auditors should work carefully on the evidence related to accounts receivable valuation.

- *Question:* Could the inventory be overstated? (*Alternative:* Could the cost of the goods sold be understated?) Overstatement of the ending inventory would cause the cost of goods sold to be understated. The percentage of cost of goods sold to sales shows a decrease. If 75 percent of the prior year represents a more accurate cost of goods sold

EXHIBIT 4.12
Dunder-Mifflin, Inc.—Selected Financial Ratios

	Prior Year	Current Year	Percent Change
Balance-Sheet Ratios			
Current ratio	4.57	2.23	−51.29%
Days' sales in receivables	18.40	30.91	67.98
Doubtful accounts ratio	0.0800	0.0556	−30.56
Days' sales in inventory	80.00	80.00	0.00
Debt/equity ratio	0.40	0.49	21.93
Operations Ratios			
Receivables turnover	19.57	11.65	−40.47
Inventory turnover	4.50	4.50	0.00
Cost of goods sold/Sales	75.00%	72.73%	−3.03
Gross margin percentage	25.00%	27.27%	9.09
Return on beginning equity	6.62%	12.76%	92.80
Financial Distress Ratios (Altman)			
Working capital/Total assets	0.49	0.30	−38.89
Retained earnings/Total assets	0.22	0.26	17.20
EBIT/Total assets	0.09	0.14	54.87
Market value of equity/Total debt	2.59	1.89	−27.04
Net sales/Total assets	2.22	2.04	−7.92
Discriminant Z-score	4.96	4.35	−12.32

amount, then the income before taxes could be overstated by $225,000 (75 percent of $9.9 million minus $7.2 million unaudited cost of goods sold). The days' sales in inventory and the inventory turnover remained the same, but you could expect them to change in light of the larger volume of sales. Careful work on the physical count and valuation of inventory appears to be needed.

Other questions can be asked and other relationships derived when industry statistics are available. Industry statistics can be obtained from such services as Yahoo! Finance, Dun & Bradstreet, and Standard & Poor's. These statistics include industry averages for important financial benchmarks such as gross profit margin, return on sales, current ratio, debt/net worth, and various others. A comparison with client data can reveal out-of-line statistics, indicating a relatively strong feature of the company, a weak financial position, or possibly an error or misstatement in the client's financial statements. However, care must be taken with industry statistics. A particular company could or could not be well represented by industry averages.

Comparing reported financial results with internal budgets and forecasts also can be useful. If the budget or forecast represents management's estimate of probable future outcomes, planning questions can arise for items that fall short of or exceed the budget. If a company that expected to sell 10,000 units of a product sold only 5,000 units, the auditors would want to plan a careful lower-of-cost-or-market study of the inventory of unsold units (*valuation*). If 15,000 were sold, an auditor would want to audit for sales validity (*occurrence*). Budget comparisons can be tricky, however. Some companies use budgets and forecasts as goals rather than as expressions of probable outcomes. Also, meeting the budget with little or no shortfall or excess can result from managers' manipulating the numbers to "meet the budget." Auditors must be careful to know something about an entity's business conditions from sources other than the internal records when analyzing comparisons with budgets and forecasts to determine inherent risk.

Cash flow analysis enables the auditors to see the crucial information of cash flow from operating, investing, and financing activities. A cash flow deficit from operations can signal financial difficulty. Companies fail when they run out of cash (no surprise) and are unable to pay their debts when they become due. Professional auditing standards state that auditors are responsible for letting financial statement users know whether they have substantial doubts as to whether the client will be able to survive into subsequent periods (i.e., whether the company can remain a *going concern*), and cash flow analysis is a good starting place.

AUDITING INSIGHT — Some Examples of Analytical Procedures

- Auditors noticed large quantities of rolled steel in the company's inventory. Several 60,000-pound rolls were entered in the inventory list. The false entries were detected because the auditor knew the company's forklift trucks had a 20,000-pound lifting capacity.
- Auditors could have compared the total quantity of vegetable oils the company claimed to have inventoried in its tanks to the storage capacity reported in national export statistics. The company's "quantity on hand" amounted to 90 percent of the national supply and greatly exceeded its own tank capacity.
- Last year's audit documentation showed that company employees had failed to accrue wages payable at the year-end date. A search for the current accrual entry showed it had again been forgotten.
- Auditors developed a complex regression model to estimate the electric utility company's total revenue. They used empirical relations of fuel consumption, meteorological reports of weather conditions, and population census data in the area. The regression model estimated revenue within close range of the reported revenue.
- Auditors for a small regional airline calculated an estimate of airline revenue by multiplying the number of company planes times an estimate of the number of flights made by each plane in a year times the number of seats on each plane times an estimate of the average ticket price. The revenue reported by the airline was significantly higher than the auditors' estimate, meaning that either more than one person was sitting in the same seat at the same time (!) or that the auditors needed to more closely examine recorded revenue transactions. Additional investigation discovered that the airline was fraudulently overstating its revenues.

Analytical procedures are required (1) at the beginning of an audit—the planning stage application of analytical procedures discussed in this chapter and (2) at the end of an audit when the partners in charge review the overall quality of the work and look for apparent problems. They can also be used as substantive procedures for predictable accounts such as interest expense. Problems (unexpected relationships) identified at the beginning of the audit may be later corrected by adjusting entries when additional substantive procedures are conducted. However, those same adjusting entries can result in other balances becoming unreasonable. Auditors conclude their analytical procedures testing by documenting the team's findings (step 5).

AUDIT INSIGHT — Analytical Procedures in Practice

Recent interviews with 36 practicing auditors found that recent corporate scandals and the ensuing Sarbanes Oxley Act, along with the advent of improved technology, have led to the following changes in how firms perform analytical procedures:

- Increased use of analytical procedures.
- Development of more precise, quantitative expectations.
- Gathering broader industry and company information, including nonfinancial information.
- Reliance on analytical procedures more to decrease substantive tests of detail.
- Less experienced staff conduct (but do not design) a larger portion of analytical procedures.
- Increased consideration of underlying controls.

Source: G. Trompeter and A. Wright, "The World Has Changed - Have Analytical Procedure Practices?", *Contemporary Accounting Research* 27 (2), 2010 669–700.

Audit Team Discussions (Brainstorming)

The risk assessment process includes *required* audit team brainstorming sessions in which critical audit areas are discussed. These sessions update audit team members on important aspects of the audit and heighten team members' awareness of the potential for fraud and errors in the engagement. Items typically discussed include previous experiences with the client, how a fraud might be perpetrated and concealed by the client, and procedures that might detect fraud. When studying a business operation, auditors' ability to think like a crook and devise ways to steal can help in creating procedures to determine whether fraud has happened. Often imaginative extended procedures can be employed to unearth evidence of fraudulent activity.

A secondary objective of the discussions is to set a proper tone for the engagement. These sessions address not only fraud risk but also other client business and audit-related risk assessments. While these brainstorming sessions typically begin during the planning phase of the engagements, they should be held on a continual basis through the conclusion of the engagement.

Many firms have fraud specialists that assist audit teams throughout the risk assessment process. If such a specialist is assigned to the audit, their involvement during brainstorming sessions is particularly important because they are particularly adept at identifying critical audit areas and how these areas influence the risk of misstatement due to fraud.

AUDITING INSIGHT — Brainstorming Best Practices

- An engagement partner or forensic specialist is the best choice to lead the brainstorming session, but the use of group decision software (which protects individuals' identities) allows each engagement team member to participate freely without fear of intimidation or repercussion. Managers and partners should be active participants.
- Audit team members should be reminded of the purpose of the brainstorming session and stress the importance of professional skepticism.
- A good strategy is to discuss material misstatements found in previous audits and/or frauds found on similar engagements.
- Checklists should be used sparingly so as not to inhibit discussion with client staff. However, if they are used, fully discuss each item on the list and don't limit discussions solely to items on the checklist. In other words, consider what might have been left off the checklist.
- The idea-generation phase should be separated from the idea-evaluation phase. Considering each threat as it is brought up may cause individuals to feel slighted and may inhibit further idea generation. Engagement team members should be encouraged to discuss why they feel an identified risk is important.
- Time should be set aside at the end of the session to indicate how the audit plan should be modified as a result of the discussions.
- An IT audit specialist should attend.
- The session should be held during preplanning or early in the planning stage.
- It should include discussion of how management might perpetrate fraud and audit responses to fraud risk.

Sources: M. Landis, S. Jerris, and M. Braswell, "Better Brainstorming," *Journal of Accountancy*, October 2008, pp. 70–73; J. F. Brazel, T. D. Carpenter, and J. G. Jenkins," *The Accounting Review* 85 (4), 2010: 1273–1301.

Inquiry of Audit Committee, Management, and Others within the Company

Interviewing the entity's management, internal auditors, directors, the audit committee, and other employees is a required audit process that can bring auditors up to date on changes in the business and the industry. Such inquiries of client personnel have the multiple purposes of building personal working relationships, observing the competence and integrity of client personnel, obtaining a general understanding, and probing for problem areas that could harbor financial misstatements. Issues to discuss include selection of accounting principles; susceptibility to errors and fraud, including known or suspected fraud; and how management controls and monitors fraud risks. Other company employees to question might include operations or marketing managers or those involved in complex or unusual transactions.

Another source of information is company discussion boards (such as those found on Yahoo.com) where anonymous whistle-blowers can post information that management may not wish to disclose to auditors.

> ### AUDITING INSIGHT Auditors Fail to Respond to Warning Signs at HealthSouth
>
> After failing to get the auditors' attention through direct e-mail, former **HealthSouth** bookkeeper Michael Vines tried to expose HealthSouth's accounting fraud on Yahoo's bulletin board forum devoted to the company. He wrote, "What I know about the accounting at [HealthSouth] will bring [the company] to its knees . . . what is going on at [HealthSouth], if discovered by the right people will bring change to the accounting department if not the entire company." Although it was prophetic, the auditors did not heed his warnings. They were, however, noticed by HealthSouth security personnel who were able to identify Vines through his Yahoo ID (which contained some digits from his social security number). What HealthSouth officials intended to do with the information never came to light. One month later, the SEC filed a civil lawsuit alleging "massive accounting fraud" followed quickly by criminal indictments of key executives.
>
> Source: "Ex-Employee Took His Case to Auditors, Then Internet—but Convinced No One," *The Wall Street Journal*, May 20, 2003, pp. A1, A13.

Assessing Risk Factors

Once risk factors have been identified, auditors have a better understanding of the potential for material misstatement. This includes evaluating the risk that a significant disclosure might be misleading or omitted. The auditors' next task is to assess the types of risk present, the likelihood that material misstatement has occurred, the magnitude of the risk (usually measured in dollars), and the pervasiveness of the potential for misstatement (how widespread the threat is). Auditors should evaluate how risks at the financial statement level could affect risks of misstatement at the assertion level. Auditors also consider controls evaluated in the assessment of control risk and the expected results of tests of controls (Chapter 5) in determining the likelihood of material misstatement.

In addition to the risk assessment based on factors identified, *auditing standards* require several other fraud risk assessments. First, auditors must presume that *improper revenue recognition* is a fraud risk. Another risk is that, despite the existence of controls, *management* might *override* the controls through force of authority. Because several major frauds were committed through year-end adjusting entries (such as **WorldCom**'s capitalization of telephone line expenses), auditors must examine journal entries and other adjustments (especially those made close to year-end). If any significant unusual accounting entries are identified, auditors must evaluate the business rationale for the transactions. Team members gather information necessary to identify key fraud risk factors (red flags) indicating an increased potential for fraud to occur.

Respond to Significant Risks *(AU 330, AS 15)*

Significant risks are those risks that require special audit consideration because of the nature of the risk or the likelihood and potential magnitude of misstatement related to the risk. By definition, fraud risks are significant risks. Auditors should specifically examine controls and design tests to address significant risks. Auditors should evaluate quantitative and qualitative risk factors on the likelihood and potential magnitude of misstatements. They should consider whether the risk is related to recent significant economic, accounting, or other developments; the complexity of transactions; whether the risk involves related parties; the degree of complexity or judgment required and uncertainty involved; and whether the risk involves significant transactions that are unusual or outside the company's normal course of business.

Auditors must next respond to the results of the risk assessments. Using the audit risk model, the auditor adjusts detection risk for *significant accounts* and *relevant disclosures*. Additional considerations must be made for risks identified as *significant risks*. For example, if the potential for fraud is high, auditors should include more experienced team members. Other responses include examining more transactions, performing **extended procedures**, including targeting tests toward higher risk areas, performing more tests of transactions at year-end rather than at interim points, and gathering higher quality evidence. Finally, the auditors should use less predictable audit procedures such as "surprise" inventory observations in which management is not told at which company warehouse locations auditors will show up to watch the client counting inventory or extended procedures such as using larger sample sizes.

Evaluate Accumulated Results of Audit Procedures

When collecting corroborating evidence to support the financial statements, auditors must remain vigilant to the potential for fraud. Discrepancies in the accounting records, conflicting evidence, and missing documentation are all symptomatic of financial statement fraud. When such instances are identified, auditors must follow up with management to identify the source of the problems. Management's response is a key source of evidence; vague, implausible, or inconsistent responses to inquiries can be a key indicator of the pervasiveness of the fraud. Similarly, problematic or unusual reactions such as refusal to cooperate, hostility, or management delays in responding to the auditors are often present in financial statement frauds. The evaluation for potential fraud continues throughout the audit. Audit team members must be on the lookout for unusual findings or events and, upon discovery, not simply write them off as isolated occurrences.

Communicate Fraud Risks

Auditors must always exercise technical and personal care because accusations of fraud are always taken very seriously. For this reason, if preliminary findings indicate fraud possibilities, auditors should enlist the cooperation of management and assist fraud examination professionals when bringing an investigation to a conclusion.

Standards for external auditors contain materiality thresholds related to auditors reporting their knowledge of frauds. Auditors may consider some minor frauds clearly inconsequential, especially when they involve misappropriations of assets by employees at low organizational levels. Auditors should report these to management at least one level above the people involved. The idea is that small matters can be kept in the management family. Having said this, fraud has often been compared to an iceberg: most of it can be hidden from sight. For this reason, auditors should be extremely cautious in deciding whether a fraud is "clearly inconsequential."

On the other hand, frauds involving senior managers or employees with significant internal control roles are never inconsequential and should be reported (along with any frauds that cause material misstatement in the financial statements) directly to those charged with governance, usually the entity's *audit committee* of its board of directors. All companies with securities traded on the exchanges (e.g., New York, American, and NASDAQ) are required to have audit committees. **Audit committees** are composed of independent, outside members of the board of directors (those not involved in the company's day-to-day operations) who can provide a buffer between the audit firm and management. *Auditing standards* set forth requirements intended to ensure that audit committees are informed about the scope and results of the independent audit.[6] External

---

[6] Audit standards have broadened communications to include groups that serve in a similar role for private companies and refers to such groups as "those charged with governance." Audit committees serve in this role for public companies.

auditors are required to make oral or written communications about other topics, including the discovery of fraud.

Auditors are normally required to keep client information confidential. However, under AICPA auditing standards, limited disclosures to outside agencies of frauds and clients' noncompliance are permitted. If the audit firm resigns or is fired, the firm can cite these matters in the letter attached to SEC Form 8-K, which requires explanation of an organization's change of auditors. An ex-auditor may tell the successor auditor about the client when the successor makes the inquiries required by auditing standards. Auditors must respond when answering a subpoena issued by a court or other agency with authority. When performing work under GAO-mandated generally accepted government auditing standards, auditors are required to report frauds and noncompliance to the client agency under the audit contract.

Document Risk Assessment

The last step involves documenting the risk assessment process in writing to provide a record of the procedures performed. Items that must be documented include these:

- Discussions with engagement personnel.
- Procedures to identify and assess risk.
- Significant decisions during discussion.
- Specific risks identified and audit team responses.
- Explanation of why improper revenue recognition is *not* a risk.
- Results of audit procedures, particularly procedures regarding management override.
- Other conditions causing auditors to believe that additional procedures are required.
- Communications to management and those charged with governance, such as the audit committee.

↳ REVIEW CHECKPOINTS

4.13 What are some types of knowledge and understanding about a client's business and industry that an auditor is expected to obtain? What are some of the methods and sources of information for understanding a client's business and industry?

4.14 What is the purpose of performing preliminary analytical procedures in the audit planning stage?

4.15 What are the five steps involved with the use of preliminary analytical procedures?

4.16 What are some of the ratios that can be used in preliminary analytical procedures?

4.17 When are analytical procedures required, and when are they optional?

▽ AUDITORS' RESPONSIBILITIES FOR NONCOMPLIANCE WITH LAWS AND REGULATIONS (AU 350, AS 17)

LEARNING OBJECTIVE 4-6
Explain auditors' responsibilities with respect to a client's failure to comply with laws or regulations.

In addition to errors and fraud, a client's noncompliance with laws and regulations can cause financial statements to be materially misstated, and external auditors are advised to be aware of circumstances that could indicate noncompliance (Exhibit 4.13). Auditors are not required to be legal experts, but they must understand the legal and regulatory framework under which their client operates and how the entity is compliant with that framework. *Auditing standards* deal with two types of *noncompliance:* (1) **direct-effect noncompliance,** which produces direct and material effects on financial statement amounts (e.g., violations of tax or pension laws or government contracting regulations

EXHIBIT 4.13
Indicators of NonCompliance

The following can be indicators of a company's noncompliance:
- Investigations, fines, or penalties
- Payments for unspecified services or loans to consultants, related parties, employees, or government employees
- Excessive sales commissions or agent's fees
- Purchases significantly above or below market
- Unusual payments in cash, cashiers' checks to bearer, or transfers to numbered accounts
- Unusual transactions with companies in tax havens
- Payments to countries other than origination
- Inadequate audit trail
- Unauthorized or improperly recorded transactions
- Media comment
- Noncompliance cited in reports of examinations
- Failure to file tax returns or pay government duties or fees

for cost and revenue recognition) that require the same assurance as errors and frauds (i.e., auditors must plan their work to provide reasonable assurance there are no material misstatements), and (2) **indirect-effect noncompliance**, which refers to violations of laws and regulations that are not directly connected to financial statements (e.g., violations relating to insider securities trading, occupational health and safety, food and drug administration regulations, environmental protection, and equal employment opportunity).

Indirect effect compliance may be fundamental to operations, fundamental to the company's ability to continue business or necessary to avoid material penalties (e.g., terms of operating licenses, regulatory solvency requirements, or environmental regulations). Auditor responsibility for detecting *indirect-effect noncompliance* is limited to performing specified audit procedures that may identify noncompliance with those laws and regulations that may have a material effect on the financial statements, making inquiry of management and those charged with governance, and inspection of correspondence with relevant licensing or regulatory authorities

Auditors must respond to noncompliance or suspected noncompliance identified during the audit. First, they must gain an understanding of the nature and circumstances of the noncompliance and then evaluate the possible effect on financial statements. The noncompliance should be discussed with management at a level above the person responsible for the noncompliance. If noncompliance is "clearly inconsequential," that may be the extent of the follow up. Noncompliance or suspected noncompliance having financial statement effects of more than this threshold should be reported to those charged with governance such as the audit committee, and the financial statements should contain adequate disclosures about the organization's noncompliance. Discussion with the client's legal counsel may also be necessary. External auditors always have the option to withdraw from an engagement if management and directors do not take satisfactory action under the circumstances.

The Private Securities Litigation Reform Act of 1995 imposed another reporting obligation. Under this law, when auditors believe an illegal act that is more than "clearly inconsequential" has or could have occurred, the auditors must inform the organization's board of directors. When the auditors believe the illegal act has a material effect on the financial statements, the board of directors has one business day to inform the U.S. Securities and Exchange Commission (SEC). If the board decides not to inform the SEC, the auditors must (1) within one business day give the SEC the same report they gave the board of directors or (2) resign from the engagement and, within one business day, give the SEC the report. If the auditors do not fulfill this legal obligation, the SEC can impose a civil penalty (e.g., monetary fine) on them.

AUDITING INSIGHT — Chiquita Caught Supporting Paramilitary Operations?

In early 2003, the head of **Chiquita Brands International Inc.**'s audit committee confessed to the U.S. Department of Justice that the company had been making illegal payments to a violent Colombian terrorist group. In March 2007, Chiquita pled guilty to engaging in transactions with a terrorist group and agreed to pay $25 million in fines, marking the first time that a major U.S. company has been charged with having financial dealings with terrorists. It seems that the company continued to make illegal payments for almost a year after its confession to the Department of Justice. The company began the illegal payments (estimated at around $1.7 million over seven years) after a Colombian paramilitary organization threatened to kidnap or kill employees on Chiquita's banana farms.

Chiquita is not the only company facing charges with engaging in illegal activity. **Schnitzer Steel Industries** pleaded guilty and paid $7.5 million in fines for offering kickbacks to its Chinese customers, **Baker Hughes Inc.** paid $21 million in fines to settle a Nigerian bribery scandal, and officials from **Siemens AG** traveled the globe with suitcases full of cash, paying more than a billion dollars in bribes to win lucrative public works contracts in countries such as Argentina, Bangladesh, and Venezuela. The German engineering company has been fined a total of $1.6 billion in fines to U.S. and German authorities. The company pleaded guilty to charges under the Foreign Corrupt Practices Act for failing to maintain proper internal controls and keeping required records. The fine is the largest ever under that statute.

Source: "Chiquita under the Gun," *The Wall Street Journal*, August 2, 2007, p. A1; http://www.washingtontimes.com/news/2008/dec/16/siemens-guilty-of-global-fraud/

REVIEW CHECKPOINT

4.18 How do the standards differ for (a) errors, (b) frauds, (c) direct-effect noncompliance, and (d) indirect-effect noncompliance?

AUDIT STRATEGY MEMORANDUM

LEARNING OBJECTIVE 4-7
Describe the content and purpose of an audit strategy.

The *audit plan* discussed in Chapter 3, which summarizes all of the important planning information and serves to document that auditors have followed generally auditing standards, includes a description of the **audit strategy**. After assessing the overall financial statement risks, determining which accounts are significant, and which assertions are relevant to those accounts, the auditor should establish an overall audit strategy that sets the scope, timing, and direction for auditing each relevant assertion. The strategy is a result of the audit risk model. If auditors believe they can rely on company controls to mitigate risks, they test the controls as described in Chapter 5. Depending on the results of such tests, the auditors determine the nature, timing, and extent of substantive procedures. If the auditors identified fraud risk or other significant risks or noncompliance with laws and regulations, they specifically address them in the strategy, including the possibility of adding fraud specialists to the team or by expanding testing.

In establishing the overall audit strategy, the auditor should take into account (1) the reporting objectives of the engagement and the nature of the communications required by auditing standards, (2) the factors that are significant in directing the activities of the engagement team, and (3) the results of preliminary engagement activities and the auditor's evaluation risk assessment. Also, various laws or regulations may require other matters to be communicated. The strategy should outline the nature, timing, and extent of *resources* necessary to perform the engagement. Planned tests of controls, substantive procedures, and other planned audit procedures required to be performed so that the engagement complies with auditing standards should be documented with specific directions about the effect on the audit.

The strategy becomes a basis for preparing the audit plans for each significant account and disclosure (often called *audit programs*), which list the audit procedures to be performed by auditors to gather sufficient appropriate evidence on which to base their opinion on the financial statements. The professional auditing standards require a *written* audit plan that documents the audit strategy on each engagement. An example of an audit strategy memorandum is presented in Appendix 4B.

> ↳ **REVIEW CHECKPOINT**
>
> 4.19 What is the purpose of an audit strategy? What information should it contain?

Summary

Risk assessment is the common language of auditing. *Business risk* is the risk that the client will not meet its objectives. Managers may use the ERM framework developed by COSO to identify and mitigate such risks. *Information risk* is the risk the financial statements will be inaccurate or misleading and can be reduced by having the financial statements audited. *Audit risk* is the risk assumed by the auditors that they could express an incorrect opinion on financial statements that are materially misstated as a result of errors or fraud. The audit risk model decomposes audit risk into three components: *inherent risk, control risk,* and *detection risk.* Inherent risk involves the susceptibility of accounts to misstatement (assuming that no controls are present). Control risk addresses the effectiveness (or lack thereof) of the controls in preventing or detecting misstatements. Inherent and control risk are often combined and referred to as the *risk of material misstatement.* Detection risk involves the effectiveness of the auditors' procedures in detecting fraud or misstatement. Solving for detection risk in the audit risk model yields guidance for the preparation of the audit plan and the nature, timing, and extent of audit procedures to be performed.

Risk assessment starts with knowledge of the types of errors and frauds that can be perpetrated. It involves understanding the company, its industry, and its environment. Auditors assess risk by obtaining public and internal information, holding team brainstorming discussions, performing analytical procedures and inquiring of management, directors, and key employees. Auditors respond to identified risks by increasing the effectiveness of their procedures and employing specialists and experienced personnel when necessary. Audit strategies are the auditors' summary of their assessment and how they will respond to identified risks, particularly significant risks, which include the risk of fraud. Audit strategies are documented in the audit plan.

Key Terms

accounting estimates: The approximations of financial statement numbers often included in financial statements, 135

analytical procedures: The reasonableness tests used to gain an understanding of financial statement accounts and relationships, 138

audit committee: A subset of a company's board of directors composed of outside members (those not involved in the day-to-day operations of the company) who can provide a buffer between the audit firm and management, 145

audit risk: The risk that the auditor will express an inappropriate audit opinion when the financial statements are materially misstated (e.g., giving an unqualified opinion on financial statements that are misleading because of material misstatements the auditors failed to discover), 127

audit strategy: The scope, timing, and direction for auditing each relevant assertion based on the results of the audit risk model, 148

business risks: The risks that result from significant conditions, events, circumstances, actions, or inactions that could adversely affect a company's ability to achieve its objectives and execute its strategies as well as from setting inappropriate objectives and strategies or from changes or complexity in the company's operations or management, 118

control risk: The probability that the client's internal control activities will *fail* to prevent or detect material misstatements provided that they enter or would have entered the accounting system in the first place, 128

defalcation: Another name for employee fraud and embezzlement, 126

detection risk: The probability that audit procedures will *fail* to produce evidence of material misstatements, provided any have entered or would have entered the accounting system in the first place and have not been prevented or detected and corrected by the client's control activities, 128

direct-effect noncompliance: The violations of laws or government regulations by the entity or its management or employees that produce direct and material effects on dollar amounts in financial statements, 146

embezzlement: A type of fraud involving employees or nonemployees wrongfully taking money or property entrusted to their care, custody, and control, often accompanied by false accounting entries and other forms of lying and cover-up, 126

employee fraud: The use of fraudulent means to take money or other property from an employer. It consists of three phases: (1) the fraudulent act, (2) the conversion of the money or property to the fraudster's use, and (3) the cover-up, 126

enterprise risk management (ERM): A process effected by an entity's board of directors, management, and other personnel applied in strategy setting and across the enterprise that is designed to identify potential events that may affect the entity and to manage risks to be within its risk appetite to provide reasonable assurance regarding the achievement of entity objectives, 119

errors: The unintentional misstatements or omissions of amounts or disclosures in financial statements, 126

extended procedures: The audit procedures used in response to heightened fraud awareness as the result of the identification of significant risks, 145

fraud: The act of knowingly making material misrepresentations of fact with the intent of inducing someone to believe the falsehood and act on it and, thus, suffer a loss or damage, 122

fraudulent financial reporting: The intentional or reckless conduct, whether by act or omission, that results in materially misstated financial statements, 123

horizontal analysis: The comparative analysis of year-to-year changes in balance-sheet and income-statement accounts, 139

indirect-effect noncompliance: The violation of laws and regulations that does not directly affect specific financial statement accounts or disclosures (e.g., violations relating to insider securities trading, occupational health and safety, food and drug administration regulations, environmental protection, and equal employment opportunity), 147

information risk: The probability that the information circulated by an entity will be false or misleading, 121

inherent risk: The probability that in the absence of internal controls, material errors or frauds could enter the accounting system used to develop financial statements, 127

larceny: The simple theft of an employer's property that is not entrusted to an employee's care, custody, or control, 126

management fraud: The deliberate fraud committed by management that injures investors and creditors through materially misleading information, 123

relevant assertion: A financial statement assertion that has a reasonable possibility of containing a misstatement or misstatements that would cause the financial statements to be materially misstated, 127

related parties: Those individuals or organizations that are closely tied to the auditee, possibly through family ties or investment relationships, 134

risk of material misstatement (RMM): The combined inherent and control risk; in other words, the likelihood that material misstatements may have entered the accounting system and not been detected and corrected by the client's internal control, 127

significant account or disclosure: An account or disclosure that has a reasonable possibility of containing a material misstatement individually or when aggregated with others regardless of the effect of controls, 127

significant risk: A risk of material misstatement that requires special audit consideration. Fraud risk is always considered significant risk, 144

vertical analysis: The common-size analysis of financial statement amounts created by expressing amounts as proportions of a common base such as sales for the income-statement accounts or total assets for the balance-sheet accounts, 139

white collar crime: Fraud perpetrated by people who work in offices and steal a pencil or a computer terminal. The contrast is blue-collar crime (violent street crime), 125

Multiple-Choice Questions for Practice and Review

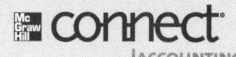 All applicable Exercises and Problems are available with McGraw-Hill's *Connect® Accounting*

LO 4-1

4.20 Enterprise risk management is the responsibility of:
   a. Company management.
   b. The external auditors.
   c. The company's insurance providers.
   d. All of the above.

LO 4-1

4.21 Failure to meet company objectives is a result of
   a. information risk.
   b. audit risk.
   c. business risk.
   d. inherent risk.

LO 4-2

4.22 Auditing standards do not require auditors of financial statements to
   a. Understand the nature of errors and frauds.
   b. Assess the risk of occurrence of errors and frauds.
   c. Design audits to provide reasonable assurance of detecting errors and frauds.
   d. Report all errors and frauds found to police authorities.

LO 4-2

4.23 If sales were overstated by recording a false credit sale at the end of the year, where could you find the false "dangling debit"?
   a. Inventory.
   b. Cost of goods sold.
   c. Bad debt expense.
   d. Accounts receivable.

LO 4-2

4.24 One of the typical characteristics of management fraud is
   a. Falsification of documents in order to misappropriate funds from an employer.
   b. Victimization of investors through the use of materially misleading financial statements.
   c. Illegal acts committed by management to evade laws and regulations.
   d. Conversion of stolen inventory to cash deposited in a falsified bank account.

LO 4-2

4.25 Which of the following circumstances would most likely cause an audit team to perform extended procedures?
   a. Supporting documents are produced when requested.
   b. The client made several large adjustments at or near year-end.
   c. The company has recently hired a new chief financial officer after the previous one retired.
   d. The company maintains several different petty cash funds.

LO 4-3

4.26 The likelihood that material misstatements may have entered the accounting system and not been detected and corrected by the client's internal control is referred to as
   a. Inherent risk.
   b. Control risk.
   c. Detection risk.
   d. Risk of material misstatement.

LO 4-3 4.27 The risk of material misstatements is composed of which audit risk components?
a. Inherent risk and control risk.
b. Control risk and detection risk.
c. Inherent risk and detection risk.
d. Inherent risk, control risk, and detection risk.

LO 4-3 4.28 The risk that the auditors' own procedures will lead to the decision that material misstatements do not exist in the financial statements when in fact such misstatements do exist is
a. Audit risk.
b. Inherent risk.
c. Control risk.
d. Detection risk.

LO 4-3 4.29 The auditors assessed risk of material misstatement at 0.50 and said they wanted to achieve a 0.05 risk of failing to express a correct opinion on financial statements that were materially misstated. What detection risk do the auditors plan to use for planning the remainder of the audit work?
a. 0.20.
b. 0.10.
c. 0.75.
d. 0.00.

LO 4-3 4.30 If tests of controls induce the audit team to change the assessed level of control risk for fixed assets from 0.4 to 1.0 and audit risk (0.05) and inherent risk remain constant, the acceptable level of detection risk is most likely to
a. Change from 0.1 to 0.04.
b. Change from 0.2 to 0.3.
c. Change from 0.25 to 0.1.
d. Be unchanged.

LO 4-4 4.31 Which of the following is a specific procedural response to a particular fraud risk in an account balance or class of transactions?
a. Exercising more professional skepticism.
b. Carefully avoiding conducting interviews with people in the fraud-rich areas.
c. Performing procedures such as inventory observation and cash counts on a surprise or unannounced basis.
d. Studying management's selection and application of accounting principles more carefully.

LO 4-4 4.32 Analytical procedures are generally used to produce evidence from
a. Confirmations mailed directly to the auditors by client customers.
b. Physical observation of inventories.
c. Relationships among current financial balances and prior balances, forecasts, and nonfinancial data.
d. Detailed examination of external, external-internal, and internal documents.

LO 4-4 4.33 Which of the following relationships between types of analytical procedures and sources of information are most logical?

Type of Analytical Procedure	Source of Information
a. Comparison of current account balances with prior periods	Physical production statistics
b. Comparison of current account balances with expected balances	Company's budgets and forecasts
c. Evaluation of current account balances with relation to predictable historical patterns	Published industry ratios
d. Evaluation of current account balances in relation to nonfinancial information	Company's own comparative financial statements

LO 4-4   4.34 Analytical procedures can be used in which of the following ways?

a. As a means of overall review at the end of an audit.

b. As "attention-directing" methods when planning an audit at the beginning.

c. As substantive audit procedures to obtain evidence during an audit.

d. All of the above.

LO 4-5   4.35 Analytical procedures used when planning an audit should concentrate on

a. Weaknesses in the company's internal control activities.

b. Predictability of account balances based on individual transactions.

c. Management assertions in financial statements.

d. Accounts and relationships that can represent specific potential problems and risks in the financial statements.

LO 4-5   4.36 When a company that sells its products for a (gross) profit increases its sales by 15 percent and its cost of goods sold by 7 percent, the cost of goods sold ratio will

a. Increase.

b. Decrease.

c. Remain unchanged.

d. Not be able to be determined with the information provided.

LO 4-5   4.37 Auditors are not responsible for accounting estimates with respect to

a. Making the estimates.

b. Determining the reasonableness of estimates.

c. Determining that estimates are presented in conformity with GAAP.

d. Determining that estimates are adequately disclosed in the financial statements.

LO 4-7   4.38 An audit strategy contains

a. Specifications of auditing standards relevant to the financial statements being audited.

b. Specifications of procedures the auditors believe appropriate for the financial statements under audit.

c. Documentation of the assertions under audit, the evidence obtained, and the conclusions reached.

d. Reconciliation of the account balances in the financial statements with the account balances in the client's general ledger.

LO 4-3   4.39 It is acceptable under generally accepted auditing standards for an audit team to

a. Assess risk of material misstatement at high and achieve an acceptably low audit risk by performing extensive detection work.

b. Assess control risk at zero and perform a minimum of detection work.

c. Assess inherent risk at zero and perform a minimum of detection work.

d. Decide that audit risk can be 40 percent.

LO 4-6   4.40 Under the Private Securities Litigation Reform Act, independent auditors are required to first

a. Report in writing all instances of noncompliance to the client's board of directors.

b. Report to the SEC all instances of noncompliance they believe have a material effect on financial statements if the board of directors does not first report to the SEC.

c. Report clearly inconsequential noncompliance to the audit committee of the client's board of directors.

d. Resign from the audit engagement and report the instances of noncompliance to the SEC.

LO 4-4 4.41 When evaluating whether accounting estimates made by management are reasonable, auditors would be most interested in which of the following?
a. Key factors that are consistent with prior periods.
b. Assumptions that are similar to industry guidelines.
c. Measurements that are objective and not susceptible to bias.
d. Evidence of a conservative systematic bias.

LO 4-5 4.42 An audit committee is
a. Composed of internal auditors.
b. Composed of members of the audit team.
c. Composed of members of a company's board of directors who are not involved in the day-to-day operations of the company.
d. A committee composed of persons not associating in any way with the client or the board of directors.

LO 4-6 4.43 When auditors become aware of noncompliance with a law or regulation committed by client personnel, the primary reason that the auditors should obtain a better understanding of the nature of the act is to
a. Recommend remedial actions to the audit committee.
b. Evaluate the effect of the noncompliance on the financial statements.
c. Determine whether to contact law enforcement officials.
d. Determine whether other similar acts could have occurred.

LO 4-6 4.44 Which of the following statements best describes auditors' responsibility for detecting a client's noncompliance with a law or regulation?
a. The responsibility for detecting noncompliance exactly parallels the responsibility for errors and fraud.
b. Auditors must design tests to detect all material noncompliance that indirectly affects the financial statements.
c. Auditors must design tests to obtain reasonable assurance that all noncompliance with direct material statement effects is detected.
d. Auditors must design tests to detect all noncompliance that directly affects the financial statements.

LO 4-5 4.45 Auditors perform analytical procedures in the planning stage of an audit for the purpose of
a. Deciding the matters to cover in an engagement letter.
b. Identifying unusual conditions that deserve more auditing effort.
c. Determining which of the financial statement assertions are the most important for the client's financial statements.
d. Determining the nature, timing, and extent of audit procedures for auditing the inventory.

Exercises and Problems

 All applicable Exercises and Problems are available with McGraw-Hill's *Connect® Accounting*

LO 4-5 4.46 **Analytical Procedures and Interest Expense.** Weyman Z. Wannamaker is the chief financial officer of Cogburn Company. He prides himself on being able to manage the company's cash resources to maximize the interest expense. Consequently, on the second business day of each month, Weyman pays down or draws cash on Cogburn's revolving line of credit at First National Bank in accordance with his cash requirements forecast.

You are the auditor. You find the information on this line of credit in the following table. You inquired at First National Bank and learned that Cogburn Company's loan agreement specifies payment on the first day of each month for the interest due on the previous month's outstanding balance at the rate of "prime plus 1.5 percent." The bank gave you a report that showed the prime rate of interest was 8.5 percent for the first six months of the year and 8.0 percent for the last six months.

Cogburn Company Notes Payable Balances	
Date	Balance
Jan 1	$150,000
Feb 1	200,000
Apr 1	225,000
May 1	285,000
Jun 1	375,000
Aug 1	430,000
Sep 1	290,000
Oct 1	210,000
Nov 1	172,000
Dec 1	95,000

Required:
a. Prepare an audit estimate of the amount of interest expense you expect to find as the balance of the interest expense account related to these notes payable.
b. Which of the types of analytical procedures did you use to determine this estimate?
c. Suppose that you find that the interest expense account shows expense of $23,650 related to these notes. What could account for this difference?
d. Suppose that you find that the interest expense account shows expense of $24,400 related to these notes. What could account for this difference?
e. Suppose that you find that the interest expense account shows expense of $25,200 related to these notes. What could account for this difference?

LO 4-4

4.47 **Appropriateness of Evidence and Related Parties.** Johnson & Company, CPAs, audited Guaranteed Savings & Loan Company. M. Johnson had the assignment of evaluating the collectibility of real estate loans. Johnson was working on two particular loans: (1) a $4 million loan secured by Smith Street Apartments and (2) a $5.5 million construction loan on Baker Street Apartments now being built. The appraisals performed by Guaranteed Appraisal Partners, Inc., showed values in excess of the loan amounts. On inquiry, Mr. Bumpus, the S&L vice president for loan acquisition, stated, "I know the Smith Street loan is good because I myself own 40 percent of the partnership that owns the property and is obligated on the loan."

Johnson then wrote in the audit documentation: (1) the Smith Street loan appears collectible; Mr. Bumpus personally attested to knowledge of the collectibility as a major owner in the partnership obligated on the loan; (2) the Baker Street loan is assumed to be collectible because it is new and construction is still in progress; and (3) the appraised values all exceed the loan amounts.

Required:
a. Do you perceive any problems with related-party involvement in the evidence used by M. Johnson? Explain.
b. Do you perceive any problems with M. Johnson's reasoning or the appropriateness of evidence used in that reasoning?

LO 4-2

4.48 **Risk of Misstatement in Various Accounts.** Based on information you have available in Chapter 4:
a. In general, which accounts are most susceptible to overstatement? To understatement?
b. Why do you think a company could permit asset accounts to be understated?
c. Why do you think a company could permit liability accounts to be overstated?
d. Which direction of misstatement is most likely: income overstatement or income understatement?

156 Part Two *The Financial Statement Audit*

LO 4-2

4.49 **Analysis of Accounting Estimates.** Oak Industries, a manufacturer of radio and cable TV equipment and an operator of subscription TV systems, had a multitude of problems. Subscription services in a market area, for which $12 million of cost had been deferred, were being terminated and the customers were not paying on time ($4 million receivables in doubt). The chances are 50–50 that the business will survive another two years.

An electronic part turned out to have defects that needed correction. Warranty expenses are estimated to range from $2 million to $6 million. The inventory of this part ($10 million) is obsolete, but $1 million can be recovered in salvage, or the parts in inventory can be rebuilt at a cost of $2 million (selling price of the inventory on hand would then be $8 million with 20 percent of the selling price required to market and ship the products, and the normal profit expected is 5 percent of the selling price). If the inventory were scrapped, the company would manufacture a replacement inventory at a cost of $6 million, excluding marketing and shipping costs and normal profit.

The company has defaulted on completion of a military contract, and the government is claiming a $2 million refund. Company attorneys think the dispute might be settled for as little as $1 million.

The auditors had previously determined that an overstatement of income before taxes of $7 million would be material to the financial statements. These items were the only ones left for audit decisions about possible adjustment. Management has presented the following analysis for the determination of loss recognition:

Write off deferred subscription costs	$ 3,000,000
Provide allowance for bad debts	4,000,000
Provide for expected warranty expense	2,000,000
Lower-of-cost-or-market inventory write-down	2,000,000
Loss on government contract refund	
Total write-offs and losses	$11,000,000

Required:

Prepare your own analysis of the amount of adjustment to the financial statements. Assume that none of these estimates have been recorded yet and give the adjusting entry you would recommend. Give any supplementary explanations you believe necessary to support your recommendation.

LO 4-5

4.50 **Horizontal and Vertical Analysis.** *Horizontal analysis* refers to changes of financial statement numbers and ratios across two or more years. *Vertical analysis* refers to financial statement amounts expressed each year as proportions of a base such as sales for the income-statement accounts and total assets for the balance-sheet accounts. Exhibit 4.50.1 contains Retail Company's prior-year (audited) and current-year (unaudited) financial statements, along with amounts and percentages of change from year to year (horizontal analysis) and common-size percentages (vertical analysis). Exhibit 4.50.2 contains selected financial ratios based on these financial statements. Analysis of these data can enable auditors to discern relationships that raise questions about misleading financial statements.

Required:

Study the data in Exhibits 4.50.1 and 4.50.2. Write a memorandum identifying and explaining potential problem areas where misstatements in the current year financial statements could exist. Additional information about Retail Company is as follows:

- The new bank loan, obtained on July 1 of the current year, requires maintenance of a 2:1 current ratio.
- Principal of $100,000 plus interest on the 10 percent long-term note obtained several years ago in the original amount of $800,000 is due each January 1.
- The company has never paid dividends on its common stock and has no plans for a dividend.

EXHIBIT 4.50.1 Retail Company

	Prior Year (Audited)		Current Year (Unaudited)		Change	
	Balance	Common Size	Balance	Common Size	Amount	Percent
Assets:						
Cash	$ 600,000	14.78%	$ 484,000	9.69%	$ (116,000)	−19.33%
Accounts receivable	500,000	12.32	400,000	8.01	(100,000)	−20.00
Allowance doubt. accts.	(40,000)	−0.99	(30,000)	−0.60	10,000	−25.00
Inventory	1,500,000	36.95	1,940,000	38.85	440,000	29.33
Total current assets	2,560,000	63.05	2,794,000	55.95	234,000	9.14
Fixed assets	3,000,000	73.89	4,000,000	80.10	1,000,000	33.33
Accum. depreciation	(1,500,000)	−36.95	(1,800,000)	−36.04	(300,000)	20.00
Total assets	$4,060,000	100.00%	$4,994,000	100.00%	$ 934,000	23.00%
Liabilities and equity:						
Accounts payable	$ 450,000	11.08%	$ 600,000	12.01%	$ 150,000	33.33%
Bank loans, 11%	0	0.00	750,000	15.02	750,000	NA
Accrued interest	50,000	1.23	40,000	0.80	(10,000)	−20.00
Accruals and other	60,000	1.48	10,000	0.20	(50,000)	−83.33
Total current liab.	560,000	13.79	1,400,000	28.03	840,000	150.00
Long-Term debt, 10%	500,000	12.32	400,000	8.01	(100,000)	−20.00
Total liabilities	1,060,000	26.11	1,800,000	36.04	740,000	69.81
Capital stock	2,000,000	49.26	2,000,000	40.05	0	0
Retained earnings	1,000,000	24.63	1,194,000	23.91	194,000	19.40
Total liabilities and equity	$4,060,000	100.00%	$4,994,000	100.00%	934,000	23.00%
Statement of operations:						
Sales (net)	$9,000,000	100.00%	$8,100,000	100.00%	$ (900,000)	−10.00%
Cost of goods sold	6,296,000	69.96	5,265,000	65.00	(1,031,000)	−16.38
Gross margin	2,704,000	30.04	2,835,000	35.00	131,000	4.84
General expense	2,044,000	22.71	2,005,000	24.75	(39,000)	−1.91
Depreciation	300,000	3.33	300,000	3.70	0	0
Operating income	360,000	4.00	530,000	6.54	170,000	47.22
Interest expense	50,000	0.56	40,000	0.49	(10,000)	−20.00
Income taxes (40%)	124,000	1.38	196,000	2.42	72,000	58.06
Net income	$ 186,000	2.07%	$ 294,000	3.63%	$ 108,000	58.06%

NA means not applicable.

EXHIBIT 4.50.2 Retail Company

	Prior Year (Audited)	Current Year (Unaudited)	Percent Change
Balance-sheet ratios:			
Current ratio	4.57	2.0	−56.34%
Days' sales in receivables	18.40	16.44	−10.63
Doubtful accounts ratio	0.0800	0.0750	−6.25
Days' sales in inventory	85.77	132.65	54.66
Debt/equity ratio	0.35	0.56	40.89
Operations ratios:			
Receivables turnover	19.57	21.89	11.89
Inventory turnover	4.20	2.71	−35.34
Cost of goods sold/sales	69.96%	65.00%	−7.08
Gross margin %	30.04%	35.00%	16.49
Return on equity	6.61%	9.80%	48.26

LO 4-4

4.51 **Analysis and Judgment.** As part of your regular year-end audit of a public client, you must estimate the probability of success of its proposed new product line. The client has experienced financial difficulty during the last few years and, in your judgment, a successful introduction of the new product line is necessary for the client to remain a going concern.

Five elements are necessary for the successful introduction of the product: (1) successful labor negotiations before the strike deadline between the construction firms contracted to build the necessary addition to the present plant and the building trades unions, (2) successful defense of patent rights, (3) product approval by the Food and Drug Administration (FDA),

(4) successful negotiation of a long-term raw material contract with a foreign supplier, and (5) successful conclusion of distribution contract talks with a large national retail distributor.

In view of the circumstances, you contact experts who have provided your public accounting firm with reliable estimates in the past. The labor relations expert estimates that there is an 80 percent chance of successfully concluding labor negotiations. Legal counsel advises that there is a 90 percent chance of successfully defending patent rights. The expert on FDA product approvals estimates a 95 percent chance of new product approval. The experts in the remaining two areas estimate the probability of successfully resolving (1) the raw materials contract and (2) the distribution contract talks to be 90 percent in each case. Assume that these estimates are reliable.

Required:

What is your assessment of the probability of successful product introduction? (*Hint:* You can assume that each of the five elements is independent of the others.)

4.52 **Analytical Procedures.** Kelly Griffin, an audit manager, had begun preliminary analytical procedures of selected statistics related to the Majestic Hotel. Her objective was to obtain an understanding of the hotel's business in order to draft a preliminary audit plan. She wanted to see whether she could detect any troublesome areas or questionable accounts that could require special audit attention. Unfortunately, Griffin caught the flu and was hospitalized. From her sickbed, she sent you the schedule she had prepared (Exhibit 4.52.1) and

EXHIBIT 4.52.1
Analytical Procedure Documentation

AP-6

Prepared by _____
Reviewed by _____

MAJESTIC HOTEL
Preliminary Analytical Procedures
FYE 3/31/13

The Majestic Hotel, East Apple, New Jersey, compiles operating statistics on a calendar-year basis. Hotel statistics, below, were provided by the controller, A. J. Marcello, for 2013. The parallel column contains industry average statistics obtained from the National Hotel Industry Guide.

	Majestic (percent)	Industry (percent)
Sales:		
Rooms	60.4%	63.9%
Food and beverage	35.7	32.2
Other	3.9	3.9
Costs:		
Rooms department	15.2	17.3
Food and beverage	34.0	27.2
Administrative and general	8.0	8.9
Management fee	3.3	1.1
Advertising	2.7	3.2
Real estate taxes	3.5	3.2
Utilities, repairs, maintenance	15.9	13.7
Profit per sales dollar	17.4	25.4
Rooms dept. ratios to room sales dollars:		
Salaries and wages	18.9	15.7
Laundry	1.1	3.7
Other	5.3	7.6
Profit per rooms sales dollar	74.8	73.0
Food/beverage (F/B) ratios to F/B sales dollars:		
Cost of food sold	42.1	37.0
Food gross profit	57.9	63.0
Cost of beverages sold	43.6	29.5
Beverages gross profit	56.4	70.5
Combined gross profit	57.7	64.6
Salaries and wages	39.6	32.8
Music and entertainment	—	2.7
Other	13.4	13.8
Profit per F/B sales dollar	4.7	15.3
Average annual percent of rooms occupied	62.6	68.1
Average room rate per day	$160	$120
Number of rooms available per day	200	148

has asked you to write a memorandum identifying areas of potential misstatements or other matters that the preliminary audit plan should cover.

Required:

Write a memorandum describing Majestic's operating characteristics compared to the industry average insofar as you can tell from the statistics. Do these analytical procedures identify any areas that could represent potential misstatements in the audit?

LO 4-5

4.53 **Preliminary Analytical Procedures.** Dunder-Mifflin, Inc. wanted to expand its manufacturing and sales facilities. The company applied for a loan from First Bank, presenting the prior year audited financial statements and the forecast for the current year shown in Exhibit 4.53.1. (Dunder-Mifflin, Inc.'s fiscal year-end is December 31.) The bank was impressed with the business prospects and granted a $1,750,000 loan at 8 percent interest to finance working capital and the new facilities that were placed in service July 1 of the current year. Because Dunder-Mifflin, Inc. planned to issue stock for permanent financing, the bank made the loan due on December 31 of the following year. Interest is payable each calendar quarter on October 1 of the current year and January 1, April 1, July 1, October 1, and December 31 of the following year.

The auditors' interviews with Dunder-Mifflin, Inc. management near the end of the current year produced the following information: The facilities did not cost as much as previously anticipated. However, sales were slow and the company granted more liberal return privilege terms than in the prior year. Officers wanted to generate significant income to impress First Bank and to preserve the company dividend ($120,000 paid in the prior year). The production managers had targeted inventory levels for a 4.0 turnover ratio and were largely successful even though prices of materials and supplies had risen about 2 percent relative to sales dollar volume. The new facilities were depreciated using a 25-year life from the date of opening.

Dunder-Mifflin, Inc. has now produced the current-year financial statements (Exhibit 4.53.1, Current Year column) for the auditors' work on the current audit.

EXHIBIT 4.53.1
Dunder-Mifflin, Inc.

	Prior Year (Audited)	Forecast	Current Year (Unaudited)
Revenue and Expense:			
Sales (net)	$9,000,000	$9,900,000	$9,720,000
Cost of goods sold	6,296,000	6,926,000	7,000,000
Gross margin	2,704,000	2,974,000	2,720,000
General expense	2,044,000	2,000,000	2,003,000
Depreciation	300,000	334,000	334,000
Operating income	360,000	640,000	383,000
Interest expense	60,000	110,000	75,000
Income taxes (40%)	120,000	212,000	123,200
Net income	180,000	318,000	184,800
Assets:			
Cash	600,000	880,000	690,800
Accounts receivable	500,000	600,000	900,000
Allowance for doubtful accounts	(40,000)	(48,000)	(90,000)
Inventory	1,500,000	1,500,000	1,350,000
Total current assets	2,560,000	2,932,000	2,850,800
Fixed assets	3,000,000	4,700,000	4,500,000
Accum. depreciation	(1,500,000)	(1,834,000)	(1,834,000)
Total assets	$4,060,000	$5,798,000	$5,516,800
Liabilities and Equity:			
Accounts payable	$ 450,000	$ 450,000	$ 330,000
Bank loans, 8%	0	1,750,000	1,750,000
Accrued interest	60,000	40,000	40,000
Accruals and other	50,000	60,000	32,000
Total current liabilities	$ 560,000	$2,300,000	$2,152,000
Long-Term debt, 10%	600,000	400,000	400,000
Total liabilities	$1,160,000	$2,700,000	$2,552,000
Capital stock	2,000,000	2,000,000	2,000,000
Retained earnings	900,000	1,098,000	964,800
Total liabilities and equity	$4,060,000	$5,798,000	$5,516,800

Required:

Perform preliminary analytical procedures on the current-year unaudited financial statements for the purpose of identifying accounts that could contain errors or frauds. Use your knowledge of Dunder-Mifflin, Inc. and the forecast in Exhibit 4.53.1. Calculate comparative and common-size financial statements as well as relevant ratios (assume that the market value of the equity for the company is $3 million). Once your calculations are complete, identify the accounts that could be misstated. (*Note:* This assignment is available in the student section of the textbook website in Excel format.)

LO 4-3

4.54 **Audit Risk Model.** Audit risks for particular accounts and disclosures can be conceptualized in the model: Audit risk (AR) = Inherent risk (IR) × Control risk (CR) × Detection risk (DR). Use this model as a framework for considering the following situations and deciding whether the auditor's conclusion is appropriate.

  a. Paul, CPA, has participated in the audit of Tordik Cheese Company for five years, first as an assistant accountant and the last two years as the senior accountant. Paul has never seen an accounting adjustment recommended and believes the inherent risk must be zero.

  b. Hill, CPA, has just (November 30) completed an exhaustive study and evaluation of the internal controls of Edward Foods, Inc. (fiscal year ending December 31). Hill believes the control risk must be zero because no material errors could possibly slip through the many error-checking procedures and review layers that Edward used.

  c. Fields, CPA, is lazy and does not like audit jobs in Philadelphia. On the audit of Philly Manufacturing Company, Fields decided to use substantive procedures to audit the year-end balances very thoroughly to the extent that the risk of failing to detect material errors and irregularities should be 0.02 or less. Fields gave no thought to inherent risk and conducted only a very limited review of Philly's internal control system.

  d. Shad, CPA, is nearing the end of a "dirty" audit of Allnight Protection Company. Allnight's accounting personnel all resigned during the year and were replaced by inexperienced people. The comptroller resigned last month in disgust. The journals and ledgers were a mess because the one computer specialist was hospitalized for three months during the year. "Thankfully," Shad thought, "I've been able to do this audit in less time than last year when everything was operating smoothly."

(AICPA adapted)

LO 4-5

4.55 **Auditing an Accounting Estimate.** Suppose management estimated the market valuation of some obsolete inventory at $99,000; this inventory was recorded at $120,000, which resulted in recognizing a loss of $21,000. The auditors obtained the following information: The inventory in question could be sold for an amount between $78,000 and $92,000. The costs of advertising and shipping could range from $5,000 to $7,000.

Required:

  a. Would you propose an audit adjustment to the management estimate? Prepare the appropriate accounting entry.

  b. If management's estimate of inventory market (lower than cost) had been $80,000, would you propose an audit adjustment? Prepare the appropriate accounting entry.

LO 4-2

4.56 **Risk Assessment.** This question consists of a number of items pertaining to an auditor's risk analysis for a company. Your task is to tell how each item affects overall audit risk—that is, the probability of issuing an unqualified audit report on materially misleading financial statements.

Bond, CPA, is considering audit risk at the financial statement level in planning the audit of Toxic Waste Disposal (TWD) Company's financial statements for the year ended December 31, 2012. TWD is a privately owned company that contracts with municipal governments to remove environmental wastes. Audit risk at the overall financial statement level is influenced by the risk of material misstatements, which may be indicated by a combination of factors related to management, the industry, and the company.

Required:

Based only on the following information, indicate whether each of the following factors (Items 1 through 15) would most likely increase overall audit risk, decrease overall audit risk, or have no effect on overall audit risk. Discuss your reasoning.

Company Profile
1. This was the first year TWD operated at a profit since 2005 because the municipalities received increased federal and state funding for environmental purposes.
2. TWD's board of directors is controlled by Mead, the majority stockholder, who also acts as the chief executive officer.
3. The internal auditor reports to the controller, and the controller reports to Mead.
4. The accounting department has experienced a high rate of turnover of key personnel.
5. TWD's bank has a loan officer who meets regularly with TWD's CEO and controller to monitor TWD's financial performance.
6. TWD's employees are paid biweekly.
7. Bond has audited TWD for five years.

Recent Developments
8. During 2012, TWD changed the method of preparing its financial statements from the cash basis to the accrual basis under generally accepted accounting principles.
9. During 2012, TWD sold one-half of its controlling interest in United Equipment Leasing (UEL) Co. TWD retained significant interest in UEL.
10. During 2012, the state dropped litigation filed against TWD in 2010 alleging that the company discharged pollutants into state waterways. Loss contingency disclosures that TWD included in prior years' financial statements are being removed for the 2012 financial statements.
11. During December 2012, TWD signed a contract to lease disposal equipment from an entity owned by Mead's parents. This related-party transaction is not disclosed in TWD's notes to its 2012 financial statements.
12. During December 2012, TWD completed a barter transaction with a municipality. TWD removed waste from a municipally owned site and acquired title to another contaminated site at below-market price. TWD intends to service this new site in 2013.
13. During December 2012, TWD increased its casualty insurance coverage on several pieces of sophisticated machinery from historical cost to replacement cost.
14. Inquiries about the substantial increase in revenue that TWD recorded in the fourth quarter of 2012 disclosed a new policy. TWD guaranteed several municipalities that it would refund the federal and state funding paid to it if any municipality fails federal or state site cleanup inspection in 2013.
15. An initial public offering of TWD's stock is planned for late 2013.

LO 4-2

4.57 **Auditing Standards Review.** Management fraud (fraudulent financial reporting) is not the expected norm, but it happens from time to time. In the United States, several cases have been widely publicized. They happen when motives and opportunities overwhelm managerial integrity.

  a. What distinguishes management fraud from a defalcation?
  b. What are an auditor's responsibilities under auditing standards to detect management fraud?
  c. What are some characteristics of management fraud that an audit team should consider to fulfill the responsibilities under auditing standards?
  d. What factors might an audit team notice that should heighten the concern about the existence of management fraud?
  e. Under what circumstances might an audit team have a duty to disclose management's frauds to parties other than the company's management and its board of directors?

(AICPA adapted)

LO 4-5

4.58 **Analytical Procedures: Ratio Relationships.** The following situations represent errors and frauds that could occur in financial statements.

Required:
State how the ratio in question would compare (higher, equal, or lower) to what the ratio should have been had the error or fraud not occurred.

  a. The company recorded fictitious sales with credits to sales revenue accounts and debits to accounts receivable. Inventory was reduced, and cost of goods sold was increased for the profitable "sales." Is the current ratio higher than, equal to, or lower than what it should have been?

b. The company recorded cash disbursements by paying trade accounts payable but held the checks past the year-end date, meaning that the "disbursements" should not have been shown as credits to cash and debits to accounts payable. Is the current ratio higher than, equal to, or lower than what it should have been? Consider cases in which the current ratio before the improper "disbursement" recording was (1) higher than 1:1, (2) equal to 1:1, and (3) lower than 1:1.

c. The company uses a periodic inventory system for determining the balance-sheet amount of inventory at year-end. Very near the year-end, merchandise was received, placed in the stockroom, and counted, but the purchase transaction was neither recorded nor paid until the next month. What was the effect of this on inventory, cost of goods sold, gross profit, and net income? How were these ratios affected compared to what they would have been without the error: current ratio (remember three possible cases), gross margin ratio, cost of goods sold ratio, inventory turnover, and receivables turnover?

d. The company is loathe to write off customer accounts receivable even though the financial vice president makes entirely adequate provision for uncollectible amounts in the allowance for bad debts. The gross receivables and the allowance both contain amounts that should have been written off long ago. How are these ratios affected compared to what they would have been if the old receivables had been properly written off: current ratio, days' sales in receivables, doubtful account ratio, receivables turnover, return on beginning equity, and working capital/total assets?

e. Since last year, the company has reorganized its lines of business and placed more emphasis on its traditional products while selling off some marginal businesses merged by the previous management. Total assets are 10 percent less than they were last year, but working capital has increased. Retained earnings remained the same because the disposals created no gains, and the net income after taxes is still near zero, which is the same as last year. Earnings before interest and taxes (EBIT) remained the same, a small positive EBIT. The total market value of the company's equity has not increased, but that is better than the declines of the past several years. Proceeds from the disposals have been used to retire long-term debt. Net sales have decreased 5 percent because the sales' decrease resulting from the disposals has not been overcome by increased sales of the traditional products. Is the discriminant Z-score of the current year higher or lower than the one of the prior year? (See Appendix 4A for the Z-score formula.)

LO 4-1

4.59 **Enterprise Risk Management.** The enterprise risk management (ERM) framework was developed by COSO to provide managers a formalized methodology to evaluate risk in their businesses.

Required:
Explain how management would use the ERM framework to manage business risk.

LO 4-7

4.60 **Audit Strategy Memorandum.** The auditor should establish an overall audit strategy that sets the scope, timing, and direction of the audit and guides the development of the audit plan. In establishing the overall audit strategy, the auditor should develop and document an audit plan that includes a description of (a) the planned nature, timing, and extent of the risk assessment procedures, (b) the planned nature, timing, and extent of tests of controls and substantive procedures, and (c) other planned audit procedures that must be performed so that the engagement complies with auditing standards.

Required:
Select a public company and determine a significant risk that could affect its financial statements. (*Hint:* Go to the EDGAR database at SEC.gov and select the company's form 10-K. The 10-K will have a list of risk factors the company faces). Describe the risk and how it could affect the financial statements, including what assertions might be misstated. Prepare an audit strategy memorandum for the risk describing what controls the company might use to mitigate the risk, how you could test the controls, and what substantive procedures you might use to determine whether there is a misstatement. Because this is early in your auditing class, do not worry about specific procedures; just be creative and think about a general strategy an auditor might use.

LO 4-1

4.61 **Errors and Frauds.** Give an example of an error or fraud that would misstate financial statements to affect the accounts as follows, taking each case independently. (*Note:* "Overstate" means the account has a higher value than would be appropriate under GAAP and "understate" means it has a lower value.)

a. Overstate one asset; understate another asset.
b. Overstate an asset; overstate stockholders' equity.
c. Overstate an asset; overstate revenue.
d. Overstate an asset; understate an expense.
e. Overstate a liability; overstate an expense.
f. Understate an asset; overstate an expense.
g. Understate a liability; understate an expense.

LO 4-6

4.62 **Compliance with Laws and Regulations.** Audit standards distinguish auditors' responsibility for planning procedures for detecting noncompliance with laws and regulations having a direct effect on financial statements versus planning procedures for detecting noncompliance with laws and regulations that do not have a direct effect on financial statements.

Required:

a. What are the requirements for auditors to plan procedures to detect direct-effect compliance versus indirect-effect compliance?
b. For each of the following instances of noncompliance, explain why they are either direct-effect (D) or indirect-effect (I) noncompliance:
   1. A manufacturer inflates expenses on its corporate tax return.
   2. A retailer pays men more than women for performing the same job.
   3. A coal mining company fails to place proper ventilation in its mines.
   4. A military contractor inflates the overhead applied to a combat vehicle.
   5. An insurance company fails to maintain required reserves for losses.
   6. An exporter pays a bribe to a foreign government official so that government will buy its products.
   7. A company backdates its executive stock options to lower the exercise price.
   8. A company fails to fund its pension plan in accordance with ERISA.

LO 4-2

4.63 **Kaplan CPA Exam Simulation: Audit Risk.**

Required:
Go to the Kaplan website link at www.mhhe.com/Louwers5e, click on Bestwood Furniture (Audit Risk) AUD TBS, and complete your answer.

4.64 **Mini-Case: Red Flags.** Refer to the mini-case "Unhealthy Accounting at HealthSouth" shown on page C14 and respond to Questions 1 and 2.

4.65 **Mini-Case: Red Flags.** Refer to the mini-case "Something Went Sour at Parmalat" shown on page C20 and respond to Question 3.

Appendix 4A

Selected Financial Ratios

Balance-Sheet Ratios	Formula*
Current ratio	$\dfrac{\text{Current assets}}{\text{Current liabilities}}$
Days' sales in receivables	$\dfrac{\text{Ending net receivables}}{\text{Credit sales}/360}$
Doubtful account ratio	$\dfrac{\text{Allowance for doubtful accounts}}{\text{Ending gross receivables}}$
Days' sales in inventory	$\dfrac{\text{Ending inventory}}{\text{Cost of goods sold}/360}$
Debt-to-equity ratio	$\dfrac{\text{Current and long-term debt}}{\text{Stockholder equity}}$

Operations Ratios	
Receivables turnover	$\dfrac{\text{Credit sales}}{\text{Ending net receivables}}$
Inventory turnover	$\dfrac{\text{Cost of goods sold}}{\text{Ending inventory}}$
Cost of goods sold ratio	$\dfrac{\text{Cost of goods sold}}{\text{Net sales}}$
Gross margin ratio	$\dfrac{\text{Net sales} - \text{Cost of goods sold}}{\text{Net sales}}$
Return on beginning equity	$\dfrac{\text{Net income}}{\text{Stockholder equity (beginning)}}$

Financial Distress Ratios (Altman)

The discriminant Z-score is an index of a company's financial health. The higher the score, the healthier the company. The lower the score, the closer financial failure approaches. The score that predicts financial failure is a matter of dispute. Research suggests that companies with scores above 3.0 never go bankrupt. Generally, companies with scores below 1.0 experience financial difficulty of some kind. The score can be a negative number.

(X_1) Working capital/Total assets	$\dfrac{\text{Current assets} - \text{Current liabilities}}{\text{Total assets}}$
(X_2) Retained earnings/Total assets	$\dfrac{\text{Retained earnings (ending)}}{\text{Total assets}}$
(X_3) Earnings before interest and taxes/Total assets	$\dfrac{\text{Net income} + \text{Interest expense} + \text{Income tax expense}}{\text{Total assets}}$
(X_4) Market value of equity/Total debt	$\dfrac{\text{Market value of common and preferred stock}}{\text{Current liabilities and long-term debt}}$
(X_5) Net sales/Total assets	$\dfrac{\text{Net sales}}{\text{Total assets}}$
Discriminant Z-score (Altman)	$1.2 \times X_1 + 1.4 \times X_2 + 3.3 \times X_3 + 0.6 \times X_4 + 1.0 \times X_5$

*These ratios are shown to be calculated using year-end, rather than year-average, numbers for balances such as accounts receivable and inventory. Other accounting and finance reference books could contain formulas using year-average numbers. As long as no dramatic changes have occurred during the year, the year-end numbers can have much audit relevance because they reflect the most current balance data. For comparative purposes, the ratios should be calculated on the same basis for all years being compared.

Appendix 4B

Sample Abridged Audit Plan

INTEGRATED CARE HEALTH INSURANCE, INC
Audit Plan (Abridged)

OVERVIEW

Integrated Care Health Insurance, Inc (Integrated) offers a variety of valuable products and services ranging from medical, dental, and behavioral health coverage to life insurance and disability plans as well as management services for Medicaid plans. Purchasing health coverage ensures future security with respect to high and unexpected costs of health care for individuals, families, and businesses. Benefits offered by Integrated include not only coverage for medical expenses but access to a wide network of doctors, hospitals, and specialists.

PRODUCT PRICING

Integrated uses a special process to calculate premiums charged for services offered. The method involves pooling customers with similar characteristics into a single risk group based on age, gender, medical history, lifestyle, and other factors such as benefits desired, administration costs, and tax obligations. After Integrated pools customers into their respective risk groups, Integrated has the responsibility to balance projected future costs with premiums charged. The most important factor in determining financial success for Integrated is its ability to predict trends and future medical costs. Therefore, faulty forecasts can lead to huge risks and downfalls for Integrated if expectations fall short of actual results. Competing in an industry where new technology and medical breakthroughs are discovered almost daily means that sustaining profitability is an increasing concern.

GOVERNMENT INFLUENCES

Along with a great deal of risk being inherent in its business, Integrated has also been experiencing a strain in its operations due to the declining U.S. economy and increasing unemployment rate. Additionally, the health care reform legislation passed in 2009 will cause significant changes to many facets of the industry's operation according to analysts. However, certain parts of the legislation leave providers with the hope of positive changes. For example, given that the new legislation will require coverage for those who are currently uninsured, the insurance companies will acquire millions of new customers virtually overnight. Nevertheless, the total effect on the reform is still uncertain because a bulk of the legislation passed will not become effective until 2012 to 2014.

CUSTOMERS, SUPPLIERS AND COMPETITORS

Integrated's customers include employer groups, self-employed individuals, part-time and hourly workers, governmental organizations, labor groups, and immigrants. Although there are a considerable number of companies competing, experts have noted a trend that competition is virtually disappearing due to the domination of markets by only a few providers. In a study published by the American Medical Association, 24 of 43 states have one or two insurers comprising a market share of a staggering 70 percent.[7] These statistics may suggest that there is essentially no competition in the market. However,

---

[7] D W. Emmons, J. R. Guardado, C K. Kane Competition in Health Insurance: A comprehensive study of U.S. markets, 2010 update American Medical Association.

1,300 companies are competing in the health insurance industry, and Integrated faces significant competition in highly concentrated markets. In addition to the competition and governmental influences already present, Integrated is also facing competition from hospitals that play a pertinent role in determining the amounts billed for services provided.

RISK ASSESSMENT

The following analysis provides an overview of the identified risks and expected controls for Integrated for one accounting cycle.

REVENUE AND COLLECTION CYCLE

Risks

Due to the contract nature of the insurance industry, revenue recognition is not a high-risk area when compared to other industries. Integrated has set contracts with commercial organizations, individuals, and the government. Therefore, large fluctuations throughout the year do not typically occur. However, one area of significant risk involves the Medicare risk adjustment. The Centers for Medicare & Medicaid Services (CMS) determines Medicare and Medicaid premium payments employing a risk-based formula using coding provided by the insurance companies based on data from the diagnosis. Members with Medicare and Medicaid benefits associated with the health insurance entity is given a risk category based on their health conditions. However, because these contracts are preset for a year, patients' risk categories might fluctuate, causing an increase in needed payment from the CMS. Integrated must ensure that revenue is recognized properly by recording a risk adjustment for the difference between what CMS paid and what should have been paid based on the appriopriate risk categories. CMS also performs audits known as *RADV audits* to ensure CMS remits premium payments to insurance organizations appropriately.

Another area of significant risk around revenue recognition involves the Medicare Part D risk-sharing provision. With Medicare Part D, insurance entities contract with CMS for set premiums on an annual basis. The ultimate payment of total premiums, however, depends on certain thresholds that might require additional payment by CMS or reimbursement to CMS. A reconciliation (true-up) is performed after year-end to account for these differences. However, because this true-up process might occur six to nine months after year-end, Integrated must account for this process by recording receiveables or payables that estimate these differences. Significant estimates are used to develop these adjustments and requires the company to plan the audit procedures to provide reasonable assurance that these estimates do not include material mistatements.

Controls

The difficulty in predicting revenue adjustment amounts from these two programs concerns Integrated management's assertions of completeness, accuracy, valuation of financial statement accounts, and proper disclosure of required revenue recognition elements. To meet disclosure assertions, Integrated established a disclosure committee to determine what revenue-related disclosures should be made regarding Medicare and Medicaid. This committee meets prior to the release of each quarter's financial statements or as often as management requires. Valuation and accuracy assertions are met by requiring that qualified personnel utilize acceptable models commonly used in industry practice when estimating the amounts for the varying revenues. Appropriate supervisors review all estimates for accuracy and verify that estimates conform to the company's operational objectives.

AUDIT APPROACH

Due to the high-risk nature of the unique business and audit risks detailed here, an audit plan for Integrated must include both test of controls and substantive procedures to provide for the appropriate level of detection risk. As mentioned, significant estimates are included in the financial statements for almost every accounting cycle within the health insurance industry. The amount of management judgment needed to determine these estimates requires the use of extensive substantive testing to provide reasonable assurance that material misstatements do not exist within the financial statements. The following detailed audit plan provides guidance on the types of control testing and substantive testing that would provide reasonable assurance that material misstatements do not exist in relation to the risks outlined within this report.

AUDIT STRATEGY
Integrated Care Health Insurance, Inc.

Overview
This audit strategy is intended to provide our responses to the risks identified for Integrated and generally detail the associated tests of controls and substantive procedures that will be required during the audit.

Risks
Revenue recognition related to participation in Medicare and Medicaid programs (Revenue and Collection Cycle)

Assertions	Tests of Controls	Substantive Procedures
Valuation or allocation	Test IT and manual controls relative to calculation of revenues from Medicare and Medicaid contracts	Reperform revenue calculations for a sampling of Medicare- and Medicaid-issued contracts
	Confirm that management estimates for risk-sharing and risk-adjustment provisions (reviews include determining whether qualified personnel perform the estimates, making estimates conform to industry practices, and verifying that estimates are accurate)	Reperform estimates for risk-sharing and risk-adjustment provisions
	Confirm that assumptions and methodologies for estimates of risk-sharing and risk-adjustment provisions are documented and approved by management	Produce independent estimates for risk-sharing and risk-adjustment provisions
	Obtain an understanding of assumptions and methodology of estimates for risk-sharing and risk-adjustment provisions	
Presentation and disclosure	Confirm that disclosure committee has been established	Review disclosure committee meeting minutes
	Confirm that comparisons of actual and budgeted Medicare and Medicaid revenues are conducted by management and significant variances are monitored	Review board of directors meeting minutes, agreements, budgets, and plans for Medicare and Medicaid revenues that should be included in financial statements
		Test whether disclosures and classifications conform to accounting principles

Source: Mark Fedewa, Emily O'Bryan, Amela Pajazetovic, and Susan Schmidt, "An Analysis of Business and Audit Risk for a Health Insurance Provider," unpublished working paper, University of Kentucky. February 28, 2011.

Risk Assessment: Internal Control Evaluation

Bernie doesn't want you to use the words "internal controls" in any more of your audit reports . . . it aggravates him.

> Cynthia Cooper (in Nowhere to Go but Up), referring to advice given her by a colleague on how best to deal with Bernie Ebbers, the then-CEO of **WorldCom**, before she uncovered an $11 billion fraud that Ebbers directed. Ebbers is currently serving a 25-year prison term in connection with the fraud.

Professional Standards References

Topic	AU/ISA Section	PCAOB Reference*
Consideration of Internal Control in an Integrated Audit		AS 5
Reporting on Whether a Previously Reported Material Weakness Continues to Exist		AS 4
Overall Objectives of the Independent Auditor	200	AU 110, AU 150, AU 201, AU 201, AU 220, AU 230
Audit Documentation	230	AS 3
Consideration of Fraud in a Financial Statement Audit	240	AU 316
Communications with Those Charged with Governance	260	AU 380
Communicating Internal Control Matters Identified in an Audit	265	AU 325
Audit Planning	300	AS 10
Identifying and Assessing the Risks of Material Misstatement	315	AS 12
Materiality	320	AS 11
Auditors' Responses to Risks of Material Misstatement	330	AS 13
Audit Considerations Relating to an Entity Using a Service Organization	402	AS 5
Audit Evidence	500	AS 15
Audit Evidence—Specific Considerations for Selected Items	501	AU 331, AU 332
Consideration of the Internal Audit Function in a Financial Statement Audit	610	AU 341
Compliance Audits of Governmental Entities and Recipients of Governmental Assistance	935	AU 801

*AU, AT, and QC references represent standards issued by the ASB prior to April 16, 2003, that have not been superseded or amended by the PCAOB.

LEARNING OBJECTIVES

An important objective of the internal control system is to help ensure that the financial statement information being presented by an organization is credible and reliable. It is therefore essential that an auditor take the time to understand whether an entity's internal control system has been designed appropriately. In fact, the fundamental principles of auditing state that, to fulfill auditors' responsibility "[t]o obtain reasonable assurance, . . . the auditor *identifies and assesses risks of material misstatement, whether due to fraud or error, based on an understanding of the entity and its environment, including the entity's internal control*" [emphasis added]. The responsibility is even greater for public companies because PCAOB *Auditing Standard No. 5* (*AS 5*) requires that the auditor express an opinion on the effectiveness of the client's internal control system. As a result, the evaluation of an entity's internal control system is a critical phase of every audit engagement.

Beyond its importance in the production of reliable financial statement information and the audit, the establishment of an internal control system is an important management function to help ensure the effectiveness and efficiency of operations and the entity's compliance with laws and regulations. As a result, understanding the elements of internal control and how to evaluate their effectiveness is an important skill that every accountant should have. Even if you do not go into auditing, you probably will have responsibility for maintaining internal controls at some point in your accounting career.

This chapter presents a general introduction to the theory and definitions you will find useful for internal control evaluation and control risk assessment. The chapter uses the payroll cycle to provide specific examples of control activities and related audit procedures.

Your objectives are to be able to:

LO 5-1 Define and describe *internal control* and explain the limitations of all internal control systems.

LO 5-2 Distinguish between the responsibilities of management and auditors regarding an entity's internal control.

LO 5-3 Define and describe the five basic components of internal control and specify some of their characteristics.

LO 5-4 Explain the process the audit team uses to assess control risk, understand its impact on the risk of material misstatement, and, ultimately, to know how it affects the nature, timing, and extent of substantive testing to be performed on the audit.

LO 5-5 Describe additional responsibilities for management and auditors of public companies required by Sarbanes-Oxley and *Auditing Standard No. 5*.

LO 5-6 List the major components of the auditors' report on internal control over financial reporting.

LO 5-7 Describe situations in which the auditors' report on internal control over financial reporting would be modified.

LO 5-8 Explain the communication of internal control deficiencies to those charged with governance such as the audit committee and other key management personnel.

INTRODUCTION

In response to the significant number of major corporate accounting scandals that had rocked the financial world (e.g., **Enron, WorldCom, Xerox, Kmart**), Congress passed the Sarbanes-Oxley Act on July 30, 2002 (the most comprehensive financial reporting legislation since the Securities Acts of 1933 and 1934). The Sarbanes-Oxley Act was passed in an attempt to strengthen corporate financial reporting by assessing harsher criminal penalties for white-collar crimes, increasing management accountability, and enhancing public accounting firm independence.

Central among the provisions of this act is the emphasis that is placed on the internal control system as an important means to prevent or detect material misstatements in the financial statements due to fraud. The feeling is that by holding both management and the auditor responsible for evaluating the effectiveness of the internal control system, the act has imposed the necessary oversight to improve the accuracy and reliability of the financial statements reported by the entity. Simply stated, the intense scrutiny on both the design and operating effectiveness of internal control systems over financial reporting will improve the reliability of the financial statements.

INTERNAL CONTROL DEFINED

LEARNING OBJECTIVE 5-1
Define and describe *internal control* and explain the limitations of all internal control systems.

In response to a report by the National Commission on Fraudulent Financial Reporting (referred to as the *Treadway Commission* after its first chairman, former SEC Commissioner James Treadway), a group of professional organizations met to determine what business entities could do to improve financial reporting. Representatives from the Financial Executives Institute (FEI), the American Accounting Association (AAA), the Institute of Internal Auditors (IIA), the Institute of Management Accountants (IMA), and the AICPA (collectively referred to as the *Committee of Sponsoring Organizations*, or *COSO*) debated internal control theory and definitions. The resulting report (the COSO Report) defined **internal control** as follows:

> Internal control is a process, effected by an entity's board of directors, management and other personnel, designed to provide reasonable assurance regarding the achievement of objectives in the following three categories:

- Reliability of financial reporting.
- Effectiveness and efficiency of operations.
- Compliance with applicable laws and regulations.

Internal control is designed to achieve *management objectives* in three categories. In the *financial reporting category,* the management objectives are related to producing reliable financial reports and safeguarding assets. In the *operations category,* some examples of management objectives are maintaining a good business reputation, ensuring a positive return on investment, increasing market share, promoting new product innovation, and using assets effectively and efficiently. In the *compliance category,* the broad management objective is compliance with laws and regulations that affect the entity.

External auditors are primarily concerned with the financial reporting category. For example, consider the control activity implemented by credit card companies that requires retailers such as **Walmart** to "swipe" a customer's credit card before approving a sale. The control is designed to ensure that a customer's account balance does not exceed its credit limit. This, of course, helps to ensure that the customer's account balance listed as an asset on the credit card company's balance sheet remains collectable. However, some controls related to operations and compliance can also be relevant to the external audit. For example, controls over the completeness and accuracy of key nonfinancial information such as scrap reports can be relevant if the audit team uses such information in completing their analytical procedures or to provide evidence about the valuation assertion for inventory. Compliance controls related to laws and regulations directly affecting the financial statements (e.g., income taxes) are also relevant to the external audit.

The preceding definition of internal control identifies several important concepts. Internal control provides *reasonable* assurance, not *absolute* assurance, that management's objectives will be achieved. Because people operate the controls, breakdowns can occur. Internal control can help prevent and detect many errors, but it cannot guarantee that they will never happen. Several limitations to internal control systems prevent management from obtaining complete assurance that controls are absolutely effective. They are:

- Human error due to mistakes in judgment, fatigue, and carelessness can still occur.
- Although controls are implemented to prevent and detect errors, deliberate circumvention by people in the system can still occur.
- Because most internal controls are directed at lower-level employees, *management override* can occur. For example, it is often possible for management to override controls by force of authority (i.e., if the CEO says to do something, most employees will).
- Although separation of duties can be extremely effective in an internal control system, *collusion* among people who are supposed to act independently can lead to a failure in the achievement of relevant internal control objectives.

Additionally, internal control is subject to cost–benefit considerations. Internal control could be made perfect, or nearly so, but at great expense. An inventory could be left completely unlocked and unguarded (no control at all) or a fence could be used; locks could be installed; lighting could be used at night; television monitors could be put in place; armed guards could be hired. Each of these successive safeguards costs additional money as does extensive supervision of clerical personnel in an office. At some point, the cost of protecting the inventory from theft (or of supervisors catching every clerical error) exceeds the benefit of the internal control activity. In the professional auditing standards, the concept of **reasonable assurance** recognizes that the costs of controls should not exceed the benefits that are expected from the controls. Hence, an entity can decide that certain controls are too costly considering the risk of loss that can occur. Finally, internal control is a *process,* a means to ends (i.e., the management objectives), not an end in itself. It is also dynamic, operating every day within an entity's operating structure, which evolves as the entity and its environment constantly change.

AUDITING INSIGHT | Sarbanes-Oxley Definition of Internal Control

The Sarbanes-Oxley Act of 2002 defines "internal control over financial reporting," which is very similar to the COSO definition, although it focuses primarily on internal control over financial reporting. This definition notes that control policies and procedures should allow:

1. Records to be maintained in reasonable detail to accurately reflect transactions.
2. Transactions to be recorded to permit financial statements to be prepared in accordance with GAAP.
3. Transactions to be executed in accordance with authorization of the entity's management.
4. Unauthorized acquisition, use, or disposition of the entity's assets to be prevented or detected on a timely basis.

Source: U.S. Congress, *Sarbanes-Oxley Act of 2002,* Pub. L. No. 107-204, 116 Stat. 745 (2002).

↳ REVIEW CHECKPOINT

5.1 What are the three goals of an internal control system, according to the COSO Report? Which of the three is most important to auditors?

5.2 What types of control breakdowns can cause a failure to achieve the goals?

5.3 What is the concept of reasonable assurance? Who is responsible for assessing reasonable assurance?

MANAGEMENT VERSUS AUDITORS' RESPONSIBILITY FOR INTERNAL CONTROL

LEARNING OBJECTIVE 5-2
Distinguish between the responsibilities of management and auditors regarding an entity's internal control.

Section 302 of the Sarbanes-Oxley Act stipulates criminal penalties for CEOs and CFOs if they issue materially misleading financial statements. A clear intention of this section of the act is to make sure that management at the top sets the proper tone for the internal control system. In fact, the act is specific about management's responsibility for the organization's internal control system: Management is responsible for establishing a control environment; assessing risks it wishes to control; specifying information and communication channels and content (including the accounting system and its reports); designing and implementing appropriate control activities; and monitoring, supervising, and maintaining the control activities. Management is also in a position to estimate the benefits to be derived from specific controls and then weigh them against the costs. They are expected to make their own judgments about the necessity of specific controls.

In addition to certifying the entity's financial statements and disclosures under Section 302, Sarbanes-Oxley requires management to assess and report on the entity's internal control over financial reporting in Section 404. Specifically, the entity's annual report must include the following (see Exhibit 5.1 for an example):

- A statement that management is responsible for establishing and maintaining adequate internal control over financial reporting.
- A statement identifying the framework (e.g., the COSO framework) that management uses as a benchmark for evaluating the effectiveness of the entity's internal control.
- A statement providing management's assessment of the effectiveness of the entity's internal control.

Under Section 302, management must also disclose any material weaknesses in internal control. If any material weaknesses exist, management may not be able to conclude that the entity's internal control over financial reporting is effective. See Exhibit 5.1 for excerpts from a **Krispy Kreme** management report on internal control over financial reporting, which identified numerous material weaknesses in its internal control. This report was issued on January 28, 2007; since that time, Krispy Kreme has taken actions to improve its internal control and the most recent report (dated March 31, 2011) does not mention any material weaknesses.

Auditors' Internal Control Responsibilities

The audit team has at least three reasons for conducting an evaluation of an entity's internal control. First, Sarbanes-Oxley requires an audit of the effectiveness of internal control over financial reporting for public companies. The internal control audit is conducted along with the financial statement audit as part of an overall **integrated audit process**. In essence, the public accounting firm employs one integrated audit process that culminates in the issuance of two opinions: one on the entity's financial statements and one on the effectiveness of the entity's internal control system.

Second, for each fraud risk identified during the planning stage, the audit team should evaluate whether the client has implemented control activities that are specifically designed to address the risk of fraud that has been identified. These might include control activities that are designed to address risks of fraud to specific financial statement accounts or more generally control activities that are designed to promote a culture of honest and ethical behavior. For example, the audit team should evaluate the controls related to the use of period-end journal entries, which have been used in the past to commit frauds at companies such as WorldCom and **Dell, Inc.** The use of period-end journal entries to manipulate income is illustrated in the following Auditing Insight.

EXHIBIT 5.1 Excerpts from Krispy Kreme's Management's Report on Internal Control over Financial Reporting

Our *management is responsible for establishing and maintaining adequate internal control over financial reporting*... Internal control over financial reporting is a process, effected by an entity's board of directors, management and other personnel, designed to provide *reasonable assurance* regarding the reliability of financial reporting and the preparation of consolidated financial statements for external purposes in accordance with GAAP. Internal control over financial reporting includes those policies and procedures which pertain to the maintenance of records that, in reasonable detail, accurately and fairly reflect the transactions and dispositions of assets; provide reasonable assurance *that transactions are recorded as necessary* to permit preparation of consolidated financial statements in accordance with GAAP; provide reasonable assurance that *receipts and expenditures are being made only in accordance with our and/or our Board of Directors' authorization;* and provide reasonable assurance regarding *prevention or timely detection of unauthorized acquisition, use or disposition of our assets* that could have a material effect on our consolidated financial statements.

Because of its inherent limitations, internal control over financial reporting may not prevent or detect misstatements. Also, projections of any evaluation of the effectiveness of our internal control over financial reporting to future periods are subject to the risk that controls may become inadequate because of changes in conditions, or that the degree of compliance with the policies or procedures may deteriorate.

Management assessed the effectiveness of our internal control over financial reporting as of January 28, 2007, *using the criteria established in Internal Control—Integrated Framework issued by the Committee of Sponsoring Organizations of the Treadway Commission* (COSO).

A *material weakness* is a control deficiency, or combination of control deficiencies, that results in *more than a remote likelihood that a material misstatement of the annual or interim consolidated financial statements will not be prevented or detected.* As of January 28, 2007, management identified the material weaknesses described below.

We did not maintain an effective control environment based on the criteria established in the COSO framework. The following material weaknesses were identified related to our control environment:

- We did not establish a formal enterprise risk assessment process.
- We did not formalize lines of communication among legal, finance and operations personnel. Specifically, procedures were not designed and in place to ensure sharing of financial information within and across our corporate and divisional offices and other operating facilities such that significant issues are brought to the attention of appropriate level of accounting and financial reporting personnel.
- We did not maintain certain written accounting policies and procedures including those over critical accounting policies.
- We did not have an effective process for monitoring the appropriateness of user access and segregation of duties related to financial applications.

These control environment material weaknesses contributed to the material weaknesses described below.

We did not maintain effective control over our financial closing and reporting processes....

We did not maintain effective controls over the completeness and accuracy of certain franchisee revenue....

We did not maintain effective controls over the completeness and accuracy of our accounting for lease related assets, liabilities and expenses....

We did not maintain effective controls over the accuracy and completeness of our property and equipment accounts...

These control deficiencies contributed to the previously reported restatement of our consolidated financial statements for fiscal 2003 and fiscal 2004 and all quarterly periods in fiscal 2004 and the first three quarters of fiscal 2005. Management has concluded that each of the control deficiencies above could result in a misstatement of account balances or disclosures that would be material to our annual or interim consolidated financial statements that would not be prevented or detected. Accordingly, management has concluded that each of the control deficiencies listed above constitutes a material weakness as of January 28, 2007. *Because of these material weaknesses, management has concluded that we did not maintain effective internal control over financial reporting* as of January 28, 2007, based on the COSO criteria. Management's assessment of the effectiveness of our internal control over financial reporting as of January 28, 2007 has been audited by PricewaterhouseCoopers LLP, an independent registered public accounting firm, as stated in their report which appears in this Annual Report on Form 10-K [emphasis added].

The final reason for evaluating an entity's internal control is to assess the risk of material misstatement (RMM) for each relevant assertion. The assessment of RMM at the assertion level is completed for all financial statement audits to give the audit team a basis for planning the audit and determining the *nature, timing,* and *extent* of substantive audit procedures to be conducted for the financial statement audit. RMM

> ### AUDITING INSIGHT — Dell Doesn't Compute
>
> In August 2005, the SEC's Division of Enforcement notified Dell, Inc. that it had commenced an investigation of the company and was seeking documents and information regarding certain accounting and financial reporting practices. The attorneys advising Dell's audit committee hired **KPMG LLP** to serve as independent forensic accountants.
>
> Using a proprietary software tool designed to identify potentially questionable journal entries based on selected criteria (for example, entries made late in the quarterly closing process, entries containing round dollar line items between $3 million and $50 million, and liability-to-liability transfers), KPMG selected and reviewed more than 2,600 journal entries.
>
> The investigation raised questions relating to numerous accounting issues, most of which involved adjustments to various reserve and accrued liability accounts, and identified evidence that certain adjustments appear to have been motivated by the objective of attaining financial targets. These activities typically occurred in the days immediately following the end of a quarter when the accounting books were being closed and the results of the quarter were being compiled. KPMG found evidence that, in that timeframe, account balances were reviewed, sometimes at the request or with the knowledge of senior executives, with the goal of seeking adjustments so that quarterly performance objectives could be met. They concluded that a number of these adjustments were improper, including the creation and release of accruals and reserves that appear to have been made for the purpose of enhancing internal performance measures or reported results as well as the transfer of excess accruals from one liability account to another and the use of the excess balances to offset unrelated expenses in later periods. KPMG also found that sometimes business unit personnel did not provide complete information to corporate headquarters and, in a number of instances, purposefully incorrect or incomplete information about these activities was provided to internal or external auditors.
>
> KPMG identified evidence that accounting adjustments were viewed at times by Dell's management team as an acceptable device to compensate for earnings shortfalls that could not be closed through operational means. Often these adjustments were for several hundred thousand or even several million dollars.
>
> **Source:** Dell, Inc. 8-K, August 13, 2007.

is composed of *inherent risk* and *control risk*. *Inherent risk,* the susceptibility of an account to misstatement, was discussed in Chapter 4; this chapter focuses on control risk assessment. Recall that **control risk** is the probability that an entity's controls will fail to prevent or detect material misstatements due to errors or frauds that would otherwise have entered the system. Remember that the audit team assesses *control risk* to determine RMM for each relevant assertion identified in the audit plan; the higher the assessment of control risk, the higher the assessment of RMM. Most audit teams express their control risk assessment decision with descriptive terminology (e.g., high, moderate, low), which recognizes the imprecise nature of evaluating risk. Audit teams' assessment of control risk as high implies that the controls are not effective at preventing or detecting material misstatements and could not be relied upon by audit teams. In this situation, audit teams would likely use substantive tests of details designed to obtain the highest quality of external evidence (*nature*) at or near the entity's fiscal year-end (*timing*) with large sample sizes (*extent*). On the other hand, audit teams' assessment of control risk as low implies that the controls are effective at preventing or detecting material misstatements and could possibly be relied upon by auditors. In this situation, the audit teams might be able to use tests of detail or a less time-consuming substantive analytical review to obtain external evidence (nature) at an interim date before the entity's fiscal year-end (*timing*) with much smaller sample sizes (*extent*). Of course, audit teams may assess control risk between low and high and adjust the substantive procedures accordingly in order to obtain enough evidence to mitigate the risk of material misstatement to a low level for the relevant assertion being tested. Exhibit 5.2 illustrates the trade-off between testing and relying on internal controls and how it impacts the nature, timing, and extent of substantive procedures performed.

EXHIBIT 5.2
Relationship between Internal Control Reliance and Audit Procedures

	Less Reliance on Internal Control (higher control risk; lower detection risk)	More Reliance on Internal Control (lower control risk; higher detection risk)
Nature	More effective tests (for example, use of direct external evidence)	Less effective tests (for example, use of internal evidence)
Timing	Testing performed at year-end	Testing can be performed at interim
Extent	Higher sample size	Lower sample size

REVIEW CHECKPOINTS

5.4 What are management's and auditors' respective responsibilities regarding internal control?

5.5 Define *control risk* and explain the role of control risk assessment in audit planning.

5.6 What are the primary reasons for conducting an evaluation of an audit client's internal control?

5.7 How does control risk affect the *nature, timing,* and *extent* of substantive procedures?

COMPONENTS OF INTERNAL CONTROL

LEARNING OBJECTIVE 5-3
Define and describe the five basic components of internal control and specify some of their characteristics.

The COSO Report defined each of the three management objectives and stated that management should enact the five components related to each of them (Exhibit 5.3). The interrelated components of internal control are relevant for each of the management objective categories (Exhibit 5.4). The financial reporting management objectives (shaded area of Exhibit 5.3) are the focus of the rest of the material in this chapter.

EXHIBIT 5.3
Internal Control—Integrated Framework (COSO)

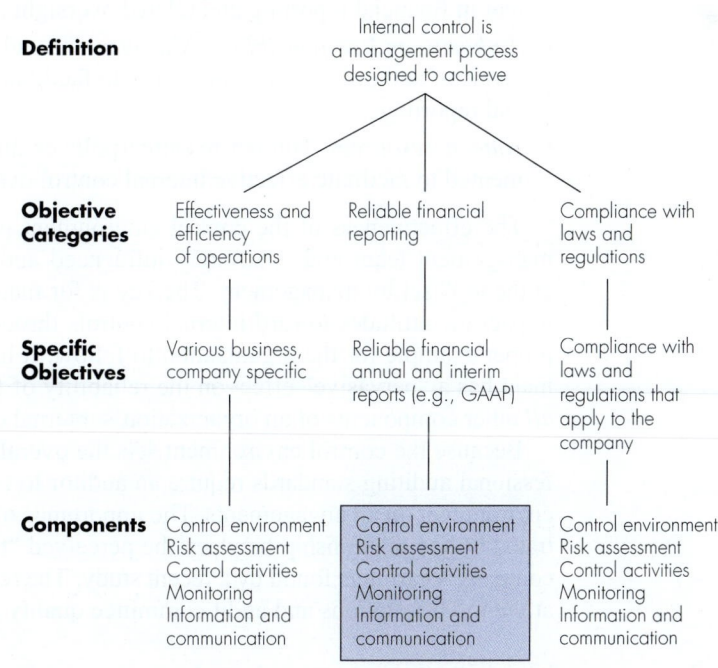

EXHIBIT 5.4
Interrelated Components of Internal Control

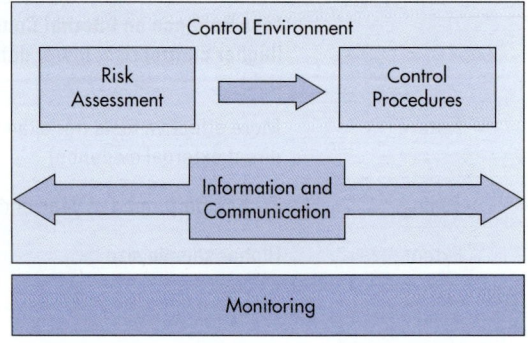

Control Environment

The control environment sets the tone of the organization. It is the foundation for all other components of internal control. It provides discipline and structure to all participants and stakeholders. Control environment factors include the integrity, ethical values, and competence of the entity's people. COSO *Internal Control over Financial Reporting. Guidance for Smaller Public Companies,* January 23, 2009, provides basic principles for each of the components of internal control. The following are general principles of an effective internal control environment:

- *Integrity and ethical values.* Sound integrity and ethical values, particularly of top management, are developed and understood and set the standard of conduct for financial reporting.
- *Board of directors.* The board of directors understands and exercises oversight responsibility related to financial reporting and related internal control.
- *Management's philosophy and operating style.* Management's philosophy and operating style support achieving effective internal control over financial reporting.
- *Organizational structure.* The company's organizational structure supports effective internal control over financial reporting.
- *Financial reporting competencies.* The company retains individuals who are competent in financial reporting and related oversight roles.
- *Authority and responsibility.* Management and employees are assigned appropriate levels of authority and responsibility to facilitate effective internal control over financial reporting.
- *Human resources.* Human resource policies and practices are designed and implemented to facilitate effective internal control over financial reporting.

The effectiveness of the control environment is influenced heavily by a company's management team and is strongly influenced and unquestionably related to the "tone at the top" set by management. The key is for management to be deliberate in trying to impact the attitudes toward internal controls throughout the organization by setting the proper example for the organization to follow. It has been said that the control environment has a "pervasive" effect on the reliability of financial reporting because it impacts *all* other components of an organization's internal control system.

Because the control environment sets the overall foundation for internal control, professional auditing standards require an auditor to obtain an understanding of the control environment on all engagements. The importance of the control environment is also illustrated by the relationship between the perceived "tone at the top" and the quality of the company's earnings found by a recent study. The results of the study found that both tone at the top perceptions and audit committee quality are associated with earnings quality.[1]

---

[1] J. Hunton, R. Hoitash, and J. Thibodeau, "The Relationship between Perceived Tone at the Top and Earnings Quality," *Contemporary Accounting Research,* Forthcoming, 2011.

The results emphasize the importance of both the tone at the top and the functioning of its board of directors and the audit committee of that board to the control environment.

> ### AUDITING INSIGHT — Assessing the Control Environment
>
> To assess employee understanding of its control environment, internal auditors of a large privately held manufacturing and distribution company used the following survey items:
>
> **BUSINESS ETHICS SURVEY RESULTS**
> The following are survey questions presented with the percentage of respondents from the study who actually selected each response when completing the survey. The complete list of survey questions and results can be found in the article referenced in the source note. Each respondent was asked to respond in the following manner:
>
> Please indicate the extent to which you agree or disagree with each of the following statements by circling the appropriate letters. All survey responses will remain strictly anonymous.
>
> SA = Strongly agree   A = Agree   D = Disagree   SD = Strongly disagree   DK = Don't know
>
> | | SA | A | D | SD | DK |
> |---|---|---|---|---|---|
> | 1. My immediate supervisor places a lot of emphasis on doing the right thing. | 52.7% | 44.1% | 2.2% | 1% | 0% |
> | 2. My immediate supervisor behaves ethically in the performance of his/her job. | 50.5 | 41.9 | 5.4 | 0 | 2.2 |
> | 3. The company provides adequate guidance for me to determine what behaviors are appropriate in performing my job (e.g., policies or guidelines that define appropriate behavior). | 30.4 | 65.2 | 3.3 | 0 | 1.1 |
> | 4. The company has a code of business ethics. | 48.4 | 51.6 | 0 | 0 | 0 |
> | 5. I am expected to strictly adhere to company policies and procedures in the performance of my job. | 50.5 | 46.2 | 2.2 | 1.1 | 0 |
>
> **Source:** S.S. Lightle, J. F. Castellana, and B.T. Cutting, "Assessing the Control Environment," *The Internal Auditor,* December 2007, pp. 51.

The **audit committee** is a subcommittee of the board of directors that is generally composed of three to six "outside" members (those not involved in the entity's day-to-day management) of the organization's board of directors. Each member must be *financially literate,* and one member must be a "financial expert." The purpose of including outside members is to provide a buffer between the audit team and the operating management team of the company. The buffer allows the audit team (and the corporate internal audit department) to report any controversial findings to members of the board of directors without fear of reprisal. For example, should the internal auditors find wrongdoing in the CEO's office, it would do no good to report the matter to the CEO. Similarly, if management does not have control over appointing auditors, management is prevented from threatening to dismiss the auditors if they do not agree with an inappropriate accounting practice. Some of the more important duties of the audit committee follow:

- Appointment, compensation, and oversight of the public accounting firm conducting the entity's audit.
- Resolution of disagreements between management and the audit team.
- Oversight of the entity's internal audit function.
- Approval of nonaudit services provided by the public accounting firm performing the audit engagement.

Small and midsize entities may implement the control environment factors differently than larger entities. For example, smaller entities might not have a written code of conduct but instead develop a culture that emphasizes the importance of integrity and ethical behavior through oral communication and by management example. Similarly, a smaller entity may not have an independent or outside member on its board of directors.

Risk Assessment

To use the ill-fated White Star liner *Titanic* as an analogy, corporate management has often been accused of spending too much time making sure that the deck chairs are properly arranged rather than worrying about their biggest risk by peering over the bow looking for icebergs. The "icebergs" for an audit client represent **business risks** that they face: factors, events, and conditions that can prevent the organization from achieving its business objectives, including effective financial reporting. To identify and assess the risk of failure for the company to meet its objectives, management must first clearly articulate its objectives. These range from overall strategy to specific entity and activity-level objectives.

Management should take steps to identify risks, estimate their significance and likelihood, and consider how to manage the risks. By setting management objectives, management can identify critical success factors and institute policies and procedures to ensure that they are met. The enterprise risk management framework discussed in Chapter 4 is an effective method for performing this function. (*Note:* The risk assessment element of the COSO framework is *management's* responsibility and is *not related* to an auditor's assessment of inherent risk, control risk, and the overall risk of material misstatement at the assertion level.) Although an audit client's risk assessment process should relate to all its objectives, the professional standards require the auditor to "obtain an understanding of management's process for (1) risks relevant to financial reporting objectives, including risks of material misstatement due to fraud ('fraud risks'); (2) assessing the likelihood and significance of misstatements resulting from those risks; and (3) deciding about actions to address those risks."[2]

In completing their work, the audit team members seek to understand whether management is specifying financial reporting objectives with sufficient clarity and criteria to enable the identification of risks of material misstatement in financial reporting, in particular due to fraud. Once identified, the audit team also would like to see that management has a basis for determining how to manage the identified risks. For smaller entities, the risk assessment process is likely to be less formal and less structured. Although all entities should have established financial reporting management objectives, they may be recognized implicitly rather than explicitly in smaller entities.

> ### ↳ REVIEW CHECKPOINTS
>
> 5.8 What are the five components of management's internal control?
> 5.9 What is the *control environment*?
> 5.10 What is an audit committee? What are its duties?
> 5.11 What is the purpose of risk assessment for an entity?

Control Activities

Once risks to management's objectives have been identified, internal control activities need to be established to eliminate, mitigate, or compensate for the risks. **Control activities** are specific actions a client's management and employees take to help ensure that management's directives are carried out.

---

[2] PCAOB Auditing Standard No. 12, "Identifying and Assessing Risks of Material Misstatement," August, 2010.

The professional standards require the audit team to document their understanding of the internal control system, which includes their understanding of whether management has implemented control activities that are sufficient to address the risks of material misstatement for each relevant assertion. To answer this important question, the audit team begins the process by considering what they learned about the internal control activities as they were gaining an understanding of the other components of the COSO framework, in particular, the control environment and risk assessment.

Simply stated, these components have an impact on the audit team's understanding of the control activities. For example, in the late 1990s and up through its bankruptcy in December 2001, Enron's corporate culture was characterized by a brutal performance evaluation culture that was executed on a quarterly basis by its now infamous performance review committee (PRC) implemented by company president, Jeffrey Skilling. The PRC promoted a culture that focused inordinately on performance-based compensation and keeping your job. As a result, it can be said that Enron's management team seemingly selected and applied accounting procedures that were designed explicitly to improve its reported financial condition and performance and ultimately mask the company's true underlying financial condition and performance. Clearly, the tone at the top set by Skilling had an impact on the control activities at Enron.

The next step in the process requires the audit team to document their understanding of the extent to which each of the client's control activities have been designed to support a relevant financial statement assertion by mitigating a risk of material misstatement. If their assessment is positive, the audit team might want to consider testing the control activity in the hopes of relying on it to reduce substantive testing for the relevant assertion that was supported. For now, see Exhibit 5.5 for several examples of this step, which will be covered in more depth later in the chapter.

Importantly, when documenting their understanding of the internal control system, the audit team should keep in mind the following principles related to control activities:

- *Information technology.* Has the audit client taken full advantage of significant advances in information technology by using entirely automated control activities whenever it is efficient and effective.
- *Level of integration with their risk assessment process.* Has the audit client's management team taken the action necessary to address the identified risks to the achievement of financial reporting objectives.
- *Selection and development of control activities.* Control activities are selected and developed considering their cost and their potential effectiveness in mitigating the risks identified.
- *Policies and procedures.* Have the policies related to reliable financial reporting been documented and communicated throughout the company?

Ultimately, financial reporting control activities are imposed on the accounting system for the purpose of *preventing, detecting,* and *correcting* errors and frauds that could enter

EXHIBIT 5.5 Risk, Controls, and Testing of Controls

Risk of Material Misstatement	Control Activity	Test of Control Activity
Sales revenue is recorded when the goods had not been shipped to the customers.	All sales invoices are matched to shipping documents before recording in general ledger.	For a sample of sales revenue entries in general ledger, vouch to proper shipping document.
Goods will be shipped to a new customer that is unable to pay for the goods	Credit department performs a detailed credit check for all new customers.	For a sample of new customers, examine documentation that indicates a proper credit check was performed.
Goods will be shipped to a customer, and the revenue is not recorded.	All shipping documents are matched to sales invoices that have been recorded in general ledger.	For a sample of shipping documents, trace amount shipped to a sales invoice recorded in the general ledger.

and flow through to the financial statements. Clearly, **preventive controls**, procedures that prevent misstatements before they occur (those that ensure hiring competent people, limiting access, requiring approval, separating duties, etc.), are preferable to **detective controls**, procedures that detect misstatements after they occur. In some sense, all control activities can be thought of as *preventive controls* because the possibility of being caught by a *detective control* might prevent someone from committing an error or a fraud. Control activities include *performance reviews, separation of duties, physical controls,* and *information-processing controls.*

Performance Reviews

Management has primary responsibility for ensuring that the organization's objectives are being met. Performance reviews require management's active participation in the supervision of operations. Management's study of budget variances with follow-up action is an example of a performance review. Management that performs frequent performance reviews has more opportunities to detect errors in the records than management that does not. The frequency, of course, is governed by the costs and benefits.

Subsequent action to investigate or correct differences is also important. Periodic comparison and action to correct errors lowers the risk that material misstatements due to error or fraud exist in the financial statement accounts. Such comparisons are frequently assigned to internal auditors and other employees. Research has shown that companies with active internal auditors have fewer accounting errors.

Separation of Duties

A very important characteristic of effective internal control is an appropriate separation of duties or functional responsibilities. Four types of functional responsibilities should be performed by different departments (see Exhibit 5.6), or at least by different persons on the entity's accounting staff:

1. *Authorization to execute transactions.* This duty belongs to people who have the authority and the responsibility for initiating or approving transactions. Authorization may be *general,* referring to a class of transactions (e.g., all purchases up to $100,000), or it may be *specific* (e.g., sale of a major asset).
2. *Recording transactions.* This duty refers to the accounting and record-keeping function, which in most organizations is delegated to a computerized information system. People who control computerized processing are the record keepers.
3. *Custody of assets involved in the transactions.* This duty refers to the actual physical possession or effective physical control of property.
4. *Periodic reconciliation of existing assets to recorded amounts.* This duty refers to making comparisons at regular intervals and taking appropriate action with respect to any differences.

Incompatible responsibilities are combinations of responsibilities that place a person alone in a position to *create* and *conceal* misstatements due to errors or frauds in her or his normal job. Duties should be divided so that no one person can control two or more of these responsibilities. If different departments or persons are forced to deal with these different facets of transactions, frauds are more difficult to commit because they would

EXHIBIT 5.6
Separation of Duties

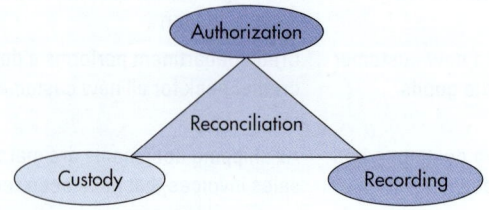

then require collusion of two or more persons, and most people hesitate to seek the help of others to conduct wrongful acts.

A second benefit of separating duties is that by acting in a coordinated manner (handling different aspects of the same transaction), innocent errors are more likely to be found and corrected. The old saying is "Two heads are better than one."

Many control activities once performed by different individuals in manual systems are, of course, now handled in an automated manner. This typically reduces the number of people who handle a transaction, often to just the individual employee who enters the data into the computer application (e.g., SAP). Therefore, individuals who have access to the computer application might be in a position to perform incompatible functions. As a result, companies have to design internal control activities that will effectively limit opportunities for any one individual to both perpetrate and conceal misstatements or losses due to errors or fraud. These often include password access controls that are designed to align the computer access rights to transactions, data, key documents, and assets with only those employees who require such access to complete their clearly defined role in the internal control system.

Physical Controls

Physical access to assets and important records, documents, and blank forms should be limited to authorized personnel. Such assets as inventory and securities should not be available to persons who have no need to handle them. Likewise, access to records should be denied to people who do not have a record-keeping responsibility for them. Some blank forms are very important for accounting and control, and their availability should be restricted. For example, someone not involved in accounting for payroll should not be able to pick up blank time cards. Only authorized persons should be able to obtain blank checks after signing for them. Sometimes access to blank forms is the equivalent of access to an important asset. For example, someone who has access to blank checks has a measure of actual custody and access to cash.

In a computerized processing environment, physical security of computer equipment and limited access to computer program files and data files are at least as important as restricting access to blank checks or inventory. Access controls help prevent improper use or manipulation of data files, unauthorized or incorrect use of computer programs, and improper use of the computer equipment. Locked doors, security passes, passwords, and check-in logs can be used to limit access to the computer system hardware. Having definite schedules for running computerized applications is another way to detect unauthorized access because the computer system software can produce reports that can be compared to the planned schedule. Applications being run at unauthorized times then can be investigated for illicit use of computer resources.

Information Processing Control Activities

Information processing control activities are essential to the effectiveness of an internal control system. Largely all organizations employ computerized information processing on a routine basis. When entities use computerized information processing, the professional standards make clear that information technology (IT) poses specific risks to an entity's internal control system. And, although the focus of this chapter is on providing a broad understanding of internal control, you should be aware that the use of computerized information processing requires entities to implement additional control activities to enable it to support its relevant financial statement assertions (see Exhibit 5.7). The special auditing considerations in a computerized information processing environment are discussed in detail in Module H. We have also provided an Auditing Insight about spreadsheet control activities to exemplify the importance of this issue, which can be found on the next page.

Although largely all organizations employ computerized information processing, some manual controls over information processing remain important in most systems. For example, important manual control activities over the purchasing and cash

EXHIBIT 5.7
Information Processing Controls and Financial Statement Assertions

Information Processing Control	Financial Statement Assertion Supported
Purchase orders must be authorized by purchasing department before any purchase is made.	Occurrence
All invoices received from vendors for payment must be matched to receiving report and purchase order to ensure that the quantity billed agrees with the quantity ordered and received at previously agreed-upon prices.	Accuracy
Prenumbered documents (checks, purchase orders, and receiving reports) must be used and accounted for to ensure that all transactions have been recorded.	Completeness

disbursement cycle include using purchase orders to ensure proper authorization (the *occurrence* assertion), matching vendor invoices with receiving reports and purchase orders to ensure that the quantity billed agrees with the quantity ordered and received at previously agreed-upon prices (the *accuracy* assertion), and using *and accounting for* prenumbered documents (checks, purchase orders, and receiving reports) to ensure that all transactions have been recorded (the *completeness* assertion). (*Note*: Failure to account for numeric sequence of documents eliminates the benefit of prenumbering.) The specific manual control activities for each cycle are discussed in more detail in Chapters 6 through 10.

AUDITING INSIGHT — Spreadsheet Goofs

- **TransAlta Corp.** confessed that a "clerical error" was a costly one—$24 million, to be exact—for the power producer. The Calgary-based company said a spreadsheet goof by an employee caused the company to pay higher than intended rates to ship power in New York. CEO Steve Snyder explained via a conference call that a "cut-and-paste" foul-up within an Excel spreadsheet on a bid to New York's power grid operator led TransAlta to secure 15 times the capacity of power lines at 10 times the price. The costly human error couldn't be reversed by the grid operator and while TransAlta has since tried to recoup the mammoth losses, it was left with a $24 million lesson.

- In October 2003, about two weeks after releasing its third-quarter earnings figures, **Fannie Mae** had to restate its unrealized gains account by $1.2 billion for errors in "mark-to-market" calculations required by *SFAS 149*. This was apparently the result of "honest mistakes made in a spreadsheet used in the implementation of the new accounting standard."

Sources: "Cut-and-Paste Oops Costly for TransAlta," *Canadian Press*, June 4, 2003; "Fannie Mae Corrects Mistakes in Results," *The New York Times*, October 30, 2003, p. C1.

↳ REVIEW CHECKPOINTS

5.12 What is a control activity?

5.13 What is the difference between preventive controls and detective controls? Give an example of each.

5.14 What kinds of functional responsibilities should be performed by different departments or persons in a control system with good separation of duties?

Information and Communication

When evaluating the information and communication component of internal control, the "auditor should obtain an understanding of the **information system**, [emphasis added] including the related business processes, relevant to financial reporting. As part of that process, the auditor must seek to understand the nature of the underlying accounting records, supporting information and the accounts that are used to fully execute a transaction." The auditor should also understand "how the information system captures events and conditions, other than transactions, that are significant to the financial statements."[3] The standards recognize that to make effective decisions, managers must have access to *timely, reliable,* and *relevant* information.

Information systems should be devised to identify data from external sources such as suppliers, customers, economic databases, and so on, as well as internal sources. Having superior information systems can be a part of an entity's strategy and competitive advantage (e.g., **Amazon.com, eBay,** and **Walmart**). Management evaluates the quality of information by determining whether the content is appropriate and the information is timely, current, accurate, and accessible. Note that these sometimes are contradictory. For example, waiting to ensure that information is *accurate* can cause it not to be *timely*.

Communication includes report production and distribution. The account balances are summarized in internal management reports and external financial statements. The internal reports are management's feedback for monitoring operations. The external reports are the financial information for outside investors, creditors, and others. Communication also involves expectations, responsibilities of individuals and groups, and other important matters. Specific duties must be made clear, and people need to know how their activities relate to the work of others. People also need to know what behavior is expected. In addition, personnel also need a means of communicating significant information upstream in an organization. Outsiders also should know that fraudulent and unethical behavior by entity personnel is unacceptable and should be reported to management.

The information system produces a trail of activities (often referred to as an *audit trail*) from data identification to reports. You can visualize that the audit trail begins with the *source documents* (purchase orders, sales orders, etc.) and proceeds through to the financial reports. Auditors often follow this trail frontward and backward, identifying and testing relevant control activities along the way (Exhibit 5.8). They follow it backward from the financial reports to the source documents to determine whether everything in the financial reports is supported by appropriate source documents (the *occurrence* assertion). They follow it forward from source documents to reports to determine whether everything that happened (transactions) was recorded in the accounts and reported in the financial statements (the *completeness* assertion).

EXHIBIT 5.8 Occurrence and Completeness of a Sales Transaction

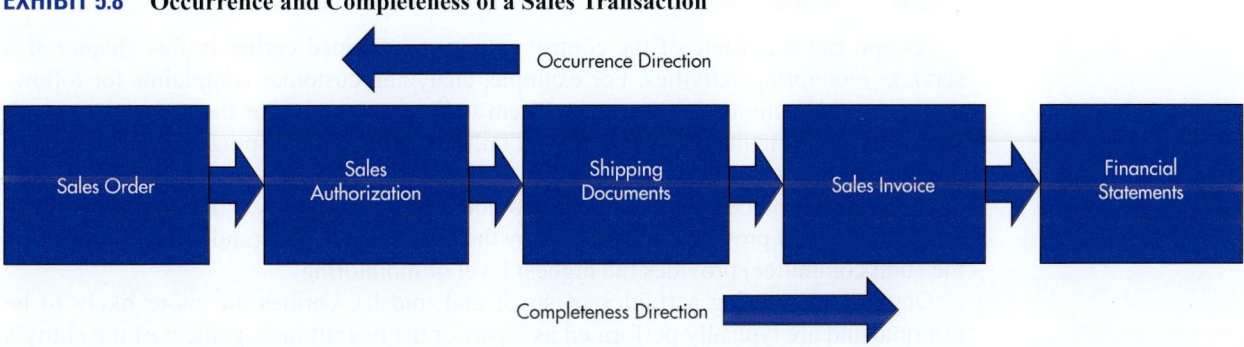

[3] PCAOB Auditing Standard 12, *"Identifying and Assessing Risks of Material Misstatement,"* August, 2010.

Information systems in small or midsize organizations are likely to be less formal than in larger organizations, but their role is just as significant. Smaller entities with active management involvement may not need extensive descriptions of accounting procedures, sophisticated accounting records, or written policies. Communication may be less formal and easier to achieve in a small or midsize company than in a larger enterprise because the smaller organization has fewer levels, and management has more visibility and availability.

One final and very important consideration made by the audit team when gaining an understanding of this component relates to the use of information produced by the company during the audit. The professional standards are clear that an auditor cannot merely rely on information produced by the company's information system without investigation. Instead, the audit team is required to perform audit procedures that are designed either to test the controls that have been designed to ensure that the information is complete and accurate or to test the completeness and accuracy of the information using substantive testing procedures.

Monitoring

To allow for continuous improvements and consider changes in the entity's operating environment, management needs to monitor its internal control systems. The fundamental principles of monitoring include:

- *Ongoing and separate evaluations.* Ongoing evaluations of controls that are separate from other types of evaluations (e.g. operational) enable management to determine whether the other components of internal control continue to function over time.
- *Reporting deficiencies.* Internal control deficiencies are identified and communicated in a timely manner to those parties for taking corrective action and to management and the board as appropriate.

It is important to note that monitoring *does not include* regular management and supervisory control activities and other actions that employees take in performing their everyday duties. Effective monitoring involves ongoing evaluation of the *controls*. Some common monitoring controls include:

- Periodic evaluation of controls by internal audit.
- Analysis of and appropriate follow-up of operating reports or metrics that might identify anomalies indicative of a control failure.
- Supervisory review of controls, such as reconciliation reviews as a normal part of processing.
- Self-assessments by boards and management regarding the tone they set in the organization and the effectiveness of their oversight functions.
- Audit committee inquiries of internal and external auditors.
- Quality assurance reviews of the internal audit department.[4]

As you can see, some of the control activities explained earlier in this chapter also serve as monitoring activities. For example, analyzing customer complaints for follow-up is a control activity, but analyzing them to determine whether the complaints result from a weakness in other controls (e.g., a failure to compare shipping documents to customer orders) is a monitoring activity.

Although the preceding procedures provide management daily monitoring opportunities, the oversight provided to the entity by the board of directors (and, more specifically, the audit committee) provides the highest level of monitoring.

Ongoing monitoring activities of small and midsize entities are more likely to be informal and are typically performed as a part of the overall management of the entity's operations. Management's close involvement in operations often will identify significant variances from expectations and inaccuracies in financial data.

[4] *Guidance on Monitoring Internal Control Systems,* COSO, January 2009.

REVIEW CHECKPOINTS

5.15 What is an *audit trail?* Of what use is it in the audit process?

5.16 Give some examples of everyday work an entity's management can use to enact the monitoring component of internal control. When are such activities control activities and when are they monitoring activities?

INTERNAL CONTROL EVALUATION

LEARNING OBJECTIVE 5-4
Explain the process the audit team uses to assess control risk, understand its impact on the risk of material misstatement, and, ultimately, to know how it affects the nature, timing, and extent of substantive testing to be performed on the audit.

To this point, we have defined internal control, identified management's and the audit team's responsibility for internal control, and described the five components of internal control defined by COSO. These components are considered to be criteria for evaluating an entity's financial reporting controls and the bases for auditors' assessment of control and inherent risk at the financial statement assertion level. In assessing control risk, audit teams use a three-phase procedure that is illustrated in Exhibit 5.9. It is important to note that these phases must be completed at the relevant financial statement assertion level if the auditor plans to rely on a control activity to modify the nature, timing, and extent of substantive tests.

Phase 1: Understand and Document the Client's Internal Control

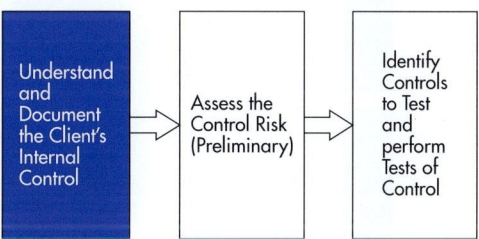

The process of obtaining an understanding of internal controls should occur early in the audit engagement. On every audit engagement, the audit team should evaluate the design of internal control and determine whether controls have been implemented over all relevant assertions related to each material account balance, class of transactions, or disclosures. The procedures used to gain an understanding provide the audit team an overall acquaintance with the control environment and management's risk assessment, the flow of transactions through the accounting system, and the design of some client control activities. Gaining an understanding should be performed in a "top-down" risk-based manner that first identifies *significant accounts* and disclosures and their *relevant assertions*. An account's *significance* is based on its *inherent risk* (i.e., the likelihood of containing a material misstatement before the consideration of internal control or "what could go wrong"). Thus, audit teams focus on likely sources of significant misstatements. This determination is not based on quantitative measures alone, but it is unlikely that a large account could be omitted from consideration. *Relevant assertions* are those that represent the possibility of a material misstatement. Thus, an assertion that does not represent meaningful risk of misstatement is not relevant (e.g., valuation of cash) and should not be considered by the audit team.

Identifying Entity-Level Controls

For all significant accounts and relevant assertions, audit teams begin by examining **entity-level controls (ELCs)**, controls that are pervasive to the internal control system and the reliability of the financial statements taken as a whole. See Exhibit 5.10 for the PCAOB's list of ELCs and the audit team's methods of obtaining an understanding

EXHIBIT 5.9
Phases of Internal Control Evaluation

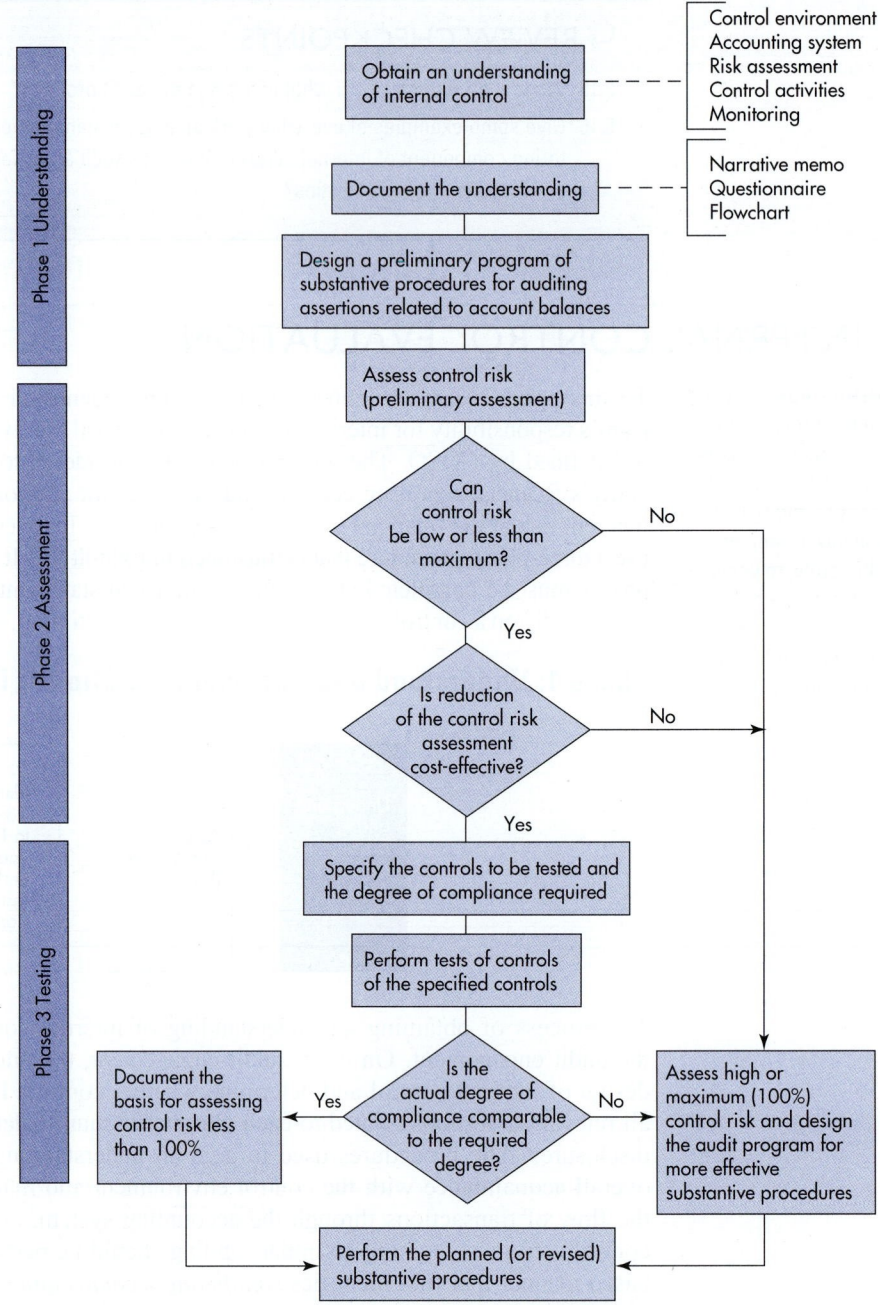

of such controls. Notice that the PCAOB explicitly includes parts or all of the COSO framework elements. If the audit team decides that an entity-level control sufficiently reduces a specific risk of material misstatement for a relevant assertion, they may not need to delve further into transaction-level controls (discussed next) related to that risk. For example, if a chief financial officer who is very familiar with the company's payroll process performs reviews of weekly payroll reports and investigates discrepancies thoroughly, this may provide a control that is sufficient to meet the internal control objectives for payroll reporting.

In addition to entity-level controls, the audit team also identifies **transaction-level controls**, controls that pertain to specific classes of transactions, account balances, and disclosures. The most effective method used to gain an understanding of the flow of transactions, the points at which a misstatement could occur, and the controls that management

EXHIBIT 5.10 Entity-Level Controls and Their Assessment

Types of Entity-Level Controls	Assessment
• Controls related to the control environment • Controls related to management override • Centralized processing and controls including shared service environments • Controls to monitor results of operations • Controls to monitor other controls.	The primary evidence to test these controls is gathered through observation and inquiry and some document examination. The phase 1 work should produce general knowledge of whether management's integrity, values, and operating style promote effective control consciousness throughout the entity.
• Management's risk assessment	The audit team next needs to gain an understanding of how the client assesses the control environment and responds to risk. If the client uses ERM, inquiring and obtaining documentation about other processes should suffice.
• Period-end financial reporting process	After the audit team gains an understanding of the control environment and the client's risk assessment, the next task is to obtain an understanding of the accounting system's flow of transactions and other processes that mitigate financial reporting risk. This review should produce general knowledge about (1) the various classes of significant accounting transactions, (2) the types of material errors and frauds that could occur and (3) the methods by which each significant class of transactions is authorized and initiated, documented and recorded, processed in the accounting system, and placed in financial reports and disclosures.
• Policies that address significant business control and risk management practices	Accounting manuals should contain statements of management objectives and policies. Management should approve statements of specific accounting and management objectives and ensure that appropriate steps are taken to accomplish them. An entity's internal auditors and systems staff often review and evaluate this documentation. Independent auditors may review and study their work instead of doing the same tasks over again. Other sources of information include (1) previous experience with the entity as found in the prior-year audit, (2) responses to inquiries directed to client personnel, and (3) examination of documents and records.

has implemented to address potential misstatements is by observing activities and operations made in a *walkthrough* of one or a few transactions. The purpose of gaining an understanding of internal control is to evaluate *design effectiveness*. **Design effectiveness** determines whether the controls over financial reporting, *if operating effectively,* would be expected to prevent or detect errors or fraud that could result in a material misstatement in the financial statements. A **walkthrough** consists of a combination of inquiry of personnel, observation of an entity's operations, and document examination while tracing one or more transactions through the audit trail from initiation of the transaction to its inclusion in the financial statements. Each client employee involved is asked to demonstrate the procedures that he or she follows in processing the transaction. The walkthrough is an important step in gaining an understanding because often the information that is contained in manuals and understood by supervisors may not be the same as the procedures actually being performed. People could change procedures to make them more efficient, they can forget to perform procedures, they may intentionally not perform procedures, or the procedures may not be passed along when new people are placed in the positions.

At this point, the audit team has obtained an understanding of the *design* of controls (or how those controls are intended to function). However, this does not provide the audit team with evidence as to the *operating effectiveness* of controls unless there is some automation that provides for the consistent application of the operation of the control. Additionally, reperformance of critical controls along the transaction trail can take place at this time to provide evidence of *operating effectiveness*. **Operating effectiveness** refers to whether the control is *operating as designed* and whether the person performing the control possesses the necessary authority and qualifications to perform the control effectively. Evidence of this nature will be obtained in a subsequent phase of the audit team's study of internal control.

Document the Internal Control Understanding

Once the audit team has gained an understanding of the design of the entity's controls, they are required to document that understanding. The understanding can be summarized and documented effectively in the form of questionnaires, narratives, and flowcharts (discussed below).

Internal Control Questionnaires Perhaps the most efficient means to begin gathering evidence about an entity's internal control is to conduct a formal interview with knowledgeable managers using the checklist form of **internal control questionnaire** illustrated in Exhibit 5.11. This questionnaire is organized under headings that identify questions

EXHIBIT 5.11 Internal Control Questionnaire—Payroll Processing

	Yes/No	Comments
Control Environment		
1. Are all employees paid by check or direct deposit?		
2. Is a special payroll bank account used?		
3. Are payroll checks signed by persons who do not prepare checks or keep cash funds or accounting records?		
4. If a check-signing machine is used, are the signature plates controlled?		
5. Is the payroll bank account reconciled by someone who does not prepare, sign, or deliver paychecks?		
6. Are payroll department personnel rotated in their duties? Required to take vacations? Bonded?		
7. Is there a timekeeping department (function) independent of the payroll department?		
8. Are authorizations for deductions signed by the employees on file?		
Occurrence		
9. Are time cards or piecework reports prepared by the employee approved by her or his supervisor?		
10. Is a time clock or other electromechanical or computerized system used?		
11. Is the payroll register sheet signed by the employee preparing it and approved prior to payment?		
12. Are names of terminated employees reported in writing to the payroll department?		
13. Is the payroll periodically compared to personnel files?		
14. Are checks distributed by someone other than the employee's immediate supervisor?		
15. Are unclaimed wages deposited in a special bank account or otherwise controlled by a responsible officer?		
16. Do internal auditors conduct occasional surprise distributions of paychecks?		
Completeness		
17. Are names of newly hired employees reported in writing to the payroll department?		
18. Are blank payroll checks prenumbered and the numerical sequence checked for missing documents?		
Accuracy		
19. Are all wage rates determined by contract or approved by a personnel officer?		
20. Are timekeeping and cost accounting records (such as hours, dollars) reconciled with payroll department calculations of hours and wages?		
21. Are payrolls audited periodically by internal auditors?		
22. Are individual payroll records reconciled with quarterly tax reports?		
Classification		
23. Do payroll accounting personnel have instructions for classifying payroll debit entries?		
Cutoff		
24. Are monthly, quarterly, and annual wage accruals reviewed by an accounting officer?		

related to relevant management assertions, as well as the overall control environment. Not all questionnaires are organized like this, so audit teams need to know the general objectives in order to know whether the questionnaire is complete. Likewise, if you are assigned to prepare an internal control questionnaire, you will need to be careful to include questions about each relevant assertion.

Internal control questionnaires are designed to help the audit team obtain evidence about the control environment and the accounting and control activities that are considered appropriate for normal circumstances. All organizations have unique features, and answers to the questions should not be taken as final and definitive evidence about how well controls actually function. Evidence obtained through the interview process is categorized as inquiry-level information that is not sufficient to demonstrate the operating effectiveness of a control activity. The interviewee could always give answers that reflect what the system should be rather than what it really is. The person can be unaware of informal ways in which duties have been changed or can be innocently ignorant of the system details. Nevertheless, interviews and questionnaires are useful for detecting control weaknesses. An auditor should always consider the possibility that a respondent admits that a control is weak.

An advantage of using internal control questionnaires is that audit teams are less likely to forget to cover some important point. Questions generally are worded such that a "no" answer points out some weakness or control deficiency, thus making analysis easier. However, audit teams should be aware that entity personnel often fully understand that "yes" answers are "good" and "no" answers are "bad," so they tend to tell audit teams "yes" all the time. Also, internal control questionnaires tend to be inflexible. If a key question is not included on the list because the question is unique to a client, the auditor might not even know to ask the question. Thus, for new clients, other methods of gaining an understanding that are tailored to the client are preferable. In practice, audit teams typically use a combination of methods to document their understanding of the client's internal control.

A second method for documenting the audit team's understanding of internal control is to tailor inquiry-type procedures to a particular entity is to write a **narrative description** of each important control subsystem. Such a narrative simply describes all environmental elements, the accounting system, and all control activities. The narrative description can be efficient in audits of very small businesses. However, for a large entity, this description may be difficult to comprehend and might not readily identify potential weaknesses in internal control in a manner that "no" responses do in an internal control questionnaire.

A third method for documenting the auditors' understanding of accounting and control is to construct an accounting and control system flowchart. Many control-conscious companies have their own flowcharts that the audit team may use instead of constructing their own. The advantages of flowcharts can be summarized by an old adage: "A picture is worth a thousand words." Flowcharts tend to help the audit team assess the key control points in the process and can be helpful in identifying missing controls.

Construction of a flowchart takes time because an auditor must take the time to learn about the operating personnel involved in the system and gather samples of relevant documents. Thus, the information for the flowchart, like the narrative description, involves a lot of effort and observation. When the flowchart is complete, however, the result is an easily evaluated, informative description of the system. Showing the various duties performed by one individual or group also provides graphic evidence of any conflicting responsibilities (i.e., lack of separation of duties).

For any flowcharting application, the chart must be understandable to an audit supervisor. Flowcharts are now created with audit-specific flowcharting software but also can be created rather easily in Excel or PowerPoint. The flowchart should communicate all relevant information and evidence about separation of responsibilities, authorization, and accounting and control activities in an understandable, visual form. The starting point in the system, if possible, should be placed at the upper-left-hand corner. The flow of procedures and documents should be from left to right and from top to bottom as much as possible. The shapes of the symbols are commonly understood and fairly obvious. For example, rectangles are processes, circles are connectors, quadrilaterals are manual processes, and so on. Narrative explanations should be written on the face of the chart as annotations or in a readily available reference key.

Refer to Exhibit 5.12 for a partial flowchart representation of the beginning stages of a payroll processing system. The connectors shown by the circled numbers indicate continuation on the flowchart. Ultimately, the flowchart ends showing entries in accounting journals and ledgers. In Exhibit 5.12, you can see some characteristics of both flowchart construction and this specific accounting system. By reading down the columns for each department, you can see that transaction-initiation authority (both hiring and time card preparation) and custody of checks are separated.

Key Decision: Deciding Whether to Continue to Test Controls At this point, the audit team has documented their understanding of the entity's internal control. Then an important decision needs to be made: Should the audit team perform tests of the operating effectiveness of those controls? Audit teams may choose *not* to do so for one of two reasons. First, the audit team could conclude that the internal control system is too ineffective in preventing or detecting misstatements to rely upon to justify reductions of subsequent audit procedures for the relevant assertions. This conclusion is equivalent to assessing control risk at the highest level and specifying extensive substantive procedures such as confirmation of all customer accounts as of year-end. Consider for a moment the Krispy Kreme management report presented earlier that identified significant material

EXHIBIT 5.12 Payroll System Flowchart

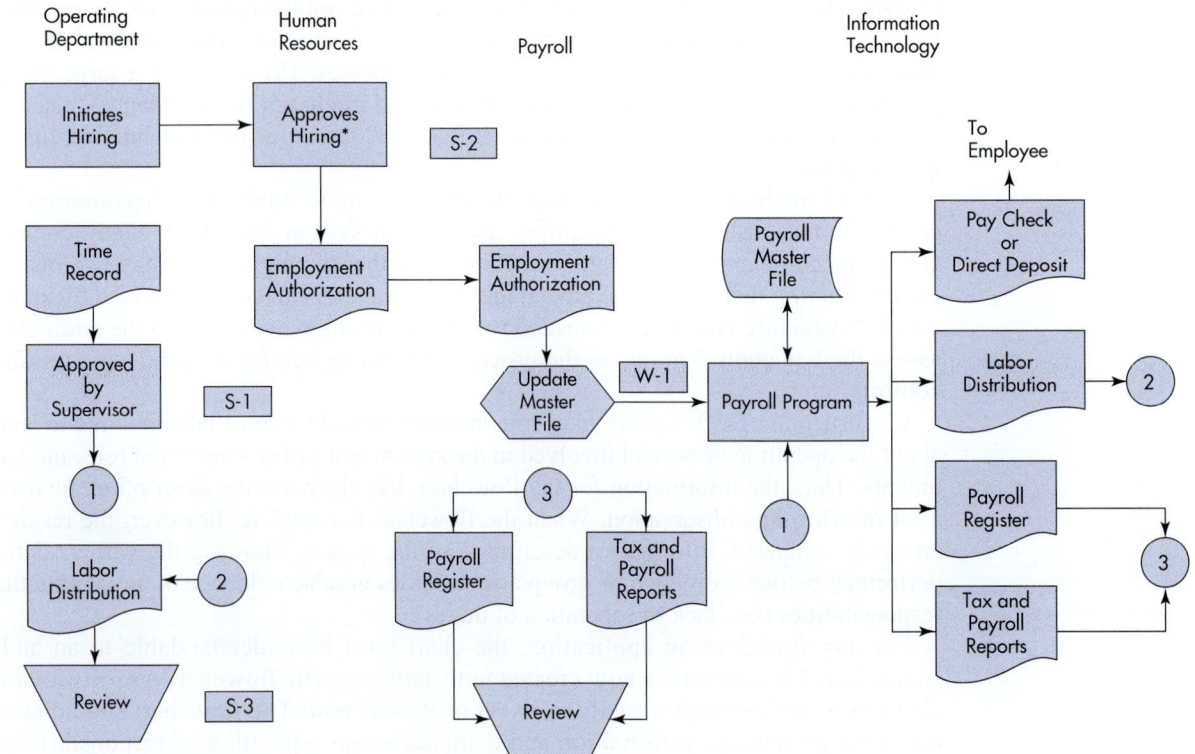

weaknesses in the internal control system. *In such a situation, the audit team would have to make* sure that the audit is conducted in an effective manner by conducting significant substantive testing.

A second reason that audit teams might not test controls would be the team's decision that it would take more time to test the operating effectiveness of the control activities than it would take to perform the substantive tests necessary for a relevant assertion (even if the controls turn out to be working well). In this situation, the cost of obtaining a low control risk assessment can be high. In this case, the conclusion is also equivalent to assessing control risk at 100 percent, but this time it is because the audit team has not conducted the tests of *operating effectiveness* of control activities, not because they have decided controls are ineffective.

For either reason, however, the result is the same: More extensive and effective substantive procedures are required to be completed in order to reduce the risk of material misstatement for a relevant assertion to an acceptably low level. For example, suppose the extensive testing of controls over the accuracy of payroll expenses is estimated to take 40 hours. Also suppose that, if controls were excellent, the substantive tests of payroll accuracy (e.g., confirmation sent to employees) could be reduced by 30 hours. The additional work on testing controls is not economical. The decision to stop work on control risk assessment in this case is a matter of audit *efficiency*—it doesn't make sense to spend 40 hours testing controls to reduce substantive tests by 30 hours. Note again that this decision is appropriate only for nonpublic companies; audit teams must extensively test internal control over financial reporting for public companies. In any event, the auditors' reasoning must be documented.

↳ REVIEW CHECKPOINTS

5.17 What is a "top-down" approach to evaluation of internal controls?

5.18 Must the overall understanding of internal control in phase 1 always be followed by assessment and testing phases? Explain.

5.19 Where can an auditor find a client's documentation of the accounting system?

5.20 What are the advantages and disadvantages of documenting internal control by using (1) an internal control questionnaire, (2) a narrative memorandum, and (3) a flowchart?

Phase 2: Assess the Control Risk (Preliminary)

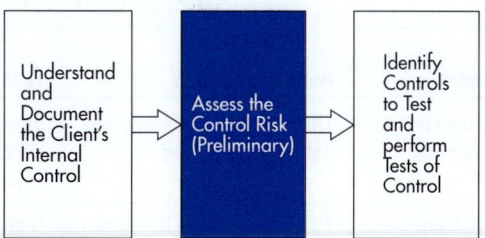

After completing phase 1—understanding and documenting internal control—the audit team should be able to make a preliminary assessment of control risk. At this preliminary stage, the audit team also may use their internal control findings from the previous year's audit. In making and documenting this assessment, the audit term should document internal control strengths and weaknesses in a *bridge workpaper,* so called because it connects ("bridges") the control evaluation to subsequent audit procedures. The major strengths and weaknesses apparent in the flowchart (Exhibit 5.12) can be summarized as in Exhibit 5.13. On the flowchart, the strengths are indicated by the S number and the weaknesses by the W number. You will note that in the bridge workpaper, tests of controls are performed for control strengths (to test their operating effectiveness). However, audit teams should not perform tests of controls on weaknesses because there is no need to prove that they are weaknesses. Doing so would be inefficient. Instead, the audit team identifies substantive procedures that compensate for the control weakness to obtain sufficient appropriate evidence that would allow the auditor to reach a conclusion for relevant assertions. The additional tests are shown in the last column of Exhibit 5.13 as Compensating Substantive Procedures.

The three control strengths relate to good control over payroll. The audit team probably wants to rely on these controls to reduce the substantive procedures related to payroll. Tests of controls must be performed to obtain evidence about whether controls that are apparent strengths actually operate as described. The Test of Controls Audit Plan column of Exhibit 5.13 for each of the strengths is a statement of tests of controls, which consist of procedures designed to produce evidence of how effectively the controls operate in practice. If they operate with the required level of frequency (i.e., control activities are followed by employees a high percentage of the time), control risk can be assessed below the maximum. If they do not operate with the required level of effectiveness, the final conclusion is to assess a high or maximum control risk, revise the audit plan to consider the control weakness, and then proceed with the substantive testing procedures.

Apparent weaknesses in control activities are matters of concern. However, absence of a control at one stage may be offset by *compensating controls* at another stage. For example, the supervisor's review of the labor distribution (S-3) can be sufficient to detect any master file errors (W-1). Of course, it usually is more efficient to *prevent* errors before they occur rather than *detect* them after they occur, but control activities can still be considered effective for the accounting records and financial statements.

The distinction between the understanding and documenting phase and the preliminary control risk assessment phase is useful for understanding the audit team's study and evaluation of internal control. However, the audit team typically performs these phases together, not as separate and distinct audit tasks. For nonpublic entities, the audit team can halt the control evaluation process for efficiency or effectiveness reasons. However, if the audit team wants to justify a low-risk assessment to reduce the substantive audit procedures, the evaluation must be continued in phase 3, the testing phase.

EXHIBIT 5.13 Bridge Workpaper

DUNDER-MIFFLIN, INC
Payroll Processing Controls
December 31, 2012

Prepared by RJR 10/20/12
Reviewed by TJL 10/22/12

	Strength/Weakness	Audit Implication	Test of Controls Audit Plan	Compensating Substantive Procedures
S-1	Supervisor approval is indicated on time card.	This ensures that work was actually performed.	Select a sample of time cards and examine for supervisor signature.	
S-2	Personnel department approves hiring of employees by.	This ensures that hiring is authorized and based on company policies.	Using the S-1 sample, examine personnel file for approval.	
S-3	Supervisor examines labor distribution.	Additional unauthorized payroll costs will not be charged to an operating department.	Using the S-1 sample, examine labor distribution for supervisor initials.	
W-1	Payroll master file update summaries are not returned to Personnel Department for review.	Errors in master file updates, which could result in incorrect payroll, will not be identified before processing.		Test information used in payroll calculations.

At this stage, the audit team has established an assessment of the level of control risk based on their understanding of internal control and identified control strengths and weaknesses. If this assessment is at a level less than the maximum level (i.e., the audit team wishes to rely on internal controls to modify the nature, timing, and extent of substantive procedures), they must next perform tests of controls. This final phase is discussed in the next section.

Phase 3: Identify Controls to Test and Perform Tests of Controls

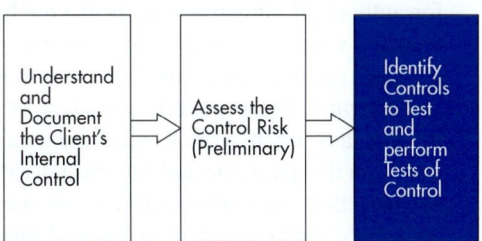

When audit teams reach the third phase of an evaluation of internal control, they already have identified specific control activities for relevant assertions on which risk could be assessed below the maximum (100 percent). This is often referred to as *controls on which the audit team intends to rely*. To support the reduced control risk assessment and the reduction of related substantive procedures for each relevant assertion, audit teams must test the control activities to determine whether they are operating effectively throughout the period. The required level of effectiveness is a matter of professional judgment. Audit teams know that compliance cannot realistically be expected to be perfect. They could decide, for example, that evidence that 96 percent of recorded payroll is supported by validated time cards is sufficient to assess a "low" control risk for the occurrence assertion. Most public accounting firms have internal guidelines to determine the acceptable rate of compliance for an internal control activity to be considered effective. Generally, if a control is judged to be more important and would result in a more significant reduction in substantive testing, the level of compliance must be higher. Factors to consider in determining appropriate levels of compliance are discussed in greater detail in Module F.

Tests of controls, when performed, should be applied to samples of transactions and control activities executed *throughout the period* under audit. The reason for this requirement is that the conclusions about controls will be generalized to the whole period under audit. If the auditor obtains audit evidence about the operating effectiveness of controls during an interim period, additional audit evidence should be obtained for the remaining period. There are cases when audit teams can rely on tests from previous periods if they have evidence that the procedure has not changed and the auditor does not believe there is a significant risk of material misstatement. However, all controls on which the auditor is relying should be tested at least once every three years, and the auditor should test at least some controls every year. In an annual audit, the auditor may not rely on audit evidence about the operating effectiveness of controls obtained in prior audits for controls that have changed since they were last tested or for controls that mitigate a significant risk.

Perform Tests of Controls

The four methods of testing controls are inquiry, observation, document examination, and reperformance. Generally, audit teams use *inquiry* about the existence of control activities and then corroborate the oral evidence by observing that the client-described control activities are actually being performed. *Observation* occurs when auditors have eyewitness observation of employees at their jobs performing control activities. Observation is typically used when certain control activities, such as separation of employees' duties leave no documentary evidence for subsequent examination. Observation also can produce evidence of access controls such as the use of password-secured access to the computerized information system, locked doors, and security guards. The limitation of observation is that this test of control is performed as of one point in time (usually near year-end) and what is observed at that point in time may not be representative of prior time periods.

Some tests of controls depend on documentary evidence such as a payroll entry supported by a time card. In these cases, *document examination* for evidence of signatures, initials, checklists, reconciliations, and the like provides better evidence than procedures that leave no documentary tracks. Document examination might be enough; the audit team may look to see whether the documents were marked with an initial, signature, or stamp to indicate they had been checked. For example, audit teams could examine canceled checks for authorized signatures, inspect voucher packets for the initials of the employee who matched vendor invoices with supporting purchase orders and receiving reports, or examine bank reconciliations to make sure that they have been performed on a timely basis.

Generally, the most effective test of controls is reperformance. *Reperformance* can involve any client control activity (such as recalculating "number of hours × wage rate"). In this case, the audit teams perform the arithmetic calculations and compare them to those that the entity's employees were supposed to have made. The key difference between document examination and reperformance is that with the former, audit teams inspect documents for evidence that employees have performed the control activity; reperformance provides evidence that the control activity was (or was not) done correctly. Exhibit 5.14 puts control testing within the perspective of the payroll function with

EXHIBIT 5.14 Assertions about Classes of Transactions and Events for the Period: Payroll Cycle

ASB Assertion	Controls	Tests of Controls
Occurrence. Payroll and related events that have been recorded have occurred and pertain to the entity.	Payroll accounting is separated from personnel and supervision. Labor usage reports are compared to job time tickets or lists of amount of time clocked. Payroll supervisor approved labor usage.	Observe separation of duties. Vouch labor costs to labor reports. Vouch labor reports to time tickets authorized by management. Examine documentary evidence of supervisor approval.
Completeness. All payroll events that occurred should have been recorded.	All documents are prenumbered and numerical sequence reviewed. Labor costs were reviewed by supervisors and compared to budgets. The personnel department notified the payroll department of new hires to include in payroll.	Account for numerical sequence of selected job cost tickets and paychecks. Examine documentary evidence of supervisor review of labor costs. Trace a sample of employees in the personnel file to payroll time logs and the payroll register.
Accuracy. Payroll amounts and related data have been recorded accurately.	Payroll entries are reviewed by a person independent of their preparation. Budgeted payroll expenses by department are compared to actual expenses.	Examine evidence of review and ensure that a party independent of preparation conducted the review. Examine documentary evidence of budget comparison.
Classification. Payroll-related events are recorded in the proper accounts.	Job cost sheets are posted weekly and summary journal entries of work-in-process and of work completed prepared monthly. Payroll supervisor is required to approve distribution of payroll expense accounts and to compare payroll costs to budget.	Verify that payroll account distribution and job cost sheets agree. Examine supervisor signature on payroll reports. Note evidence of comparison to budget.
Cutoff. Payroll events have been recorded in the correct accounting period.	Payroll reports are prepared weekly and transmitted to cost accounting.	Check that the date of payroll reports agrees with dates in weekly journal entries.

examples of specific assertions being supported. Appendix 5A illustrates a sample audit plan for these tests.

Overall, the audit teams' choice of which test of controls to use depends on the nature and importance of the control activity being tested. Not surprisingly, certain types of tests produce more evidence about the operating effectiveness of a control activity than others. The following hierarchy lists the type of control tests from the least persuasive (inquiry) to the most persuasive type of evidence:

- Inquiry of client personnel.
- Observation of the control activity being performed.
- Inspection of relevant documentation.
- Reperformance of the control activity.

To conclude that an internal control activity is operating effectively if the control activity has high risk, the audit team needs more persuasive evidence about its operating effectiveness than it would for a lower risk control. As a result, if the audit team wants to obtain a lower control risk and rely on a higher risk control, the team needs to obtain more persuasive forms of evidence.

Direction of the Tests of Controls   The tests of controls in Exhibit 5.14 are designed to test the payroll accounting in two directions. One is the *completeness* direction, which the audit team is interested in ensuring that all valid hours are included in the entity's payroll; as a result, time logs (which represent valid hours worked) are traced to payroll department files and the payroll register (which represents hours included in the payroll). Exhibit 5.15 shows that the sample for this direction is taken from the population of time logs (including listings of electronic clock ins).

The purpose of the *occurrence* test of payroll is to ensure that all labor hours included in the payroll (represented by the payroll register) were actually worked (represented by time logs). Because payroll provides access to cash, this cycle is highly susceptible to fraudulent activity on the part of an organization's employees. If a fictitious employee were created and added to the payroll, his or her pay could be deposited into another person's account. This is relatively difficult to detect in the era of direct deposit of paychecks.

Reassess the Control Risk

The audit team should evaluate the evidence obtained from an understanding of the client's internal control and from the related tests of control activities. If control risk (and the related RMM) is assessed very low, the substantive procedures on the relevant assertions

EXHIBIT 5.15
Dual-Direction Test of Payroll Controls

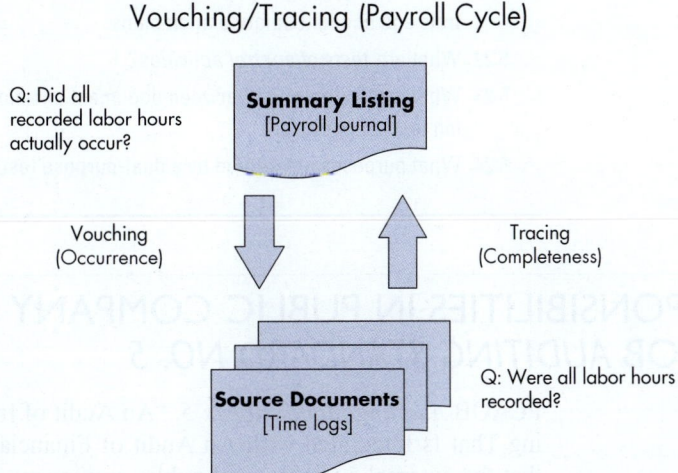

for significant account balances can be limited in cost-saving ways. For example, a surprise payroll distribution as a substantive test might be considered unnecessary or the audit team might decide it is appropriate to place considerable reliance on control activities in the payroll system. On the other hand, if tests of control activities reveal weaknesses (e.g., improper separation of duties, inaccurate cost reports, inaccurate tax returns, or lax personnel policies), the RMM would be assessed at higher levels and substantive procedures would need to be increased to lower the risk of failing to detect material misstatements in the financial statements.

Final assessment of control risk (and consequently, the RMM) is complicated. In the sampling modules (Modules E and F), you will find explanations of sampling methods for performing tests of controls of the type illustrated in Exhibit 5.14. Further discussion of assessing the RMM (including control risk) are saved for those modules. However, recognize that the final evaluation of an entity's internal control is the assessment of the control risk related to each relevant assertion. These assessments are the auditors' expression of the effectiveness of control activities for preventing, detecting, and correcting specific errors and frauds in management's relevant financial statement assertions.

An assessment of control risk should be coordinated with the final audit plan, which includes the list of **substantive procedures** to detect material misstatements in account balances and financial statement disclosures for each relevant assertion. Note that the reassessment of control risk can go only one direction: upward. If the controls are not functioning as described, they cannot be relied upon. On the other hand, even if weak controls are functioning, they are still weak and do not reduce the risk of material misstatement. There is one exception: You find that you were in error during the understanding of controls phase; there are additional controls about which you were unaware. In that case, lowering control risk could be justified.

Thus far, our discussion of tests of control activities and substantive procedures has assumed that these are easily distinguishable. Be advised, however, that general audit procedures can at times be used as **dual-purpose tests**. That is, a single audit test can produce both control testing and substantive testing evidence and, thus, serve both purposes. For example, a selection of recorded payroll entries could be used to (1) vouch payroll to time cards and (2) calculate the correct dollar amount of payroll. The first procedure provides relevant information about an important control activity. The second provides dollar value information that can help provide substantive evidence to support the account balance in the financial statements.

⌕ REVIEW CHECKPOINTS

5.21 What is a *bridge workpaper*? Describe its content and its connection to the tests of controls and account balance audit plans.

5.22 What are *tests of control activities*?

5.23 What is the difference between document examination and reperformance when conducting tests of controls?

5.24 What purposes are served by a dual-purpose test?

▽ RESPONSIBILITIES IN PUBLIC COMPANY AUDITS REQUIRED BY PCAOB *AUDITING STANDARD NO. 5*

PCAOB *Auditing Standard No. 5*, "An Audit of Internal Control Over Financial Reporting That Is Integrated with An Audit of Financial Statements" (*AS 5*) details the work that the external audit team of public entities must perform to comply with section 404

LEARNING OBJECTIVE 5-5
Describe additional responsibilities for management and auditors of public companies required by Sarbanes-Oxley and *Auditing Standard No. 5*.

of Sarbanes-Oxley. The audit team must plan and perform the audit to obtain *reasonable assurance* about whether the entity maintained effective control over financial reporting. The SEC understands reasonable assurance not to be absolute but a "high level of assurance." The focus in *AS 5* is whether a *material weakness* exists at the *end of the year* being reported on. If a material weakness exists, the entity's internal control over financial reporting cannot be considered effective. For the audit team, this duty entails an increased amount of testing for the internal control system.

According to GAAS, when auditing nonpublic entities, the audit team must obtain an understanding of internal controls to determine the *nature, timing,* and *extent* of audit procedures to be performed. If they plan to rely on controls to reduce substantive procedures, they must test the controls for operating effectiveness. However, if they do not plan to rely on controls, tests of operating effectiveness are not required. Under Sarbanes-Oxley, an audit of the internal control system over *financial reporting* is required. The audit of internal controls must be integrated with the financial statement audit and cannot be performed as a separate engagement. Thus, the procedures related to internal control in an integrated audit performed under *AS 5* are far more extensive than those in a GAAS audit for a nonpublic entity.

Requirements

Much of the initial work, including documenting and testing controls, is done by employees of the client, management, the internal audit staff, and outside parties hired by management. *AS 5* encourages the audit team to use the work of internal auditors and others, but the audit team must evaluate the internal auditors' *competence* and *objectivity* and must perform some tests of their work. For more risky areas, audit teams should perform more of the work and the assessment of likely sources of misstatement themselves or supervise any others who assist them in the evaluation.

Another important difference between *AS 5* internal control audits and GAAS financial statement audits is that the audit of internal control is *as of the end of the fiscal year,* whereas, for audits of the financial statements, the audit team must understand and evaluate internal control for the *entire period* to determine its effect on the nature, timing, and extent of substantive procedures.

	Internal Control Audit	Financial Statement Audit
Scope	Test each relevant control activity each year	Test relevant control activities if relying on them
Reporting	Opinion on the effectiveness of internal control	No opinion on internal control
Timing	Evaluate effectiveness of internal control as of the fiscal year-end	Evaluate effectiveness of internal control throughout the fiscal year

AS 5 emphasizes the use of a six-step audit process that is designed to evaluate the effectiveness of the internal control system over financial reporting:

1. *Planning the engagement.* The audit team must evaluate controls for all *relevant assertions* and for all *significant accounts or disclosures.* Thus, significant accounts, locations, and assertions must be identified. A difficult decision in auditing controls of global organizations is determining which locations are significant and must be visited. Each location is evaluated based on size, risks, and whether risks are mitigated by entity-wide controls. The key to determining whether an account, location, or assertion is significant is whether there is a more than remote possibility that a material misstatement could be associated with it. Just as *control risk* is used to determine the nature, timing, and extent of substantive procedures, *inherent risk* is used to determine the nature, timing, and extent of tests of controls.

2. *Using a top-down approach.* As mentioned earlier, the top-down approach focuses on the threats to the integrity of the external financial reporting process. The audit team's first step in gaining an understanding should focus on ELCs that have a pervasive impact on control activities at the process, transaction, or application level. The team next moves down to the significant accounts and disclosures and their *relevant* assertions. By relevant, we mean that the assertion has a reasonable possibility of containing a material misstatement. The audit team is required to understand the internal control process over financial reporting. This aspect of the standard emphasizes performing a *walkthrough* of the internal control process by the audit team members. The top-down approach recommended in *AS 5* is illustrated in Exhibit 5.16.

3. *Testing controls.* After identifying significant controls over financial reporting in the previous step, the audit team decides which controls to test. The evaluation and testing for each assertion must be performed on an annual basis. After an understanding of internal controls is gained through inquiry, document examination, and observation, the controls are evaluated for the possibility that they would not prevent or detect a misstatement. The tests of *operating effectiveness* are similar to a test of controls discussed previously. A sample of transactions is examined using inquiry, observation, document examination, and reperformance. The more risk associated with a control, the more evidence is required. Tests of controls are not performed if the internal control system design is not considered effective. Only the control activies for each relevant assertion that the auditor is relying on to mitigate the risk of material misstatement need to be tested.

4. *Evaluating identified deficiencies.* An **internal control deficiency**—whether resulting from a design or an operating deficiency—exists when either the design or operation of the control under consideration does not allow the entity's management or employees to detect or prevent misstatements in a timely fashion. A *design deficiency* is a problem relating to either a necessary control that is missing or an existing control that is so poorly designed that it fails to satisfy the control's objective. An *operating deficiency,* on the other hand, occurs when a properly designed control is either ignored or inappropriately applied (possibly because employees are poorly trained). More serious internal control deficiencies can be categorized into one of two groups, significant deficiencies or material weaknesses, depending on their severity.

- A **material weakness** in internal control is defined as a deficiency, or combination of deficiencies, that results in a *reasonable possibility* that a *material misstatement*

EXHIBIT 5.16
Top-Down Process

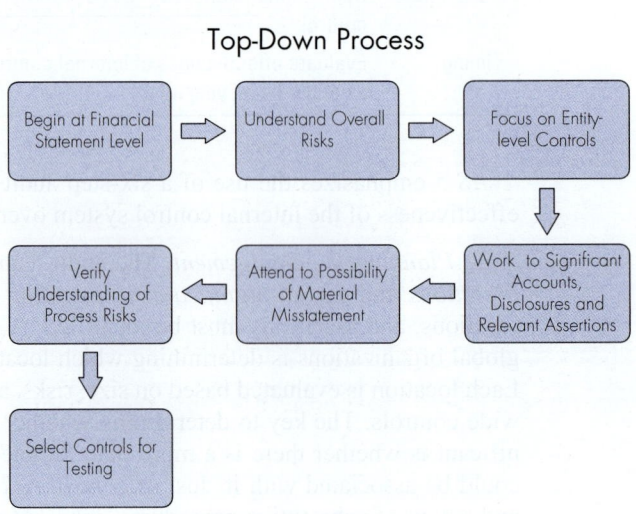

would not be prevented or detected on a timely basis. The following circumstances should be regarded as strong indicators that a material weakness exists:

- Restatement of previously issued financial statements to reflect the correction of a misstatement.
- Evidence of material misstatements (identified by the audit team) that were not prevented or detected by the client's internal controls.
- Ineffective oversight of the financial reporting process by the entity's audit committee.
- Indication of fraud (either material or immaterial) by senior management.

- A **significant deficiency** is a deficiency or a combination of deficiencies in internal control that is less severe than a material weakness yet important enough to merit attention by those charged with governance.

The difference between a significant deficiency and a material weakness involves the (1) *likelihood* and (2) *materiality* that a potential (or actual) misstatement would not be detected on a timely basis.

5. *Wrapping up.* Audit teams are required to issue an opinion on the effectiveness of internal controls. They do so by evaluating evidence obtained from all sources, including the team's testing of controls, any misstatements detected during the financial statement audit, and any identified control deficiencies and material weaknesses. They then form an opinion on the effectiveness of internal control over financial reporting. Audit teams can issue one of three types of opinions on internal controls:

- *Unqualified.* No material weaknesses exist.
- *Disclaimer of opinion.* The audit team cannot perform all of the procedures considered necessary and is unable to determine whether material weaknesses exist.
- *Adverse opinion.* One or more material weaknesses exist.

Note that because the opinion on internal controls is as of the end of the fiscal year, the entity may be able to correct or remediate deficiencies or weaknesses after they have been detected. However, the audit team must have sufficient time to test the design effectiveness and operating effectiveness of the remediated control before providing an unqualified opinion.[5]

In addition to expressing an opinion on the effectiveness of the entity's internal control over financial reporting, the audit team also should evaluate the completeness and presentation of **management's annual report on internal control over financial reporting**. Among other factors, the audit team also must obtain written representations from management that explicitly acknowledges:

- Its responsibility for effective internal control over financial reporting.
- It has evaluated the effectiveness of the internal control over financial reporting.
- It has disclosed all internal control deficiencies and frauds to the audit team.

6. *Reporting on internal control.* The next step in the process is reporting on internal control over financial reporting. For the auditors' report on internal control, two options are available. One option is to have two separate reports: one on the fairness of the entity's financial statements (presented earlier in Chapter 2) and a separate report on internal control over financial reporting. Each report would be separately titled, dated (although using the same date), and signed. The auditors' separate report on internal control is discussed in detail in the following section. The second option is to prepare a *combined report* that expresses one opinion on the financial statements and a second on the effectiveness of internal control over financial reporting. An example of a combined auditors'

---

[5] Clients may request auditors to report separately on the elimination of material weaknesses. Guidance on preparing such a report is provided by PCAOB's *AS 4*.

report on internal control over financial reporting and financial statements is shown in Chapter 12.

> ### AUDITING INSIGHT | The Cost of Section 404
>
> A recent opinion piece published by *The Wall Street Journal* blames the excessive costs associated with the Sarbanes-Oxley Act of 2002 for the significant reduction in initial public offerings (IPOs) in recent years. In particular, the piece argues that "the pace of initial public offerings has never recovered since the enactment of Sarbox," citing that prior to the enactment, there were three times as many IPOs in the first half of the 1990s as there have been since the legislation was enacted. It specifically highlights that Section 404 is primarily to blame, "chewing up more than $2.3 million each year in direct compliance costs at the average public company." Of course, in 2009, the number of financial statement restatements fell for the third consecutive year, so there appears to be some benefit to Sarbanes-Oxley as well.
>
> Sources: "Stock Exchanges and Sarbox," *The Wall Street Journal*, May 6, 2011, p. A14; "Restatements on the Decline," *CFO.com*, March 4, 2010.

> ### ↳ REVIEW CHECKPOINTS
>
> 5.25 What is management's responsibility for reporting on internal control over financial reporting?
>
> 5.26 What steps do audit teams follow in examining internal control over financial reporting?
>
> 5.27 What are (a) an *internal control deficiency*, (b) a *significant deficiency*, and (c) a *material weakness*?
>
> 5.28 What options are available to the auditor for presenting reports on the entity's financial statements and internal control over financial reporting?

▽ AUDITOR REPORTS ON INTERNAL CONTROL OVER FINANCIAL REPORTING

LEARNING OBJECTIVE 5-6
List the major components of the auditors' report on internal control over financial reporting.

As noted earlier in this chapter, in addition to the auditors' report on the entity's financial statements, *AS 5* imposes the following reporting requirements for SEC registrants related to the entity's internal control over financial reporting at the date of the financial statements:

- Management's report on its assessment of the internal control over financial reporting.
- The auditors' report on internal control over financial reporting.

The **auditors' report on internal control over financial reporting** provides an opinion on the effectiveness of the entity's internal control over financial reporting. This opinion is based on tests of the operating effectiveness of the entity's internal control policies and procedures over financial reporting. See Exhibit 5.17 for an example of a standard, unqualified report.

As the exhibit indicates, the auditors' report includes the following key components:

- A title that includes the word *independent*.
- Statements regarding the responsibility of the auditors and management with respect to the assessment and evaluation of internal control as well as the title of management's report on internal control over financial reporting.

EXHIBIT 5.17 Standard Report on Internal Control over Financial Reporting

Title	Report of Independent Registered Public Accounting Firm
Address	To the Board of Directors and Shareholders Dunder-Mifflin, Inc.
Introductory paragraph	We have audited Dunder-Mifflin, Inc.'s internal control over financial reporting as of December 31, 2012, based on control criteria established in Internal Control—Integrated Framework issued by the Committee of Sponsoring Organizations of the Treadway Commission (COSO). Dunder-Mifflin, Inc.'s management is responsible for maintaining effective internal control over financial reporting, and for its assessment of the effectiveness of internal control over financial reporting, included in the accompanying Management's Report on Internal Control over Financial Reporting. Our responsibility is to express an opinion on the company's internal control over financial reporting based on our audits.
Scope paragraph	We conducted our audits in accordance with the standards of the Public Company Accounting Oversight Board (United States). Those standards require that we plan and perform the audits to obtain reasonable assurance about whether effective internal control over financial reporting was maintained in all material respects. Our audit of internal control over financial reporting included obtaining an understanding of internal control over financial reporting, assessing the risk that a material weakness exists, and testing and evaluating the design and operating effectiveness of internal control based on the assessed risk. Our audits also included performing such other procedures as we considered necessary in the circumstances. We believe that our audit provides a reasonable basis for our opinion.
Definition paragraph	A company's internal control over financial reporting is a process designed to provide reasonable assurance regarding the reliability of financial reporting and the preparation of financial statements for external purposes in accordance with generally accepted accounting principles. A company's internal control over financial reporting includes those policies and procedures that (1) pertain to the maintenance of records that, in reasonable detail, accurately and fairly reflect the transactions and dispositions of the assets of the company; (2) provide reasonable assurance that transactions are recorded as necessary to permit preparation of financial statements in accordance with generally accepted accounting principles, and that receipts and expenditures of the company are being made only in accordance with authorizations of management and directors of the company; and (3) provide reasonable assurance regarding prevention or timely detection of unauthorized acquisition, use, or disposition of the company's assets that could have a material effect on the financial statements.
Inherent limitations paragraph	Because of its inherent limitations, internal control over financial reporting may not prevent or detect misstatements. Also, projections of any evaluation of effectiveness to future periods are subject to the risk that controls may become inadequate because of changes in conditions, or that the degree of compliance with the policies or procedures may deteriorate.
Opinion paragraph	In our opinion, Dunder-Mifflin, Inc. maintained, in all material respects, effective internal control over financial reporting as of December 31, 2012, based on control criteria established in Internal Control—Integrated Framework issued by the Committee of Sponsoring Organizations of the Treadway Commission (COSO).
Paragraph on financial statement report	We have also audited, in accordance with the standards of the Public Company Accounting Oversight Board (United States), the balance sheets of Dunder-Mifflin, Inc. as of December 31, 2012 and 2011, and related statements of income, comprehensive income, shareholders' equity, and cash flows for each of the three years in the period ended December 31, 2012, and our report dated March 7, 2013, expressed an unqualified opinion thereon.
Signature	*Michael Scarn, LLP, CPAs* Scranton, PA
Date	March 7, 2013

- A paragraph indicating that the engagement was conducted in accordance with standards established by the PCAOB with a brief description of the procedures performed in the engagement.
- The definition of internal control over financial reporting.
- An identification of the inherent limitations of internal control over financial reporting.
- The auditors' opinion on whether the entity maintained effective internal control over financial reporting. The opinion in Exhibit 5.17 represents an **unqualified opinion on internal control over financial reporting**.
- A reference to the auditors' opinion on the financial statements, indicating the type of opinion expressed.
- The date of the report.

> ### ⌐ REVIEW CHECKPOINT
>
> 5.29 Describe the major components of the auditors' standard, unqualified report on internal control over financial reporting.

MODIFICATIONS TO THE AUDITORS' STANDARD REPORT ON INTERNAL CONTROL OVER FINANCIAL REPORTING

LEARNING OBJECTIVE 5-7
Describe situations in which the auditors' report on internal control over financial reporting would be modified.

As noted earlier, in most situations, the audit team issues an integrated report that includes both the opinion on the financial statements and the opinion on the effectiveness of the internal control system. This report is illustrated as part of our detailed coverage of reports on audits of financial statements in Chapter 12. However, the audit team may also choose to issue separate reports for both the financial statements and the internal control system. In this chapter, we focus solely on internal control reporting.

The report in Exhibit 5.17 expresses an unqualified opinion on the effectiveness of the entity's internal control over financial reporting. The standard unqualified report on internal control may be modified for two reasons: (1) the existence of material weaknesses in internal control over financial reporting and/or (2) the existence of a limitation in the scope of the engagement. These modifications, along with those for other factors, are discussed in the following subsections.

Material Weaknesses in the Entity's Internal Control over Financial Reporting

Recall that a *material weakness* in internal control is defined as a deficiency or combination of deficiencies that results in a reasonable possibility that a material misstatement would not be prevented or detected on a timely basis. If the audit team identifies a material weakness in internal control, the firm expresses an *adverse opinion* on the effectiveness of the entity's internal control over financial reporting. As shown in Exhibit 5.18, the standard report on internal control over financial reporting would be modified (in the exhibit, modifications are shown in bold italic color type) as follows:

- Include a paragraph immediately following the inherent limitations paragraph that defines a material weakness.
- Describe any material weakness(es) identified during the audit as well as an identification of the material weakness(es) described in management's assessment. (*Note*: If any identified material weakness has been omitted from or not presented fairly in management's assessment, the auditors' report should so state, as well as disclose any information necessary to fairly describe the material weakness.) The description should provide specific information about the nature of the material weakness and its effect on the presentation of the company's financial statements issued during the existence of the weakness.

EXHIBIT 5.18 *Modified* **Report on Internal Control over Financial Reporting if a Material Weakness Exists**

Title	Report of Independent Registered Public Accounting Firm
Address	To the Board of Directors and Shareholders Dunder-Mifflin, Inc.
Introductory paragraph	[Standard introductory paragraph]
Scope paragraph	[Standard scope paragraph]
Definition paragraph	[Standard definition paragraph]
Inherent limitations paragraph	[Standard inherent limitations paragraph]
Explanatory paragraphs	*A material weakness in internal control is defined as a deficiency, or combination of deficiencies, that results in a reasonable possibility that a material misstatement would not be prevented or detected on a timely basis.* *During the fiscal year ended December 31, 2012, Dunder-Mifflin, Inc. senior managers were able to override internal controls over financial reporting. This material weakness resulted in accounting errors that were corrected prior to the issuance of the financial statements for the year ended December 31, 2012. Given the nature of the transactions and processes involved and the potential for a misstatement to occur as a result of the internal control deficiency existing on December 31, 2012, we have concluded that there is a reasonable possibility that a material misstatement in the annual or interim financial statements would not have been prevented or detected by internal controls over financial reporting.* *This material weakness was considered in determining the nature, timing, and extent of audit tests applied in our audit of the 2012 financial statements, and this report does not affect our report dated March 7, 2013, on those financial statements.*
Opinion paragraph	*In our opinion, because of the effect of the material weakness described above on the achievement of the objectives of the control criteria, Dunder-Mifflin, Inc. has **not maintained** effective* internal control over financial reporting as of December 31, 2012, in all material respects, based on the COSO criteria.
Paragraph on financial statement report	[Standard financial statement report paragraph]
Signature	*Michael Scarn, LLP, CPAs* Scranton, PA
Date	March 7, 2013

- Modify the opinion paragraph to indicate that because of the effect of the material weakness(es) identified, the company has *not* maintained effective internal control over financial reporting. This is referred to as an **adverse opinion on internal control over financial reporting**.

The audit team also may express an adverse opinion if management's report on internal control is incomplete or improperly presents a disclosure about a material weakness. In addition to the adverse opinion, the auditors' report would include an explanatory paragraph describing the situation.

AUDITING INSIGHT — Material Weaknesses

Restatements of financial results, which soared shortly after the Sarbanes-Oxley Act was passed, dropped in 2007 for the first time in five years. This trend has continued all the way into 2009 when only 630 companies filed a total of 674 restatements, which represented a decline of 27% from the prior year. In addition, the average impact on net income declined from $7.2 million in 2008 to $4.6 million in 2009.

Sources: "Compliance Week; Material Weaknesses Plunge at Large U.S. Companies, Exclusive Compliance Week Analysis Shows," *Marketing Business Weekly,* August 18, 2008; "Restatements on the Decline," *CFO.com,* March 4, 2010.

Effect of an Adverse Opinion on Internal Control on the Auditor's Opinion on the Financial Statements

One issue raised by the preceding discussion concerns how a material weakness that results in an adverse opinion on the effectiveness of the entity's internal control over financial reporting affects the opinion on the financial statements. For example, could the auditor still issue an unqualified opinion on the entity's financial statements? Assuming that no material misstatements were detected, the auditor could issue an unqualified opinion on the entity's financial statements. In addition, as shown in Exhibit 5.18, the following language would be included in the report in the paragraph describing the material weakness(es): "This material weakness was considered in determining the nature, timing, and extent of audit tests applied in our audit of the 2012 financial statements, and this report does not affect our report dated January 29, 2013, on those financial statements."

Restriction on the Scope of the Engagement

During the engagement, audit teams could encounter scope limitations on their ability to evaluate the effectiveness of the entity's internal control over financial reporting, such as failure to obtain written management representations. An additional scope limitation related to internal control over financial reporting could arise when management has implemented new controls (or remediated existing controls) in response to previously identified material weaknesses. If the auditor believes the time period is not sufficient to evaluate the operating effectiveness of the new controls, a scope limitation exists.

A scope limitation may result in the issuance of a **disclaimer of opinion on internal control over financial reporting** or a withdrawal from the engagement, depending on the significance of the limitation (Exhibit 5.19). The standard report on internal control over

EXHIBIT 5.19 Modified Report on Internal Control over Financial Reporting If a Scope Limitation Exists

Title	Report of Independent Registered Public Accounting Firm
Address	To the Board of Directors and Shareholders Dunder-Mifflin, Inc.
Introductory paragraph	Change "we have audited" to "we *were engaged* to audit" because an audit could not be completed. Delete the sentence describing the auditors' responsibility for internal control over financial reporting. (It is inappropriate to indicate that the auditors' responsibility is to express an opinion, and then later say that an opinion could not be expressed.)
Scope paragraph	Delete the scope paragraph.
Definition paragraph	No change
Inherent limitations paragraph	No change
Explanatory paragraphs	Provide an explanatory paragraph describing the scope limitation. If the scope limitation is related to the inability to gather sufficient evidence with respect to a potential material weakness, this paragraph also should include the definition of a material weakness.
Opinion paragraph	Modify the opinion paragraph to disclaim an opinion ("the scope of our work was not sufficient to enable us to express, and we do not express, an opinion . . .").
Signature	Michael Scarn, LLP, CPAs Scranton, PA
Date	March 7, 2013

financial reporting would have to be modified as well. It is important to note that the audit team can still issue an opinion on the entity's financial statements if a disclaimer of opinion is issued on internal control over financial reporting.

Other Report Modifications

AS 5 identifies other situations that may result in modification to the auditors' report on internal control over financial reporting:

- If component audit teams have audited the financial statements and internal control over financial reporting of one or more subsidiaries of the group financial statements, the group audit teams need to determine whether to refer to the component auditors' report in their own report on internal control.
- If management's report on internal control contains additional information (such as corrective actions taken by the entity or the entity's plan to implement new controls), the audit team should disclaim an opinion on this information if they have not had an opportunity to evaluate the information.
- If the audit team believes that management's annual certification (section 302) is misstated, they should include an explanatory paragraph describing the reasons the audit team believes management's disclosures should be modified.
- If changes in internal control over financial reporting occur that materially and adversely affect the effectiveness of the entity's internal control subsequent to the date of the financial statements but prior to the issuance of the report, the audit team should issue an adverse opinion (if the subsequently discovered fact indicates a material weakness) or a disclaimer of opinion (if the auditor is unable to determine whether the subsequently discovered fact indicates a material weakness) on the effectiveness of the entity's internal control over financial reporting.

AUDITING INSIGHT — PricewaterhouseCoopers (PwC) Issues Disclaimer on Krispy Kreme

Recall the material weaknesses identified by Krispy Kreme's management in its 2007 report on internal controls in Exhibit 5.1. Things were worse in 2005. PwC found the following in its 2005 integrated audit of the company's internal control:

a. Krispy Kreme's management did not complete its assessment of internal control over financial reporting.
b. A total of 10 material weaknesses were identified, some of which represented very basic elements of the control environment.
c. The auditors acknowledged that these weaknesses resulted in financial statement restatements.
d. Krispy Kreme's management restricted PwC from completing its own assessment, resulting in a disclaimer of opinion on the effectiveness of internal control.

As a result, PwC was forced to issue the following disclaimer in its 2005 auditors' report on internal control over financial reporting at Krispy Kreme:

Since (a) the Company was unable to complete its assessment of the effectiveness of internal control over financial reporting as of January 30, 2005 and (b) management further restricted the scope of our work by directing that we not complete our (i) testing and evaluation of the effectiveness of the design of the Company's internal control over financial reporting, (ii) testing of operating effectiveness of the Company's internal control over financial reporting, and (iii) review and evaluation of the results of management's testing and of the control deficiencies noted in management's incomplete assessment, and because we were unable to complete our procedures to satisfy ourselves as to the effectiveness of the Company's internal control over financial reporting, the scope of our work was not sufficient to enable us to express, and we do not express, an opinion either on management's assessment or on the effectiveness of the Company's internal control over financial reporting, including identifying all material weaknesses that might exist as of January 30, 2005.

Exhibit 5.20 summarizes situations in which modifications are appropriate for the auditors' report on internal control over financial reporting.

EXHIBIT 5.20 Summary of Modifications to Auditors' Report on Internal Control over Financial Reporting

Situation	Effect on Opinion on Effectiveness of Internal Control
Material weaknesses in internal control over financial reporting	Issue an adverse opinion on internal control
Restriction on the scope of the engagement	Issue a disclaimer of opinion or withdraw from the engagement, depending on the severity of the scope limitation
Refer to report of component auditors as the basis for the auditors' opinion	No effect, assuming other auditors' opinion is consistent with principal auditors' opinion (would refer to report of other auditors)
Other information contained in management's report on internal control	No effect, but should disclaim an opinion on other information
Management's annual certification (section 302) is misstated	Include an explanatory paragraph describing the reasons why management's disclosures should be modified
Significant subsequently discovered fact related to internal control	Issue either adverse opinion (if subsequently discovered fact adversely affects the effectiveness of internal control) or disclaimer of opinion (if auditor is unable to determine effects of subsequently discovered fact)

⌐ REVIEW CHECKPOINTS

5.30 What are some major reasons for departing from the standard, unqualified report on internal control over financial reporting?

5.31 What type of opinion(s) would the audit team issue on the effectiveness of internal control over financial reporting if a material weakness in internal control exists? How would the standard report be modified?

5.32 What type of opinion would be issued by the audit team as the result of a scope limitation on the examination of internal control over financial reporting?

▽ INTERNAL CONTROL COMMUNICATIONS

LEARNING OBJECTIVE 5-8
Explain the communication of internal control deficiencies to those charged with governance such as the audit committee and other key management personnel.

Whether auditing a nonpublic entity under GAAS or a public entity in an examination conducted under PCAOB standards, the audit team must communicate significant deficiencies and material weaknesses in internal control that come to their attention during the performance of the audit. Auditors' communications of significant deficiencies and material weaknesses are intended to help management carry out its responsibilities for internal control monitoring and change. However, external auditors' observations and recommendations are usually limited to external financial reporting matters.

For public entities, the auditors' report must be in writing and presented to those in charge of governance (usually the audit committee) before its report on internal control over financial reporting is issued to the public. The report is to be addressed to the management, the board of directors, or its audit committee. See Exhibit 5.21 for an illustration of such a report. In addition, all deficiencies noted must be communicated in writing to management.

If the audit team does not identify any significant deficiencies, they should not issue a report stating that "no significant deficiencies were noted during the audit." Doing so might be misleading because an integrated audit is not designed to detect all significant deficiencies. A manager receiving such a report could conclude (incorrectly) that the audit team is stating positively that the entity has no internal control problems.

EXHIBIT 5.21
Internal Control Letter

> Michael Scarn, LLP, CPAs
> Scranton, PA
>
> March 7, 2013
>
> Board of Directors
> Dunder-Mifflin, Inc.
> Scantron, Maine
>
> In planning and performing our audit of the financial statements of Dunder-Mifflin, Inc. for the year ended December 31, 2012, we considered its internal control in order to determine our audit procedures for the purpose of expressing our opinion on the financial statements as well as the effectiveness of the company's internal control over financial reporting. Our consideration of internal control would not necessarily disclose all deficiencies in internal control that might be significant deficiencies. However, we noted a certain matter involving the internal control and its operation that we consider to be a significant deficiency under standards established by the Public Company Accounting Oversight Board. A significant deficiency is a deficiency, or a combination of deficiencies, in internal control that is less severe than a material weakness, yet important enough to merit attention by those charged with governance.
>
> The matter noted is that shipping personnel have both transaction-initiation and alteration authority as well as custody of inventory assets. If invoice/shipping copy documents are altered to show a shipment of smaller quantities than actually shipped, customers or accomplices can receive your products without charge. The sales revenue and accounts receivable could be understated, and the inventory could be overstated. This deficiency caused us to spend more time auditing your inventory quantities.
>
> A material weakness in internal control is defined as a deficiency, or combination of deficiencies, that results in a reasonable possibility that a material misstatement would not be prevented or detected on a timely basis. We do not believe that the significant deficiency described above is a material weakness.
>
> This report is intended solely for the information and use of the board of directors and its audit committee, and is not intended to be, and should not be, used by anyone other than these specified parties.
>
> Respectfully yours,
> **Michael Scarn, LLP, CPAs**

Audit teams often issue another type of report to management called a *management letter*. This letter may contain commentary and suggestions on a variety of matters in addition to internal control matters. Examples include issues identified during the audit related to operational and administrative efficiency, business strategy, and profit-making possibilities. Auditing standards do not require management letters, but they represent a type of value-added management advice rendered as a part of an audit.

↳ REVIEW CHECKPOINT

5.33 What reports (other than auditors' report) on internal control do audit teams give to an entity's management, board of directors, or audit committee?

Summary

The purposes of the audit team's evaluation of internal control are to assess the control risk (as part of the overall assessment of the RMM) in order to make the substantive audit plan and to report control deficiencies to management and the board of directors. The PCAOB's *AS 5* defines additional responsibilities for management and public accounting firms' reports on internal control stipulated by the Sarbanes-Oxley Act.

Internal control consists of five components: management's control environment, management's risk assessment, management's information and communication system, management's control activities, and management's monitoring of the control system. The auditor is required to gain an understanding of each of these components and to document this understanding in the audit files. The control environment and management's risk assessment are explained in terms of understanding the client's business. Elements of the accounting system are explained in conjunction with control activities designed to prevent, detect, and correct misstatements that occur in transactions. Documentation of an entity's internal control system is accomplished through the use of questionnaires, flowcharts, and narratives.

Internal control is assessed in a top-down manner by which audit teams first identify accounts that may contain significant risks of material misstatement. They then identify which relevant assertions may be misstated. After determining what could go wrong, audit teams examine entity-level controls that might mitigate the risk of material misstatement. Finally, they identify transaction level controls that would mitigate any residual risks. If the auditor relies on controls are relied on by, they must be tested to ensure they are operating effectively. Where controls are not in place to reduce the risk, or if testing the controls would not be cost effective, substantive tests are designed to identify any material misstatements.

Control evidence is linked to substantive audit plans with a "bridge workpaper" presentation. It is important to distinguish the "client's control activities" from the "audit teams' tests of controls." Control activities are part of the internal control designed and operated by the entity. The audit teams' procedures are the audit teams' own evidence-gathering work performed to obtain evidence about the client's control activities.

Sarbanes-Oxley requires that management of public companies report on their assessments of the effectiveness of their financial reporting controls, and that audit teams provide opinions on the controls over financial reporting. This may involve more extensive procedures than those required by GAAS.

Key Terms

adverse opinion on internal control over financial reporting: The opinion issued when the company has *not* maintained an effective internal control over financial reporting, 203

audit committee: A subcommittee of the board of directors that is generally composed of three to six "outside" members of the organization's board of directors, 177

auditors' report on internal control over financial reporting: A report required by the Sarbanes-Oxley Act that provides an opinion on the effectiveness of the entity's internal control over financial reporting, 200

business risk: Those factors, events, and conditions that could prevent the organization from achieving its business objectives, 178

control activities: The specific actions taken by a client's management and employees to help ensure that management directives are carried out, 178

control risk: The probability that an entity's controls will fail to prevent or detect errors and frauds that would otherwise have entered the system, 174

design effectiveness: A condition expressing whether controls would be expected to prevent or detect errors or fraud that could result in a material misstatement in the financial statements, 187

detective controls: The activities that detect misstatements after they occur, 180

disclaimer of opinion on internal control over financial reporting: The situations in which auditors cannot provide assurance on the effectiveness of internal control over financial reporting; issued when a significant scope limitation exists, 204

dual-purpose test: An audit procedure that can be used as both a test of controls and a substantive test, 196

entity-level controls (ELCs): The controls that are pervasive to the financial statements taken as a whole, 185

information system: An entity's system, usually built on some type of technological platform that has been designed to produce the information necessary for the entity to operate and control its business operations, 183

integrated audit process: The term used to describe an audit process that is designed to provide an opinion on both the financial statements and internal control system of an entity, 172

internal control: A process, effected by an entity's board of directors, management, and other personnel, designed to provide reasonable assurance regarding the achievement of objectives in the reliability of financial reporting, the effectiveness and efficiency of operations, and compliance with applicable laws and regulations, 170

internal control deficiency: A condition that exists when the design or operation of a control does not allow the entity's management or employees to detect or prevent misstatements in a timely fashion, 198

internal control questionnaire: A checklist of internal control–related questions used to gain and document an understanding of the client's internal control, 188

management's annual report on internal control over financial reporting: A report required by the Sarbanes-Oxley Act that states that management is responsible for establishing and maintaining adequate internal control over financial reporting, identifies the framework management uses to evaluate the effectiveness of the entity's internal control, and provides management's assessment of the effectiveness of the entity's internal control, 199

material weakness: A deficiency or combination of deficiencies that results in a reasonable possibility that a material misstatement would not be prevented or detected on a timely basis, 198

narrative description: The audit documentation that describes the environmental elements, the accounting system, and the control activities in an entity's internal control, 189

operating effectiveness: A condition expressing whether a control is operating as designed and whether the person performing the control possesses the necessary authority and qualifications to perform the control effectively, 187

preventive controls: The activities that prevent misstatements before they occur, 180

reasonable assurance: The concept that recognizes that the costs of control activities should not exceed the benefits that are expected from the control activities, 171

significant deficiency: A deficiency or a combination of deficiencies in internal control that is less severe than a material weakness yet important enough to merit attention by those charged with governance, 199

substantive procedures: The detailed audit and analytical procedures designed to detect material misstatements in account balances and footnote disclosures, 196

transaction-level controls: The controls that relate to specific classes of transactions, account balances, and disclosures, 186

unqualified opinion on internal control over financial reporting: The report issued when no material weaknesses in internal control over financial reporting are identified and no scope limitations on the audit of internal control exist, 202

walkthrough: The tracing of one or more transactions through the audit trail from initiation of the transaction to its inclusion in the financial statements, 187

Multiple-Choice Questions for Practice and Review

 All applicable Exercises and Problems are available with McGraw-Hill's *Connect® Accounting*

LO 5-3

5.34 The most important fundamental component of an entity's internal control is
   a. Effectiveness and efficiency of operations.
   b. People who operate the control system.
   c. Reliability of financial reporting.
   d. Compliance with applicable laws and regulations.

LO 5-4

5.35 The primary purpose for obtaining an understanding of a nonpublic audit client's internal control is to
   a. Provide a basis for making constructive suggestions in a management letter.
   b. Determine the nature, timing, and extent of tests to be performed in the audit.
   c. Provide the rational for the inherent risk assessment at the financial statement assertion level.
   d. Provide information for a communication of internal control–related matters to management.

LO 5-4

5.36 Effectiveness of audit procedures would be reduced by
   a. Selecting larger sample sizes for audit.
   b. Performing audit procedures at the fiscal year-end date as opposed to the interim period.
   c. Deciding to obtain external evidence instead of internal evidence.
   d. Performing procedures during the interim period as opposed to at the fiscal year-end date.

LO 5-5   5.37 According to the PCAOB, during the audit of internal controls for an issuer, the ultimate objective of testing the design effectiveness of internal controls is to
- a. Determine whether the company's controls are processing company data effectively.
- b. Determine that the company's controls will satisfy the company's control objectives and can effectively prevent or detect errors or fraud that could result in material misstatements, if they operate as prescribed.
- c. Determine that the company's employees are processing the controls according to the policy and procedure manuals at the company.
- d. None of the above.

LO 5-4   5.38 To test the operating effectiveness of a control, an audit team might use a combination of each of the following tests *except* for:
- a. Inquiry of client personnel.
- b. Observation of company operations.
- c. Confirmation of balances.
- d. Inspection of documentation.

LO 5-4   5.39 Which of the following is a preventive control?
- a. Reconciliation of a bank account.
- b. Recalculation of a sample of payroll entries by internal auditors.
- c. Separation of duties between the payroll and personnel departments.
- d. Detailed fluctuation analysis completed by the CFO for revenue.

LO 5-4   5.40 In most audits of large entities, control risk assessment contributes to audit efficiency, which means that
- a. The cost of substantive procedures will exceed the cost of control evaluation work.
- b. Auditors will be able to reduce the cost of substantive procedures by an amount more than the control evaluation costs.
- c. The cost of control evaluation work will exceed the cost of substantive procedures.
- d. Auditors will be able to reduce the cost of substantive procedures by an amount less than the cost of tests of controls.

LO 5-4   5.41 Which of the following is a device designed to help the audit team obtain evidence about the accounting and control activities of an audit client?
- a. A narrative memorandum describing the control system.
- b. An internal control questionnaire.
- c. A flowchart of the documents and procedures used by the company.
- d. All of the above.

LO 5-4   5.42 A bridge workpaper shows the connection between
- a. Control evaluation findings and subsequent audit procedures.
- b. Management objectives and accounting system procedures.
- c. Management objectives and entity control activities.
- d. Financial statement assertions and tests of controls.

LO 5-4   5.43 Tests of controls in a GAAS audit are required for
- a. Obtaining evidence about the financial statement assertions.
- b. Accomplishing control over the occurrence of recorded transactions.
- c. Applying analytical procedures to financial statement balances.
- d. Obtaining evidence about the operating effectiveness of client control activities.

LO 5-4   5.44 A transaction-level internal control activity is best described as
- a. An action taken by auditors to obtain evidence.
- b. An action taken by client personnel for the purpose of preventing, detecting, and correcting errors and frauds in transactions to eliminate or mitigate risks identified by the company.
- c. A method for recording, summarizing, and reporting financial information.
- d. The functioning of the board of directors in support of its audit committee.

LO 5-5   5.45 When planning the audit of internal controls for an issuer, the audit team should
  a. Identify significant accounts, locations, and assertions.
  b. Conduct a walkthrough of the internal control process.
  c. Make inquiries of employees regarding the existence of control activities.
  d. Reperform control activities performed by client employees to determine their effectiveness.

LO 5-5   5.46 A material weakness is a situation in which
  a. It is probable that an immaterial financial statement misstatement would not be detected on a timely basis.
  b. There is a remote likelihood that a material misstatement would be detected on a timely basis.
  c. It is reasonably possible that a material misstatement would not be detected on a timely basis.
  d. It is reasonably possible that an immaterial misstatement would not be detected on a timely basis.

LO 5-5   5.47 When completing the audit of internal controls for an issuer, the severity of an internal control deficiency depends on:
  a. Whether there is a reasonable possibility that the company's controls will fail to prevent or detect a misstatement of an account balance or disclosure.
  b. Whether the account has a history of errors.
  c. The magnitude of the potential misstatement resulting from the deficiency or the deficiencies.
  d. Both a and c are correct.
  e. All of the above are correct.

LO 5-5   5.48 Which of the following does *not* accurately summarize auditors' requirements regarding internal control?

	Public Entity	Nonpublic Entity
a. Understanding	Yes	Yes
b. Documenting	Yes	Yes
c. Evaluating control risk	Yes	Yes
d. Test Controls	Yes	Yes

LO 5-5   5.49 When completing the audit of internal controls for an issuer, the PCAOB requires auditors of public companies to audit internal controls over
  a. Operations.
  b. Compliance with regulations.
  c. Financial reporting.
  d. All of the above.

LO 5-5   5.50 When completing the audit of internal controls for an issuer, *AS 5* requires auditors of public companies to report on

	Management's Report on Internal Control	An Audit of Internal Control
a.	No	No
b.	Yes	No
c.	No	Yes
d.	Yes	Yes

LO 5-5 5.51 When completing the audit of internal controls for an issuer, *AS 5* requires auditors to test
   a. Operating effectiveness only.
   b. Design effectiveness only.
   c. Both operating and design effectiveness.
   d. Neither operating nor design effectiveness

LO 5-5 5.52 Which of the following would probably *not* be considered an indication of a material weakness?
   a. Evidence of a material misstatement.
   b. Ineffective oversight by the audit committee.
   c. Immaterial fraud committed by senior management.
   d. Overproduction by the manufacturing plant.

LO 5-7 5.53 Which report would *not* be appropriate for a public accounting firm to provide on financial reporting controls?
   a. Unqualified—no material weaknesses found.
   b. Disclaimer of opinion—unable to perform all necessary procedures.
   c. Disclaimer of opinion—significant deficiencies exist.
   d. Adverse—material weaknesses exist.

LO 5-4 5.54 The purpose of separating the duties of hiring personnel and distributing payroll checks is to separate the
   a. Authorization of transactions from the custody of related assets.
   b. Operational responsibility from the record-keeping responsibility.
   c. Human resources function from the controllership function.
   d. Administrative controls from the internal accounting controls.

(AICPA adapted)

LO 5-6 5.55 Which of the following statements is *not* true with respect to the auditors' report on internal control over financial reporting?
   a. The report will be dated as of the date of the financial statements.
   b. The report will express an opinion on the effectiveness of internal control over financial reporting.
   c. The auditor will issue an adverse opinion if one or more material weaknesses exist.
   d. The report may be presented with the report on the entity's financial statements as a combined report.

LO 5-7 5.56 If the auditors encounter a significant scope limitation in evaluating a public company's internal control over financial reporting, which of the following types of opinions on the effectiveness of the company's internal control over financial reporting would be appropriate?
   a. Unqualified opinion or adverse opinion.
   b. Qualified opinion or adverse opinion.
   c. Unqualified opinion or disclaimer of opinion.
   d. Disclaimer of opinion.

LO 5-6 5.57 Which of the following information would be included in the introductory paragraph of the auditors' report on internal control over financial reporting if the report is presented separately from the auditors' report on the entity's financial statements?
   a. The fact that the auditors conducted an audit of the entity's financial statements.
   b. The definition of a material weakness in internal control over financial reporting.
   c. Statements identifying the responsibility of the auditors and management for internal control over financial reporting.
   d. A reference to the auditors' report and opinion on the entity's financial statements.

Exercises and Problems

 All applicable Exercises and Problems are available with McGraw-Hill's *Connect® Accounting*

LO 5-2

5.58 **Internal Control Audit Standards.** Auditors are required to obtain a sufficient understanding of each component of a client's internal control. This understanding is used to assess control risk and plan the audit of the client's financial statements.

Required:
a. For what purposes should an auditors' understanding of the internal control components be used in planning an audit?
b. What is required for an audit team to assess control risk below the maximum level?
c. What should an audit team consider when seeking to reduce the planned assessed level of control risk below the maximum?
d. What are the documentation requirements concerning a client's internal control components and the assessed level of control risk?

(AICPA adapted)

LO 5-3

5.59 **Separation of Duties.** Your small business client, Phillip's Computer Repair Shop, is experiencing financial difficulties and has to lay off one of its four employees in the accounting area. Phillip has asked you to determine what duties should be assigned to the three remaining employees—Abigail, Bryan, and Chris—to maintain the best separation of duties.

Required:
Assign the following 10 duties to each of the three employees.
a. Reconcile bank statement.
b. Open mail and list checks.
c. Prepare checks for Phillip's signature.
d. Prepare payroll checks.
e. Maintain personnel records.
f. Prepare deposit and take to bank.
g. Maintain petty cash.
h. Maintain accounts receivable records.
i. Maintain general ledger.
j. Reconcile accounts receivable records to general ledger account.

LO 5-4

5.60 **Types of Audit Tests.** Indicate whether each of the following audit procedures is a test of controls, a substantive test, or dual-purpose test. Next, indicate the financial statement assertion most closely related to each audit procedure.
a. Vouch recorded sales invoices to supporting shipping documents.
b. Inspect recorded sales invoices for credit approval.
c. Vouch recorded sales invoices prices to the approved price list.
d. Send confirmations to all customers regarding accounts receivable.
e. Recalculate the arithmetic accuracy of the recorded sales invoices.
f. Compare the shipment date of recorded sales invoices with the invoice record date.
g. Trace recorded sales invoices to posting in the general ledger control account and in the correct customer's account.
h. Select a sample of shipping documents from the shipping department file and trace shipments to recorded sales invoices.
i. Scan recorded sales invoices and shipping documents for missing numbers in sequence.
j. Vouch sales invoices and shipping documents.
k. Evaluate the adequacy of the allowance for doubtful accounts.

l. Obtain financial statements or credit reports on large past due accounts and inquire of the credit manager about collections.

m. Calculate an estimate of the allowance for doubtful accounts using prior relations of write-offs and sales.

LO 5-5

5.61 **Impact of Sarbanes-Oxley Act.** Your long-time client, Central Office Supply, has been rapidly expanding, and the board of directors is considering taking the company public. CEO Terry Puckett has heard that costs of operating a public company have increased significantly as a result of the Sarbanes-Oxley Act. Puckett is particularly concerned with reports that audit fees have doubled because of internal control provisions of the act and *AS 5*. Puckett has asked you to explain the possible effects on the audit of complying with the requirements of Sarbanes-Oxley.

Required:
Draft a letter to Puckett outlining the changes in the company's responsibilities for internal control and changes in the audit due to Sarbanes-Oxley and *Auditing Standard 5*.

LO 5-4

5.62 **Internal Control Questionnaire Items: Assertions, Tests of Controls, and Possible Errors or Frauds.** Following is a selection of items from the payroll processing internal control questionnaire in Exhibit 5.11.

1. Are names of terminated employees reported in writing to the payroll department?
2. Are authorizations for deductions signed by the employee on file?
3. Is there a timekeeping department (function) independent of the payroll department?
4. Are timekeeping and cost accounting records (such as hours, dollars) reconciled with payroll department calculations of hours and wages?

Required:
For each of the four preceding questions:

a. Identify the assertion to which the question applies.

b. Specify one test of controls an auditor could use to determine whether the control was operating effectively.

c. Provide an example of an error or fraud that could occur if the control were absent or ineffective.

d. Identify a substantive auditing procedure that could detect errors or frauds that could result from the absence or ineffectiveness of the control items.

LO 5-4

5.63 **Obtaining a "Sufficient" Understanding of Internal Control.** The 12 partners of a regional public accounting firm met in special session to discuss audit engagement efficiency. Jones spoke up, saying, "We all certainly appreciate the firmwide policies set up by Martin and Smith, especially in connection with the audits of the large clients that have come our way recently. Their experience with a large public accounting firm has helped build our practice. But I think the standard policy of conducting reviews and tests of internal control on all audits is raising our costs too much. We can't charge our smaller clients fees for all of the time the staff spends on this work. I would like to propose that we give engagement partners discretion to decide whether to do a lot of work on assessing control risk. I may be old-fashioned, but I think I can finish a competent audit without it." Discussion on the subject continued but ended when Martin said, with some emotion, "But we can't disregard generally accepted auditing standards like Jones proposes!"

Required:
What do you think of Jones's proposal and Martin's view of the issue? Discuss.

LO 5-4

5.64 **Fraud Opportunities.** Simon Blfpstk Construction Company has two divisions. The president (Chris Simon) manages the roofing division. Simon delegated authority and responsibility for management of the modular manufacturing division to John Gault. The company has a competent accounting staff and a full-time internal auditor. Unlike Simon's procedures, however, Gault and his secretary handle all bids for manufacturing jobs, purchase all materials without competitive bids, control the physical inventory of materials, contract for shipping by truck, supervise the construction activity, bill the customer when the job is finished, approve all bid changes, and collect the payment from the customer. With Simon's tacit approval, Gault has asked the internal auditor not to interfere with his busy schedule.

Required:
Discuss this situation in terms of internal control and identify frauds that could occur.

LO 5-4

5.65 **Internal Control Questionnaire Items: Errors that Could Occur from Control Weaknesses.** Refer to the internal control questionnaire on a payroll system (Exhibit 5.11).

a. Assume that the answer to each question is no. Prepare a table matching the questions to errors or frauds that could occur because of the absence of the control. Your column headings should be

Question	Possible Error or Fraud Due to Weakness

b. Which controls are preventive controls and which are detective?

LO 5-7

5.66 **Reports on Internal Control over Financial Reporting (Report Modifications).** For each of the following situations, describe how the auditors' report on internal control over financial reporting would be modified from the standard, unqualified report. Do *not* write the actual reports.

a. The auditors have identified a material weakness in the processing of sales transactions.

b. Because of a relatively short period of time has passed since a control weakness was remediated, the auditors do not believe that sufficient evidence can be obtained with respect to the operating effectiveness of the entity's internal control over financial reporting.

c. Component auditors have audited a significant component of the group financial statements, including internal control over financial reporting relating to that component. They did not find a material weakness in internal control, and the group auditor believes the component auditor's work can be relied on.

d. The auditors believe that the entity's management has not adequately disclosed a material weakness in its internal control over financial reporting.

LO 5-7

5.67 **Reports on Internal Control over Financial Reporting (Identify Report Deficiencies).** Sorrell, CPA, is auditing the financial statements of Van Dyke as of December 31, 2012. Sorrell's substantive procedures and other tests indicated that Van Dyke's financial statements were prepared in accordance with generally accepted accounting principles and, accordingly, Sorrell expressed an unqualified opinion on those financial statements. Because Van Dyke's securities are registered with the Securities and Exchange Commission, Van Dyke is subject to the reporting requirements of *AS 5*. During its assessment of internal control over financial reporting, Van Dyke's management identified material weaknesses related to (1) the method of accounting for sales commissions and (2) separation of duties related to purchase transactions. Sorrell was able to gather sufficient evidence and did not encounter any limitations with respect to the evaluation of Van Dyke's internal control over financial reporting. Sorrell prepared the following draft report on Van Dyke's internal control over financial reporting:

Required:
Identify the deficiencies in the audit report drafted by Sorrell. Group the deficiencies by paragraph and in the order in which they appear. Do not rewrite the report. Cite the relevant sections from the professional standards.

Report of Independent Registered Public Accounting Firm

To the Board of Directors and Shareholders of Van Dyke:

We have audited management's assessment, included in the accompanying Management's Report on Internal Control over Financial Reporting, that Van Dyke has not maintained effective internal control over financial reporting as of December 31, 2012, based on criteria established in Internal Control—Integrated Framework issued by the Committee of Sponsoring Organizations of the Treadway Commission (COSO criteria). Van Dyke's management is responsible for assessing the effectiveness of internal control over financial reporting. Our responsibility is to express an opinion on management's assessment and an opinion on the effectiveness of the company's internal control over financial reporting based on our audit.

We conducted our audits in accordance with the standards of the Public Company Accounting Oversight Board (United States). Those standards require that we plan and perform the audit to obtain reasonable assurance about whether effective internal control over financial reporting was maintained in all material respects. Our audit included obtaining an understanding of internal control over financial reporting, evaluating management's assessment, testing and evaluating the design and operating effectiveness of internal control, and performing such other procedures as we considered necessary in the circumstances. We believe that our audit provides a reasonable basis for our opinion.

A company's internal control over financial reporting is a process designed to provide reasonable assurance regarding the reliability of financial reporting and the preparation of financial statements for external purposes in accordance with generally accepted accounting principles. A company's internal control over financial reporting includes those policies and procedures that (1) pertain to the maintenance of records that, in reasonable detail, accurately and fairly reflect the transactions and dispositions of the assets of the company; (2) provide reasonable assurance that transactions are recorded as necessary to permit preparation of financial statements in accordance with generally accepted accounting principles and that receipts and expenditures of the company are being made only in accordance with authorizations of management and directors of the company; and (3) provide reasonable assurance regarding prevention or timely detection of unauthorized acquisition, use, or disposition of the company's assets that could have a material effect on the financial statements.

Two material weaknesses were identified in the design and operation of internal controls over the accounting for sales commissions and separation of duties related to purchases of inventory. Given the nature of the transactions and processes involved and the potential for a misstatement to occur as a result of the internal control deficiencies existing on December 31, 2012, we have concluded that there is more than a remote likelihood that a material misstatement in the annual or interim financial statements would not have been prevented or detected by internal controls.

These material weaknesses were considered in determining the nature, timing, and extent of audit tests applied in our audit of the 2012 financial statements.

In addition to the material weaknesses noted above, we identified several deficiencies in internal control over financial reporting that we deemed to be less significant than a material weakness. These deficiencies have been separately communicated to Van Dyke's management.

In our opinion, because Van Dyke has not maintained an effective internal control over financial reporting, we are unable to evaluate management's assessment that Van Dyke did not maintain effective internal control over financial reporting as of December 31, 2012. Also in our opinion, because of the effect of the material weaknesses described above on the achievement of the objectives of the control criteria, Van Dyke has not maintained, in all material respects, effective internal control over financial reporting as of December 31, 2012, based on the COSO criteria.

We have also audited, in accordance with the standards of the Public Company Accounting Oversight Board (United States), the balance sheets of Van Dyke as of December 31, 2012 and 2011, and related statements of income, shareholders' equity, and cash flows for each of the three years in the period ended December 31, 2012.

Sorrell, CPA
December 31, 2012

LO 5-3

5.68 **Role of a Board of Directors in Internal Control.** *Audit: Ky. airport execs racked up $500K in lavish expenses, concert tickets, and even strip club tabs*

LEXINGTON, Ky. (AP)—A small commercial airport in Kentucky—and the taxpayers who support it—picked up top executives' tabs in recent years for Hannah Montana concert tickets, Nintendo Wii video game bundles and even a $4,400 strip club check, according to a state auditor's report.

The report released Wednesday outlines indulgences ranging from pricey electronics and exercise equipment to lavish meals and champagne. In three years, officials tallied more than $500,000 in questionable personal expenses [Author's note: general fund expenses were approximately $10,000,000 annually].

Kentucky Auditor Crit Luallen said the former executive director at Lexington's **Blue Grass Airport** created a culture of wasteful spending so vast, employees sometimes were paid twice for the same expense and used airport credit cards as if they were personal checkbooks.

"I don't think we have ever seen an audit where so many different individuals involved in the management of a public agency abused the trust with such arrogance and lack of ethical standards," she said.

Luallen says she has forwarded the case to the Kentucky attorney general, the U.S. attorney's office and the FBI.

Although the audit only covered the past three years, it does refer to one of the more glaring examples reported by the *Herald-Leader:* a $4,400 charge Gobb and two other directors incurred at a Dallas strip club in 2004.

The charge, which appeared on the credit card statement of the airport's director of planning, was listed as going to Millennium Restaurant. The word "marketing" was handwritten next to the amount. The Associated Press obtained that receipt and others through an open records request.

Excerpted from *Ky. Airport Execs Racked Up Lavish Expenses* Jeffrey McMurray, Associated Press writer

Thursday February 26, 2009

The audit found that airport employees also used the coffers for tuxedos and other expensive clothing; more than 400 DVDs—many of them currently missing—for the internal airport library; $14,000 in holiday hams given out as gifts; and $7,400 for a NASCAR driving experience excursion for staff described as "team building."

More than 92 percent of the things Gobb charged to his airport card lacked proper documentation, Luallen said.

While Luallen acknowledged that Gobb was responsible for the free-spending culture, she said the board and its public accounting firm should have supervised the airport more closely.

Required:

a. Discuss the role of the board of directors in monitoring the behavior of a chief executive officer.
b. If the chief executive officer has subordinates incur expenses that he or she approves, how can the board prevent abuse?
c. Should external auditors be expected to detect abuses such as these?
d. How should the use of credit cards be controlled?

LO 5-6

5.69 **Is Sarbanes-Oxley Working?** Since its inception in 2002, the Sarbanes-Oxley Act has been criticized for its rigorous internal control requirements (section 404), which detractors have argued are too burdensome and costly. Ultimately, the question arises as to whether Sarbanes-Oxley is working as intended.

The following are some early effects of section 404 on financial reporting:

- The provisions of Sarbanes-Oxley have resulted in a doubling of audit fees among the Big Four public accounting firms. A survey of 43 companies (40 of which are Fortune 500 companies) indicated that these companies spent an average of $5 to $8 million in new audit fees related solely to Sarbanes-Oxley.
- More than 60 companies requested an additional 15 days to file their 2004 annual reports, citing issues relating to documenting internal controls as required under Sarbanes-Oxley.

These companies included **American International Group,** Fannie Mae, **HealthSouth, EDS, Veritas Software,** and **Impax Laboratories.**

- Reviews of the first year of internal disclosures under Sarbanes-Oxley indicate that nearly 12 percent of companies (mostly smaller ones) reported material weaknesses. The most common general issues were deficiencies in documentation, weaknesses resulting in adjustments or restatements, and inadequate personnel competence. Specific areas related to tax accounting, revenue recognition, leases, and inventory.
- Compared to the general stock market, companies disclosing a material weakness in internal control over financial reporting experienced a decline in their stock prices of 0.67 percent on the day of disclosure; this decline increased to 4.06 percent during the next 60 days. The market performance was even worse when the company missed its filing deadline with the SEC.

Required:
a. What are some of the benefits of the Sarbanes-Oxley Act?
b. What is your opinion of the Act? Do the benefits justify the costs? Justify your answer.

Sources: "Audit Fees Double Due to Sarbox," *CFO.com,* February 11, 2005; "Five Dozen Companies Seek Filing Delay," *CFO.com,* March 21, 2005; Deloitte & Touche, *Internal Control Disclosures: Key Trends to Watch,* May 11, 2005; "How Markets Punish Material Weaknesses," *CFO.com,* July 21, 2005; "Restatements Still Bedevil Firms," *The Wall Street Journal,* February 12, 2007, p. C7; "Study: Costs of 404 Drop 23 Percent," *CFO.com,* May 17, 2007; "Costs to Comply with Sarbanes Decline Again," *The Wall Street Journal,* May 16, 2007, p. C7.

LO 5-3 5.70 **Mini-Case: Control Environment.** Refer to the mini-case "Unhealthy Accounting at HealthSouth" shown on page C14 and respond to Questions 3 and 4.

LO 5-1 5.71 **Mini-Case: Effect of Internal Control Evaluation on Auditors' Fees.** Refer to the mini-case "How Much Are Auditors Paid?" shown on page C23 and respond to Questions 5 and 6.

LO 5-8 5.72 **Kaplan CPA Exam Simulation: Internal Control Matters.**

Required:
Go to the Kaplan website link at www.mhhe.com/Louwers5e, click on Audit Client Letter (Internal Control Matters) AUD TBS, and complete your answer.

CPA REVIEW

Appendix 5A

Audit Plan

DUNDER-MIFFLIN, INC. Audit Plan for Tests of Controls in the Payroll Cycle 12/31/12		
	Performed by	**Ref.**

1. Observe the separation of duties between the personnel, timekeeping, and payroll departments.
2. Select a sample of payments from the payroll distribution for the year.
   a. Vouch labor costs to labor reports.
   b. Vouch labor reports to time tickets or computerized listing.
   c. Examine documentary evidence of supervisor review of labor costs.
   d. Examine documentary evidence of supervisor approval.
3. Account for numerical sequence of selected job cost tickets and paychecks. Trace a sample of employees in the personnel file to payroll department files and the payroll register.
4. Examine documentary evidence of budget comparison.
5. Verify that payroll account distribution and job cost sheets agree.
6. Examine supervisor signature on payroll reports. Note evidence of comparison to budget.		

Employee Fraud and the Audit of Cash

Rather fail with honor than succeed by fraud.

Sophocles, philosopher (496–406 BC)

Professional Standards References

Topic	AU/ISA Section	PCAOB Reference*
Overall Objectives of the Independent Auditor	200	AU 110, AU 150, AU 201, AU 201, AU 220, AU 230
Supervision of the Audit Engagement	220, 300	AS 11
Audit Documentation	230	AS 3
Consideration of Fraud in a Financial Statement Audit	240	AU 316
Consideration of Laws and Regulations	250	AU 317
Communications with Those Charged with Governance	260	AU 380
Audit Planning	300	AS 10
Consideration of Internal Control in an Integrated Audit		AS 5
Identifying and Assessing the Risks of Material Misstatement	315	AS 12
Materiality	320	AS 11
Auditors' Responses to Risks of Material Misstatement	330	AS 13
Audit Considerations Relating to an Entity Using a Service Organization	402	AS 5
Audit Evidence	500	AS 15
External Confirmations	505	AU 330
Analytical Procedures	520	AU 329
Accounting Estimates	540	AU 342
Related Parties	550	AU 334
Using the Work of an Audit Specialist	620	AU 336

*AU, AT, and QC references represent standards issued by the ASB prior to April 16, 2003, that have not been superseded or amended by the PCAOB.

LEARNING OBJECTIVES

Fraud auditing can be very exciting. It has the aura of detective work—finding things people want to keep hidden. However, fraud auditing and fraud examination are not easy and are not activities to be pursued without special training, experience, and care. In Chapter 4, we discussed the auditor's role in detecting fraud in the financial statements and related footnote disclosures. In this chapter, we focus on the auditor's role in detecting the other category of fraud, referred to generally as *misappropriation* (or *theft*) of assets or employee fraud. Additionally, because cash is often the primary target of employee theft, we also focus on the control and substantive testing procedures that are typically performed during the audit of cash balances.

Your objectives are to be able to:

LO 6-1 Define and explain the differences among several kinds of employee fraud that might occur at an audit client.

LO 6-2 Identify and explain the three conditions (i.e., the fraud triangle) that often exist when a fraud occurs.

LO 6-3 Describe techniques that can be used to prevent employee fraud.

LO 6-4 Describe the control activities over the receipt and disbursement of cash.

LO 6-5 Describe the types of substantive procedures that are conducted during the audit of cash.

LO 6-6 Discuss actual cash fraud cases and describe how the schemes were uncovered.

LO 6-7 Describe some extended procedures for detecting employee fraud schemes involving cash.

EMPLOYEE FRAUD OVERVIEW

LEARNING OBJECTIVE 6-1
Define and explain the differences among several kinds of employee frauds that might occur at an audit client.

It is essential that auditors maintain their professional skepticism at all times throughout the engagement. In fact, professional standards require that when auditors brainstorm about the potential for fraud in an engagement that the activity should "occur with an attitude that includes a questioning mind, and the key engagement team members should set aside any prior beliefs they might have that management is honest and has integrity."[1] Why is it so important that auditors maintain such a high degree of skepticism at all times? Because a fraud is often committed by a person that an auditor least expects. Consider a Little League coach ripping off the league to buy expensive jewelry by using a routing number from a league payroll check.[2] Or, consider an executive assistant at a large public accounting firm that wrote more than $1 million in checks payable, drawn on a client's bank account, to herself.[3] You just never know where the next fraud might originate!

AUDITING INSIGHT — Employee Fraud Typically Increases in a Down Economy

Employee fraud ranging from check forgery to petty cash theft tends to increase while the economy struggles as employees feel financial pressure in their personal lives. At small companies lacking rigorous internal controls, stolen cash is often attributed to lower sales. Jim Ratley, president of the Association of Certified Fraud Examiners (ACFE) notes that "[a] lot of times a small business will close its doors, and may never know they were defrauded—that the problem wasn't a declining economy, [it was] that employees were stealing."

Source: "Small Businesses Face More Fraud in Downturn," *The Wall Street Journal,* February 19, 2009, B5.

---

[1] *PCAOB Auditing Standard No. 12,* "Identifying and Assessing Risks of Material Misstatement," September, 2010.
[2] "Little League Coach Accused of Fraud," *St. Petersburg Times,* Page 3B, July 4, 2009.
[3] "Aide Gets 2 Years in Fraud Case," *San Francisco Chronicle,* p. D2, October 28, 2010.

An entity's internal control cannot thwart or detect all fraud schemes. Inherent limitations in internal control (such as *collusion* among employees) prevent complete assurance that every fraud scheme will be detected before a loss is incurred. For this reason, the entity's auditors, accountants, and security personnel must be acquainted with the basics of fraud awareness. Although the professional auditing standards concentrate on fraudulent financial reporting—the production of materially false and misleading financial statements—the standards also require auditors to pay attention to employee fraud perpetrated against a client. Attention to employee fraud is also important because it is possible that financial statement misstatements may occur when the fraudster tries to cover up the crime.

Fraud consists of knowingly making material misrepresentations of fact with the intent of inducing someone to believe the falsehood and act upon it and, thus, suffer a loss or damage. This definition encompasses all ways by which people can lie, cheat, steal, and deceive other people. **Employee fraud** (often referred to as **misappropriation of assets**) is the use of fraudulent means to take money or other property from an employer. It usually involves falsifications of some kind—false documents, lying, exceeding authority, or violating an employer's policies. Employee frauds generally consist of (1) the fraudulent act itself, (2) the conversion of assets to the fraudster's use (very easy if cash is involved), and (3) the cover-up. Catching people in the fraudulent act is difficult to accomplish. The act of conversion is equally difficult to observe because it typically takes place in secret away from the entity's offices (e.g., selling stolen inventory). By noticing signs and signals of fraud and then following the trail of missing, mutilated, or false documents that are part of the accounting records cover-up, alert auditors uncover many frauds. Being able to notice red flags, oddities, and unusual events takes some experience, but this chapter provides you with some ideas about where and when to look.[4]

Other Definitions Related to Fraud and Illegal Acts

Management fraud is an intentional deception that is orchestrated by management and is designed to injure investors and creditors by providing materially misleading information.

Errors are unintentional misstatements or omissions of amounts or disclosures in financial statements.

Direct-effect illegal acts are violations of laws or government regulations by the company, or its management or employees that produce direct and material effects on dollar amounts in financial statements.

Embezzlement is a type of fraud that typically involves an employee wrongfully stealing assets that were entrusted to their care, custody, and/or control. In many situations, embezzlement is accompanied by false accounting entries or lying to try to cover-up the crime.

Employee Fraud Red Flags

Employee fraud can involve all types of employees from high-level executives to hourly employees in the warehouse. For most people, committing a fraudulent act is stressful. Observation of changes in a person's habits and lifestyles may reveal some red flags. Fraudsters often exhibit these behaviors:

- Experience sleeplessness.
- Drink too much.
- Take drugs.
- Become irritable easily.

---

[4] Long lists of red flags can be found in G. J. Bologna and R. J. Lindquist, *Fraud Auditing and Forensic Accounting* (New York: John Wiley & Sons, 1995), pp. 49–56; W. S. Albrecht et al., in R. K. Elliott and J. J. Willingham, *Management Fraud: Detection and Deterrence* (New York: Petrocelli Books, Inc., 1980), pp. 223–226; *Statement on Auditing Standards No. 99* (New York: AICPA, 2002); Auditing for Fraud\ courses of the Association of Certified Fraud Examiners; and courses offered by other organizations such as the AICPA and The Institute of Internal Auditors.

- Can't relax.
- Get defensive, argumentative.
- Can't look people in the eye.
- Sweat excessively.
- Go to confession (e.g., priest, psychiatrist).
- Find excuses and scapegoats for mistakes.
- Work standing up.
- Work alone.
- Work late frequently.

Personality red flags are difficult because (1) honest people often show them as well, (2) they often are hidden from view, and (3) auditors are not in a good position to notice these characteristics. Managers are in the best position to notice changes, especially when a person varies his or her lifestyle or spends more money than the salary seems to justify—for example, on homes, furniture, jewelry, clothes, boats, autos, vacations, and the like. Therefore, it is imperative that the auditor make specific inquiries of management regarding changes in an employee's demeanor and lifestyle.

AUDITING INSIGHT — High Style in the Mailroom

A female mailroom employee started wearing designer clothes (and making a big deal about it). She drove a new BMW to work. An observant manager who had known her as an employee for seven years and knew she had no outside income became suspicious. He asked the internal auditors to examine her responsibilities extra carefully. They discovered she had stolen $97,000 over a two-year period.

Source: Association of Certified Fraud Examiners (ACFE), "Auditing for Fraud."

Characteristics of Fraudsters

White-collar criminals are not like typical bank robbers who are often described as "young and dumb." Bank robbers and other strong-arm criminals often make comical mistakes such as writing their holdup note on the back of a probation identification card, leaving the getaway car keys on the convenience store counter, using a zucchini as a holdup weapon, going through a fast-food restaurant's drive-through window backward, and timing the holdup to get stuck in rush hour traffic. Then there's the classic story about the robber who ran into his own mother at the bank (she turned him in!).

Burglars and robbers average about $400–$500 for each hit. Employee frauds often range from $20,000 up to $500,000 or even in the millions if a computer is used. Yet employee frauds are not usually the intricate, well-disguised ploys you find in espionage novels. Who are these thieves wearing ties? What do they look like? Unfortunately, they look like most everybody else, including you and me. They have these characteristics:

- Has education beyond high school.
- Is likely to be married.
- Is member of a mosque, temple, or church.
- Ranges in age from teens to over 60.
- Is socially conforming.
- Has an employment tenure from 1 to 20 years (although the scale of the fraud typically increases with tenure as the employee becomes more trusted).
- Has no arrest record.
- Usually acts alone (70 percent or more of incidents).

> ### AUDITING INSIGHT Who Does It?

Alex W was a 47-year-old treasurer of a credit union. Over a seven-year period, he stole $160,000 from it. He was a good husband and the father of six children, and he was a highly regarded official of the credit union. His crime came as a stunning surprise to his associates. Why did he do it? He owed significant amounts on his home, cars, college for two children, two side investments, and five credit cards. His monthly payments significantly exceeded his take-home pay.

Source: Association of Certified Fraud Examiners (ACFE), "Auditing for Fraud."

White-collar criminals do not make themselves obvious, although they may leave telltale signs, or red flags. Older individuals (usually over 50) who hold high executive positions, have long tenure, and are respected and trusted employees, often have gained the trust and confidence of others and, therefore, are in the position to commit the largest frauds. After all, these are the people who have access to the largest amounts of money and have the power to give orders and override controls. When managers minimize the significance of a weak or missing control by rationalizing that the employee involved is a *"long-time trusted employee,"* most experienced auditors will actually escalate their level of fraud risk awareness. You should as well.

> ### AUDITING INSIGHT Trusted Employees?

- A small business owner hired his best friend to work as his accountant. The friend was given full, unlimited access to all aspects of the business and was completely responsible for the accounting. Five years later, the owner finally terminated the friend because the business was not profitable. Upon taking over the accounting responsibilities, the owner's wife found that cash receipts from customers were twice the amounts formerly recorded by the accountant "friend." An investigation revealed that the friend had stolen $450,000 in cash sales receipts from the business while the owner had never made more than $16,000 a year. (The friend had even used the stolen money to make loans to the owner to keep the business going!)
- An electrical supply company employed only one bookkeeper. She wrote the checks and reconciled the bank account. In the cash disbursements journal, she coded some checks as inventory, but she wrote the checks to herself, using her own name. When the checks were returned with the bank statement, she simply destroyed them. Confronting continuous guilt over doing something she knew was wrong, she contacted a lawyer and turned herself in but not before she had stolen $416,000 over a five-year period. Because of the lack of separation of duties and her trusted status in the company, the fraud might have continued indefinitely (or at least until she bankrupted the company).

Source: Association of Certified Fraud Examiners (ACFE), "Auditing for Fraud."

> ### ↳ REVIEW CHECKPOINTS
>
> 6.1 What are the defining characteristics of employee fraud? **embezzlement**?
>
> 6.2 What does a fraud perpetrator look like? How does one act?
>
> 6.3 Is there anything odd about these two situations? (a) A check to Larson Electric Supply was endorsed with "Larson Electric" above the signature of "Eloise Garfunkle." (b) Numerous checks were issued dated September 7, November 26, December 25, January 1, May 25, and July 4.

EXHIBIT 6.1

Fraud Elements

Source: W. Hillison, D. Sinason, and C. Pacini, "The Role of the Internal Auditor in Implementing SAS 82," *Corporate Controller*, July/August 1998, p. 20.

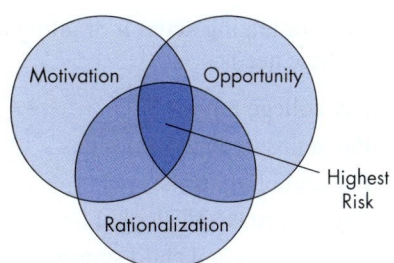

THE FRAUD TRIANGLE (AU/ISA 315, AS 12)

LEARNING OBJECTIVE 6-2
Identify and explain the three conditions (i.e., the fraud triangle) that often exist when a fraud occurs.

The three conditions that are likely to be present when a fraud occurs (Exhibit 6.1) are commonly referred to as the *fraud triangle*. The first condition (motivation) recognizes that an employee or manager of a company is likely to either have incentives in place (e.g., bonus compensation) or be under significant pressure to meet specific estimates, forecasts, or expectations about net income. The second condition (opportunity) recognizes that in order for a fraud to be perpetrated, there must be a weakness in the system of internal control to allow the fraud to occur. Finally, the third condition (rationalization) recognizes that for an employee or a manager of a company to perpetrate a fraud, the individual must possess an "attitude" that allows her or him to rationalize why they are knowingly committing a crime. Each of these conditions is now discussed.[5]

Motivation

A **motive** is some type of pressure experienced by a person that is believed to be unshareable with friends and confidants. Psychotic motivation is relatively rare, but it is characterized by the habitual criminal who steals simply for the sake of stealing. In general, egocentric motivations drive people to steal to achieve more personal prestige. Ideological motivations are held by people who think their cause is morally superior and they are justified in making someone else a victim. However, economic benefits are by far the most common motivations in business frauds.

AUDITING INSIGHT | I Couldn't Tell Anyone

A young unmarried woman stole $300 from her employer to pay for an abortion. Coming from a strict religious family, she felt her only alternative was to have the secret abortion. Once she realized how easy it was to steal, however, she took another $86,000 before being caught.

Source: W. S. Albrecht, "How CPAs Can Help Clients Prevent Employee Fraud," *Journal of Accountancy*, 1988, pp. 110–14.

The economic motive is simply a need for money, and at times it can be intertwined with egocentric and ideological motivations. Ordinary honest people can experience circumstances in which they have a new or unexpected need for money and the normal

---

[5] For further reference, see D. R. Cressey, "Management Fraud, Accounting Controls, and Criminological Theory," pp. 117–147, and Albrecht et al., "Auditor Involvement in the Detection of Fraud," pp. 207–261, both in R. K. Elliott and J. J. Willingham, *Management Fraud: Detection and Deterrence* (New York: Petrocelli Books, Inc., 1980); J. K. Loebbecke, M. M. Eining, and J. J. Willingham, "Auditors' Experience with Material Irregularities: Frequency, Nature, and Detectability," *Auditing: A Journal of Practice and Theory*, Fall 1989, pp. 1–28.

options for talking about it or going through legitimate channels seem to be closed. Consider these needs:

- Pay college tuition.
- Pay uninsured medical bills.
- Pay gambling debts.
- Pay for drugs and alcohol.
- Pay alimony and child support.
- Pay for high lifestyle (homes, cars, boats).
- Finance business or stock speculation losses.

AUDITING INSIGHT — When Facing Adversity, Become a Model Employee

A supervisor for a state university health service was facing great financial difficulty. Her husband had permanently injured his back and no longer worked. One of her children was in a serious automobile accident requiring large payments to cover the uninsured portion of the medical bills.

Despite these personal problems, the supervisor was considered a model employee. She would come to work early, stay late, never call in ill, and took vacation time only between semesters when the health service facility was closed. When she was ill with something contagious, she would come in to work after all other employees had left.

A newly hired director of health services noticed that although the number of students and number of services had increased, health services was having unexplained cash flow problems. An investigation revealed that the supervisor had embezzled $757,000 over a 13-year period. She was sentenced to five years in prison and ordered to repay the university $208,000 and perform 250 hours of community service.

Source: "Catching Fraudsters with Their Hands in the Till," *CPA Journal*, May 2005, pp. 13–15.

Opportunity

An opportunity is an open door for solving the unshareable problem by violating some type of trust. The violation may be a circumvention of existing internal control activities, or it may be simply taking advantage of an absence or lapse of a control activity in an entity. In many cases, the opportunity is nothing more than the absence of an important internal control activity. In general, the higher the position in an organization, the higher the degree of trust, the more likely that controls can be overridden, and, hence, the greater the opportunity for larger frauds. Here are some examples:

- Inventory is not counted on a regular basis, so inventory shortages and losses are not known.
- The petty cash box is left unattended.
- The vice president of finance has investment authority without any review.
- Frequent emergency jobs leave a lot of excess material in a manufacturing plant just lying around.

AUDITING INSIGHT — No Locks on the Door

Perini Corporation kept blank checks in an unlocked storeroom to which every clerk and secretary had access. The automatic check-signing machine was also in the storeroom. The prenumbered checks were not logged when used. The bookkeeper was very surprised to open the bank statement one month and find that $1.5 million in stolen checks had been paid on the account.

Source: Association of Certified Fraud Examiners (ACFE), "Auditing for Fraud."

Rationalization

Practically everyone, even the most violent criminal, knows the difference between right and wrong. Unimpeachable integrity is the ability to act in accordance with the highest moral and ethical values all the time. Thus, it is the lapses in integrity that permit motive and opportunity to commit a fraud. But people normally do not make deliberate decisions to "lack integrity today while I steal some money." They find a way to describe (rationalize) the act in words that make it acceptable for their self-image. Here are some of these rationalizations:

- I need it more than other people (also known as the *Robin Hood theory*).
- I'm borrowing the money and will pay it back.
- Nobody will get hurt.
- The company is big enough to afford it.
- A successful image is the name of the game.
- Everybody is doing it.
- I am underpaid, so this is due compensation.

AUDITING INSIGHT — What's Your Excuse?

A manager at Accenture stole $240,000 by abusing the expense reimbursement procedures in her company. She claimed that she suffered from severe depression and her only remedy was shopping sprees for exorbitant jewelry and fine clothing.

Source: M.F. Zimbelman, "Student Shares Insights about Expense Fraud," *Fraud Magazine*, December 2004, pp. 15–19.

REVIEW CHECKPOINTS

6.4 What are some pressures that can cause honest people to contemplate fraud? List some egocentric and ideological ones as well as economic ones.

6.5 What conditions provide opportunities for employee fraud?

6.6 Give some examples of rationalizations that people have used to excuse fraud. Can you imagine using them?

6.7 Is capability required to commit a fraud? Is capability part of opportunity, or should it be considered a separate element of fraud?

FRAUD PREVENTION

LEARNING OBJECTIVE 6-3
Describe techniques that can be used to prevent employee fraud.

Building a good fraud prevention program is an extremely difficult task. Most day-to-day business activities require some trust in the processes where controls will never be absolute. For example, if we entrust an individual with check authorization, at the instant that person signs the check he or she has physical custody of the asset. As a result, taking steps to "fraud proof" an organization is a tall order.

Accountants and auditors have often been exhorted to be the leaders in fraud prevention by employing their skills in designing "tight" control systems. This strategy is, at best, a short-run solution to a large and pervasive problem. Business activity is built on the trust that people at all levels will do their jobs properly. As a result, it is essential that management establish a strong control environment. A strong control environment and tone at the top can have a pervasive effect on the prevention of fraud at an entity because it can impact all components of an organization's internal control system. For example, a CEO who always acts with ethics and integrity sends a strong message to all employees that management is serious about internal controls and fraud prevention. Beyond a strong control environment, management must be sensitive to the needs of the business by instituting controls that will prevent or detect fraud without impeding business activity. Control systems limit trust and, in the extreme, can strangle business in bureaucracy. The challenge is to have useful controls and to avoid picky rules that are "fun to beat." Managers and employees must have freedom to do business, which may mean giving them some freedom that can result in committing frauds. Effective long-run prevention measures are complex and difficult, involving the elimination of the causes of fraud by mitigating the effect of motive, opportunity, and lack of integrity.

Managing People Pressures in the Workplace

From time to time, people experience financial and other pressures. The pressures cannot be eliminated, but forums and facilities for sharing such pressures can and have been created by leading organizations. Some companies have "ethics officers" to serve this purpose. Their job is to be available to talk over various ethical dilemmas faced in the workplace and help employees identify legitimate responses. However, it is important to remember that the ethics officers are not normally psychological counselors.

Many companies have anonymous hotlines for reporting ethical problems. Indeed, companies that must comply with the Sarbanes-Oxley Act of 2002 were required to implement an employee hotline. Usually, the best kind of hotline arrangement is to have the responding party be a third-party agency outside the organization. In the United States, some external providers are in the business of being the recipients of hotline calls and coordinating their activities with the audit committee of the internal audit department of various organizations to whom they provide this service.

Another method of long-run fraud prevention, however, lies in the practice of management by caring for people. Managers and supervisors at all levels can exhibit a genuine concern for the personal and professional needs of their subordinates and fellow managers, and subordinates can show the same concern for each other and their managers. Many companies facilitate this caring attitude with an organized employee assistance program (EAP). They offer a range of counseling referral services dealing with substance abuse, mental health issues, family problems, crisis help, legal matters, health education, retirement, career paths, job loss troubles, and family financial planning.

When external auditors are engaged in the audit of an entity's financial statements, they must obtain an understanding of and evaluate the control environment. In so doing, the audit team should consider how management addresses these types of employee issues. Using devices such as those discussed here enhances an entity's control environment and represents the start of an effective control system.

Internal Control Activities and Employee Monitoring

As discussed in Chapter 5, internal control activities may include job descriptions and performance specifications that help people know the specific tasks they are supposed to accomplish. An entity whose only control is "trustworthy employees" has no control.[6] The possibility of being detected by a control activity can be an effective deterrent to a potential fraudster. Stated simply, control activities often provide the "opportunity" for a fraudster to get caught.

As previously discussed, concealment of the crime is a distinguishing attribute of a fraud. Often the audit team's first indication of a fraud is the identification of a control

---

[6] W. S. Albrecht, "How CPAs Can Help Clients Prevent Employee Fraud," *Journal of Accountancy,* December 1988, pp. 110–114.

violation. Cover-up attempts generally appear in the accounting records. The key for an auditor is to be aware of and notice exceptions and oddities such as the following:

- Transactions recorded at unusual times of the day, month, or year.
- An unusual (either large or small) number or dollar amount of transactions.
- Transactions for "round" dollar amounts (e.g., $50,000).
- Transactions associated with unusual branches or locations of a multilocation entity.
- Cash shortages and overages.
- Excessive voids and credit memos.
- General ledgers that do not balance.
- An increase in past due receivables.
- Inventory shortages.
- Unexplained adjustments to inventory or accounts receivable balances, especially without adequate supporting documentation.
- Increased scrap or waste in a manufacturing plant.
- Alterations on official documents.
- Duplicate payments made to the same vendor.
- Employees who cannot be found.
- Use of copies instead of originals for supporting documentation.
- Missing documentation to support transactions.
- Unusual endorsements on checks.
- Unusual patterns in deposits in transit.
- Common names or addresses for refunds.
- Consistent customer complaints about account balances or missing shipments.

AUDITING INSIGHT — When Assessing Fraud Risk, Answer These Questions

According to fraud experts Joseph Wells and John Gill of the Association of Fraud Examiners, when assessing fraud risk, answering a set of 15 questions is a good starting point for sizing up a company's vulnerability to fraud and creating an action plan from lessening the risks. Their key questions are:

1. Is the company dominated by one or two key employees?
2. Do any key employees appear to have a close association with vendors?
3. Do any key employees have outside business interests that might conflict with their job duties?
4. Does the organization conduct pre-employment background checks to identify previous dishonest or unethical behavior?
5. Does the organization educate employees about the importance of ethics and antifraud programs?
6. Does the organization have antifraud policies and provide an anonymous way to report suspected violations of ethics?
7. Is job or assignment rotation mandatory for employees who handle cash receipts and accounting duties?
8. Has the company established positive pay controls with its bank by supplying the bank with a daily list of checks issued and authorized for payment?
9. Are refunds, voids, and discounts evaluated on a routine basis to identify patterns of activity among employees, departments, shifts, or merchandise?
10. Are purchasing and receiving functions separate from invoice processing, accounts payable, and general ledger functions?
11. Is the employee payroll list periodically reviewed for duplicate or missing Social Security numbers?
12. Are there policies and procedures that address the identification, classification, and handling of proprietary information?
13. Do employees who have access to proprietary information sign nondisclosure agreements?
14. Is there a company policy that addresses the receipt of gifts, discounts, and services offered by a supplier or customer?
15. Are the organization's financial goals and objectives realistic?

Source: Joseph T. Wells and John D. Gill, "Assessing Fraud Risk," *Journal of Accountancy,* October 2007: 63–65.

As noted previously in Chapter 5, an important feature of an effective internal control system is the separation of duties and responsibilities for (1) transaction authorization, (2) record keeping, (3) custody of or access to assets, and (4) reconciliation of actual assets to the accounting records. Not surprisingly, for cash disbursements, effective internal control also begins with appropriate separation of duties. Proper separation involves different people and different departments handling the cash disbursement *authorization*; *custody* of blank documents (checks); *record keeping* for payments; and bank *reconciliation*. Generally, a person acting alone or in a conspiracy who can perform two or more of these functions also can commit a fraud by taking assets, converting them, and covering up. Auditing with fraud awareness often involves the combination of observing client control activities that were put in place and trying to "think like a crook" and imagine ways that theft could occur. When controls are missing, the ways and means for theft may be obvious. Otherwise, it might take significant planning and collusion to figure out how to steal from an employer.

When collecting corroborating evidence to support the financial statements, the audit team must remain vigilant to the potential for fraud. Discrepancies in the accounting records, conflicting evidence, and missing documentation are all symptomatic of financial statement fraud. When the audit team identifies such instances, members must follow up with management to identify the source of the problems. Management's response is a key source of evidence; vague, implausible, or inconsistent responses to inquiries can be a key indicator of the pervasiveness of the fraud. Similarly, problematic or unusual relationships between the audit team and management are often present in financial statement frauds.

The collection of evidence concerning fraud (which can lead to prosecution and court scrutiny) is different from the collection of evidence to support the auditor's opinion. If the auditors do come across questionable documents or other evidence of fraud, they should know how to preserve the chain of custody of evidence. The *chain of custody* is the crucial link of the evidence to the suspect, called the *relevance of evidence* by attorneys and judges. If documents are lost, mutilated, coffee stained, or otherwise compromised (so a defense attorney can argue that they were altered to frame the suspect), they lose their effectiveness for the prosecution. Auditors should learn to mark the evidence, writing an identification of the location, condition, date, time, and circumstances as soon as it appears to be a signal of fraud. This marking should be on a separate tag or page; the original document should be put in a protective (plastic) envelope for preservation and locked away for protection. Then audit work should proceed with copies of the documents instead of originals. A record should be made of the safekeeping and of all persons who use the original. Any eyewitness observations should be recorded in a timely manner in a memorandum or on tape (audio or video) with corroboration of colleagues, if possible. Other features of the chain of custody relate to interviews, interrogations, confessions, documents obtained by subpoena, and other matters, but auditors usually do not conduct these activities.

Integrity by Example and Enforcement

The key to integrity in business is accountability—that is, each person must be willing to put his or her decisions and actions in the open for all to see. Many organizations begin by publishing codes of conduct. Some of these codes are simple and some are very elaborate. Government agencies and defense contractors typically have the most elaborate rules for employee conduct. Sometimes these codes are effective; sometimes they are not. A code can be effective only if the control environment and tone at the top support it. When the chairman of the board and the president make themselves visible examples of the code, other people will then believe it is real. Subordinates tend to follow the boss's lead.

Hiring and firing are important. Background checks on prospective employees are advisable and very good business practice. A new employee who has been a fraudster in some other organization's accounting department has a higher probability to be a fraudster in a new organization. As a result, organizations have even been known to hire

AUDITING INSIGHT You're Not Supposed to Audit Me!

One of the large public accounting firms was conducting an "ethical compliance" audit of a Fortune 500 company. An ethical compliance audit is an attestation engagement to ensure, among other things, that client personnel are following the company's code of ethical conduct. Believing that the control environment and tone at the top were the most important elements of the client's ethical compliance control system, the assurance team started in the CEO's office. They found that the CEO was using the company plane to fly his fashion designer wife and her friends back and forth to Paris on a regular basis. When confronted in a board of directors meeting with the evidence, the CEO chastised the assurance team: "You weren't supposed to check on me; you were supposed to check on the employees." The board of directors disagreed and then requested the CEO's resignation.

---

private investigators to make background checks. Fraudsters should be fired and, in most cases, prosecuted. Experience has shown that they have a low rate of repeat offenses if they are prosecuted, but they have a high rate if not. Prosecution has the added benefit of sending the message that management does not believe that fraudulent activity is acceptable.

AUDITING INSIGHT Where Did He Come From?

The controller defrauded the company for several million dollars. As it turned out, he was not even a controller. He did not know a debit from a credit. The fraudster had been fired from five previous jobs where money had turned up missing in each situation. He was exposed one evening when the president showed up unexpectedly at the company and found a stranger in the office with the controller. It was later learned that the stranger had been doing all of the accounting work for the bogus controller.

Source: Association of Certified Fraud Examiners (ACFE), "Auditing for Fraud."

↳ REVIEW CHECKPOINT

6.8 What are some red flags that may indicate a cover-up or concealment of a fraud?

CASH INTERNAL CONTROL CONSIDERATIONS

LEARNING OBJECTIVE 6-4
Describe the control activities over the receipt and disbursement of cash.

Cash is highly liquid, not easily identifiable as company property, and highly portable. For these reasons, cash is the favorite target of employee thieves, although theft of inventory is a close second. As a consequence, controls over cash must be unusually strong. It is essential that the organization set up a robust set of control activities for both cash receipts and cash disbursements to "fraud-proof" an organization. Because a detailed discussion of these control activities is also needed to gain an understanding of how auditors complete their work on the cash balance in the financial statements, we now cover the full range of audit procedures used to audit the balance in the cash account.

Additionally, because cash is important to each of a client's accounting cycles, the discussion of cash should naturally precede the audits of the different cycles in the following chapters. For example, the basic activities in the revenue and collection cycle (Chapter 7) are (1) receiving and processing customer orders, including credit granting, (2) delivering goods and services to customers, (3) billing customers and accounting for accounts receivable, (4) *collecting and depositing cash received from customers*, and (5) *reconciling bank statements*. The basic acquisition and expenditure activities

(Chapter 8) are (1) purchasing goods and services and (2) *paying the bills.* Similarly, the production and conversion cycle (Chapter 9) and the investing and financing cycle (Chapter 10) also feature the collection or expenditure of cash. We now turn our attention to the control activities related to cash.

Control Activities for Cash Receipts

Cash can be received in several ways—over the counter, through the mail, and by electronic funds transfer. It can also be received in a **lockbox** arrangement in which payments are remitted by customers to an external location (i.e., a lockbox). In a lockbox arrangement, a fiduciary (usually a bank) opens the box on a daily basis, lists the receipts, deposits the money, and sends the remittance advices (stubs showing the amount received from each customer) to the company. Refer to Exhibit 6.2 for some cash receipts processing procedures in a manual accounting setting.

An individual employee always initially receives cash and checks and thus has custody of the physical cash for a short time. Because this initial custody cannot be avoided, it is always a good control to (1) have two people open the mail containing customer receipts, if possible, resulting in joint custody, (2) restrictively endorse the checks immediately after removing them from the envelope, (3) prepare a list of the cash receipts as early in the process as possible, and then (4) separate the actual cash from the record-keeping documents. The cash should be sent to the cashier or treasurer's office where a bank deposit is prepared and the money is sent to the bank *daily* and *intact* (no money should be withheld from the deposit). The list or remittance advices go to the

EXHIBIT 6.2 Cash Receipts Processing

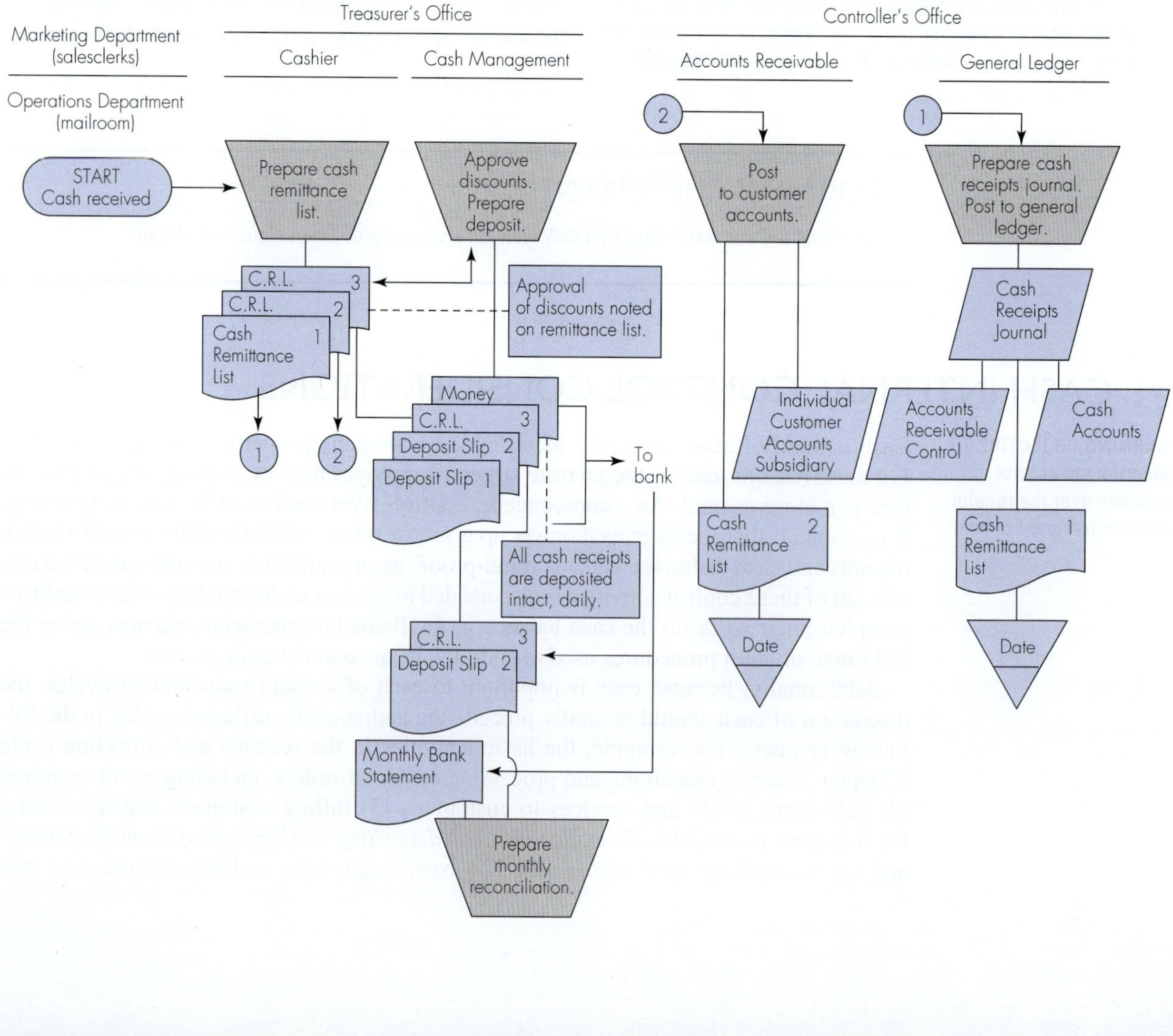

accountants (controller's office), who record the cash receipts. (You have prepared a "remittance advice" each time you write the amount enclosed on part of your credit card bill, tear it off, and enclose it with your check.)

The accountants who record cash receipts and credits to customer accounts should never handle the cash. They should use the remittance list or remittance advice to make the entries to the cash and accounts receivable control accounts and to the customers' accounts receivable subsidiary account records. A good internal control activity is to have control account and subsidiary account entries made by different people, and later the accounts receivable entries and balances can be compared (reconciled) to determine whether they agree in total. Most computerized accounting programs post the customers' accounts automatically by keying in the customer identification number, and the computer program controls agreement.

At the end of the day, an independent person should receive (1) a copy of the check listing, (2) a report of payments recorded in accounts receivable, and (3) a copy of the deposit slip from the bank. Commercial deposit slips have multiple copies. The bank runs these copies through the teller machine, which imprints the time, date, account, and amount on each copy. At least one copy is returned to the person making the deposit, who returns the copy to the company as evidence that the deposit was made. If the cash received during the day is maintained intact, the information on all three items should match.

Take a close look at Exhibit 6.2. Suppose that the cashier who prepares the remittance list had misappropriated and converted Customer A's checks to personal use. It might work for a short time until Customer A complained that the entity had not credited the account for payments. The cashier of course knows this. So the cashier later puts Customer B's check in the bank deposit, but shows Customer A on the remittance list; thus, the accountants give Customer A credit. So far, so good for preventing Customer A's complaint. But now Customer B needs to be covered. To detect this **lapping** scheme, a detailed audit should include comparison of the checks listed on a sample of deposit slips (Customer B) to the detail of customer remittances recorded to customer accounts (Customer A). Doing so is an attempt to find credits given to customers for whom no payments were received on the day in question.

AUDITING INSIGHT Lapping up the Profits

Stephan Winkler was the controller and director of accounting for a beverage distributing company in Florida. Some customers paid the route drivers by cash or check when beverages were delivered; other customers mailed payments directly to the company. Winkler performed the final accounting before the bank deposits were made and was able to skim cash collected by the route drivers by covering the customers' account with payments received in the mail from other customers. In this manner, Winkler stole approximately $350,000 from his employer.

Source: A. McNeal, "Lapping up the Profits," *Internal Auditor,* December 2006, pp. 85–87.

Employees outside the normal cash operations (recording and custody) should prepare bank account reconciliations on a timely basis. Deposit slips should be compared to the details on cash remittance lists and the total should be traced to the general ledger accounts receivable entries. (This reconciliation would reveal whether money was withheld from the deposit.) This care is required to establish that all the receipts recorded in the books were deposited and that credit was given to the right customer.

A common feature of cash management is to require that persons who handle cash be insured under a **fidelity bond**, which is an insurance policy that covers most kinds of cash embezzlement losses. Fidelity bonds do not prevent or detect embezzlement, but the failure to carry the insurance exposes the company to complete loss if embezzlement occurs. Moreover, bonding companies often perform their own background checks of employees before bonding them. Auditors often recommend fidelity bonding to small companies that might not know about such coverage.

Information about a company's internal control activities often is gathered by completing an internal control questionnaire. A selection of other questionnaires for both general (manual) controls and computer controls over cash receipts is found in Appendix 6A at the end of this chapter. You can study these questionnaires for details of other desirable control activities. They are organized under headings that identify the important control objectives over cash transactions—occurrence, accuracy, completeness, classification, and cutoff.

Another way to obtain general information about controls can be achieved by conducting a *walkthrough*. In conducting walkthroughs, the auditors select examples of a transaction (in this case, customer remittance advices) and "walk them through" the information-processing system from their initial receipt all the way to their recording in the accounting records. Sample documents are collected, and employees in each department are questioned about their specific duties. The walkthrough, combined with inquiries, can contribute evidence about appropriate separation of duties, which might be a sufficient basis for a preliminary assessment of control risk. However, a walkthrough is too limited in scope to provide evidence of whether the client's control activities were operating effectively during the period under audit. Rather, to justify a low control risk assessment and a reduction of substantive testing procedures, an auditor would have to conduct a test of operating effectiveness for the control activity under consideration.

Tests of Controls over Cash Receipts

An entity should establish input, processing, and output control activities to prevent, detect, and correct accounting errors. Auditors can perform tests of controls to determine whether the internal control activities related to the correct handling of cash receipts are operating effectively. If the internal control activities are not operating effectively (e.g., because personnel in the organization are not performing the cash control activities very well), auditors need to expand substantive audit procedures to ensure that the cash balance is not materially misstated and to identify possible fraudulent acts related to cash.

Exhibit 6.3 contains a selection of tests of controls for cash receipts transactions. Many of these procedures can be characterized as steps taken to verify the content and character of sample documents from one file with the content and character of documents in another file. These steps are designed to enable the audit team to obtain objective evidence about the *effectiveness* of control activities and about the *reliability* of accounting records. Exhibit 6.3 also shows the management assertions that are supported by the internal control activity and ultimately the test of control. Thus, the test of controls procedures are designed to produce evidence that helps auditors determine whether the specific management assertions were supported.

EXHIBIT 6.3
Test of Controls for Cash Receipts

Internal Control	Test of Control	Management Assertion Supported
• Cash receipts are deposited intact and daily.	1. Observe the opening of the mail and ensure that:	
	a. Two employees are opening the mail, remittance advice is received, and check is restrictively endorsed.	Occurrence
	b. A listing of all checks is being prepared and compared to total of deposit ticket for total of checks.	Accuracy
	c. Trace the deposit ticket to the bank statement to ensure that the deposit was recorded in the proper period.	Cutoff
• Deposits are reconciled with totals posted to the accounts receivable subsidiary ledger.	2. For a sample of daily postings to the accounts receivable subsidiary ledger, trace the amount to the amount of cash deposited in bank on that day as per the bank statement.	Completeness

Control Considerations for Cash Disbursements

For cash disbursements, effective internal control begins with appropriate separation of duties. Proper separation involves different people and different departments handling *custody* of blank documents (checks); cash disbursement *authorization; record keeping* for payments; and bank *reconciliation:*

- *Custody.* Blank documents such as blank checks should be kept secure at all times. If unauthorized persons can obtain a blank check, they can be in another country before an embezzlement is detected.
- *Authorization.* Cash disbursements are typically authorized by an accounts payable department's assembly of purchase orders, vendor invoices, and internal receiving reports to demonstrate a valid obligation to pay. This assembly of supporting documents is called a *voucher* and will be discussed in more detail in Chapter 8. (Accounts payable obligations usually are recorded when the purchaser receives the goods or services ordered.) A person authorized by management signs the checks. A company may have a policy to require two signatures on checks over a certain amount (e.g., $50,000). Vouchers should be marked "PAID" or otherwise stamped to show that they have been processed completely so they cannot be paid a second time.
- *Recording.* When checks are prepared, entries are made to debit accounts payable and credit cash. Someone without access to the check-writing function should perform the recording function.
- *Reconciliation.* Monitoring of the internal control over cash can be provided by timely bank reconciliations made by individuals outside of the normal cash operations.

Combinations of two or more of these responsibilities in one person, one office, or one computerized system may open the door for errors and frauds. In addition, the control system should provide for detailed information-processing control activities.

Tests of Controls over Cash Disbursements

An entity should have detailed control activities in place and operating to prevent, detect, and correct accounting errors. Auditors can perform tests of controls to determine whether the internal control activities related to the correct handling of cash disbursements are operating effectively. If the internal control activities are not operating effectively (e.g., because personnel in the organization are not performing the cash control activities very well), auditors need to expand substantive audit procedures to ensure that the cash balance is not materially misstated and to identify possible fraudulent acts related to cash. Exhibit 6.4 identifies common tests of control activities, the management assertions that are supported, and the typical test of control. Thus, the test of control procedures are designed to produce evidence that helps auditors determine whether the specific management assertions were supported.

EXHIBIT 6.4 Tests of Controls over Cash Disbursements

Internal Control	Test of Control	Management Assertion Supported
• Checks are not printed until voucher packets are prepared.	a. For a sample of recorded cash disbursements from the cash disbursements journal, vouch to supporting documentation for evidence of mathematical accuracy, correct classification, proper approval, and proper date of entry.	Occurrence
• An employee compares amounts on printed checks with voucher packets prior to submission for signature.		Accuracy
• Only authorized signers are permitted to sign checks.		Occurrence
• Checks are prenumbered and accounted for.	b. Scan checks for sequence. Look for gaps in sequence and duplicate numbers.	Completeness
• Bank reconciliations are prepared on a timely basis.	c. Review bank reconciliations to ensure that they were prepared on a timely basis.	Cutoff

> **AUDITING INSIGHT** | **Too Much Trouble**
>
> A trucking company self-insured claims of damage to goods in transit, processed claims vouchers, and paid customers from its own bank accounts. Several persons were authorized to sign checks. One person thought it "too much trouble" to stamp the vouchers PAID and said: "That's textbook stuff anyway." Numerous claims were recycled to other check signers and $80,000 was paid for duplicate claims before the problem was discovered.

Risk of Material Misstatement at the Relevant Assertion Level

Recall that from our study of audit planning in Chapter 3, the professional standards clearly focus the auditor's attention on the importance of careful identification of each relevant financial statement assertion related to significant accounts and disclosures. It is clear that certain financial statement assertions have a higher risk of material misstatement than others and are thus "more" relevant for a particular financial statement account. For cash, existence is always a relevant assertion in the audit plan. Other assertions may also be relevant depending on the facts and circumstances of the engagement.

Once the relevant assertions have been identified for cash (e.g., existence) and the tests of control activities are complete, the auditor must evaluate the evidence obtained from risk assessment activities and controls tests to determine the risk of material misstatement for each relevant assertion. Recall from Chapters 3 and 4 that the risk of material misstatement comprises inherent risk and control risk for each relevant management assertion. For example, if the inherent risk for existence of cash is high, but the control activities were found to be operating effectively and control risk is assessed low, the substantive testing procedures to be conducted for the existence assertion might be limited in cost-saving ways. Perhaps the auditors might be able to rely on test work performed by internal auditors when they tested bank reconciliations. On the other hand, if tests of controls reveal weaknesses, control risk would be evaluated to be higher and the substantive procedures need to be more effective to lower the risk of failing to detect material misstatement related to the existence of cash.

> **REVIEW CHECKPOINTS**
>
> 6.9 What is the basic sequence of activities in the cash collection process?
>
> 6.10 Why should a list of cash remittances be made and sent to the accounting department? Wouldn't it be easier to send the cash and checks to the accountants so they can enter the credits to customers' accounts accurately?
>
> 6.11 What is *lapping?* What procedures can auditors employ to detect lapping?
>
> 6.12 What feature of the acquisition and expenditure control would be expected to prevent an employee from embezzling cash by creating fictitious vouchers?

AUDIT EVIDENCE USED TO TEST CASH

Audit evidence can be found in a number of different management reports, documents, and data files. The sources of evidence are discussed in this section.

Cash Receipts Journal

The cash receipts journal contains all of the detailed entries for all receipts of cash by the entity (debits to the cash account), including cash deposits. It contains the population of credit entries that should be reflected in the credits to accounts receivable for customer payments. It also contains the adjusting and correcting entries that can result from the bank account reconciliation. These entries are important because they may signal the types of accounting errors or manipulations that occur in the cash receipts accounting.

Cash Disbursements Journal

The cash disbursements journal is the company's checkbook. It contains all detailed entries for checks written during the period being audited (cash disbursements). Because all cash disbursements (other than those from a petty cash account) should be made via check or electronic transfer, the cash disbursements journal contains the cash credit entries that provide a population for testing cash disbursements. It also contains the adjusting and correcting entries that can result from the bank account reconciliation. These entries are important because they may signal the types of accounting errors or manipulations that occur in the cash disbursements accounting. The cash disbursements journal is usually scanned for suspect items such as checks made out to "cash" or "bearer." In addition, company procedures should require that "voided" checks be retained and auditors should review these checks to ensure they were in fact actually voided and have not been recorded in any bank statements.

Bank Reconciliations

The company's bank reconciliation is the primary document used to test the cash balance in the financial statements. The amount of cash in the bank is almost always different from the amount in the general ledger (financial statements), and the reconciliation is designed to explain the difference between these two amounts. In addition, a bank account reconciliation that compares the book cash balance to the bank cash balance provides management with an opportunity to monitor the separation of duties for cash receipts and cash disbursements as well. The timely preparation of bank reconciliations is therefore an important element of a company's internal control activities over cash.

Canceled Checks

Exhibit 6.5 describes the information found on a typical check. Whether the auditor examines the actual check or a scanned image obtained from the bank, knowledge of the codes for Federal Reserve districts, offices, states, and bank identification numbers could enable an auditor to spot a crude check forgery. A forger's mistakes with the optional identification printing or the magnetic check number might provide a tip-off. If the amount of a check is altered after it has cleared the bank, the alteration would be noted by comparing the

AUDITING INSIGHT — Who Was That Check from Again?

Naomi, an employee at a check-cashing business in Brooklyn, New York, received only the basics of detecting check fraud from her supervisors: look for watermarks, compare encoded check numbers, and question customers to see whether they can keep their stories straight if a check looks suspicious.

Earlier in the month, the main office of Naomi's business warned workers to look for a Roberta Kane who had been successfully passing false checks in other branches. When Roberta walked into Naomi's branch, Naomi closely examined her ID and the $200 check. The check's routing numbers were larger than they should be, the check felt softer than others, and there was no watermark. Naomi asked Roberta how she had received the check and Roberta said it was a paycheck from her employer. Naomi called the number of the company that supposedly wrote the check. When the number appeared to be out of service,

Naomi told Roberta that she had presented a false check and that the police would have to get involved. Roberta frantically ran for the door, leaving behind her fake check and ID. Even with the most basic knowledge of detecting check fraud, this teller was able to deter a thief. As you can see, it is important for auditors to review the fundamentals of check fraud detection.

In an unrelated case, four people were under investigation for an easily discovered counterfeit check-cashing scheme. Despite using high-tech computer equipment to generate the counterfeit checks, the fraudsters mistakenly misspelled the payer (Broyhill Furniture) as "Boryhill Furniture."

Sources: Suzanne Mahadeo, "Check Fraud: Separating Money from Worthless Paper," *Fraud Magazine,* September/October 2005, pp. 21–23, 50; "News of the Weird," *Funny Times,* May 2003.

EXHIBIT 6.5 How to Read a Canceled Check and Endorsement

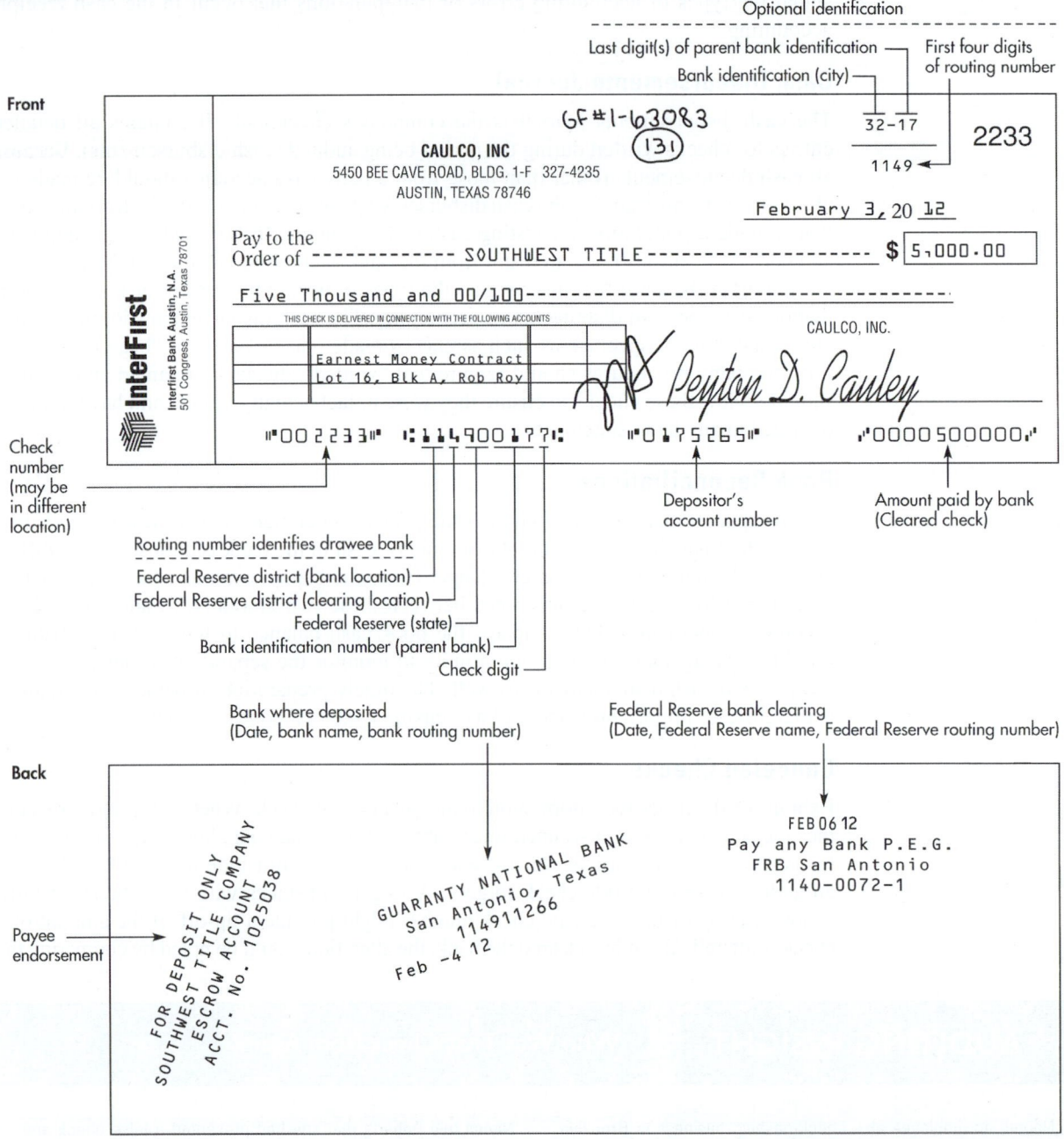

magnetic imprint of the amount paid to the amount written on the check face. The reverse side of a check carries the endorsement(s) of the payees and holders in due course; the date and the name and routing number of the bank where the check was deposited; and the date, identification of the Federal Reserve office, and its routing number for the Federal Reserve check clearing. (Sometimes there is no Federal Reserve clearing identification when regional checks are cleared locally without going through a Federal Reserve office.) Auditors can follow the path of a canceled check by following the banks where it was deposited and cleared. This route may or may not correspond with the characteristics of the payee. (For example, ask why a check to a local business in Texas was deposited in a small Missouri bank and cleared through the St. Louis Federal Reserve office.)

Individuals engaging in fraudulent schemes involving cash often try to conceal their crimes by removing canceled checks they made payable to themselves or endorsed on the back with their own names. Missing canceled checks are a red flag. However, many banks no longer return the canceled checks to their customers. Instead, they send photocopies of the front of the checks. While this information is sufficient for reconciling an account, it does not provide the information that may assist a company or auditor in detecting or investigating possible frauds. Many banks will return the canceled checks to the company for a small fee. Other banks retain images of checks (front and back) on their Internet sites. Auditors, controllers, and CFOs should strongly recommend that their client or company pay to ensure that access to canceled checks is available, even if additional fees are required.

Bank Statements

Most of the information shown on the bank statement in Exhibit 6.6 is self-explanatory. However, auditors should not overlook the usefulness of some of the information: the number and dollar amount of deposits and checks can be compared to the detail data on

EXHIBIT 6.6
Small Business Bank Statement

```
                                                                              27
     ⊠ First RepublicBank
     FIRST REPUBLICBANK AUSTIN, N.A.                         ACCOUNT
     P.O. BOX 908                       ---               604017-526-5
     AUSTIN, TEXAS  78781               ---   ---
                                              ---                 PAGE
                                              ---                    1

     CAULCO INC                                           SSN/TAX ID
     BLDG 1 OFFICE F                                      74-2076251
     5450 BEE CAVE RD
     AUSTIN,  TX                                          CYC MC FREQ
     78746                                                01 01 M0000

     **  YOUR CHECKING ACCOUNT       01-29-12 THRU 02-28-12  **

     TO YOUR PREVIOUS BALANCE OF - - - - - - - -        7,559.06
     YOU ADDED         1 DEPOSITS FOR  - - - - -        5,654.16
     YOU SUBTRACTED   25 WITHDRAWALS FOR - - - - -      5,838.29
     GIVING YOU A CURRENT BALANCE OF - - - - - - -      7,374.93

     NUMBER OF DAYS USED FOR AVERAGES - - - - - -              31
     YOUR AVERAGE LEDGER BALANCE - - - - - - - - -       4,014.67
     YOUR LOW BALANCE OCCURRED ON 02-22 AND WAS  -       2,374.93

                            THANK YOU


     ---------------------------------------------------------------
     ---------------------------------------------------------------
                     DEPOSITS AND OTHER ADDITIONS

             DATE     AMOUNT
             0204     5654.16
     ---------------------------------------------------------------
                     CHECKS AND OTHER WITHDRAWALS

     CHECK DATE    AMOUNT  CHECK DATE    AMOUNT  CHECK DATE    AMOUNT
     2201  0211    57.83   2214  0203    403.92  2225  0217    182.77
      **                   2215  0203    135.59   **
     2205  0222    16.72   2216  0216      6.16  2231  0205    254.37
     2206  0203   533.28   2217  0217    138.43  2232  0210     60.61
     2207  0203  1312.15   2218  0217    131.92   **
      **                   2219  0217     82.97  2234  0217     64.69
     2209  0203   247.10   2220  0217     87.49  2235  0218    279.97
     2210  0203   249.98   2221  0217     85.68   **
     2211  0203   255.26   2222  0217     84.69  2238  0219     90.00
     2212  0203   242.09    **
     2213  0203   384.91   2224  0217    449.71
```

the bank statement; the account holder's federal business identification number is on the statement, and this can be used in other databases; and the statement itself can be studied for alterations.

> ### REVIEW CHECKPOINTS
>
> 6.13 How can you tell whether the amount on a check was altered after it was paid by a bank?
>
> 6.14 Take a closer look at Exhibit 6.6. Is there anything wrong with the bank statement? What are some ways to tell whether any of the amounts have been altered?

THE AUDIT OF CASH

LEARNING OBJECTIVE 6-5
Describe the types of substantive procedures that are conducted during the audit of cash.

The first procedure in an audit of cash is to obtain the entity-prepared bank reconciliations and audit them, focusing on some of the reconciling items discussed in the preceding section. In a well-functioning control environment, auditors should never have to perform the company's internal control activity of preparing the bank reconciliation. Rather, this is clearly the responsibility of management.

Bank Reconciliation

A client-prepared bank reconciliation is shown in Exhibit 6.7. When auditing the bank reconciliation, the auditor should begin by confirming the account balance listed as the "balance per bank" on the top of the bank reconciliation for each bank account from each bank that the client utilizes in the business. A confirmation letter is required to be sent by the auditor and received in the mail directly back from each bank at the offices of the public accounting firm. This procedure is important because the auditor needs to make sure that the confirmation request was actually completed by an independent professional at a third-party bank. In fact, a failure to adhere to professional standards in this area was cited by the SEC and PCAOB when announcing financial statement fraud charges against **Satyam,** an information technology company based in India. A description is found in this auditing insight.

> ### AUDITING INSIGHT — The Dangers of Bank Confirmations
>
> The Securities and Exchange Commission recently charged "India-based Satyam Computer Services Limited with fraudulently overstating the company's revenue, income and cash balances by more than $1 billion over five years." The SEC's complaint states that "former senior officials at Satyam—an information technology services company based in Hyderabad, India—used false invoices and forged bank statements to inflate the company's cash balances and make it appear far more profitable to investors." In addition, "Satyam employees also created bogus bank statements to reflect payment of the sham invoices. This resulted in more than $1 billion in fictitious cash and cash-related balances." In addition, the SEC instituted administrative proceedings against the auditors, **Price Waterhouse India** for "failure to properly execute third-party confirmation procedures" to test the existence of cash at Satyam.
>
> Source: "SEC Charges Satyam Computer Services with Financial Fraud," www.sec.gov, *Case 2011-81,* April 5, 2011.

The standard bank confirmation form, approved by the AICPA, the American Bankers Association, and the Bank Administration Institute, is shown in Exhibit 6.8. This form is used to obtain confirmation of deposit balances. You will note in Exhibit 6.8 that the

EXHIBIT 6.7
Bank Reconciliation

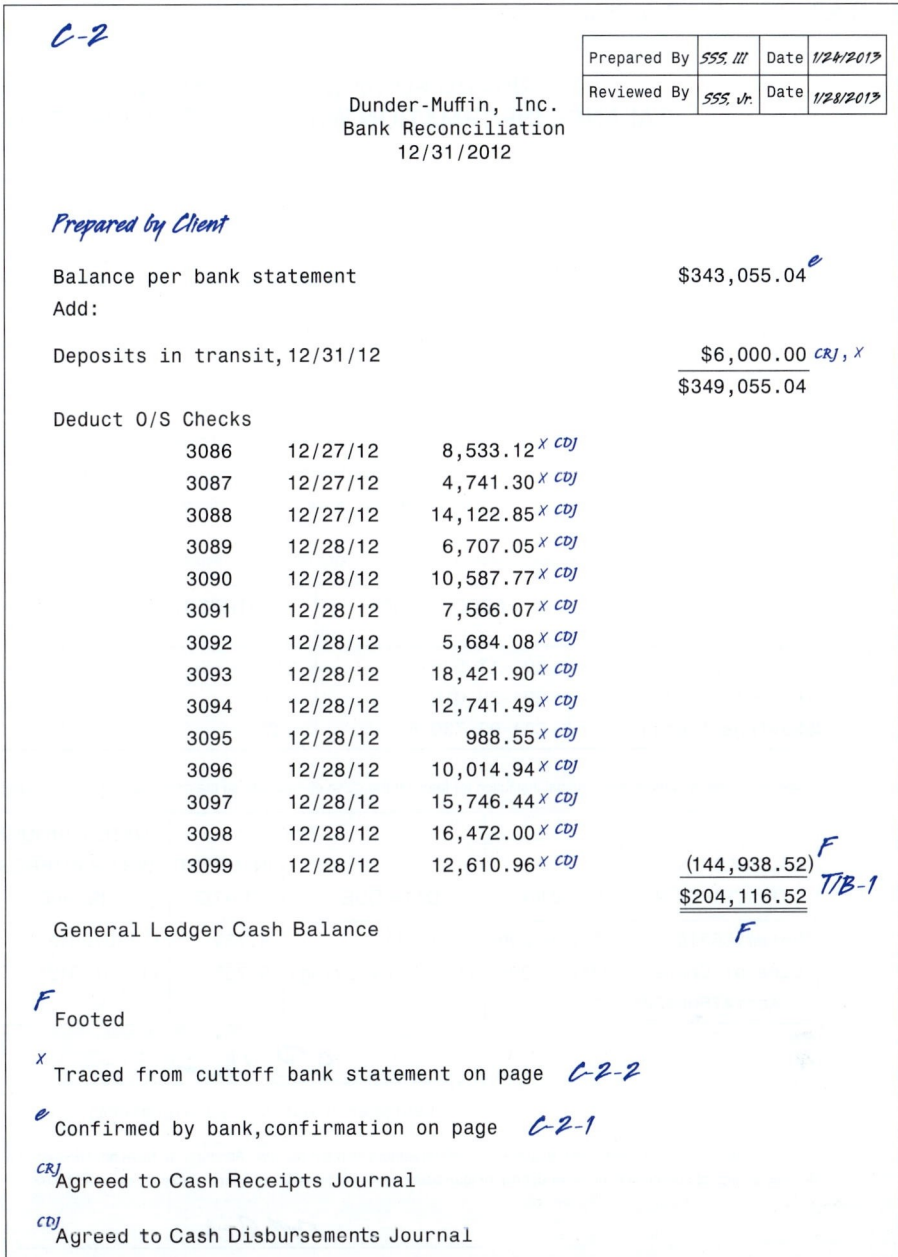

auditor can also use the confirmation letter to confirm outstanding loan balances listed on the balance sheet. As shown, a bank's response to question 2 would provide the auditor with evidence to test the existence assertion for liabilities. Alternatively, in regard to question 2, the auditor may choose to leave out the detailed information about outstanding loan balances and instead ask the bank to list any loans or commitments made by the client at that bank. In this way, the auditors would be gathering evidence to test the completeness assertion for liabilities, as the auditor would trace the information provided by the bank to loan balances listed on the balance sheet. We will discuss substantive tests of the loan balance in more detail in Chapter 10.

A couple of words of caution are in order. First, while financial institutions may note exceptions to the information typed in a confirmation and may confirm items omitted from it, the AICPA warns auditors that sole reliance on the form to satisfy the completeness assertion for cash and liabilities is unwarranted. Employees of financial institutions

EXHIBIT 6.8 Bank Confirmation

C-2-1

STANDARD FORM TO CONFIRM ACCOUNT BALANCE INFORMATION WITH FINANCIAL INSTITUTIONS

Dunder-Muffin, Inc.
CUSTOMER NAME

FINANCIAL INSTITUTION'S NAME AND ADDRESS

Twenty-First National Bank
Post Office Box 1
Shoetown, ME 00002

We have provided to our accountants the following information as of the close of business on 12/31/2012, regarding our deposit and loan balances. Please confirm the accuracy of the information, noting any exceptions to the information provided. If the balances have been left blank, please complete this form by furnishing the balance in the appropriate space below.* Although we do not request nor expect you to conduct a comprehensive, detailed search of your records, if during the process of completing this confirmation additional information about other deposit and loan accounts we may have with you comes to your attention, please include such information below. Please use the enclosed envelope to return the form directly to our accountants.

1. At the close of business on the date listed above, our records indicated the following deposit balance(s):

ACCOUNT NAME	ACCOUNT NO.	INTEREST RATE	BALANCE*	
Checking Account	604-17-526-5	n/a	343,055.04	C-2
Payroll Account	604-29-016-3	n/a	0	C-3
Savings Account	604-03-739-8	1.2%	4,150,947.95	C-4

2. We were directly liable to the financial institution for loans at the close of business on the date listed above as follows:

ACCOUNT NO./ DESCRIPTION	BALANCE*	DATE DUE	INTEREST RATE	DATE THROUGH WHICH INTEREST IS PAID	DESCRIPTION OF COLLATERAL	
Note#106316	10,000,000	1/1/2014	8.75%	11/30/2012	None	I-3
Line of Credit, Acct#7500438	44,053,000	2014 (revolving)	9.75%	11/30/2012	None	I-4

E.P. Unum   1/3/2013
(Customer's Authorized Signature)   (Date)

The information presented above by the customer is in agreement with our records. Although we have not conducted a comprehensive, detailed search of our records, no other deposit or loan accounts have come to our attention except as noted below.

I.M Rich   1/10/2013
(Financial Institution Authorized Signature)   (Date)

Account Confirmation Specialist
(Title)

EXCEPTIONS AND OR COMMENTS

No exceptions noted.

Please return this form directly to our accountants:

Smith & Smith, CPAs
31st Financial Avenue
Shoetown, ME 00002

*Ordinarily, balances are intentionally left blank if they are not available at the time this form is prepared.
Approved 1990 by American Bankers Association, American Institute of Certified Public Accountants, and Bank Administration Institute. Additional forms available from: AICPA–Order Department, P.O. Box 1003 NY, NY 10108-1003.

cannot be expected to search their information systems for balances and loans that may not be immediately evident as assets and liabilities of the client company. And second, even if the auditor properly controls the mailing and receipt of the confirmation request, the auditor cannot be absolutely certain that a competent and independent professional at the bank has completed the response.

To help improve the control of both delivery and receipt of the confirmation request, authenticate the identity of the person completing the request and to improve efficiency, many public accounting firms use electronic audit confirmations when testing cash (e.g., www.confirmations.com). In fact, many of the largest banks such as Bank of America, JP Morgan Chase, and Wells Fargo complete all of their confirmation responses electronically. The professional standards do allow auditors to use secure electronic audit confirmations as a substantive auditing procedure.[7]

Once the "balance in the bank" has been confirmed and cross-referenced to the balance in the bank reconciliation, the following additional procedures are typically used in auditing the bank reconciliation:

- Verify the mathematical accuracy of the reconciliation, including the listing of outstanding checks and deposits in transit.
- Examine reconciling items to ensure they are appropriately classified (e.g., that they were legitimate outstanding checks that were written but not paid by the bank at the statement date).
- Agree the book balance to the trial balance, which has been traced to the general ledger.

The auditors' information source for validating the bank reconciliation items is typically a **cutoff bank statement**, which is a complete bank statement including all paid checks and deposit slips. The client requests the bank to send this bank statement directly to the auditor. It is usually for a 10- to 20-day period following the date of the financial statements. (It also can be the next regular monthly statement received directly by the auditors.) The cutoff bank statement is important because it (1) is sent directly to the auditors (which qualifies as *external evidence*) and (2) documents important bank transactions occurring early in the subsequent period so that the audit team doesn't have to wait for the normal bank statement to be sent to the client (which qualifies only as *external-internal evidence*). These transactions subsequent to the date of the financial statements are important for testing the completeness of the client's outstanding check list as well as the existence of any deposits in transit. The bank cutoff statement can also be used in a *search for unrecorded liabilities* discussed in more detail in Chapter 8.

Deposits in transit should be *vouched* from the bank reconciliation to the bank cutoff statement (*existence*) and should have been recorded by the bank in the first business days of the cutoff period. If recorded later, the inference is that the deposit may have been composed of receipts of the period after the date of the financial statements.

When auditing negative reconciling items (i.e., outstanding checks) listed on the bank reconciliation and because the audit team is most concerned about the existence of cash (i.e., overstatement) rather than the completeness of cash (i.e., understatement), the completeness of the outstanding checks listing is more critical than their existence. Comparably, when auditing positive reconciling items (i.e., deposits in transit) listed on the bank reconciliation, the *completeness* of the deposits-in-transit listing is more critical than their *existence* because the audit team is most concerned about the existence of cash (i.e., overstatement) rather than the completeness of cash (i.e., understatement). As a result, the audit team *traces* outstanding checks that cleared on the cutoff bank statement (and were either returned with that statement or identified in that statement) to the client's list of outstanding checks for evidence that all checks that were written prior

---

[7] The PCAOB recently solicited public comment on a proposed standard, Confirmation. The new standard is designed to provide additional guidance to auditors related to the performance of confirmation procedures. The new standard is expected to be issued at the end of 2011 or in 2012 (www.pcaobus.org).

to the reconciliation date were included on the list of outstanding checks. Additionally, canceled checks should be traced to the cash disbursements listing (journal). For large outstanding checks not clearing in the cutoff period, other documentation supporting the disbursement may be used. These procedures are key and described by tick marks in Exhibit 6.7. As the next Auditing Insight suggests, it is important to pay close attention to possible errors in the bank reconciliation.

AUDITING INSIGHT — The Darn Stuff Is So Easy to Count

Through the use of discretionary estimates, **HealthSouth,** one of the largest health care providers in the United States, inflated its assets by $1.5 billion. In an even more bizarre twist, prosecutors allege that the company overstated its cash by more than $300 million. Because auditors use standardized forms to confirm cash balances with financial institutions, how the auditors missed the cash overstatement is a mystery. "I'm shocked that cash is manipulated and overstated, because the darn stuff is so easy to count," states one audit expert. Nevertheless, auditors must never take the cash balance for granted when conducting the audit.

Source: "Did HealthSouth Auditor Ernst Miss Key Clues to Fraud Risks?" *The Wall Street Journal,* April 10, 2003.

Schedule of Interbank Transfers

Auditors usually prepare a **schedule of interbank transfers** to determine whether transfers of cash from one bank to another were recorded properly (correct amount and correct date). The audit team should also be alert to the possibility of a company's practice of illegal "kiting." **Check kiting** is the deliberate floating of funds between two or more bank accounts in order to make it appear that more cash is present than is really the case. When a check is deposited in one bank, the cash receipts journal immediately includes that deposit. At the same time, the check, drawn on a different bank account, does not appear in the cash disbursements journal for several days. By this method, an entity can use the time required for checks to clear to inflate the cash amount on the entity's books. Advances in information technology and increased bank scrutiny have reduced the incidences of check kiting in recent years. However, auditors must still be aware of the possibility, and the schedule of bank transfers is a technique designed to detect the practice.

These are some characteristic signs of check-kiting schemes:

- Frequent deposits and checks in rounded and the same amounts.
- Frequent deposits with checks written on the same (other) banks.
- Short time lags between deposits and withdrawals.
- Frequent ATM account balance inquiries.
- Many large deposits made on Thursday or Friday to take advantage of the weekend.
- Large periodic balances in individual accounts with no apparent business explanation.
- Low average balance compared to high level of deposits.
- Many checks made payable to other banks.
- Banks' willingness to pay against uncollected funds.
- "Cash" withdrawals with deposit checks drawn on another bank.
- Checks drawn on foreign banks with lax banking laws and regulations.

Auditors can detect the preceding signs of check kiting by reviewing an audit client's bank account activity. The only trouble is that criminal check kiters often destroy the banking documents. A company should provide the auditor access to all deposit slips and canceled checks. However, in today's computerized banking environment, many documents exist only in electronic form or as scanned images. The auditor may need to review the client's account activity directly on the bank's website.

Of course, if each of these cash transfers is recorded in the books, a company will show the negative balances that result from checks drawn on insufficient funds. However, perpetrators may try to hide the kiting by not recording the deposits and checks. Such maneuvers may be detected by using a schedule of interbank transfers.

Today, banks have implemented the Check Clearing for the 21st Century Act, referred to as Check 21. In this system, checks are converted to digital images allowing for a dramatic increase in speed in check clearing. The benefit is that the "float" on the check is virtually eliminated and kiting becomes difficult to perform and conceal. However, in the Check 21 system, the paper check is usually destroyed, a hard copy of the check is never returned to the customer or its bank, and consequently, the nature of the audit trail is significantly different. In investigating possible fraud, the audit team is able to obtain only an electronic copy of the check and the controls over the safeguarding of the imaging files will be of great importance.

AUDITING INSIGHT — As Simple as Flying a Kite

Four employees of Detroit-based **Simplified Employment Services** were charged with defrauding banks of at least $32 million in a complex check-kiting scheme. Using seven corporate entities holding 21 separate checking accounts, the fraudsters were able to commingle legitimate company transactions with fraudulent ones to conceal overdrawn bank accounts.

Source: "4 Charged in $32 Million Check-Kiting Scheme," *Detroit News*, January 24, 2002.

Proof of Cash

Auditors can use another method to discover unrecorded cash transactions. It is called a *proof of cash*. You may have studied this method in your intermediate accounting course under the name of "four-column bank reconciliation." The **proof of cash** is a reconciliation in which the bank balance, the bank report of cash deposited, and the bank report of cash paid are all reconciled to the corresponding records maintained in the entity's general ledger, cash receipts journal, and cash disbursements journal. Exhibit 6.9 illustrates a proof of cash.

The proof of cash attempts to reconcile the deposits and payments reported by the bank to the deposits and payments recorded in the cash receipts and cash disbursements journals, respectively, as well as the final general ledger totals. The proof of cash is a very effective procedure to verify cash transactions but is usually used only when controls over cash are weak.

↳ REVIEW CHECKPOINTS

6.15 What is a cutoff bank statement? How do auditors use it?

6.16 What is *check kiting*? How might auditors detect kiting?

6.17 How does a schedule of interbank transfers show improper cash transfer transactions?

6.18 How can a *proof of cash* reveal unrecorded cash deposit and cash payment transactions?

EXHIBIT 6.9 Illustration of Proof of Cash—First National Bank

	Balance June 30	Month of July Deposits	Month of July Payments	Balance July 31
Bank statement amounts	$264,322	$398,406	$390,442	$272,286
Deposits in transit				
June 30	76,501	(76,501)		
July 31		79,721		79,721
Outstanding checks				
June 30	(89,734)		(89,734)	
July 31			62,958	(62,958)
Unrecorded bank interest (recorded in the next month)				
June 30	(162)	162		
July 31		(155)		(155)
Unrecorded service charges (recorded in the next month)				
June 30	118		118	
July 31			(129)	129
Unrecorded transfers received from Last National Bank		(37,000)		(37,000)
Unrecorded transfers to Last National Bank			(42,000)	42,000
General ledger amounts	$251,045	$364,633	$321,655	$294,023

AUDIT CASES: MORE SCHEMES AND WAYS TO DETECT THEM

LEARNING OBJECTIVE 6-6
Discuss actual cash fraud cases and describe how the schemes were uncovered.

As discussed previously, many cases of fraud occur in the cash collections and disbursements areas. In this section, we try a new approach. Instead of discussing lists of schemes and detection procedures in the abstract, the following illustrative cases tell the actual stories of some of these cash embezzlement schemes. The cases follow a standard format in two major parts: (1) case situation and (2) audit approach. Some problems at the end of the chapter will give the case situation and you will be assigned to write the audit approach section.

Case 6.1

Case of the Missing Petty Cash

PROBLEM

The petty cash custodian (1) brought postage receipts from home and paid them from the fund, (2) persuaded the supervisor to sign blank authorization slips the custodian could use when the supervisor was away and used them to pay for fictitious meals and minor supplies, and (3) took cash to get through the weekend, replacing it the next week. Postage receipts were from a distant post office station the company did not use. The blank authorization slips were dated on days the supervisor was absent. The fund was cash short during the weekend and for a few days the following week. The fund was small ($500), but the custodian replenished it about every two working days, stealing about $50 each time. With about 260 working days per year and 130 reimbursements, the custodian was stealing about $6,500 per year. The custodian was looking forward to getting promoted to general cashier and bigger and better things!

AUDIT APPROACH

The audit team should discuss petty cash procedures with the custodian and supervisor, especially those that relate to situations in which the custodian or supervisor is not available to provide needed petty cash. Next a sample of petty cash reimbursement check copies with receipts and authorization slips attached should be studied for evidence of authorization and validity. On Friday, an audit team member should count the petty cash and receipts to see that they total $500. Then the fund should be recounted later in the afternoon. (The second count should be a surprise.) The custodian or supervisor should be present at all times so that the auditor will not be accused of theft.

DISCOVERY SUMMARY

Knowing the location of the nearby post office branch used by the company, the auditor noticed the pattern of many receipts from a distant branch, which was near the custodian's apartment. Several authorizations were dated during the supervisor's vacation and he readily admitted signing the forms in blank so his own supervisor "wouldn't be bothered." The second count on the same day was a real surprise: The fund was found $65 short.

Case 6.2

The Laundry Money Skim

PROBLEM

Albert owned and operated 40 coin laundries around town. As the business grew, he could no longer visit each one, empty the cash boxes, and deposit the receipts. Each location grossed about $140 to $160 per day, operating 365 days per year—gross receipts of about $2 million per year.—Each of four part-time employees visited 10 locations, collecting the cash boxes and delivering them to Albert's office where he would count the coins and currency (from the change machine) and prepare a bank deposit. One of the employees skimmed $5 to $10 from each location visited each day.

The daily theft does not seem like much, but at an average of $7.50 per day from each of 10 locations, totaled about $27,000 per year. If all four of the employees had stolen the same amount, the loss could have been over $100,000 per year.

AUDIT APPROACH

Controls over the part-time employees were nonexistent. There was no overt or covert surprise observation and no times when two people went to collect cash (thereby needing to agree, in collusion, to steal). There was no rotation of locations or other indications to the employees that Albert was concerned about control. With no controls, there is no test of control activities. Obviously, however, "thinking like a crook" leads to the conclusion that the employees could simply pocket money.

Assuming that some employees are honest, periodically rotating the stores assigned to each employee and performing revenue comparisons (analytical procedures) on a store-by-store basis may be helpful. If revenues consistently decline for stores assigned to a specific employee, further investigation may be warranted.

The "balance" in this case is the total revenue that should have been deposited, and auditing for completeness is always difficult. Albert marked a quantity of coins with an etching tool and marked some $1 and $5 bills with ink. Unknown to the employees, he put these in all the locations, carefully noting the coins and bills in each.

DISCOVERY SUMMARY

Sure enough, a pattern of missing money emerged. When confronted, the employee confessed.

⌕ REVIEW CHECKPOINTS

6.19 In Case 6.1, if the petty cash custodian were replaced and the frequency of fund reimbursement decreased from every two days to every four days, what might you suspect?

6.20 Give some examples of control omissions that would make it easy to "think like a crook" and see opportunities for fraud.

"EXTENDED PROCEDURES" TO DETECT FRAUD

LEARNING OBJECTIVE 6-7
Discribe some extended procedures for detecting employee fraud schemes involving cash.

The auditing literature often refers to "extended procedures," which are "specific responses to fraud risk factors." Although the professional standards list a few of these procedures, an exhaustive list would be very lengthy. Moreover, authorities fear that a definitive list might limit the range of such procedures, so extended procedures are generally identified as whatever is necessary in the circumstances. This section describes some of the extended procedures and warns that (1) some auditors may consider them ordinary and (2) other auditors may consider them unnecessary in any circumstances. They are useful detective procedures in either event.

Count and Recount Petty Cash on the Same Day

A second petty cash count is unexpected, and auditors might catch an embezzling custodian who incorrectly believes that "the auditors are gone, so now it's safe!" Auditors should always make sure a client employee is present during the count and that the employee signs for the returned cash so the auditor cannot be blamed for any shortages. Another "trick of the trade" is to make sure that the auditor's pockets are empty (leave wallets locked up safely elsewhere) when counting client cash on hand. This is especially important when counting cash at a financial services client like a bank or credit union. All cash should be counted simultaneously to prevent embezzling employees from substituting cash from other places. If this is not possible (e.g., the employee claims that he or she does not have the safe combination), there is audit tape (similar to police tape) to seal the safe until it can be opened with the auditor present. If the seal is broken, your suspicions should be raised.

Examine Endorsements on Canceled Checks

Most business payments are deposited with one (usually stamped) endorsement. Look for handwritten endorsements and second endorsements, especially those of employees. The second endorsee indicates that the payee (possibly a "ghost employee") may not have received the benefit of the payment. Be sure to include checks payable to "cash" or to a bank for purchase of cashiers' checks.

> ### AUDITING INSIGHT Who Endorsed That Check?
>
> The distribution manager called internal audit and asked why his predecessor's endorsement was on a $600 check payable to the company and why it appeared to be deposited in his personal account. Further investigation revealed that the former manager had been selling company inventory without recording the sale and keeping the payments when received. The result?
>
> More than 60 payments totaling approximately $70,000 were identified. However, a count of physical inventory revealed an inventory variance of more than $200,000. Keep an eye on those endorsements!
>
> Source: "Purchasing Below the Radar," *Internal Auditor,* August 2003, pp. 95–97.

Retrieve Customers' Checks

If an employee has diverted customer payments for his or her own use, the canceled checks showing endorsements and deposits to a bank where the company has no account are not available because they are returned to the issuing customer. Ask the customer to give originals or copies (front and back) or to provide access for examination.

Use Marked Coins and Currency

Plant marked money in locations where cash collections should be gathered and turned over for deposit.

Analyze the Mix of Cash and Checks in Deposits

This procedure is most effective for retail operations in which cashiers receive significant amounts of both cash and checks. Unless there is a marked change in consumer behavior, one should expect the mix of cash and checks to be relatively consistent over time. A decrease in the proportion of cash in the mix is often a sign of skimming.

AUDITING INSIGHT — Mixing It Up

Noting a significant change in the mix of cash and checks on bank deposit slips over time, a government auditor became suspicious enough to set up a hidden camera. The camera caught a county tax clerk "skimming" cash from daily property tax deposits. The clerk would pocket most of the cash, leaving the checks to be deposited. The fraud perpetrator was able to conceal the theft by replacing the missing cash with checks written to the county for other, miscellaneous purposes for which established procedures were not closely followed.

In an unrelated fraud, **Ocean World Seafood** was recently charged with food stamp fraud. According to investigators, a store of Ocean World's size would normally make approximately $3,000 a month in sales paid with food stamps. Over a 13-month period, Ocean World accepted more than $1 million in food stamps. Apparently the store would provide cash for food stamps, paying approximately 50 cents for $1 of food stamps.

Source: "Store Owner Charged in $1 Million Food Stamp Fraud," *Associated Press Wire,* April 15, 2005.

Measure Deposit Lag Time

Compare the dates of the deposit slip to the date recorded as a debit in the general ledger to the date the deposit was credited in the account by the bank. Someone who takes cash and then holds the deposit for the next cash receipts to make up the difference causes a delay between the date of recording and the bank's date of deposit.

Document Examination

Look for erasures, alterations, copies where originals should be filed, telltale lines from a copier when a document has been pieced together, handwriting, and other oddities. Auditors should always insist on seeing original documents instead of photocopies. Professional document examination is a technical activity that requires special training (e.g., by the IRS, FBI), but crude alterations may be observed and at least enough to bring them to specialists' attention.

Inquiry

Be careful not to discuss fraud possibilities with the managers who might be involved. It gives them a chance to cover up their fraud or even resign from the organization prior to the fraud being detected. Described as a nonaccusatory method of asking key questions of personnel during a regular audit, *fraud audit questioning* (FAQ) provides employees an opportunity to furnish information about possible misdeeds. Fraud possibilities are addressed in a direct manner, so the FAQ approach must have the support of management. Example questions are: "Do you think fraud is a problem for business in general?" "Do you think this company has any particular problem with fraud?" "In your department, who is beyond suspicion?" "Is there any information you would like to furnish regarding possible fraud within this organization?"[8]

Covert Surveillance

Observe activities while not being seen. Audit team members might watch employees clocking onto a work shift, observing whether they use only one time card. Casino auditors actually get paid to gamble so they can observe cash-handling procedures. Traveling hotel auditors may check in unannounced, use the restaurant and entertainment

---

[8] Joseph T. Wells, "From the Chairman: Fraud Audit Questioning," *The White Paper,* National Association of Certified Fraud Examiners, May–June 1991, p. 2. This technique must be used with extreme care and practice.

facilities, and watch the employees skimming receipts and tickets. (Trailing people on streets, undercover surveillance, and maintaining a "stake-out" should be left to trained investigators.)

AUDITING INSIGHT — The Case of the Extra Checkout

The district grocery store manager could not understand why receipts and profitability had fallen and inventory was hard to manage at one of the largest stores in her area. She hired an investigator who covertly observed the checkout clerks and reported that no one had shown suspicious behavior at any of the nine checkout counters. Nine? That store only has eight, she exclaimed! As it turns out, the store manager had installed another checkout aisle, not connected to the cash receipts and inventory maintenance central computer and was pocketing all the receipts from that register.

Source: Association of Certified Fraud Examiners (ACFE), "Auditing for Fraud."

Horizontal and Vertical Analyses

Horizontal and vertical ratio analysis procedures are very similar to preliminary analytical procedures explained in earlier chapters. *Horizontal analysis* refers to changes of financial statement numbers and ratios across several years. *Vertical analysis* refers to financial statement amounts expressed each year as proportions of a base such as sales for the income statement accounts and total assets for the balance sheet accounts. Auditors look for relationships that do not appear logical as indicators of potential large misstatement and fraud.

Net Worth Analysis

This analysis is used when fraud has been discovered or strongly suspected and the information to calculate a suspect's net worth can be obtained (e.g., asset and liability records, bank accounts). The method involves calculating the suspect's net worth (known assets minus known liabilities) at the beginning and end of a period (months or years) and then trying to account for the difference as (1) known income less living expenses and (2) unidentified difference. The unidentified difference may be the best available approximation of the amount of a theft.

Expenditure Analysis

This analysis is similar to net worth analysis except the data are the suspect's spending for all purposes compared to known income. If spending exceeds legitimate and explainable income, the difference may be the amount of a theft.

Reasonableness Tests

Often auditors become so involved in ticking and tying numbers that they forget to ask themselves the simplest questions: Where is the cash going? For what purpose? Is this reasonable? The answers to these often motivate the auditor to ask more penetrating questions of management and to dig for more evidence.

AUDITING INSIGHT — Thank Goodness It's Payday!

Five individuals have been charged with tax and insurance fraud in the operation of a temporary employment agency in southeastern Massachusetts. From January 1993 through June 2001, the agency paid a large portion of its payroll in cash in order to avoid employment taxes (e.g., Social Security and Medicare) and to reduce payments for workers' compensation insurance.

Why would a company pay its employees in cash? Is there a legitimate reason to do this? Even if the employees wanted cash, would there be a better way to provide it?

Source: "Five Charged in $30 Million 'Under-the-Table' Payroll Fraud, Reports U.S. Attorney," *PR Newswire*, January 27, 2005.

REVIEW CHECKPOINTS

6.21 What is the difference between a *normal* procedure and an *extended* procedure?

6.22 What might two endorsements on a canceled check indicate?

6.23 What can an auditor find using net worth analysis? Expenditure analysis?

Summary

Although auditing standards concentrate on management fraud—the production of materially false and misleading financial statements (i.e., fraudulent financial reporting), professional standards also require auditors to consider employee fraud perpetrated against an entity. Attention to employee fraud is important in the context that the cover-up may create financial statement misstatements (e.g., overstating inventory to disguise unauthorized removal of valuable products). The three conditions that are likely to be present when a fraud occurs (Exhibit 6.1) are commonly referred to as the "fraud triangle." The first condition (motivation) recognizes that an employee or a manager of a company is likely to either have incentives in place (e.g., bonus compensation) or be under significant pressure to meet specific estimates, forecasts, or expectations about net income. The second condition (opportunity) recognizes that in order for a fraud to be perpetrated, there must be a weakness in the system of internal control to allow the fraud to occur. Finally, the third condition (rationalization) recognizes that for an employee or a manager of a company to perpetrate a fraud, the individual must possess an "attitude" that allows her or him to rationalize that she or he is knowingly committing a crime.

Audit team members need to know about the red flags, those telltale signs and indications that have accompanied many frauds. When studying a business operation, members' ability to "think like a crook" to devise ways to steal can help in planning procedures designed to determine whether fraud has happened. Often imaginative "extended procedures" can be employed to unearth evidence of fraudulent activity. Audit team members must always exercise technical and personal care, however, because accusations of fraud are taken very seriously. For this reason, after preliminary findings indicate fraud possibilities, the audit team should enlist the cooperation of management and assist fraud examination professionals when bringing an investigation to a conclusion.

Once the relevant assertions have been identified for cash (e.g., existence) and the tests of control activities are complete, the auditor must evaluate the evidence obtained from risk assessment activities and control tests to determine the risk of material misstatement for each relevant assertion. Cash is highly liquid, very portable, and not easily identifiable. For these reasons, cash is often the primary target of fraudulent activities and must be carefully controlled and monitored. Accordingly, controls over cash receipts and disbursements must be strong. With respect to auditing the cash balance, the detailed procedures performed on the bank reconciliation provide evidence about the existence of cash.

Additional procedures can be performed to try to detect attempts at lapping accounts receivable collections and kiting checks. For lapping, these procedures include comparing the details of customer payments listed in bank deposits to the details of customer payment postings (remittance lists). For kiting, these procedures include being alert to the signs of kiting activity and preparing a schedule of interbank transfers. If controls are weak, a proof of cash is an effective procedure to verify that recorded cash transactions have occurred and are complete.

Key Terms

check kiting: The practice of building up balances in one or more bank accounts based on uncollected (floating) checks drawn against similar accounts in other banks, 244

cutoff bank statement: A client bank statement (usually sent directly to the auditor) that includes all paid checks and deposits slips through a certain date, usually the middle of the month, 243

direct-effect illegal acts: The violations of laws or government regulations by a company or its management or employees that produce direct and material effects on dollar amounts in financial statements, 222

embezzlement: A type of fraud involving employees or nonemployees wrongfully taking money or property entrusted to their care, custody, and control, often accompanied by false accounting entries and other forms of lying and cover-up, 222

employee fraud (also called **misappropriation of assets**)**:** The use of fraudulent means to take money or other property from an employer. It consists of three phases: (1) the fraudulent act, (2) the conversion of the money or property to the fraudster's use, and (3) the cover-up, 222

errors: The unintentional misstatements or omissions of amounts or disclosures in financial statements, 222

fidelity bond: An insurance policy that covers most kinds of cash embezzlement losses, 233

fraud: The act of knowingly making material misrepresentations of fact with the intent of inducing someone to believe the falsehood and act upon it and, thus, suffer a loss or damage, 222

lapping: The theft of a payment and the application of subsequent payments to cover the theft, 233

lockbox: An arrangement in which a fiduciary (e.g., a bank) receives the payments, lists the receipts, deposits the money, and sends the remittance advices (stubs showing the amount received from each customer) to the company, 232

management fraud: The deliberate fraud committed by management that injures investors and creditors through materially misleading information, 222

misappropriation of assets: (See **employee fraud.**)

motive: The pressure experienced by a person and believed to be unshareable with friends and confidants, 225

proof of cash: A reconciliation in which the bank balance, the bank report of cash deposited, and the bank report of cash paid are all reconciled to the company's general ledger and cash receipts and disbursements journals, 245

schedule of interbank transfers: An analysis used to determine whether transfers of cash from one bank to another were recorded properly (correct amount and correct date), 244

Multiple-Choice Questions for Practice and Review

 All applicable Exercises and Problems are available with McGraw-Hill's *Connect® Accounting*

LO 6-2

6.24 When auditing with "fraud awareness," auditors should especially notice and follow up employee activities under which of these conditions?
   a. The company always estimates the inventory but never takes a complete physical count.
   b. The petty cash box is always locked in the desk of the custodian.
   c. Management has published a company code of ethics and sends frequent communication newsletters about it.
   d. The board of directors reviews and approves all investment transactions.

LO 6-3

6.25 The best way to enact a broad fraud-prevention program is to
   a. Install airtight control systems of checks and supervision.
   b. Name an "ethics officer" who is responsible for receiving and acting on fraud tips.
   c. Place dedicated hotline telephones on walls around the workplace with direct communication to the company ethics officer.
   d. Practice management "of the people and for the people" to help them share personal and professional problems.

LO 6-3

6.26 A good fraud prevention program should address employees' motivation to steal from the company. The best method for doing this is to
   a. Establish employee assistance programs.
   b. Require a fidelity bond on all employees.
   c. Require reconciliations of all accounts to be reviewed by a supervisor.
   d. Ensure that all accounts with high inherent risk of fraud are audited.

LO 6-3 6.27 A code of ethics is an important element of a fraud [prevention program]. Which of the following would diminish the effectiveness of a company's code of ethics?
   a. The establishment of a chief ethics officer.
   b. The establishment of a hotline for reporting unethical behavior.
   c. The violation of the code of ethics by senior management.
   d. The posting of the code of ethics in the company workplace.

LO 6-6 6.28 Which of the following is *least* indicative of fraudulent activity?
   a. Numerous cash refunds have been made to different people at the same address.
   b. Internal auditors cannot locate several credit memos to support reductions of customer balances.
   c. Bank reconciliation has no outstanding checks or deposits older than 15 days.
   d. Three people were absent the day the auditors handed out the paychecks and have not picked them up four weeks later.

LO 6-6 6.29 Which of the following combinations is a good way to conceal employee fraud but an ineffective means of perpetrating management (financial reporting) fraud?
   a. Overstating sales revenue and overstating customer accounts receivable balances.
   b. Overstating sales revenue and overstating bad debt expense.
   c. Understating interest expense and understating accrued interest payable.
   d. Omitting the disclosure information about related-party sales to the president's relatives at below-market prices.

LO 6-5 6.30 Allison Everhart, an employee in accounts payable, believes she can run a fictitious invoice through the accounts payable system and collect the money. She knows payments are subject to an audit. Which account would be the best place to hide the fraud?
   a. Inventory.
   b. Wage expense.
   c. Consulting service expense.
   d. Property tax expense.

LO 6-2 6.31 Which of these arrangements of duties could most likely lead to an embezzlement or theft?
   a. The inventory warehouse manager has responsibility for making the physical inventory observation and reconciling discrepancies to the perpetual inventory records.
   b. The cashier prepared the bank deposit, endorsed the checks with a company stamp, and delivered the cash and checks to the bank for deposit (no other bookkeeping duties).
   c. The accounts receivable clerk received a list of payments received by the cashier so he could make entries in the customers' accounts receivable subsidiary accounts.
   d. The financial vice president received checks made out to suppliers and the supporting invoices, signed the checks, and mailed the checks.

LO 6-4 6.32 Which of the following would the auditor consider to be an incompatible operation if the cashier receives remittances?
   a. The cashier prepares the daily deposit.
   b. The cashier makes the daily deposit at a local bank.
   c. The cashier posts the receipts to the accounts receivable subsidiary ledger cards.
   d. The cashier endorses the checks.

LO 6-5 6.33 Which of the following is an effective audit procedure that an auditor might use to detect kiting between intercompany banks?
   a. Review the composition of authenticated deposit slips.
   b. Review subsequent bank statements.
   c. Prepare a schedule of the bank transfers.
   d. Prepare a year-end bank reconciliation.

6.34 Immediately upon receipt of cash, a responsible employee should
   a. Record the amount in the cash receipts journal.
   b. Prepare a remittance listing.
   c. Update the subsidiary accounts receivable records.
   d. Prepare a deposit slip in triplicate.

(AICPA adapted)

LO 6-4

6.35 Each morning the controller gets the prior day's list of remittances, a copy of the payment report, and a copy of the deposit slip returned from the bank. When comparing these items, the controller would be able to determine that
   a. No checks were returned for insufficient funds.
   b. The cash received and remittance advice received were maintained in a single batch.
   c. The accounts receivable system has controls over unauthorized access.
   d. The assistant controller does not also reconcile the subsidiary accounts payable.

LO 6-4

6.36 Upon receipt of customers' checks in the mail room, a responsible employee should prepare a remittance list that is forwarded to the cashier. A copy of the list should be sent to the
   a. Internal auditor to investigate the list for unusual transactions.
   b. Treasurer to compare the list with the monthly bank statement.
   c. Accounts receivable bookkeeper to update the subsidiary accounts receivable records.
   d. Entity's bank to compare the list with the cashier's deposit slip.

(AICPA adapted)

LO 6-6

6.37 Cash receipts from sales on account have been misappropriated. Which of the following acts would conceal this defalcation and be least likely to be detected by an auditor?
   a. Understating the sales journal.
   b. Overstating the accounts receivable control account.
   c. Overstating the accounts receivable subsidiary ledger.
   d. Overstating the sales journal.

LO 6-1

6.38 Embezzlement is a type of fraud that involves
   a. An employee's misappropriating an employer's money or property not entrusted to him or her.
   b. A manager's falsification of financial statements for the purpose of misleading investors and creditors.
   c. An employee's mistaken representation of opinion that causes incorrect accounting entries.
   d. An employee misappropriating an employer's money or property entrusted to the employee's control in the employee's normal job.

LO 6-4

6.39 Which of the following control activities would best protect against the preparation of improper or inaccurate cash disbursements?
   a. All checks must be signed by an officer designated by the board of directors.
   b. All signed checks must be reviewed and compared with supporting documentation by the treasurer before mailing.
   c. All checks must be sequentially numbered and accounted for by internal auditors.
   d. All checks must be perforated or otherwise effectively canceled when they are returned with the bank statement.

LO 6-5

6.40 During an audit of cash, the auditor is most concerned with the management assertion of
   a. Existence.
   b. Rights and obligations.
   c. Valuation or allocation.
   d. Occurrence.

LO 6-5

6.41 In preparing for the audit of cash, the auditors perform analytical procedures concerning cash balances. Which of the following would be the best source of information for use in the estimate of cash?
   a. Prior-years' balances.
   b. Management inquiry.
   c. Cash budgets.
   d. Aged accounts receivable reports.

LO 6-4

6.42 Which of the following control activities could prevent a paid disbursement voucher from being presented for payment a second time?

a. Vouchers should be prepared by individuals who are responsible for signing disbursement checks.

b. Disbursement vouchers should be approved by at least two responsible management officials.

c. The date on a disbursement voucher should be within a few days of the date the voucher is presented for payment.

d. The official signing the check should compare it with the voucher and should stamp "paid" on the voucher documents.

Exercises and Problems

 All applicable Exercises and Problems are available with McGraw-Hill's *Connect*® *Accounting*

LO 6-4

6.43 **Tests of Controls over Cash Disbursements.** The Runge Controls Corporation manufactures and markets electrical control systems: temperature controls, machine controls, burglar alarms, and the like. The company acquires electrical and semiconductor parts from outside vendors, and assembles systems in its own plant. The company incurs other administrative and operating expenditures. Liabilities for goods and services purchased are entered in a vouchers payable journal, at which time the debits are classified to the asset and expense accounts to which they apply.

The company has specified control activities for approving vendor invoices for payment, for signing checks, for keeping records, and for reconciling the checking accounts. The procedures appear to be well specified and in operation.

You are the senior auditor on the Runge engagement and need to specify a list of test of control procedures to evaluate the effectiveness of the controls over cash disbursements.

Required:

Using management's assertions over transactions as a guide, specify two or more test of control procedures to audit the effectiveness of typical control activities. (*Hint:* From one sample of recorded cash disbursements, you can specify procedures related to several objectives. See Exhibit 6.4 for examples of test of control procedures over cash disbursements.) Organize your list according to the example shown below for the "completeness" assertion.

Completeness Assertion	Test of Controls
All valid cash disbursements are recorded and none are omitted.	Determine the numerical sequence of checks issued during the period and scan the sequence for missing numbers.

(AICPA adapted)

LO 6-4

6.44 **Internal Control Questionnaire for Book Buy-Back Cash Fund.** Taylor, a CPA, has been engaged to audit the financial statements of University Books, Incorporated. University Books maintains a large cash fund exclusively for the purpose of buying used books from students for cash. The cash fund is active all year because the nearby university offers a large variety of courses with varying starting and completion dates throughout the year.

Receipts are prepared for each purchase. Reimbursement vouchers periodically are submitted to replenish the fund.

Required:

Construct an internal control questionnaire to be used in evaluating the internal control over University Books' repurchasing process using the revolving cash fund. The internal control questionnaire should elicit a yes or no response to each question. *Do not discuss the internal controls over books that are purchased from publishers.*

(AICPA adapted)

LO 6-4

6.45 **Test of Controls over Cash Receipts.** You are the in-charge auditor examining the financial statements of the Gutzler Company for the year ended December 31. During late October, with the help of Gutzler's controller, you completed an internal control questionnaire and prepared the appropriate memoranda describing Gutzler's accounting procedures. Your comments relative to cash receipts are as follows:

- All cash receipts are sent directly to the accounts receivable clerk with no processing by the mail department. The accounts receivable clerk keeps the cash receipts journal, prepares the bank deposit slip in duplicate, posts from the deposit slip to the subsidiary accounts receivable ledger, and mails the deposit to the bank.
- The controller receives the validated deposit slips directly (unopened) from the bank. She also receives the monthly bank statement directly (unopened) from the bank and promptly reconciles it.
- At the end of each month, the accounts receivable clerk notifies the general ledger clerk by journal voucher of the monthly totals of the cash receipts journal for posting to the general ledger.
- With regard to the general ledger cash account, the general ledger clerk makes an entry each month to record the total debits to cash from the cash receipts journal. In addition, the general ledger clerk, on occasion, makes debit entries in the general ledger cash account from sources other than the cash receipts journal, for example, funds borrowed from the bank.

Certain standard audit procedures that follow already have been performed by you in the audit of cash receipts:

- All columns in the cash receipts journal have been totaled and cross-totaled.
- Postings from the cash receipts journal have been traced to the general ledger.
- Remittance advices and related correspondence have been traced to entries in the cash receipts journal.

Required:

Considering Gutzler's internal control over cash receipts and the standard audit procedures already performed, list all other audit procedures that should be performed to obtain sufficient appropriate audit evidence regarding controls over cash and give the reasons for each procedure. Do not discuss the procedures for cash disbursements and cash balances. Also, do not discuss the extent to which any of the procedures are to be performed. Assume that adequate controls exist to ensure that all sales transactions are recorded. Organize your answer sheet as follows:

Other Audit Procedure	Reason for Other Audit Procedures

(AICPA adapted)

LO 6-3

6.46 **Internal Control over Sales Returns.** You are the auditor for Konerko's Office supply store, which is opening for business next week. The owner of the store has established all the controls you have recommended for ensuring that sales are recorded properly and cash is accounted for. The owner has heard from other small business owners that employees often used returned goods as means of skimming money from the register.

Required:

a. How might an employee use returned goods to skim money from the register?
b. What controls would you recommend to prevent or detect fraudulent returns?
c. What audit procedures might you perform to detect fraudulent returns?

LO 6-5

6.47 Procedures for Auditing a Client's Bank Reconciliation. Auditors typically will find the items lettered A–F in a client-prepared bank reconciliation.

GENERAL COMPANY
Bank Reconciliation: 1st National Bank
September 30

A. Balance per bank				$28,375
B. Deposits in transit				
Sept 29			$ 4,500	
Sept 30			1,525	6,025
				34,400
C. Outstanding checks:				
988	Aug 31		$ 2,200	
1281	Sept 26		675	
1285	Sept 27		850	
1289	Sept 29		2,500	
1292	Sept 30		7,255	(11,450)
				20,950
D. Customer note collected by the bank:				(3,000)
E. Error: Check #1282, written on Sept. 26 for $270, was erroneously charged by bank as $720; bank was notified Oct. 2				450
F. Balance per books				$20,400

Required:

Assume these facts: On October 11, the auditor received a cutoff bank statement dated October 7. The September 30 deposit in transit; the outstanding checks 1281, 1285, 1289, and 1292; and the correction of the bank error regarding check 1282 appeared on the cutoff bank statement.

a. For each of the preceding lettered items A–F, select one or more of the following procedures 1–10 that you believe the auditor should perform to obtain evidence about the item. These procedures may be selected once, more than once, or not at all. Be prepared to explain the reasons for your choices.

   1. Trace to cash receipts journal.
   2. Trace to cash disbursements journal.
   3. Compare to the September 30 general ledger.
   4. Confirm directly with the bank.
   5. Inspect bank credit memo.
   6. Inspect bank debit memo.
   7. Ascertain reason for unusual delay, if any.
   8. Inspect supporting documents for reconciling items that do not appear on the cutoff bank statement.
   9. Trace items on the bank reconciliation to the cutoff bank statement.
   10. Trace items on the cutoff bank statement to the bank reconciliation.

b. Auditors ordinarily foot a client-prepared bank reconciliation. If the auditors had performed this recalculation on the preceding bank reconciliation, what might they have found? Be prepared to discuss any findings.

(AICPA adapted)

LO 6-5

6.48 Proof of Cash. You can use the computer-based *Electronic Audit Documentation* on the textbook's website to prepare the proof of cash required in this problem.

The auditors of Steffey, Ltd., decided to study the cash receipts and disbursements for the month of July of the current year under audit. They obtained the bank reconciliations and the cash journals prepared by the company accountants, which revealed the following:

June 30: Bank balance, $355,001; deposits in transit, $86,899; outstanding checks, $42,690; general ledger cash balance, $399,210.

July 1: Cash receipts journal, $650,187; cash disbursements journal, $565,397.

July 31: Bank balance, $506,100; deposits in transit, $51,240; outstanding checks, $73,340; general ledger cash balance, $484,000. Bank statement record of deposits: $835,846; of payments: $684,747.

Required:

Prepare a four-column proof of cash (see Exhibit 6.9 for an example) covering the month of July of the current year. Identify problems, if any.

LO 6-5

6.49 **Interbank Transfers.** You can use the computer-based *Electronic Workpapers* on the textbook website to prepare the schedule of interbank transfers required in this problem.

EverReady Corporation is in the home building and repair business. Construction business has been in a slump and the company has experienced financial difficulty over the past two years. Part of the problem lies in the company's desire to avoid laying off its skilled crews of bricklayers and cabinetmakers. Meeting the payroll has been a problem.

The auditors are engaged to audit the 2012 financial statements. Knowing of EverReady's financial difficulty and its business policy, the auditors decided to prepare a schedule of interbank transfers covering the 10 days before and after December 31, which is the company's balance sheet date.

First, the auditors used the cash receipts and disbursements journals to prepare part of the schedule shown in Exhibit 6.49.1. They obtained the information for everything except the dates of deposit and payment in the bank statements (disbursing date per bank and receiving date per bank). The auditors learned that EverReady always transferred money to the payroll account at 1st National Bank from the general account at 1st National Bank. This transfer enabled the bank to clear the payroll checks without delay. The only bank accounts in the EverReady financial statements are the two at 1st National Bank.

Next, the auditors obtained the December 2012 and January 2013 bank statements for the general and payroll accounts at 1st National Bank. They recorded the bank disbursement and receipt dates in the schedule of interbank transfers. For each transfer, these dates are identical because the accounts are in the same bank. An alert auditor noticed that the 1st National Bank general account bank statement also contains deposits received from Citizen National Bank and canceled check 1799 dated January 5 payable to Citizen National Bank. This check cleared the 1st National Bank account on January 8 and was marked "transfer of funds." This led to the auditors' decision to inquire about this of EverReady's chief financial officer.

Asked about the Citizen National Bank transactions, EverReady's chief financial officer readily admitted the existence of an off-books bank account. He explained that it was used for financing transactions in keeping with normal practice in the construction industry. He gave the auditors the December and January bank statements for the account at Citizen National Bank. In it, the auditors found the following:

EXHIBIT 6.49.1 Schedule of Interbank Transfers

C-5

EVERREADY CORPORATION
Schedule of Interbank Transfers
December 31, 2012

Prepared _____
Date _____
Reviewed _____
Date _____

	Disbursing Account				Receiving Account		
Check	Bank	Amount	Date per Books	Date per Bank	Bank	Date per Books	Date per Bank
1417	1st National	10,463✓	24-Dec	24-Dec m	1st National Payroll	24-Dec t	24-Dec n
1601	1st National	11,593✓	31-Dec ɫ	31-Dec m	1st National Payroll	31-Dec t	31-Dec n
1982	1st National	9,971✓	08-Jan	08-Jan m	1st National Payroll	08-Jan t	08-Jan n

✓ Traced from cash disbursements journal.
ɫ Check properly listed as outstanding on bank reconciliation.
m Vouched to check cleared in bank statement.
t Traced from cash receipts journal.
n Vouched deposit cleared in bank statement.
Note: We scanned the cash disbursements and cash receipts journals for checks to and deposits from other bank accounts.

Citizen National Bank

Check	Payable to	Amount	Dated	Cleared Bank
4050	1st National	$10,000	23-Dec	29-Dec
4051	Chase Bank	12,000	28-Dec	31-Dec
4052	1st National	12,000	30-Dec	05-Jan
4053	Chase Bank	14,000	4-Jan	07-Jan
4054	1st National	20,000	8-Jan	13-Jan

Deposits

Received from	Amount	Date
Chase Bank	$11,000	22-Dec
Chase Bank	15,000	30-Dec
1st National	10,000	05-Jan
Chase Bank	12,000	07-Jan

When asked about the Chase Bank transactions, EverReady's chief financial officer admitted the existence of another off-books bank account, which he said was the personal account of the principal stockholder. He explained that the stockholder often used it to finance EverReady's operations. He gave the auditors the December and January bank statements for this account at Chase Bank; in it, the auditors found the following:

Chase Bank

Payments

Check #	Payable to	Amount	Dated	Cleared Bank
2220	Citizen National Bank	11,000	22-Dec	28-Dec
2221	Citizen National Bank	15,000	30-Dec	05-Jan
2222	Citizen National Bank	12,000	7-Jan	12-Jan

Deposits

Received from	Amount	Dated
Citizen National Bank	12,000	28-Dec
Citizen National Bank	14,000	04-Jan

An abbreviated calendar for the period is in Exhibit 6.49.2.

EXHIBIT 6.49.2

	S	M	T	W	T	F	S
December 2010	20	21	22	23	24	25	26
	27	28	29	30	31		
January 2011						1	2
	3	4	5	6	7	8	9
	10	11	12	13	14	15	16

Required:

a. Complete the Schedule of Interbank Transfers (document C-5, Exhibit 6.49.1) by entering the new information.

b. What is the actual cash balance for the three bank accounts combined, considering only the amounts given in this case information as of December 31, 2012 (before any of the December 31 payroll checks are cashed by employees)? As of January 8, 2013 (before any of the January 8 payroll checks are cashed by employees)? (*Hint*: Prepare a schedule of bank and actual balances.)

LO 6-5

6.50 **Manipulated Bank Reconciliation.** You can use the computer-based *Electronic Workpapers* on the textbook website to prepare the bank reconciliation solution.

Caulco, Inc., is the audit client. You have obtained the client-prepared bank reconciliation as of February 28 (see the following). The February bank statement is shown in Exhibit 6.6 in the text.

Required:

Check 2231 was the first check written in February. All earlier checks cleared the bank, some during January and some during February. Assume that the only February-dated canceled checks returned in the March bank statement are 2239 and 2240 showing the amounts listed in the February bank reconciliation. They cleared the bank on March 3 and March 2, respectively. The first deposit on the March bank statement was $1,097.69 credited on March 3. Assume also that all checks entered in Caulco's cash disbursements journal through February 29 have either cleared the bank or are listed as outstanding checks in the February bank reconciliation.

Determine whether any errors exist in the following bank reconciliation. If errors exist, prepare a corrected reconciliation and explain the problem.

CAULCO, INC.
Bank Reconciliation
February 28

Balance per bank			$7,374.93
Deposit in transit			1,097.69

Outstanding Checks

Number	Date	Payee	Amount
2239	Feb 26	Alpha Supply	500.00
2240	Feb 28	L.C. Stateman	254.37
Total outstanding			(754.37)
General ledger balance Feb. 28			$7,718.25

LO 6-7

6.51 **Investigating a Fraud.** Suppose you are auditing cash disbursements and discover several payments to a company you were unfamiliar with and cannot find information about this company on the Internet or in the local telephone directory. The invoices from this company have numbers very close to each other in the sequence, there is no phone number on the invoice, and each bill is for a dollar amount just under the amount that would require additional approvals before payment. Based on this information, you now suspect this may be a fraud.

Required:

Based on your suspicions, how would you change the audit procedures you would perform and how might you change the evidence you gather?

LO 6-7

6.52 **Fraud in Purchasing.** Consider the following scenario:

Adam worked for the local hardware store as an outside sales representative. His job was to visit local companies and contractors in an attempt to identify their needs for tools and materials and provide a bid to supply those items. When a local contractor accepted a new job, Adam would get its material requirements, come back to the store, and prepare and submit a proposal for the items. After some initial success with Big Builder, a large contractor, the number of jobs awarded to Adam had decreased dramatically.

One day Adam was back at the store after losing a bid to Big Builder when he noticed someone in the store purchasing the exact items and quantities that were in the specification for that bid. The combination of items was unusual and it would be an unlikely coincidence for someone else to want such a combination in that exact quantity. The customer paid the retail price for the merchandise and left.

Adam decided to contact Big Builder, but he knew he could not do so and make any accusations. Adam set up a meeting with the president of Big Builder and inquired as to how Adam might "increase his business and better meet the needs of Big Builder." Eventually, the recent bid entered the conversation. Adam showed his copy of the bid to the president. The president retrieved a copy of the purchase order and recognized that the amount on it was more than the bid Adam had submitted. The company that submitted the bid was K. A. Supplies, Inc. Adam had never heard of K. A. Supplies and noted the address of K. A. Supplies on the purchase order. The president of Big Builder promised to investigate the bidding process.

Adam drove to the address of K. A. Supplies and found a packaging and shipping store at that address. Furthermore, Adam went to the county courthouse and inquired about K. A. Supplies. The company was listed in the county records and one of the purchasing agents for Big Builder was listed as an officer.

Required:
a. Given the information that Adam knows, what do you believe is occurring at Big Builder?
b. What other information would you want to obtain and how might you retrieve that information?
c. What controls might be instituted at Big Builder to prevent improprieties in the bidding and purchasing process?

6.53 **The Perfect Crime?** Consider the following story of an actual embezzlement.

This was the ingenious embezzler's scheme: (a) He hired a print shop to print a private stock of Ajax Company checks in the company's numerical sequence. (b) In his job as an accounts payable clerk at Ajax, he intercepted legitimate checks written by the accounts payable department and signed by the Ajax treasurer and destroyed them. (c) He substituted the same numbered check from the private stock, payable to himself in the same amount as the legitimate check, and he "signed" it with a rubber stamp that looked enough like the Ajax Company treasurer's signature to fool the paying bank. (d) He deposited the money in his own bank account. The bank statement reconciler (a different person) was able to agree the check numbers and amounts listed in the cleared items in the bank statement to the recorded cash disbursement (check number and amount) and thus did not notice the embezzler's scheme. The embezzler was able to process the vendor's "past due" notice and the next month's statement with complete documentation, enabling the Ajax treasurer to sign another check the next month paying both the past due balance and current charges. The embezzler was careful to scatter the double-expense payments among numerous accounts (telephone, office supplies, inventory, etc.) so the double-paid expenses did not distort any accounts very much. As time passed, the embezzler was able to recommend budget amounts that allowed a large enough budget so his double-paid expenses in various categories did not often pop up as large variances from the budget.

Required:
List and explain the ways and means you believe someone might detect the embezzlement. Think first about the ordinary everyday control activities. Then think about extensive detection efforts assuming a tip or indication of a possible fraud has been received. Is this a "perfect crime"?

6.54 **Select Effective Extended Procedures.** The following are some "suspicions"; you have been requested to select some effective extended procedures designed to confirm or deny the suspicions.

Required:
Write the suggested procedures for each case in definite terms so another person can know what to do.
a. The custodian of the petty cash fund may be removing cash on Friday afternoon to pay for weekend activities.

b. A manager noticed that eight new vendors were added to the purchasing department's approved vendor list after the assistant purchasing agent was promoted to chief agent three weeks ago. She suspects all or some of them might be fictitious companies set up by the new chief purchasing agent.

c. The payroll supervisor may be stealing unclaimed paychecks of employees who resigned and did not collect their last check.

d. Although no customers have complained, cash collections on accounts receivable have decreased and the counter clerks may have stolen customers' payments.

e. The cashier may have "borrowed" cash receipts, covering it by holding each day's deposit until cash from the next day(s) collection is enough to make up the shortage from an earlier day and then sends the deposit to the bank.

LO 6-6 6.55 **Forensic Accounting: Assurance Engagement 1: Expenditure Analysis.** Expenditure analysis is used when fraud has been discovered or strongly suspected and the information to calculate a suspect's income and expenditures can be obtained (e.g., asset and liability records, bank accounts). Expenditure analysis consists of establishing the suspect's known expenditures for all purposes for the relevant period, subtracting all known sources of funds (e.g., wages, gifts, inheritances, bank balances), and identifying the difference as "expenditures financed by unknown sources of income."

The law firm of Gleckel and Morris has hired you. The lawyers have been retained by Blade Manufacturing Company in a case involving a suspected kickback by a purchasing employee, E. J. Cunningham. Cunningham is suspected of taking kickbacks from Mason Varner, a salesman for Tanco Metals. Cunningham has denied the charges, but Lanier Gleckel, the lawyer in charge of the case, is convinced the kickbacks have occurred.

Gleckel filed a civil action and subpoenaed Cunningham's financial records, including last year's bank statements. The beginning bank balance January 1 was $3,463 and the ending bank balance December 31 was $2,050. Over the intervening 12 months, Cunningham's gross salary was $3,600 per month with a net of $2,950. His house payments were $1,377 per month. In addition, he paid $2,361 per month on a new Mercedes 500 SEL and a total of $9,444 last year toward a new Nissan Maxima (including $5,000 down payment). He also purchased new state-of-the-art audio and video equipment for $18,763, with no down payment and made total payments of $5,532 on the equipment last year. A reasonable estimate of his household expenses during the period is $900 per month ($400 for food, $200 for utilities, and $300 for other items).

Required:
Using expenditure analysis, calculate the amount of income, if any, from "unknown sources."

LO 6-6 6.56 **Forensic Accounting: Assurance Engagement 2: Net Worth Analysis.** You can use the computer-based *Electronic Workpapers* on the textbook website to prepare the net worth analysis required in this problem.

Net worth analysis is performed when fraud has been discovered or strongly suspected and the information to calculate a suspect's net worth can be obtained (e.g., asset and liability records, bank accounts). The procedure used is to calculate the person's change in net worth (excluding changes in market values of assets) and to identify the known sources of funds to finance the changes. Any difference between the change in net worth and the known sources of funds is called *funds from unknown sources,* which might include ill-gotten gains.

Nero has worked for Bonne Consulting Group (BCG) as the executive secretary for administration for nearly 10 years. Her dedication has earned her a reputation as an outstanding employee and has resulted in increasing responsibilities. Nero is also a suspect in a fraud.

During Nero's first five years of employment, BCG subcontracted all of its feasibility and marketing studies through Jackson & Company. This relationship was terminated because Jackson & Company merged with a larger, more expensive consulting group. At the time of termination, Nero and her supervisor were forced to select a new firm to conduct BCG's market research. However, Nero never informed the accounting department that the Jackson & Company account had been closed.

Because her supervisor allowed Nero to sign the payment voucher for services rendered, she was able to continue to process checks made payable to Jackson's account. Nero was trusted to be the only signature required to authorize payments less than $10,000. The accounting department continued to write the checks and Nero took responsibility for delivering the checks. She opened a bank account in a nearby city under the name of Jackson & Company, where she made the deposits.

Nero's financial records have been obtained by subpoena. Exhibit 6.56.1 provides a summary of the data obtained from Nero's records.

EXHIBIT 6.56.1
Nero's Subpoenaed Records

	Year 1	Year 2	Year 3
Assets:			
Residence	$100,000	$100,000	$100,000
Stocks and bonds	30,000	30,000	42,000
Automobiles	20,000	20,000	40,000
Certificate of deposit	50,000	50,000	50,000
Cash	6,000	12,000	14,000
Liabilities:			
Mortgage balance	90,000	50,000	—
Auto loan	10,000	—	—
Income:			
Salary		34,000	36,000
Other		6,000	6,000
Expenses:			
Scheduled mortgage payments		6,000	6,000
Auto loan payments		4,800	—
Other living expenses		20,000	22,000

Required:
You have been hired to estimate the amount of loss by estimating Nero's "funds from unknown sources" that financed her comfortable life style. (*Hint*: Set up a working paper like the following:)

	End Year 1	End Year 2	End Year 3
Assets (list)			
Liabilities (list)			
Net worth (difference)			
Change in net worth			
Add total expenses			
= Change plus expenses			
Subtract known income			
= Funds from unknown sources			

LO 6-5

6.57 **Employee Embezzlement via Cash Receipts and Payment of Personal Expenses.** This case is designed in a manner similar to the cases in the chapter. In this case, you can assume you have received a message from an informant regarding the following case. Your assignment is to write the "audit approach" portion of the case.

a. Write a brief explanation of desirable controls, missing controls, and especially the kinds of "deviations" that might arise from the situation described in the case. (Refer to controls explained in Chapter 5.)

b. Develop some procedures for obtaining evidence about existing controls, especially procedures that could discover deviations from controls. If there are no controls to test, then there are no procedures to perform. Then, just move on to letter c. below. (Refer to test of controls procedures explained in this chapter.) An audit "procedure" should instruct someone about the source(s) of evidence to obtain and the work to perform.

c. Write some procedures for gathering evidence in this case.

d. Write a short statement about the discovery you expect to accomplish with your procedures.

The Extra Bank Account

The Ourtown Independent School District, like all others, had formal, often bureaucratic, procedures regarding school board approval of cash disbursements. To get around the rules and to make possible timely payment of selected bills, the superintendent of schools had a school bank account that was used in the manner of a petty cash fund. The board knew about it and had given blanket approval in advance for its use to make timely payment of minor school expenses. The board, however, never reviewed the activity in this account. The business manager had sole responsibility for the account subject to the annual audit. The account received money from transfers from other school accounts and from deposit of cafeteria cash receipts. The superintendent did not like to be bothered with details and often signed blank checks so the business manager would not need to obtain a signature all the time. The business manager sometimes paid her personal **American Express** credit card bills, charged personal items to the school's VISA account, and pocketed some cafeteria cash receipts before deposit.

An informant called the state education audit agency and told the story that this business manager had used school funds to buy hosiery. When told of this story, the superintendent told the auditor to place no credibility in the informant, who was "out to get us." The business manager had, in fact, used the account to write unauthorized checks to "cash," put her own American Express bills in the school files (the school district had a VISA card, not American Express), and signed on the school card for gasoline and auto repairs during periods of vacation and summer when school was not in session. (As for the hosiery, she purchased $700 worth with school funds one year.) The superintendent was genuinely unaware of the misuse of funds. The business manager had been employed for six years, was trusted, and embezzled an estimated $25,000.

LO 6-6

6.58 **Mini-Case: Cash Confirmations.** Refer to the mini-case "Something Went Sour at Parmalat" on page C20 and respond to question 1.

Appendix 6A

Internal Control Questionnaires

EXHIBIT 6A.1 Internal Control Questionnaire—Cash Receipts Processing

	Yes	No	Comments
1. Are cash receipts deposited daily, intact, and without delay?			
2. Does someone other than the cashier or accounts receivable bookkeeper take the deposits to the bank?			
3. Are the duties of the cashier entirely separate from record keeping for notes and accounts receivable? From general ledger record keeping?			
4. Is the cashier denied access to receivables records or monthly statements?			
5. Is a bank reconciliation performed monthly by someone who does not have cash custody or record-keeping responsibility?			
6. Are the cash receipts journal entries compared to the remittance lists and deposit slips regularly?			
7. Does the person who opens the mail make a list of cash received (a remittance list)?			
8. Are currency receipts controlled by mechanical devices? Are machine totals checked by the internal auditor?			
9. Are prenumbered cash receipts listings used? Is the numerical sequence checked for missing documents?			
10. Does the accounting manual contain instructions for dating cash receipts entries the same day as the date of receipt?			
11. Is a duplicate deposit slip retained by someone other than the employee preparing the deposit?			
12. Is the remittance list compared to the deposit by someone other than the cashier?			
13. Does the accounting manual contain instructions for classifying cash receipts credits?			
14. Does someone reconcile the accounts receivable subsidiary to the control account regularly (to determine whether all entries were made to customers' accounts)?			

EXHIBIT 6A.2 Internal Control Questionnaire—Cash Disbursements Processing

	Yes	No	Comments
1. Are persons with cash custody or check-signing authority denied access to accounting journals, ledgers, and bank reconciliations?			
2. Is access to blank checks denied to unauthorized persons?			
3. Are all disbursements except petty cash made by check?			
4. Are check signers prohibited from drawing checks to cash?			
5. Are signing blank checks prohibited?			
6. Are voided checks mutilated and retained for inspection?			
7. Are invoices, receiving reports, and purchase orders reviewed by the check signer?			
8. Are the supporting documents stamped "paid" (to prevent duplicate payment) before being returned to accounts payable for filing?			
9. Are checks mailed directly by the signer and not returned to the accounts payable department for mailing?			
10. Do checks require two signatures? Is there dual control over machine signature plates?			
11. Are blank checks prenumbered and the numerical sequence checked for missing documents?			

(continued)

EXHIBIT 6A.2 *(continued)*

	Yes	No	Comments
12. Are checks dated in the cash disbursements journal with the date of the check?			
13. Are bank accounts reconciled by personnel independent of cash custody or record keeping?			
14. Do internal auditors periodically conduct a surprise audit of bank reconciliations?			
15. Does the chart of accounts and accounting manual give instructions for determining debit classifications of disbursements not charged to accounts payable?			
16. Is the distribution of charges checked periodically by an official? Is the budget used to check on gross misclassification errors?			
17. Are special disbursements (e.g., payroll and dividends) made from separate bank accounts?			
18. Is the bank reconciliation reviewed by an accounting official with no conflicting cash receipts, cash disbursements, or record keeping responsibilities?			

Appendix 6B

Audit Plans

EXHIBIT 6B.1 Audit Plan—Tests of Controls—Cash

	Documentation Reference	Performed by

1. Inquire of management concerning employees who
   a. Receive remittances from customers.
   b. Record payments in accounts payable.
   c. Prepare and deliver payments to the bank.		

2. Observe the opening of the mail and ensure that
   a. Two employees are opening the mail.
   b. Checks are restrictively endorsed.
   c. A listing of all checks is being prepared.		

3. Observe the flow of checks and remittance advices and ensure that
   a. Checks are delivered directly to the cashier.
   b. Remittance advices are delivered to the accounting department.		

4. Review reconciliations of cash listings, accounts receivable payments, and bank deposits.		

5. Review reconciliations of bank statements for
   a. Initials of proper review.
   b. Investigation of all outstanding items reviewed for propriety.		

EXHIBIT 6B.2 Audit Plan—Selected Substantive Procedures—Cash

	Documentation Reference	Performed by
1. Obtain confirmations from banks (standard bank confirmation).		

2. Obtain reconciliations of all bank accounts.
   a. Trace the bank balance on the reconciliation to the bank confirmation.
   b. Trace the reconciled book balance to the general ledger.
   c. Recompute the bank reconciliation for mathematical accuracy.		

3. Review the bank confirmation for evidence of loans and collateral.		

4. Ask the client to request a cutoff bank statement for each account, to be mailed directly to the audit firm.
   a. Vouch deposits in transit on the reconciliation to the bank cutoff statement.
   b. Trace the outstanding checks that have cleared the cutoff statement back to the list of outstanding checks on the bank reconciliation.		

5. Prepare a schedule of interbank transfers for a period of 10 business days before and after the year-end date. Document dates of book entry transfer and correspondence with bank entries and reconciliation items, if any.		
6. Count cash funds in the presence of a client representative.		
7. Obtain management representations concerning compensating balance agreements.		

Revenue and Collection Cycle

What at first was plunder assumed the softer name of revenue.

Thomas Paine

Professional Standards References

Topic	AU/ISA Section	PCAOB Reference
Audit Documentation	230	AS 3
The Auditor's Responsibilities Related to Fraud	240	AU 316
Audit Planning	300	AS 10
Identifying and Assessing the Risks of Material Misstatement	315	AS 12
The Auditor's Responses to Assessed Risks	330	AS 13
Audit Evidence	500	AS 15
The Confirmation Process	505	AU 330[1]
Analytical Procedures	520	AU 329[1]*
Auditing Accounting Estimates	540	AU 342[1]
Related Parties	550	AU 334[1]
Management Representations	580	AU 333[1]

*AU sections under the PCAOB reference refer to interim standards that have not been superseded by the PCAOB.

LEARNING OBJECTIVES

This is the first of four "cycle chapters" in which you will go through the steps of the audit risk model. First, we discuss the inherent risks particular to the revenue cycle. Many recent frauds have consisted of improper revenue recognition, which also results in overstatement of assets, usually receivables. Next, we examine controls normally included in the cycle. Finally, we discuss substantive procedures, including common analytical procedures. Accounts receivable confirmations are a central part of accounts receivable auditing and are required by GAAS. You will see examples of confirmations and a discussion of procedures auditors perform when sending those confirmations.

Your objectives are to be able to:

LO 7-1 Discuss inherent risks related to the revenue and collection cycle with a focus on improper revenue recognition.

LO 7-2 Describe the revenue and collection cycle, including typical source documents and control procedures.

LO 7-3 Give examples of tests of controls over customer credit approval, delivery, and recording of accounts receivable.

LO 7-4 Give examples of substantive procedures in the revenue and collection cycle and relate them to assertions about account balances at the end of the period.

LO 7-5 Describe some common errors and frauds in the revenue and collection cycle and design some audit and investigation procedures for detecting them.

INTRODUCTION

Rather than attend an **Ernst & Young** banquet honoring him as Denmark's "Entrepreneur of the Year," Stein Bagger, the dynamic CEO of the **IT Factory,** a Danish computer software company, was attempting to flee the country ahead of law enforcement officials investigating what has become known as "Denmark's Enron." Experts suggest that approximately 95 percent ($200 million) of his company's sales were fictitious. Bagger inflated his company's profits by setting up fictitious corporations that borrowed money from Danish banks. With the borrowed money, these companies "purchased" software from the IT Factory. Although audits by Big 4 firms failed to uncover the fictitious sales, red flags were apparent. A competitor had sent out warnings that the IT Factory "simply didn't have enough known customers to explain its explosive growth."

Bagger went to great lengths to cover his tracks. To throw off a journalist who had questioned his credentials, he claimed to have a PhD in International Business from San Francisco Technological University (a bogus educational institution). He hired an actress to play an official at San Francisco State University who would disclose that San Francisco Tech had been absorbed by San Francisco State University and verify his degree.[1]

On June 11, 2009, Stein Bagger was convicted of fraud and forgery and was sentenced to seven years in prison.

OVERALL AUDIT APPROACH FOR THE REVENUE AND COLLECTION CYCLE

Chapter 4 introduced the audit risk model. As noted there, this model allows auditors to control audit risk to desired levels. *Audit risk* is defined as the risk that auditors will issue an unqualified opinion on financial statements that contain a material misstatement. Audit risk is manifested when a material misstatement enters the financial reporting process (inherent risk) that the client's internal controls do not prevent or detect (control risk) and that the auditors' substantive procedures do not detect (detection risk). Recall the basic three-step approach for using the audit risk model to plan an engagement:

1. Set audit risk at desired levels (normally, low).
2. Assess risk of material misstatement, which incorporates inherent risk based on the nature of the account balance or class of transactions and control risk based on gaining an understanding of internal control. Remember that audit standard *240* requires

---
[1] Source: "For Denmark's Entrepreneur of Year, Something Was Rotten," *The Wall Street Journal,* December 17, 2008, pp. A1, A16.

consideration of revenue as a fraud risk and documentation if the auditors conclude that revenue is not a fraud risk.

3. Determine detection risk based on the level of audit risk and risk of material misstatement.

The components of the audit risk model are assessed on an assertion-by-assertion basis. This assessment recognizes that certain assertions assume an increased level of importance and are of more interest to auditors than others. For example, because of the tendency to use fictitious sales to overstate assets and revenues, the *existence* assertion is relatively important in the audit of accounts receivable, and *occurrence* is important for sales. Because material mistakes happen, auditors need to examine revenue and accounts receivable for completeness. However, there is no advantage for the client to intentionally omit these items. Thus, auditors may assess inherent risk for the *existence* assertion to be higher than for the *completeness* assertion for these accounts, all other things being equal. Exhibit 7.1 shows the AICPA assertions for sales and receivables with their relative risks.

After considering the inherent risk associated with each assertion, the auditors identify important control activities implemented by the client for each relevant assertion. Once the control activities have been determined to be in place through inquiry, observation, and walkthrough, auditors estimate the control risk. Based on the combined inherent and control risk assessments (referred to as *the risk of material misstatement*), auditors calculate detection risk and determine the nature, timing, and extent of evidence to gather by substantive procedures. If the audit team estimates that control risk is below the maximum, they need to perform tests of controls to confirm that the control

EXHIBIT 7.1 Relative Assertion Risks for Revenue and Receivables

AICPA Assertions	Revenues	Receivables	Explanation
Transaction assertions			Management may overstate both sales and receivables by adding fictitious transactions or inflating actual sales. This can be done by holding the books open past the end of the period. There is no advantage to omitting sales or receivables transactions.*
• Occurrence	High	High	
• Completeness	Low	Low	
• Cutoff	High	High	
• Accuracy	High	High	
• Classification	Medium	Medium	
Balance assertions			Management may overstate balances in both sales and receivables by including fictitious transactions or inflating actual balances. Therefore, the risk of overstated balances in both sales and receivables is high. Management can include sales or receivables for which it does not have the rights to collect (e.g., remaining performance). Omitting existing sales or receivables from account balances provides no advantage.
• Existence	High	High	
• Rights and obligations	Medium–High	Medium–High	
• Completeness	Low	Low	
• Valuation and allocation	High	High	
Presentation and disclosure assertions			Frauds have occurred through the misapplication of revenue recognition principles resulting in nonexistent and overvalued revenues and receivables or the misclassification of items (e.g., unearned revenue as earned). The auditors must carefully review footnotes regarding revenues, receivables, and returns and allowances.
• Occurrence	High	High	
• Rights and obligations	Medium–High	Medium–High	
• Completeness	Low	Low	
• Accuracy and valuation allocations	High	High	
• Classification and understandability	Medium	Medium	

Note: The risks listed are for a typical entity engaged in manufacturing, retail, and other similar industries. Some specialized industries may have risks that vary from those indicated in this table.

* In some cases, clients could understate revenues; however, the greater risk to auditors is the overstatement of revenues.

activities are operating effectively and that the auditors' initial strategy is sound.[2] If the tests of controls reveal that control risk is higher than originally estimated, the audit team would *decrease* detection risk and modify the *nature, timing, and extent* of substantive procedures. Using a matrix such as the following one (which assumes a low desired overall audit risk), the maximum allowable level of detection risk can be determined by finding the intersection of the row (representing inherent risk) and column (representing control risk).

		CONTROL RISK		
		Low	Moderate	High
INHERENT RISK	Low	High Detection Risk	Moderate to High Detection Risk	Moderate Detection Risk
	Moderate	Moderate to High Detection Risk	Moderate Detection Risk	Low to Moderate Detection Risk
	High	Moderate Detection Risk	Low to Moderate Detection Risk	Low Detection Risk

Later in the chapter, we present a specific example of how the audit team might go through this process.

INHERENT RISKS IN THE REVENUE AND COLLECTION CYCLE

LEARNING OBJECTIVE 7-1
Discuss inherent risks related to the revenue and collection cycle with a focus on improper revenue recognition.

Revenue Recognition

The IT Factory is an extreme example of the violation of accounting standards related to **revenue recognition** (recording revenues in the entity's books). To be recognized, revenues must be (1) realized or realizable and (2) earned.[3]

An entity's revenue-earning activities involve delivering or producing goods, rendering services, or performing other activities that constitute its ongoing major or central operations, and revenues are considered to have been earned when the entity has substantially accomplished what it must do to be entitled to the benefits represented by the revenues.[4]

Similarly, the SEC believes that revenue generally is realized or realizable and earned when *all* of the following criteria are met:

- Persuasive evidence of an arrangement exists.
- Delivery has occurred or services have been rendered.

---

[2] Note that PCAOB *AS 5* requires auditors of public companies to test *all relevant* controls over *significant accounts* for design and operating effectiveness.
[3] **SFAC** *No. 5*, "Recognition and Measurement in Finance Statements."
[4] Ibid., ¶ 83(b).

- The seller's price to the buyer is fixed or determinable.
- Collectability is reasonably ensured.[5]

The SEC and the popular press have expressed concern about appropriate recognition of revenue in financial statements. A study by the Association of Certified Fraud Examiners indicates that the typical organization loses 5 percent of its annual revenue to fraud. If we applied that percentage to the gross world product, it is estimated that more than $2.9 trillion is lost.[6] Some recent restatements are listed in Exhibit 7.2. The fact that the financial statements were restated means that the auditors missed the original misstatement or went along with the company's accounting treatment. In some cases, predecessor auditors accepted the accounting treatment, but the current auditors demanded the restatement.

AUDITING INSIGHT — Revenue Recognition Issues Are Important

Ernst & Young failed to note when two clients strayed from revenue-recognition rules, according the 2008 Public Company Accounting Oversight Board inspection report. Those clients had to restate their previously issued financial statements to make up for the departure from GAAP. According to the report, these companies "failed" to follow Accounting Standards Codification 605 (ASC 605), Revenue Recognition. The rule calls on companies to make reasonable estimates of how many products customers will return as a factor in deciding when revenue can be recorded. Additionally, EY was criticized for not obtaining objective evidence in determining whether a client's revenue recognized for individual parts of a technology contract was reasonable. These deficiencies were linked to the firm's national office in New York and 22 of its 85 U.S. offices. These errors were significant enough for the oversight board to conclude that the firm "had not obtained sufficient competent evidential matter to support its opinion on the issuer's financial statements or internal control over financial reporting."

Source: "PCAOB Rips E&Y on Revenue Recognition," CFO.com, May 27, 2009.

Risks of improper revenue recognition are higher in developing companies that financial analysts often value at a multiple of total revenues. In addition, companies with complex transactions, related-party transactions, and reciprocal transactions have a higher likelihood of inflating revenues. An example of the latter occurred in the telecom industry in which **Global Crossing** and other companies are alleged to have traded line rights in one geographic area to other companies for rights in another area. The rights given up were recorded in revenue while the rights received were capitalized and the expense was spread over several years. Clearly, the issues in revenue recognition and accounts receivable are complex and can be difficult for the auditors.

AUDITING INSIGHT — Net or Gross Revenue?

Under its Name Your Own Price® services, **Priceline.com** takes bids from customers for airline tickets, rental cars, hotel rooms, and other services. If the supplier agrees to the price, the customer pays Priceline, which deducts its commission and pays the airline, hotel, or car rental company. If Priceline receives $175 for a ticket and pays the airline $150, what should the company record as revenue? Priceline contends they should record $175 because it takes ownership of the ticket and does not receive a fee or commission. Moreover, Priceline argues that it assumes the risk of uncollectable accounts, even though it receives the customer's credit card number before it awards the ticket. The SEC staff generally believes companies should report this type of transaction on a net basis (i.e., $25), but they have agreed with Priceline so far. For the year ended December 31, 2010, Priceline reported $1,691 million of "merchant" revenues and $1,175 million as the cost of "merchant" revenues.

Source: Priceline.com Annual Report 2010.

---

[5] Association of Certified Fraud Examiners, *Report to the Nations on Occupational Fraud and Abuse*, 2010.

[6] *Staff Accounting Bulletin No. 104*, "Securities and Exchange Commission."

EXHIBIT 7.2 Revenue Recognition Rogues

Company	Cause of Misstatement	Alleged Amount
Bristol-Myers	Company offered incentives to wholesalers to build their inventories so Bristol-Meyers could meet sales forecasts (*channel stuffing*).*	$2.5 billion
Computer Associates	Company recognized revenue from several contracts in which it had either (1) agreed to make offsetting purchases (*round trips*) or (2) had contracts that contained undisclosed side letters that could have canceled the contracts.	$2.2 billion
Qwest Communication	Company used fiber-optic "swaps." It recorded sales of equipment when it agreed to pay hundreds of millions of dollars for Internet services. It recognized the revenue for the equipment, but deferred the cost of the Internet services.	$2.2 billion
Nortel	Company prematurely recorded revenue from equipment sales before the buyer had taken title to the equipment.	$1.5 billion
Sea View Video Technology	Company prematurely recorded revenues and accounts receivable for customer orders for security camera products prior to shipping.	$1.4 billion
AOL (now Time Warner)	AOL recorded advertising revenue, some of which included one-time payments, stock sales, and "round-trip" deals in which money flowed both ways between AOL and the advertiser.	$1 billion
Royal Ahold	Company induced third parties to provide false confirmations to auditors relating to sales and accounts receivable.	$700 million
Safety-Kleen Corporation	Company recorded contingent revenues and contract claims that were not probable and recorded revenue for property not yet sold.	$534 million
Household International	Company employed incorrect timing of recognizing costs and revenues related to its MasterCard and Visa cobranding and affinity credit card relationships as well as a credit card marketing agreement with a third party.	$386 million
Xerox	Several senior managers colluded to circumvent company's accounting policies and administrative procedures. The restatement related to uncollectable long-term receivables, failure to record liabilities for amounts due to concessionaires, and, to a lesser extent, recording revenue for contracts that did not fully meet the requirements of sales-type leases.	$207 million
Interpublic	Company improperly booked credits, creating double counting; included insurance proceeds that had not been realized; and understated liabilities.	$181 million
Gemstar	Subsidiary TV Guide recorded $113 million in patent-licensing revenue from an expired Scientific-Atlanta Inc. contract.	$113 million

Channel stuffing is a deceptive business practice that inflates sales and earnings by forcing more products along a company's distribution channel without actual sales taking place.

Collectability of Accounts Receivable

In most companies, a portion of accounts receivable will not be paid. GAAP requires the client to provide an estimate of the amount that will likely be uncollectable and provide an allowance for this amount. Estimation of the allowance for doubtful accounts can be subjective and difficult for the client and the auditor. This is particularly true when the client has changed products or its customer base, so there is little experience on which to base estimates. Changing economic conditions also make it difficult to estimate collectability.

Customer Returns and Allowances

In some industries, customers have a right to return unused or unsold merchandise. For example, the university bookstore can usually return unsold textbooks to the publisher. When these agreements are in the purchase contract and disclosed to the auditor, an appropriate evaluation of revenue can be performed. However, clients may enter into informal right of return agreements with customers unknown to the auditors. Liabilities for known rights of return, warranties, and other potential obligations are often very difficult to estimate. Companies with new products or technologies have an even higher inherent risk in these areas.

AUDITING INSIGHT — Are You Stuffed?

For each of 14 quarters between September 2001 and April 2006, **Vitesse Semiconductor Corporation** engaged in an elaborate channel stuffing scheme to improperly recognize revenue on product shipments. Vitesse immediately recognized revenue and recorded invalid accounts receivable for product shipped at period-end to its largest distributor even though the distributor had an unconditional right to return the entire product. For September 2001, Vitesse recognized more than $40 million in improper revenue representing 10.4 percent of its annual revenue and nearly 108 percent of its fourth quarter revenue. The right of return was accomplished through an undisclosed side letter and several oral agreements. In addition, Vitesse failed to record credits relating to accounts receivable in a timely manner when the distributor returned the product. Furthermore, Vitesse misapplied payments received from customers to conceal the age of the uncollected fraudulent receivable from the auditors.

As a result of the fraud, NASDAQ delisted Vitesse's stock; four of its topic executives were indicted for fraud[*]; and the company has paid $8.75 million to settle shareholder lawsuits.

[*] In addition to the fraud described, management is accused of backdating stock options for personal gain.

Sources: "SEC Charges Vitesse Semiconductor Corporation and Four Former Vitesse Executives in Revenue Recognition and Options Backdating Schemes," Tech Zone 360°, December 10, 2010; "Two Former High-Technology Company Executives in Accounting and Securities Fraud Scheme," StopFraud.gov, December 10, 2010; "Ex-Vitesse Chief Tomasetta Charged with Fraud in Options Backdating Case," Bloomberg, December 10, 2010.

REVIEW CHECKPOINTS

7.1 What do we mean by *revenue recognition*? What does GAAP say about proper revenue recognition?

7.2 Why do you think companies use revenue recognition as a primary means for inflating profits?

7.3 Why is revenue recognition riskier for a new company?

REVENUE AND COLLECTION CYCLE: TYPICAL ACTIVITIES

LEARNING OBJECTIVE 7-2
Describe the revenue and collection cycle, including typical source documents and control procedures.

STAGES OF AN AUDIT

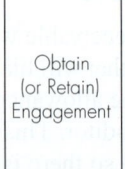 Obtain (or Retain) Engagement
 Engagement Planning
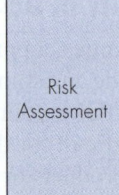 Risk Assessment
 Audit Evidence
Reporting

The basic activities in the revenue and collection cycle are (1) receiving and processing customer orders, including credit approval; (2) delivering goods and services to customers; (3) billing customers and accounting for accounts receivable; and (4) collecting and depositing cash received from customers. See Exhibit 7.3 for the activities and transactions involved in a revenue and collection cycle. As you follow the exhibit, you can track some of the highlighted elements of internal control. The numbers listed next to the headings correspond to the numbers in Exhibit 7.3.

EXHIBIT 7.3 Revenue and Collection Cycle

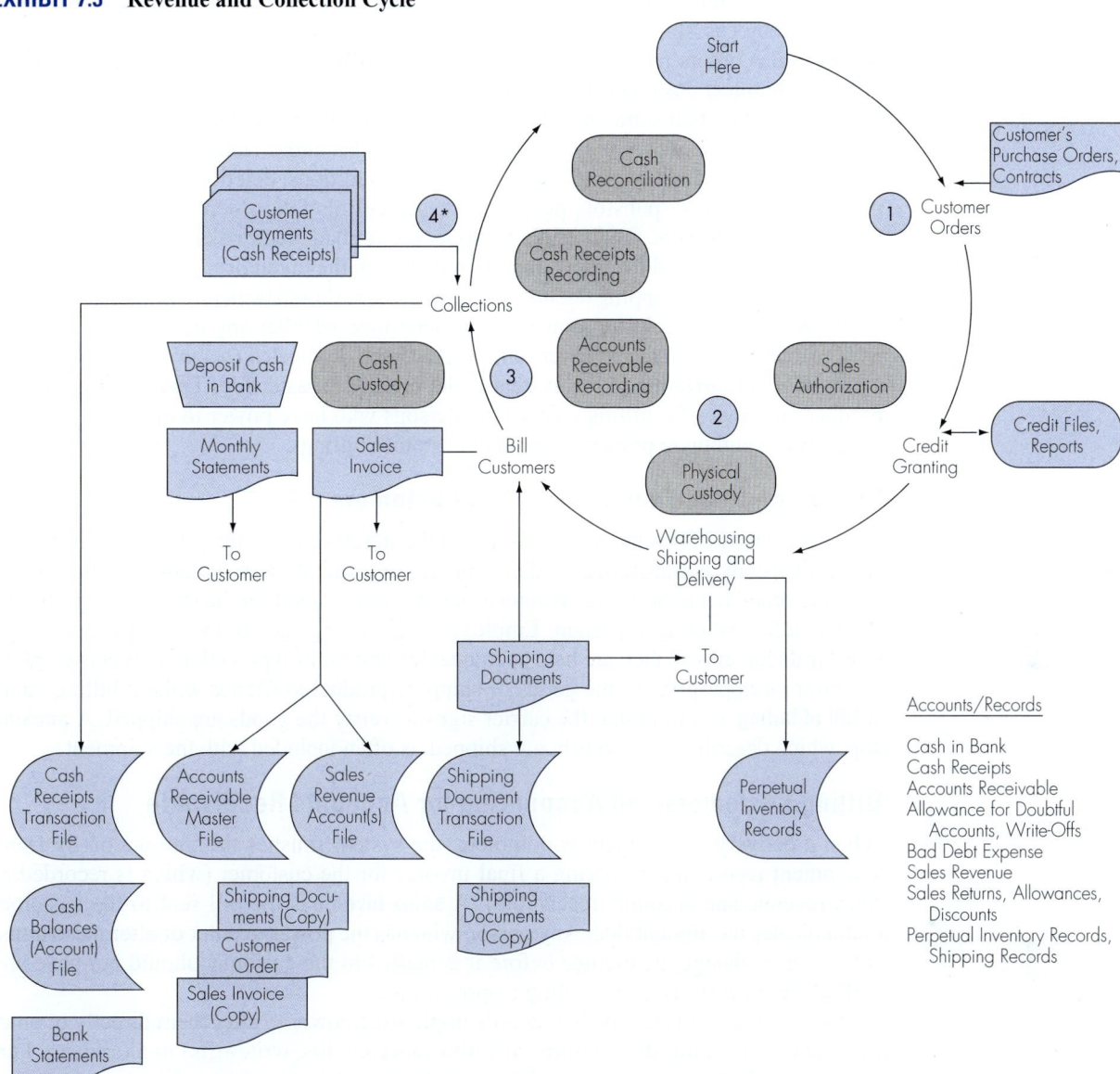

*Processing customer payments is discussed in the Cash Receipts section of Chapter 6.

Entity-Level Controls

It is important that auditors consider the entity-level controls in all processes and procedures. In the revenue process, management should have a process for continually reviewing revenue and comparing it to budgets and forecasts. Management should constantly scrutinize total write-offs of accounts receivable, merchandise returns, and the timeliness of collections. Physical controls over inventory and warehouses must include entity-level controls such as identification badges, restricting access to facilities, and further restricting access within the facilities (e.g., office employees restricted from inventory areas).

Receiving and Processing Customer Orders, Including Credit Granting ①

Customers initiate sales orders in a variety of ways. They can mail purchase orders, call or fax orders, e-mail orders, place orders on a website, or simply come to the company's place of business and buy their goods. In some cases, companies are directly linked to production schedules in their customers' computer files (via electronic data interchange, EDI), so they can ship goods automatically as the customer needs them. Electronic or Internet sales orders require special software controls that protect against unauthorized orders and protect customer information.

It is important that someone authorize credit sales to ensure that the customer will be able to pay for the goods or services. Because various authorizations are imbedded in a computerized system, access to the master file for additions, deletions, and other changes must be limited to responsible people. If these controls fail, orders might be processed for fictitious customers, credit might be approved for bad credit risks, and shipping documents might be created for goods that do not exist in the inventory.

Customer orders, shipping documents, and invoices should be in prenumbered sequence so the system can check the sequence and determine whether any transactions have not been recorded (*completeness* assertion) or have been duplicated (*occurrence* assertion).

Another authorization in the system is the price list master file. This file contains the product unit prices for billing customers. Persons who have power to alter this file have the power to authorize price changes and customer billings.

Delivering Goods and Services to Customers ②

Physical custody of inventory goods starts in the storeroom or warehouse where inventory is kept. Custody is transferred to the shipping department upon the authorization of the shipping order that permits the inventory clerk to release goods to the shipping department. Proper authorization is important: Employees performing each of these steps should sign transfer documents so they are held accountable. This control procedure prevents employees from misappropriating the goods or shipping product to friends without billing them. A **bill of lading** is a form that the carrier signs to verify the goods are shipped. A **packing slip**, which describes the goods being shipped, is often included with the shipment.

Billing Customers and Accounting for Accounts Receivable ③

When a delivery or shipment is complete, the system finishes the transaction by filing a shipment record and preparing a final invoice for the customer (which is recorded as sales revenue and accounts receivable). A **sales invoice** is the bill sent to the customer that indicates the amount due. Any person who has the power to enter or alter these transactions or to change the invoice before it is mailed to the customer should not have any authorization, custody, or recording responsibilities.

Access to accounts receivable records implies the power to alter them directly or enter transactions (e.g., transfers, returns and allowance credits, write-offs) to alter them. Personnel with this power have a combination of authorization and recording responsibility. Another important facet of control is physical protection of the files. If the files are lost or destroyed, it is unlikely the accounts will be collected, so the records are truly assets. Limited access, frequent backup, and disaster recovery plans are important controls to ensure the availability of information. Moreover, customer and employee information must be protected.

AUDITING INSIGHT   Maxed Out?

TJX, operator of discount chains including **T.J. Maxx** and **Marshalls**, said its computers had been hacked, putting shoppers at risk of identity fraud. Intruders accessed systems used to process and store customer transaction data. "It is pretty obvious that it was a very well orchestrated, targeted attack," said Avivah Litan, a stock analyst. Litan suspects the perpetrators are the same people who have broken into systems at other retailers. "These people are piecing together information on millions of Americans. It is quite scary."

Source: "T.J. Maxx Hack Exposes Consumer Data," C-Net News.com, January 18, 2007.

The most frequent reconciliation is the comparison of the sum of customers' unpaid balances (customer database or subsidiary ledger) kept in the accounts receivable department) with the accounts receivable control account total (maintained in corporate accounting). This reconciliation is accomplished by preparing a trial balance of the accounts receivable subsidiary ledger, adding it, and comparing its total with the control account balance. Internal auditors can perform periodic comparisons of the customers' balances by sending confirmations to the customers.

Audit Evidence in Management Reports and Data Files

Exhibit 7.4 represents a computerized system for processing customer orders. Computerized processing of revenue and cash receipts transactions enables management to generate several reports that can provide important audit evidence.

Pending Order Master File

Sales transactions that were initiated but are not yet completed, and thus not yet recorded as sales, are kept in the *pending order master file.* Long-standing orders may represent unfilled sales to a customer, which results in ill will and lack of revenue. They also may represent shipments that actually were made but for some reason were not recorded in the sales journal or could not be matched to a customer order. The pending orders should be reviewed for evidence of the *completeness* of recorded sales and accounts receivable.

Credit Check Files

The computerized system may make automatic credit checks, but up-to-date maintenance of the credit information is very important. Credit checks based on dated or incomplete information are not good credit checks. A sample of the *credit check files* can be tested for current status. Alternatively, the company's data change controls can be reviewed to ensure the files are accurately maintained.

EXHIBIT 7.4 Computerized Sales and Accounts Receivable Processing

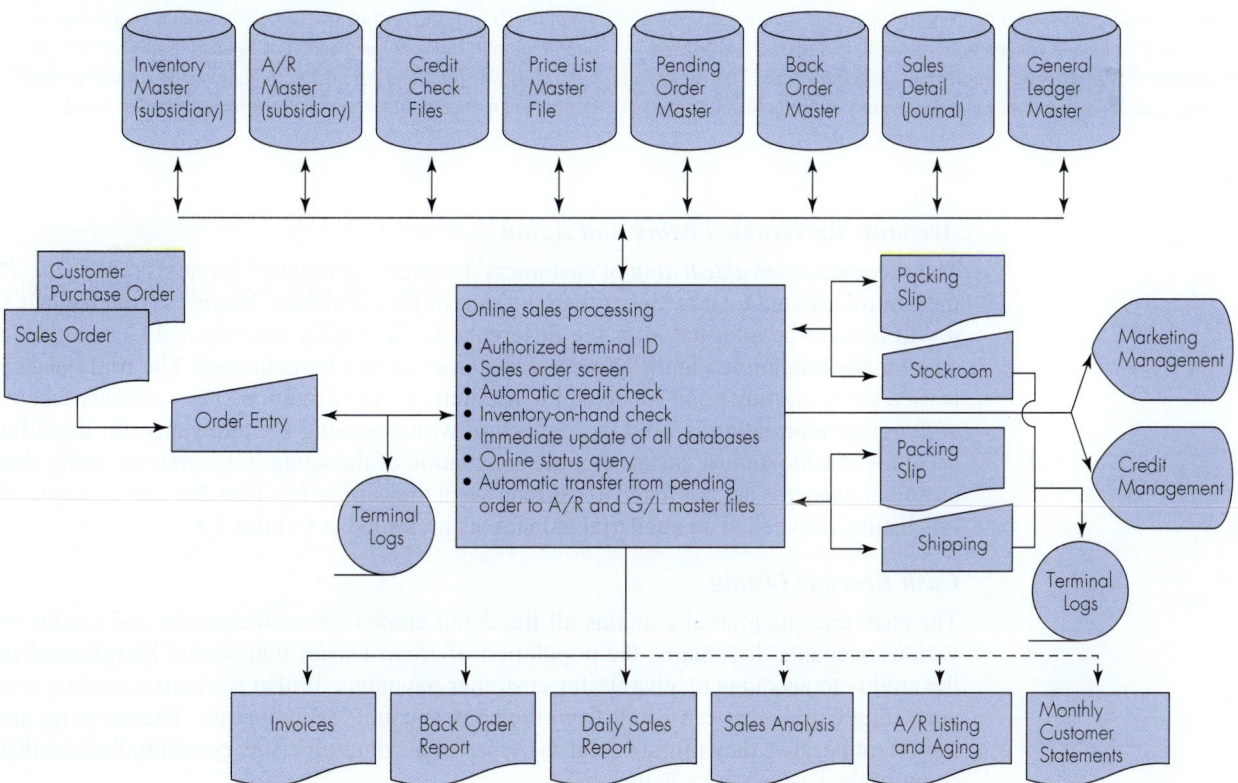

Price List Master File

The computerized system may produce customer invoices automatically, but if the *price list master file* is incorrect, the billings will be incorrect. The computer file can be compared to an official price source for accuracy. The company should perform this comparison every time it changes its prices. Remember that prices may change over the year. Therefore, when vouching invoices and sales journal entries to price lists, it is important to make certain you have the price list that was in effect at the time of the customer's order.

Sales Detail (Journal) File

The detailed sales entries, including the shipping references and dates, should be in the *sales detail (journal) file*. The file can be scanned using computer-assisted auditing techniques (CAATs) for checking entries without shipping references (fictitious sales?) and for matching recording dates with shipment dates (sales recorded before shipment?). Daily totals should be compared to a computer-generated list of debits to accounts receivable.

Sales Analysis Reports

A variety of *sales analysis reports* can be produced. Sales that are classified by product lines provide required information for the business segment disclosures. Sales classified by sales employee or region can show unusually high or low volume that might bear further investigation if an error or fraud is suspected. Analytical procedures, such as trend analysis or comparison among sales units, can be a great help to the auditor as illustrated by the following Audit Insight.

AUDITING INSIGHT | **Peaks and Valleys**

During the year-end audit, the independent auditors reviewed the weekly sales volume reports classified by region. They noticed that sales volume was very high in Region 2 the last two weeks of March, June, September, and December. The volume was unusually low in the first two weeks of April, July, October, and January. In fact, the peaks far exceeded the volume in all the other six regions. Further investigation revealed that the manager in Region 2 was holding open the sales journal at the end of each quarterly reporting period (i.e., including sales from the next period) in an attempt to make the quarterly reports look good.

Accounts Receivable Listing and Aging

The *accounts receivable listing* of customers' balances is the actual accounts receivable. If the control account total is higher than the sum of the customers' balances (trial balance), it will have to be adjusted after the difference is thoroughly investigated. A receivable amount that cannot be identified with a customer cannot be collected! The trial balance is used as the starting point for selecting accounts for confirmation. The *accounts receivable aging* information is used in connection with assessing the allowance for doubtful accounts. Auditors must ensure that the calculation of the aging is accurate to verify that customer accounts are not listed as current when they are in fact past due. An example of this listing, also called an **aged trial balance**, is presented at Exhibit 7.8.

Cash Receipts Listing

The cash receipts journal contains all the detail entries for cash deposits and credits to various accounts. It contains the population of credit entries that should be reflected in the credits to accounts receivable for customer payments. It also contains adjusting and correcting entries that can result from the bank account reconciliation. These entries are important because they might signal the types of accounting errors or manipulations that occur in the *cash receipts listing*.

Customer Statements

Probably the best control over whether cash is received and recorded is the customer. Therefore, sending on a monthly basis *customer statements* of what has been billed, what has been paid, and ending monthly balances enables customers to spot discrepancies and notify the company. Statements should be sent if there is *any* activity in the account, even if the ending balances are zero.

> ### ↪ REVIEW CHECKPOINTS
>
> 7.4 What is the basic sequence of activities and accounting in a revenue and collection cycle?
>
> 7.5 What purpose is served by prenumbering sales orders, shipping documents, and sales invoices?
>
> 7.6 What controls should be implemented to safeguard accounts receivable files?
>
> 7.7 What computer-based files might auditors examine to find evidence of unrecorded sales? Of inadequate credit checks? Of incorrect product unit prices?
>
> 7.8 Suppose that you selected a sample of customers' accounts receivable and wanted to find supporting evidence for the entries in the accounts. Where would you go to vouch the debit entries? What would you expect to find? Where would you go to vouch the credit entries? What would you expect to find?

▽ CONTROL RISK ASSESSMENT

LEARNING OBJECTIVE 7-3
Give examples of tests of controls over customer credit approval, delivery, and recording of accounts receivable.

Control risk assessment is important because it governs the nature, timing, and extent of substantive procedures that will be applied in the audit of account balances in the revenue and collection cycle. These account balances (listed in the corner of Exhibit 7.3) include

- Cash in bank.
- Accounts receivable.
- Allowance for doubtful accounts.
- Bad debts expense.
- Sales revenue.
- Sales returns, allowances, and discounts.

Control Considerations

Controls for proper separation of responsibilities should be in place and operating. By referring to Exhibit 7.3, you can see that proper separation involves different people and different departments performing the sales and credit authorization; custody of goods and cash; and record keeping for sales, receivables, inventory, and cash receipts. Combinations of two or more of these responsibilities in one person, one office, or one computerized system might open the door for errors and fraud.

It is not always possible to have complete separation of duties in a small business with few employees because the benefits of controls do not outweigh the costs involved. To obtain *reasonable assurance* that financial controls are intact, the owner must have active involvement in the accounting process—approving credit and discounts, reviewing the aged accounts receivable listing, and occasionally opening mail. The owner usually is in direct contact with customers and can ensure that shipments are received. The owner also can follow up on past due accounts.

In addition, the following control activities should be in place to prevent and detect errors:

- No sales order should be entered without a customer order.
- A credit check code or manual signature should be recorded for authorization.
- Access to inventory and the shipping area should be restricted to authorized persons.
- Access to billing terminals and blank invoice forms should be restricted to authorized personnel.
- Accountants should be instructed to record sales and accounts receivable when all supporting documentation of shipment is in order.
- Care should be taken to record sales and receivables as of the date the goods and services were shipped and the cash receipts on the date the payments were received.
- Customer invoices should be compared with bills of lading and customer orders to determine that the customer is sent the goods ordered at the proper location for the proper prices and that the quantity being billed is the same as the quantity shipped.
- Pending order files should be reviewed frequently to avoid failure to bill and record shipments.

Finally, procedures must be in place to ensure that errors noted by these steps are properly corrected. An error control log monitored by the information systems supervisor ensures that this is done. Such a log may aid in the identification of patterns that indicate either control weaknesses or possible fraudulent activities.

Information about a company's controls often is gathered by completing an internal control questionnaire. Questionnaires for both manual controls and computerized controls over the revenue and collection cycle are in Appendix 7A. You can study these questionnaires for details of desirable control activities. They are organized under headings that address the assertions regarding classes of transactions. Auditors should perform a *walkthrough* to verify that they understand the activities. The revenue and collection cycle walkthrough involves following a sale from the initial customer order through credit approval, billing, and delivery of goods to the entry in the sales journal and subsidiary accounts receivable records and then its subsequent collection and cash deposit.

Tests of Controls

An organization should have control activities in place and operating to prevent, detect, and correct accounting errors. Exhibit 7.5 puts these in the perspective of revenue cycle activity with examples of specific assertions.

Auditors can perform tests of controls to determine whether company personnel are properly performing controls that are said to be in place. In general, the actions in tests of controls involve vouching, tracing, observing, scanning, and recalculating. If personnel in the organization are not performing their control activities effectively, auditors need to design substantive procedures to try to detect whether control failures have produced materially misstated account balances.

AUDITING INSIGHT Is Everyone Control Conscious?

Clearly, a first line of defense against accounting fraud is to ensure that everyone is control conscious.... unless you work at NutraCea. NutraCea faked a $2.6 million sale in the second quarter of 2007 and a $1.9 million deal later that year. These deals made it look like the company had met its sales forecast when in fact it had not. The Securities and Exchange Commission alleges the fraud was so blatant that one executive, when told about the accounting problems by a colleague, covered his ears and said "No, no, no, no, I don't want to hear it."

Source: "NutreaCea Ex-Execs Accused of Fraud," *Arizona Business & Money,* January 15, 2011.

EXHIBIT 7.5 Assertions about Classes of Transactions and Events for the Period: Revenue and Collection Cycle

Assertion	Control Activity	Tests of Controls
Occurrence—Sales and related events that have been recorded have occurred and pertain to the entity.	Invoices supported by customer purchase orders. Bills of lading or other shipping documents exist for all invoices.	Check agreement of sales in sales detail file to invoices, supporting shipping documents, and customer purchase orders for customer name, product description, terms, dates, and quantities.
	Recorded sales in Sales Revenue account file are supported by invoices.	Vouch debits from Accounts Receivable accounts to supporting sales invoices.
Completeness—All sales and related events that should have been recorded have been recorded.	Invoices, shipping documents, and sales orders are prenumbered and the numerical sequence is checked.	Scan documents for numerical sequence. Observe client-checking sequence. Trace shipping document to recording in sales detail file.
	Overall comparisons of sales are made periodically by a statistical or product line analysis.	Examine evidence of client review and follow-up of analytical sales data.
Accuracy—Amounts and other data related to sales transactions and events have been recorded properly.	Credit sales are approved by the credit department.	Examine invoice for credit approval.
	Prices used to prepare invoices are from the authorized price schedule.	Compare prices to approved price listing.
	Invoice quantities are compared to shipment and customer order quantities.	Observe client comparing shipping quantities. Examine evidence of client making the comparison.
	Prices and mathematical accuracy are independently checked after the invoice is prepared.	Recalculate price extensions and discounts. Examine evidence of client checking prices.
Cutoff—Sales and related events have been recorded in the correct period.	Date of shipping document is compared to invoice date.	Check agreement of date of shipment to sales invoice date. Check FOB terms.
Classification—Sales and related events have been recorded in the proper accounts.	Sales to subsidiaries and affiliates are classified as intercompany sales and receivables.	Trace posting of intercompany sales, sales returns, etc. to sales.
	Credit sales are posted to customers' individual accounts.	

Tests of controls can be used to audit the accounting for transactions in two directions (see Exhibit 7.6). This dual-direction testing involves selecting samples to obtain evidence about control over *completeness* in one direction and control over *occurrence* in the other direction. The completeness direction determines whether all transactions that occurred were recorded (none omitted), and the occurrence direction determines

EXHIBIT 7.6
Dual Direction of Test Audit Samples

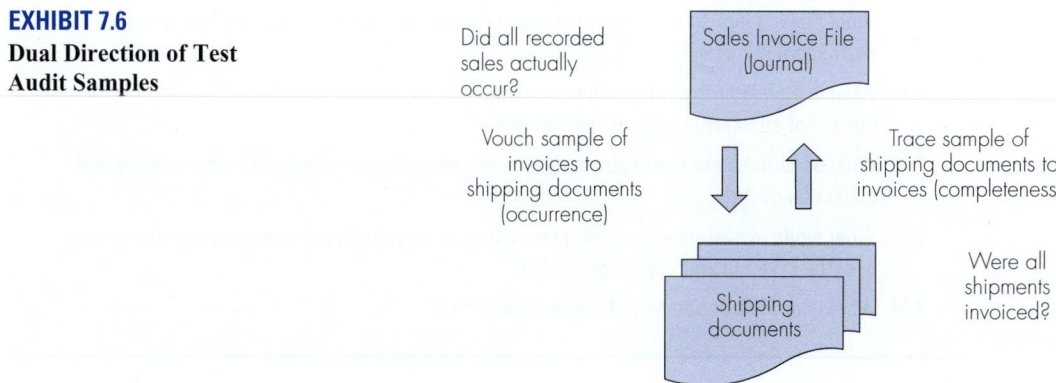

whether recorded transactions represent valid economic events (actual sales). An example of the *completeness* direction is the examination of a sample of shipping documents (from the file of all shipping documents) to determine whether invoices were prepared and recorded. An example of the *occurrence* direction is the examination of a sample of entries in the sales journal to determine whether supporting bills of lading and customer order exist to verify the actual shipment and that the shipment was made of an existing sales order. The content of each document or file is compared with its related supporting document or file.

See Appendix Exhibit 7B.1 for a test of controls audit plan. These steps are designed to direct the audit team in obtaining objective evidence about the effectiveness of controls and about the reliability of accounting records. Thus, the tests of controls produce evidence that helps auditors determine whether the specific control was properly designed and has been effectively implemented.

When the business receives many payments from customers, a detailed audit should include comparison of the checks listed on a sample of deposit slips to the customer credits listed on the day's posting to customer accounts receivable (daily remittance list or other record of detail postings). This procedure is a test for accounts receivable—*lapping* (see Chapter 6). Auditors look for credits given to customers for whom no payments were received on the day in question.

Summary: Control Risk Assessment

Auditors must evaluate the evidence obtained from an understanding of internal control and from tests of controls. The initial process of obtaining an understanding of the company's controls and the later process of obtaining evidence from actual tests of controls are two of the phases of control risk assessment. If the control risk is assessed to be very low, the substantive procedures on the account balances can be reduced, resulting in audit efficiencies. For example, the accounts receivable confirmations can be sent on a date prior to the year-end and the sample size can be small.

On the other hand, if tests of controls reveal weaknesses (such as posting sales without shipping documents, charging customers the wrong prices, or recording credits to customers without supporting documentation), the substantive procedures need to be designed to lower the risk of failing to detect material misstatement in the account balances. For example, the confirmation procedure may need to be scheduled on the year-end date with a large sample of customer accounts.

⤷ REVIEW CHECKPOINTS

7.9 What account balances are included in a revenue and collection cycle?

7.10 What specific control procedures (in addition to separation of duties and responsibilities) should be in place and operating in internal controls governing revenue recognition and cash accounting?

7.11 What is a *walkthrough* of a sales transaction? How can the walkthrough work complement the use of an internal control questionnaire?

7.12 What assertions are made about classes of transactions and events in the revenue and collection cycle?

7.13 What types of evidence-gathering procedures are typically performed in testing controls over the revenue and collection cycle?

7.14 What is *dual-direction test of controls sampling*?

▽ SUBSTANTIVE PROCEDURES IN THE REVENUE AND COLLECTION CYCLE

LEARNING OBJECTIVE 7-4
Give examples of substantive procedures in the revenue and collection cycle and relate them to assertions about account balances at the end of the period.

STAGES OF AN AUDIT

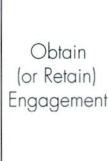   

Obtain (or Retain) Engagement — Engagement Planning — Risk Assessment — Audit Evidence — Reporting

Refer to Exhibit 7.7 for information concerning the assertions about the account balances in the revenue and collection cycle and some substantive procedures the audit team might use to test those assertions. When considering assertions and obtaining evidence about accounts receivable and other assets, auditors must emphasize the *existence* assertion. This emphasis on existence is appropriate because companies and auditors have found themselves in malpractice lawsuits by issuing unqualified reports on financial statements that overstated assets and revenues. For example, credit sales recorded too early or fictitious sales result in overstated accounts receivable and overstated sales revenue.

Discerning the population of assets to audit for existence is easy because the company has asserted their existence by putting them on the balance sheet. The audit procedures described in the following sections can be used to obtain evidence about the existence of accounts receivable.

EXHIBIT 7.7
Assertions and Substantive Procedures in the Revenue and Collection Cycle

Assertions about Account Balances	Substantive Procedures
Existence—Accounts receivable exist.	Confirm a sample of accounts receivable and perform follow-up procedures.
Rights and obligations—The entity holds or controls the rights to accounts receivable.	Inquire whether any receivables have been sold or factored. Review bank confirmations, loan agreements, and minutes of the board for indications of pledged, discounted, or assigned receivables.
Completeness—All receivables that should have been recorded are recorded.	Perform sales cutoff tests. Include a sample of zero-balance accounts in the confirmation process.
Valuation or allocation—Receivables are included in the financial statements at appropriate amounts and any resulting valuation adjustments are properly recorded.	Obtain an aged trial balance of individual customer accounts and test the aging. Compare current-year write-off experience to the prior-year allowance for bad debts. Examine cash receipts after the balance sheet date for collections on past due accounts. For large past due accounts, obtain financial statements or credit reports and discuss with the credit manager. Calculate an allowance estimate using prior relations of write-offs and sales, taking current economic events under consideration.

> ### AUDITING INSIGHT — Fraud 101?
>
> *Koss Corporation,* a Milwaukee company with sales of $38 million dollars in 2009, was the victim of a $31 million fraud. It is believed that Sujata Sachdeva, vice president of finance, circumvented the books and did not record revenues and was able to siphon the unrecorded revenue to her own personal accounts. This case could be a primer for fraud auditors.
>
> Sachdeva was a long-time trusted employee of Koss and was promoted to vice president of finance in 1992. Koss viewed her as so valued an employee that when her family decided to move to Texas, Sachdeva was allowed to telecommute to her job. This is extremely unusual for someone in her position and with the type of responsibilities associated with being vice president of finance. Most auditors with fraud experience are very skeptical of any employee known to be a *long time trusted* employee. Such a designation often comes with an ability to have controls waived or circumvented. Place this person in a remote, unsupervised situation, and trouble is likely around the corner.
>
> Many fraud auditors will tell you that there is no such thing as an immaterial fraud. Although fraud may start as quantitatively immaterial, it can grow in nature and should be viewed as qualitatively material in all instances. Follow the numbers in the Koss fraud:
>
> 2005: $2,195,477
> 2006: $2,227,669
> 2007: $3,160,310
> 2008: $5,040,968
> 2009: $8,485,937
> 2010: $10,243,310 (two quarters).
>
> Finally, there is Michael Koss, vice chairman, chief executive officer, president, and chief financial officer of Koss Corporation. Even in small companies, each of these posts is a full-time position. An auditor should not be surprised that a person with such responsibilities would have difficulty adequately supervising employees that report to him or her. In addition, each of these executive positions is instrumental in the establishment and/or execution of sound corporate governance, which was likely insufficient at Koss Corporation.
>
> In the aftermath of the discovery of fraud, shareholder lawsuits have been filed against Koss Corporation, its management, and its auditors, Grant Thornton. A retired partner with KPMG stated, "The fraud is so large, in relation to the size of the company, that I have got to believe that it is going to make it difficult for Grant Thornton to prove that they conducted an audit in accordance with generally accepted auditing standards."
>
> Sources: "Koss Financial Records Will Get More Scrutiny in 2010," *Milwaukee Journal Sentinel,* December 28, 2009; "Koss Corp: Anatomy of an Alleged $31 Million Fraud," Dailyfinanci.com, January 18, 2010; "Koss Fraud May Have Been Due, In No Small Part, to Michael Koss Holding Five Executive Positions," Goingconcern.com, March 22, 2010; "Koss Auditor Faces Lawsuit, Questions," *Milwaukee Journal Sentinel,* March 28, 2010.

Analytical Procedures

During an audit, a variety of analytical comparisons might be employed, depending on the circumstances and the nature of the business. Comparisons of asset and revenue balances with recent history might help detect overstatements. Such relationships as receivables turnover, days' sales in receivables, receivables aging, gross margin ratio, and sales/asset ratios can be compared to historical data and industry statistics for evidence of overall reasonableness. Account interrelationships also can be used in analytical procedures. For example, sales returns and allowances and sales commissions generally vary directly with dollar sales volume, bad debt expense usually varies directly with credit sales, and freight expense varies with the physical sales volume. Accounts receivable write-offs should be compared with estimates of doubtful accounts.

> ### AUDITING INSIGHT — Simple Analytical Comparison
>
> The auditors prepared a schedule of the monthly credit sales totals for the current and prior years. They noticed several variations, but one in November of the current year stood out in particular. The current-year credit sales were almost twice as large as in any prior November. Further investigation showed that a computer error had caused the November credit sales to be recorded twice in the control accounts. The accounts receivable and sales revenue were materially overstated as a result.

Confirmation of Accounts and Notes Receivable

In general, the use of confirmations for accounts receivable is considered a required audit procedure by audit standards. If auditors decide not to use them, the burden of proof is on the auditors to justify their position. Auditors should document justifications for the decision not to use confirmations for accounts receivable in a particular audit. Justifications might include (1) receivables are not material; (2) confirmations would be ineffective, based on prior years' experience or knowledge that responses could be unreliable; and (3) analytical procedures and other substantive procedures provide sufficient, competent evidence.

> **AUDITING INSIGHT** — **A Decision Not to Use Accounts Receivable Confirmations**
>
> **Sureparts Manufacturing Company** sold all its production to three auto manufacturers and six aftermarket distributors. All nine of these customers typically paid their accounts in full by the 10th of each following month. The auditors were able to vouch the cash receipts for the full amount of the accounts receivable in the bank statements and cash receipts records in the month following the Sureparts year-end. Confirmation evidence was not considered necessary in these circumstances.

Confirmations provide evidence of *existence* and, to a limited extent, *valuation* of accounts and notes receivable. Remember that just because a customer owes an amount does not mean it will pay that amount. Customers in bankruptcy routinely confirm amounts owed although the receivable's value may be only a small fraction of that amount. The accounts and notes to be confirmed should be documented with an aged trial balance. (An aged trial balance annotated to show the auditors' work is shown in Exhibit 7.8.) Accounts for confirmation can be selected at random or in accordance with another sampling method consistent with the audit objectives. Statistical methods may be useful for determining the sample size. Audit software can be used to access computerized receivables files, select, and even print the confirmations.

Two widely used confirmation forms are positive confirmations and negative confirmations. A **positive confirmation** asks the customer to respond whether the balance is correct or incorrect. See Exhibit 7.9 for an example of a positive confirmation. A variation of the positive confirmation is the *blank form.* A blank confirmation does not contain the balance; customers are asked to fill it in themselves. The blank positive confirmation may produce better evidence because the recipients need to get the information directly from their own records instead of just signing the form and returning it with no exceptions noted. (However, the effort involved on the part of the recipient may cause a lower response rate.) As illustrated in several of the Audit Insights, the auditors must follow up on all exceptions. For example, they may choose to examine the bank deposit that includes a check mentioned by the customer. The reason for any discrepancy will have to be investigated by the client, and the audit team will examine corroborative evidence of the client's resolution.

See Exhibit 7.10 for the **negative confirmation** form for the same request in Exhibit 7.9. The positive form asks for a response. The negative form asks for a response *only if something is wrong with the balance;* thus, lack of response to negative confirmations is considered evidence that the account is fairly stated.

The positive form is by far the most common and is used when individual balances are relatively large or when accounts are in dispute. Positive confirmations may ask for information about either the account balance or specific invoices, depending on knowledge about how customers maintain their accounting records. The negative form is used mostly when the risk of material misstatement is considered low, when a large number of small balances is involved, and when the client's customers can be expected to consider

286 Part Two *The Financial Statement Audit*

EXHIBIT 7.8 Accounts Receivable Aged Trial Balance

DUNDER-MIFFLIN
Accounts Receivable Aged Trial Balance
For Year Ended 12/31/2012
(Prepared by Client)

C-2

	2012 Total Balance	Conf. No.	Date Mailed	Date Rec'd	Current < 30 Days	30–60 Days	Past Due 60–90 Days	> 90 Days
Pay More Paper	$ 173,406.37					$173,406.37		
Nuke Me Office Supplies	11,630.14				$ 11,630.14			
Bet Your Life Printing	718,986.45	1 C	1/15	1/22	718,986.45			
Paper Shack	242,568.88				242,568.88		$ 461.09	
Shreadables	461.09							
Mall-Wart	6,822,725.10	2 C	1/15	1/27	γ5,765,081.85			$1,057,643.25
House of Paper	3,181.49						3,181.49	
Sunshine Office Supplies	1,644.41				1,644.41			
Imelda's Printing	32,023.89	3 E	1/15	1/21	32,023.89			
Hip Hop Invitations	230,932.95					230,932.95		
The Paper Federation	405,846.10				405,846.10			
Office Least	15,026.57	4 E	1/15	1/25	γ(1,388.75)	γ16,415.32		
Lamour Glamor Printing	127,907.18β	5 NR	1/15α	n/a			127,907.18	
Bullseye	1,013,239.57	6 E	1/15	2/2	1,013,239.57			
Peyton's Paper	879.43				879.43			
Total	$16,410,902.71CF				$10,233,296.72	$536,874.60	$746,034.56	$4,894,696.83
	u TB				u	u	u	u

α Second request mailed 2/1.
γ Tested calculation of aging.
C Confirmation received without exception
E Confirmation received with exception. See C-2.1 for follow-up.

β Examined related invoices and shipping documents.
u Footed
CF Crossfooted
TB Agreed to trial balance.

NR Confirmation not returned. See C-3 for application of subsequent cash receipts.

EXHIBIT 7.9
Positive Confirmation Form

Dunder-Mifflin
Scranton, PA

Bullseye
1359 Central Boulevard
Derma, MS 39530
Attn: Accounts Payable Dept.

Our auditor, M. Chael Smith, is making his regular audit of our financial statements. Part of this audit includes direct verification of customer balances.

PLEASE EXAMINE THE DATA BELOW CAREFULLY AND EITHER CONFIRM ITS ACCURACY OR REPORT ANY DIFFERENCES DIRECTLY TO OUR AUDITORS USING THE ENCLOSED REPLY ENVELOPE.

This is not a request for payment. Please do not send your remittance to our auditors.

Your prompt attention to this request will be appreciated.

Samuel Carboy
Samuel Carboy, Controller

The balance due Dunder-Mifflin as of December 31, 2012, is $1,013,239.57 C-2

This balance is correct except as noted below:

Our records indicate that we wrote a check to Dunder-Mibblin on 12/28 for this amount. ✓

Date: 1/21/13   By: Rudy Robinson
                  Title: Accounts Payable

✓ Check Received 1/3/13 RJR

---

the confirmations properly. Auditors must use these confirmations with great care. Occasionally, they use both forms by sending positive confirmations on some (large) customers' accounts and negative confirmations on others (usually smaller account balances).

Getting confirmations delivered to the intended recipient requires auditors' careful attention. Auditors need to control the mailing of the confirmations, including the addresses to which they are sent, and the confirmations should be returned directly to the auditors. The confirmations should normally be addressed to the customer's accounts payable department. There have been cases in which confirmations were mailed to company accomplices, who provided false responses. The auditors should carefully consider features of the reply, such as postmarks, fax and telephone responses, letterhead, e-mail, or other characteristics that may indicate a false response. Auditors should follow up electronic and telephone responses to determine their origin (e.g., returning the telephone call to a known number, looking up telephone numbers to determine addresses, or using a directory to determine the location of a respondent). On the other hand, an electronic confirmation process that creates a secure confirmation environment may mitigate the risks of human intervention and misdirection. For example, encryption, electronic digital

EXHIBIT 7.10
Negative Confirmation Form

Bullseye
1359 Central Boulevard
Derma, MS 39530
Attn: Accounts Payable Dept.

Our auditor, M. Chael Smith, is making his regular audit of our financial statements. Part of this audit includes direct verification of customer balances.

PLEASE EXAMINE THE DATA BELOW CAREFULLY AND COMPARE THEM TO YOUR RECORDS OF YOUR ACCOUNT WITH US. IF THE INFORMATION IS NOT IN AGREEMENT WITH YOUR RECORDS, PLEASE STATE ANY DIFFERENCES BELOW AND RETURN DIRECTLY TO OUR AUDITORS IN THE RETURN ENVELOPE PROVIDED. **IF THE INFORMATION IS CORRECT, NO REPLY IS NECESSARY.**

This is not a request for payment. Please do not send your remittance to our auditors.

Your prompt attention to this request will be appreciated.

Samuel Carboy
Samuel Carboy, Controller

The balance due Dunder-Mufflin as of December 31, 2012, is $1,013,239.57 C-2

This balance is correct except as noted below:
Our records indicate that we wrote a check to Dunder-Mibblin on 12/28 for this amount. ✓

Date: 1/21/13   By: *Rudy Robinson*
                       Title: *Accounts Payable*

✓ *Check Received 1/3/13 RJR*

---

signatures, and procedures to verify website authenticity may improve the security of the electronic confirmation process (AU 9330). Second and third requests should be sent to motivate responses to positive confirmations, and auditors should audit nonresponding customers by alternative procedures. Furthermore, the lack of response to a negative confirmation is no guarantee that the intended recipient received it or read it. Exhibit 7.11 illustrates some common confirmation responses and the appropriate follow-up action.

If an exception cannot be resolved or it appears to indicate a misstatement, auditors should (1) determine the cause of the misstatement, (2) extrapolate the misstatements over the population, and (3) consider whether fraud may have occurred. If similar misstatements could exist, additional procedures are generally necessary to determine the extent of misstatements. In the case of fraud, an extensive investigation may be necessary.[7]

---

[7] "AICPA Practice Alert 03-1: Audit Confirmations," June 2007.

EXHIBIT 7.11
Responses to Positive Confirmations (December 31)

Response	Follow-Up Action
"This amount was paid on December 28th."	This account is probably valid because the check was probably received after year-end. However, it should be treated as an exception and the date of the receipt should be verified.
"We are unable to confirm this amount."	This is treated the same way as a nonresponse and alternative procedures should be performed.
"We returned these items."	This is an exception that should be discussed with the client. The auditor should verify that there are no other returns included in receivables.
"We received these goods on January 3rd."	This is also probably valid because the shipment was probably made in late December. However, this should also be treated as an exception and the shipment should be verified. The auditor should also make sure the goods were removed from the year-end inventory.

Confirmation of receivables may be performed at a date other than the year-end. When confirmation is done at an interim date, the audit firm is able to spread work throughout the year and avoid the pressures of overtime that typically occur during "busy season." In addition, the audit can be completed sooner after the year-end date if confirmations have been done earlier. The primary consideration when planning confirmation of receivables before the balance sheet date is the client's internal control over transactions affecting receivables. When confirmation is performed at an interim date, the following additional procedures should be considered:

1. Obtain a summary of receivables transactions from the interim date to the year-end date and review them for unusual items.
2. Vouch a selected sample of transactions for the period.
3. Obtain a year-end trial balance of receivables, compare it to the interim trial balance, and obtain evidence and explanations for large variations.
4. Consider the necessity for additional confirmations as of the balance sheet date if balances have significantly increased.

Alternative Procedures

Often the client's customers are not willing or able to return the confirmation. They may not be able if, for example, they are on a voucher system that lists payables by invoice instead of by vendor account. The U.S. government is notorious for not returning confirmations because records may be kept at various agencies. In these cases, auditors have to perform alternative procedures to ensure existence. These include examining (1) subsequent cash receipts, (2) sales orders, invoices, and shipping documents, and (3) correspondence files for past due accounts. Examining subsequent cash receipts is a particularly effective test because if the customer paid the account, it provides strong evidence the receivable existed. This examination is often performed even when the customer has confirmed the account. The cash receipt should be traced to the remittance advice and the deposit into cash.

Review for Collectability

Even if the customer confirms that the account exists, this does not necessarily mean that the customer can or will pay it! Therefore, the primary evidence gained from confirmations relates to existence. However, the audit team must review accounts for collectability and determine the adequacy of the allowance for doubtful accounts in support of the *valuation* assertion. To do this, auditors review subsequent cash receipts from the customer, discuss unpaid accounts with the credit manager, and examine the credit files. These should contain the customer's financial statements, credit reports, and correspondence between the client and the customer. Based on this evidence, the audit team estimates the likely amount of nonpayment for the customer, which is included in the estimate of the allowance for doubtful accounts. In addition, an allowance should be estimated for all other customers, perhaps as a percentage of the current accounts with a higher percentage of past due accounts. The auditors compare their estimate to the recorded balance in the allowance account and propose an adjusting entry for the difference.

Cutoff and Sales Returns

Auditors must make sure that sales are recorded in the proper period. To do this, they employ **sales cutoff tests.** Procedures include tracing shipping documents before and after year-end to the sales journal to ensure the sale was recorded in the proper period. Credit memos for returns after year-end are vouched to receiving reports. Any goods returned after year-end that were sold during the year being audited should be deducted from sales.

AUDITING INSIGHT — Time Doesn't Fly

The Securities and Exchange Commission filed an action alleging that **Sirena Apparel Group, Inc.**, a women's swimwear manufacturer, held open the March fiscal quarter until the company had reached its sales target for that period. The fraud was accomplished by resetting the date on the company's computer clock to the end of the month. Manipulation of the computer clock allowed April shipments to be recorded as March revenue because the computer clock controlled the date that was printed on the company's invoices. The computerized system also automatically recorded revenue earned as of the date of the invoice. The bills of lading for the out-of-period shipments reflected April shipping dates. When management learned that the company's independent auditors would be testing shipping cutoff for the March 31 quarter, they instructed a subordinate to create false bills of lading to reflect March shipping dates to conceal the fraud from the auditors.

Source: SEC Accounting and Auditing Enforcement Release No. 1325, September 27, 2000.

Adjusting entries for cutoff errors (i.e., sales recorded for next month's shipments) must be considered carefully because not only are Accounts Receivable and Sales overstated, but also Inventory is understated and Cost of Goods Sold is overstated.

Rights and Obligations

Companies may sell or **factor** their accounts receivable to a financial institution to obtain cash immediately. It is difficult to determine whether receivables have been sold because the customers usually do not know that someone else actually owns their account. The cash goes to the original seller, who passes it on to the factor. Inquiring of management and examining support for large cash receipts is the best way to detect these transactions.

AUDITING INSIGHT — Ambassador to Fraud

The SEC has settled financial fraud charges with Raymond Green, former treasurer and principal financial accounting officer and Barry Budilov, former president, director, and chief executive at defunct **Ambassador Eyewear Group** (an eyeglass frame distributor), which allegedly overstated assets by as much as 35 percent. To compensate for Ambassador's large cash shortfalls, Budilov obtained an asset-based collateralized line of credit. Under the line of credit terms, Ambassador could borrow up to a percentage of the total value of accounts receivable and inventory value. Ambassador continued to encounter cash shortfalls and subsequently began to falsify accounts receivable and inventory values. On November 26, 2004, Green pleaded guilty to two counts of fraud and was sentenced to five years' probation, including eight months of home custody and an order to pay restitution of nearly $17.5 million. On July 12, 2005, Budilov pleaded guilty to four counts of fraud and was sentenced to 27 months in prison, five years' probation, and ordered to repay nearly $17.5 million.

Source: "Mentor to Fraud? Two Former Execs Settle with SEC," CFO.com, September 17, 2007.

Presentation and Disclosure

Once auditors are satisfied that controls have been examined and transactions and balances have been appropriately tested, the job is not over. The accounts in the revenue cycle require certain disclosures. Revenue recognition policies and the amount of the allowance for doubtful accounts are some of the items requiring specific presentation and disclosures. These disclosures must ensure that the presentation and disclosure assertions of *occurrence, rights and obligations, completeness, classification, accuracy and valuation,* and *understandability* have been met.

Some notes about confirmations

- Confirmations of accounts, loans, and notes receivable may not produce sufficient evidence of ownership by the client (rights assertion). Debtors may not be aware that the client sold the accounts, notes, or loans receivable to financial institutions or to the public (collateralized securities). Auditors need to perform additional inquiry and detailed procedures to get evidence of the ownership of the receivables and the appropriateness of disclosures related to financing transactions secured by receivables.
- Although confirmations are most often used for account balances, experienced auditors recognize that confirming a specific transaction, especially a large one, may be more effective. This is especially true if the balance consists primarily of a few large transactions. In your own life, you probably do not know what your current balance is on your credit cards, but you likely remember a recent large purchase (e.g., for textbooks).
- In today's business environment, the receipt of confirmation information by e-mail or fax is becoming more common. Such responses involve additional detection risk relating to the reliability of evidence since the origin and identity of the respondent may be difficult to establish. If the auditor has concerns about the reliability of the information that was received electronically, the auditor should contact the purported sender directly (e.g., by telephone).
- It is also possible for an auditor to receive an oral response to a confirmation. Such a response does not meet the definition of an external confirmation because there is no *direct written response* to the auditor. The auditor should request a written response, and, if one is not forthcoming, the auditor should determine whether alternative audit procedures are warranted.

REVIEW CHECKPOINTS

7.15 Why is it important to emphasize the *existence* assertion when auditing accounts receivable?

7.16 Which audit procedures are usually the most useful for auditing the existence assertion?

7.17 What analytical procedures might be informative regarding the existence assertion?

7.18 Distinguish between positive and negative confirmations. Under what conditions would you expect each type of confirmation to be appropriate?

7.19 What are some justifications for not using confirmations of accounts receivable on a particular audit?

7.20 What special care should be taken with regard to examining the sources of accounts receivable confirmation responses?

7.21 What alternative procedures should be applied to accounts that do not return confirmations?

7.22 What procedures should be performed to determine the adequacy of the allowance for doubtful accounts?

AUDIT RISK MODEL SUMMARY

Now that the control and inherent risk elements for the revenue and collection cycle along with some of the important substantive procedures have been presented, let's examine how an audit team might apply the audit risk model for the *existence* assertion.

Healthy Delights Ice Cream, Inc.

Healthy Delights is a publicly held company that sells health-based ice cream to grocery store chains in the United States. Annual sales have steadily remained at around $100 million. Marsha Fields had been assigned as the senior auditor. Her firm's policy is always to set overall audit risk as low. She knows previous years' errors were few and the food industry is sound. The company is generally profitable; management's compensation is based on long-term performance, not short-term goals; and the overall economy is strong at the time of the audit, so she assesses inherent risk as low to moderate. Controls have been historically strong including hiring of competent people; maximum use of computer technology, which is reviewed by internal auditors; and careful reviews of detailed sales analyses by management. Testing of controls in accordance with *AS 5* found no design or operating deficiencies. Thus, Fields assesses the risk of material misstatement as low. In this situation, she can be comfortable setting detection risk at a moderate to high level. This will allow her to limit her sample of accounts for confirmation to the largest accounts with a small random sample of smaller accounts. The confirmations will be sent at an interim date. She also can rely heavily on analytical procedures. This combination of low risk of material misstatement and moderate to high detection risk should lead Fields to an acceptably low overall audit risk.

FRAUD CASES: EXTENDED AUDIT PROCEDURES (AU 240)

LEARNING OBJECTIVE 7-5
Describe some common errors and frauds in the revenue and collection cycle and design some audit and investigation procedures for detecting them.

The audit processes to gather evidence on the assertions in account balances are called *substantive procedures*. Some amount of substantive procedures must be performed in all audits. Auditors should not totally rely on controls to the exclusion of other procedures. Substantive procedures differ from tests of controls in their basic purpose. Substantive procedures are designed to obtain direct evidence about the dollar amounts in account balances while tests of controls are designed to obtain evidence about the company's performance of its own control activities. Sometimes an audit procedure can be used for both purposes, and when it is, it is called a **dual-purpose procedure**.

Dual-Purpose Nature of Accounts Receivable Confirmations

Accounts receivable confirmation is a substantive procedure designed to obtain evidence of the existence and gross amount (valuation) of customers' balances directly from the customer. If such confirmations show numerous exceptions, auditors are concerned with the controls over the details of sales and cash receipts transactions even if previous control evaluations seemed to show little control risk.

The goal in performing substantive procedures is to detect evidence of any material misstatement due to errors or fraud. If there is a risk of material misstatement involving revenue recognition, auditors should consider confirming contract terms and the absence of side agreements with customers. Items to be considered would be acceptance criteria, delivery and payment terms, and the absence of future or continuing vendor obligations, rights of return, guaranteed resale, and cancellation or refund provisions.

The remainder of this part of the chapter uses a set of cases that provide specific examples of tests of controls and substantive procedures (recalculation, observation, confirmation, inquiry, vouching, tracing, scanning, and analytical procedures). The case stories are better than listing schemes and detection procedures in the abstract.

The cases follow a standard format that first tells about an error or fraud situation in terms of the problem, the audit approach, and the discovery. The first part of each case gives you the "inside story" that auditors seldom know before they perform the audit work. The next part is an "audit approach" section, which discusses the audit objective (assertion), controls, tests of controls, and substantive procedures that could be considered in approaching the situation. The audit approach section presumes that the auditors do not know everything about the situation.

At the end of the chapter, some similar discussion cases are presented and you can write the audit approach to test your ability to design audit procedures for detecting errors and frauds. Appendix 7B is a substantive audit plan for reference.

Case 7.1

The Canny Cashier

PROBLEM

D. Bakel was the assistant controller of Sports Equipment, Inc. (SEI), an equipment retailer. SEI maintained accounts receivable for school districts in the region; otherwise, customers received credit by using their own credit cards.

As company cashier, Bakel received all incoming mail payments on school accounts, credit card accounts, and cash and checks taken over the counter. He prepared the bank deposit, listing all checks and currency, and prepared a remittance worksheet (daily cash report) that showed amounts received, discounts allowed on school accounts, and amounts to credit to the accounts receivable. Another accountant used the remittance worksheet to post credits to the accounts receivable. Bakel delivered the deposit to the bank and reconciled the bank statement. No one else reviewed the deposits or the bank statements except the independent auditors.

Bakel opened a bank account in the name of Sport Equipment Company (SEC) after properly incorporating the company in the secretary of state's office. Over-the-counter cash, checks, and school district payments were taken from the SEI receipts and deposited in the SEC account. (None of the customers noticed the difference between the rubber stamp endorsements for the two similarly named corporations, and neither did the bank.) SEC kept the money a while, earning interest, and then Bakel wrote SEC checks to SEI to replace the "borrowed" funds, in the meantime taking new SEI receipts for deposit to SEC.

Bakel also stole payments made by the school districts, depositing them to SEC. Later he deposited SEC checks in SEI, giving the schools credit, but approved an additional 2 percent discount in the process. Thus, the schools received proper credit later and SEC paid less by the amount of the extra discount.

SEI's bank deposits systematically showed small currency deposits. Bakel was nervous about taking too many checks, so he preferred cash. The deposit slips had to include the SEC checks because bank tellers compare the deposit slip listing to the checks submitted. The remittance worksheet showed different details: Instead of showing SEC checks, it showed receipts from school districts and currency but not many over-the-counter checks from customers.

The transactions became complicated enough that Bakel had to use the office computer to keep track of the school districts that needed to receive credit. There were no vacations for this hardworking cashier because a substitute might notice the discrepancies, and Bakel needed to give the districts credit later.

Over a six-year period, Bakel built up a $150,000 average balance in the Sport Equipment Company (SEC) account that earned a total of $67,500 interest that Sports Equipment, Inc. (SEI) should have earned. By approving the "extra" discounts, Bakel skimmed 2 percent of $1 million in annual sales, for a total of $120,000. Because SEI would have had net income before taxes of about $1.6 million over these six years (about 9 percent of sales), Bakel's embezzlement took about 12.5 percent of the income.

AUDIT APPROACH

Authorization related to cash receipts, custody of cash, recording cash transactions, and bank statement reconciliation should be separate duties designed to prevent errors and frauds. Some supervision and detail review of one or more of these duties should be performed as a next-level control designed to detect errors and frauds, if they have occurred. For example, someone else should prepare the remittance worksheet, or at least the controller should approve the discounts; someone else should prepare the bank reconciliation.

Bakel performed incompatible duties. (While he did not actually perform the recording, Bakel provided the source document—the remittance worksheet—the other accountant used to make the cash and accounts receivable entries.) According to the company president, the "control" was the diligence of "our long-time, trusted, hard-working assistant controller." (*Note:* A vigilant auditor who "thought like a crook" might have been able to imagine ways Bakel could have committed fraud and thus prevented or detected this cash embezzlement and accounts receivable lapping scheme.)

Because the "control" purports to be Bakel's honest and diligent performance of the accounting and control activities that might have been performed by two or more people, the test of controls is an audit of cash receipts transactions as they relate to accounts receivable credit. The dual-direction samples and procedures are these:

Occurrence direction. The auditors selected a sample of customer accounts receivable and vouched payment credits to remittance worksheets and bank deposits, including recalculation of discounts allowed in comparison to sales terms (2 percent), classification (customer name) identification, and correspondence of receipt date to recording date.

Completeness direction. The auditors selected a sample of remittance worksheets (or bank deposits), vouched details to bank deposit slips (trace details to remittance worksheets if the sample is bank deposits), and traced to complete accounting posting in customer accounts receivable.

Because there was a control risk of incorrect accounting, accounts receivable were confirmed as of year-end using positive confirmations. The sample included all school district accounts.

When prompted by notice of an oddity (noted in the following discovery summary), the audit team can use the telephone book, chamber of commerce directory, local criss cross directory, and a visit to the secretary of state's office to determine the location and identity of Sport Equipment Company.

DISCOVERY SUMMARY

The test of controls samples showed four cases of discrepancy, one of which is discussed here.

The auditors sent positive confirmations on all 72 school district accounts. Three of the responses stated the districts had paid the balances before the confirmation date. Follow-up procedures on their accounts receivable credit in the next period showed they had received credit in remittance reports and the bank deposits had shown no checks from the districts but had contained a check from Sports Equipment Company.

Investigation of SEC revealed the connection of Bakel, who was confronted and then confessed.

Bank Deposit Slip		Cash Remittance Report				
		Name	Amount	Discount	AR	Sales
Jones	25	Jones	25	0	0	25
Smith	35	Smith	35	0	0	35
Hill District	980	Hill District	980	20	1,000	0
Sport Equipment	1,563	Marlin District	480	20	500	0
Currency	540	Waco District	768	32	800	0
Deposit	3,143	Currency	855	0	0	855
		Totals	3,143	72	2,300	915

Case 7.2

The Taxman Always Rings Twice

PROBLEM

J. Shelstad was the tax assessor-collector in the Ridge School District, serving a large metropolitan area. The staff processed tax notices on a computerized system and generated 450,000 tax notices each October. An office copy was printed and used to check off "paid" when payments were received. Payments were processed by computer and a master file of "accounts receivable" records (tax assessments, payments) was kept on the computer hard disk.

Shelstad was a good personnel manager and often took over the front desk at lunchtime so the teller staff could enjoy lunch together. During these times, she took payments over the counter, gave the taxpayers a counter receipt, and pocketed some of the money, which was never entered in the computerized system.

Shelstad resigned when she was elected to the Ridge school board. The district's assessor-collector office was eliminated upon the creation of a new countywide tax agency.

The computerized records showed balances due from many taxpayers who had actually paid their taxes. The book of printed notices was not marked "paid" for many taxpayers who had received counter receipts. These records and the daily cash receipts reports (cash receipts journal) were available when the independent auditors had performed the most recent annual audit in April. When Shelstad resigned in August, a power surge permanently destroyed the hard disk receivables file, and the cash receipts journals could not be found.

The new county agency managers noticed that the total of delinquent taxes disclosed in the audited financial statements was much larger than the total turned over to the county attorney for collection and foreclosure.

Shelstad had been the assessor-collector for 15 years. The "good personnel manager" pocketed 100–150 counter payments each year in amounts of $500–$2,500, stealing about $200,000 a year for a total of approximately $2.5 million. The district had assessed about $800–$900 million per year, so the annual theft was less than 1 percent. Nevertheless, the taxpayers got mad.

AUDIT APPROACH

The school district had a respectable system for establishing the initial amounts of taxes receivable. The professional staff of appraisers and the independent appraisal review board established the tax base for each property. The school board set the price (tax rate). The computerized system authorization for billing was validated on these two inputs.

The cash receipts system was well designed, calling for preparation of a daily cash receipts report (cash receipts journal that served as a source input for computerized entry). The "boss," Shelstad, always reviewed this report.

Unfortunately, Shelstad had the opportunity and power to override the controls and become both cash handler and supervisor. She made the decisions about sending delinquent taxes to the county attorney for collection and withheld the ones known to have been paid but stolen.

The auditors performed dual-direction sampling to test the processing of cash receipts.

Occurrence direction. The auditors selected a sample of receivables from the computer hard disk and vouched (1) charges to the appraisal record, recalculating the amount using the authorized tax rate and (2) payments, if any, to the cash receipts journal and bank deposits. (The auditors found no exceptions.)

Completeness direction. The auditors selected a sample of properties from the appraisal rolls and determined that tax notices had been sent and tax receivables (charges) recorded in the computer file. They next selected a sample of cash receipts reports, vouched them to bank deposits of the same amount and date, and traced the payments forward to credits to taxpayers' accounts. They also selected a sample of bank deposits and traced them to cash receipts reports of the same amount and date. Finally, they compared the details on bank deposits to the details on the cash receipts reports to determine whether the same taxpayers appear on both documents. (The auditors found no exceptions.)

The auditors confirmed a sample of unpaid tax balances with taxpayers. In such cases, response rates may not be high, and follow-up procedures determining the ownership (county title files) may need to be performed and new confirmations may need to be sent.

DISCOVERY SUMMARY

Shelstad persuaded the auditors that the true "receivables" were the delinquencies turned over to the county attorney. The confirmation sample and other work were based on this population. Thus, confirmations were not sent to fictitious balances that Shelstad knew had been paid, and the auditors never had the opportunity to receive "I paid" complaints from taxpayers.

Shelstad did not influence the new managers of the countywide tax district. They questioned the discrepancy between the delinquent taxes in the audit report and the lower amount turned over for collection. Because the computer file was not usable, the managers had to use the printed book of tax notices in which paid accounts had been marked "paid." (Shelstad had not marked the stolen ones "paid," so the printed book would agree with the computer file.) Tax due notices were sent

Case 7.3

Bill Often, Bill Early

PROBLEM

McGossage Company experienced profit pressures for two years in a row. Actual profits were squeezed in a recessionary economy, but the company reported net income decreases that were not as severe as other companies' in the industry were.

Sales for orders that had been prepared for shipment but not actually shipped until later were recorded in the grocery products division. Employees backdated the shipping documents. Gross profit on these "sales" was about 30 percent. Customers took discounts on payments, but the company did not record them, leaving the debit balances in the customers' accounts receivable instead of charging them to the sales discounts and allowances account. Company accountants were instructed to wait 60 days before recording discounts taken.

The division vice president and general manager knew about these accounting practices as did a significant number of the 2,500 employees in the division. The division managers were under orders from headquarters to achieve profit objectives they considered unrealistic.

The customers' accounts receivable balances contained amounts due for discounts the customers already had taken. The cash receipts records showed payments received without credit for discounts. Discounts were entered monthly by a special journal entry.

The unshipped goods were on the shipping dock at year-end with papers showing earlier shipping dates.

As misstatements go, some of these were on the materiality borderline. Sales were overstated 0.3 percent and 0.5 percent in the prior and current year, respectively. Accounts receivable were overstated 4 percent and 8 percent, respectively. The combined effect was to overstate the division's net income by 6 percent and 17 percent. Selected data follow:

	One Year Ago*		Current Year*	
	Reported	Actual	Reported	Actual
Sales	$330.0	$329.0	$350.0	$348.0
Discounts expense	1.7	1.8	1.8	2.0
Net income	6.7	6.3	5.4	4.6

*Dollars in millions.

AUDIT APPROACH

The accounting manual should provide instructions to record sales on the date of shipment (or when title passes, if later). Management subverted this control procedure by having shipping employees date the shipping papers incorrectly.

Cash receipts procedures should provide for authorizing and recording discounts when customers take them. Management overrode this control instruction by giving instructions to delay the recording.

Tests of Controls

Questionnaires and inquiries should be used to determine the company's accounting policies. It is possible that employees and managers would lie to the auditors to conceal the policies. It is also possible that pointed questions about revenue recognition and discount recording policies would elicit answers to reveal the practices.

For detail procedures, the auditors select a sample of cash receipts, examine them for authorization, recalculate the customer discounts, and trace them to accounts receivable input for recording the proper amount on the proper date. They select a sample of shipping documents and vouch them to customer orders and then trace them to invoices and to the accounts receivable account with proper amounts on the proper date. These tests follow the tracing direction—starting with data that represent the beginning of transactions (cash receipts, shipping) and tracing them through the company's accounting process.

The audit team should confirm a sample of customer accounts and use analytical procedures to determine relationships of past years' discount expense to a relevant base (sales, sales volume) to calculate an overall test of the discounts expense.

DISCOVERY SUMMARY

The managers lied to the auditors about their revenue and expense timing policies. The sample of shipping documents showed no dating discrepancies because the employees had inserted incorrect dates. The analytical procedures on discounts did not show the misstatement because the historical relationships were too erratic to show a deficient number. However, the sample of cash receipts transactions showed that discounts had not been calculated and recorded at time of receipt. Additional inquiry led to the discovery of the special journal entries and knowledge of the recording delay. Two customers in the sample of 65 confirmations responded with exceptions that turned out to be unrecorded discounts.

Two other customers in the confirmation sample complained that they did not owe for late invoices on December 31. Follow-up showed that the shipments were noticed on the shipping dock. Auditors taking the physical inventory noticed the goods on the shipping dock during the December 31 inventory taking. Inspection revealed the shipping documents dated December 26. When the auditors traced these shipments to the sales recording, they found them recorded **bill and hold** on December 29. (These procedures were performed and the results obtained by a new audit firm in the third year!)

Case 7.4

Thank Goodness It's Friday

PROBLEM

Alpha Brewery Corporation generally has good controls related to authorization of transactions for accounting entry, and the accounting manual has instructions for recording sales transactions in the proper accounting period. The company regularly closes the accounting process each Friday at 5 P.M. to prepare weekly management reports. The year-end date (cutoff date) is December 31, and this year, December 31 was a Monday. However, the accounting was performed through Friday as usual and the accounts were closed for the year on January 4.

AUDIT TRAIL

All entries were properly dated after December 31, including the sales invoices, cash receipts, and shipping documents. However, the trial balance from which the financial statements were prepared was dated December 31, (this year). Nobody noticed the slip of a few days because the Friday closing was normal.

Alpha recorded sales of $672,000 and gross profit of $268,800 over the January 1–4 period. Cash collections on customers' accounts were recorded in the amount of $800,000.

AUDIT APPROACH

The company had in place the proper instructions for people to date transactions on the actual date on which they occurred, to enter sales and cost of goods sold on the day of shipment, and to enter cash receipts on the day received in the company offices. An accounting supervisor should have checked the entries through Friday to make sure the dates corresponded with the actual events and that the accounts for the year were closed with Monday's transactions.

In this case, the auditors need to be aware of the company's weekly routine closing and the possibility that the December 31 date might cause a problem. Asking the question: "Did you cut off the accounting on Monday night this week?" might elicit the "Oh, we forgot!" response.

Otherwise, it is normal to sample transactions around the year-end date to determine whether they were recorded in the proper accounting period.

The Procedure

Select transactions 7–10 days before and after the year-end date and inspect the dates on supporting documentation for evidence of accounting in the proper period.

The audit for sales overstatement is partly accomplished by auditing the cash and accounts receivable at December 31 for overstatement. Confirm a sample of accounts receivable. If the accounts are too large, the auditors expect the debtors to say so, thus leading to detection of sales overstatements.

Cash overstatement is audited by auditing the bank reconciliation to see whether deposits in transit (the deposits sent late in December) actually cleared the bank early in January. Obviously, the January 4 cash collections could not reach the bank until at least Monday, January 7. That is too long for a December 31 deposit to be in transit to a local bank.

The completeness of sales recordings is audited by selecting a sample of sales transactions (and supporting shipping documents) in the early part of the next accounting period (January next year). One way this year's sales could be incomplete would be to postpone recording December shipments until January, and this procedure will detect those deffered sales if the shipping documents are dated properly.

The completeness of cash collections (and accounts receivable credits) is examined by auditing the cash deposits early in January to see whether there is any sign of holding cash without entry until January.

In this case, the existence objective is more significant for discovery of the problem than the completeness objective. After all, the January 1–4 sales, shipments, and cash collections did not "exist" in December this year.

DISCOVERY SUMMARY

The test of controls sample from the days before and after December 31 quickly revealed the problem. Company accounting personnel were embarrassed, but there had been no effort to misstate the financial statements. This was a simple error. The company readily made the following adjustment:

	Debit	Credit
Sales	$672,000	
Inventory	403,200	
Accounts receivable	800,000	
Accounts receivable		$672,000
Cost of goods sold		403,200
Cash		800,000

REVIEW CHECKPOINTS

7.23 What are the goals of dual-direction testing regarding an audit of the accounts receivable and cash collection system?

7.24 In the case of The Canny Cashier, name one control that could have revealed signs of the embezzlement.

7.25 What feature(s) could SEI have installed in its cash receipts internal controls that would have been expected to prevent the cash receipts journal and recorded cash sales from reflecting more than the amount shown on the daily deposit slips?

7.26 In the case of The Taxman Always Rings Twice, what information could have been obtained from confirmations directed to the real population of delinquent accounts?

7.27 In the case of Bill Often, Bill Early, what information might have been obtained from inquiries? From tests of controls? From observations? From confirmations?

7.28 With reference to the case of Thank Goodness It's Friday, what contribution could an understanding of the business and the management reporting system have made to discovery of the open cash receipts journal cutoff error?

AUDITING INSIGHT — PCAOB Inspections and the Revenue and Collections Cycle

- In this audit, due to deficiencies in auditing revenue and the fair value of investments, the Firm failed to obtain sufficient competent evidential matter to support its audit opinions on the issuer's financial statements and internal control over financial reporting.
- The Firm's level of reliance on internal controls when testing revenue was not supported adequately because the Firm failed to identify and test certain relevant controls over the existence and valuation assertions.
- The issuer allocated revenues . . . based upon the issuer's list prices, which, according to the Firm, the issuer asserted were indicative of the relative fair values of each of the elements. Data in the Firm's work papers, however, indicated that the issuer sold separate elements at amounts that varied significantly from its price list. The Firm failed to test the issuer's assertion that the list prices were representative of the fair value.
- In addition, while the Firm tested certain revenue transactions that occurred during the first seven months of the year, it failed to perform roll-forward procedures for the remaining five months of the year or to adequately test revenues and accounts receivable at year end as the year-end procedures were limited to analytical procedures and certain cash receipts testing.
- The Firm failed . . . to obtain sufficient competent evidential matter to support its audit opinion—The issuer entered into multiple-element software sales contracts that generally included a license fee and a maintenance element. Documentation of the issuer's revenue recognition policies was limited to an issuer-prepared memorandum dated in 2002. Since that time, the issuer has acquired three additional entities; however, the Firm failed to consider the appropriateness of the issuer's methods of recognizing revenues with respect to each acquired entity's unique software license and maintenance contracts. In addition, there was no evidence in the audit documentation, and no persuasive other evidence, that the Firm had assessed whether a change in a maintenance renewal rate on its standard price list affected the timing of the issuer's recognition of revenue.
- The Firm sent confirmations to test accounts receivable and identified errors based on the responses; however, the Firm failed to adequately evaluate the extent of the errors. The Firm noted errors both in invoices with debit balances and in invoices with credit balances. The Firm estimated the total amount of the errors in the debit balances and performed certain procedures to evaluate the errors noted in the credit balances; however, the Firm failed to estimate a total amount of the errors noted in the credit balances in order to adequately evaluate the issuer's assertion that the errors netted to an immaterial amount.
- The Firm failed to perform sufficient procedures to test the issuer's allowance for notes and accounts receivable. The Firm failed to test the reasonableness of the issuer-applied specific reserve percentages, other than by comparing them to prior years, obtaining issuer-prepared schedules, and holding discussions with management. While the Firm also performed analytical procedures in support of its testing, these procedures lacked sufficient precision to detect misstatements that might, individually or in aggregate, be material. In addition, there was no evidence in the audit documentation, and no persuasive evidence, that the firm had tested the issuer's aging of notes receivable.
- The Firm failed in the following respects to obtain sufficient competent evidential matter to support its audit opinion:
  1. The Firm's audit procedures to test revenue consisted primarily of analytical procedures. The Firm analyzed revenue at the companywide level, even though the issuer operated in more than 250 locations and provided different products and services. The Firm's analytical procedures were therefore not disaggregated to a level that would provide the Firm with reasonable assurance of detecting misstatements that are material, individually or when aggregated with other misstatements. Further, the Firm failed to seek corroboration of management's explanation for a difference from the Firm's expectation that was greater than its threshold of significant differences.
  2. To test accounts receivable, the Firm performed substantive analytical procedures rather than sending confirmation requests. These analytical procedures consisted primarily of comparing reported subsequent cash receipts to the Firm's expectation of subsequent cash receipts. The reported subsequent cash receipts differed from the Firm's expectation by an amount greater than the Firm's established threshold of significant differences. The Firm revised its expectation based upon its discussions with the issuer. The reported cash receipts were within this revised expectation; however, the Firm failed to obtain corroboration of management's explanations that resulted in the revised expectation.
- One issuer had numerous foreign locations, which accounted for over 20 percent of the issuer's revenue. The Firm did not visit any of the foreign locations in connection with the audit, nor did it use the work of its international affiliates or other auditors in reporting on the issuer's financial statements in the year under audit.
- The Firm limited its tests of the existence and accuracy of accounts receivable to tests of controls and analytical procedures. The analytical procedures did not qualify as substantive analytical procedures because there was no evidence in the audit documentation, and no persuasive other evidence, that the Firm had established precise enough expectations or obtained corroboration of management's explanations of certain significant differences. Further, the Firm failed to perform other substantive tests of significant receivables.

Source: 2010 PCAOB Inspection of BDO Seidman; 2005 PCAOB Inspection of Deloitte & Touche; 2006–2008 PCAOB Inspection of Ernst & Young; 2005–2008, 2010 Inspection of KPMG; and 2005 and 2010 Inspection of PricewaterhouseCoopers. All reports can be found on the PCAOB's website www.pcaob.org/Inspections/Public_Reports/index.aspx.

Summary

The revenue and collection cycle consists of customer order processing, credit checking, shipping goods, billing customers, accounting for accounts receivable, and collecting and accounting for cash receipts. Companies reduce control risk by having a suitable separation of authorization, custody, recording, and periodic reconciliation duties. Error-checking activities of comparing customer orders and shipping documents are important for billing customers the correct prices for the delivered quantities. Otherwise, many things could go wrong—ranging from making sales to fictitious customers or customers with bad credit to erroneous billings for the wrong quantities at the wrong prices at the wrong time.

Confirmation is the primary substantive audit procedure accompanied by analytical procedures, application of subsequent cash receipts, and other alternative procedures. Confirmations of loans, accounts receivable, and notes receivable are required unless auditors can justify substituting other procedures in the circumstances of a particular audit. Confirmations for accounts and notes receivable can be in positive or negative form, and the positive form may be a blank confirmation. Confirmations yield evidence about *existence* and gross *valuation*. Other procedures must be undertaken to audit the collectability of the accounts. Nevertheless, confirmations can give some clues about collectability when customers tell about balances in dispute. Confirmations of accounts, notes, and loans receivable should not be used as the only evidence of the ownership (*rights* assertions) of these financial assets.

Although these procedures may seem like common sense, auditing the revenue and collection cycle is not straightforward. The following Auditing Insight discusses some deficiencies the PCAOB noted in its inspections of Big Four audit firms regarding audits of this cycle. Note that these issues can involve more than a slap on the wrist and added staff training. In December 2007, the PCAOB fined Deloitte & Touche $1 million for failing to exercise due professional care and obtain sufficient evidential matter regarding revenues in the audit of **Ligand Pharmaceuticals.**

Key Terms

aged trial balance: A schedule that lists each individual receivable and indicates whether it is current or past due and if past due, for how long. The total should equal the accounts receivable general ledger balance, 278

bill and hold: A fraudulent financial reporting activity by which a company recognizes a sale even though it does not ship the merchandise to the customer but holds it in its own warehouse, 297

bill of lading: A contract between a seller and a common carrier to verify shipment of goods, 276

dual-purpose procedure: An audit procedure that simultaneously serves the substantive purpose (obtain direct evidence about the dollar amounts in account balances) and the test of controls purpose (obtain evidence about the company's performance of its own control activities), 292

factor: The action to sell accounts receivable to another party (the factor) at a discount from face value, 290

negative confirmation: A form sent to a customer by auditors requesting that the customer respond only if the balance shown on it is incorrect, 285

packing slip: A document included with a shipment that shows the description and quantity of the goods being shipped, 276

positive confirmation: A letter sent to a customer by auditors requesting that the customer respond whether the balance shown on it is correct or not, 285

revenue recognition: The recording of revenues in the general ledger, often done fraudulently by schemes such as bill and hold, 271

sales cutoff tests: The tests that ensure that sales are recorded in the proper period—generally, when they are shipped—and that the cost of sales is recorded and removed from inventory, 290

sales invoice: A bill sent to customers for payment showing the amount due and payment terms, 276

Multiple-Choice Questions for Practice and Review

 All applicable Exercises and Problems are available with McGraw-Hill's *Connect® Accounting*

LO 7-1
7.29 Revenues are normally considered to have been earned when
 a. All possibility of return has expired.
 b. The company has substantially accomplished what it must to be entitled to the benefits.
 c. The cash is collected.
 d. Goods have been shipped.

LO 7-3
7.30 Sales are normally recorded on the date of the
 a. Customer purchase order.
 b. Bill of lading.
 c. Sales invoice.
 d. Payment check.

LO 7-2
7.31 When auditing the revenue and collection cycle, auditors normally select balances to confirm from the
 a. Sales journal.
 b. Accounts receivable listing.
 c. General ledger.
 d. Cash receipts listing.

LO 7-2
7.32 Which of the following accounts is not normally part of the revenue and collection cycle?
 a. Sales
 b. Accounts Receivable.
 c. Cash.
 d. Purchases Returns and Allowances

LO 7-3
7.33 The control procedure "credit sales approved by credit department" is directed toward which transaction assertion?
 a. Occurrence
 b. Completeness
 c. Accuracy
 d. Cutoff

LO 7-3
7.34 Which of the following would be the best protection for a company that wishes to prevent the "lapping" of trade accounts receivable?
 a. Separate duties so that the bookkeeper in charge of the general ledger has no access to incoming mail.
 b. Separate duties so that no employee has access to both checks from customers and currency from daily cash receipts.
 c. Have customers send payments directly to the company's depository bank.
 d. Request that customer's payment checks be made payable to the company and addressed to the treasurer.

LO 7-3
7.35 Which of the following internal control activities will most likely prevent the concealment of a cash shortage by improperly writing off a trade account receivable?
 a. Write-offs must be approved by a responsible officer after review of credit department recommendations and supporting evidence.
 b. Write-offs must be supported by an aging schedule showing that only receivables overdue several months have been written off.
 c. Write-offs must be approved by the cashier who is in a position to know whether the receivables have, in fact, been collected.
 d. Write-offs must be authorized by company field sales employees who are in a position to determine customers' financial standing.

LO 7-4

7.36 Auditors sometimes use comparisons of ratios as audit evidence. An unexplained decrease in the ratio of gross profit to sales may suggest which of the following possibilities?

a. Unrecorded purchases.

b. Unrecorded sales.

c. Merchandise purchases being charged to selling and general expense.

d. Fictitious sales.

LO 7-3

7.37 An audit team is auditing sales transactions. One step is to vouch a sample of debit entries from the accounts receivable subsidiary ledger back to the supporting sales invoices. The purpose of this audit procedure is to establish that

a. Sales invoices represent bona fide sales.

b. All sales have been recorded.

c. All sales invoices have been properly posted to customer accounts.

d. Entries in the accounts receivable subsidiary ledger were properly invoiced.

Use the following information to answer questions 7.38 and 7.39:

An auditor noted that client sales increased 10 percent for the year. At the same time, Cost of Goods Sold as a percentage of sales had decreased from 45 percent to 40 percent and year-end accounts receivable had increased by 8 percent.

LO 7-4

7.38 Based on this information, the auditor is most likely concerned about

a. Unrecorded costs.

b. Improper credit approvals.

c. Improper sales cutoff.

d. Fictitious sales.

LO 7-2

7.39 Based on this information, the auditor interviewed the sales manager, who stated that the increase in sales without a corresponding increase in cost of goods sold was due to a price increase enacted by the company during the year. How would the auditor test the sales manager's representation?

a. Perform additional inquiries with sales personnel.

b. Obtain copies of all price lists in use during the year and vouch the prices to sales invoices.

c. Send confirmations asking customers about unit prices paid for product.

d. Vouch vender invoices to payments made after year-end.

LO 7-5

7.40 To conceal defalcations involving receivables, a dishonest bookkeeper might charge which of the following accounts?

a. Miscellaneous income.

b. Petty cash.

c. Miscellaneous expense.

d. Sales returns.

LO 7-4

7.41 Which of the following responses to an accounts receivable confirmation at December 31 would cause an audit team the most concern?

a. "This amount was paid on December 30."

b. "We received this shipment on January 2."

c. "These goods were returned for credit on November 15."

d. "The balance does not reflect our sales discount for paying by January 5."

LO 7-4

7.42 A client has a separate sales group for its largest "preferred" customers, a select group of customers that normally make purchases in excess of $250,000 and often have accounts receivable balances in excess of $1 million. Which of the following audit procedures would the auditor most likely perform?

a. Prepare a schedule of purchases and payments for these customers.

b. Send out negative confirmations on a large sample of these customers.

c. Inquire of the sales manager regarding the accounts receivable terms.

d. Send out positive confirmations on a large sample of these customers.

LO 7-2 7.43 Audit documentation often includes a client-prepared, aged trial balance of accounts receivable as of the balance sheet date. The audit team uses this aging primarily to
   a. Evaluate internal control over credit sales.
   b. Test the accuracy of recorded charge sales.
   c. Estimate credit losses.
   d. Verify the existence of the recorded receivables.

LO 7-4 7.44 Which of the following might be detected by auditors' cutoff review and examination of sales journal entries for several days prior to the balance sheet date?
   a. Lapping year-end accounts receivable.
   b. Inflating sales for the year.
   c. Kiting bank balances.
   d. Misappropriating merchandise.

LO 7-4 7.45 Confirmation of individual accounts receivable balances directly with debtors will, of itself, normally provide the strongest evidence concerning the
   a. Collectability of the balances confirmed.
   b. Ownership of the balances confirmed.
   c. Existence of the balances confirmed.
   d. Internal control over balances confirmed.

LO 7-2 7.46 Which of the following is the best reason for prenumbering in numerical sequence documents such as sales orders, shipping documents, and sales invoices?
   a. Enables company personnel to determine the accuracy of each document.
   b. Enables personnel to determine the proper period recording of sales revenue and receivables.
   c. Enables personnel to check the numerical sequence for missing documents and unrecorded transactions.
   d. Enables personnel to determine the validity of recorded transactions.

LO 7-3 7.47 When a sample of customer accounts receivable is selected for vouching debits, auditors will vouch them to
   a. Sales invoices with shipping documents and customer sales invoices.
   b. Records of accounts receivable write-offs.
   c. Cash remittance lists and bank deposit slips.
   d. Credit files and reports.

LO 7-4 7.48 In the audit of accounts receivable, the most important emphasis should be on the
   a. Completeness assertion.
   b. Existence assertion.
   c. Rights and obligations assertion.
   d. Presentation and disclosure assertion.

LO 7-4 7.49 When accounts receivable are confirmed at an interim date, auditors need not be concerned with
   a. Obtaining a summary of receivables transactions from the interim date to the year-end date.
   b. Obtaining a year-end trial balance of receivables, comparing it to the interim trial balance, and obtaining evidence and explanations for large variations.
   c. Sending negative confirmations to all customers as of the year-end date.
   d. Considering the necessity for some additional confirmations as of the balance sheet date if balances have increased materially.

LO 7-4 7.50 The negative request form of accounts receivable confirmation is useful particularly when the

Assessed Level of Risk of Material Misstatement Relating to Receivables Is	Number of Small Balances Is	Proper Consideration by the Recipient Is
a. Low	Many	Likely
b. Low	Few	Unlikely
c. High	Few	Likely
d. High	Many	Likely

(AICPA adapted)

LO 7-3

7.51 When an audit team traces a sample of shipping documents to the related sales invoice copies, they are trying to find relevant evidence that
   a. Shipments to customers were invoiced.
   b. Shipments to customers were recorded as sales.
   c. Recorded sales were shipped.
   d. Invoiced sales were shipped.

(AICPA adapted)

LO 7-2

7.52 Write-offs of doubtful accounts should be approved by
   a. The salesperson.
   b. The credit manager.
   c. The treasurer.
   d. The cashier.

LO 7-4

7.53 When an audit team does not receive a response on a positive accounts receivable confirmation, auditors should do all of the following except
   a. Send a second request.
   b. Do nothing for immaterial balances.
   c. Examine shipping documents.
   d. Examine client correspondence files.

LO 7-5

7.54 Cash receipts from sales on account have been misappropriated. Which of the following acts would conceal this defalcation and be least likely to be detected by an auditor?
   a. Understating the sales journal.
   b. Overstating the accounts receivable control account.
   c. Overstating the accounts receivable subsidiary ledger.
   d. Understating the cash receipts journal.

(AICPA adapted)

LO 7-3

7.55 Which of the following internal control activities most likely would deter lapping of collections from customers?
   a. Independent internal verification of dates of entry in the cash receipts journal with dates of daily cash summaries.
   b. Authorization of write-offs of uncollectable accounts by a supervisor independent of credit approval.
   c. Separation of duties between receiving cash and posting the accounts receivable ledger.
   d. Supervisory comparison of the daily cash summary with the sum of the cash receipts journal entries.

(AICPA adapted)

LO 7-4

7.56 The financial records of the Movitz Company show that R. Dennis owes $4,100 on an account receivable. An independent audit is being carried out, and the auditors send a positive confirmation to R. Dennis. What is the most likely reason as to why a positive confirmation rather than a negative confirmation was used here?
   a. Control risk was particularly low for accounts receivable.
   b. Inherent risk was particularly high for accounts receivable.
   c. Dennis's account was not yet due.
   d. Dennis's account was not with a related party.

Exercises and Problems

 All applicable Exercises and Problems are available with McGraw-Hill's *Connect® Accounting*

LO 7-2

7.57 **Control Objectives and Procedures Associations.** Exhibit 7.57.1 contains an arrangement of examples of transaction errors (lettered a–g) and a set of client control procedures and devices (numbered 1–15). You should photocopy the exhibit page or obtain a full-size copy from your instructor to complete the following requirements.

Required:
   a. Opposite the examples of transaction errors lettered a–g, write the name of the transaction assertion clients wish to achieve to prevent, detect, or correct the error.
   b. Opposite each numbered control procedure, place an "X" in the column that identifies the error(s) the procedure is likely to control by prevention, detection, or correction.

EXHIBIT 7.57.1

a.	Sales recorded, goods not shipped
b.	Goods shipped, sales not recorded
c.	Goods shipped to a bad credit risk customer
d.	Sales billed at the wrong price or wrong quantity
e.	Product line A sales recorded as Product line B
f.	Failure to post charges to customers for sales
g.	January sales recorded in December

CONTROL PROCEDURES

1. Sales order approved for credit
2. Prenumbered shipping doc prepared. sequence checked
3. Shipping document quantity compared to sales invoice
4. Prenumbered sales invoices, sequence checked
5. Sales invoice checked to sales order
6. Invoiced prices compared to approved price list
7. General ledger code checked for sales product lines
8. Sales dollar batch totals compared to sales journal
9. Periodic sales total compared to same period accounts receivable postings
10. Accountants have instructions to date sales on the date of shipment
11. Sales entry date compared to shipping doc date
12. Accounts receivable subsidiary totaled and reconciled to accounts receivable control account
13. Intercompany accounts reconciled with subsidiary company records
14. Credit files updated for customer payment history
15. Overdue customer accounts investigated for collection

LO 7-3

7.58 **Control Assertion Associations.** Exhibit 7.57.1 contains an arrangement of examples of transaction errors (lettered a–g) and a set of client control procedures and devices (numbered 1–15).

Required:
For each error/control objective, identify the assertion about classes of transactions and events most benefited by the control.

LO 7-3

7.59 **Client Control Procedures and Audit Tests of Controls.** Exhibit 7.57.1 contains an arrangement of examples of transaction errors (lettered a–g) and a set of client control procedures and devices (numbered 1–15).

Required:
For each client control procedure numbered 1–15, write a test of controls that could produce evidence on the question of whether the client's control procedure has been implemented and is in operation.

LO 7-4

7.60 **Confirmation of Trade Accounts Receivable.** L. King, CPA, is auditing the financial statements of Cycle Company, a client that has receivables from customers arising from the sale of goods in the normal course of business. King is aware that the confirmation of accounts receivable is a generally accepted auditing procedure.

Required:
a. Under what circumstances could King justify omitting the confirmation of Cycle's accounts receivable?
b. In designing confirmation requests, what factors are likely to affect King's assessment of the reliability of confirmations that King sends?
c. What alternative procedures could King consider performing when replies to positive confirmation requests are not received?

LO 7-4

7.61 Audit Objectives and Procedures for Accounts Receivable. In the audit of accounts receivable, auditors develop specific audit assertions related to the receivables. They then design specific substantive procedures to obtain evidence about each of these assertions. Here is a selection of accounts receivable assertions:

a. Accounts receivable represent all amounts owed to the client company at the balance sheet date.

b. The client company has a legal right to all accounts receivable at the balance sheet date.

c. Accounts receivable are stated at net realizable value.

d. Accounts receivable are properly described and presented in the financial statements.

Required:

For each of these assertions, select the following audit procedure (numbered 1–7) that is best suited for the audit plan. Select only one procedure for each audit objective. A procedure may be selected once, not at all, or more than once.

1. Analyze the relationship of accounts receivable and sales and compare with relationships for preceding periods.

2. Perform sales cutoff tests to obtain assurance that sales transactions and corresponding entries for inventories and cost of goods sold are recorded in the same and proper period.

3. Review the aged trial balance for significant past due accounts.

4. Obtain an understanding of the business purpose of transactions that resulted in accounts receivable balances.

5. Review loan agreements for indications of whether accounts receivable have been factored or pledged.

6. Review the accounts receivable trial balance for amounts due from officers and employees.

7. Analyze unusual relationships between monthly accounts receivable and monthly accounts payable balances.

(AICPA adapted)

LO 7-5

7.62 Overstated Sales and Accounts Receivable. This case is designed like the ones in the chapter. Your assignment is to write the "audit approach" portion of the case, organized around these sections:

Objective. Express the objective in terms of the facts supposedly asserted in financial records, accounts, and statements.

Control. Write a brief explanation of desirable controls, missing controls, and especially the kinds of "deviations" that might arise from the situation described in the case.

Tests of controls. Write some procedures for getting evidence about existing controls, especially procedures that could discover deviations from controls. If there are no controls to test, then there are no procedures to perform; go then to the next section. A "procedure" should instruct someone about the source(s) of evidence to tap and the work to do.

Audit of balance. Write some procedures for getting evidence about the existence, completeness, valuation, ownership, or disclosure assertions identified in your objective section above.

Discovery summary. Write a short statement about the discovery you expect to accomplish with your procedures.

Ring around the Revenue

Mattel Toy Manufacturing Company had experienced several years of good business. Income had increased steadily and the common stock was a favorite among investors. Management had confidently predicted continued growth and prosperity. However, business turned worse instead of better. Competition became fierce.

In earlier years, Mattel had accommodated a few large retail customers with the practice of field warehousing coupled with a "bill and hold" accounting procedure. These large retail customers executed noncancelable written agreements, asserting their purchase of toys and their obligation to pay. The toys were not actually shipped because the customers did not have available warehouse space. They were set aside in segregated areas on the Mattel premises and identified as the customers' property. Mattel would later ship the toys to various retail locations upon instructions from the customers. The "field warehousing" was explained as Mattel's serving as a temporary warehouse and storage location for the customers' toys. In the related bill and hold accounting procedure, Mattel prepared invoices billing the customers, mailed the invoices to the customers, and recorded the sales and accounts receivable.

When business took a downturn, Mattel expanded its field warehousing and its bill and hold accounting practices. Invoices were recorded for customers who did not execute the written agreements used in previous arrangements. Some customers signed the noncancelable written agreements with clauses permitting subsequent inspection, acceptance, and determination of discounted prices. The toys were not always set aside in separate areas, and this failure later gave shipping employees problems with identifying shipments of toys that had been "sold" earlier and those that had not.

Mattel also engaged in overbilling. Customers who ordered closeout toys at discounted prices were billed at regular prices, even though the customers' orders showed the discounted prices agreed by Mattel sales representatives.

In a few cases, the bill and hold invoices and the closeout sales were billed and recorded in duplicate. In most cases, the customers' invoices were addressed and mailed to specific individuals in the customers' management instead of the routine mailing to the customers' accounts payable departments.

Audit trail. The field warehousing arrangements were well known and acknowledged in the Mattel accounting manual. Related invoices were stamped "bill and hold." Customer orders and agreements were attached in a document file. Sales of closeout toys also were stamped "closeout," indicating the regular prices (basis for salespersons' commissions) and the invoice prices. Otherwise, the accounting for sales and accounts receivable was unexceptional. Efforts to record these sales in January (last month of the fiscal year) caused the month's sales revenue to be 35 percent higher than the January of the previous year.

In the early years of the practice, inventory sold under the field warehousing arrangements (both regular and closeout toys) was segregated and identified. The shipping orders for these toys left the "carrier name" and "shipping date" blank, even though they were signed and dated by a company employee in the spaces for the company representative and the carrier representative signatures.

The lack of inventory segregation caused problems for the company. After the fiscal year-end, Mattel solved the problem by reversing $6.9 million of the $14 million bill and hold sales. This caused another problem because the reversal was larger than the month's sales, causing the sales revenue for the first month of the next year to be a negative number!

Amount. Company officials gave persuasive reasons for the validity of recognizing sales revenue and receivables on the bill and hold procedure and field warehousing. After considering the facts and circumstances, the company's auditors agreed that the accounting practices appropriately accounted for revenue and receivables.

Mattel's abuse of the practices caused financial statements to be materially misstated. In January of the year in question, the company overstated sales by about $14 million, or 5 percent of the sales that should have been recorded. The gross profit of $7 million on these sales caused the income to be overstated by about 40 percent.

LO 7-4 7.63 **CAATs Application—Receivables Confirmation.** You are using computer audit software to prepare accounts receivable confirmations during the annual audit of the Eastern Sunrise Services Club. The company has the following data files:

Master file—debtor credit record.

Master file—debtor name and address.

Master file—account detail:

    Ledger number.

    Sales code.

    Customer account number.

    Date of last billing.

    Balance (gross).

    Discount available to customer (memo account only).

    Date of last purchase.

The discount field represents the amount of discount available to the customer if the customer pays within 30 days of the invoicing date. The discount field is cleared for expired amounts during the daily updating. You have determined that this is properly executed.

Required:

From the data files shown, list the information that you would include on the confirmation requests. Identify the file from which the information can be obtained.

LO 7-2

7.64 **Rock Island Quarry—Evidence Collection in an Online System.** Your firm has audited the Rock Island Quarry Company for several years. Rock Island's main revenue comes from selling crushed rock to construction companies from several quarries owned by the company in Illinois and Iowa. The rock is priced by weight, quality, and crushed size.

Past procedure. Trucks owned by purchasing contractors or by Rock Island needed to display a current certified empty weight receipt or be weighed in. The quarry yard weigh master recorded the empty weight on a handwritten "scale ticket" along with the purchasing company name, the truck number, and the date. After the truck was loaded, it was required to leave via the scale where the loaded weight and rock grade were recorded on the scale tickets. The scale tickets were sorted weekly by grade and manually recorded on a summary sheet that was forwarded to the home office. Scale tickets were prenumbered and an accountant in the home office checked the sequence for missing numbers.

Revenue (and receivables) audit procedures involved evaluating the controls at selected quarries (rotated each year) and vouching a statistical sample of scale tickets to weekly summaries. Weekly summaries were traced through pricing and invoicing to the general ledger on a sample basis, and general ledger entries were vouched back to weekly summaries on a sample basis. Few material discrepancies were found.

New procedures. At the beginning of the current year, Rock Island converted to a local area network of personal computers to gather the information formerly entered manually on the scale ticket. This conversion was done with your knowledge but without your advice or input. Now all entering trucks must weigh in. The yard weigh master enters "NEW" on the terminal keyboard and a form appears on the screen that is similar to the old scale ticket except that the quarry number, transaction number, date, and incoming empty weight are automatically entered. Customer and truck numbers are keyed in. After the weigh-in, the weigh master enters "HOLD" through the terminal. The weight ticket record is stored in the computer until weigh-out.

When a truck is loaded and stops on the scale, the weigh master enters "OLD" and a directory of all open transactions appears on the screen. The weigh master selects the proper one and enters "OUT." The truck out-weighs and the rock weights are computed and entered automatically. The weigh master must enter the proper number for the rock grade but cannot change any automatically entered field. When satisfied that the screen weight ticket is correct, the weigh master enters "SOLD," and the transaction is automatically transmitted to the home office computer, and the appropriate accounting database elements are updated. One copy of a scale ticket is printed and given to the truck driver. Rock Island keeps no written evidence of the sale.

Required:

It is now midyear for Rock Island, and you are planning for this year's audit.

a. What control procedures (manual and computerized) should you expect to find in this system for recording quarry sales?

b. The computer programs that process the rock sales and perform the accounting reside at the home office and at the quarries. What implication does this have for your planned audit procedures?

c. What are you going to do to gather substantive audit evidence now that there are no written scale tickets?

LO 7-1

7.65 **Organizing a Risk Analysis.** You are the director of internal auditing of a large municipal hospital. You receive monthly financial reports prepared by the accounting department and your review of them has shown that total accounts receivable from patients has steadily and rapidly increased over the past eight months.

Other information in the reports shows the following conditions:

a. The number of available hospital beds has not changed.

b. The bed occupancy rate has not changed.

c. Hospital billing rates have not changed significantly.

d. The hospitalization insurance contracts have not changed since the last modification 12 months ago.

Your internal audit department audited the accounts receivable 10 months ago. The audit file for that assignment contains financial information, a record of the risk analysis, documentation of the study and evaluation of management and internal risk mitigation controls, documentation of the evidence-gathering procedures used to produce evidence about the existence and collectability of the accounts, and a copy of your report, which commented favorably on the controls and collectability of the receivables.

However, the current increase in receivables has alerted you to a need for another audit so that things will not get out of hand. You remember news stories last year about the manager of the city water system who got into big trouble because his accounting department double-billed all the residential customers for three months.

Required:

You plan to perform a risk analysis to get a handle on the problem if one indeed exists. Write a memo to your senior auditor listing at least eight questions to use to guide and direct the risk analysis. (*Hint*: The questions used last year were organized under these headings: (1) Who does the accounts receivable accounting? (2) What information processing procedures and policies are in effect? and (3) How is the accounts receivable accounting done? This time, you will add a fourth category: What financial or economic events have occurred in the last 10 months?)

(CIA adapted)

LO 7-5

7.66 **Study and Evaluation of Management Control.** The study and evaluation of management risk mitigation control is not easy. First, auditors must determine the risks and the controls subject to audit. Then they must find a standard by which performance of the control can be evaluated. Next they must specify procedures to obtain the evidence on which an evaluation can be based. Insofar as possible, the standards and related evidence must be quantified. The following description gives certain information (in italics) that internal auditors would know about or be able to determine on their own. Fulfilling the requirement thus amounts to taking some information from the scenario and figuring out other things by using accountants' and auditors' common sense.

The Scenario

Ace Corporation ships building materials to more than a thousand wholesale and retail customers in a five-state region. The company's normal credit terms are net/30 days and no cash discounts are offered. Fred Clark is the chief financial officer, and he is concerned about risks related to maintaining control over customer credit. In particular, he has stated two management control principles for this purpose.

1. Sales are to be billed to customers accurately and promptly. *Fred knows that errors will occur but thinks company personnel ought to be able to hold quantity, unit price, and arithmetic errors down to 3 percent of the sales invoices. He considers an invoice error of $1 or less not to matter.* He believes prompt billing is important because customers are expected to pay within 30 days. *Fred is very strict in thinking that a bill should be sent to the customer one day after shipment.* He believes he has staffed the billing department well enough to be able to handle this workload. The relevant company records consist of an accounts receivable control account; a subsidiary ledger that enters customers' accounts by billing (invoice) date and credits and by date of payment receipts; a sales journal that lists invoices in chronological order; and a file of shipping documents cross-referenced by the number on the related sales invoice copy kept on file in numerical order.

2. Accounts receivable are to be aged and followed up to ensure prompt collection. *Fred has told the accounts receivable department to classify all customer accounts in categories of (a) current, (b) 31–59 days overdue, (c) 60–90 days overdue, and (d) more than 90 days overdue. He wants this trial balance to be complete and to be transmitted to the credit department within five days after each month-end. In the credit department, prompt follow-up means sending a different (stronger) collection letter to each category, cutting off credit to customers over 60 days past due (putting them on cash basis), and giving the over-90-days accounts to an outside collection agency. These actions are supposed to be taken within five days after receipt of the aged trial balance.* The relevant company records, in addition to the others listed, consist of the aged trial balance, copies of the letters sent to customers, copies of notices of credit cutoff, copies of correspondence with the outside collection agent, and reports of results—statistics of subsequent collections.

Required:

Take the role of a senior internal auditor and write a memo to the internal audit staff to inform them about comparison standards for the study and evaluation of these two management control policies. You also need to specify two or three procedures for gathering evidence about performance of the controls. The body of your memo should be structured as follows:

1. Control: Sales are billed to customers accurately and promptly.
   a. Accuracy.
      (1) Policy standard . . .
      (2) Audit procedures . . .
   b. Promptness.
      (1) Policy standard . . .
      (2) Audit procedures . . .
2. Control: Accounts receivable are aged and followed up to ensure prompt collection.
   a. Accounts receivable aging.
      (1) Policy standard . . .
      (2) Audit procedures . . .
   b. Follow-up prompt collection.
      (1) Policy standard . . .
      (2) Audit procedures . . .

LO 7-2

7.67 **Cash Receipts and Billing Control.** The following narrative description of a company's cash receipts and billing system is in the auditors' audit files:

Rural Building Supplies, Inc., is a single-store retailer that sells a variety of tools, garden supplies, lumber, small appliances, and electrical fixtures. About half of the sales are to walk-in customers and about half to construction contractors. Rural employs 12 salaried sales associates, a credit manager, three full-time clerical workers, and several part-time cash register clerks and assistant bookkeepers. The full-time clerical workers are the cashier who handles the cash and the bank deposits, the accounts receivable supervisor who prepares invoices and does the accounts receivable work, and the bookkeeper who keeps journals and ledgers and sends customer statements. Their work is described more fully in the narrative.

Control Narrative

Rural's retail customers pay for merchandise by cash or credit card at cash registers when they purchase merchandise. A building contractor can purchase merchandise on account if approved by the credit manager. The credit manager bases approvals on general knowledge of the contractor's reputation. After credit is approved, the sales associate files a prenumbered charge form with the accounts receivable (A/R) supervisor to set up the contractor's account receivable.

The A/R supervisor independently verifies the pricing and other details on the charge form by reference to a management-authorized price list, corrects any errors, prepares the sales invoice, and supervises a part-time employee who mails the invoice to the contractor. The A/R supervisor electronically posts the details of the invoice in customer database, and the computerized system simultaneously transmits the transaction details to the bookkeeper. The A/R supervisor also prepares (1) a monthly computer-generated A/R subsidiary ledger without reconciliation to the A/R control account and (2) a monthly report of overdue accounts.

The cashier performs the cash receipts functions, including supervising the cash register clerks. The cashier opens the mail, compares each check with the enclosed remittance advice, stamps each check "for deposit only," and lists the checks for the deposit slip. The cashier then gives the remittance advices to the bookkeeper for recording. The cashier deposits the checks each day and prepares a separate deposit of the cash from the cash registers. The cashier retains the verified bank deposit slips (stamped and dated at the bank) to use in reconciling the monthly bank statements. The cashier sends to the bookkeeper a copy of the daily cash register summary. The cashier does not have access to the bookkeeper's journals or ledgers.

The bookkeeper receives information for journalizing and posting to the general ledger from the A/R supervisor (details of credit transactions) and from the cashier (cash reports).

After recording the remittance advices received from the cashier, the bookkeeper electronically transmits the information to the A/R supervisor for subsidiary ledger updating. Upon receipt of the A/R supervisor's report of overdue balances, the bookkeeper sends monthly statements of account to contractors with unpaid balances. The bookkeeper authorizes the A/R supervisor to write off accounts as uncollectable six months after sending the first overdue notice. At this time, the bookkeeper notifies the credit manager not to approve additional credit to that contractor.

Required:
Take the role of the supervising auditor on the Rural engagement. Your assistants prepared the narrative description. Now you must analyze it and identify the internal control weaknesses. Organize them under the heading of employee job functions: credit manager, accounts receivable supervisor, cashier, and bookkeeper. (Do not give advice about correcting the weaknesses.)

Optional Requirement:
Discuss the possibilities for fraud you notice in this control system.

LO 7-5

7.68 **Tests of Controls and Errors/Frauds.** The following four questions are taken from an internal control questionnaire. For each question, state (a) one test of controls procedure you could use to find out whether the control technique was really functioning and (b) what error or fraud could occur if the question were answered "no" or if you found the control was not effective.

1. Are blank sales invoices available only to authorized personnel?
2. Are sales invoices checked for the accuracy of quantities billed? Prices used? Mathematical calculations?
3. Are the duties of the accounts receivable bookkeeper separate from all cash functions?
4. Are customer accounts regularly balanced with the control account?

LO 7-1

7.69 **Revenue Recognition and Ethics.** The following article was published in *Newsday* on February 9, 2009:

Call for Probe of Ticket Sales

Bruce Springsteen fans were victims of a "classic bait and switch" scam by the nation's largest concert ticket seller, Senator Charles Schumer said yesterday, as he called for a federal investigation into the company, Ticketmaster. Schumer wants the Federal Trade Commission to look into whether the Ticketmaster website withheld the best tickets from the public and then shuttled fans to TicketsNow, a fully owned subsidiary. TicketsNow had the best seats available immediately—at sky-high prices—after Springsteen tickets went on sales at 10 A.M. on February 2.

A federal investigation would look into whether Ticketmaster was instantly scalping the tickets, never giving fans a chance to buy them at face value, Schumer said. Customers who tried to buy tickets originally priced at $95 on Ticketmaster's website were directed to TicketsNow where they were priced at more than $2,000

Since buying TicketsNow in February, Ticketmaster has faced similar criticism for its handling of Elton John tickets in Canada and numerous U.S. concert tours, including Radiohead. Law enforcement agencies in Connecticut and New Jersey have also launched investigations.

Required:
a. During the course of an audit, do you believe that the auditor should look into how revenues are being generated? Do you think the auditors should have looked at the business practices of Ticketmaster?
b. Assume that Ticketmaster had properly accounted for the revenue it received from the Springsteen concert. Should the auditors have asked Ticketmaster to make adjustments or disclosures regarding its sales practices?
c. Should Ticketmaster disclose the investigations being conducted in Connecticut and New Jersey?

7.70 Kaplan CPA Exam Simulation: Turnover Ratios

LO 7-4

Required:
Go to the Kaplan website link at www.mhhe.com/Louwers5e, click on Matsworth Co. (Turnover Ratios) AUD TBS and complete your answers.

CPA REVIEW

LO 7-4

7.71 Kaplan CPA Exam Simulation: Adjusting Entry

Required:
Go to the Kaplan website link at www.mhhe.com/Louwers5e, click on Chester Co. (Adjusting Entry) AUD TBS and complete your answers.

LO 7-4

7.72 **Mini-Case: Confirmations.** Refer to the mini-case "Something Went Sour at Parmalat" on page C20 and respond to Question 2.

Appendix 7A

Internal Control Questionnaires

APPENDIX EXHIBIT 7A.1 Internal Control Questionnaire—Revenue and Collection Cycle

	Yes/No	Comments
Occurrence		
1. Is the customer database maintained by someone who has no access to cash?		
2. Is access to sales invoice blanks restricted?		
3. Are prenumbered bills of lading or other shipping documents prepared or completed in the shipping department?		
4. Are customers' statements mailed monthly by the accounts receivable department?		
5. Are direct confirmations of accounts and notes obtained periodically by the internal auditor?		
6. Are differences reported by customers routed to someone outside the accounts receivable department for investigations?		
7. Are returned goods checked against receiving reports?		
8. Are returned sales credits and other credits supported by documentation as to receipt, condition, and quantity and approved by a responsible officer?		
9. Are write-offs, returns, and discounts allowed after discount date subject to approval by a responsible officer?		
10. Are large loans or advances to related parties approved by the directors?		
Completeness		
11. Are sales invoice forms prenumbered?		
12. Is the sequence checked for missing invoices?		
13. Is the shipping document numerical sequence checked for missing bills of lading numbers?		
14. Are credit memo documents prenumbered and the sequence checked for missing documents?		
Accuracy		
15. Is customer credit approved before orders are shipped?		
16. Are delinquent accounts listed periodically for review by someone other than the credit manager?		
17. Is the credit department separated from the sales department?		
18. Are sales prices and terms based on approved standards?		
19. Are shipped quantities compared to invoice quantities?		
20. Are sales invoices checked for error in quantities, prices, extensions and footings, and freight allowances, and checked with customers' orders?		
21. Do the internal auditors confirm customer accounts periodically to determine accuracy?		
22. Does someone reconcile the accounts receivable subsidiary to the control account regularly?		
Cutoff		
23. Does the accounting manual contain instructions to date sales invoices on the shipment date?		
Classification		
24. Does the accounting manual contain instructions for classifying sales?		
25. Are summary journal entries approved before posting?		
26. Are sales of the following types controlled by the same procedures described: sale to employees, COD sales, disposals of property, cash sales, and scrap sales?		
27. Are receivables from officers, directors, and affiliates identified separately in the accounts receivable records?		

APPENDIX EXHIBIT 7A.2 Internal Control Questionnaire—Sales and Accounts Receivable Computerized Controls

	Yes/No	Comments
1. Does each terminal perform only designated functions? For example, the terminal at the shipping dock cannot be used to enter initial sales information or to access the payroll database.		
2. Are an identification number and password (issued on an individual person basis) required to enter the sale and each command that a subsequent action has been completed? Unauthorized entry attempts are logged and immediately investigated. Furthermore, certain passwords have "read-only" (cannot change any data) authorization. For example, the credit manager can determine the outstanding balance of any account or view online "reports" summarizing overdue accounts receivable but cannot enter credit memos to change the balances.		
3. Is all input information immediately logged to provide restart processing should any terminal become inoperative during the processing?		
4. Does a transaction code call up on the terminals a full-screen "form" that appears to the operator in the same format as the original paper documents? Each clerk must enter the information correctly or the computer will not accept the transaction. This is called *online input validation* and utilizes validation checks such as missing data, check digit, and limit tests.		
5. Are all documents prepared by the computer numbered with the number stored as part of the sales record in the accounts receivable database?		
6. Is a daily search of the pending order database made by the computer with sales orders outstanding more than seven days listed on the terminal in marketing management?		

Appendix 7B

Audit Plan

APPENDIX EXHIBIT 7B.1

DUNDER-MIFFLIN
Audit Plan for Tests of Controls in the Revenues and Collection Cycle
12/31/12

	Performed by	Ref.

Sales
1. Select a sample of recorded sales from the sales journal.
   a. Vouch to supporting shipping documents.
   b. Vouch to supporting sales order
   c. Inspect sales orders for credit approval.
   d. Vouch prices to the approved price list.
   e. Compare the quantity billed to the quantity shipped.
   f. Recalculate the invoice arithmetic.
   g. Compare the shipment date with the sales journal record date.
   h. Trace the invoice to posting in the general ledger control account and in the correct customer's account.
   i. Inspect for proper revenue account classification.
2. Select a sample of shipping documents from the shipping department file and trace shipments to entries in the sales journal.
3. Scan recorded sales invoices and shipping documents for missing numbers in sequence.
 	
Accounts Receivable
1. Select a sample of customers' accounts from the accounts receivable database.
   a. Vouch recorded sales to supporting sales invoices.
   b. Vouch recorded payments to supporting cash receipts documents
2. Select a sample of credit memos.
   a. Review for proper approval.
   b. Trace to posting in customers' accounts.
3. Scan the accounts receivable control for postings from sources other than the sales and cash receipts journals (e.g., general journal adjusting entries, credit memos). Vouch a sample of such entries to supporting documents.		

APPENDIX EXHIBIT 7B.2

DUNDER-MIFFLIN
Audit Plan for Accounts and Notes Receivable and Revenue
12/31/12

	Performed by	Ref.

A. Accounts and Notes Receivable
1. Obtain an aged trial balance of individual customer accounts. Recalculate the total and trace to the general ledger control account.
2. Review the aging for large and unusual items.
3. Send confirmations to all accounts over $X. Select a random sample of all remaining accounts for confirmation.
   a. Investigate exceptions reported by customers.
   b. Investigate any confirmations returned by the post office as undeliverable.
   c. Perform alternative procedures on accounts that do not respond to positive confirmation requests.
      (1) Vouch cash receipts after the confirmation date for subsequent payment.
      (2) Vouch sales invoices and shipping documents.		

(continued)

APPENDIX EXHIBIT 7B.2 *(continued)*

DUNDER-MIFFLIN
Audit Plan for Accounts and Notes Receivable and Revenue
12/31/12

	Performed by	Ref.

4. Review the adequacy of the allowance for doubtful accounts.
   a. Inquire of management regarding assumptions used in calculating the allowance for doubtful accounts.
   b. Vouch a sample of current amounts in the aged trial balance to sales invoices to determine whether amounts aged current should be aged past due.
   c. Compare the current-year write-off experience to the prior-year allowance.
   d. Vouch cash receipts after the balance sheet date for collections on past due accounts.
   e. Obtain financial statements or credit reports and inquire of the credit manager about collections on large past due accounts.
   f. Calculate an allowance estimate using prior relations of write-offs and sales, taking under consideration current economic events.
5. Inspect the bank confirmations, loan agreements, and minutes of the board for indications of pledged, discounted, or assigned receivables.
6. Inspect or obtain confirmation of notes receivable.
7. Recalculate interest income and trace to the income account.
8. Obtain management representations regarding pledge, discount, or assignment of receivables, and about receivables from officers, directors, affiliates, or other related parties.
9. Review the adequacy of control over recording all charges to customers (completeness) audited in the sales transaction test of controls audit plan.
B. Revenue
1. Select a sample of sales recorded in the sales journal and vouch to underlying shipping documents.
2. Select a sample of shipping documents and trace to sales invoices.
3. Obtain production records of physical quantities sold and calculate an estimate of sales dollars based on average sale prices.
4. Compare revenue dollars and physical quantities with prior-year data and industry economic statistics.
5. Select a sample of sales invoices prepared a few days before and after the balance sheet date and vouch to supporting documents for evidence of proper cutoff.		

Acquisition and Expenditure Cycle

> *Show those numbers to the damn auditors and I'll throw you out the $%*@@ window.*
>
> Buddy Yates, director of WorldCom, Inc. general accounting, to an employee asking for an explanation of a large accounting discrepancy

Professional Standards References

Topic	AU/ISA Section	PCAOB* Reference
Consideration of Internal Control in a Financial Statement Audit	NA#	AS 5
Audit Documentation	230	AS 3
Consideration of Fraud in Financial Statement Audits	240	AS 13
Audit Planning	300	AS 10
Risks of Material Misstatement	315	AS 12
Materiality	320	AS 11
Audit Considerations Relating to an Entity Using a Service Organization	402	AU 324
Audit Evidence	500	AS 15
External Confirmations	505	AU 330[1]
Analytical Procedures	520	AS 15
Auditing Accounting Estimates	540	AU 342[1]
Written Representations	580	AU 333[1]

*AU references represent standards issued by the ASB prior to April 16, 2003 that have not been superseded pr amended by the PCAOB
#Internal controls are covered under numerous Audit Standards

LEARNING OBJECTIVES

This chapter contains a concise overview of the cycle for the acquisition of goods and services as well as the expenditure of cash in connection with paying for the purchases and acquisitions.

This cycle affects more general ledger accounts than any other cycle. Major accounts discussed include accounts payable and long-term assets. For accounts payable, the focus shifts from the *existence* assertion to the *completeness* assertion. A series of short cases is used to show the application of audit procedures in situations in which errors and frauds might be discovered. Payroll is a subcycle related to the acquisition and expenditure cycle and to the production cycle. A discussion of payroll controls and audit tests is included in Appendix 8C.

Your objectives are to be able to:

LO 8-1 Identify significant inherent risks in the acquisition and expenditure cycle.

LO 8-2 Describe the acquisition and expenditure cycle, including typical source documents and controls.

LO 8-3 Give examples of tests of controls over purchases of inventory and services.

LO 8-4 Explain the importance of the *completeness* assertion for the audit of accounts payable and list some procedures for a *search for unrecorded liabilities*.

LO 8-5 Discuss audit procedures for other accounts affected by the acquisition and expenditure cycle.

LO 8-6 Specify some ways fraud can be found in accounts payable and cash disbursements.

LO 8-7 Describe some common errors and frauds in the acquisition and expenditure cycle and design some audit and investigation procedures for detecting them.

LO 8-8 Describe the payroll cycle, including typical source documents and controls. [Appendix 8C]

INTRODUCTION

A headline in the March 14, 2003, issue of *The Wall Street Journal* announced that **WorldCom, Inc.** was going to write down assets by more than $70 *billion* to correct the company's accounting records for a massive fraud that had been uncovered. To put this number in perspective, the amount of the write-off almost equaled the entire gross domestic product for the country of Ireland.[1] How did WorldCom's books become so inflated? A large part of the restatement was a result of the company's practice of capitalizing (rather than properly expensing) certain transactions to fixed asset accounts. The improper charges were not part of the regular system but were hidden in computerized files of adjusting entries to intercompany receivables. Only the dogged pursuit of the facts, led by the company's director of internal audit and 2002 *Time* Person of the Year Cynthia Cooper, uncovered the massive fraud. The internal auditors' search included midnight hacking into the computerized system to sort through hundreds of thousands of transactions—a process that discovered $2 billion of questionable items in the first week! When **Andersen**, the company's public accounting firm, was first apprised of the problems, the firm allegedly told Ms. Cooper that it had approved some of the very accounting practices she questioned.[2]

At the time of its discovery, the WorldCom fraud represented the largest fraud ever perpetrated in the United States. However, as you will see, understating or capitalizing expenses is a means often used to mislead financial statement users. GAAP prescribes that expenses be charged to income to reflect the consumption of economic benefits. The FASB *Statement of Concepts* discusses three ways to recognize expenses:

1. They are recognized when they can be **matched** with related revenues (e.g., cost of goods sold with sales) and those revenues are recognized.
2. They are recognized in the period in which they are incurred.
3. They are allocated to the future periods benefited by a "systematic and rational" process (e.g., depreciation).[3]

It is imperative that the auditor understand these concepts of expense recognition and ascertain that the client is correctly applying the appropriate concept to the expense at hand and is properly valuing the expense.

---

[1] www.infoplease.com/IPA/A0874911.html.
[2] S. Pulliam and D. Soloman, "Uncooking the Books," *The Wall Street Journal,* October 10, 2002, p. A1.
[3] *SFAC No. 5,* "Recognition and Measurement in Finance Statements."

INHERENT RISKS IN THE ACQUISITION AND EXPENDITURE CYCLE

LEARNING OBJECTIVE 8-1
Identify significant inherent risks in the acquisition and expenditure cycle.

The report of the Government Accountability Office (GAO) on financial statement restatements between 2002 and 2005 found that the most common reason for restatements was misstated costs and expenses. In addition, Audit Analytics reported that, for 2008, debt (including accounts payable) and payroll were among the top reasons for financial statement restatements.[4] The most recent reports indicate that although restatements as a whole have declined since 2007 (a finding attributed to the PCAOB), expense recognition errors were still the second leading cause of restatements accounting for over 14 percent of all restatements.[5] This category included improperly recognizing costs or expenses, improperly **capitalizing** expenditures, and improperly accounting for taxes.[6] WorldCom, Inc. is an example of a company that simply placed expenses in capital accounts (accounts that would be expensed over a number of years as depreciation or amortization expense). Although the expenses do not go away, capitalizing them increases net income in the year when they should have been completely expensed. These restatements led to nearly $5 billion in immediate market losses when they were restated. (Some recent restatements are summarized in Exhibit 8.1. Note that in at least one case (**Cablevision**), expenses were *accelerated* to an earlier period.

In addition to improperly recognizing expenses, other concerns (inherent risks) in the acquisition and expenditure cycle include *unrecorded liabilities* and *noncancelable purchase agreements*. Exhibit 8.2 shows the AICPA assertions for sales and receivables with their relative risks.

In many accounting systems, liabilities are not recorded until receiving reports have been matched to purchase orders and invoices. Often when there is a problem in matching the documents, the liability is not recorded, thus understating costs and overstating profits. Under noncancelable purchase agreements, companies order goods for future delivery to obtain volume discounts or favorable pricing. However, if market forces or technology cause a permanent decline in the value of those goods, the company must recognize any related losses immediately.

EXHIBIT 8.1 Cost and Expense Capers

Company	Alleged Fraud Strategy	Restatement Amount
MCI (WorldCom)	The telecommunications company improperly capitalized expense items.	$74.4 billion
Waste Management, Inc.	The waste disposal giant used "top-level adjustments" to improperly eliminate and defer current period expenses and avoided depreciation on garbage trucks by assigning unsupported, inflated, and arbitrary salvage values and extending the useful lives.	$1.1 billion
Adelphia Communications Corporation	The cable company did not report off-balance-sheet liabilities.	$210.0 million
Orbital Sciences Corporation	The satellite manufacturer improperly capitalized costs.	$124.0 million
Aurora Foods, Inc.	The food company did not record trade marketing expenses (e.g., case discounts to induce grocery stores to stock its goods).	$81.5 million
Collins and Aikman	The automotive supply company booked rebates as lump sums that should have been spread out over time.	$16.0 million
Cablevision	The cable company improperly *accelerated* marketing expenses in the programming division.	$15.0 million

[4] Tammy Whitehouse, "Restatements Tumble, As Internal Controls Hit Stride," *Compliance Week,* May 2009.
[5] Audit Analytics, "2009 Financial Restatements: A nine Year Comparison" (February 2010).
[6] GAO, *Financial Statement Restatements* (GAO, October 2002).

EXHIBIT 8.2 Relative Assertion Risks for Procurement and Payables

AICPA Assertions	Procurement	Payables	Explanation
Transaction assertions			Frauds may occur when items are purchased for personal use or payables are recorded for payments made to inappropriate parties. In addition, management may wish to delay the recording of expense and, therefore, need to delay the recording of the corresponding payable. This may include recording the payable in a subsequent period. Not recording a purchase may occur when an individual has used a purchase order to procure personal property; therefore, a missing purchase order may indicate a fraud. The cutoff risk in procurement occurs in receiving when items received prior to year-end are dated after year-end to delay the payable.
• Occurrence	High	High	
• Completeness	Medium	Medium	
• Cutoff	High	High	
• Accuracy	High	High	
• Classification	Medium	Medium	
Balance assertions			Management may understate the accounts payable balance to reduce the liabilities of the entity by recording the liability in a subsequent period (completeness). The failure to record a liability in the proper period, the inclusion of purchases and payable for personal items, and the risk of fraud in the purchasing function make the valuation of these accounts high risk.
• Existence	Medium	Medium	
• Rights and obligations	Medium	Medium	
• Completeness	High	High	
• Valuation and allocation	High	High	
Presentation and disclosure assertions			There is little incentive for management to present purchases or payables that do not exist or for which the entity does not have an obligation. As discussed, management may present accounts that are incomplete and therefore improperly valued.
• Occurrence	Medium	Low	
• Rights and obligations	Medium	Low	
• Completeness	Medium	High	
• Accuracy and valuation allocations	High	High	
• Classification and understandability	Low	Low	

Note: These risks are for a typical entity engaged in manufacturing, retail, and other similar industries. Some specialized industries may have risks that vary from those indicated in this table.

↳ REVIEW CHECKPOINT

8.1 What are the short-term effect and the long-term effect on the financial statements for improperly capitalizing expenditures?

ACQUISITION AND EXPENDITURE CYCLE: TYPICAL ACTIVITIES

LEARNING OBJECTIVE 8-2
Describe the acquisition and expenditure cycle, including typical source documents and controls.

STAGES OF AN AUDIT

Obtain (or Retain) Engagement → Engagement Planning → **Risk Assessment** → Audit Evidence → Reporting

The basic acquisition and expenditure activities include (1) purchasing goods and services, (2) receiving the good or service, (3) recording the asset or expense and related liability, and (4) paying the vendor. See Exhibit 8.3 for the activities and transactions involved in an

EXHIBIT 8.3 Acquisition and Expenditure Cycle

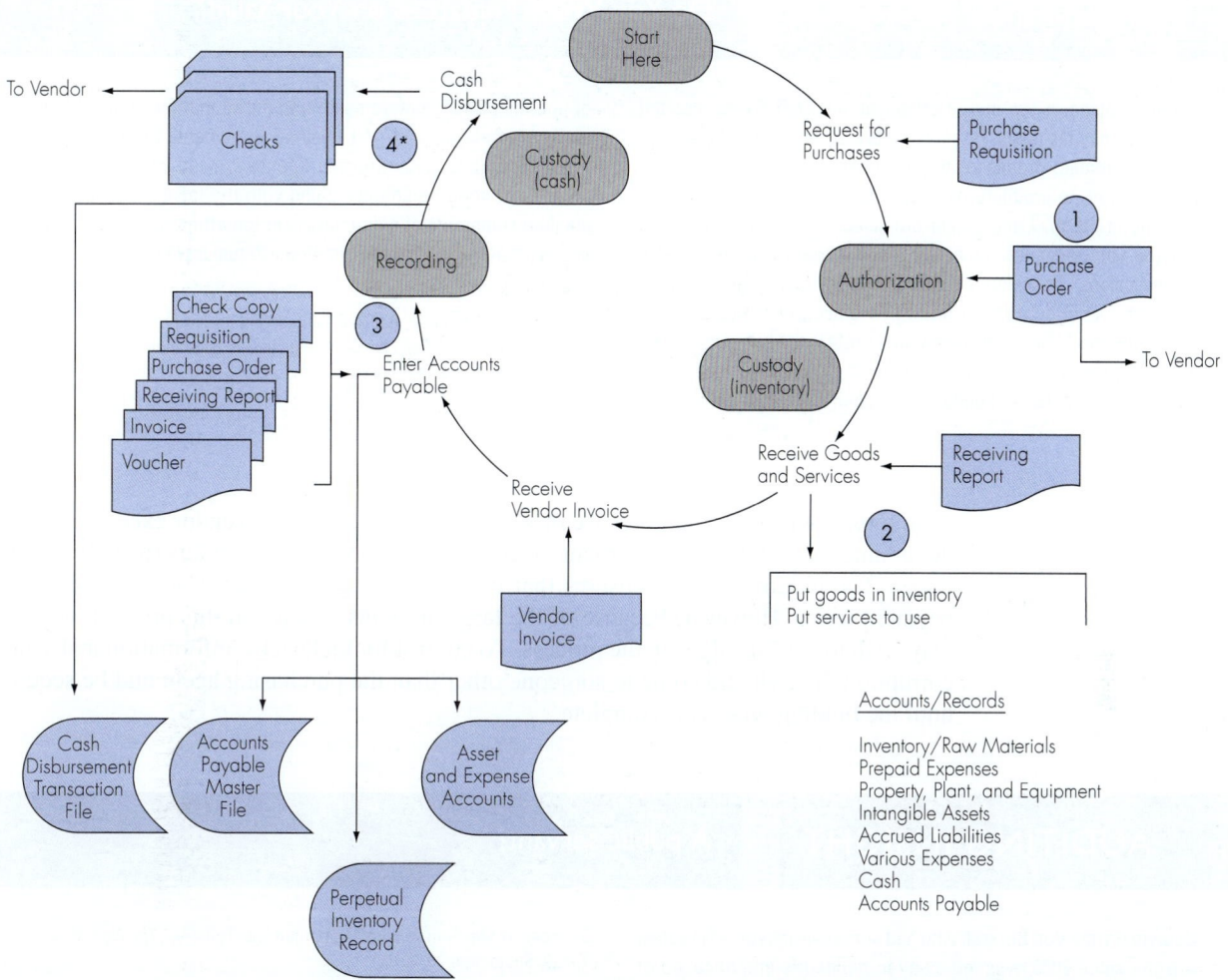

*Paying the vendor is discussed in the Cash Disbursements section of Chapter 6.

acquisition and expenditure cycle. The exhibit also lists the accounts and records typically found in this cycle. As you follow the exhibit, you can track the elements of internal control described in the following sections.

Purchasing Goods and Services ①

Purchases are requested via a **purchase requisition** by people who know the needs of the organization. A purchasing department seeks the best prices and quality and issues a **purchase order** to a selected vendor from an **approved vendor list**. Obtaining competitive bids is a good practice because it tends to produce the best prices and involves several legitimate suppliers in the process. Inventory is often ordered automatically from approved vendors through **electronic data interchange (EDI)**. When production plans indicate a need for the inventory, automatic links to the vendor's computerized system generate a purchase order.

The purchasing department is an area of high fraud risk because employees who have authority to purchase assets and services for the company are in a unique position to take advantage of their authority to enrich themselves or their friends. The abuse can simply be to give business to vendors that do not supply the best quality or price to the company. This may occur because of a conflict of interest (employee has an ownership interest in a supplier), a kickback (the vendor provides the purchasing agent a gift or payment), or a "shell" company (a company created by the employee to provide fictitious invoices and receipt of payment). The abuse can extend to misdirecting purchases to the employee's personal benefit. These abuses are difficult to detect because vendors are often reluctant to lose favor with purchasing decision makers.

> **AUDITING INSIGHT** — Do You Want Tomatoes on Your Salad?

Robert Watson, a top ingredient buyer for **Kraft Foods**, needed $20,000 to pay his taxes. He called a broker for **SK Foods**, a large California tomato processor that for years had been paying him bribes to get its products Into Kraft factories. The check would soon be in the mail, the broker promised. "We'll have to deduct it out of your commissions as we move forward," using the term "commissions" as a euphemism for bribes. Days later, U.S. government agents descended on Kraft's offices near Chicago and confronted Mr. Watson. He admitted his role in the bribery scheme.

Now prosecutors have taken aim at SK Foods. Prosecutors state that for years, SK Foods had shipped its customers millions of pounds of bulk tomato paste and puree that fell short of basic quality standards and had falsified documentation to hide the practice. Bribes to purchasing agents at Kraft Foods and three other large food companies along with the false documentation masked shipments of old tomatoes or tomatoes with mold counts so high that the sale of the tomatoes should have been prohibited under U.S. laws.

Source: "Bribes Let Vendor Sell Tainted Tomato Products, U.S. Says; Admission by Buyer Exposes Corruption in U.S. Food Industry," *The International Times,* February 26, 2010.

In most companies, if a purchase or series of purchases from a vendor exceed a certain dollar amount, there is a requirement to receive bids from several vendors (usually at least three). The bidding process ensures that the company gets the best price, delivery, and payment terms. However, because of the large amounts at stake in this process, vendors may wish to get "an edge" in the process. To control for kickbacks, information leaks, and corruption, bids should come to someone other than the purchasing agent and be secured until the bidding process is complete.

> **AUDITING INSIGHT** — A public servant?

Octavio Garcia Von Borstal, who had served as mayor of Nogales, Arizona since 2008, was led away in handcuffs and accused of soliciting Nogales businesses to hire him as a consultant. One business owner told the FBI that it paid the mayor to obtain a city contract without going through the bidding process.

Source: "A Mayor in Arizona Is Charged with Bribery," *The New York Times,* September 29, 2010

Receiving the Goods or Services ②

When goods arrive at a company, the trucker will have a **bill of lading** (which should include the purchase order number), it is imperative that the bill of landing be matched to the purchase order on file at receiving. If a company obtains a reputation for receiving any goods that show up at its receiving department, any "undeliverable" item on a truck may find its way to the company's receiving docks. After the delivery has been verified as the company's purchase, the receiving department inspects the goods received for quantity and quality (producing a receiving report) and then puts them in the hands of other responsible persons (e.g., inventory warehousing, fixed asset installation). A **receiving report** is completed to indicate the quantity and description of the item. Receiving departments should receive a "blind" purchase order that has all purchase information except the quantity, which is left blank for the receiving department to fill in after an independent inspection and count. Services are not "received" in this manner, but responsible persons indicate that the service was satisfactorily performed by signing the invoice or some other form that can be used like a receiving report to verify that the service was completed.

Recording the Asset or Expense and Related Liability ③

Accounts payable usually are recorded when the purchaser receives the goods or services ordered. The accounts payable department attaches a **voucher** to the purchase order, **vendor's invoice**, and receiving report. The combined documents are often called the **voucher package**. The voucher shows the accounts that are debited and indicates who checked the invoice for proper date, price, math, and reconciled the voucher package. After the voucher package has been completed, accountants enter the accounts (or vouchers) payable with debits to proper inventory, fixed asset, and expense accounts and with a credit to accounts payable.

AUDIT EVIDENCE IN MANAGEMENT REPORTS AND DATA FILES

Computerized processing of acquisition and payment transactions enables management to generate several reports that can provide important audit evidence.

Open Purchase Orders

Purchase orders are "open" from the time they are issued until all goods and services have been received. They are held in an *open purchase order file*. Generally, no liability exists until the transactions have been completed (i.e., the merchandise or services are received). However, auditors can find evidence of losses on purchase commitments in this file if market prices have fallen below the purchase price shown in purchase orders.

AUDITING INSIGHT — Thinking Ahead

Lone Moon Brewing purchased bulk aluminum sheets and manufactured its own cans. To ensure a source of raw materials supply, the company entered into a long-term purchase agreement for 6 million pounds of aluminum sheeting at 40 cents per pound. At the end of the year, it had purchased and used 1.5 million pounds, but the market price had fallen to 32 cents per pound. Lone Moon was on the hook for a $360,000 (4.5 million pounds at 8 cents) purchase commitment in excess of current market prices that should be recognized as a loss in the period.

Unmatched Receiving Reports

Liabilities should be recorded on the date the goods and services are received and accepted by the receiving department or by another responsible person. Sometimes, however, vendor invoices arrive later. In the meantime, the accounts payable department holds the purchase order and receiving reports *unmatched* with invoices, awaiting enough information to record an accounting entry. Auditors can inspect the unmatched receiving report file to determine whether the company has material unrecorded liabilities on the financial statement date for goods that were received but not matched to invoices.

Unmatched Vendor Invoices

Sometimes vendor invoices arrive in the accounts payable department before the receiving activity is complete. Such invoices are held *unmatched* with receiving reports, awaiting information that the goods and services were actually received and accepted. Auditors can inspect the *unmatched invoice file* and compare it with the *unmatched receiving report file* to determine whether liabilities are unrecorded. Systems failures and human coding errors can cause unmatched invoices and related unmatched receiving reports to sit around unnoticed when all of the information for recording a liability is actually in hand. Sometimes, however, unmatched invoices are indicators of fraudsters looking for an easy score as noted in the following Auditing Insight.

> ### AUDITING INSIGHT Paying for Nothing
>
> A Toronto man received more than $7 million by mailing thousands of phony invoices to companies around the world. Emanuel Medeiros mailed fake "renewal notices" in the amount of $297.83 and received payments from more 25,000 companies. Medeiros hired a commercial mailing company in New York to send out 200 to 400 bills stamped "RENEWAL" in large, bold letters every two weeks. The bills were sent in the name of two companies, Bradstreet International and Boom Global Media. One company tried to contact Boom to cancel the service. When the next bill arrived for twice the amount and threatened that the account would be turned over for collection, the company immediately sent a check for $595.66.
>
> After receiving complaints, the U.S. Postal Service stopped the mailing and after some communications, Medeiros agreed to come to New York. He plead guilty to fraud, agreed to pay $300,000 and serve 46 months in prison. In addition, the U.S. Attorney's Office in New York has notified victim companies who may file for restitution.
>
> Source: "Fake Invoices Net $7M and Four Years," *National Post*, January 29, 2009.

Accounts (Vouchers) Payable Trial Balance

This trial balance is a list of payable amounts by vendor, and the total should agree with the accounts payable control account. (Some organizations keep records by individual vouchers instead of vendor names, so the trial balance is a list of unpaid vouchers. The total still should agree with the control account balance.) The best type of trial balance for audit purposes is one that contains the names of *all* vendors with whom the organization has done business, even those whose balances are zero. The *search for unrecorded liabilities* should emphasize accounts with small and zero balances, especially for regular vendors, because these accounts can be the places where unrecorded liabilities may exist.

Purchases Journal

A list of all purchases may or may not be printed out. It may exist only in a computer transaction file. In either event, it provides information for (1) the analysis of purchasing patterns that can exhibit characteristics of errors and frauds and (2) the sample selection of transactions for tests of controls. (A company could have already performed analyses of purchases that auditors can use for analytical procedures, provided the analyses are produced under reliable control activities.)

Fixed Asset Reports

Many large purchases are for fixed assets. Auditors should trace large purchases to the fixed asset reports and ensure that the details of fixed assets in control accounts are consistent with purchase orders. Furthermore, additions to fixed assets should be vouched to the purchasing documents to ensure that items were acquired in accordance with policy and procedure.

> ### ↳ REVIEW CHECKPOINTS
>
> 8.2 What is a *voucher*?
>
> 8.3 How can purchasing managers use their position to defraud the company? What can be done to prevent it?
>
> 8.4 Why is a "blind" purchase order used as a receiving report document?
>
> 8.5 Where could an auditor look to find evidence of (a) losses on purchase commitments or (b) unrecorded liabilities to vendors?
>
> 8.6 List the management reports and data files that can be used for audit evidence. What information in them can be useful to auditors?

CONTROL RISK ASSESSMENT

LEARNING OBJECTIVE 8-3
Give examples of tests of controls over purchases of inventory and services.

Control risk assessment is important because it governs the nature, timing, and extent of substantive procedures that will be applied in the audit of account balances in the acquisition and expenditure cycle. These account balances include

- Inventory.
- Prepaid and other assets.
- Fixed assets.
- Accounts payable.
- Accrued liabilities.
- Cash.
- Various expenses.

Entity-Level Controls

It is important that auditors consider entity-level controls in all processes and procedures. In the expenditure process, management should have a process for continually reviewing expenses and comparing them to budgets and forecasts. Proper authorization for all expenditures should be established and included in company policy and procedures. Corporate values and ethics that have been established should be communicated to suppliers and other partners of the entity along with a place to which inappropriate behavior (such as the solicitation of a bribe or kickback) may be reported. The security of items such as blank purchase orders is an important control, as well as the proper delivery and safeguarding of all material received by the entity.

Control Considerations

Control activities for proper separation of responsibilities should be in place and operating. By referring to Exhibit 8.3, you can see that proper separation involves different people and different departments performing the purchasing, receiving, and cash disbursement authorization; custody of inventory, fixed assets, and cash; record keeping for purchases and payments; and reconciliation of assets, cash, and accounts payable. Combinations of two or more of these responsibilities in one person, one office, or one computerized system can open the door for errors and frauds. Specifically, the persons authorizing purchases should not be responsible for recording them. Persons who actually handle the receipt and storage of goods should neither authorize nor account for them. The persons who sign checks should not prepare the vouchers, nor should they mail the checks.

In addition, the internal controls should provide for detailed control-checking activities. For example, purchase requisitions and purchase orders should be signed or initialed by authorized personnel. (Computer-generated purchase orders should come from a system whose master file specifications for reordering and vendor identification are restricted to changes by authorized persons.)

Accountants should be instructed to record accounts payable only when all supporting documentation is in order, and care should be taken to record purchases and payables as of the date goods and services are received. Vendor invoices should be compared to purchase orders and receiving reports to determine that the vendor is charging the approved price and that the quantity being billed is the same as the quantity received.

Custody

Access to inventory and other physical assets must be restricted by placing them in locked areas when possible. Responsibility must be established by having someone sign for receipt of the assets when they are moved. Cash "custody" rests largely in the hands of the person or persons authorized to sign checks.

Another aspect of custody involves access to blank documents such as purchase orders, receiving reports, and checks. If unauthorized persons can obtain blank copies of these internal business documents, they can forge a false purchase order to a fictitious vendor, forge a false receiving report, send a false invoice from a fictitious supplier, and prepare a company check to the fictitious supplier, thereby accomplishing embezzlement. In addition, a blank purchase order can be used to order merchandise, material, or services for personal use. If this material can be diverted and sound controls are not in place, the company may end up paying for an employee's home improvement project.

Periodic Reconciliation

A periodic comparison or reconciliation of existing assets to recorded amounts is not shown in Exhibit 8.3, but it occurs in several ways, including the following:

- Taking physical inventory to compare inventory on hand to perpetual inventory records.
- Inspecting fixed assets to compare to detailed fixed asset records.
- Preparing an accounts payable trial balance to compare the detail of accounts payable to the control account.
- Confirming accounts payable to compare vendors' reports and monthly statements to recorded liabilities.
- Review unmatched purchase orders, receiving reports, and invoices.

Information about the control system is often gathered by completing an *internal control questionnaire*. See Appendix 8A for a selection of questionnaires for both manual controls and computer controls. These questionnaires can be studied for details of desirable control activities. They are organized under headings that identify the management assertions.

Tests of Controls

An organization should have controls in place and operating to prevent, detect, and correct accounting errors. Exhibit 8.4 puts controls in the perspective of purchasing activity with examples of specific assertions. You should study this exhibit carefully. It expresses the general control assertions in specific examples related to purchasing.

Auditors can perform tests of controls to determine whether company controls actually are in place and operating effectively. Tests of controls consist of identification of (1) the control that will be relied on to reduce assessed control risk and (2) the data population from which a sample of items will be selected for audit. In general, the actions in tests of controls involve vouching, tracing, observing, scanning, and recalculating.

Procedures such as matching, recalculating, and scanning for unusual items often can be performed electronically using computer-assisted audit techniques (CAATs). If personnel in the organization are not performing control activities effectively, auditors need to design substantive procedures to try to detect whether control failures have produced materially incorrect account balances.

Tests of controls over *occurrence* involve tests of the additions to the expense accounts. The chart in Exhibit 8.5 shows the *direction of the test* for tests of controls in the acquisition and expenditure cycle. The samples from the source documents (receiving reports, invoices) meet the *completeness* direction requirement to determine whether everything received was recorded as an addition to the balance. The sample from the purchase records meets the *occurrence* direction requirement to determine whether receiving reports and invoices supports everything recorded as an addition.

Summary: Control Risk Assessment

The auditor should evaluate the evidence obtained from understanding internal controls and from the tests of controls. This evaluation of control risk along with the auditor's understanding of the inherent risk leads to the auditor's determination of the risk of material misstatement (RMM). If the control risk is assessed below the maximum, the substantive procedures can be reduced in cost-saving ways. For example, if *completeness*

EXHIBIT 8.4 Assertions about Classes of Transactions and Events for the Period: Acquisition and Expenditure Cycle

Assertion	Controls	Tests of Control
Occurrence—Purchases and related events that have been recorded have occurred and pertain to the entity.	• Separation of duties between purchasing, receiving, and accounting. • Purchase orders support by invoices. • Existence of receiving documents for all invoices. • Recorded purchases and expenditures supported by invoices. • Comparison by managers of actual expenses with budgeted amounts. • Invoices canceled with a PAID stamp when paid.	• Observe separation of duties. • Review and reconcile voucher packages for purchase order, receiving reports, and invoice. Check documents for correct customer name, product description, terms, dates, and quantities. • Examine evidence of managers' reviews of actual versus budget and of follow-up on unusual items. • Examine paid vouchers for PAID stamp.
Completeness—All purchases and related events that should have been recorded have been recorded.	• Use of prenumbered vouchers, receiving reports, purchase orders, and checks and the numerical sequence checked. • Overall comparisons of purchases by a statistical or product line analysis made periodically.	• Trace receiving reports to recording in purchases journal. • Scan documents for numerical sequence. • Observe client checking sequence. • Examine evidence that managers review statistical analyses and follow up on unusual relationships.
Accuracy—Amounts and other data related to purchase transactions and events have been recorded properly.	• Purchase contracts are authorized at the appropriate level and accounting made aware of all significant terms. • Comparison of invoice quantities and prices with purchase orders and receiving reports • Prices and mathematical accuracy independently checked before preparing voucher. • Journal entries reviewed at the appropriate level. • Individual accounts payable reconciled to general ledger. • Statements reviewed and approved at senior level.	• Examine contracts for authorization. Inquire how accounting is notified of pending contracts. • Observe client comparing receiving quantities and insect documentary evidence of comparison. • Compare prices to approved price listing. • Inspect evidence of client checking. • Recalculate price extensions and discounts. • Inspect evidence of approval for purchase requisitions and purchase contracts. • Review reconciliation and support for reconciling items. • Inspect evidence of financial statement review by senior officials.
Cutoff—Purchases and related events have been recorded in the correct period.	• Date of receiving report compared with invoice date.	• Compare the date of receipt to date recorded in voucher journal. • Inspect evidence of client comparison of dates. • Inspect purchases occurring near year-end for recording in appropriate period.
Classification—Purchases and related events have been recorded in the proper accounts.	• Chart of accounts is used for classifying purchase entries. • Purchases from subsidiaries and affiliates are classified as intercompany purchases and payables. • Purchases returns and allowance properly classified. • Journal entries reviewed at the appropriate level.	• Observe use of chart of accounts. • Observe correct account classification. • Inspect evidence of journal entry review.

EXHIBIT 8.5
Direction of Tests

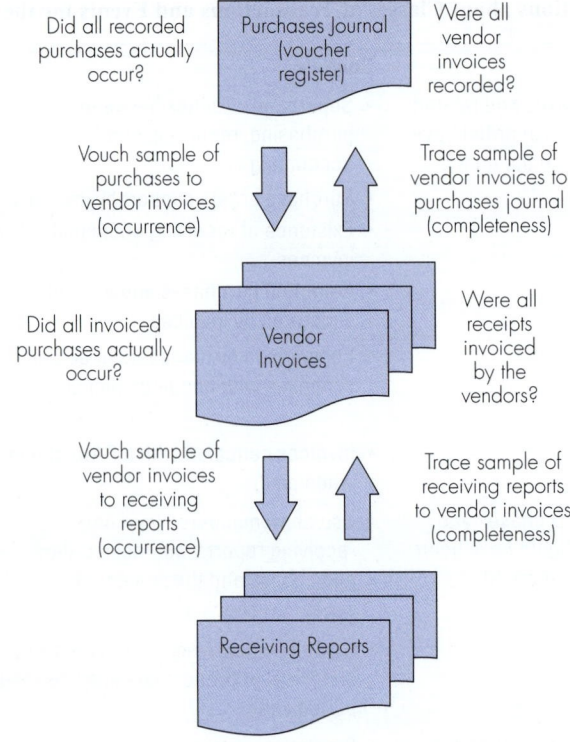

controls are strong, only large items in purchases, cash disbursements, and fixed assets may be examined in the search for unrecorded liabilities in accounts payable, and if *occurrence* controls are strong, vouching of expenses can be limited to significant items. On the other hand, if the tests of controls reveal weaknesses, the substantive procedures need to be designed to lower the detection risk for the account balances. For example, if *completeness* controls are weak, the auditor might send confirmation letters to vendors with small or zero balances. If *occurrence* controls are weak, the auditor may have to perform substantive tests of transactions by recalculating and testing a sample of payments for the period for monetary errors rather than just evidence of control effectiveness. Other substantive procedures that can be affected include vouching of debits to assets and expenses.

↳ REVIEW CHECKPOINTS

8.7 What primary functions should be separated in the acquisition and expenditure cycle?

8.8 What feature of the acquisition and expenditure control would be expected to prevent an employee's embezzling cash through creation of fictitious vouchers?

8.9 How would substantive procedures for accounts payable be affected by (a) a low risk of material misstatement or (b) a high risk of material misstatement?

SUBSTANTIVE PROCEDURES IN THE ACQUISITION AND EXPENDITURE CYCLE

The Completeness Assertion

Exhibit 8.6 lists assertions related to account balances in the acquisition and expenditure cycle and some illustrative substantive procedures. When considering assertions and obtaining evidence about accounts payable and other liabilities, auditors must emphasize

LEARNING OBJECTIVE 8-4
Explain the importance of the *completeness* assertion for the audit of accounts payable and list some procedures for a *search for unrecorded liabilities.*

STAGES OF AN AUDIT

the *completeness* assertion. (Remember from Chapter 7 that the emphasis is on the *existence* assertion for asset and revenue accounts.) This emphasis on completeness is rightly placed because financial statement users are typically more concerned if a company understates expenses and liabilities than if management overstates those accounts. Additional procedures are included in a sample audit plan in Appendix 8B.

Evidence is much more difficult to obtain to verify the *completeness* assertion than the *existence* assertion. Auditors cannot rely entirely on a management assertion of *completeness,* even in combination with a favorable assessment of the risk of material misstatement. The **search for unrecorded liabilities** is the set of procedures designed to yield audit evidence of liabilities that were not recorded in the reporting period. Such a search normally should be performed from the audit client's balance sheet date to the date of the auditors' report.

The following is a list of procedures useful in the *search for unrecorded liabilities.* The audit objective is to search all places where evidence of liabilities could exist.

- Inquire of client personnel about their procedures for ensuring that all liabilities are recorded.
- Scan the open purchase order file at year-end for indications of material purchase commitments at fixed prices. Obtain current prices and determine whether any adjustments for loss and liability for purchase commitments are needed.
- Examine the unmatched vendor invoices and determine when the goods were received, focusing on the unmatched receiving reports and receiving reports prepared around year-end. Determine which invoices, if any, should be recorded by tracing them to the payables listing.
- Review the unmatched receiving reports and determine whether entries are recorded in the proper accounting period.
- Select a sample of cash disbursements from the accounting period following the balance sheet date. Vouch them to supporting documents (invoice, receiving report) to determine whether the related liabilities were recorded in the proper accounting period.

EXHIBIT 8.6 Assertions about Account Balances at the Period-End and Substantive Procedures in the Acquisition and Expenditure Cycle

Assertions about Account Balances	Substantive Procedures
Existence—Accounts payable exist.	• Vouch recorded payables to vendor invoices, receiving reports, and purchase orders. • Confirm high-risk accounts payable with vendors.
Rights and obligations—The company has all rights to items purchased. Liabilities are obligations of the entity.	• Review bank confirmations, loan agreements, and minutes of the board for indications that property has been pledged as collateral.
Completeness—All payables that should have been recorded are recorded.	• Perform search for unrecorded liabilities.
Valuation or allocation—Purchases and related transactions have been recorded at the proper amount.	• Test mathematical accuracy of payables listing. • Select accounts due and test arithmetical accuracy and terms on invoices.

- Confirm accounts payable with vendors, especially those most likely to be understated (regular suppliers showing small or zero balances in the year-end accounts payable ledger). Unlike accounts receivable confirmations, accounts payable confirmations are not required by auditing standards. Such confirmations are not commonly used because they are primarily directed at the *existence* assertion, and the main concern regarding liabilities is *completeness*. However, accounts payable confirmations might be used under the following circumstances:
  - Internal controls are weak.
  - The company is in a tight cash position and bill paying is slow.
  - Physical inventories exceed general ledger inventory balances by significant amounts.
  - Certain vendors do not send statements.
  - Vendor accounts are pledged by assets.
  - Vendor accounts include unusual transactions.
- Perform analytical procedures appropriate in the circumstances. In general, accounts payable volume and period-end balances should increase when the company experiences increases in physical production volume or engages in inventory stockpiling. Some liabilities can be functionally related to other activities; for example, sales taxes are functionally related to sales dollar totals, payroll taxes to payroll totals, excise taxes to sales dollars or volume, and income taxes to income.
- Purchase cutoff must be tested both at year-end and in conjunction with the observation of the physical inventory count. Receiving reports issued and unissued at the end of the period are examined and listed. Later, auditors check to ensure that the goods received on the issued reports are included in inventory and payables and to ensure that no goods are recorded for the unissued receiving reports.

↳ REVIEW CHECKPOINTS

8.10 Describe the purpose and give examples of audit procedures in the search for unrecorded liabilities.

8.11 In substantive procedures, why is the emphasis on the *completeness* assertion for liabilities instead of on the *existence* assertion as in the audit of assets?

Auditing Other Accounts in the Acquisition and Expenditure Cycle

Prepaid Expenses and Accrued Liabilities

LEARNING OBJECTIVE 8-5
Discuss audit procedures for other accounts affected by the acquisition and expenditure cycle.

Some of the other accounts affected by the acquisition and expenditure cycle are listed in Exhibit 8.3. Performing substantive procedures for cash and inventory accounts are discussed in other chapters. Many accounts, particularly expense accounts, can be tested using analytical procedures, such as horizontal and vertical analyses. Other accounts such as prepaid expenses can be analyzed by a schedule similar to Exhibit 8.7. In addition to vouching payments, related expense accounts are cross referenced to expense workpapers (X-10, 11, 12 in Exhibit 8.7). A sample audit plan for prepaid, deferred, and accrued expenses is shown at Appendix Exhibit 8B.2.

Accrued Income Taxes

Income taxes are a special audit area because the accounting and underlying federal tax laws are so complex. State and local tax differences add to the complexity. Approximately one-third of the first round of adverse opinions on internal controls under Sarbanes-Oxley requirements cited tax accounting control weaknesses.[7] In addition, income tax expense is

---
[7] K. Frieswick, *CFO Magazine,* November 7, 2005, www.cfo.com/article.cfm/5077959/c_2984354/?f=archives.

EXHIBIT 8.7 Account Analysis for Prepaid Expenses

DUNDER-MIFFLIN
Prepaid Expenses
For Year Ended 12/31/2012
Prepared by Client

E-1

| Prepared by | RJR 1/16/13 |
| Reviewed by | TJL 1/18/13 |

Acct #	Account Title	(Audited) Balance 12/31/2011	Additions	Amortization/ Disposals	Unaudited Balance 12/31/2012
14100	Prepaid insurance	$706,148.66 PY	$941,531.55 v	$904,365.83 C X-10	$743,314.38
14200	Prepaid rent	190,000.00 PY	760,000.00 v	750,000.00 C X-11	200,000.00
14300	Office supplies	7,036.48 PY	26,025.00 v	25,654.66 C X-12	7,406.82
		$903,185.14	$1,727,556.55	$1,680,020.59	$950,721.20 CF
		F	F	F	F TB

PY = Agreed to prior-year documentation
v = Vouched to policies or agreements and vendor invoice
F = Footed
CF = Cross-footed
C = Calculated
TB = Agreed to Trial Balance

one of the largest items on the income statement. *Accounting Standard Codification 740 (ASC 740)* requires companies to estimate deferred income tax assets and liabilities, both of which are very subjective. An important aspect of *ASC 740* requires a higher standard for tax benefits before they can be recognized in a company's financial statements. Public accounting firms normally include tax specialists on the audit team to assess tax liabilities and estimates. The procedures for auditing estimates (discussed in detail in Chapter 10) are generally followed, including evaluating controls over management's procedures for determining assumptions and calculating the amounts. Basic audit procedures are similar to those discussed for accrued liabilities: Auditors vouch payments, test the expense, and recalculate the liability. All tax returns and government communications are carefully reviewed.

AUDITING INSIGHT — H&R Block Accounting Is Taxing

As part of its ongoing work to remediate control weaknesses in its corporate tax function, **H&R Block** restated its results for fiscal years 2005 and 2004 as well as previously reported quarterly results for fiscal 2006. The restatement pertains principally to errors in determining the company's state income tax rate, resulting in a cumulative understatement of its state income tax liability of approximately $32 million as of April 30, 2005.

Source: H&R Block press release, February 23, 2006.

Property, Plant, and Equipment and Intangible Assets

Assertions Management makes assertions about *existence, completeness, rights and obligations,* and *valuation and allocation.* Typical specific assertions relating to property, plant, and equipment (PP&E) and intangible assets include these:

- Recorded PP&E exist.
- All PP&E are recorded (completeness).

- PP&E are owned (rights).
- Repairs and maintenance expense does not include items that should have been capitalized (completeness).
- Freight-in is included as part of purchase and added to equipment costs (valuation).
- Purchased goodwill is properly valued (valuation).
- Goodwill is not impaired (valuation).
- Capitalized intangible costs relate to intangibles acquired in exchange transactions (existence).
- Amortization and depreciation expenses are properly allocated (valuation).
- Items listed in PP&E are used in operations (presentation and disclosure)

Audit Procedures

The two primary means of gathering evidence supporting management's assertions with respect to PP&E are physical inspection and vouching. The principal goal of the physical inspection of PP&E is to determine actual *existence* and condition of the property (*valuation*). The inspection of equipment should be compared to detailed PP&E records. Unlike current assets, most of the items in PP&E were also in the account in the previous year. Therefore, if the company was audited last year, the audit team can trace existing items to the previous-year audit documentation. The cost of newly acquired PP&E can be vouched to invoices, purchase documents and/or physically inspected (*existence, valuation*), and title documents (such as on land, buildings) may be inspected (*rights and obligations*). Disposals of items that were on last year's list also should be traced to cash receipts records if they were sold or to other documentation if they were traded in or abandoned. Auditors also should prepare or obtain a schedule of casualty insurance on buildings and equipment and determine the adequacy of insurance in relation to asset market values. Auditors should always keep their eyes open for buildings or equipment not in use. Equipment not in use with no intention of being used in the future (e.g. held for disposal or sale) should not be included in PP&E.

The depreciation schedule is audited by recalculating the depreciation expense (*valuation or allocation*), using the company's methods, estimates of useful life, and estimates of residual value. Auditors also must evaluate the useful lives and residual values assigned by the client for reasonableness. Industry groups often publish tables of useful lives of assets commonly found in the industry. The asset acquisition and disposition information in the schedule gives auditors some key information for auditing the asset additions and disposals. When the schedule covers hundreds of assets and numerous additions and disposals, auditors can use (1) CAATs to recalculate the depreciation expense and (2) sampling to choose additions and disposals for tests of controls and substantive procedures. See Exhibit 8.8 for an abbreviated illustration of audit documentation for PP&E and depreciation. Note that the ending balances of PP&E, accumulated depreciation, and depreciation expense are carried forward to the trial balance.

With respect to intangible assets, official documents of patents, copyrights, and trademark rights can be inspected to see that they are recorded in the client's name. Currently, goodwill is of special interest to companies and auditors. A recent study by **KPMG** in the United States indicates that goodwill impairment in 2008 more than doubled to $339.6 billion with the median charge going up tenfold. The number of companies in the U.S. study that had goodwill impairment in 2008 increased to nearly 20 percent, up almost threefold from the previous year.[8] The client must review goodwill for impairment. The auditors must review and evaluate management's calculations and decisions to ensure that goodwill is correctly valued and impairments are properly recorded. Amortization of other intangibles should be recalculated. Similar to depreciation expense, this expense owes its existence to a calculation, and recalculation based on audited costs and rates is sufficient appropriate audit evidence.

---

[8]"Goodwill Impairment in 2009," Press Release, http://www.kpmg.com/global/pressroom/pressreleases/Pages/Goodwill-impairment-in-2009.aspx.

EXHIBIT 8.8 Sample PP&E and Depreciation Documentation

DUNDER-MIFFLIN
Building and Land Improvements
for Year Ended 12/31/2012
Prepared By Client

F-1

| Prepared by | RJR 2/18/13 |
| Reviewed by | TJL 2/20/13 |

	Asset Cost ($s)				Accumulated Depreciation ($s)			
Description	Beginning Balance	Added	Sold	Ending Balance	Beginning Balance	Depreciation Expense	Sold	Ending Balance
Building 1	$218,367 PY	$0	$0	$218,367	$54,591 PY	$10,918 C	$0	$65,509
Building 2	0	155,976 v	0	155,976	0	1,050 C	0	1,050
Building 1 improvements	149,737 PY	109,825 v	10,000 E	249,562	37,434 PY	10,232 C	2,500 C	45,166
Total buildings and improvements	$368,104	$265,801	$10,000	$623,905 TB	$92,025	$22,200 TB	$2,500	$111,725 TB
	F	F	F	F/CF	F	F	F	F/CF

PY = Agreed to prior-year documentation.
v = Vouched to purchase contract.
E = Examined sales agreement and related cash receipts.
F = Footed.
CF = Cross-footed.
C = Recalculated.
TB = Carried forward to the Trial Balance.

AUDITING INSIGHT — How Good Is Goodwill?

Northrop Grumman Corporation announced a fourth quarter noncash, after-tax charge of $3.0 to $3.4 billion for impairment of goodwill in accordance with *Accounting Standards Codification 350 (ASC 350)*, "Goodwill and Other Intangible Assets." As a result of this charge, the company reported a net loss for the fourth quarter and in 2008. The company performed its required annual testing of goodwill as of November 30, 2008, using a discounted cash flow analysis supported by comparative market multiples to determine the fair values of its businesses versus their book values. Testing as of November 30, 2008, indicated that book values for shipbuilding and space technology exceeded the fair values of these businesses. The charge is attributable to goodwill recorded in connection with acquisitions made in 2001 and 2002.

Source: Northrop Grumman press release, January 22, 2009, http://www.irconnect.com/noc/press/pages/news_releases.html?d=158124.

Auditors inquire of company counsel about knowledge of any lawsuits or defects relating to patents, copyrights, trademarks, or trade names. Questions about lawsuits challenging patents, copyrights, or trade names can produce early knowledge of problem areas for further investigation. Likewise, discussions and questions about research and development successes and failures can alert the audit team to problems of valuation of intangible assets and related amortization expenses. Responses to questions about licensing of patents can be used in the audit of related royalty revenue accounts. Auditors can confirm royalty income from patent licenses received from a single licensee and review licensing and royalty contracts. However, such income amounts usually are audited by vouching the licensee's reports and the related cash receipt.

Vouching may be extensive in the areas of research and development (R&D) and deferred software development costs. The principal evidence problem is to determine whether costs are properly classified as assets or as R&D expenses. Recorded amounts generally are selected on a sample basis and the purchase orders, receiving reports, payroll records, authorization notices, and management reports are compared with them. Some R&D costs can resemble non-R&D cost (such as supplies, payroll costs), so auditors must be very careful in the vouching to be alert for costs that appear to relate to other operations.

Merger and acquisition transactions should be reviewed in terms of the appraisals, judgments, and allocations used to assign portions of the purchase price to tangible assets, intangible assets, liabilities, and goodwill. In the final analysis, nothing really substitutes for the inspection of transaction documentation, but verbal inquiries can help auditors to understand the circumstances of a merger. An illustrative plan of substantive procedures for PP&E and related accounts can be found in Appendix Exhibit 8B.3.

AUDITING INSIGHT | The Sign of the Credit Balance

Auto Parts & Repair, Inc., kept perpetual inventory records and equipment records on a computerized system. Because of the size of the files (8,000 parts in various locations and 1,500 asset records), the company never printed reports for visual inspection. Auditors ran a computer-audit "sign test" on inventory balances and equipment net book balances that called for a printed report for all balances less than zero. The auditors discovered 320 negative inventory balances that were caused by employees' failure to record purchases and 125 negative net asset balances caused by depreciating assets more than their cost.

Other Expenses

As mentioned earlier, most expense accounts can be tested in conjunction with tests of related assets and liabilities (e.g., depreciation) or through analytical procedures. However, if risk of material misstatement is high, expenses can be tested by **substantive tests of transactions** by which a sample of transactions is tested much like a test of controls except that auditors look for evidence that the transactions are properly recorded rather than that controls are operating. Payroll expense is usually audited by testing controls or using substantive tests of transactions and performing analytical procedures (see Appendix 8C). Some expenses should be examined separately because of their unique nature. For example, the client should list legal and professional expenses, and significant amounts should be vouched so the auditors can determine what legal and professional services the client is using. Miscellaneous expenses likewise should be listed and examined for significant unusual items. Finally, maintenance and repairs should be examined to determine whether any items should be capitalized.

Presentation and Disclosure

Once auditors are satisfied that controls have been examined and transactions and balances have been appropriately tested, the job is not over. The accounts in the acquisition and expenditure cycle require many disclosures. Depreciation methods, asset impairments, leases, and details about income taxes are only a few of the essential items with specific presentation and disclosures requirements. These disclosures must ensure that the presentation and disclosure assertions of *occurrence* and *rights and obligations, completeness, classification and understandability,* and *accuracy and valuation* are all met.

↳ REVIEW CHECKPOINTS

8.12 How do audit procedures for prepaid expenses and accrued liabilities also provide audit evidence about related expense accounts?

8.13 What assertions found in PP&E, investments, and intangibles accounts are of interest to an auditor during the examination of the expenditure and acquisition cycle?

8.14 What items in a client's PP&E and depreciation schedule give auditors points of departure (assertions) for audit procedures?

8.15 What four methods are used to audit other expense accounts?

AUDIT RISK MODEL SUMMARY

Now that the elements of risk of material misstatement for the acquisition and expenditure cycle as well as some of the important substantive procedures have been presented, let's examine how auditors might apply the audit risk model for the completeness and classification assertions.

Chi-Chi's Clothing Stores, Inc. Example

Chi-Chi's Clothing Stores, Inc. is a chain of women's clothing stores that sells upscale fashions, mostly in the northeastern United States. Chi-Chi's is a public company with annual sales increasing at a rate of almost 30 percent per year. David Escobar has been assigned as the senior auditor. The policy of his firm is to always set overall audit risk as low. Chi-Chi's accounting department and systems have not kept up with the rapid growth. As a result, numerous audit adjustments have been required every year, and the company received an adverse report on internal controls in the previous year. One problem has been that invoices do not come from the stores on a timely basis. The company has been very profitable, causing enormous increases in management stock options, which are a significant part of management compensation. Although the economy has taken a downturn, management and analyst forecasts still project a 30 percent growth rate. Escobar is concerned that management could be biased toward understating costs and liabilities and therefore sets inherent risk at high.

As mentioned, controls have not kept pace with company growth. Chi-Chi's has been working to improve the systems, but the accounting department and internal audit department are overworked. Their staff members have not had time to sufficiently test new systems or train new personnel. Thus, Escobar assesses control risk as high and plans to test only year-end controls sufficiently to comply with *AS 5*. In this situation, Escobar believes he must set risk of material misstatement as high and set detection risk at low. He will perform an extensive search for unrecorded liabilities, examining a large sample of disbursements after the balance sheet date, and he will send confirmations to vendors that historically have had activity but have small or zero year-end balances. Escobar also will vouch a sample of additions to PP&E accounts to ensure they are not items that should be properly expensed. The combination of high inherent risk, high control risk, and low detection risk should lead Escobar to an acceptably low overall audit risk.

FINDING FRAUD SIGNS IN ACCOUNTS PAYABLE

LEARNING OBJECTIVE 8-6
Specify some ways fraud can be found in accounts payable and cash disbursements.

Fraudsters can have a field day generating false payments through a company's acquisition and expenditure systems. A common scheme is to send false invoices on the letterhead of a fictitious vendor to the company and have an insider manipulate supporting documents or controls to make payments. Sometimes a company's own employees engage in unauthorized "business" as suppliers to their employers. In these cases, the perpetrators receive company payments from these "vendors" for personal use.

AUDIT INSIGHT — Did we take him to the hospital?

Olaronke Fakunle pleaded guilty to defrauding **Star Air Ambulance Service** of $210,000 between September 7, 2007, and October 9, 2008. Fakunle was able to divert money from the organization by setting up Blackbaud, a false corporation, and creating fictitious invoices for that company. A week after the controller at Star began an internal investigation into payments to Blackbaud, Fakunle gave her two weeks notice. She then went to work for **Rosen Canada Ltd.** where she fraudulently received $54,885 using a similar fictitious vendor scheme.

Source: "Stars Bilked for $210,000," *The Daily Herald-Tribune* (Grande Prairie, Alberta, Canada), November 9, 2010.

These frauds can proceed undetected for a long time as long as auditors and managers do not identify the signs and signals the perpetrators leave behind. If the review for fraud risk indicates that a potential significant risk of fraud exists in the acquisition and expenditure cycle, auditors can try several types of searches and matches in the company's records. These searches and matches are often performed using CAATs.

- *Look for photocopies of invoices in the files.* Fraudsters alter real invoices for false or duplicate payments and make photocopies to hide whiteout and cut-and-paste changes.
- *Look for a vendor's invoices submitted in numerical order.* False vendors sometimes use the same pad of prenumbered invoices (standard office supply store printing) to send bills to the company. Either the company is the vendor's only customer or the company is a victim of a false billing scheme.
- *Look for a vendor's invoices that always are in round numbers.* Prices, shipping charges, and taxes too often come in penny amounts, making a vendor's invoice in even dollars an unusual occurrence.
- *Look for vendor's invoices that are always slightly lower than a review threshold.* Insiders know that a company gives special attention and approval to invoices over a specified dollar amount (e.g., $10,000). Therefore, the fraudster always avoids invoices for more than that amount.
- *Look for vendors with only post office box addresses.* Although many businesses use post office box addresses for receiving payments, invoices also should show a street address location.
- *Look for vendors with no listed telephone number.* Legitimate businesses normally do not hide behind unlisted telephone numbers. Also, cheap fraudsters sometimes do not buy a phone line for their false companies.
- *Match vendor and employee addresses and telephone numbers.* Many companies have policies that their employees cannot also be vendors. Insiders (employees) often know how to circumvent controls when their business with the employer could be suspicious.
- *Look for multiple vendors at the same address and telephone number.* Many invoices from the same location, especially invoices for different kinds of products and services, could simply come from a front organization conducting a false invoice scheme. However, legitimate suppliers often operate under several company names and conduct business from the same location.
- *Look for vendors not on the approved vendor list.*
- *Know the addresses of the local mail drops (e.g. shipping and packaging stores that accept client mail).* These stores provide a street address for fraudulent companies, adding false legitimacy to their fraudulent invoices.

↳ REVIEW CHECKPOINTS

LEARNING OBJECTIVE 8-7
Describe some common errors and frauds in the acquisition and expenditure cycle and design some audit and investigation procedures for detecting them.

8.16 What items could indicate a significant risk of fraud in the acquisition and expenditure cycle (i.e., be red flags)?

8.17 Describe the purpose and give examples of specific fraud detection procedures in the acquisition and expenditure cycle.

8.18 Are these specific fraud detection procedures designed to detect fraudulent financial reporting or misappropriation of assets? Explain.

▽ FRAUD CASES: EXTENDED AUDIT PROCEDURES (ISA/AU 320)

The audit of account balances consists of procedural efforts to detect errors and frauds that could exist in the balances, thus making them misleading in financial statements.

Case 8.1

Printing (Copying) Money

PROBLEM

Argus Productions, Inc., a motion picture and commercial production company, assigned M. Welby the authority and responsibility for obtaining copies of scripts used in production. Established procedures permitted Welby to arrange for outside script-copying services, receive the copies, and approve the bills for payment. In effect, Welby was the "purchasing department" and the "receiving department" for this particular service. To a certain extent, Welby was also the "accounting department" by virtue of approving bills for payment and coding them for assignment to projects. Welby did not make the actual accounting entries or sign the checks.

Welby set up a fictitious company under the registered name Quickprint Company with himself as the incorporator and stockholder complete with a post office box number, letterhead stationery, and nicely printed invoices but no printing equipment. Legitimate copy services were "subcontracted" by Quickprint to perform the actual printing and then billed Quickprint. Welby then prepared Quickprint invoices billing Argus, usually at the legitimate shop's rate, but for a few extra copies each time. Welby also submitted Quickprint bills to Argus for fictitious copying jobs on scripts for movies and commercials that never went into production. As the owner of Quickprint, Welby endorsed Argus's checks with a rubber stamp and deposited the money in the business bank account, paid the legitimate printing bills, and took the rest for personal use.

Argus's production cost files contained all of the Quickprint bills sorted under the names of the movie and commercial production projects. Welby even created files for proposed films that never went into full production and thus should not have had script-copying costs. There were no copying service bills from any shop other than Quickprint Company.

Welby conducted this fraud for five years, embezzling $475,000 in false and inflated billings. (Argus's net income was overstated a modest amount because copying costs were capitalized as part of production cost and then amortized over a two- to three-year period.)

AUDIT APPROACH

Management should assign the authority to request copies and the purchasing authority to different responsible employees. Other persons also should perform the accounting, including coding cost assignments to projects. Managerial review of production results could result in notice of excess costs.

The request for the quantity (number) of copies of a script should come from a person involved in production who knows the number needed. This person also should sign off for the receipt (or approve the bill) for this requested number of copies, thus acting as the "receiving department." This procedure could prevent waste (excess cost), especially if the requesting person also were held responsible for the profitability of the project. A company agent always performs actual purchasing, and, in this case, the agent was Welby. Purchasing agents generally have latitude to seek the best service at the best price with or without bids from competitors. A requirement to obtain bids is usually a good idea, but much legitimate purchasing is done without bid. However, an approval process should be employed before vendors are placed on the approved vendor list.

Someone in the accounting department should be responsible for coding invoices for charges to authorized projects, thus making it possible to detect costs charged to projects not actually in production. Someone with managerial responsibility should review project costs and the purchasing practices. However, this is an expensive use of executive time. It was not spent in the Argus case.

In gaining an understanding of the internal controls, auditors could learn of the trust and responsibility vested in Welby. Because the embezzlement was about $95,000 per year, the total copying cost under Welby's control must have been around $1 million or more. (It might attract unwanted attention to inflate a cost more than 10 percent.)

Controls were very weak, especially in the combination of duties performed by Welby and in the lack of managerial review. For all practical purposes, there were no controls to test other than to see whether Welby had approved the copying cost bills and coded them to active projects. This provides an opportunity because proper classification is a control objective.

The auditors should select a sample of project files and vouch costs charged to them to support in source documents (*occurrence* direction of the test). Select a sample of expenditures and trace them to the project cost records shown coded on the expenditures (*completeness* direction of the test).

Substantive procedures are directed to obtaining evidence about the *existence* of film projects, *completeness* of the costs charged to them, *valuation* of the capitalized project costs, *rights* in copyright and ownership, and proper *disclosure* of amortization methods. The most important procedures are the same as the tests of control activities; thus, when performed at the year-end date on the capitalized cost balances, they are dual-purpose audit procedures. Either of the procedures described earlier as tests of controls should show evidence of projects that had never gone into production. (Auditors should be careful to obtain a list of actual projects before they begin the procedures.) Chances are good that the discovery of bad project codes with copying cost will reveal a pattern of Quickprint bills.

Knowing that controls over copying cost are weak, auditors could be tipped off to the possibility of a Welby-Quickprint connection. Efforts to locate Quickprint should be taken (telephone book, chamber of commerce, other directories). Inquiry with the secretary of state for names of the Quickprint incorporators should reveal Welby's connection. The audit findings can then be turned over to a trained investigator to arrange an interview and confrontation with Welby.

DISCOVERY SUMMARY

In this case, internal auditors performed a review of project costs at the request of the manager of production, who was worried about profitability. The auditors performed the procedures described earlier, noticed the dummy projects and the Quickprint bills, investigated the ownership of Quickprint, and discovered Welby's association. They had first tried to locate Quickprint's shop but could not find it in the telephone, chamber of commerce, or other city directories. They were careful not to direct any mail to the post office box for fear of alerting the then-unknown parties involved. A sly internal auditor already had used a ruse at the post office and learned that Welby rented the box, but the auditors did not know whether anyone else was involved. Alerted, the internal auditors gathered all Quickprint bills and determined the total charged for nonexistent projects. Carefully, under the covert observation of a representative of the local district attorney's office, Welby was interviewed and readily confessed.

Case 8.2
Real Cash Paid to Phony Doctors

PROBLEM

As manager of the claims processing department, Martha Lee was considered one of Beta Magnetic's best employees. She had never missed a day of work in 10 years and her department had one of the company's best efficiency ratings. Controls were considered good, including the verification by a claims processor that (1) the patient was a Beta employee, (2) medical treatments were covered in the plan, (3) the charges were within approved guidelines, (4) the cumulative claims for the employee did not exceed $50,000 (paid all claims less than $50,000 but submitted claims more than $50,000 to an insurance company), and (5) the calculation for payment was correct. After verification processing, claims were sent to the claims payment department to pay the doctor directly. No payments ever went directly to employees.

Lee prepared false claims on real employees, forging the signatures of various claims processors, adding her own review approval, and naming bogus doctors who would be paid by the payment department. The payments were mailed to various post office box addresses and to her husband's business address.

Nobody ever verified claims information with the employees. The employees received no reports of medical benefits paid on their behalf. Although the department had performance reports by claims processors, these reports did not show claim-by-claim details. No one verified the credentials of the doctors. As noted, Martha never missed a day of work for vacation or sickness. She was considered an ideal employee.

The falsified claim forms were in Beta's files, containing all fictitious data on employee names, processor signatures, doctors' bills, and phony doctors and addresses. The canceled checks were returned by the bank and were kept in Beta's files, containing "endorsements" by the doctors. Lee and her husband were clever: They deposited the checks in various banks in accounts opened in the names of the "doctors."

Lee did not stumble on the audit trail. She drew the attention of an auditor who saw her take her 24 claims processing employees out to an annual staff appreciation luncheon in a fleet of stretch limousines.

Over the seven years, Lee and her husband had stolen $3.5 million and, until the last, no one noticed anything unusual about the total amount of claims paid.

AUDIT APPROACH

The controls were good as far as they went. The claims processors used internal data in their work: employee files for identification, treatment descriptions submitted by doctors with comparisons with plan provisions, and mathematical calculations. This work amounted to all approval necessary for the claims payment department to prepare a check. No controls connected the claims data with outside sources such as employee acknowledgment or doctor investigation. Employees certainly should be notified of any payments made on their behalf.

By never taking a day off, Lee was able to make sure she saw all documents related to her scheme. The company needed an enforced vacation and employee rotation policy.

The processing and control work in the claims payment department can be audited for deviations from controls. The auditors should select a sample of paid claims and reperform the claims processing procedures to verify the employee status, coverage of treatment, proper guideline charges, cumulative amount of less than $50,000, and accurate calculation. However, this procedure would not help answer the question "Does Martha Lee steal the money to pay for the limousines?"

"Thinking like a crook" points out the holes in the controls. Nobody seeks to verify data with external sources. However, the audit team must be careful in an investigation not to cast aspersions on a manager by letting rumors start when interviewing employees to find out whether they actually had the medical attention whose claim is paid on their behalf. If money is being taken, the company check must be intercepted in some manner.

The balance under audit is the sum of the charges in the employee medical benefits expense account and the objective relates to the valid existence of the payments.

The first procedure can be as follows: Obtain a list of doctors paid by the company and look them up in the state medical society directory. Look up their business addresses and determine whether they are valid. You could try comparing claims processors' signatures on various forms, but this is difficult and requires training. An extended procedure would be as follows: Compare the doctors' addresses to addresses known to be associated with Lee and other claims processing employees.

DISCOVERY SUMMARY

The comparison of doctors to the medical society directory showed eight "doctors" who were not licensed in the current period. Five of these eight had post office box addresses, and discrete inquiries and surveillance showed that Lee rented theme. The other three had the same mailing address as her husband's business. Further investigation involving the district attorney and police was necessary to obtain personal financial records and reconstruct the thefts from prior years.

↳ REVIEW CHECKPOINTS

8.19 What key control concept was missing at Argus Productions?

8.20 What evidence could the *verbal inquiry* audit procedure provide in "Printing (Copying) Money"?

8.21 If Lee had not been seen taking employees out in a limousine, how else could she have been caught?

8.22 How would a policy of mandatory vacations have helped discover the Beta fraud?

AUDIT ISSUES IN THE EXPENSE AND ACQUISITION CYCLE

Auditing the acquisition and expenditure cycle is not straightforward. Because it is ripe for fraud, an auditor must be aware that inappropriate policies and procedures or poor execution of processes can lead to problems for the client as illustrated by the following Audit Insight.

AUDITING INSIGHT — It's Not Fraud—It's Just a Mess

When Jim Farrelly took over as executive director of the **Pasco Hernando Early Learning Coalition,** arranging for an audit was at the top of his to-do list. The CPA firm of **Woodruff, Wardlow, Nelson & Cash** found the following:

- Purchases costing more than $5,000 were made without board approval in violation of the agency's policy.
- An American Express card used by staffers was in the name of a director rather than the Coalition.
- Invoices submitted to the State Office of Early Learning did not match amounts on invoices submitted for payment.
- The financial records used to report expenditures incurred for services provided for school readiness and voluntary prekindergarten programs cannot be relied upon and are inaccurate.
- Sloppy record keeping did not reflect employees' paid leave time.
- Methods of recording fixed assets were inadequate.
- Backup documentation for transactions in accounts payable was lacking.
- One staffer handles bills *and* paid them.
- No staffers were qualified in applying generally accepted accounting practices to record financial transactions and prepare financial statements.

The firm's recommendations include:

- Accounts payable should be coordinated by the fiscal manager, office manager, and executive director.
- Invoices should not be paid without purchase documentation.
- All transactions exceeding $5,000 should be noted with the date of board approval.
- A computer-based system of inventory control using bar codes should be established.
- A computer system should be established for tracking employees' accrued time off.
- Invoices submitted for state reimbursement should require paperwork showing that the amount matches the invoices.

Source: "Board 'Disturbed' by Audit Findings," *St. Petersburg Times,* May 17, 2008, p.8

AUDITING INSIGHT — PCAOB Inspections and the Acquisition and Expenditure Cycle

- The audit documentation did not evidence sufficient testing of . . . fair values allocated to certain assets and liabilities, useful lives assigned to the acquired assets, and the amount of the asset retirement obligation. In addition, there was no evidence that the Firm (1) evaluated the qualifications and relationships to the issuer of the specialists used to determine the fair values of certain of the acquired assets and liabilities, (2) obtained an understanding of the methods and assumptions used by the specialists, or (3) tested the data used by the specialists.
- The Firm's analytical procedures to test operating expenses did not meet the requirements for substantive analytical procedures because, in one procedure, the Firm did not set a threshold for investigation and evaluation that allowed it to achieve the desired level of assurance and, in another procedure, there was no evidence in the audit documentation, and no persuasive other evidence, that the Firm had obtained corroboration of management's explanations for significant differences from the Firm's expectations.
- The issuer completed a significant acquisition during the year. The Firm failed to perform audit procedures regarding the revenues and expenses of the acquired company from the date of acquisition to year end.
- In connection with an acquisition . . . one issuer engaged a valuation specialist who provided the issuer with an estimated enterprise value for the acquired business, which approximated the purchase price. Later in the year, the issuer settled a contingent liability of the acquired business under terms that were significantly less favorable from a cash flow perspective than had been expected at the time of the acquisition. In the fourth quarter...the issuer estimated the fair value of the acquired entity based on the lower projected cash flows. In this fair value estimate, certain of the issuer's other assumptions, including the discount rate and terminal growth rate, were significantly more favorable than those that the valuation specialist had used earlier that year. The effect of these more favorable assumptions more than offset the effect of the decrease in projected cash flows, and, had these other assumptions not been changed, the estimated fair value of the acquired business would have been less than its carrying value. There was no evidence in the audit documentation, and no persuasive other evidence, that the Firm had addressed the inconsistencies between the assumptions used to estimate the values on the two dates.

Sources: 2005, 2008 PCAOB Inspection of Deloitte & Touche (November 30, 2006; April 16, 2009); 2006, 2008 PCAOB Inspection of Ernst & Young (May 2, 2007, May 19, 2009); 2005 Inspection of KPMG (January 11, 2007); and 2009 Inspection of PricewaterhouseCoopers (March 25, 2009). All reports can be found on the PCAOB's Web site, www.pcaob.org/Inspections/Public_Reports/index.aspx.

Even with proper diligence and due professional care it may be difficult to identify all issues related to expenses, purchases, and unrecorded items. This is illustrated in the Auditing Insight on the preceding page that lists matters identified by the Public Company Accounting Oversight Board (PCAOB) during its annual inspections for audits conducted by the Big Four firms.

Summary

The acquisition and expenditure cycle consists of purchase requisitioning, purchase ordering, receiving goods and services, recording vendors' invoices, accounting for accounts payable, and making cash disbursements. Companies reduce control risk by having a suitable separation of authorization, custody, recording, and periodic reconciliation duties. Error-checking procedures of comparing purchase orders and receiving reports with vendor invoices are important for recording proper amounts of accounts payable liabilities. Having a separation of duties between preparing cash disbursement checks and actually signing them provides supervisory control. Otherwise, many things—ranging from processing false or fictitious purchase orders to failing to record liabilities for goods and services received—could go wrong.

Purchases are executed for a myriad of items including inventory; property, plant, and equipment; supplies; and all other items necessary for a business to operate. Large purchases for capital equipment may be significant items requiring the auditors' inspection and review. Reviewing the accruals for income taxes may be complex, especially if the organization is operating in multiple tax jurisdictions. The use of a tax specialist may be appropriate in auditing income tax expense.

The *completeness* assertion is important in the audit of liabilities because misleading financial statements often have involved unrecorded liabilities and expenses. The search for unrecorded liabilities is an important set of audit procedures. The section "Finding Fraud Signs in Accounts Payable" suggests some methods for finding signs that could indicate false payments to fictitious vendors.

Key Terms

approved vendor list: A record of vendors that have been vetted to ensure that vendors meet company policy and procedure in terms of price, quality, delivery, etc. This control activity provides evidence to auditors of vendor existence, 321

bill of lading: A contract between the shipper and the carrier; includes shipping information such as ship dates and origination, purchase order number, and signatures for receipt of merchandise, 322

capitalizing: The recording of expenditures as assets and charging them to expense by a systematic allocation over a number of years, 319

clearing accounts [Appendix 8C]: The temporary storage places for transactions awaiting final accounting that should eventually have zero balances, 360

electronic data interchange (EDI): The transfer of data between/among different companies using networks such as the Internet, 321

ghost employees [Appendix 8C]: The fictitious or separated employees fraudulently maintained on the payroll to obtain checks, 356

imprest bank account [Appendix 8C]: An account used for special purposes such as payroll or branch banking that is maintained at a zero or fixed balance in the general ledger. Checks written on the account are offset by deposits of the same amount, 359

matching: The recognition od expenses in the same period as associated revenues, 318

purchase order: A formal contractual document (may be a computer document) between a buyer and seller issued by the buyer establishing price, delivery point, delivery dates, and other information pertinent to the purchase, 321

purchase requisition: An internal document initialed by a department or person within the entity asking the purchasing department to buy specific goods or services, 321

receiving report: The documentation completed by the receiving department that includes receiving date and time, purchase order number, condition of material received, and amount of material received; provides evidence regarding the receipt of materials by the entity, 322

search for unrecorded liabilities: A substantive procedure to test the completeness assertion for liability accounts, 329

substantive tests of transactions: The tests of a sample of transactions during the period for monetary errors, 334

vendor's invoice: A bill sent from the vendor to the entity purchasing the goods or services, 323

voucher/voucher package: A document used as a source for recording payables. It shows approvals, accounts, and amounts to be recorded, usually attached to the supporting purchase order, receiving report, and vendor invoice, 323.

W-2 [Appendix 8C]: The annual report of gross salaries and wages and the income, Social Security, and Medicare taxes withheld, 361

Multiple-Choice Questions for Practice and Review

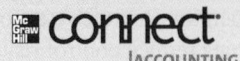 All applicable Exercises and Problems are available with McGraw-Hill's Connect® Accounting

LO 8-2
8.23 Which of the following accounts does *not* appear in the acquisition and expenditure cycle?
a. Cash.
b. Purchases Returns.
c. Sales Returns.
d. Prepaid Insurance.

LO 8-3
8.24 For which of the following accounts would the matching concept be the most appropriate?
a. Cost of Goods Sold.
b. Research and Development.
c. Depreciation Expense.
d. Sales.

LO 8-1
8.25 Which of the following would *not* overstate current period net income?
a. Capitalizing an expenditure that should be expensed.
b. Failing to record a liability as an expense.
c. Failing to record a check paying an item in Vouchers Payable.
d. All of the above would overstate net income.

LO 8-4
8.26 A client's purchasing system ends with the recording of a liability and its eventual payment. Which of the following best describes auditors' primary concern with respect to liabilities resulting from the purchasing system?
a. Accounts payable are not materially understated.
b. Authority to incur liabilities is restricted to one designated person.
c. Acquisition of materials is not made from one vendor or one group of vendors.
d. Commitments for all purchases are made only after established competitive bidding procedures are followed.

LO 8-3
8.27 Which of the following is an internal control activity that could prevent a paid disbursement voucher from being presented for payment a second time?
a. Vouchers should be prepared by individuals who are responsible for signing disbursement checks.
b. Disbursement vouchers should be approved by at least two responsible management officials.
c. The date on a disbursement voucher should be within a few days of the date the voucher is presented for payment.
d. The official who signs the check should compare the check with the voucher and should stamp "PAID" on the voucher documents.

LO 8-3
8.28 Budd, the purchasing agent of Lake Hardware Wholesalers, has a relative who owns a retail hardware store. Budd arranged for hardware to be delivered by manufacturers to the retail store on a cash-on-delivery (COD) basis, thereby enabling his relative to buy at Lake's wholesale prices. Budd was probably able to accomplish this because of Lake's poor internal control over
a. Purchase requisitions.
b. Cash receipts.
c. Perpetual inventory records.
d. Purchase orders.

LO 8-4 8.29 Which of the following is the best audit procedure for determining the existence of unrecorded liabilities?
a. Examine confirmation requests returned by creditors whose accounts are on a subsidiary trial balance of accounts payable.
b. Examine a sample of cash disbursements in the period subsequent to year-end.
c. Examine a sample of invoices a few days prior to and subsequent to the year-end to ascertain whether they have been properly recorded.
d. Examine unusual relationships between monthly accounts payable and recorded purchases.

LO 8-4 8.30 Which of the following procedures is *least* likely to be performed before the balance-sheet date?
a. Observation of inventory.
b. Review of internal control over cash disbursements.
c. Search for unrecorded liabilities.
d. Confirmation of receivables.

LO 8-4 8.31 To determine whether accounts payable are complete, auditors perform a test to verify that all merchandise received has been recorded. The population for this test consists of all
a. Vendors' invoices.
b. Purchase orders.
c. Receiving reports.
d. Canceled checks.

(AICPA adapted)

LO 8-3 8.32 When verifying debits to the perpetual inventory records of a nonmanufacturing company, auditors would be most interested in examining a sample of purchase
a. Approvals.
b. Requisitions.
c. Invoices.
d. Orders.

LO 8-3 8.33 A furniture company ordered 84 tables from a supplier. The supplier accidentally sent only 48 tables, but the receiving department at the furniture company accepted the tables. The invoice was eventually received but was for the original 84 tables. The furniture company paid the entire amount. Which of the following controls would have been *least* likely to have prevented this erroneous payment?
a. The copy of the purchase order sent to the furniture company's receiving department should not have shown an expected quantity.
b. Personnel in the furniture company's accounts payable department should compare the receiving report to the purchase invoice before creation of the voucher.
c. Personnel in the furniture company's cash disbursements department should compare the check that is prepared to all of the backup documentation.
d. Personnel in the furniture company's purchasing department should compare the purchase requisition with the purchase order.

LO 8-2 8.34 Curtis, a maintenance supervisor, submitted maintenance invoices from a phony repair company and received the checks at a post office box. This should have been prevented by
a. Comparison of the company name to the approved vendor list by the check signer.
b. Recognition of the excess maintenance costs by Curtis's supervisor.
c. Refusal by the purchasing department to approve the vendor.
d. All of the above.

LO 8-5 8.35 An audit team would most likely examine the detail support for charges to which of the following accounts?
a. Payroll expense.
b. Cost of goods sold.
c. Supplies expense.
d. Legal expense.

LO 8-5

8.36 Which of the following accounts would most likely be audited in connection with a related balance-sheet account?
   a. Property Tax Expense.
   b. Payroll Expense.
   c. Research and Development.
   d. Legal Expense.

LO 8-4

8.37 When auditing account balances of liabilities, auditors are most concerned with management's assertion about
   a. Existence.
   b. Rights and obligations.
   c. Completeness.
   d. Valuation and allocation.

LO 8-3

8.38 In a test of controls, auditors may trace receiving reports to vouchers recorded in the voucher register. This is a test for
   a. Occurrence.
   b. Completeness.
   c. Classification.
   d. Cutoff.

Exercises and Problems

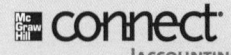 All applicable Exercises and Problems are available with McGraw-Hill's *Connect® Accounting*

8.39 **Payable ICQ Items: Assertions, Tests of Controls, and Possible Errors or Frauds.** Following is a selection of items from internal control questionnaires.

   1. Are purchase orders above a certain level approved by an officer?
   2. Are the quantity and quality of goods received determined at the time of receipt by receiving personnel independent of the purchasing department?

LO 8-1,2,3,4,5,6,7

   3. Are vendors' invoices matched against purchase orders and receiving reports before a liability is recorded?
   4. Are journal entries authorized at appropriate levels?

Required:

For each preceding item:
   a. Identify the management assertion to which it applies.
   b. Specify one test of controls auditors could use to determine whether the control was operating effectively.
   c. Give an example of an error or fraud that could occur if the control were absent or ineffective.
   d. Write a substantive procedure that could find errors or frauds that could result from the absence or ineffectiveness of the control items.

LO 8-4

8.40 **Unrecorded Liabilities Procedures.** You are in the final stages of your audit of the financial statements of Ozine Corporation for the year ended December 31, 2012, when the corporation's president consults you. The president believes there is no point to your examining the 2013 voucher register and testing data in support of 2013 entries. She stated that any bills pertaining to 2012 that were received too late to be included in the December voucher register were recorded by a year-end journal entry and the internal auditor tested for unrecorded liabilities after the year-end. The president will provide you a letter certifying that there are no unrecorded liabilities.

Required:

   a. Should your procedures for unrecorded liabilities be affected by the fact that the client made a journal entry to record 2012 bills that were received later? Explain.
   b. Should your test for unrecorded liabilities be affected by the fact that a letter is obtained in which a responsible management official certifies that, to the best of that person's knowledge, all liabilities have been recorded? Explain.
   c. Should your test for unrecorded liabilities be eliminated or reduced because of the internal audit work? Explain.

d. What sources, in addition to the 2013 voucher register, should you consider for locating possible unrecorded liabilities?

(AICPA adapted)

LO 8-4

8.41 **Accounts Payable Confirmations.** Partners Clark and Kent, both CPAs, are preparing their audit plan for the audit of accounts payable on Marlboro Corporation's annual audit. Saturday afternoon they reviewed the thick file of last year's documentation and they both remembered too well the six days they spent last year on accounts payable.

Last year, Clark had suggested that they mail confirmations to 100 of Marlboro's suppliers. The company regularly purchases from about 1,000 suppliers and these account payable balances fluctuate widely, depending on the volume of purchase and the terms Marlboro's purchasing agent is able to negotiate. Clark's sample of 100 was designed to include accounts with large balances. In fact, the 100 accounts confirmed last year covered 80 percent of the total dollars in accounts payable. Both Clark and Kent had spent many hours tracking down minor differences reported in confirmation responses. Nonresponding accounts were investigated by comparing Marlboro's balance with monthly statements received from suppliers.

Required:
a. Identify the accounts payable audit objectives that auditors must consider in determining the audit procedures to be performed.
b. Identify situations when auditors should use accounts payable confirmations and discuss whether they are required to use them.
c. Discuss why the use of large dollar balances as the basis for selecting accounts payable for confirmation is not the most effective approach and indicate a more effective sample selection procedure that could be followed when choosing accounts payable for confirmation.

LO 8-4

8.42 **Search for Unrecorded Liabilities.** C. Marsh, CPA, is the independent auditor for Compufast Corporation (Compufast), which sells personal computers, peripheral equipment (printers, data storage), and a wide variety of programs for business and games. From experience on Compufast's previous audits, Marsh knew that the company's accountants were very much concerned with timely recording of revenues and receivables and somewhat less concerned with keeping up-to-date records of accounts payable and other liabilities. Marsh knew that the control environment was strong in the asset area and weak in the liability area.

Required:
List substantive procedures that Marsh and the audit staff can perform to obtain reasonable assurance that Compufast's unrecorded liabilities are discovered and adjusted in the financial statements currently under audit.

LO 8-7

8.43 **Fictitious Vendors, Theft, and Embezzlement.** The following cases are designed like the ones in the chapter. Your assignment is to write the audit approach portion of the cases organized around these sections:

Objective. Express the objective in terms of the facts supposedly asserted in financial records, accounts, and statements.

Control. Write a brief explanation of desirable controls, missing controls, and especially the kinds of "deviations" that could arise from the situation described in the case.

Tests of controls. Write some procedures for getting evidence about existing controls, especially procedures that could discover deviations from controls. If there are no controls to test, then there are no procedures to perform; go to the next section. A "procedure" should instruct someone about the source(s) of evidence to tap and the work to do.

Audit of balance. Write some procedures for getting evidence about the existence, completeness, valuation or allocation, or rights and obligations assertions identified in your objective section.

Discovery summary. Write a short statement about the discovery you expect to accomplish with your procedures.

Purchasing Stars

Bailey Books, Inc. is a retail distributor of upscale books, periodicals, and magazines. Bailey has 431 retail stores throughout the southeastern states. Three full-time purchasing agents work at corporate headquarters. They are responsible for purchasing all inventory at the best prices available from wholesale suppliers. They can purchase with or without obtaining competitive bids. The three purchasing agents are R. McGuire in charge of purchasing books, M. Garza in charge of purchasing magazines and periodicals, and L. Collins (manager of purchasing) in charge of ordering miscellaneous items such as paper products and store supplies.

One of the purchasing agents is suspected of taking kickbacks from vendors. In return, Bailey is thought to be paying inflated prices, which first are recorded in inventory and then in cost of goods sold and other expense accounts as the assets are sold or used.

The duties of L. Collins, the manager in charge, do not include audit or inspection of the performance of the other two purchasing agents. No one audits or reviews Collins's performance.

The purchasing system is computerized and detail records are retained. An extract from these records is in Exhibit 8.43.1.

This kickback scheme has been going on for two or three years. Bailey Books could have overpaid by several hundred thousand dollars.

(ACFE adapted)

LO 8-2

8.44 **Bidding Process.** Maine Construction builds office buildings. The buildings generally cost between $5 million and $8 million to build, and the plumbing can cost between $300,000 and $600,000 depending on the building requirements. Therefore, Maine always sends the plumbing work out for bid before deciding on whom to use as a subcontractor. the company has had 21 projects over the last five years with $10 million dollars in plumbing contracts being sent out for bids.

Over the past five years Maine has asked for bids from three contractors: Beltran Plumbing; Delgado Plumbing Services; Wright Contracting—Plumbing Specialists. Each vendor has been reviewed by Maine and is on Maine's approved vendor list.

For each of the following situations (each situation is independent), determine whether the auditor should be concerned about the controls over the bidding process. If yes, what control would you recommend to Maine to ensure a fair and honest bidding process?

a. Of the 21 projects sent out for bid, Wright had the winning bid on 12 of the projects.

b. Of the 21 projects sent out for bid Wright had the winning bid on 12 of the projects. In each of these bidding processes, Wright's bid was the last bid received.

c. Of the 21 projects sent out for bid each, vendor had the winning bid on 7 of the projects.

d. Of the 21 projects sent out for bid, Delgado was awarded 5 contracts even though he did not have the lowest bid.

EXHIBIT 8.43.1

BAILEY BOOKS, INCORPORATED
Selected Purchases 2010–2012

Vendor	Items Purchased	2010	2011	2012	Date of Last Bid	Percent of Purchases Bid (3-yr. period)
Armour	Books	$ 83,409	$ 02,929	$ 810,103	12/01/10	87%
Burdick	Sundries	62,443	70,949	76,722	—	—
Canon	Magazines	1,404,360	1,947,601	2,361,149	11/03/10	94
DeBois, Inc.	Paper	321,644	218,404	121,986	06/08/10	57
Elton Books	Books	874,893	781,602	649,188	07/21/10	91
Fergeson	Books	921,666	1,021,440	1,567,811	09/08/10	88
Guyford	Magazines	2,377,821	2,868,988	3,262,490	10/08/10	81
Hyman, Inc.	Supplies	31,640	40,022	46,911	10/22/10	—
Intertec	Books	821,904	898,683	949,604	11/18/10	86
Jerrico	Paper	186,401	111,923	93,499	10/04/10	72
Julian-Borg	Magazines	431,470	589,182	371,920	02/07/10	44
King Features	Magazines	436,820	492,687	504,360	11/18/10	89
Lycorp	Sundries	16,280	17,404	21,410	—	—
Medallian	Books	—	61,227	410,163	12/15/10	99
Northwood	Books	861,382	992,121	—	12/07/09	—
Orion Corp.	Paper	86,904	416,777	803,493	11/02/09	15
Peterson	Supplies	114,623	—	—	N/A	N/A
Quick	Supplies	—	96,732	110,441	11/03/10	86
Robertson	Books	2,361,912	3,040,319	3,516,811	12/01/10	96
Steele	Magazines	621,490	823,707	482,082	11/03/10	90
Telecom	Sundries	81,406	101,193	146,316	—	—
Union Bay	Books	4,322,639	4,971,682	5,368,114	12/03/10	97
Victory	Magazines	123,844	141,909	143,286	06/09/10	89
Williams	Sundries	31,629	35,111	42,686	—	—

LO 8-3, 8-6, 8-7

8.45 **Grounds for Dismissal.** This case is designed like the ones in the chapter. Your assignment is to write the "audit approach" portion of the case organized around these sections:

Objective. Express the objective in terms of the facts supposedly asserted in financial records, accounts, and statements.

Control. Write a brief explanation of desirable controls, missing controls, and especially the types of "deviations" that might arise from the situation described in the case.

Tests of controls. Write some audit procedures for getting evidence about existing controls, especially procedures that could discover deviations from controls. If there are no controls to test, then there are no procedures to perform; go to the next section. A "procedure" should instruct someone about the source(s) of evidence to tap and the work to do.

Audit of balance. Write some procedures for getting evidence about the existence, completeness, valuation or allocation, or rights and obligations assertions identified in your objective section above.

Discovery summary. Write a short statement about the discovery you expect to accomplish with your procedures.

A. Doe, IT application manager for The Coffee Company, signed a consulting services agreement with Fictitious Consulting Company (FCC). Doe was required to obtain written approval of the contract from a supervisor but forged the supervisor's signature. More than 100 invoices came in, which were approved with Doe's initials. Even though Doe's approval authority was only $5,000, many of the invoices were for more than $40,000.

FCC was not registered in the state or listed in telephone directories. The phone number was for a cell phone registered to Doe and the mailing address was a post office box. When Doe's supervisor asked to meet the FCC consultants, Doe was evasive, saying they "had just left" or "they were working away from the office." Ultimately, Doe told her supervisor that she had dismissed FCC, but she simply moved the charges to capital accounts that the supervisor did not monitor.

The Coffee Co. paid more than $3.7 million to FCC between December 1999 and August 2000. (Source: M. Atkinson and M. Biliske, "Grounds for Dismissal," *Internal Auditor*, February 2005.)

LO 8-5

8.46 **Audit the PP&E and Depreciation Schedule.** Bart's Company has prepared the PP&E and depreciation schedule shown in Exhibit 8.46.1.

The following information is available (assume the beginning balance has been audited):

- The land was purchased eight years ago when building 1 was erected. The location was then remote but now is bordered by a major freeway. The appraised value of the land is $35 million.
- Building 1 has an estimated useful life of 35 years and no residual value.
- Building 2 was built by a local contractor this year. It also has an estimated useful life of 35 years and no residual value. The company occupied it on May 1 this year.
- Computer A system was purchased January 1 six years ago when the estimated useful life was eight years with no residual value. It was sold on May 1 for $500,000.

EXHIBIT 8.46.1 PP&E and Depreciation

	Asset Cost (000s)				Accumulated Depreciation (000s)			
Description	Beginning Balance	Added	Sold	Ending Balance	Beginning Balance	Added	Sold	Ending Balance
Land	10,000			10,000				
Building 1	30,000			30,000	6,857	857		7,714
Building 2		42,000		42,000		800		800
Computer A	5,000		5,000	0	3,750	208	3,958	0
Computer B		3,500		3,500		583		583
Press	1,50			1,500	300	150		450
Auto 1	15		15	0	15		15	0
Auto 2		22		22		2		2
Total	46,515	45,522	5,015	87,022	10,922	2,600	3,973	9,549

- Computer B system was placed in operation as soon as Computer A system was sold. It is estimated to be in use for six years with no residual value at the end.
- The company estimated the useful life of the press at 20 years with no residual value.
- Auto 1 was sold during the year for $1,000.
- Auto 2 was purchased on July 1. The company expects to use it five years and then sell it for $2,000.
- All depreciation is calculated on the straight-line method using months of service.

Required:

a. Verify the depreciation calculations. Are there any errors? Put the errors in the form of an adjusting journal entry, assuming that 90 percent of the depreciation on the buildings and the press has been charged to Cost of Goods Sold and 10 percent is still capitalized in the inventory, and the other depreciation expense is classified as General and Administrative Expense (i.e., building and press depreciation is considered a product cost; inventory on hand includes 10 percent of the depreciation expense for buildings and the press: $180,700; Cost of Goods Sold contains the other 90 percent: $1,626,300).

b. List two audit procedures for auditing the additions to PP&E.

c. What will auditors expect to find in the Gain and Loss on Sale of Assets account? What amount of cash flow from investing activities will be in the statement of cash flows?

8.47 **PP&E Assertions and Substantive Procedures.** This question contains three items that are management assertions about property and equipment. Following them are several substantive procedures for obtaining evidence about management's assertions.

Assertions

1. The entity has legal right to property and equipment acquired during the year.
2. Recorded property and equipment represent assets that actually exist at the balance-sheet date.
3. Net property and equipment are properly valued at the balance-sheet date.

Substantive Procedures

a. Trace opening balances in the summary schedules to the prior-year audit documentation.
b. Review the provision for depreciation expense and determine whether depreciable lives and methods used in the current year are consistent with those used in the prior year.
c. Determine whether the responsibility for maintaining the property and equipment records is separated from the responsibility for custody of property and equipment.
d. Examine deeds and title insurance certificates.
e. Perform cutoff tests to verify that property and equipment additions are recorded in the proper period.
f. Determine whether property and equipment are adequately insured.
g. Physically examine all major property and equipment additions.

Required:

For each of the three assertions (1, 2, and 3), select the one best substantive audit procedure (a–g) for obtaining competent evidence. A procedure may be selected only once or not at all.

(AICPA adapted)

8.48 **Assertions and Substantive Procedures for Property, Plant, and Equipment (PP&E).** Following are the four assertions about account balances that can be applied to the audit of a company's PP&E, including assets the company has constructed itself: existence, rights and obligations, completeness, and valuation and allocation.

Required:

For each of the following substantive procedures, (1) cite one assertion most closely related to the evidence the procedure will produce (the primary assertion) and (2) when appropriate, cite one or more other assertions that also are related to the evidence the procedure will produce—the secondary assertion(s).

a. For major amounts charged to PP&E and a sample of smaller charges, examine supporting documentation for expenditure amounts, budgetary approvals, and capital work orders.

b. For a sample of capitalized PP&E, examine construction work orders in detail.

c. For a sample of construction work orders, vouch time and material charges to supporting payroll and material usage records. Review the reasonableness of the hours worked, the work description, and the material used.

d. Evaluate the policy and procedures for allocating overhead to the work orders and recalculate their application.

e. Determine whether corresponding retirements of replaced PP&E have occurred and have been properly entered in the detail records.

f. Select major additions for the year and a random sample of other additions and inspect the physical assets.

g. Vouch a sample of charges in the Repairs account and determine whether they are proper repairs, not capital items.

h. Review the useful lives, depreciation methods, and salvage values for reasonableness. Recalculate depreciation.

i. Study loan documents for terms and security of loans obtained for purchase of PP&E.

j. Inspect title documents for automotive and real estate assets.

k. Analyze the productive economic use of PP&E to determine whether any other-than-temporary impairment is evident.

(AICPA adapted)

LO 8-5

8.49 CAATs Application—PP&E. You are supervising the audit fieldwork of Sparta Springs Company and need certain information from Sparta's equipment records, which are maintained on a computer file. The particular information is (1) net book value of assets so that your assistant can reconcile the subsidiary ledger to the general ledger control accounts (the general ledger contains an account for each asset type at each plant location) and (2) sufficient data to enable your assistant to find and inspect selected assets. The record layout of the master file follows:

Asset number.
Description.
Asset type.
Location code.
Year acquired.
Cost.

Accumulated depreciation, end of year (includes accumulated depreciation at the beginning of the year plus depreciation for year to date).

Depreciation for the year to date.
Useful life.

Required:

From the data file described earlier,

a. List the information needed to verify correspondence of the subsidiary detail records with the general ledger accounts. Does this work complete the audit of PP&E?

b. What additional data are needed to enable your assistant to inspect the assets?

LO 8-4

8.50 **Search for Unrecorded Liabilities.** The list of vouchers payable for Potter's Magic Shoppe at December 31 is as follows:

Vendor	Invoice Date	Amount
Hagrid Cleaning Services	11/15	$ 4,322.43
Hermione's Hats	12/02	2,167.76
Lockhart Magic Books	12/31	6,489.11
Malfoy Financial Consultants	12/28	23,752.63
McGonagall Veterinary Supplies	12/23	4,590.60
Moaning Myrtle's Mystical Capes	10/14	11,529.88
Nicholas Fancy Headwear	12/29	51,268.62
Snape's Snakes	12/28	36,152.45
Weasley's Wands	12/28	6,400.55
Hogwart's Rentals	12/15	53,000.00
Total vouchers payable		$199,674.03

Checks written in the following January are:

Check Number	Payee	Description	Invoice Date	Amount
1842	Malfoy Financial Consultants	Professional services	12/28	$23,752.63
1843	Hagrid Cleaning Services	October monthly cleaning	11/15	4,322.43
1844	Hogwart's Rentals	January rent	12/15	53,000.00
1845	Lockhart Magic Books	Inventory	12/31	6,489.11
1846	Dudley Pastries	Catering for office Christmas party	1/15	6,300.00
1847	Weasley's Wands	Inventory	12/28	6,400.55
1848	Rowlin's Enterprises	Trademark	1/1	10,000.00
1849	McGonagall Veterinary Supplies	Inventory	12/23	4,590.60
1850	Nicholas Fancy Headwear	Inventory	12/29	51,268.62
1851	Weasley's Wands	Inventory	12/31	6,400.55
1852	Hermione's Hats	Inventory	12/02	2,167.76
1853	Lockhart Magic Books	Inventory	12/31	5,932.89
1854	Hagrid Cleaning Service	November monthly cleaning	12/15	4,322.43
1855	Malfoy Financial Consultants	Professional services	1/28	13,888.56

Required:

a. Prepare an audit plan for the audit of unrecorded liabilities for Potter's Magic Shoppe.

b. Prepare an adjusting journal entry to correct accounts payable. Potter's maintains perpetual inventory records and the inventory was counted and adjusted on December 31.

8.51 **Kaplan CPA Exam Simulation:** Unrecorded Liabilities

Required

LO 8-4

Go to the Kaplan website link at www.mhhe.com/Louwers5e, click on Client's Check Register (Unrecorded Liabilities) AUD TBS, and complete your answers.

Appendix 8A

Internal Control Questionnaires

APPENDIX EXHIBIT 8A.1 Internal Control Questionnaire—Acquisitions and Expenditures

	Yes/No	Comments
Occurrence		
1. Are the purchasing department, accounting department, receiving department, and shipping department independent of each other?		
2. Are receiving reports prepared for each item received and copies transmitted to inventory custodians? To purchasing? To the accounting department?		
3. Are purchases made by employees authorized through standard purchases procedures?		
4. Are quantity and quality of goods received determined at the time of receipt by receiving personnel independent of the purchasing department?		
5. Are vendors' invoices reconciled against purchase orders and receiving reports before a liability is recorded?		
6. Do managers compare actual expenses to budget?		
7. Are all documents in the vouchers package canceled with a PAID stamp when paid?		
8. Are shipping documents authorized and prepared for goods returned to vendors?		
9. Are invoices approved for payment by a responsible officer?		
Completeness		
1. Are the purchase order forms prenumbered and the numerical sequence checked for missing documents?		
2. Are receiving report forms prenumbered and the numerical sequence checked for missing documents?		
3. Is the accounts payable department notified of goods returned to vendors?		
4. Are vendors' invoices recorded immediately on receipt?		
5. Are unmatched receiving reports reviewed frequently and investigated for proper recording?		
6. Is statistical analysis used to examine overall purchasing levels?		
7. Are vendors' monthly statements reconciled with individual accounts payable accounts?		
Accuracy		
1. Are competitive bids received and reviewed for certain items?		
2. Are all purchases made only on the basis of approved purchase requisitions?		
3. Are all purchases, whether for inventory or expense, routed through the purchasing department for approval?		
4. Does the accounts payable department check invoices against purchase orders and receiving reports for dates, quantities, prices, and terms?		
5. Does the accounting department check invoices for mathematical accuracy?		
6. Is the accounts payable listing balanced periodically with the general ledger control account?		
7. Are purchase prices approved by a responsible purchasing officer?		
8. Is accounts payable reconciled to the general ledger every period?		
9. Are monthly statements reviewed by senior officials?		
Classification		
1. Do the chart of accounts and the accounting manual give instructions for classifying debit entries when purchases are recorded?		
2. Are journal entries authorized at appropriate levels?		
Cutoff		
1. Does the accounting manual give instructions to date purchase/payable entries on the date of receipt of goods?		

APPENDIX EXHIBIT 8A.2 Selected Computerized Questionnaire Items—General and Application Controls

	Yes/No	Comments
General Controls		
1. Are computer operators and programmers excluded from participating in the input and output control functions?		
2. Are programmers excluded from entering transactions or performing other routine computer operations?		
3. Is there a database administrator who is independent of computer operations, systems, programming, and users?		
4. Are computer personnel restricted from initiating, or authorizing, transactions or adjustments to the general ledger master database or the subsidiary ledger master database?		
5. Is access to the computer room restricted to authorized personnel?		
6. Is online access to data and programs controlled with the use of department account codes, personal ID numbers, and passwords?		
7. Are systems, programs, and documentation stored in a fireproof area?		
8. Can current files, particularly master files, be reconstructed from files stored in an off-site location?		
Application Controls		
1. Are process manuals for purchasing and accounts payable current?		
2. Are process documents (e.g. purchase requisitions, purchase orders, bills of lading) signed as evidence of review and authorization?		
3. Are all data fields subject to input validation tests—missing data tests, limit and range tests, check digits, valid codes, and so forth?		
4. Are input error reports generated daily? Are they returned to the accounting department for correction of errors?		
5. Is an accounting department person assigned the responsibility for promptly correcting input errors and reentering the data for inclusion with the next report?		
6. Are controls used to reconcile computerized output to input control data?		
7. Are reports reviewed for reasonableness, accuracy, and legibility by the responsible department personnel?		

APPENDIX EXHIBIT 8A.3 Acquisitions and Expenditures—Computerized Controls

	Yes/No	Comments
1. Is each terminal restricted to designated functions? For example, the receiving clerk's terminal cannot accept a purchase order entry.		
2. Are identification numbers and passwords (used on an individual basis) required to enter purchase orders, vendors' invoices, and the receiving report information?		
3. Are certain personnel authorized to determine the status of various records, such as an open voucher, but not authorized to enter data. Do these personnel have "read only" authorization?		
4. Is all input immediately logged to provide restart processing should any terminal become inoperative during the processing?		
5. Do transaction codes call up a full screen "form" on the terminals that appears to the operators in the same format as the original paper documents?		
6. Does the system reject incomplete or incorrect information (online input validation)?		
7. Are all printed documents computer numbered and are the numbers stored as part of the record?		
8. Do all records in the open databases have the vendor's number as the primary search and matching field key?		
9. Can status searches be made by another field? For example, the inventory number can be the search key to determine the status of a purchase of an item in short supply.		
10. Is a daily search of the open databases made—for example, open purchase orders more than 10 days past the delivery date?		
11. Is the check signature printed, using a signature plate that is installed on the computer printer only when checks are printed?		
12. Does a designated person in the treasurer's office maintain custody of this signature plate and take it to the computer room to be installed when checks are printed?		
13. Is this person restricted from access to blank check stock?		
14. Are the printed checks taken immediately from the computer room for mailing?		

APPENDIX EXHIBIT 8A.4 Internal Control Questionnaire—PP&E and Related Transactions Processing

	Yes/No	Comments
Occurrence		
1. Is the accounting department notified of actions of disposal, dismantling, or idling a productive asset? For terminating a lease or rental?		
2. Are assets inspected periodically and physically counted?		
Completeness		
1. Are detailed property records maintained for the various assets included in PP&E?		
2. Are property tax assessments periodically analyzed? When was the last analysis?		
3. Are purchase contracts for major assets provided to the accounting department?		
Accuracy		
1. Are capital expenditure and leasing proposals prepared for review and approval by the board of directors or by responsible officers?		
2. When actual expenditures exceed authorized amounts, is the excess approved?		
3. Is there a uniform policy for assigning depreciation rates, useful lives, and salvage values?		
4. Are depreciation calculations checked by internal auditors or other officials?		
5. Are subsidiary records periodically reconciled to the general ledger accounts?		
Classification		
1. Does the accounting manual contain policies for capitalization of assets and expensing repair and maintenance?		
2. Are memorandum records of leased assets maintained?		
Cutoff		
1. Does the accounting manual give instructions for recording PP&E additions on a proper date of acquisition?		

Appendix 8B

Audit Plans

APPENDIX EXHIBIT 8B.1

DUNDER-MIFFLIN, INC Audit Plan for Accounts Payable 12/31/12	Performed by	Ref.

1. Obtain a trial balance of recorded accounts payable as of year-end.
   a. Foot and trace the total to the general ledger account.
   b. Vouch a sample of balances to vendors' statements. Review the trial balance for related-party payables.
2. Send confirmations to creditors, especially those with small or zero balances and those with which the company has done significant business.
3. Inquire of client personnel about their procedures for ensuring that all liabilities are recorded.
4. Scan the open purchase order file at year-end for indications of material purchase commitments at fixed prices. Obtain current prices and determine whether any adjustments for loss are needed.
5. Obtain a list of unmatched vendor invoices and determine when the goods were received.
6. For goods received before year-end, trace the unmatched receiving reports to accounts payable and determine whether items recorded in the next accounting period need to be adjusted.
7. Select a sample of cash disbursements from the accounting period following the balance-sheet date. Vouch them to supporting documents (invoice, receiving report) to determine whether the related liabilities were recorded in the proper accounting period.		

APPENDIX EXHIBIT 8B.2

DUNDER-MIFFLIN Audit Plan for Prepaid, Deferred, and Accrued Expenses 12/31/12	Performed by	Ref.

1. Obtain a schedule of all prepaid expenses, deferred costs, and accrued expenses.
2. Review documentation to determine whether each item is properly allocated to the current or future accounting periods.
3. Select significant additions to deferred and accrued amounts and vouch them to supporting invoices, contracts, or calculations.
4. Determine the basis for deferral and accrual and recalculate the recorded amounts.
5. Review the nature of each item, inquire of management, and determine whether the remaining balance will be recovered from future operations.
6. Scan income and expense items for items that should be considered prepaid, deferred, or accrued and allocated to current or future accounting periods.
7. Scan the expense accounts in the trial balance and compare to prior year.
   a. Investigate unusual difference that could indicate failure to account for a prepaid or accrual item.
   b. Review each item to determine the proper current or noncurrent balance sheet classification.		

APPENDIX EXHIBIT 8B.3

DUNDER-MIFFLIN **Audit Plan for PPE and Related Accounts** **12/31/12**	**Performed by**	**Ref.**

Property, Plant, and Equipment
1. Summarize and foot detailed asset subsidiary records and reconcile to general ledger control account(s).
2. Select a sample of detail asset subsidiary records:
   a. Perform a physical observation (inspection) of the assets recorded.
   b. Inspect title documents, if any, to ensure ownership by the client.
3. Prepare, or have client prepare, a schedule of asset additions and disposals for the period:
   a. Vouch to documents indicating proper approval.
   b. Vouch costs to invoices, contracts, or other supporting documents.
   c. Review all costs of shipment, installation, testing, and other appropriate cots for proper capitalization.
   d. Vouch proceeds (on dispositions) to cash receipts or other asset records.
   e. Recalculate gain or loss on dispositions.
   f. Trace amounts to detail asset records and general ledger control account(s).
4. Observe the taking of a physical inventory of the assets and compare with detailed asset records.
5. Obtain written representations from management regarding pledge of assets as security for loans and leased assets.
6. Select a sample of repair and maintenance expense entries and vouch them to supporting invoices for evidence of property that should be capitalized.
 	
Depreciation
1. Review depreciation expense for overall reasonableness with reference to costs of assets and average depreciation rates.
2. Prepare, or have client prepare, a schedule of accumulated depreciation showing beginning balance, current depreciation, disposals, and ending balance.
   a. Review the schedule for appropriate asset costs, useful life, and salvage value.
3. Trace to depreciation expense and asset disposition analyses.
4. Recalculate depreciation expense and trace to general ledger account(s).
5. Trace amounts to general ledger account(s).
 	
Other Accounts
1. Review prepaid insurance for proper recording and adequacy of coverage.
2. Review accrued property taxes to determine whether taxes due on assets have been paid or accrued.
3. Recalculate prepaid and/or accrued insurance and tax expenses.
4. Select a sample of rental expense entries and vouch to rent/lease contracts to determine whether any leases qualify for capitalization.
 	
Intangibles and Related Expenses
1. Review merger documents for proper calculation of purchased goodwill.
2. Inquire of management about legal status of patents, leases, copyrights, and other intangibles.
3. Review documentation of new patents, copyrights, leaseholds, and franchise agreements.
4. Select a sample of recorded research and development expenses. Vouch to supporting documents for evidence of proper classification.
5. Recalculate amortization of goodwill, patents, and other intangibles.
6. Perform tests for goodwill impairment.		

Appendix 8C

The Payroll Cycle

Martin Bodner, the former finance chief of **Tommy Hilfiger Group Handbags and Small Leather Goods Inc.**, pleaded guilty to mail fraud and wire fraud for allegedly stealing more than $19 million, according to Michael Garcia, U.S. attorney for the Southern District of New York. According to Garcia, Bodner began working at the Hilfiger licensee in March 2000, eventually rising to CFO. Among his responsibilities was to supervise the company's payroll. Beginning in 2000, Bodner began stealing money from his employer by secretly increasing the amount of money that he was to be paid in salary and bonus and arranging to be reimbursed by the handbag and leather goods unit for phony expenses he purportedly had incurred. In addition, during 2004 and 2005, Bodner added one of his sons, who did not work for the company, to the company's payroll. He arranged for his son to be paid about $225,500 during those years. Bodner was fired on December 21, 2007.

Bodner entered into a plea deal in which he agreed to forfeit a home in Sands Point, New York, along with a Manhattan apartment, three cars, and various other properties. Bodner also was accused of causing hundreds of checks to be issued to various recipients for the purpose of paying off his personal credit card bills; purchasing a luxury automobile for himself; paying for insurance for a home, apartments, and automobiles owned by Bodner; and paying for decorating services.

LEARNING OBJECTIVE 8-8
Describe the payroll cycle, including typical source documents and controls.

Every company has payroll. It can include manufacturing labor, research scientists, administrative personnel, or all of these. Payroll may take different forms. Personnel management and the payroll accounting cycle not only include transactions that affect the wage and salary accounts but also the transactions that affect pension benefits, deferred compensation contracts, compensatory stock option plans, employee benefits (such as health insurance), payroll taxes, and related liabilities for these costs. An important aspect of the payroll cycle is that it is self-policing. If employees are not paid, they will complain. If someone commits fraud by overpaying an employee and then diverts the difference, the employee will complain because his or her W-2 will be overstated and the employee will owe too much tax. As a result, company employees report many misstatements (both intentional and unintentional).

Typically, balance-sheet accounts such as accrued payroll and accrued taxes are not material to companies' financial position. Also, because of the self-policing nature of the accounts and the regulatory restrictions of the Internal Revenue Service and the Department of Labor, controls over payroll are normally stronger than of other areas. Therefore, most audit procedures related to payroll consist of evaluation of internal control and analytical procedures.

INHERENT RISKS

The major risks in the payroll cycle include
- Paying **ghost employees**, employees who do not exist (invalid transactions).
- Paying terminated employees (who have not been removed from payroll) whose paychecks are then endorsed with forged signatures by their supervisors.
- Overpaying for time or production (inaccurate transactions, improper valuation).
- Accounting incorrectly for costs and expenses (incorrect classification, improper or inconsistent presentation and disclosure).
- Ensuring that related taxes are appropriately paid.

Source: "Hilfiger Unit Ex-CFO Pleads Guilty to $19M Fraud," CFO.com, September 16, 2008.

> ### AUDITING INSIGHT | A Dedicated Employee
>
> Prosecutors told the Winchester Crown Court in southern England that Jaswinder Bains, 45, was "blatantly dishonest" on the time cards for his job as a social worker on at least 24 occasions. In one instance, Bains allegedly claimed he worked 23 hours in one day on 29 case files even though his credit card records show he was on a shopping spree in Paris that day. Bains testified that he did not falsify his work hour records. "I was working very long hours without sleep," he said. "I do not need a lot of sleep." He didn't explain what was behind his records on another day, when he claimed he worked 28 hours.
>
> Source: SocietyGuardian.co.UK, May 9, 2005.

TYPICAL ACTIVITIES

Appendix Exhibit 8C.1 shows a payroll cycle. It starts with hiring (and firing) people and determining their wage rates and deductions, then proceeds to attendance and work (timekeeping), and ends with payment followed by preparation of governmental (tax) and internal reports.

The elements that follow are part of the payroll internal control system.

Personnel ①

A human relations department that is independent of the other functions should have authority to add new employees to the payroll, delete terminated employees, obtain authorizations for deductions, and transmit authority for pay rate changes to the payroll

APPENDIX EXHIBIT 8C.1 Typical Activities in the Payroll Cycle

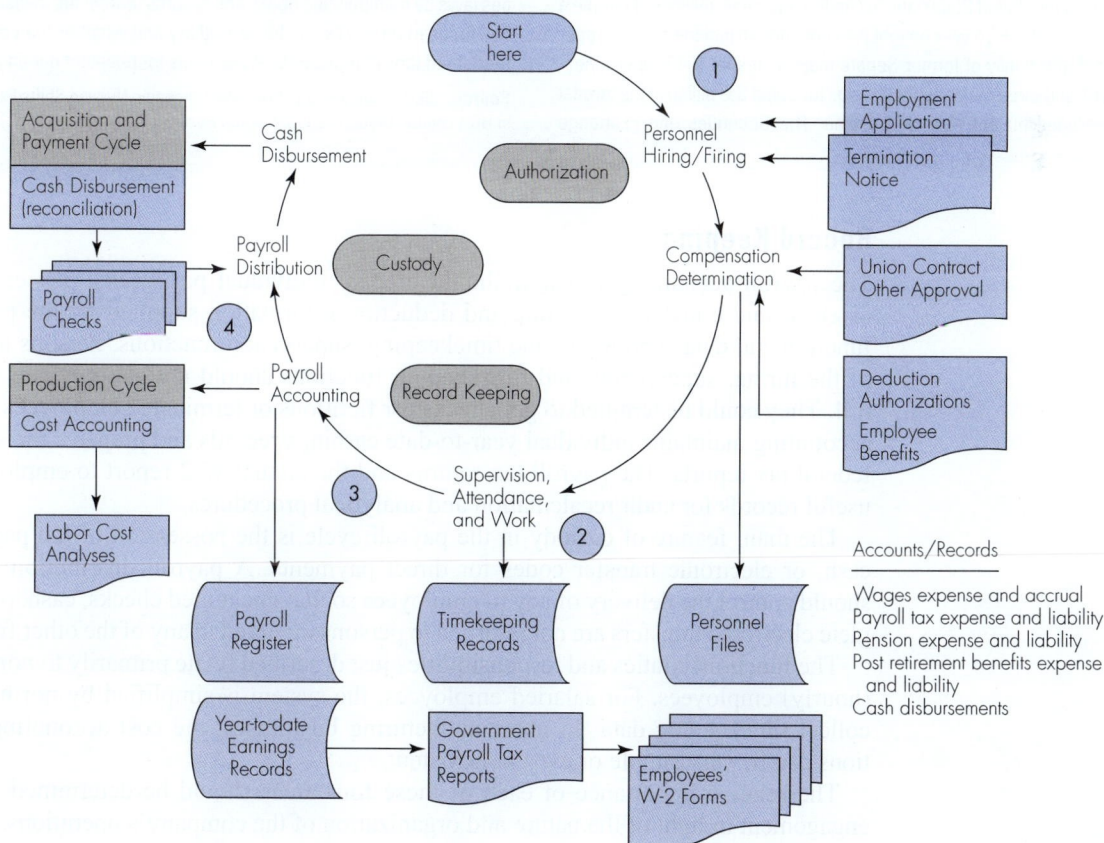

department. A process should exist to ensure that terminated employees are removed from the payroll. This is often done in conjunction with an exit interview performed by human resources. Final checks and W-2s should be mailed to the employee's home.

Supervision ②

Supervisors assign the employees to their jobs and approve any overtime. The immediate supervisor should approve all employee activity data (number of hours worked, job number, absences, time off allowed for emergencies, and the like). Finally, supervisors compare production plans and budget reports to actual employee costs for discrepancies.

Timekeeping ③

Employees paid by the hour or on various incentive systems require records of time, production, piecework, or other measures of the basis for their pay. (Salaried employees do not require such detailed records.) Timekeeping or similar records are collected in a variety of ways. The traditional time clock is still used. More sophisticated computerized systems perform the same function without the paper time card. Production employees may clock in for various jobs or production processes in the system for assigning labor cost to various stages of production.

Supervisors should approve timekeeping records. In computerized systems, this approval may be automatic by virtue of the supervisory passwords used to input data into a computerized payroll system.

AUDIT INSIGHT — Nurse, I need you?

Hospital Corporation of America (HCA) runs more than 160 facilities across the United States and in London and treats millions of people a year. In 2006, HCA was bought by a consortium including its management, the family of former Senate majority leader Bill First (Tennessee), and three major financial firms for about $33 billion in the largest leveraged buyout ever at the time. The Securities and Exchange Commission has opened a probe into whether HCA violated securities laws by manipulating books and records. Part of the investigation has focused on HCA's London subsidiary and whether the company fabricated tens of thousands of payments for phantom nursing shifts.

Source: "SEC Probing Biggest Hospital Company: Nursing Shifts Examined in HCA London Unit," *The Washington Post,* October 7, 2009

Record Keeping ④

The payroll accounting function should prepare individual paychecks, pay envelopes, or electronic transfers using rate and deduction information supplied by the personnel function and data supplied by the timekeeping–supervision functions. Persons in charge of the hiring, supervision, and timekeeping functions should not also prepare the payroll. They could be tempted to get checks for fictitious or terminated employees. Payroll accounting maintains individual year-to-date earnings records and prepares the state and federal tax reports. The payroll tax returns and the annual W-2 report to employees are useful records for audit recalculation and analytical procedures.

The main feature of custody in the payroll cycle is the possession of the paychecks, cash, or electronic transfer codes for direct payments. A payroll distribution function should control the delivery of pay to employees so that unclaimed checks, cash, or incomplete electronic transfers are not returned to persons involved in any of the other functions.

The functional duties and responsibilities just described relate primarily to nonsalaried (hourly) employees. For salaried employees, the system is simplified by not having to collect timekeeping data. In nonmanufacturing businesses, the cost accounting operations can be very simple or even nonexistent.

The relative importance of each of these four areas should be determined for each engagement in light of the nature and organization of the company's operations.

AUDITING INSIGHT — Not Enough Control, No Feedback, Bye-Bye Money

Homer had been in payroll accounting for a long time. He knew it was not uncommon to pay a terminated employee severance benefits and partial pay after termination. Homer received the termination notices and the data for the final paychecks. However, he also knew how to keep the terminated employee on the payroll for another week, pay a full week's compensation, change the electronic transfer code, and take the money for himself. The only things he could not change were the personnel department's copy of the termination notices, the payroll register, and the individual employee pay records used for withholding tax and W-2 forms.

Fortunately, nobody reconciled the cost accounting labor charges to the payroll. The supervisors did not get a copy of the payroll register for post payment approval, so they did not have any opportunity to notice the extra week. Nobody ever reviewed the payroll with reference to the termination notices. Former employees never complained about more pay and withholding reported on their W-2s than they actually received.

Homer and his wife retired comfortably to a villa in Spain on a nest egg that had grown to $450,000. After his retirement, the company experienced an unexpected decrease in labor costs and higher profits.

REVIEW CHECKPOINTS

8C.1 What functional responsibilities are associated with the payroll cycle?

8C.2 Which duties should be separated in the payroll cycle?

8C.3 How does a company ensure that terminated employees are removed from the payroll?

8C.4 Describe a walkthrough of the payroll transaction flow from hiring authorization to payroll check disbursement. (a) What document copies would be collected? (b) What controls should be noted?

AUDIT EVIDENCE IN MANAGEMENT REPORTS AND FILES

Payroll systems produce numerous reports. Some are internal reports and bookkeeping records. Others are government tax reports.

Personnel Files

The personnel, human relations, or labor relations department keeps individual employee files. The files usually include an employment application, a background investigation report, a notice of hiring, a job classification with pay rate authorization, and employee authorizations for deductions. When employees retire, resign, or are otherwise dismissed, appropriate notices of termination are filed.

A personnel file should establish a person's existence and employment. The background investigation report is important for employees in such sensitive areas as accounting, finance, and asset custody positions. News reports are rich with reports of errors and frauds perpetrated by people who falsified their credentials.

Payroll Register

The *payroll register* is a special journal. It typically contains a row for each employee with columns for the gross regular pay, gross overtime pay, income tax withheld, Social Security and Medicare tax withheld, other deductions, and net pay. The net pay amount usually is transferred from the general bank account to a special **imprest bank account** that maintains a zero or fixed balance.

Payroll department records contain the canceled checks (or a similar computerized deposit record). The checks have the employees' endorsements on the back.

> ### AUDITING INSIGHT | Look at the Endorsements
>
> Marsha Marston, an assistant accountant, was instructed to look at the endorsements on the back of a sample of canceled payroll checks. She noticed three occurrences of the payee's signature followed by a second signature. Although scrawled almost illegibly, the second signatures were identical and were later identified as the handwriting of Fred Holmes (the payroll accountant). Holmes had taken unclaimed checks and converted (stolen) them. When cashing these "third-party checks," banks and stores had required him to produce identification and endorse the checks that already had been "endorsed" by the employee payee. The lesson is that second endorsements are a red flag.

Labor Cost Analysis

One of the internal reports in the payroll cycle is a report of labor cost to the cost accounting department, thus linking the payroll cycle with cost accounting in the production cycle. The cost accounting department can receive its information in more than one way. Some companies have systems that independently report time and production work data from the production floor directly to the cost accounting department. Other companies let their cost accounting department receive labor cost data from the payroll department. When the data are received independently, they can be reconciled with a report from the payroll department.

The cost accounting department (or a similar accounting function) is responsible for labor distribution. This is the most important part of the presentation and disclosure assertion with respect to payroll. Labor distribution is an assignment of payroll to the accounts where it belongs for internal and external reporting.

Payroll data flow from the hiring process, through the timekeeping function, into the payroll department, then to the cost accounting department, and finally to the accounting entries that record the payroll for inventory cost determination and financial statement presentation. The same data are used for various governmental and tax reports.

Beware the "Clearing Account"

Clearing accounts are temporary storage places for transactions awaiting final accounting. All clearing accounts should have zero balances after the accounting is completed. A balance in a clearing account means that some amounts have not been classified properly in the accounting records.

Governmental and Tax Reports

One of the main objectives of a payroll system is to calculate the payments due to third parties including insurance fees, union dues, retirement funds, and so on. Of most importance is the calculation of payroll taxes due to the federal, state, and local governments. Large fines, mounting interest, or business closure is a possible ramification if these taxes are not paid timely and accurately. These issues cause payroll systems to be complicated and change almost every year as tax law and tax rates change. The payroll system produces several reports. Auditors can use these reports in tests of controls and substantive procedures produced by accumulating numerous payroll transactions.

Companies in financial difficulty have been known to try to postpone payment of employee taxes withheld. However, the consequences can be serious. The IRS can and will padlock the business and seize its assets for nonpayment.

Year-to-Date Earnings Records

The year-to-date (YTD) earnings records are the cumulative subsidiary records of each employee's gross pay, deductions, and net pay. Each time a periodic payroll is produced, the YTD earnings records are updated for the new information. The YTD earnings records are a subsidiary ledger of the wages and salaries cost and expense in the financial statements. Like any subsidiary and control account relationship, their sum (i.e., the gross pay amounts) should be equal to the costs and expenses in the financial statements. These YTD records provide the data for periodic governmental tax forms. They can be reconciled to the tax reports. Details can be compared to the company's YTD earnings records.

Employee W-2 Reports

The **W-2** is the annual report of gross salaries and wages and the income, Social Security, and Medicare taxes withheld. Copies are filed with the Social Security Administration and the IRS, and copies are sent to employees for use in preparing their income tax returns. The W-2s contain the annual YTD accumulations for each employee. Auditors can use the name, address, Social Security number, and dollar amounts in certain procedures to obtain evidence about the existence of the employees. The W-2s can be reconciled to the payroll tax reports.

W-2s should be mailed directly to employees' homes so if someone has been collecting additional pay in an employee's name (for example, if an employee leaves and the supervisor continues to send in a time card), the employee can spot the added income.

The assessment of payroll cycle control risk normally takes on added importance because most companies have fairly elaborate and well-controlled personnel and payroll functions. The transactions in this cycle are numerous during the year yet result in small amounts in balance sheet accounts at year-end. Therefore, in most audit engagements, the review of controls, tests of controls, and substantive tests of transactions constitute the major portion of the evidence gathered for these accounts. On most audits, the substantive procedures devoted to auditing the payroll-related account balances are limited.

Control Considerations

Control activities for proper separation of responsibilities should be in place and operating. By referring to Exhibit 8C.1, you can see that proper separation involves authorization (personnel department hiring and termination, pay rate, and deduction authorizations) by persons who do not have payroll preparation, paycheck distribution, or reconciliation duties. Payroll distribution (custody) is in the hands of persons who do not authorize employees' pay rates or time or prepare the payroll checks. Record keeping is performed by payroll and cost accounting personnel who do not make authorizations or distribute pay. Combinations of two or more of the duties of authorization, payroll preparation and record keeping, and payroll distribution in one person, one office, or one computerized system can open the door for errors and frauds.

In addition, the internal controls should provide for detailed control checking procedures. Examples of these controls follow:

- Periodic comparison of the payroll register to the personnel department files to check hiring authorizations and any terminated employees who have not been deleted.
- Periodic rechecking of wage rate and deduction authorizations.
- Reconciliation of time and production paid to cost accounting calculations.
- Quarterly reconciliation of YTD earnings records with tax returns.
- Payroll bank account reconciliation.

Some companies send each supervisor a copy of the payroll register, showing the employees paid under the supervisor's authority and responsibility. The supervisor has a chance to reapprove the payroll after it has been completed. Managers also should receive a comparison of actual labor costs to standards to review any unusual differences.

The payroll report sent to cost accounting can be reconciled to the labor records used to charge labor cost to production. The cost accounting function should determine whether the labor paid is the same as the labor cost used in the cost accounting calculations. Finally, the payroll bank account can be reconciled like any other bank account.

Information about the payroll cycle control often is gathered initially by completing an internal control questionnaire (ICQ). An example of an ICQ for payroll controls is in Exhibit 5.11 on page 188. You can study this questionnaire for details of desirable controls. It is organized with headings that identify the important assertions.

COMPUTERIZED PAYROLL

Complex computerized systems that gather payroll data, calculate payroll amounts, print checks, and transfer computerized deposits are found in many companies. Even though the technology is complex, the basic management and control functions of ensuring a flow of data to the payroll department should be in place. Various paper records and approval signatures may not exist. They may be imbedded in computerized payroll systems. Companies often use computer service organizations to process their payroll because it is a specialized function that can be performed effectively and efficiently by an organization whose specialty is to keep up with and apply changes in tax laws and rates. Thus, auditors should refer to the requirements of *AU/ISA 402 and AU 324* ("Service Organizations") in addressing this function.

Service Organizations

Service organizations are widely used for payroll preparation. This process can range from the calculation of payroll including the amounts due to third parties and to the actual payment of the payroll to individuals and third parties. Even when service bureaus are used to process payroll, the client is still responsible for payroll. For example, if the calculation for federal taxes is incorrect, the IRS will be auditing the client, not the service bureau payroll provider. Therefore, the auditor must review the payroll controls both at the client and the service organization for the processing of payroll. This would include getting a report on controls from the service bureau's auditor and ensuring that controls at the client are in place. The client should verify that the number of checks issued by the service bureau equals the number of employees eligible for compensation during the period. The client should review reports from the third party such as a payroll register, a listing of changes made to the payroll file, and a report of payments due to third parties should be reviewed by the client. The auditor should ensure that payroll numbers are reasonable given the activity level at the client. Analytical procedures can be a powerful test in these situations.

AUDITING INSIGHT — Who Is Your Help Helping?

Robert Kenneth Dromm, owner of **Pay + Plus Payroll Administrators,** admitted to siphoning money from clients who hired his company to process quarterly payroll tax payments. Dromm's Clearwater firm processed quarterly payroll tax payments for hundreds of clients around the Tampa Bay area. The clients would send Dromm's company their estimated tax payments. **Pay + Plus Payroll** was supposed to handle the paperwork and send the money to the IRS. Between 1999 and 2004, Dromm submitted false, understated filings to the IRS but gave many clients what appeared to be correct payroll tax returns. That allowed him to skim off money and direct it to his personal accounts. According to the plea deal concerning this, Dromm used these accounts for personal and business expenses as well as real estate investments.

Defense attorney Anthony LaSpada said the diversion began as a way to pay off old tax debts, not to defraud anyone. Some of Dromm's clients had financial needs (to pay debts, rents, wages, taxes etc.) in the mid-1990s, LaSpada said, and Dromm advanced them money. When a number of these clients went out of business, **Pay + Plus Payroll** was left in a precarious position, and Dromm began to divert funds. During that time, he paid $1.3million in old tax debts to the IRS, LaSpada said, but, he added, the company hit another snag in 2003 with the discovery that chief bookkeeper Robert M. Crawford Jr. had embezzled $1.5million to $2 million on his own. "I strongly believe that had it not been for that embezzlement by Mr. Crawford, that he would have been able to pay," LaSpada said. Dromm pleaded guilty and was sentenced to four years in federal prison and ordered to pay $1.6million in restitution.

Source: "Payroll Tax Scam Nets 4-year Term," *St. Petersburg Times,* November 3, 2007.

> ### ⌕ REVIEW CHECKPOINTS
>
> 8C.5 What documents should be included in an employee's personnel file?
>
> 8C.6 What features of a payroll system could be expected to prevent or detect the (a) payment of a fictitious employee and (b) omission of payment to an employee?
>
> 8C.7 What are the most common errors and frauds in the personnel and payroll cycle? Which control characteristics are auditors looking for to prevent or detect these errors and frauds?

FRAUD CASE: EXTENDED AUDIT PROCEDURES (AU/ISA 240, AS 13)

Case 8C.1

Time Card Forgeries

PROBLEM

A personnel agency assigned Nurse Jane Kent to work at County Hospital. She claimed payroll hours on agency time cards that showed approval signatures of a hospital nursing shift supervisor. The hospital had terminated the shift supervisor several months prior to the periods covered by the time cards in question. Kent worked one or two days per week but submitted time cards for a full 40-hour workweek. The leasing agency paid Kent and then billed County Hospital for the wages and benefits. Supporting documents were submitted with the leasing agency's bills.

Each hospital workstation keeps ward shift logs, which are sign-in sheets showing nurses on duty at all times. Nurses sign in and sign out when going on and going off duty. County Hospital maintains personnel records showing, among other things, the period of employment of its own nurses, supervisors, and other employees.

Kent's wages and benefits were billed to the hospital at $22 per hour. False time cards overcharging about 24 extra hours per week cost the hospital $528 per week. Kent was assigned to County Hospital for 15 weeks during the year, so she caused overcharges of about $7,900. However, she told three of her friends about the procedure and they overcharged the hospital another $24,000.

AUDIT APPROACH

Control activities should include a hiring authorization to put employees on the payroll. When temporary employees are used, this authorization includes contracts for nursing time, conditions of employment, and terms including the contract reimbursement rate. Control records of attendance and work should be kept (ward shift log). Supervisors should approve time cards or other records used by the payroll department to prepare paychecks. In this case, the contract with the leasing agency provided that approved time cards had to be submitted as supporting documentation for the agency billings.

Although the activities and documents for control were in place, the controls did not operate because no one at the hospital ever compared the ward shift logs to time cards and no one examined the supervisory approval signatures for their validity. The fraud was easy in the personnel agency situation because the nurses submitted their own time cards to the agency for payment. The same fraud could be operated by the hospital's own employees if they, too, could write their time cards and submit them to the payroll department.

Auditors should make inquiries (e.g., internal control questionnaire) about the error-checking activities performed by hospital accounting personnel. Tests of controls are designed to determine whether control activities are followed properly by the organization. Because the comparison and checking activities were not performed, there is nothing to test.

Select a sample of leasing agency billings and their supporting documentation (time cards). Vouch rates billed by the agency to the contract for agreement to proper rate. Vouch time claimed to hospital work attendance records (ward shift logs). Obtain handwriting examples of supervisors' signatures and compare them to the approval signatures on time cards. Use personnel records to determine whether supervisors were actually employed by the hospital at the time they approved the time cards. Use available work attendance records to determine whether supervisors were actually on duty at the time they approved the time cards.

DISCOVERY SUMMARY

The auditors quickly found that Kent (and others) had not signed in on ward shift logs for days they claimed to have worked. Further investigation showed that the supervisors who supposedly signed the time cards were not even employed by the hospital at the time their signatures were used for approvals. Handwriting comparison showed that the signatures were not by the supervisors.

The leasing agency was informed and refunded the $31,900 overpayment that the auditors had proved. The auditors continued to comb the records for more!

Source: **Adapted from vignette published in *Internal Auditor*.**

Multiple-Choice Questions for Practice and Review

All applicable Exercises and Problems are available with McGraw-Hill's Connect® Accounting

LO 8-8

8C.8 An audit team most likely would assess control risk at the maximum if the payroll department supervisor is responsible for
  a. Examining authorization forms for new employees.
  b. Comparing payroll registers with original batch transmittal data.
  c. Authorizing payroll rate changes for all employees.
  d. Hiring all subordinate payroll department employees.

(AICPA adapted)

LO 8-8

8C.9 Which of the following departments most likely would approve changes in pay rates and deductions from employee salaries?
  a. Personnel.
  b. Treasurer.
  c. Controller.
  d. Payroll.

(AICPA adapted)

LO 8-8

8C.10 Matthew Corp. has changed from a system of recording time worked on clock cards to a computerized payroll system in which employees record time in and out with magnetic cards. The computerized system automatically updates all payroll records. Because of this change
  a. A generalized computer audit program must be used.
  b. Part of the audit trail is altered.
  c. The potential for payroll-related fraud is diminished.
  d. Transactions must be processed in batches.

(AICPA adapted)

LO 8-8

8C.11 Effective control over the cash payroll function would mandate which of the following?
  a. The payroll clerk should fill the envelopes with cash and a computation of the net wages.
  b. Unclaimed payroll envelopes should be retained by the paymaster.
  c. Each employee should be asked to sign a receipt.
  d. A separate checking account for payroll should be maintained.

LO 8-8

8C.12 A large retail enterprise has established a policy that requires the paymaster to deliver all unclaimed payroll checks to the internal audit department at the end of each payroll distribution day. This policy was most likely adopted to
  a. Ensure that employees who were absent on a payroll distribution day are not paid for that day.
  b. Prevent the paymaster from cashing checks that are unclaimed for several weeks.

c. Prevent a bona fide employee's check from being claimed by another employee.

d. Detect any fictitious employee who may have been placed on the payroll.

(AICPA adapted)

LO 8-8   8C.13 Auditors ordinarily ascertain whether payroll checks are properly endorsed during the audit of

a. Clock cards.

b. The voucher system.

c. Cash in bank.

d. Accrued payroll.

(AICPA adapted)

LO 8-8   8C.14 In determining the effectiveness of an entity's policies and procedures relating to the occurrence assertion for payroll transactions, auditors most likely would inquire about and

a. Observe the separation of duties concerning personnel responsibilities and payroll disbursement.

b. Inspect evidence of accounting for prenumbered payroll checks.

c. Recompute the payroll deductions for employee fringe benefits.

d. Verify the preparation of the monthly payroll account bank reconciliation.

(AICPA adapted)

LO 8-8   8C.15 Which of the following activities most likely would be considered a weakness in an entity's internal control over payroll?

a. A voucher for the amount of the payroll is prepared in the general accounting department based on the payroll department's payroll summary.

b. Payroll checks are prepared by the accounts payable department and signed by the treasurer.

c. The employee who distributes payroll check returns unclaimed payroll checks to the payroll department.

d. The personnel department sends employees' termination notices to the payroll department.

Exercises and Problems

 All applicable Exercises and Problems are available with McGraw-Hill's *Connect® Accounting*

8C.16 **Major Risks in Payroll Cycle.** Prepare a schedule of the major risks in the payroll cycle. Identify the financial statement assertions related to each. Create a two-column schedule like this:

LO 8-8

Payroll Cycle Risk	Assertion

LO 8-8   8C.17 **Payroll Authorization in a Computerized System.** Two accountants were discussing control activities and tests of controls for payroll systems. The senior accountant in charge of the engagement said: "It is impossible to determine who authorizes transactions when the payroll account is computerized."

Required:

Evaluate the senior accountant's statement about control in a computerized payroll system. List the points in the flow of payroll information where authorization takes place.

LO 8-8   8C.18 **Payroll Processed by a Service Organization.** Assume that you are the audit senior conducting a review of a new client's payroll system. In the process of interviewing the payroll department manager, she makes the following statement: "We don't need many controls because our payroll is done outside the company by Automated Information Processing, a service bureau."

Required:

Evaluate the payroll department manager's statement and describe how a service organization affects an auditors' review of controls.

LO 8-8

8C.19 Payroll Audit Procedures, Computers, and Sampling. You are the senior auditor in charge of the annual audit of Onward Manufacturing Corporation for the year ending December 31. The company is of medium size with only 300 employees. All 300 employees are union members paid by the hour at rates set forth in a union contract, a copy of which is furnished to you. Job and pay rate classifications are determined by a joint union–management conference, and a formal memorandum is placed in each employee's personnel file.

Every week, clock cards prepared and approved in the shop are collected and transmitted to the payroll department. The total of labor hours is summed on a calculator and entered on each clock card. Batch and hash totals are obtained for the following: (1) labor hours and (2) last four digits of Social Security numbers. These data are input into a disk file, batch balanced, and batch processed. The clock cards (with cost classification data) are sent to the cost accounting department.

The payroll system is computerized. As each person's payroll record is processed, the Social Security number is matched to a table (in a separate master file) to obtain job classification and pay rate data, then the pay rate is multiplied by the number of hours, and the check is printed. (Ignore payroll deductions for the following requirements.)

Required:

a. What audit procedures would you recommend to obtain evidence that payroll data are accurately totaled and transformed into machine-readable records? What deviation rate might you expect? What tolerable deviation rate would you set? What "items" would you sample? What factors should be considered in setting the size of your sample?

b. What audit procedures would you recommend to obtain evidence that the pay rates are appropriately assigned and used in figuring gross pay? In what way, if any, would these procedures be different if the gross pay were calculated by hand instead of on a computer?

LO 8-8

8C.20 Payroll Tests of Controls. The diagram in Exhibit 8C.20.1 describes several payroll tests of controls. It shows the direction of the tests, leading from samples of clock cards, payrolls, and cumulative year-to-date earnings records to blank squares.

Required:

For each blank square in Appendix Exhibit 8C.20.1, write a payroll test of controls procedure and describe the evidence it can produce. (*Hint*: Refer to Exhibit 5.12.)

APPENDIX EXHIBIT 8C.20.1
Diagram of Payroll Tests of Controls

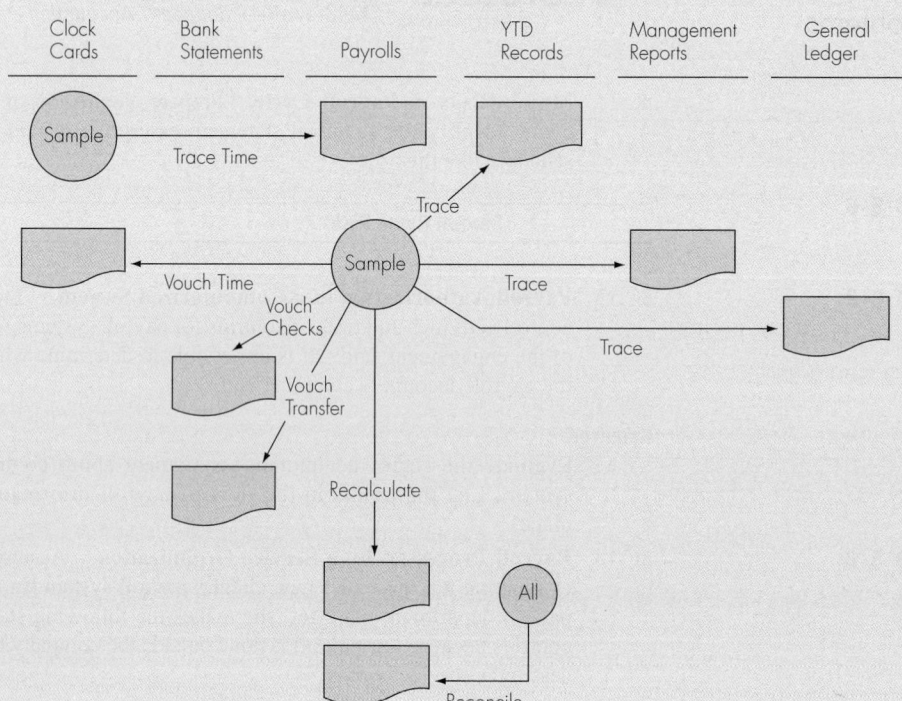

Production Cycle

> *There is one rule for industrialists and that is: Make the best-quality of goods possible at the lowest cost possible, paying the highest wages possible.*
>
> Henry Ford

Professional Standards References

Topic	AU/ISA Section	PCAOB Reference*
An Audit of Internal Control over Financial Reporting	*Various*	AS 5
Audit Documentation	230	AS 3
The Auditor's Responsibilities Related to Fraud	240	AS 13
Audit Planning	*300*	AS 10
Risks of Material Misstatement	315	AS 12
Materiality	320	AS 11
Audit Considerations Relating to an Entity Using a Service Organization	402	AU 324
Audit Evidence	500	AS 15
Analytical Procedures	520	AS 15
Auditing Accounting Estimates	540	AU 342
Written Representations	580	AU 333

*AU sections under the PCAOB reference refer to interim standards that have not been superseded by the PCAOB.

LEARNING OBJECTIVES

In the production cycle, materials, labor, and overhead are converted into finished goods (inventory) and services. Even companies that do not sell products sell services generated solely from the labor of employees. These services still represent costs that have to be accounted for and recovered by revenues. This chapter covers the production cycle, focusing on determining inventory valuation and cost of goods sold. Observation of the client's physical inventory count is such an important audit procedure that auditing standards require it. This chapter discusses procedures to be followed in observing the physical inventory count. It also discusses procedures for auditing the accumulation and pricing of the inventory and recording it in the financial statements.

This chapter includes several short cases to illustrate the application of audit procedures in situations in which errors and frauds can be discovered.

367

Your objectives are to be able to:

LO 9-1 Describe the production cycle, including typical source documents and controls.

LO 9-2 Give examples of tests of controls over conversion of materials and labor in a production process.

LO 9-3 Identify and describe considerations involved in the observation of physical inventory and tests of inventory pricing and compilation.

LO 9-4 Describe some common errors and frauds in the accounting for production costs and related cost of goods sold and design some audit and investigation procedures for detecting these errors and frauds.

PHAR-MOR, INC.

From his childhood, Mickey Monus loved all sports, especially basketball. However, with limited talents and height (5 foot 9 on a good day), he would never play on a professional team. Monus did have one trait, however, shared by top athletes: an unquenchable thirst for winning.

Monus transferred his boundless energy from the basketball court to the boardroom. He acquired a single drugstore in Youngstown, Ohio, and, within 10 years, he had built 299 more stores and formed the national chain **Phar-Mor.** Unfortunately, it was all built on nonexistent inventory and phony profits that eventually would be the downfall of Monus and his company and would cost the company's auditors millions of dollars. Here is how it happened.

After acquiring the first drugstore, Monus dreamed of building his modest holdings into a large pharmaceutical empire using *power buying*, that is, offering products at deep discounts. First, he took his one unprofitable, unaudited store and increased the profits with the stroke of a pen by adding phony inventory figures. Armed only with his gift of gab and a set of inflated financials, Monus bilked money from investors, bought eight stores within a year, and began the miniempire that grew to 300 stores. Monus became a financial icon ,and his organization gained near-cult status in Youngstown.

With his newly found wealth, Momus decided to fulfill a sports fantasy by starting the World Basketball League (WBL) in which no players would be more than six feet five inches tall. He pumped $10 million of Phar-Mor's money into the league. However, the public did not like short basketball players and were not buying tickets, so Monus poured more Phar-Mor money into the WBL. One day a travel agent who booked flights for league players received a $75,000 check for WBL expenses, but it was disbursed from a Phar-Mor bank account. The employee thought it odd that Phar-Mor would be paying the team's expenses. Because she was an acquaintance of one of Phar-Mor's major investors, she showed him the check. Alarmed, the investor began conducting his own investigation into Monus's illicit activities and helped expose an intricate financial fraud that caused losses of more than $1 billion.

Generating phony profits over an entire decade was no easy feat. Phar-Mor's CFO said the company was losing serious money because it was selling goods for less than it had paid for them. A significant mantra of Phar-Mor was "We will not be undersold by Walmart." (Remember that a highly competitive industry can be an important red flag for management fraud.) Nevertheless, Monus argued that through Phar-Mor's *power buying*, it would become so large that it could sell its way out of trouble. Eventually, the CFO caved in—under extreme pressure from Monus—and for the next several years, he and some of his staff kept two sets of books: the ones they showed the auditors and the ones that reflected the awful truth.

Phar-Mor's management dumped the losses into the "bucket account" and then used "blow-out" entries to reallocate the sums to the company's hundreds of stores in the form of increases in inventory costs. They issued fake invoices for merchandise purchases, made phony journal entries to increase inventory and decrease cost of sales, recognized inventory purchases but failed to accrue a liability, and overcounted and double counted merchandise. The finance department was able to conceal the inventory shortages because the auditors, **Coopers & Lybrand**, observed inventory in only four of 300 stores and informed Phar-Mor months in advance which stores they would visit. Phar-Mor executives fully stocked the four selected stores and allocated the phony inventory increases to the other stores. Regardless of the accounting tricks, Phar-Mor was heading for collapse. During its last audit, cash was so tight suppliers threatened to cut the company off for nonpayment of bills.

The auditors never uncovered the fraud, for which they paid dearly. This failure cost the audit firm more than $300 million in civil judgments. The CFO, who did not profit personally, was sentenced to 33 months in prison. Monus himself went to jail for five years.[1]

INHERENT RISKS IN THE PRODUCTION CYCLE

The Phar-Mor case illustrates how even a relatively simple inventory can be manipulated and misstated. Many other corporate frauds such as those at **Crazy Eddie's, Leslie Fay,** and **Health Management** were concealed by creating nonexistent or overvalued inventory. Inventory is often the largest current asset on a company's balance sheet, and it is likely to be the most complex account. Imagine trying to value the cars at **General Motors**, the computers at **IBM**, or the oil reserves at **ExxonMobil**. How about the 230 thousand hogs listed as inventory by **Tyson Foods**? Even inventories of simple commodities present issues of measurement and valuation. Inventories of more complex items such as electronics or biochemicals can require specialists.

A number of problems can arise in accounting for inventory. Some inventories are very susceptible to theft. Others require complex cost build-ups (especially if they are valued at LIFO). GAAP require inventory to be stated at the lower of cost or market. Cost is the total price paid, including freight-in, or estimates of actual costs using LIFO, FIFO, or an average. Market is replacement cost limited by a ceiling [as defined by the **net realizable value (NRV)**] or floor, (as defined by NRV less a normal profit). Items should be added to inventory when the company has title to them and removed to cost of goods sold when the related revenue is recognized.[2] These multiple and often subjective evaluations make inventory a high-risk area that management often uses to overstate assets. The inherent risk for inventory is shown in Exhibit 9.1

Unethical managers might prefer to manipulate cost of goods sold (and the related inventory account) instead of other expenses because of the double effect on the financial statements. When ending inventory is overstated, assets are overstated and cost of goods sold is understated, thereby increasing both total assets and income. Analysts often look at a company's profit margins to determine how well it is managing costs and to determine whether the company can maintain sufficient markup to cover other operating and nonoperating costs and be competitive. Another reason that inventory is an inviting target for manipulation is the complexity and subjectivity involved in accounting for it.

TYPICAL ACTIVITIES IN THE PRODUCTION CYCLE

LEARNING OBJECTIVE 9-1
Describe the production cycle, including typical source documents and controls.

When auditing a manufacturer, whether it is a small entity producing specialty goods or a Fortune 100 corporation manufacturing millions of units each year, it is paramount that an auditor understand all stages involved with converting raw materials into finished goods. If this process is not properly controlled, not only are financial statement misstatements likely, but also mismanagement can quickly put a company out of business.

The production cycle links the acquisition cycle in which goods and services are purchased to the revenue cycle, in which the inventory is sold (see Exhibit 9.3). These cycles, along with the payroll cycle, account for all additions and reductions of inventory

---
[1] J. T. Wells, "Ghost Goods: How to Spot Phantom Inventory," *Journal of Accountancy,* June 2001.
[2] FASB, *Revenue Recognition, 605,* June 30, 2009.

EXHIBIT 9.1 Relative Assertion Risks for Inventory Accounts

AICPA Assertions	Raw Material Inventory	Work-in-Process Inventory	Finished Goods Inventory	Explanation
Transaction assertions				Management may overstate all inventories: *Raw material* and *finished goods inventories* are most often overstated by adding numbers to counts or stating that items' costs are higher than actual costs. *Work-in-process* inventory is difficult to value and may be overstated by adding labor and material that have not been actually applied to the product. In addition, it might be easy to miss items within the manufacturing process.
• Occurrence	High	Low	High	
• Completeness	Low	Medium	Low	
• Cutoff	Medium	Low	Medium	
• Accuracy	Medium	High	High	
• Classification	Low	Low	Low	
Balance assertions				As stated, fictitious inventory may exist in *raw materials and finished goods inventory*. *Raw material inventory* may contain goods not owned by the client. *Finished goods inventory* may include consignment goods. Inventory costs may be overstated in all three inventories. Significant disclosures are required for inventory balances that may be manipulated to management's advantage.
• Existence	High	Low	High	
• Rights and Obligations	Medium	Low	Medium	
• Completeness	Low	Low	Low	
• Valuation and allocation	High	High	High	
Presentation and disclosure assertions				Inventory disclosures concerning valuation method as well as lower of cost or market are required. Disclosures concerning inventory returns and obsolescence may also be required.
• Occurrence	Medium	Low	Medium	
• Rights and obligations	Medium	Medium	Medium	
• Completeness	Low	Low	Low	
• Accuracy, valuation and allocation	High	High	High	
• Classification and understandability	Low	Medium	Low	

Note: These risk are for a typical entity engaged in manufacturing, retail, and other similar industries. Some specialized industries may have risks that vary from those indicated in this table.

items. Thus, the production cycle is mostly concerned with accounting for inventory as it moves through the production stages from raw materials to work-in-process to finished goods and for accumulating accurate costs of the inventory items.

Sales Forecasts ①

Production activities start with a **sales forecast**, a marketing projection of product sale, based on past performance and marketing initiatives. Based on this forecast and other pertinent factors (e.g., production setup costs, scheduled equipment maintenance, finished goods inventories, and raw material inventories), the production planner can determine both the type and quantity of products that need to be produced to meet anticipated demand and can schedule the products in a production plan.

Production Planning ①

The goal of production planning is to provide a schedule for manufacturing, called the **production plan**, so that quality products will be available at the appropriate time for the least cost. For example, production planners must balance the finished goods

EXHIBIT 9.2 Production cycle

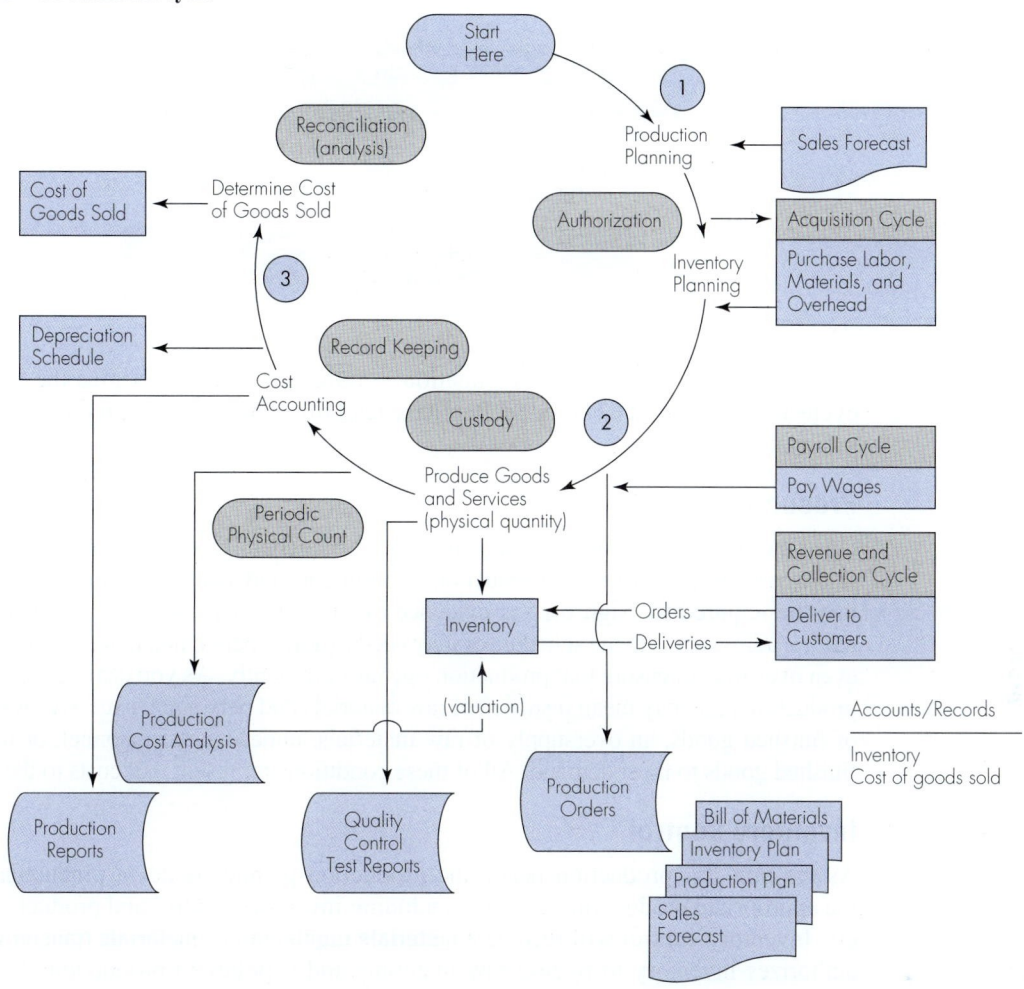

warehousing costs associated with making large (high-quantity) production runs with the changeover costs of making several smaller (low-quantity) production runs. In addition, production planners must integrate corporate strategies such as long-range plans and just-in-time (JIT) inventory management. Refer to Exhibit 9.2 for the activities and accounting involved in a production cycle. As you follow the exhibit, you can track the elements of a control system that are described in the following sections.

The physical output of a production cycle is inventory (starting with raw materials, proceeding to work-in-process and then to finished goods). Exhibit 9.2 shows the connection of inventory to the revenue and collection cycle in terms of orders and deliveries.

Most of the transactions in a production cycle are cost accounting allocations, unit cost determinations, and standard cost calculations. These are internal transactions produced entirely within the company's accounting system. Exhibit 9.2 also includes the elements of depreciation cost calculation, cost of goods sold determination, and production cost analysis as examples of these transactions.

The job of the production planner is one of the most critical in any manufacturing operation. The production planner not only creates a production plan but also must identify the total quantity of raw materials necessary for production based on the production plan and the **bill of materials** (a specification of the type and quantity of component materials authorized for the production). Once what raw materials are required (from the bill of materials) is known, the planner uses the **raw material inventory status report** to determine whether enough raw materials are in stock to complete production. If insufficient raw materials exist, additional materials must be purchased and, if required, the

EXHIBIT 9.3
Relationship of Business Cycles

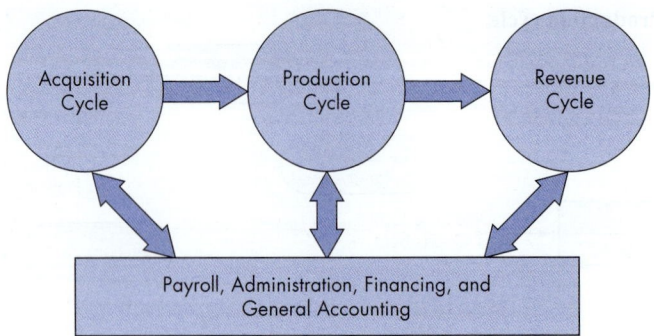

planner must send a purchase requisition to purchasing (which begins the expenditure cycle as discussed in Chapter 8). Purchase lead times must be factored into the production plan.

Production ②

Once the production plan has been finalized, it is generally shared with managers in the sales/marketing department, production department, and possibly human resources who may be required to "sign off" as evidence of their approval of the plan. Managers may request adjustments to the schedule or may need to adjust personnel, maintenance schedules, even overtime, to ensure that production operates efficiently. As you can see, an error in the production plan may mean insufficient raw materials and personnel, excessive warehousing of finished goods, an oversupply of raw materials, unnecessary personnel, or insufficient finished goods to meet demand. All of these conditions represent real costs to the entity.

Inventory Control

As the time for production nears, the production planner issues a **production order** to the appropriate production personnel including inventory control and production managers. Inventory control will receive a **materials requisition** or **materials transfer ticket** that authorizes inventory to release raw materials and supplies to production. These documents are the inventory record keepers' authorizations to update the raw materials inventory files to record the reductions of the raw materials inventory.

Cost Accounting ③

When production is completed, production orders and the related records of materials and labor used are sent to the cost accounting department. Labor is reported by various means from time sheets to computerized clocks. Employees designate what job or product they worked on, or the labor is automatically assigned based on the department or machinery to which the employee is assigned. Because these accounting documents may come from the production workers, there may be an independent verification of hours worked from other sources (e.g., notifications of materials from the inventory custodian or labor costs assigned from the payroll department).

Cost accounting generally records finished goods at **standard costs**. Developing standard costs is a difficult, time-consuming process, even for relatively simple products. All materials, supplies, labor, and overhead that go into the product must be measured based on the bill of materials and associated with a cost. Differences between standard costs and actual costs are recorded in variance accounts and reviewed by supervisors. (*Note:* GAAP recognizes specific-item, first-in, first-out [FIFO], last-in, first-out [LIFO], and weighted-average costing but does not recognize standard costs per se. The auditor must ensure that standard costs are not materially different from the GAAP method that the client has adopted.)

AUDITING INSIGHT — Overhead Allocation

The cost accounting department at Pointed Publications, Inc. routinely allocated overhead to book printing runs at the rate of 40 percent of materials and labor cost. The debit was made initially to the finished goods (books) inventory, and the credit went to an "overhead allocated" account that was offset against other entries in the cost of goods sold calculation, which included all actual overhead incurred. During the year, the company produced 10 million books to which $40 million of overhead were allocated. The auditors noticed that actual overhead expenditures were $32 million and 3 million books remained in the ending inventory. This finding resulted in the conclusion that inventory was overstated by $2.4 million, the cost of goods sold was understated by $2.4 million, and the income before taxes was overstated by 8.2 percent.

Overhead Allocation	Company Accounting	Proper Accounting
Books produced	10 million	10 million
Books sold	7 million	7 million
Labor and materials cost	$100 million	$ 100 million
Overhead allocated	$40 million	$32 million (actual cost)
Cost per book	$14.00	$13.20
Cost of goods sold:		
Labor and materials cost	$100 million	$ 100 million
Overhead allocated to books	40 million	
Overhead incurred	32 million	32 million
Overhead credited to cost	(40 million)	
Ending inventory	(42 million)	(39.6 million)
Total cost of goods sold	$ 90 million	$92.4 million

The cost accounting department produces analyses of actual cost per unit, standard cost, and variances. Cost accounting also may determine the **overhead allocation** to production in general, to production orders, and to finished units. Depending on the design of the company's cost accounting system, these costs are used to value inventory and ultimately to determine the cost of goods sold. In addition, production reports are authorization for the finished goods inventory custodian to place the units in the finished goods inventory. The reports also authorize the inventory record keepers to update the finished goods inventory. In many cases, the cost accounting department is also responsible for calculating the depreciation of fixed assets and the amortization of intangibles.

REVIEW CHECKPOINTS

9.1 What functions are normally associated with the production cycle?
9.2 What inventory costing methods does GAAP recognize?

AUDIT EVIDENCE IN MANAGEMENT REPORTS AND FILES

Most production systems produce timely reports that managers need for monitoring and controlling production. Auditors can use these reports as supporting evidence for assertions about raw materials inventories, work-in-process inventories, finished goods inventories, and cost of goods sold.

Sales Forecast

Management's sales forecast provides the basis for several aspects of business planning, notably of production and inventory levels. Forecasts can be used in gaining an understanding of management's plans for the year under audit, some of which will have already been completed when the audit work begins. Forecasts help auditors understand the nature and volume of production orders and management's strategy and rationale for inventory levels. Forecasts for the following year can be used in valuing the inventory at lower of cost or market (e.g., identifying slow-moving and potentially obsolete inventory). Special care must be taken when using the forecast for the next year in valuing inventory because an overly optimistic forecast can lead to a failure to write down inventory, accelerate the depreciation of fixed assets, and account for more cost of goods sold.

If the auditors want to use the forecast for audit decisions, they should perform some work to obtain assurance about its reasonableness. For example, the auditor can inquire about how the forecast was prepared, what assumptions were made, and how the client ensures its accuracy. The auditor also can compare previous forecasts with actual results. In addition, some work on the mechanical accuracy of the forecast should be performed to avoid relying on faulty calculations. This work can usually be limited to overall tests for reasonableness.

AUDITING INSIGHT — The SALY Forecast

The auditors were reviewing the inventory items that had not been issued for 30 days or more, considering the need to write some items down to market lower than cost. The production manager showed them the SALY forecast that indicated continuing need for the materials in products that are expected to have reasonable demand. The auditors agreed that the forecasts supported the prediction of future sales of products at prices that would cover the cost of the slow-moving material items.

Unfortunately, the auditors neglected to ask the meaning of *SALY* in the designation of the forecast and therefore did not learn that it meant "same as last year." It was not a forecast at all. The products did not sell at the prices expected, and the company experienced losses the following year that should have been charged to cost of goods sold earlier.

Inventory Reports

Companies can produce a wide variety of inventory reports useful to auditors in conducting analytical procedures. These reports should include a list of the items in inventory and their costs and should agree with the inventory control account. Auditors can use this list (1) to scan for unusual conditions (e.g., negative item balances, overstocking, and valuation problems) and (2) as a population for sample selection for a physical inventory observation. The scanning and sample selection may be performed by computer-assisted audit techniques (CAATs) on the computerized inventory report file.

Production Plans and Reports

Based on the sales forecast, management should develop a plan for the amount and timing of production. The production plan provides general information to the auditors, but the production orders and inventory plan associated with the production plan are even more important. The production orders carry the information about requirements for raw materials, labor, and overhead, including the requisitions for purchase and use of materials and labor. These documents are the initial authorizations for control of the inventory and production.

Production reports record the completion of production quantities. When coupled with the related cost accounting reports, they are the company's record of the cost of goods placed into the finished goods inventory. In most cases, auditors examine the cost reports in connection with determining the cost valuation of inventory and cost of goods sold.

AUDITING INSIGHT Do You Want a Lamborghini Cheap?

By all appearances, 45-year-old Viken Keuylian's business ventures were thriving. Keuylian once sold 5 percent of the world's Lamborghinis to a star-studded clientele that included the likes of NBA star Kobe Bryant. In 2007, he appeared at fund-raisers with actress Sharon Stone and singer-songwriter Elton John. In April of that year, Keuylian gave actors Eric Roberts and Luke Perry a helicopter ride to one of his dealership parties. And photos of the grand opening of the Calabasas (California) store in November 2007 show him with Natalie Maines of the Dixie Chicks and actors Kristen Bell, Hayden Panettiere, and Milo Ventimiglia. In May 2008, Keuylian told *The Orange County Register*, "Other dealers are turning down cars, and we're picking them up and selling them at a profit."

In fact, by the fall of 2007, Keuylian had become "financially overextended" and could not meet his debt obligations. So he began selling superluxury cars without reporting the transactions to his floor planner (*floor plan* is the industry term that refers to the dealer's inventory). He pled guilty to bilking **Volkswagen Credit Inc.** of at least $6 million in floor plan loans by keeping sold items on the floor plan. Keuylian used the proceeds from sales to pay for his Southern California vineyard, Newport Beach commercial property, and a Lotus dealership in Beverly Hills. In October 2008, in a desperate move to stay afloat, Keuylian sold 54 vehicles in two weeks, mostly to other dealers and auto auctions. He steeply discounted most of the vehicles, which included 45 Lamborghinis, 4 Bentleys, 2 Mercedes, a Ferrari, a Jaguar, and a Dodge Sprinter van. As an example, Volkswagen Credit had loaned him $336,320 to buy a 2008 Lamborghini Murcielago, which he sold for $90,000. He had a $387,720 floor plan loan for a 2009 Lamborghini LP640, which he sold for $60,430. Seventeen other vehicles had discounts of at least $100,000. Keuylian showed Volkswagen Credit inventory reports that included these sold vehicles. Records show that Keuylian received $8.1 million for vehicles that Volkswagen Credit had financed for $12.6 million.

In an agreement with the District Attorney, Keuylian pled guilty to numerous charges and was sentenced to five years in prison. The FBI impounded 14 of the vehicles sold in connection with the scheme. The cars will either be returned to their new owners or be given to Volkswagen Credit, depending on the circumstances surrounding each car's sale. "You can draw your own conclusions about whether someone getting a Lamborghini at $60,000 would get suspicious or not," said Andrew Stolper, the assistant U.S. attorney handling the case.

Source: "Star Lambo Dealer Played Fast, Loose with Funds," *Automotive News,* April 20, 2009.

REVIEW CHECKPOINTS

9.3 Describe a walkthrough of a production transaction from receiving production orders to making an entry in the finished goods perpetual inventory records. What document copies would be collected? What controls noted? What duties separated?

9.4 When auditors want to use a client's sales forecast for general familiarity with the production cycle or for evaluation of slow-moving inventory, what kind of procedures should be performed with respect to the forecast?

9.5 If the actual sales for the year are substantially lower than the sales forecasted at the beginning of the year, what potential valuation problems could arise in the production cycle accounts?

CONTROL RISK ASSESSMENT

LEARNING OBJECTIVE 9-2
Give examples of tests of controls over conversion of materials and labor in a production process.

Control risk assessment is important because it governs the *nature, timing,* and *extent* of substantive procedures that will be performed in the audit of account balances in the production cycle. These account balances include

- Raw materials inventory.
- Work-in-process inventory.
- Finished goods inventory.
- Cost of goods sold.

With respect to inventory valuation, this chapter discusses the cost accounting function and its role in determining the cost valuation of manufactured finished goods.

Entity-Level Controls

It is important that auditors consider entity-level controls in all processes and procedures. In the production cycle, controls over access to the production facility including inventory are essential. The prevention of theft of inventory and equipment begins with a facility that requires escorts for visitors and ensures that only authorized personnel have access to inventory and production areas. Furthermore, adequate security must be enforced when the facility is not in operation. Finally, production reports should be adequate to ensure that only authorized operations are performed and that performance statistics are reviewed on a timely basis and anomalies investigated promptly.

Control Considerations

Control activities for proper separation of responsibilities should be in place and operating. By referring to Exhibit 9.2, you can see that proper separation involves authorization (production planning, inventory planning, and purchase requisitions) by persons who do not have custody, record-keeping, cost accounting, or reconciliation duties. Custody of inventories (raw materials, work-in-process, and finished goods) is in the hands of persons who do not authorize the amount or timing of production or the purchase of materials and labor, perform the cost accounting record keeping, or prepare cost analyses (reconciliations). Persons who do not authorize production or have custody of assets in the production process perform cost accounting (a recording function). Combinations of two or more of the duties of authorization, custody, and accounting in one person, one office, or one computerized system could open the door for errors and frauds.

In addition, the controls should provide for detailed checking activities, for example:

- Production orders should contain a list of materials and their quantities, and they should be approved by a production planner/scheduler.
- Materials requisitions should be compared in the cost accounting department with the list of materials on the production orders and the production operator and the materials inventory storekeeper should sign the materials requisitions.
- All material requisitions should be accounted for. Material requisitioned is either used in production, unusable (scrap), or excess material returned to raw material inventory. Documentation for material returned to raw material inventory should accompany the returned items with a copy going to inventory control for use in adjusting the perpetual raw material inventory.
- Production supervisors should sign (or review if the time is kept electronically) labor time records on jobs, and the cost accounting department should reconcile these cost amounts with the labor report from the payroll department.
- The production supervisor and finished goods inventory custodian should review production reports of finished units and then forward them to cost accounting.
- Inventory should be periodically counted with the counts agreed to perpetual inventory records.

These control activities track the raw materials and labor from the beginning of production to completion in the production process. With each internal transaction, the responsibility and accountability for assets are passed from one person or location to another.

Many entities have complex computer systems to manage production and materials flow. Even though the technology is complex, the basic management and control functions of ensuring the flow of labor and materials to production and the control of waste should be in place. Manual signatures, paper production orders, and paper requisitions might not exist, but computer system equivalents should be in place.

Custody

Supervisors and production workers have physical custody of materials and labor documents (time cards, job tickets, etc.) while the production work is being performed. Authorized employees can requisition materials from the raw materials inventory, assign people to jobs, and control the pace of work. In a sense, they have custody of a "moving inventory." The work-in-process (WIP) is literally "moving" and changing form in the process of being transformed from raw materials into finished goods.

Inventory warehouses and fixed asset locations should be under adequate physical security (storerooms, fences, locks, and the like). However, control over goods in process is more difficult than control over a warehouse of raw materials or finished goods where unauthorized individuals cannot gain access. Control over WIP can be exercised by holding supervisors and workers accountable for the use of materials specified in the production orders, for the timely completion of production, and for the quality of the finished goods. This accountability can be achieved with effective cost accounting, cost analysis, and quality control testing. Accountability may be evident by ensuring that supervisors and management are analyzing the costs of production orders, comparing the costs to prior experience or to standard costs, and determining lower-of-cost-or-market (LCM) valuations. When costs of material or labor, scrap rates for materials, or production numbers do not meet expectations, management should require a documented assessment by cost accounting or internal audit to determine the cause and corrective action required.

AUDITING INSIGHT — Is Your Inventory on eBay?

Kevin Lee Ruff, a warehouse supervisor for **Sacred Heart Medical Center**, was given access to the computerized inventory system. Ruff took boxes of inventory including medical and office supplies and sold them on eBay. In court, Ruff said, "I took several inventory items and sold them... Made adjustments to the inventory... so they would not be shown as missing." The FBI solved the case by investigating Ruff's PayPal account, which identified each **eBay** transaction he made. His take? More than $664,000.

Source: Thomas Clouse, "Man Pleads Guilty to Fraud: Stolen Items Were Sold on eBay," *Spokane-Review* (Spokane, Washington), December 21, 2006.

Internal Control Questionnaire

Information about the production cycle control often is gathered initially by completing an *internal control questionnaire (ICQ)*. An ICQ for control activities commonly found in the production cycle is included in Appendix Exhibit 9A.1. You can study this questionnaire for details of desirable control activities. The ICQ is organized with headings that identify the important transaction assertions: *occurrence, completeness, accuracy, cutoff,* and *classification.*

Tests of Controls

An entity should have detailed control activities in place and operating to prevent, detect, and correct accounting errors. Exhibit 9.4 puts controls in the perspective of production activity with examples of specific assertions. This exhibit identifies the transaction assertions in specific examples related to production.

Auditors can perform tests of controls to determine whether company personnel are effectively performing control activities that are said to be in place and operating properly. Exhibit 9.4 includes a selection of tests of controls for the accumulation of costs for WIP inventory. This is the stage of inventory that is in the production process. Upon completion, the accumulated costs become the value of the finished goods inventory. The illustrative procedures presume the existence of production cost reports that are updated as production takes place, labor reports that assign labor cost to the job, materials used and materials requisitions charging raw materials to the production order, and overhead allocation calculations. Some or all of these documents may be in the form of computerized records.

EXHIBIT 9.4 Assertions about Classes of Transactions and Events: Production Cycle

Transaction Assertion	Controls	Tests of Controls
Occurrence—Production and related events that have been recorded have occurred and pertain to the entity.	• Cost accounting is separated from production, payroll, and inventory control. • Material usage reports are reconciled with raw material stores' issue slips, scrap reports, and documentation of unused material returned to inventory.	• Observe separation of cost accounting function from production, payroll, and inventory control. • Inspect evidence of reconciliations.
Completeness—All production events that should have been recorded have been recorded.	• All documents are prenumbered and numerical sequence reviewed. • Periodic count of inventory is compared to perpetual records. • Open production cost reports are reconciled to the WIP inventory cost report. • Receiving reports and material usage are posted to perpetual inventory records. • Job cost sheets are posted weekly, and summary journal entries of work in process and work completed are prepared monthly.	• Inspect evidence of review of numerical sequence. Select a sample of documents and examine numerical sequence. • Inspect evidence that inventory counts are compared to perpetual records. • Inspect reconciliation of production cost reports to WIP inventory control report. • Trace receiving reports to perpetual inventory. Trace materials used reports to production cost reports. • Inspect journal entries and agree with approved cost sheets. Compare costs to standard cost listing.
Accuracy—Production information including costs has been properly calculated and recorded.	• Labor usage reports are compared to job time tickets. • Material usage and labor usage are prepared by floor supervisor and approved by production supervisor. • Periodic count of inventory is compared to perpetual records. • Receiving reports are posted to perpetual inventory on a timely basis.	• Inspect evidence of comparison by client. • Inspect evidence of approval of material and labor usage reports. • Compare inventory counts with perpetual records. • Compare dates on receiving reports to posting in perpetual inventory records.
Cutoff—Production events have been recorded in the correct accounting period.	• Receiving reports are posted to perpetual inventory in the proper period. • Finished goods are recorded in the proper period. • Production reports of material and labor are prepared weekly and transmitted to cost accounting.	• Compare the dates of inventory records with receiving reports. • Inspect production data and agree with finished goods inventory status reports. • Inspect production reports and agree dates with dates in weekly journal entries.
Classification—Classification-related events are recorded in the proper accounts.	• Production supervisor is required to account for all material and labor as direct or indirect and to identify appropriate job classifications.	• Observe supervisor allocation. Test allocation. Examine supervisor signature.

It is important for the auditor performing tests of controls in the production cycle to recognize that most of the company's documentation is internal. The entity's reporting system generates production reports, inventory reports, material and labor distribution reports, and other documents auditors rely on. The auditor must pay close attention to general and application controls over the production reporting system in order to have some assurance that reports can be relied on for testing.

EXHIBIT 9.5
Test of Production Cost Controls: Completeness Direction

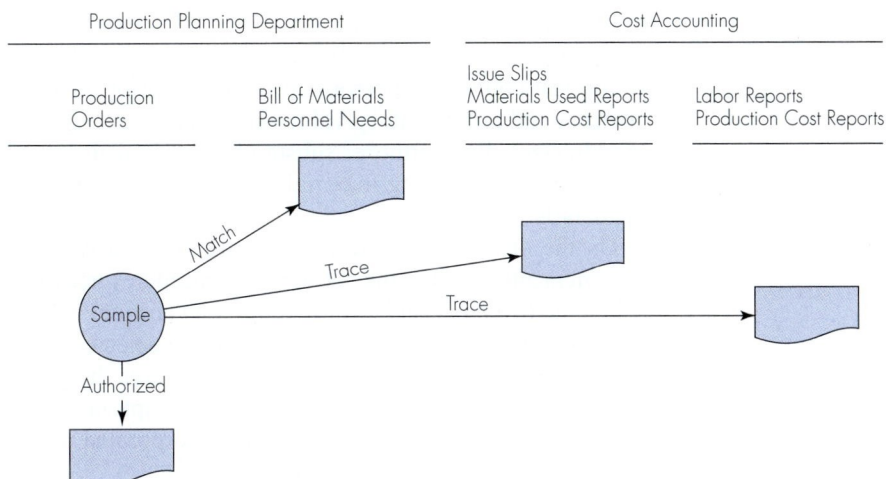

Direction of Tests of Controls

The tests of controls in Exhibit 9.5 are designed to test production accounting in two directions. One is the *completeness* direction, in which the auditors are interested in determining that all production that was started was recorded. Exhibit 9.5 shows that the sample for this direction is taken from the population of production orders found in the production-planning department. The procedures trace the cost accumulation forward to the production cost reports in the cost accounting department.

Testing the other direction relates to the *occurrence* of production. The auditors are interested in determining that items composing WIP and finished goods inventories recorded in the general ledger were produced. Exhibit 9.6 shows that the sample for this test is from the general ledger. This sample is vouched to the production reports (quantity and cost) recorded in the inventory accounts. Additional testing may include vouching from the production reports to the recorded material, labor, and payroll reports. Potential findings include errors in the *accuracy* of the recorded inventory cost. Of course, CAATs could be used to perform a 100 percent match that would accomplish both goals.

Summary: Control Risk Assessment

The audit team should evaluate the evidence obtained from an understanding of the internal controls and from the tests of controls. The evaluation of control risk with the assessment of inherent risk provides the auditors an assessment of the risk of material

EXHIBIT 9.6
Test of Production Cost Controls: Occurrence Direction

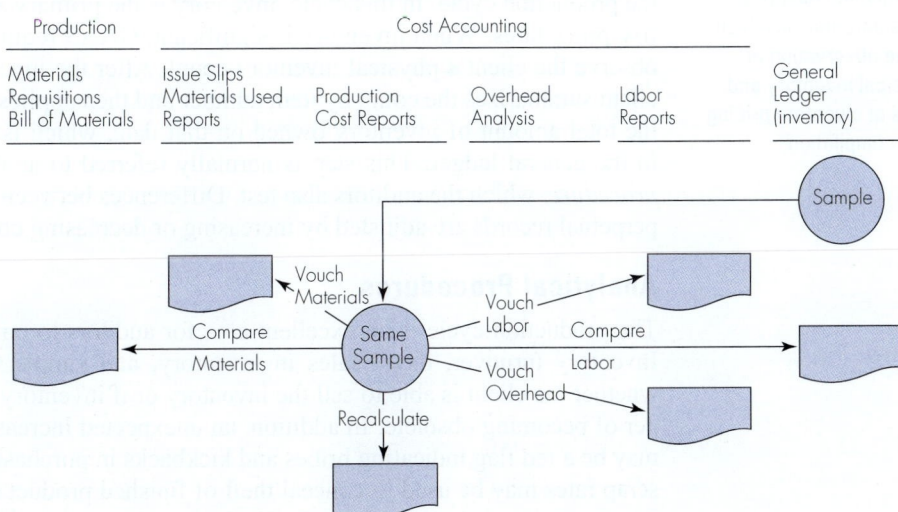

misstatement. If the risk of material misstatement is relatively low, the substantive procedures on the account balances can be reduced. For example, if inventory observation test counts are performed on a date prior to the year-end, fewer counts would be made and the inventory valuation procedures can be reduced in scope (i.e., smaller sample size). Furthermore, substantive analytical procedures can be used with more confidence in detecting material misstatements not otherwise evident in the accounting details.

On the other hand, if tests of controls reveal weaknesses and the risk of material misstatement is higher, the substantive procedures need to be designed to lower detection risk in the inventory and cost of goods sold account balances. For example, a large number of inventory production reports may be selected for valuation calculations and the inventory observation may be scheduled nearer the year-end date with the audit team making a large number of test counts. Descriptions of significant deficiencies, control weaknesses, and inefficiencies may be incorporated in a letter to the client and must be communicated to the audit committee.

↳ REVIEW CHECKPOINTS

9.6 What features of the cost accounting system would be expected to prevent the omission of recording materials used in production?

9.7 Describe how the functions of (a) authorization of production transactions, (b) recording of these transactions, and (c) physical custody of inventories can be separated among the production, inventory, and cost accounting departments.

9.8 How does the production order record provide a control over the quantity of materials used in production?

9.9 From what population of documents would an auditor sample to determine whether (a) all authorized production was completed and placed in inventory or recorded as scrap and (b) finished goods inventory was actually produced and the costs were accounted for properly?

▽ SUBSTANTIVE PROCEDURES IN THE PRODUCTION CYCLE

LEARNING OBJECTIVE 9-3
Identify and describe considerations involved in the observation of physical inventory and tests of inventory pricing and compilation.

See Exhibit 9.7 for the assertions and primary substantive procedures used for accounts in the production cycle. In this cycle, inventory is the primary account balance for substantive procedures. When inventory is significant, GAAS requires auditors to be present to observe the client's physical inventory count. After the inventory has been counted, the client summarizes the count by item number and then applies standard costs to determine the total amount of inventory owned on that date, which is compared with the amount in the general ledger. This step is normally referred to as the *compilation and pricing procedure,* which the auditors also test. Differences between the inventory count and the perpetual records are adjusted by increasing or decreasing cost of goods sold.

Analytical Procedures

The production cycle is an excellent area for auditors to employ analytical procedures. Inventory turnover, days' sales in inventory, and simple trend analysis can indicate whether the client is able to sell the inventory or if inventory is slow moving and in danger of becoming obsolete. In addition, an unexpected increase in raw material inventory may be a red flag indicating bribes and kickbacks in purchasing or production. Increased scrap rates may be used to conceal theft of finished product at the end of the production process (prior to the transfer to finished goods inventory). The gross margin percentage

EXHIBIT 9.7 Account Balance Assertions and Substantive Procedures in the Production Cycle

Balance Assertions	Substantive Procedures
Existence—Inventory exists.	• Observe client's physical inventory count. • Confirm inventory held by others on consignment. • Vouch items on inventory listing to inventory count tags. • *Analytical procedures.* Compare inventory turnover and gross margin to budget and previous periods and discuss differences with client personnel.
Rights and obligations—The entity holds or controls the rights to inventory.	• Inquire whether any inventory is on consignment. • Inquire whether inventory has been pledged as collateral or security.
Completeness—All inventory that should have been recorded has been recorded.	• Review inventory subsidiary accounts and trace to inventory control account. • Review physical inventory to ensure all items were counted. • Trace test inventory counts to inventory subsidiary accounts and control account.
Valuation and allocation—Inventory is included in the financial statements at appropriate amounts and any resulting valuation adjustments are properly recorded.	• Perform lower-of-cost-or-market tests. • Review cost of goods sold calculations. • Check that inventory cost agrees with standard costs or purchase invoices. • Inquire whether any inventory is obsolete or unsalable. • Examine loans and other agreements for the use of inventory as collateral.

reveals whether the client is able to price the inventory to earn an acceptable profit. Moreover, comparing current-year gross margin to that of prior years can uncover fraudulent inventory accounting. These ratios should be disaggregated to specific product lines or geographic regions to make them more meaningful. The results can be compared to the amounts budgeted, results in previous years, results of competitors, and industry averages.

AUDITING INSIGHT   Really Gross Margins

A popular move among online retailers has been to include shipping costs and discounts in selling expenses to inflate their gross margins. Placing these costs in selling expense instead of cost of goods sold has a big effect on gross margin. Say a company sells a $1,200 bicycle that cost $600 but takes a $500 coupon for it. Gross margin is 14 percent—right? Not if you bury the coupon in selling costs; then the margin becomes 50 percent, a number sure to catch Wall Street's eye. According to **Lehman Brothers**, **Amazon.com** inflated its gross margin in the first quarter of 2000 from 10 to 22.9 percent, **Etoys** reported 20.5 percent when it should have reported a negative 6.5 percent, and **Drugstore.com** reported 5 percent instead of a negative 15 percent. Because analysts value new companies more on their potential than their results, inflating gross margins can make a big difference in stock prices. Accounting rules have been adopted to prevent the abuse, but these actions illustrate the importance companies place on gross margins.

Source: "Fess-Up Time," *Forbes*, September 18, 2000.

Physical Inventory Observation

The auditing procedures for inventory and related cost of sales accounts frequently are extensive in an audit engagement. A material error or fraud in inventory has a pervasive effect on financial statements. Misstatements in inventory also cause misstatements in many other important financial statement elements (such as current assets, working capital, total assets, cost of sales, gross margin, and net income). Although analytical procedures may indicate inventory misstatements, the auditor's best opportunity to detect inventory errors and frauds is during a **physical inventory observation**, an observation of the client's **physical inventory count** taken by company personnel. (Auditors observe the inventory taking and make test counts, but they seldom actually count the entire inventory.)

This section gives details about inventory procedures and auditors' responsibilities during the observation of the physical inventory count. The first task is to review the client's inventory-taking instructions, which should include the following:

1. Names of client personnel responsible for the count.
2. Dates and times of inventory taking.
3. Names of client personnel who will participate in the inventory taking.
4. Instructions for recording accurate descriptions of inventory items, for count and double count, and for measuring physical quantities (such as counting by measures of gallons, barrels, feet, dozens).
5. Instructions for making notes of obsolete or worn items.
6. Instructions for the use of tags, punched cards, count sheets, computers, or other media devices and for their collection and control (a typical inventory count sheet is illustrated at Exhibit 9.8).
7. Plans for shutting down plant operations or for taking inventory after store closing hours and plans for having goods in proper places (such as on store shelves instead of on the floor, or of raw materials in a warehouse rather than in transit to a job).

EXHIBIT 9.8
Inventory Count Sheet

DUNDER-MIFFLIN
Inventory Count Sheet
12/31/2012

SHEET NO. 3

COUNT TEAM

J. Morris, T. Peters

ENTERED BY

H.R. Samuels

REVIEWED BY

A. Jacobs

Pallet Location	SKU#	Style	Type	Size	Quantity Counted
A10	10030	Siren	Men's	8	1080
A11	10030	Siren	Men's	8	1080
A12	10030	Siren	Men's	8	1080
A13	10030	Siren	Men's	8	890

8. Plans for counting or controlling movement of goods in receiving and shipping areas if those operations are not shut down during the count.
9. Instructions for computer compilation of the count media (such as tags, count sheets) into final inventory lists or summaries.
10. Instructions for review and approval of the inventory count; supervisory personnel notations of obsolescence or other matters.
11. Instructions for making changes and corrections to count tickets.

These instructions characterize a well-planned counting operation. As the plan is carried out, the auditors should be present to hear the count instructions being given to the client's count teams and to observe the instructions being followed. In addition, the auditor should make selected test counts and record these in the audit documentation.

Manual Physical Inventory

Refer to Appendix Exhibit 9B.1 for an example of an audit plan for observing a physical inventory count. Note the requirement for obtaining tag numbers. It is critically important to know which tag numbers or count sheets were and were not used to prevent the client from simply adding inventory items by creating more tags at a later date. Also, note the cutoff procedures of examining shipping and receiving documents issued immediately before and after the count. The items that are included in the count must be the same as those recorded in the inventory records, and any items that have been sold or are not yet received must be excluded from the count and the records.

The auditors can perform dual-direction testing by (1) selecting inventory items from a perpetual inventory master file, going to the location, and obtaining a test count, which produces evidence for the *existence* balance assertion, and (2) selecting inventory from locations on the warehouse floor, obtaining a test count, and tracing the count to the final inventory compilation, which produces evidence for the *completeness* balance assertion. If the company does not have perpetual records and a file to test for *existence,* the auditors must be careful to obtain a record of all counts and use it for the existence-direction tests. In addition to the test counts, the auditor should document whether client personnel were following the inventory instructions, the tag or count sheet numbers used and unused, the last shipping and receiving reports issued before the inventory count, the condition of the inventory, any inventory on hand that the client does not own, and any unusual items noticed during the count.

Inventory Count and Measurement Challenges		
Examples	**Challenges**	**Special Procedures**
Lumber	Problem identifying quality or grade	Employ a specialist.
Piles of sugar, coal, scrap steel	Use of geometric computations, aerial photos	Employ a specialist.
Items weighed on scales	Accuracy of scales	Examine certification.
Bulk materials (oil, grain, liquids in storage tanks)	Measurement of volume, ensuring composition of content	Climb the tanks. Dip measuring rods. Sample for assay or chemical analysis.
Diamonds, jewelry	Identification and quality determination problems	Employ a specialist.
Pulp wood	Quantity measurement estimation	Examine aerial photos.
Livestock	Movement not controllable	Use chutes to control animals.

EXHIBIT 9.9

Example of Inventory Bar Code Scanners
Phaser memory scanners P360 and P460 by Barcoding Incorporated

Using Bar Codes and Computers in Physical Inventory

Many organizations are now using the bar codes located on products to improve the efficiency and effectiveness of monitoring the movement of physical inventory. Perhaps on a trip to the grocery store or department store you have seen an individual with a handheld device scanning the store shelves. This device (see Exhibit 9.9) is designed to scan the bar code located on the front of the shelf. That bar code records the product type, manufacturer, and size in the hand unit. Once the individual counts the number of units in inventory, the count can be entered and stored in the scanner by using the number pad located on the top of the scanner. When the counts are completed, the unit can be brought back to the physical inventory supervisor, who can download the data to the computer program being used to manage the physical inventory.

Although the use of scanners and computers greatly improves the accuracy (all product descriptions are identical) and efficiency (product descriptions and counts do not need to be written), there is still a need to follow the basic elements of a physical inventory count. For example, all items still should be counted twice. However, the computer program can match first and second counts and, if they are identical, accept and record the count. If the counts are not identical, the item can be flagged for review by the physical inventory supervisor.

RFID Physical Inventory

Many people driving in cities with toll roads and bridges now bypass the toll booths by using the technology of radio frequency identification (RFID). Its devices send a signal to an RFID reader that identifies the automobile or truck as it travels and charges the driver's account for the toll. This same technology is being used in some warehouses and stores around the world. As more and more products are tagged with RFID chips, most about the size of a nickel, companies will automatically scan each product as it enters or leaves the warehouse or store, or count the inventory by using portable RFID readers. For example, **Sam's Club** uses an electronic product code (EPC) system designed to track goods using RFID technology. When a case of products tagged with RFID labels arrives in a warehouse, it is detected by readers on the door. A staff member can then use a handheld RFID reader to trace the case and process the product. If every product is tagged with individual RFID labels, inventory levels can be recorded automatically and out-of-stock situations reduced. **Walmart** expects the system to be widely adopted by its suppliers and competitors in the near future.

Will this eliminate the need for a physical inventory? Probably not. But it will change the focus of the audit of the physical inventory. If the RFID reader is connected to a computer, a completely accurate count of the RFID signals can be made without the need for a second count. The major focus may be a sampling of items to ensure the actual goods are contained in the shipping container, not just an empty container with only a RFID chip.

Difficult Circumstances

The following are some unusual circumstances that present difficulties for the auditors.

Physical Inventory Not on Year-End Date Clients usually count the inventory before or after the balance-sheet date. When the auditors are present to make their physical observation, they follow the procedures outlined for observation of the physical count. However, with an intervening period between the count date and the year-end,

> ### AUDITING INSIGHT | Using RFID in Inventory Management
>
> RFID (radio frequency identification) is a tiny computer chip that Walmart has been using since 2006 to keep track of pallets of goods flowing in and out of its warehouses and stores.
>
> Each tag broadcasts a radio signal that beams 10 times as much information as a bar code to sensors deployed in doorways and store fixtures. With the price at 8 cents a tag and dropping, merchants are now starting to hang RFID tags on individual high-dollar items such as apparel so they can pinpoint every item in their stock down to the shelf.
>
> Walmart started putting RFID tags in the jeans and men's underwear departments in stores in July. After a test at one **Bloomingdale's**, corporate parent **Macy's Inc**. will expand its first RFID steps this year to basic men's apparel in all its New York department stores.
>
> The tags empower chains to identify each garment by size, style, and color in a real-time inventory. That dramatically enhances their ability to be fully stocked with the right goods at the right store more often.
>
> It's part of an industrywide initiative aimed at curing the apparel industry's abysmal 60 to 65 percent inventory accuracy.
>
> "In our test, the accuracy improved to 95 percent," said Peter Longo, who heads Macy's logistics and co-chairs GS1, a retail/apparel industry effort to shepherd RFID inventory control to common use. "The sales (people) like it because it gives them a handheld device that leads them to the exact item the customer is looking for."
>
> Retailers hope to wring $60 billion from annual expenses once RFID is widespread.
>
> "This is no longer a science experiment," wrote Mark Roberti, editor of the *RFID Journal*, a trade publication.
>
> The upside for shoppers is lower prices and fewer missing sizes thanks to technology-driven efficiencies. The downsides: fewer markdown sales to unload unsold inventory mistakes deployed in the wrong place or store. And, because RFID tags can keep broadcasting after the sale, potentially lost privacy to customers who forget to throw tags away if a store doesn't deactivate them or opt for a passive system.
>
> Source: "Stores Gather Instant Feedback," *St. Petersburg Times*, January 18, 2011, p. 4B.

additional **inventory roll-forward** auditing procedures must be performed on transactions during that period. The inventory on the count date is reconciled to the year-end inventory by appropriate addition or subtraction of the subsequent receiving and shipping transactions.

Cycle Inventory Counting **Cycle counts** are physical counts of selected inventory throughout the year (i.e., different parts of the inventory throughout the year). They are most appropriate when internal control over inventory is effective (that is, a low level of control risk is present). Other companies use a statistical counting plan. In these circumstances, the auditors must understand the cycle or sampling plan and evaluate its appropriateness. In this situation, the auditors are present for only some of the physical inventory counts. Only under unusual circumstances and as an "extended procedure" are auditors present every month (or more frequently) to observe all counts. Businesses that count inventory using cycle counts purport to have accurate perpetual records and carry out the counting as a means of testing the records and maintaining their accuracy.

The auditors must be present during some counting operations to evaluate the counting plans and their execution. The same procedures enumerated for an annual count are used, test counts are made, and the audit team is responsible for making a determination concerning the accuracy of perpetual records.

Professional Inventory Teams Some clients with large numbers of operating facilities (e.g., retail store chains) may have a professional inventory team(s) or hire a professional inventory company. These teams go from one facility to another performing physical inventory counts all year long. In addition, these inventory companies may have their own standard inventory procedures, minimal qualification requirements, and substantial training for inventory count supervisors and employees. These types of operations add an air of professionalism and expertise to the physical inventory count. Auditors should review inventory team qualifications, training requirements, and standard policies and procedures.

When counts go on all year long, the auditors are present for only a few counts. Auditors should review annual inventory schedules and carefully select the inventories to observe. These observations may be performed during interim periods, but good inventory observation procedures should always be followed.

Auditors Not Present for Client's Inventory Count This situation can arise on a first audit when the accounting firm is appointed after the beginning inventory already has been counted. Because the beginning inventory amount affects cost of goods sold, the auditors must disclaim an opinion on the income statement and may have substantial concerns with stockholders' equity, the statement of cash flows, and additional items affect by net income. The auditor can utilize alternative procedures to provide sufficient, appropriate evidence that the beginning inventory number is not materially misstated. For example, the auditors must review the client's plan for the already completed count as described earlier. Some test counts of current inventory should be made and traced to current records to determine the reliability of perpetual records. If the actual count was recent, intervening transaction activity might be reconciled back to the inventory count. The reconciliation of more than a few months' transactions to unobserved beginning inventories could be very difficult. The auditors can employ analytical procedures using such interrelationships as sales activity, physical volume, price variation, standard costs, and gross profit margins for the decision about beginning inventory reasonableness. Nevertheless, much care must be exercised in "backing into" the audit of inventory previously taken.

Inventories Located off the Client's Premises The auditors must determine where and in what dollar amounts inventories are located off the client's premises, in the custody of consignees, or in public warehouses. If amounts are material and if control activities are not exceptionally strong, the audit team may wish to visit these locations and conduct on-site test counts. However, if amounts are not material, alternative evidence (such as periodic reports, cash receipts, receivables records, shipping records) is adequate or control risk is low, then direct confirmation with the custodian may be considered sufficient appropriate evidence of the existence of quantities.

Pricing and Compilation

The physical observation procedures are designed to audit for *existence* and *completeness* (physical quantities). The **pricing and compilation** tests examine *valuation* (recalculation of appropriate FIFO, LIFO, or other pricing at cost, and lower of cost or market, and write-down of obsolete or worn inventory). After the observation is complete, auditors should have sufficient appropriate evidence of the following physical quantities and valuations:

- Goods in the perpetual records but not owned were excluded from the inventory compilation.
- Goods on hand were counted and included in the inventory compilation.
- **Consignment** (consigned-out) **goods** or goods stored in outside warehouses (goods owned but not on hand) were included in the inventory compilation.
- Goods in transit (goods actually purchased and recorded but not received) were added to the inventory count and included in the inventory compilation.
- Goods on hand that have been recorded as sold but have not been delivered were not counted and were excluded from the inventory compilation.
- Consignment (consigned-in) goods were excluded from the inventory compilation.

The compilation and pricing stage starts by listing all inventory items counted. The auditor foots[3] the list and tests the mathematical accuracy by multiplying the quantities and the price to get the total value for each item. Test counts taken by the auditor during the physical count are traced to the list and other items from the list are vouched back to inventory count tags. The unit price is vouched to the vendor invoices for the purchase

---

[3] *Foots* is an accounting term meaning to add up a column.

> ### AUDITING INSIGHT — Whose Inventory Is It?
>
> James E. Lorenz, former corporate controller of **Electro Scientific Industries (ESI)**, pled guilty to federal charges that he lied to auditors in connection with a scheme to falsely increase the company's profits. Lorenz, who was charged in a 17-count indictment in September 2004, pled guilty to 1 count of making false statements to a public company's accountants in connection with his role in the scheme. He faces a maximum penalty of 20 years in prison and a $5 million fine.
>
> According to the indictment, on December 10, 2002, Lorenz lied on a quarterly review questionnaire that **KPMG** had asked him to complete. Lorenz knew that he had recently changed the way in which consignment inventory was valued on the books of ESI. Before the second quarter of fiscal 2003, consignment inventory was not recorded as an asset, but in the second quarter of 2003, Lorenz changed ESI's accounting practice to treat the inventory as an asset. The change, which was concealed from the auditors, falsely increased quarterly net income by $650,564.
>
> Lorenz admitted to lying to auditors by telling them that he had made no changes in company accounting practices in the second quarter of fiscal 2003. Former ESI CEO James T. Dooley also pled guilty to lying to auditors about a separate accounting transaction.
>
> **Source:** "Electro Scientific's Ex-Controller Pleads Guilty," *CFO.com*, August 8, 2007.

price for raw materials and to standard cost for in-process and finished goods. Many of these tests can be performed automatically using CAATs.

Lower-of-cost-or-market testing is an important step toward the *valuation* assertion. Market price can be obtained by examining the client's catalogue and actual sales in the subsequent period. Items that are slow moving or obsolete can be spotted during the inventory observation if they demonstrate evidence of unsalability (e.g., old inventory tags, dust, and rust). Appendix Exhibit 9B.2 illustrates an audit plan for inventory pricing and compilation tests.

> ### AUDITING INSIGHT — Sometimes Things Are Worth What They Were
>
> **Worthington Industries** is a diversified metals processing company focused on steel processing and manufactured metal products. On December 3, 2008, Worthington announced that market weakness and decline in steel pricing have left it with inventories in excess of demand with reduced market values.
>
> As a result, Worthington wrote down the value of its inventories by approximately $100 million.
>
> **Source:** "Worthington Industries Announces Inventory Write-Down and Declares Quarterly Dividend," Worthington Industries Press Release, December 3, 2008, Worthington Industries website.

Inventory—A Ripe Field for Fraud

These problems have occurred in entities' inventory frauds:

- Auditors were fooled as a result of taking a small sample for test counting, thus missing important information.
- Entities included inventory they pretended to have ordered.
- Entities stacked inventory on pallets in such a manner that "empty spaces" were not visible to auditors, resulting in overstatements of inventory.
- Auditors permitted company officials to follow them and note their counts. Then the managers falsified counts for inventory the auditors did not count.
- Shipments between plants (transfers) were reported as inventory at both plant locations.
- Auditors spotted a barrel whose contents management had valued at thousands of dollars, but it was filled with sawdust. The auditors required management to exclude the value from the inventory, but it never occurred to them that they had found just one instance in an intentional and pervasive overstatement fraud.

- Auditors observed inventory at five store locations and told the management in advance of the specific stores. Management took care not to make fraudulent entries in these five stores but instead made fraudulent adjustments in many of the other 236 stores.
- After counting an inventory of computer chips, the auditors received a call from the client's controller: "Just hours after you left the plant, 2,500 chips arrived in a shipment in transit." The auditors included them in inventory but never checked to see whether the chips were actually received.[4]

Accounting Firm Tips

To help detect inventory fraud, **Grant Thornton,** a large national accounting firm, advises its audit personnel:

- Focus test counts on high-value items and sample lower-value items. Test count a sufficient dollar amount of the inventory.
- If all locations will not be observed, do not follow an easily predictable pattern. Advise client personnel as late as possible of the locations to be visited.
- Be skeptical of large and unusual test count differences or of client personnel making notes or displaying particular interest in our procedures and test counts.
- Be alert for inventory not used for some time, stored in unusual locations, or showing signs of damage, obsolescence, or excess quantities.

Presentation and Disclosure Assertions

Once the auditor is satisfied that controls have been examined and transactions and balances are fairly presented according to GAAP, the job is not over. The aspects of production, especially inventory, require many disclosures. The components of inventory (raw materials, work in process, finished goods), inventory valuation method, lower of cost or market, and allocation of fixed costs are only a few of the essential items with specific presentation and disclosure requirements. These disclosures must ensure that the presentation and disclosure assertions of *occurrence, rights and obligations, completeness, classification and understandability,* and *accuracy and valuation* are all met. See Exhibit 9.10 for excerpts from the footnote contained in **Boeing Corporation's** 2009 financial statements.

EXHIBIT 9.10 Excerpts from Inventory Footnote in Boeing Aircraft 2009 Annual Report

Disclosure Assertion	Excerpt from Boeing Footnote
Completeness	Inventoried costs on commercial aircraft programs and long-term contracts include direct engineering, production and tooling costs, and applicable overhead, which includes fringe benefits, production-related indirect and plant management salaries and plant services, not in excess of estimated net realizable value.*
Classification of items included in inventory costs	To the extent a material amount of such costs are related to an abnormal event or are fixed costs not appropriately attributable to our programs or contracts, they are expensed in the current period rather than inventoried. Inventoried costs include amounts relating to programs and contracts with long-term production cycles, a portion of which is not expected to be realized within one year. Included in inventory for federal government contracts is an allocation of allowable costs related to manufacturing reengineering.*
Accuracy and valuation of inventoried parts	Spare parts inventory is stated at lower of average unit cost or market. We review our commercial spare parts and general stock materials quarterly to identify impaired inventory, including excess or obsolete inventory, based on historical sales trends, expected production usage, and the size and age of the aircraft fleet using the part. Impaired inventories are charged to cost of products in the period the impairment occurs.

*These items are one single paragraph in the annual report It has been separated for illustrative purpose. Items can be found in the annual report, pp. 60–61.

[4] Examples cited in this list have been taken from *The Wall Street Journal*.

> ## ⤷ REVIEW CHECKPOINTS
>
> 9.10 What characteristics do auditors consider in reviewing a client's inventory-taking instructions?
>
> 9.11 Explain dual-direction sampling in the context of inventory test counts.
>
> 9.12 Why is it important for auditors to obtain control information over inventory count sheets or tickets?
>
> 9.13 What inventory information should auditors document?
>
> 9.14 Why is it important to obtain shipping and receiving cutoff information during the inventory observation?
>
> 9.15 What procedures do auditors employ to audit inventory when the physical inventory is taken on a cycle basis or on a statistical plan but never a complete count on a single date?
>
> 9.16 What could be happening when a client's managers take notes of auditors' test counts while an inventory is being counted?
>
> 9.17 What analytical procedures might reveal obsolete or slow-moving inventory?

▽ AUDIT RISK MODEL SUMMARY

Now that the control and inherent risk elements for the production cycle and some of the important substantive procedures have been presented, let's examine how an auditor might apply the audit risk model for the account balance assertion of existence. First, we show a table relating levels of detection risk to extent of substantive procedures; note that the level of detection risk influences the nature (use of analytical procedures), timing (year-end counts versus interim counts versus cycle counts), and extent (number of inventory purchases vouched) of substantive tests. Then we provide an example of how they might be employed in practice. It is important to note that similar examples could be provided for the remaining material financial statement assertions related to inventory.

Extent of Substantive Inventory Procedures for Balance Assertion of Existence	
Low detection risk	Observe physical inventory count at year-end. Take substantial number of test counts and use large sample for vouching inventory purchases. Perform analytical procedures during planning and at audit completion.
Moderate detection risk	Observe inventory count at interim date. Test roll-forward to year-end. Use moderate vouching of purchases. Perform analytical procedures during planning and at audit completion.
High detection risk	Rely heavily on analytical procedures. Observe cycle counts of inventory. Rely on roll-forward procedures with minimal testing.

▽ FRAUD CASE: EXTENDED AUDIT PROCEDURES (STANDARD 240)

LEARNING OBJECTIVE 9-4
Describe some common errors and frauds in the accounting for production costs and related cost of goods sold and design some audit and investigation procedures for detecting these errors and frauds.

The case refers to the Phar-Mor incident discussed at the beginning of this chapter. "The Problem" section reiterates the "inside story," which auditors seldom know before they perform the audit procedures. The second part of the case under the heading "Audit Approach," tells a structured story about the audit objective, controls, tests of controls, substantive procedures, and discovery summary. At the end of the chapter, some similar discussion cases are presented, and you can prepare the audit approach to test your ability to design audit procedures for the detection of errors and frauds.

World Electronics LLC

Martin Phelps has been assigned as audit manager for **World Electronics LLC,** a medium-size publicly held manufacturer of semiconductors used in the computer industry. It has four manufacturing facilities located in Lexington, Kentucky; Dublin, Ireland; Barcelona, Spain; and Bangkok, Thailand. World uses just-in-time inventory management at all plants so that when a plant receives a customer order, it electronically forwards a purchase order for the materials to vendors. The company takes cycle counts of its inventory so it will not disrupt production. When World receives goods, the receiving clerk enters the receipt into the system, which automatically updates the perpetual inventory. Likewise, as semiconductors are completed, they are scanned and automatically moved from in-process to finished goods. The computerized controls were reviewed and tested by the audit firm's computer audit specialist, who noted no exceptions. Therefore, Phelps has set control risk as low. Control risk also has been set as low in the acquisition cycle and the revenue cycle.

The company is a leader in the industry, and management has a very good reputation. The semiconductor industry is experiencing strong growth, and the company is consistently profitable. There have been only minor audit adjustments in previous years, and the company has moved quickly to correct the cause of the adjustments. Consequently, Phelps also has set inherent risk as low. Therefore, considering these factors and the assessment of control risk, the risk of material misstatement is assessed as low and detection risk has been set as high. As a result, Phelps can select a sample of the cycle counts to observe on a surprise basis. He can record limited test counts and rely on limited testing of the computer records that roll forward the perpetual inventory until year-end. Because risk of material misstatement is low in the acquisition cycle, Phelps can limit vouching of invoices to test the prices of raw materials. Finally, Phelps can rely heavily on analytical procedures, particularly gross margin percentages, to ensure that no serious errors or frauds have occurred. The combination of a low risk of material misstatement and a high detection risk combine to give Phelps an acceptably low audit risk.

Case 9.1

The Players Weren't All That Was Short![5]

PROBLEM

Mickey Monus, the CEO of Phar-Mor, stated on many occasions that he would "not let Walmart undersell Phar-Mor." To that end, Phar-Mor would actually sell many products at a loss resulting in corporate net losses. Phar-Mor dumped these losses in a "bucket account" and spread them over the individual stores by increasing inventory amounts. When company personnel found out which stores the auditors would be visiting for inventory observation, they simply moved goods from the stores that were not visited to make up for shortages. Phar-Mor used an outside service for inventory counting, but after receiving the results, Phar-Mor personnel would inflate the amounts during the pricing and compilation process. In some cases, the compilations were altered after the auditors tested them. When Phar-Mor rolled forward the inventory from the count date, the inventory showed large increases right at year-end. These increases were due to the "blow-out" entries allocating the losses in the bucket account to stores' inventory. One entry was as high as $139 million. Finally, Phar-Mor did not have perpetual records but used the retail inventory method instead. Employees used distorted margin percentages to increase the estimated cost of the inventory on hand.

Phar-Mor issued fictitious invoices for purchases, made fictitious journal entries to increase inventory and decrease cost of sales, recognized purchases but failed to record the liabilities, and overcounted the merchandise.

The fraud lasted over a 10-year period, resulting in a financial statement fraud of more than $1 billion.

AUDIT APPROACH

The primary control should have been an environment that discouraged false accounting. However, this clearly was not the case. Other controls that should have prevented or detected these misstatements include a review of nonstandard journal entries, comparison of inventory records to actual periodic counts, and management analysis of gross margins and cash flows. Senior management can easily override any controls. Doing so requires only employees who can be bribed, threatened, or intimidated into going along.

[5] Additional data taken from D. Cottrell and S. Glover, "Finding Auditors Liable for Fraud: What the Jury Heard in the Phar-Mor Case," *CPA Journal,* July 1997, pp. 14–21.

How does one test the control environment? In the client acceptance/continuation stage of planning, the auditors should obtain evidence about management's reputation for integrity. In this case, many vendors were complaining because they were "squeezed" by Phar-Mor to provide rebates and promotion allowances, and some were threatening to cut the company off for nonpayment of bills. Many employees, including the controller, were very concerned about the company's practices and might have been persuaded to come clean had the auditors approached the audit with skepticism. However, because the client's chief financial officer was a former partner of the audit firm, the auditors appeared to lack skepticism.

It is not practical to observe inventory at all stores. However, because the auditors had identified inventory valuation as a high-risk area, they probably should have visited more than four stores! Moreover, the actual stores that the auditors visited for inventory observation should have been kept secret until the day of the count to prevent movement of goods and randomized from one year to the next.

The auditors performed only a reasonableness test of the margins used in the retail method. They selected a sample of items in a "haphazard" method that turned out not to be representative. When the sample margins differed from the company's margins, the auditors explained the difference away without expanding their sample. In vouching the costs of inventory, the auditors should have been alert to phony documentation. Finally, large nonstandard journal entries at the end of the year should have been thoroughly scrutinized.

DISCOVERY SUMMARY

When a travel agent noticed that a bill for the World Basketball League (WBL) was paid with a Phar-Mor check, she asked a neighbor, who was a major shareholder, why Phar-Mor would pay the WBL's expenses. The neighbor phoned a board member, who initiated the investigation that uncovered the fraud.

↳ REVIEW CHECKPOINTS

9.18 What steps should auditors take if the client has multiple locations being counted?

9.19 What is an inventory roll forward? What roll-forward tests should be performed?

Summary

Production involves production planning; inventory planning; acquiring labor, materials, and overhead (acquisition and payment cycle); custody of assets; and cost accounting. Production information systems produce many internal documents, reports, and files that are sources of audit information as described in the chapter. The production cycle is characterized by having mostly internal documentation as evidence and having relatively little external documentary evidence; therefore, the systems that produce these documents must be evaluated to ensure the validity of the information.

Companies reduce control risk by having a suitable separation of authorization, custody, recording, and periodic reconciliation duties. Error-checking procedures, including analyzing production orders and finished production cost reports, are important for the proper determination of inventory values and proper valuation of cost of goods sold. Otherwise, many things could go wrong, ranging from overvaluing the inventory to understating costs of production by deferring costs that should be expensed.

Cost accounting is a central feature of the production cycle. The illustrative case in the chapter tells the stories of financial reporting manipulations and the audit procedures that will detect them. The physical inventory observation audit work was discussed because actual contact with inventories provides auditors direct eyewitness evidence of important tangible assets.

It may appear that production and related activities offer little risk, especially if the nature of inventory does not lend itself to high inherent risk (e.g., steel I-beams), even when production material is not highly susceptible to theft, but many frauds have been hidden in the inventory accounts. Therefore, the auditors should pay attention to the inventory balance assertions of *existence* and *valuation and allocation*. The Auditing Insight on the previous page presents deficiencies noted in the PCAOB inspection reports of some of the largest audit firms regarding audits of this cycle.

AUDITING INSIGHT — PCAOB Inspections and the Production Cycle

- The Firm failed in the following respects to adequately test the valuation assertion regarding inventory:
    a. There was no evidence in the audit documentation that the firm sufficiently tested the raw materials and/or labor and overhead components of inventory at certain of its manufacturing locations.
    b. Specific analytical procedures performed by the Firm failed to meet the requirements for substantive analytical procedures.
- The Firm failed to evaluate the assumptions that management had used to determine the reserve for obsolete inventory.
- Substantially all of the revenue from a significant location of the issuer had been recognized on a bill-and-hold basis, and the inventory subject to this arrangement was shipped periodically to the buyer. At this location, the Firm failed to test that the bill-and-hold inventory at year-end physically existed, was complete and ready for shipment, and that delivery dates for this inventory were reasonable and consistent with the buyer's business purpose. In addition, the Firm failed to identify and appropriately address that the issuer had not disclosed that it recognized revenue on a bill-and-hold basis for a major customer.
- The Firm failed to adequately audit the valuation of the inventory. The issuer performed a reasonableness test of the valuation of its ending inventory by computing historical cost to retail value using aggregated companywide data. The Firm used that reasonableness test as its primary substantive test of inventory valuation. However, the Firm did not investigate a significant difference between the ratio computed using aggregate data and the ratio computed using store-level data. In addition, where significant unexpected differences were identified, the Firm's procedures were limited to inquiry of management and did not include obtaining corroboration of management's explanations. Furthermore, the Firm failed to adequately test the completeness and accuracy of the data used in computing the ratios.
- When testing inventory, the Firm applied a controls reliance strategy, which included reliance on IT controls. The Firm's audit documentation indicated that the issuer's information technology general controls did not support a conclusion that the issuer's information processing was reliable. The Firm, however, did not perform any additional procedures to address its finding, nor did it modify its audit strategy.
- Other than reviewing certain untested reports for reasonableness, there was no evidence that the Firm performed audit procedures, such as examination, observation, or reperformance, to obtain corroboration of management's explanations regarding a significant portion of the inventory controls identified for testing.
- The Firm observed certain inventory counts at various times during the year but did not test inventory transactions between the dates of the interim physical inventory observations and year-end, nor did it compare the interim balances with the year-end inventory balances.

- The Firm failed to perform sufficient procedures to test the valuation and existence assertions related to certain portions of the inventory. The deficiencies included
    a. The failure to test certain key factors used in calculating the LIFO cost of the inventory;
    b. The failure to perform inventory price testing;
    c. The failure to perform substantive procedures on the activity in inventory between the date of interim audit procedures and the issuer's fiscal year-end;
    d. The failure to establish a precise expectation, and to appropriately investigate or evaluate significant differences, when performing substantive analytical procedures; and
    e. The failure to test certain assumptions and underlying data used to calculate the inventory obsolescence reserve.
- The Firm failed to perform adequate audit procedures to test the valuation of the issuer's inventory and investments in joint ventures (the primary assets of which were inventory). Specifically, the Firm:
    a. Failed to reevaluate, in light of a significant downturn in the issuer's industry and the general deterioration in economic conditions, whether the issuer's assumption, which it had also used in prior years, that certain inventory required no review for impairment was still applicable in the year under audit;
    b. Excluded from its impairment testing a significant portion of the inventory that may have been impaired, because the Firm selected inventory items for testing from those for which the issuer already had recorded impairment charges;
    c. Failed to evaluate the reasonableness of certain of the significant assumptions that the issuer used in determining the fair value estimates of inventory and investments in joint ventures;
    d. Failed to obtain support for certain of the significant assumptions that the Firm used when developing an independent estimate of the fair value of one category of inventory; and
    e. Failed to test items in a significant category of inventory, which consisted of all items with book values per item below a Firm-specified amount that was more than 70 percent of the Firm's planning materiality.
- The Firm used positive confirmations to test the existence of inventory held by consignees. The Firm, however, failed to evaluate the authenticity of the confirmations returned through facsimile or email and also failed to perform alternative procedures on certain other confirmations that were not returned.

Sources: 2006 PCAOB Inspection of PricewaterhouseCoopers (December 14, 2006); 2006 & 2010 PCAOB Inspection of Deloitte & Touche (November 30, 2006; May 4, 2010); 2007 & 2008 PCAOB Inspection of KPMG (January 11, 2007; August 12, 2008); 2007 & 2008 PCAOB Inspection of Grant Thornton (June 28, 2007; April 4, 2008); 2008 PCAOB Inspection Report BDO Seidman (May 6, 2008).

Key Terms

bill of materials: A list of raw materials and supplies used to build a product that is used to develop standard costs, 371

consignment goods: The goods that are given by one party, the consignor, to another party, the consignee, to sell; however, the consignee retains title until the goods are sold, 386

cycle counts: A method of physically counting different areas of inventory throughout the year, 385

inventory roll-forward: An accounting process from date of physical inventory count to the end of the period; includes additions for purchases and production and reductions for sales, scrap, and so on, 385

materials requisition (materials transfer ticket): A form used to obtain raw materials and supplies from inventory custodian, 372

net realizable value (NRV): The selling price less costs to sell (e.g., sales commissions), 369

overhead allocation: An accounting procedure used to assign indirect costs to various products, 373

physical inventory count: The client's procedure for determining actual amount of inventory on hand, 382

physical inventory observation: The auditor's procedures during client's physical inventory count; includes observing inventory procedures and performing test counts on selected inventory items, 382

pricing and compilation: The procedure for translating units counted in the physical inventory count to amounts recorded in the accounting records, including gains or losses for shortages or overages; involves mathematically accumulating counts and applying standard costs, 386

production order: A document that communicates to production personnel the specific product, product quantity, and date a product is to be produced, 372

production plan: A schedule of goods to be produced for a period based on sales forecasts, 370

raw material inventory status report: A periodic report (usually daily or weekly) that includes a list of all raw materials and the inventoried quantity of each material, 371

sales forecast: A report, usually prepared by marketing, predicting future sales of product, 370

standard costs: The estimates of cost to produce a product; used for transferring products between departments and to finished goods and to record cost of goods sold; compared to actual costs to obtain variances, 372

Multiple-Choice Questions for Practice and Review

 All applicable Exercises and Problems are available with McGraw-Hill's *Connect® Accounting*

LO 9-1

9.20 Which of the following methods for determining inventory cost is not allowed by GAAP?
 a. Average cost.
 b. FIFO.
 c. LIFO.
 d. Standard cost.

LO 9-1

9.21 Which cycle is *not* directly linked to the production cycle?
 a. Acquisition and expenditure cycle.
 b. Payroll cycle.
 c. Revenue and collection cycle.
 d. Finance and investment cycle.

LO 9-1

9.22 To determine the client's planned amount and timing of production of a product, the auditor reviews the
 a. Sales forecast.
 b. Inventory reports.
 c. Production plan.
 d. Purchases journal.

LO 9-2 9.23 An auditor reviews job cost sheets to test which *transaction assertion*?
a. Occurrence
b. Completeness
c. Accuracy
d. Classification

LO 9-2 9.24 Which of the following is an internal control weakness for a company whose inventory of supplies consists of a large number of individual items?
a. Supplies of relatively little value are expensed when purchased.
b. The cycle basis is used for physical counts.
c. The warehouse manager is responsible for maintenance of perpetual inventory records.
d. Perpetual inventory records are maintained only for items of significant value.

LO 9-3 9.25 To make a year-to-year comparison of inventory turnover *most* meaningful, the auditor performs the analysis
a. For the company as a whole.
b. By division.
c. By product.
d. All of the above.

LO 9-2 9.26 Which of the following procedures would best prevent or detect the theft of valuable items from an inventory that consists of hundreds of different items selling for $1 to $10 and a few items selling for hundreds of dollars?
a. Maintain a perpetual inventory of only the more valuable items with frequent periodic verification of the accuracy of the perpetual inventory record.
b. Have an independent accounting firm prepare an internal control report on the effectiveness of the controls over inventory.
c. Have separate warehouse space for the more valuable items with frequent periodic physical counts and comparison to perpetual inventory records.
d. Require a manager's signature for the removal of any inventory item with a value of more than $50.

LO 9-3 9.27 An auditor usually traces the details of the test counts made during the observation of physical inventory counts to a final inventory compilation. This audit procedure is undertaken to provide evidence that items physically present and observed by the auditor at the time of the physical inventory count are
a. Owned by the client.
b. Not obsolete.
c. Physically present at the time of the preparation of the final inventory schedule.
d. Included in the final inventory schedule.

(AICPA adapted)

LO 9-3 9.28 A retailer's physical count of inventory was higher than that shown by the perpetual records. Which of the following could explain the difference?
a. Inventory items had been counted but the tags placed on the items had not been taken off and added to the inventory accumulation sheets.
b. Credit memos for several items returned by customers had not been recorded.
c. No journal entry had been made on the retailer's books for several items returned to its suppliers.
d. An item purchased FOB shipping point had not arrived at the date of the inventory count and had not been reflected in the perpetual records.

LO 9-3 9.29 From the auditors' point of view, inventory counts are more acceptable prior to the year-end when
a. Internal control is weak.
b. Accurate perpetual inventory records are maintained.
c. Inventory is slow moving.
d. Significant amounts of inventory are held on a consignment basis.

LO 9-2 9.30 Which of the following internal control activities most likely addresses the completeness assertion for inventory?
   a. The Work-in-Process account is periodically reconciled with subsidiary inventory records.
   b. Employees responsible for custody of finished goods do not perform the receiving function.
   c. Receiving reports are prenumbered, and the numbering sequence is checked periodically.
   d. There is a separation of duties between the payroll department and inventory accounting personnel.
   (AICPA adapted)

LO 9-3 9.31 When auditing inventories, an auditor would *least* likely verify that
   a. All inventory owned by the client is on hand at the time of the count.
   b. The client has used proper inventory pricing.
   c. The financial statement presentation of inventories is appropriate.
   d. Damaged goods and obsolete items have been properly accounted for.
   (AICPA adapted)

LO 9-3 9.32 A client maintains perpetual inventory records in quantities and in dollars. If the assessed control risk is high, an auditor would probably
   a. Apply gross profit tests to ascertain the reasonableness of the physical counts.
   b. Increase the extent of tests of controls relevant to the inventory cycle.
   c. Request the client to schedule the physical inventory count at the end of the year.
   d. Insist that the client perform physical counts of inventory items several times during the year.
   (AICPA adapted)

LO 9-3 9.33 An auditor selected items for test counts while observing a client's physical inventory. The auditor then traced the test counts to the client's inventory listing. This procedure most likely obtained evidence concerning management's balance assertion of
   a. Rights and obligations.
   b. Completeness.
   c. Existence.
   d. Valuation and allocation.
   (AICPA adapted)

LO 9-3 9.34 Which of the following auditing procedures probably would provide the most reliable evidence concerning the entity's assertion of rights and obligations related to inventories?
   a. Trace test counts noted during the entity's physical count to the entity's summarization of quantities.
   b. Inspect agreements to determine whether any inventory is pledged as collateral or subject to any liens.
   c. Select the last few shipping documents used before the physical count and determine whether the shipments were recorded as sales.
   d. Inspect the open purchase order file for significant commitments that should be considered for disclosure.
   (AICPA adapted)

LO 9-3 9.35 An auditor most likely would analyze inventory turnover rates to obtain evidence concerning management's balance assertions about
   a. Existence.
   b. Rights and obligations.
   c. Completeness.
   d. Valuation and allocation.

LO 9-3 9.36 An auditor would vouch inventory on the inventory status report to the vendor's invoice to obtain evidence concerning management's balance assertions about
   a. Existence.
   b. Rights and obligations.
   c. Completeness.
   d. Valuation.

LO 9-2 9.37 When evaluating inventory controls, an auditor would be *least* likely to
  a. Inspect documents.
  b. Make inquiries.
  c. Observe procedures.
  d. Consider policy and procedure manuals.

LO 9-1 9.38 When testing a company's cost accounting system, the auditor uses procedures that are primarily designed to determine that
  a. Quantities on hand have been computed based on acceptable cost accounting techniques that reasonably approximate actual quantities on hand.
  b. Physical inventories agree substantially with book inventories.
  c. The system is in accordance with generally accepted accounting principles and is functioning as planned.
  d. Costs have been properly assigned to finished goods, work-in-process, and cost of goods sold.

LO 9-2 9.39 The auditor tests the quantity of materials charged to work-in-process by vouching these quantities to
  a. Cost ledgers.
  b. Perpetual inventory records.
  c. Receiving reports.
  d. Material requisitions.

LO 9-3 9.40 Your client counts inventory three months before the end of the fiscal year because controls over inventory are excellent. Which procedure is not necessary for the roll-forward?
  a. Check that shipping documents for the last three months agree with perpetual records.
  b. Trace receiving reports for the last three months to perpetual records.
  c. Compare gross margin percentages for the last three months.
  d. Request the client to recount inventory at the end of the year.

LO 9-2 9.41 An auditor is examining a nonpublic company's inventory procurement system and has decided to perform tests of controls. Under which of the following conditions do GAAS require tests of controls be performed by an auditor?
  a. Significant weaknesses were found in the company's internal control.
  b. The auditor hopes to reduce the amount of work to be done in assessing inherent risk.
  c. The auditor believes that testing the controls could lead to a reduction in overall audit time and cost.
  d. Tests of controls are always performed when the auditor begins to assess control risk.

Exercises and Problems

 All applicable Exercises and Problems are available with McGraw-Hill's *Connect®* Accounting

LO 9-1, 9-4 9.42 **Internal Control Questionnaire Items: Possible Error or Fraud Due to Weakness.** Refer to the internal control questionnaire for the production cycle (Appendix Exhibit 9A.1) and assume that the answer to each question is "no." Prepare a table matching questions to errors or frauds that could occur because of the absence of the control. Your column headings should be as follows:

Question	Possible Error or Fraud Due to Weakness

LO 9-2 9.43 **Tests of Controls Related to Controls and Assertions.** Each of the following tests of controls could be performed during the audit of the controls in the production cycle.

Required:
For each procedure, identify (a) the internal control activity (strength) being tested and (b) the assertion(s) being addressed.
  1. Balance and reconcile detailed production cost sheets to the work-in-process inventory control account.
  2. Scan closed production cost sheets for missing numbers in the sequence.

3. Vouch a sample of open and closed production cost sheet entries to (a) labor reports and (b) issue forms and materials used reports.
4. Locate the material issue forms and determine whether they are (a) prenumbered, (b) kept in a secure location, and (c) available to unauthorized persons.
5. Select several summary journal entries in the work-in-process inventory and (a) vouch them to weekly labor and material reports and to production cost sheets and (b) trace them to the control account.
6. Select a sample of the material issue forms in the production department file. Examine them for
   a. Issue date and materials used report date.
   b. Production order number.
   c. Floor supervisor's signature or initials.
   d. Name and number of material.
   e. Raw material stores clerk's signature or initials.
   f. Material requisition in raw material stores file, noting the date of requisition.
7. Determine by inquiry and inspection whether cost clerks review dates on reports of units completed for accounting in the proper period.

LO 9-2

9.44 **Cost Accounting Tests of Controls.** The diagram in Exhibit 9.44.1 describes several cost accounting tests of controls. It shows the direction of the tests, leading from samples of cost accounting analyses, management reports, and the general ledger to blank squares.

Required:
For each blank square in Exhibit 9.44.1, write a cost accounting test of controls procedure and describe the evidence it can produce. (*Hint:* Refer to Exhibits 9.4 and 9.6)

EXHIBIT 9.44.1
Diagram of Cost Accounting Tests of Controls

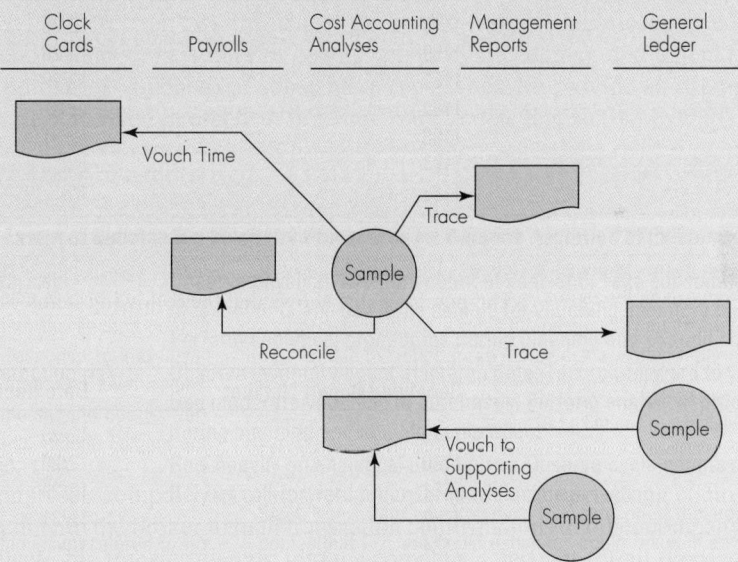

LO 9-3

9.45 **Inventory Count Observation: Planning and Substantive Procedures.** Sammy Smith is the partner in charge of the audit of Blue Distributing Corporation, a wholesaler that owns one warehouse containing 80 percent of its inventory. Smith is reviewing the audit documentation that was prepared to support the firm's opinion on Blue's financial statements and wants to be certain that essential audit procedures are well documented.

Required:
a. What evidence should Smith expect to find indicating that the observation of the client's physical count of inventory was well planned and that assistants were properly supervised?
b. What substantive procedures should Smith find in the audit documentation of management's balance assertions about existence and completeness of inventory quantities at the end of the year? (Refer to Appendix 9B for the audit plan's procedures.)

(AICPA adapted)

398 Part Two *The Financial Statement Audit*

LO 9-3

9.46 **Sales/Inventory Cutoff.** Your client took a complete physical inventory count under your observation as of December 15 and adjusted the inventory control account (perpetual inventory method) to agree with the physical inventory. After considering the count adjustments as of December 15 and after reviewing the transactions recorded from December 16 to December 31, you are almost ready to accept the inventory balance as fairly stated. However, your review of the sales cutoff as of December 15 and December 31 disclosed the following items not previously considered:

Sales		Date		
Cost	Price	Shipped	Billed	Credited to Inventory Control
$28,400	$36,900	12/14	12/16	12/16
39,100	50,200	12/10	12/19	12/10
18,900	21,300	1/2	12/31	12/31

Required:
What adjusting journal entries, if any, would you make for each of these items? Explain why each adjustment is necessary.

(AICPA adapted)

LO 9-3

9.47 **Purchasing Cutoff.** When tracing using the cutoff information from the December 31 inventory count of Thermo-Tempur Mattresses, you note the following information:

Receiving Report Number	Date Received	Total Cost
1179	12/28	$12,433.61
1180	12/28	8,923.34
1181	12/29	15,448.22
1182	12/31	14,109.33
1183	12/31	11,482.57
1184	1/2	17,852.56
1185	1/3	8,753.95

The purchases list shows that the following items were recorded in December.

Receiving Report Number	Date Received	Total Cost
1179	12/28	$12,433.61
1180	12/28	8,923.34
1181	12/29	15,448.22
1182	12/31	14,109.33
1184	1/2	17,852.56

The documentation indicates that the last receiving report included in the inventory count was Receiving Report 1182. Receiving Reports 1183 and 1184 were for goods received on the company's truck but not unloaded. Receiving report 1185 was for goods received on January 3.

Required:
Prepare a correcting journal entry assuming that Thermo-Tempur uses (a) a periodic inventory system and (b) a perpetual inventory system that was updated for the inventory count.

LO 9-3

9.48 **Statistical Sampling Used to Estimate Inventory.** ACE Corporation does not conduct a complete annual physical count of purchased parts and supplies in its principal warehouse but uses statistical sampling to estimate the year-end inventory. ACE maintains a perpetual inventory record of parts and supplies. Management believes that statistical sampling is highly effective in determining inventory values and is sufficiently reliable, making a physical count of each item of inventory unnecessary.

Required:
  a. List at least 10 normal audit procedures that should be performed to verify physical quantities whenever a client conducts a periodic physical count of all or part of its inventory (see Appendix Exhibit 9B.1 for procedures).
  b. Identify the audit procedures you should use that change or are in addition to normal required audit procedures (in addition to those listed in your solution to part a) when a client utilizes statistical sampling to determine inventory value and does not conduct a 100 percent annual physical count of inventory items.

(AICPA adapted)

LO 9-3

9.49 **Inventory Procedures Using Computer-Assisted Audit Techniques (CAATs).** You are conducting an audit of the financial statements of a wholesale cosmetics distributor with an inventory consisting of thousands of individual items. The distributor keeps its inventory in its own distribution center and in two public warehouses. A perpetual inventory computer database is maintained on a computer disk. The database is updated at the end of each business day. Each individual record of the perpetual inventory database contains the following data:

Item number.

Location of item.

Description of item.

Quantity on hand.

Cost per item.

Date of last purchase.

Date of last sale.

Quantity sold during year.

You are planning to observe the distributor's physical count of inventories as of a given date. The client will provide a computer file of the preceding items taken from its database as of the date of the physical count. Your firm has a computer audit program that will be ideal for analyzing the inventory records.

Required:
List the basic inventory auditing procedures and, for each, describe how the use of CAATs and the computerized perpetual inventory database might be helpful to the auditor in performing such auditing procedures. (See Appendix 9B for substantive procedures for inventory.)

Organize your answer as follows:

Basic Inventory Auditing Procedures	How CAATs and Copy of the Inventory Data File Might Be Helpful
Conduct an observation of the company's physical count.	Determine which items are to be test counted by selecting a random sample of a representative number of items from the inventory file as of the date of the physical count.

(AICPA adapted)

LO 9-3

9.50 **CAATs Application: Inventory.** Your client, Boos & Becker, Inc., is a medium-size manufacturer of products for the leisure-time activities market (camping equipment, scuba gear, bows and arrows, and the like). During the past year, a computer system was installed, and inventory records of finished goods and parts were converted to computerized processing. Each record of the inventory master file contains the following information:

Item or part number.
Description.
Size.
Quantity on hand.
Cost per unit.
Total value of inventory on hand at cost.
Date of last sale or usage.
Quantity used or sold this year.
Reorder point (quantity).
Economic order quantity.
Code number of major vendor or code number of secondary vendor.

In preparation for year-end inventory, the client has two identical sets of preprinted inventory cards prepared from the master file. One set is for the client's inventory counts and the other is for your use to make audit test counts. The following information has been included on the preprinted cards:

Item or part number.
Description.
Size.
Unit of measure code.

In taking the year-end count, the client's personnel will write the actual counted quantity on the face of each card. When all counts are complete, the counted quantity will be processed against the master file, and quantity-on-hand figures will be adjusted to reflect the actual count. A computer list will be prepared to show any missing inventory count cards and all quantity adjustments of more than $100 in value. Client personnel will investigate these items and will make all required adjustments. When adjustments have been completed, the final year-end balances will be computed and posted to the general ledger.

Your firm has available an audit software package that will run on the client's computer and can process both cards and disk master files.

Required:

a. In general and without regard to the preceding facts, discuss the nature of CAATs and list the various audit uses of such packages.

b. List and describe at least five ways CAATs can be used to assist in all aspects of the audit of the inventory of Boos & Becker, Inc. (For example, CAATs can be used to read the inventory master file and list items and parts with a high unit cost or total value. Such items can be included in the test counts to increase the dollar coverage of the audit verification.) (*Hint:* Think of the normal audit procedures in gathering evidence on inventory when the client makes a periodic count; then think of how these could help in this particular client situation.)

(AICPA adapted)

LO 9-3

9.51 **Inventory Evidence and Long-Term Purchase Contracts.** During the audit of Mason Company, Inc., for the calendar year 2012, you noted that the company produces aluminum cans at the rate of about 40 million units annually. On the plant tour, you noticed a large stockpile of raw aluminum in storage. Your inventory observation and pricing procedures showed this stockpile to be the raw materials inventory of 400 tons valued at $240,000 (LIFO cost). Inquiry with the production chief yielded the information that 400 tons was about a four-month supply of raw materials.

Suppose you learn that Mason had executed a firm long-term purchase contract with All Purpose Aluminum Company to purchase raw materials on the following schedule:

Delivery Date	Quantity (Tons)	Total Price
January 30, 2011	500	$300,000
June 30, 2011	700	420,000
December 30, 2011	1,000	500,000

Because of recent economic conditions, principally a decline in the demand for raw aluminum and a consequent oversupply, the price stood at 20 cents per pound as of January 15, 2013. Commodities experts predict that this low price will prevail for 12 to 15 months or until there is a general economic recovery.

Required:

a. Describe the procedures you would employ to gather evidence about this contract (including its initial discovery).
b. What facts recited in the problem would you have to discover for yourself in an audit?
c. Discuss the effect this contract has on the financial statements.

LO 9-3

9.52 **Tracing the Inventory Count.** You have been assigned to trace the results of the observation of Brightware China's physical inventory count to its pricing and compilation. You note the following conditions.

1. The last inventory tag documented by Mark Hulse, the auditor who observed the inventory, was 1732, but you notice a number of items with count ticket numbers higher than 1732. You contact the client's controller, Marcia Vines, who tells you the client found a storage room full of a new product that Brightware had just produced and added it to the inventory.

2. The count tickets recorded by Hulse agree to the inventory list, but some of the other count tickets you select are substantially different from it. Vines tells you these are input errors and she will have them corrected.

3. Hulse described several boxes of goods as being dusty and even broken. They are included in the inventory at cost. Vines's explanation is that china never "goes bad" and the goods themselves were not broken.

Required:

a. Prepare an audit plan for tracing the information from the inventory count to the compilation.
b. What might have caused the conditions you found? What effect might they have on the financial statements?
c. What steps will you take to follow up on Vines's explanations?

LO 9-3

9.53 **FIFO Inventory Pricing.** You are auditing Martha's Prison Clothes, Inc., as of December 31, 2012. The inventory for orange jumpsuits shows 1,263 suits at $782 for a total of $987,666. When you look at the invoices for the jumpsuits, you see the following:

Inventory Number	Date	Quantity	Unit Price	Total
12732	11/22/10	1,000	$765	$765,000
12844	12/03/10	800	777	621,600
12905	12/28/10	600	782	469,200

Required:

a. Determine the adjusting entry, if any, for the cost of inventory at December 31, 2012.
b. Would your answer to part (a) be different if you saw an invoice dated January 9, 2013, for 500 suits at $750?

Instructions for Problems 9.54, 9.55, and 9.56

The cases in Problems 9.54, 9.55, and 9.56 are similar to the one in the chapter. They give the problem and the amount. Your assignment is to write the audit approach portion of the case organized around these sections:

Objective. Express the objective in terms of the facts supposedly asserted in the financial records, accounts, and statements.

Control. Write a brief explanation of desirable controls, missing controls, and especially the types of deviations that might arise from the situation described in the case.

Tests of controls. Write some procedures for obtaining evidence about controls, especially procedures that could discover control deviations. If there are no controls to test, there are no procedures to perform; go to the next section. A *procedure* should instruct someone about the source(s) of evidence to tap and the work to do.

Audit of balance. Write some procedures for obtaining evidence about the balance assertions of existence, rights and obligations, completeness, valuation, and accuracy identified in your objective section.

Discovery summary. Write a short statement about the discovery you expect to accomplish with your procedures.

Inventory and deferred cost overstatement. Follow the preceding instructions. Write the audit approach section following the cases in the chapter.

LO 9-4

9.54 **Toying around with the Numbers. Mattel, Inc.,** a manufacturer of toys, failed to write off obsolete inventory, thereby overstating inventory and improperly deferred tooling costs, both of which understated cost of goods sold and overstated income.

"Excess" inventory was identified by comparing types of toys (wheels, general toys, dolls, and games), parts, and raw materials with the forecasted sales or usage; lower-of-cost-or-market (LCM) determinations then were made to calculate the obsolescence write-off. Obsolescence was expected and the target for the year was $700,000. The first comparison computer run showed $21 million "excess" inventory! The company "adjusted" the forecast by increasing the quantities of expected sales for many toy lines. (Forty percent of items had forecasted sales more than their actual recent sales.) Another "adjustment" was to forecast toy closeout sales not at reduced prices but at regular prices. In addition, certain parts were labeled "interchangeable" without the normal reference to a new toy product. These adjustments to the forecast reduced the excess inventory exposed to LCM valuation and write-off.

The cost of setting up machines, preparing dies, and other preparations for manufacture are tooling costs. They benefit the lifetime run of the toy manufactured. The company capitalized them as prepaid expenses and amortized them in the ratio of current-year sales to expected product lifetime sales (much like a natural resource depletion calculation). To lower the amortization cost, the company transferred unamortized tooling costs from toys with low forecasted sales to ones with high forecasted sales. This caused the year's amortization ratio to be lower, the calculated cost write-off lower, and the cost of goods sold lower than it should have been.

The computerized forecast runs of expected usage of interchangeable parts provided a space for a reference to the code number of the new toy where the part would be used. Some of these references contained the code number of the part itself, not a new toy. In other cases, the forecast of toy sales and parts usage contained the quantity on hand, not a forecast number.

In the tooling cost detailed records, unamortized cost was classified by lines of toys (similar to classifying asset cost by asset name or description). Unamortized balances were carried forward to the next year. The company changed the classifications shown at the prior year-end to other toy lines that had no balances or different balances. In other words, the balances of unamortized cost at the end of the prior year did not match the beginning balances of the current year except for the total prepaid expense amount.

For lack of obsolescence write-offs, inventory was overstated at $4 million. The company recorded a $700,000 obsolescence write-off. It should have been about $4.7 million, as later determined. The tooling cost manipulations overstated the prepaid expense by $3.6 million.

The company reported net income (after taxes) of $12.1 million in the year before the manipulations took place. If pretax income were in the $20 to $28 million range in the year of the misstatements, the obsolescence and tooling misstatements alone amounted to about 32 percent income overstatement.

LO 9-4

9.55 **No Defense for These Charges.** Follow the instructions preceding Problem 9.54. Write the audit approach section following the case in the chapter.

SueCan Corporation manufactured electronic and other equipment for private customers and government defense contracts. It deferred costs under the heading of defense contract claims for reimbursement and deferred tooling labor costs, thus overstating assets, understating cost of goods sold, and overstating income.

Near the end of the year, the company used a journal entry to remove $110,000 from cost of goods sold and defer it as deferred tooling cost. This $110,000 was purported to be labor cost associated with preparing tools and dies for large production runs.

The company opened a receivables account for "cost overrun reimbursement receivable" as a claim for reimbursement on defense contracts ($378,000).

The company altered the labor time records for the tooling costs in an effort to provide substantiating documentation. Company employees prepared new work orders numbered in the series used late in the fiscal year and attached labor time records dated much earlier in the year. The production orders originally charged with the labor cost were left completed but with no labor charges!

The claim for reimbursement on defense contracts did not have documentation specifically identifying the labor costs as being related to the contract. There were no work orders. (Auditors know that Defense Department auditors insist on documentation and justification before approving such a claim.)

SueCan reported net income of about $442,000 for the year, an overstatement of approximately 60 percent.

LO 9-4

9.56 **Chips Ahoy.** Follow the instructions preceding Problem 9.54. Write the audit approach section following the cases in the chapter.

The following is an excerpt from an article, "Memory Chip Trader Gets 14 Years for Bank Fraud," in *The Straits Times* (Singapore), February 13, 2009:

> Through most of the 1990s, entrepreneur Kelvin Ang Ah Peng rode the crest of a wave as his company traded in memory chips and recycled used ones for sale at a good price. His story, which follows the ebb and flow of the integrated circuit (IC) chip business, started at **EC-Asia International (ECI)** in 1993. Computer chips were expensive, so his business did well. A major earthquake in Taiwan in 1999 totaled the computer chip factories there. Production halted and the market price of computer chips soared even higher. The bubble burst the following year, when the Taiwan factories recovered and several computer chip businesses folded. In 2001, as ECI struggled to keep afloat, Ang started abusing its credit facilities. Between that year and early 2007, he bought and sold worthless memory chips and created fake orders and invoices to receive payment from banks.
>
> He was charged in October 2008 on 687 charges involving US$290 million; last month, he pleaded guilty to 30 charges—28 for cheating and 2 for money laundering and falsifying revenues in ECI's initial public offering (IPO) prospectus. Deputy Public Prosecutor David Chew Siong Tai said that, to secure credit in the absence of incoming orders, Ang fashioned an elaborate scheme with the help of Hong Kong firms. He got ECI's partners to issue the necessary trade documents and to circulate computer chips and money between Hong Kong and Singapore. Chips were actually shipped in these sham transactions as if they were bona fide business trades. In reality these were worthless, defective chips due for scrapping by ECI. In November 2006 when asked about ECI's unusually large inventory in Hong Kong and the huge debts owed by the firm's Hong Kong "customers," Ang confessed to an ECI subsidiary's director that 90 per cent of the inventory did not exist and that its billings were all faked.
>
> Yesterday, Ang, 44, was jailed for 14 years for having swindled banks of US$23 million (S$35 million) and laundering these proceeds through Hong Kong. The Australian-listed ECI is now being liquidated, and Ang was declared a bankrupt last year.

LO 9-3

9.57 **Detection of Errors and Fraud.** For each of the following independent events, indicate the (1) effect of the error or fraud on the financial statements and (2) what auditing procedures could have detected the misstatement resulting from error or fraud.

a. The physical inventory count of J. Payne Enterprises, which has a December 31 year-end, was conducted on August 31 without incident. In September, the perpetual inventory was not reduced for the cost of sales.

b. Holmes Drug Stores counted its inventory on December 31, which is its fiscal year-end. The auditors observed the count at 20 of Holmes's 86 locations. The company falsified the inventory at 20 of the locations not visited by the auditors by including fictitious goods in the counts.

c. Pope Automotive inadvertently included in its inventory automobiles that it was holding on consignment for other dealers.

d. Peffer Electronics, Inc. overstated its inventory by pricing wiring at $200 per hundred feet instead of $200 per thousand feet.

e. Goldman Sporting Goods counted boxes of baseballs as having one dozen baseballs per box when they had only six per box.

Appendix 9A

Internal Control Questionnaires

APPENDIX EXHIBIT 9A.1 Production Cycle

	Yes/No	Comments
Occurrence 1. Is cost accounting separate from production, payroll, and inventory control? 2. Is access to blank production order forms restricted to authorized persons? 3. Is access to blank bills of materials and labor needs forms restricted to authorized persons? 4. Is access to blank material requisition forms restricted to authorized persons? 5. Are production orders prepared by authorized persons? 6. Are bills of materials and labor needs prepared by authorized persons? 7. Are material usage reports compared to raw material stores issue forms? 8. Are labor usage reports compared to job time tickets? 9. Are material requisitions and job time tickets reviewed by the production supervisor after the floor supervisor prepares them? 10. Are the weekly direct labor and materials used reports reviewed by the production supervisor after preparation by the floor supervisor? **Completeness** 1. Are production orders prenumbered and the numerical sequence checked for missing documents? 2. Are bills of materials and labor needs forms prenumbered and the numerical sequence checked for missing documents? 3. Are material requisitions and job time tickets prenumbered and the numerical sequence checked for missing documents? 4. Are inventory issue forms prenumbered and the numerical sequence checked for missing documents? 5. Is accounting notified of terms on purchase agreements? 6. Is accounting notified of orders received on consignment? **Accuracy** 1. Are differences between inventory issue forms and materials used reports recorded and reported to the cost accounting supervisor? 2. Are differences between job time tickets and the labor report recorded and reported to the cost accounting supervisor? 3. Are standard costs used? If so, are they reviewed and revised periodically? 4. Are reports for materials issued to production reconciled with finished goods reports? **Cutoff** 1. Does the accounting manual give instructions to date cost entries on the date of use? 2. Does an accounting supervisor review monthly, quarterly, and year-end cost accruals? **Classification** 1. Are summary entries reviewed and approved by the cost accounting supervisor? 2. Does the accounting manual give instructions for proper classification of cost accounting transactions?		

APPENDIX EXHIBIT 9A.2 Inventory Transaction Processing

	Yes/No	Comments

Occurrence
1. Are perpetual inventory records kept for raw materials? Supplies? Work-in-process? Finished goods?
2. Is merchandise or materials held on consignment (not the property of the company) physically segregated from goods owned by the company?
3. Are additions to inventory quantity records made only on receipt of a receiving report copy?
4. Do inventory custodians notify inventory records of reductions of inventory?

Completeness
1. Are reductions of inventory record quantities made only on receipt of inventory issuance documents?
2. Do inventory custodians notify the records department of additions to inventory?
3. Are separate records maintained for consignment inventory?

Accuracy
1. Are perpetual records reconciled to general ledger control accounts?
2. Do the perpetual records show both quantities and prices?
3. Are inventory records maintained by someone other than the inventory stores custodian?
4. Are the inventory records compared to physical counts?
5. Are production reports of material and labor prepared weekly and transmitted to cost accounting?
6. Are job cost sheets posted weekly and summary journal entries of work-in-process and work completed prepared monthly?
7. Are job cost sheet entries reviewed by a person independent of the preparer?
8. If standard costs have been used for inventory pricing, have they been reviewed for reasonableness and current applicability?
9. Is there a periodic review for overstocked, slow-moving, or obsolete inventory? Have any adjustments been made during the year?
10. Are periodic counts of physical inventory made to correct errors in the individual perpetual records?

Cutoff
1. Does the accounting manual give instructions to record inventory additions on the date of the receiving report?
2. Does the accounting manual give instructions to record inventory issues on the issuance date?

Classification
1. Are perpetual inventory records kept in dollars periodically reconciled to general ledger control accounts?

Appendix 9B

Audit Plans

APPENDIX EXHIBIT 9B.1

DUNDER-MIFFLIN, INC.
Audit Plan for Physical Inventory Observation
December 31, 2012

	Performed by	Ref.
1. Obtain client's inventory-counting instructions and review for completeness. 2. Tour facility before the inventory count looking for out-of-the-way items, obsolete items, and patterns of inventory flow. 3. Observe client personnel taking inventory counts for compliance with instructions. 4. Test count a selection of items throughout the facility and record a sample of your test counts. Note description, stage of completion, counting unit, and condition. 5. Obtain and record tag numbers used and ensure all tag numbers are accounted for. 6. Select sample of used tags and trace them to the items on the floor. 7. Record the last five receiving reports and last five shipping documents and the numbers of next five unused items in sequence. Vouch the recorded items to inventory count to determine that the item was appropriately included (or excluded) from the inventory count. 8. Tour facilities to ensure all items have been counted.		

APPENDIX EXHIBIT 9B.2

DUNDER-MIFFLIN, INC.
Audit Plan for Inventory Pricing and Compilation
December 31, 2012

	Performed by	Ref.

Inventory
1. Obtain client's inventory list, recalculate, and check it against the general ledger.
2. Trace test counts from inventory observation to the final inventory compilation.
3. Select a sample of inventory items.
   a. Vouch unit prices to vendors' invoices or other cost records.
   b. Recalculate the inventory valuation for sampled items.
4. Scan the inventory compilation for items added from sources other than the physical count and items that appear to be large round numbers or systematic fictitious additions.
5. Recalculate the extensions and footings of the final inventory compilation for mathematical accuracy. Reconcile the total to the adjusted trial balance.
6. For selected inventory items and categories, determine the replacement cost and the applicability of lower-of-cost-or-market valuation.
7. Determine whether obsolete or damaged goods should be written down.
8. Inquire about obsolete, damaged, slow-moving, and overstocked inventory.
9. Scan the perpetual records for slow-moving items.
10. During the physical observation, be alert to notice damaged or scrap inventory.
11. Compare the list of obsolete, slow-moving, damaged, or unsalable inventory from last-year's audit to the current inventory compilation.
12. At year-end, identify the numbers of the last shipping and receiving documents for the year. Compare these to the sales, inventory/cost of sales, and accounts payable entries for proper cutoff.
13. Read bank confirmations, debt agreements, and minutes of the board and make inquiries about pledge or assignment of inventory to secure debt.
(continued)		

APPENDIX EXHIBIT 9B.2 *(continued)*

	Performed by	Ref.
14. Inquire about inventory held by third parties on consignment and inventory on hand on consignment from vendors.		
15. Confirm or inspect inventories held in public warehouses.		
16. Recalculate the amount of intercompany profit to be eliminated in consolidation.		
17. Obtain management representations concerning pledging of inventory as collateral, intercompany sales, and other related-party transactions.		
Cost of Sales		
1. Select a sample of recorded cost of sales entries and vouch to supporting documentation.		
2. Select a sample of basic transaction documents (such as sales invoices, production reports) and determine whether the related cost of goods sold was figured and recorded properly.		
3. Determine whether the accounting costing method used by the client (such as FIFO, LIFO, standard cost) was applied properly.		
4. Compute the gross margin rate and compare to prior years.		
5. Compute the ratio of cost elements (such as labor, material) to total cost of goods sold and compare this ratio to that for prior years.		

Finance and Investment Cycle

Credit has done a thousand times more to enrich mankind than all the goldmines in the world. It has exalted labor, stimulated manufacture and pushed commerce over every sea.

Daniel Webster, statesman, lawyer, and orator

Professional Standards References

Topic	AU/ISA Section	PCAOB Reference*
An Audit of Internal Control over Financial Reporting That Is Integrated with an Audit of Financial Statements		AS 5
Audit Documentation	230	AS 3
Consideration of Fraud in a Financial Statement Audit	240	AU 316
Planning	300	AS 10
Risks of Material Misstatement	315	AS 12
Materiality	320	AS 11
Responses to Risks of Material Misstatements	330	AS 11
Audit Evidence	500	AS 15
Audit Evidence—Specific Consideration for Selected Items	501	AU 332
External Confirmations	505	AU 330
Analytical Procedures	520	AU 329, AS 15
Accounting Estimates, Including Fair Value Accounting Estimates	540	AU 342
Related Parties	550	AU 334
Written Representations	580	AU 333
Using the Work of an Audit Specialist	620	AU 336

*AU references represent standards issued by the ASB prior to April 16, 2003, that have not been superseded or amended by the PCAOB

LEARNING OBJECTIVES

The finance and investment cycle consists of planning for capital requirements and raising the required money by borrowing, selling stock, and entering into acquisitions and joint ventures. The finance part of the cycle involves obtaining money through stock or debt issues. The investment portion of the cycle encompasses using the funds for investments in property, plant, and equipment (covered in the acquisition and expenditure cycle chapter 8), marketable securities, joint ventures and partnerships, and subsidiaries. The transactions discussed in this chapter generally involve large dollar amounts and occur relatively infrequently. They can involve complex accounting issues and generally receive significant attention from management and the auditors.

Your objectives are to be able to:

LO 10-1 Describe the finance and investment cycle, including typical source documents and controls.

LO 10-2 Give examples of tests of control activities over debt and stockholders' equity transactions and investment transactions.

LO 10-3 Describe substantive testing procedures for finance and investment accounts.

LO 10-4 Describe common errors and frauds in the accounting for investment and financing transactions and investments, and design audit procedures for detecting them.

INTRODUCTION

Enron used hundreds of off-the-book arrangements known as **special purpose entities (SPEs)** ostensibly to create joint ventures for new businesses such as energy trading and on-demand movies. (The company created so many SPEs that officers named them after Star Wars characters [Chewco and Jedi], animals [raptors and bobcats], and even officers' children.) In point of fact, however, they were used to enrich company officers and hide more than $1 billion of debt from the company's creditors, investors, and auditors. Rather than vehicles to fund expansion into new innovative markets, the SPEs essentially brought down the company. Many of the SPEs were financed by pledges of Enron stock as collateral, and their viability depended on the company's stock price. When the company's stock started to fall, the SPEs collapsed. When the firm's stock price dropped from $80 to less than $1 in less than a year, millions of investors suffered losses, and thousands of current and former company employees had their retirement plans wiped out. The restatement of the company's financial statements totaled $586 million. Although Andersen's obstruction of justice conviction for shredding Enron audit documentation was later overturned by the U.S. Supreme Court, the 86,000-employee accounting firm had been ruined.

Enron appeared to be a spectacular, greatly successful business therefore, and the audit failure captured the attention of the country. However, hidden behind all of the headlines was the enormous difficulty the auditors faced in unraveling Enron's complex financing arrangements. Enron management had paid millions of dollars to Wall Street firms to design the SPEs so that they could be kept off the balance sheet. Early knowledge of the extent of Enron's deception might have caused its auditors to insist on consolidating the SPEs on Enron's books and thereby might have saved both Enron and Andersen.

This example illustrates the potential size and complexity of transactions in the finance and investment cycle. Transactions in this cycle are much less frequent than in the other cycles; however, they tend to be large and complex. Thus, the focus of control activities is on the authorization of transactions and making sure that the client has competent accounting personnel who can understand the transactions and related accounting standards. Auditors must examine with professional skepticism all aspects of the transactions in the finance and investment cycle, but the focus of substantive procedures is gaining an understanding of the transactions, verifying the amounts and calculations, and ensuring proper presentation and disclosure. Finance and investment cycle transactions have become a leading cause of recent financial statement restatements. Some of the largest recent restatements are described in Exhibit 10.1.

EXIHIBIT 10.1 Finance and Investment Shenanigans

Company	Cause of Misstatement	Amount
Bernard Madoff Investments	Great Ponzi scheme used to defraud thousands of investors including individuals, charities, and pension funds.	$65.0 billion
Fannie Mae	The mortgage lending giant used questionable methodology, assumptions, and documentation for applying cash flow hedge accounting.	$9.18 billion
Freddie Mac	The other mortgage lending giant similarly used improper accounting techniques and financial transactions structured to push unwanted earnings into the future and hide gains senior management thought would make the entity appear too volatile.	$4.5 billion
AIG	The insurance giant hid deferred compensation that some executives received through an investment entity, Starr International Co., with long ties to AIG. AIG disclosed the amounts in prior filings but did not run the cost through its financial statements, as it now admits it should have. In addition, the company had problems with accounting for investments by AIG's subsidiaries in synthetic-fuel production facilities, wrongly booked tax credits from the investments as net investment income or other revenue when it should have used them to reduce tax expenses, and accounted for syndication transactions from low-cost housing as sales, boosting net income by $209 million over five years.	$2.7 billion
El Paso	The energy company used improper hedges of anticipated natural gas production.	$2.4 billion
Tyco	Most of the substantive accounting changes centered on $50.6 million in pretax credits that it took to reverse merger reserves set up in prior periods but never used. The SEC said the reserves should either never have been set up or should have been reversed earlier. Additionally, a subsidiary, ADT, improperly carried canceled alarm accounts on its books.	$1.15 billion
Goodyear Tire Company	The company changed the way it accounted for income taxes and the costs of retirees' health and life insurance benefits.	$1.03 billion
General Electric	The company misapplied a rule on how to account for certain derivative deals.	$460 million
Millennium Chemicals	The company changed the accounting treatment on a five-year agreement for its requirements for gold used for production of acetyls that should have been accounted for as a secured financing rather than as an operating lease, underestimated the obligation due to its largest domestic pension plan, and understated deferred taxes.	$400 million
Xerox	Over a period of years, several senior managers in Mexico collaborated to circumvent Xerox's accounting policies and administrative procedures. The restatement related to uncollectible long-term receivables, a failure to record liabilities for amounts due to concessionaires, and, to a lesser extent, for contracts that did not fully meet the requirements to be recorded as sales-type leases.	$207 million
Gap, Inc.	The popular clothier used improper lease accounting related to accounting for rent holidays and tenant allowances.	$200 million
Nikko Cordial	The company falsified information on the timing of a derivative deal.	$119 million
Provident Financial Group	Auto leases were reported off the company's balance sheet as sale and leasebacks of operating leases, but after a review, the company determined that none of the transactions should have been recorded that way. Instead, they should have been recorded as financing leases with all assets and liabilities appearing on the company's balance sheet.	$114.7 million
Kroger	The grocery giant used improper lease accounting.	$25 million
Starbucks Corp.	The chain of popular coffee houses used lease accounting practices that were not consistent with generally accepted accounting principles.	$12.6 million

INHERENT RISKS IN THE FINANCE AND INVESTMENT CYCLE

As previously mentioned, the transactions in the financing and investing cycle do not occur in most firms on a daily, or even weekly basis and are often for large amounts. Therefore, there is a premium on ensuring that transactions are properly authorized.

In addition, Accounting Standards Update (No. 2010-067) has amended ASC 820 requiring more disclosure regarding the fair market value of these items. Therefore, presentation and disclosure have increased in inherent risk. Refer to Exhibit 10.2 for the likely inherent risks in a typical corporation.

Lease Accounting

A company can make an investment by purchasing property, plant, or equipment. These transactions were discussed in the acquisition and expense cycle in Chapter 8. Often companies do not want to purchase assets because of cash considerations or the flexibility in changing assets as the business changes. Leases may offer businesses a better

EXHIBIT 10.2 Relevant Inherent Risks for Finance and Investment Accounts

AICPA Assertions	Assets (e.g., investments)	Long-Term Liabilities (e.g., bonds, loans)	Equity	Derivatives and Hedges	Explanation
Transaction assertions					Management may record fictitious purchases for investments or fail to disclose taking on long-term liabilities: Liabilities may be recorded in the subsequent period although they were occurred in the current period. Determining fair market value may be difficult for investments and derivatives and hedges. New disclosure rules may effect classification investments.
• Occurrence	High	Medium	Medium	Medium	
• Completeness	Low	High	Low	Medium	
• Cutoff	Low	Medium	Low	Low	
• Accuracy	High	Medium	Low	High	
• Classification	High	Medium	Low	High	
Balance assertions					As with transactions, management may overstate investments. Management may overstate long-term liabilities by failing to record all transactions or incorrectly recording the liability in the subsequent period. Determining fair market value may be difficult for investments and derivatives and hedges. New disclosure rules may affect valuation for investments or derivatives.
• Existence	High	Low	Medium	Medium	
• Rights and obligations	High	Medium	Low	Medium	
• Completeness	Medium	High	Low	Low	
• Valuation and allocation	High	Low	Low	High	
Presentation and disclosure assertions					Issues here relate to substantial and complex disclosure requirements especially for derivative and investments
• Occurrence	High	Medium	Medium	Medium	
• Rights and obligations	High	Medium	Medium	Medium	
• Completeness	Low	High	Low	Low	
• Accuracy and valuation allocations	High	Medium	Low	High	
• Classification and understandability	High	Low	Low	High	

Note: These risks are for a typical entity engaged in manufacturing, retail, and other similar industries. Some specialized industries may have risks that vary from those indicated in this table.

cash flow situation or the ability to easily terminate or modify an asset. However, the accounting for leases is more complex than a direct purchase of an asset. The classification of leases as either operating or capitalized is based on assumptions delineated in *ASC 840*. However, management can easily manipulate these assumptions. For example, if the present value of lease payments is 90 percent or more of the property's value, the lease is capitalized; however, if it is only 89.9 percent of the value, the lease is classified as operating and is not reported as a liability on the balance sheet. This provides an opportunity for management to structure the deal in a way that allows for the lease not to be capitalized. Indeed, the SEC has estimated that Fortune 500 companies have $482 billion of off-balance-sheet leases.[1] With the SEC providing additional scrutiny to lease accounting, more than 200 companies recently announced restatements due to their lease accounting.

AUDITING INSIGHT — Watch Out for Leases!!!

In a 2005 review of internal control disclosures conducted by *Financial Executive* magazine, 58 companies disclosed material weaknesses in their internal controls over financial reporting. The largest type of disclosed weaknesses? Leases accounted for 22.6 percent of the disclosed weaknesses.

Source: "Internal Control Weaknesses in April Highlight Leases," *Financial Executive* 21 (5), June 2005, p. 14.

Loan Covenants

To protect themselves, banks usually insert clauses in loan agreements intended to keep the borrower's financial position at a level that will ensure repayment of the loan. These **loan covenants** may restrict payment of dividends, additional borrowings, or use of assets for collateral on other debt. They often require the borrower to maintain certain ratio levels (e.g., a current ratio of no less than 2:1). If borrowers violate these restrictions, the debt can be called (payment demanded) immediately. If the borrower cannot pay the debt when called, the lender can force the borrower into bankruptcy. Auditors must check to see that their clients are not in violation of their loan covenants. An additional risk is that companies' managements will misstate their other accounts to meet the covenant requirements.

Related-Party Transactions

Many of the examples of fraud in this chapter occurred through related-party transactions. *ASC 850* provides the definition for related parties and the appropriate disclosure and accounting. Essentially, a **related party** is one that can exert significant influence over another party. Related parties are frequently used in fraudulent activity because they can conceal activities that the auditors would normally be aware of if the activity occurred between unrelated parties. *AU 316*, "Consideration of Fraud in a Financial Statement Audit," specifically lists significant transactions with related parties not in the ordinary course of business as risk factors relating to fraudulent financial reporting. The auditor must make certain that a transaction between "related parties" was consummated at "arm's length." An *arm's length* transaction is performed between entities at a fair and equitable value, that is, terms that any individual could obtain in similar circumstances.

---

[1] D. Gullapali, "Lease Restatements Are Surging," *The Wall Street Journal,* April 20, 2005.

> **AUDITING INSIGHT** — The Importance of Disclosure
>
> Bobby L. Jolly was the director of the **War Fighting Center** at I Corps at Fort Lewis, Washington. John P. Doran, Jolly's friend, was the owner of **Walking D Ranch Adventures** in Twisp, Washington. On May 16, 2006, the procurement fraud branch of the army's Legal Services Agency suspended Jolly and banned Doran from doing business with the government. The army alleged that Jolly had shared sensitive bidding information with Doran leading to a contract for the Walking D Ranch valued at $65,190. A major part of the allegations is that Jolly served as president of the U.S. Cavalry School, which is part of the Walking D Ranch Adventures, and this relationship was not disclosed.
>
> **Source:** "Trading in Gray Areas," *Governmental Executive* 38, December 2006, pp. 28, 30.

Complex Transactions

In the past, clients have worked with investment bankers to create investing and financing transactions that are structured to get around GAAP rules. Management may want to keep risky ventures off the financial statements to make the company look better. These transactions are usually complex, are difficult to audit, and can be used as vehicles to hide fraud.

> **AUDITING INSIGHT** — Don't Just Look at the Balance Sheet
>
> Bloomberg.com estimates that off-balance-sheet assets at the four largest U.S. Banks—**Bank of America, Citigroup, JP-Morgan Chase,** and **Wells Fargo**—were approximately $5.2 trillion dollars according to their 2008 10-K reports. These hidden items consist of mortgages, credit card debts, auto loans, and other items.
>
> **Source:** "Banks' Hidden Junk Menaces $1 Trillion Purge," *Bloomberg.com*, May 25, 2009.

Impairments

When auditing large investment balances, auditors must be aware of the risk of material misstatement related to the valuation assertion. GAAP requires that impairments to asset values should normally be taken as losses when they occur. Valuing investments and determining possible impairment of related goodwill is very complex. Moreover, companies have been accused of taking a "big bath," which means writing off assets and building up reserves to reduce expenses in future years. This is more likely to happen when a company is experiencing a bad year or when it hires a new CEO (like a football coach going 1-11 his first year and blaming it on his predecessor's players). Thus, auditors must always consider whether assets are overstated due to a possible impairment or whether impairment write-offs have been delayed.

Presentation and Disclosure

As previously mentioned, it is important for auditors to determine whether a lease is a capital or operating lease. In part, the importance stems from different disclosures for these types of leases. Capital leases are presented in a manner identical to purchased assets. Operating leases are disclosed solely in the footnotes to the financial statements. In addition, fixed assets not used in the operations or projected for future use in the operations should not be classified as property, plant, and equipment. For example, if a company owns a warehouse that is no longer in use and has no projected future use (possibly awaiting a buyer), it should be presented in the "other assets" category. Impairments of tangible and intangible assets also must be disclosed in the proper places. These subtle but important distinctions make the review of proper disclosure a greater risk for long-lived assets.

> **AUDITING INSIGHT**   Not Disclosing Information Can Hurt
>
> According to the SEC, five former San Diego city officials knew that the city had been intentionally underfunding its pension obligations so that it could increase pension benefits but defer the costs. They were aware that the city would face severe difficulty funding its future pension and retiree health care obligations unless new revenues were obtained, pension and health care benefits were reduced, or city services were cut. They specifically knew that the city's unfunded liability to its pension plan was projected to dramatically increase from $284 million at the beginning of fiscal year 2002 to an estimated $2 billion by 2009 and that the city's liability for retiree health care was another estimated $1.1 billion. But the officials failed to disclose these and other material facts to rating agencies or to investors in bond-offering documents and continuing disclosures.
>
> Specifically, the SEC alleges that the city manager signed the closing letter for one of the bond offerings, falsely certifying that it was accurate and did not contain any misleading statements. The city auditor and comptroller signed letters falsely representing that the city's audited financial statements included in the securities offerings were accurate. The deputy city manager of finance regularly reviewed and revised the false and misleading disclosure documents and signed the closing letter for two of the five bond offerings. She falsely certified that the disclosures were accurate and did not contain any misleading statements, and she reviewed and made presentations to the rating agencies. The assistant auditor and comptroller reviewed the city's financial statements that contained some of the false and misleading disclosures, and the city treasurer participated in drafting the city's false and misleading disclosures. Additionally, the city treasurer and the assistant auditor and comptroller both knew that in 2003, the rating agencies had concerns about the city's growing pension obligations and that those obligations could negatively affect the city's credit rating. Nevertheless, they withheld material facts from the rating agencies.
>
> In October 2010, four of the accused officials agreed to pay a total of $80,000 to settle the fraud charges with the Securities and Exchange Commission. The fifth defendant's case is still ongoing. Regulators have pointed to this case as an indication that they intend to pursue individuals engaged in perceived abuses in the $2.8 billion municipal bond market.
>
> **Sources:** "SEC Charges Five Former San Diego Officials with Securities Fraud," SEC Press Release 2008-57, April 7, 2008; Nicole Bullock, "Ex-San Diego Officials Fined in Fraud Case," FT.Com, October 28, 2010.

FINANCE AND INVESTMENT CYCLE: TYPICAL ACTIVITIES

LEARNING OBJECTIVE 10-1
Describe the finance and investment cycle, including typical source documents and controls.

The finance and investment cycle contains a large number of accounts and records ranging across tangible (e.g., property, plant, and equipment—PP&E) and intangible assets (e.g., goodwill, patents), long-term liabilities, deferred credits, stockholders' equity, gains and losses, expenses, and income taxes. See Exhibit 10.3 for a list of the major accounts and records. These include some of the more complicated topics in accounting: equity method accounting for investments, consolidation accounting, goodwill, income taxes, and derivatives, to name a few. The purpose of this chapter is to focus on the auditing issues associated with each of these accounting topics, not to explain how to account for these balances and transactions. Because the cycle generally involves large, infrequent transactions, auditors usually employ more substantive testing procedures in this cycle.

Exhibit 10.3 is an illustration of the finance and investment cycle, which interacts with all of the other cycles. Its major functions are financial planning; raising capital; and entering into mergers, acquisitions, and other investments. As you follow the exhibit, you can use the numbers to track the elements of internal control described in the following sections.

Financing the Entity through Debt and Stockholder Equity

Transactions in debt and stockholder equity are normally few in number but large in monetary amount. The highest levels of corporate governance authorize and execute these transactions. The control-related duties and responsibilities reflect this high-level attention.

Financial Planning   ①

Financial planning starts with the cash flow forecast by the chief financial officer (CFO). This forecast informs the board of directors and management of the business plans, the prospects for cash inflows, and the needs for cash outflows. The cash flow forecast usually is

416 Part Two *The Financial Statement Audit*

EXHIBIT 10.3
Finance and Investment Cycle

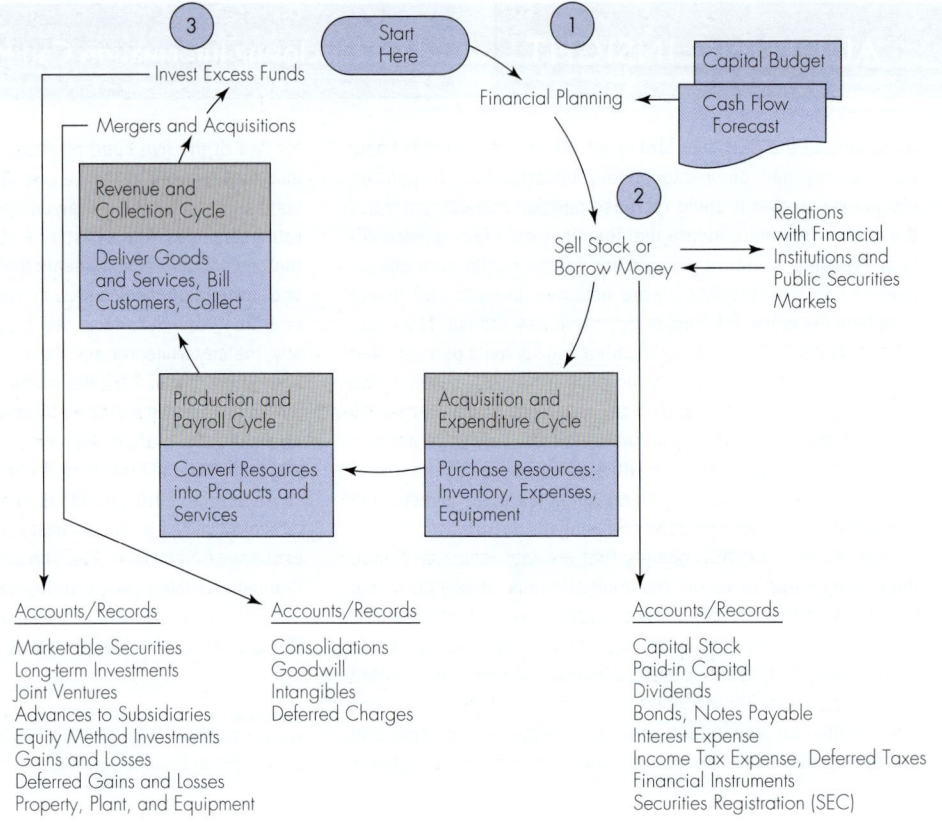

integrated with the capital budget, which contains the plans for asset purchases and business acquisitions. A **capital budget** approved by the board of directors constitutes the authorization for major capital asset acquisitions (acquisition cycle) and investments. Cash flow planning and capital budgeting are important controls over major management decisions.

Raising Capital ②

The board of directors usually authorizes sales of capital stock and debt financing transactions. All directors must sign registration documents for public securities offerings. However, authority normally is delegated to the CFO or treasurer to complete such transactions (e.g., periodic renewals of notes payable and other ordinary types of financing transactions without specific board approval of each transaction). Auditors should expect to find the authorizing signatures of the chief executive officer (CEO), CFO, treasurer, chair of the board of directors, and perhaps other high-ranking officers on financing documents.

Company bonds and stocks are normally handled by an intermediary called a **transfer agent**, generally a bank or trust company. The transfer agent tracks securities' owners for payment of interest or dividends. The certificate records are kept by a **registrar** who updates the records based on information from the transfer agent. Often the registrar and transfer agent are the same company.

In the past, many financing transactions have been off the balance sheet. Companies entered into obligations and commitments that did not require recording in the accounts. Examples of transactions that did not necessitate recording in the accounts include operating leases and endorsements on discounted notes or on other companies' obligations, letters of credit, guarantees, repurchase or remarketing agreements, commitments to purchase at fixed prices, commitments to sell at fixed prices, and certain kinds of stock options. As noted previously, the Enron debacle was a case of using SPEs to keep certain transactions off the company's balance sheet. Off-balance-sheet transactions often cause problems in financial reporting and disclosure. Although new accounting standards will reduce the number of off-balance-sheet transactions (e.g., new rules make it harder to create SPEs and have mandated more disclosure), auditors must still be aware of their existence and ensure their proper use and adequate disclosure.

Record Keeping for Long-Term Liabilities

The accounting department and the CFO or controller maintain records of notes and bonds payable. The record-keeping procedures should be similar to those used to account for vendor accounts payable: comparing payment notices from lenders to the accounting records, monitoring due dates, setting up interest in vouchers for payment, and making accruals for unpaid interest on financial reporting dates. If the company has only a few bonds and notes outstanding, it usually does not keep subsidiary records of them. All information is in the general ledger accounts. However, many large companies, especially in industries such as utilities, have large numbers of bonds and notes and may keep control and subsidiary accounts as is done for accounts payable. Exhibit 10.4 shows debentures of Consolidated Edison, Inc. on its 2010 financial statement. With 36 debentures totaling more than $9 billion dollars, record keeping and the auditing of records represent a formidable task. But add to this two other categories of long-term debt consisting of 12 other long-term debt items, and the total debt exceeds $10 billion. Also, when all or parts of the notes become due within the next year, the CFO and controller have the necessary information for properly classifying current and long-term amounts.

Another class of credit balances is treated in this section under the heading "Record Keeping," for which the functions of authorization, custody, and reconciliation are not easy to describe. They are the "calculated liabilities and credits": lease obligations, deferred income taxes, pension and postretirement benefit liabilities, and foreign currency translation gains and losses, to name a few. These are accounting transactions calculated according to accounting rules using basic data from company plans and operations. Management usually has considerable discretion in structuring leases, tax strategies, pension plan and employee benefit terms, foreign holdings, and the like. These accounting calculations often involve significant accounting estimates made by management. Company accountants try to capture the economic reality of these calculated liabilities by following generally accepted accounting principles, which are often complex and difficult to understand. Auditors need to discuss these transactions at length and ensure that the fundamental economic and business assumptions underlying these transactions are reasonable.

Periodic Reconciliation

Most public entities use registrars and transfer agents to issue certificates and track stock ownership. Reports can be obtained from registrars and transfer agents to verify that the company's record of the number of shares outstanding agrees with the registrar's number. (Without this reconciliation, counterfeit shares handled by the transfer agent and recorded by the registrar might go unnoticed.) A **trustee** having duties and responsibilities similar to those of registrars and transfer agents can handle ownership of bonds. Confirmations and reports from bond trustees can be used to reconcile the trustee's records to the company's records.

Some small, especially closely held, corporations may issue stock certificates themselves. These companies utilize a stock certificate book to issue certificates as authorized by the board of directors. A responsible independent person should periodically inspect the stock certificate book to determine whether all certificates are recorded and in the possession of bona fide owners. If necessary, officials in very small companies can confirm the ownership of shares with the holders of record.

Investing Transactions: Investments and Intangibles ③

Company investments can take many shapes. Management invests in the company through the purchase or lease of PP&E, which was discussed in the acquisition and expenditure cycle chapter. Investments in intangible assets may be in the form of purchased assets (e.g., patents, trademarks) or accounting allocations (e.g., goodwill, deferred charges). Finally, a company can have a variety of types of investments in marketable securities.

EXHIBIT 10.4
Consolidated Edison Inc.
2010 Financial Statements

Consolidated Edison, Inc.
Consolidated Statement of Capitalization

LONG-TERM DEBT (Millions of Dollars)

Maturity	Interest Rate	Series	At December 31, 2010	2009
DEBENTURES:				
2010	8.125%	2000A	$ —	$ 325
2010	7.50	2000A	—	55
2010	7.50	2000B	—	300
2012	5.625	2002A	300	300
2013	4.875	2002B	500	500
2013	3.85	2003B	200	200
2014	4.70	2004A	200	200
2014	5.55	2008A	275	275
2015	2.50	2010A	56	—
2015	5.375	2005C	350	350
2015	5.30	2005A	40	40
2016	5.45	2006A	75	75
2016	5.50	2006C	400	400
2016	5.30	2006D	250	250
2016	5.85	2008A	600	600
2018	7.125	2008C	600	600
2018	6.15	2008A	50	50
2019	4.96	2009A	60	60
2019	6.65	2009B	475	475
2020	4.45	2010A	350	—
2027	6.50	1997F	80	80
2029	7.00	1999G	—	45
2033	5.875	2003A	175	175
2033	5.10	2003C	200	200
2034	5.70	2004B	200	200
2035	5.30	2005A	350	350
2035	5.25	2005B	125	125
2036	5.85	2006A	400	400
2036	6.20	2006B	400	400
2036	5.70	2006E	250	250
2037	6.30	2007A	525	525
2038	6.75	2008B	600	600
2039	6.00	2009B	60	60
2039	5.50	2009C	600	600
2040	5.70	2010B	350	—
2040	5.50	2010B	115	—
TOTAL DEBENTURES			**9,210**	**9,065**
TRANSITION BONDS:				
2019*	5.22%	2004-1	32	34
TOTAL TRANSITION BONDS			**32**	**34**

Consolidated Edison, Inc.
Consolidated Statement of Capitalization

LONG-TERM DEBT (Millions of Dollars)

Maturity	Interest Rate	Series	At December 31, 2010	2009
TAX-EXEMPT DEBT — Notes issued to New York State Energy Research and Development Authority for Facilities Revenue Bonds[†]:				
2014	0.40%	1994[‡]	—	55
2015	0.34	1995[‡]	44	44
2032	0.595	2004B Series 1	127	127
2034	0.548	1999A	293	293
2035	0.525	2004B Series 2	20	20
2036	1.45	2010A	225	—
2036	4.70	2001A	—	225
2036	0.49	2001B	98	98
2039	0.525	2004A	98	98
2039	0.307	2004C	99	99
2039	0.29	2005A	126	126
TOTAL TAX-EXEMPT DEBT			**1,130**	**1,185**
Other long-term debt			323	326
Unamortized debt discount			(19)	(25)
TOTAL			**10,676**	**10,585**
Less: long-term debt due within one year			5	731
TOTAL LONG-TERM DEBT			**10,671**	**9,854**
TOTAL CAPITALIZATION			**$21,945**	**$20,316**

* The final date to pay the entire remaining unpaid principal balance, if pay of all outstanding bonds is May 17, 2021,
[†] Other than Series 2001A and Series 2010A (the proceeds of which were used to shown the Series 2001A), rates reset weekly or by suction held every 35 days: December 31, 2010 rates shown (August 16, 2010 not shown for Series 1964).
[‡] Issued for O&R pollution control financis.

The following sections are phrased in the context of a manufacturing or service company; however, financial institutions (banks, thrifts), investment companies (mutual funds, small business investment companies), and insurance companies have more elaborate systems for managing their investments and intangibles.

Authorization

Those in the entity charged with governance (e.g., board of directors or investment committee) should approve all investment policies. It is not unusual to find board or executive committee approval required for major investment transactions. However, auditors should expect to find a great deal of variation across companies about the nature and amount of transactions that must have specific high-level approval. It is imperative that auditors understand the approval process and vouch major acquisitions to the appropriate documented approval.

AUDITING INSIGHT — **Authorization: Here Today, Gone Tomorrow**

The chief financial officer of Travum County invested several million dollars of county funds with a California-based investment money manager. Soon thereafter, news stories of the money manager's expensive personal lifestyle and questionable handling of clients' funds began to circulate, indicating that clients could lose much of their investments. At the same time, news stories about the county treasurer's own credit card spending habits were published locally, indicating that she had obtained a personal credit card by using the county's name. Although no county funds were lost and no improper credit card bills were paid, the county commissioners temporarily suspended the treasurer's authority to choose investment vehicles for county funds.

Custody

Negotiable certificates such as stocks and bonds may be kept in a brokerage account. Other negotiable certificates (such as titles to real estate) may be in the actual possession of the client. If the company keeps them, they should be in a safe or a bank safe deposit box. Only high-ranking officers (e.g., CFO, CEO, president, and chairman of the board) should have access, which should require two people (**dual control**) to these documents. This may require two signatures to enter a safe deposit box or ensuring that no one person knows the complete combination to the safe. When it is not possible for one person to enter a safe, cabinet or drawer, as in two locks and no one has both keys, or no one knows the entire combination, a strict form of dual custody, known as **joint custody** is implemented as a control.

Patents, trademarks, copyrights, and similar legal intangible rights can be evidenced in legal documents and contracts. These seldom are negotiable and they usually are kept in ordinary company files. However, these intangible assets are highly valued and entities make every effort to protect these assets as indicated in the following Audit Insight.

AUDITING INSIGHT — **Don't Use Our Logo**

The **University of Texas at Austin** has trademark rights over the "longhorn" symbol and a particular school color (burnt orange). The university actively prohibits businesses from using these symbols without permission. For example, a local cleaning business and a trash-hauling business were informed that they must cease and desist using the longhorn head logo on their buildings, signs, and trucks. The businesses complied by repainting and finding other ways to promote their business.

The **Coalition to Advance the Protection of Sports Logos** (CAPS), whose members are colleges and the professional leagues (NFL, NBA, MLB, and NHL), uses a national network of investigators to scour flea markets, customs ports, and parking lots on game days to ferret out unlicensed T-shirts, caps, and other gear. Since 1993, CAPS, working with local law enforcement, has seized more than 9 million illegal products valued at more than $329 million.

Source: "Stopping Knockoffs an Elusive Goal for Flyers," *The Philadelphia Inquirer,* May 15, 2008, p. C01.

Record Keeping for Investments

The procedures for purchase of most investments involve the voucher system previously described in the acquisition and expenditure cycle chapter. Unauthorized transactions can be a major risk for investments and intangibles. The board of directors or other responsible officials should authorize large transactions. These authorizations provide the approval for the purchasing department to acquire the assets and for the accounting department to prepare the voucher and the check. The treasurer or CFO signs the check to purchase the investment.

The record keeping for many types of investments and intangibles can be complicated. The complications arise not so much from the original recording of transactions but from the maintenance of the accounts over time. This is where complex accounting standards for marketable securities, equity method accounting, consolidations, goodwill, intangibles' amortization and valuation, depreciation, deferred charges, deferred taxes, pension and postretirement benefit liabilities, and various financial instruments enter the picture. High-level accountants who prepare financial statements are involved with the accounting rules and the management estimates required to account for such investments and intangibles. Management plans and estimates of future events and interpretations of the accounting standards often become elements of the accounting maintenance of these balances. These decisions are ripe areas for overstatement of assets, understatement of liabilities, and understatement of expenses.

Periodic Reconciliation

Investment accounts may be overstated by recording marketable securities that the entity does not own. The most significant reconciliation opportunity for the investments in marketable securities is the inspection and count of negotiable securities certificates. This reconciliation is similar to a physical inventory count consisting of an inspection of certificates on hand and comparison with the information recorded in the accounts. (When a brokerage firm holds the securities, the inspection is accomplished with a written confirmation.) As in all cases concerning the inspection or counting of marketable assets, a representative of the client should be present at all times.

A securities count is not a mere handling of bits of paper. A securities count should include a record of the name of the company represented by the certificate, the interest rate for bonds, the dividend rate for preferred stocks, the due date for bonds, the serial numbers on the certificates (known as the *CUSIP number*), the face value of bonds, the number of stock shares or face amount of bonds, and notes on the name of the owner shown on the face of the certificate or on the endorsements on the back (should be the client company). Companies should perform this reconciliation reasonably often and not wait for an annual visit by the independent auditors. A securities count in a financial institution that holds thousands of shares in multibillion-dollar asset accounts is a major undertaking. A surprise count by the auditors may be done during the interim testing. As with other assets, the auditor should insist that client personnel are present during the entire count.

↳ REVIEW CHECKPOINTS

10.1 Who is normally responsible for the authorization of investment activities? Why is the authorization normally performed at this level?

10.2 What constitutes the authorization for notes payable? What documentary evidence could auditors examine as evidence of this authorization?

10.3 What documents would auditors inspect in the audit of investment securities and what information would they obtain from these documents?

10.4 Describe the activities and documentation of a controlled count of the client's investment securities.

CONTROL RISK ASSESSMENT

LEARNING OBJECTIVE 10-2
Give examples of tests of control activities over debt and stockholders' equity transactions and investment transactions.

In the finance and investment cycle, auditors look for control activities such as authorization, appropriate custody, record keeping, and periodic reconciliation. They especially look for information about the level of management that is involved in these functions. Tests of controls generally begin with inquiries and observations related to these features. Inspection of documents, primarily looking for proper authorizations, and a walkthrough of controls over the determination of the fair value of assets should be performed.

Because finance and investment transactions are often individually material, each transaction usually is audited using substantive procedures. Auditors do not normally examine samples of transactions for tests of controls as they do in the other cycles because reliance on controls does not normally reduce the extent of substantive procedures on finance and investment cycle accounts. However, lack of control can lead to performance of significant extended procedures. Of particular importance are the entitywide controls that restrict access to systems, documents, and assets, many of which are key in the performance of investment cycle activities. Establishing appropriate procedures, including adequate controls, for determining the fair market value of investments, derivatives, hedges, and other investment instruments is imperative in accessing the overall control structure for any company that maintains a material amount of such instruments. Of course, for public companies in which the auditors must issue a report on the effectiveness of controls over the financial reporting process, evaluation of controls over these transactions is essential.

Control Considerations

Control activities for suitable handling of responsibilities should be in place and operating. By referring to the discussion accompanying Exhibit 10.3, you can tell that these responsibilities are primarily in the hands of senior management officials. You also can tell that different companies may have widely different policies and activities.

It is difficult to have a strict separation of functional responsibilities when the principal officers of a company authorize, execute, and control finance and investment activities. It is not realistic to have the CEO authorize investments but not have access to stockholder records, securities certificates, and the like. Real separation of duties can be found in middle management and lower ranks, but it is difficult to create and enforce among upper managers.

Because of this control problem, a company should have *compensating control activities*. A **compensating control** is a control activity used because a specific standard control activity is not in place. The compensating control reduces the risk due to the missing control. For example, the board of directors may delegate the execution of investment purchases to the CFO. The CFO would call the company's broker to execute authorized transactions. Because the CFO is authorized to instruct the broker to buy and sell securities, the CFO is in a position to sell company securities for personal use. A compensating control might be an agreement with the broker to mail transaction confirmations to other company personnel or to use electronic transfer directly into the company's account for all proceeds from the sale of investments. In the area of finance and investment, the compensating control feature often involves two or more persons in each area of important functional responsibility.

If involvement by multiple persons is not specified, an oversight or review can be substituted. For example, the board of directors can authorize the purchase of securities or the creation of a partnership. The CFO or CEO can carry out the transactions, have custody of certificates and agreements, manage the partnership or the portfolio of securities, oversee the record keeping, and make the decisions about valuations and accounting (authorizing the journal entries). These are normal management activities, and they combine several responsibilities. The compensating control can exist in the form of periodic reports to the board of directors, oversight by the investment committee of the board, and internal audit involvement in making a periodic reconciliation of securities certificates in a portfolio with the amounts and descriptions recorded in the accounts.

Control over Accounting Estimates

An **accounting estimate** is an approximation of a financial statement element, item, or account. Estimates often are included in basic financial statements because (1) the measurement of some amount of valuation is uncertain, perhaps depending on the outcome of future events, or (2) relevant data cannot be accumulated on a timely, cost-effective basis (*AU 342*). Some examples of accounting estimates in the finance and investment cycle include the following:

- *Plant and equipment depreciation.* Useful lives, salvage values.
- *Financial instruments.* Valuation of securities, including fair values assigned to debt and equity securities; classification into held-to-maturity, available-for-sale, and trading securities investment portfolios; probability of a correlated hedge; sales of securities with puts and calls; investment model assumptions; and impairments. The issue of valuation may be especially difficult if the investment was received in a noncash transaction and is not readily marketable. Appraisals, financial modeling or other methods may be necessary to estimate the investment's value.
- *Accruals.* Compensation in stock option plans, actuarial assumptions in pension costs.
- *Leases.* Initial direct costs, useful lives, executory costs, and residual values; capitalization interest rate.
- *Rates.* Imputed interest rates on receivables and payables.
- *Other.* Losses and net realizable value on segment disposal and business restructuring, fair values in nonmonetary exchanges, and impairment of goodwill.

A client's management is responsible for making estimates and should have processes and controls designed to reduce the likelihood of material misstatements in them. According to auditing standards (*AU 342*), specific relevant aspects of such controls include the following:

- Management communication of the need for proper accounting estimates.
- Accumulation of relevant, sufficient, and reliable data for estimates.
- Preparation of estimates by qualified personnel.
- Adequate review and approval by appropriate levels of authority.
- Comparison of prior estimates with subsequent results to assess the reliability of the estimation outcomes.
- Consideration by management as to whether particular accounting estimates are consistent with the company's operational plans.

Auditors' tests of controls over the estimation process include making inquiries and observations. Inquiries would include such questions as: Who prepares estimates? When are they prepared? What data are used? Who reviews and approves the estimates? Have prior estimates been compared with subsequent actual events? Observations include study of data documentation, study of comparisons of prior estimates with subsequent actual experience, and study of intercompany correspondence concerning estimates and operational plans. The audit of a valuation estimate starts with the tests of controls, much of which have a bearing on the quality of the estimation process and of the estimate itself.

AUDITING INSIGHT — OOPS!

A large television manufacturer decided to extend its 90-day warranty on labor to one year. Because the company had no experience with such an extended warranty, it devised a complex formula to take into account the increased likelihood of repair and the associated cost. While going through the pages and pages of calculations with the warranty accountant to obtain an understanding, the auditor noticed that one fraction used in the calculation was inverted. The error resulted in a $20 million understatement of the warranty reserve.

Authorization

Most of the transactions in the financing and investing cycle involve large amounts of cash or other assets. Therefore, authorization is a critical issue when examining these transactions. The issuance, sale, or purchase of company stock and bonds, the obtaining of large bank loans, and the purchase or sale of large assets generally are discussed at the highest levels of the organization. Auditors must review minutes of the board of directors meetings, finance committee meetings, or other appropriate committee meetings for the authorization of these transactions. In addition, the authorization for the purchase of large assets may reside in the capital budget, which should have been approved by senior management and the board. Absent tangible evidence of the authorization of these transactions, the auditor should make inquires at the highest levels to ensure that these major transactions have been approved.

Record Keeping

Transactions that occur on a daily basis are usually recorded in a special journal designed especially for those transactions (e.g., sales journals, purchase journals, payroll journals). Generally, the transactions in this cycle occur infrequently and are recorded in the general journal. In addition, because the transactions are infrequent, vary greatly in type, and are for large dollar amounts, controls over the proper recording of the transaction must be implemented. The competency of the individuals making these journal entries and the review and reconciliation of the general ledger are essential controls that the auditor should review.

Custody

In large companies, custody of **stock certificate books** is not a significant management problem because of the use of registrars and transfer agents. Small companies often keep their own stockholder records. A stock certificate book looks like a checkbook. It has perforated stubs for recording the number of shares, the owner's name and other identification, and the date of issue. Actual unissued share certificates are attached to the stubs, like blank checks in a checkbook. The company should have a record of certificates that are outstanding in the possession of owners. Custody of the stock certificate book is important because the unissued certificates are like money or collateral. If improperly removed, they can be sold to buyers who think they are genuinely issued or can be used as collateral with unsuspecting lenders.

Lenders have custody of debt instruments (e.g., leases, bonds, and notes payable). However, when a company repurchases its bonds or pays off its debt, the debt instruments are returned to the company. These documents could be misused by improperly reselling them to unsuspecting investors. Auditors should inspect documentation indicating the extinguishment of debt and should inspect returned bonds or notes for appropriate cancelation or evidence of destruction.

AUDITING INSIGHT — A New Meaning for "Recycling"

Something strange must have happened on the way to the dump. Hundreds of long-term bonds were redeemed early and presented to **Citibank** in New York, which acted as the agent for the issues. Many of the bonds still had not reached the maturity date marked on them. Citibank sent about $1 billion of the canceled U.S. corporate bonds to a landfill dump in New Jersey, but some of them turned up at banks in Europe and the United States. Although the bonds are worthless, they still might look genuine to a layman or even to some bankers. The FBI traced the canceled bonds to a defunct company in New Jersey that had a contract to destroy the bonds. (*Note:* Companies obtain a destruction certificate when bonds and stock certificates are canceled. The certificates obtained by Citibank apparently was fraudulent.)

Source: *Securities Exchange Act Release No. 31612,* December 17, 1992. www.sec.gov/news/digest/1992/dig121792.pdf.

Summary: Control Risk Assessment

From the preceding discussion, you can tell that tests of controls take a variety of forms: inquiries, observations, studies of documentation, comparisons with related data, and detail audits of some transactions. However, because of the nature of finance and investment transactions (i.e., few in number and high in dollar amount), auditors often focus on substantive tests rather than tests of controls. For example, a company may have only 10 security investment transactions during the year. The most efficient use of audit time may be to review all 10 transactions for all pertinent assertions. Conversely, some companies may have numerous debt-financing transactions and a more detailed evaluation of control risk may be pertinent, including the selection of a sample of transactions for control risk assessment evidence.

See Appendix 10A for internal control questionnaires for the finance and investment cycle. They illustrate typical questions about the assertions. These inquiries give auditors insights into the client's specifications for review and approval of major investing and financing transactions, the system of accounting for them, and the provision for error-checking review activities.

The audit team should evaluate the evidence obtained from an understanding of internal control and from tests of controls. These tests can take many forms because management systems for finance and investment accounts can vary a great deal among clients. The involvement of senior officials in a relatively small number of high-dollar transactions makes control risk assessment a process tailored specifically to the company's situation. Some companies enter into complicated financing and investment transactions while others keep to the simple transactions.

AUDITING INSIGHT — Goodwill Impairment

Damage from goodwill impairment continued to hit the books in 2008.

- **US Airways** took a $622 million noncash charge in 2008 to write off impaired goodwill relating to its September 2005 merger with America West Holdings Corp.
- Toronto-based **Celestica Inc.** reported an $822 million fourth-quarter net loss. The contract electronics maker said it wrote off $850.5 million of goodwill established primarily as a result of an acquisition in 2001.
- **Flextronics,** a Singapore-based electronics manufacturer, recorded a noncash charge of $5.9 billion in its December third quarter to write off the entire carrying value of its goodwill. **Flextronics ConocoPhillips Boston Scientific Corp. Valero Energy Corp. Colonial BancGroup**
- **ConocoPhillips** reported in its fourth-quarter earnings that it had recorded a $25.4-billion impairment of all exploration & production segment goodwill.
- **Boston Scientific Corp.** recorded a $2.7 billion goodwill impairment charge associated with its acquisition of Guidant.
- **Valero Energy Corp.** recorded a noncash loss of $4.1 billion from the impairment of goodwill.
- **Colonial BancGroup** took a goodwill impairment charge of $575 million in the fourth quarter while **Banner Corp.**, the parent company of **Banner Bank** and **Islanders Bank**, reported a $71.1 million noncash impairment charge in writing off the remaining balance of goodwill.

Source: "More Earnings Overwhelmed by Impairments," CFO.com, January 29, 2009.

REVIEW CHECKPOINTS

10.5 What is a compensating control? Give some examples for finance and investment cycle accounts.

10.6 What are some of the specific relevant aspects of management's control over the estimation process? What are some inquiries auditors can make?

10.7 When a company has produced an estimate of an investment valuation based on a non-monetary exchange, what source of comparative information can auditors use to audit the estimate's reasonableness?

10.8 What documentation should an auditor inspect when a client has paid off a bank note? How could an employee defraud the company if the bank note has no indication of being paid?

FINANCING ACTIVITIES: ASSERTIONS AND SUBSTANTIVE PROCEDURES

This part of the chapter covers the audit of various account balances and transactions. It is presented in two sections: (1) financing activities (such as stockholders' equity, long-term liabilities, and related accounts) and (2) investing activities (PP&E, investments, and intangibles). This section provides some assertions and procedures related to accounts in each portion of the financing and investing cycle. As in previous chapters, some cases illustrating errors and frauds are used to describe useful audit approaches.

Long-Term Liabilities and Related Accounts

A list of assertions for debt and equity accounts and some illustrative procedures for each assertion are in Exhibit 10.5. The primary audit concerns with the verification of long-term liabilities is that all of them are recorded and that the interest expense is properly paid or accrued. Therefore, the balance sheet assertion of *completeness* is paramount. Alertness to the possibility of unrecorded liabilities during the performance of procedures in other areas frequently uncovers liabilities that have not been recorded. For example, when PP&E are acquired during the year under audit, auditors should inquire about the source of funds to finance the new assets. Auditors also should be alert for large cash disbursements and maintenance expenses for electrical, plumbing, and air-conditioning systems upgrades. Often all of these are indicators of the purchase and installation of equipment. In addition, the auditors must ensure that the liability accounts are recorded at their fair market value.

When auditing long-term liabilities, auditors usually obtain independent written confirmations for notes and bonds payable. In the case of notes payable to banks, the standard bank confirmation may be used and should include a request to list any banking relationships not listed on the confirmation request. The amount and terms of bonds payable, mortgages payable, and other formal debt instruments can be verified by reading the bond **indenture**, the written agreement with the bondholders, and confirmed by requests to bond holders or the bond trustee. The confirmation request should include questions

EXHIBIT 10.5 Account Balance and Presentation and Disclosure Assertions and Substantive Procedures for Debt and Equity Accounts

Account Balance Assertions	Substantive Procedures
Existence—Items in the debt and equity accounts exist.	Confirm debt balances with debtors, including terms, collateral, interest, etc. Confirm stock certificates issued and outstanding with registrar.
Completeness—All debt and equity that should have been recorded have been recorded.	Confirmations with debt and equity holders should include an inquiry into other debts or equities not listed. Examine large cash receipts for related debt or equity transactions.
Rights and obligations—Obligations related to debt or equity are recorded.	Examine debt agreements and include information about restrictions, terms, and collateral on debt confirmations.
Valuation and allocation—Debt and equity are included in the financial statements at appropriate amounts and any resulting valuation adjustments are properly recorded.	Recalculate amortization of discount or premiums on debt.

Presentation and Disclosure Assertions	Substantive Procedures
Classification—Debt is properly classified as current or noncurrent. Leasing arrangements are properly classified in the financial statements.	Inquire and obtain representations from management. Read footnote disclosures and agree to debt instruments.
Completeness—Debt terms, collateral, leasing arrangements, and debt covenants are disclosed in footnotes.	Calculate ratios and balances required by debt covenants.

not only of amount, interest rate, and due date but also of collateral, restrictive covenants, and other items of agreement between lender and borrower. Confirmation requests should be sent to lenders with whom the company has done business in the recent past, even if no liability balance is shown at the confirmation date. Such extra coverage is a part of the search for unrecorded liabilities. An illustration of typical audit documentation for auditing long-term debt and interest expense is in Exhibit 10.6. Note that the interest expense consists of additions to the accrual account as well as amortization of premiums or discounts on long-term debt. An illustrative audit plan of substantive procedures for notes payable and long-term debt is in Appendix Exhibit 10B.1.

Confirmation and inquiry procedures may be used to obtain responses on a class of items loosely termed *off-balance-sheet information*. Within this category are terms of loan agreements, leases, endorsements, guarantees, and insurance policies (whether issued by a client insurance company or owned by the client). Among these items is the difficult-to-define set of commitments and contingencies that often pose evidence-gathering problems. See Exhibit 10.7 for some common types of commitments.

Footnote disclosure should be considered for the types of commitments shown in Exhibit 10.7. Some of them can be estimated and valued and, thus, can be recorded in the accounts and shown in the financial statements themselves (such as losses on fixed-price purchase commitments and losses on fixed-price sales commitments). Interest expense generally is related item by item to interest-bearing liabilities. Based on the evidence of long-term liability transactions (including those that have been retired during the year), the related interest expense amounts can be recalculated. The amount of debt, the interest rate, and the time period are used to determine whether the interest expense and accrued interest are properly recorded. Interest expense also may be estimated by the analytical procedure of multiplying average debt outstanding by the average interest rate.

EXHIBIT 10.6 Audit Documentation—Long-Term Debt and Interest Expense

DUNDER-MIFFLIN
Long-Term Debt, Accrued Interest Payable, and Interest Expense
For Year Ended 12/31/2012
Prepared by Client

Prepared by RJR 3/10/2013
Reviewed by DHS 3/12/2013

		Long-Term Debt				Accrued Interest Payable			
	Date Due	Balance 12/31/2016	Additions	Amortization/ Payments	Balance 12/31/2012	Balance 12/31/2011	Interest Expense	Payments	Balance 12/31/2010
5.25% senior subordinated debt	6/30/21	$2,500,000 PY	0	$250,000 v	$2,250,000 CF TB	$66,750	$131,437 C	$143,750 v	$54,437 CF
4% note payable— Bank One	9/30/14	0	$500,000 u	0	$ 500,000 CF TB	$ 5,000	$ 20,000 C $151,437	$ 20,000 v	$ 5,000 CF
Premium on long-term debt		$ 354,128 PY	0	$ 18,266 C	$ 335,862 CF TB		$ 18,266 C		
						$71,750 F PY	$169,703 F/TB	$163,750 F	$59,437 CF F/TB

PY = Agreed to prior year workpapers
u = Agreed to copy of note and cash receipts journal
v = Vouched to cash disbursement
F = Footed

CF = Cross-Footed
C = Recalculated
TB = Carried forward to the trial balance

EXHIBIT 10.7 Off-Balance-Sheet Commitments

Type of Commitment	Typical Audit Procedures
Repurchase or remarketing agreements	Vouching of contracts, confirmation by customer, and inquiry of client management
Commitments to purchase at fixed prices	Vouching of open purchase orders, inquiry of purchasing personnel, and confirmation by supplier
Commitments to sell at fixed prices	Vouching of sales contracts, inquiry of sales personnel, and confirmation by customer
Loan commitments (as in a savings and loan association)	Vouching of open commitment file, inquiry of loan officers
Lease commitments	Vouching of lease agreement, confirmation with lessor or lessee

Stockholders' Equity: Substantive Procedures

Stockholders' equity transactions usually are well documented in the minutes of the meetings of the board of directors, proxy statements, and securities offering registration statements. For publicly traded companies, stock transactions usually require a filing with the SEC (e.g., an offering of stock to raise capital). Transaction authorization can be vouched to these documents, and the cash proceeds can be traced to the bank accounts. Capital stock may be subject to confirmation when independent registrars and transfer agents are employed. Such agents are responsible for knowing the number of shares authorized and issued and for keeping lists of stockholders' names. The basic information about capital stock—such as number of shares, classes of stock, preferred dividend rates, conversion terms, dividend payments, shares held in the company name, expiration dates, and terms of warrants and stock dividends and splits—can be confirmed with the independent agents. The audit team's own inspection and reading of stock certificates, charter authorizations, directors' minutes, and registration statements can corroborate many of these items. However, when the client company does not use independent agents, most audit evidence is gathered by inspecting and vouching stock record documents (such as certificate book stubs). When circumstances call for extended procedures, information on outstanding stock in very small corporations having only a few stockholders may be confirmed directly with the holders. See Appendix Exhibit 10B.2 for an illustrative audit plan of substantive procedures for stockholders' equity.

⤷ REVIEW CHECKPOINTS

10.9 What are some of the important assertions found in stockholders' equity account balances and disclosures?

10.10 What are some of the important assertions found in the long-term liability accounts?

10.11 How can confirmations be used in auditing (a) stockholder capital accounts and (b) notes and bonds payable?

10.12 What information about capital stock could be confirmed with outside parties? How could the auditors corroborate this information?

10.13 Define and give five examples of off-balance-sheet information. Why should auditors be concerned with such items?

10.14 If a company does not monitor notes payable for due dates and interest payment dates in relation to financial statement dates, what misstatements can appear in the financial statements?

INVESTING ACTIVITIES: ASSERTIONS AND SUBSTANTIVE PROCEDURES

Refer to Exhibit 10.8 for a list of assertions for investment accounts and related substantive procedures. In general, substantive procedures on finance and investment accounts are extensive. As previously stated, the number of transactions is usually not large and therefore the audit cost is not high for complete coverage. Auditors often perform substantive procedures on most or all transactions and components within these accounts. Nevertheless, control deficiencies and unusual or complicated transactions can cause auditors to adjust the nature and timing of audit procedures. For example, if separation of duties is lacking in the execution of investment transactions, the auditor may include a positive confirmation of securities held by the broker and a year-end count of securities held by the company (as opposed to interim testing). Complicated financial instruments, pension plans, exotic equity securities, related-party transactions, and nonmonetary exchanges of investment assets call for procedures designed to find evidence of errors and frauds in the finance and investment accounts.

Companies can have a wide variety of investments and relationships with affiliates. Investment accounting may be on the market value method, cost method, equity method, or full consolidation, depending on the nature, size, and influence represented by the investment. Consolidations usually create problems of accounting for the fair value of acquired assets and the related goodwill. Auditors must identify the appropriate accounting method for each investment and ensure that investments are properly valued. The next section deals with some of the finance and investment cycle assertions and presents some cases for your review.

Substantive procedures for estimates include determining whether (1) the valuation principles are acceptable under the financial reporting framework, (2) the valuation principles are consistently applied, (3) the valuation principles are supported by the underlying documentation, and (4) the method of estimation and the significant assumptions are properly disclosed according to GAAP. When auditors perform the securities inspection and count, all of this information should be recorded in the audit documentation. *Existence* is established by inspecting the securities, ownership (*rights*) is established by viewing the client name as owner, and *valuation* evidence is determined by finding the cost and market value. If a security certificate is pledged as collateral for a loan, it may not be available for inspection. It can be confirmed or inspected if the extended procedure of visiting the creditor is necessary. The pledge as collateral may be important for a footnote disclosure.

EXHIBIT 10.8 Assertions and Substantive Procedures in Investment Accounts

Assertions about Account Balances	Substantive Procedures
Existence—Items in investment accounts exist.	Confirm stock investments with brokerage.
Completeness—All investment activity should have been recorded.	Examine documentation for large expenditures. Confirm stock investments with brokerage.
Rights and obligations—The entity holds or controls the rights to investments.	Examine documents for acquisitions.
Valuation and allocation—Investments are included in the financial statements at appropriate amounts and any resulting valuation adjustments are properly recorded.	Obtain client documentation for the calculations of goodwill and test. Inquire whether management is aware of any impairment to investment securities. Obtain audited financial statements of investments accounted for by equity method and recalculate investment amount. Perform walkthrough procedures for determining the fair market value of investment instruments
Presentation and disclosure—Investments are properly classified as current or noncurrent and as trading, available for sale, or hold to maturity. Hedging terms are properly disclosed in footnotes.	Inquire of management as intent for holding investments. Read footnote disclosures and agree to investment documents. Calculate footnote disclosures required for derivatives. Ensure that hedges meet requirements for hedging treatment.

A securities count and reconciliation is important for management and auditors because companies have tried to substitute others' securities for missing ones. If securities have been sold and then replaced without any accounting entries, the serial numbers will show that the certificates recorded in the accounts are not the same as the ones on hand.

Derivative Instruments, Hedging Activities, and Investments in Securities (*AU 332*)

Derivative instruments are those that take their value from another asset or index. For example, an option to buy Disney stock is a derivative instrument. Interest rate swaps, options, futures contracts, and foreign currency options are also derivatives. Derivatives can be used as **hedging instruments** to protect companies from uncertainties in the marketplace. For example, a clothing manufacturer could buy futures contracts on cotton to lock the price of its main raw ingredient so that it can predict the future cost of goods sold. Likewise, companies selling overseas use currency futures to lock in the exchange rate for their sales. Accounting for derivatives is extremely complex, and new ones are constantly being developed. There are even derivatives to protect against bad weather!

Depending on why a company engages in derivative activities, the company may have only a few derivatives (e.g., foreign currency hedges to protect a few large contracts where foreign currency is the method of payment) or a large number of derivatives (commodity options to protect the company from price swings in essential raw materials). In the latter case, the auditor may need to focus on control activities and adjust the substantive testing based on the control risk assessment. When derivative activity is characterized by few transactions, the auditors likely focus on the transaction authorization and perform substantive tests on most or all of the transactions. Auditors must ensure that derivatives are recorded at their fair market value at the balance sheet date and should review derivative activities after the balance sheet date in a search for unrecorded derivatives.

AUDIT INSIGHT — Trimming the hedge?

J.M. Smucker Co., the maker of Smuckers jams, and JIF peanut butter, saw a strong first quarter on higher volumes in its key brands and expects the momentum to continue into the second quarter helped by its hedging activities taken in response to increasing coffee prices. The company said it has protected itself against exposure to coffee price fluctuations for the second quarter very well. Indeed, Smucker, whose coffee brands include Folgers and Dunkin' Donuts, said the coffee segment, which accounts for about 38 percent of its revenue, surpassed its expectations with a 7 percent increase in sales for the quarter, but the margin took a beating due to higher green coffee costs. Coffee futures have rallied about 40 percent since the beginning of March.

Source: "JM Smucker Sees Strong Q2 on Coffee Price Hedging," Reuters, August 20, 2010.

An illustrative audit plan of substantive procedures for investments and related accounts is presented in Appendix Exhibit 10B.3. Part B of this audit plan covers portfolio classification, fair value determination, and evidence about impairment.

Auditing Fair Value Measurements (*AU 328*)

GAAP pronouncements increasingly require the use of fair value for measurement of transactions and disclosure amounts. In addition, recent FASB pronouncements have required more stringent determination and more complete disclosures for investments, derivatives, and other assets and liabilities that are measured at fair value on a recurring basis. A fair value hierarchy has been established at three different levels:

Level 1. Quoted prices in active markets for identical assets.
Level 2. Significant other observable inputs.
Level 3. Significant unobservable inputs.

Disclosure is required not only as to the level for assets and liabilities but also to specific information if an item is moved between levels. For level 3 assets and liabilities, a reconciliation of the beginning and ending balances is required. These additional disclosure requirements increase the risk for assets and liabilities measured at fair value.

Auditing fair value measurements is similar to auditing accounting estimates. As with other estimates, management has primary responsibility for determining fair value in accordance with GAAP. Observable market-based values are generally preferred (level 1). However, if market prices are not readily available, clients should incorporate assumptions that would have been used by the marketplace (Level 2). If information about the assumptions is not readily available, management can use their own assumptions "as long as there are no contrary data . . ." (*AU 342*) (level 3). Thus, auditors first must determine whether a market-based value is available; if not, they must evaluate whether clients' assumptions would have been used by the marketplace or there are data contrary to what the client used—very murky waters, indeed. The auditor must take considerable care when auditing fair value calculations for level 3. These calculations use a considerable amount of judgment and estimates resulting in an increased risk of improper valuation.

AUDIT INSIGHT Another GE Innovation?

The SEC settled its long investigation into **GE's** accounting practices in August 2009, citing GE for four separate accounting violations related to derivatives and revenue recognition and fining the company $50 million. GE has wrestled with the accounting issues since 2004 and ultimately had to restate more than two years' worth of financial results—results that repeatedly won clean audit opinions from **KPMG** when first issued.

One of GE's accounting problems focused on a departure from generally accepted accounting principles to fix a misstep in GE's hedging program in which GE found itself overhedged and tried to bend its hedge plan to fit accounting requirements.

The SEC complaint describes numerous exchanges between GE and its auditors over GE's plan to alter the hedge program to achieve an accounting objective—namely, to avoid a $200 million pretax charge to earnings. The SEC said KPMG's national office was consulted when hedge problems became apparent and confirmed the company's worst fears: The hedge approach had failed and the company had to disclose it.

An accounting failure does not automatically mean there was an audit failure, says auditing consultant Douglas Carmichael, a former chief auditor for the PCAOB. "Auditing standards have a provision that essentially says that," he says. "The auditor gets reasonable assurance, not absolute assurance" that financial statements are fairly stated.

But the "reasonable assurance" threshold doesn't fully explain why KPMG gave a clean audit opinion to GE's failed accounting, at least for GE's hedge accounting problems. "Reasonable assurance usually relates to a failure to detect something," Carmichael says. "It doesn't have anything to do with not reporting something once you know about it."

Source: Tammy Whitehouse, "GE Restatement, Part II: What about the Auditors?" www.complianceweek.com, October 2009.

Trouble Spots in Audits of Investments and Intangibles

To some it might appear that the audit of investments and intangibles presented in this chapter is straightforward. After all, in many instances, we have stated that the auditor can test most, if not all, of the transactions in these areas; finding documentation for authorization is the key control. The following are some of the complex issues in the audit of investments and intangibles:

- Valuation of investments at cost or market, or impairment that is other than temporary.
- Determination of significant influence relationship for equity method investments.
- Impairment of goodwill.
- Capitalization and continuing valuation of intangibles and deferred charges.
- Propriety, effectiveness, and risk disclosure of derivative securities used as hedges of exposure to changes in fair value (fair value hedge), variability in cash flows (cash flow hedge), or fluctuations in foreign currency.
- Determination of the fair value of derivatives and securities, including valuation models and the reasonableness of key assumptions.
- Realistic distinctions of research, feasibility, and production milestones for capitalization of software development costs.
- Adequate disclosure of restrictions, pledges, or liens related to investment assets.

The practice of obtaining independent written confirmation from outside parties is fairly limited in the area of investments, intangibles, and related income and expense accounts. Securities held by trustees or brokers should be confirmed and the confirmation request should seek the same descriptive information as that obtained in a physical inspection by the auditors.

Investment costs should be vouched to brokers' confirmations, monthly statements, or other documentary evidence of cost. At the same time, the amounts of investment sales are traced to gain or loss accounts, and the amounts of sales prices and proceeds are vouched to the brokers' statements and the cash receipts journal. Auditors should determine what method of cost-out assignment was used (i.e., FIFO, specific identification, or average cost) and whether it is consistent with prior years' transactions.

Market valuation of securities is required for securities classified in trading portfolios and available-for-sale portfolios. While management may assert that an investment valuation is not impaired, subsequent sale at a loss before the end of audit fieldwork will indicate otherwise. Auditors should review investment transactions subsequent to the balance-sheet date for this kind of evidence about value impairment.

Classification of marketable securities is another management judgment that auditors must evaluate. If management classifies securities as trading securities, net income includes unrealized gains. When the market is doing well, these gains can provide significant additions to the bottom line. When the market is down, management can classify the securities as available for sale, which removes the losses from net income. Similar management judgments can move securities from noncurrent to current, thus affecting current ratios. Auditors must use their professional judgment to ensure that management is basing its classifications on sound business judgments, not their financial statement effect. However, there is often little tangible evidence in support of management responses to these audit inquiries. By consulting quoted market values for securities, auditors can calculate market values and determine whether investments should be written down in value. If quoted market values are not available, financial statements related to investments must be obtained and analyzed for evidence of basic value. If such financial statements are unaudited, they provide extremely weak evidence.

Income amounts can be verified by consulting published or online dividend records for quotations of dividends actually declared and paid during a period (e.g., Moody's and Standard & Poor's dividend records). Because auditors know the holding period of securities, dividend income can be calculated and compared to the amount in the account. Any difference could indicate a cutoff error, misclassification, defalcation, or failure to record a dividend receivable. In a similar manner, application of interest rates to bond or note investments produces a calculated interest income figure (considering amortization of premium or discount if applicable).

Inquiries should deal with the nature of investments and the reasons for holding them, especially derivative securities used for hedging activities. The classification affects the accounting treatment of market values and the unrealized gains and losses on investments. Due to the complexity of *ASC 815,* "Derivative and Hedging," auditors may need special skills or knowledge to understand clients' hedging transactions, to ensure that effective controls are in place to monitor them, and to audit the transactions.

When equity method accounting is used for investments, auditors need to obtain financial statements of the investee company. These should be audited statements. The inability to obtain financial statements from a closely held investee could indicate that the client investor does not have the significant controlling influence required by *APB Opinion No. 18.* When available, these statements are used as the basis for recalculating the amount of the client's share of income to recognize in the accounts. In addition, these statements can be used to

↳ REVIEW CHECKPOINTS

10.15 What are some of the important assertions found in investment accounts?

10.16 What are some of the typical areas of concern to auditors involving investment accounts?

10.17 How can confirmations be used in auditing investments in stocks?

audit the disclosure of investees' assets, liabilities, and income presented in footnotes, a disclosure recommended when investments accounted for by the equity method are material.

FRAUD CASES: EXTENDED AUDIT PROCEDURES (AU 316)

LEARNING OBJECTIVE 10.4
Describe common errors and frauds in the accounting for investment and financing transactions and investments, and design audit procedures for detecting them.

These cases first set the stage with a story about an accounting error or fraud. The first part of each case gives you the "inside story," which auditors seldom know before they perform this audit work. The second part of each case, under the heading "Audit Approach," tells a structured story about the audit objective, desirable controls, test of control activities, and audit of balance procedures. The third part wraps up the case with a discovery summary. At the end of the chapter, some similar discussion cases are presented, and you can write the audit approach to test your ability to design audit procedures for the detection of mistaken accounting estimates, errors, and frauds. Some substantive audit plans are in Appendix 10B.

Case 10.1

Unregistered Sale of Securities

PROBLEM

A.T. Bliss & Company (Bliss) salespeople contacted potential investors and sold limited partnership interests in the company. The setup deal called for these limited partnerships to purchase solar hot water heating systems for residential and commercial use from Bliss. All partnerships entered into arrangements to lease the equipment to Nationwide Corporation, which then rented the equipment to end users. The limited partnerships were, in effect, financing conduits for obtaining investors' money to pay for Bliss's equipment. The investors depended on Nationwide's business success and ability to pay under the lease terms for their return of capital and profit.

Bliss published false and misleading financial statements, which used a non-GAAP revenue recognition method and failed to disclose cost of goods sold. Bliss overstated Nationwide's record of equipment installation and failed to disclose that Nationwide had little cash flow from end users (resulting from rent-free periods and other inducements). Bliss knew—and failed to disclose to prospective investors—the fact that numerous previous investors had filed petitions with the U.S. tax court to contest the disallowance by the IRS of all their tax credits and benefits claimed in connection with their investments in Bliss's tax-sheltered equipment lease partnerships.

All of the money put up by the limited partnership investors was at risk but was not disclosed to investors.

AUDIT APPROACH

Management should employ experts—attorneys, underwriters, and accountants—who can determine whether securities and investment contract sales require registration. Auditors should learn the business backgrounds and securities industry expertise of the client's senior managers. They should study the minutes of board of directors meetings for authorization of the fund-raising method, obtain and study opinions rendered by attorneys and underwriters about the legality of the fund-raising methods, and inquire about management's interaction with the SEC in any presale clearance. (The SEC gives advice about the necessity for registration.)

Auditors should study the offering documents and literature used in the sale of securities to determine whether financial information is being used properly. In this case, the close relationship with Nationwide and the experience of earlier partnerships give reasons for extended procedures to obtain evidence about the representations concerning Nationwide's business success (in this case, lack of success).

DISCOVERY SUMMARY

The auditors gave unqualified reports on Bliss's materially misstated financial statements. The auditors apparently did not question the legality of the sales of the limited partnership interests as a means of raising capital. They apparently did not perform procedures to verify representations made in offering literature reflecting Bliss or Nationwide finances. Two partners in the audit firm were enjoined because of violations of the securities laws. The partners resigned from practice before the SEC and were ordered not to perform any attest services for companies making filings with the SEC. According to SEC Litigation Release 10274, AAER 20, and AAER 21, they later were expelled from the AICPA as reported in *The CPA Letter,* for failure to cooperate with the Professional Ethics Division in its investigation of alleged professional ethics violations.

Case 10.2

Off-Balance-Sheet Inventory Financing

PROBLEM

Verity Distillery Company's president incorporated the Veritas Corporation, making him and two other Verity officers the sole stockholders. The president arranged to sell $40 million of Verity's inventory of whiskey in the aging process to Veritas, showing no gain or loss on the transaction. The officers negotiated a 36-month loan with a major bank to get the money Veritas used for the purchase, pledging the inventory as collateral. Verity pledged to repurchase the inventory for $54.4 million, which amounted to the original $40 million plus 12 percent interest for three years.

The contract of sale was in the files, specifying the name of the purchasing company, the $40 million amount, and the cash consideration. Nothing mentioned the relationship of Veritas to the officers. Nothing mentioned the repurchase obligation. However, the sale amount was unusually large for a company the size of Verity.

The $40 million amount was 40 percent of the normal inventory. Veritas's cash balance increased 50 percent. The current asset total was not changed, but the inventory ratios (e.g., inventory turnover, days' sales in inventory) and quick ratio were materially altered. Long-term liabilities were understated by not recording the liability. The ploy was actually a secured loan with inventory pledged as collateral, but this reality was neither recorded nor disclosed. The total effect would be to keep debt off the books, to avoid recording interest expense, and later to record inventory at a higher cost. Subsequent sale of the whiskey at market prices would not affect the ultimate income results, but the unrecorded interest expense would be buried in the cost of goods sold. The net income in the first year when the "sale" was made was not changed, but the normal relationship of gross margin to sales was distorted by the zero-profit transaction.

	Before Transaction	Recorded Transaction	Pro forma
Assets	$530 million	$530 million	$570 million
Liabilities	390	390	430
Stockholder equity	140	140	140
Debt/equity ratio	2.79	2.79	3.07

AUDIT APPROACH

The relevant control in this case would rest with the integrity and accounting knowledge of the senior officials who arranged the transaction. Authorization in the board minutes might detail the arrangements, but, if the officials wanted to hide it from the auditors, they also would suppress the telltale information in the board minutes.

Inquiries should be made about large and unusual financing transactions. This might not elicit a response because the event is a sales transaction according to Veritas. Other audit work on controls in the revenue and collection cycle might reveal the large sale. Fortunately, this one sticks out as a large one.

Analytical procedures to compare monthly or seasonal sales probably will identify the sale as large and unusual. This identification should lead to an examination of the sales contract. Auditors should discuss the business purpose of the transaction with knowledgeable officials. If being this close to discovery does not result in an admission of the loan and repurchase arrangement, the auditors nevertheless should investigate further. Even if the "customer" names were not a giveaway, a quick inquiry of the corporation records office at the secretary of state will show the names of the officers, and the auditors will know the related-party nature of the deal. A request for the financial statements of Veritas should therefore be made.

DISCOVERY SUMMARY

The auditors found the related-party relationship between the officers and Veritas. Confronted, the president admitted the attempt to make the cash position and the debt/equity ratio look better than they were. The financial statements were adjusted to reflect the pro forma set of figures shown earlier.

Case 10.3

Go for the Gold

PROBLEM

In 2009, Alta Gold Company was a public "shell" corporation that was purchased for $1,000 by the Blues brothers. Operating under the corporate names of Silver King and Pacific Gold, the brothers purchased numerous mining claims in auctions conducted by the U.S. Department of the Interior. They invested a total of $40,000 in 300 claims. Silver King sold limited partnership interests in its 175 Nevada silver claims to local investors, raising $20 million to begin mining production. Pacific Gold then traded its 125 Montana gold mining claims for all of the Silver King assets and partnership interests, valuing the silver claims at $20 million. (Silver King valued the gold claims received at $20 million as the fair value in the exchange.) The brothers then put $3 million obtained from dividends into Alta Gold and, with the aid of a bank loan, purchased half of the Silver King gold claims for $18 million. The Blues brothers then obtained another bank loan of $38 million to merge the remainder of Silver King's assets and all of Pacific Gold's mining claims by purchase. They paid off the limited partners. At the end of 2009, Alta Gold had cash of $16 million and mining assets valued at $58 million and liabilities on bank loans of $53 million.

Alta Gold had in its files the partnership-offering documents, receipts, and other papers showing partners' investment of $20 million in the Silver King limited partnerships. The company also had Pacific Gold and Silver King contracts for the exchange of mining claims. The $20 million value of the exchange was justified in light of the limited partners' investments.

Appraisals in the files showed one appraiser's report that there was no basis for valuing the exchange of Silver King claims other than the price limited partner investors had been willing to pay. The second appraiser reported a probable value of $20 million for the exchange based on proved production elsewhere, but no geological data on the actual claims had been obtained. The $18 million paid by Alta to Silver King also had similar appraisal reports.

The transactions occurred over a period of 10 months. The Blues brothers had $37 million of cash in Silver King and Pacific Gold as well as the $16 million in Alta (all of which was the gullible bank's money, which the bank had loaned to Alta with the mining claims and production as security). The mining claims that had cost $40,000 were now in Alta's balance sheet at $58 million, the $37 million was about to flee, and the bank was about to be left holding the bag containing 300 mining claim papers.

AUDIT APPROACH

Alta Gold, Pacific Gold, and Silver King had no internal controls. The Blues brothers engineered all transactions and hired friendly appraisers. The only control that might have been effective was at the bank in the loan-granting process, but the bank failed.

The only vestige of control could have been the engagement of competent, independent appraisers. Because the auditors need to use (or try to use) the appraisers' reports, the procedures involve investigating the reputation, engagement terms, experience, and independence of the appraisers. The auditors can use local business references, local financial institutions that keep lists of approved appraisers, membership directories of the professional appraisal associations, and interviews with the appraisers themselves (AU 336).

The procedures for auditing the asset values include analyses of each of the transactions through all of the complications, including obtaining knowledge of the owners and managers of the several companies and the identities of the limited partner investors. If the Blues brothers did not disclose their connection with the other companies (and perhaps with the limited partners), the auditors need to inquire at the secretary of state's offices where Pacific Gold and Silver King are incorporated and try to discover the identities of the players in this flip game. Numerous complicated premerger transactions in small corporations and shells often signal manipulated valuations.

Loan applications and supporting papers should be examined to determine the representations Alta made in connection with obtaining the bank loans. These papers may reveal some contradictory or exaggerated information.

Ownership of the mining claims might be confirmed with the Department of Interior auctioneers or be found in the local county deed records (spread all over Nevada and Montana).

DISCOVERY SUMMARY

The inexperienced audit staff were unable to unravel the Byzantine exchanges and never questioned the relation of Alta Gold to Silver King and Pacific Gold. They never discovered the Blues brothers' involvement in the other side of the exchange, purchase, and merger transactions. They accepted the appraisers' reports because they had never worked with appraisers before and thought all appraisers were competent and independent. The bank lost $37 million. The Blues brothers changed their names.

Case 10.4
No Treasure in This Treasure Planet[2]

PROBLEM

In 2002, **Disney** had to take a last-minute write-down of motion picture production costs for the movie *Treasure Planet*. The set-in-space version of Robert Louis Stevenson's *Treasure Island* cost $140 million to make, but opening five-day revenues were only $16.7 million, compared to relatively successful *Lilo & Stitch*, which grossed $35.3 million in its first weekend.

Revenue forecasts are based on many factors, including facts and assumptions about number of theaters, ticket prices, receipt-sharing agreements, domestic and foreign reviews, and moviegoer tastes. Several publications track the box office records of movies. You can find them in newspaper entertainment sections and in industry trade publications. Of course, the production companies themselves are the major source of the information. However, company records also show the revenue realized from each movie. Revenue forecasts can be checked against actual experience and the company's history of forecasting accuracy can be determined by comparing actual to forecast over many films and many years.

The write-down in 2002 was $74 million.

AUDIT APPROACH

Revenue forecasts should be prepared in a controlled process that documents the facts and underlying assumptions built into the forecast. Forecasts should break down the revenue estimate by years, and the accounting system should produce comparable actual revenue data so that forecast accuracy can be assessed after the fact. Forecast revisions should be prepared in as much detail and documentation as original forecasts.

The general procedures and methods used by personnel responsible for revenue forecasts should be studied (inquiries and review of documentation), including their sources of information, both internal and external. Procedures for review of mechanical aspects (arithmetic) should be tested: Select a sample of finished forecasts and recalculate the final estimate.

Specific procedures for forecast revision also should be studied in the same manner. A review of the accuracy of forecasts for other movies with hindsight on actual revenues helps in a circumstantial way, but past accuracy on different film experiences do not directly influence the forecasts on a new, unique product.

The audit of motion picture development costs concentrates on the content of the forecast itself. The preparation of forecasts used in the impairment calculation should be studied to distinguish underlying reasonable expectations from hypothetical assumptions. A hypothetical assumption is a

[2] F. Ahrens, "Is Disney Losing Its Boy Appeal?" *The Washington Post,* December 19, 2002.

statement of a condition that is not necessarily expected to occur but nonetheless is used to prepare an estimate. For example, a hypothetical assumption is like an "if-then" statement: "If *Treasure Planet* sells 15 million tickets in the first 12 months of release, then domestic revenue and product sales will be $40 million, and foreign revenue can eventually reach $10 million." Auditors need to assess the reasonableness of the basic 15-million-ticket assumption. It helps to have some early actual data from the film's release in hand before the financial statements need to be finished and distributed. For actual data, auditors should review industry publications and pay special attention to competing films and critics' reviews (yes, movie reviews!).

DISCOVERY SUMMARY

The company was too optimistic in its revenue forecasts, and management did not weigh unfavorable actual/forecast history comparisons heavily enough. Apparently, management let itself be convinced that the movie was comparable to recent animated hits from other studios such as *Shrek* and *A Bug's Life*. One of the possible problems was the long development time—17 years from conception. The audit of forecasts and estimates used in accounting determinations is very difficult, especially when company personnel have incentives to hype the numbers, seemingly with conviction about the artistic and commercial merit of their productions. The high production costs finally came home to roost in big write-offs when the film was released.

REVIEW CHECKPOINTS

10.18 What unfortunate lesson did the auditors learn from the situation in Case 10.1, "Unregistered Sale of Securities"? What should auditors do when a violation of U.S. securities laws is suspected?

10.19 How could auditors have discovered the off-balance-sheet financing described in Case 10.2, "Off-Balance-Sheet Inventory Financing"?

10.20 What effect can related-party transactions have in some cases of asset valuation? (Refer to Case 10.3, "Go for the Gold.")

10.21 How should an audit team assess the reasonableness of a film studio's estimate of film revenues? (Refer to Case 10.4, "No Treasure in This Treasure Planet.")

Summary

The finance and investment cycle contains a wide variety of accounts: Capital Stock, Dividends, Long-Term Debt, Interest Expense, Income Tax Expense and Deferred Taxes, financial instruments, marketable securities, equity method investments, related gains and losses, consolidated subsidiaries, goodwill, and other intangibles. These accounts involve some of the most technically complex accounting standards. They create many of the difficult judgments for financial reporting.

Senior officials generally authorize these transactions and maintain control of them in these accounts. Therefore, internal control is centered on the integrity and accounting knowledge of these officials. The procedural controls over details of transactions are not very effective because senior managers can override them and order their own desired accounting presentations. As a consequence, auditors' work on the assessment of control risk is directed toward the senior managers and the board of directors, focusing on authorization and design of finance and investment activities. Because of the threat of management override and the high dollar value of many of these transactions, auditors ensure the occurrence and valuation of transactions as well as the existence and valuation of year-end balances. Many accounts consist of a relatively few high-dollar transactions, and, therefore, the auditor often relies on substantive testing of most, if not all, of the transactions that occurred during the audit period. See the following Auditing Insight for some deficiencies the PCAOB noted in its inspections of the Big Four audit firms regarding audits of this cycle.

AUDITING INSIGHT — PCAOB Inspections and the Finance and Investment Cycle

- Regarding the issuer's off-balance-sheet structures, the Firm failed to perform adequate tests of controls over, or perform other procedures (beyond inquiry of management) to test, the issuer's process for identifying events affecting continued off-balance-sheet accounting treatment and the completeness of the issuer's inventory of off-balance-sheet structures. Specifically, the controls tested were entity-level controls that were not precise enough to identify all such events or structures. In addition, the Firm failed to test the issuer's ongoing compliance with certain of the qualifications for the off-balance-sheet accounting used for Qualifying Special Purpose Entities, including servicing activities, clean-up calls, limits on asset sales, amendments, and events of default.
- The issuer exchanged certain of its debt for debt at a lower interest rate and extended maturity and for cash. There was no evidence in the audit documentation that the firm had performed procedures to test the issuer's accounting for the debt exchange, including testing the issuer's assumptions and calculations and analyzing the terms of the new debt.
- In connection with a merger, the issuer assumed convertible debt securities, and as a result of the merger, certain terms and features of the convertible debt securities were changed. The Firm failed to evaluate the effect of the changes on the accounting for securities. These changes include changes to the conversion and settlement options and certain contingent features.
- The Firm's audit documentation did not address whether the issuer's investments in marketable securities or U.S. government securities were appropriately classified, and the Firm did not test the issuer's evaluation of a financial derivative, even though the issuer used different inputs for that evaluation than the forward price curve would indicate.
- The Firm failed to test the fair market values of marketable securities, beyond obtaining a confirmation from the investment broker.
- The issuer held investments in certain illiquid securities. The Firm failed to perform sufficient procedures to evaluate the issuer's valuation of these securities, including the failure to evaluate the reasonableness of certain of the assumptions related to the underlying information used to develop and support the estimated fair values.
- The issuer reported a significant net equity loss from its equity-method investments. The Firm failed to apply, or request that the issuer arrange with the investees to have another auditor apply, appropriate auditing procedures to the financial results of the equity-method investees.
- The Firm failed to perform sufficient procedures concerning the valuation of the issuer's investment securities. Specifically:
    a. The Firm retained a specialist to estimate certain difficult-to-value investment securities. During interim testing, the specialist's initial fair value estimates were significantly lower than the issuer's recorded values. The specialist later increased its fair value estimates, though they remained significantly lower than the recorded values. The Firm used the specialist's work as evidence in the Firm's interim audit procedures. The Firm failed to (i) obtain an understanding of the valuation methods and assumptions used by the specialist; and (ii) evaluate whether the specialist's findings supported the related investment securities valuation assertion. Further, the Firm did not obtain an understanding of the reason for the specialist's change in fair value estimates. Also, the Firm failed to perform audit procedures to provide a reasonable basis for extending its conclusions regarding the valuation of investment securities reached at an interim date to year end.
    b. In evaluating management's conclusion that the impairment of certain available for sale securities was temporary, the Firm failed to assess what a reasonable period of time would be for the securities to recover their values.

Sources: 2006 PCAOB Inspection of Ernst & Young (January 11, 2007); 2006 PCAOB Inspection of PricewaterhouseCoopers (December 14, 2006); 2009 PCAOB Inspection of Deloitte & Touche (April 16, 2009); 2008 PCAOB Inspection of KPMG (August 12, 2008); 2009 PCAOB Inspection of McGladrey & Pullen (May 6, 2009); and 2010 PCAOB Inspection of KPMG (October 5, 2010).

Key Terms

accounting estimate: An approximation of a financial statement element, item, or account, 422

capital budget: A listing of the proposed expenditures for property, plant, and equipment or other capital items for a period of time (usually annually). The capital budget is submitted to senior management with corporate governance responsibilities for approval; is often a part of the annual budget, 416

compensating control: A control activity instituted by a company to offset the risk imposed by a weakness in another activity, 421

derivative instrument: A financial instrument whose value is based on an index or value of another financial instrument, 429

dual control: Having two people perform a task (e.g., open the mail) as a control over the process, 419

hedging instrument: An investment made to reduce the risk of adverse price movements in a security or future transaction by taking an offsetting position in a related security such as an option or a short sale, 429

indenture: A written agreement between the issuers of bonds and the bondholders, usually specifying interest rate, maturity date, convertibility, and other terms, 425

joint custody: The safeguarding of assets by placing them in a secured area that requires two people to access (e.g., a cabinet with two locks to which no individual has both keys), 419

loan covenant: A provision in a loan agreement that requires the borrower to undertake or refrain from specified actions and to maintain specified financial levels and ratios, 413

registrar: A financial institution appointed to record issue and ownership of company securities, 416

related party: A relationship between two businesses that have a personal or other association that might destroy the self-interest of one of the parties to an extent that one of them might be prevented from fully pursuing its own separate interests, 413

special purpose entity (SPE) sometimes referred to as qualified special purpose entity **(QSPE):** A partnership formed by a company to pursue particular lines of business, often used to keep risky enterprises off the company's books. QSPE is the newer term instated by the FASB, 410

stock certificate book: A book (similar to a check book) with prenumbered stock certificates. These certificates are issued to investors with the custodian of the book recording the number of shares, the owner's name, the date of issue, and other identification information; basically used only by small companies that are not traded publicly, 423

transfer agent: A bank or other company employed by a corporation to maintain shareholder records, including purchases, sales, and account balances, 416

trustee: Agent of a bond issuer who handles the administrative aspects of a loan and ensures that the borrower complies with the terms of the bond indenture, 417

Multiple-Choice Questions for Practice and Review

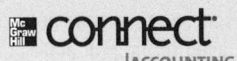 All applicable Exercises and Problems are available with McGraw-Hill's *Connect® Accounting*

LO 10-2

10.22 Which of the following approaches is most suitable for auditing the finance and investment cycle?
  a. Perform extensive tests of controls and limit substantive procedures to analytical procedures.
  b. Ignore internal controls and perform extensive substantive procedures.
  c. Gain an understanding of internal controls and perform extensive substantive procedures.
  d. Ignore internal controls and limit substantive procedures to analytical procedures.

LO 10-1

10.23 Loan covenants are used for which of the following reasons?
  a. To protect the lender from the borrower's substantially weakening of the latter's financial position.
  b. To protect the borrower from the lender's calling the loan early.
  c. To protect the auditors from false information by the borrower.
  d. To protect shareholders from management taking on too much debt.

LO 10-1

10.24 A related party is a person or entity that
  a. Has a family tie to a management member.
  b. Does business with the company.
  c. Can exert significant influence over or be influenced by the company.
  d. Is a member of the company's management team or board of directors.

LO 10-3

10.25 Jones was engaged to examine the financial statements of Gamma Corporation for the year ended June 30. Having completed an examination of the investment securities, which of the following is the best method of verifying the accuracy of recorded dividend income?
  a. Tracing recorded dividend income to cash receipts records and validated deposit slips.
  b. Performing analytical procedures and statistical sampling.
  c. Comparing recorded dividends with amounts appearing on federal information Form 1099.
  d. Comparing recorded dividends with a standard financial reporting service's record of dividends.

LO 10-1 10.26 When the client holds a large amount of negotiable securities, auditors need to plan to guard against
   a. Unauthorized negotiation of the securities before they are counted.
   b. Unrecorded sales of securities after they are counted.
   c. Substitution of securities already counted for other securities that should be on hand but are not.
   d. Substitution of authentic securities with counterfeit securities.

LO 10-3 10.27 In connection with the audit of an issue of long-term bonds payable, the audit team should
   a. Determine whether bondholders are persons other than owners, directors, or officers of the company issuing the bond.
   b. Calculate the effective interest rate to see whether it is substantially the same as the rates charged for similar issues.
   c. Decide whether the bond issue was made without violating state or local laws or regulations.
   d. Ascertain that the client has obtained the opinion of counsel on the legality of the issue.

LO 10-3 10.28 Which of the following is the most important audit consideration when examining the stockholders' equity section of a client's balance sheet?
   a. Changes in the capital stock account are verified by an independent stock transfer agent.
   b. Stock dividends and stock splits during the year under audit were approved by the stockholders.
   c. Stock dividends are capitalized at par or stated value on the dividend declaration date.
   d. Entries in the capital stock account can be traced to resolutions in the minutes of meetings of the board of directors.

LO 10-3 10.29 If the auditors discover that the carrying amount of a client's investments is overstated because of a loss in value that is other than a temporary decline in market value, they should insist that
   a. The approximate market value of the investments be shown in parentheses on the face of the balance sheet.
   b. The investments be classified as long term for balance sheet purposes with full disclosure in the footnotes.
   c. The loss in value be recognized in the financial statements.
   d. The equity section of the balance sheet separately show a charge equal to the amount of the loss.

LO 10-3 10.30 The primary reason for preparing a reconciliation between interest-bearing obligations outstanding during the year and interest expense in the financial statements is to
   a. Evaluate internal control over securities.
   b. Determine the validity of prepaid interest expense.
   c. Ascertain the reasonableness of imputed interest.
   d. Detect unrecorded liabilities.

LO 10-1 10.31 The auditors should insist that a representative of the client be present during the inspection and count of securities to
   a. Lend authority to the auditors' directives.
   b. Detect forged securities.
   c. Coordinate the return of all securities to proper locations.
   d. Acknowledge the receipt of securities returned.

LO 10-2 10.32 When independent stock transfer agents are not employed and the corporation issues its own stock and maintains stock records, canceled stock certificates should
   a. Be defaced to prevent reissuance and attached to their corresponding stubs.
   b. Not be defaced but be segregated from other stock certificates and retained in a canceled certificates file.
   c. Be destroyed to prevent fraudulent reissuance.
   d. Be defaced and sent to the secretary of state.

LO 10-3   10.33 When a client company does not maintain its own capital stock records, the auditors should obtain written confirmation from the transfer agent and registrar concerning
   a. Restrictions on the payment of dividends.
   b. The number of shares issued and outstanding.
   c. Guarantees of preferred stock liquidation value.
   d. The number of shares subject to agreements to repurchase.

(AICPA adapted)

LO 10-3   10.34 All corporate capital stock transactions should ultimately be traced to the
   a. Minutes of the meetings of the board of directors.
   b. Cash receipts journal.
   c. Cash disbursements journal.
   d. Numbered stock certificates.

LO 10-3   10.35 An audit plan for the examination of the retained earnings account should include a step that requires verification of the (choose two steps)
   a. Market value used to charge retained earnings to account for a 2-for-1 stock split.
   b. Approval of the adjustment to the beginning balance as a result of a write-down of account receivables.
   c. Authorization for both cash and stock dividends declared and paid.
   d. Gain or loss resulting from disposition of treasury shares.

LO 10-4   10.36 When an entity uses a trust company as custodian of its marketable securities, the possibility of concealing fraud most likely would be reduced if the
   a. Trust company has no direct contact with the entity employees responsible for maintaining investment accounting records.
   b. Securities are registered in the name of the trust company rather than the entity itself.
   c. Interest and dividend checks are mailed directly to an entity employee who is authorized to sell securities.
   d. The trust company places the securities in a bank safe deposit vault under the custodian's exclusive control.

(AICPA adapted)

LO 10-3   10.37 An audit team would most likely verify the interest earned on bond investments by
   a. Vouching the receipt and deposit of interest checks.
   b. Confirming the bond interest rate with the issuer of the bonds.
   c. Recomputing the interest earned on the basis of face amount, interest rate, and period held.
   d. Testing internal controls relevant to cash receipts.

(AICPA adapted)

LO 10-3   10.38 A client has a large and active investment portfolio that is kept in a bank safe deposit box. If the auditors are unable to count securities at the balance sheet date, they most likely will
   a. Request the bank to confirm to the auditors the contents of the safe deposit box at the balance sheet date.
   b. Examine supporting evidence for transactions occurring during the year.
   c. Count the securities at a subsequent date and confirm with the bank whether securities were added or removed since the balance sheet date.
   d. Request the client to have the bank seal the safe deposit box until the auditors can count the securities at a subsequent date.

(AICPA adapted)

LO 10-3   10.39 An audit team testing long-term investments would ordinarily use analytical procedures to ascertain the reasonableness of the
   a. Existence of unrealized gains or losses.
   b. Completeness of recorded investment income.
   c. Classification as available-for-sale or trading securities.
   d. Valuation of trading securities.

(AICPA adapted)

LO 10-3   10.40 In auditing for unrecorded long-term bonds payable, an audit team most likely will
  a. Perform analytical procedures on the bond premium and discount accounts.
  b. Examine documentation of assets purchased with bond proceeds for liens.
  c. Compare interest expense with the bond payable amount for reasonableness.
  d. Confirm the existence of individual bondholders at year-end.

(AICPA adapted)

LO 10-3   10.41 An audit plan to examine long-term debt most likely would include steps that require
  a. Comparing the carrying amount of held-to-maturity securities with their year-end market values.
  b. Correlating interest expense recorded for the period with outstanding debt.
  c. Verifying the existence of the holders of the debt by direct confirmation.
  d. Inspecting the accounts payable subsidiary ledger for unrecorded long-term debt.

(AICPA adapted)

LO 10-2   10.42 Which of the following questions would auditors most likely include on an internal control questionnaire for notes payable?
  a. Are assets that collateralize notes payable critically needed for the entity's continued existence?
  b. Are two or more authorized signatures required on checks that repay notes payable?
  c. Are the proceeds from notes payable used for the purchase of noncurrent assets?
  d. Are direct borrowings on notes payable authorized by the board of directors?

(AICPA adapted)

LO 10-3   10.43 An audit team's purpose in reviewing the documentation concerning the renewal of a note payable shortly after the balance-sheet date most likely is to obtain evidence concerning management's assertions about
  a. Existence.
  b. Valuation.
  c. Completeness.
  d. Classification.

(AICPA adapted)

LO 10-3   10.44 Which of the following audit procedures would *not* likely be performed for audits of investments?
  a. Read board of directors' minutes for authorization of investment strategies.
  b. Confirm investments with registrar.
  c. Confirm investments with broker or trustee.
  d. Compare valuation to published market prices.

LO 10-3   10.45 Which of the following audit procedures would *not* likely be performed for audits of shareholders' equity?
  a. Read board of directors' minutes for authorization of equity transactions.
  b. Confirm outstanding common and preferred stock with stock registrar.
  c. Compare valuation of stock to published market prices.
  d. Obtain management representation about number of shares issued and outstanding.

LO 10-3   10.46 ABC Company has 100 shares of IBM stock that it holds as an investment. The stock was purchased three years ago and has been in the client's safe deposit box along with other investment securities. During an inspection of securities held by the client, the auditor noted the 100 shares of IBM stock had a different CUSIP number than the number listed when purchased and the number verified during the previous audit. Which of the following would be the auditor's main concern about this discovery?
  a. The certificates in the safe deposit box were forgeries.
  b. There had been unauthorized buying and selling of investment securities.
  c. The securities may be misclassified on the balance sheet.
  d. ABC Company no longer own the securities.

Exercises and Problems

 All applicable Exercises and Problems are available with McGraw-Hill's *Connect® Accounting*

LO 10-2

10.47 **Internal Control Questionnaire for Equity Investments.** Cassandra Corporation, a manufacturing company, periodically invests large sums in marketable equity securities. The investment committee of the board of directors established the investment policy. The treasurer is responsible for carrying out the investment committee's directives. All securities are stored in a bank safe deposit vault. Your internal control questionnaire with respect to Cassandra's investments in equity securities contains the following three questions:

1. Is investment policy established by the investment committee of the board of directors?
2. Is the treasurer solely responsible for carrying out the investment committee's directive?
3. Are all securities stored in a bank safe deposit vault?

Required:

In addition to these three questions, what questions should your internal control questionnaire include with respect to the company's investment in marketable equity securities? (*Hint:* Prepare questions to cover management's transaction assertions of *occurrence, completeness, cutoff, accuracy, classification.*)

(AICPA adapted)

LO 10-3, 10-4

10.48 **Investment Securities.** You are engaged in the audit of the financial statements of Bass Corporation for the year ended December 31 and you are about to begin an audit of the investment securities. Bass's records indicate that the company owns various bearer bonds as well as 25 percent of the outstanding common stock of Commercial Industrial, Inc. All securities in Bass's portfolio are actively traded in a broad market. You are satisfied with evidence that supports the presumption of significant influence over Commercial Industrial, Inc. The various securities are at two locations as follows:

1. Recently acquired securities are in the company's safe in the custody of the treasurer.
2. All other securities are in the company's bank safe deposit box.

Required:

a. Assuming that the internal controls over securities are satisfactory, what are the objectives (specific assertions) for the audit of the held-to-maturity securities?
b. What audit procedures should you undertake with respect to obtaining audit evidence for the existence and cost valuation of Bass's securities in the held-to-maturity classification?
c. What audit procedures should you undertake with respect to obtaining audit evidence against Bass's investment in Commercial Industrial, Inc.?
d. What audit procedures should you undertake with respect to obtaining audit evidence about the classification of held-to-maturity securities in the Bass portfolio? (*Hint:* Review the audit plan in Appendix Exhibit 10B.3.)
e. Suppose that the held-to-maturity portfolio (excluding the investment in Commercial Industrial, Inc.) is carried at cost in the amount of $3,450,000. What audit procedures should you undertake with respect to obtaining audit evidence about the fair market value of this portfolio?
f. Suppose that the auditors determine that the held-to-maturity portfolio (excluding the investment in Commercial Industrial, Inc.) has an aggregate fair market value of $2,970,000. What audit procedures should they undertake with respect to obtaining audit evidence regarding a value impairment that might be "other than temporary?" (*Hint:* Review the audit plan in Appendix Exhibit 10B.3.)

(AICPA adapted)

LO 10-3

10.49 **Lease Accounting. Union Pacific Corp.** opened its new 19-story, $260 million headquarters in Omaha, Nebraska. The railroad operator is the owner of the city's largest building, the Union Pacific Center. Under an initial operating lease, Union Pacific guaranteed 89.9 percent of all construction costs through the building's completion date. After completing the building, the company signed a new operating lease, which guarantees 85 percent of the building's costs. Both were "synthetic" leases, which allow the company to take income tax deductions for interest and depreciation while maintaining complete operational control (Jonathan Weil, "Open Secrets: How Leases Play a Shadowy Role in Accounting," *The Wall Street Journal,* September 22, 2004).

Required:

a. Explain why Union Pacific would want to structure the lease to be an operating lease.

b. What audit evidence would you require for testing the appropriate accounting for this lease?

LO 10-3, 10-4

10.50 **Securities Examination and Count.** You are in charge of the audit of the financial statements of Demot Corporation for the year ended December 31. The corporation has a policy of investing its surplus funds in marketable securities. Its stock and bond certificates are kept in a safe deposit box in a local bank. Only the president and the treasurer of the corporation have access to the box.

You were unable to obtain access to the safe deposit box on December 31 because neither the president nor the treasurer was available. Arrangements were made for your assistant to accompany the treasurer to the bank on January 11 to examine the securities. Your assistant should be able to inspect all securities on hand in an hour. Your assistant has never examined securities in the safe deposit box and requires instructions.

Required:

a. List the instructions that you should give to your assistant regarding the examination of the stock and bond certificates kept in the safe deposit box. Include in your instructions the details of the securities to be examined and the reasons for examining these details.

b. After returning from the bank, your assistant reports that the treasurer had entered the box on January 4 to remove an old photograph of the corporation's original building. The photograph was loaned to the local chamber of commerce for display purposes. List the additional audit procedures that are required because of the treasurer's action.

(AICPA adapted)

LO 10-3

10.51 **Audit Objectives and Procedures for Investments.** In the audit of investment securities, auditors develop specific audit assertions related to the investments. They then design specific substantive procedures to obtain evidence about each of these assertions. Following is a selection of investment securities assertions:

1. Investments are properly described and classified in the financial statements.
2. Recorded investments represent investments actually owned at the balance-sheet date.
3. Investments are properly valued at the balance-sheet date.

Required:

For each of these assertions, select the following audit procedure that is best suited for the audit plan. Select only one procedure for each assertion. A procedure may be selected once or not at all.

a. Trace opening balances in the general ledger to prior-year audit documentation.

b. Determine whether employees who are authorized to sell investments have access to cash.

c. Examine supporting documents for a sample of investment transactions to verify that prenumbered documents are used.

d. Determine whether any other-than-temporary impairments in the carrying value of investments have been properly recorded.

e. Verify that transfers from the trading portfolio to the held-to-maturity investment portfolio have been properly recorded.

f. Obtain positive confirmations as of the balance sheet date of investments held by independent custodians.

g. Trace investment transactions to minutes of the board of directors meetings to determine that transactions were properly authorized.

(AICPA adapted)

LO 10-3, 10-4

10.52 **Intangibles.** Sorenson Manufacturing Corporation was incorporated on January 3, 2011. The corporation's financial statements for its first year's operations were not examined by a CPA. You have been engaged to audit the financial statements for the year ended December 31, 2012, and your work is substantially completed. A partial trial balance of the company's accounts follows:

SORENSON MANUFACTURING CORPORATION
Trial Balance
at December 31, 2012

	Debit	Credit
Cash	$11,000	
Accounts receivable	42,500	
Allowance for doubtful accounts		$ 500
Inventories	38,500	
Machinery	75,000	
Equipment	29,000	
Accumulated depreciation		10,000
Patents	85,000	
Leasehold improvements	26,000	
Prepaid expenses	10,500	
Organization expenses	29,000	
Goodwill	24,000	
Licensing Agreement No. 1*	50,000	
Licensing Agreement No. 2*	49,000	

*An intangible asset representing the right to use a patent.

The following information relates to accounts that may yet require adjustment:

1. Patents for Sorenson's manufacturing process were purchased January 2, 2012, at a cost of $68,000. An additional $17,000 was spent in December 2010 to improve machinery covered by the patents and charged to the Patents account. The patents had a remaining legal term of 17 years.

2. On January 3, 2011, Sorenson purchased two licensing agreements; at that time they were believed to have unlimited useful lives. The balance in the Licensing Agreement No. 1 account included its purchase price of $48,000 and $2,000 in acquisition expenses. Licensing Agreement No. 2 also was purchased on January 3, 2011, for $50,000, but it has been reduced by a credit of $1,000 for the advance collection of revenue from the agreement.

3. In December 2011, an explosion caused a permanent 60 percent reduction in the expected revenue-producing value of Licensing Agreement No. 1 and, in January 2012, a flood caused additional damage, which rendered the agreement worthless.

4. A study of Licensing Agreement No. 2 made by Sorenson in January 2012, revealed that its estimated remaining life expectancy was only 10 years as of January 1, 2012.

5. The balance in the Goodwill account includes $24,000 paid December 30, 2011, for an advertising program, which it is estimated will assist in increasing Sorenson's sales over a period of four years following the disbursement.

6. The Leasehold Improvement account includes (a) the $15,000 cost of improvements with a total estimated useful life of 12 years, which Sorenson, as tenant, made to leased premises in January 2011; (b) movable assembly-line equipment costing $8,500, which was installed in the leased premises in December 2012; and (c) real estate taxes of $2,500 paid by Sorenson, which, under the terms of the lease, should have been paid by the landlord. Sorenson paid its rent in full during 2012. A 10-year nonrenewable lease was signed January 3, 2011, for the leased building that Sorenson used in manufacturing operations.

7. The balance in the Organization Expenses account includes preoperating costs incurred during the organizational period.

Required:

For each of the items 1–7:

a. Prepare adjusting entries as necessary.
b. Identify the substantive audit procedures you would perform to test the transactions.

(AICPA adapted)

LO 10-1, 10-3

10.53 **Loan Covenants.** A *loan covenant* is a condition requiring the borrower to comply with the terms of a loan agreement. If the borrower does not act in accordance with the covenants, the loan can be considered in default and the lender has the right to demand payment (usually in full).

Required:

a. Why do banks add covenants to loan agreements?

b. The following is a list of common loan covenants. For each covenant, indicate what the bank is trying to accomplish by requiring it.

   (1) Maintain hazard insurance/content insurance.

   (2) Maintain key-person life insurance.

   (3) Make all payments of taxes/fees /licenses.

   (4) Provide financial information on borrower and guarantor.

   (5) Maintain a certain level in key financial ratios such as

      (a) Minimum quick and current ratios (liquidity).

      (b) Minimum return on assets and return on equity (profitability).

      (c) Minimum equity and minimum working capital.

      (d) Maximum debt to worth (leverage).

   (6) Make no change of management or merger without prior approval.

   (7) Obtain no more loans without prior approval.

   (8) Make no dividends/withdrawals or limited dividend withdrawals.

c. For each item 1–7, indicate where the auditor would be most likely to find evidence of the company's adherence with the covenant.

d. Why is it important for an auditor to review the covenants and review documents related to each item listed in (b)?

LO 10-3

10.54 **Long-Term Financing Agreement.** You have been engaged to audit the financial statements of Broadwall Corporation for the year ended December 31, 2012. During the year, Broadwall obtained a long-term loan from a local bank pursuant to a financing agreement, which provided the following:

1. The loan is to be secured by the company's inventory and accounts receivable.

2. The company is to maintain a debt:equity ratio not to exceed 2:1.

3. The company is not to pay dividends without permission from the bank.

4. Monthly installment payments are to commence July 1, 2012.

In addition, during the year, the company also borrowed, on a short-term basis, substantial amounts just prior to the year-end from the president of the company.

Required:

a. For the purposes of your audit of the Broadwall Corporation's financial statements, what procedures should you employ in examining the described loans? Do not discuss internal control.

b. What are the financial statement disclosures that you should expect to find with respect to the loan from the president?

LO 10-3

10.55 **Bond Indenture Covenants.** The following covenants are extracted from the indenture of a bond issue. The indenture provides that failure to comply with its terms in any respect automatically advances the due date of the loan to the date of noncompliance (the stated date is 20 years hence).

Give any audit steps or reporting requirements you believe should be taken or recognized in connection with each of the following:

1. "The debtor company shall endeavor to maintain a working capital ratio of 2:1 at all times and, in any fiscal year following a failure to maintain said ratio, the company shall restrict compensation of officers to a total of $500,000. Officers for this purpose shall include the board chair, president, all vice presidents, secretary, and treasurer."

2. "The debtor company shall keep all property that is security for this debt insured against loss by fire to the extent of 100 percent of its actual value. Policies of insurance comprising this protection shall be filed with the trustee."

LO 10-3

10.56 Common Stock and Treasury Stock: Substantive Audit Procedures. You are the continuing auditor of Sussex, Inc. and are beginning the audit of the common stock and treasury stock accounts. You have decided to design substantive procedures with reliance on internal controls.

Sussex has no-par, no-stated-value common stock and acts as its own registrar and transfer agent. During the past year, Sussex both issued and reacquired shares of its own common stock, some of which the company still owned at year-end. Additional common stock transactions occurred among the shareholders during the year.

Common stock transactions can be traced to individual shareholders' accounts in a subsidiary ledger and to a stock certificate book. The company has not paid any cash or stock dividends. There are no other classes of stock, stock rights, warrants, or option plans.

Required:

What substantive procedures should you apply in examining the common stock and treasury stock accounts? Organize your answer as a list of audit procedures organized by the financial statement assertions. (See Appendix 10B for examples of substantive procedures for stockholders' equity.)

(AICPA adapted)

LO 10-3

10.57 Stockholders' Equity. You are a CPA engaged in an audit of the financial statements of Pate Corporation for the year ended December 31. The financial statements and records of Pate Corporation have not been audited by a CPA in prior years.

The stockholders' equity section of Pate Corporation's balance sheet at December 31 follows:

Pate Corporation was founded in 1985. The corporation has 10 stockholders and serves as its own registrar and transfer agent. There are no capital stock subscription contracts in effect.

Required:

a. Prepare the detailed audit plan for the examination of the three accounts composing the stockholders' equity section of Pate Corporation's balance sheet. Organize the audit plan under broad financial statement assertions. (Do not include in the audit plan the audit of the results of the current-year operations.)

b. After every other figure on the balance sheet has been audited, it might appear that the retained earnings figure is a balancing figure and requires no further audit work. Why do auditors audit retained earnings as they do the other figures on the balance sheet? Discuss.

(AICPA adapted)

LO 10-4

10.58 Intercompany and Interpersonal Investment Relations. You have been engaged to audit the financial statements of Hardy Hardware Distributors, Inc., as of December 31. In your review of the corporate nonfinancial records, you have found that Hardy Hardware owns 15 percent of the outstanding voting common stock of Hardy Products Corporation. Upon further investigation, you learn that Hardy Products Corporation manufactures a line of hardware goods, 90 percent of which is sold to Hardy Hardware.

James L. Hardy, president of Hardy Hardware, has supplied you objective evidence that he personally owns 30 percent of the Hardy Products voting stock and the remaining 70 percent is owned by Juana Hardy Lewis, his sister and president of Hardy Products. Hardy also owns 20 percent of the voting common stock of Hardy Hardware Distributors, another 20 percent is held by an estate of which Hardy and Lewis are beneficiaries, and the remaining 60 percent is publicly held. The stock is listed on the American Stock Exchange.

Hardy Hardware consistently has reported operating profits higher than the industry average. Hardy Products Corporation, however, has a net return on sales of only 1 percent. The Hardy Products investment always has been reported at cost and no dividends have been paid by the company. During the course of your conversations with the Hardy siblings, you learn that you were appointed as auditor because they had a heated disagreement with the former auditors over the issues of accounting for the Hardy Products investment and the prices at which goods have been sold to Hardy Hardware.

Required:

Discuss the following.

a. Identify the issues in this situation as they relate to (1) conflicts of interest and (2) controlling influences among individuals and corporations.

b. Should the investment in Hardy Products Corporation be accounted for using the equity method?

c. What evidence should the auditor seek with regard to the prices paid by Hardy Hardware for products purchased from Hardy Products Corporation?

d. What information would you consider necessary for adequate disclosure in the financial statements of Hardy Hardware Distributors?

Instructions for Discussion Cases 10.59–10.61

These cases are designed to be similar to the ones in the chapter. They give the problem, and your assignment is to write the audit approach portion of the case organized around these sections:

Objectives. Express the objective in terms of the facts supposedly asserted in financial records, accounts, and statements.

Control. Write a brief explanation of control considerations, especially the kinds of manipulations that could arise from the situation described in the case.

Tests of controls. Write some procedures for getting evidence about existing controls, especially procedures that could discover management manipulations. If there are no controls to test, there are no procedures to perform; go on then to the next section. A *procedure* should instruct someone about the source(s) of evidence to tap and the work to do.

Audit of balance. Write some procedures for getting evidence about the *existence, completeness, valuation, rights,* and *disclosure* assertions identified in your objective section above.

Discovery summary. Write a short statement about the discovery you expect to accomplish with your procedures.

LO 10-1, 10-4

10.59 **Related-Party Transaction "Goodwill."** Write the audit approach section like the cases in the chapter.

Hide the Loss under the Goodwill

Gulwest Industries, a public company, decided to discontinue its unprofitable line of business of manufacturing sporting ammunition. Gulwest had capitalized the startup cost of the business, and with its discontinuance, the $7 million deferred cost should have been written off. Instead, Gulwest formed a new corporation, Amron, and transferred the sporting ammunition assets (including the $7 million deferred cost) to it in exchange for all Amron stock. In the Gulwest accounts, the Amron investment was carried at $12.4 million, which was the book value of the assets transferred (including the $7 million deferred cost).

Gulwest and a different public company (Big Industrial) created another company (BigShot Ammunition). Gulwest transferred all Amron assets to BigShot in exchange for (1) common and preferred stock of Big Industrial valued at $2 million and (2) a note from BigShot in the amount of $3.4 million. Big Industrial thus acquired 100 percent of the stock of BigShot. Gulwest management reasoned that it had "given" Amron stock valued at $12.4 million to receive stock and notes valued at $5.4 million, so the difference must be goodwill. Thus, the Gulwest accounts carried amounts for Big Industrial Stock ($2 million), BigShot's note receivable ($3.4 million), and Goodwill ($7 million).

Gulwest directors included in the minutes of board meetings an analysis of the sporting ammunition business's lack of profitability. The minutes showed approval of a plan to dispose of the business, but they did not use the words *discontinue the business.* The minutes also showed approval of the creation of Amron, the deal with Big Industrial, the formation of BigShot, and the acceptance of Big's stock and BigShot's note in connection with the final exchange and merger.

LO 10-1, 10-4

10.60 **Related-Party Transaction Valuation.** Follow the instructions in the preceding the case in 10.59. Write the audit approach section like the cases in the chapter.

In Plane View

Whiz Corporation owned 160,000 shares of Wing Company stock, carried on the books as an investment in the amount of $6,250,000. Whiz bought a used airplane from Wing, giving in exchange (1) $480,000 cash and (2) the 160,000 Wing shares. Even though the quoted market value of the Wing stock was $2,520,000, Whiz valued the airplane received at $3,750,000, indicating a stock valuation of $3,270,000. Thus, Whiz recognized a loss on disposition of the Wing stock in the amount of $2,980,000.

Whiz justified the airplane valuation with another transaction. On the same day it was purchased, Whiz sold the airplane to the Mexican subsidiary of one of its subsidiary companies (two layers down, but Whiz owned 100 percent of the first subsidiary, which in turn owned 100 percent of the Mexican subsidiary). The Mexican subsidiary paid Whiz with US$25,000 cash and a promissory note for US$3,725,000 (market rate of interest).

The transaction was within the authority of the chief executive officer, and company policy did not require a separate approval by the board of directors. A contract of sale and correspondence with Wing detailing the terms of the transaction were in the files. Likewise, a contract of sale to the Mexican subsidiary, a copy of the deposit slip, and a memorandum of the promissory note were on file. The note itself was kept in the company vault. None of the Wing papers cited a specific price for the airplane.

Whiz overvalued the Wing stock and justified it with a related-party transaction with its own subsidiary company. The loss on the disposition of the Wing stock was understated by $750,000.

LO 10-4

10.61 **Lack of Controls over Investments.** Follow the instructions in the preceding the case 10.59. Write the audit approach section like the cases in the chapter.

Rogue Trader

In February 1989, 22-year-old Nicholas Leeson joined Barings Investment Bank. In 1993, he began trading on behalf of the Barings group as a "proprietary trader" on the Singapore International Monetary Exchange (SIMEX). By 1995, he had wiped out the 233-year-old bank, which had counted Queen Elizabeth as a client. He left behind liabilities totaling $1.3 billion. As a proprietary trader, Leeson was to arbitrage or take advantage of differences between the prices quoted for identical contracts on SIMEX and on other exchanges. This was supposed to be achieved by entering into matching purchase and sale contracts simultaneously to capture favorable price differences. Unfortunately, Leeson entered into very large contracts that were not matched with offsetting contracts, exposing the bank to enormous potential losses from even small market movements. These trades were hidden in a separate account 88888. Transactions were transferred from other Barings accounts into account 88888 to artificially generate a profit for the other accounts.

During the period, Barings was reorganizing and Leeson reported to local managers in Singapore and product managers in London. Neither set of managers checked Leeson's activities. An internal audit report had criticized the reporting structure, but its recommendations were never implemented. Funds to finance Leeson's trades were requested from him to ostensibly fund client positions and were recorded as receivables from clients. The credit control group never reviewed the creditworthiness of the clients because they said they were never informed of the remittances.

Leeson's managers accepted reports of his profitability with admiration. They did not question the unusually large profits from his trading that would have been unlikely from an arbitrage operation.

Appendix 10A

Internal Control Questionnaires

APPENDIX EXHIBIT 10A.1 Internal Control Questionnaire: Notes Payable

	Yes/No	Comments
Environment 1. Are notes payable records kept by someone who cannot sign notes or checks? 2. Are direct borrowings on notes payable authorized by the directors? By the treasurer or by the chief financial officer? 3. Are two or more authorized signatures required on notes? **Occurrence** 4. Are paid notes canceled, stamped PAID, and filed? **Completeness** 5. Is all borrowing authorization by the directors checked to determine whether all notes payable are recorded? **Accuracy** 6. Are loan documents forwarded to accounting for review? 7. Are bank due notices compared with records of unpaid liabilities? 8. Is the subsidiary ledger of notes payable periodically reconciled with the general ledger control account(s)? Are interest payments and accruals monitored for due dates and financial statement dates? **Cutoff** 9. Are new notes recorded in the appropriate period? **Classification** 10. Is sufficient information available in the accounts to enable financial statement preparers to classify current and long-term debt properly?		

APPENDIX EXHIBIT 10A.2 Internal Control Questionnaire: Investments

	Yes/No	Comments
Environment 1. Does the board of directors authorize investment strategies? 2. Are investment structures based on legitimate business goals? 3. Are trading guidelines and limits established by company policy? 4. Are derivatives used for legitimate company objectives? 5. Are brokerage relationships reviewed for potential conflicts of interests? 6. Are personnel recording investments competent and appropriately trained to ensure the accuracy and appropriateness of journal entries? **Occurrence** 7. Are brokerage statements reconciled to the general ledger monthly? **Completeness** 8. Are company traders monitored in their discussions with brokers? **Accuracy** 9. Does accounting review all significant transactions? 10. Are purchases and sales of investments listed on brokerage statements compared to changes in the investment account? *(continued)*		

APPENDIX EXHIBIT 10A.2 *(continued)*

	Yes/No	Comments
11. Are purchases and sales of investments listed on brokerage statements compared to receipts and disbursements?		
12. Are changes in investments accounted for on the equity method monitored and recorded in the financial statements?		
13. Are accounting personnel trained in standards for hedge accounting?		
Cutoff		
14. Are purchases and sales of investments listed on brokerage statements compared to changes in the investment account to ensure they were recorded in the proper period?		
Classification		
15. Are investment classifications based on legitimate management intentions?		
16. Are disclosures reviewed by senior management?		

Appendix 10B

Substantive Audit Plans

APPENDIX EXHIBIT 10B.1

DUNDER-MIFFLIN, INC.
Audit Plan for Notes Payable and Long-Term Debt
December 31, 2013

	Performed by	Ref.
1. Obtain a schedule of notes payable and other long-term debt (including capitalized lease obligations) showing beginning balances, new notes/issuances, repayment, and ending balances. Trace to general ledger accounts. 2. Confirm liabilities with creditor: amount, interest rate, due date, collateral, and other terms. Some of these confirmations may be standard bank confirmations. 3. Review the standard bank confirmation for evidence of assets pledged as collateral and for unrecorded obligations. 4. Review loan agreements for terms and conditions that need to be disclosed and for pledge of assets as collateral. 5. Recalculate the current portion of long-term debt classified as a current liability and trace to the trial balance. 6. Inspect lease agreements for indications of need to capitalize leases. Recalculate the capital and operating lease amounts for required disclosures. 7. Recalculate interest expense on debts and trace to the interest expense and accrued interest accounts. 8. Obtain written representations from management concerning notes payable, collateral agreements, and restrictive covenants.		

APPENDIX EXHIBIT 10B.2

DUNDER-MIFFLIN, INC.
Audit Plan for Stockholders' Equity
December 31, 2012

	Performed by	Ref.

1. Obtain an analysis of stockholders' equity transactions. Trace additions and reductions to the general ledger.
   a. Vouch additions to directors' minutes and cash receipts.
   b. Vouch reductions to directors' minutes and other supporting documents.
2. Read the directors' minutes for stockholders' equity authorization. Trace to entries in the accounts. Determine whether related disclosures are adequate.
3. Confirm outstanding common and preferred stock with stock registrar.
4. Vouch stock option and profit-sharing plan disclosures to contracts and plan documents.
5. Vouch treasury stock transactions to cash receipts and cash disbursement records and to directors' authorization. Inspect treasury stock certificates.
6. When the company keeps its own stock records:
   a. Inspect the stock record stubs for certificate numbers and number of shares.
   b. Inspect the unissued certificates.
7. Obtain management representations about the number of shares issued and outstanding.		

APPENDIX EXHIBIT 10B.3

DUNDER-MIFFLIN, INC.
Audit Plan for Investments and Related Accounts
December 31, 2010

	Performed by	Ref.
A. Investments and Related Accounts		
1. Obtain a schedule of all investments, including purchase and disposition information for the period. Reconcile with investment accounts in the general ledger.		
2. Inspect or confirm with a trustee or broker the name, number, identification, interest rate, and face amount (if applicable) of securities held as investments.		
3. Vouch the cost of recorded investments to brokers' reports, contracts, canceled checks, and other supporting documentation.		
4. Vouch recorded sales to brokers' reports and bank deposit slips and recalculate gain or loss on disposition.		
5. Recalculate interest income and verify dividend income from a dividend-reporting service (such as Moody's or Standard & Poor's annual dividend record).		
6. Obtain market values of investments and determine whether any write-down or write-off is necessary. Scan transactions soon after the client's year-end to see if any investments were sold at a loss. Recalculate the unrealized gains and losses required for fair value securities accounting.		
7. Read loan agreements and minutes of the board of directors and inquire of management about pledges of investments as security for loans.		
8. Obtain audited financial statements of joint ventures, investee companies (equity method of accounting), subsidiary companies, and other entities in which an investment interest is held. Evaluate indications of significant controlling influence. Determine proper balance sheet classification. Determine appropriate consolidation policy in conformity with accounting principles.		
9. Obtain management representations concerning pledge of investment assets as collateral.		
B. Investments in Debt and Equity Securities		
1. Review the proper classification of securities in the categories of held-to-maturity, available-for-sale, and trading securities.		
a. Inquire about management's intent regarding classifications.		
b. Inspect written records of investment strategies.		
c. Review records of past investment activities and transactions.		
d. Review instructions to portfolio managers.		
e. Inspect minutes of the investment committee of the board of directors.		
2. Review whether facts support management's intent to hold securities to maturity.		
a. Consider the company's financial position, working capital requirements, results of operations, debt agreements, guarantees, and applicable laws and regulations.		
b. Inspect the company's cash flow forecasts.		
c. Obtain management representations confirming proper classification with regard to intent and ability.		
3. Review the value of debt and equity securities by performing the following:		
a. Obtain published market quotations.		
b. Obtain market prices from broker-dealers who are market makers in particular securities.		
c. Obtain valuations from expert specialists.		
d. Determine whether proprietary market valuation models are reasonable and the data and assumptions in them are appropriate.		
4. Review whether value impairments are "other than temporary," considering evidence of the following:		
a. Fair market is materially below cost.		
b. The value decline is due to specific adverse conditions.		
c. The value decline is industry or geographically specific.		
d. Management does not have both the intent and ability to hold the security long enough for a reasonable hope of value recovery.		
e. The fair value decline has existed for a long time.		
f. A debt security has been downgraded by a rating agency.		
g. The financial condition of the issuer has deteriorated.		
h. Dividends of interest payments have been reduced or eliminated.		
Stockholders' Equity		
Capital stock—10,000 shares of $10 par value authorized; 5,000 shares issued and outstanding	$ 50,000	
Capital contributed in excess of par value of capital stock	32,580	
Retained earnings	47,320	
Total stockholders' equity	$129,900	

Completing the Audit

> *It ain't over till it's over.*
>
> Yogi Berra, former catcher for the New York Yankees

Professional Standards References

Topic	AU/ISA Section	PCAOB Reference*
Terms of Engagement	210	AU 310, PCAOB Exposure Draft
Engagement Partner Review	220	AS 7
Communication with Those Charged with Governance	260	AU 380, AS 5, PCAOB Exposure Draft
Communicating Internal Control Related Matters	265	AU 325, AS 5
Evaluation of Misstatements Identified during the Audit	450	AS 13
Inquiry of a Client's Lawyer	501	AU 337
Analytical Procedures	520	AU 329
Accounting Estimates	540	AU 342
Subsequent Events and Subsequently Discovered Facts	560	AU 560, 561
Going Concern (Exposure Draft)	570	AU 341
Written Representations	580	AU 333, AS 5
Omitted Procedures	585	AU 390

*AU references represent standards issued by the ASB prior to April 16, 2003, that have not been superseded or amended by the PCAOB.

LEARNING OBJECTIVES

This chapter discusses the completion of the audit examination and identifies major events and auditors' responsibilities in the completion stage of the audit.

Your objectives are to be able to:

LO 11-1 Identify major activities performed by auditors in completing the substantive procedures following the date of the financial statements.

LO 11-2 Understand the role of attorney letters in evaluating litigation, claims, and assessments.

LO 11-3 Explain why auditors obtain written representations and identify the key components of written representations.

LO 11-4 Identify the final steps in the completion of an audit.

LO 11-5 Understand auditors' responsibility for subsequent events and subsequently discovered facts.

LO 11-6 Identify important activities and communications following the completion of the audit and audit report release date.

INTRODUCTION[1]

Dell Inc. is one of America's greatest success stories. Founded by Michael Dell in his college dormitory room in 1984 as "PCs Limited," Dell rose from humble beginnings to make its founder the youngest billionaire (at that time) at the age of 26. In 2005, Dell had a market capitalization of more than $100 billion and was recognized as "American's Most Admired Company" by *Fortune*. In popularizing the "Dell model" (where computers were built to customer specifications), Dell had the highest share of the personal computer market (19 percent). It seemed as though the future was bright and the sky was the limit.

Then everything changed. In August 2006, Dell announced an inquiry into its accounting practices by the Securities and Exchange Commission and initiated an independent investigation into these practices. The extensive scope of this investigation is illustrated by the following:[2]

- An investigation team of 125 lawyers and 250 accountants.
- Evaluation of more than 5 million documents and 2,600 journal entries.
- Completion of 233 interviews conducted with 146 individuals.

Largely because of this investigation, Dell was unable to meet its deadline for filing its fiscal year 2007 financial statements (and auditors' report on those financial statements) with the SEC. In its "Notification of Late Filing" with the SEC, Dell disclosed:[3]

> The Audit Committee is working with the management and the company's independent auditors to determine whether the accounting errors necessitate any restatements of prior period financial statements, and to assess whether the control deficiencies constitute a material weakness in Dell's internal control over financial reporting.

On August 17, 2007, Dell announced that it would restate its financial statements from 2002 to 2006 with a cumulative reduction in net income of $92 million over that period.[4] Following the investigation, Dell's auditors (**PricewaterhouseCoopers**) were able to complete their examination and filed their reports on Dell's financial statements and internal control over financial reporting on October 30, 2007 . . . more than six months after the required filing deadline of April 2, 2007 (Dell had a February 2, 2007, fiscal year-end). By that time, Dell's market capitalization had declined by more than 50 percent to $41 billion. PricewaterhouseCoopers' report on Dell's internal control over financial reporting indicated that material weaknesses in internal control existed.

Since 2007, Dell has met its filing deadlines, and their auditors encountered no issues in completing their examinations. In 2010, Dell paid $100 million to settle the SEC's fraud charges related to these restatements, apparently closing this chapter in Dell's history.

Under current rules, public companies are required to file audited financial statements with the SEC within 60 days of their fiscal year-ends. This deadline requires auditors to complete their work within a relatively short time period and ensure that all important matters are addressed and promptly resolved with clients. In this chapter, we discuss important

---
[1] Much of the background in this section is drawn from "Dell in the Penalty Box," *Fortune*, September 18, 2006, p. 72.
[2] Dell Form 8-K, August 13, 2007.
[3] Dell Form 12b-25, April 4, 2007.
[4] "Dell Details Accounting Woes," *The Wall Street Journal*, October 31, 2007, p. B3.

procedures performed by auditors in completing the audit as well as addressing matters that may arise following its completion. While the Dell case is obviously unusual, it illustrates that the completion of the audit is not always a straightforward, "check-the-boxes" activity.

Thus far in this text, we have discussed auditors' use of the audit risk model to limit exposure to audit risk, auditors' tests of controls to determine the operating effectiveness of internal control and to assess control risk (and the risk of material misstatement), and auditors' substantive procedures to determine the fairness of the account balances and classes of transactions. At this point, it seems as though little work remains to be done! Although the audit is concluding, the potential for audit failure is at its highest. Consider just a few of these questions that auditors may be asking as the audit is concluding:

- Have year-end misstatements been identified that significantly affect the financial statements?
- What events that occur after the date of the financial statements could affect the current-year financial statements?
- What potential exposure does the client have for pending litigation?
- Has the client provided all relevant information to auditors during the engagement?
- What matters need to be discussed with the individuals charged with governance of the client (normally, the audit committee)?

As shown in the following Auditing Insight, the completion of the audit is far from a straightforward, checking-the-boxes matter but involves significant auditor judgment and attention. The Public Company Accounting Oversight Board (PCAOB) identified these matters during its annual inspections for audits conducted by the Big Four firms (**Deloitte, Ernst & Young, KPMG,** and **PwC**). In this excerpt, "the firm" refers to one of these firms.

AUDITING INSIGHT — PCAOB Inspections and Completing the Audit

- The firm identified known errors that it concluded did not warrant further investigation, discussion, or adjustment to the financial statements. Some of these errors were left in the audit documentation without final disposition, despite the fact that they exceeded the firm's posting threshold.
- The firm's analytical procedures for testing operating expenses did not appropriately set a threshold for investigation of significant differences between the recorded balance and the firm's expectations; further, the firm did not document its corroboration of management's explanations for significant differences between the recorded balance and the firm's expectations.
- The firm did not perform sufficient audit procedures with respect to income tax contingencies (assessing the likelihood of occurrence, testing the amount of the estimate accrued by the client, evaluating whether the client's policy on establishing reserves was consistent with GAAP, and evaluating the client's conclusion that no reserve was required for items that were disallowed in a report received in connection with an Internal Revenue Services' audit).
- While the firm tested certain revenue transactions that occurred during the first seven months of the year, it failed to perform roll-forward procedures for the remaining five months of the year or otherwise adequately test revenues at year-end.
- While the firm obtained responses to attorneys' letters, the responses did not include an evaluation from the attorneys regarding the probability of an unfavorable outcome and the firm failed to perform additional procedures to evaluate the contingency.
- Firms did not sufficiently test or challenge management's forecasts, views, or representations that constituted critical support for amounts recorded in the financial statements.
- Deficiencies raised questions about the sufficiency, rigor, and effectiveness of the review of audit documentation, including engagement quality review. In some of these instances, the amount of time committed to an engagement quality review did not appear sufficient, given the difficulty and complexity of the engagement.

All four of the firms performed additional auditing procedures in response to PCAOB inspection findings; in all but one instance, the additional procedures did not affect the firms' conclusions, the client's financial statements, or the firms' reports on the financial statements. In the one exception, the firm's failure to identify departures from GAAP resulted in the client restating its financial statements.

Sources: 2005–2010 PCAOB Inspection of Deloitte, Ernst & Young, KPMG, and PwC. All reports can be found on the PCAOB's Website.

AUDIT TIMELINE

This chapter discusses the completion (or wrap-up) of the audit. During this time, many important issues arise and many other issues that have served as the focus of the auditors' work need to be documented. To provide an overview of the general time frame of the audit and the potential emergence of issues and matters for the auditors' consideration, consider the following broad timeline:

Beginning of Year January 1, 2012	Yaer-End Date (date of the financial statements) December 31, 2012	Date of the Auditors' Report (audit completion date) February 15, 2013	Audit Report Release Date February 17, 2013
Interim testing • Test of controls • Substantive procedures	Completing substantive procedures Attorneys' letters Written representation Going-concern assessment Adjusting journal entries Audit documentation review Subsequent events	Subsequently discovered facts	Subsequently discovered facts Omitted audit procedures Management letter Communications with those charged with governance

The preceding schematic suggests four important time periods; the first of these is prior to the year-end date under audit. Auditors often do a significant amount of tests of controls and substantive procedures prior to year-end to "spread" the audit work over a more extended period. This *interim testing* occurs between the beginning of the year (January 1, 2012) and the year-end date under audit (December 31, 2012). The year-end date is also referred to as the **date of the financial statements**, which represents the year-end date of the latest period covered by the client's financial statements.

The second time period of interest is the period from the date of the financial statements (December 31, 2012) through the completion of the audit (February 15, 2013). Although a significant amount of audit evidence is typically gathered prior to the date of the financial statements, auditors will continue to perform other procedures and gather evidence following this date. At some point, auditors will have gathered sufficient appropriate evidence on which to base their reports on the financial statements and internal control over financial reporting; this includes the review of audit documentation, preparation of the financial statements and related disclosures, and management's assertion that they take responsibility for the financial statements and disclosures. We refer to this as the **date of the auditors' report**, which is the date auditors use for their reports on the client's financial statements and internal control over financial reporting. (This date is also referred to as the *audit completion date* and, in our example, would be February 15, 2013.) Recall that the auditors' report on the entity's financial statements covers all events that occur up to this date, and, as a result, auditors need to continue to be alert for developments affecting the client.

In some instances, auditors become aware of a development affecting the client *after* the date of the auditors' report (in our example, February 15, 2013) but *prior* to the **audit report release date** (date on which auditors allow the client to use the auditors' reports in conjunction with the financial statements, in our example, February 17, 2013).[5] This is the third time period of interest to the auditor. Although this time period normally is fairly short, events occurring between the date of the auditors' report and audit report release date present significant challenges to auditors, who are no longer actively obtaining audit evidence; however, their reports have yet to be issued. The auditors' dilemma is simple: how to report on the new development without increasing the responsibility for other (unknown) developments. As discussed later in this chapter, auditors may consider dual dating the report on the financial statements to limit responsibility for other developments.

---

[5] These reports include opinions on the financial statements and the effectiveness of internal control over financial reporting. As noted in Chapter 12, both auditors' reports are dated on the audit completion date and included with the 10-K filed with the U.S. Securities and Exchange Commission (SEC).

Finally, some issues can come to auditors' attention after the audit report release date and the issuance of the client's financial statements (in our example, February 17, 2013); this is the fourth time period of interest.[6] Although Form 10-K and auditors' reports have been released, it is important that auditors take important steps to ensure that third parties do not inappropriately rely on the reports. In addition, following the audit report release date, auditors make other communications to the client and individuals charged with governance based on observations during the audit examination.

To illustrate the timing of these various activities, consider **Merck & Co.'s** 2010 financial reporting process. The following dates should be considered in light of the timeline presented earlier in this section:

- Year-end date (date of the financial statements): December 31, 2010.
- Date of the auditors' report: February 25, 2011. (The fieldwork performed by Merck's auditor, PricewaterhouseCoopers, occurred through February 25, 2011. This is the date that PricewaterhouseCoopers uses on its report on Merck's financial statements.)
- Audit report release date: February 28, 2011. (Merck filed its financial statements and auditors' reports with the SEC on February 28, 2011.)

This chapter focuses on a number of the topics addressed in the preceding timeline. In considering auditors' responsibility for various matters, it is important to consider the timing of these topics in the above timeline.

↳ REVIEW CHECKPOINTS

11.1 Identify four primary time periods in an audit examination and the tasks and activities that occur in each time period.

▽ PROCEDURES PERFORMED DURING FIELDWORK

LEARNING OBJECTIVE 11-1
Identify major activities performed by auditors in completing the substantive procedures following the date of the financial statements.

Completing Substantive Procedures

Roll-Forward Procedures

Obviously, auditors cannot issue an opinion on financial statements without examining the entire time period covered by these statements. Thus, auditors extend the work from the interim period through the date of the financial statements. For example, assume that that work was carefully planned in such a manner that auditors' interim work satisfied them that the financial statements were fairly presented as of October 15, 2012. In this case, auditors would perform additional tests of controls and substantive procedures on transactions occurring from October 16, 2012, through December 31, 2012, (assuming the client has a December 31, 2012, fiscal year-end). These procedures are often referred to as **roll-forward procedures** work because they allow auditors to *roll* the conclusion *forward* to the year-end date under audit.

Common roll-forward procedures include conducting confirmations of accounts receivable with customers, confirmations of cash balances with banks, searches for unrecorded liabilities, price tests and test counts for inventory, and so on. These procedures are often performed after the date of the financial statements out of necessity; for example, the final balances in significant customer accounts may not be known with certainty until after the date of the financial statements and, thus, cannot be confirmed with the customer until that time.

Analytical Procedures and Review of Accounts (AU 520)

Throughout the text, we have discussed the use of **analytical procedures**, which allow auditors to evaluate financial information by studying relationships among both financial

---

[6] Public entities must file annual reports with the SEC within 60 days after the date of the financial statements. Thus, audit fieldwork must be completed and auditors' reports for these companies must be dated earlier than 60 days after the date of the financial statements.

and nonfinancial data. Under the provisions of AU 520, analytical procedures can be used in three stages of the audit:

1. In the planning stage to assist auditors in planning the nature, timing, and extent of other auditing procedures.
2. In the substantive testing stage, to obtain audit evidence about particular assertions related to account balances or classes of transactions.
3. In the review stage of the audit, as an overall review of the financial information.

It is this latter use of analytical procedures that is of interest to auditors in completing the audit. In this use, auditors review the financial statements and footnotes to the financial statements to evaluate (1) the adequacy of evidence gathered in response to unexpected account balances or relationships among account balances identified during the audit and (2) unusual or unexpected account balances or relationships among account balances that were not previously identified in other stages of the audit. To illustrate, in the early 2000s, **WorldCom's** ratio of line expenses to revenues (an important metric in the telecommunications industry) was stable despite the fact that the industry was experiencing a significant downturn and industry ratios were increasing (becoming less favorable). An overall review of WorldCom's ratios, along with the auditors' knowledge of the economic conditions facing the industry, would have suggested a potential issue and triggered the need to gather additional audit evidence. In hindsight, had WorldCom's auditors (**Arthur Andersen**) performed this relatively simple analytical procedure in the review stage of the audit, one of the largest corporate frauds in history could have been averted! AU 520 requires auditors to use analytical procedures in the final review stages of the audit to assess the conclusions reached and evaluate the overall financial statement presentation.

In addition to the preceding, auditors should be alert for "miscellaneous," "other," and "clearing" accounts classified as revenues or expenses, particularly when they result from adjustments made at the end of the year or quarter. These items can be identified by scanning accounts for large and unusual entries. In many cases, these items reflect adjustments made to meet analysts' earnings expectations (known as *earnings management*) and should be more appropriately classified as *deferred items, assets, liabilities, contra-assets,* or *contra-liabilities*. **HealthSouth, Sunbeam,** and WorldCom used adjustments (which did not comply with generally accepted accounting principles) near the end of a reporting period to improve their reported earnings. If items of this nature are identified, auditors should examine related documentation and inquire of the client to verify that classification as a revenue or expense is appropriate. Recent inquiries into **Lehman Brothers'** practice of using "Repo 105s" (accounting maneuvers that involve the sale and subsequent repurchase of debt within a short period of time) to reduce reported debt near the end of fiscal quarters further illustrates the importance of auditors carefully evaluating transactions occurring near the end of the year or quarter.[7]

Review of Accounting Estimates (AU 540)

Chapters 6 through 10 discuss auditing procedures performed in the examination of various cycles. As noted in these chapters, the entity's account balances and financial statements are affected by many significant estimates that must be made by management. For example, **Best Buy** (a retailer of consumer electronics, home office products, entertainment software, appliances, and related services) identifies the following as some of the critical accounting estimates necessary in preparing its financial statements:

- Future markdown and loss reserves for valuing its inventories.
- Future cash flows from long-lived assets for evaluating potential impairment.
- Sales returns for recognizing net revenues.
- Allowance for doubtful accounts for determining the balance of accounts receivable.
- Potential benefits earned by customers under loyalty programs for accruing potential liabilities related to those programs.
- Gift card usage for determining revenue earned from the sale of gift cards.

[7] "Debt 'Masking' Under Fire," *The Wall Street Journal,* April 21, 2010, p. A1.

Because estimates, by their very nature, reflect uncertainty and future outcomes, auditors cannot "audit," "corroborate," or "verify" accounting estimates. However, auditors should consider whether estimates are *reasonable* in the circumstances. For example, it is not likely that assigning computer equipment a 20-year useful life for purposes of depreciation would be considered reasonable. Although the reasonableness of accounting estimates is assessed to some extent on an account-by-account basis throughout the audit, auditors will evaluate management's process for developing estimates as well as the overall *reasonableness* of management's estimates during the completion stage of the audit. With respect to reasonableness, auditors should ensure that estimates are consistent with one another, historical data, and industry data. In addition, auditors should consider how events occurring after the date of the financial statements may impact the reasonableness of accounting estimates. For example, a significant economic downturn may suggest that previous estimates related to uncollectible accounts are insufficient and a higher percentage of uncollectible accounts should be estimated. In a sense, this overall review of the reasonableness of accounting estimates is similar in nature and purpose to the role of analytical procedures conducted in the final stages of the audit.

↳ REVIEW CHECKPOINTS

11.2 What are roll-forward procedures? Provide some examples of them.

11.3 How are analytical procedures used in the completion stage of the audit?

11.4 What additional issues are involved with miscellaneous, other, and clearing accounts?

11.5 What are auditors' responsibilities with respect to accounting estimates made by management in the completion stages of the audit?

Attorney Letters

LEARNING OBJECTIVE 11-2
Understand the role of attorney letters in evaluating litigation, claims, and assessments.

For financial statements to be presented according to an applicable financial reporting framework (such as GAAP), all material contingencies (contingent gains or losses) must be properly accounted for and disclosed in the financial statements. According to *Accounting Standards Codification 450 (ASC 450)*, a **contingency** is [8]

> an existing condition, situation, or set of circumstances involving uncertainty as to possible gain ("gain contingency") or loss ("loss contingency") to an enterprise that will ultimately be resolved when one or more future events occur or fail to occur.

Examples of contingent liabilities include potential payments related to warranties for products and services sold by the entity, income taxes in disputes with the Internal Revenue Service, and guarantees of debt on behalf of another party. With respect to contingencies, auditors should ensure that (1) all contingencies have been appropriately identified and (2) any client disclosure of contingencies reflects the most current information and all recent developments, both favorable and unfavorable to the client. These contingencies are normally evaluated as part of the audit of the related account balances and classes of transactions and have been discussed in previous chapters of this text.

A contingent liability that requires special consideration by auditors is the uncertain outcome of litigation, claims, and assessments pending against the entity. From the auditors' standpoint, two important issues relating to pending litigation, claims, and assessments are ensuring that all pending litigation, claims, and assessments (1) have been disclosed to auditors and (2) are properly presented and disclosed in the client's financial statements. Because the client's attorneys are most familiar with the existence and classification of pending litigation, claims, and assessments, they play a very important role in auditors' evaluation of these matters.

---

[8] A current proposal would greatly expand disclosures of contingent liabilities by requiring the amount of potential monetary claims to be disclosed unless the likelihood of occurrence is judged to be "remote." However, the potential future passage of this proposal is uncertain because significant concerns have been expressed that such expanded disclosures might adversely impact potential legal judgments or cash settlements (see "Will FASB's Breadcrumb Trail Remain?" *CFO.com*, August 17, 2010).

Auditors should inquire of management and discuss potential litigation, claims, and assessments. Once this inquiry has identified litigation, claims, and assessments, auditors perform the following procedures:

- Obtain from management a description and evaluation of litigation, claims, and assessments.
- Examine documents in the client's possession concerning litigation, claims, and assessments, including correspondence and invoices from attorneys.
- Obtain assurance from management that it has disclosed all material unasserted claims the attorney has advised them are likely to be litigated.
- Read minutes of meetings of stockholders, directors, and appropriate committees.
- Read contracts, loan agreements, leases, and correspondence from taxing or other governmental agencies.
- Obtain information concerning guarantees from bank confirmations.
- Review the legal expense account, cash disbursements records, and invoices related to legal services.

The client's responsibility is to respond to auditors' inquiries and provide auditors with a description and evaluation of litigation, claims, and assessments. When auditors assess a risk of material misstatement from pending litigation, claims, and assessments, they will request that the client send an **attorney letter** (or letter of inquiry) to all attorneys who worked for the client during the period under audit. It is important to note that the client should make this request because it informs the attorney that the client is waiving the attorney-client privilege and is authorizing the attorney to provide information to auditors. The attorney letter should contain the following information (prepared from the client's perspective):

- A list of pending or threatened litigation, claims, or assessments.
- A description of each item, including the nature of the case and management responses or intended responses to the case.
- An evaluation of the likelihood of an unfavorable outcome.
- An estimate of the range of potential loss.

Review the following diagram for the flow of correspondence related to the attorney letter. The process begins when auditors request the client to send a letter to its attorney(s) (step 1). In step 2, the attorney receives the letter from the client asking the attorney to respond to the letter (step 3). The *attorney's response* should be provided *directly* to auditors for purposes of control and should explain any matters noted in the attorney letter in which the attorney's view differs from the information in the letter. For example, the client may indicate that the likelihood of an unfavorable outcome is "remote," but the attorney may believe that it is higher than "remote." In addition, the attorney may inform auditors of pending litigation, claims, or assessments not included in the attorney letter.

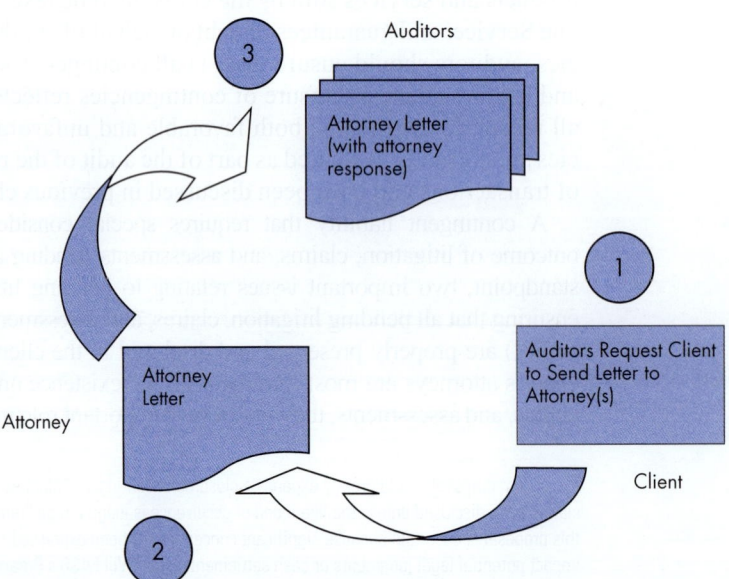

EXHIBIT 11.1
Role of Various Parties in Audit of Litigation, Claims, and Assessments

Party	Responsibilities
Auditors	• Inquire of client regarding the existence of litigation, claims, and assessments. • Perform various procedures regarding litigation, claims, and assessments. • Initiate request to the client for attorney letter.
Client	• Respond to auditors' inquiries regarding litigation, claims, and assessments. • Provide auditors a list, description, and evaluation of litigation, claims, and assessments. • Send letter to attorney (attorney letter) that includes information related to litigation, claims, and assessments.
Attorney	• Respond to auditors regarding client's description of litigation, claims, and assessments contained in the attorney letter.

The general roles of the client, auditors, and attorney(s) in this process are summarized in Exhibit 11.1.

See Exhibit 11.2 for a sample attorney letter.

Unasserted claims raise additional issues for attorney letters. An **unasserted claim** represents that no formal lawsuit or claim has been filed or threatened on behalf of others but that circumstances such as a catastrophe, accident, or other physical occurrence could result in a suit or claim being filed in the future. In these cases, attorneys must consider the likelihood that a lawsuit or claim will be filed as well as the possibility of an unfavorable outcome when responding to the attorney letter.

Because unasserted claims have not been filed, the issue of client disclosure of these matters to auditors is less clear. Attorneys should encourage their clients to disclose this information to auditors when the assertion of a claim is at least *probable.* However, the American Bar Association's guidelines to attorneys do not require them to disclose unasserted claims to auditors unless the client specifically lists them in the attorney letter. Thus, auditors must rely on the attorney to inform the client (not the auditors) if an unasserted claim must be disclosed. As shown in Exhibit 11.2, the attorney letter explicitly asks that this understanding be communicated to the client's auditors through the attorney's response.

AUDITING INSIGHT — Microsoft's Contingencies

In its 2010 10-K, **Microsoft**, a company that develops, manufactures, licenses, and supports software and other computer-related products, disclosed the following contingencies in its footnotes to the financial statements:

- The appeal of a fine paid to the European Commission related to pricing terms on Microsoft's products licensed to competitors.
- An investigation by the European Commission related to the interoperability of Microsoft Office products.
- Numerous antitrust and unfair competition lawsuits related to sales of Microsoft's operating system and other software products.
- An appeal by Novell on dismissals of antitrust claims against Microsoft related to Novell's ownership of a competing product (WordPerfect).
- Various patent and intellectual property claims (a total of 54, 10 of which were set for trial in the upcoming year).

In response to these contingencies, Microsoft accrued more than $1.2 billion in liabilities. However, Microsoft notes that adverse outcomes that "... we could estimate" could result in an additional $800 million of liabilities. To the extent that external auditors are involved in this litigation, issues related to these actions would be included in attorney letters.

Source: Microsoft 2010 10-K, July 30, 2010.

⤷ REVIEW CHECKPOINTS

11.6 What are the responsibilities of (a) client management, (b) auditors, and (c) the client's attorneys with respect to obtaining evidence regarding litigation, claims, and assessments?

11.7 What is the typical content of attorney letters?

11.8 In addition to obtaining responses to attorney letters, what other procedures can be used to gather audit evidence regarding litigation, claims, and assessments?

EXHIBIT 11.2 Sample Attorney Letter

DUNDER-MIFFLIN
1725 Slough Avenue
Scranton, PA 18501

March 2, 2013

Jackie Childs
Childs and Dunn
280 East 23rd Street
New York, NY 21005

> *Information is provided by management*

In connection with an audit of our financial statements at December 31, 2012, and for the year then ended, management of Dunder-Mifflin has prepared, and furnished to Michael Scarn, LLP, P.O. Box 10024, Scranton, PA 18501, a description and evaluation of certain contingencies, including those set forth below involving matters with respect to which you have been engaged and to which you have devoted substantive attention on behalf of Dunder-Mifflin in the form of legal consultation or representation. These are regarded by the management of Dunder-Mifflin as material for this purpose. Your response should include matters that existed at December 31, 2012, and during the period from that date to the date of your response.

[Add description of pending or threatened litigation]

Please furnish to our auditors such explanation, if any, that you consider necessary to supplement the foregoing information, including an explanation of those matters as to which your views may differ from those stated and an identification of the omission of any pending or threatened litigation, claims, and assessments or a statement that the list of such matters is complete.

> *Attorneys indicate whether view differs from management's views*

[Add description of unasserted claims and assessments]

Please furnish to our auditors such explanation, if any, that you consider necessary to supplement the foregoing information, including an explanation of those matters as to which your views may differ from those stated.

We understand that whenever, in the course of performing legal services for us with respect to a matter recognized to involve an unasserted possible claim or assessment that may call for financial statement disclosure, if you have formed a professional conclusion that we should disclose or consider disclosure concerning such possible claim or assessment, as a matter of professional responsibility to us, you will so advise us and will consult with us concerning the question of such disclosure and the applicable requirements of Financial Accounting Standards Board (FASB) Accounting Standards Codification (ASC) 450, *Contingencies*. Please specifically confirm to our auditors that our understanding is correct.

Please specifically identify the nature of and reasons for any limitation on your response.

Signed:

Cosmo Kramer
Cosmo Kramer, Chief Executive Officer

Source: Adapted from AU 501.A69.

Written Representations

LEARNING OBJECTIVE 11-3
Explain why auditors obtain written representations and identify the key components of written representations.

Under section 302 of the Sarbanes-Oxley Act of 2002 (Sarbanes-Oxley), all 10-Q and 10-K filings with the SEC are required to include certifications from the chief executive officer and chief financial officer related to the fairness of the financial statements and effectiveness of the internal control over financial reporting. However, these are only some representations that the client makes. As noted in previous chapters, an important source of audit evidence is inquiries of client personnel. Many of the responses to these inquiries are very important. To the extent that additional evidence is obtainable through other procedures, auditors should corroborate these representations.

AU 580 requires that auditors obtain **written representations** (also known as *management representations* or *client representations*) to confirm certain matters and support other evidence obtained during the audit. The representations take the form of a letter on the client's letterhead addressed to auditors and signed by responsible officers of the client (normally the chief executive officer [CEO], chief financial officer [CFO], and other appropriate officers). These representations are dated as of the date of the auditors' reports, which is the date the audit is completed (in fact, the completion of the audit depends on auditors' receipt of assertions from management regarding its responsibility for the fairness of the financial statements and related disclosures through written representations). Thus, written representations cover events and representations running beyond the date of the financial statements up to this date.

It is important to note that written representations are not substitutes for corroborating evidence obtained by applying other substantive procedures. That is, auditors cannot substitute client inquiry (and representations regarding that inquiry) for substantive procedures. For example, the representation that "management told us that the inventory costing method was FIFO and adequate allowance for obsolescence was provided" is not a good excuse for failing to obtain the evidence from the records and other sources.

However, in some cases, written representations are the only available evidence about important matters of management intent. For example, the following representations (written by the client's management) provide auditors important audit evidence regarding presentation and disclosure matters:

- "We will discontinue the parachute manufacturing business, wind down the operations, and sell the remaining assets" (classification of the parachute manufacturing business as a discontinued operation).
- "We will exercise our option to refinance the maturing debt on a long-term basis" (classification of the maturing debt as long-term debt).

Exhibit 11.3 is a sample written representations in the form of a letter from the client to auditors. As noted earlier, it is written by the client (specifically, key officers) to auditors and is dated March 2, 2013 (the date of the auditors' report). Notice from Exhibit 11.3 that the representations are organized into three sections that discuss:

1. The entity's financial statements, including:
   - Management's responsibilities for the financial statements and internal control over financial reporting.
   - The appropriate disclosure, presentation, and reasonableness of certain items (accounting estimates, related parties, subsequent events, and litigation and claims).
   - A statement that uncorrected misstatements are immaterial to the financial statements taken as a whole.
2. Information provided to the auditors, both in general and related to sensitive areas (fraud, noncompliance with laws and regulations, litigation, and related-party transactions).
3. Internal control over financial reporting (for audits of public entities).

EXHIBIT 11.3 Sample Written Representations

DUNDER-MIFFLIN
1725 Slough Avenue
Scranton, PA 18501

To: Michael Scarn LLP *— Representations addressed to auditors*

March 2, 2013

This representation letter is provided in connection with your audit of the financial statements of Dunder-Mifflin, which comprise the balance sheet as of December 31, 2012, and the related statements of income, changes in stockholders' equity and cash flows for the year then ended, and the related notes to the financial statements, for the purpose of expressing an opinion as to whether the financial statements are presented fairly, in all material respects, in accordance with accounting principles generally accepted in the United States (U.S. GAAP).

Certain representations in this letter are described as being limited to matters that are material. Items are considered material, regardless of size, if they involve an omission or misstatement of accounting information that, in the light of surrounding circumstances, makes it probable that the judgment of a reasonable person relying on the information would be changed or influenced by the omission or misstatement.

Except where otherwise stated below, immaterial matters are not considered to be exceptions that require disclosure for the purpose of the following representations. This amount is not necessarily indicative of amounts that would require adjustment to or disclosure in the financial statements.

We confirm that, to the best of our knowledge and belief, having made such inquiries as we considered necessary for the purpose of appropriately informing ourselves as of March 2, 2013:

Financial Statements

- We have fulfilled our responsibilities, as set out in the terms of the audit engagement dated March 1, 2012, for the preparation and fair presentation of the financial statements in accordance with U.S. GAAP.
- We acknowledge our responsibility for the design, implementation, and maintenance of internal control relevant to the preparation and fair presentation of financial statements that are free from material misstatement, whether due to fraud or error.
- We acknowledge our responsibility for the design, implementation, and maintenance of internal control to prevent and detect fraud.

[Detail omitted; see AU 580.A36]

Information Provided

- We have provided you with:
  — Access to all information, of which we are aware that is relevant to the preparation and fair presentation of the financial statements such as records, documentation and other matters;
  — Additional information that you have requested from us for the purpose of the audit; and
  — Unrestricted access to persons within the entity from whom you determined it necessary to obtain audit evidence.
- All transactions have been recorded in the accounting records and are reflected in the financial statements.
- We have disclosed to you the results of our assessment of the risk that the financial statements may be materially misstated as a result of fraud.

[Detail omitted; see AU 580.A36]

Representations related to financial statements and disclosures

Internal Control over Financial Reporting [for audits of public entities under *AS 5*]:

- We have performed an assessment of the effectiveness of internal control over financial reporting based on criteria established in Internal Control — Integrated Framework issued by the Committee on Sponsoring Organizations of the Treadway Commission (COSO criteria).
- Based on this assessment, we conclude that we have maintained an effective internal control over financial reporting as of December 31, 2012.
- We have disclosed to you all deficiencies in the design or operation of internal control over financial reporting, including separate disclosure of any deficiencies that we believe to be significant deficiencies or material weaknesses.
- There are no subsequent changes in internal control over financial reporting or other factors that may significant affect internal control over financial reporting.

Representations related to internal control over financial reporting

Signed:

Cosmo Kramer
Cosmo Kramer, Chief Executive Officer

Newman Post
Newman Post, Chief Financial Officer

Representations provided and signed by management

Source: *AS 5* and AU 580.A36.

Although representations should be limited to matters that are material, professional standards note that materiality guidelines do not apply for representations not related to amounts included in the financial statements (such as management's responsibility for the financial statements) or for management's acknowledgement regarding its responsibility for designing, implementing, and maintaining internal control to prevent and detect fraud.

Clearly, written representations are a critical part of auditors' overall ability to support the opinion on the financial statements. As a result, management's refusal to furnish representations constitutes a scope limitation, which requires a qualification in the auditors' report on the entity's financial statements or a disclaimer of opinion. Auditors should be very skeptical of any situation in which the client's management refuses to furnish representations.

In addition to those discussed, auditors may obtain representations related to specific transactions or activities, particularly if they have a material effect on the companies' financial statements. See the accompanying Auditing Insight for an example of such a representation (although in this case, some questions as to the validity of the representation were raised).

AUDITING INSIGHT — Can You Trust Written Representations?

Gemstar-TV Guide International, Inc., a media, entertainment, and technology company headquartered in Los Angeles, California, engaged in a massive scheme to inflate its revenue; the most significant fraudulent transaction was $100 million in revenue from an expired contract with **Scientific-Atlanta, Inc.** Gemstar's auditor (**KPMG**) raised specific questions about the Scientific-Atlanta transaction and received written assurance from Henry Yuen (then CEO of Gemstar) and Elsie Leung (then CFO) that the revenue from Scientific-Atlanta was legitimate and would be received. Brian Palbaum, the KPMG partner involved with this audit, indicates that Yuen and Leung "may have misled [him] about the status of the settlement negotiations with Scientific-Atlanta."

Source: "As Fraud Case Unravels, Executive Is at Large," *The Wall Street Journal*, April 25, 2007, pp. A1, A9.

↳ REVIEW CHECKPOINTS

11.9 What are the major categories of information contained in written representations?

11.10 If the entity is subject to the requirements of *AS 5*, what written representations should auditors obtain from the client with respect to internal control over financial reporting?

11.11 Why are written representation and attorney letters obtained near the end of the evidence-gathering process and dated on the date of the auditors' report?

11.12 How should auditors respond if the client refuses to furnish written representations?

LEARNING OBJECTIVE 11-4
Identify the final steps in the completion of an audit.

Ability to Continue as a Going Concern

As auditors gather evidence throughout the engagement, information may be encountered that raises questions as to the client's ability to continue as a going concern, such as:

- Negative trends, including recurring operating losses, working capital deficiencies, and negative cash flow from operations.
- Indications of financial difficulties, including default on loans, denial of trade credit from suppliers, restructuring of debts, or arrearages in dividends.

- Internal matters, including work stoppages or substantial dependence on the success of a particular project or activity.
- External matters, including legal proceedings; loss of a key franchise, license, or patent; or loss of a major customer or supplier.

Auditors are not expected to design and perform procedures solely for the purpose of identifying conditions that indicate going-concern uncertainties. However, procedures performed during the normal course of the audit might reveal such situations. For example, performing analytical procedures may reveal deteriorating profitability and cash flows, which may indicate the client's inability to continue as a going concern. Also, communications received from client attorneys (discussed earlier in this chapter) might reveal litigation that could significantly threaten the client's ability to continue to exist.

Auditors are required to consider whether any evidence that comes to their attention during the examination provides "*substantial doubt*" about the client's ability to continue as a going concern for a period of time not to exceed one year beyond the date of the financial statements being audited. Once again, auditors are not required to perform additional procedures during the completion stages designed to assess going-concern status. However, they are required to consider evidence obtained and accumulated throughout the audit and make an overall evaluation as to whether substantial doubt exists with respect to the ability of the client to continue as a going concern.

If the auditor's evaluation suggests going-concern uncertainties, auditors should obtain information about management's plans to mitigate the effect of these factors and assess the likelihood that these plans can be effectively implemented. For example, clients may have the ability to delay or reduce expenditures, restructure existing debt on more favorable terms, or access additional sources of financing. If so, and these actions would allow the client to continue in operations, auditors may conclude that the likelihood of going-concern uncertainties is low. In this instance, auditors would likely conclude that substantial doubt about going concern *does not* exist and no further financial statement disclosures or audit report modifications would be necessary.

In contrast, if after this evaluation, auditors still believe that substantial doubt exists about the client's ability to continue as a going concern, they should ensure that appropriate disclosures related to going concern are provided in the financial statements and modify their opinion on the client's financial statements. Depending upon the severity of the going-concern uncertainty, an unqualified opinion, qualified opinion, or disclaimer of opinion may be issued; the specific report modifications for going-concern uncertainties are discussed in Chapter 12.

In all cases, audit documentation should include information related to the (1) conditions or events that suggested going-concern uncertainties, (2) management's plans to mitigate going-concern uncertainties and the audit procedures performed to evaluate management's plans, and (3) the auditors' conclusion as to whether substantial doubt exists about the client's ability to continue as a going concern and whether the audit report needs to be modified to reflect that substantial doubt.

AUDITING INSIGHT | Going Concerns at Borders

In early 2011, **Borders Group, Inc.,** (the second largest bookstore chain in the United States) announced it was seeking to delay payments to some of its publishers as part of efforts to refinance its debt. Borders indicated that "there can be no assurance" that their refinancing efforts will be successful and, if they are not, they could experience a liquidity shortfall in the first quarter of 2011. Borders has also experienced net losses in 9 of the last 11 quarters. Both issues suggest potential going-concern uncertainties. On April 13, 2011, Borders notified the SEC that, because of these financial difficulties, it would delay filing its 2010 financial statements; these statements were ultimately filed on April 29, 2011 and Borders' auditors (**Ernst & Young**) modified their opinion to acknowledge Borders' going-concern uncertainties. On July 19, 2011, Borders announced that it would liquidate and close its remaining 399 stores.

Sources: "Borders Delays Payments to Publishers," *The Wall Street Journal,* December 31, 2010, p. B1; "Borders to Ask Publishers to Agree to Longer IOUs," *The Wall Street Journal,* January 5, 2011, p. B1; "Borders Forced to Liquidate, Close All Stores," *The Wall Street Journal,* July 19, 2011, p. B1.

Adjusting Entries and Financial Statement Disclosure

The financial statements, including the accompanying footnotes, are the responsibility of the client's management, although auditors frequently draft them. Thus, although auditors could detect some misstatements in the financial statements during the examination, it is the client's responsibility to adjust the financial statements. Even when the failure to adjust the financial statements would result in materially misstated financial statements, it is the client's decision as to whether to accept auditors' proposed adjustments.

Exhibit 11.4 is a summary worksheet ("score sheet") showing the effect of proposed adjusting journal entries. In this example, three potential adjustments were noted during the audit: (1) recording payments on account to vendors made prior to year-end, (2) reversing sales entries that were incorrectly recorded in the current year, and (3) recording items discovered during the auditors' search for unrecorded liabilities. In addition, a fourth adjustment reflects the income tax effects of these adjustments (if recorded by the client). These adjustments are considered to be *proposed* to indicate the responsibility of management

EXHIBIT 11.4
Proposed Adjusting Journal Entries (Score Sheet)

	Income Statement	Balance Sheet		
	Increase (Decrease) Net Income	Increase (Decrease) Assets	Increase (Decrease) Liabilities	Increase (Decrease) Equity
(1) Unrecorded cash disbursements				
Accounts payable			($42,000)	
Cash		($42,000)		
(2) Improper sales cutoff:				
Sales	($13,000)			($13,000)
Inventory		7,800		
Cost of goods sold	7,800			7,800
Accounts receivable		(13,000)		
(3) Unrecorded liabilities:				
Utilities expense	(700)			(700)
Commissions expense	(3,000)			(3,000)
Wage expense	(2,500)			(2,500)
Accounts payable			700	
Accrued expenses payable			5,500	
Net effect before taxes	($11,400)	($47,200)	($35,800)	($11,400)
(4) Reduction in income taxes ($11,400 × 0.35)				
Income tax expense	3,990			3,990
Income taxes payable			(3,990)	
Current-year effects	($7,410)	($47,200)	($39,790)	($7,410)
Uncorrected misstatements from prior audits	($18,000)			($18,000)
Cumulative effect of uncorrected misstatements	($25,410)			($25,410)

Conclusion: Uncorrected misstatements from previous audits had a net debit effect of $18,000 on the income statement (decrease in net income) and a net credit effect on the balance sheet (decrease in net assets, or equity). When considered with the $7,410 effect noted in the current year, the cumulative uncorrected misstatements ($25,410) are less than performance materiality ($100,000). As a result, no adjustment to the financial statements is considered necessary.

for the financial statements. This summary indicates how the proposed adjustments would affect the financial statements and helps auditors decide which adjustments must be made to support an unqualified opinion on the financial statements and which adjustments may be waived (or not corrected). An **uncorrected misstatement** is a misstatement that the auditor has identified and accumulated during that audit that the client has not corrected (or adjusted). Prior to the issuance of Sarbanes-Oxley, evidence suggests that a large number of misstatements were not corrected.[9]

As shown in Exhibit 11.4, the misstatements have a current year $7,410 debit (decrease) effect on net income and a $7,410 credit (decrease) effect on net assets. In addition, note that $18,000 of uncorrected misstatements was identified in previous audits. If performance materiality were established at $100,000, auditors could decide not to require adjustment of these misstatements because doing so would not result in materially misstated financial statements. However, *Staff Accounting Bulletin No. 99* notes that auditors and clients should not simply decline to adjust "apparently" immaterial misstatements without giving consideration to a number of other factors (such as the effect of adjusting the misstatement on debt covenants).

An important issue with respect to the auditors' adjustment recommendation is whether a number of uncorrected misstatements in previous years will accumulate over time to have a material effect on an entity's financial statements in a future year. For example, if performance materiality is $100,000 and an entity fails to accrue a $25,000 liability for unused sick pay (which will not be paid until employees retire) each year for four years, this matter will not have a material effect on the income statement in any individual year. However, assuming this obligation has not been paid, at least in part, by the end of year 4, the cumulative effect on the entity's balance sheet would become material ($100,000).

Auditors may use either of two methods to evaluate the materiality of uncorrected misstatements. The **rollover method** considers only the current-period income effect(s); in the example shown in Exhibit 11.4, when using the rollover method, auditors would consider the misstatement to be $7,410. In contrast, the **iron curtain method** considers the aggregate effect of the misstatements on the entity's balance sheet; when using the iron curtain method, auditors would consider the misstatement to be $25,410 (the $7,410 of current-year adjustments and the $18,000 of uncorrected prior-year adjustments). In September 2006, the Securities and Exchange Commission issued *Staff Accounting Bulletin No. 108,* which requires auditors to evaluate misstatements using both methods and propose an adjustment if either method indicates that the misstatement is material. Because neither the amount of the current-year uncorrected misstatement in Exhibit 11.4 ($7,410) nor the cumulative effect of uncorrected misstatements ($25,410) exceeds performance materiality of $100,000, the auditors would conclude that the financial statements are not materially misstated. Although auditors could recommend the client adjust its financial statements for all known adjustments, no adjustment is required in this situation.

Auditors are required to communicate all misstatements detected during the audit to the client's audit committee (or other individuals charged with governance). These should be communicated regardless of whether they have a material effect on the financial statements. A recent report issued by the PCAOB noted that a common deficiency observed by inspection teams was the failure of audit teams to accumulate all uncorrected misstatements and communicate these to the audit committee.[10] Auditors' identification of material misstatements is

---

[9] For example, an academic study of audits performed by Deloitte & Touche (then Deloitte, Haskins & Sells) reported that 75 percent of all detected errors were not corrected; see C. Houghton and J. Fogarty, "Inherent Risk," *Auditing: A Journal of Practice & Theory* Spring 1991, pp. 1–21. A similar study of audits conducted by an unnamed international public accounting firm found a corresponding rate of 65 percent ; see A. Wright and S. Wright, "An Examination of Factors Affecting the Decision to Waive Audit Adjustments," *Journal of Accounting, Auditing, & Finance* Winter 1997, pp. 15–36. However, J. Joe et al. concluded that the additional scrutiny faced by auditors from the Sarbanes-Oxley Act may, in part, account for a much lower percentage of uncorrected misstatements in their study (24.2%); see "The Impact of Client and Misstatement Characteristics on the Disposition of Proposed Audit Adjustments," *Auditing: A Journal of Practice and Theory,* May 2011, pp. 103–124.

[10] *Report on the PCAOB's 2004, 2005, 2006, and 2007 Inspections of Domestic Annually Inspected Firms,* PCAOB Release No. 2008-008, December 5, 2008.

normally considered to be a "strong indicator" of a material weakness in internal control over financial reporting even if these misstatements are ultimately adjusted by the client.

> ### AUDITING INSIGHT | Auditors and Restatements

XEROX

In 2003, the Securities and Exchange Commission filed suit against **KPMG** for civil fraud and accused the firm of "knowingly and recklessly" misleading investors on its audits of **Xerox**. However, when it came to adjustments, KPMG's main partner on the Xerox audit (Ronald Safan) was extremely stringent. Safan insisted that virtually every audit adjustment be recorded, including immaterial amounts that were not required for the financial statements to be prepared in conformity with generally accepted accounting principles. In fact, during 2001, Xerox had to delay filing its annual report due to a disagreement with KPMG over accounting issues.

Epilogue: On April 11, 2002, Xerox agreed to a $10 million fine with the SEC and restated its financial statements from 1997 to 2001; on April 21, 2005, KPMG agreed to pay $22.5 million to the SEC to settle charges related to its audits of Xerox. On March 28, 2008, Xerox agreed to pay $670 million and KPMG $80 million to settle shareholder lawsuits.

Sources: "KPMG's Auditing with Xerox Tests Toughness of SEC," *The Wall Street Journal*, May 6, 2002, p. A10; "Xerox: New Lease on Life," *CFO.com*, October 24, 2003; "KPMG Settles Xerox Charges with SEC," *CFO.com*, April 21, 2005; "Xerox to Pay $670 Million to Settle Securities Suit," *The Wall Street Journal*, March 28, 2008, p. B3.

ACADEMIC INSIGHTS

A significant amount of academic research has evaluated the process through which auditors and clients "negotiate" with respect to adjustments identified during the audit examination. These studies demonstrate that this process is prevalent; Gibbins et al. (2001) found that 67 percent of audit partners entered into some level of negotiation with more than one-half of their clients and that all partners have negotiated with at least one client. Some interesting conclusions in these studies include:

- While approximately one-third of surveyed chief financial officers (CFOs) and audit partners indicated they "won" the negotiation (34 percent for CFOs and 32 percent for auditors), both groups indicated that negotiations resulted in a compromise (26 percent for CFOs and 41 percent for auditors) or a new solution generated during the negotiation (17 percent for CFOs and 16 percent for auditors) (Gibbins et al., 2005). (Each group was asked to recall an auditor–client negotiation and was not necessarily considering the same negotiation).

- Factors considered as important by CFOs in the outcome of the negotiation include accounting and disclosure standards, the prior relationship with the audit partner, the organization's (client's) accounting expertise, and the audit firm's accounting expertise; auditors primarily considered accounting and disclosure standards and the audit firm's accounting expertise as important in influencing the outcome of the negotiation (Gibbins et al., 2005).

- The (income-decreasing) adjustments proposed by auditors are smaller in cases in which the magnitude of the audit difference is higher and when the client has previously conceded with respect to an audit issue (Hatfield et al., 2010).

Sources: M. Gibbins, S. Salterio, and A. Webb, "Evidence about Auditor–Client Management Negotiation Concerning Client's Financial Reporting," *Journal of Accounting Research,* December 2001, pp. 535–563; M. Gibbins, S. McCracken, and S. Salterio, "Negotiations over Accounting Issues: The Congruency of Audit Partner and Chief Financial Officer Recalls," *Auditing: A Journal of Practice & Theory,* Supplement 2005, pp. 171–193; R.C. Hatfield, R.W. Houston, C.M. Stefaniak, and S. Usrey, "The Effect of Magnitude of Audit Differences and Prior Client Concessions on Negotiations of Proposed Adjustments," *The Accounting Review,* September 2010, pp. 1647–1668.

Audit Documentation Review

During fieldwork, the audit supervisor—and sometimes the audit manager—reviews the audit documentation soon after the audit staff complete it. The general purpose of this review is to ensure that all appropriate steps in the audit plan were performed, the referencing among audit documentation is clear, and the explanations contained in the audit documentation are understandable. In general, the supervisor is attempting to determine that the work was performed with due care and that, if necessary, the work can be reperformed or verified by another party. A common outcome of this review is a set of "review notes" prepared by the audit supervisor that are to be completed or addressed by the audit staff; these notes address the procedures performed, the referencing among audit documentation, and the appropriateness of the audit staff member's conclusions based upon the procedures performed. This review process provides evidence of compliance with the performance principle, which requires proper planning and supervision.

When this initial review has been completed, the audit manager and audit partner review the audit documentation. This review focuses more on the overall scope of the audit and whether the overall conclusions in the audit documentation are sufficient to provide support for the opinion on the financial statements.

Current GAAS requires the audit documentation to be reviewed by an additional person (normally, a partner or equivalent with the firm) who has not been involved with the audit (known as an *engagement quality reviewer*). This review focuses on the significant judgments made by the engagement team and the conclusions reached by the engagement team in preparing the auditors' report. *AS 7* notes that this **engagement quality review** (formally known as a *second-partner review* or *concurring-partner review*) is undertaken to ensure that the quality of audit work and reporting is in keeping with the public accounting firm's quality standards. In addition, the engagement quality review provides a very-high-level review of whether the evidence obtained during the audit is sufficient to support the opinion on the client's financial statements. The use of electronic audit documentation and the accompanying search capabilities has enhanced the efficiency and effectiveness of audit documentation review. Audit documentation review provides a number of benefits to the firm, including these:

- Because audit documentation is the primary evidence of the audit procedures performed and conclusions reached by auditors, the review ensures that the audit is conducted in accordance with GAAS.
- Audit documentation review provides the firm an opportunity to evaluate the overall quality of the firm's audit practices as a method of quality control.
- Audit documentation review often serves as an important component of the training and evaluation of audit staff members.
- Audit documentation review allows the firm to adhere to the performance principle, which requires that auditors adequately plan the work and properly supervise any assistants.

REVIEW CHECKPOINTS

11.13 What responsibility do auditors have for evaluating a client's ability to continue as a going concern?

11.14 What factors may indicate that substantial doubt exists about the client's ability to continue as a going concern?

11.15 What actions should auditors take if evidence suggests that substantial doubt exists about the client's ability to continue as a going concern?

11.16 Why are adjusting entries and note disclosures labeled "proposed"?

11.17 What is an uncorrected misstatement? What is the auditors' responsibility for communicating misstatements detected during the audit?

11.18 Identify the two methods of evaluating the performance materiality of uncorrected misstatements. What are the requirements of *Staff Accounting Bulletin No. 108* for evaluating the performance materiality of these misstatements?

11.19 Describe the audit documentation review process in a public accounting firm.

11.20 What is an engagement quality review?

11.21 What are some of the benefits of audit documentation review to a public accounting firm?

SUBSEQUENT EVENTS AND SUBSEQUENTLY DISCOVERED FACTS

LEARNING OBJECTIVE 11-5
Understand auditors' responsibility for subsequent events and subsequently discovered facts.

What is the auditors' responsibility for events occurring after the date of the financial statements but before the audit report is released? In early 2008, after their fiscal-year end, real estate investments held by **UBS** (a global financial services firm) declined in value by 19 billion Swiss francs ($16 billion). On one hand, because this decline in value occurred *after* December 31, 2007 (the date of UBS's financial statements), it did not affect the financial position or results of operations as of December 31, 2007. However, it would clearly be misleading for UBS to fail to disclose this decline in market value if it occurred and was known prior to the issuance of their financial statements. As a result, auditors not only should evaluate the fairness of the entity's financial statements based on facts and circumstances that exist as of the date of the financial statements but also should consider the impact of events occurring after the date of the financial statements.

Subsequent Events

Events occurring between the date of the financial statements and the date of the auditors' report are referred to as **subsequent events**. The auditors' primary objective with respect to subsequent events is to ensure that any major events that affect the fairness of the client's financial statements and disclosures are properly identified and disclosed in the client's financial statements. AU 560 identifies the following two types of subsequent events; examples of these events from recent SEC filings are shown in the accompanying Auditing Insight[11]:

- Events that provide additional evidence of conditions that existed *at the date of the financial statements* (for example, the deteriorating financial condition of the client's customer that had a large accounts receivable balance at the date of the financial statements)
- Events that provide evidence of conditions that arose *following the date of the financial statements* (for example, a major acquisition occurring after the date of the financial statements).

AUDITING INSIGHT — The Real-World of Subsequent Events

The following are examples of subsequent events disclosed by companies in their footnotes to the financial statements.

- In early 2010, **Citigroup, Dupont, Praxair**, and **Federal Mogul** disclosed the decision by the Venezuelan government to devalue its currency (the Bolivar) and the potential financial statement impacts of this devaluation.
- In 2010, **Hewlett-Packard** disclosed that it sold land and buildings, which resulted in a gain $280 million.
- In January 2009, **Kellogg Company** announced a hold on sales of products and recall of a number of products because of potential salmonella contamination; it estimated total costs associated with this recall of $34 million, or $0.06 per share.
- In January 2009, **Pfizer** announced a merger agreement to acquire Wyeth for $68 billion.

Sources: Citigroup, Dupont, Praxair, Federal Mogul, Hewlett-Packard, Kellogg, and Pfizer 10-K filings.

Auditors may learn of subsequent events through audit procedures performed in obtaining evidence related to account balances or classes of transactions. For example, the deterioration of a customer's financial condition may be identified through accounts receivable confirmations obtained after the date of the financial statements. Other procedures performed during the completion stage of the audit (such as attorney letters and written representations) may provide auditors information about the existence of subsequent events. AU 560 identifies the following procedures that should be specifically performed to identify the existence of subsequent events:

- Obtain an understanding of procedures management performed to identify subsequent events.
- Inquire of management and those charged with governance as to the existence of subsequent events (this inquiry should subsequently be corroborated through written representations).
- Read minutes of meetings of owners, management, or those charged with governance held after the date of the financial statements.
- Review the entity's latest interim financial statements, if applicable.

---

[11] Until recently, events that provide additional evidence of conditions that existed at the date of the financial statements were known as Type I subsequent events and events that provide evidence of conditions that arose following the date of the financial statements were known as Type II subsequent events.

When subsequent events are identified, auditors are required to ensure that the financial statement disclosure of these events reflects all current information and is according to GAAP. This might require adjustment to the financial statements to reflect new information (for conditions existing at the date of the financial statements) or disclosure of the information in the financial statements or footnotes accompanying the financial statements (for conditions that arose after the date of the financial statements).

Subsequently Discovered Facts

In the preceding discussion, we assumed that auditors identified subsequent events prior to the date of the auditors' report. This assumption is noteworthy because the auditors are still conducting fieldwork and can obtain evidence regarding the appropriate presentation and disclosure of the subsequent events. However, in some situations, auditors learn of events or facts following the date of the auditors' report. The dilemma for auditors in these situations is that the fieldwork is complete and, in some cases, the financial statements and auditors' report may have been issued. Facts that become known to auditors after the date of the auditors' report that, had they been known at that time, may have caused the auditors to revise their report, are known as **subsequently discovered facts**.

The auditors' response to subsequently discovered facts depends on when the facts are identified. In some circumstances, auditors could learn of these facts *after the date of the auditors' report* but *prior to the audit report release date.* The issue this raises for the auditors is that auditing procedures have been performed only through the date of the auditors' report, yet the facts are discovered prior to the release of the financial statements and auditors' reports. As a result, the financial statements, or auditors' report, or both could still be revised prior to issuance. If these facts require revision of the financial statements or footnote disclosures, auditors should perform additional procedures and evaluate the appropriateness of the disclosure of these events. One option would be to do so and change the date on the auditors' report to reflect the new (later) date. However, a disadvantage of this approach is that the auditors' responsibility for *all events* is now extended to this later date.

When facts are discovered following the date of the auditors' report but prior to the audit report release date, auditors normally choose to **dual date** the report (that is, to give it two dates). For example, **Ernst & Young** completed the fieldwork of its 2001 audit of **Hewlett-Packard** on November 13, 2001 (Hewlett-Packard had an October 31 year-end). On December 6, 2001, Hewlett-Packard made an offering of $1 billion of debt, which it disclosed in Note 19 to its financial statements. The date used by Ernst & Young in its 2001 auditors' report of Hewlett-Packard was as follows:

> November 13, 2001, except for Note 19, as to which the date is December 6, 2001.

As this date noted, Ernst & Young has full responsibility for all subsequent events through November 13, 2001, except for the issuance of debt. Ernst & Young has responsibility for this event through December 6, 2001.

Dual dating serves two important functions. First, it provides a way to modify the financial statements and disclosures for information discovered by auditors after the date of the auditors' report. This provides financial statement users the most complete set of information about the entity. Second, it limits auditors' liability for events after the date of the auditors' report to the event(s) specifically identified in the report date. In some cases (particularly if facts become known immediately before a filing deadline), auditors may choose not to evaluate the effect of subsequently discovered facts on the financial statements. For example, in January 2011, **American International Group (AIG)** disclosed the impact of the recapitalization of AIG through the distribution of 92.2 percent of its outstanding shares of common stock to the **U.S. Department of the Treasury**. This event was disclosed in the footnotes to AIG's financial statements and was marked as "unaudited."

Alternatively, auditors may learn of facts following the issuance of the financial statements and auditors' report. Obviously, this situation presents additional challenges because the financial statements and auditors' reports cannot be revised prior to issuance. If these facts would

AUDITING INSIGHT — How Long Does It Take?

For Fortune 100 companies in 2010, the average lag between the date of the financial statements and the date of the auditors' report is 52.8 days and from the date of the auditors' report to the filing of the 10-K with the SEC is 0.44 days. Interestingly, 87.4 percent of the Fortune 100 companies file their 10-K with the SEC on the same date as the date of the auditors' report. Clearly, the length of the period between the date of the auditors' report and the audit report release date is quite short for the largest companies (this same period is 0.38 days for the Fortune 500 and 0.34 days for the Fortune 1000). (This may be a conservative measure because the auditors' report may be released even earlier than this through inclusion in an 8-K or other filing).

Source: Drawn from Wharton Research Data Services *Audit Analytics* database.

---

result in either the revision of the auditors' report or the financial statements and individuals are continuing to rely on these financial statements, the client should take the following actions:

1. Notify individuals known to be relying on the financial statements or likely to rely on the financial statements that (a) the financial statements should not be relied upon and (b) revised financial statements and a new auditors' report will be issued.
2. Issue revised financial statements as soon as practicable with appropriate disclosure of the matter related to the subsequently discovered facts.

In the event that management refuses to take either of these actions, auditors should notify management, regulatory agencies, or any individuals known to be relying on the financial statements that the auditors' report cannot be relied upon. If auditors determine that the subsequently discovered facts would require revision to the financial statements, the nature of the matter and effect on the financial statements should also be included in the auditors' notification.

The audit timeline and actions for subsequent events and subsequently discovered facts follow:

Year-End Date (December 31, 2012)	Date of the Auditors' Report (audit completion date) (February 15, 2013)	Audit Report Release Date (February 17, 2013)
• Perform procedures related to subsequent events • Adjust financial statements or disclose subsequent events	• Perform procedures related to subsequently discovered facts • Adjust financial statements or disclose subsequently discovered facts • Extend date of the auditors' report or dual date auditors' report on financial statements	• Request client to take action to reduce reliance on financial statements and auditors' report and reissue financial statements • If client refuses to take above actions, notify client, regulatory agencies, and users that auditors' report is not to be relied upon

AUDITING INSIGHT — Don't Rely?

On August 13, 2007, **Dell** filed a Form 8-K with the Securities and Exchange Commission indicating that its previously issued financial statements for fiscal 2003, 2004, 2005, and 2006 (including interim financial statements) should no longer be relied upon because of certain accounting errors and irregularities in those financial statements.

Source: *Dell Form 8-K*, August 13, 2007.

In June 2011, **Ernst & Young** notified the Securities and Exchange Commission that it was withdrawing its opinion on **Life Partners** Holdings Inc.'s 2010 financial statements because they were "no longer able to rely on management's representations" and are not willing to be associated with Life Holdings' financial statements. This decision was based, in part, on disagreements related to Life Partners' recognition of revenue and the potential need for a restatement of prior results that arose following the audit report release date.

Source: "Auditor Is Exiting from Life Partners," *The Wall Street Journal*, June 9, 2011, p. C3.

> ### ↳ REVIEW CHECKPOINTS
>
> 11.22 What is a *subsequent event*?
>
> 11.23 What procedures do auditors perform to identify subsequent events?
>
> 11.24 Identify the two types of subsequent events. How should information about these events be reflected in the financial statements?
>
> 11.25 What are subsequently discovered facts?
>
> 11.26 What are auditors' responsibilities for subsequently discovered facts if these are identified (a) prior to the audit report release date and (b) following the audit report release date?
>
> 11.27 What is the purpose of dual dating the auditors' report?

▽ RESPONSIBILITIES FOLLOWING THE AUDIT REPORT RELEASE DATE

LEARNING OBJECTIVE 11-6
Identify important activities and communications following the completion of the audit and audit report release date.

Omitted Procedures

Although auditors have no responsibility to continue to review their work after the audit report release date, auditors' reports and audit documentation may be subjected to a PCAOB inspection, external peer review, or the firm's own internal inspection program as part of its system of quality control. Section 104 of Sarbanes-Oxley requires inspections to be conducted annually by the PCAOB (if the firm provides services for more than 100 public audit clients) or every three years (if the firm provides services for 100 or fewer public audit clients). These inspections could reveal situations in which an audit was not performed in accordance with generally accepted auditing standards. In particular, auditors could have failed to perform necessary audit procedures prior to the audit report release date. This situation is referred to as **omitted procedures**.

AU 585 provides guidance for such situations. If (1) the omitted procedures are important in supporting the auditors' opinion and (2) individuals are currently relying on the client's financial statements (and auditors' reports), auditors should perform the omitted procedure or alternative procedure(s). Assuming that the procedures allow auditors to support the previously-expressed opinion, no further action is necessary. However, if they do not, auditors should formally withdraw the original report, issue revised reports, and inform persons currently relying on the financial statements. This course of action is illustrated in actions by **PwC** (or an affiliate firm's) actions in its audits of **OAO Yukos** and **Satyam Computer Services** included in the accompanying Auditing Insight.

▽ AUDITING INSIGHT │ Discovering Facts . . . 10 Years Later

A Russian unit of PwC recently withdrew its audits and reports from 1995–2004 for oil company OAO Yukos. PwC officials indicated that Yukos's management may have provided inaccurate information to auditors and that PwC only recently became aware of new evidence that suggested Yukos's management had misled PwC auditors. PwC indicated that its decision to formally withdraw the reports "was influenced by the fact that some former shareholders and management of Yukos are continuing to encourage others to rely on PwC's audit reports."

Following the $1 billion accounting scandal at India's Satyam Computer Services, **Price Waterhouse India** (an affiliate of PwC's international network) has notified the company's board that, while the firm followed appropriate audit procedures, its reports from 2000 through 2008 could no longer be relied upon.

Source: "PwC Withdraws a Decade of Yukos Audits," *The Wall Street Journal*, June 25, 2007, p. A3; "Satyam Overlooked Oversight," *CFO.com*, January 20, 2009.

Communications with Individuals Charged with Governance (AU 260, AU 265, *AS 5*)

During the engagement, matters can arise that are of such importance that they must be communicated with "individuals charged with governance." **Individuals charged with governance** are person(s) responsible for overseeing the client's financial reporting process, including the internal control over financial reporting. While this phrase can include the client's management and full board of directors, for public entities it is typically the audit committee of the board of directors. Audit committees are required for registrants under Sarbanes-Oxley and must be composed of only independent directors. Audit committees are an important element in the governance process because they are directly responsible for the appointment, compensation, and oversight of auditors and the audit examination.

Sections 204 and 404 of Sarbanes-Oxley both address required communications between auditors and the client's audit committee; these communications have been formally incorporated into professional standards relating to the communication of internal control–related issues (AU 265 and *AS 5*) and communication of other matters (AU 260). AU 265 and *AS 5* require auditors to communicate (*in writing*) all significant internal control deficiencies and material weaknesses to the client and individuals charged with governance. For public entities, *AS 5* requires the communication to be made prior to the audit report release date. For nonpublic entities, AU 265 notes that it is preferable to provide this communication prior to the audit report release date, but it should be made no later than 60 days following the audit report release date. Although auditors may decide to communicate significant deficiencies and material weaknesses to the client as they are discovered during the audit, if the client has not corrected (or remediated) these deficiencies or weaknesses, they must be communicated again in writing at the conclusion of the audit.

For nonpublic entities, auditors' communication would acknowledge that the purpose of the audit is to express an opinion on the financial statements, not on internal control over financial reporting; furthermore, the communication would explicitly state that auditors are not expressing an opinion on internal control over financial reporting. For public entities subject to the reporting requirements of Sarbanes-Oxley, this communication would parallel the form and content of the auditors' report on internal control over financial reporting, which expresses an opinion on internal control over financial reporting. These communications are governed by *AS 5*.

In addition to internal control deficiencies, AU 260 requires auditors to communicate various other matters to the client. As with internal control communications, auditors ordinarily make these communications with individuals charged with governance after the conclusion of the audit; however, if the matters are particularly significant, they should be communicated during the audit. These communications may be made either orally or in writing (however, because of the important nature of these matters, one would anticipate that they be made in writing).

Auditors should communicate the following information to individuals charged with governance:

- Auditors' responsibility under generally accepted auditing standards.
- An overview of the planned scope and timing of the audit.
- Auditors' judgment about the quality of the client's accounting policies, accounting estimates, and financial statement disclosures.
- Any significant difficulties encountered during the audit.
- Any uncorrected misstatements identified during the audit other than those auditors believe to be trivial.
- Any disagreements with management.
- Material, corrected misstatements that were brought to the attention of management.

- Representations requested from the client's management.
- Any management consultations with other auditors.
- Any significant issues arising from the audit that were discussed with management.
- Other findings or issues that are significant and relevant to individuals charged with governance.

Auditors also should determine that individuals charged with governance have received copies of written communications regarding material issues between auditors and management such as engagement letters, written representations, and reports on deficiencies in internal control over financial reporting. However, as the accompanying Auditing Insight reveals, such communication does not ensure that all relevant issues will be handled appropriately.

Because of its important role, auditors communicate frequently with the audit committee throughout the engagement. A recent study by Cohen et al referred to in the accompanying Auditing Insight summarizes the nature of this communication.

AUDITING INSIGHT Meetings with Audit Committees?

Based on interviews with auditors, an academic study by Cohen et al. provided the following insights into auditors' meetings with client audit committees:

- The frequency of meetings has increased from two to three times per year prior to Sarbanes-Oxley to more than six times per year.
- The most frequent issues discussed in audit committee meetings relate to accounting/auditing issues encountered in the engagement, the audit plan, the results of the audit, and other mandated disclosures (discussed in this section).
- A relatively small percentage of auditors (52 percent) indicated that audit committees played an important role in resolving auditor disputes with management.

Source: J. Cohen, G. Krishnamoorthy, and A. Wright, "Corporate Governance in the Post-Sarbanes-Oxley Era: Auditors' Experiences," *Contemporary Accounting Research* 27 (Fall 2010), pp. 751–786.

Management Letter

During the engagement (particularly the study and evaluation of the client's internal control, assessment of the risk of material misstatement, and evaluation of the effectiveness of internal control over financial reporting), auditors note matters that can be made as recommendations to the client. These recommendations may allow the client to improve the efficiency and effectiveness of their operations. After the conclusion of the audit, these matters are summarized in a letter (commonly referred to as the **management letter**) that is delivered to and discussed with the client. Management letters are not required by generally accepted auditing standards but are considered an important method of adding value to clients beyond that provided by the audit examination. In this spirit, some firms encourage consulting and tax professionals to participate in preparing the management letter.

Management letters are a service provided as a by-product of the audit. The management letter is an excellent opportunity to develop rapport with the client and to make the client aware of other business services offered by the public accounting firm.

Summary of Audit Communications

This text has mentioned many types of formal communications. Because you are learning the final procedures to complete the audit, this is a good place to summarize these various communications. See Exhibit 11.5 for a summary of audit correspondence other than auditors' reports on the financial statements (discussed in Chapter 12) and internal control over financial reporting (discussed in Chapter 5).

EXHIBIT 11.5 Audit Communications

Type	From	To	Timing	Reference	Method
Engagement letter	Auditors	Client	Before engagement	AU 210	Written
Acceptance letter (signed copy of engagement letter)	Client	Auditors	Before engagement	AU 210	Written
Attorney letter response	Attorney	Auditors	Near date of the auditors' reports	AU 501	Written
Written representations	Client	Auditors	Date of the auditors' reports (audit completion date)	AU 580	Written
Internal control deficiencies	Auditors	Individuals charged with governance (audit committee)	Prior to audit report release date (for public entities) or within 60 days of audit report release date (for nonpublic entities)*	AU 265 and *AS 5*	Written
Communications with individuals charged with governance	Auditors	Individuals charged with governance (audit committee)	After audit*	AU 260 and *AS 5*	Oral or written
Management letter	Auditors	Client	After audit	None	Oral or written

*May be communicated during the audit if matters are significant.

REVIEW CHECKPOINTS

11.28 What steps should auditors take if, after the audit report release date, they discover that an important audit procedure was omitted?

11.29 Identify information that auditors are required to communicate to individuals charged with governance of the client.

11.30 What is a *management letter?* Are management letters required by generally accepted auditing standards?

Summary

This chapter began by identifying four major time periods during an audit: (1) prior to the date of the financial statements, (2) between the date of the financial statements and the date of the auditors' report, (3) between the date of the auditors' report and the audit report release date, and (4) following the audit report release date. As various matters are discussed, it is important to determine the time period in which auditors identify issues because this will affect auditors' responsibility for these matters.

Within the context of the four time periods, the chapter discussed several aspects of completing an audit. These events include (1) completing substantive procedures, (2) obtaining responses to attorney letters, (3) obtaining written representations, (4) evaluating the entity's ability to continue as a going concern, (5) summarizing proposed adjustments to the financial statements, (6) reviewing audit documentation, (7) considering the effects of subsequent events and subsequently discovered facts, (8) evaluating omitted audit procedures identified following the audit examination, and (9) providing communications at the conclusion of the audit. The purpose of these procedures is to enable auditors to issue and support opinions on financial statements and internal control over financial reporting.

Key Terms

analytical procedures: Procedures that allow auditors to evaluate financial information by studying relationships among both financial and nonfinancial data. When used in the completion stage of the audit, analytical procedures allow auditors to assess the conclusions reached during the audit and evaluate the overall financial statement presentation, 457

attorney letter: A communication sent from the client to its attorneys that details all pending litigation, claims, and assessments against the client and that requests the attorneys to comment on these matters directly to the client's auditors, 460

audit report release date: The date on which auditors allow the client to use their reports in conjunction with the financial statements; also the date on which the client's financial statements are issued, 456

contingency: An existing condition, situation, or set of circumstances involving uncertainty as to possible gain ("gain contingency") or loss ("loss contingency") to an enterprise that will ultimately be resolved when one or more future events occur or fail to occur, 459

date of the auditors' report: The date on which auditors have gathered sufficient appropriate evidence on which to base their opinions on the financial statements and internal control over financial reporting; the date that will be used for auditors' reports on the client's financial statements and internal control over financial reporting, 456

date of the financial statements: The year-end date of the latest period covered by the client's financial statements, 456

dual date: The use of two dates in the auditors' report to limit the responsibility beyond the date of the auditors' report to a specific subsequent event identified in the report, 472

engagement quality review: A review of audit documentation by an additional person (normally, a partner or equivalent with the firm) who has not been involved with the audit to ensure that the quality of the audit work and reporting is consistent with the quality standards of the public accounting firm, 470

individual(s) charged with governance: The person(s) responsible for overseeing the client's financial reporting process, including the internal control over financial reporting; individuals charged with governance may include the client's management and full board of directors, but typically refers to public entities' audit committee of the board of directors, 475

iron curtain method: The process used when evaluating the effect of uncorrected misstatements that considers the aggregate effect of current and prior misstatements in the entity's balance sheet, 468

management letter: A communication that provides a summary of auditors' recommendations resulting from the audit engagement that allows the client to improve the effectiveness and efficiency of its operations, 476

omitted procedures: The inadvertent failure of auditors to perform necessary audit procedures prior to the audit report release date, 474

roll-forward procedure(s): The procedure(s) performed by auditors to extend the conclusions from an interim date to the date of the financial statements, 457

rollover method: The process used when evaluating the effect of uncorrected misstatements that considers only the current-period income effect(s) of the potential adjustment, 468

subsequent events: Events occurring between the date of the financial statements and the date of the auditors' report, 471

subsequently discovered fact: Information that becomes known to auditors after the date of their report that, had it been known at that time, may have caused the auditors to revise their report, 472

unasserted claim: A representation that no formal lawsuit or assertion has been filed or threatened on behalf of others against the audit client but that circumstances such as a catastrophe, accident, or other physical occurrence could result in a suit or assertion being filed in the future, 461

uncorrected misstatement: A misstatement that the auditor identified and accumulated during the audit that has not been corrected (or adjusted) by the client, 468

written representation A written assertion provided by management to auditors related to the entity's financial statements, the information provided to the auditors, and management's internal control over financial reporting to confirm certain matters and support other evidence obtained during the audit, 463

Multiple-Choice Questions for Practice and Review

 All applicable Exercises and Problems are available with McGraw-Hill's Connect® Accounting

LO 11-1

11.31 Which of the following best describes the role of analytical procedures in the review stages of the audit engagement?
 a. To identify possible deficiencies in the client's internal control over financial reporting.
 b. To identify accounts that appear to be misstated with the intention of planning the nature, timing, and extent of other substantive procedures.
 c. To gather evidence to support one or more assertion(s) related to the account balance or class of transactions.
 d. To provide an overall review of the financial information and assessment of the adequacy of evidence gathered during the audit engagement.

LO 11-3

11.32 A major objective of written representations is to
 a. Shift responsibility for financial statements from the management to auditors.
 b. Provide a substitute source of audit evidence for substantive procedures that auditors would otherwise perform.
 c. Provide management an opportunity to make assertions about the quantity and valuation of the physical inventory.
 d. Impress on management its ultimate responsibility for the financial statements and disclosures.

LO 11-2

11.33 Which of these substantive procedures is *not* used to obtain evidence about contingencies?
 a. Scanning expense accounts for credit entries.
 b. Obtaining a letter from the client's attorney.
 c. Reading the minutes of the board of directors' meetings.
 d. Examining terms of sale in sales contracts.

LO 11-5

11.34 Subsequent knowledge of which of the following would cause the entity to adjust its December 31 financial statements?
 a. Sale of an issue of new stock for $500,000 on January 30.
 b. Settlement of a damage lawsuit for a customer's injury sustained February 15 for $10,000.
 c. Settlement of litigation in February for $100,000 that had been estimated at $12,000 in the December 31 financial statements.
 d. Storm damage of $1 million to the entity's buildings on March 1.

LO 11-5

11.35 A. Griffin audited the financial statements of Dodger Magnificat Corporation for the year ended December 31, 2012. She completed gathering sufficient appropriate evidence on January 30 and later learned of a stock split voted by the board of directors on February 5. The financial statements were changed to reflect the split, and she now needs to dual date the report on the entity's financial statements. Which of the following is the proper form?
 a. December 31, 2012, except as to Note X, which is dated January 30, 2013.
 b. January 30, 2013, except as to Note X, which is dated February 5, 2013.
 c. December 31, 2012, except as to Note X, which is dated February 5, 2013.
 d. February 5, 2013, except for the date of the auditors' report, for which the date is January 30, 2013.

LO 11-5

11.36 Auditors have a responsibility related to management's disclosure of new information related to subsequent events until
 a. The date of the financial statements.
 b. The date of the auditors' report.
 c. The audit report release date.
 d. The following year's date of the financial statements.

LO 11-5

11.37 The auditing standards regarding subsequently discovered facts refers to knowledge obtained after
 a. The date the fieldwork began.
 b. The date of the auditors' report.
 c. The date of the financial statements.
 d. The date interim audit work was complete.

LO 11-6   11.38 Which of the following is *not* required by generally accepted auditing standards?
   a. Written representations.
   b. Attorney letter.
   c. Management letter.
   d. Engagement letter.

LO 11-6   11.39 Which of these persons generally does *not* participate in writing the management letter?
   a. Client's outside attorneys.
   b. Client's accounting and production managers.
   c. Public accounting firm's audit team on the engagement.
   d. Public accounting firm's consulting and tax experts.

LO 11-1   11.40 Which of the following is ordinarily performed *last* in the audit examination?
   a. Securing a signed engagement letter from the client.
   b. Performing tests of controls.
   c. Performing a review for subsequent events.
   d. Obtaining signed written representations.

LO 11-1   11.41 Which of the following normally occurs *earliest* in the audit examination?
   a. Discovery of an omitted audit procedure.
   b. Dual dating the auditors' report on the entity's financial statements for subsequent events that exist at the date of the financial statements.
   c. Preparation of the management letter.
   d. Review of audit documentation.

LO 11-5   11.42 Ambrose is auditing the financial statements of Mays (dated December 31, 2012). The date of the auditors' report is February 17, 2013, and the audit report release date is February 20, 2013. For which of the following matters would Ambrose have the *least* responsibility?
   a. The obsolescence of inventory held on December 31, 2012, that was identified on January 20, 2013.
   b. A customer's deteriorating financial condition that was identified on February 19, 2013.
   c. A merger that was announced by Mays and known by Ambrose on February 12, 2013.
   d. A major loss due to a catastrophe that occurred and was known by Ambrose on March 1, 2013.

LO 11-2   11.43 Which of the following statements is *most likely* to be included in an attorney letter?
   a. "Certain representations in this letter are described as being limited to matters that are material."
   b. "If any unasserted claims or assessments are omitted from this disclosure, please provide this information directly to our auditors."
   c. "Our work enabled us to notice some actions that could enhance the profitability of the Company."
   d. "Please furnish to our auditors such explanation, if any, that you consider necessary to supplement the foregoing information."

LO 11-6   11.44 After the audit report release date, the auditors determine that an important auditing procedure was omitted. Which of the following initial courses of action is most appropriate?
   a. Perform the omitted procedure or an alternative procedure.
   b. Notify the board of directors and regulatory agencies that are currently relying on auditors' reports.
   c. Determine whether the omitted procedure is important in supporting the auditors' opinion on the entity's financial statements.
   d. Engage another public accounting firm to conduct a quality assurance review.

LO 11-3   11.45 Which of the following statements is *not* true with respect to written representations?
   a. The failure of management to furnish them is a significant scope limitation, resulting in either an adverse opinion or a disclaimer of opinion.
   b. They should address management's responsibility for designing internal control to prevent and detect fraud.
   c. Auditors use them to corroborate information received during the audit from the client and its employees.
   d. They are dated the same date as the auditors' reports.

LO 11-3   11.46 Hall accepted an engagement to audit the year 1 financial statements of XYZ Company. XYZ completed the preparation of the year 1 financial statements on February 13, year 2, and its auditors began the fieldwork on February 17, year 2. Hall completed gathering sufficient appropriate evidence on March 24, year 2; Hall's report and XYZ's financial statements were released on March 28, year 2. The written representations normally would be dated
   a. February 13, year 2.
   b. February 17, year 2.
   c. March 24, year 2.
   d. March 28, year 2.

(AICPA adapted)

LO 11-2   11.47 A charge following the date of the financial statements to a notes receivable account from the cash disbursements journal should alert auditors to the possibility that a
   a. Contingent asset has come into existence following the date of the financial statements.
   b. Contingent liability has come into existence following the date of the financial statements.
   c. Provision for contingencies is required.
   d. Contingent liability has become a real liability and has been settled.

(AICPA adapted)

LO 11-5   11.48 Which of the following substantive procedures should auditors ordinarily perform regarding subsequent events?
   a. Compare the latest available interim financial statements with the financial statements being audited.
   b. Send second requests to the client's customers who failed to respond to initial accounts receivable confirmation requests.
   c. Communicate material weaknesses in internal control to the client's audit committee.
   d. Review the cutoff bank statements for several months after the date of the financial statements.

(AICPA adapted)

LO 11-5   11.49 Which of the following substantive procedures would auditors most likely perform to obtain evidence about the occurrence of subsequent events?
   a. Recompute a sample of large-dollar transactions occurring after the date of the financial statements for arithmetic accuracy.
   b. Investigate changes in shareholders' equity occurring after the date of the financial statements.
   c. Send confirmations to vendors with whom the client normally does business but for which no balance in accounts payable is noted.
   d. Confirm bank accounts established after the date of the financial statements.

(AICPA adapted)

LO 11-2   11.50 The primary reason auditors request responses to attorney letters is to provide auditors
   a. The probable outcome of asserted claims and pending or threatened litigation.
   b. Corroboration of the information furnished by management about litigation, claims, and assessments.
   c. The attorney's opinions of the client's historical experiences in recent similar litigation.
   d. A description and evaluation of litigation, claims, and assessments that existed at the date of the financial statements.

(AICPA adapted)

LO 11-2   11.51 The scope of an audit is *not* restricted when an attorney letter limits the response to
   a. Matters to which the attorney has given substantive attention in the form of legal representation.
   b. An evaluation of the likelihood of an unfavorable outcome of the matters disclosed by the entity.
   c. The attorney's opinion of the entity's historical experience in recent similar litigation.
   d. The probable outcome of asserted claims and pending or threatened litigation.

(AICPA adapted)

Exercises and Problems

 All applicable Exercises and Problems are available with McGraw-Hill's *Connect® Accounting*

LO 11-3

11.52 **Written Representations.** Hart, an assistant accountant with the firm of Better & Best, CPAs, is auditing the financial statements of Tech Consolidated Industries, Inc. The firm's audit plan calls for the preparation of written representations.

Required:

a. In an audit of financial statements, in what circumstances are auditors required to obtain written representations?

b. What are the major categories of items covered by written representations?

c. To whom should the representations be addressed and as of what date should they be dated?

d. Who should sign the representations and what would be the effect of a refusal to sign them?

e. In what respects may auditors' other responsibilities be relieved by obtaining written representations?

(AICPA adapted)

LO 11-3

11.53 **Written Representations Omissions.** During the audit of the annual financial statements of Amis Manufacturing, Inc., the company's president, Vance Molar, and Wanda Dweebins, the engagement partner, reviewed matters that were supposed to be included in written representations. Amis Manufacturing is not subject to the reporting requirements of *AS 5*. Upon receipt of the following representations, Dweebins contacted Molar to state that they were incomplete.

To John & Wayne, CPAs:

In connection with your examination of the balance sheet of Amis Manufacturing, Inc., as of December 31, 2012, and the related statements of income, retained earnings, and cash flows for the year then ended, for the purpose of expressing an opinion on whether the financial statements present fairly the financial position, results of operations, and cash flows of Amis Manufacturing, Inc., in conformity with generally accepted accounting principles, we confirm, to the best of our knowledge and belief, the following representations made to you during your audit. There were no

- Plans or intentions that could materially affect the carrying value or classification of assets or liabilities.
- Communications from regulatory agencies concerning noncompliance with, or deficiencies in, financial reporting practices.
- Agreements to repurchase assets previously sold.
- Violations or possible violations of laws or regulations whose effects should be considered for disclosure in the financial statements or as a basis for recording a contingent liability.
- Unasserted claims or assessments that our lawyer has advised are probable of assertion that must be disclosed in accordance with *Accounting Standards Codification (ASC) 450*.
- Capital stock purchase options or agreements or capital stock reserved for options, warrants, conversions, or other requirements.
- Compensating balance or other arrangements involving restrictions on cash balances.

Vance Molar, President
Amis Manufacturing, Inc.
March 14, 2013

Required:
Identify the other matters that Molar's representations should specifically confirm.

(AICPA adapted)

LO 11-3   11.54 **Written Representations.** Each of the following statements is a communication from management. Indicate whether the inclusion of each statement in written representations is appropriate. Provide your rationale for any statements whose inclusion in written representations is *not* appropriate.

a. "Certain representations in this letter are described as being limited to matters that are material."

b. "No frauds involving management, employees who have significant roles in internal control, or other frauds that could have a material effect on the financial statements have occurred during the year under audit."

c. "Based on our assessment, we conclude that the Company has maintained an effective internal control over financial reporting as of December 31, 2012."

d. "We have prepared a description and evaluation of certain contingencies for which our attorneys have devoted substantive attention on our behalf in the form of legal representation."

e. "There are no significant deficiencies, including material weaknesses, in the design or operation of internal controls that could adversely affect our ability to record, process, summarize, and report financial data."

f. "Summarized below are important actions taken in response to comments provided by you in the management letter dated March 22, 2013, based on your prior audit."

g. "Our assessment of internal control over financial reporting provides us absolute assurance that no material misstatements will occur and be undetected by our internal control."

h. "We have made available to you all financial records and related data."

LO 11-3   11.55 **Written Representations.** For each of the following issues, classify them according to whether they will be (1) included in written representations in all audits, (2) included in written representations in audits of public entities (under *AS 5*), or (3) not included in written representations:

a. Management acknowledgement of its responsibility for the fairness of the financial statements in accordance with U.S. GAAP.

b. A list of pending or threatened litigation, claims, or assessments currently outstanding against the client.

c. A description of recommendations that allow the client to improve the efficiency and effectiveness of its operations.

d. Availability of all financial records and related data.

e. Information related to the presentation and disclosure of items within the financial statements.

f. Disclosure of all significant deficiencies and material weaknesses in internal control.

g. Information concerning fraud involving management and employees who have significant roles in internal control.

h. Auditors' judgment about the quality of the client's accounting principles.

i. Management's conclusion about the effectiveness of its internal control over financial reporting.

j. A statement that the financial statements are prepared according to U.S. generally accepted accounting principles.

LO 11-2   11.56 **Client Request for Attorney Letter.** The firm of Cole & Cole, CPAs, is auditing the financial statements of Consolidated Industries Co. for the year ended December 31, 2012. On May 6, 2013, C. R. Brown, Consolidated's chief financial officer, gave the auditors a draft of an attorney letter for Cole's review before mailing it to J. J. Young, Consolidated's outside counsel. This letter is intended to elicit the attorneys' responses to corroborate information furnished to the auditors by management concerning pending and threatened litigation, claims, assessments, and unasserted claims and assessments.

Client's Attorney Letter Request
May 6, 2013
J. J. Young, Attorney at Law
123 Main Street, Anytown, USA
Dear J. J. Young:

In connection with an audit of our financial statements at December 31, 2012, and for the year then ended, management of the Company has prepared, and furnished to our auditors, Cole & Cole, CPAs, a description and evaluation of certain contingencies, including those set forth below, involving matters with respect to which you have been engaged and to which you have devoted substantive attention on behalf of the Company in the form of legal consultation or representation. Your response should include matters that existed at December 31, 2012. Because of the confidentiality of all these matters, your response may be limited.

In November 2012, an action was brought against the Company by an outside salesman alleging breach of contract for sales commissions and asking an accounting with respect to claims for fees and commissions. The causes of action claim damages of $3,000,000, but the Company believes it has meritorious defenses to the claims. The possible exposure of the Company to a successful judgment on behalf of the plaintiff is slight.

In July 2012, an action was brought against the Company by Industrial Manufacturing Company (Industrial) alleging patent infringement and seeking damages of $20,000,000. On October 16, 2012, the U.S. District Court decided that the Company had infringed on seven Industrial patents and awarded damages of $14,000,000. The Company vigorously denies these allegations and has filed an appeal with the U.S. Court of Appeals. The appeal process is expected to take approximately two years, but there is some chance that Consolidated may ultimately prevail.

Please furnish to our auditors such explanation, if any, that you consider necessary to supplement this information, including an explanation of those matters as to which your views may differ from those stated, and an identification of the omission of any pending or threatened litigation, claims, and assessments or a statement that the list of such matters is complete. Your response may be quoted or referred to in the financial statements without further correspondence with you.

You also consulted on various other matters considered to be pending or threatened litigation. However, you may not comment on these matters because publicizing them may alert potential plaintiffs to the strengths of their cases. In addition, various other matters probable of assertion that have some chance of an unfavorable outcome, as of December 31, 2012, are presently considered unasserted claims and assessments.

Respectfully,
C. R. Brown
Chief Financial Officer

Required:

Describe the omissions, ambiguities, and inappropriate statements and terminology in Brown's letter. Remember that this is Brown's letter requesting a response to auditors, but it must request responses in the manner most useful to auditors.

(AICPA adapted)

LO 11-2

11.57 **Attorney Letters.** Faye Jaworski, CPA, is auditing the financial statements of Fulbright Company. As she is nearing the audit completion date, Jaworski realizes that she needs to evaluate whether all material contingencies are properly accounted for and disclosed in Fulbright's financial statements. Because of its size, Fulbright has retained external counsel (Vinson, LLP) to handle its various legal matters.

Required:

a. List some common procedures that Jaworski will perform with respect to Fulbright's litigation, claims, and assessments.

b. What are the responsibilities of Jaworski, Fulbright, and Vinson with respect to litigation, claims, and assessments?

c. Attorney letters are used to provide corroboration of litigation, claims, and assessments against the client. Briefly describe the process through which attorney letters are prepared, sent, and used in the audit examination.

d. What information is normally included in an attorney letter?

LO 11-4

11.58 Uncorrected Misstatements and Performance Materiality. Aaron Rivers, CPA is auditing the financial statements of Charger Company, a client for the past five years. During past audits of Charger, Rivers identified some immaterial misstatements (most of which relate to isolated matters and do not have common characteristics). A summary of these misstatements follows (to illustrate, in 2007, the misstatements would have reduced net income by $13,200 if corrected):

Year	Effect on Net Income	Effect on Assets	Effect on Liabilities	Effect on Equity
2007	($13,200)	($20,000)	($6,800)	($13,200)
2008	5,000	12,000	7,000	5,000
2009	(9,250)	(11,000)	(1,750)	(9,250)
2010	(2,000)	(5,500)	(3,500)	(2,000)
2011	1,000	1,000	0	1,000

During the most recent audit, Rivers concluded that sales totaling $11,000 were recognized as of December 31, 2012, that did not meet the criteria for recognition until 2013. When Rivers discussed these sales with Chris Turner, Charger Company's chief financial officer, Turner asked Rivers about the performance materiality level used in the audit, which was $25,000. Upon learning of this, Turner remarked, "Then there's no need to worry . . . it's not a material amount. Why should we bother with this item?"

Required:

a. How does the misstatement identified in 2012 affect net income, assets, liabilities, and equity in 2012? (Assume a 35 percent tax rate for Charger.)

b. Comment upon Turner's remark to Rivers. Is Turner's reasoning correct?

c. Upon doing some research, Rivers learned of the rollover method and iron curtain method for evaluating the performance materiality of misstatements. Briefly define each of these methods.

d. How would Rivers evaluate the performance materiality of the $11,000 sales cutoff error in 2012 under the *rollover method* and *iron curtain method?*

e. Based on your response to (d), what adjustments (if any) would Rivers propose to Charger Company's financial statements under the rollover method and iron curtain method?

LO 11-4

11.59 Uncorrected Misstatements and Performance Materiality. During the conduct of an audit, auditors may identify misstatements as a result of the completion of their substantive procedures. An important activity performed in the completion stages of the audit is considering the materiality of misstatements identified during the audit.

Required:

a. What is an *uncorrected misstatement?* What is the auditors' responsibility for uncorrected misstatements during the completion stage of the audit engagement?

b. How do auditors use the *rollover method* and *iron curtain method* to evaluate uncorrected misstatements?

c. Assume that auditors have identified misstatements during the current audit that had a net impact of $100,000 on expenses and payables (both were understated). If the cumulative effect of prior uncorrected misstatements was $120,000 (overstatement of net income and understatement of liabilities) and materiality was $150,000, what would the auditors' conclusion be with respect to the misstatements under the rollover method and iron curtain method?

d. Based on your response to (c), what adjustments (if any) would the auditors propose to the client's financial statements?

e. What requirements do auditors have for communicating uncorrected misstatements identified during the audit engagement?

LO 11-4

11.60 Uncorrected Misstatements and Performance Materiality. Pat Colt is auditing the financial statements of Manning Company. The following is a summary of the uncorrected misstatements that Colt has identified during the last three years. These misstatements are immaterial and have related to isolated matters. In this summary, parentheses imply that the misstatements would have reduced balances if they were corrected (for example, in 2009, the misstatements would have reduced net income by $82,500, assets by $100,000, liabilities by $17,500, and equity by $82,500 if corrected).

Year	Effect on Net Income	Effect on Assets	Effect on Liabilities	Effect on Equity
2009	$(82,500)	$(100,000)	$(17,500)	$(82,500)
2010	(22,000)	(25,500)	(3,500)	(22,000)
2011	30,000	30,000	0	30,000

During the most recent audit, Colt concluded that expenses totaling $130,000 were recognized in January 2013 (when Manning paid them) but should have been recognized in 2012.

Required:

a. How does the misstatement identified in 2012 affect net income, assets, liabilities, and equity? (Assume a 35 percent tax rate for Manning.)

b. Describe the *rollover method* of evaluating uncorrected misstatements. Assume that performance materiality was set at $170,000. How would Colt evaluate the materiality of the misstatement under the rollover method? What adjustments (if any) would Colt propose to Manning's financial statements?

c. Describe the *iron curtain method* of evaluating uncorrected misstatements. Assume that performance materiality was set at $170,000. How would Colt evaluate the materiality of the $130,000 misstatement in 2012 under the iron curtain method? What adjustments (if any) would Colt propose to Manning's financial statements?

d. If performance materiality were established at $100,000 for Manning, how would Colt evaluate the materiality of the misstatement in 2012 under the rollover method and iron curtain method?

e. Based on your response to (d), what adjustments (if any) would Colt propose to Manning's financial statements under the rollover method and the iron curtain method?

LO 11-5

11.61 **Subsequent Events—Internet Exercise.** The following subsequent event was disclosed in **Dole Food Company**'s 2009 annual report:

Note 24: Subsequent Event
On February 27, 2010, a significant earthquake struck the country of Chile. Although Dole's Chilean operations resumed business after the earthquake in a matter of days, Dole is currently evaluating its impact, if any, to its financial results. Preliminary reports indicate no major structural damage to the Dole facilities. Dole maintains customary insurance for its properties, including business interruption and extra related expense.

Required:

a. What is a subsequent event?

b. Access Dole's 2009 10-K (filed in 2010) from the SEC's website (www.sec.gov).
   1. What is Dole's fiscal year-end?
   2. What is the date of the auditors' report?
   3. When was Dole's 10-K filed with the SEC?

c. Given your answers in (b), does it appear that this event meets the definition of a "subsequent event"? Why or why not?

d. Assuming that this event did meet the definition of a subsequent event, would you classify it as a subsequent event that relates to a condition that existed at the date of the financial statements or one that arose after the date of the financial statements?

e. Given the preceding disclosure, what procedures do you think Dole's auditors (Deloitte & Touche) performed with respect to this event?

LO 11-2

11.62 **Attorney Letters and Litigation—Internet Exercise.** From the SEC's website (www.sec.gov), access any company's 10-K and review its footnote disclosures related to pending litigation.

Required:

a. Briefly summarize the nature of pending litigation facing the company you selected.

b. From the auditors' perspective, what is the primary concern with respect to the disclosure of pending litigation?

c. Identify the responsibility of the company, the auditor, and its attorneys with respect to the presentation and disclosure of this pending litigation.

d. What information included in the disclosure you selected would have been included in attorney letters? What is the attorney's responsibility with respect to this information?

LO 11-5 11-6

11.63 **Omitted Procedures and Subsequently Discovered Facts—Internet Exercise.** From the "Inspections" section of the PCAOB's website, access the most recent inspection reports for each of the Big Four firms (Deloitte, Ernst & Young, KPMG, and PwC). Each inspection report contains the following information:

- An introductory preface.
- Inspection procedures and observations, which include specific findings related to issuers (clients) (Part I).
- A summary of the inspection process (Appendix B; note that Parts II, III, and Appendix A are not publicly available).
- The firm's response to the inspection report (Appendix C).

Occasionally, the PCAOB's inspection process identifies situations in which necessary audit procedures were not performed or in which the auditors did not identify departures from GAAP.

Required:

a. What is the auditors' responsibility with respect to subsequently discovered facts and omitted procedures?

b. If one is provided, review and briefly summarize the firm's response to the inspection report (Appendix C). Comment on whether you believe the firm's response to omitted procedures and subsequently discovered facts was consistent with generally accepted auditing standards.

LO 11-5

11.64 **Subsequent Events and Subsequently Discovered Facts.** Michael Ewing is auditing the financial statements of Dallas Company for the year ended December 31, 2012. In concluding the process of gathering sufficient appropriate evidence, Michael has asked to meet with his supervisor on the audit (John Ross) to discuss responsibility for events occurring after the date of the financial statements.

Required:

a. What is a *subsequent event?* During what time period is Michael Ewing responsible for subsequent events?

b. List some procedures that Michael may perform to assist him in identifying subsequent events.

c. What are two types of subsequent events? How should information related to these types of subsequent events be reflected in Dallas's financial statements?

d. Assume that on January 8, 2013, Dallas Company agreed to acquire Houston, Inc., in a significant transaction. The date of Michael's report was February 7, 2013, and Dallas issued its financial statements (and Michael's reports on its financial statements and internal control over financial reporting) on February 14, 2013. How would Michael proceed if he became aware of this subsequent event on the following dates?

1. January 10, 2013.
2. February 10, 2013.
3. February 20, 2013.

e. On March 2, 2013, Dallas announced that it also will acquire San Antonio Company in a significant transaction. What is Michael Ewing's responsibility with respect to this acquisition in the audit of Dallas's financial statements for the year ended December 31, 2012?

LO 11-2 11-5

11.65 **Subsequent Events and Contingent Liabilities.** Crankwell, Inc. is preparing its annual financial statements and annual report to stockholders. Management wants to be sure that all of the necessary and proper disclosures have been incorporated into the financial statements and the annual report. Two classes of items that have an important bearing on the financial statements are subsequent events and contingent liabilities. The financial statements could be materially inaccurate or misleading if proper disclosure of these items is not made.

Required:

a. With respect to subsequent events
   1. Define what is meant by a *subsequent event*.
   2. Identify two types of subsequent events and explain the appropriate financial statement presentation of each type.
   3. What are the procedures that should be performed to ascertain the existence of subsequent events?
b. With respect to contingent liabilities
   1. Identify the essential elements of a contingent liability.
   2. Explain how a contingent liability should be disclosed in the financial statements.
c. Explain how a subsequent event may relate to a contingent liability. Give an example to support your answer.

(CMA adapted)

LO 11-5

11.66 **Subsequent Events Procedures.** You are in the process of completing the gathering of sufficient appropriate evidence for Top Stove Corporation, a company engaged in the manufacture and sale of kerosene space heaters. To date there has been every indication that the financial statements of the client present fairly the position of the company at December 31 and the results of its operations and cash flows for the year then ended. Top Stove had total assets at December 31 of $4 million and a net profit for the year (after deducting federal and state income taxes) of $285,000. The principal records of the company include a general ledger, cash receipts record, voucher register, sales register, check register, and general journal. Financial statements are prepared monthly. Your audit report is dated February 20 and you plan to deliver the reports to the client by March 12.

Required:

a. Write a brief statement about the purpose and period to be covered in a review of subsequent events.
b. Outline the program you would follow to determine what transactions involving material amounts, if any, have occurred since the date of the financial statements.

(AICPA adapted)

LO 11-5

11.67 **Subsequent Events—Cases.** In connection with your examination of the financial statements of Olars Manufacturing Corporation for the year ended December 31, your postbalance-sheet substantive procedures disclosed the following items:

1. *January 3.* The state government approved a plan for the construction of an express highway. The plan will result in the appropriation of a portion of the land area owned by Olars. Construction will begin late next year. No estimate of the condemnation award is available.
2. *January 4.* Yang Olars (president of Olars Manufacturing Corporation) loaned the company $25,000. He obtained these funds on July 15 by borrowing against a personal life insurance policy. The loan from Olars to Olars Manufacturing Corporation was recorded in the account Loan Payable to Officers. Olars's source of the funds was not disclosed in the company records. The corporation pays the premiums on the life insurance policy and the president's wife is the owner and beneficiary of the policy.
3. *January 7.* The mineral content of a shipment of ore in transit on December 31 was determined to be 72 percent. The shipment was recorded at year-end at an estimated content of 50 percent by a debit to Raw Materials Inventory and a credit to Accounts Payable in the amount of $20,600. The final liability to the vendor is based on the actual mineral content of the shipment.
4. *January 15.* A series of personal disagreements have arisen between Olars and Zane Tweedy, his brother-in-law, the treasurer. Tweedy resigned, effective immediately, under an agreement whereby the corporation would purchase his 10 percent stock ownership at book value as of December 31. Payment is to be made in two equal amounts in

cash on April 1 and October 1. In December, the treasurer had obtained a divorce from Olars's sister.

5. *January 31.* As a result of reduced sales, production was curtailed in mid-January and some workers were laid off. On February 5, all remaining workers went on strike. To date the strike is unsettled.

Required:

Assume that the preceding items came to your attention prior to completion of your audit work on February 15. For each item

a. Give the substantive procedures, if any, that would have brought the item to your attention. Indicate other sources of information that could have revealed the item.

b. Discuss the disclosure that you would recommend for the item, listing all details that should be disclosed. Indicate those items or details, if any, that should not be disclosed. Give your reasons for recommending or not recommending disclosure of the items or details.

(AICPA adapted)

LO 11-5

11.68 **Subsequently Discovered Facts.** On June 1, Sidney Faultless of A. J. Faultless & Co., CPAs, noticed some disturbing information about the firm's client, Hopkirk Company. A story in the local paper mentioned the indictment of Tony Baker, whom Faultless knew as the assistant controller at Hopkirk. The charge was mail fraud. Faultless made discreet inquiries with the controller at Hopkirk's headquarters and learned that Baker had been speculating in foreign currency futures. In fact, part of Baker's work at Hopkirk involved managing the company's foreign currency. Unfortunately, Baker had violated company policy, lost a small amount of money, and then decided to speculate some more, lost some more, and eventually lost $7 million in company funds.

The mail fraud was involved in Baker's attempt to cover his activity until he recovered the original losses. Most of the events were in process on March 1, when Faultless had signed and dated the unqualified opinion on Hopkirk's financial statements for the year ended on the previous December 31.

Faultless determined that the information probably would affect the decisions of external users and advised Hopkirk's chief executive to make the disclosure. She flatly refused to make any disclosure, arguing that the information was immaterial. On June 17, Faultless provided the subsequent information in question to a news reporter, and it was printed in *The Wall Street Journal* with a statement that the financial statements and accompanying auditors' report on the company's financial statements could not be relied on.

Required:

Evaluate the actions of Faultless & Co., CPAs, with respect to the information discovered. What other action could Faultless & Co. have taken? What are the possible legal effects of the firm's actions, if any?

LO 11-6

11.69 **Omitted Audit Procedures.** The following are independent situations that have occurred in your public accounting firm, Arthur Hurdman[12]:

Case 1

During the internal inspection by a regional office of Arthur Hurdman, one of its clients, Wildcat Oil Suppliers, was selected for review. The reviewers questioned the thoroughness of inventory obsolescence procedures, especially in light of the depressed state of the oil exploration industry at the time. They believed that specific substantive procedures, which they considered appropriate, were not performed by your audit team.

Case 2

Top Stove, one of your clients, installed an automated system in July 2012 to process part of its accounting transactions. You completed the audit of Top Stove's December 31, 2012, statements on February 15, 2013. During the April 2013 review work on Top Stove's first-quarter financial information, you discovered that during the audit of the 2012 statements, only the manual records had been investigated in the search for unrecorded liabilities.

[12] Situation derived from examples given in Thomas R. Weirich and Elizabeth J. Ringelberg, "Omitted Audit Procedures," *CPA Journal,* March 1984, pp. 34–39.

Required:

a. Without regard to the specific situation given, answer the following questions:

1. What are the proper steps auditors should take if it is discovered, after the report date, that an important substantive procedure was omitted?

2. How are auditors' decisions affected if, after review of the audit documentation, they determine that other substantive procedures produced the sufficient appropriate audit evidence?

3. If, in subsequently applying the omitted procedure, auditors become aware of material new information that should have been disclosed in the financial statements, how should they proceed?

b. Describe the proper action to take in each of the preceding situations, given the following additional information:

Case 1. You thoroughly consider the scope of the audit of Wildcat Oil Suppliers and made a detailed review of the audit documentation. You have concluded that sufficient compensating procedures were conducted to support the valuation of inventory.

Case 2. Your subsequent investigation of the automated system's records of Top Stove revealed that material liabilities were not recorded as of December 31.

LO 11-5 11-6

11.70 **Subsequent Events, Subsequently Discovered Facts, and Omitted Procedures.** Jay Ralph completed the December 31, 2012, audit of Raider Company on February 3, 2013; Raider's financial statements, and Ralph's reports on Raider's financial statements and internal control over financial reporting were released on February 12, 2013. During April 2013, Ralph's firm conducted a quality review over selected audits that had been completed during the most recent year and the audit of Raider Company was randomly selected for review. The reviewer identified the following matters that Ralph had not addressed during the audit of Raider:

a. On February 9, 2013, Ralph learned of the following events during his post-audit meeting with Raider's chief operating officer.

1. A class action lawsuit was brought against Raider Company by some of its former employees for workplace discrimination. An attorney on behalf of a class of employees filed the lawsuit on January 10, 2013. The letter from Raider's attorneys did not identify this lawsuit.

2. One of Raider's major customers is experiencing significant financial difficulties; this customer's account receivable balance on December 31, 2012, was $1.2 million, which represented 2 percent of Raider's total accounts receivable on that date.

Because of an important deadline for submitting the financial statements to lenders for evaluation, Raider did not modify its financial statements for the preceding events despite the fact that they were material. Their justification was that because the events occurred after the date of the financial statements, they were not required to be disclosed in the financial statements. Ralph acquiesced to Raider's wishes and did not modify the report on Raider's financial statements.

b. On March 16, 2013, Ralph initially learned of the following events affecting Raider Company, neither of which was disclosed in Raider's financial statements:

1. Raider Company declared a significant dividend payable to its shareholders. This dividend was declared on March 14, 2013, to be paid to Raider's shareholders of record on May 16, 2013.

2. Raider Company activated a portion of its line of credit on February 1, 2013, by borrowing $2.5 million. This additional obligation increased Raider Company's long-term liabilities by 10 percent.

c. Reviewing Ralph's audit documentation, it does not appear that any tests were conducted to evaluate the need for impairment of the carrying value of Raider Company's property, plant, and equipment.

Required:

For each of the preceding items, describe what actions Ralph should take after the firm's quality review identified these issues.

LO 11-3, 11-4, 11-5, 11-6

11.71 **Various Completion Matters.** For each of the following independent situations, describe the most appropriate course of action that the auditors should take.

a. Drew Allison is conducting the audit of Anderson, Inc. as of December 31, 2012. At the beginning of completing the evidence gathering, Allison becomes aware that one of Anderson's major customers (Jones) is experiencing significant financial difficulties. Jones normally accounts for 5 percent of Anderson's net sales. After performing the necessary procedures, Allison believes that $2.8 million of Jones's receivable balance will ultimately become uncollectible. Allison further believes this amount is material to Anderson's financial condition and results of operations.

b. Nagan Carmelo is completing the December 31, 2012, audit of Nugget Company. As part of the final procedures, Carmelo has requested representations from Nugget's management regarding their assertion as to the fairness of the financial statements and other important matters addressed by professional standards. Because Nugget's management is attending an analyst briefing in the upcoming week, Carmelo receives these signed representations dated February 6, 2013. Carmelo has a few remaining items to complete, does so, and dates the auditors' report February 9, 2013.

c. Pat Colt completed the December 31, 2012, audit of Manning and issued an unqualified opinion on Manning's financial statements dated March 15, 2013. Colt's opinion was released, along with Manning's financial statements, on March 21, 2013. During a review of Manning's first quarter 10-Q in late April, Colt became aware of the company's settlement with a customer over a product warranty lawsuit; this case had been settled on March 13, 2013. Although Colt had received the necessary letter from Manning's attorneys, the letter was arrived prior to the settlement of the case and did not mention this development. After reviewing the information related to the settlement, Colt does not believe that the settlement is material to Manning's financial condition or results of operations and believes the opinion on Manning's financial statements is still supportable.

d. Cameron Alta completed the December 31, 2012, audit of Saxe Company on February 10, 2013. Saxe is planning to release its financial statements, along with Alta's opinion on these financial statements and internal control over financial reporting, on February 17, 2013. On February 12, 2013, a flood in one of Saxe's warehouses located in the Gulf Coast region destroyed more than $10 million of inventory. Although the extent to which this loss is recoverable through Saxe's insurance is uncertain at this time, Alta believes that this loss could have a material impact on Saxe's financial condition and results of operations.

e. During the audit of Glomco, Angel Myron identified a number of misstatements. These misstatements are not material in dollar amount, do not appear to represent any discernable pattern, and do not represent fraudulent activity. As a result, Myron has decided that Glomco's financial statements do not need to be adjusted to reflect the effect of these misstatements.

f. Following the completion of the 2012 audit of Blankenship Corporation and release of the financial statements and auditors' reports, Reese Jill met with the manager on the engagement to conduct a postmortem on the engagement and identify how changes in Blankenship's operations noted during the most recent audit may affect future audits. During this review, Jill became aware that Blankenship's process for evaluating goodwill related to an acquisition made by Blankenship during the most recent year for potential impairment had not been considered. Jill believes that the omitted procedure is important in supporting the opinion on Blankenship's financial statements and that users continue to rely on the financial statements and the auditors' reports.

LO 11-2

11.72 **Attorney Letter Responses.** Omega Corporation is involved in a lawsuit brought by a competitor for patent infringement. The competitor is asking $14 million actual damages for lost profits and unspecified punitive damages. The lawsuit has been in progress for 15 months, and Omega has worked closely with its outside counsel preparing its defense. Omega recently requested its outside attorneys with the firm of Wolfe & Goodwin to provide information to its auditors.

The managing partner of Wolfe & Goodwin asked four different lawyers who have worked on the case to prepare a concise response to auditors. The auditors received these responses from the lawyers:

1. The action involves unique characteristics in which authoritative legal precedents bearing directly on the plaintiff's claims do not seem to exist. We believe the plaintiff will have

serious problems establishing Omega's liability; nevertheless, if the plaintiff is successful, the damage award may be substantial.

2. In our opinion, Omega will be able to defend this action successfully, but, if not, the possible liability to Omega in this proceeding is nominal in amount.

3. We believe the plaintiff's case against Omega is without merit.

4. In our opinion, Omega will be able to assert meritorious defenses and has a reasonable chance of sustaining an adequate defense with a possible outcome of settling the case for less than the damages claimed.

Required:

a. Interpret each of the four responses separately. Decide whether each is (i) adequate to conclude that the likelihood of an adverse outcome is "remote," requiring no disclosure in financial statements or (ii) too vague to serve as adequate information for a decision, requiring more information from the lawyers or from management.

b. What response do you think auditors would receive if they asked the plaintiff's counsel about the likely outcome of the lawsuit? Discuss.

LO 11-2

11.73 **Accounting for a Contingency: Attorney Letter Information.** Central City was involved in litigation brought by Mexican-American Legal Defense Fund (MALDEF) over the creation of single-member voting districts (which require candidates to receive only the highest number of votes, even if not a majority) for city council positions. Auditors were working on the financial statements for the year ended December 31, 2012, and had almost completed gathering sufficient appropriate evidence by February 12, 2013.

The court heard final arguments on February 1 and rendered its judgment on February 10. The ruling was in favor of MALDEF and required the creation of certain single-member voting districts. This ruling did not impose a monetary loss on Central City, but the court also ruled that MALDEF would be awarded a judgment of court costs and attorney fees to be paid by Central City.

Local newspaper reports stated that MALDEF would seek a $250,000 recovery from the city. Auditors obtained an attorney letter dated February 15 that stated the following:

In my opinion, the court will award some amount for MALDEF's attorney fees. In regard to your inquiry about an amount or range of possible loss, I estimate that such an award could be anywhere from $30,000 to $175,000.

Required:

a. What weight should be given to the newspaper report of the $250,000 amount that MALDEF might ask? What weight should be given to the attorney's estimate?

b. How should this subsequent event be reflected in the 2012 financial statements of Central City?

LO 11-4

11.74 **Mini-Case: Going-Concern Reporting.** Refer to the mini-case "GM: Running on Empty" and respond to questions 1–6.

LO 11-2

11.75 **Kaplan CPA Exam Simulation: Attorney Letters.**

CPA REVIEW

Required:

Go to the Kaplan website link at www.mhhe.com/Louwers5e, click on XYZ Co. (Attorney Letters) AUD TBS, and complete your answer. Only complete the column related to "Audit Response (report)."

Reports on Audited Financial Statements

The television industry doesn't like to see the complexity of the world. It prefers simple reporting, with simple ideas: this is white, that's black; this is good, that's bad.
    Filmmaker Krzysztof Kieslowski

In our opinion, the financial statements referred to above present fairly, in all material respects, the financial position of Enron Corp. and subsidiaries as of December 31, 2000 and 1999, and the results of their operations, cash flows, and changes in shareholders' equity for each of the three years in the period ended December 31, 2000, in conformity with accounting principles generally accepted in the United States.
    The opinion paragraph from Arthur Andersen's final audit of Enron Corp. dated February 23, 2001

Professional Standards References

Topic	AU/ISA Section	PCAOB Reference*
Association with Financial Statements	504	AU 504
Going Concern (Exposure Draft)	570	AU 341
Audits of Group Financial Statements	600	AU 543
Reporting on Financial Statements	700	AS 1, AS 5
Modifications to Reports on Financial Statements	705	AU 508
Emphasis-of-Matter Paragraphs	706	AU 508
Consistency	708	AS 6
Other Information	720	AU 550
Required Supplementary Information	730	AU 558
Summary Financial Statements	810	AU 552

*AU references represent standards issued by the ASB prior to April 16, 2003, that have not been superseded or amended by the PCAOB.

LEARNING OBJECTIVES

Management has the primary responsibility for the effectiveness of the entity's internal control over financial reporting and fair presentation of financial statements in conformity with generally accepted accounting principles (GAAP) or other applicable reporting framework. Auditors have primary responsibility for expressing an opinion, based on their audits, on internal control over financial reporting and the fairness of the financial statements in auditors' reports. The accounting firm partner's signature on these reports concludes the last stage of the audit engagement, as shown here:

Obtain (or Retain) Engagement → Engagement Planning → Risk Assessment → Substantive Procedures → **Reporting**

While the vast majority of audits involve "clean" reports (unqualified opinions), this chapter covers the most frequent variations in auditors' reports. The *standard report* is a starting place, and you must understand the reasons for modifying the standard language when auditors cannot issue a "clean" opinion.

Your objectives are to be able to:

LO 12-1 Provide an overview of the types of reports that accompany an entity's financial statements.

LO 12-2 Identify three general functions of the auditors' report on an entity's financial statements.

LO 12-3 Explain the significance of each of the paragraphs in the auditors' standard report on an entity's financial statements.

LO 12-4 Describe the types of auditors' reports that may be issued if an entity's financial statements contain a departure from GAAP.

LO 12-5 Describe the types of auditors' reports that may be issued if scope limitations exist.

LO 12-6 Describe how the standard report is modified when auditors issue unqualified opinions but reference other matters affecting the audit or the client.

LO 12-7 Identify other circumstances affecting auditors' reporting responsibilities and explain how they affect auditors' reports on an entity's financial statements.

INTRODUCTION[1]

Founded in 1908, **General Motors (GM)** is truly an iconic American corporation. From 1931 through 2008, GM was the world's largest automobile manufacturer; in 1955, it became the first company to report more than $1 billion in revenues and reached a peak market share of 51 percent in 1962. GM's domination in the market was such that many recommended the company be subject to scrutiny under antitrust laws. In 1971, former President Lyndon Johnson made the statement "now what's good for General Motors really is good for America."[2]

GM's net income reached an all-time high of $6.7 billion in 1997, and the automaker continued to generate positive net income through 2004. In 2005, things began to change. GM reported a net loss of over $10 billion and has continued to post annual losses since

---

[1] With the exception of items that are directly footnoted, facts in this section were drawn from "GM Seeks $16.6 Billion More in U.S. Aid," *The Wall Street Journal,* February 18, 2009, p. A1; "GM Will Replace at Least Six Others on Board," *The Wall Street Journal,* March 31, 2009, p. A8; "A Company's Saga of Decline and Denial," *The Wall Street Journal,* June 2, 2009, p. A1, A15; "GM Set to Exit Bankruptcy," *The Wall Street Journal,* July 10, 2009, p. A1.

[2] "The Black on GM's Board," *Time,* September 6, 1976.

that time with losses reaching $30.8 billion in 2008. (GM's cash flow from operations in 2008 was a negative $12 billion.)

Because of concerns with the ultimate impact of GM's financial struggles on the world economy, GM received $13.4 billion in government loans in December 2008 and requested an additional $16.6 billion. President Barak Obama's administration pledged interim financing to allow GM to develop a restructuring plan, requested then-CEO Rick Wagoner to resign, and announced a plan to replace at least 6 of the 12 members of GM's board of directors. All of these events occurred in a market in which the economic conditions sharply decreased demand for automobile purchases. Not surprisingly, GM's stock reached a low (at that time) of $1.45 per share on March 6, 2009. (With one brief exception, GM's stock traded between $30 per share and $82 per share between 1983 and 2008.)

What should GM's auditors (**Deloitte & Touche**) do in this situation? Clearly, some significant questions existed about GM's ability to continue to exist as a going concern. However, if GM's management disclosed these going-concern uncertainties, would this affect the conformity of GM's financial statements with GAAP[3]? And how should Deloitte's report have reflected these uncertainties?

In its March 4, 2009, report on GM's financial statements, Deloitte & Touche concluded that GM's financial statements were fairly presented in conformity with GAAP. However, Deloitte expanded its report to include the recognition of GM's going-concern uncertainties to users of GM's financial statements:

> The accompanying consolidated financial statements for the year ended December 31, 2008, have been prepared assuming that the Corporation [GM] will continue as a going concern. As discussed in Note 2 to the consolidated financial statements, the Corporation's recurring losses from operations, stockholders' deficit, and inability to generate sufficient cash flow to meet its obligations and sustain its operations raise substantial doubt about its ability to continue as a going concern. Management's plans concerning these matters are also discussed in Note 2 to the consolidated financial statements. The consolidated financial statements do not include any adjustments that might result from the outcome of this uncertainty.

On June 1, 2009, the once unthinkable happened: GM filed for Chapter 11 bankruptcy, from which it exited on July 10, 2009 (just 40 days later). On November 18, 2010, GM returned to public company status with an "initial public offering" that raised $23.1 billion, one of the largest in the history of the United States.[4] Deloitte & Touche's opinion on GM's 2010 financial statements (issued on March 1, 2011) concluded that the financial statements were presented in conformity with GAAP and made no reference to the going-concern uncertainties that GM had previously faced. In addition, 2010 was GM's most profitable year since 1999.[5]

As the preceding vignette indicates, the auditors' report on an entity's financial statements does more than simply report on whether the financial statements are fairly presented in conformity with GAAP. In this case, professional standards required Deloitte & Touche to inform users about GM's potential going-concern problems despite the fact that this information was disclosed by GM and that its financial statements were in conformity with GAAP. Interestingly, while **Ford's** audit report did not provide a going-concern uncertainty, its auditor (**PricewaterhouseCoopers**) expanded the audit report to refer to the effect of the financial crisis and recession on the automotive industry as well as the viability plans submitted by two unnamed competitors (presumably GM and **Chrysler**).

This chapter discusses auditors' reports on an entity's financial statements. As with the GM example discussed, auditors' reports serve as an important tool to communicate to third-party users both the conformity of the entity's financial statements with GAAP as well as other important matters affecting the entity.

---

[3] Throughout this chapter, we assume U.S. GAAP to be the applicable financial reporting framework.
[4] "Total for GM Offering Rises to $23.1 Billion," *The Wall Street Journal*, November 27, 2010, p. B4.
[5] "GM Rebounds with Best Year Since 1999," *The Wall Street Journal*, February 25, 2011, p. B1.

REPORTS ACCOMPANYING THE ENTITY'S FINANCIAL STATEMENTS

LEARNING OBJECTIVE 12-1
Provide an overview of the types of reports that accompany an entity's financial statements.

Within 60 days of their fiscal year-end, large public entities subject to the reporting requirements of the Securities and Exchange Commission (SEC) are required to file certain financial information with the SEC. This information, which includes the entity's audited financial statements and footnotes and other required disclosures related to the financial statements, is filed using Form 10-K.

Until 2004, this financial information was accompanied by a single report, the auditors' **report on financial statements and related disclosures**. It provides (or disclaims) an opinion on whether the entity's financial statements and related disclosures are presented in conformity with GAAP. This opinion is based on the tests of controls and substantive procedures that have been performed during the audit engagement and discussed throughout this text.

The Sarbanes-Oxley Act of 2002 and *Accounting Standard 5 (AS 5)* have mandated two additional types of reports for SEC registrants:

1. A report, prepared by the entity's management, on the effectiveness of the entity's internal control over financial reporting.
2. A report, prepared by the auditors, on the effectiveness of the entity's internal control over financial reporting.

Management's **report on internal control over financial reporting** was discussed in Chapter 5. As noted there, management's report includes the following major components:

- A statement indicating that management is responsible for establishing and maintaining adequate internal control over financial reporting.
- A statement identifying the framework used by management to assess the effectiveness of the entity's internal control over financial reporting.
- Management's opinion on the effectiveness of the entity's internal control over financial reporting, including an explicit statement as to whether the internal control over financial reporting is effective.
- A statement that the registered accounting firm auditing the financial statements (auditor) has issued a report on the entity's internal control over financial reporting (see following paragraph).

The auditors' **report on internal control over financial reporting** provides an opinion on the effectiveness of the entity's internal control over financial reporting. This opinion is based on tests of the operating effectiveness of the entity's internal control policies and procedures over financial reporting.

Refer to Exhibit 12.1 for a summary of the reports that accompany an entity's financial statements. Note that auditors can issue either two separate reports (one related to the financial statements and one related to internal control over financial reporting) or a single combined report addressing both the financial statements and internal control over financial reporting. Note also that management's report on internal control over financial reporting accompanies the entity's financial statements. It is important to reiterate that *AS 5* reports on internal control over financial reporting are required *only for SEC registrants*.

The focus in this chapter is auditors' reports on an entity's annual financial statements based on an audit of these financial statements. In addition to the reports in Exhibit 12.1, public entities are required to prepare and file interim (quarterly) financial statements (through Form 10-Q) with the SEC within 30 days of the end of each fiscal quarter. Auditors perform a less comprehensive examination (referred to as a *review engagement*) on these financial statements. Reviews of interim financial information, and the auditors' report based on these reviews, are discussed in Module A of this text.

EXHIBIT 12.1
Reports Accompanying the Entity's Financial Statements

Prepared by Management:
- Financial Statements and Other Disclosures
- Management's Report on Internal Control over Financial Reporting(*)

Prepared by Auditors:
- Auditors' Report on Financial Statements and Other Disclosures
- Auditors' Report on Internal Control over Financial Reporting(*)

OR

- Combined Report on Financial Statements and Other Disclosures and Internal Control over Financial Reporting(*)

* Presented only if required to comply with *AS 5* (SEC registrants).

> ### ↳ REVIEW CHECKPOINTS
>
> 12.1 List the reports that accompany a public entity's financial statements along with the party or parties that prepare each report.
>
> 12.2 What are the major elements included in management's report on internal control over financial reporting?

REPORTING ON THE ENTITY'S FINANCIAL STATEMENTS

LEARNING OBJECTIVE 12-2
Identify three general functions of the auditors' report on an entity's financial statements.

Purpose of the Report

In its discussion of the overall objectives of an audit conducted in accordance with generally accepted auditing standards (GAAS), the AICPA notes that the purpose of an audit is

> ... to enhance the degree of confidence that intended users can place in the financial statements. This is achieved by the *expression of an opinion* by the auditor on whether the financial statements are prepared, in all material respects, in accordance with an applicable financial reporting framework [emphasis added].[6]

The auditors' report serves to communicate to users three specific elements with respect to the financial statements, the conduct of the audit, and the entity in general:

1. The report indicates *whether the financial statements are presented in conformity with GAAP (or other applicable financial reporting framework, such as International Financial Reporting Standards [IFRS]).* If the entity's financial statements do not conform with GAAP, the auditors must indicate how the financial statements would appear if they did. Additionally, the auditors must disclose any material omissions from the financial statements. For example, if the entity omits a footnote, the auditors must disclose the GAAP departure in the report as well as the information that was omitted.

2. Auditors use their reports to *highlight any unusual aspects of the audit examination.* The audit team may not have been able to examine all facets of the entity due either to the timing of the audit, the nature of the entity, or entity-imposed restrictions. For example, if the entity has never been audited before, the auditors have the nearly

---
[6] Proposed Preface to *Codification of Statements on Auditing Standards, Principles Governing an Audit Conducted in Accordance with Generally Accepted Auditing Standards* (AICPA, 2009), paragraph 1.

impossible task of recreating financial statements from the previous year. In a more ominous scenario, the entity may not allow the auditors access to all relevant information, thereby prohibiting the auditors from gathering sufficient evidence to express an opinion on the financial statements. Auditors also may use their reports to indicate a division of responsibility when components of group financial statements are audited by auditors affiliated with another firm.

3. Even if the financial statements are fairly presented in conformity with GAAP and the audit was conducted in accordance with GAAS, *auditors may wish to reference other matters affecting the audit or the client.* Auditors, for example, can highlight a change in an entity's accounting principles that could result in a comparability problem when comparing prior-years' results with those of the current year. When an entity is experiencing significant financial difficulties, auditors can express their concerns ("substantial doubt") about the entity's ability to continue as a going concern. Auditors also can use their reports to emphasize matters such as subsequent events, significant related-party transactions, or other events and transactions that they believe are material to financial statement users.

In the following sections of this chapter, we discuss how the various conditions, events, and transactions just mentioned affect the auditors' report.

↳ REVIEW CHECKPOINT

12.3 What are three general functions of the auditors' report?

The Standard Report

LEARNING OBJECTIVE 12-3
Explain the significance of each of the paragraphs in the auditors' standard report on an entity's financial statements.

Auditors issue a standard report when (1) the financial statements present fairly the financial condition, results of operations, and cash flows of the entity in conformity with GAAP; (2) there are no unusual issues related to the conduct of the audit; and (3) the auditors do not need to highlight any entity transactions or events to financial users. The auditors' standard report contains four basic components: (1) the **introductory paragraph**, (2) the **scope paragraph**, (3) the **opinion paragraph**, and (4) the **internal control paragraph**. See Exhibit 12.2 for an example.

The report shown in Exhibit 12.2 would be issued for public entities subject to the requirements of *AS 5;* this report, and modifications to the report, will be the focus of this chapter. The report issued for a nonpublic entity (which is largely similar to that shown in Exhibit 12.2) is shown in Appendix 12A.

All standard reports contain these features:

1. *Title.* The title should contain the word *independent,* as in "independent registered public accounting firm" (for public entities) or "independent auditors" (for nonpublic entities).

2. *Address.* The report should be addressed to the client, which occasionally may be different from the auditee. A **client** is the person (entity, board of directors, agency, or some other person or group) who retains the auditors and pays the fee. In financial audits, the client and the auditee usually are the same economic entity. An **auditee** is the actual designation of the entity or other entity whose financial statements are being audited. Occasionally, the client and the auditee are different. For example, if Conglomerate Corporation hires and pays the auditors to audit Newtck Company in connection with a proposed acquisition, Conglomerate is the client and Newtck is the auditee.

3. *Notice of audit.* A sentence should identify the financial statements and declare that they were audited. This appears in the *introductory paragraph.*

EXHIBIT 12.2 Auditors' Standard Report

Title	Report of Independent Registered Public Accounting Firm
Address	To the Board of Directors and Shareholders Dunder-Mifflin, Inc.
Introductory Paragraph	We have audited the accompanying balance sheets of Dunder-Mifflin, Inc. as of December 31, 2012 and 2011, and the related statements of income, shareholders' equity, and cash flows for each of the years in the three-year period ended December 31, 2012. These financial statements are the responsibility of Dunder-Mifflin, Inc.'s management. Our responsibility is to express an opinion on these financial statements based on our audits.
Scope Paragraph	We conducted our audits in accordance with the standards of the Public Company Accounting Oversight Board (United States). Those standards require that we plan and perform the audit to obtain reasonable assurance about whether the financial statements are free of material misstatement. An audit includes examining, on a test basis, evidence supporting the amounts and disclosures in the financial statements. An audit also includes assessing the accounting principles used and significant estimates made by management, as well as evaluating the overall financial statement presentation. We believe that our audits provide a reasonable basis for our opinion.
Opinion Paragraph	In our opinion, the financial statements referred to above present fairly, in all material respects, the financial position of Dunder-Mifflin, Inc. at December 31, 2012 and 2011, and the results of its operations and its cash flows for each of the years in the three-year period ended December 31, 2012, in conformity with accounting principles generally accepted in the United States of America.
Internal Control Paragraph	We have also audited, in accordance with the standards of the Public Company Accounting Oversight Board (United States), the effectiveness of Dunder-Mifflin, Inc.'s internal control over financial reporting as of December 31, 2012, based on criteria established in *Internal Control—Integrated Framework* issued by the Committee of Sponsoring Organizations of the Treadway Commission and our report dated January 29, 2013, expressed an unqualified opinion thereon.
Signature	*Michael Scarn, LLP* Scranton, PA
Date	January 29, 2013

4. *Responsibilities.* The report should state management's responsibility for the financial statements and the auditors' responsibility for the report. These statements are also in the *introductory paragraph.*

5. *Description of the audit.* The second paragraph (*scope paragraph*) should indicate that the audit was conducted in accordance with the standards of the Public Company Accounting Oversight Board (PCAOB) (which represent GAAS for the audits of public entities). The scope paragraph also should describe the characteristics of an audit, including a statement that the audit provides a reasonable basis for the opinion.

6. *Opinion.* The report should express an opinion (*opinion paragraph*) regarding conformity of the financial statements with GAAP. In this example, the conclusion that Dunder-Mifflin, Inc.'s financial statements are presented in conformity with GAAP is referred to as an *unqualified opinion.*

7. *Internal control.* The report should reference the auditors' report and opinion on the client's internal control over financial reporting (*internal control paragraph*). These reports and engagements were initially discussed in Chapter 5. As noted later in this chapter, auditors may prepare a combined report that expresses opinions on both the financial statements and internal control over financial reporting.

8. *Signature.* The auditors (partner of the audit team) should sign the firm name to the report, manually or otherwise.

9. *Date.* The date of the report should be the date when the auditors have obtained sufficient appropriate evidence to support the opinion (the **date of the auditors' report**).

> ### AUDITING INSIGHT   What's That Date?
>
> In **Hertz Global Holdings'** 10-K filed with the SEC on February 26, 2010, **PricewaterhouseCoopers'** audit report was dated March 3, 2009 (almost 10 months *before* the date of the financial statements covered by the report!). Without identifying the reason for the discrepancy (other than the report contained a "typographical error in the opinion date"), Hertz subsequently filed an amended 10-K that contained the correct report date of February 26, 2010.
>
> Source: *Hertz Global Holdings 2010 10-K*

Introductory Paragraph

The introductory paragraph indicates that an audit has been conducted and identifies the financial statements that the auditors examined. Identifying the financial statements is important because the opinion paragraph expresses an opinion on these financial statements. The introductory paragraph also explicitly states that the financial statements are the responsibility of management. This statement was added to ensure that users did not mistakenly attribute responsibility for the preparation and presentation of the financial statements to the auditors. Instead, auditors are responsible for expressing an opinion on the financial statements based on the audit work performed.

In some instances, entities engage auditors to audit and report on only one of the financial statements but not on the others (although GAAP requires that an income statement always be accompanied by a statement of cash flows). Most often, such an engagement is for the audit of the balance sheet only. Audit standards make a special exception for this type of engagement referred to as a *limited reporting engagement*. A report on only one financial statement is permitted. In the introductory paragraph, the auditors state that only one statement (e.g., the balance sheet) has been audited. In the opinion paragraph, the opinion on presentation in conformity with GAAP is limited to one characteristic (e.g., financial position). If one or more of the basic financial statement(s) is not identified in the introductory paragraph, the opinion paragraph likewise should not express an opinion on these statement(s).

Scope Paragraph

The scope paragraph is the description of the character of the work in the audit. The sentence "We conducted our audits in accordance with the standards of the Public Company Accounting Oversight Board (United States)" refers to GAAS and the responsibilities and performance principles discussed in Chapter 2. As you read this paragraph, phrases such as "reasonable assurance," "material misstatement" and "evidence" clearly relate to elements within these principles. However, by following GAAS, it is implicit that the auditors (1) had competence and capabilities to perform the audit, (2) complied with relevant ethical requirements, including independence and due care, (3) maintained professional skepticism and exercised professional judgment, (4) planned and supervised the work, (5) identified and assessed risks of material misstatement based on an understanding of the entity, including internal control, and (6) gathered sufficient appropriate evidence.

To the extent that one or more of the elements of the responsibilities and performance principles is not actually satisfied during an audit, the scope paragraph must be modified to identify which standard was not satisfied. Such modifications can be caused by a lack of independence, lack of sufficient appropriate evidence, or restrictions on procedures that the auditors could perform. In practice, auditors also modify the standard opinion paragraph language when the scope paragraph is modified.

Opinion Paragraph

Users of audited financial statements are generally most interested in the opinion paragraph. This long sentence contains the conclusions about the financial statements. This conclusion is in the form of an *opinion* on whether the entity's financial statements present its financial condition, the results of operations, and cash flows in conformity with GAAP.

Auditors may issue four types of opinions:

1. An **unqualified opinion**, in which the conclusion is that the financial statements present the financial condition, results of operations, and cash flows in conformity with GAAP. The *auditors' standard report* in Exhibit 12.2 is an example of an unqualified opinion; however, unqualified opinions can be issued in forms other than the standard report. Interestingly, while the term *unqualified* normally has a negative connotation, an unqualified opinion is the most favorable opinion auditors can issue.

2. A **qualified opinion**, in which the conclusion is that, with the exception of one or more issues, the financial statements present the financial condition, results of operations, and cash flows in conformity with GAAP. Qualified opinions use the phrase *except for* in describing the issues that give rise to the qualification. Interestingly, although the term *qualified* normally has a positive connotation, qualified opinions are issued when one or more issues are encountered during the audit.

3. An **adverse opinion**, in which the conclusion is that the financial statements *do not* present the financial condition, results of operations, and cash flows in conformity with GAAP.

4. A **disclaimer of opinion**, in which the auditors do not express an opinion on the fairness of the entity's financial statements.

AU 705 refers to qualified opinions, adverse opinions, and disclaimers of opinion as **modified opinions**.

Internal Control Paragraph

As noted in Chapter 5, *AS 5* requires auditors to evaluate and report on the operating effectiveness of the entity's internal control over financial reporting. Auditors can fulfill their reporting responsibility in two ways. First, they can issue two separate reports (one on the financial statements and one on internal control over financial reporting); if this option is selected, each of these reports will include a reference to the other report. As a result, the auditors' report on the entity's financial statements references the auditors' opinion on the effectiveness of internal control over financial reporting. In Exhibit 12.2, the last paragraph of the auditors' report on the financial statements states that Dunder-Mifflin, Inc.'s internal control over financial reporting was effective based on criteria established by the Committee of Sponsoring Organizations of the Treadway Commission (COSO) and refers to the auditors' report expressing an unqualified opinion on internal control. This report (not shown) would, in turn, refer to Michael Scarn LLP's audit of Dunder-Mifflin, Inc.'s financial statements and refer to the unqualified opinion issued on those financial statements.

The second option for Michael Scarn would be to issue a single report that expresses opinions on both Dunder-Mifflin, Inc.'s financial statements and internal control over financial reporting. This report (sometimes referred to as an **integrated report**) is shown in Exhibit 12.3. This report essentially combines the report on Dunder-Mifflin, Inc.'s financial statements (shown in Exhibit 12.2) with a report on its internal control (for examples, see Chapter 5). A review of this report in Exhibit 12.3 reveals that the introductory, scope, and opinion paragraphs are modified to describe the additional responsibilities assumed (introductory paragraph), engagement scope (scope paragraph), and conclusions (opinion paragraph) resulting from the examination of Dunder-Mifflin, Inc.'s internal control over financial reporting. In addition, two additional paragraphs (the definition and inherent limitations paragraphs) are included to provide readers with additional information about Dunder-Mifflin, Inc.'s internal control over financial reporting.

EXHIBIT 12.3 Combined Report on Financial Statements and Internal Control over Financial Reporting

Title	**Report of Independent Registered Public Accounting Firm**
Address	To the Board of Directors and Shareholders Dunder-Mifflin, Inc.
Introductory Paragraph	We have audited the accompanying balance sheets of Dunder-Mifflin, Inc. as of December 31, 2012 and 2011, and the related statements of income, shareholders' equity, and cash flows for each of the years in the three-year period ended December 31, 2012. We have also audited Dunder-Mifflin, Inc.'s internal control over financial reporting as of December 31, 2012, based on criteria established in *Internal Control—Integrated Framework* issued by the Committee of Sponsoring Organizations of the Treadway Commission (COSO criteria). Dunder-Mifflin, Inc.'s management is responsible for these financial statements, for maintaining effective internal control over financial reporting, and for its assessment of internal control over financial reporting, included in the accompanying "Management's Report to Shareholders" under the caption "Report on Internal Control over Financial Reporting." Our responsibility is to express an opinion on these financial statements and an opinion on the company's internal control over financial reporting based on our audits.
Scope Paragraph	We conducted our audits in accordance with the standards of the Public Company Accounting Oversight Board (United States). Those standards require that we plan and perform the audits to obtain reasonable assurance about whether the financial statements are free of material misstatement and whether effective internal control over financial reporting was maintained in all material respects. Our audits of the financial statements included examining, on a test basis, evidence supporting the amounts and disclosures in the financial statements, assessing the accounting principles used and significant estimates made by management, and evaluating the overall financial statement presentation. Our audit of internal control over financial reporting included obtaining an understanding of internal control over financial reporting, assessing the risk that a material weakness exists, and testing and evaluating the design and operating effectiveness of internal control based on the assessed risk. We believe that our audits provide a reasonable basis for our opinions.
Definition Paragraph	A company's internal control over financial reporting is a process designed to provide reasonable assurance regarding the reliability of financial reporting and the preparation of financial statements for external purposes in accordance with generally accepted accounting principles. A company's internal control over financial reporting includes those policies and procedures that (1) pertain to the maintenance of records that, in reasonable detail, accurately and fairly reflect the transactions and dispositions of the assets of the company; (2) provide reasonable assurance that transactions are recorded as necessary to permit preparation of financial statements in accordance with generally accepted accounting principles and that receipts and expenditures of the company are being made only in accordance with authorizations of management and directors of the company; and (3) provide reasonable assurance regarding prevention or timely detection of unauthorized acquisition, use, or disposition of the company's assets that could have a material effect on the financial statements.
Inherent Limitations Paragraph	Because of its inherent limitations, internal control over financial reporting may not prevent or detect misstatements. Also, projections of any evaluation of effectiveness to future periods are subject to the risk that controls may become inadequate because of changes in conditions, or that the degree of compliance with the policies or procedures may deteriorate.
Opinion Paragraph	In our opinion, the financial statements referred to above present fairly, in all material respects, the financial position of Dunder-Mifflin, Inc. as of December 31, 2012 and 2011, and the results of its operations and cash flows for each of the years in the three-year period ended December 31, 2012, in conformity with accounting principles generally accepted in the United States of America. Also, in our opinion, Dunder-Mifflin, Inc. maintained, in all material respects, effective internal control over financial reporting as of December 31, 2012, based on the COSO criteria.
Signature	*Michael Scarn LLP* Scranton, PA
Date	January 29, 2013

Information on the audit reports of 476 of the Fortune 500 companies (largest 500 U.S. companies based on revenues) are available on the Audit Analytics database. Of these, 177 (37 percent) used a single report and 299 (63 percent) used two separate reports. Because the focus of this chapter is on reports on the fairness of the entity's financial statements, we illustrate report modifications assuming that separate reports are prepared.

Reports Other Than the Standard Report

Subsequent sections of this chapter explain the major variations on the standard report on the financial statements. There are three reasons for issuing a report other than the standard report.

1. If the financial statements contain a *departure from GAAP,* including inadequate disclosure, the auditors must choose between an *unqualified opinion* (including the standard report), a *qualified opinion,* or an *adverse opinion.* The choice depends on the nature and materiality of the effects of the GAAP departure.

2. If matters affect the auditors' ability to conduct a GAAS audit, the auditors may deviate from the standard report. For example, when the audit has a *scope limitation* (a departure from GAAS in which the extent of audit work was limited) and the auditors have not been able to obtain sufficient appropriate evidence on a particular account balance or disclosure, the auditors must choose between an *unqualified opinion* (including the standard report), a *qualified opinion,* or a *disclaimer of opinion.* The choice again depends on the significance of the scope limitation and materiality of the affected account balances.

3. If the auditors believe it is important to *bring certain information to financial statement users' attention,* the auditors may highlight the information by adding an explanatory paragraph to or otherwise modifying the language in the standard report. These situations include changes in an entity's accounting methods, financial difficulties facing the entity, justified departures from accounting principles, the involvement of component auditors in an audit of group financial statements, and the desire to emphasize some matter with respect to the entity. In many of these cases, the fairness of the entity's financial statements is not affected, so an *unqualified opinion* is still appropriate. However, the modifications made to the report to address these issues would result in this report differing from the standard report.

It is clear from the preceding sections that various reporting alternatives are permissible to reflect departures from GAAP and scope limitations. Although the details are discussed in subsequent sections, auditors issue adverse opinions or disclaimers of opinion when GAAP departures and scope limitations are highly material and pervasive (i.e., affect a substantial portion of the financial statements) with qualified opinions issued when these matters are material but not as pervasive.

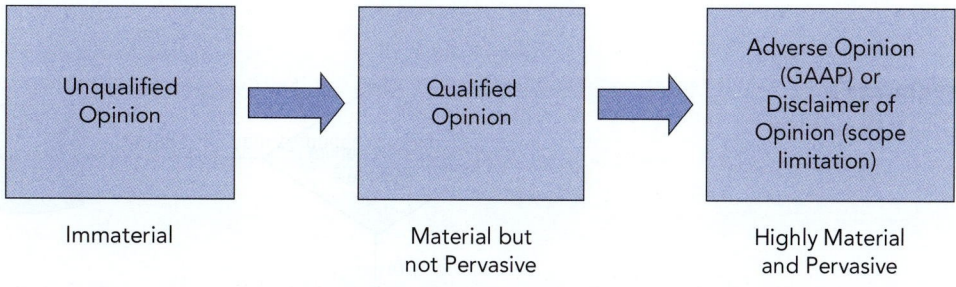

REVIEW CHECKPOINTS

12.4 What are the important elements of the auditors' standard report?

12.5 Regarding the standard introductory and scope paragraphs, (a) what do they identify as the objects of the audit and (b) what does the sentence "We conducted our audit in accordance with the standards of the Public Company Accounting Oversight Board" mean?

12.6 Under what circumstances would auditors issue qualified opinions, adverse opinions, and disclaimers of opinion?

12.7 What are the major reasons for deviating from the wording in the auditors' standard report?

AUDITORS' REPORTS ON DEPARTURES FROM GAAP

LEARNING OBJECTIVE 12-4
Describe the types of auditors' reports that may be issued if an entity's financial statements contain a departure from GAAP.

Audit examinations frequently identify transactions that have not been recorded according to GAAP. In most of these situations, assuming that the results are material to the financial statements, entities adjust their financial statements to reflect the proper accounting treatment for the transactions. As discussed later in this section, public entities are not permitted to file financial statements with the SEC if these statements are "false and misleading"; departures from GAAP would constitute such a filing. The process through which auditors propose adjustments to financial statements for misstatements identified during the audit was discussed in Chapter 11.

An entity's management may decide to present financial statements containing an accounting treatment or disclosure that is not in conformity with GAAP. Situations in which an entity does not follow GAAP in preparing its financial statements are referred to as **departures from GAAP**. Exhibit 12.4 summarizes auditors' reporting options when departures from GAAP are noted.

As with any issue, a departure from GAAP may not be material to the entity's financial statements. Recall the wording of the opinion paragraph in the auditors' standard report: "In our opinion, the financial statements referred to above present fairly, *in all material respects . . .*" [emphasis added]. As a result, if a departure from GAAP is immaterial, the auditors would treat the departure as if it did not exist. In this case, the auditors can express an unqualified opinion and issue the standard report.

If the departure is sufficiently material to affect users' decisions based on the financial statements but can be "compartmentalized," the auditors must *qualify* the opinion. By "compartmentalized," we mean that the departure can be isolated to a particular account group (e.g., accounts receivable not valued at net realizable value) or transactions (e.g., failure to capitalize leases) without affecting other accounts to a material extent. In other words, this departure would not be considered *pervasive*. This qualification isolates a particular departure but indicates that the financial statements are otherwise in conformity with GAAP. The nature of the GAAP departure must be explained in a separate paragraph in the report, as shown in Exhibit 12.5.

On the other hand, if the GAAP departure is pervasive, affecting numerous accounts and financial statement relationships, or is material to the point that the financial statements as a whole are misleading, the auditors must issue an adverse opinion. As noted earlier, in an adverse opinion, auditors conclude that the financial statements *do not*

EXHIBIT 12.4
GAAP Departures

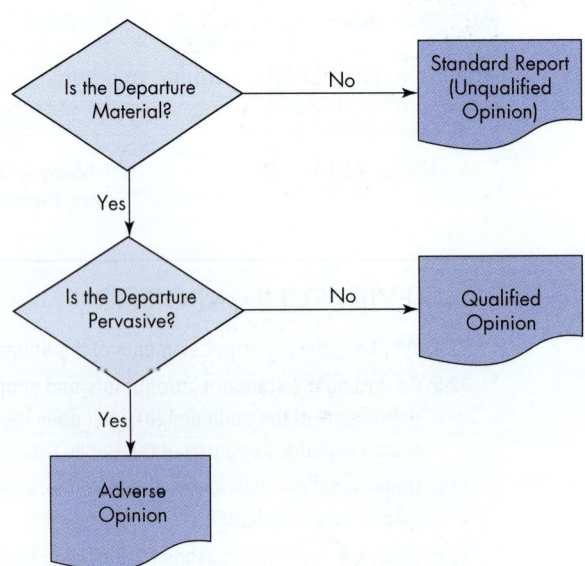

EXHIBIT 12.5
Qualified Opinion

Report of Independent Registered Public Accounting Firm*

To the Board of Directors and Shareholders, Dunder-Mifflin, Inc.

[Standard Introductory Paragraph]

[Standard Scope Paragraph]

As discussed in Note 16, an additional provision in the amount of $30,000,000 for possible uncollectible receivables at December 31, 2011, was charged to operations during the year ended December 31, 2012, which, in our opinion, should have been reflected in the financial statements for 2011. Had this provision been properly recorded in the 2011 financial statements, the net loss in that year would have been increased by $30,000,000 and shareholders' equity would have been decreased by that amount, and Dunder-Mifflin, Inc., would have reported net earnings of $700,000 for the year ended December 31, 2012, rather than the net loss of $29,300,000 as reflected in the statements of income, shareholders' equity, and cash flows for that period.

In our opinion, *except for the effects of the provision for possible uncollectible receivables reported in the preceding paragraph,* the financial statements referred to above present fairly, in all material respects, the financial position of Dunder-Mifflin, Inc., at December 31, 2012 and 2011, and the results of operations and cash flows for each of the years in the three-year period ended December 31, 2012, in conformity with accounting principles generally accepted in the United States of America.

[Standard Internal Control Paragraph]

Michael Scarn LLP
Scranton, PA
January 29, 2013

---

present fairly the financial position, results of operations, and cash flows in conformity with GAAP. The introductory and scope paragraphs should not be modified because, in order to decide to issue an adverse opinion, the audit team must possess all evidence necessary to reach the decision. When this opinion is issued, all substantive reasons must be disclosed in the report in the report.

The example in Exhibit 12.6 assumes that the same departure in GAAP that served as the focus of the qualified opinion in Exhibit 12.5 reached a level of materiality and pervasiveness to warrant an adverse opinion. The adverse opinions relate to the results of operations and cash flows for 2011 and 2012 and to the financial position as of December 31, 2011. However, as noted in the last paragraph, the balance sheet for 2012 and statements of income, shareholders' equity, and cash flows for 2010 were presented in conformity with GAAP. This report illustrates the fact that auditors can issue different opinions on different financial statements in the same report.

The report in Exhibit 12.6 illustrates how different opinions on financial statements in comparative years can be issued (i.e., an unqualified opinion on the statements of income, shareholders' equity, and cash flows in 2010 and adverse opinions on these statements in 2011 and 2012). This report also illustrates how different opinions on different financial statements within the same year may be appropriate. For example, because the timing of the provision for uncollectible accounts did not affect the ending account receivable balance in 2012, an unqualified opinion on the 2012 balance sheet is appropriate. However, because the timing of recognizing this provision did materially impact the results of operations for both 2011 and 2012, Michael Scarn's report appropriately expressed an adverse opinion on the 2012 statements of income, shareholders' equity, and cash flows.

---

[7] For easier reference, all revisions to the auditors' standard report in Exhibit 12.2 are shown in color and italicized in reports presented throughout this chapter.

EXHIBIT 12.6
Adverse Opinion

> **Report of Independent Registered Public Accounting Firm**
>
> To the Board of Directors and Shareholders, Dunder-Mifflin, Inc.:
>
> [Standard Introductory Paragraph]
>
> [Standard Scope Paragraph]
>
> As discussed in Note 16, an additional provision in the amount of $30,000,000 for possible uncollectible receivables at December 31, 2011, was charged to operations during the year ended December 31, 2012, which, in our opinion, should have been reflected in the financial statements for 2011. Had this provision been properly recorded in the 2011 financial statements, the net loss in that year would have been increased by $30,000,000 and shareholders' equity would have been decreased by that amount, and Dunder-Mifflin, Inc., would have reported net earnings of $700,000 for the year ended December 31, 2012, rather than the net loss of $29,300,000 as reflected in the statements of income, shareholders' equity, and cash flows for that period.
>
> In our opinion, *because of the effects of the matters discussed above,* the aforementioned balance sheet as of December 31, 2011, and the statements of income, shareholders' equity, and cash flows for the years ended December 31, 2011 and 2012, *do not* present fairly the financial position of Dunder-Mifflin, Inc., as of December 31, 2011, or the results of its operations or its cash flows for the years ended December 31, 2011 and 2012, in conformity with accounting principles generally accepted in the United States of America.
>
> However, in our opinion, the balance sheet as of December 31, 2012, presents fairly, in all material respects, the financial position of Dunder-Mifflin, Inc., as of December 31, 2011, and the statements of income, shareholders' equity, and cash flows present fairly the results of operations and cash flows for the year ended December 31, 2010, in conformity with accounting principles generally accepted in the United States of America.
>
> [Standard Internal Control Paragraph]
>
> *Michael Scarn LLP*
> Scranton, PA
> January 29, 2013

Modifications to the auditors' standard report for departures from GAAP (assuming such departures are material) are summarized below:

	Qualified Opinion	**Adverse Opinion**
Introductory Paragraph	No modification	No modification
Scope Paragraph	No modification	No modification
Opinion Paragraph	Modified to note that "except for" a specific departure, financial statements are presented according to GAAP	Modified to note that financial statements are not presented according to GAAP
Additional Paragraph	Identifies departure from GAAP and dollar effect(s)	Identifies departure from GAAP and dollar effect(s)

Although the reports shown in Exhibit 12.5 and 12.6 reflect the appropriate wording if departures from GAAP necessitate the issuance of qualified and adverse opinions, under the provisions of Regulation S-X, public companies are not permitted to file financial statements with the SEC if these statements would be false or misleading. As a result, if a material departure from GAAP is noted during an audit examination, the auditors' report must be modified to identify that departure as noted in the preceding subsections. However, the entity's financial statements and accompanying auditors' report would be classified as a "deficient" filing by the SEC and would not satisfy its reporting requirements.

> ### ⤷ REVIEW CHECKPOINTS
>
> 12.8 Explain the effect of pervasiveness on the auditors' report when the entity uses an accounting method that departs from GAAP.
>
> 12.9 What are the major differences in wording for qualified opinions and adverse opinions issued as a result of departures from GAAP?

▽ AUDITORS' REPORTS WHEN SCOPE LIMITATIONS EXIST

LEARNING OBJECTIVE 12-5
Describe the types of auditors' reports that may be issued if scope limitations exist.

Auditors use reports not only to document unusual issues related to the entity's financial statements (i.e., GAAP departures) but also to document unusual aspects related to the conduct of the audit. In this section, we discuss the two unusual aspects of the audit (scope limitations and lack of independence) that may be highlighted in the report.

Scope Limitation Reports

Auditors are most comfortable when they have all of the evidence they need to reach their conclusion as to whether the financial statements present the financial condition, results of operations, and cash flows in conformity with GAAP. However, two situations may create **scope limitations** when auditors are unable to obtain sufficient appropriate evidence. The two arise from (1) management's deliberate refusal to let auditors perform auditing procedures (known as a **client-imposed scope limitation**) and (2) circumstances beyond the auditors' and client's control such as the late appointment of the auditors that lead to auditors' inability to perform certain auditing procedures (known as a **circumstance-imposed scope limitation**). The nature of auditors' reports depends on the nature and materiality of the scope limitation (see Exhibit 12.7).

EXHIBIT 12.7
Scope Limitations

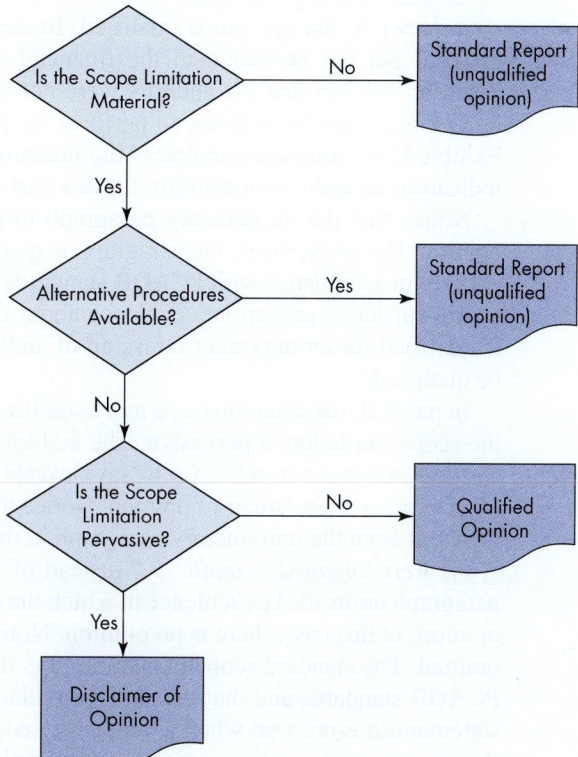

If management's refusal or the circumstances affect the scope of the audit in an immaterial manner, the audit can be considered unaffected and the auditors can issue the standard report as if the limitation had never occurred. This response is consistent with auditors' actions when they identified an immaterial departure from GAAP. Similarly, if alternative procedures are available to the auditors and they can obtain sufficient evidence despite the scope limitation, the auditors may still issue the standard report. For example, assume that a large chain of funeral homes did not want its auditors to send confirmations to its (deceased) customers' families. This request would normally be considered a scope limitation, but the audit team was able to gather sufficient evidence by examining supporting documentation (signed contracts, newspaper obituaries, and subsequent cash receipts) to support the entity's accounts receivable balance. In this situation, because the auditors were able to gather sufficient appropriate evidence, they can issue a standard report (and an *unqualified opinion*). The auditors' report should not mention the alternative procedures.

While the funeral home chain's request in the previous scenario was reasonable under the circumstances, management's deliberate refusal to give auditors access to documents or otherwise limit the application of auditing procedures is a most serious condition. It casts doubt on management's integrity. (Why would management refuse access or limit the work?) Assuming that the audit is affected in a material manner, these *client-imposed scope limitations* result in the issuance of either a qualified opinion or disclaimer of opinion, depending on the materiality of the financial items affected. Because of the significant implications of a client-imposed limitation, auditors would normally either issue a disclaimer of opinion or withdraw from the engagement. This disclaimer reflects the auditors' inability to gather sufficient appropriate evidence in cases in which clients feel it necessary to limit the nature of the auditors' examination. In addition, auditors should communicate client-imposed scope limitations to those charged with the entity's governance.

Refer to Exhibit 12.8 for examples of two reports that illustrate reporting alternatives when scope limitations are encountered. The failure to take physical counts of inventory could have been based on a request from the client's management *(client imposed)*, or it could have resulted from other circumstances such as the entity's not anticipating the need for an audit and appointing the auditors after the latest year-end *(circumstance imposed)*.

In panel A, the opinion is qualified. In this case, the lack of evidence is considered material but not pervasive to the financial statements. Note that the qualification is based on the fact that the auditors were not able to determine whether the inventory is fairly stated, not the inability to perform the procedure *per se*. The report in panel A of Exhibit 12.8 "compartmentalizes" the inventory from the audit reporting responsibility, indicating no audit responsibility for this part of the financial statements.

Notice that the introductory paragraph in panel A is the same as for an unqualified opinion. However, the scope paragraph is qualified because the audit was not conducted entirely in accordance with PCAOB standards. Specifically, the audit team was unable to obtain sufficient appropriate evidence about the inventories. When the scope paragraph is qualified for an important omission of audit work, the opinion paragraph also should be qualified.

In panel B, the situation has a more significant impact on the auditors' opinion; that is, the scope limitation is pervasive. The auditors believe that the inventories are too large and too important in this case to say "except for adjustments, if any." The report then must express a disclaimer of opinion. Notice that the introductory paragraph in panel B is different from the introductory paragraph in the standard report. This paragraph indicates "[w]e *were engaged to audit* . . ." instead of "[w]e have audited. . . ." The introductory paragraph omits the last sentence in which the auditors normally take responsibility for an opinion; in this case, there is no opinion. Notice also that the scope paragraph is entirely omitted. The standard scope paragraph says the audit was conducted in accordance with PCAOB standards and that the audit provided a reasonable basis for the opinion. These statements are not true when a pervasive scope limitation exists. It is important to note that this scope limitation does not necessarily preclude auditors from reporting on the

EXHIBIT 12.8
Scope Limitation Reports

Panel A: Qualified Opinion

Report of Independent Registered Public Accounting Firm

To the Board of Directors and Shareholders, Dunder-Mifflin, Inc.:

[Standard Introductory Paragraph]

Except as discussed in the following paragraph, we conducted our audits in accordance with the standards of the Public Company Accounting Oversight Board (United States). [Remainder of paragraph the same as the standard unqualified scope paragraph] . . .

Dunder-Mifflin, Inc., did not make a count of its physical inventory in 2012 or 2011, stated in the accompanying financial statements at $10 million as of December 31, 2012, and at $15 million as of December 31, 2011, and we were unable to observe the physical quantities on hand. Dunder-Mifflin, Inc.'s records do not permit the application of other auditing procedures to the audit of the inventories.

In our opinion, *except for the effects of such adjustments, if any, as might have been determined to be necessary had we been able to examine evidence regarding the inventories described above,* the financial statements referred to above present fairly, in all material respects, the financial position of Dunder-Mifflin, Inc., at December 31, 2012 and 2011, and the results of operations and cash flows for each of the years in the three-year period ended December 31, 2012, in conformity with accounting principles generally accepted in the United States of America.

[Standard Internal Control Paragraph]

Michael Scarn LLP
Scranton, PA
January 29, 2013

Panel B: Disclaimer of Opinion

Report of Independent Registered Public Accounting Firm

To The Board of Directors and Shareholders, Dunder-Mifflin, Inc.:

We were engaged to audit the accompanying balance sheets of Dunder-Mifflin, Inc. as of December 31, 2012 and 2011, and the related statements of income, shareholders' equity, and cash flows for the years then ended. These financial statements are the responsibility of Dunder-Mifflin, Inc.'s management. *[Sentence on auditors' responsibility is omitted.]*

[Standard Scope Paragraph Omitted]

Dunder-Mifflin, Inc. did not make a count of its physical inventory in 2012 or 2011, stated in the accompanying financial statements at $10 million as of December 31, 2012, and at $15 million as of December 31, 2011, and we were unable to observe the physical quantities on hand. Dunder-Mifflin, Inc,'s records do not permit the application of other auditing procedures to the audit of the inventories.

Since Dunder-Mifflin, Inc, did not take physical inventories and we were not able to apply other auditing procedures to satisfy ourselves as to inventory quantities and cost, the scope of our work was not sufficient to enable us to express, and we do not express, an opinion on these financial statements.

[Standard Internal Control Paragraph]

Michael Scarn LLP
Scranton, PA
January 29, 2013

client's internal control over financial reporting (see the reference to the internal control paragraph in panel B of Exhibit 12.8).

The following summarizes modifications to the auditors' standard report for scope limitations (assuming that such limitations are material and alternative auditing procedures are not available):

	Qualified Opinion	Disclaimer of Opinion
Introductory Paragraph	No modification	• Modified to note that auditor was engaged to audit the financial statements • Sentence identifying auditors' responsibility is omitted
Scope Paragraph	Modified to note that "except for" the scope limitation, a PCAOB audit was conducted	Paragraph is omitted
Opinion Paragraph	Modified to note that "except for" the effects of adjustments that might have been identified, financial statements are presented according to GAAP	Modified to indicated that an opinion cannot be expressed on the financial statements
Additional Paragraph	Identifies scope limitation and dollar effect(s)	Identifies scope limitation and dollar effect(s)

Lack of Independence

When auditors lack independence, performing an audit in accordance with PCAOB standards is impossible. An audit is not just the application of tools, techniques, and procedures of auditing; it also requires the independence in the auditors' mental attitude. This idea is set forth clearly in the following excerpt from AU 504:

> When an accountant is not independent, any procedures he might perform would not be in accordance with generally accepted auditing standards, and he would be precluded from expressing an opinion on such statements. Accordingly, he should disclaim an opinion with respect to the financial statements and should state specifically that he is not independent.

This standard applies to the financial statements of public entities. In keeping with this standard, evidence obtained by auditors who are not independent is not considered sufficient appropriate evidence. In such cases, a disclaimer like the one in Exhibit 12.9 is appropriate.

Notice that the report in Exhibit 12.9 is not titled or addressed to specific users because the auditors did not complete the engagement. When financial statements are unaudited, the following additional guidelines should be observed:

1. If a disclaimer is issued because of a lack of independence, the report should not mention any reasons for not being independent because the readers might erroneously interpret them as unimportant.

EXHIBIT 12.9
Disclaimer of Opinion When Auditors Are not Independent

> We are not independent with respect to the Dunder-Mifflin, Inc. and the accompanying balance sheet as of December 31, 2012, and the related statements of income, shareholders' equity, and cash flows for the year then ended were not audited by us and, accordingly, we do not express an opinion on them.
>
> *Michael Scarn LLP*
> Scranton, PA
> January 29, 2013

2. The report should not mention any auditing procedures performed because readers might erroneously conclude that they were sufficient to enable an opinion to be expressed on the financial statements.
3. If the auditors should learn that the financial statements are not in conformity with GAAP (including adequate disclosures), the departures should be explained in the disclaimer.
4. If prior-years' unaudited financial statements are presented, the disclaimer should cover them as well as the current-year statements.
5. Each page of the financial statements should be labeled clearly as being "unaudited."

The report in Exhibit 12.9 for situations in which auditors are not independent provides guidance for unusual circumstances. Clearly, a public entity would not hire auditors who are not independent. However, issues can arise during the audit that impair independence. For example, in an actual case, an unnamed bank's management disagreed with its auditors over the auditors' insistence on increasing the allowance for loan losses. The bank's management filed a lawsuit against the auditors. Under ethics interpretations, such circumstances impair the auditors' independence and the disclaimer described in Exhibit 12.9 is the appropriate report. Because it needed the report to meet a reporting deadline, the bank had to forgo its lawsuit and the auditors were able to issue a standard report (after the bank recorded additional charges for loan losses that the auditors believed necessary).

Regulation S-X requires SEC registrants to file financial statements accompanied by an auditors' report that clearly expresses an opinion on the financial statements. As a result, financial statements accompanied by a disclaimer of opinion issued as a result of a material and pervasive scope limitation or a lack of auditor independence would represent a substantial deficiency in the SEC filing and would not satisfy the SEC's reporting requirements.

↳ REVIEW CHECKPOINTS

12.10 Distinguish between client-imposed scope limitations and circumstance-imposed scope limitations. Which of these scope limitations is generally of more concern to auditors?

12.11 When a scope limitation exists, how would the standard report be modified to express (1) a qualified opinion and (2) a disclaimer of opinion?

12.12 If auditors are not independent with respect to an entity, what type of opinion must be issued? Why?

▽ AUDITORS' REPORTS REFERENCING OTHER MATTERS ENCOUNTERED DURING THE AUDIT

LEARNING OBJECTIVE 12-6
Describe how the standard report is modified when auditors issue unqualified opinions but reference other matters affecting the audit or the client.

Several circumstances may permit an unqualified opinion paragraph but require additional information to be added to the standard report. This section presents five such situations:

1. *Consistency.* A paragraph identifies a change in accounting principles.
2. *Going concern.* A paragraph draws attention to questions about the entity's ability to continue as a going concern.
3. *Justified departures from GAAP.* A paragraph describes a departure from GAAP, which the auditors believe to be appropriate because following GAAP would be misleading.

4. *Division of responsibility in the audit of group financial statements.* The introductory paragraph, scope paragraph, and opinion paragraph are modified to note a division of responsibility when component auditors are involved in the audit of group financial statements.
5. *Emphasis paragraph(s).* One or more paragraphs emphasize matter(s) of importance.

If the only change is the addition of a fourth paragraph appended to an otherwise standard report (or, in the case of an audit of group financial statements, modifications to three paragraphs of the standard report), these reports would still conclude that the financial statements are presented fairly according to GAAP and the audit team would still issue an unqualified opinion.[8] Paragraphs providing information that is fundamental to users' understanding of the financial statements (such as consistency, going-concern uncertainties, or justified departures from GAAP) are known as **emphasis-of-matter paragraphs**. Alternatively, if paragraphs provide information that relates to users' understanding of the audit, the auditors' responsibility, or auditors' report, these are known as **other-matter paragraphs**. We refer to additional paragraphs added to an unqualified opinion on the financial statements collectively as **explanatory paragraphs**. It is not unusual to see the report express an unqualified opinion with an additional explanatory paragraph (most commonly for a consistency exception because of changes in the requirements of GAAP).

Consistency (*AS 6*, AU 708)

GAAS requires that the auditors' report be modified to disclose (1) changes in accounting principles in any of the year(s) presented and (2) adjustments to correct misstatements in previously-issued financial statements. Doing so ensures that the auditors give users appropriate notice if the comparability of an entity's financial statements from year to year has been materially affected by a change in accounting principles (such as depreciation methods or inventory cost flow assumptions). In addition, specifically identifying restatements of previously-issued financial statements makes users aware that prior-years' financial statements (as restated) will differ from previously-issued financial statements for those year(s).

Accounting Standards Codification 250 (ASC 250), "Accounting Changes and Error Corrections," specifies the accounting requirements regarding changes in principles, estimates, the accounting entity, and correction of errors. Auditing standards parallel the requirements of *ASC 250* and require the addition of a notification to the auditors' report for changes in

1. Accounting principles (from one GAAP method to another GAAP method).
2. The form of the reporting entity (other than that resulting from a transaction or event).
3. Accounting principles from an accounting principle that is not GAAP to one that is GAAP (which is considered to be an adjustment to correct a misstatement in previously-issued financial statements).
4. Changes in accounting principles inseparable from changes in estimates.

Changes in accounting estimates, corrections in errors not involving accounting principles, and changes in classification and reclassifications do not involve the consistency standard and are not recognized in the report.

The following is an excerpt from Deloitte & Touche's 2011 report on **Fannie Mae's** financial statements related to consistency.

> As discussed in Notes 1 and 2 to the consolidated financial statements, on January 1, 2010, the Company prospectively adopted the Financial Accounting Standards Board (FASB) new accounting standards on the transfers of financial assets and the consolidation of variable interest entities.

---

[8] It should be noted that the explanatory paragraphs discussed in this section could be added to a qualified opinion, adverse opinion, or disclaimer of opinion although such situations are rare in practice.

As discussed in Note 1 to the consolidated financial statements, on April 1, 2009, the Company adopted the FASB modified standard on the model for assessing other-than-temporary impairments, applicable to existing and new debt securities.

Changes in accounting principle may result from the issuance of new accounting standards (as noted in the preceding example) or from management's selection of alternatives provided under existing accounting standards. When evaluating a change in accounting principle, the audit team must be satisfied that:

- The newly-adopted accounting principle is a generally accepted accounting principle.
- The method of accounting for the effect of the change (i.e., restating prior-years' financial statements versus accounting for the change prospectively) is in conformity with GAAP.
- Disclosures related to the change are adequate.
- The alternative accounting principle is *preferable* to the previous principle (for example, an entity's decision to change from accelerated depreciation to the straight-line method "to increase profits" could be preferable from management's viewpoint, but such a reason is not a reasonable justification for most auditors).

If any of these criteria are not met, the audit team should treat the change in principle as a departure from GAAP and modify the report accordingly. In auditors' reports on financial statements in years following the change in accounting principle, an appropriate consistency reference must be included as long as the financial statements for the year of the change are included in the years presented.

Reporting on "Going-Concern" Uncertainties (AU 341, AU 570)

GAAP are based on the *going-concern* principle, which means the entity is expected to continue in operation and meet its obligations as they become due without substantially disposing of its assets outside the ordinary course of business, restructuring its debt, significantly revising its operations based on external forces (e.g., a bank reorganization forced by the Federal Deposit Insurance Corporation), or similar actions. Hence, an opinion that financial statements are in conformity with GAAP means that continued existence may be presumed for a "reasonable time" not to exceed one year beyond the date of the financial statements. As noted in Chapter 11, one of the activities performed by auditors during the completion of the audit is assessing the entity's ability to continue as a going concern.

Questions raised about the entity's ability to continue in operation and meet its obligations as they become due are known as **going-concern uncertainties.** Managers and auditors view news of financial troubles in the auditors' report (an attention-directing paragraph or a disclaimer based on going-concern uncertainty) as a *self-fulfilling prophecy* that causes bankruptcy because of the disclosure's effect on the actions of investors, suppliers, and creditors. However fallacious this view might be, it still prevails and sometimes inhibits auditors' appropriate consideration of going-concern questions. Auditors are responsible for determining any substantial doubt about an entity's ability to continue as a going concern. Careful auditors should not ignore signs of financial difficulty and operate entirely on the assumption that the entity will continue indefinitely. Financial difficulties, labor problems, loss of key personnel, litigation, and other such matters may be important signals of financial distress. Likewise, elements of financial flexibility (salability of assets, availability of lines of credit, debt extension, and dividend elimination) may be available as survival strategies. (In the auditing standards, these elements of financial flexibility and management strategy are known as **mitigating factors** that may reduce the financial difficulty problems.)

The most common report issued when going-concern uncertainties exist is an unqualified opinion with an explanatory paragraph following the opinion paragraph that directs users' attention to management's disclosures about going-concern uncertainties and specifically includes the words "substantial doubt" and "going concern." Auditing standards recommend this paragraph when the audit team concludes that the entity may not be able to continue in existence as a going concern (for example, see the paragraph included by Deloitte & Touche in its report on General Motors in the introduction to this chapter). However, in practice, an entity in financial distress may present explanatory notes describing its financial problems and its auditors may decide that they are not serious enough to warrant modification of the report. For very severe going-concern uncertainties, professional standards (AU 341.12, footnote 4) indicate that auditors may issue a disclaimer of opinion with the auditors' report providing all substantive reasons for the disclaimer.

Recent economic circumstances have resulted in a higher preponderance of going-concern opinions than in previous years. For fiscal 2008, in addition to General Motors, seven other Fortune 500 companies (**Asbury Automotive Group, Charter International, Lear Corp, MGM Mirage, Pilgrim's Pride Corporation, Sonic Automotive, Inc.,** and **TRW Automotive Holdings Corp.**) received going-concern opinions; no Fortune 500 companies had received such opinions in 2007, and two (Pilgrim's Pride Corporation and **YRC Worldwide**) received such opinions in fiscal 2009. For a broader universe of companies, the number of all companies filing financial statements with the SEC that received going-concern uncertainties declined by over 13 percent from its high in 2008.[9]

These reporting options assumed that the entity has properly disclosed matters related to the going-concern uncertainty. If they have not done so, auditors would issue a qualified or adverse opinion on the entity's financial statements, similar to actions taken for other departures from GAAP.

AUDITING INSIGHT — Research on Going-Concern Reports

An academic study by Joe found that negative media coverage (from *The Wall Street Journal* as well as other media outlets) of a company's potential bankruptcy increased the likelihood that auditors would issue reports modified for going-concern uncertainties. The author concluded that the closer scrutiny and awareness of these cases influenced auditors' reporting decisions despite the fact that auditors' perceptions of the probability of bankruptcy were not influenced.

An analysis by Geiger et al. of 226 companies entering into bankruptcy between 2000 and 2003 revealed that auditors were more likely to issue reports modified for going-concern uncertainties after December 2001 (70 percent) than prior to December 2001 (40 percent). This tendency is attributed to legislative and media scrutiny resulting from the scandals at **Enron** and **WorldCom** as well as the regulation brought by the Sarbanes-Oxley Act of 2002.

Geiger and Rama found that the going-concern reporting decisions of Big Four firms were more accurate regarding the company's ability to continue in existence compared to the decisions of non–Big Four firms. In other words, for companies that ultimately experienced bankruptcy, Big Four firms were more likely to issue going-concern modifications prior to that bankruptcy than were non–Big Four firms. Geiger and Rama attribute these differences to higher-quality reporting decisions made by the largest international accounting firms.

Menon and Williams studied initial going-concern reports for 1,194 firms from 1995–2006 and evaluated how the receipt of those opinions affected investors' perceptions (through changes in stock prices). They found that the stock market's reaction to a going-concern report was more negative if the report mentioned difficulties in obtaining financing and if the company had debt covenants that were related to the receipt of a going-concern report.

Sources: J. Joe, "Why Press Coverage of a Client Influences the Audit Opinion," *Journal of Accounting Research,* March 2003, pp. 109–33; M. A. Geiger, K. Raghunandan, and D. V. Rama, "Recent Changes in the Association between Bankruptcies and Prior Audit Opinions," *Auditing: A Journal of Practice & Theory,* May 2005, pp. 21–35; M. A. Geiger and D. V. Rama, "Audit Firm Size and Going-Concern Reporting Accuracy," *Accounting Horizons,* March 2006, pp. 1–17; and K. Menon and D.D. Williams, "Investor Reaction to Going Concern Audit Reports," *The Accounting Review,* November 2010, pp. 2075–2105.

Justified Departures from GAAP

Although an *unqualified opinion* is normally issued only when the entity's financial statements are presented in conformity with GAAP, Rule 203 of the AICPA Code of

---
[9] "Auditors' Somewhat Raised Confidence, *CFO.com,* July 25, 2011.

Professional Conduct provides for the possibility (although remote) that adherence to GAAP might create misleading financial statements:

> *Rule 203.* A member [auditor] shall not (1) express an opinion or state affirmatively that financial statements or other financial data of an entity are presented in conformity with GAAP or (2) state that he or she is not aware of any material modifications that should be made to such statements or data in order for them to be in conformity with GAAP, if such statements or data contain any departure from an accounting principle promulgated by bodies designated by Council to establish such principles that has a material effect on the statements taken as a whole. *If, however, the statements or data contain such a departure and the member can demonstrate that due to unusual circumstances the financial statements or data would otherwise have been misleading, the member can comply with the rule by describing the departure, its approximate effects, if practicable, and the reasons why compliance with the principle would result in a misleading statement* [emphasis added].

Earlier, we discussed auditors' reports when departures from GAAP exist. However, in some highly unusual circumstances, the use of GAAP may result in misleading financial statements. These situations are sometimes referred to as **justified departures from GAAP**. Rule 203 has the effect of allowing financial statements to contain a departure from a Financial Accounting Standards Board (FASB) or Governmental Accounting Standards Board (GASB) (or their predecessors') accounting standard, permitting the auditors to explain why the departure was necessary and then allowing the departure to be "in conformity with GAAP" as indicated by the unqualified opinion. An example of such a report that refers to a FASB statement is presented in Exhibit 12.10; current auditing standards permit the explanatory paragraph to be placed either prior to or following the opinion paragraph. Notice that the standard opinion paragraph would be used in this report, indicating an unqualified opinion.

It is important to note that the PCAOB did not adopt Rule 203. As a result, a report modification of this nature would not be appropriate for a public entity subject to PCAOB standards.

EXHIBIT 12.10
Report Conforming to Rule 203

Report of Independent Registered Public Accounting Firm

To the Board of Directors and Shareholders of Dunder-Mifflin, Inc.

[Standard Introductory Paragraph]

[Standard Scope Paragraph]

As described in Note 3, in May 2012, Dunder-Mifflin, Inc. exchanged shares of its common stock for $5,060,000 of its outstanding public debt. The fair value of the common stock issued exceeded the carrying amount of the debt by $466,000, which has been shown as an extraordinary loss in the 2012 income statement. Because a portion of the debt exchanged was convertible debt, a literal application of Accounting Standards Codification 470-20 "Debt with conversion and other options" would have resulted in a further reduction in net income of $3,611,000, which would have been offset by a corresponding $3,611,000 increase in additional paid-in capital; accordingly, there would have been no net effect on shareholders' equity. In the opinion of Dunder-Mifflin, Inc.'s management, with which we agree, a literal application of accounting standards would have resulted in misleading financial statements that do not properly portray the economic consequences of the exchange.

[Standard Opinion Paragraph]

[Standard Internal Control Paragraph]

Michael Scarn LLP
Scranton, PA
January 29, 2013

Group Financial Statements (AU 600)

Many large entities have financial statements that are composed of more than one component (division, subsidiary, or other segment); these financial statements are referred to as **group financial statements**. In some cases, principal auditors (known as the *group engagement team* or **group auditors**) perform the audit of a material portion of the entity's assets, liabilities, revenues, and expenses while other independent auditors (known as **component auditors**) may be engaged to audit divisions, subsidiaries, or components that are included in the group financial statements.

Situations such as this are not common for the largest public accounting firms (which have offices located throughout the world) but may occur if clients have significant remote subsidiaries or if clients have an investment in another entity that is accounted for using the equity method. Because the group engagement partner's signature appears in the report on the financial statements of a consolidated or parent entity, the group auditors must make decisions regarding the use of the work and reports of the component auditor(s).

The group auditors must first obtain information about the independence and professional reputation of the component auditors. If the group auditors are satisfied with these qualities, they must next communicate with the component auditors and decide whether to refer to their work in the group auditors' report. The group auditors may decide to make no reference and issue a report following the form and wording of the standard report. In this case, the group auditors assume full responsibility for the component auditors' work.

On the other hand, the group auditors may decide to refer to the work and reports of the component auditors; this is referred to as a **division of responsibility**. Such a reference is not in itself a scope limitation and the report should not be considered to be substandard to a standard report that does not contain such a reference. The explanation should show very clearly the extent of the *division of responsibility* by disclosing the percent or amount of assets, revenues, and expenses covered by component auditors' work. However, the opinion paragraph must be consistent with the sufficiency and appropriateness of evidence gathered by all auditors. If component auditors have rendered opinions that are qualified in some way, the group auditors must consider the circumstances when deciding whether to qualify, modify, or expand the report on the consolidated financial statements.

When the group auditors refer to the component auditors' work, the component auditors are ordinarily not identified by name. In fact, the component auditors may be named in the group auditors' report only by express permission and with publication of their report along with the group auditors' report. Refer to Exhibit 12.11 for a summary of the options available to group auditors for reporting a division of responsibility.

EXHIBIT 12.11
Reporting Options for Division of Responsibility

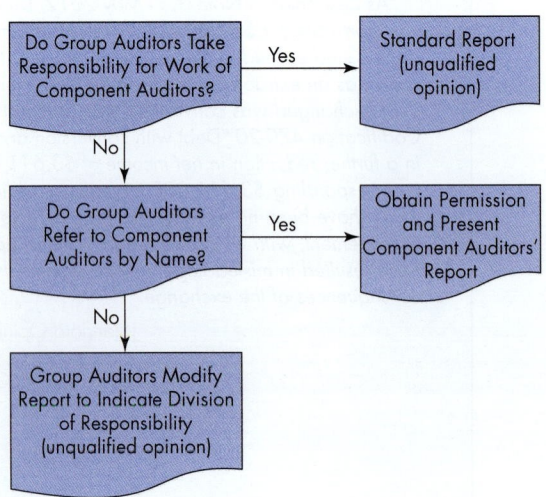

EXHIBIT 12.12
Report Modified for Division of Responsibility

> **Report of Independent Registered Public Accounting Firm**
>
> To the Board of Directors and Shareholders, Dunder-Mifflin, Inc.
>
> We have audited the accompanying consolidated balance sheets of Dunder-Mifflin, Inc. and subsidiaries as of December 31, 2012 and 2011, and the related consolidated statements of income, shareholders' equity, and cash flows for each of the years in the three-year period ended December 31, 2012. These financial statements are the responsibility of Dunder-Mifflin, Inc.'s management. Our responsibility is to express an opinion on these financial statements based on our audits. *We did not audit the financial statements of American Reserve Company, a consolidated subsidiary, which statements reflect total assets constituting 35 percent in 2012 and 36 percent in 2011, and total revenues constituting 13 percent in 2012, 14 percent in 2011, and 17 percent in 2010 of the related consolidated totals. Those statements were audited by other auditors whose reports have been furnished to us, and our opinion, insofar as it relates to the amounts included for American Reserve Company, is based solely on the reports of the other auditors.*
>
> We conducted our audits in accordance with the standards of the Public Company Accounting Oversight Board (United States). Those standards require that we plan and perform the audit to obtain reasonable assurance about whether the financial statements are free of material misstatement. An audit includes examining, on a test basis, evidence supporting the amounts and disclosures in the financial statements. An audit also includes assessing the accounting principles used and significant estimates made by management, as well as evaluating the overall financial statement presentation. We believe that our audits *and the reports of other auditors* provide a reasonable basis for our opinion.
>
> In our opinion, *based on our audits and the reports of other auditors,* the financial statements referred to above present fairly, in all material respects, the consolidated financial position of Dunder-Mifflin, Inc., and subsidiaries at December 31, 2012 and 2011, and the consolidated results of operations and their cash flows for each of the years in the three-year period ended December 31, 2012, in conformity with accounting principles generally accepted in the United States of America.
>
> [Standard Internal Control Paragraph]
>
> *Michael Scarn LLP*
> Scranton, PA
> January 29, 2013

Exhibit 12.12 is an example of a group auditors' report that has been modified to express an unqualified opinion on financial statements while indicating a division of responsibility. Note in this report that the group auditors do not identify the "other auditors" by name.

AUDITING INSIGHT — Reverse Mergers and Component Auditors

The SEC has begun investigating the audits of Chinese companies that are created through a process known as a "reverse merger." Many of these audits are conducted by small U.S. firms that outsource some of the work to Chinese firms; the PCAOB claims that the U.S. firms are not properly verifying that the work of the component auditors meets U.S. auditing standards. Thus far, two U.S. firms (**Clancy & Co. PLLC** and **Chisholm Bierwolf Nilson & Morrill LLC**) have been barred from auditing public companies because of deficiencies identified in these types of audits.

Source: "Auditors Facing 'Reverse' Inquiry," *The Wall Street Journal*, June 3, 2011, p. C1, C2.

Other Modifications

Beyond the wording in the standard report, auditors can enrich the information content in their reports by adding one or more paragraphs to emphasize something they believe readers should consider important or useful. The matters addressed in these paragraphs are not mentioned in the opinion paragraph because the financial statements as presented may be in conformity with GAAP and there were not any issues in the conduct of the audit engagement.

Although auditing standards place no official limits on the content of explanatory paragraphs, auditors often use them to describe circumstances that present some business or information risk. Matters that may be emphasized include a warning that a bankruptcy filing may be imminent, a description of the auditee as a subsidiary of a larger entity, the effects of business events on the comparability of financial statements, the interaction of the auditee with related parties, and the effect of events that occur after the date of the financial statements (commonly referred to as *subsequent events*). The accompanying Auditing Insight summarizes some explanatory paragraphs related to ongoing effects of the 2008–2009 financial crisis.

AUDITING INSIGHT — Emphasis on the Economy

AMERICAN INTERNATIONAL GROUP (AIG)
As described in Note 1 to the consolidated financial statements, AIG completed a series of integrated transactions to recapitalize AIG with the Department of Treasury, the Federal Reserve Bank of New York and the AIG Credit Facility Trust on January 14, 2011.

FANNIE MAE
As also discussed in Note 1 to the consolidated financial statements, the Company is currently under the control of its conservator and regulator, the Federal Housing Finance Agency ("FHFA"). Further, the Company directly and indirectly receives substantial support from various agencies of the United States Government, including the United States Department of Treasury and FHFA. The Company is dependent upon the continued support of the United States Government, various United States Government agencies and the Company's conservator and regulator, FHFA.

Source: AIG 2010 10-K, Fannie Mae 2010 10-K.

The following is a summary of report modifications for issues discussed in this section:

Consistency	Add explanatory paragraph (assuming auditor concurs with the change and the change has been accounted for correctly)
Going concern	Add explanatory paragraph (assuming that going-concern uncertainties are properly disclosed in the financial statements)
	Issue a disclaimer of opinion in very serious going-concern circumstances
Justified departures from GAAP	Add explanatory paragraph
Emphasis of a matter	Add explanatory paragraph
Division of responsibility (assume responsibility for component auditors' work)	Issue the standard report
Division of responsibility (do not assume responsibility for components auditors' work)	• Modify introductory, scope, and opinion paragraphs to indicate division
	• To name component auditors, obtain their permission and present their report

> ### ↳ REVIEW CHECKPOINTS
>
> 12.13 What types of changes would result in the auditors' report being modified for consistency matters?
>
> 12.14 What circumstances lead auditors to have substantial doubt about an entity's ability to continue as a going concern?
>
> 12.15 What are auditors' reporting options when going-concern uncertainties are noted?
>
> 12.16 What is the purpose of the Code of Professional Conduct Rule 203, and how does the rule affect audit reporting?
>
> 12.17 What options are available to group auditors when component auditors are involved in the examination of a subsidiary or division?
>
> 12.18 Is the reference in the auditors' report to work performed by component auditors a scope limitation? Explain.
>
> 12.19 Define *emphasis-of-matter* and *other-matter* paragraphs. What type of information do auditors provide in these paragraphs?

OTHER REPORTING TOPICS

LEARNING OBJECTIVE 12-7
Identify other circumstances affecting auditors' reporting responsibilities and explain how they affect auditors' reports on an entity's financial statements.

A great deal of financial and nonfinancial information is included in annual reports, SEC filings, and other documents containing audited financial statements. The president's letter to shareholders, management's discussion and analysis of results of operations, interim financial statements, and supplementary schedules contain information that is not mentioned explicitly in the auditors' report. Auditors have professional responsibilities, however, with regard to much of this information. When this other information is inaccurate, inconsistent, or unusual, auditors should expand their reports. In this section, we discuss this and several other reporting topics that are somewhat outside the mainstream of the basic auditors' report modification topics covered to this point in this chapter.

Association with Financial Statements

In some cases, auditors may consent to the use of their name in some form of communication containing the entity's financial statements. In other situations, auditors may submit to their clients or others (such as third-party users) financial statements they have prepared or assisted in preparing. These situations are referred to as being **associated with financial statements**. In these cases, we refer to the financial statements of public entities subject to audit requirements, *not* to the financial statements of nonpublic entities (whose financial statements may either be compiled or reviewed by independent accountants). Those engagements for nonpublic entities are discussed more in Module A.

When auditors are associated with the financial statements of a public entity, they must specifically disclaim an opinion (see Exhibit 12.13).

EXHIBIT 12.13
Disclaimer of Opinion on Unaudited Financial Statements

> The accompanying balance sheet of Dunder-Mifflin, Inc. as of December 31, 2012, and the related statements of income, shareholders' equity, and cash flows for the year then ended were not audited by us and, accordingly, we do not express an opinion on them.
>
> *Michael Scarn LLP*
> Scranton, PA
> January 29, 2013

As with disclaimers when the auditors were not independent (see Exhibit 12.9), a disclaimer of opinion when auditors are associated with financial statements but did not conduct an audit is not titled or addressed to specific users because the auditors were not engaged to conduct an audit. In addition, similar to disclaimers for a lack of independence, the report should observe the following additional guidelines:

1. The report should not mention any auditing procedures applied because readers might erroneously conclude that they were sufficient to enable an opinion to be expressed on the financial statements.
2. If the auditors should learn that the financial statements are not in conformity with GAAP (including adequate disclosures), the departures should be explained in the disclaimer.
3. If prior-years' unaudited financial statements are presented, the disclaimer should cover them as well as the current-year statements.
4. Each page of the financial statements should be labeled clearly as being "unaudited."

Reporting on Comparative Statements

The SEC requires public entities to present comparative balance sheets for two years and comparative statements of income, shareholders' equity, and cash flows for three years. Financial statement footnotes contain disclosures in comparative form for two or three years. Together, these comparative financial statements and footnotes are the subject of the auditors' work and report.

When auditors issue a report on the current-year financial statements, they are required to update the report previously-issued on the prior-years' financial statements by considering whether the opinions on the prior-years' financial statements are still appropriate. For example, consider Exhibit 12.2; Dunder-Mifflin, Inc.'s auditors previously expressed opinions and issued reports (not shown in the exhibit) on the 2011 and 2010 financial statements. As shown in the report in Exhibit 12.2, after the most recent audit, the auditors' report dated January 29, 2013, covers the 2012 and 2011 financial statements (for all financial statements) and 2010 financial statements (for the statements of income, shareholders' equity, and cash flows). The **updated report** on the 2011 and 2010 financial statements is based not only on the prior-year audits but also on information that has come to the auditors' attention since then (particularly in the course of the most recent audit). An updated report may express the same opinion as that originally expressed or a different opinion if current information causes a change in the auditors' reporting decision. An updated report carries the most recent date of the auditors' report, and the auditors' responsibility for the comparative financial statements now extends to this date.

An updated report differs from a **reissued report**. When auditors reissue a report, they simply provide additional copies of a previously-issued report or grant clients permission to use a previously-issued report in another document sometime after its original date. However, auditors do not attempt to update the report or otherwise consider events that have occurred since the date of the original report. The report date of a reissued report is the same as that for the original report, indicating a cutoff date for the auditors' responsibility.

The situation in which the same auditors audited the comparative years' financial statements (Exhibit 12.2) is a common one. If the entity has changed auditors, the introductory paragraph would have identified only the current financial statements examined by the new auditors. If Michael Scarn were engaged by Dunder-Mifflin, Inc. for the 2012 audit, a sentence would be added to the introductory paragraph providing facts about the former (predecessor) auditors' report: "The financial statements of Dunder-Mifflin, Inc. as of December 31, 2011 and 2010, were audited by other auditors whose report dated February 4, 2012, expressed an unqualified opinion on those statements." The opinion paragraph would cite only the current-year financial statements audited by Michael Scarn (the new auditors). As one example, in 2006, **Best Buy** changed auditors from **Ernst & Young** to **Deloitte & Touche**. Deloitte & Touche's 2006 audit report on Best Buy expresses an opinion on the 2006 financial statements and the introductory paragraph identifies that "other auditors" examined the 2005 and 2004 financial statements and expressed an unqualified opinion on those statements.

Alternatively, companies can present both auditors' reports, with each report specifically identifying that auditors' responsibility. For example, **Apple** changed auditors from **KPMG** to **Ernst & Young** in 2009; Apple's 2009 annual report presents KPMG's report on the 2007 and 2008 financial statements (using the original report date) and Ernst & Young's report on the 2009 financial statements.

AUDITING INSIGHT — Audit Them? No, You Audit Them

In the wake of the Enron debacle, **PricewaterhouseCoopers** (PwC) required one of its clients, **Amerco** (the holding company for **U-Haul International**), to restate its prior-year financial statements to consolidate a number of special purpose entities (SPEs). Unfortunately for PwC, prior to the consolidation, **Ernst & Young** had audited the unconsolidated SPEs. Because the SPEs were to be consolidated into Amerco's financial statements, PwC simply needed to obtain permission from Ernst & Young to allow its report to be included in Amerco's 10-K report to the SEC. However, because of a misunderstanding between Ernst & Young and PwC, Ernst & Young declined. Consequently, PwC was forced to reperform auditing procedures related to the (already audited) SPEs prior to issuing an opinion on Amerco's consolidated financial statements, thereby delaying the submission of Amerco's 10-K to the SEC.

Source: "PricewaterhouseCooper's Goof Is Now U-Haul's Big Problem," *Fortune*, June 23, 2003, pp. 110–11.

Auditors can express different opinions on comparative-years financial statements in the same report. For example, the adverse opinion in Exhibit 12.6 shows the situation in which the prior-year financial statements were considered materially misstated, but the most recent balance sheet was presented in conformity with GAAP. You can see that the opinion on the misstated financial statements is an adverse opinion and the opinion on the most recent balance sheet is an unqualified opinion.

Auditors also can change the opinion expressed on prior-years' financial statements if circumstances have changed in the intervening period. The auditors must have good reasons for such a change, which must be explained in the report. For example, consider again the adverse opinion issued in Exhibit 12.6. Suppose that Dunder-Mifflin, Inc. had originally failed to record the additional $30 million provision for uncollectible receivables in the 2011 financial statements and Michael Scarn issued an adverse opinion in that year. Assume that, in 2012, Dunder-Mifflin, Inc. restated its 2011 financial statements, recording the additional provision in the proper period. The report on the 2012 and 2011 comparative financial statements should contain the explanation in Exhibit 12.14.

Reporting on Summary Financial Statements (AU 810)

Published financial statements are lengthy and often complex. Entities sometimes have occasion to present the financial statements in considerably less detail (for example, summarize totals of current assets, current liabilities, long-term liabilities, operating income, or present other subtotals). Generally, such summary financial statements (sometimes referred to as *condensed financial statements*) are derived directly from the full audited financial statements. However, summary financial statements are not a fair presentation of financial position, results of operations, and cash flows in conformity with GAAP. Auditors who report on such statements cannot issue the standard report even if an unqualified opinion was issued on the full financial statements.

Auditors may issue a report on summary financial statements derived from full financial statements that have been audited. The report must refer to the auditors' report on the full financial statements, giving the date and the type of opinion, and state whether the information in the summary financial statements is fairly stated in all material respects in relation to the complete financial statements.

EXHIBIT 12.14
Comparative Financial Statement Opinion Changed from Adverse to Unqualified

Report of Independent Registered Public Accounting Firm

To the Board of Directors and Shareholders, Dunder-Mifflin, Inc.:

[Standard Introductory Paragraph]

[Standard Scope Paragraph]

In our report dated January 30, 2012, we expressed an opinion that the balance sheet as of December 31, 2011, and the statements of income, shareholders' equity, and cash flows for the year then ended did not fairly present financial position, results of operations, and cash flows in conformity with accounting principles generally accepted in the United States of America because Dunder-Mifflin, Inc. did not record an additional $30,000,000 provision for uncollectible receivables as of December 31, 2011. As described in Note 2 in these financial statements, Dunder-Mifflin, Inc. has restated its 2011 financial statements to record the provision in conformity with accounting principles generally accepted in the United States of America. Accordingly, our present opinion on the 2011 financial statements, as presented herein, is different from the opinion we expressed in our previous report.

In our opinion, the financial statements referred to above present fairly, in all material respects, the financial position of Dunder-Mifflin, Inc. as of December 31, 2012 and 2011, and the results of its operations and its cash flows for each of the years in the two-year period ended December 31, 2012 in conformity with accounting principles generally accepted in the United States of America.

[Standard Internal Control Paragraph]

Michael Scarn LLP
Scranton, PA
January 29, 2013

Alternatively, if summary financial statements are presented in a document with the audited financial statements (such as the entity's annual report or Form 10-K), auditors may report on summary financial statements within their report on the entity's complete financial statements. In this case, the auditors would expand their report on the entity's financial statements to include their conclusion as to the fairness of the summary financial statements in relation to the complete financial statements.

Other Information Accompanying Audited Financial Statements (AU 720)

All annual reports to shareholders and SEC filings contain such sections as a president's letter and management's discussion and analysis (MD&A) of operations. These sections are separate from the audited financial statements and are not covered by the auditors' opinion. Nevertheless, auditors have an obligation to read the other information and determine whether (1) it is consistent with the audited financial statements or (2) it contains material misstatements.

Other information accompanying audited financial statements is subject to "exception-based" reporting (that is, auditors' reports mention the other information only if inconsistencies or misstatements exist). For example, consider the following remark from a president's letter: "Earnings increased from $1 million to $2 million, an increase of 50 cents per share." This statement can be corroborated by comparison to the audited financial statements. The president's comment would be considered inconsistent if the $1 million was income before an extraordinary loss and the $2 million was income after an extraordinary gain, or if the 50 cent change in earnings per share (EPS) was the difference between last year's fully diluted EPS and this year's basic EPS.

If misstatements or inconsistencies exist with respect to other information accompanying audited financial statements and the client chooses not to revise the other information, the auditors should (1) notify the client in writing of their views, (2) consult with legal counsel about appropriate action to take, and (3) consider whether this inconsistency affects the opinion on the financial statements. If it does affect the opinion, the auditors should revise their opinion on the financial statements; if not, the auditors should expand their report to add an explanatory paragraph (similar to an *emphasis-of-matter* paragraph). It is important to note that, in this latter case, auditors may still conclude that the financial statements are presented in conformity with GAAP but are emphasizing that material inconsistencies exist between the other information accompanying the audited financial statements and the financial statements themselves.

Required Supplementary Information (AU 730)

In addition to the financial statements and footnotes accompanying the financial statements, accounting standard-setting bodies (such as the FASB) may require companies to provide supplementary information that is not part of the basic financial statements. This information is necessary to allow users to place the basic financial statements in an appropriate operational, economic, or historical context. It is important to note that standards-setting bodies have established authoritative guidelines for measuring and presenting this information. For example, the FASB requires energy companies to present oil, gas, and other mineral reserve information as supplementary information. Other examples of such information related to specific industries or types of companies (construction, development stage entities, financial services, and real estate) can be found in *ASC 235*.

Auditors are required to perform limited procedures (inquiry of management, comparison of information for consistency with the financial statements, and obtain written representations from management) with respect to the supplementary information. Problems with supplementary information arise when (1) required information is omitted (either in its entirety or in part), (2) the information departs materially from presentation guidelines, (3) the information contains material departures from GAAP, or (4) the auditors cannot perform necessary procedures to evaluate the information. When companies present supplementary information, auditors are required to expand their report on the financial statements to include a paragraph that identifies the supplementary information, describes any procedures performed with respect to this information, and identifies any issues related to this information. However, the paragraph specifically disclaims an opinion or any form of assurance on the supplementary information.

REVIEW CHECKPOINTS

12.20 What is meant when auditors are "associated with" a public entity's financial statements? In connection with unaudited statements, which general reporting guidelines should the auditors follow for public entities?

12.21 What is an updated report? What is a reissued report?

12.22 What two types of disclosure problems must auditors be alert to detect when reading "other information" in an annual report?

12.23 Why do you think auditors are prohibited from issuing a standard report on summary financial statements?

12.24 What issues may arise with respect to required supplementary information? How does the auditors' report address these issues?

THE FUTURE OF AUDIT REPORTING

The auditors' report is the single most important communication that emerges from the audit examination. As such, its wording has continued to be evaluated and critiqued by users, standards setters, auditors, and entities whose financial statements are subject to the audit. Revisions to the ASB version of the auditors' report, which is issued in the audit of nonpublic entities (see Appendix 12A), have recently been undertaken to more clearly communicate its intended message. The Auditing Insight "Are Changes Coming?" describes a current proposal that would modify the nature of the PCAOB version of the auditors' report discussed in this chapter.

> ### AUDITING INSIGHT — Are Changes Coming?
>
> A recent concept release by the PCAOB identified the following possible changes to its version of the auditors' report:
>
> 1. The addition of a supplemental narrative report that would discuss auditors' views about significant matters, such as risks identified in the audit and the auditors' perceptions regarding the entity's financial statements and management's judgments and estimates (known as *"auditors' discussion and analysis"*).
> 2. The required inclusion of an explanatory paragraph that would highlight the most significant matters disclosed in the financial statements.
> 3. The expansion of auditors' responsibility to include providing assurance on information outside the financial statements, such as management's discussion and analysis, non–GAAP information, and earnings releases.
> 4. Clarification of language and concepts, such as reasonable assurance, auditors' responsibility for fraud, auditors' responsibility for financial statement disclosures, management's responsibility for the preparation of the financial statements, auditors' responsibility for information outside of the financial statements, and auditor independence.

Two academic studies[10] evaluated perceptions of the ASB report (which is very similar to the PCAOB version). Some results from these studies are:

- Users felt that the report is important in investing and lending decisions and provided a high level of confidence that the entity will remain viable. One lender indicated that "[unaudited] financial statements would just be junk."
- Users focus on the opinion paragraph to determine that the entity received an unqualified opinion and to see whether the audit firm is a Big 4 firm. If it is not a Big 4 firm, users may do some research to determine the firm's reputation.
- Compared to auditors, the two user groups (investors and lenders) felt the report provides higher confidence that the entity's financial statements are free of material fraud; the entity is more effectively managed, is a sounder investment, and is more likely to meet its strategic goals; and the auditors are more likely to have detected material fraud.
- Most preparers, users, and auditors believe a PCAOB-based audit is superior to an ASB-based audit. Preparers and users believe that PCAOB audits are more thorough than ASB audits.

Summary

This chapter has discussed a wide range of reporting issues. While the array and variety of reports may seem confusing, several simple rules will enable you to remember the basics of auditors' reports on financial statements. First, begin with the standard report in Exhibit 12.2. Keeping the four paragraphs in mind, remember that the following basic rules apply (modifications to the *internal control paragraph* were previously discussed in Chapter 5):

- The *introductory paragraph* is modified when the financial statements examined or responsibility assumed by auditors changes (for example, in a limited reporting

---

[10] S.K. Asare and A. Wright, "Investors', Auditors', and Lenders' Understanding of the Message Conveyed by the Standard Audit Report," Unpublished working paper, 2009; T.J. Mock, J. L. Turner, G. L. Gray, and P.J. Coram, "Perceptions and Misperceptions Regarding the Unqualified Auditor's Report by Financial Statement Preparers, Users, and Auditors," Unpublished working paper, 2009.

EXHIBIT 12.15 Summary of Reporting Issues

	Significance of the Matter		Paragraphs Modified				Other Comments
	Material	**Pervasive**	Introductory	Scope	Opinion	Additional	
Departure from GAAP	Qualified opinion	Adverse opinion			X	X	
Scope limitation	Qualified opinion	Disclaimer of opinion		X	X	X	Auditors can issue standard report if alternative procedures are available and performed; should consider disclaimer if client-imposed limitation.
Lack of independence	Disclaimer of opinion	Disclaimer of opinion					Auditors would issue single-paragraph disclaimer of opinion.
Consistency	Unqualified opinion	Unqualified opinion				X	
Going-concern uncertainty	Unqualified opinion	Disclaimer of opinion			X	X	The opinion paragraph is modified only if a disclaimer is issued.
Justified departure from GAAP	Unqualified opinion	Unqualified opinion				X	The explanatory paragraph can be placed before or following opinion paragraph.
Division of responsibility	Unqualified opinion	Unqualified opinion	X	X	X		Auditors can issue a standard report if group auditors assume responsibility for component auditors' work.
Emphasis of a matter	Unqualified opinion	Unqualified opinion				X	
Association with unaudited financial statements	Disclaimer of opinion	Disclaimer of opinion					Auditors would issue single-paragraph disclaimer of opinion.

engagement to audit the balance sheet, for a division of responsibility, or for a pervasive scope limitation).

- The *scope paragraph* is modified when the scope of the audit is not in accordance with GAAS or PCAOB standards (most notably, when a scope limitation exists).
- The *opinion paragraph* is modified when an opinion other than an unqualified opinion is issued.
- An *additional paragraph* is added to the report when an opinion other than an unqualified opinion is issued or when some other matter arises. A general rule for the placement of the additional paragraph is that, if an unqualified opinion is issued, the paragraph follows the opinion paragraph; if an opinion other than unqualified is issued, the paragraph precedes the opinion paragraph.

Like all general guidelines, exceptions to these rules can be found. For example, when a division of responsibility is encountered, an additional paragraph *would not* be added, which contradicts the general rule related to additional paragraphs (however, the introductory, scope, and opinion paragraphs are modified in this situation!). See Exhibit 12.15 for a comprehensive summary of auditors' reports discussed in this chapter. In reviewing Exhibit 12.15, it is important to note that if any of the issues does not have a material effect on the financial statements, auditors can issue the standard report without any reference to the issue (except for a lack of independence, which can never be immaterial).

Key Terms

adverse opinion: Opinion issued when the auditors conclude that the financial statements do not present the financial condition, results of operations, and cash flows in conformity with GAAP, 501

associated (association) with financial statements: Cases when auditors consent to the use of their name in some form of communication containing the entity's financial statements or submit to their clients or others (such as third-party users) financial statements they have prepared or assisted in preparing. Auditors should issue a one-paragraph disclaimer when they are associated with (but did not audit) financial statements, 519

auditee: The company or other entity whose financial statements are being audited, 498

circumstance-imposed scope limitation: A restriction on auditors from gathering sufficient appropriate evidence because of a situation beyond control of both the auditors and client, such as late appointment of the auditors, 507

client: The person (entity, board of directors, agency, or some other person or group) who retains the auditors and pays the fee, 498

client-imposed scope limitation: A restriction on auditors from gathering sufficient appropriate evidence because of the client's deliberate refusal to provide them access to documents or to otherwise limit the auditors' application of auditing procedures, 507

component auditor: The auditor who audits divisions, subsidiaries, or components that are included in the group financial statements, 516

date of the auditors' report: The date on which auditors have obtained sufficient appropriate evidence to support their opinion, 499

departure from GAAP: Situation in which an entity does not follow GAAP in preparing its financial statements. Auditors can issue qualified or adverse opinions for material departures from GAAP, 504

disclaimer of opinion: Issued when auditors do not express an opinion on the fairness of the entity's financial statements. Disclaimers of opinion are issued for pervasive going-concern uncertainties, pervasive scope limitations, situations in which auditors' are associated with financial statements, and situations in which the auditors are not independent, 501

division of responsibility: Situation in which the component auditors are involved with the examination of a subsidiary, branch, component, or investment that is included in the financial statements audited by group auditors 516

emphasis-of-matter paragraph: A paragraph added to an auditors' report that provides information fundamental to users' understanding of the financial statements (such as consistency, going-concern uncertainties, or justified departures from GAAP), 512

explanatory paragraph: A paragraph added to an auditors' report that either provides information fundamental to users' understanding of the financial statements (emphasis-of-matter paragraph) or relevance to users' understanding of the audit, the auditor's responsibility, or auditors' report (other-matter paragraph), 512

going-concern uncertainty: Situation in which questions are raised about an entity's ability to continue operations and meet its obligations as they become due, 513

group auditors: Also known as principal auditors, these auditors perform the audit of a material portion of the assets, liabilities, revenues, and expenses of an entity's group financial statements, 516

group financial statements: The financial statements of more than one component (division, subsidiary, or other segment), 516

integrated report: A single report issued by auditors expressing their opinion on the fairness of the financial statements and effectiveness of internal control over financial reporting, 501

internal control paragraph: Paragraph in the auditors' report that refers to the auditors' report on the effectiveness of the entity's internal control over financial reporting, 498

introductory paragraph: The paragraph in the auditors' report that identifies the financial statements examined by the auditors and the responsibility of auditors and management with respect to the financial statements, 498

justified departure from GAAP: Situation in which an entity does not follow GAAP in preparing its financial statements because the use of GAAP would result in materially misleading financial statements. If auditors agree with the departure, an unqualified opinion is issued, 515

mitigating factors: Elements of financial flexibility (salability of assets, lines of credit, debt extensions, dividend elimination) available as survival strategies in circumstances of going-concern uncertainty that may reduce financial difficulty problems, 513

modified opinions: Any opinion other than an unqualified opinion on an entity's financial statements (qualified opinion, adverse opinion, or disclaimer of opinion), 501

opinion paragraph: A paragraph in the auditors' report that expresses the auditors' opinion on whether the financial statements are presented in conformity with GAAP, 498

other-matter paragraph: A paragraph added to the auditors' report that is relevant to users' understanding of the audit, the auditor's responsibility, or the auditors' report, 512

qualified opinion: Issued when the auditors conclude that, with the exception of one or more issue(s), the financial statements present the financial condition, results of operations, and cash flows in conformity with GAAP. Qualified opinions can be issued for material departures from GAAP and material scope limitations, 501

reissued report: A copy of a previously-issued report that auditors provide or grant clients permission to use in another document after its original date; the report is not modified to consider events occurring subsequent to the date of the original report, 520

report on financial statements and related disclosures: A report prepared by the auditors that expresses an opinion on whether the entity's financial statements and disclosures are prepared and presented in conformity with GAAP, 496

report on internal control over financial reporting (prepared by auditors): Report that expresses an opinion on the effectiveness of the entity's internal control over financial reporting, 496

report on internal control over financial reporting (prepared by management): Report that describes the process through which management assesses its internal control over financial reporting and that provides management's conclusion with respect to the effectiveness of its internal control over financial reporting, 496

scope limitation: A situation in which the auditors are unable to obtain sufficient appropriate evidence. If material, a scope limitation results in the issuance of either a qualified opinion or disclaimer of opinion, 507

scope paragraph: A paragraph in the auditors' report indicating that the engagement was performed in accordance with the standards of the PCAOB and provides a general description of an audit, 498

unqualified opinion: Issued when the auditors conclude that the financial statements present the financial condition, results of operations, and cash flows in conformity with GAAP, 501

updated report: Auditors' report on prior-year financial statements that is based on both the prior-year audit and information that has come to the auditors' attention in the most recent audit, 520

Multiple-Choice Questions for Practice and Review

 All applicable Exercises and Problems are available with McGraw-Hill's Connect® Accounting

LO 12-3

12.25 When reporting under GAAS, certain statements are required in all auditors' reports ("explicit") and others are required only under certain conditions ("implicit"). Which combination that follows correctly describes the auditors' responsibilities for reporting?

	(a)	(b)	(c)	(d)
1. GAAP	Explicit	Explicit	Implicit	Implicit
2. Consistency	Implicit	Explicit	Explicit	Implicit
3. Disclosure	Implicit	Implicit	Explicit	Explicit
4. Opinion	Explicit	Explicit	Implicit	Implicit

LO 12-4

12.26 Auditors found that the entity has not capitalized a material amount of leases in the financial statements. When considering the materiality of this departure from GAAP, the auditors would choose between which reporting options?
   a. Unqualified opinion or disclaimer of opinion.
   b. Unqualified opinion or qualified opinion.
   c. Explanatory paragraph with unqualified opinion or an adverse opinion.
   d. Qualified opinion or adverse opinion.

LO 12-6

12.27 The auditors determined that the entity is suffering financial difficulty and the going-concern status is seriously in doubt. Assuming the entity adequately disclosed this matter in the financial statements, the auditors must choose between which of the following auditors' report alternatives?
   a. Unqualified opinion with a going-concern explanatory paragraph or disclaimer of opinion.
   b. Standard report or a disclaimer of opinion.
   c. Qualified opinion or adverse opinion.
   d. Standard report or adverse opinion.

LO 12-6

12.28 An entity accomplished an early extinguishment of debt and the auditors believe that literal application of GAAP would cause recognition of a loss that would materially distort the financial statements and cause them to be misleading. Given these facts, the auditors would probably choose which reporting option?
   a. Explain the situation and issue an adverse opinion.
   b. Explain the situation and issue a disclaimer of opinion.
   c. Explain the situation and issue an unqualified opinion, relying on Rule 203 of the AICPA Code of Professional Conduct.
   d. Issue the standard report.

LO 12-6

12.29 Which of these situations would require auditors to append an explanatory paragraph about consistency to an otherwise unqualified opinion?
   a. Entity changed its estimated allowance for uncollectible accounts receivable.
   b. Entity corrected a prior mistake in accounting for interest capitalization.
   c. Entity sold one of its subsidiaries and consolidated six subsidiaries this year compared to seven last year.
   d. Entity changed its inventory costing method from FIFO to LIFO.

LO 12-7

12.30 R. Wolfe became the new auditor for Royal Corporation, succeeding C. Mason, who audited the financial statements last year. Wolfe needs to report on Royal's comparative financial statements and should disclose in the report an explanation about other auditors having audited the prior year
   a. Only if Mason's opinion last year was qualified.
   b. Describing the prior audit and the opinion but not naming Mason as the predecessor auditor.
   c. Describing the audit but not revealing the type of opinion Mason gave.
   d. Describing the audit and the opinion and naming Mason as the predecessor auditor.

LO 12-6   12.31   When other independent auditors are involved in the current audit of parts of the entity's business, the group auditors may issue a report that
- a. Mentions the component auditors, describes the extent of the component auditors' work, and expresses an unqualified opinion.
- b. Does not consider or evaluate the component audiors' work, but expresses an unqualified opinion in a standard report.
- c. Places primary responsibility for the reporting on the component auditors.
- d. Names the component auditors, describes their work, and presents only the group auditors' report.

LO 12-6   12.32   When auditors wish to issue an unqualified opinion but highlight that the entity changed its method of accounting for software development costs, what type of report modification would be most appropriate?
- a. Identify the change in accounting methods in the introductory paragraph.
- b. Identify the change in accounting methods in the opinion paragraph.
- c. Identify the change in accounting methods in an emphasis-of-matter paragraph.
- d. Identify the change in accounting methods in an other-matter paragraph.

LO 12-3   12.33   Under which of the following conditions can a disclaimer of opinion *never* be issued?
- a. The entity's going-concern problems are highly material and pervasive.
- b. The entity does not allow the auditors access to evidence about important accounts.
- c. The auditors own stock in the entity.
- d. The auditors have determined that the entity uses the NIFO (next-in, first-out) inventory costing method.

LO 12-3   12.34   How is the auditors' own responsibility for expressing the opinion on financial statements disclosed in the report?
- a. Stated explicitly in the introductory paragraph of the standard report.
- b. Unstated but understood in the introductory paragraph of the standard report.
- c. Stated explicitly in the opinion paragraph of the standard report.
- d. Stated explicitly in the scope paragraph of the standard report.

LO 12-3   12.35   Company A hired Samson & Delilah, CPAs, to audit the financial statements of Company B and deliver the report to Megabank. Who is the client?
- a. Megabank.
- b. Samson & Delilah.
- c. Company A.
- d. Company B.

LO 12-3   12.36   Which of the following is *not* included in the standard report on the financial statements?
- a. An identification of the financial statements that were audited.
- b. A general description of an audit.
- c. An opinion that the financial statements present financial position in conformity with GAAP.
- d. An explanatory paragraph commenting on the effect of economic conditions on the entity.

LO 12-3   12.37   If the auditors decide to present separate reports on the entity's financial statements and internal control over financial reporting, which of the following reports should be modified to refer to the other report?

	Report on Financial Statements	Report on Internal Control over Financial Reporting
a.	Yes	Yes
b.	Yes	No
c.	No	Yes
d.	No	No

Exercises and Problems

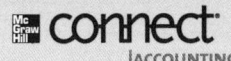 All applicable Exercises and Problems are available with McGraw-Hill's *Connect® Accounting*

LO 12-4, 12-5, 12-6

12.38 **Basic Reports.** Auditors' alternatives for reporting on financial statements offer many choices among unqualified, qualified, adverse, and disclaimers.

Required:
a. List the report(s) that require fully sufficient appropriate evidence.
b. List the report(s) that would be issued because of pervasive evidence deficiencies.
c. List the report(s) that would be issued because of "compartmentalized" (or material, but not pervasive) evidence deficiencies.

LO 12-4, 12-5

12.39 **Basic Reports.** The concept of materiality is important to auditors in examinations of financial statements and expressions of opinion on these statements.

Required:
How will materiality influence auditors' reporting decisions in the following circumstances?
a. The entity prohibits confirmation of accounts receivable, and sufficient and appropriate evidence cannot be obtained using alternative procedures.
b. The entity is a gas and electric utility company that follows the practice of recognizing revenue when it is billed to customers. At the end of the year, amounts earned but not yet billed are not recorded in the accounts or reported in the financial statements.
c. The entity leases buildings for its chain of transmission repair shops under terms that qualify as capital leases under *ASC 840*. These leases are not capitalized as leased property assets and lease obligations.
d. The entity has lost a lawsuit in federal district court. The case is on appeal in an attempt to reduce the amount of damages awarded to the plaintiffs. No loss amount is recorded.

LO 12-4

12.40 **Departures from GAAP.** Following are three possible scenarios relating to a departure from generally accepted accounting principles noted during the audit of Pathways Company. All of these departures are related to accounting for leases that should be capitalized under GAAP and have a material effect on Pathways' financial condition, results of operations, and cash flows.

Scenario A. Pathways has decided not to capitalize the lease agreements because of a highly unusual feature of these agreements. Pathways' auditors agree with Pathways' treatment of these lease agreements because they feel that this treatment is consistent with the nature of the agreements and that classifying these leases as capital leases (as required by GAAP) would be misleading. Pathways has fully disclosed their treatment of these lease agreements, the fact that it departs from GAAP, and the approximate effects of this departure in the footnotes accompanying the financial statements.

Scenario B. Pathways has decided not to capitalize the lease agreements because of a highly unusual feature of these agreements. Pathways' auditors agree with the treatment of these lease agreements because they believe that it is consistent with the nature of the agreements and that classifying them as capital leases (as required by GAAP) would be misleading. Pathways has not provided any disclosures regarding their treatment of these lease agreements in the footnotes accompanying the financial statements and refuses to do so, fearing that this disclosure will confuse investors and lenders.

Scenario C. Pathways has decided not to capitalize the lease agreements because of a highly unusual feature of these lease agreements. Pathways' auditors do not agree with this treatment and believe that they should be capitalized under GAAP.

Required:
For each of these scenarios, indicate the reporting option(s) and factors Pathways' auditors should consider in deciding which type of opinion to issue in the circumstances. (Do *not* draft the report on Pathway's financial statements for the year ended December 31, 2012.)

LO 12-5

12.41 Scope Limitations. Situations in which auditors are unable to obtain sufficient appropriate evidence necessary to support their opinion on the entity's financial statements are referred to as *scope limitations*.

Required:

a. Distinguish between *client-imposed* scope limitations and *circumstance-imposed* scope limitations. Which of these scope limitations is generally of more concern to auditors?

b. Why do scope limitations impact the auditors' ability to express an opinion on the entity's financial statements?

c. Assume that a circumstance-imposed scope limitation prevented auditors from performing procedures they considered to be necessary. How would each of the following factors independently influence the opinion expressed on the entity's financial statements?

1. The account balances affected by the scope limitation are not material to the entity's financial position, results of operations, or cash flows.

2. The account balances affected by the scope limitation are material to the entity's financial position, results of operations, and cash flows. However, the auditors are able to perform alternative procedures that provide evidence supporting the accounts affected by the scope limitation.

3. The account balances affected by the scope limitation are material to the entity's financial position, results of operations, and cash flows. Because of a lack of supporting documentation and key accounting records, auditors are unable to perform alternative procedures that provide evidence supporting the accounts affected by the scope limitation.

d. For each of the situations in (c), briefly describe how the auditors' report on the entity's financial statements would be affected. (Do *not* rewrite or draft the report that would be issued in each of these circumstances.)

LO 12-5

12.42 Scope Limitations. Following are four possible scenarios that reflect scope limitations encountered by J. Bruce, CPA, during the audit of Weaver, Inc. In all cases, assume that the ending balance in inventory is material to the financial position, results of operations, and cash flows of Weaver, Inc.

Scenario A. Because of the late appointment to the audit engagement, Bruce is unable to observe Weaver's physical inventory for the year ended December 31, 2012. However, Weaver maintains extensive perpetual inventory records and Bruce has been able to perform other substantive procedures and became satisfied as to the fairness of the ending inventory balance for December 31, 2012.

Scenario B. Because of the late appointment to the audit engagement, Bruce is unable to observe Weaver's physical inventory for the year ended December 31, 2012. Because Weaver's accounting records are not complete, Bruce is unable to perform other substantive procedures and is not satisfied as to the fairness of the ending inventory balance for December 31, 2012.

Scenario C. Because of a direct request by Weaver's management, Bruce did not observe Weaver's physical inventory for the year ended December 31, 2012. However, Weaver maintains extensive perpetual inventory records, and Bruce has been able to perform other substantive procedures and is satisfied as to the fairness of the ending inventory balance for December 31, 2012.

Scenario D. Because of a direct request by Weaver's management, Bruce did not observe Weaver's physical inventory for the year ended December 31, 2012. Weaver's accounting records are not complete, so Bruce is unable to perform other substantive procedures and is not satisfied as to the fairness of the ending inventory balance for December 31, 2012.

Required:

For each of these scenarios, indicate what reporting option(s) and factors Bruce should consider in deciding which type of opinion to issue in the circumstances. (Do *not* draft Bruce's report on Weaver Inc.'s financial statements for the year ended December 31, 2012.)

LO 12-5 12.43 **Scope Limitations.** D. Brady has been engaged as the auditor of Patriot Company and is currently planning the year-end physical inventory counts. Patriot is a retailer that holds significant inventories in its warehouses and stores in six regions across the United States. Because of timing and logistics, Brady is able to observe the physical inventory at only one of Patriot's warehouses, which accounts for 20 percent of Patriot's inventories.

In Brady's professional judgment, the fact that inventories held at only one warehouse can be observed does not provide sufficient evidence with respect to Patriot's inventory balances at the date of the financial statements. Although physical inventory counts could be delayed at the remaining warehouses for Brady to observe the counts, the flow of goods in and out of the warehouses would result in a discrepancy between the inventory quantities on hand at year-end and the inventory quantities on hand at the date of the count.

Required:
a. Assume that Brady observes physical inventory at only the one warehouse and does not perform alternative procedures related to inventories held at the other warehouses. Does a scope limitation exist in this situation? If so, is this a client-imposed or circumstance-imposed scope limitation?
b. What type of opinion would Brady likely issue for the situation in (a)? How would the wording in the standard report be modified to reflect this opinion?
c. What alternative procedures might be available to Brady with respect to this scope limitation? (*Hint:* You may wish to refer to Chapter 9 to identify alternative procedures for inventory.)
d. Assume that Brady performs one or more of the alternative procedures in (c) and is able to gather evidence to support the recorded balance in inventory. What type of opinion would Brady issue on Patriot's financial statements (assuming that no other issues were identified in the audit examination)?

LO 12-6 12.44 **Consistency.** Various types of "accounting changes" can affect the auditors' reporting responsibility under generally accepted auditing standards. This standard indicates that the auditors' report should be modified to identify situations in which accounting principles have not been consistently observed in relation to prior years.

Assume that the following list describes changes that have a material effect on an entity's financial statements for the current year:

1. A change from the completed-contract method to the percentage-of-completion method of accounting for long-term construction-type contracts.
2. A change in the estimated useful life of previously recorded fixed assets based on newly acquired information.
3. The correction of a mathematical error in inventory pricing made in a prior period.
4. A change from prime costing to full absorption costing for inventory valuation.
5. A change from presentation of statements of individual entities to presentation of consolidated statements.
6. A change from deferring and amortizing preproduction costs to recording such costs as an expense when incurred because future benefits of the costs have become doubtful. The new accounting method was adopted in recognition of the change in estimated future benefits.
7. A change to include the employer's share of FICA taxes in "retirement benefits" on the income statement rather than in "other taxes."
8. A change from the FIFO method of inventory pricing to the LIFO method of inventory pricing.

Required:
Identify the type of change described in each preceding item as a change in accounting principle, change in the reporting entity, error correction, combined error correction and change in principle, or change in an accounting estimate. State whether any explanatory paragraph is required in the auditors' report. Organize your answer sheet as in the following table. For example, a change from the LIFO method of inventory pricing to the FIFO method of inventory pricing would appear as follows:

Item No.	Type of Change	Should the Auditors' Report Be Modified?
Example	An accounting change from one generally accepted accounting principle to another generally accepted accounting principle	Yes
1.		
2.		
3.		
4.		
5.		
6.		
7.		
8.		

LO 12-6

12.45 **Division of Responsibility.** Lando Corporation is a domestic company with two wholly-owned subsidiaries. Michaels, CPA, has been engaged to audit the financial statements of the parent company and one of the subsidiaries and to act as the group auditor. Thomas, CPA, has audited the financial statements of the other subsidiary whose operations are material in relation to the consolidated financial statements.

The work performed by Michaels is sufficient for serving as the group auditor and to report as such on the financial statements. Michaels has not yet decided whether to refer to the part of the audit performed by Thomas.

Required:
a. What responsibilities does Michaels have with respect to Thomas when deciding on whether a division of responsibility is appropriate?
b. What are the reporting requirements with which Michaels must comply in naming Thomas and referring to the work done by Thomas?
c. What report should be issued if Michaels can neither assume responsibility for Thomas's work nor indicate a division of responsibility by referring to Thomas's work?

LO 12-4, 12-5, 12-6, 12-7

12.46 **Various Reporting Situations.** Assume that the auditors encountered the following separate situations when deciding on the report to issue for the current-year financial statements.

1. The auditors decided that sufficient appropriate evidence could not be obtained to complete the audit of significant investments the entity held in a foreign entity.
2. The entity failed to capitalize lease assets and obligations but explained them fully in the notes to the financial statements.
3. The entity is defending a lawsuit on product liability claims. (Customers allege that power saw safety guards were improperly installed.) All facts about the lawsuit are disclosed in the notes to the financial statements, but the auditors believe the entity should record a loss based on a probable settlement mentioned by the entity's attorneys.
4. The entity hired the auditors after taking inventory on December 31. The accounting records and other evidence are not reliable enough to enable the auditors to have sufficient evidence about the proper inventory amount.
5. The oil company is required by the FASB to present supplementary oil and gas reserve information outside the basic financial statements. The auditors find that this information, which is not required as a part of the basic financial statements, has been omitted.

6. The auditors are group auditors of the parent company, but they reviewed the component auditors' work and reputation and decide not to take responsibility for the work of the component auditors on three subsidiary companies included in the consolidated financial statements. The component auditors' work amounts to 32 percent of the consolidated assets and 39 percent of the consolidated revenues.

7. The entity changed its depreciation method from units of production to straight line, and its auditors believe the straight-line method is the more appropriate method in the circumstances. The change, fully explained in the notes to the financial statements, has a material effect on the year-to-year comparability of the comparative financial statements.

8. Because the entity has experienced significant operating losses and has had to obtain waivers of debt payment requirements from its lenders, the auditors decide that there is substantial doubt that the entity can continue as a going concern. The entity has fully described all problems in a note in the financial statements and the auditors believe that, while material, the uncertainty is not serious enough to warrant a disclaimer of opinion.

Required:
a. What kind of opinion should the auditors express in each separate case?
b. What other modification(s) or addition(s) to the standard report is (are) required for each separate case?

LO 12-4, 12-6, 12-7   12.47 **Various Reporting Situations.** Assume that Stanford CPAs encountered the following issues during its various audit engagements in 2012:

1. It conducted the audit of Luck, a new client this past year. Last year, Luck was audited by another CPA, who issued an unqualified opinion on Luck's financial statements. Luck is presenting balance sheets for 2011 and 2012 and income statements, statements of shareholders' equity, and statements of cash flows for 2010–2012 in comparative form.

2. One of Stanford's clients is RealCo, a real estate holding company. Assume that RealCo experienced a significant decline in the value of its investment properties during the past year because of a downturn in the economy and has appropriately recognized that decline in market value under GAAP. Stanford wishes to emphasize the decline in the economy and its impact on RealCo's financial position and results of operations for 2012 in its audit report.

3. For the past five years, Stanford has conducted the audits of TechTime, a company that provides technology consulting services, and has always issued unqualified opinions on its financial statements. Based on its 2012 audit, Stanford believes that an unqualified opinion is appropriate; however, Stanford did note that TechTime reported its third consecutive operating loss and has experienced negative cash flows because of the inability of some of its customers to promptly pay for services received.

4. Stanford has assisted Cardinal, Inc. with the preparation of its financial statements, but has not audited, compiled, or reviewed those financial statements. Cardinal wishes to include these financial statements in a communication that would describe Stanford's involvement in the preparation of the financial statements. Stanford believes that Cardinal's communication is adequate and appropriately describes Stanford's role in the preparation of the financial statements.

5. Trees, Inc. presents summary financial information along with its financial statements. The summary financial information has been derived from the complete set of financial statements that have been audited by Stanford (which issued an unqualified opinion on the complete financial statements). Stanford believes that the summary financial information is fairly stated in relation to Trees' complete financial statements.

6. Stanford believes that some of the verbiage in Plunkett's Management Discussion & Analysis section is inconsistent with the firm's financial statements. Stanford has concluded that Plunkett's financial statements present its financial position, results of operations, and cash flows in accordance with GAAP and has decided to issue an unqualified opinion on Plunkett's financial statements.

7. Oil Patch is a client in the energy industry that is required to present supplementary oil and gas reserve information. Stanford has performed certain procedures regarding this information and concluded that it is presented in conformity with FASB presentation guidelines and does not appear to depart from GAAP. Based on Stanford's audit, it plans to issue an unqualified opinion on Oil Patch's financial statements.

Required:

How would each of these issues affect Stanford's report on the client's financial statements? (Do *not* draft the report that Stanford would issue in each situation).

LO 12-4, 12-5, 12-6 12.48 **Various Reporting Situations.** For each of the following situations, indicate the type of opinion(s) that could be issued by auditors (more than one opinion may be appropriate in each circumstance). Unless otherwise noted, assume that no departures from GAAP were identified in the audit engagement. In addition, indicate how the standard report would be modified, if appropriate.

1. Auditors have identified an immaterial departure from GAAP in their examination. They have not requested the client to adjust its financial statements for this departure because they believe this situation is unusual and that accounting for the related transactions under the provisions of GAAP would be misleading to investors and creditors.

2. Because they were appointed to the engagement after the date of the financial statements, the auditors have experienced a significant scope limitation and were unable to perform standard auditing procedures used in their engagements. The account(s) affected by this scope limitation were material and pervasive. However, they have been able to completely satisfy themselves as to the fairness of the related account balances and classes of transaction by performing alternative procedures.

3. During the year, the entity changed its method of accounting for inventories from FIFO to LIFO and has disclosed this change in the footnotes to the financial statements and accounted for the change properly. However, the auditors do not agree with the rationale for the change and believe that it was made to improve the company's earnings.

4. Subsequent to accepting the audit engagement, the auditors have determined that they are not independent with respect to the client because of a financial interest a newly-admitted partner to the audit firm held in the client.

5. Evidence gathered during the audit examination and inquiry of the client's management revealed substantial doubt about the client's ability to continue in existence. The auditors believe that the client has appropriately disclosed the going-concern uncertainties in its financial statements and footnotes.

6. The auditors wish to emphasize the company's acquisition of two large subsidiaries during the most recent year.

7. The auditors have engaged component auditors to conduct a portion of the audit but do not wish to assume responsibility for the component auditors' work. The auditors have not approached the component auditors about presenting their reports along with the company's financial statements and do not plan to do so.

8. The client has not recognized a material loss related to a decline in the market value of its investments. Because the auditors believe this decline in value is not temporary, they believe the financial statements do not present the client's results of operations in conformity with GAAP.

9. The auditors have experienced a significant scope limitation and are unable to satisfy themselves as to the fairness of the affected account balances through alternative procedures.

LO 12-3 12.49 **Audit Report Deficiencies.** On September 23, 2013, Betsy Ross drafted the following report on Continental Corporation's financial statements.. Continental's stock is publicly traded, and accordingly, the corporation is subject to the reporting requirements of *AS 5*. Ross has decided to present separate reports on Continental's financial statements and internal control over financial reporting.

536 Part Two *The Financial Statement Audit*

> To Whom It May Concern:
>
> The accompanying balance sheet of Continental Corporation and the related statements of income, and shareholders' equity as of July 31, 2013, are the responsibility of management.
>
> In accordance with your instructions, we have conducted a complete audit. We planned and performed the audit to obtain reasonable assurance about whether the financial statements are free of material misstatement. An audit includes examining, on a test basis, evidence supporting the amounts and disclosures in the financial statements. An audit also includes assessing the accounting principles used and significant estimates made by management, as well as evaluating the overall financial statement presentation. We believe that our audit provides a reasonable basis for our opinion.
>
> In many respects this was an unusual year for the Continental Corporation. The weakening of the economy in the early part of the year and the strike of plant employees in the summer led to a decline in sales and net income. After making several tests of the sales records, nothing came to our attention that would indicate sales have not been properly recorded.
>
> In our opinion, with the explanation given above, and with the exception of some minor errors we consider immaterial, the aforementioned financial statements present the financial position of Continental Corporation at July 31, 2013, and the results of its operations, and its cash flows for the year then ended in conformity with pronouncements of the Financial Accounting Standards Board.
>
> We have also audited, in accordance with the standards of the Public Company Accounting Oversight Board (United States), the effectiveness of Continental Corporation's internal control over financial reporting as of July 31, 2013, based on criteria established in *Internal Control – Integrated Framework* issued by the Committee of Sponsoring Organizations of the Treadway Commission and our report dated July 31, 2013, expressed an unqualified opinion thereon.
>
> *Betsy Ross & Co., CPA*
> July 31, 2013

Required:
List and explain the deficiencies and omissions in Ross's report on Continental Company's financial statements.

LO 12-4

12.50 **Audit Report Deficiencies: Adverse Opinion.** The board of directors of Cook Industries, Inc. engaged Brown & Brown, CPAs, to audit the financial statements for the year ended December 31, 2012. Because Cook is publicly traded, Brown & Brown will issue reports on the financial statements and internal control over financial reporting; they will present separate reports on each of these areas. M. Brown agrees with Cook's management's assessment that the company has maintained an effective internal control over financial reporting but has decided an adverse opinion is appropriate on its financial statements.

Brown also became aware of a March 14, 2013, matter that Cook's financial vice president properly disclosed in the notes to the financial statements. Brown wants responsibility for subsequently discovered facts such as this to be limited to this specific event after March 7.

Required:
Identify the deficiencies in the following draft of the report. Do *not* rewrite the report.

> **Report of Independent Registered Public Accounting Firm**
>
> To the President of Cook Industries, Inc.:
> We have audited the accompanying financial statements of Cook Industries, Inc., for the year ended December 31, 2012. We conducted our audits in accordance with the standards of the Public Company Accounting Oversight Board (United States). Those standards require that we plan and perform the audit to obtain reasonable assurance about whether the financial statements are free of material misstatement. An audit includes examining, on a test basis, evidence supporting the amounts and disclosures in the financial statements. An audit also includes assessing the accounting principles used and significant estimates made by

> management as well as evaluating the overall financial statement presentation. We believe that our audit provides a reasonable basis for our opinion.
>
> As discussed in Note K to the financial statements, the Company has properly disclosed a subsequently discovered fact dated March 14, 2013.
>
> As discussed in Note G to the financial statements, the Company carries its property and equipment at appraisal values and provides depreciation on the basis of such values. Furthermore, the Company does not provide for income taxes with respect to differences between financial income and taxable income arising from the use, for income tax purposes, of the installment method of reporting gross profit from certain types of sales.
>
> In our opinion, the financial statements referred to above do not present fairly the financial position of Cook Industries, Inc., as of December 31, 2012, and the results of its operations and its cash flows for the year then ended in conformity with accounting principles generally accepted in the United States of America.
>
> We have also audited, in accordance with the standards of the Public Company Accounting Oversight Board (United States), the effectiveness of Cook Industries' internal control over financial reporting as of December 31, 2012, based on criteria established in *Internal Control—Integrated Framework* issued by the Committee of Sponsoring Organizations of the Treadway Commission; because of our adverse opinion on Cook Industries' financial statements, our report dated March 14, 2013, does not express an opinion thereon.
>
> *Brown & Brown, CPAs*
> March 14, 2013

(AICPA adapted)

LO 12-7

12.51 **Audit Report Deficiencies: Comparative Reporting.** An assistant drafted the following auditors' report at the completion of the audit of Cramdon, Inc., on March 5, 2013. The partner in charge of the engagement has decided the opinion on the 2012 financial statements should be modified only with reference to the change in the method of computing the cost of inventory. In 2011, Cramdon used the next-in, first-out (NIFO) method, which is not permissible under GAAP, but in 2012 changed to FIFO and restated the 2011 financial statements. (The auditors' report on the 2011 financial statements expressed an adverse opinion.) The 2011 auditors' report (prepared by the same firm) was dated March 5, 2012.

> **Report of Independent Registered Public Accounting Firm**
>
> To the Board of Directors of Cramdon, Inc.:
>
> We have audited the accompanying financial statements of Cramdon, Inc., as of December 31, 2012 and 2011. These financial statements are the responsibility of Cramdon, Inc.'s management. Our responsibility is to express an opinion on these financial statements based on our audits.
>
> We conducted our audits in accordance with the standards established by the Public Company Accounting Oversight Board (United States). Those standards require that we plan and perform the audit to obtain reasonable assurance about whether the financial statements are free of material misstatement. An audit includes examining, on a test basis, evidence supporting the amounts and disclosures in the financial statements. An audit also includes assessing the accounting principles used and significant estimates made by management as well as evaluating the overall financial statement presentation. We believe that our audit provides a reasonable basis for our opinion.
>
> As discussed in Note 7 to the financial statements, the company changed its method of accounting for inventory cost from NIFO to FIFO. The 2011 financial statements have been restated to reflect this change. Accordingly, our present opinion on the 2011 financial statements, as presented herein, is different from the opinion we expressed in our previous report dated December 31, 2011.
>
> *(continued)*

> In our opinion, based on the preceding, the financial statements referred to above present fairly, in all material respects, the financial position of Cramdon, Inc., as of December 31, 2012, and the results of its operations and its cash flows for the period then ended in conformity with accounting principles generally accepted in the United States of America, consistently applied, except for the changes in the method of computing inventory cost as described in Note 7 to the financial statements.
>
> We have also audited, in accordance with the standards of the Public Company Accounting Oversight Board (United States), the effectiveness of Cramdon, Inc.'s internal control over financial reporting as of December 31, 2012, based on criteria established in *Internal Control—Integrated Framework* issued by the Committee of Sponsoring Organizations of the Treadway Commission and our report dated March 5, 2013, expressed an unqualified opinion thereon.
>
> *George Costanza, CPA*
> March 5, 2013

Required:

Identify the deficiencies and errors in the draft report and write an explanation of the reasons they are errors and deficiencies. Do *not* rewrite the report.

LO 12-6

12.52 **Audit Report Deficiencies: Audits of Group Financial Statements and Other Operating Matters.** Following is Rex Wolf's report on Bonair Corporation's financial statements. Bonair is profit oriented and publishes general-purpose financial statements for distribution to owners, creditors, potential investors, and the general public.

> **Report of Independent Registered Public Accounting Firm**
>
> To the Board of Directors and Shareholders, Bonair Corporation:
>
> We have audited the accompanying consolidated balance sheet of Bonair Corporation and subsidiaries as of December 31, 2012, and the related statements of income and shareholders' equity for the year then ended. Our responsibility is to express an opinion on these financial statements based on our audit. We did not examine the financial statements of Caet Company, a major consolidated subsidiary. These statements were examined by Nero Stout, CPA, whose report thereon has been furnished to us, and our opinion expressed herein, insofar as it relates to Caet Company, is based solely upon the component auditors' report on Caet Company.
>
> Except as stated in the preceding paragraph, we conducted our audit in accordance with the standards established by the Public Company Accounting Oversight Board (United States). Those standards require that we plan and perform the audit to obtain reasonable assurance about whether the financial statements are free of material misstatement. An audit includes assessing control risk and examining on a test basis evidence supporting the amounts and disclosures in the financial statements. An audit also includes assessing the accounting principles used and significant estimates made by management, as well as evaluating the overall financial statement presentation. We believe that our audit provides a reasonable basis for our opinion.
>
> In our opinion, except for the matter of the report of the component auditors, the financial statements referred to above present fairly, in all material respects, the financial position of Bonair Corporation and subsidiaries as of December 31, 2012, and the results of its operations and its cash flows for the year then ended.
>
> We have also audited, in accordance with the standards of the Public Company Accounting Oversight Board (United States), the effectiveness of Bonair Corporation's internal control over financial reporting as of December 31, 2012, based on criteria established in *Internal Control—Integrated Framework* issued by the Committee of Sponsoring Organizations of the Treadway Commission and our report dated March 5, 2013, expressed an unqualified opinion thereon.
>
> *Rex Wolf, CPA*
> March 5, 2013

Required:
Describe the reporting deficiencies and explain why they are considered deficiencies. Organize your response according to each of the paragraphs in the standard report.

LO 12-7

12.53 Audit Report Deficiencies: Disclaimer of Opinion. Your partner drafted the following auditors' report yesterday. You need to describe the reporting deficiencies, explain the reasons for them, and discuss with the partner how the report should be corrected. You have decided to prepare a three-column worksheet showing the deficiencies, reasons, and corrections needed. Your partner's report follows:

> I made my examination in accordance with standards of the Public Company Accounting Oversight Board (United States). However, I am not independent with respect to Mavis Corporation because my wife owns 5 percent of the outstanding common stock of the company. The accompanying balance sheet as of December 31, 2012, and the related statements of income, shareholders' equity, and cash flows for the year then ended were not audited by me. Accordingly, I do not express an opinion on them.

Required:
Prepare the three-column worksheet described.

LO 12-6

12.54 Audit Report Deficiencies: Accounting Change and Uncertainty. The following auditors' report was drafted by Quinn Moore, a staff auditor with Tyler & Tyler, CPAs, at the completion of the audit of the financial statements of Park Publishing Company for the year ended September 30, 2012. The engagement partner reviewed the audit documentation and properly decided to issue an unqualified opinion. In drafting the report, Moore considered the following:

- During fiscal year 2012, Park changed its depreciation method. The engagement partner concurred with this change in accounting principles and its justification, and Moore included an explanatory paragraph in the report.
- The 2012 financial statements are affected by an uncertainty concerning a lawsuit, the outcome of which cannot presently be estimated. Moore included an explanatory paragraph in the report to emphasize this uncertainty.
- The financial statements for the year ended September 30, 2011, are to be presented for comparative purposes. Tyler & Tyler previously audited these statements and expressed an unqualified opinion.
- Because Park Publishing Company is publicly traded, Tyler & Tyler also prepared a separate report on Park Publishing's internal control over financial reporting. This report expressed an unqualified opinion on the effectiveness of Park's internal control over financial reporting.

> **Report of Independent Registered Public Accounting Firm**
>
> To the Board of Directors of Park Publishing Company:
> We have audited the accompanying balance sheets of Park Publishing Company as of September 30, 2012 and 2011, and the related statements of income, shareholders' equity, and cash flows for each of the years in the three-year period ended September 30, 2012. These financial statements are the responsibility of Park Publishing Company's management.
> We conducted our audits in accordance with the standards of the Public Company Accounting Oversight Board (United States). Those standards require that we plan and perform the audit to obtain reasonable assurance about whether the financial statements are fairly presented. An audit includes examining, on a test basis, evidence supporting the amounts and disclosures in the financial statements. An audit also includes assessing significant estimates made by management as well as evaluating the overall financial statement presentation.
>
> *(continued)*

> We believe that our audits provide a basis for determining whether any material modifications should be made to the accompanying financial statements.
>
> As discussed in Note X to the financial statements, the company changed its method of computing depreciation in fiscal 2012.
>
> In our opinion, except for the accounting change, with which we concur, the financial statements referred to above present fairly, in all material respects, the financial position of Park Publishing Company as of September 30, 2012, and the results of its operations and its cash flows for each of the years in the three-year period ended September 30, 2012, in conformity with accounting principles generally accepted in the United States of America.
>
> As discussed in Note Y to the financial statements, the company is a defendant in a lawsuit alleging infringement of certain copyrights. The company has filed a counteraction, and preliminary hearings on both actions are in progress. Accordingly, any provision for liability is subject to adjudication of this matter.
>
> We have also audited, in accordance with the standards of the Public Company Accounting Oversight Board (United States), the effectiveness of Park Publishing Company's internal control over financial reporting as of September 30, 2012, based on criteria established in *Internal Control—Integrated Framework* issued by the Committee of Sponsoring Organizations of the Treadway Commission and our report dated November 5, 2012, expressed an unqualified opinion thereon.
>
> *Tyler & Tyler, CPAs*
> November 5, 2012

Required:

Identify the deficiencies in the auditors' report as drafted by Moore. Group the deficiencies by paragraph and in the order in which they appear. Do *not* rewrite the report.

(AICPA adapted)

LO 12-3

12.55 **Internet Exercise: Reports on Financial Statements.** One of the great resources on the World Wide Web for auditors is the SEC's Electronic Data Gathering, Analysis and Retrieval (EDGAR) system database at www.sec.gov. Public companies file SEC-required documents electronically. The SEC makes this information available on its web page.

Required:

Choose five public companies with which you are familiar. After accessing the EDGAR database, download copies of auditors' reports from the Form 10-K filings and check the boxes in the following table that apply. The first has been done for you. (*Hint:* Search the 10-K filing by using the key word "independent," as in "Report of Independent Registered Public Accounting Firm.") Do *not* evaluate the auditors' report on internal control over financial reporting.

(*Note:* U = unqualified opinion; Q = qualified opinion; D = disclaimer of opinion; A = adverse opinion; C = consistency; GC = going concern; E = explanatory paragraph; IC = reference to report on internal control over financial reporting)

Company Name	Type of Opinion				Additional Paragraph?			
	U	Q	D	A	C	GC	E	IC
Walmart (2011)	X				X			X

LO 12-3

12.56 **Internet Exercise: Reports on Internal Control over Financial Reporting.** One of the great resources on the World Wide Web for auditors is the SEC's Electronic Data Gathering, Analysis and Retrieval (EDGAR) system database at www.sec.gov. Public companies file SEC-required documents electronically. The SEC makes this information available on its web page.

Required:

Choose five public companies with which you are familiar. After accessing the EDGAR database, download copies of auditors' reports on the financial statements from the Form 10-K filings and check the boxes in the following table that apply. The first has been done for you. *(Hint:* Search the 10-K filing by using the key word "independent," as in "Report of Independent Registered Public Accounting Firm.")

(*Note:* U = unqualified opinion; Q = qualified opinion; D = disclaimer of opinion; A = adverse opinion)

Company Name	Auditors' Opinion on Internal Control over Financial Reporting				Separate or Combined Report
	U	Q	D	A	
Walmart (2011)	X				Separate

Report-Writing Cases

Cases 12.57 through 12.63 require you to draft auditors' reports. The *Electronic Workpapers* (available on the textbook website listed on the back cover of the text) has a Word file (file name AUDIT) containing the standard report, which can be used as the starting place for a nonstandard report requirement. You can read this file in many word-processing programs to make your report-writing task easier and more professional.

Unless instructed otherwise, assume the following in drafting your reports: (1) your firm Anderson, Olds, & Watershed (AOW) conducted the audit examination of the identified client; (2) the fiscal year-end is December 31, 2012; (3) the date of the auditors' report is February 10, 2013; and (4) the client is publicly traded and, therefore, subject to the auditing and reporting requirements of *AS 5*.

LO 12-6

12.57 **Financial Difficulty: The "Going-Concern" Problem.** Pitts Company has experienced significant financial difficulty. Current liabilities exceed current assets by $1 million, cash has decreased to $10,000, the interest on the long-term debt has not been paid, and a customer has brought a lawsuit against Pitts for $500,000 on a product liability claim. Significant questions concerning the going-concern status of the company exist. The lawsuit and information about the going-concern status have been appropriately described in footnote 3 to the financial statements.

Required:

a. Draft AOW's report, assuming that the auditors decide that an unqualified opinion instead of a disclaimer of opinion is appropriate in the circumstances.

b. Draft AOW's report, assuming that the auditors decide the uncertainties are so overwhelming that they do not wish to express an opinion on Pitts' financial statements (assume they are still able to express an opinion on Pitts' internal control over financial reporting).

LO 12-7

12.58 **Disagreement with Auditors.** Officers of Richnow Company do not wish to disclose information about a product liability lawsuit filed by a customer seeking $500,000 in damages. They believe the suit is frivolous and without merit. Outside counsel is more cautious. The auditors insist on disclosure. Angered, the chair of the board of Richnow Company threatens to sue AOW if a standard report is not issued within three days.

Required:

Draft AOW's report appropriate under the circumstances.

12.59 **Late Appointment of Auditors.** Anderson, Olds, & Watershed (AOW) has completed the audit of the financial statements of Musgrave Company for the year ended December 31, 2012, and is now preparing the report.

AOW has audited Musgrave's financial statements for several years, but this year Musgrave delayed the start of the audit work, so AOW was not present to observe the taking of the physical inventory on December 31, 2012. The inventory balance is $194,000, which represents 39 percent of Musgrave's total assets and 69 percent of its current assets. However, AOW performed alternative procedures including (1) examination of shipping and receiving documents with regard to transactions since the date of the financial statements, (2) extensive review of the inventory count sheets, and (3) discussion of the physical inventory procedures with responsible company personnel. AOW also is satisfied about the propriety of the inventory valuation calculations and the consistency of the valuation method. Musgrave determines year-end inventory quantities solely by means of physical count.

Required:

Draft AOW's report on the balance sheet at the end of the current year and on the statements of operations, shareholders' equity, and cash flows for the year then ended. (*Hint:* Did the alternative procedures produce sufficient appropriate evidence?)

12.60 **Audits of Group Financial Statements.** The firm of Anderson, Olds, & Watershed (AOW) is the group auditor for the December 31, 2012, consolidated financial statements of Ferguson Company and subsidiaries. However, component auditors perform the work on certain subsidiaries for the year under audit amounting to

	2012	2011
Total assets	29%	31%
Total revenues	36	41

AOW investigated the component auditors, as required by auditing standards, and they furnished AOW their reports. AOW has decided to rely on their work and to refer to the component auditors in their report. None of the audit work revealed any issues with respect to Ferguson Company or its subsidiaries.

Required:

Draft AOW's report indicating the division of responsibility.

12.61 **Other Information in a Financial Review Section of an Annual Report.** Gustav Humphreys (chair of the board) and Ingrid VanEns (vice president, finance) prepared the draft of the financial review section of the annual report. You are reviewing it for consistency with the audited financial statements. The draft contains the following explanation about income coverage of interest expense:

Last year, operating income before interest and income taxes covered interest expense by a ratio of 6:1. This year, on an incremental basis, the coverage of interest expense increased to a ratio of 6.59:1.

The relevant portion of the audited financial statements showed the following:

	Current Year	Prior Year
Operating income	$400,000	$360,000
Extraordinary gain from realization of tax benefits	100,000	
Interest expense	(81,250)	(60,000)
Income taxes	(127,500)	(120,000)
Net income	$291,250	$180,000

Required:

a. Determine whether the financial review section statement about coverage of interest is or is not consistent with the audited financial statements. Be able to show your conclusion with calculations.

b. Assume that you find an inconsistency and the officers disagree with your conclusions. Draft the explanatory paragraph you should put in your auditors' report.

LO 12-4

12.62 **Departures from GAAP.** On January 1, Graham Company purchased land (the site of a new building) for $100,000. Soon thereafter, the state highway department announced that a new feeder road would run next to the site. The effect was a dramatic increase in local property values. Comparable land located nearby sold for $700,000 in December of the current year. Graham presents the land at $700,000 in its accounts and, after reduction for implicit taxes at 33 percent, the fixed asset total is $400,000 higher than historical cost with the same amount shown separately in the shareholder equity account Current Value Increment. The valuation is fully disclosed in a footnote to the financial statements with a letter from a certified property appraiser attesting to the $700,000 value.

Required:

a. Draft the appropriate auditors' report, assuming that you believe the departure from GAAP is material but not pervasive enough to cause you to issue an adverse opinion.

b. Draft the appropriate auditors' report, assuming that you believe an adverse opinion is necessary.

c. Discuss whether you should (could) issue a report conforming to Rule 203 of the AICPA Code of Professional Conduct.

LO 12-6

12.63 **Reporting on an Accounting Change.** In December of the current year, Williams Company changed its method of accounting for inventory and cost of goods sold from LIFO to FIFO. The account balances shown in the trial balance have already been recalculated and adjusted retroactively as required by *ASC 250*. The accounting change and the financial effects are described in Note 2 in the financial statements.

Required:

a. Assume that you believe the accounting change is justified as required by *ASC 250*. Draft the report appropriate in the circumstances.

b. Assume that you believe the accounting change is not justified and causes the financial statements to be materially distorted. Inventories that would have been reported at $1.5 million (LIFO) are reported at $1.9 million (FIFO); operating income before tax that would have been $130,000 is reported at $530,000. As a result of this change, current assets, total assets, and shareholders' equity have increased by 17 percent, 9 percent, and 14 percent, respectively. Draft the report appropriate in the circumstances.

LO 12-6

12.64 **Mini-Case: Component Auditors.** Refer to the mini-case "Something Went Sour at Parmalat" and respond to question 4.

LO 12-6

12.65 **Mini-Case: Going-Concern Reporting.** Refer to the mini-case "GM: Running on Empty" and respond to questions 1, 2, and 3.

Appendix 12A

Auditing Standards Board Report for Nonpublic Entities (AU 700)

See Exhibit 12A.1 for the standard form of report that would be issued in the audit of a nonpublic entity. This report was recently revised by the Auditing Standards Board through the issuance of AU 700. Some significant differences (other than minor wording changes) between this report and the PCAOB report related to the audit of public entities include:

PCAOB Report	ASB Report
Titled "Report of Independent Registered Public Accounting Firm"	Title does not contain the phrase "Independent Registered Public Accounting Firm"
Introductory paragraph • Identifies financial statements examined • Identifies responsibility of management and auditors in the financial reporting process	Information presented in three separate sections: • "Report on the Financial Statements" • "Management's Responsibility for Financial Statements" • "Auditor's Responsibility"
Scope paragraph • Provides a general description of an audit • Concludes that the audit provides a reasonable basis for the opinion	• Information presented in the "Auditor's Responsibility" section, along with the auditor's responsibility in the financial reporting process • Refers to "standards generally accepted in the United States of America" rather than "standards of the Public Company Accounting Oversight Board" • Specifically refers to auditor's responsibility for internal control
Opinion paragraph • Provides auditors' conclusion as to the fair presentation of the financial statements	No major differences
Internal control paragraph	Omitted because it is not applicable in the audit of a nonpublic entity

EXHIBIT 12A.1
Auditors' Report for Nonpublic Entities

Independent Auditor's Report

To the Board of Directors and Shareholders Dunder-Mifflin, Inc.

Report on the Financial Statements

We have audited the accompanying consolidated financial statements of Dunder-Mifflin, Inc., which comprise the consolidated balance sheets as of December 31, 2012 and 2011, and the related consolidated statements of income, changes in shareholders' equity, and cash flows for the years then ended, and the related notes to the financial statements.

Management's Responsibility for the Financial Statements

Management is responsible for the preparation and fair presentation of these consolidated financial statements in accordance with accounting principles generally accepted in the United States of America; this includes the design, implementation, and maintenance of internal control relevant to the preparation and fair presentation of consolidated financial statements that are free from material misstatement, whether due to fraud or error.

Auditor's Responsibility

Our responsibility is to express an opinion on these consolidated financial statements based on our audits. We conducted our audits in accordance with auditing standards generally accepted in the United States of America. Those standards require that we plan and perform the audit to obtain reasonable assurance about whether the consolidated financial statements are free from material misstatement.

An audit involves performing procedures to obtain audit evidence about the amounts and disclosures in the consolidated financial statements. The procedures selected depend on the auditor's judgment, including the assessment of the risks of material misstatement of the consolidated financial statements, whether due to fraud or error. In making those risk assessments, the auditor considers internal control relevant to the entity's preparation and fair presentation of the consolidated financial statements in order to design audit procedures that are appropriate in the circumstances, but not for the purpose of expressing an opinion on the effectiveness of the entity's internal control. Accordingly, we express no such opinion. An audit also includes evaluating the appropriateness of accounting policies used and the reasonableness of significant accounting estimates made by management, as well as evaluating the overall presentation of the consolidated financial statements.

We believe that the audit evidence we have obtained is sufficient and appropriate to provide a basis for our audit opinion.

Opinion

In our opinion, the consolidated financial statements referred to above present fairly, in all material respects, the financial position of Dunder-Mifflin, Inc. and its subsidiaries as of December 31, 2012 and 2011, and the results of their operations and their cash flows for the years then ended in accordance with accounting principles generally accepted in the United States of America.

Michael Scarn, LLP
Scranton, PA
January 29, 2013

Other Public Accounting Services

There's no business like show business, but there are several businesses like accounting. —David Letterman

Professional Standards References

Topic	AU/ISA Section*	PCAOB Reference†
Attestation Engagements		
Defining Professional Requirements in Statements on Standards for Attestation Engagements	AT 20	N/A
SSAE Hierarchy	AT 50	N/A
Attestation Engagements	AT 101	AT 101
Agreed-upon Procedures Engagements	AT 201 ISAE 4400	AT 201
Financial Forecasts and Projections	AT 301 ISAE 4400	AT 301
Reporting on Pro Forma Financial Information	AT 401	AT 401
An Examination of an Entity's Internal Control in an Audit of Its Financial Statements	AT 501	AS 5
Compliance Attestation	AT 601	AT 601
Management's Discussion and Analysis	AT 701	AT 701
Reporting on Controls at a Service Organization	AT 801 ISAE 3402	AU 324
Review and Compilation of Unaudited Financial Statements		
Framework for Compilation and Review Engagements	AR 60	N/A
Compilation of Financial Statements	AR 80 ISAE 4410	N/A
Review of Financial Statements	AR 90 ISRE 2400	N/A
Compilation of Specified Elements, Accounts, or Items of a Financial Statement	AR 110	N/A
Compilation of Pro Forma Financial Information	AR 120	N/A

Reporting on Comparative Financial Statements	AR 200	N/A
Compilation Reports on Financial Statements Included in Certain Prescribed Forms	AR 300	N/A
Communications between Predecessor and Successor Accountants	AR 400	N/A
Personal Financial Statements	AR 600	N/A
Special Reports		
Audits of Financial Statements Prepared in Accordance with Special Purpose Frameworks	AU 800	AU 544
Special Considerations—Audits of Single Financial Statements and Specific Elements, Accounts, or Items of a Financial Statement	AU 805	AU 508 AU 623
Reporting on Compliance with Aspects of Contractual Agreements or Regulatory Requirements in Connection with Audited Financial Statements	AU 808	AU 623
Reports on Application of Requirements of an Appropriate Financial Reporting Framework	AU 915	AU 625
Other Information in Documents Containing Audited Financial Statements	AU 720	AU 550
Interim Financial Information	AU 930 ISRE 2410	AU 722

*Any unmarked references are AU/ISA. Others are as follows: ISAE (International Standards on Assurance Engagements), ISRE (International Standards for Review Engagements), SOP (Statements of Position—Auditing and Attestation). ISREs (International Standards on Review Engagements) are to be applied in the review of historical financial information. ISAEs (International Standards on Assurance Engagements) are to be applied in assurance engagements dealing with subject matters other than historical financial information.

†AU, AT, and QC references represent standards issued by the ASB prior to April 16, 2003, that have not been superseded or amended by the PCAOB.

LEARNING OBJECTIVES

Certified public accountants (CPAs) are trusted professionals with a reputation for objectivity and integrity. The reputation has its foundation in a long history of service to the business community and the general public. Despite recent problems (such as the Madoff scandal and the banking crisis), individuals and businesses still view their CPAs as trusted business professionals who add value to their businesses and provide valuable guidance concerning difficult business decisions. In this tradition, CPAs and other accountants offer numerous assurance and attestation services on information other than audited financial statements. These services result from consumer demand for assurance by objective experts. This module covers several areas of public accounting practice related to accountants' association with information other than audited historical financial statements discussed in Chapter 12.

This module is broken into five parts. The first part is devoted to (nonaudit) attestation engagements. The second part deals with reviews and compilations of unaudited financial statements. The third part discusses the auditors' responsibility related to interim financial information. The fourth part addresses other topics, including special and restricted-use reports. The final part defines and further explores other type of assurance services.

Your objectives are to be able to:

LO A-1 Explain and provide examples of attestation engagements.

LO A-2 Describe reviews and compilations of unaudited financial statements and prepare appropriate reports given specific factual circumstances.

LO A-3 Explain auditors' responsibilities related to reporting on interim financial information.

LO A-4 Define, explain, and give examples of other special reports provided by auditors, including specified elements of financial statements, special purpose frameworks and application of requirements of appropriate financial reporting frameworks.

LO A-5 Explain and provide examples of assurance services engagements.

INTRODUCTION

The major banks in Louisville, Kentucky, wondered how their various services, such as ATM transactions, mortgage loans, credit card transactions, and so on were doing compared with those of their competitors. Because banking regulations prevented the banks from sharing the information, they approached a CPA to help. They asked the CPA to take reports of the transactions from the banks each month and combine them into a total. The CPA was also asked to verify the numbers in each bank's report to supporting documents. Thus, the banks were able to confidently know how their market shares were changing on a month-to-month bases. This is an example of an *attestation* engagement—one of a number discussed in this Module—in which a CPA can provide a needed service to businesses, beyond examining financial statements or preparing tax returns

ATTESTATION ENGAGEMENTS

LEARNING OBJECTIVE A-1
Explain and provide examples of attestation engagements.

Introduction to Attestation Engagements

Although the majority of this textbook is devoted to the audit of financial statements, audit services are really a subset of a larger group of services referred to as *attestation services*. An **attestation** is defined as an engagement

> in which a practitioner is engaged to issue or does issue an examination, a review, or an agreed-upon procedures report on subject matter, or an assertion about the subject matter . . . that is the responsibility of another party [AT 101.01].

The subject matter of an attest engagement may take many forms, including the following:

a. Historical or prospective performance or condition (for example, backlog data).
b. Physical characteristics (for example, narrative descriptions, square footage of facilities).
c. Historical events (for example, the price of a market basket of goods on a certain date).
d. Analyses (for example, break-even analyses).
e. Systems and processes (for example, internal control).
f. Behavior (for example, corporate governance, compliance with laws and regulations, and human resource practices) [AT 101.07].

The subject matter of an attest engagement may be as of a point in time or for a period of time. The **responsible party** is the person at the client who is accountable for the information (e.g., the company's controller for financial information.). The accountant[1] should obtain written acknowledgment or other evidence of the party's responsibility for the subject matter or the written assertion. The responsible party can acknowledge responsibility in a number of ways, for example, in an engagement letter or a representation letter. If the accountant is not able to directly obtain written acknowledgment, the practitioner should obtain other evidence of the party's responsibility for the subject matter (for example, by reference to legislation, a regulation, or a contract).

The preceding definition of **attestation** identifies three types of attestation engagements:

- An **examination** is similar in substance to an audit. Accountants evaluate internal controls and assess the risk of material misstatement, gather evidence in support of the assertions, and render opinions that represent a high level of assurance.

---

[1] Because this module discusses a wide variety of engagements, the word accountant is used to refer to practitioners performing non audit engagements rather than the word auditor, which has been used to this point in the text.

- A **review** provides only a limited level of assurance. The procedures performed in a review engagement are generally limited to making inquiries and performing analytical procedures although the accountants may decide that other procedures are necessary.
- In an **agreed-upon procedures** engagement (discussed in more detail later in this module), the client delineates exactly what procedures it wants accountants to perform. Therefore, the level of assurance provided by such an engagement varies depending on the procedures requested.

The purpose of differentiating attestation engagements from audits is to provide accountants a framework that allows them to perform other services often requested by their clients. For example, clients may want a public accounting firm to lend its name to a report on compliance with a contract or an environmental regulation. Public accounting firms have even attested to success rates at fertility clinics!

Professional standards for performing attest engagements are provided by *Statements on Standards for Attestation Engagements* (*SSAEs*) in the AT section of the AICPA's Professional Standards in the opening of this chapter. *SSAE 10* lists standards similar to the fundamental auditing principles on which *Statements on Auditing Standards* (*SASs*) are based (see Exhibit 2.A.1 in Appendix A of Chapter 2).

Attestation standards are similar to the fundamental auditing principles; however, some important differences exist. The general standards concern the *practitioner's* knowledge about the *subject matter* of the engagement and having suitable *criteria by which to measure* the subject matter. To be suitable, the criteria must be objective, measurable, complete, and relevant. The attestation standards do not require an evaluation of internal controls although such an evaluation may be necessary, particularly in an examination engagement. In financial statement audits, the measurement criteria or **appropriate financial reporting framework** is the financial reporting framework adopted by management and, when appropriate, those charged with governance in the preparation of the financial statements that is acceptable in view of the nature of the entity and the objective of the financial statements, or that is required by law or regulation. They include generally accepted accounting principles (GAAP), international financial reporting standards (IFRS), and special purpose frameworks (discussed later in this module); therefore, the determination of suitable measurement criteria has already been established.[2] In engagements in which GAAP, IFRS, or special purpose framework are not suitable measurement criteria, the identification of the appropriate criteria may be difficult and time consuming. The reporting standards restrict the distribution of the reports to persons who will understand the subject matter.

Attestation engagements include engagements related to

- Agreed-upon procedures.
- Financial forecasts and projections.
- Pro forma financial information.
- An entity's internal control over financial reporting.
- Compliance attestation.
- Management's discussion and analysis.
- Service organizations.

We briefly discuss these types of attestation engagements in the following sections.

Applying Agreed-Upon Procedures (AT 201)

Clients sometimes engage accountants to perform specified procedures, known as *agreed-upon procedures,* to examine a particular element, account, or item in financial statements or to perform a special engagement. For example, restaurant managers may

---

[2] In this chapter, we use *GAAP* to refer to appropriate frameworks other than special purpose frameworks.

ask their accountants to classify and summarize customer comment cards, or a composer might ask an accountant to verify the mathematics on a royalty report. The banking report discussed in the "Introduction" was an agreed-upon procedures engagement. Such engagements should not be considered audits because the specified sets of agreed-upon procedures are usually not sufficient to be considered as audits in accordance with auditing standards. Agreed-upon procedures engagements have a limited scope, so the performance principles (assessing the risk of material misstatement and obtaining sufficient appropriate evidence for an opinion) and the reporting principle do not apply.

Under attestation standards for agreed-upon procedures engagements, accountants must reach a clear understanding with the client and the report users about the users' needs and the procedures to be performed. For these types of engagements, clearly worded engagement letters specifically delineating the desired procedures to be performed are of utmost importance. Reports are to be restricted to the specified users who participate in and take responsibility for defining the work on the engagement.

A report on an agreed-upon procedures engagement is quite different from the standard audit report. In particular, the report should identify the specified users and describe in detail the procedures the users decided were necessary; state that the work is not an audit or review that results in an overall opinion or assurance; and describe each of the agreed-upon procedures and the specific findings related to each procedure. No overall "opinion" or "negative assurance" is given as a conclusion to the report. Instead, the report provides the accountant's findings based on the procedures performed. An example agreed-upon procedures report is provided in Exhibit A.1.

Financial Forecasts and Projections (AT 301) and Pro Forma Financial Information (AT 401)

Prospective financial information is financial information representing the financial position, results of operations, and cash flows for some period of time in the future. A **financial projection** is prospective financial information based on the occurrence of one or more *hypothetical* events that change the entity's existing business structure (e.g., possible addition of a new distribution center, potential new product line). A **financial forecast** is prospective financial information based on *expected* conditions and courses of action. In contrast, **pro forma** financial information shows the effect of a proposed or consummated transaction on the *historical* financial statements "as if" that transaction had occurred by a specific date.

In many cases, the entity is negotiating directly with a single user (*limited use*) that has requested prospective financial information for use in making economic decisions. Both financial projections and financial forecasts can be used for limited purposes because users directly requested the information and are aware of the nature of this information. In other instances, the entity may be preparing financial statements that it intends to present to a large number of users (*general use*), none of whom it is negotiating with at the current time. Only financial forecasts can be provided for general use because the users may not be familiar with the hypothetical event(s) underlying a financial projection.

The prospective financial information may contain amounts similar to historical financial statements (single-point estimates, for example, forecast revenues of $10 million) or ranges of amounts (for example, $10 million to $14 million). If ranges are used, care should be taken to indicate that the endpoints of this range do not represent best- and worst-case scenarios. In addition, the prospective financial information should disclose the significant accounting policies and procedures used to generate the statements. If the basis in the prospective financial information is different from that used in the historical financial statements, a reconciliation of the two bases must be shown. In addition, the entity must disclose all significant assumptions used to prepare prospective financial statements, indicate that actual events or conditions may not be consistent with these assumptions, and for financial projections, indicate the limited usefulness of the projection.

EXHIBIT A.1
Example Agreed-Upon Procedures Report

GRABOWSKI, SPARANO & VINCELETTE

Certified Public Accountants
1814 Newport Gap Pike
Wilmington, Delaware 19808

TELEPHONE (302) 999-7300
TELEFAX (302) 999-7183

Thomas J. Grabowski, CPA
Joseph C. Sparano, CPA
Charles J. Vincelette, CPA

Member American Institute of CPA's
Delaware Society of CPA's

INDEPENDENT ACCOUNTANT'S REPORT ON APPLYING AGREED-UPON PROCEDURES

Town of Ocean View
32 West Avenue
Ocean View, Delaware

We have performed the procedures enumerated below, which were agreed to by the Town of Ocean View, State of Delaware's Office of the Auditor of Accounts, Department of Homeland Security, and the Office of the State Treasurer, solely to assist the specified parties with respect to determining the Town's compliance with Delaware's applicable laws, regulations, financial reporting and the effectiveness of the internal control structure related to the municipal grant funds received for the year ended June 30, 2008. The Town of Ocean View's management is responsible for compliance with those requirements.

This agreed-upon procedures attestation engagement was performed in accordance with *Government Auditing Standards*, issued by the Comptroller General of the United States and the attestation standards established by the American Institute of Certified Public Accountants. The sufficiency of these procedures is solely the responsibility of those parties specified in this report. Consequently, we make no representation regarding the sufficiency of the procedures described below either for the purpose for which this report has been requested of for any other purpose.

Our procedures and findings were as follows:

1. Complete the State of Delaware Office of Auditor of Accounts municipal grants agreed-upon procedures program to determine the Town of Ocean View's compliance with applicable laws, regulations and financial reports related to municipal grant funds received for the year ended June 30, 2008 and detail any instances of noncompliance.

   The Town of Ocean View received municipal grant funds under the following programs for the year ended June 30, 2008:

   Municipal Street Aid
   Police Pension
   State Aid to Local Law Enforcement

   During the completion of the agreed-upon procedures checklists as provided by the State of Delaware Auditor of Accounts, there were no findings or recommendations relating to any of the municipal grant funds indicated above.

2. Address the status of any findings and recommendations disclosed in previous reports.

   There were no findings or recommendations relating to any municipal grant funds administered by the Town of Ocean View in previous reports.

We were not engaged to and did not conduct an examination, the objective of which would be the expression of an opinion on compliance with specified laws. Accordingly, we do not express such an opinion. Had we performed additional procedures, other matters might have come to our attention that would have been reported to you.

This report is intended solely for the information and use of the Town of Ocean View's management and council members, the State of Delaware's Office of Auditor of Accounts, Department of Homeland Security, and the Office of the State Treasurer and should not be used by those who have not agreed to the procedures and have not taken responsibility for the sufficiency of the procedures for their purposes. However, this report is a matter of public record and its distribution is not limited.

Grabowski, Sparano & Vincelette, CPA's

Wilmington, Delaware
January 9, 2009

To perform an attestation engagement on either prospective financial information or pro forma information, accountants must evaluate the preparation of the financial information, the support underlying the assumptions, and the presentation of the information. To accomplish these objectives, accountants must (1) obtain knowledge about the entity's business, accounting principles, and factors affecting the events and transactions in question, (2) obtain an understanding of the process through which the information was developed (e.g., determine whether all relevant information was considered in developing assumptions), (3) evaluate the assumptions (and their underlying support) used to prepare the information, (4) identify key factors affecting the information, and (5) evaluate the preparation and presentation of the financial information (e.g., consistency with AICPA guidelines).

AUDITING INSIGHT — Attestation Expectation Gap?

The results of an academic study indicate significant differences in beliefs among accountants, users, and preparers of prospective financial information concerning forecast reliability and the role and responsibilities of accountants and management. Contrary to the usual published studies on the expectation gap between accountants and the public, researchers found that accountants believe that forecasts are *more* reliable than users or preparers do. Accountants also believe that they have a higher level of responsibility and accountability than is attributed to them by users or preparers.

Source: P. Schelluch and G. Gay, "Assurance Provided by Auditors' Reports on Prospective Financial Information: Implications for the Expectation Gap," *Accounting and Finance* 46 (December 2006), p. 653.

An Examination of an Entity's Internal Control over Financial Reporting that Is Integrated with an Audit of Its Financial Statements (AT 501)

Auditing Standard 5 (AS 5) requires the management of public companies to assess and report on their internal control over financial reporting and the auditors to express an opinion on the effectiveness of internal control based on established criteria (generally, based on criteria established by the Committee of Sponsoring Organizations, or COSO) in conjunction with the financial statement audits. These reports are covered in Chapter 5.

Regulators, boards, or management of non-SEC companies may engage accountants to examine and report on the effectiveness of internal controls over financial reporting in their organization in conjunction with their financial statement audit. Accountants should not accept an engagement to *review* an entity's internal control or an assertion thereon. The attestation standard that governs accountants' examination of an entity's internal control AT 501 is very similar to *AS 5*. It calls for an examination of internal controls using a top-down, risk-based approach and control testing comparable to the approach discussed in Chapter 5. The following conditions must be met before accountants can conduct an examination on an entity's internal control:

- Management accepts responsibility for the effectiveness of its internal control.
- Management's evaluation of control is based on suitable and available criteria (e.g., the Committee of Sponsoring Organizations (COSO) Report; see Chapter 5).
- Management's evaluation of control is supported by sufficient evidence.
- Management presents its assertion about the effectiveness of its internal control in a written report that accompanies the accountants' report.

Reports on examination of internal controls under AT 501 are also similar to those required by *AS 5*. A material weakness requires an adverse report. The inability to complete the engagement requires a disclaimer of opinion. A written report of significant deficiencies and material weaknesses must also be given to those charged with governance.

Compliance Attestation (AT 601)

Management often must report its compliance with contractual obligations to third parties. For example, entities may have restrictive covenants in loan agreements, and lenders may require a periodic report on whether the entity has complied with these covenants. Contractual agreements could include dividend limitations, loan limitations, prescribed debt/equity ratios, or limitations on geographic operations. In addition, companies and governmental agencies must comply with applicable laws and regulations. Accountants may accept engagements to attest to (1) an entity's compliance with the requirement of the laws, regulations, rules, and so forth, and to (2) the effectiveness of an entity's internal controls that ensure compliance with the requirements. In addition to these examination engagements, accountants also can perform *agreed-upon procedures* regarding compliance. (*Reviews* of compliance are not appropriate engagements).

For a compliance attestation, three conditions must be met: (1) management accepts responsibility for compliance, (2) compliance or the controls over compliance is capable of evaluation and measurement against reasonable criteria, and (3) sufficient evidence must be available to support management's evaluation. Management may either make an assertion in a written report or as a written representation to the accountants. The accountants then *examine* or perform *agreed-upon procedures* that evaluate management's written assertion about the entity's compliance with the criteria.

Attestation standards require accountants to consider inherent risk, control risk, and detection risk in connection with *examination* engagements for compliance. These considerations are very similar to the risk elements in financial statement audits. However, consideration of materiality in compliance engagements may be difficult; sometimes monetary measures can be applied; sometimes they cannot. Nevertheless, risk and materiality are as important in compliance attestation as they are in financial statement audits.

Exercise of due care and professional skepticism about noncompliance are prerequisites for a compliance examination. Otherwise, the major steps in a compliance examination are these:

- Understand the specific compliance requirements and assess planning materiality.
- Plan the engagement and assess inherent risk.
- Understand relevant controls over compliance, assess control risk, and design tests of compliance with detection risk in mind.
- Obtain sufficient evidence of compliance with specific requirements, including a written letter of management representations.
- Consider subsequent events: subsequent information that bears on the management assertion and subsequent events of noncompliance after the assertion date.
- Form an opinion and prepare the report.

These standards call for work that is directly parallel to that in financial statement audits. The standard unqualified report in a compliance examination engagement (Exhibit A.2) expresses the accountant's opinion as to compliance. Accountants can issue an unqualified report or, if findings dictate (1) a report modified to disclose a noncompliance event, (2) a qualified report stating material noncompliance, or (3) an adverse report stating that the entity is not in compliance.

Accountants may also be asked to provide similar assurance with regard to federal and state regulatory requirements. Examples include limitations on investments for mutual funds or state insurance department regulations about the nature of insurance company investments. Regulatory agencies may seek assertions in prescribed report language that go beyond acceptable professional reporting responsibilities and involve accountants in areas outside their function and responsibility. In such cases, accountants should insert additional wording in the prescribed report language or write a completely revised report that adequately reflects their position and responsibility.

EXHIBIT A.2
Standard Unqualified Compliance Attestation Report

Independent Accountant's Report

To the Agency:

We have examined the Agency's compliance with Department of Employment Regulation JR-52 during the year ended December 31, 2012. Management is responsible for the Agency's compliance with those requirements. Our responsibility is to express an opinion on the Agency's compliance based on our examination.

Our examination was conducted in accordance with attestation standards established by the American Institute of Certified Public Accountants and, accordingly, included examining, on a test basis, evidence about the Agency's compliance with those requirements and performing such other procedures as we considered necessary in the circumstances. We believe that our examination provides a reasonable basis for our opinion. Our examination does not provide a legal determination on the Agency's compliance with specified requirements.

In our opinion, the Agency complied, in all material respects, with the aforementioned requirements for the year ended December 31, 2012.

Smith and Smith, CPAs
February 15, 2013

Management's Discussion and Analysis (AT 701)[3]

Accountants also can examine or review **management's discussion and analysis** (MD&A) that usually accompanies the audited financial statements in corporate annual reports. Under existing audit standards (AU 720), auditors are required to read the MD&A section to ensure that this information accompanying the audited financial statements is consistent with them. For example, MD&A should not indicate that operating income increased by 10 percent from the prior year if this is not consistent with information in the company's audited income statement. Attestation standards allow accountants to undertake engagements to additionally *examine* or *review* the MD&A section. The performance of the attestation engagement and subsequent reporting responsibilities are similar to other attestation engagements and result in accountants issuing an opinion on the MD&A based on the engagement performed.

Service Organizations (AT 801)

Often, a **service organization** that provides services to *user entities* processes clients' transactions that are likely to be relevant to user entities' internal control over financial reporting. Examples of service organizations include payroll processing companies, computerized information processing service centers, trust departments of banks, insurers that maintain the accounting records for reinsurance transactions, mortgage bankers and savings and loan associations that service loans for owners, and transfer agents that handle the shareholder accounting for mutual and money market investment funds. The fact that management is *outsourcing* some of its noncore functions does not absolve management of its responsibility for internal control over those functions. Management (as well as the audit team) of *user entities* must somehow gain comfort that controls are in place and effective. The solution to this dilemma is a special purpose report on internal control (formerly referred to as a *SAS 70* report) in which the service organization's auditors report on the effectiveness of the service organization's internal control to the user entities (and their auditors).

---

[3] A recent PCAOB proposal would have auditors commenting on this in their report on the financial statements.

> **AUDITING INSIGHT** Increase in SAS 70 (now SSAE 16) Reports Tied to Sarbanes-Oxley
>
> With increased outsourcing of activities that are not company core competencies, the emphasis on *SAS 70* (now *SSAE 16*) reports takes on greater significance. Take, for example, **Service Corporation International (SCI)**, the largest provider of funeral, cemetery, and cremation services in North America. SCI's funeral homes are spread across 48 states, Canada, and Puerto Rico. The company outsources both generic activities (e.g., payroll) and some activities specific to its industry (e.g., the management of trust accounts held for future funeral and cremation services).
>
> Although it would not be cost effective for the company's management to examine the controls over all of these activities (as required by Sarbanes-Oxley), management relies on service auditors to do the work for them—the company collects more than 40 SAS 70 reports a year.
>
> **Source:** "*SAS 70* Reports Continue to Grow in Demand and Utility for Sarbanes-Oxley Compliance," Protiviti, Inc. 2006, (accessed July 13, 2011).

There are two types of service organization reports:

- A *type 1 report* describes the service organization's internal controls placed in operation at a specific point in time but does not report on the effectiveness of the controls.
- A *type 2 report* not only includes a description of the controls but also reports on the service organization's auditors' *testing* of the controls over a minimum six-month period.

Only the type 2 reports are useful with respect to meeting Sarbanes-Oxley's rigorous internal control requirements. Ordinarily, service auditors' reports are not public reports on internal controls but are used only by user entities' auditors to assess internal controls at the service organization.

As a condition of the engagement, management of the service organization is required to provide the auditor with a written assertion about (1) the fairness of the presentation of the description of the service organization's system, (2) the suitability of the design controls to achieve the related control objectives and, in a type 2 engagement, (3) the operating effectiveness of those controls. In a type 2 report, the service auditor expresses an opinion on the fairness of the description and on the suitability of the design and operations of the controls throughout the period covered by the report. The service auditor should inquire whether management is aware of any subsequent events that could have a significant effect on the controls at the service organization or on the service auditor's report. The service auditor also should modify the report if information comes to the service auditor's attention that causes him or her to conclude that (1) design deficiencies exist and (2) user organizations would not be expected to have controls in place to mitigate such design deficiencies. See Exhibit A.3 for an example of a type 2 report.

The report in Exhibit A.3 is part of a set of new reports called *service organization control reports* or SOCs.

- *SOC 1* is the AT 801 report illustrated in Exhibit A.3 for controls over financial reporting.
- *SOC 2* report is a "report on controls at a service organization relevant to security, availability, processing integrity, confidentiality or privacy," which may be requested by a user but does not apply directly to the user's financial statements. The report contents are the same as *SOC 1* reports.
- *SOC 3* is a trust services report. It is used in marketing organizations' control effectiveness. A *SOC 3* report basically covers the same subject matter as *SOC 2* does but in less detail and in a format that lends itself to a general-use report.

EXHIBIT A.3
Service Auditor's type 2 report

Service Organizations Controls

Independent Service Auditor's Report on a Description of a Service Organization's System and the Suitability of the Design and Operating Effectiveness of Controls

To: XYZ Service Organization

We have examined XYZ Service Organization's description of its Global Development Center system for processing user entities' transactions throughout the year ended December 31, 2012, and the suitability of the design and operating effectiveness of controls to achieve the related control objectives stated in the description.

On page 22 of the description, XYZ Service Organization has provided an assertion about the fairness of the presentation of the description and suitability of the design and operating effectiveness of the controls to achieve the related control objectives stated in the description. XYZ Service Organization is responsible for preparing the description and for the assertion, including the completeness, accuracy, and method of presentation of the description and the assertion, providing the services covered by the description, specifying the control objectives and stating them in the description, identifying the risks that threaten the achievement of the control objectives, selecting the criteria, and designing, implementing, and documenting controls to achieve the related control objectives stated in the description.

Our responsibility is to express an opinion on the fairness of the presentation of the description and on the suitability of the design and operating effectiveness of the controls to achieve the related control objectives stated in the description based on our examination. We conducted our examination in accordance with attestation standards established by the American Institute of Certified Public Accountants. Those standards require that we plan and perform our examination to obtain reasonable assurance about whether, in all material respects, the description is fairly presented and the controls were suitably designed and operating effectively to achieve the related control objectives stated in the description throughout the year ended December 31, 2012.

An examination of a description of a service organization's system and the suitability of the design and operating effectiveness of the service organization's controls to achieve the related control objectives stated in the description involves performing procedures to obtain evidence about the fairness of the presentation of the description and the suitability of the design and operating effectiveness of those controls to achieve the related control objectives stated in the description. Our procedures included assessing the risks that the description is not fairly presented and that the controls were not suitably designed or operating effectively to achieve the related control objectives stated in the description. Our procedures also included testing the operating effectiveness of those controls that we consider necessary to provide reasonable assurance that the related control objectives stated in the description were achieved. An examination engagement of this type also includes evaluating the overall presentation of the description and the suitability of the control objectives stated therein, and the suitability of the criteria specified by the service organization and described at page 22. We believe that the evidence we obtained is sufficient and appropriate to provide a reasonable basis for our opinion.

Because of their nature, controls at a service organization may not prevent, or detect and correct, all errors or omissions in processing or reporting transactions. Also, the projection to the future of any evaluation of the fairness of the presentation of the description, or conclusions about the suitability of the design or operating effectiveness of the controls to achieve the related control objectives is subject to the risk that controls at a service organization may become inadequate or fail.

In our opinion, in all material respects, based on the criteria described in XYZ Service Organization's assertion on page 22.

a. the description fairly presents the system that was designed and implemented throughout the year ended December 31, 2012.
b. the controls related to the control objectives stated in the description were suitably designed to provide reasonable assurance that the control objectives would be achieved if the controls operated effectively throughout the year ended December 31, 2012.
c. the controls tested, which were those necessary to provide reasonable assurance that the control objectives stated in the description were achieved, operated effectively throughout the year ended December 31, 2012.

The specific controls tested and the nature, timing, and results of those tests are listed on pages 10-20.

This report, including the description of tests of controls and results thereof on pages 10–20 is intended solely for the information and use of XYZ Service Organization, user entities of XYZ Service Organization's system during some or all of the year ended December 31, 2012, and the independent auditors of such user entities, who have a sufficient understanding to consider it, along with other information including information about controls implemented by user entities themselves when assessing the risks of material misstatements of user entities' financial statements. This report is not intended to be and should not be used by anyone other than these specified parties.

Smith and Smith CPAs
March 15, 2013
New York, NY

AUDITING INSIGHT — SOC Report Logos

Auditors and their clients can use SOC logos to market their services. The logos for CPAs and their clients look like this:

In addition, the Canadian Institute of Chartered Accountants provides a Seal for SOC 3 reporting service organizations to use as a marketing tool. The seal is part of the SysTrust program described in the following "Assurance Services" section.

For CPAs who provide the services that result in a SOC 1^{SM}, SOC 2^{SM} or SOC 3^{SM} report

For service organizations that had a SOC 1^{SM}, SOC 2^{SM} or SOC 3^{SM} engagement within the past year

Certification Mark of the AICPA, used by consent for informational purposes only.

Source: http://www.aicpa.org/_catalogs/masterpage/Search.aspx?S=soc&L=4294965113:4294965104||1, (accessed July 13, 2011).

This section discussed engagements and reports related to attestation services. A brief summary of these services is shown in Exhibit A.4.

EXHIBIT A.4 Summary of Attestation Reports

Services	Description	Type(s) of Engagements	Report Distribution
Agreed-upon procedures engagement	Perform procedures requested by specified users	Agreed-upon procedures	Distribution limited to users participating in determining scope of the engagement
Financial forecast	Expected conditions	Examination or agreed-upon procedures	General or limited use
Financial projections	Hypothetical conditions	Examination or Agreed-upon procedures	Limited use
Pro forma	Historical statements "as-if" a transaction had occurred	Examination or review	General use
Internal control	Similar to PCAOB *AS 5*	Examination	General use
Compliance	Compliance or controls over compliance	Examination or agreed-upon procedures	General use for examinations
Management's discussion and analysis	Compared to rules and regulations of the SEC	Examine or review	General or limited use
Service organizations	Examine controls over financial information	Type 1—design effectiveness Type 2—operating effectiveness	Limited to user organizations and their auditors

> ### ◐ REVIEW CHECKPOINTS
>
> A.1 What is *attestation?* Provide some examples of attestation engagements.
>
> A.2 What is a "responsible party"? Why is it necessary for the accountant to identify one?
>
> A.3 What is the difference between an examination, a review, and agreed-upon procedures?
>
> A.4 Identify several points of similarity between a compliance examination and an audit of financial statements.
>
> A.5 What is a service organization? Why would it engage an auditor to report on its controls?
>
> A.6 Why should distribution be limited for reports on projections, agreed-upon procedures, and service organizations?

▽ UNAUDITED FINANCIAL STATEMENTS: REVIEWS AND COMPILATIONS

LEARNING OBJECTIVE A-2
Describe reviews and compilations of unaudited financial statements and prepare appropriate reports for given specific factual circumstances.

Many CPAs perform bookkeeping, financial statement preparation, and other services to help nonpublic entities prepare financial communications for banks and other parties. Because these entities are not required to have an audit performed, banks and other parties may request a lower level of assurance than that provided by an audit. A subset of *attestation engagements*, these services are collectively referred to as *accounting and review services*. The Accounting and Review Services Committee (ARSC) has continuing responsibility for developing and issuing pronouncements of standards concerning the services and reports that accountants may render in connection with unaudited financial statements. This committee issues *Statements on Standards for Accounting and Review Services* (*SSARS*), which apply to accountants' services on unaudited financial statements of *nonissuers*.[4] The AICPA's Code of Professional Conduct and Statements on Quality Control Standards also govern these engagements. Accountants who perform accounting and review services should possess a level of knowledge of the accounting principles and practices of the industry. Their reports should compare financial statements to the *appropriate financial accounting framework*.

Review Services

A review is a service performed by accountants to obtain limited assurance that there are no material modifications that should be made to the financial statements in order for the statements to be in conformity with GAAP (AR 60). Because some assurance is provided in a review engagement, accountants must be independent in order to perform review services.

Procedures performed during a review of unaudited financial statements consist primarily of obtaining **review evidence** by:

1. *Obtaining* a written understanding with management about the nature and limitations of a review engagement (engagement letter).
2. Obtaining knowledge of the entity's business, accounting principles in the entity's industry, and the entity's organization and operations.
3. Inquiring of management about the entity's accounting system; actions taken at meetings of shareholders, directors, and other important executive committees; and issues surrounding the preparation and presentation of the financial statements, such as accounting principles used, unusual or complex transactions, significant transactions near the end of the period, subsequent events, and communications with regulatory agencies.

---

[4] According to *SSARS*, nonissuers are all entities except those whose securities are registered under the Securities Exchange Act of 1934 or are required to file reports under the Securities Act of 1933.

4. Conducting analytical procedures.
5. Obtaining written representations from management.

Professional standards require accountants to provide adequate documentation for the review engagement. Accountants are required to describe the procedures they performed and the results obtained. While the information gained through these procedures is similar to audit evidence, they are much more limited in scope than the typical auditing procedures for assessing the risk of material misstatement, conducting physical observation of tangible assets, sending confirmations, or examining documentary details of transactions. In addition, a review does not contemplate obtaining an understanding of internal control. As a result, a review engagement does *not* provide a basis for expressing an opinion on financial statements. In a standard unqualified report for an *audit* engagement, auditors provide *positive assurance* (a forthright and factual statement of the auditors' opinion based on an audit) that the financial statements are fairly presented.

For engagements that are less than an audit, accountants do not provide positive assurance but provide *negative assurance* through a phrase such as "we are not aware of any material modifications" that are necessary for the financial statements to be in conformity with an appropriate financial reporting framework. While *auditing* standards prohibit the use of negative assurance in reports on audited financial statements (because it is considered too weak a conclusion for the audit effort), negative assurance is permitted in reviews of unaudited financial statements, in letters to underwriters, and in reviews of interim financial information.

When accountants perform a review engagement, each page of the company's financial statements should be marked "See accountants' review report." This clearly indicates to users that an audit engagement was not performed. An example of a review report is provided in Exhibit A.5.

EXHIBIT A.5
Example Review Report (Income Tax Basis)

Accountant's Review Report

To the Board of Directors and Shareholders of Apollo Shoes, Inc.:

We have reviewed the accompanying statement of assets, liabilities, and equity—income tax basis of, Apollo Shoes, Inc. as of December 31, 2012, and the related statement of revenue and expenses—income tax basis for the year then ended. A review includes primarily applying analytical procedures to management's financial data and making inquiries of company management. A review is substantially less in scope than an audit, the objective of which is the expression of an opinion regarding the financial statements as a whole. Accordingly, we do not express such an opinion.

Management is responsible for the preparation and fair presentation of the financial statements in accordance with the income tax basis for accounting and for designing, implementing, and maintaining internal control relevant to the preparation and fair presentation of the financial statements.

Our responsibility is to conduct the review in accordance with Statements on Standards for Accounting and Review Services issued by the American Institute of Certified Public Accountants. Those standards require us to perform procedures to obtain limited assurance that there are no material modifications that should be made to the financial statements. We believe that the results of our procedures provide a reasonable basis for our report.

Based on our review, we are not aware of any material modifications that should be made to the accompanying financial statements in order for them to be in conformity with the income tax basis of accounting, as described in note 1.

Smith and Smith, CPAs
Shoetown, Maine
March 1, 2013

Compilation Services

In your first principles of accounting course, you were probably given a list of account balances and accounting information and asked to prepare basic financial statements. In essence, you were being asked to do a compilation engagement. Compilation is a synonym for an older term, *write up*. Both terms refer to accountants helping clients summarize (or "write up") their financial information in the form of financial statements. The purpose of a **compilation** engagement is to assist management in presenting financial information (including prospective financial information) that is the representation of management in the form of financial statements without providing any assurance on the accuracy or completeness of that information.

When performing a compilation engagement, the accountant has no responsibility to assess the conformity of the entity's financial statements with GAAP. However, accountants should obtain an engagement letter, understand the entity's business and applicable accounting standards, read the financial statements looking for obvious clerical or accounting principle errors, and follow up on information that is incorrect, incomplete, or otherwise unsatisfactory. Accountants are *not* required to assess control risk or to perform any other evidence-gathering procedures. Documentation should provide a clear understanding of the work performed, the engagement letter, significant findings or issues, the resolution of those issues, and any oral or written communications with management regarding fraud or illegal acts.

In a compilation engagement, given the very limited procedures performed, accountants explicitly state that no opinion and no assurance are expressed, thus taking no responsibility for a report on the fair presentation of financial statements in conformity with GAAP. Because no assurance is provided, accountants are *not* required to be independent to perform compilation engagements or issue compilation reports.

Each page of the financial statements should be marked "See accountants' compilation report." An example report for a compilation engagement is presented in Exhibit A.6.

Three types of reports on compiled financial statements can be issued:

1. The management or owners may not wish to present all footnote disclosures required by GAAP (believing such disclosures are not needed for their purposes). Accountants can issue a compilation report that notifies users of the omission and states that if they

EXHIBIT A.6
Example Compilation Report

Accountant's Compilation Report

To the Board of Directors and Shareholders of Apollo Shoes, Inc.:

We have compiled the accompanying balance sheet of Apollo Shoes, Inc. as of December 31, 2012, and the related statements of income, retained earnings, and cash flows for the year then ended. We have not audited or reviewed the accompanying financial statements and, accordingly, do not express an opinion or provide any assurance about whether the financial statements are in accordance with accounting principles generally accepted in the United States of America.

Management is responsible for the preparation and fair presentation of the financial statements in accordance with accounting principles generally accepted in the United States of America and for designing, implementing, and maintaining internal control relevant to the preparation and fair presentation of the financial statements.

Our responsibility is to conduct the compilation in accordance with Statements on Standards for Accounting and Review Services issued by the American Institute of Certified Public Accountants. The objective of a compilation is to assist management in presenting financial information in the form of financial statements without undertaking to obtain or provide any assurance that there are no material modifications that should be made to the financial statements.

Smith and Smith, CPAs
March 1, 2013

were included, they might influence users' conclusions about the business (provided the accountant has no reason to believe the footnotes were omitted to mislead the financial statement user).
2. If accountants are not independent, their report should specifically state their lack of independence. Unlike audits or reviews, accountants may provide a general description of the reason for impaired independence (e.g., providing internal control services) in their compilation report if they choose.
3. The management or owners can also choose to present the financial statements complete with all disclosures required by GAAP.

If the financial statements are not expected to be used by a third party, accountants can perform compilation engagements in which no compilation report is necessary (referred to as *plain-paper* engagements). Instead of issuing a compilation report, accountants have the option to document an understanding with the entity through an engagement letter regarding the services to be performed and the limitations on the use of those financial statements. The restricted use should be indicated on each page of the financial statements.

AUDITING INSIGHT — Do Plain-Paper Financial Statements Have Any Value?

A survey of practicing CPAs and bankers found that both groups reported confidence and were likely to place some reliance on plain-paper statements. This confidence was even greater when a CPA was involved with the financial statements.

Source: A. Reinstein, B. P. Green, and C. L. Miller, "Evidence of Perceived Quality of 'Plain-Paper Statements,'" *Auditing: A Journal of Practice & Theory* 25 (2), November 2006, pp. 85–94.

Other Review and Compilation Topics

Additional *SSARS* statements explain standards for review and compilation engagements and reports that differ from audit standards. These topics point out some of the different problems in dealing with unaudited financial statements and are briefly discussed next.

Reviews, Compilations, and Fraud

SSARS require accountants to establish an understanding with the entity in an engagement letter that the accountants will inform the appropriate level of management if any evidence of fraud or illegal acts comes to the accountants' attention during the performance of compilation or review procedures. However, the accountants need not report matters regarding illegal acts that are clearly inconsequential.

Comparative Financial Statements

AR 200, "Reporting on Comparative Financial Statements," deals with reporting variations that turn out to be rather complex. The complexity arises from the several possible combinations of prior and current services. For example, the accountant should not issue a report on comparative financial statements when statements for one or more, but not all, of the periods presented omit substantially all of the disclosures required by GAAP. The following sections contribute some organization to the technical details found in AR 200. If the level of service does not change, the comparative report is similar to comparative audit reports discussed in Chapter 12.

Same or Higher Level of Service These combinations are (in prior-year/current-year order) (1) compilation followed by compilation, (2) compilation followed by review, and (3) review followed by review. The essence of comparative reporting is to report on the results from the current engagement and *update* the report on the engagements from the prior period. In an update, accountants must consider facts and circumstances that have occurred since the date of the report and evaluate whether the report is still appropriate. When the current-year work is an audit, the report is governed by auditing standards, not by SSARS.

When *successor* accountants are performing the current-year service, they cannot update the predecessors' report. In this case, the successors can request that the predecessors reissue the prior report and distribute it and the current report. Alternatively, the successors can simply indicate in the current report a paragraph describing the predecessors' report on the prior period. The paragraph (1) states that prior-period financials were compiled or reviewed by other accountants, (2) gives the date of the previous report, (3) describes the compilation disclaimer or review report with negative assurance rendered last year, and (4) describes any modifications written in the prior-year report.

Lower Level of Service These combinations are (in prior-year/current-year order) (1) review followed by compilation, (2) audit followed by compilation, and (3) audit followed by review. In these cases, the accountant should either (*a*) include as a separate paragraph of the report a description of the responsibility assumed for the financial statements of the prior period or (*b*) *reissue* the report on the financial statements of the prior period. When reissuing a report, accountants do *not* consider events and circumstances that have occurred since their last report and do *not* evaluate whether that report is still appropriate. The underlying theory calling for reissuance in such cases is that accountants cannot update a previous report when currently performing a lower level of work compared to that performed in the prior year.

When the current-year service is being performed by successor accountants, the predecessors can be asked to reissue the prior report. When the predecessors' report is not presented, the descriptive paragraph about the report can be added to the current-year report.

Other Matters

1. *Prescribed forms.* If standard, preprinted forms used by industry trade associations, banks, government agencies, and other regulatory agencies would result in information not being presented in conformity with an appropriate financial reporting framework, an additional paragraph can be added to an accountant's compilation report.
2. *Communication with predecessor accountants.* Unlike audits, accountants are not required to communicate with predecessors in compilation and review engagements. However, AR 400 points out that such communication is desirable in certain situations (such as when the accountant has limited knowledge of the client's industry).
3. *Additional paragraphs.* Accountants can include additional paragraph(s) in their reports to indicate potential going-concern uncertainties, situations in which financial statements are not prepared in conformity with an appropriate financial reporting framework, or emphasize other matters related to the client or engagement.
4. *Personal financial plans.* Personal financial planning provides a significant source of business for CPAs. Most personal financial plan documentation includes personal financial statements. Ordinarily, accountants associated with such statements would need to issue the standard compilation report, which seems rather awkward in a personal financial planning engagement when the client is the only one using the statements. "Reporting on Personal Financial Statements Included in Written Personal Financial Plans" (AR 600.05) exempts such personal financial statements from the AR 80 reporting requirement when the accountant establishes an understanding that the financial statements will be used solely to develop the client's personal financial goals and objectives but for no other purposes.

Summary of Audits, Reviews, and Compilations

Exhibit A.7 provides a comparison of Audits to Reviews and Compilations.

EXHIBIT A.7
Summary of Differences among Audits, Reviews, and Compilations

	Audit	Review	Compilation
Objective	To provide a reasonable basis for expressing an opinion regarding the financial statements taken as a whole	To provide a reasonable basis for expressing limited assurance that there are no material modifications that should be made to the financial statements in order for the statements to be in conformity with GAAP or, if applicable, special purpose framework	To present in the form of financial statements information that is the representation of the management or owners
Procedures	Audit procedures required by generally accepted auditing standards (GAAS)	Inquiry Analytical procedures Obtain management representation letter	Read the financial statements and look for obvious errors
Assurance	Positive	Limited (Negative)	No assurance
Independence required?	Yes	Yes	No
Professional standards	PCAOB *Auditing Standards* (*ASs*) ASB *Statements on Auditing Standards* (*SASs*)	AICPA *Statements on Standards for Accounting and Review Services* (*SSARS*)	

↳ REVIEW CHECKPOINTS

A.7 In what area(s) of practice are the Accounting and Review Service Committee pronouncements applicable?

A.8 What is the difference between a review service engagement and a compilation service engagement regarding historical financial statements? Compare both of these with an audit engagement.

Responsibilities Related to Reporting on Interim Financial Information (AU 930)

LEARNING OBJECTIVE A-3
Explain auditors' responsibilities related to reporting on interim financial information.

Interim financial information refers to financial information or statements covering a period less than a full year or for a 12-month period ending on a date other than the entity's fiscal year end. Entities often provide interim financial information to owners and other financial statement users or include such information in documents containing their audited annual financial statements. Companies that are under the jurisdiction of the SEC are required to engage independent accountants to review internal control over financial reporting and interim financial information filed with the SEC. In addition, when a nonissuer entity is required to file financial information with a regulatory agency in preparation for a public offering or listing, the interim information included in the filing must be reviewed. In each case, the accountants performing the review must also be engaged to perform the audit of the annual financial statements for the current year. (If they audited the financial statements in the previous year, they need only *expect* to be engaged to audit the current year.)

A review of interim financial information differs considerably from an audit. According to AU 930, the objective of a review of interim financial information is to provide the accountants a basis for communicating whether material modifications should be made to interim financial information to ensure conformity with GAAP. In this respect, the interim information review is very similar to a review of unaudited financial statements of a nonissuer. The interim review does not require a complete assessment of control risk each quarter or gathering sufficient appropriate evidential matter on which to base an opinion on interim financial information. The objective of an interim review of *internal controls* for public companies is to provide a basis for determining whether material modifications should be made to management's quarterly certifications about changes in internal control, which are required by the Sarbanes-Oxley Act.

In reviewing interim financial information, the accountants need to acquire a sufficient knowledge of the entity's business and its internal control. This information helps the accountants identify the types of potential misstatements and select the inquiries and analytical procedures that allow the accountants to communicate any modifications that must be made for the information to conform to GAAP. Basically, the extent of review procedures depends on the accountants' professional judgment about deficiencies in the internal control, the severity of unique accounting problems, and the errors that have occurred in the past. With knowledge of these areas, the accountants can direct and fine-tune the review procedures. Procedures include performing analytical procedures; reading minutes; inquiring of management and obtaining written representation about accounting issues, changes in internal controls, and the entity's ability to continue as a going concern; and reconciling the financial statements with accounting records. Procedures for reviews of internal controls include inquiring of management about significant changes in internal control, evaluating the implications of any misstatements found through other procedures that relate to internal control, and determining through observation and inquiry whether any change might materially affect internal control over financial reporting.

A written report is not required unless the entity refers to the accountant's review in writing; however, accountants may report on interim information presented separately from audited financial statements provided that a review has been satisfactorily completed. If a report is prepared, each page of the financial statements should be marked "Unaudited."

A report on reviewed interim information presented in a quarterly report (not within an annual report) is shown in Exhibit A.8

EXHIBIT A.8
Report on Interim Financial Statements

Independent Accountant's Report

We have reviewed the accompanying unaudited condensed balance sheets of Dunder-Mifflin, Inc. as of March 31, 2013, and the related consolidated statements of income and comprehensive income for the three-month period then ended. This interim financial information is the responsibility of the company's management.

We conducted our review in accordance with standards established by the American Institute of Certified Public Accountants. A review of interim financial information consists principally of applying analytical procedures and making inquiries of persons responsible for financial and accounting matters. It is substantially less in scope than an audit conducted in accordance with auditing standards generally accepted in the United States, the objective of which is the expression of an opinion regarding the financial information taken as a whole. Accordingly, we do not express such an opinion.

Based on our review, we are not aware of any material modifications that should be made to the accompanying interim financial information for it to be in conformity with accounting principles generally accepted in the United States of America.

Michael Scarn, LLP
May 1, 2013

Report on Interim Information in a Company's Annual Report

The preceding section relates to auditors' responsibilities for interim financial information filed throughout the year with the SEC. In addition, in their Form 10-Ks, companies provide interim information for their fourth quarter as well as a summary of interim information for the entire year. This information may be presented as supplementary information accompanying audited financial statements or in a note to audited annual financial statements and should be clearly labeled "Unaudited." The auditors' report for the entity's financial statements need not refer to the reviewed information unless this information

- Has not been marked "Unaudited" (in this case, the auditor should disclaim an opinion on the interim financial information).
- Is not in conformity with GAAP (in this case, the opinion on the audited statements is not modified but the departure is discussed in a separate paragraph).
- Is required and has been omitted.
- Has not been reviewed by the accountant.

> ### ↳ REVIEW CHECKPOINTS
>
> A.9 In what respects is a review of interim financial information similar to a review of the unaudited annual financial statements of a nonissuer
>
> A.10 Is interim financial information required to be presented by (a) U.S. GAAP and (b) SEC filing requirements?

▽ OTHER TOPICS: SPECIAL AND RESTRICTED-USE REPORTS

LEARNING OBJECTIVE A-4
Define, explain, and give examples of other special reports provided by auditors, including specified elements of financial statements, special purpose frameworks, and application of requirements of appropriate financial reporting frameworks.

Auditors may issue special reports in connection with the following:

- Conducting engagements to report on specified elements, accounts, or items of a financial statement.
- Reporting on accounting using a special purpose framework.
- Reporting on the requirements of appropriate financial reporting frameworks.

Specified Elements, Accounts, or Items (AU 805)

Entities may have a lender or another user request an audit of an element, account, or item within the financial statements. Auditors may be requested to render special reports on a single financial statement (e.g. balance sheet only) or such elements as rentals, royalties, profit participations, or a provision for income taxes. Usually, the auditor has performed an audit of the complete set of financial statements. These engagements are different than attestation engagements in that the accountant follows the fundamental auditing principles instead of attestation standards and should consider any disclosures related to the element.

The auditors' report on a single statement or elements, accounts, or items is very similar to the standard auditors' report on the complete set of financial statements. The auditors express an opinion on whether the element, account, or item is fairly stated in accordance with GAAP. Refer to Exhibit A.9 for an illustrative report on a company's accounts receivable. If an adverse opinion or disclaimer of opinion is issued for the financial statements taken as a whole, the public accounting firm may separately report only on an element, account, or item in the financial statements if that report is *not* published with the report containing the adverse or disclaimer of opinion, and the element is not a major portion of the financial statements and is not based on stockholders' equity or

EXHIBIT A.9
Report on a Financial Element

Independent Auditor's Report

The Board of Directors and Stockholders
Dunder-Mifflin, Inc.

We have audited the accompanying schedule of accounts receivable of Dunder Mifflin, Inc. as of December 31, 2012, and the related notes (the schedule).

Management is responsible for the preparation and fair presentation of this schedule in accordance with accounting principles generally accepted in the United States of America; this includes the design, implementation, and maintenance of internal control relevant to the preparation and fair presentation of the schedule that is free from material misstatement, whether due to fraud or error.

Our responsibility is to express an opinion on the schedule based on our audit. We conducted our audit in accordance with auditing standards generally accepted in the United States of America. Those standards require that we plan and perform the audit to obtain reasonable assurance about whether the schedule is free from material misstatement.

An audit involves performing procedures to obtain audit evidence about the amounts and disclosures in the schedule. The procedures selected depend on the auditor's judgment, including the assessment of the risks of material misstatement of the schedule, whether due to fraud or error. In making those risk assessments, the auditor considers internal control relevant to the entity's preparation and fair presentation of the schedule in order to design audit procedures that are appropriate in the circumstances, but not for the purpose of expressing an opinion on the effectiveness of the entity's internal control. Accordingly, we express no such opinion. An audit also includes evaluating the appropriateness of accounting policies used and the reasonableness of significant accounting estimates made by management, as well as evaluating the overall presentation of the schedule.

We believe that the audit evidence we have obtained is sufficient and appropriate to provide a basis for our audit opinion.

In our opinion, the schedule referred to above presents fairly, in all material respects, the accounts receivable of Dunder-Mifflin, Inc. as of December 31, 2012, in accordance with accounting principles generally accepted in the United States of America.

We have audited, in accordance with auditing standards generally accepted in the United States of America, the financial statements of Dunder-Mifflin, Inc. as of and for the year ended December 31, 2012, and our report thereon, dated March 11, 2013, expressed an unmodified opinion on those financial statements.

Michael Scarn, LLP
Scranton, PA
March 11, 2013

---

net income. Auditors cannot express an unqualified opinion on a single financial statement if they expressed a disclaimer or adverse opinion on the complete set of financial statements.

Special Purpose Frameworks

Often small companies choose to report on a framework other than U.S. GAAP or IFRS, using instead **special purpose frameworks,** also known as *other comprehensive bases of accounting or OCBOA.* A special purpose framework in this context refers to a coherent accounting treatment in which substantially all important financial measurements are governed by criteria other than GAAP. Some examples include (1) statements conforming to regulatory agency accounting rules, (2) tax basis accounting, (3) **cash basis framework** accounting (i.e., no accruals) or **modified cash basis framework** accounting (i.e., limited accruals such as long-term assets and liabilities or inventory), and (4) some other method required for contractual purposes.

The Private Companies Practice Section (PCPS) of the AICPA Division for Firms has promoted special purpose frameworks to its members as a way to accomplish simplified reporting. The position is that special purpose framework financial statements can be less expensive to produce and easier to interpret than full GAAP statements. Surveys report that 50 percent of special purpose framework financial statements are on the tax basis of accounting and 49 percent are on the cash basis. However, PCPS also notes that special purpose frameworks are appropriate *only* when they meet user needs. Companies that are not subject to SEC regulations and filing requirements can choose to present financial information in accordance with special purpose frameworks.

AU 800 warns that special purpose framework financial statements should not use the titles normally associated with GAAP statements such as balance sheet, statement of financial position, statement of operations, income statement, statement of comprehensive income, and statement of cash flows. Even the titles are said to suggest GAAP financial statements. Instead, special purpose framework statements should use titles such as statement of assets and liabilities and statement of revenue and expenses with a designator for the basis used (regulatory, cash, income tax, etc.):

- Statement of assets and liabilities—regulatory basis.
- Statement of admitted assets, liabilities, and surplus—statutory basis required by the insurance department of the state of (name).
- Statement of income—regulatory basis.
- Statement of revenue collected and expenses paid—cash basis.
- Statement of changes in partners' capital accounts—income tax basis.

Special purpose framework statements can be audited, reviewed, or compiled like any other financial statements. All auditing standards apply, and the standards for review and compilation apply just as they do for GAAP financial statements. Special purpose frameworks do not reduce disclosure requirements. The only difference introduced is that a basis of accounting different from GAAP is used in the preparation of the financial statements. The standard requires that auditors of special purpose framework statements

- Obtain an understanding of (1) the purpose for which the financial statements are prepared, (2) the intended users, and (3) the steps taken by management to determine that the special purpose framework is acceptable in the circumstances.
- Obtain the agreement of management that it acknowledges and understands its responsibility to include all informative disclosures that are appropriate for the special purpose framework used to prepare the financial statements, including, but not limited to, additional disclosures beyond those required by GAAP that may be necessary to achieve fair presentation. The auditor is required to evaluate whether such disclosures are necessary.
- In the case of special purpose financial statements prepared in accordance with a contractual basis of accounting, obtain an understanding of any significant interpretations of the contract that management made in the preparation of those financial statements and to evaluate whether the financial statements adequately describe such interpretations.
- When management has a choice of financial reporting frameworks in the preparation of the financial statements, explain management's responsibility for the financial statements in the auditor's report and refer to management's responsibility for determining that the applicable financial reporting framework is acceptable in the circumstances.
- In the case of financial statements prepared in accordance with a regulatory or contractual basis of accounting, describe in the auditor's report the purpose for which the financial statements are prepared or refer to a note in the special purpose financial statements that contains that information.

When special purpose frameworks are audited, the auditors' report is modified as follows: (1) the introductory paragraph of the report includes a sentence that identifies the special purpose framework basis of accounting, (2) the scope paragraph is modified to "auditing standards generally accepted in the United States of America," not PCAOB standards, and (3) the opinion sentence refers to the special purpose framework instead of to GAAP. Unless the financial statements are prepared under a regulatory basis for general use, the report should include an emphasis-of-matter paragraph under an appropriate heading that, among other things, states that the financial statements are prepared in accordance with a special purpose framework, which is a basis of accounting other than GAAP and refers to the note to the financial statements that describes the framework. If the special purpose framework relates to a contractual or regulatory basis of accounting, it also should be restricted to those within the entity, parties to the agreement, or a regulatory agency. If the financial statements are prepared on a regulatory basis for general use, the emphasis of a matter paragraph is not required, but the auditor should provide two opinion paragraphs, one about whether the financial statements are prepared in accordance with GAAP and another about whether the financial statements are prepared in accordance with the special purpose framework. Exhibit A.10 (AU 800) summarizes the reporting requirements.

Disclosures in the financial statements should (1) contain an explanation of the special purpose framework and (2) describe in general how the special purpose framework differs from GAAP. However, the differences between GAAP and the special purpose framework do not have to be quantified; that is, the special purpose framework does not need to be reconciled to GAAP with dollar amounts. For all practical purposes, GAAP criteria are replaced by criteria applicable to the special purpose framework. See Exhibit A.11 for an example of an auditor's report on modified cash basis statements.

Reports on Application of Requirements of an Appropriate Financial Reporting Framework (AU 915)

The subject of reporting on the application of requirements of an appropriate financial reporting framework touches a sensitive nerve in the public accounting profession. The issue arose from entities searching for a public accounting firm that would agree to give an unqualified audit report on a questionable accounting treatment. *Opinion shopping* often involved auditor–client disagreements, after which the client said, "If you won't agree with my accounting treatment, then I'll find an auditor who will." These disagreements often involved early revenue recognition and unwarranted expense or loss deferral. A few cases of misleading financial statements occurred after opinion shopping resulted in clients switching to more agreeable auditors. On the other hand, obtaining "second opinions" on complex accounting matters may be helpful to both clients and auditors in resolving these issues.

EXHIBIT A.10 Overview of Reporting Requirements

	Cash Basis	Tax Basis	Regulatory Basis	Regulatory Basis (general use)	Contractual Basis
Opinion(s)	Single opinion on special purpose framework	Single opinion on special purpose framework	Single opinion on special purpose framework	Dual opinion on special purpose framework and generally accepted accounting principles	Single opinion on special purpose framework
Description of purpose for which special purpose financial statements are prepared	No	No	Yes	Yes	Yes
Emphasis of matter paragraph alerting readers as to the preparation in accordance with a special purpose framework	Yes	Yes	Yes	No	Yes
Other matter paragraph restricting the use of the auditor's report	No	No	Yes	No	Yes

EXHIBIT A.11
Special Report on Special Purpose Framework (cash basis statements)

Independent Auditor's Report

The Board of Directors and Stockholders
Apollo Shoes, Inc.

Report on the Financial Statements

We have audited the accompanying financial statements of Apollo Shoes, Inc., which comprise the statement of assets and liabilities arising from cash transactions as of December 31, 2012, and the related statement of revenue collected and expenses paid for the year then ended, and the related notes to the financial statements.

Management is responsible for the preparation and fair presentation of these financial statements in accordance with the cash basis of accounting described in Note 1; this includes determining that the cash basis of accounting is an acceptable basis for the preparation of the financial statements in the circumstances. Management is also responsible for the design, implementation and maintenance of internal control relevant to the preparation and fair presentation of financial statements that are free from material misstatement, whether due to fraud or error.

Our responsibility is to express an opinion on these financial statements based on our audit. We conducted our audit in accordance with auditing standards generally accepted in the United States of America. Those standards require that we plan and perform the audit to obtain reasonable assurance about whether the financial statements are free from material misstatement.

An audit involves performing procedures to obtain audit evidence about the amounts and disclosures in the financial statements. The procedures selected depend on the auditor's judgment, including the assessment of the risks of material misstatement of the financial statements, whether due to fraud or error. In making those risk assessments, the auditor considers internal control relevant to the partnership's preparation and fair presentation of the financial statements in order to design audit procedures that are appropriate in the circumstances, but not for the purpose of expressing an opinion on the effectiveness of the partnership's internal control. Accordingly, we express no such opinion. An audit also includes evaluating the appropriateness of accounting policies used and the reasonableness of significant accounting estimates made by management as well as evaluating the overall presentation of the financial statements.

We believe that the audit evidence we have obtained is sufficient and appropriate to provide a basis for our audit opinion.

In our opinion, the financial statements referred to above present fairly, in all material respects, the assets and liabilities arising from cash transactions of Apollo Shoes, Inc. as of December 31, 2012, and its revenue collected and expenses paid during the year then ended in accordance with the cash basis of accounting described in Note 1.

We draw attention to Note 1 of the financial statements, which describes the basis of accounting. The financial statements are prepared on the cash basis of accounting, which is a basis of accounting other than accounting principles generally accepted in the United States of America. Our opinion is not modified with respect to this matter.

Smith and Smith, CPAs
Shoetown, Maine
March 1, 2013

The auditing standard establishes procedures for dealing with requests for consultation from parties other than auditors' own clients. These parties can include other companies (nonclients who are shopping), attorneys, investment bankers, and others. AU 915 is applicable in these situations:

- When preparing a written report or giving oral advice on specific transactions, either completed or proposed.
- When preparing a written report or giving oral advice on the type of audit opinion that might be rendered on specific financial statements.

Providing a written report on a hypothetical transaction (as opposed to a specific proposal) is prohibited. Also, the standard does not apply to conclusions about accounting requirements offered in connection with litigation support engagements or expert witness work, nor does it apply to advice given to another CPA in public practice. Nor does it apply to an accounting firm's expressions of positions in newsletters, articles, speeches, lectures, and the like, provided that the positions do not give advice on a specific transaction or apply to a specific company.

When auditors evaluate the requirements of GAAP, they are not required to issue written reports. However, a written report or oral advice that is provided to an entity regarding the requirements of an appropriate financial reporting framework should

- Describe the engagement and state that it was performed in accordance with appropriate standards.
- Identify the entity and describe the transactions, circumstances, and sources of information.
- Provide the conclusion about the requirements of the appropriate financial reporting framework or the type of audit report, including reasons for the conclusions, if appropriate.
- State that the entity's management is responsible for proper accounting treatments in consultation with its own auditors.
- State that any differences in facts, circumstances, or assumptions might change the conclusions.
- Include a separate paragraph that indicates (1) the report is for the sole use of specified parties, (2) the specified parties for whom the report is intended, and (3) the restriction that the information should not be used by anyone else.

The purpose of AU 905 is to impose some discipline on the process of shopping/consultation and to erect a barrier to some companies' quest for willing auditors. The reporting accountant should always consult with the continuing auditor of the entity to ascertain all the available facts relevant to forming a professional judgment.

↳ REVIEW CHECKPOINTS

A.11 Why would a client ask a CPA to report on a financial statement element?

A.12 Regarding special purpose frameworks, (a) why do they exist and (b) can financial statements prepared using special purpose frameworks be audited?

A.13 What are some examples of special purpose framework?

A.14 How could "opinion shopping" be (a) suspect or (b) helpful?

A.15 What must a CPA do when reporting on the application of requirements of an appropriate financial reporting framework?

▽ ASSURANCE SERVICES

LEARNING OBJECTIVE A-5
Explain and provide examples of assurance services engagements.

Why Develop New Assurance Services?

While auditing courses focus on the role of auditors in the financial reporting process, students should not lose sight of the fact that CPAs require sufficient revenue to cover expenses, provide profit, and provide funds for continued growth. One of the objectives of the AICPA has been to identify additional niche services that accountants might offer to enhance their value to clients, attract new clients, and improve the potential for growth as a business. Such services include tax and consulting, personal financial planning, forensic, and valuation services. One broad area of services falls under the heading of Assurance Services.

The AICPA's Assurance Services Executive Committee (ASEC) identified five megatrends that can affect CPAs' business. Each presents opportunities to provide assurance service products, and each presents business risks:

1. *The shift from the industrial age to the knowledge age.* The current knowledge-based economy emphasizes management of intangible assets and decreases the focus on physical assets, measured largely in terms of historical cost. Market values may significantly differ from book values, hindering optimal capital allocation.

2. *Information technology.* The proliferation of tools (for example, cloud technology, file sharing, notepads, and smart phones) that make data digital, mobile, personal, and virtual, will amplify and empower collaboration. These tools should make open source innovation more open because they will enable more individuals to collaborate with one another in more ways and from more places than ever before. These tools will enhance outsourcing because they will make it much easier for a single department of any company to collaborate with another company. They will enhance supply chaining because headquarters will be able to be connected in real time with every individual employee stocking the shelves, every individual package, and every factory manufacturing the goods. The tools will enhance insourcing—having a company such as **UPS** come deep inside a retailer and manage its whole supply chain and use drivers who can interact with its warehouses and with every customer carrying a smart phone. And most obviously, they will enhance informing—the ability to manage your own knowledge supply chain.[5]

3. *Globalization.* One consequence of the globalization of capital markets is that organizations have facilities in different jurisdictions with different cultural principles, affiliations, ownership, accountability, and auditing standards. Domestic demand for international capital sources drives demand for a common language and global consistency in accounting and auditing standards, hence, the recent focus on convergence of international auditing and accounting standards.

4. *Demands for transparency and new focus on corporate governance.* The call for more relevant information echoes externally from investors, creditors, analysts, regulatory agencies, and standards setters and internally from boards of directors and management. Regulatory bodies around the world are also facing pressure for, and consequently demanding, more granular levels of assessment.

5. *New social structures.* The final category of change involves new socioeconomic structures, such as the democratization of the capital markets, the aging population, and the increasing social pressures. Increasing social pressures have manifested themselves in a growing global focus on corporate social responsibility and sustainability whereby investors are demanding increased accountability from companies via regular responsibility or sustainability business reports and are often basing investment decisions on them.[6]

Definition: Assurance Services

Assurance services are "independent professional services that improve the quality of information, or its context, for decision makers."[7] A large group of activities can fit within this definition. In addition, although attestation and audit services are highly structured and intended to be useful for large groups of decision makers (e.g., investors, lenders), assurance services are more customized and intended to be useful to smaller, targeted groups of decision makers. In this sense, assurance services resemble consulting services.

---

[5] T. L. Friedman, *The World Is Flat* (New York: Farrar, Straus & Giroux, 2005).
[6] AICPA Assurance Services Executive Committee White Paper, "The Shifting Paradigm in Business Reporting and Assurance," 2008.
[7] Ibid.

Reporting-related services currently being studied by the AICPA to determine how CPAs can provide value are *XBRL, enhanced business reporting,*[8] and *Trust Services*: *CPA WebTrust* and *CPA SysTrust.*

Extensible Business Reporting Language (XBRL)

The SEC has mandated financial reporting using **eXtensible Business Reporting Language (XBRL),** which provides a computer-readable identifying tag for each individual item of data. For example, "company net profit" has its own unique tag. The introduction of XBRL tags enables automated processing of business information by computer software. Computers can treat XBRL data "intelligently": They can recognize the information in a XBRL document, select it, analyze it, store it, exchange it with other computers, and present it automatically in a variety of ways for users. XBRL greatly increases the speed of handling financial data, reduces the chance of error, and permits automatic checking of information.

XBRL can handle data in different languages and prepared according to different accounting standards. It can flexibly be adapted to meet different requirements and uses. Data can be transformed into XBRL by suitable mapping tools or can be generated in XBRL by appropriate software.

Although the SEC does not require auditor involvement with the XBRL tagged data or related controls, at some point it may be necessary for auditors to provide some degree of assurance on XBRL-coded data. Issues to be addressed will include the appropriate levels of assurance for various scenarios and the subject matter of assurance.[9] The ASEC has established the *XBRL Assurance Task Force* to develop guidance that will assist CPAs in public practice who are requested to provide assurance on XBRL-related documents, and the ASEC and the Auditing Standards Board have released *Statement of Position 09-1,* "Performing Agreed-Upon Procedures Engagements That Address the Completeness, Accuracy, or Consistency of XBRL-Tagged Data" that provides recommendations and guidance for practitioners who perform an attest engagement under AT 201 to provide assurance on XBRL reports. In addition, the Center for Audit Quality issued Alert #2009-55 "Potential Audit Firm Service Implications Raised by the SEC Final Rule on XBRL" to raise auditors' level of awareness of the implications of XBRL, including potential services that may be provided.

Enhanced Business Reporting

Enhanced business reporting focuses on improving business reporting by developing an internationally recognized, voluntary framework for presentation and disclosure of value drivers, nonfinancial performance measures, and qualitative information.[10] Benefits would include better allocation of capital by investors, reduced financing costs of companies and more efficient and effective regulatory processes, strengthened global competitiveness, and stability in the capital markets.

Trust Services

Electronic commerce (or e-commerce), the sale of goods and services via the Internet, is exploding. According to the U.S. Census Bureau, U.S. e-commerce revenues totaled $145 billion in 2009.[11] Although the growth of e-commerce continues unabated, security issues, both real and perceived, have prevented many potential customers from

---

[8] Ibid.

[9] Ibid.

[10] http://www.aicpa.org/InterestAreas/AccountingAndAuditing/Resources/EBR/Pages/EBRFramework.aspx (accessed July 13, 2011).

[11] "E-Stats Reports," U.S. Census Bureau, May 26, 2011, available at http://www.census.gov/econ/estats/ (accessed July 13, 2011).

purchasing goods and services via the Internet. Many customers and business owners distrust the Internet as a medium of conducting business. Indeed, a general lack of security is the top reason nonbuyers give for not purchasing products online and the top concern among current online buyers. Specifically, prospective buyers have expressed concerns about ascertaining whether an e-commerce company is authentic, is trustworthy (the e-tailer will do what it says it will do), and will safeguard buyers' personal information. Customers also want to be reassured that they can get their products, services, and repairs on a timely basis. Despite growing familiarity with doing business on the Internet, these security issues have not diminished for potential customers.

For significant customer–supplier business relationships, company computers are often directly linked through Internet-based virtual private networks. Purchase orders for goods are made and sent via computer, and payment is made automatically through electronic funds transfer directly to the vendor's bank. The primary benefit of such a relationship is an increase in the timeliness of the process; transactions that once took several weeks to complete manually (from customer purchase order generation to final payment being deposited to the supplier's bank account) now take only as long as it takes to ship and receive the goods. However, just as Internet customers are wary of purchasing online, business customers are often cautious about entering into such relationships with other businesses.

The AICPA and the Canadian Institute of Chartered Accountants developed the *WebTrust* Service to provide assurance to the consumer on the reliability of Internet Web sites and the *SysTrust* Service to focus on a company's systems as a means of increasing the reliability of business-to-business (B-to-B) computer transactions. Because these two services have a common framework to address risks and technological opportunities, the AICPA has adopted the term **trust services** to define a set of professional attestation and advisory services based on a core set of principles and criteria that addresses the risks and opportunities of IT-enabled systems and privacy programs.[12] The ASEC Trust Services/Data Integrity Task Force is focused on updating and maintaining the Trust Services Principles and Criteria (TSPC) and creating a framework of principles and criteria to provide assurance on the integrity of information.

Trust Services comprise a set of professional attestation and advisory services based on a core set of principles and criteria that address the risks and opportunities of IT-enabled systems and privacy programs. Practitioners use the following principles and related criteria in the performance of Trust Services engagements:

- *Security*. The system is protected against unauthorized access (both physical and logical).
- *Availability*. The system is available for operation and use as committed or agreed.
- *Processing integrity*. System processing is complete, accurate, timely, and authorized.
- *Confidentiality*. Information designated as confidential is protected as committed or agreed.
- *Privacy*. Personal information is collected, used, retained, disclosed and destroyed in conformity with the commitments in the entity's privacy notice and with criteria set forth in Generally Accepted Privacy Principles issued by the AICPA and CICA.[13]

Accountants offering **WebTrust Services** and **SysTrust Services** can issue opinions and corresponding "seals of assurance" on individual principles or a combination of the principles. An actual *WebTrust* report is reproduced in Exhibit A.12.

---

[12] AICPA TSP 100 2009, para. 3.

[13] http://www.aicpa.org/interestareas/frc/assuranceadvisoryservices/pages/trustdataintegritytaskforce.aspx (accessed September 21, 2011)

EXHIBIT A.12
Example of Independent Practitioner's WebTrust Report

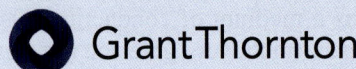

Independent Practitioner's WebTrust Report

To the Management of Google Inc.:

We have examined Postini, Inc.'s management assertion that, during the period of April 1, 2007 through March 31, 2008, Postini, Inc. and its wholly owned subsidiaries, Postini UK Limited and Postini Switzerland GmbH, collectively referred to as "Postini" maintained effective controls in its Postini Email Security System (the "System") to provide reasonable assurance that security (the System was protected against unauthorized access, both physical and logical), availability (the System was available for operation and use as committed or agreed) and privacy (personal information obtained as a result of e-commerce was collected, used, retained and disclosed in conformity with its commitments in its privacy notice) are in conformity with the Trust Services criteria issued by the American Institute of Certified Public Accountants (AICPA) and the Canadian Institute of Chartered Accountants (CICA) (AICPA/CICA Trust Services) and that Postini complied with the security, availability and privacy criteria set forth in AICPA/CICA Trust Services. Postini is a wholly owned subsidiary of Google Inc.

This assertion is the responsibility of Postini's management. Our responsibility is to express an opinion based on our examination.

Our examination was conducted in accordance with attestation standards established by the American Institute of Certified Public Accountants and, accordingly, included (1) obtaining an understanding of Postini's controls over security, availability, and privacy, (2) testing and evaluating the operating effectiveness of the controls, (3) testing compliance with security, availability and privacy criteria and (4) performing such other procedures as we considered necessary in the circumstances. We believe that our examination provides a reasonable basis for our opinion.

In our opinion, Postini management's assertion referred to above is fairly stated, in all material respects, based on the AICPA/CICA Trust Services Criteria for Security, Availability and Privacy.

Because of inherent limitations in controls, error or fraud may occur and not be detected. Furthermore, the projection of any conclusions, based on our findings, to future periods is subject to the risk that the validity of such conclusions may be altered because of changes made to the system or controls, the failure to make needed changes to the system or controls, or a deterioration in the degree of effectiveness of the controls.

Postini's use of the WebTrust Seal on their Web Site constitutes a symbolic representation of the contents of this report and it is not intended, nor should it be construed, to update this report or provide any additional assurance.

Grant Thornton LLP
San Jose, California
September 26, 2008

Sustainability Reporting

Sustainability (also called *corporate social responsibility*) is defined by the AICPA as "the triple-bottom-line of 1) economic viability, 2) social responsibility, and 3) environmental responsibility."[14] KPMG surveyed 378 senior executives of companies and found 62 percent have a strategy for sustainability, and 55 percent have either issued at least one public report on sustainability or plan to do so soon.[15] Various assurance approaches are currently being used for sustainability reports by CPA firms, engineering firms, stakeholder panels, and other groups. Standard setters are also developing standards. The AICPA and Canadian Institute of Chartered Accountants have developed SOP 03-2

---

[14] "Sustainability Accounting and Reporting-FAQ, AICPA 6/28/2011 http://www.aicpa.org/InterestAreas/BusinessIndustryAnd Government/Resources/Sustainability/Pages/SustainabilityFAQs.aspx (accessed July 13, 2011).

[15] "Corporate Sustainability: A progress report." KPMG.com 2011.

"Attest Engagements on Greenhouse Gas Emissions Information," and the IAASB has proposed a similar new standard. See Exhibit A.13 for an illustration of an assurance report on **Starbucks**'s sustainability report.

> ### ↳ REVIEW CHECKPOINTS
>
> A.16 What makes CPAs qualified to perform the assurance services discussed here?
>
> A.17 Briefly describe the two trust services in terms of those provided and of intended customers.
>
> A.18 What is *sustainability reporting?* Why would a company choose to provide a sustainability report? Why would they pay for independent assurance?

EXHIBIT A.13
Starbucks's Assurance Report

Independent Assurance Report

To the Stakeholders of Starbucks Coffee Company:

We have examined the data identified below (the Data) contained within the Starbucks Coffee Company's Global Responsibility Annual Report (the Report) for the year ended October 3, 2010. Starbucks Coffee Company's management is responsible for the Data. Our responsibility is to express an opinion on the Data listed below based on our examination.

- Green coffee purchases and average price per pound as contained in the **Coffee Purchasing** section
- C.A.F.E. Practices coffee purchases and purchases as a percentage of total coffee purchased as contained in the **Coffee Purchasing** section
- Fair trade certified green coffee purchases and purchases as a percentage of total coffee purchased as contained in the **Coffee Purchasing** section
- Certified organic coffee purchases and purchases as a percentage of total coffee purchased as contained in the **Coffee Purchasing** section
- Amount of commitment to investment in farmer loans and number of farmers as contained in the **Farmer Support** section

The Criteria used to evaluate the Data are contained in the sections of the Report indicated above.

Our examination was conducted in accordance with attestation standards established by the American Institute of Certified Public Accountants, and accordingly, included examining, on a test basis, evidence supporting the Data and performing such other procedures as we considered necessary in the circumstances. Those procedures are described in more detail in the paragraph below. We believe that our examination provides a reasonable basis for our opinion.

Our evidence-gathering procedures included, among other activities, the following:

- Testing the effectiveness of the internal reporting system used to collect and compile information on the Data which is included in the Report;
- Performing specific procedures, on a sample basis, to validate the Data, on site at Starbucks Coffee Trading Company buying operations in Lausanne, Switzerland and Corporate headquarters in Seattle, Washington;
- Interviewing partners (employees) responsible for data collection and reporting;
- Reviewing relevant documentation, including corporate policies, management and reporting structures;
- Performing tests, on a sample basis, of documentation and systems used to collect, analyze and compile the Data that is included in the Report, and
- Confirming certain of the Data to third party confirmations and reports.

In our opinion, the Data for the fiscal year ended October 3, 2010, is fairly presented, in all material respects, based on the Criteria indicated above.

Moss Adams LLP
Seattle, Washington
March 7, 2011
www.mossadams.com

Summary

Public accounting firms are highly regarded for their attestation services. Many forms of services, in addition to audits of historical financial statements, have arisen or have been proposed. Managers of companies often develop innovative financial presentations and want to give the public some assurance about them, so they engage independent CPAs. Regulators and other users, such as service organization users, also often rely on entities' communication of information and press regarding CPA attestation. Guided by the general attestation standards, auditing standards, and accounting and review services standards, auditors offer services and render reports in several areas.

Accountants have provided services related to unaudited financial statements for some time. Work of this nature is known in public practice as *review and compilation.* The differences lie in the amount of work performed and the level of assurance provided in an accountants' report. Review engagements involve less work than an audit, and reports give a limited level of assurance instead of an audit opinion. Compilation engagements merely involve reading the financial statements, which is less work than a review, and the report gives no assurance as expressed by an outright disclaimer.

Another type of review is of interim financial information (e.g., quarterly financial reports). This review is technically similar to a review of unaudited financial statements, and the report on free-standing interim financial statements gives negative assurance.

Some entities have the option to prepare their statements for public use on special purpose frameworks. Auditors can audit and report on such financial statements. This option gives managers an opportunity to avoid the complications of many of the GAAP rules. Special purpose framework audits and reporting are discussed in the auditing standards under the heading of special reports. Other types of special audit reports can be given on particular elements, accounts, or items in a financial statement.

Because of the shift to the knowledge age and new developments in information technology, globalization, social structures and demands for transparency and governance, assurance services offer new ways for CPAs to provide service to their clients by improving the quality of information, or its context, for decision makers. CPAs currently provide assurance on XBRL, enhanced business reporting, sustainability, and trustworthiness of electronic commerce. The AICPA is exploring other ways CPAs can provide value to their clients in the new business environment.

Key Terms

agreed-upon procedures: The methods used in an engagement in which users participate in determining the scope of procedures performed by the accountants, 549

appropriate financial reporting framework: The financial reporting treatment (i.e. GAAP, IFRS, etc.) adopted by management and, when appropriate, those charged with governance in the preparation of the financial statements that is acceptable in view of the nature of the entity and the objective of the financial statements, or that is required by law or regulation, 549

assurance services: The independent professional functions that improve the quality of information, or its context, for decision makers, 571

attestation: An accounting service resulting in a report on subject matter or an assertion about subject matter that is the responsibility of another party, 548

cash basis framework: A special purpose framework that includes no accruals, 566

compilation: An accounting service in which the practitioner assists in assembling information that is the representation of management but provides no assurance, 560

examination: An attestation engagement similar in nature to an audit, 548

eXtensible Business Reporting Language (XBRL): The communication terminology required by the Securities and Exchange Commission for companies to use to provide financial statement information that has a computer-readable identifying tag for each individual item of data, 572

financial forecast: The prospective financial information reflecting an entity's estimates of what is likely to occur in a future period, 550

financial projection: The prospective financial information reflecting a transaction or event that may occur in the future, 550

interim financial information: refers to financial information or statements covering a period less than a full year or for a 12-month period ending on a date other than the entity's fiscal year end. 563

management's discussion and analysis: A required section of financial reports of public companies in which management analyzes the results of operations and cash flows for the periods presented, 554

modified cash basis accounting: A special purpose framework that provides limited accruals for items such as fixed assets and/or inventories and long-term debt, 566

pro forma: The description of financial information reflecting historical data as if a certain transaction had occurred, 550

responsible party: The person or persons, either as individuals or representatives of the entity, responsible for the subject matter of an attestation engagement, 548

review: An engagement in which a practitioner provides limited assurance about financial information, 549

review evidence: The evidence required to provide limited assurance obtained by (1) inquiring of management, (2) conducting analytical procedures, and (3) obtaining written representations from management, 558

service organization: An organization or segment of it that provides services to user entities that are likely to be relevant to user entities' internal control as it relates to financial reporting, 554

special purpose framework: A coherent accounting framework in which substantially all important financial measurements are governed by criteria other than GAAP or IFRS, 566

sustainability: The triple-bottom-line of economic viability, social responsibility, and environmental responsibility, 574

SysTrust Services: An assurance function that reviews an entity's computer system to provide confidence to business partners and customers concerning the security, privacy, and confidentiality of information in addition to system availability and processing integrity, 573

trust services: A set of professional attestation and advisory functions based on a core set of principles and criteria that addresses the risks and opportunities of IT-enabled systems and privacy programs, 573

WebTrust Services: An assurance function designed to reduce the concerns of Internet users regarding the existence of a company and the reliability of key business information placed on its website, 573

Multiple-Choice Questions for Practice and Review

All applicable Exercises and Problems are available with McGraw-Hill's *Connect® Accounting*

LO A-1

A.19 To perform an attestation engagement on prospective information or pro forma information, accountants must do all of the following *except*
 a. Obtain knowledge about the entity's business and accounting principles.
 b. Understand the internal controls used in the processes that generated the information.
 c. Obtain an understanding of the process through which the information was developed.
 d. Evaluate the assumptions used to prepare the information.

LO A-1

A.20 If a nonissuer wants an accountant to perform an examination of its internal controls, the accountant should follow:
 a. PCAOB *AS 5,* "An Audit of Internal Control over Financial Reporting That Is Integrated with an Audit of Financial Statements."
 b. AICPA AT 501, "An Examination of an Entity's Internal Control over Financial Reporting That Is Integrated with an Audit of Its Financial Statements."
 c. AICPA AU 315, "Understanding the Entity and Its Environment and Assessing the Risks of Material Misstatement."
 d. *FASB Concepts Statement No. 1,* "Objectives of Financial Reporting by Business Enterprises."

LO A-2

A.21 A review service engagement involving unaudited financial statements involves
 a. More work than a compilation and an audit.
 b. Less work than an audit but more work than a compilation.
 c. Less work than a compilation but more work than an audit.
 d. More work than an audit but less work than a compilation.

LO A-2

A.22 When accountants are not independent, which of the following reports can they nevertheless issue?
   a. Compilation report.
   b. Standard unqualified audit report.
   c. Examination report on a forecast.
   d. Examination of internal control over financial reporting.

LO A-1

A.23 For a compliance engagement, three conditions must be met. Which of the following is *not* one of the three conditions?
   a. Management accepts responsibility for compliance.
   b. Management's evaluation of compliance is capable of evaluation and is measured against reasonable criteria.
   c. Sufficient evidence is available to support management's evaluation.
   d. Management provides a report attesting to satisfactory compliance.

LO A-2

A.24 Accountants are permitted to express "negative assurance" in which of the following reports?
   a. Standard unqualified audit report on financial statements.
   b. Compilation report on unaudited financial statements.
   c. Review report on unaudited financial statements.
   d. Adverse opinion report on financial statements.

LO A-1

A.25 Which of the following conditions must be met before an accountant can conduct an examination of an entity's internal control?
   a. Management must present its assertion about the effectiveness of its internal control in a written report.
   b. Management must represent that there are no internal control deficiencies.
   c. The accountant must represent that he or she has not conducted an audit of the financial statements.
   d. The accountant must have designed a significant portion of the internal controls.

LO A-3

A.26 When interim financial information is presented in a footnote to annual financial statements, the standard audit report on the annual financial statements should
   a. Not mention the interim information unless there is an exception that the auditors need to include in the report.
   b. Contain an audit opinion paragraph that specifically mentions the interim financial information if it is not in conformity with GAAP.
   c. Contain an extra paragraph that gives negative assurance on the interim information if it has been reviewed.
   d. Contain an extra explanatory paragraph if the interim information note is labeled "Unaudited."

LO A-2

A.27 During a review of a nonissuer's financial statements, accountants are required to make certain inquiries of management. Which of the following inquiries is *not* required by the *SSARS*?
   a. The basis for the preparation of financial statements.
   b. Internal control deficiencies.
   c. Significant transactions occurring near the end of the reporting period.
   d. Material subsequent events.

LO A-4

A.28 According to auditing standards, financial statements presented on a special purpose framework should *not*
   a. Contain a note describing the special purpose framework.
   b. Describe in general how the special purpose framework differs from generally accepted accounting principles.
   c. Be accompanied by an audit report that gives an unqualified opinion with reference to the special purpose framework.
   d. Contain a note with a quantified dollar reconciliation of the assets based on the special purpose framework with the assets based on generally accepted accounting principles.

LO A-1 A.29 To be useful, an audit of a service organization's controls should cover a minimum of
   a. Three months.
   b. Six months.
   c. One year.
   d. The user entity's fiscal period.

LO A-5 A.30 In providing assurance services to clients, CPAs are building on their reputations for
   a. Knowledge and integrity.
   b. Objectivity and integrity.
   c. Independence and due professional care.
   d. Professionalism and trust.

LO A-5 A.31 The AICPA Special Committee on Assurance Services identified five global "mega trends" that can affect a CPA's business. Which of the following is *not* one of these mega trends?
   a. The decreasing supply of natural resources.
   b. Information technology.
   c. New social structures.
   d. Demands for transparency.

LO A-5 A.32 An *assurance service* is defined as a service that
   a. Provides auditing services to nonfinancial information.
   b. Reviews unaudited financial information.
   c. Improves the quality of information for decision makers.
   d. Reduces the risk in management decision making.

LO A-5 A.33 B. Harper is surfing the Internet and finds a great pair of rollerblades at a really low price but he has never heard of the company and is concerned that the product he ordered may not be the product he receives. Harper may be more willing to place an order with this company if
   a. The website displays the WebTrust seal.
   b. The company provides its annual report and the report of the independent auditors on its website.
   c. The company provides a money-back guarantee.
   d. Only a partial payment is required prior to receiving the product.

LO A-5 A.34 Which of the following is *not* a principle of Trust Services?
   a. Security.
   b. Authentication.
   c. Privacy.
   d. Confidentiality.

LO A-2 A.35 Services in connection with unaudited historical cost financial statements may be provided by
   a. International accounting firms only.
   b. Regional and local CPAs.
   c. Local CPAs only.
   d. All CPAs.

LO A-2 A.36 The official *Statements on Standards for Accounting and Review Services* are applicable to practice with
   a. Audited financial statements of public companies.
   b. Unaudited financial statements of public companies.
   c. Unaudited financial statements of nonissuers.
   d. Audited financial statements of nonissuers.

LO A-1 A.37 Which of the following is a generally accepted attestation standard but is *not* a fundamental auditing principle?
   a. Appropriate competence and capability.
   b. Adequate knowledge of the subject matter.
   c. Independence.
   d. Due care.

LO A-1

A.38 The performance of an attestation engagement on prospective financial information does *not* require which of the following?

a. If the basis of the prospective financial information is different than the financial statements, a reconciliation of the two must be provided.

b. Management must disclose all significant assumptions used in generating the prospective financial information.

c. Management must disclose significant accounting policies and procedures used in generating the prospective financial information.

d. Management must disclose the probability of obtaining the results included in the prospective financial information.

LO A-4

A.39 If the auditor expresses an adverse or disclaimer of opinion on the complete set of financial statements, she or he is not permitted to:

a. Express an unqualified opinion on a single financial statement.

b. Express an unqualified opinion on an element of the financial statements.

c. Express a similar opinion on a single financial statement.

d. Perform any of the above.

LO A-1

A.40 An accountant may allow general distribution of reports based on

a. An agreed-upon-procedures engagement.

b. An examination of prospective financial information.

c. An examination of forecasted financial information.

d. None of the above.

Exercises and Problems

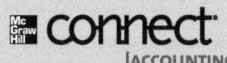

All applicable Exercises and Problems are available with McGraw-Hill's *Connect® Accounting*

LO A-2

A.41 **Errors in an Accountants' Review Report.** M. Jordan & E. Stone, CPAs, audited the financial statements of Tech Company, a nonissuer, for the year ended December 31, 2011, and expressed an unqualified opinion. For the next year, ended December 31, 2012, Tech issued comparative financial statements. Jordan & Stone reviewed Tech's 2012 financial statements and B. Kent, an assistant on the engagement, drafted the accountants' review report that follows. Stone, the engagement supervisor, decided not to reissue the prior-year audit report but instructed Kent to include a separate paragraph in the current-year review report describing the responsibility assumed for the prior-year audited financial statements. This is an appropriate reporting procedure.

Stone reviewed Kent's draft and indicated in the following supervisor's review notes that the draft contained several deficiencies (assume that U.S. GAAP is the appropriate reporting framework).

Accountants' Review Report—Kent's Draft

We have reviewed and audited the accompanying balance sheets of Tech Co. as of December 31, 2012 and 2011, and the related statements of income and comprehensive income, retained earnings, and cash flows for the years then ended, in accordance with Statements on Standards for Accounting and Review Services issued by the American Institute of Certified Public Accountants and generally accepted auditing standards. All information included in these financial statements is the representation of the management of Tech Company.

A review consists principally of inquiries of company personnel and analytical procedures applied to financial data. It is substantially less in scope than an audit in accordance with generally accepted auditing standards, the objective of which is the expression of an opinion regarding the financial statements taken as a whole.

Based on our review, we are not aware of any material modifications that should be made to the accompanying financial statements. Because of the inherent limitations of a review engagement, this report is intended for the information of management and should not be used for any other purpose.

We audited the financial statements for the year ended December 31, 2011, and our report was dated March 2, 2012. We have no responsibility for updating that report for events and circumstances occurring after that date.

Jordan and Stone, CPAs

March 1, 2013

Required:

These supervisor's review notes may or may not be correct. For each item a-n, indicate whether Stone is correct (C) or incorrect (I) in the criticism of Kent's draft.

a. The report should contain no reference to the prior-year audited financial statements in the first (introductory) paragraph.

b. All current-year basic financial statements are not properly identified in the first (introductory) paragraph.

c. The report should contain no reference to the American Institute of Certified Public Accountants in the first (introductory) paragraph.

d. Accountants' review and audit responsibilities should follow management's responsibilities in the first (introductory) paragraph.

e. The report should contain no comparison of the scope of a review to an audit in the second (scope) paragraph.

f. Negative assurance should be expressed on the current-year reviewed financial statements in the second (scope) paragraph.

g. The report should contain a statement that no opinion is expressed on the current-year financial statements in the second (scope) paragraph.

h. The report should contain a reference to "conformity with generally accepted accounting principles" in the second paragraph.

i. The report should not express a restriction on the distribution of the accountants' review report in the third paragraph.

j. The report should not contain a reference to "material modifications" in the third paragraph.

k. The report should indicate the type of opinion expressed on the prior-year audited financial statements in the last paragraph.

l. The report should indicate that no auditing procedures were performed after the date of the report on the prior-year financial statements in the fourth (separate) paragraph.

m. The report should not contain a reference to "updating the prior-year auditors' report for events and circumstances occurring after that date" in the fourth (separate) paragraph.

n. The description of procedures performed in a review engagement in the second (scope) paragraph incomplete.

(AICPA adapted)

LO A-1

A.42 **Review of Forecast Assumptions.** Dodd Manufacturing Corporation has engaged you to attest to the reasonableness of the assumptions underlying its forecast of revenues, costs, and net income for the next calendar year, 2013. Four of the assumptions follow.

1. The company intends to sell certain real estate and other facilities held by Division B at an after-tax profit of $600,000; the proceeds of this sale will be used to retire outstanding debt.

2. The company will call and retire all outstanding 9 percent subordinated debentures (callable at 108). The debentures are expected to require the full call premium given present market interest rates of 8 percent on similar debt. A rise in market interest rates to 9 percent would reduce the loss on bond retirement from the projected $200,000 to $190,000.

3. Current labor contracts expire on September 1, 2013, and the new contract is expected to result in a wage increase of 5.5 percent. Given the forecasted levels of production and sales, after-tax operating earnings would be reduced approximately $50,000 for each percentage point of wage increase in excess of the expected contract settlement.

4. The sales forecast for Division A assumes that the new Portsmouth facility will be complete and operating at 40 percent of capacity on February 1, 2013. It is highly improbable that the facility will be operational before January 2013. Each month's delay would reduce Division A sales by approximately $80,000 and operating earnings by $30,000.

Required:

For each assumption, state the evidence sources and procedures you would use to determine the reasonableness of that assumption.

LO A-1

A.43 **Internet Exercise: Reporting on Service Organization Controls.** Search for a service organization auditor's report on internal controls on the Web. (*Hint*: You may have to look under the old name "*SAS 70* reports.") If you cannot find an auditor's report, find a company's news release describing its auditor's service organization report.

Required:
a. Why do you think it is so difficult to find an actual report?
b. If you found an auditor's report, were any deficiencies noted? If so, what were they?
c. Why would a service organization publicize the results of its auditor's report?

LO A-2

A.44 **Compilation and Review Procedures.** The following numbered items 1–10 state procedures accountants should consider in review engagements and compilation engagements on the annual financial statements of nonissuers (performed in accordance with AICPA *Statements on Standards for Accounting and Review Services*).

Required:

For each item (taken separately), tell whether the item is (a) required in all review engagements, (b) *not* required in review engagements, (c) required in all compilation engagements, (d) *not* required in compilation engagements. For each item, give two responses, one regarding review engagements and the other regarding compilation engagements.

1. The accountants should establish an understanding in writing with the entity's management regarding the nature and limitations of the services to be performed.
2. The accountants should make inquiries concerning actions taken at the board of directors' meetings.
3. The accountants, as the entity's successor accountants, should communicate with the predecessor accountants to obtain access to the predecessors' audit documentation.
4. The accountants should obtain a level of knowledge of the accounting principles and practices of the entity's industry.
5. The accountants should obtain an understanding of the entity's internal control.
6. The accountants should perform analytical procedures designed to identify relationships that appear to be unusual.
7. The accountants should assess the risk of material misstatement.
8. The accountants should obtain a letter from the entity's attorney to corroborate the information furnished by management concerning litigation.
9. The accountants should obtain management representations from the entity.
10. The accountants should study the relationship of the financial statement elements that would be expected to conform to a predictable pattern.

(AICPA adapted)

LO A-2

A.45 **Compilation Presentation Alternatives.** Jimmy C. operates a large service station, garage, and truck stop on Interstate 95 near Plainview. His brother, Bill, has recently joined him as a partner, even though he will continue his small CPA practice. One slow afternoon, they were discussing financial statements with Bert, the local CPA who operates the largest public practice in Plainview.

Jimmy: The business is growing, and sometimes I need to show financial statements to parts suppliers and the loan officers at the bank.
Bert: That so?
Jimmy: Yea-boy, and they don't like the way I put 'em together.
Bert: That so?
Bill: Heck, Jimmy, I know all about that. I can compile a jim-dandy set of financial statements for us.
Jimmy: What does Jim Dan over at the cafe have to do with it?
Bert: Never mind, Jimmy. Bill can't do compiled financial statements for you. He's not independent.
Jimmy: I know. Momma didn't let him outa the house 'til he was 24. The neighbors complained.
Bert: That so?
Bill: Shucks.
Jimmy: But, Bert, those fellas are always asking me about accounting policies, contingencies, and stuff like that. Said something about "footnotes." I don't want to fool with all that small print.

Required:
Think about the financial disclosure problems of Jimmy and Bill's small business.
a. Why does Jimmy need a compilation service?
b. What types of compiled financial statements can be prepared for them and by whom?

LO A-2

A.46 **Negative Assurance in Review Reports.** One portion of the report on a review services engagement is the following: "Based on my review, I am not aware of any material modifications that should be made to the accompanying financial statements in order for them to be in conformity with generally accepted accounting principles [or another framework for financial reporting]."

Required:
- a. Is this paragraph a "negative assurance" given by the accountants?
- b. Why is negative assurance generally prohibited in audit reports?
- c. What justification is there for permitting negative assurance in a review services report on unaudited financial statements and on interim financial information?

(AICPA adapted)

LO A-4

A.47 **Reporting on a Special Purpose Framework.** The following abstracted report is a report on a trust fund that refers to a statutory basis of accounting (special purpose framework) as well as to generally accepted accounting principles (GAAP).

Independent Auditor's Report

To Natalia National Bank Association (Trustee)
and the Unit Holders of the Mega Offshore Trust:

We have audited the accompanying statements of assets, liabilities, and trust corpus—cash basis, of the Mega Offshore Trust as of December 31, 2012 and 2011, and the related statements of changes in trust corpus—cash basis, for each of the three years in the period ended 12 December, 2012. These financial statements are the responsibility of the Company's management. Our responsibility is to express an opinion on these financial statements based on our audits.

(Standard scope and responsibility paragraphs here)

As described in Note 2, these financial statements were prepared on the cash receipts and disbursements basis of accounting, which is a comprehensive basis of accounting other than generally accepted accounting principles.

In our opinion, the financial statements referred to above present fairly, in all material respects, the assets, liabilities, and trust corpus arising from cash transactions of the Mega Offshore Trust as of December 31, 2012 and 2011, and the related changes in trust corpus arising from cash transactions for each of the three years in the period ended December 31, 2012, on the basis of accounting described in Note 2.

George Costanza, CPA
March 18, 2013

Required:
Write Note 2 to Mega Offshore Trust's 2012 financial statements.

LO A-2

A.48 **Prepare a Compilation Report.** The Coffin brothers have engaged you to compile their financial schedules from books and records maintained by James Coffin. The brothers own and operate three auto parts stores in Central City. Even though their business is growing, they have not wanted to employ a full-time bookkeeper. James specifies that all he wants is a balance sheet, a statement of operations, and a statement of cash flows. He does not have time to write up footnotes to accompany the financial statements.

James directed the physical count of inventory on June 30 and adjusted and closed the books on that date. You find that he actually is a good accountant, having taken some night courses at the community college. The accounts appear to have been maintained in conformity with generally accepted accounting principles. At least you have noticed no obvious errors.

Required:
You are independent with respect to the Coffin brothers and their Coffin Auto Speed Shop business. Prepare a report on your compilation engagement.

LO A-2

A.49 **Reporting on Comparative Unaudited Financial Statements.** A. Jones, CPA, performed a review service for the Independence Company in 2012. He wants to present comparative financial statements. However, the 2011 statements were compiled by Able and Associates, CPAs, and Able does not want to cooperate with Jones by reissuing the prior-year compilation report. Jones has no indication that any adjustments should be made to either the 2012 or 2011 statements, which are to be presented with all necessary disclosures. However, he does not have time to perform a review of the 2011 statements. Jones completed his work on January 15, 2013, for the statement dated December 31, 2012.

Required:

Write Jones's review report and include the paragraph describing the report on the 2011 statements. List any assumptions you need to make to write the report.

LO A-3

A.50 **Interim Financial Information.** June's Java provides coffee services (coffee, cups, cream, sugar, and coffee makers) to local companies for use in their offices. Each of five drivers has a truck with inventory and has a different route each day to replenish coffee supplies to the companies on the route. In past audits, the accountant found that June's Java was having difficulty properly recognizing revenue, usually due to timing issues. In addition, the internal control over inventory on each driver's truck was weak.

June's Java has prepared its third-quarter financial statements and the owners want a review of the information. The accountants have audited the financial statements for the past three years but have never been asked to review any interim financial information until now.

Required:

Prepare a review plan that lists the procedures that accountants should perform to do a professional review in accordance with AU 930. Be as specific as possible in planning your procedures.

LO A-3

A.51 **Erroneous Reporting on Interim Financial Information.** Baker & Baker, CPAs, prepared the following report on the interim financial information of Micro Mini Company. The interim financial information was presented in the first quarterly report for the three-month period ended March 31, 2013. No comparative quarterly information of the first quarter of the prior year was presented. Baker & Baker completed a review in accordance with standards established by the AICPA and found that, to the best of their knowledge, the information was presented in conformity with GAAP. In an audit report dated January 21, 2013, Baker & Baker had given a standard unqualified audit report on Micro Mini's 2012 and 2011 annual financial statements.

Report of Independent Auditors

Board of Directors and Stockholders,
Micro Mini Company:

We have made a review of the balance sheet of Micro Mini Company at March 31, 2013, the related statement of income and comprehensive income for the three-month period ended March 31, 2013, and the statement of cash flows for the three-month period ended March 31, 2013, in accordance with standards established by the American Institute of Certified Public Accountants.

A review of interim financial information consists principally of obtaining an understanding of the system for the preparation of the interim financial information, applying analytical review procedures to financial data, and making inquiries to persons responsible for financial and accounting matters.

In our opinion, the accompanying interim financial information presents fairly, in all material respects, the financial position of Micro Mini Company at March 31, 2013, and the results of its operations and its cash flows for the three-month period then ended in conformity with generally accepted accounting principles.

Baker & Baker, CPAs
March 31, 2013

Required:
a. Review the report and list, with explanation, the erroneous portions in it.
b. Rewrite the report.

LO A-4

A.52 **Report on Special Purpose Framework.** Brooklyn Life Insurance Company prepares its financial statements on a statutory basis in conformity with the accounting practices prescribed and permitted by the Insurance Department of the State of New York. This statutory basis produces financial statements that differ materially from statements prepared in conformity with generally accepted accounting principles. On the statutory basis, for example, agents' first-year commissions are expensed instead of being partially deferred.

The company engaged its auditors, Major and Major Associates, to audit the statutory basis financial statements and report on them. Footnote 10 in the statements contains a narrative description and a numerical table explaining the differences between the statutory basis and GAAP accounting. Footnote 10 also reconciles the statutory basis assets, liabilities, income, expense, and net income (statutory basis) to the measurements that would be obtained using GAAP.

Required:

Write the audit report appropriate in the circumstances. The year-end date is December 31, 2012, and the audit fieldwork was completed on February 20, 2013. (The company plans to distribute this report to persons other than the department of insurance regulators, so the auditors need to follow AU 700.)

LO A-5

A.53 **Internet Exercise: CPA WebTrust.** Visit the AICPA WebTrust site (www.webtrust.org).

Required:
a. What is WebTrust?
b. Why is WebTrust needed?
c. How does an Internet user know that a website has received the WebTrust service?
d. Where can a person obtain copies of the Trust service principles?

LO A-5

A.54 **Assurance Services.** In 2008, the AICPA Assurance Services Executive Committee identified five global "mega trends" that can affect a CPA's business.

Required:
a. Review the mega trends that were identified. Are these trends still viable in today's society and economy? Which trends, if any, need to be reconsidered because of current conditions in society and the economy?
b. Are there additional trends in the marketplace that could affect a public accounting firm's business?

LO A-5

A.55 **Assurance Services.** Davis has a store that sells old baseball cards. To expand the business, he has decided to open an Internet site where potential customers can view the cards and place orders. Davis hires Johnson, who is an expert in constructing Web sites for small businesses. She explains that even with a quality website and pictures of the merchandise for sale, customers may be reluctant to purchase baseball cards from Davis's website.

Required:
a. Explain the reasons for Johnson's concerns.
b. What steps can Davis and Johnson take to reduce customer's reluctance to make purchases on the Internet?

LO A-5

A.56 **Assurance Services.** Henry's Health Food Store maintains a perpetual inventory on its computer. The sales representative from A-Plus Vitamins has recommended the following to Henry:
- All the files should have password protection.
- A-Plus Vitamins should be given the URL and the password for Henry's inventory file on the computer, which can be accessed from outside.
- A-Plus Vitamins will search the inventory for items that fall below an established reorder point and will automatically ship a set amount of product to Henry's.

Required:
a. What are the advantages of this arrangement for Henry's? For A-Plus Vitamins?
b. What concerns might Henry's have in this arrangement?
c. How might these concerns be addressed?

LO A-5

A.57 **Internet Assignment: Try XBRL.** Go to the TryXBRL website and examine the sample XBRL EDGAR filing. EDGAR is the SEC's electronic financial reporting format that allows downloads of financial reports of public companies.

Required:

How can CPAs provide assurance for XBRL reporting as a service to their clients?

LO A-1 A.58 **Attestation Evaluation Criteria.** The local high school experienced trouble two years ago. Its graduation rates had declined to the bottom 10 percent in the state, college admission rates were low, and graduates had a high unemployment rate. The school board and administration have notified the state Department of Education and the taxpayers in the school district that these problems have been fixed. Graduation rates have increased, a higher percentage of students are continuing with their education, and a higher percentage of graduates have jobs. The Department of Education wants an independent attestation to these assertions. It is concerned not only about the numbers claimed by the school board and administration but also about the underlying process and means used to obtain these numbers.

Required:

Establish a list of criteria you would use to validate the claim of the school board and administration and to determine the processes and means used to obtain these numbers.

Professional Ethics

Auditors must approach their jobs with independence and skepticism. How do we instill those necessary traits in auditors? This may be the most important auditing question of our time.

> James Doty, PCOAB Chairman, remarks made at SEC Reporting Conference, June 2, 2011

To educate a person in mind and not in morals is to educate a menace to society.

> Theodore "Teddy" Roosevelt, 26th President of the United States

Always do right—this will gratify some and astonish the rest.

> Mark Twain, famous American novelist

There is nothing so powerful as truth.

> Daniel Webster, Secretary of State for three different U.S. presidents in the period after the American Revolution

Professional Standards References

Topic	AU/ISA Section	PCAOB Reference*
Overall Objectives of the Independent Auditor and the Conduct of an Audit	200	AU 110, AU 150, AU 201, AU 201, AU 220, AU 230
Quality Control	220	AU 161
Responsibility Not to Knowingly or Recklessly Contribute to Violations		Rule 3502
Auditor Independence		Rule 3520
Contingent Fees		Rule 3521
Tax Transactions		Rule 3522
Tax Services for Persons in Financial Reporting Oversight Roles		Rule 3523

Topic	AU/ISA Section	PCAOB Reference*
Audit Committee Pre-approval of Certain Tax Services		Rule 3524
Audit Committee Pre-approval of Nonaudit Services Related to Internal Control over Financial Reporting		Rule 3525
Communication with Audit Committees Concerning Independence		Rule 3526
	ET/BL Section†	
Principles of Professional Conduct	ET 51–57	
Rules: Applicability and Definitions	ET 91–92	
Independence, Integrity, and Objectivity	ET 101–191	
General Standards Accounting Principles	ET 201–291	
Responsibilities to Clients	ET 301–391	
Other Responsibilities and Practices	ET 501-591	
Resolution Designating Bodies to Promulgate Technical Standards (Rules 201, 202, and 203)	ET Appendix A	
Resolution Concerning Form of Organization and Name (Rule 505)	ET Appendix B	
Bylaws of the AICPA	BL 100–900	

*AU references represent standards issued by the ASB prior to April 16, 2003, that have not been superseded or amended by the PCAOB.
† ET references represent sections in the AICPA Code of Professional Conduct. BL references represent sections of the AICPA bylaws.

LEARNING OBJECTIVES

As described in Chapter 2, the responsibilities principle identifies three specific responsibilities. Two of the responsibilities, (1) having appropriate competence and capabilities to perform the audit and (2) maintaining professional skepticism and exercising professional judgment throughout the planning and performance of the audit, have been focused on in other chapters of this book. This module focuses on the third responsibility, complying with relevant ethical requirements. In this spirit, this module is designed to teach you about the AICPA Code of Professional Conduct and demonstrate why it is so important to your success as a professional accountant. As you will soon learn, regulation of the profession, including any discipline for violations, depends on the prevailing published codes of ethics and enforcement practices. As a result, we believe this module is essential to your success.

Your objectives are to be able to:

LO B-1 Understand general ethics and a series of steps for making ethical decisions.

LO B-2 Reason through an ethical decision problem using the imperative, utilitarian, and generalization principles of moral philosophy.

LO B-3 Identify the different entities that make ethics rules for CPAs and public accounting firms.

LO B-4 With reference to American Institute of Certified Public Accounting (AICPA), Government Accountability Office (GAO), Public Company Accounting Oversight Board (PCAOB), and Securities and Exchange Commission (SEC) rules, analyze factual situations and decide whether an accountant's conduct does or does not impair independence.

LO B-5 With reference to AICPA rules on topics other than independence, analyze factual situations and decide whether an accountant's conduct does or does not conform to the AICPA Rules of Conduct.

LO B-6 Explain the types of penalties that can be imposed on accountants.

INTRODUCTION

When the U.S. Senate passed the Sarbanes-Oxley Act in July 2002 (by a vote of 99–0), the investing public was outraged by the magnitude of the financial statement frauds at both **Enron** and **WorldCom** (among many other frauds). The audacity of these frauds is mind boggling. Consider that in 2000, Enron was the seventh largest company on the Fortune 500 with reported assets of $65 billion and sales revenues of $100 billion. However, just a year later, Enron filed for bankruptcy, and billions of shareholder dollars were lost. In June 2002, WorldCom announced that it would be restating its financial statements due to improper accounting that took two major forms: the overstatement of revenue by at least $958 million and the understatement of line costs, its largest category of expenses, by more than $7 billion. As you will soon see, the passage of Sarbanes-Oxley was a direct response to these financial statement frauds. Indeed, a number of the sections of the act are specifically targeted to prevent the threats to auditor independence that existed on both the Enron and WorldCom audit engagements.

For example, Section 201 of Sarbanes-Oxley makes it unlawful for a public accounting firm to provide most consulting type services to its audit clients, including information systems design and implementation (e.g., SAP) and internal audit outsourcing. This was clearly designed to prevent the type of relationship that existed between Enron and **Arthur Andersen (Andersen).** In 2000, Enron paid Andersen $25 million for financial statement audit services and $27 million for consulting and other services, such as internal audit services. The significant amount of revenue generated on consulting services was considered a threat to independence by many, especially considering that the compensation of audit partners at Andersen depended, in part, on consulting sales to its audit clients.

As you will soon learn, the AICPA Code of Professional Conduct (the Code) is crystal clear about the importance of independence. The responsibilities principle requires auditors to maintain independence *in mental attitude;* that is, auditors are expected to be unbiased and impartial with respect to all professional judgments and to the financial statements they audit. This "state of mind" is often referred to as the auditor's possessing independence in fact. It is important for auditors not only to be unbiased but also to *appear* to be unbiased. Independence in appearance relates to financial statement users' perceptions of auditors' independence. For example, even if the auditor does not have any direct or indirect financial interest or obligation with the audit client, they must ensure that no part of their behavior or actions appears to affect their independence in the opinion of the public.

Simply stated, audit quality and the value of the profession depend on independence. If an auditor's independence is doubted, users of audited financial statements are likely to question the motives of the public accounting firm in completing the audit, greatly diminishing the value of the audit. As a result of its importance, public accounting firms now spend a substantial amount of time making sure they maintain their independence at all times. And, although independence is clearly the cornerstone of professional ethics, studying professional ethics goes beyond the subject of independence. We therefore begin this module with a discussion of ethical philosophy before our focus on the standards of ethical conduct for auditors.

GENERAL ETHICS

LEARNING OBJECTIVE B-1
Understand general ethics philosophy and a series of steps for making ethical decisions.

What is ethics? Wheelwright defined *ethics* as "that branch of philosophy which is the systematic study of reflective choice, of the standards of right and wrong by which it is to be guided, and of the goods toward which it may ultimately be directed."[1] In this definition, you can detect three key elements: ethics (1) involves questions requiring reflective choice (*decision problems*), (2) involves guides of right and wrong (*moral principles*), and (3) is concerned with the consequences (*good or bad*) of decisions.

---

[1] Philip Wheelwright, *A Critical Introduction to Ethics,* 3rd ed. (Indianapolis, IN: Odyssey Press, 1959).

What is an ethical problem? A *problem situation* exists when an individual must make a choice among alternative actions and the right choice is not absolutely clear. An *ethical problem situation* may be described as one in which the choice of alternative actions affects the well-being of other persons. While these are technical definitions of ethical dilemmas, we are often faced with situations in which what we want to do conflicts with what we know is the right course of action. While ethicists may argue that these are not ethical dilemmas, that fact does not make the decisions any easier.

What is *ethical behavior?* You can find two standard philosophical answers to this question: ethical behavior is that which (1) produces the greatest good and (2) conforms to moral rules and principles. The most difficult problem situations arise when two or more rules conflict or when a rule and the criterion of "greatest good" conflict. However, as a professional auditor, you must always conform to the code of ethical behavior that applies to your jurisdiction or face the possibility of being formally sanctioned by the profession.

Why does an individual or group need a code of ethical conduct? A *code* makes explicit some of the criteria for conduct unique to the profession. *Codes of professional ethics* provide guidance in addressing situations that may not be specifically available in general ethics theories. An individual is better able to know what the profession expects. From the viewpoint of the organized profession, a *code* is a public declaration of principled conduct and a means of facilitating *enforcement* of standards of conduct. Once again, you can see the value of ethical behavior. Remember that accounting is the only business discipline that is considered a profession similar to those of doctors and lawyers. As a student of auditing, you must commit yourself to knowing and understanding the code of professional conduct.

Ethical Example 1

In a famous experiment conducted by Stanley Milgram (a psychologist at Yale University), subjects were told to ask questions of an individual in another room. If the individual answered incorrectly, the subjects were told to inflict an electric shock as punishment. In reality, no shock was actually administered; however, the subjects believed they were administering one and could hear shouts, cries, and appeals to stop emanating from the next room. The experimenter ordered the subjects to continue to apply the shocks at ever increasing amounts. Many subjects increased the voltage to intensities labeled as dangerous and continued even after the individual in the next room asked for a doctor. Why do you think the subjects continued to apply shocks? What would you have done in this circumstance? Many have used the Milgram study result as an explanation for why good people often get caught up in wide-reaching frauds such as Enron and WorldCom because they allow authority figures to subvert their better judgments.

AN ETHICAL DECISION PROCESS

LEARNING OBJECTIVE B-2
Reason through an ethical decision problem using the imperative, utilitarian, and generalization principles of moral philosophy.

When considering general ethics, your primary goal is to arrive at a personal framework for making ethical decisions. Consequently, an understanding of some of the general principles of ethics can provide background for a detailed consideration of standards for professional conduct.

In the earlier definition of ethics, one of the key elements was *reflective choice*. This involves engaging in an important sequence of events beginning with the recognition of a decision problem. Collection of evidence, in the ethics context, refers to thinking about rules of behavior and outcomes of alternative actions. The process ends with analyzing the situation and taking an action. Ethical decision problems almost always involve projecting yourself into the future to live with your decisions. Professional ethics decisions usually turn on these questions: "What written and unwritten rules govern my behavior?" and "What are the possible consequences of my choices—whom will my decision affect?" *Principles of ethics* can help you think about these two questions in real situations.

A good way to approach ethical decision problems is to think through several steps:

1. Define all facts and circumstances known at the time you need to make the decision. They are the "who, what, where, when, and how" dimensions of the situation. Identify the actor who needs to decide what to do.

2. a. Because ethical decision problems are defined in terms of their effects on people, identify the people involved in the situation or affected by it. These are the "stakeholders"; be careful not to expand the number of stakeholders beyond the bounds of reasonable analysis.
   b. Identify and describe the stakeholders' rights and obligations in general and to each other.
3. Specify the actor's major alternative decision actions and their consequences (good, bad, short run, long run).
4. The actor must choose among the alternative actions.

Let's apply the preceding ethical framework to Ethical Example 2.

Ethical Example 2

Step 1: Kathy Ellis (the chief financial officer) ordered Jorge Santos (a staff accountant) to "enhance" the financial statements in a loan application to Spring National Bank by understating the allowance for uncollectible accounts receivable saying, "It's an estimate anyway and we need the loan for a short time to keep from laying off loyal employees." What should Santos do?

Step 2a: The stakeholders include the direct participants—Ellis, Santos, and Luis Perez (Spring National Bank's loan officer)—and some indirect participants—bank stockholders and loyal employees. Other people may be affected— Santos's mother, citizens who depend on the solvency of the banking system as a whole, taxpayers who eventually need to bail out the insolvent banking system, and others—but identifying them probably will not improve the analysis.

Step 2b: *Obligations:* Ellis and Santos should act with integrity, and Ellis should not pressure Santos to cut corners with financial statements. Perez should make careful loan approval decisions. *Rights:* Santos should not be subject to pressures to cut corners with "enhanced financial statements." Perez should receive information that is not materially misstated or manipulated. (Some rights of employees and bank stockholders also could be identified.)

Step 3: (a) Santos can follow orders: Ellis is happy, he keeps his job, Perez gets fooled and approves the loan, the employees keep their jobs, the company fails, the bank is unable to collect the loan, the employees are laid off anyway, Ellis and Santos are prosecuted and convicted of making false statements to a federal institution and go to federal prison. (2) Santos can refuse to "enhance" the financial statements: Ellis is not happy, Santos is fired, Ellis prepares the financial statements herself, and so on. (3) Santos persuades Ellis of the potential problems and Perez refuses the loan, and the company must find another way to survive, or Perez approves the loan anyway and the bank takes the risk; or Ellis does not agree, and Santos must again face alternatives (1) and (2) anyway.

In addition to weighing the consequences, Santos also should consider general and professional rules. If he is a CPA, some of the relevant professional rules relate to maintaining integrity (AICPA rule 102), application of accounting standards (AICPA rule 203), and the prohibition of discreditable acts (AICPA rule 501). Santos needs to decide whether to follow rules or balance the expected consequences in the particular situation.

Step 4: As the actor, Santos must choose one of the alternative actions and justify it by presenting a convincing argument for its superiority. He can base the argument on rules, consequences, or a combination of both.

PHILOSOPHICAL PRINCIPLES IN ETHICS

We could skip a discussion of ethical theories if we were willing to accept a simple rule: "Let your *conscience* be your guide." Such a rule is appealing because it calls on an individual's own judgment, which may be based on wisdom, insight, adherence to custom, or an authoritative code. However, it also might be based on caprice, immaturity, ignorance, stubbornness, or misunderstanding. Often, as in the Milgram experiments, undue pressures might cause us to act in a way that we will later regret. The problem with using conscience as a guide is that it tells you about a wrong decision *after* you act!

In a similar manner, reliance on the opinions of others or on the weight of opinions of a particular social group is not always enough. Another person or a group of persons may perpetuate a custom or habit that is wrong. To adhere blindly to custom or to group habits is to abdicate individual responsibility. Titus and Keeton summarized this point succinctly: "Each person capable of making moral decisions is responsible for making his own decisions. The ultimate locus of moral responsibility is in the individual."[2] This does not mean you should not consult with friends, colleagues, or family members when facing a dilemma, but that only *you* have the final responsibility.

Thus, the function of *ethical principles* is not to provide a simple and sure rule but to provide some guides for your individual decisions and actions. Of course, as a professional auditor, you are required to follow the code of professional conduct. So, in that sense, professional auditors always must first apply the imperative principle. However, because many decisions go beyond the code, the principle of utilitarianism and the generalization argument are also considered.

The Imperative Principle

The *imperative principle* directs a decision maker to act according to the requirements of an ethical rule. Strict versions of imperative ethics maintain that a decision should be made without trying to predict whether an action will create the greatest balance of good over evil. Ethics in the *imperative* sense is a function of moral rules and principles and does not involve a situation-specific calculation of the consequences.[3]

The philosopher Immanuel Kant (1724–1804) was perhaps the foremost advocate of the imperative school. Kant maintained that *reason* and the strict *duty to be consistent* should govern our actions. He believed that individuals should act only as they think everyone should act all of the time. This law of conduct (in moral philosophy) is known as Kant's **categorical imperative**, meaning that it specifies an *unconditional obligation*. One such maxim (rule), for example, is "Lying is wrong."

Suppose you believe that Santos (from Ethical Example 2) should agree with Ellis and do everything she asked for "enhancing the financial statements," thus participating in a lie (knowingly misrepresenting the facts about the allowance for uncollectible accounts receivable). The Kantian test of the morality of such a lie is this: Can this maxim be a moral rule that should be followed without exception by all persons who have the opportunity to fool a bank loan officer for a good cause? If Santos refuses to manipulate the financial statements and the loan is refused, the result may be economic hardship and employee layoffs. Kant maintained that motive and duty alone define a moral act, not the consequences of the act. This reasoning places the highest value on the duty to be consistent and a lower value on the consequences, in this case the fate of the employees.

The general objection to the imperative principle is the belief that so-called universal rules always turn out to have exceptions. The general response to this objection is that if the rule is stated properly to include the exceptional cases, the principle is still valid. The problem with this response, however, is that human experience is complicated, and extremely complex universal rules would have to be constructed to try to cover all possible cases.[4]

Most professional codes of ethics have characteristics of the imperative type of theory. As a general matter, professionals are expected to act in a manner in conformity with the rules. As it relates to your work as an audit professional, this principle would lead you to follow the code of professional conduct to the letter of the law. This, of course, is what you must do to avoid being sanctioned by the profession. However, society frequently questions not only conduct itself but also the rules on which conduct is based. Thus, a dogmatic imperative approach to ethical decisions may not be completely sufficient for the maintenance of professional standards. Society may question the rules, and conflicts among them are always possible. A means of estimating the consequences of alternative actions may be useful; see Ethical Example 3.

---

[2] Harold H. Titus and Morris Keeton, *Ethics for Today*, 4th ed. (New York: American Book–Stratford Press, 1966), p. 131.

[3] I. Kant, *Foundations of the Metaphysics of Morals*, trans. Lewis W. Beck (Indianapolis, IN: Bobbs-Merrill, 1959; originally published in 1785).

[4] Several rules in the AICPA Rules of Conduct are explicitly phrased to provide for exceptions to the general rules, notably Rules 203 and 301. Imperative rules also seem to generate borderline cases, so the AICPA Ethics Division issues interpretations and rulings to explain the applicability of the rules.

Ethical Example 3

Consolidata, Inc., was a tax client of **Alexander Grant & Company, CPAs** (AG). Consolidata prepared payrolls for 38 customers, received the customers' money, and then paid the payrolls. AG learned that Consolidata was in serious financial difficulty and advised the company to inform its customers, but company officials did not do so. When AG learned that the company's officers and directors had resigned, AG telephoned 12 Consolidata customers who were also AG clients, told them of the situation, and advised them not to entrust further payroll funds to Consolidata. The 12 were spared the risk of losing their money when Consolidata went out of business one month later.

Consolidata accused AG of breach of contract for breaking an obligation of confidentiality required by the AICPA Code of Professional Conduct. One SEC attorney said she thought AG should have alerted all 38 customers, not just the 12 AG clients. Accountants and SEC officials viewed the situation as a balancing of confidentiality (AICPA rule) against the public interest (Consolidata customers who needed a warning).

The Principle of Utilitarianism

The *principle of utilitarianism* emphasizes examining the *consequences* of action rather than following some rules. The criterion of producing the greater good is made an explicit part of the decision process. The *principle* is very useful, but be sure to notice that it does not specify the *values* that enable you to determine the good or evil of an action. In **act-utilitarianism**, the center of attention is the *individual act* as it is affected by the specific circumstances of a situation. The general difficulty with act-utilitarianism is that it seems to permit too many exceptions to well-established rules. By focusing attention on individual acts, the long-run effect of setting examples for other people appears to be ignored. If an act-utilitarian decision is to break a moral rule, the decision's success usually depends on everyone else's adherence to the rule, which is highly unlikely in auditing.

Rule-utilitarianism, on the other hand, emphasizes the centrality *of rules for ethical behavior* while still maintaining the criterion of the greatest universal good. This kind of utilitarianism means that decision makers must first determine the rules that will promote the greatest general good for the largest number of people. The initial question is not which *action* has the greatest utility but which *rule.*

The Generalization Argument

The generalization argument may be considered a judicious combination of the imperative and utilitarian principles. Basically, the **generalization argument** considers the consequences of a decision made by similar persons acting under similar circumstances.[5] A more everyday expression of the argument is this question: "What would happen if everyone acted in that certain way?" If the answer to the question is that the consequences would be undesirable, the conclusion, according to the generalization test, is that the way of acting is unethical and should not be done.

The key ideas in the generalization test are *similar persons* and *similar circumstances*. These features provide the needed flexibility to consider the many variations that arise in real problem situations. They also demand considerable judgment in determining whether persons and circumstances are genuinely different or are just arbitrarily rationalized as different so that a preconceived preference can be "explained" as right.

In Ethical Example 2, Santos's problem as a professional accountant and as an employee arose when Ellis asked him to "enhance the financial statements" and he saw the enhancement as a lie. His generalization question may be something like this: "What if all accountants fudged financial statements and fooled loan officers when their companies needed to obtain loans?" Most people will see an easy answer: The result would be undesirable (because it might succeed often and cause considerable losses to banks along with other undesirable personal consequences for the actors in addition to the problem of having broken a rule that requires truth telling). Another kind of conflict subject to the generalization test is illustrated by a public accounting firm's desire for service and need for independence (see the Auditing Insight "Service versus Independence").

---

[5] Marcus G. Singer, *Generalization in Ethics* (New York: Atheneum, 1961, 1971), esp. pp. 5, 10–11, 61, 63, 73, 81, 105–122.

> ### AUDITING INSIGHT | Service versus Independence
>
> For many years, a national public accounting firm encouraged its professionals to become active members of the boards of directors of corporations. The purpose was to provide expertise to businesses in the metropolitan area and to enable the public accounting firm to become well known and well respected. The public accounting firm changed its policy to prohibit such service after it had to refuse the opportunity to obtain some of these corporations as audit clients because of independence concerns.
>
> The public accounting firm's audit independence was considered impaired when a member of the firm had served in a director or management capacity during the period covered by the financial statements the corporations wanted the firm to audit. The generalization test was this: If members of the firm serve on the boards of directors of all corporations that may become audit clients, none of these corporations can be accepted as audit clients—a result that is undesirable.

This brief review of ethical principles provides some important background to the ways that many people approach difficult ethical decision problems. As a professional auditor, you are required to adhere to the prevailing code of conduct in all your duties. However, there will be times in your career when the code does not go far enough. In those situations, it is important to consider the general notions of ethics—the imperative, utilitarian, and generalization—and apply them to decisions. Deciding how you will behave (i.e., what ethical principle you will follow) *before* you find yourself in an ethical dilemma can inoculate you from the kind of pressures the Milgram subjects and our hypothetical Santos experienced and allow you to make decisions of which you will be proud.

> ### ↳ REVIEW CHECKPOINTS
>
> B.1 What roles must a professional accountant be prepared to perform in regard to ethical decision problems?
>
> B.2 When might the rule "Let your conscience be your guide" *not* be a sufficient basis for (a) your personal ethical decisions and (b) your professional ethical decisions?
>
> B.3 Assume that you accept the following ethical rule: "Failure to tell the whole truth is wrong." In the textbook illustration about Santos's problem with Ellis's instructions, (a) what would this rule require Santos to do and (b) why is an unalterable rule such as this classified as an element of imperative ethical theory?
>
> B.4 How do utilitarian ethics differ from imperative ethics?

ETHICAL CODES OF CONDUCT

LEARNING OBJECTIVE B-3
Identify the different entities that make ethics rules for CPAs and public accounting firms.

Independence, professionalism, and integrity have long been concerns of the accounting profession, but the scandals of Enron, WorldCom, and the financial crisis have brought renewed cries and placed additional emphasis on these issues. The PCAOB was created, in part, to help bring a new level of independence and integrity to the profession. In that spirit, the PCAOB has issued a number of rules that apply to auditors that serve clients that are public entities. Furthermore, public accounting firms and CPAs also must follow rules set forth by the SEC and the AICPA Professional Ethics Executive Committee (PEEC). Public accounting firms and CPAs completing multinational audits also must comply with the International Federation of Accountants (IFAC) Code of Ethics for Professional Accountants. If you are an internal auditor, you will be expected to observe the rules of conduct of the Institute of Internal Auditors (IIA). As a management accountant, the standards of ethical conduct for management accountants of the Institute of Management Accountants (IMA) will apply to you. Certified fraud examiners are expected to observe the Association of Certified Fraud Examiners (ACFE) Code of Ethics. If you find this "alphabet soup" of ethics rule makers confusing, imagine those CPAs who have to deal with complex and often conflicting rules on a daily basis. As a CPA, you will be expected to observe rules of conduct published in several codes of ethics, depending on the jurisdiction. In summary, if you join the AICPA and a state society of CPAs and practice before the U.S. Securities and Exchange Commission (SEC) on a multinational audit client, you will be subject to the following:

Source of Rules of Conduct	Applicable to
U.S. Securities and Exchange Commission (SEC)	Persons who practice before the SEC as accountants and auditors for SEC-registered companies
Public Company Oversight Accounting Board (PCAOB)	Registered firms and individuals who perform audits of companies under the jurisdiction of the PCAOB
International Federation of Accountants (IFAC)	Public accounting firms and CPAs performing audits of multinational companies
American Institute of CPAs (AICPA)	Members of AICPA
Applicable state society of CPAs	Members of a state society of CPAs
Applicable state board of accountancy	Persons licensed by the state to practice accounting

AUDITING INSIGHT — Fraud Auditor Expelled for Committing Fraud

A trial board of the ACFE found that a member had wrongfully represented himself as a *certified internal auditor* when in fact he did not hold the CIA designation. Such conduct is in violation of Article 1.A.4 of the Certified Fraud Examiners Code of Professional Ethics, and the member was summarily expelled from the organization.

L. Jackson Shockey, CFE, CPA, CISA, chairperson of the board of regents, said: "We are saddened that a member has been expelled for such conduct. However, in order to maintain the integrity of the CFE program, the trial board vigorously investigates violations of the Code of Professional Ethics. When appropriate, the board of regents will not hesitate to take necessary action."

Source: *CFE News.*

U.S. Securities and Exchange Commission (SEC)

The SEC has federal statutory authority to regulate the public accounting profession for the purposes of (1) protecting the reliability and integrity of the financial statements of public companies and (2) promoting investor confidence in financial statements and the securities markets. The SEC's jurisdiction covers only public companies that are required by federal securities laws to file financial statements audited by independent accountants. In addition to the duties outlined earlier, the passage of the Sarbanes-Oxley Act in 2002 requires the SEC to oversee the PCAOB.

The Public Company Accounting Oversight Board (PCAOB)

The PCAOB has been given the responsibility to set standards for public accounting firms and to oversee quality control, ethics, and independence issues for accounting professionals who audit financial statements of public companies. Students are urged to review the PCAOB website (www.pcaobus.org) to review the latest standards and rules issued by the PCAOB.

Although the PCAOB has almost the same level of authority as the SEC, the SEC must approve all PCAOB proposed rules before they are final. Also, even though the PCAOB has authority over the audits of only public entities, it would be a mistake to believe that the PCAOB's influence ends there. Indeed, several states (e.g., California) have passed legislation that incorporates PCAOB rules into state law applicable to audits of all companies, both public and private.

The International Federation of Accountants (IFAC)

For audits of multinational companies, auditors must follow the guidelines promulgated by the IFAC. IFAC's International Ethics Standards Board for Accountants is responsible for the Code of Ethics for Professional Accountants (IESBA Code), which is the code of conduct that governs the audits of multinational companies. The most recent edition of the IESBA code was made effective on January 1, 2011, and is available at tinyurl.com/372k2wg. Although there are differences between the IESBA code and the AICPA Code of Professional Conduct used to govern the audits of U.S. companies (which will be described later in this module), the codes are actually quite similar. In general, a CPA should always comply with the more restrictive standard that is applicable on a particular audit engagement. Not surprisingly, with the dramatic increase in audits of multinational companies by public accounting firms from the United States, the importance of the IESBA code has increased. Indeed, the AICPA is in the middle of a convergence and codification project designed to align the AICPA and IESBA codes and simplify the overall structure of the AICPA code. The project is expected to be completed by the end of 2012.

The Professional Ethics Executive Committee (PEEC) of the American Institute of CPAs (AICPA)

The PEEC is the AICPA committee that makes and enforces all rules of conduct for CPAs (i.e., the AICPA Code of Professional Conduct) who are AICPA members. You might think that if you were not in public accounting and not a member of the AICPA, the rules would not apply. However, state and federal court proceedings and disciplinary bodies have consistently upheld that CPAs must adhere to professional ethical standards even if they are not members of the AICPA. The AICPA Code of Professional Conduct contains two basic sections. The first section is the Principles of Professional Conduct, a set of six positive essays expressing the profession's high ideals; the second is the Rules of Professional Conduct, described later in this module. A summary of the Principles of Conduct now follows:

I. *Responsibilities.* In carrying out their responsibilities as professionals, members should exercise sensitive professional and moral judgments in all of their activities.

II. *The public interest.* Members should accept the obligation to act in a way that will serve the public interest, honor the public trust, and demonstrate commitment to professionalism.

III. *Integrity.* To maintain and broaden public confidence, members should perform all professional responsibilities with the highest sense of integrity.

IV. *Objectivity and independence.* A member should maintain objectivity and be free of conflicts of interest in discharging professional responsibilities. A member in public practice should be independent in fact and appearance when providing auditing and other attestation services.

V. *Due care.* A member should observe the profession's technical and ethical standards, strive continually to improve competence and quality of services, and discharge professional responsibility to the best of the member's ability.

VI. *Scope and nature of services.* A member in public practice should observe the Principles of the Code of Professional Conduct in determining the scope and nature of services to be provided.

The responsibility to the public interest clearly sets accountants apart from other business professionals. It is the reason that accounting is considered a profession even beyond other professionals such as doctors and lawyers whose primary responsibility is to their patients/clients. However, this *responsibility to the public interest* demands that CPAs' work must reflect high levels of moral judgment, true commitment to the public interest, and excellent performance. The *scope and nature of services* refer to the issue of balancing public accounting firms' commitment to clients (giving business advice and consulting) and commitment to the public (giving opinions on financial statements).

Although the first section of the AICPA Code of Conduct embodies principles to which CPAs should adhere, they are very general in nature, and thus are difficult, if not impossible, to enforce on their own. The second section, however, contains the enforceable Rules of Conduct that were derived from the six Principles of Conduct.

AICPA Rules of Conduct

Section 90: Rules: Applicability and Definitions
Section 100: Independence, Integrity, and Objectivity
  Rule 101: Independence
  Rule 102: Integrity and Objectivity
Section 200: General and Technical Standards
  Rule 201: General Standards
  Rule 202: Compliance with Standards
  Rule 203: Accounting Principles
Section 300: Responsibilities to Clients
  Rule 301: Confidential Client Information
  Rule 302: Contingent Fees

Section 400: (No title or rules are in the 400 series.)*
Section 500: Other Responsibilities and Practices
  Rule 501: Acts Discreditable
  Rule 502: Advertising and Other Forms of Solicitation
  Rule 503: Commissions and Referral Fees
  Rule 504: (No Rule 504)
  Rule 505: Form of Practice and Name

*Regarding the numbering system for the Rules of Conduct, you might wonder why no rule is numbered in the 400 series (formerly "Responsibilities to Colleagues"). Rules in this section were repealed by vote of the AICPA membership in 1979 after the U.S. Department of Justice challenged them as an unwarranted restraint on competition. The AICPA simply has not changed the numbering system.

The PEEC also publishes Interpretations of Rules of Conduct, which are detailed explanations of specific rules necessary to help members understand particular applications. Finally, the PEEC also publishes "rulings" on the applicability of rules in specific situations.[6]

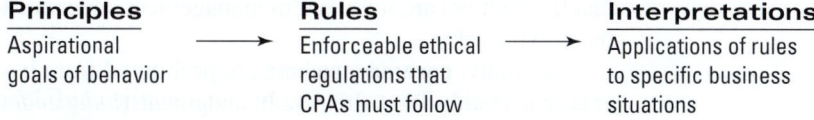

Principles → **Rules** → **Interpretations**
Aspirational goals of behavior — Enforceable ethical regulations that CPAs must follow — Applications of rules to specific business situations

↳ REVIEW CHECKPOINTS

B.5 In regard to ethics rules, what are the jurisdictions of the (a) AICPA PEEC, (b) SEC, (c) PCAOB, and (d) IFAC?

B.6 What organizations and agencies have rules of conduct that you must observe when you practice (a) public accounting, (b) internal auditing, (c) management accounting, and (d) fraud examination?

---

[6] The full text of the interpretations and rulings are available on the AICPA website (www.aicpa.org).

AN EMPHASIS ON INDEPENDENCE

LEARNING OBJECTIVE B-4
With reference to American Institute of Certified Public Accounting (AICPA), Government Accountability Office (GAO), Public Company Accounting Oversight Board (PCAOB), and Securities and Exchange Commission (SEC) rules, analyze factual situations and decide whether an accountant's conduct does or does not impair independence.

As mentioned previously, a lack of perceived independence between public accounting firms and their clients has been blamed for a number of massive financial accounting frauds, including those of Enron and WorldCom. For example, many have argued that Arthur Andersen's independence was impaired on the Enron engagement because of the large consulting fees that the firm was receiving which actually *exceeded* the audit fees for the engagement. The argument goes that Andersen partners were so concerned about losing the lucrative consulting engagement fees that they compromised their professional skepticism when dealing with Enron's questionable accounting practices. The focus on independence has resulted in a number of laws and rules that are aimed at bolstering public accounting firm independence. Not surprisingly, ethics rule-making bodies discussed in the previous section have developed their own solutions, each of which is discussed below.

American Institute of Certified Public Accountants[7]

The PEEC makes independence rules for CPAs that are applicable not only for audits of public companies but also for all other audits (audits of nonpublic companies, not-for-profit organizations, and government units) and attestation engagements. Independence is required for audit as well as attestation engagements, including reviews of financial statements. However, attestation engagements are governed by *Statements on Standards for Attestation Engagements* (*SSAEs*) dealing with assertions other than financial statements in which some form of assurance is provided (*Interpretation 101-11*). Rule 101, the independence rule, is derived from the AICPA Code of Professional Conduct's objectivity and independence principle:

Rule 101: Independence

> **Rule 101.** A member in public practice shall be independent in the performance of professional services as required by standards promulgated by bodies designated by Council.[8]

Rule 101 itself has very little substantive content. Instead, it incorporates PEEC interpretations that are explained in the following paragraphs. Exhibit B.1 summarizes the PEEC interpretations and other independence matters. The fundamental thrust of these interpretations is that auditors preserve **independence**, the mental attitude and appearance that auditors are not influenced by others in making judgments and decisions, by (1) avoiding financial connections that make it appear that the auditor's wealth depends on the outcome of the audit and (2) avoiding managerial connections that make it appear that the auditors are involved in management decisions for the audit client (thus auditing their own work).

Essentially, **covered members** are prohibited from having any financial interest in clients that could affect their audit judgment (*independence in fact*) or would appear to others to have an influence on their judgment (*independence in appearance*). In addition, immediate family members are under the same restrictions as the auditor. Again, the appearance of independence would be jeopardized if the auditor's child owned stock in a client. Similarly, if a close relative or immediate family member worked for a client in a position that could influence the audit (e.g., a controller), independence in appearance, if not in fact, is impaired. Exhibit B.2 provides important definitions (both AICPA and SEC) used in delineating these issues.

So, what do all of the definitions presented in Exhibit B.2 mean for applying the independence rules? For most practical purposes, the people who are prohibited from having

---

[7] The AICPA annually publishes a "Plain English Guide to Independence," which is designed to increase understanding of the complex independence rules. The guide can be downloaded from the AICPA website, www.aicpa.org/download/ethics/plainenglish.doc.

[8] The "bodies designated by Council" to produce them refers to the PEEC.

EXHIBIT B.1
Summary of Rule 101 Interpretations

A covered member cannot
- Have a direct financial interest in a client.
- Have a material indirect financial interest in a client.
- Be a trustee or administrator of an estate that has a direct or material indirect financial interest in a client.
- Have a joint investment with a client that is material to the covered member.
- Have a loan to or from a client, any officer of the client, or any individual owning more than 10 percent of the client (except as specifically described in interpretation 101-5).
- Participate on an attest engagement if she or he was formally employed by the client in a position to influence the audit or acted as an officer, director, promoter, underwriter, or trustee of a pension or profit-sharing trust of the client.

A covered member's immediate family cannot
- Have a direct financial interest in a client.
- Have a material indirect financial interest in a client.
- Have vested retirement benefits at a client.

A covered member's close relatives cannot
- Have a key management level position with a client.
- Have a material financial interest in a client that is known to the covered member.
- Have a financial interest in a client that allows the relative to have significant influence in a client.
- Be in a position to influence the audit.

A partner or a professional employee cannot
- Be associated with a client as a director, officer, employee, promoter, underwriter, voting trustee, or trustee of a pension or profit-sharing trust of the client.

---

financial and managerial relationships with the client are the audit engagement team, the people in the chain of command, the covered persons in the public accounting firm, their close family members, and immediate family members.

When a questionable practice or relationship arises, the PEEC evaluates whether the practice or relationship poses an unacceptable risk to a CPAs' independence.[9] The PEEC uses a three-step risk-based approach that involves (1) identifying and evaluating threats to independence, (2) determining whether safeguards eliminate or sufficiently mitigate the identified threats, and (3) determining whether independence is impaired. Identified threats to independence include the following:

1. *Familiarity threat.* CPAs having a close or longstanding relationship with a client (e.g., a spouse is in a key client position or a partner has served a prolonged tenure with the client).
2. *Adverse interest threat.* CPAs acting in opposition to clients (e.g., through litigation).
3. *Undue influence threat.* Attempts to coerce or otherwise influence the CPA member (e.g., significant gifts or threats to replace the auditor over an accounting principles disagreement).
4. *Self-review threat.* CPAs reviewing their own work.
5. *Financial self-interest threat.* CPAs having a financial relationship with a client.
6. *Management participation threat.* CPAs taking on the role of client management or otherwise performing management functions.
7. *Advocacy threat.* CPAs promoting a client's interests or position.

Next we take a closer look at threats to independence and their related interpretations that address those threats.

---

[9] In April 2006, the PEEC adopted the *Conceptual Framework for AICPA Independence Standards*, which describes the PEEC's risk-based approach to analyzing independence issues that arise.

EXHIBIT B.2 Comparison of SEC and AICPA Selected Definitions

	AICPA Definition	SEC Definition
Engagement Team	Individuals participating in the audit or attest engagement, including those who perform reviews. The audit or attest engagement team includes all employees and contractors who participate in the audit or attest engagement, irrespective of their functional classification (for example, audit, tax, or management consulting services). The audit or attest engagement team excludes specialists and individuals who perform only routine clerical functions.	All partners, principals, shareholders, and professional employees participating in an audit, review, or attestation engagement of an audit client, including those conducting reviews and all persons who consult with others on the audit engagement team during the audit, review, or attestation engagement regarding technical or industry-specific issues, transactions, or events.
Chain of Command	**Partner:** A proprietor, shareholder, equity or nonequity partner, or any individual who assumes the risks and benefits of firm ownership or who is held out by the firm to be the equivalent of an owner or partner. **Manager:** A professional employee of the firm who has either of the following responsibilities: 1. Continuing responsibility for the overall planning and supervision of engagements for specified clients. 2. Authority to determine that an engagement is complete subject to final partner approval.	All persons who (1) supervise or have direct management responsibility for the audit, (2) evaluate the performance or recommend the compensation of the audit engagement partner, or (3) provide quality control or other oversight of the audit.
Covered Person	The following are considered covered members: (1) An individual on the audit or attest engagement team; (2) An individual in a position to influence the audit or attest engagement; (3) A partner or manager who provides nonattest services to the audit or attest client beginning once he or she provides 10 hours of nonattest services to the audit or attest client within any fiscal year and ending on the later of the date (i) the firm signs the report on the financial statements for the fiscal year during which those services were provided or (ii) he or she no longer expects to provide 10 or more hours of nonattest services to the audit or attest client on a recurring basis; (4) A partner in the office in which the lead audit or attest engagement partner primarily practices in connection with the audit or attest engagement; (5) The firm, including the firm's employee benefit plans; or (6) An entity whose operating, financial, or accounting policies can be controlled (as defined by generally accepted accounting principles [GAAP] for consolidation purposes) by any of the individuals or entities described in (1) through (5) or by two or more such individuals or entities if they act together.	The following partners, principals, shareholders, and employees of an accounting firm are considered covered members: (1) An individual on the audit engagement team, (2) An individual in the chain of command, (3) Any other partner, principal, shareholder, or managerial employee of the firm who has provided 10 or more hours of nonaudit services to the audit client for the period beginning on the date such services are provided and ending on the date the accounting firm signs the report on the financial statements for the fiscal year during which those services are provided, or who expects to provide 10 or more hours of nonaudit services to the audit client on a recurring basis, and (4) Any other partner, principal, or shareholder from an office of the accounting firm in which the lead audit engagement partner primarily practices in connection with the audit. *Authors' Note:* In essence, the "covered members" are the firm's professionals closely connected to the audit engagement and the firm's owners who are located in the office where the lead engagement partner practices. However, the SEC added the category of manager-level professionals and owners who provide nonaudit (tax, consulting) services for the audit client. Therefore, almost everyone who provides services of any type for an audit client must observe the independence rules.
Close Family Member	Parent, sibling, or nondependent child.	Person's spouse, spousal equivalent, parent, dependent child, nondependent child, or sibling.
Immediate Family Member	Spouse, spousal equivalent, or dependents (whether or not related).	Person's spouse, spousal equivalent, or dependents.

Familiarity Threat (Interpretations 101-1 and 101-2)

An immediate family member may not hold a position of influence (key position) in an audit client. The close family member's definition comes into play in connection with (1) ownership or control of an audit client or (2) employment with an audit client. An example of (1) is the impairment of the public accounting firm's independence when a close family member of a covered person in the firm owns a material investment in an audit client or is in a position to exert significant influence over an audit client. An example of (2) is the impairment of the public accounting firm's independence when a close family member works in an accounting or financial reporting role at an audit client or was in such a role during any period covered by an audit for which the person in the firm is a covered person. (Neither an immediate family member nor a close family member can work in a capacity such as a member of the board of directors, chief executive officer, president, chief financial officer, chief operating officer, general counsel, chief accounting officer, controller, director of internal audit, director of financial reporting, treasurer, or vice president of marketing.)

We already understand that a covered member cannot have a financial relationship with a client. However, suppose the client is an investor in another company and the covered member has also invested in that company. Has independence been impaired? Under *Interpretation 101-8*, if the covered member's investment is a direct or materially indirect financial interest in a nonclient investee, independence is considered to be impaired. The reasoning for the basic rule is that the client investor, through its ability to influence a nonclient investee, can increase or decrease the CPA's financial stake in the investee by an amount material to the CPA, and therefore, the CPA may not appear to be independent. If the investment by the client is not material to the nonclient (i.e., there does not appear to be any influence over the investee), then independence is not impaired unless the covered member's investment allows the member to exercise significant influence over the nonclient.

Material cooperative arrangements with clients (i.e., joint participation in a business activity) also impair independence (*Interpretation 101-12*). Examples include joint ventures to develop or market products or to market a package of client and CPA services or one party working to market the products or services of the other.

Interpretation 101-5 prohibits most loans to or from audit clients: "Independence is considered impaired if a covered member has a loan from a client, officer, director, or any individual owning 10 percent or more of a client." Similarly, independence is impaired if there are unpaid fees or a note receivable arising from unpaid fees from the client outstanding for more than a year (ET 191.52). The only loans permitted are "grandfathered loans" and "other permitted loans."

Grandfathered loans are those loans that were obtained either (1) before the independence rules changed (but met the requirements of Rule 101 in effect at that time) or (2) from a financial institution before it became a client for services requiring independence. These grandfathered loans must at all times be current under all of their terms and the terms shall not be renegotiated. The specific types of loans that are grandfathered are home mortgages, loans not material to the CPA's net worth, and secured loans for which the collateral value must exceed the balance of the loan at all times.

Other permitted loans include

- Auto loans and leases collateralized by the automobile.
- Insurance policy loans based on policy surrender value.
- Loans collateralized by cash deposits at the same financial institution.
- Credit card balances and cash advances of $10,000 or less.

An important part of *Interpretation 101-1* is the recognition that ethics rules do not cover all circumstances in which the appearance of independence might be questioned. It is the member's responsibility to determine whether the personal and business relationships would lead a reasonable person aware of all the relevant facts to conclude that there is an unacceptable threat to the member's and the firm's independence.

Management Participation and Advocacy Threats (Interpretations 101-1, 101-3, and 101-4)

In addition to prohibitions against financial relationships with clients, *Interpretation 101-1* also prohibits a covered member from acting in the capacity of a manager, employee, promoter, or trustee of a client. Generally, independence is impaired if the public accounting firm even *appears* to outside observers to be working in the capacity of management or employees of the client. The client management (including its board of directors and audit committee) must understand that they are responsible for establishing and maintaining internal control and directing the internal audit function, if any. The board of directors and/or audit committee (i.e., those charged with governance) must understand their roles and responsibilities with regard to extended audit services including the establishment of guidelines for both management and the public accounting firm to follow in carrying out these responsibilities and monitoring how well the respective responsibilities have been met.

In addition to the guidance discussed in the previous paragraphs, *Interpretation 101-3* lists additional activities that would impair independence:[10]

- Performing ongoing monitoring or control activities.
- Determining which, if any, recommendations for improving internal control should be implemented.
- Reporting to the board of directors or audit committee on behalf of management or the individual responsible for the internal audit function.
- Authorizing, executing, or consummating transactions or otherwise exercising authority on behalf of the client.
- Preparing source documents on transactions.
- Having custody of assets.
- Approving or being responsible for the overall internal audit work plan including the determination of the internal audit risk and scope project priorities and frequency of performance of audit procedures.
- Performing forensic accounting services, litigation support work, or any other service in which it appears that the CPA is taking an advocacy position on the client's behalf. While performing tax compliance work would not normally impair independence, certain tax work in which an advocacy position is required does (e.g., representing a client in court to resolve a tax dispute).
- Being connected with the client as an employee or in any capacity equivalent to a member of client management (for example, being listed as an employee in client directories or other client publications, permitting himself or herself to be referred to by title or description as supervising or being in charge of the client's internal audit function, or using the client's letterhead or internal correspondence forms in communications).

Although this list is not all inclusive, a prohibited activity is any that would force the CPA to either act in the capacity of management or as an advocate for management.

As noted, independence is ordinarily impaired if a CPA serves on an organization's board of directors. However, members can be *honorary* directors of organizations such as charity hospitals, fund drives, symphony orchestra societies, and similar not-for-profit organizations so long as (1) the position is purely honorary, (2) the CPA is identified as an honorary director on letterheads and other literature, (3) the only form of participation is the use of the CPA's name, and (4) the CPA does not vote with the board or participate

---

[10] Although the following information does not prohibit auditors from providing internal audit and a variety of other services, it should be emphasized that the interpretation covers client companies that are public and private. Audits of public companies must comply with the rules of the SEC, the appropriate stock exchange, and the PCAOB. These agencies have rules that prohibit auditors from providing internal audit services to audit clients in most cases and have more stringent requirements regarding extended services.

in management functions (*Interpretation 101-4*). When all of these criteria are satisfied, the CPA/board member can perform audit and attest services because the appearances of independence will have been preserved.

Other Rule 101 interpretations include relationships with governmental entities (*Interpretation 101-10*) and alternative practice structures (*Interpretation 101-14*). The full list of interpretations, with accompanying detail, can be found on the AICPA's website (www.aicpa.org). As you can see, the detail is substantial, yet you have no choice but to understand the full details of the AICPA independence requirements. Lack of knowledge of the appropriate jurisdiction's ethical requirements is not a defense when facing severe sanctions and penalties.

SEC and PCAOB Independence Rules

Prior to the issuance of Sarbanes-Oxley in 2002, the SEC accepted most of the independence rules established by the PEEC. However, the SEC became concerned about the public accounting profession's emphasis on consulting fees and the resulting effect on public accounting firm independence. In fact, the SEC issued a comprehensive independence rule in November 2000. The rule is based upon two premises: (1) *independence in fact* is a mental state of objectivity and lack of bias and (2) *independence in appearance* depends on whether a reasonable investor, with knowledge of all relevant facts and circumstances, can conclude that the auditor is not capable of exercising objective and impartial judgment. Hence, an auditor's independence depends on auditors both having the proper mental state and passing the appearance test.

In a preface to the rule, the SEC stated four principles for determining whether a public accounting firm is independent of an audit client, factors the SEC will first consider when making independence determinations in controversial cases. Auditors are *not* independent if they have a relationship that

- Creates a mutual or conflicting interest between the public accounting firm and the audit client.
- Places the public accounting firm in the position of auditing its own work.
- Results in the public accounting firm personnel acting as management or employees of the audit client.
- Places the public accounting firm in a position of being an advocate for the audit client.

The SEC independence rules relating to financial relationships are very similar to the AICPA Code of Professional Conduct Rule 101 Interpretations explained earlier. The most significant categories addressed by the SEC rules are in the areas of financial and employment relationships, nonaudit services (e.g., taxation, consulting), and disclosure of fees.

AUDITING INSIGHT — PCAOB Chairman to Focus on Auditor Independence

In February 2011, former SEC General Counsel James R. Doty took over the lead role at the PCAOB and immediately made clear that he intends to make sure that auditors remain independent of their clients. In a recent interview, he stated that he wants to "consider the independence and integrity of the profession at a level that will assure the protection of investors and the importance that auditors have in our society, and in our economic system." He believes that auditors must see themselves as responsible to the investing public and bring "to the audit process real objectivity, resisting any pressure from management." He also reinforced the importance of the inspection program, commenting that he felt it very important to carry out the inspection process in a consistent, high-quality manner.

Source: "PCAOB Set to Expand under New Mandates," *Journal of Accountancy*, July 2011, pp. 36–39.

Nonaudit Services

The SEC is very concerned about the fact and appearance of independence when public accounting firms perform consulting services for audit clients. A major issue in the Enron case was that more than half of the fee it paid to Arthur Andersen was for consulting services. This fact exacerbated the concern that auditors would allow a client's improper financial reporting for the sake of preserving lucrative fees from other services. The SEC's concern in this regard is controversial, but the PCAOB has reinforced it. The SEC and PCAOB independence rules prohibit or place restrictions on the following types of nonaudit services provided to *audit* clients:

- Bookkeeping or other services related to the audit client's accounting records or financial statements (including maintaining or preparing the accounting records, preparing the financial statements, or preparing or originating source data underlying the financial statements *except* in emergency situations).
- Financial information systems design and implementation (including operating or supervising the client's information system, designing or implementing a hardware or software system that generates information that is significant to the client's financial statements *unless* the audit client's management takes full and complete responsibility for all design, implementation, internal control, and management decisions about the hardware and software).
- Appraisal or valuation services or fairness opinions (including any such services material to the financial statements when the auditor might audit the results of the public accounting firm's own work, *but* the public accounting firm's valuation experts may audit actuarial calculations, perform tax-oriented valuations, and perform nonfinancial valuations for audit clients).
- Actuarial services (including determination of actuarial liabilities *unless* the audit client management first uses its own actuaries and accepts responsibility for significant actuarial methods and assumptions).
- Internal audit services (including those related to the client's internal accounting controls, financial systems, or financial statements).
- Management functions (including acting temporarily or permanently as a director, officer, or employee of an audit client, or performing any decision-making, supervisory, or ongoing monitoring function for the audit client).
- Human resources (including all aspects of executive search activities, reference checking, status and compensation determination, and hiring advice).
- Broker-dealer services (including acting as a broker-dealer, promoter, or underwriter on behalf of an audit client; making investment decisions or otherwise having discretionary authority over investments; executing a transaction to buy or sell investments; or having custody of assets).
- Legal services (including any service under circumstances in which the person providing the service must be admitted to practice before the courts of a U.S. jurisdiction).
- Expert services (including providing expert opinions or other services to an audit client or legal representative of an audit client for the purpose of advocating that the audit client's interests in litigation, regulatory, or administrative investigations or proceedings; the auditor may perform internal investigations at the direction of the audit committee or its legal counsel).
- Any service performed for an audit client where the auditor is paid a contingent fee or commission.
- Tax services that are based on judicial proceedings or aggressive interpretations of tax law.
- Planning or opining on the tax consequence of a transaction.
- Tax services for key company executives.

The PCAOB's Rule 3526 (*Communication with Audit Committees Concerning Independence*) requires public accounting firms to discuss any independence issues with the audit committee (or those charged with governance) *prior* to accepting an initial engagement. This discussion must be documented (usually in the engagement administrative file workpapers).

AUDITING INSIGHT — E&Y, PeopleSoft, and a Loss of Independence

An administrative law judge recommended that **Ernst & Young** (E&Y) pay the government $1.7 million and be barred from taking new auditing clients for six months for violating SEC conflict-of-interest regulations involving a joint marketing agreement with **PeopleSoft,** a former audit client. The judge found that E&Y had "engaged in improper professional conduct because it violated applicable professional standards for auditors by conduct that was both reckless and negligent." Furthermore, the Big Four firm had displayed "an utter disdain for the commission's rules and regulations of auditor independence." Although no wrongdoing was alleged in its auditing of the software company, the joint marketing agreement violated SEC rules against having anything more than a "consumer" relationship with audit clients. The firm sold its consulting arm that created the conflict of interest.

Source: "Ernst & Young Hit Hard in PeopleSoft Case," April 16, 2004, available at www.TheStreet.com.

Disclosures about Fees

The SEC believes that investors who use financial statements and auditors' reports can be enlightened with information about auditors' fee arrangements with clients. Hence, SEC rules require that companies (not auditors) disclose the following in proxy statements delivered to their shareholders:

- Total audit fees to the public accounting firm for the annual audit and the reviews of quarterly financial information.
- Total fees to the public accounting firm for tax and other advisory work (over and above the audit fees).
- Whether the audit committee or the board of directors considered the public accounting firm's advisory work to be compatible with maintaining the auditor's independence.
- If more than 50 percent, the percentage of the audit hours performed by persons other than the principal auditor's full-time, permanent employees. (This disclosure refers to "leased employees" in an "alternative practice structure" arrangement.)

Other Effects of Sarbanes-Oxley on Auditor Independence

Sarbanes-Oxley required the SEC to modify its position on auditor independence in several ways. Perhaps the most important change in independence arises from the changing role of the audit committee. Since the inception of the principle of the independence for auditors, it has been the auditor who was responsible for evaluating and determining the independence of the individual and firm. While auditors still must be vigilant in establishing and monitoring independence policy to ensure that they are in fact independent, Sarbanes-Oxley has placed the responsibility for the determination of independence in appearance at the door of the audit committee. This is particularly evident by the fact that the audit committee bears the responsibility for determining the scope of services provided by the auditor and reviewing independence issues prior to the appointment of the auditor. The audit committee may do this on a case-by-case basis or may establish a set of policies and procedures that establish acceptable and unacceptable services.

In addition, Sarbanes-Oxley limits the engagement partners and concurring audit partners on an engagement to five-year terms. Other partners associated with the engagement are limited to seven-year terms with that client. Partners also are deemed as not independent if they receive compensation that is based on selling services to an audit client other than audits, reviews, or attestations.

In the past, it was not unusual for a member of an audit team, usually a manager or higher, to leave the public accounting firm to take a financial management position with a client. Under the rules established by Sarbanes-Oxley, a public accounting firm cannot perform an audit of a company in which an individual with financial reporting oversight responsibilities was a member of the audit engagement team for the audit period, up to the audit date.

Governmental Accountability Office (GAO) Independence Requirements

Many state agencies and local municipalities use public accounting firms to perform audits required by government charters, laws, or contractual obligations (usually as part of a grant). During these audits, the public accounting firm is required to follow all GAO standards included in the Government Auditing Standards manual (also called the *Yellow Book; see Module D*). These standards require the auditor to be independent with respect to the government entity. These standards differ from the SEC, AICPA, and Sarbanes-Oxley requirements in the following ways. Nonaudit services are allowed providing that the audit organization does not perform management functions, make management decisions, or audit their own work. However, the audit organization must employ the following safeguards:

1. Personnel who provide nonaudit services are prohibited from planning, conducting, or reviewing audit work related to the nonaudit services.
2. The audit organization may not reduce the scope or extent of work performed on the audit because a member of the firm performed the nonaudit work. The extent of the audit work may be reduced by an amount consistent with a reduction had the nonaudit been performed by another public accounting firm.
3. The audit organization must document its reasons that the nonaudit services do not affect the firm's independence.
4. The audit organization must document an understanding with the client regarding the objectives, scope, and work product for the nonaudit service.
5. The audit organization must have established policies and procedures to ensure that effects of nonaudit services on the present and future audits are considered.
6. The audit organization must communicate to the government entity any situation in which the nonaudit service would prohibit it from performing the audit.
7. When subjected to a peer review, the audit organization must identify all nonaudit services provided to the audited entity.

↳ REVIEW CHECKPOINTS

B.7 Yolanda is the executive in charge of the Santa Fe office of Best & Co, an international public accounting firm. She is responsible for the practice in all areas of audit, tax, and consulting, but she does not serve as a field audit partner or a reviewer. Javier is the partner in charge of the Besame, Inc. audit (an SEC filing). Is Best & Co independent if (a) Yolanda owns common stock of Besame or (b) her brother owns 10 shares of the common stock of Besame?

B.8 Can audit managers on the audit engagement team, who are also attorneys admitted to the state bar, assist in the defense of a lawsuit against an audit client for product liability defects?

B.9 Why do you think the SEC requires companies to disclose fees paid to independent accounting firms for audit and consulting services? What must be disclosed?

B.10 What do the SEC disclosure rules and PCAOB Rule 3526 have in common with auditors' relations with an audit client's board of directors and its audit committee?

B.11 Given what you have learned about independence, do you believe that there would be a perceived independence problem concerning members of an audit engagement team entertaining employment offers from audit clients? Why or why not?

AICPA RULES OF CONDUCT: INTEGRITY AND OBJECTIVITY, RESPONSIBILITIES TO CLIENTS, AND OTHER RESPONSIBILITIES

LEARNING OBJECTIVE B-5
With reference to AICPA rules on topics other than independence, analyze factual situations and decide whether an accountant's conduct does or does not conform to the AICPA Rules of Conduct.

Now that we have discussed independence (Rule 101), we can turn to the other AICPA rules of conduct. Ten such rules are in sections 100, 200, 300, and 500.

Rule 102: Integrity and Objectivity

Rule 102. In the performance of any professional service, a member shall maintain objectivity and integrity, shall be free of conflicts of interest, and shall not knowingly misrepresent facts or subordinate his or her judgment to others.

Rule 102 applies not only to CPAs in public practice but also to CPAs working in government and industry. (Santos, the staff accountant in the decision process illustration in Ethics Example 2, is a government and industry CPA.) The rule requires integrity and objectivity in all types of professional work—tax practice and consulting practice as well as audit practice for public accountants—and all types of accounting work performed by CPAs employed in corporations, not-for-profit organizations, governments, and individual practices. In addition to integrity and objectivity, Rule 102 emphasizes (1) being free from conflicts of interest between CPAs and others, (2) representing facts truthfully in reports and discussions, and (3) not letting other people dictate or influence the CPA's judgment and professional decisions.

Conflicts of interest cited in Rule 102 refer to the need to avoid having business interests in which the accountant's personal financial relationships or the accountant's relationships with other clients might tempt the accountant to fail to serve the best interests of a client or the public. Some examples of conflicts of interest are those in which the CPA

- Is engaged to perform litigation support services for a plaintiff in a lawsuit filed against a client.
- Recommends that a client makes an investment in a business in which the CPA has a financial interest.
- Provides tax services for several members of a family who have opposing interests.
- Performs management consulting for a client and has a financial or managerial interest in a major competitor.
- Serves on a city board of tax appeals, which hears matters involving clients.
- Refers a tax client to an insurance broker, who refers clients to the CPA under an exclusive agreement.
- Charges a contingent fee to a client for expert witness litigation support services when the fee can be affected by the opinion the CPA expresses.

The phrases "shall not knowingly misrepresent facts" (*Interpretation 102-1*) and "shall not subordinate his or her judgment to others" (*Interpretation 102-4*) emphasize conditions people ordinarily identify with the concepts of integrity and objectivity. Accountants who know about a client's fraudulent tax return, about false journal entries, about material misrepresentations in financial statements, and yet do nothing, have violated both the spirit and the letter of Rule 102.

The prohibition of misrepresentations in financial statements (*Interpretation 102-1*) applies to the management accountants who prepare companies' statements. Government and industry CPAs should not subordinate their professional judgment to superiors who try to produce materially misleading financial statements and fool their external auditors. Government and industry CPAs must be candid and not knowingly misrepresent facts or fail to disclose material facts when dealing with their employer's external auditor. Government and industry CPAs cannot have conflicts of interest in their jobs and their outside business interests that are not disclosed to their employers and approved. The importance of integrity and objectivity for government and industry CPAs cannot be overemphasized. Too often, CPAs relate the Code of Professional Conduct only to CPAs in public practice.

> **AUDITING INSIGHT** — You Can't Sacrifice Your Integrity When You Work in Industry
>
> On May 19, 2008, the Securities and Exchange Commission filed civil fraud charges against eight former executives of **AOL Time Warner Inc.** for their roles in a fraudulent scheme that caused the company to overstate its advertising revenue by more than $1 billion. Two of those accused, both CPAs, also are charged with misleading the company's external auditor about the fraudulent transactions, a clear violation of the Code of Professional Conduct's Objectivity and Integrity rules.
>
> **Source:** "SEC Statement on AOL Lawsuit," *The Wall Street Journal,* May 19, 2008.

Rule 102 has two other applications. One concerns serving as a client advocate (*Interpretation 102-6*), which occurs frequently in taxation and rate regulation practice as well as in supporting clients' positions in FASB and SEC proceedings. Client advocacy in support or advancement of client positions is acceptable only so long as the member acts with integrity, maintains objectivity, and does not subordinate judgment to others. (Accountants-as-advocates do not adopt the same attitude as defense attorneys in a courtroom.) The other application is directed specifically to your college professors: They are supposed to maintain integrity and objectivity, be free of conflicts of interest, and not knowingly misrepresent facts to students (*Interpretation 102-5*).

Rule 201: General Standards

Rule 201. A member shall comply with the following standards and with any interpretations thereof by bodies designated by Council:

A. *Professional competence.* Undertake only those professional services that the member or the member's firm can reasonably expect to be completed with professional competence.

B. *Due professional care.* Exercise due professional care in the performance of professional services.

C. *Planning and supervision.* Adequately plan and supervise the performance of professional services.

D. *Sufficient relevant data.* Obtain sufficient relevant data to afford a reasonable basis for conclusions or recommendations in relation to any professional services performed.

Rule 201 is a comprehensive statement of general standards that accountants are expected to observe in all areas of practice. This is the rule that enforces the various series of professional standards. The AICPA Council has authorized the following agencies, boards, and committees to issue standards enforceable under Rule 201:

- Public Company Accounting Oversight Board (PCAOB).
- Auditing Standards Board.
- Accounting and Review Services Committee.
- Tax Executive Committee.
- Management Consulting Services Executive Committee.

Rule 201 effectively prohibits the acceptance of any engagement that the CPA cannot competently complete. Such engagements may involve audits that require specialized industry knowledge or technical expertise the practioner does not possess. Practitioners are allowed to accept an engagement if, through education, hiring of additional staff, or contracting with specialists, the practitioners can obtain the required knowledge *prior to the conclusion* of the engagement. As a result, a practitioner can accept an engagement for which he or she does not possess knowledge as long as this knowledge can be obtained prior to the conclusion of the engagement. This rule covers all areas of public accounting practice except personal financial planning and business valuation. Of course, a CPA may have to do some research to learn more about a unique problem or technique and may need to engage a colleague as a consultant.

Rule 202: Compliance with Standards

Rule 202. A member who performs auditing, review, compilation, management consulting, tax, or other professional services shall comply with standards promulgated by bodies designated by Council.

Rule 202 requires adherence to duly promulgated technical standards in all areas of professional service. These areas include the ones cited in the rule: auditing, review and compilation (unaudited financial statements), consulting, tax, or "other" professional services. The "bodies designated by Council" are the Auditing Standards Board, the Accounting and Review Services Committee, the Tax Executive Committee, and the Consulting Services Executive Committee. The practical effect of Rule 202 is to make noncompliance with all technical standards (in addition to the Rule 201 general standards) subject to disciplinary proceedings. Therefore, failure to follow auditing standards, accounting and review standards, tax standards, and consulting standards is a violation of Rule 202.

Rule 203: Accounting Principles

Rule 203. A member shall not (1) express an opinion or state affirmatively that the financial statements or other financial data of any entity are presented in conformity with generally accepted accounting principles or (2) state that he or she is not aware of any material modifications that should be made to such statements or data in order for them to be in conformity with generally accepted accounting principles, if such statements or data contain any departure from an accounting principle promulgated by bodies designated by Council to establish such principles that has a material effect on the statements or data taken as a whole. If, however, the statements or data contain such a departure and the member can demonstrate that due to unusual circumstances the financial statements or data would otherwise have been misleading, the member can comply with the rule by describing the departure, its approximate effects, if practicable, and the reasons why compliance with the principle would result in a misleading statement.

The AICPA Council has designated three rule-making bodies to pronounce accounting principles under Rule 203. The Financial Accounting Standards Board (FASB) and its predecessors are designated to pronounce standards in general. Therefore, Rule 203 requires adherence to Accounting Research Bulletins of the Committee on Accounting Procedure (issued before 1959), Opinions of the Accounting Principles Board (1959–1973), and statements and interpretations of financial accounting standards adopted by the Financial Accounting Standards Board (1973 to present). The Council also has designated the Governmental Accounting Standards Board (GASB) to pronounce accounting standards for state and local government entities and the Federal Accounting Standards Advisory Board (FASAB) with respect to statements of federal accounting standards.

You may wonder about the two parts at the beginning of Rule 203: "(1) express an opinion or state affirmatively . . . or (2) state that he or she is not aware of any material modifications. . . ." These two parts are intended to cover two types of attestation reports regarding the conformity of financial statements or other information with an appropriate financial reporting framework. The first part refers to *opinions* on financial statement and other information, for example, the standard unqualified auditors' report on audited financial statements. The second part refers to reports in which *negative assurance* is permitted, for example, the review report on unaudited financial statements.

Rule 203 requires adherence to official pronouncements unless such adherence would be misleading. The consequences of misleading statements to outside decision makers would be financial harm, so presumably the greater good would be realized by explaining a departure and thereby "breaking the rule of officially promulgated accounting principles." Such an instance occurs in very rare situations and the burden of proving that following pronouncements would be misleading is the responsibility of the auditor.

Members in government and industry also can be subject to Rule 203. These accountants produce and certify financial statements and sign written management representation letters for their external auditors. They also present financial statements to regulatory authorities and creditors. Government and industry accountants generally "report" that the company's financial statements conform to GAAP and this report is taken as an expression of opinion (or negative assurance) of the type governed by Rule 203. The result is that accountants who present financial statements containing any undisclosed departures from official pronouncements face disciplinary action for violating the rule.

Rule 301: Confidential Client Information

> **Rule 301.** A member in public practice shall not disclose any confidential information without the specific consent of the client.

Confidential information is any information that is not available to the public (or in the public domain). Such information should not be disclosed to outside parties unless demanded by a court or an administrative body having subpoena or summons power. *Privileged information* is information that cannot even be demanded by a court. Common-law privilege exists for husband–wife and attorney–client relationships. While physician–patient and priest–penitent relationships have obtained the privilege through state statutes, no accountant–client privilege exists under federal law and no state-created privilege has been recognized in federal courts. In all recognized privilege relationships, the professional person is obligated to observe the privilege, which can be waived only by the client, patient, or penitent. (These persons are said to be the *holders of the privilege*.)

The rules of privileged and confidential communication are based on the belief that they facilitate a free flow of information between parties to the relationship. The nature of accounting services makes it necessary for the accountant to have access to information about salaries, products, contracts, merger or divestment plans, tax matters, and other information required for the best possible professional work. Managers would be less likely to reveal such information if they could not trust the accountant to keep it confidential. If accountants were to reveal such information, the resulting reduction of the information flow might be undesirable, so no accountant should break the confidentiality rule without a good reason.

AUDITING INSIGHT — Spies, Lies, and Client Confidentiality

What would you do if a government intelligence agent approached you to assist him in a "top secret" assignment involving national security? Guy Enright, an accountant with **KPMG**'s Financial Advisory Services Ltd. in Bermuda, said "yes" to Nick Hamilton, a British intelligence officer, and agreed to deposit confidential audit documents in plastic containers at "dead drop" sites located throughout Bermuda. Unfortunately for Enright, KPMG, and their client, **IPOC International Growth Fund Ltd.** (IPOC), "Nick Hamilton" was in fact Nick Day, a co-founder of **Diligence Inc.**, a Washington-based private intelligence firm that was gathering information for one of IPOC's business competitors.

The setup was quite elaborate. "Hamilton" required Enright to undergo a detailed background check, even producing an official-looking questionnaire with a British government seal at the top, before he could participate on "Project Yucca." The undercover mission came to an abrupt end when someone (still unknown) dropped off a package of Diligence business records and e-mails involving "Project Yucca" at KPMG's Montvale office. After KPMG sued, Diligence ended up paying $1.7 million.

Source: "Spies, Lies, and KPMG," *Business Week,* February 26, 2007.

Difficult problems arise over auditors' obligations to "blow the whistle" about clients' shady or illegal practices. Auditing standards deal with the problem this way: If a client refuses to accept an auditors' report that has been modified because of the inability to obtain sufficient appropriate evidence about a suspected illegal act, failure to account for or disclose properly a material amount connected with an illegal act, or inability to estimate amounts involved in an illegal act, the public accounting firm should withdraw from the engagement and give the reasons in writing to the board of directors. In such an extreme case, the withdrawal amounts to whistle-blowing, but the action results from the client's decision not to disclose the information. For all practical purposes, information is not considered confidential if its disclosure is necessary to prevent financial statements from being misleading.

Auditors are not, in general, legally *obligated* to blow the whistle on clients. However, circumstances in which auditors are legally *justified* in making disclosures to a regulatory agency or a third party may exist. Such circumstances include (1) when a client has intentionally and without authorization associated or involved a CPA in its misleading conduct (e.g., used the CPA's name on financial statements), (2) when a client has distributed misleading draft financial statements prepared by a CPA for internal use only, or (3) when a client prepares and distributes in an annual report or prospectus misleading information for which the CPA has not assumed any responsibility.[11] In addition, the Private Securities Litigation Reform Act of 1995 imposed another reporting requirement in connection with clients' illegal acts (see Module C).

Rule 301 possibly provides accountants the most difficulties and may be the most violated procedure. First, in its strictest interpretation, the principle of confidentiality applies to the communication of information to anyone who is not involved in the audit except as noted by the rule. Over lunch or after hours, however, you might find auditors discussing the day's work with other members of the firm or company. Second, CPAs should not view Rule 301 on confidential information as an excuse for inaction when action may be appropriate to right a wrongful act committed or about to be committed by a client. In some cases, auditors' inaction may be viewed as part of a conspiracy or willingness to be an accessory to a wrong. Such situations are dangerous and potentially damaging. A useful initial course of action is to consult an attorney about possible legal pitfalls of both whistle-blowing and silence. In both situations, the auditor's personal standard of ethics will determine the individual's course of action.

Accountants can permit other accountants to review confidential audit documentation and other information about clients in connection with arrangements to sell or merge an accounting practice. The AICPA advises accountants to have an agreement among themselves that extends the confidentiality safeguard to the prospective purchasing accountant as it existed with the original accountant.

CPAs also may disclose confidential information without the client's permission to remain in compliance with applicable laws (e.g., responding to a subpoena), as part of an ethics investigation (*of a CPA*), or as part of a peer review or PCAOB investigation of *public accounting firm* practices. The exception related to ethics violations applies only to investigative or disciplinary bodies under the AICPA's jurisdiction, namely the AICPA Professional Ethics Division, the ethics enforcement committees in the various state societies of CPAs, and state boards of accountancy. Thus, the ethics and law enforcement agencies in the United States (SEC, Internal Revenue Service [IRS], and other agencies such as the U.S. Department of Justice, Federal Trade Commission [FTC], Equal Employment Opportunity Commission, and local police and district attorneys) are not within the exception. Voluntary disclosure to these agencies is not explicitly permitted under Rule 301 (i.e., subpoenas are required).

AUDITING INSIGHT — Auditor Insider Trading? Say It Ain't So!

The SEC found that a former **PricewaterhouseCoopers** auditor profited from trading on insider information that he obtained from a co-worker who was involved in the firm's mergers and acquisitions practice. Both have resigned from the Big 4 firm and, while not admitting guilt, will pay fines of between $20,000 and $50,000.

In an unrelated case, an Ernst & Young partner was convicted of six counts of securities fraud related to insider trading arising from a relationship that began on an extramarital dating website. The principal witness against the partner was a woman who had befriended him online, and through a guessing game they played from their respective offices, guessed the impending mergers he was working on. She then traded 18 times on the insider information, netting approximately $400,000 on the transactions. Her trading was funded by another man she met on the same website. Her suspicious trading just before the mergers were announced caused her name to repeatedly appear on SEC watch lists. When confronted, she cut a deal, pleading guilty to 15 counts of securities fraud and agreeing to testify against the E&Y partner who apparently was unaware of the insider trading scheme and did not make a cent off the trades but now faces up to four years in prison.

Sources: "Insider Affair: An SEC Trial of the Heart," *The Wall Street Journal*, July 28, 2009, p. C1; "Pricewaterhouse Pair Settle SEC Trading Charges," *The Wall Street Journal*, January 16, 2008, p. C8.

---

[11] C. Chazen, R. L. Miller, and K. I. Solomon, "When the Rules Say: 'See Your Lawyer,'" *Journal of Accountancy*, January 1981.

Rule 302: Contingent Fees

Rule 302. A member in public practice shall not:

(1) Perform for a contingent fee any professional services for, or receive such a fee from, a client for whom the member or the member's firm performs:

   (a) an audit or review of a financial statement; or

   (b) a compilation of a financial statement when the member expects, or reasonably might expect, that a third party will use the financial statement and the member's compilation report does not disclose a lack of independence; or

   (c) an examination of prospective financial information; or

(2) Prepare an original or amended tax return or claim for a tax refund for a contingent fee for any client.

Suppose you are a shareholder in New Medical Corporation. You have some concerns about the company's revenue practices, but the fact that New Medical Corporation received an unqualified audit opinion reassures you. Now let's assume that you discover that New Medical Corporation's contract with its auditor paid the auditor more for an unqualified opinion than a qualified opinion. How might that affect the value you placed on the auditor's report?

A **contingent fee** is a fee established for the performance of any service in an arrangement in which no fee will be charged unless a specific finding or result is attained or the fee otherwise depends on the result of the service. (Fees are not contingent if they are fixed by a court or other public authority or, in tax matters, determined as a result of the findings of judicial proceedings or the findings of government agencies; nor are fees contingent when they are based on the complexity or time required for the work.) Under Rule 302, CPAs can charge contingent fees for work such as representing a client in an IRS tax audit and certain other tax matters, achieving goals in a consulting service engagement, or helping a person obtain a bank loan in a financial planning engagement. However, the PCAOB has proposed (but not issued at the date of publication) an independence rule that would prohibit all contingent fees for audit clients of registered public accounting firms. Rule 302 permits CPAs to receive contingent fees *except* from clients for whom the CPAs perform attest services when users of financial information may be relying on the CPAs' work. The prohibitions in item 1(a), 1(b), and 1(c) all refer to attest engagements in which independence is required. Acceptance of contingent fee arrangements during the period in which the member or the member's firm is engaged to perform any of these attestations or during the period covered by any historical financial statements involved in any of these engagements is considered an impairment of independence.

Rule 302 also prohibits contingent fees in connection with the everyday tax practice of preparing original or amended tax returns. This prohibition arose from an interesting conflict of government agencies. The Federal Trade Commission (FTC) wanted to see contingent fees permitted, but the IRS objected on the grounds that such fees might induce accountants and clients to "play the audit lottery"—understate tax improperly in the hope of escaping audit. The IRS asserted that if the AICPA permitted such contingent fees, the IRS would make its own rules prohibiting them. The FTC agreed that the AICPA rule could contain this prohibition.

Rule 501: Acts Discreditable

Rule 501. A member shall not commit an act discreditable to the profession.

Rule 501 may be called the *moral clause* of the code, but it is only occasionally the basis for disciplinary action. Penalties normally are invoked automatically under the AICPA bylaws, which provide for expulsion of members found by a court to have committed any fraud, filed false tax returns, been convicted of any criminal offense, or found by the AICPA Trial Board to have been guilty of an act discreditable to the profession.

AICPA interpretations consider discreditable acts to include these:

- Withholding a client's books and records and important documentation when the client has requested their return.
- Being found guilty by a court or administrative agency as having violated employment antidiscrimination laws, including ones related to sexual and other forms of harassment.
- Failing to follow government audit standards and guides in governmental audits when the client or the government agency expects such standards to be followed.
- Failure to follow the requirements of governmental bodies, commissions, or other regulatory bodies including the PCAOB.
- Soliciting or disclosing CPA Examination questions and answers from the closed CPA Examination.
- Failing to file tax returns or remit payroll and other taxes collected for others (e.g., employee taxes withheld).
- Making, or permitting others to make, false and misleading entries in records and financial statements.

This last item is specifically applicable to members in government and industry as well as members in public practice. Any management accountant who participates in the production of false and misleading financial statements commits a discreditable act.

AUDITING INSIGHT — Discreditable Act?

The Enforcement Committee found that Respondent drew a gun from his desk drawer during a dispute with a client in his office in contravention of Section 501.41 [discreditable acts prohibition] of the [Texas] Rules of Professional Conduct. Respondent agreed to accept a private reprimand to be printed . . . in the Texas State Board Report.

Source: Texas State Board of Accountancy Report.

Rule 502: Advertising and Other Forms of Solicitation

Rule 502. A member in public practice shall not seek to obtain clients by advertising or other forms of solicitation in a manner that is false, misleading, or deceptive. Solicitation by the use of coercion, overreaching, or harassing conduct is prohibited.

Advertising consists of messages designed to attract business that are broadcast widely to an undifferentiated audience (e.g., print, radio, television, billboards). Rule 502 permits advertising with only a few limitations. The current rule applies only to CPAs practicing public accounting and relates to their efforts to obtain clients. The guidelines basically prohibit false, misleading, and deceptive messages:

- Advertising may not create false or unjustified expectations of favorable results.
- Advertising may not imply the ability to influence any court, tribunal, regulatory agency, or similar body or official.
- Advertising may not contain a fee estimate when the CPA knows it is likely to be substantially increased unless the client is notified.
- Advertising may not contain any other representation likely to cause a reasonable person to misunderstand or be deceived.

Most CPAs carry out only modest advertising efforts, and many do no advertising at all. Public practice is generally marked by decorum and a sense of good taste. However, there are exceptions, and they tend to get much negative attention from other CPAs and the public in general. The danger in bad advertising lies in creating the image of a professional huckster, which may backfire on efforts to build a practice.

Solicitation generally refers to direct contact (e.g., in person, mail, telephone) with a specific potential client. In regard to solicitation, Rule 502 basically prohibits extreme bad behavior (coercion, overreaching, or harassing conduct). Many CPAs abhor solicitation and many state boards of accountancy try to prohibit direct, uninvited approaches to prospective clients, especially when the client already has a CPA. Nevertheless, the U.S. Supreme Court has struck down state solicitation prohibitions, declaring them to be an infringement of personal and business rights to free speech and due process.

AUDITING INSIGHT | Felicity and Solicitations

CPA Fane moved to Florida and conducted face-to-face meetings to obtain clients. The Florida Board of Accountancy brought suit to enforce its antisolicitation rule but lost in a Supreme Court decision. As a result some state boards try to discourage solicitation with restrictive rules they hope will not run afoul of the Supreme Court decision. Other state boards are trying to put antisolicitation rules into their state laws when they think they will be shielded from the U.S. Supreme Court. Currently, solicitation is legal, but be aware that your local state board may have rules or laws prohibiting it.

Source: *Edenfield v. Fane*, 507 U.S. 761 (1993).

CPAs sometimes hire marketing firms to obtain clients. In years past, this arrangement was designed to avoid direct involvement in advertising and solicitation efforts that might violate Rule 502. The AICPA permits such arrangements but warns that all such "practice development" activity is subject to Rule 502 because members cannot do through others things they are prohibited from doing themselves.

Rule 503: Commissions and Referral Fees

A. Prohibited Commissions

A member in public practice shall not recommend or refer to a client any product or service for a commission, or recommend or refer any product or service to be supplied by a client for a commission, or receive a commission, when the member or the member's firm also performs for that client:

(a) an audit or review of a financial statement; or

(b) a compilation of a financial statement when the member expects, or reasonably might expect, that a third party will use the financial statement and the member's compilation report does not disclose a lack of independence; or

(c) an examination of prospective financial information.

This prohibition applies during the period in which the member is engaged to perform any of the services listed above and the period covered by any historical financial statements involved in such listed services.

B. Disclosure of Permitted Commission

A member in public practice who is not prohibited by this rule from performing services for, or receiving a commission from, and who is paid or expects to be paid a commission, shall disclose that fact to any person or entity to whom the member recommends or refers a product or service to which the commission relates.

C. Referral Fees

Any member who accepts a referral fee for recommending or referring any service of a CPA to any person or entity or who pays a referral fee to obtain a client shall disclose such acceptance or payment to the client. A **commission** is generally defined as a percentage-based fee charged for professional services in connection with executing a transaction or performing some other business activity. Examples are insurance sales commissions, real estate sales commissions, and securities sales commissions. A CPA can earn commissions except in connection with any client for whom the CPA performs attestation services.

Part A of Rule 503 treats commissions as an impairment of independence just as Rule 302 treats contingent fees. Recall that *contingent fees* are based on attaining a specific finding or result and are prohibited for attestation clients. When involved in an attest engagement with a client, the CPA cannot receive a commission from anyone for (1) referring a product or service to the client or (2) referring to someone else a product or service supplied by the client. It does not matter which party actually pays the commission.

Part B of Rule 503 *permits commissions* provided that the engagement *does not involve attestation* of the types cited in Part A of the rule. This permission is tempered by the requirement that the CPA must disclose to clients an arrangement to receive a commission.

Most of the commission fee activity takes place in connection with personal financial planning services. CPAs often recommend insurance and investments to individuals and families. Some critics point out that clients cannot always trust commission agents (e.g., insurance salespersons, securities brokers) to have clients' best interests in mind when the agents' own compensation depends on clients' buying the product that produces commissions.

Part C of Rule 503 deals with **referral fees**, which are fees (1) a CPA receives for recommending another CPA's services and (2) a CPA pays to obtain a client. Such fees may or may not be based on a percentage of the amount of any transaction. Referral involves the practice of sending business to another CPA and paying other CPAs or outside agencies for drumming up business. Some CPAs have hired services that solicit clients on their behalf, paying a fixed or percentage fee. Many CPAs frown on these arrangements, but they are permitted. However, CPAs must disclose such fees to clients.

Rule 505: Form of Organization and Name

Rule 505. A member may practice public accounting only in a form of organization permitted by law or regulation whose characteristics conform to resolutions of Council. A member shall not practice public accounting under a firm name that is misleading. Names of one or more past owners may be included in the firm name of a successor organization. A firm may not designate itself as "Member of the American Institute of Certified Public Accountants" unless all of its CPA owners are members of the Institute.

Rule 505 allows CPAs to practice public accounting in any form of organization permitted by a state board of accountancy and authorized by law. Organization forms include sole proprietorship, partnership, limited partnership, limited liability partnership (LLP), professional corporation (PC), limited liability corporation (LLC), and ordinary corporation (Inc.). You may have noticed that the large international accounting firms now place LLP after their firm names. Many small accounting firms include PC in their names.

CPAs in public practice cannot use misleading firm names. For example, suppose CPAs Stone and Thompson, who are not in partnership, agree to share expenses for office support, advertising, and continuing education. They cannot put up a sign that states "Stone & Thompson CPAs" because this name suggests a partnership where there is none.

A member who practices public accounting also can participate in the operation of another business organization (e.g., a consulting or tax preparation firm) that offers professional services of the types offered by public accounting firms. If this business is permitted to practice public accounting under state law, the member also is considered to be in the practice of public accounting in it and must observe all rules of conduct. CPAs who work in alternative practice structures occupy an odd position. They can prepare compiled (unaudited) financial statements, which is considered a form of public accounting practice. In such a case, CPA employees of the alternative practice structure (e.g., "PublicCo") must take final responsibility for the accountants' compilation report and must sign it with their own personal names (not the name of PublicCo).

The last paragraph of Rule 505 permits a mixed accounting organization consisting of CPA and non-CPA owners to designate itself "Members of the AICPA" if all of the CPA owners are actually AICPA members. However, the AICPA Council limits this privilege of organizational form by expressing certain requirements for ownership and control, especially regarding non-CPAs who have ownership interests in an organization that practices public accounting. (See the Council Resolution provisions in the feature "Council Resolution: Form of Organization and Name." The purpose of the Council Resolution is to conform the operations of an accounting organization as closely as possible to the traditional accounting firm and to ensure control of professional services in the hands of CPAs.)

Council Resolution: Form of Organization and Name

(EXCERPTS)
The characteristics of an accounting organization under Rule 505 are as follows:

- A majority (50 percent +) ownership and voting rights must belong to CPAs.
- Non-CPA owners must be active in the firm, not passive investors.
- A CPA must have ultimate responsibility for the firm's services.
- Non-CPA owners can use titles such as "principal, owner, officer, member, and shareholder" but cannot hold out to be a CPA.
- Non-CPA owners must abide by the AICPA Code of Professional Conduct.
- Non-CPA owners must hold a bachelor's degree, and after the year 2010, must have 150 semester hours of college education.
- Non-CPA owners must complete the same continuing education requirements as CPAs who are members of the AICPA.
- Non-CPA owners are not eligible to be members of the AICPA.

The International Ethics Standards Board for Accountants (IESBA) Code

The IESBA Code must be followed by auditors whenever an audit engagement is completed for a multinational client. As a result, the importance of the IESBA code has increased dramatically in recent years. Although there are some differences between the IESBA code and the AICPA Code of Ethics, the codes are quite similar. For example, each code is highly focused on the possible threats to auditor independence, and each code provides many safeguards to mitigate these threats. However, there are differences in the way that these threats and safeguards are described.[12] Given the increased importance of the international standards, the AICPA is engaged in a project to align the two codes. The following Auditing Insight provides more detail on this process.

AUDITING INSIGHT | Codification and International Convergence Are on the Way

The PEEC has recently undertaken a project to recodify the AICPA's ethics standards. The code will be restructured into topical areas and certain provisions will be revised to reflect more of a conceptual framework approach. Importantly, the new recodified standards will be promulgated to be in convergence with the IESBA ethical standards. The new structure will include a convenient numbering system and a two-part organization. Part 1 will apply to members practicing public accounting; part 2 will apply to members working in other areas of the profession. The project is expected to be completed by the end of 2012.

Source: C. Allen, "Improving the Code of Professional Conduct," *Journal of Accountancy*, June 2011, pp. 38–43.

---

[12] For a summary of the specific differences between the IESBA and the AICPA codes, please consult C. Allen, "Comparing the Ethics Codes: AICPA and IFAC," *Journal of Accountancy*, October 2010, pp. 24–32.

⌕ REVIEW CHECKPOINTS

B.12 What ethical responsibilities do members of the AICPA have for acts of nonmembers who are under their supervision (e.g., recent college graduates who are not yet CPAs)?

B.13 What rules of conduct apply specifically to members in government and industry?

B.14 What provisions of the AICPA Council Resolution on form of organization place control of accounting services in the hands of CPAs?

B.15 What is the primary difference between commissions and referrals?

▽ CONSEQUENCES TO VIOLATING THE CODE OF PROFESSIONAL CONDUCT

LEARNING OBJECTIVE B-6
Explain the types of penalties that can be imposed on accountants.

Public accounting firms and responsible professional accountants understand the importance of ethics to the profession and seek to ensure that the organization and all employees are acting in an ethical manner. Unethical behavior by an auditor can have financial implications (e.g., fines, lawsuits) and reputation implications that may be difficult to remedy. Quality control practices and disciplinary proceedings provide the mechanisms of *self-regulation*. **Self-regulation** refers to the quality control reviews and disciplinary actions conducted by fellow CPAs—professional peers.

Self-Regulatory Discipline

Individual persons (not accounting firms) are subject to the rules of conduct of state CPA societies and the AICPA only if they choose to join these organizations. The AICPA and most of the state societies have entered into a Joint Ethics Enforcement Program through which the AICPA can refer complaints against CPAs to state societies or state societies can refer them to the AICPA. Both organizations have ethics committees to hear complaints. They can (1) acquit an accused CPA, (2) find the CPA in violation of rules and issue a letter of required corrective action, or (3) refer serious cases to an AICPA trial board. The letter of required corrective action ordinarily admonishes the CPA and requires specific continuing education courses to bring the CPA up to date in technical areas.

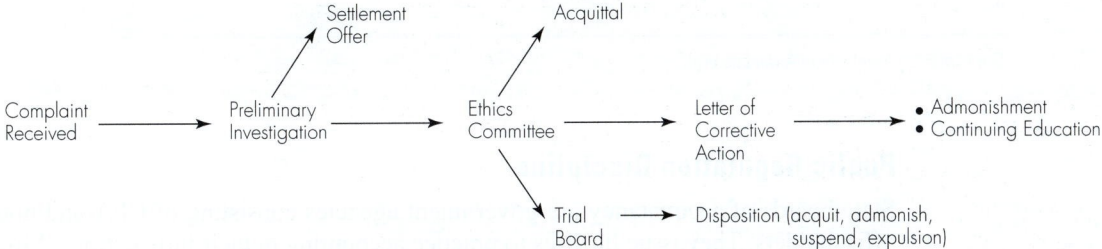

The trial board panel has the power to (1) acquit the CPA, (2) admonish the CPA, (3) suspend the CPA's membership in the state society and the AICPA for up to two years, or (4) expel the CPA from the state society and the AICPA. The AICPA bylaws (not the Code of Professional Conduct) provide for automatic expulsion of CPAs judged to have committed a felony, failed to file their tax returns, or aided in the preparation of a false and fraudulent income tax return. The trial board panels are required to publish the names of the CPAs disciplined in their proceedings. Published details about these disciplinary actions are on the AICPA website at www.aicpa.org/pubs/cpaltr/index.htm.

The AICPA also has a *settlement offer* procedure designed to impose penalties for rule violations. When the preliminary investigation of a complaint against a CPA shows clear evidence of a violation, the AICPA can (1) proceed with the full investigation and documentation leading to a trial board hearing or (2) offer the CPA the opportunity to plead and accept the penalties proposed by the Professional Ethics Executive Committee. The penalties are typically the same ones that would result from a trial board panel hearing—resignation, continuing professional education (CPE) requirement, and suspension or termination of membership with publication—but the lengthy process of investigation, documentation, and formal hearing is not carried out. When a CPA agrees, the penalty is presented to the Joint Trial Board for endorsement. The settlement offer procedure is a means of closing cases without the time-consuming investigation and trial board hearing that burdens both the CPA and the AICPA Professional Ethics Division.

The expulsion penalty, while severe, does not prevent a CPA from continuing to practice accounting. Membership in the AICPA and state societies, while beneficial, is not required. However, a CPA must have a valid state license in order to practice. State boards of accountancy are the agencies that can suspend or revoke the license to practice.

AUDITING INSIGHT — The AICPA Joint Trial Board in Action

The following is the AICPA's report on cases investigated and their resolutions for 2010 and 2009 cases:

	2010	2009
Total cases at beginning of period (including 118 and 134, respectively, deferred due to pending litigation)	844	1,065
Cases opened during period	370	226
Cases completed during period	(430)	(447)
Total cases at end of period (including 134 and 158, respectively, deferred due to pending litigation)	784	844
Summary of Disposition of Completed Cases		
Expelled or suspended	93	85
Admonished	6	11
Corrective action required	134	153
No violation/dismissed	82	93
No further action	67	62
Subsequent monitoring completed satisfactorily	33	30
Other	15	13
	430	447

Source: AICPA website (www.aicpa.org).

Public Regulation Discipline

State boards of accountancy are government agencies consisting of CPA and non-CPA officeholders. They issue licenses to practice accounting in their jurisdictions. Most state laws require a license to use the designation CPA or certified public accountant and limit the attest (audit) function to license holders only.

State boards have rules of conduct and trial board panels. They can admonish a license holder; perhaps more importantly, they can suspend or revoke the license to practice. Suspension and revocation are severe penalties because a person no longer can use the CPA title and cannot sign auditors' reports. When candidates have successfully passed the CPA examination and are ready to become CPAs, some state boards administer an ethics examination or require taking an ethics course intended to familiarize new CPAs with the state rules.

The SEC and the PCAOB also conduct public disciplinary actions. Their authority comes from their rules of practice, of which Rule 102(e) provides that the SEC can deny, temporarily or permanently, the privilege of practice before the SEC to any person found to have engaged in unethical or improper professional conduct. When conducting a "Rule 102(e) proceeding," the SEC acts in a quasi-judicial role as an administrative agency.

AUDITING INSIGHT — Be Audit You Can Be

The PCAOB instituted disciplinary proceedings against **Deloitte & Touche LLP** and a former Deloitte audit patner, James L. Fazio, CPA, for violations of the board's interim auditing standards in connection with the firm's 2003 audit for **Ligand Pharmaceuticals Incorporated**. Without admitting or denying the board's findings, Deloitte consented to an order imposing a $1 million civil penalty. In addition to the monetary fine, as described in the order, Deloitte has implemented changes to its system of quality control for identifying and addressing potential audit quality concerns regarding the performance and deployment of its audit partners. The order requires Deloitte to undertake certain documentation practices relating to these additional quality control policies and procedures. The firm also was censured. The PCAOB also sanctioned accountants with **BDO Seidman and Geisler & Oppenheimer** for failing to review the audit work of a junior member of the firm and then trying to cover up by backdating documents (including backdating initials and signatures) and independence violations, respectively.

Sources: "PCAOB Sanctions Three Auditors," *CFO.com,* December 18, 2007; "Ex-BDO Seidman Auditors Disciplined by PCAOB" *WebCPA,* December 18, 2007.

The SEC penalty bars an accountant from signing any documents filed by an SEC registered company. The penalty effectively stops the accountant's SEC practice. In a few severe cases, Rule 102(e) proceedings have resulted in settlements barring not only the individual accountant but also her or his accounting firm or certain of its practice offices from accepting new SEC clients for a period of time. The PCAOB has the authority to permanently revoke a public accounting firm's registration status for auditing public entities. In addition, the PCAOB can permanently bar an auditor from being associated with a registered public accounting firm.

AUDITING INSIGHT — What Do Other Countries Do?

Different countries have different penalties for accountants caught not honoring the public trust. In China, the *death sentences* for Zhou Limin, the former head of the China Construction Bank, and Liu Yibing, an accountant, were upheld by China's State Supreme Court. The pair was found guilty of stealing more than $60 million by offering fake accounts with high interest rates.

Source: "Accountant Gets Death Penalty," *CFO.com,* December 14, 2006.

⤷ REVIEW CHECKPOINTS

B.16 What penalties can be imposed by the AICPA and the state societies on CPAs in their "self-regulation" of ethics code violators?

B.17 What penalties can the SEC and PCAOB impose on CPAs who violate rules of conduct?

Summary

This module begins with philosophers' considerations of moral philosophy, explains the AICPA Code of Professional Conduct as well as the SEC and PCAOB rules related to auditors' independence, provides an overview of the IESBA code of conduct, and ends with a review of enforcement actions against those CPAs who choose not to follow the rules. It is important to remember that accounting is the only business discipline that is considered a profession as are doctors and lawyers. As a result, professional ethics for accountants is not simply a matter covered by a few rules in a formal code of professional conduct. Concepts of proper professional conduct permeate all areas of practice. Ethics and accompanying sanctions for ethical failures provide the foundation for public accountants' value in the marketplace.

The spirit of the AICPA Code of Professional Conduct is that, while independence is required for audit and attest services, integrity and objectivity are required in connection with all professional services. In this context, integrity and objectivity are the larger concepts and "independence" is a special condition largely defined by the matters of appearance specified in the interpretations of Rule 101. The ethics rules may appear to be restrictive, but they are intended to benefit the public the value of the profession and to allow for sanctions to those CPAs choosing not to comply with the rules.

Specific rules in the AICPA Rules of Conduct may not necessarily be classified under one of the ethics principles. Decisions based on a rule may involve imperative, utilitarian, or generalization considerations, or elements of all three. The rules have the form of imperatives because that is the nature of a code. However, elements of utilitarianism and generalization seem to be apparent in the underlying rationale for most of the rules. If this perception is accurate, auditors may use these two principles in difficult decision problems for which adherence to a rule could produce an undesirable result. Your knowledge of philosophical principles in ethics—the imperative, utilitarian, and generalization—will help you make decisions about the AICPA, SEC, and PCAOB rules. This structured approach to thoughtful decisions is important not only when you are employed in public accounting but also when you work in government, industry, and education.

Public accountants must be careful in all areas of practice. As an accountant, you must not lose sight of the nonaccountants' perspective. No matter how complex or technical a decision may be, a simplified view of it always tends to cut away the details of special technical issues to get directly to the heart of the matter. A sense of professionalism coupled with sensitivity to the effect of decisions on other people is invaluable in the practice of accounting and auditing. Remember that when you face an ethical dilemma, you are not alone. The AICPA, other professional organizations, and most accounting firms have anonymous hotlines for you to ask questions, and you always have your colleagues, friends, and family members to talk to.

Key Terms

act-utilitarianism (in moral philosophy): The emphasis on an individual act as it is affected by the specific circumstances of a situation, 593

categorical imperative (in moral philosophy): Kant's specification of an unconditional obligation to act as one thinks others should act regardless of circumstances, 592

commission: A percentage fee charged for professional services in connection with executing a transaction or performing some other business activity, 614

contingent fee: A type of compensation established for the performance of any service in an arrangement in which no amount will be charged unless a specific finding or result is attained or the fee otherwise depends on the result, 612

covered member: Broadly defined, any individual who might be in a position to compromise the integrity of an audit. In the AICPA Code of Conduct, the term is defined as any individual, among others, who is: (1) on the audit engagement team, (2) in a position to influence the audit engagement, (3) a partner or manager of a nonaudit client service team, or (4) a partner from the local office of the public accounting firm, 598

generalization argument (in moral philosophy): A judicious combination of the imperative and utilitarian principles; to act as one thinks others should act in a similar circumstance, 593

independence: A mental attitude and the appearance that the auditor is not influenced by others in judgments and decisions, 598

referral fee: The (1) compensation that a CPA receives for recommending another CPA's services and (2) that a CPA pays to obtain a client; may or may not be based on a percentage of the amount of any transaction, 615

rule-utilitarianism (in moral philosophy): The emphasis on the centrality of rules for ethical behavior while still maintaining the criterion of the greatest universal good, 593

self-regulation: The quality control reviews and disciplinary actions conducted by fellow CPAs—professional peers, 617

Multiple-Choice Questions for Practice and Review

All applicable Exercises and Problems are available with McGraw-Hill's *Connect® Accounting*

LO B-4
B.18 Auditors are interested in having independence in appearance because
   a. They want to impress the public with their independence in fact.
   b. They want the public at large to have confidence in the profession.
   c. They need to comply with the fundamental principles of GAAS.
   d. Audits should be planned and properly supervised.

LO B-4
B.19 Ensuring that the auditor is independent in appearance is the responsibility of
   a. The public accounting firm.
   b. Senior management.
   c. The audit committee.
   d. The PCAOB.

LO B-2
B.20 If a public accounting firm says it always follows the rule that requires adherence to FASB pronouncements in order to give a standard unqualified auditors' report, it is following a philosophy characterized by
   a. The imperative principle in moral philosophy.
   b. The utilitarian principle in moral philosophy.
   c. The generalization principle in moral philosophy.
   d. Reliance on members' collective conscience.

LO B-3
B.21 Which of the following agencies issues independence rules for the auditors of public companies?
   a. Financial Accounting Standards Board (FASB).
   b. Government Accountability Office (GAO).
   c. Public Company Accounting Oversight Board (PCAOB)
   d. AICPA Accounting and Review Services Committee (ARSC).

LO B-4
B.22 Audit independence in fact is most clearly lost when
   a. A public accounting firm audits competitor companies in the same industry (e.g., Coca-Cola and Pepsi).
   b. An auditor agrees to the argument made by the client's financial vice president that deferring losses on debt refinancing is in accordance with generally accepted accounting principles.
   c. An audit team fails to discover the client's misleading omission of disclosure about permanent impairment of asset values.
   d. A public accounting firm issues a standard unqualified report, but the reviewing partner fails to notice that the assistant's observation of inventory was woefully incomplete.

LO B-4
B.23 The audit committee's responsibility for auditor independence concerns
   a. Ensuring that partners of the public accounting firm are not stockholders in the company.
   b. Ensuring that nonaudit services provided by the auditor do not impair independence.
   c. Reporting on auditor independence to the PCAOB.
   d. Ensuring that all nonaudit services are provided by auditors who do not perform the financial statement audit.

LO B-5
B.24 AICPA members who work in industry and government must always uphold which two of the following AICPA rules of conduct?
   a. Rule 101—Independence.
   b. Rule 102—Integrity and Objectivity.
   c. Rule 301—Confidential Client Information.
   d. Rule 501—Acts Discreditable.

LO B-4   B.25 A public accounting firm's independence is not impaired when members of the audit engagement team does which of the following for a public company audit client?
   a. Prepares special purchase orders for active plutonium in secure national defense installations.
   b. Completes operational internal audit assignments under the directions of the client's director of internal auditing.
   c. Prepares outsourced internal audit work on the client's financial accounting control monitoring.
   d. Prepares actuarial assumptions used by the client's actuaries for life insurance actuarial liability determination.
   e. All of the above would impair the public accounting firm's independence.

LO B-4   B.26 When a public accounting firm audits FUND-A in a mutual fund complex that has sister funds FUND-B and FUND-C, independence for the audit of FUND-A is not impaired when
   a. Managerial-level professionals located in the office where the engagement audit partner is located but who are not on the engagement team own shares in FUND-B, which is not an audit client.
   b. The wife of the FUND-A audit engagement partner owns shares in FUND-C (an audit client of another of the firm's offices) and these shares are held through the wife's employee benefit plan funded by her employer, the AllSteelFence Company.
   c. Both (a) and (b).
   d. Neither (a) nor (b).

LO B-4   B.27 Which of the following is considered a close relative (but not an immediate family member) as defined by the AICPA?
   a. Spouse
   b. Spousal equivalent
   c. Parent
   d. Uncle

LO B-5   B.28 Which of the following is true if an auditor performs nonaudit services for a government entity?
   a. The scope of the audit must be reduced so that the auditor does not audit the area for which the nonaudit work was performed.
   b. The auditor is prohibited from providing nonaudit work in areas directly related to the production of accounting information.
   c. The senior members of the government entity must document their review of the nonaudit service and indicate why it is appropriate for the auditors to perform this service.
   d. The scope of the audit cannot be reduced because the nonaudit work was performed by the public accounting firm.

LO B-4   B.29 Which of the following is true?
   a. Members of an audit engagement team cannot speak with audit client officers about matters outside the scope of the audit while the audit engagement is in progress.
   b. Audit team members who leave the public accounting firm for employment with audit clients can provide audit efficiencies (next year) because they are very familiar with the firm's audit plans.
   c. Audit team partners who leave the public accounting firm for employment with audit clients can retain variable annuity retirement accounts established in the person's former firm retirement plan.
   d. The public accounting firm must discuss with the audit client's board or its audit committee the independence implications of the client's having hired the audit engagement team manager as its financial vice president.

LO B-3   B.30 Which of the following "bodies designated by Council" have been authorized to promulgate general standards enforceable under Rule 201 of the AICPA Code of Professional Conduct?
   a. AICPA Division of Professional Ethics.
   b. Financial Accounting Standards Board.
   c. Government Accounting Standards Board.
   d. Accounting and Review Services Committee.

LO B-5   B.31 Which of the following "bodies designated by Council" have been authorized to promulgate accounting principles enforceable under Rule 203 of the AICPA Code of Professional Conduct?
  a. Auditing Standards Board.
  b. Federal Accounting Standards Advisory Board.
  c. Consulting Services Executive Committee.
  d. Accounting and Review Services Committee.

LO B-5   B.32 Phil Greb has a thriving practice in which he assists attorneys in preparing litigation dealing with accounting and auditing matters. Phil is "practicing public accounting" if he
  a. Uses his CPA designation on his letterhead and business card.
  b. Is in partnership with another CPA.
  c. Practices in a professional corporation with other CPAs.
  d. Never lets his clients know that he is a CPA.

LO B-5   B.33 The AICPA removed its general prohibition of CPAs taking commissions and contingent fees because
  a. CPAs prefer more price competition to less.
  b. Commissions and contingent fees enhance audit independence.
  c. Nothing is inherently wrong about the form of fees charged to nonaudit clients.
  d. Objectivity is not always necessary in accounting and auditing services.

LO B-4   B.34 CPA Kara Rambo is the auditor of Ajax Corporation. Her audit independence will *not* be considered impaired if she
  a. Owns $1,000 worth of Ajax stock.
  b. Has a husband who owns $1,000 worth of Ajax stock.
  c. Has a sister who is the financial vice president of Ajax.
  d. Owns $1,000 worth of the stock of Pericles Corporation, which is controlled by Ajax as a result of Ajax's ownership of 40 percent of Pericles' stock, and Pericles contributes 3 percent of its total assets and income in Ajax's financial statements.

LO B-5   B.35 When a client's financial statements contain a material departure from an FASB *Statement on Accounting Standards* and the public accounting firm believes the departure is necessary to ensure that the statements are not misleading,
  a. The public accounting firm must qualify the auditors' report for a departure from GAAP.
  b. The public accounting firm can explain why the departure is necessary and then give an unqualified opinion paragraph in the auditors' report.
  c. The public accounting firm must give an adverse auditors' report.
  d. The public accounting firm can give the standard unqualified auditors' report with an unqualified opinion paragraph.

LO B-5   B.36 Which of the following would *not* be considered confidential information obtained in the course of an engagement for which the client's consent would be needed for disclosure?
  a. Information about whether a consulting client has paid the CPA's fees on time.
  b. The actuarial assumptions used by a tax client in calculating pension expense.
  c. Management's strategic plan for next year's labor negotiations.
  d. Information about material contingent liabilities relevant for audited financial statements.

LO B-5   B.37 Which of the following would probably *not* be considered an "act discreditable to the profession"?
  a. Numerous moving traffic violations.
  b. Failing to file the CPA's own tax return.
  c. Filing a fraudulent tax return for a client in a severe financial difficulty.
  d. Refusing to hire Asian Americans in an accounting practice.

LO B-5   B.38 According to the AICPA Code of Conduct, which of the following acts is generally forbidden to CPAs in public practice?
  a. Purchasing bookkeeping software from a hi-tech development company and reselling it to tax clients.
  b. Being the author of a "TaxAid" newsletter promoted and sold by a publishing company.
  c. Having a commission arrangement with an accounting software developer to receive 4 percent of the price of programs recommended and sold to audit clients.
  d. Engaging a marketing firm to obtain new financial planning clients for a fixed fee of $1,000 for each successful contact.

LO B-6 B.39 A CPA's legal license to practice public accounting can be revoked by the
  a. American Institute of Certified Public Accountants.
  b. State society of CPAs.
  c. Auditing Standard Board.
  d. State board of accountancy.

LO B-5 B.40 According to Rule 501, which of the following is *not* a "discreditable act"?
  a. Withholding a client's sales records.
  b. Failing to file or remit tax payments.
  c. Failing to follow requirements of the PCAOB during the audit of an SEC client.
  d. Advertising that indicated the firm can reduce IRS penalties.

LO B-4 B.41 An auditor's independence would *not* be considered impaired if she or he had
  a. Owned common stock of the audit client but sold it before the company became a client.
  b. Sold short the common stock of an audit client while working on the audit engagement.
  c. Served as the company's treasurer for six months during the year covered by the audit but resigned before the company became a client.
  d. Performed the bookkeeping and financial statement preparation for the company, which had no accounting personnel and for which the president had no understanding of accounting principles.

LO B-5 B.42 When a CPA knows that a tax client has skimmed cash receipts and not reported the income in the federal income tax return but signs the return as a CPA who prepared the return, the CPA has violated which of the following AICPA Rules of Conduct?
  a. Rule 301—Confidential Client Information.
  b. Rule 102—Integrity and Objectivity.
  c. Rule 101—Independence.
  d. Rule 203—Accounting Principles.

LO B-5 B.43 An auditor recommends a local computer company to a client that is trying to upgrade its computerized sales records. The client purchases $25,000 worth of equipment and sends a check to the auditor for 5 percent of the total sales. This is an example of a
  a. Commission.
  b. Contingent fee.
  c. Referral fee.
  d. Nonaudit fee.

LO B-5 B.44 Which of the following ownership situations is permissible for a public accounting firm?
  a. A partner of the firm is responsible for fraud issues related to audits and audit clients. He owns 20 percent of the firm and is not a CPA.
  b. Because the firm now specializes in fraud auditing and fraud investigation, the managing partner of the firm has a background in law enforcement and fraud investigation but is not a CPA.
  c. A partner of the firm who owns 50 shares of stock in an audit client of the firm is responsible for fraud issues related to audits and audit clients.
  d. A partner of the firm who has 20 years of experience in law enforcement and fraud investigation is responsible for fraud issues related to audits and audit clients. The partner's career began as a police officer after receiving a law enforcement degree from a local community college.

Exercises and Problems

 All applicable Exercises and Problems are available with McGraw-Hill's *Connect® Accounting*

LO B-4 B.45 **SEC Independence Rules.** Is independence impaired for the individual or the public accounting firm on these SEC filing audits according to SEC independence rules?
  a. CPA Yolanda is the Best & Co engagement partner on the Casa Construction Company (CCC) audit supervised from the Santa Fe office of the firm. Yolanda owns 100 shares of CCC.

b. CPA Yolanda sold the 100 CCC shares to CPA Javier, who is another partner in the Santa Fe office but who is not involved in the CCC audit.

c. CPA Javier transferred ownership of the 100 CCC shares to his wife.

d. CPA Javier's wife gave the shares to their 12-year-old son.

e. CPA Javier's son sold the shares to Javier's father.

f. CPA Javier's father was happy to combine the 100 CCC shares with shares he already owned because now he owns 25 percent of CCC and can control many decisions of the board of directors.

g. CPA Javier's father declared personal bankruptcy and sold his CCC stock. CCC then hired him to fill the newly created position of director of financial reporting.

LO B-4

B.46 SEC Independence and Nonaudit Services. Is independence impaired on these SEC filing audits according to SEC independence rules regarding nonaudit services?

a. CPA Dakota Tidrick is a staff assistant II auditor on the Section Co. audit. Upon the audit completion date in January, Tidrick drafted the balance sheet, income statement, comprehensive income statement, statement of cash flows, and notes for review by the engagement partner before the auditors' report was finalized.

b. CPA Mel Carnes is a manager in the firm's consulting division. He spent 100 hours with the Section Co. audit client on an accounts payable information system study, which involved selecting the preferred software and supervising Section Co.'s employees in startup operations.

c. CPA Nicky Webber, working in the public accounting firm's asset valuation consulting division located in Chicago, prepared for Section Co. an appraisal of the fair value of assets purchased in Section's merger with the Group Co. These valuations were then audited by the engagement team located in Dallas in connection with the purchase accounting for the merger.

d. CPA Fran Young is the engagement partner on the Section Co. audit and is also an actuarial consultant in the firm's consulting division. Young personally audited the client's postemployment benefits calculations, which had been prepared by Section's actuaries.

e. Section Co. appointed its own employee, certified internal auditor (CIA) Pat Mumta, to be director of internal auditing with complete responsibility for planning, management, and review of all internal audit work. Mumta engaged Section Co.'s independent public accounting firm to supply staff to perform all operational audit studies of efficiency and effectiveness in Section's domestic subsidiary companies. The public accounting firm used half of these same staff professionals to work on the audit of Section's financial statement audit.

f. CPA Dale Churyk is the partner in charge of the Dallas office where the Section Co. audit is managed (by engagement partner Jack). Churyk has no direct role on the audit engagement team. However, Section relies on Churyk to prepare the confidential papers for the board of directors' stock options and sign the release forms for option grants.

g. CPA Robin Mantzke works in the executive search department of the public accounting firm's consulting division, located in New York City. In connection with Section Co.'s hiring of its new vice president for marketing, Mantzke checked the references on the lead candidate Smith and performed a thorough background investigation that led to the firm's advice that Smith was the best person for the appointment. Section Co. board members investigated other candidates and hired Smith in Dallas without further interaction with Mantzke.

h. Section Co. completed a private placement of long-term bonds during the year under audit. The bonds were distributed to 40 qualified-exempt investors through the brokerage firm of Amalgamated Exchange, Inc., which is 50 percent owned by the public accounting firm and 50 percent owned by Lynch Merrill Investment Corporation.

i. The public accounting firm's tax consulting division prepared Section Co.'s export-import tax reports, which involved numerous interpretations of complicated export-import tax law provisions.

LO B-4

B.47 Independence, Integrity, and Objectivity Cases. Read the following cases.

Required:

For each case, state whether the action or situation shows a violation of the AICPA Code of Professional Conduct, explain why if it does, and cite the relevant rule or interpretation.

a. CPA Ellen Stout performs the audit of the local symphony society. Because of her good work, she was elected an honorary member of the board of directors.

b. CPA Darcy Wolfe practices management consulting in the area of computerized information systems under the firm name of Wolfe & Associates. The "associates" are not CPAs and the firm is not an accounting firm. However, Wolfe shows "CPA" on business cards and uses these credentials when dealing with clients.

c. CPA Alex Goodwin performs significant day-to-day bookkeeping services for Harper Corporation and supervises the work of the one part-time bookkeeper employed by Hadley Harper. This year, Harper wants to engage CPA Goodwin to perform an audit.

d. CPA H. Poirot bought a home in 1989 and financed it with a mortgage loan from Farraway Savings and Loan. Farraway was merged into Nearby S&L, and Poirot became the manager in charge of the Nearby audit.

e. Poirot inherited a large sum of money from old Mr. Giraud in 2000. Poirot sold his house, paid off the loan to Nearby S&L, and purchased a much larger estate. Nearby S&L provided the financing.

f. Poirot and Mala Lemon (a local real estate broker) formed a partnership to develop apartment buildings. Lemon is a 20 percent owner and managing partner. Poirot and three partners in the accounting firm are limited partners. They own the remaining 80 percent of the partnership but have no voice in everyday management. Lemon obtained permanent real estate financing from Nearby S&L.

g. Lemon won the lottery and purchased part of the limited partners' interests. She now owns 90 percent of the partnership and remains general partner while the CPAs remain limited partners with 10 percent interest.

h. CPA Justin Shultz purchased a variable annuity insurance contract that offered the option to choose the companies in which this contract will invest. As directed, the insurance company purchased common stock in one of Shultz's audit clients.

LO B-4

B.48 Independence, Integrity, and Objectivity Cases. Read the following cases.

Required:

For each separate case, state whether the action or situation shows a violation of the AICPA Code of Professional Conduct; if so, explain why and cite the relevant rule or interpretation.

a. Your client, Contrary Corporation, is very upset over the fact that your audit last year failed to detect an $800,000 inventory overstatement caused by employee theft and falsification of the records. The board discussed the matter and authorized its attorneys to explore the possibility of a lawsuit for damages.

b. Contrary Corporation filed a lawsuit alleging negligent audit work, seeking $1 million in damages.

c. In response to the lawsuit by Contrary, you decided to bring litigation against certain officers of the company alleging management fraud and deceit. You are asking for a damage judgment of $500,000.

d. The Allright Insurance Company paid Contrary Corporation $700,000 under a fidelity bond covering an inventory theft by employees. Allright is suing your public accounting firm for damages on the grounds of negligent performance of the audit, claiming that a proper audit would have uncovered the theft sooner and the amount of loss would have been considerably less.

e. Your audit client, Science Tech, Inc., installed a cost accounting system devised by the consulting services department of your firm. The system failed to account properly for certain product costs (according to management), and the system had to be discontinued. Science Tech management was very dissatisfied and filed a lawsuit demanding return of the $10,000 consulting fee. The audit fee is normally about $50,000 and $10,000 is not an especially large amount for your firm. However, you believe that Science Tech management operated the system improperly. While you are willing to do further consulting work at a reduced rate to make the system operate, you are unwilling to return the entire $10,000 fee.

f. A group of dissident shareholders filed a class action lawsuit against both you and your client, Amalgamated, Inc., for $30 million. They allege there was a conspiracy to present misleading financial statements in connection with a recent merger.

g. CPA Ellis Lisa, a shareholder in the firm of Eden, Benjamin, and Block, P.C. (a professional accounting corporation), owns 25 percent of the common stock of Dove Corporation (not a client of Eden, Benjamin, and Block). This year, Dove purchased a 32 percent interest in Tale Company and is accounting for the investment using the equity method of accounting. The investment amounts to 11 percent of Dove's consolidated net assets. Tale Company has been an audit client of Eden, Benjamin, and Block for 12 years.

h. CPAs Mark and Ben Saliba are the father-and-son partners of Queens, LLP. They have a 12 percent joint private investment in ownership of the voting common stock of Hydra Corporation, which is not an audit client of Queens, LLP. However, the firm's audit client, Howard Company, owns 46 percent of Hydra, and this investment accounts for 20 percent of Howard's assets (using the equity method of accounting).

i. Drew Francie and Madison Brian, CPAs, regularly perform the audit of the First National Bank and the firm is preparing for the audit of the financial statements for the year ended December 31, 2012.

   (1) Two directors of the First National Bank became partners in Francie and Brian, CPAs, on July 1, 2012, resigning their directorship on that date. They will not participate in the audit.

   (2) During 2012, the former controller of the First National Bank, now a partner in Francie and Brian, was frequently called on for assistance regarding loan approvals and the bank's minimum checking account policy. In addition, the former controller conducted a computer feasibility study for First National.

j. The Cather Corporation is indebted to a CPA for unpaid fees and has offered to give the CPA unsecured interest-bearing notes. Alternatively, Cather Corporation offered to give the CPA two shares of its common stock, after which 10,002 shares would be outstanding.

k. May Debra is not yet a CPA but is doing quite well in her first employment with a large public accounting firm. She has been on the job two years and has become an "experienced assistant." If she passes the CPA exam this year, she will be promoted to senior accountant. This month, during the audit of Row Lumber Company, Debra told the controller that she is remodeling an old house. The controller likes Debra and had a load of needed materials delivered to the house, billing Debra at a 70 percent discount—a savings over the normal cash discount of about $300. Debra paid the bill and was happy to have the materials that she otherwise could not afford on her meager salary.

l. Groaner Corporation is in financial difficulty. You are about to sign the report on the current audit when your firm's office manager informs you the audit fee for last year has not yet been paid.

m. CPA Aubrey Rowan prepared Goodwin's tax return this year. Last year, Goodwin prepared the return and paid too much income tax because the tax return erroneously contained "income" in the amount of $300,000 from an inheritance received when dear Aunt Martha died. This year, Goodwin sold the inherited property for $500,000. Goodwin argued with Rowan, who agreed to omit the sale of the property and the $200,000 gain this year on the grounds that Goodwin had already overpaid tax last year and this omission would make things even.

n. CPA Sage Watson is employed by Baker Street Company as its chief accountant. Lee Lestrade, also a CPA and the financial vice president of Baker, owns a trucking company that provides shipping services to Baker in a four-state area. The trucking company needs to buy 14 new trailers, and Lestrade authorized a payment to finance the purchase in the amount of $750,000. The related document cited repayment in terms of reduced trucking charges for the next seven years. Lestrade created the journal entry for this arrangement, charging the $750,000 to prepaid expenses. Watson and Lestrade signed the representation letter to Baker's external auditors and stated that Baker had no related-party transactions that were not disclosed to the auditors.

LO B-5

B.49 **Integrity and Objectivity.** In 1997, a disagreement arose between **Livent Inc.** and its auditor, **Deloitte and Touche.** Livent, which operated several theaters for live stage production, had sold the naming rights to one of its theaters to **AT&T** for $12.5 million. The agreement was oral and one of the theaters was under construction. The auditors for Deloitte believed that only a portion of the deal should be included in revenue, but Livent wanted to book the entire $12.5 million. Livent retained **Ernst & Young** (E&Y) to provide an opinion on the transaction. E&Y's report indicated that all $12.5 million could be recorded as revenue. Deloitte hired **Price Waterhouse** (currently **PricewaterhouseCoopers**) to review the transaction. Price Waterhouse agreed with E&Y and Livent, and Deloitte allowed Livent to book the $12.5 million. In 1998, Livent issued a series of press releases indicating the discovery of significant account irregularities and, later in 1998, declared bankruptcy.

Required:

Comment on the decision to engage E&Y and Price Waterhouse concerning the $12.5 million transaction. What would your position be on the need for other opinions? What would your position be for the disposition of the transaction?

LO B-5

B.50 **General and Technical Rule Cases.** Read the following cases. For each, state whether the action or situation shows a violation of the AICPA Code of Professional Conduct; if so, explain why and cite the relevant rule or interpretation.

a. CPA Jerry Cheese became the new auditor for Python Insurance Company. Cheese knew a great deal about insurance accounting but had never conducted an audit of an insurance company. Consequently, Cheese hired CPA Tate Gilliam, who had six years of experience with the State Department of Insurance Audit. Gilliam managed the audit and Cheese was the partner in charge.

b. CPA Mackenzie Palin practices public accounting and is a director of Comedy Company. Palin's firm performs consulting and tax services for Comedy. Palin prepared unaudited financial statements on Comedy's letterhead and submitted them to First National Bank in support of a loan application. Palin's accounting firm received a fee for this service.

c. CPA Ellery Idle audited the financial statements of Monty Corporation and gave an unqualified report. Monty is not a public company, so the financial statements did not contain the SEC-required reconciliation of deferred income taxes.

d. CPA Gwyn Chapman audited the financial statement of BTV., Ltd. These financial statements contain capitalized leases that do not meet FASB criteria for capitalization. They resemble more closely the criteria for operating leases. The effect is material, adding $4 million to assets and $3.5 million to liabilities. However, BTV has a long experience with acquiring such property as its own assets after the "lease" terms end. Chapman and BTV management believe the financial statements should reflect the operating policy of the management instead of the technical requirements of the FASB. Consequently, the auditors' report explains the accounting and gives an unqualified opinion.

LO B-5

B.51 **Responsibilities to Clients' Cases.** Read the following cases. For each case, state whether the action or situation shows a violation or potential for violation of the AICPA Code of Professional Conduct, explain why, and cite the relevant rule or interpretation.

a. CPA Sal Colt has discovered a way to eliminate most of the boring work of processing routine accounts receivable confirmations by contracting with the Cohen Mail Service. After the auditor has prepared the confirmations, Cohen stuffs them in envelopes, mails them, receives the return replies, opens the replies, and returns them to Colt.

b. Cadentoe Corporation, without consulting Jora Cramer, its CPA, has changed its accounting so that it is not in conformity with GAAP. During the regular audit engagement, Cramer discovers that the statements based on the accounts are so grossly misleading that they might be considered fraudulent. Cramer resigns the engagement after a heated argument. Cramer knows that the statements will be given to Sandy Panzer, a friend at the Last National Bank, and that Panzer is not a very astute reader of complicated financial statements. Two days later, Panzer calls Cramer and asks some general questions about Cadentoe's statements and remarks favorably on the very thing that is misrepresented. Cramer corrects the erroneous analysis and Panzer is very much surprised.

c. A CPA who had reached retirement age arranged to sell the practice to another certified public accountant. Their agreement called for the review of all audit documentation and business correspondence by the accountant purchasing the practice.

d. Martha Jacoby, CPA, withdrew from the audit of Harvard Company after discovering irregularities in Harvard's income tax returns. One week later, Jacoby received a phone call from Jake Henry, CPA, who explained that he had just been retained by Harvard Company to replace her. Henry asked Jacoby why she withdrew from the Harvard engagement, and she told him.

e. CPA Chen Wallace has two audit clients: Willingham Corporation owned by Jayden Willingham and Ward Corporation owned by Bailey Ward. Willingham Corp. sells a large proportion of its products to Ward Corp., which amounts to 60 percent of Ward Corp.'s purchases in most years. Willingham and Ward are also Wallace's tax clients as individuals. This year, while preparing Ward's tax return, Wallace discovered information that suggested Ward Corporation is in a failing financial position. In consideration of the fact that the companies and individuals are mutual clients, Wallace discussed Ward Corporation's financial difficulties with Willingham.

f. Ashley Fiddle, CPA, prepared an uncontested claim for a tax refund on Faddle Corporation's amended tax return. The fee for the service was 30 percent of the amount the IRS rules to be a proper refund. The claim was for $300,000.

g. After Faddle had won a $200,000 refund and Fiddle collected the $60,000 fee, Jordan Faddle, the president, invited Fiddle to be the auditor for Faddle Corporation.

h. Burgess Company engaged CPA Kim Philby to audit Maclean Corporation in connection with a possible initial public offering (IPO) of stock registered with the SEC. Burgess Company established a holding company named Cairncross Inc. and asked Philby to issue an engagement letter addressed to Cairncross stating that Cairncross would receive the auditors' report. Cairncross has no assets and Philby agreed to charge a fee for the audit of Maclean only if the IPO is successful.

LO B-5

B.52 **Other Responsibilities and Practices Cases.** Read the following cases. For each, state whether the action or situation shows a violation or potential for violation of the AICPA Code of Professional Conduct; if so, explain why, and cite the relevant rule or interpretation.

a. CPA Ron Stout completed a review of the unaudited financial statements of Wolfe Gifts. Arvida Wolfe was very displeased with the report. An argument ensued and she told Stout never to darken her door again. Two days later, she telephoned Stout and demanded that he return (1) Wolfe's cash disbursement journal, (2) Stout's documentation schedule of adjusting journal entries, (3) Stout's inventory analysis documentation, and (4) all other documentation prepared by Stout. Wolfe had not yet paid her bill, so Stout replied that state law gave him a lien on all of the records and he would return them as soon as she paid his fee.

b. CPA O'Dell May teaches a CPA review course at the university. He needs problem and question material for students' practice, but the CPA examination questions and answers are no longer published. He pays $5 to students who take the exam for each question they can "remember" after taking the examination.

c. CPA Kelsey Blitz has been invited to conduct a course in effective tax planning for the City Chamber of Commerce. The chamber's president said a brochure would be mailed to members giving the name of Blitz's firm, Blitz's educational background and degrees held, professional society affiliations, and testimonials from participants in the course held last year comparing Blitz's excellent performance with other CPAs who have offered competing courses in the city.

d. CPA Reece Philby is a member of the state bar whose practice is a combination of law and accounting and is heavily involved in estate planning engagements. Philby's letterhead has the following: Member, State Bar of Illinois, and Member, AICPA.

e. The public accounting firm of Burgess & Maclean (B&M) has made a deal with Brit & Company, a firm of management consulting specialists, for mutual business advantage. B&M agreed to recommend Brit to clients who need management consulting services. Brit agreed to recommend B&M to clients who need improvements in their accounting systems. During the year, both firms would keep records of fees obtained by these mutual referrals. At the end of the year, Brit and B&M would settle the net differences based on a referral rate of 5 percent of fees.

f. Jack Robinson and Archie Robertson (both CPAs) are not partners, but they have the same office, the same employees, and a joint bank account and work together on audits. A letterhead they use shows both their names and the description "Members, AICPA."

g. CPA Lou Dewey retired from the two-person firm of Dewey & Cheatham (D&C). One year later, D&C merged practices with Howe & Company to form a regional firm under the name of Dewey, Cheatham, & Howe Company.

LO B-4

B.53 **AICPA Independence and Other Services.** AICPA Interpretation 101-3 (Performance of Other Services: www.aicpa.org) cites several "other services" that do and do not impair audit independence.

Required:

Go to the AICPA website and find whether the following items impair independence (Yes) or do not impair independence (No) when performed for audit clients.

a. Post the client-approved entries to a client's trial balance.

b. Authorize the client's customer credit applications.

c. Use CPA's information-processing facilities to prepare the client's payroll and generate checks for the client treasurer's signature.

d. Sign the client's quarterly federal payroll tax return.

e. Advise client management about the application or financial effect of provisions in an employee benefit plan contract.

f. Have emergency signature authority to cosign cash disbursement checks in connection with a client's hospital benefit plan.

g. As an investment advisory service, provide analyses of a client's investments in comparison to benchmarks produced by unrelated third parties.

h. Take temporary custody of a client's investment assets each time a purchase is made as a device to reduce cash float expense.

LO B-1

B.54 **General Ethics.** Is there any moral difference between a disapproved action in which you are caught and the same action that never becomes known to anyone else? Do many persons in business and professional society make a distinction between these two circumstances? If you respond that you do (or do not) perceive a difference while persons in business and professional society do not (or do), how do you explain the differences in attitudes?

LO B-2

B.55 **Competition and Audit Proposals.** Accounting firms are often asked to present "proposals" to companies' boards of directors. These proposals are comprehensive booklets, accompanied by oral presentations, telling about the firm's personnel, technology, special qualifications, and expertise in the hope of convincing the board to award the work to the firm.

Kourtney Dena has a new job as staff assistant to Selby Michael, chairman of the board of Granof Grain Company. The company has a policy of engaging new auditors every seven years. The board will hear oral proposals from 12 accounting firms. This is the second day of the three-day meeting. Dena's job is to help evaluate the proposals. During the first day of meetings, the proposal presented by Eden, Benjamin, and Block was clearly the best.

At the end of the day, Dena sees Michael's staff chief slip a copy of Eden, Benjamin, and Block's written proposal into an envelope. He then tells Dena to take it to a friend who works for Hunt and Hunt, a public accounting firm scheduled to make its presentation tomorrow, saying, "I told him we'd let him glance at the best proposal." Michael is absent from the meeting and will not return for two hours.

Required:

What should Dena do? What should CPA Hunt do if he receives the Eden, Benjamin, and Block proposal, assuming he has time to modify the Hunt and Hunt proposal before tomorrow's presentation?

LO B-2

B.56 **Engagement Timekeeping Records.** A time budget is always prepared for audit engagements. Numbers of hours are estimated for various segments of the work, for example, internal control evaluation, cash, inventory, and report review. Audit supervisors expect the work segments to be completed "within budget" and evaluate staff accountants' performance in part on the ability to perform audit work efficiently within budget.

Jessica Sara is an audit manager who has worked hard to get promoted. She hopes to become a partner in two or three years. Finishing audits on time is heavily weighted on her performance evaluation. She assigned the cash audit work to Paul Ed, who has worked for the firm for 10 months. Ed hopes to get a promotion and salary raise this year. Twenty hours were budgeted for the cash work. Ed is efficient, but it took 30 hours to finish because the company had added seven new bank accounts. Ed was worried about his performance evaluation, so he recorded 20 hours for the cash work and put the other 10 hours under the internal control evaluation budget.

Required:

What do you think about Ed's resolution of his problem? Was his action a form of lying? What would you think of his action if the internal control evaluation work was presently under budget because it was not yet complete and another assistant was assigned to finish that work segment later?

Module B *Professional Ethics* **631**

LO B-2

B.57 **Audit Overtime.** The performance evaluation of all accountants is based in part on their ability to do audit work efficiently and within the time budget planned for the engagement. New staff accountants, in particular, usually have some early difficulty learning speedy work habits, which demand that no time be wasted.

Cynthia Elizabeth started work for Julie and Jacob CPAs in September. After attending the staff training school, she was assigned to the Rising Sun Company audit. Her first work assignment was to complete the extensive recalculation of the inventory compilation using the audit test counts and audited unit prices for several hundred inventory items. Her time budget for the work was six hours. She started at 4 P.M. and was not finished when everyone left the office at 6 P.M. Not wanting to stay downtown alone, she took all necessary audit documentation home. She resumed work at 8 P.M. and finished at 3 A.M. The next day, she returned to the CPA offices, put the completed documentation in the file, and recorded six hours in the time budget/actual schedule. Her supervisor was pleased, especially about her diligence in taking the work home.

Required:
a. What do you think about Elizabeth's diligence and her understatement of the time she took to finish the work?
b. What would you think of the case if she had received help at home from her husband Paul?
c. What would you think of the case if she had been unable to finish and had left the work at home for her husband to finish?

LO B-5

B.58 **Conflict of Client's Interests.** Jon Williams, CPA, is in the middle of the real-life soap opera, "Taxing Days of Our Lives."

The Cast of Characters

Oneway Corporation is Williams's audit and tax client. The three directors are the officers and the only three stockholders, each owning exactly one-third of the shares.

President Raul Jack founded the company and is now nearing retirement. As an individual, he is also Williams's tax client.

Vice President Jana Jill manages the day-to-day operations. She has been instrumental in increasing the business and its profits. Jill's individual tax work is done by CPA Corin Phil.

Treasurer Chris Bill has been a long-term, loyal employee and has been responsible for many innovative financial transactions and reports of great benefit to the business. He is Williams's close personal friend and an individual tax client.

The Conflict

President Jack discussed with CPA Williams the tax consequences to him as an individual of selling his one-third interest in Oneway Corporation to Vice President Jill. Later, meeting with Bill to discuss his individual tax problems, Williams learns that Bill fears that Jack and Jill will make a deal, put him in a minority position, and force him out of the company. Bill says, "Jon, we've been friends a long time. Please keep me informed about Jack's plans, even rumors. My interest in Oneway Corporation represents my life savings and my resources for the kid's college. Remember, you're little Otto's godfather."

Thinking back, Williams realized that Vice President Jill has always been rather hostile. Chances are that Phil would get the Oneway engagement if Jill acquires Jack's shares and controls the corporation. Nevertheless, Bill will probably suffer a great deal if he cannot learn about Jack's plans, and Williams's unwillingness to keep him informed will probably ruin their close friendship.

Later, on a Dark and Stormy Night:

Williams ponders the problem. "Oneway Corporation is my client, but a corporation is a fiction—only a form. The stockholders personify the real entity, so they are collectively my clients, and I can transmit information among them as though they were one person. Right? On the other hand, Jack and Bill engage me for individual tax work, and information about one's personal affairs is really no business of the other. What to do? What to do?"

Required:
Give Williams advice about alternative actions, considering the constraints of the AICPA Code of Conduct.

LO B-4

B.59 **Managerial Involvement and Audit Independence.** CPA Parker Marlowe is the partner in charge of the audit practice in the midsize public accounting firm of Marlowe & Chandler,

PC. CPA Raz Chandler is the overall managing partner of the firm. They founded the firm 20 years ago. Marlowe is also a member of the board of directors of Hobart Arms Hotel Corporation, one of the firm's tax clients. Hobart wanted to acquire the Bristol Apartment Company, and the Los Angeles National Bank insisted on an independent audit of Hobart's financial statements in connection with its loan application for $3 million. Marlowe & Chandler knew they were not independent for this audit because of Marlowe's position on the board.

To solve this problem, Hobart engaged Wilde & Associates, LLP to perform the audit. The Wilde firm was not very large, so the following arrangement was made: CPA Tai Wilde was the partner in charge of the audit, CPA Whitney Linda (a Wilde professional) was the manager of the audit, and CPAs Ron Lacosta and Rae Martinez were the staff assistants. Lacosta and Martinez were employed by Marlowe & Chandler and were loaned to Wilde & Associates for the purpose of staffing the Hobart audit. They performed almost all of the detailed fieldwork.

Wilde & Associates completed the audit and delivered an unqualified auditors' report. Fees were paid to Wilde & Associates for the work of its professionals. Marlowe & Chandler, PC billed fees separately by for the work performed by Lacosta and Martinez, and Hobart paid these directly to Marlowe & Chandler.

Required:
Analyze this situation. Do you see any lack of independence in connection with the audit? Discuss.

LO B-6

B.60 **Disciplinary Action.** Go to the website for the CPA Society and for the Department of Professional Regulation in the state where you live. Search the websites for disciplinary actions taken against CPAs for violation of the code of ethics.

Required:
Review the ethics cases and list the violations and penalties indicated in each case.

LO B-6

B.61 **Ethics Case.**[13] Sandy Sally is a sole proprietor CPA who runs a successful practice with five employees. Several years ago, Sally purchased an office building and relocated the practice in about 20 percent of the space and rented out the remaining portion. Things went well for the first few months, but then two of Sally's tenants ran into financial difficulties and had to vacate the building. Sally was unable to quickly find new tenants for the space.

Sally struggled to keep current with the mortgage payments for a few months, but the loss of tenant income combined with the expense of operating a building became a large burden. Cash flow became very tight, and Sally stopped remitting the employee payroll taxes withheld.

The IRS filed a lien for nonpayment of employee payroll taxes, which was published in a local newspaper. A concerned citizen filed an ethics complaint.

Investigation found that although the company had been delinquent in remitting employee payroll taxes and a federal tax lien had been filed, Sally had brought the tax liabilities into current status and produced evidence that the IRS lien had been released.

Required:
a. What code violation(s) have occurred in this case?
b. What is the range of penalties that could be levied against Sally?
c. What do you think is the appropriate penalty?

LO B-4

B.62 **Kaplan CPA Exam Simulation: Independence Requirements.**

KAPLAN
CPA REVIEW

Required:
Go to the Kaplan website link at www.mhhe.com/Louwers5e, click on Able, Baker & Charles, CPAs (Independence) AUD TBS and provide your answer.

LO B-5

B.63 **Mini-Case: Ethics.** Refer to the mini-case "Andersen: An Obstruction of Justice?" shown on page C1 and respond to question 6.

LO B-4

B.64 **Mini-Case: Nonaudit Services and Independence.** Refer to the mini-case "How Many Firms?" shown on page C17 and respond to questions 1, 2, and 3.

LO B-4

B.65 **Mini-Case: Nonaudit Services and Independence.** Refer to the mini-case "How Much Are Auditors Paid?" shown on page C23 and respond to questions 1 and 2.

LO B-4

B.66 **Mini-Case: Effect of Sarbanes-Oxley on Fees.** Refer to the mini-case "How Much Are Auditors Paid?" shown on page C23 and respond to questions 3 and 4.

---

[13] The following information was obtained from the *Pennsylvania CPA Journal* and is adopted from a case brought before the Pennsylvania Ethics Committee; see R. J. DePasquale and C. Williams, "The CPA's Taxes and the Code of Ethics," *Pennsylvania CPA Journal*, Winter 2004.

Legal Liability

When men are pure, laws are useless; when men are corrupt, laws are broken.

Benjamin Disraeli, former British prime minister

Professional Standards References

Topic	AU/ISA Section	PCAOB Reference*
Audit Documentation	230	AS 3
Letters for Underwriters and Certain Other Requesting Parties	920	AU 634
Filings Under the Securities Act of 1933	925	AU 711

*AU references represent standards issued by the ASB prior to April 16, 2003, that have not been superseded or amended by the PCAOB.

LEARNING OBJECTIVES

Module B on professional ethics dealt mainly with auditors' self-regulation. This module focuses on public regulation enforced by the Securities and Exchange Commission (SEC) and state and federal court systems. The discussion will help you understand auditors' legal liability for professional work.

Your objectives are to be able to:

LO C-1 Identify and describe auditors' exposure to lawsuits and loss judgments.

LO C-2 Specify the characteristics of auditors' liability under common law and cite specific case precedents.

LO C-3 Describe auditors' liability to third parties under statutory law.

LO C-4 Specify the civil and criminal liability provisions of the Securities Act of 1933.

LO C-5 Specify the civil and criminal liability provisions of the Securities Exchange Act of 1934.

LO C-6 Understand recent developments that affect auditors' liability to clients and third parties.

BDO Seidman LLP (BDO) is one of the nation's largest accounting firms (ranking seventh in the United States) with revenues of $620 million in 2010. In 2007, investors of **E.S. Bankest** (a Miami, Florida, factoring firm) brought a $170 million lawsuit against BDO for losses the investors incurred because of the alleged failure of BDO to detect a fraud that led to E.S. Bankest's collapse. BDO was not willing to settle the case out of court, but risked a trial that could lead to the demise of the entire firm. Scott Univer, BDO's general counsel, noted that "we do settle cases. But there are situations where, if we're accused of fraud or collaboration or misconduct, we have to draw a line.

We'll see you in court."[1] Prior to the Bankest case, BDO had taken six cases to trial over the preceding 12 years and had prevailed in each one.

On June 16, 2007, a Florida jury concluded that BDO had exhibited gross negligence in its audits of Bankest; subsequently, BDO was ordered to pay $521 million ($170 million in compensatory damages plus $351 million in punitive damages). In 2010, following an appeal by BDO, a Florida state appeals court overturned this verdict and ordered a new trial. BDO's chief executive, Jack Weisbaum, stated that BDO "acted at all time consistent with its professional obligations."[2] An attorney for the original claimant (**Banco Espirito Santo**) contradicted Weisbaum's comments, indicating that "the evidence of BDO Seidman's failures of even the most basic auditing procedures is so overwhelming that we expect a new jury will reach the same conclusion as the original jury."[3]

BDO's track record in court is unusual simply because most legal actions against auditors and accounting firms do not actually make it to trial. Accounting firms have generally found it preferable to settle cases out of court instead of risking a trial and significant monetary judgments. As Michael Young, an attorney who has represented the Big Four firms as well as BDO, noted, "The practical reality is that our system of justice breaks down when you're talking about the Big Four. The damages sought are often so big that a rational approach is to settle."[4] In addition to the potential monetary damages, firms consider the opportunity costs of their professionals' time as well as negative publicity surrounding an extensive legal proceeding when making decisions whether to risk a trial. Ironically, on May 5, 2011, BDO entered into a confidential settlement with the plaintiffs in the Bankest case.

Legal liability continues to be an important consideration for auditors and accounting firms as they conduct business. Recent settlements involving the largest accounting firms reveal that our litigious society has significantly impacted the auditing profession:[5]

- Deloitte & Touche (now **Deloitte**): **Adelphia Communications** ($167.5 million in 2007), **Delphi** ($38 million in 2008), **Fortress Re** ($250 million in 2006), **General Motors** ($26 million in 2008), **Parmalat, SpA** ($159 million in 2007).
- **Ernst & Young**: **Bank of New England** ($84 million in 2005), **Cendant** ($335 million in 1999), **HealthSouth** ($143 million in 2009).
- **KPMG**: **Countrywide** ($24 million in 2010), **Xerox** ($80 million in 2008).
- PricewaterhouseCoopers (now **PwC**): **American International Group (AIG)** ($97.5 million in 2008), **Amerco** ($50 million in 2004), **Safety-Kleen** ($48 million in 2005), **Tyco** ($225 million in 2007).

In addition to these settlements, in December 2010 then-New York Attorney General Andrew Cuomo brought suit against Ernst & Young for permitting **Lehman Brothers Holdings Inc.'s** use of an accounting technique known as "Repo 105," which Cuomo claims resulted in misleading perceptions of Lehman's financial condition. This lawsuit seeks damages of all audit fees Lehman paid to Ernst & Young ($150 million) plus additional unspecified damages. However, the failure of the SEC to issue a Wells

---

[1] "BDO Prepares to Fight Lawsuit, with Survival Possibly at Stake," *The Wall Street Journal,* January 24, 2007, p. C2.

[2] "Florida Court Overturns Seidman Jury Verdict," *The Wall Street Journal,* June 24, 2010, p. C3.

[3] Ibid.

[4] "BDO Prepares to Fight Lawsuit," p. C2.

[5] "Deloitte to Be Latest to Settle in Accounting Scandals," *The Wall Street Journal,* April 26, 2005, p. B1; "Deloitte Pays Insurers More than $200 Million," *The Wall Street Journal,* January 6, 2006, p. C3; "Big Accounting Firms Still Pay for Scandals," *The Wall Street Journal,* January 13, 2007, p. B5; "PwC Sets Accord in Tyco Case," *The Wall Street Journal,* July 7–8, 2007, p. A3; "Deloitte to Pay $167.5M in Adelphia Case," *CFO.com,* August 6, 2007; "Deloitte to pay $38 Million in Delphi Case," *CFO.com,* January 2, 2008; "PwC Zapped in $97.5 Million Settlement," *CFO.com,* October 6, 2008; "GM Reaches Settlement in Securities-Fraud Case," *The Wall Street Journal,* August 9, 2008, p. B5; "Xerox to Pay $670 Million to Settle Securities Suit," *The Wall Street Journal,* March 28, 2008, p. B3; "N.Y. Funds Reach Settlement with Countrywide, KPMG," *The Wall Street Journal* (Online), May 7, 2010.

notice (which is a formal signal that civil charges may be forthcoming) indicates some uncertainty as to Ernst's ultimate culpability.[6]

AUDITING INSIGHT — Did Auditors Play a Role in the Subprime Crisis?

The charges filed against Ernst & Young for its audit of Lehman Brothers raised further questions about the role auditors could have played in averting the recent financial crisis. Lynn Turner, former chief accountant at the SEC, noted that, while auditors' performance improved following Sarbanes-Oxley, the slowing economy resulted in auditors ". . . reversing course, heading down the same old road they've been on before the corporate scandals." In contrast, Michael Young, an attorney at Wilkie Farr & Gallagher noted that auditors forced many of their financial institution clients to justify their valuations and eventually, take writedowns on assets and concluded that "by and large, the accountants rose to the occasion."

Source: "Auditors Role in Crisis Gets Fresh Scrutiny," *The Wall Street Journal,* December 23, 2010, p. C1, C2.

A report conducted by the Advisory Committee on the Auditing Profession noted the following with respect to auditor liability:[7]

- The six largest auditing firms are currently defendants in 90 actions with damage claims in excess of $100 million; of these, 51 seek damages in excess of $500 million, 27 seek damages in excess of $1 billion, and seven seek damages in excess of $10 billion.
- Between 1995 and 2007, these six firms paid $5.66 billion to resolve 362 cases.
- Between 1995 and 2007, "litigation and practice protection costs" was 6.6 percent of these six firms' revenues; in 2007, this total was 15.1 percent of these firms' revenues.
- Because claims in securities class action suits can be a multiple of the largest firms' capital, the threat of failure and dissolution of a major auditing firm because of litigation is "real."

This chapter summarizes the legal liability of auditors and the burden of care they owe to various parties who rely upon their work.

THE LEGAL ENVIRONMENT

LEARNING OBJECTIVE C-1
Identify and describe auditors' exposure to lawsuits and loss judgments.

How does legal liability arise? Consider the following schematic that summarizes the relationship between auditors and two key parties: the client and third-party users.

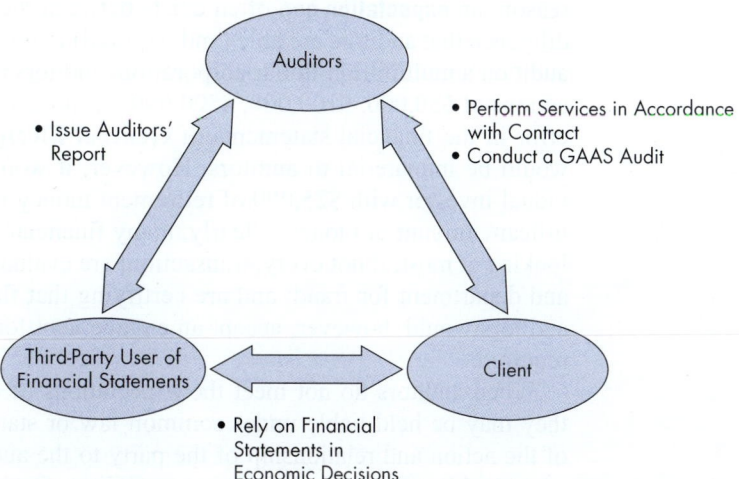

---

[6] "Ernst Accused of Lehman Whitewash," *The Wall Street Journal,* December 22, 2010, p. C1; "Lehman Probe Stalls; Chance of No Charges," *The Wall Street Journal,* March 12–13, 2011, p. B1, B2; "Lehman Auditor May Bear the Brunt," *The Wall Street Journal,* March 14, 2011, p. C1; "Suit Versus Lehman Ex-Officers Can Go On," *The Wall Street Journal,* July 28, 2011, p. C3.

[7] *Final Report of the Advisory Committee on the Auditing Profession,* October 6, 2008.

As this graphic shows, auditors owe clients a responsibility to conduct an audit in accordance with generally accepted auditing standards (GAAS) consistent with the terms in the *engagement letter* that serves as a contract between auditors and their clients. Clients may suffer losses related to these responsibilities for two reasons.

1. A breach of contract between auditors and the client (for example, auditors' failure to complete the engagement by a specified deadline) may cause economic losses to the client resulting from delays, such as failing to receive funding through loans or investments, issuing its shares through a public offering at a less favorable price or paying fines or penalties for missed deadlines.
2. Clients may suffer economic losses from acts of fraud or other misappropriation of assets by employees that *should have been identified* during a GAAS audit.

In either case, whether the client's loss is caused by the breach of contract or failure to exercise the appropriate level of professional care (substandard performance) by auditors, the client may seek legal action.

With respect to third-party users, auditors are responsible for issuing a report based on a GAAS audit that provides reasonable assurance that the financial statements on which these users base their economic decisions (lending decisions and investment decisions) are presented according to generally accepted accounting principles (GAAP). For third-party users, economic losses are either related to the inability of the client to repay loans or other obligations or to a decline in the value of the user's investment in the client (in the form of a partnership interest or publicly traded shares of stock). If the user's loss is caused by reliance on financial statements and those financial statements were not presented according to GAAP, users may seek legal action against auditors.

The main defense for auditors is that they followed GAAS and performed their audits with due professional care. In many cases, lawsuits are brought against auditors not because they are necessarily at fault, but in the case of client failure, they are the only party with resources against which recovery can be made (the **"deep pockets" theory**). As Bill Thompson, president of CPA Mutual Insurance Company of America, noted, auditors are ". . . the last men standing—and they carry insurance, which, to the attorneys, equals deep pockets."[8]

Many users of auditors' reports expect auditors to detect and report fraud, theft, and illegal acts despite the fact that a GAAS audit cannot be expected to identify all items of this nature. Some financial statement users' expectations are very high and, for this reason, an **expectation gap** often exists between the diligence that users expect and the diligence that auditors are able (and required) to provide. For example, in performing an audit on a multibillion-dollar corporation, auditors may choose to exclude testing transactions of $50,000, $100,000, $500,000, or more as immaterial. Certainly, a $1 million error in the financial statements of **General Electric** (2010 revenues of $150 billion) would be immaterial to auditors. However, it would be difficult to convince an individual investor with $25,000 of retirement money invested that $1 million is not a significant amount of money. Clearly, many financial statement users believe auditors are looking at most, if not every, transaction; are evaluating each transaction, event, person, and department for fraud; and are certifying that financial statements are accurate. No auditors would, however, accept an engagement for which any of these objectives was required.

When auditors do not meet the expectations of clients or financial statement users, they may be held liable under common law or statutory law, depending on the nature of the action and relationship of the party to the auditors. **Common law** uses legal precedent to identify the fault and responsibility of parties when there is no violation of a

---

[8] "Target: CPAS," *Accounting Today,* July 1, 2011, p. 53.

written law or statute. When no legal precedent can be found, the judge follows a sense of justice or morality, considering the prevailing customs and moral standards. Common law liability against auditors is available to clients and nonshareholder third parties; the jurisdiction for common law actions is typically a court in the state in which the alleged action occurred.

Statutory law is based on laws passed by legislative bodies and compiled in federal, state, and municipal codes. In a statutory case, the primary basis for a decision is whether the party's actions have violated the law as written in the code. A lawsuit claiming that auditors did not perform the audit in an appropriate manner is a common law action. The primary statutory laws relevant to the audit of financial statements are laws governing the purchase and sale of securities; as a result, auditors' liability under statutory law is primarily to third-party shareholders for securities issued by public entities. The Securities Act of 1933 and Securities and Exchange Act of 1934 (discussed later in this module) provide U.S. district courts with jurisdiction for violations of these acts.

> ### ↳ REVIEW CHECKPOINTS
>
> C.1 Identify the general responsibilities auditors owe to clients and third parties.
> C.2 Distinguish between *common law* liability and *statutory law* liability. Which parties generally bring suit against auditors under common law and under statutory law liability?

▽ LIABILITY UNDER COMMON LAW

LEARNING OBJECTIVE C-2
Specify the characteristics of auditors' liability under common law and cite specific case precedents.

Under common law, lawsuits may be brought against auditors based on the law of contracts or as tort actions for failure to exercise the appropriate level of professional care.

- **Breach of contract** is a claim that accounting or auditing services were not performed in the manner described in the contract. Although auditors may have contractual relationships with third parties, cases involving breach of contract are most frequently brought against auditors by their clients.
- **Tort** actions cover other civil complaints (e.g., fraud, deceit, injury) arising from auditors' failure to exercise the appropriate level of professional care (substandard performance). Clients or users of financial statements can bring tort actions against auditors.

Suits for damages under common law usually result when someone suffers a financial loss after relying on financial statements later found to be materially misstated. The popular press calls such unfortunate events *audit failures*. **Plaintiffs** in legal actions involving auditors (clients or third-party users of financial statements) generally assert all possible causes of action, including breach of contract, tort, deceit, fraud, and whatever else may be relevant to the claim. Various legal terms that will be used throughout this module are summarized in the accompanying feature for reference.

Liability to Clients

Clients may bring a lawsuit for breach of contract and other tort actions. The relationship of direct involvement between parties to a contract is known as **privity of contract**. When privity exists, plaintiffs must demonstrate all of the following:

1. They suffered an economic loss.
2. Auditors did not perform in accordance with the terms of the contract (for breach of contract).

3. Auditors failed to exercise the appropriate level of professional care (for tort actions).
4. The breach of contract or failure to exercise the appropriate level of professional care caused the loss.

The first case in the United States involving an auditor and client dispute (*Smith v. London Assurance Corp.*) established auditors' obligation for breach of contract.

LEGAL PRECEDENT

SMITH V. LONDON ASSURANCE CORP. (1905)
This was the first U.S. case involving auditors. Smith, the auditor, sued the client (**London Assurance Corp.**) for an unpaid fee. In a countersuit, London Assurance Corp. brought suit against Smith for losses resulting from employee embezzlement, which London claimed would not have occurred except for the auditors' breach of contract. The evidence indicated that Smith had indeed failed to audit the cash accounts at one branch office as stipulated in an engagement contract. The court recognized auditors as skilled professionals and held Smith liable for the embezzlement losses that could have been prevented by appropriate performance under the terms of the contract.

In addition to breach of contract, auditors also may be liable to clients for tort liability. Three levels of substandard performance that may lead to tort liability include (listed from least severe to most severe):

1. **Ordinary negligence**: An unintentional breach of duty owed to another party because of a lack of reasonable care.
2. **Gross negligence**: A breach of duty owed to another party because of a lack of minimal care.
3. **Fraud**: A misrepresentation of facts that the individual knows to be false with the intention to deceive.

Because of the very close relationship between auditors and their clients, auditors have a high level of responsibility to their clients. This responsibility is to conduct an audit in accordance with GAAS; if auditors exhibit *ordinary negligence*, clients will typically prevail in their legal actions against auditors. (Auditors are also liable to their clients for *gross negligence* and *fraud*.)

Auditors' Defenses for Client Claims

Auditors may attempt to mitigate clients' claims by using one of the following three defenses:

1. Auditors exercised the appropriate level of professional care (tort) or performed the engagement in accordance with terms of the contract (breach of contract).
2. The client's economic loss was caused by a factor other than auditors' failure to exercise appropriate levels of professional care or breach of contract (the **causation defense**).
3. Actions on the part of the client were, in part, responsible for the loss (for example, failure of the client to establish effective internal control to prevent embezzlement losses). This is referred to as **contributory negligence** and is available to auditors in certain jurisdictions.

Liability to Third Parties

In the early part of the 20th century, parties other than clients had difficulty succeeding in lawsuits against auditors. Parties not in privity of contract have no cause of action for breach of contract. However, these parties can bring lawsuits against auditors for failure to exercise appropriate levels of professional care (tort action). In these cases, third parties suffer an economic loss because of reliance on the audited financial statements and auditors' reports on those statements. Recall that the three levels of failure to exercise the appropriate level of professional care that have emerged through various cases are *ordinary negligence* (lack of reasonable care), *gross negligence* (lack of minimal care), and *fraud* (intention to deceive).

It has been well established that auditors are liable to all third parties for levels of performance representing gross negligence and fraud. However, auditors' liability to various third parties for ordinary negligence has been debated and has changed significantly over time. Furthermore, the extent of liability for ordinary negligence to third parties varies by jurisdiction (state in which the action is brought). As a result, both auditors and third-party users carefully monitor the evolution of auditors' liability to third parties for ordinary negligence through common law precedents. This is particularly important because it is relatively easier for third parties to demonstrate ordinary negligence compared to either gross negligence or fraud.

To bring a suit against auditors under common law, third parties must demonstrate all of the following:

1. They suffered an economic loss (normally, a decline in the value of an investment or failure to be repaid for a loan or other obligation).
2. The auditors failed to exercise the appropriate level of professional care (ordinary negligence, gross negligence, or fraud).
3. The financial statements contained a material misstatement.
4. The loss was caused by reliance on the materially misstated financial statements.

One early and important case involving auditors' liability to third parties was known as *Ultramares*. The *Ultramares* opinion expressed the view that, if auditors' failures to exercise the appropriate level of professional care were so great as to constitute gross negligence, grounds might exist for concluding that auditors had engaged in **constructive fraud**, which is characterized by reckless disregard for the truth. The significance of *Ultramares* is that it established an obligation to third parties and others not in privity with auditors for gross negligence and fraud. *Ultramares* has been cited in numerous third-party common law cases against auditors.

LEGAL PRECEDENT

ULTRAMARES CORP. V. TOUCHE (1931)

In 1924, **Touche, Niven & Co.** was engaged to audit the 1923 balance sheet of **Fred Stern & Co.**, a rubber importer. Based on the audited balance sheet, **Ultramares**, a factoring business, made numerous loans to Stern & Co. In January 1925, Stern & Co. went bankrupt and was unable to repay these loans to Ultramares (this represented the economic loss), and Ultramares brought suit against Touche for negligent performance. While the New York court of appeals denied Ultramares' negligence claim, the court *did not assert that privity of contract was a requirement for third parties to sue auditors*. As a result, this case recognized auditors' potential liability to third parties and the right of third parties to bring suits against auditors.

In part, the court's decision established criteria for auditors' liability to third parties for constructive fraud. To do so, third parties must prove all of the following:

1. There was a misrepresentation of a material fact (usually in the financial statements).
2. The misrepresentation was made knowingly or without adequate knowledge to know whether it was true.
3. There was knowledge (*scienter*) and intent to induce action in reliance on the information.
4. The damaged party justifiably relied on the misrepresentation.
5. There was resulting damage.

The court held that auditors could be liable when they did not have sufficient information (audit evidence) to lead to an opinion. Therefore, the auditors' opinion is deceitful when auditors claim to have knowledge that they do not possess. The court also wrote that when the degree of negligence is gross, it may amount to a constructive fraud and auditors could be liable to a third-party user.

Case conclusion: Ultramares contributed to the development of common law liability to third parties by establishing that

1. Third parties not in privity with auditors can bring suit against auditors.
2. Auditors may be liable to parties who are not in privity in cases representing constructive fraud (gross negligence) or fraud.
3. Auditors are generally not liable for ordinary negligence to parties who are not in privity.

The *Ultramares* decision was upheld in *State Street Trust Co. v. Ernst,* in which the courts identified auditors' liability to third parties for gross negligence in the following opinion:

> [Auditors], however, may be liable to third parties, even where there is lacking deliberate or active fraud. . . . A representation certified as true to the knowledge of the accountants when knowledge there is none, a reckless misstatement, or an opinion based upon grounds so flimsy, . . . In other words, heedlessness and reckless disregard of consequence may take the place of deliberate intention.[9]

Although the *Ultramares* case opened the door for lawsuits by third parties in which fraud or constructive fraud was present, for many years only parties that had privity of contract (typically, the client) could bring legal action against auditors for ordinary negligence. **Primary beneficiaries** are third parties known by name to the auditors for whose primary benefit the audit or other accounting service is performed (also referred to as *near privity*). In some legal jurisdictions, a beneficiary must be named in the contract; in other jurisdictions, the beneficiary need only be identified to auditors prior to or during the engagement. For example, an accounting firm may be informed that the report is needed for a bank loan application at the First National Bank; in this case, First National Bank is a primary beneficiary because they are known *by name* to auditors. Many cases (for example, *CIT v. Glover*) indicate that proving ordinary negligence may be sufficient to hold auditors liable for damages to primary beneficiaries. *Credit Alliance v. Arthur Andersen* identified specific criteria that must be met for primary beneficiaries to prevail against auditors for ordinary negligence.

LEGAL PRECEDENT

CREDIT ALLIANCE V. ARTHUR ANDERSEN (1985)

In this landmark case, **Credit Alliance** (a financial services firm) provided financing for equipment to **L.B. Smith, Inc.** In 1978, Credit Alliance advised Smith that any future extensions of credit would require audited financial statements, which Smith subsequently provided for fiscal years 1976 through 1979. In 1980, L.B. Smith filed for bankruptcy and was unable to repay Credit Alliance (this represented the economic loss). The New York court of appeals provided a three-pronged test for Credit Alliance's right to sue:

1. Auditors were aware that a particular party intended to rely on the auditors' opinion and financial statements.
2. The third party was specifically identified.
3. Some action by the auditors showed that they had acknowledged the third-party's identification and intent to rely on the opinion and financial statements.

This test has been used as precedent in many cases in determining whether the third party was an intended beneficiary of the auditors' work.

Case conclusion: In many jurisdictions, third parties may bring suit against auditors for ordinary negligence even if they are not in privity of the contract. However, they must meet the three-pronged test established by the New York court of appeals.

In many jurisdictions, auditors also may be liable for ordinary negligence to **foreseen parties**. In these jurisdictions, the *restatement of torts* doctrine specifies that auditors are liable if they are aware that the auditors' opinion and financial statements are to be used by some third party. Auditors need not know the exact identity of the third party but are presumed to owe a duty to persons who could reasonably be expected to rely on the auditors' work. For example, if a client informs auditors that it will be using audited financial statements to obtain financing but does not identify any specific banks, under the doctrine of *restatement of torts,* any bank that uses the audited financial statements in making lending decisions may have legal standing to sue auditors for ordinary negligence. *Rusch Factors v. Levin* concluded that auditors were liable to a lender (**Rusch Factors**) because the auditors were aware that the financial statements were to be shown to potential lenders despite the fact that the auditors were not aware of their actual identity. *Fleet National Bank v. Gloucester Co.* affirmed auditors' obligation to third parties who are foreseen parties but are not known by name to auditors (and, therefore, do not qualify as primary beneficiaries).

---

[9] *State Street Trust Co. v. Ernst,* 278 N.Y. 105, 15 N.E.2d 415 (1938).

LEGAL PRECEDENT

FLEET NATIONAL BANK V. GLOUCESTER CO. (1994)

Fleet Bank relied on financial statements audited by **Tonneson** when making loans to **Gloucester**. Upon Gloucester's default (the economic loss), Fleet brought suit against Tonneson, alleging that the basis for making the loans was the audited financial statements. Fleet made the following allegations: (1) Tonneson knew about Fleet Bank's loans to Gloucester, (2) Tonneson reviewed the loan agreements between Gloucester and Fleet Bank, (3) Tonneson knew the loan agreements required submission of audited financial statements, and (4) Tonneson believed and expected Gloucester would provide the audited financial statements to Fleet Bank. The U.S. District Court in Massachusetts found in favor of Fleet, adopting the *restatement of torts* approach.

Case conclusion: Auditors may be liable to third parties for ordinary negligence even if the third party is not named in the engagement contract. If auditors have knowledge that financial statements will be provided to third parties for the purpose of making a decision, in some jurisdiction auditors may be liable to such a third party.

Finally, in other jurisdictions auditors may be liable to reasonably **foreseeable parties**. These parties (sometimes referred to as *members of an unlimited class*) include creditors, investors, or potential investors whose decisions normally rely on audited financial statements and opinions on those financial statements. If auditors are reasonably able to *foresee* a limited class of potential users (e.g., local banks, regular suppliers) of their reports, liability may be imposed for ordinary negligence. This, however, is an uncertain area and liability in a particular case depends entirely on the unique facts and circumstances of the case and the jurisdiction of the legal action. This is the most liberal interpretation of the third-party liability and is used in only two states, Mississippi and Wisconsin. *Rosenblum, Inc. v. Adler* established auditors' liability for ordinary negligence to individuals who are "reasonably foreseeable."[10]

LEGAL PRECEDENT

ROSENBLUM, INC. V. ADLER (1983)

Giant Stores Corporation acquired the retail catalog showroom business owned by **Rosenblum**, giving stock in exchange for the business. Fifteen months after the acquisition, Giant Stores declared bankruptcy, significantly reducing the value of the shares received by Rosenblum in the acquisition (the economic loss). **Adler** had audited Giant Stores' financial statements and issued unqualified opinions on those financial statements for several prior years. These financial statements were later revealed to be misstated as a result of a fraudulent scheme perpetrated by Giant Stores. Rosenblum subsequently brought suit against the auditors (Adler) to attempt to recover the loss resulting from the decline in the value of the shares.

In finding for Rosenblum on certain motions, the New Jersey Supreme Court held, "Independent auditors have a duty of care to all persons whom the auditor should *reasonably foresee* (emphasis added) as recipients of the statements from the company for proper business purposes, provided that the recipients rely on those financial statements. . . . It is well recognized that audited financial statements are made for the use of third parties who have no direct relationship with the auditor. . . . Auditors have responsibility not only to the client who pays the fee but also to investors, creditors, and others who rely on the audited financial statements."

Case conclusion: In some jurisdictions, auditors may be liable for ordinary negligence to a large class of users that are reasonably foreseeable but may not be known to the auditor at the time of the audit.

Additional note: While the opinion in the *Rosenblum* case is an excellent example of a court opinion that extends liability to foreseeable parties, it should be noted that subsequent legislation (1995) in New Jersey has moved that state to a *near privity* standard. However, the *Rosenblum* opinion has been used as precedent in other states. This is an example of how state law can change and how court decisions can provide an impetus to legislatures to enact new law.

It should be noted that these classes of third parties are based on legislation and legal precedents. For example, for primary beneficiaries, auditors know both the name of the party and the intended use of the financial statements; for foreseen parties, auditors know the financial statements will be used by a certain type of third party; for foreseeable parties, auditors *should be* aware that the financial statements *could be used* by third parties.

---

[10] F. D. Greene, A. R. Petrocine, and R. C. FitzPatrick, "Holding Accountants Accountable: The Liability of Accountants to Third Parties," *Employee Responsibilities and Rights Journal,* March 2003, p. 27.

For example, if Grand Bank is relying on audited financial statements to decide whether to provide a loan to Prize Company, Grand Bank's classification as a third party could be as follows:

- Grand Bank would be a primary beneficiary if Prize Company informed the auditors that the audited financial statements would be used to obtain a loan from Grand Bank and Grand Bank was identified to the auditors by name.
- Grand Bank would be a foreseen party if Prize Company informed the auditors that the audited financial statements would be used to obtain a loan but did not specify the name of a third party.
- Grand Bank would be a foreseeable party in almost any situation because audited financial statements are commonly used to obtain financing.

In all jurisdictions, auditors are generally liable for acts of gross negligence and fraud; auditors' liability to third parties for ordinary negligence depends upon the doctrine in effect in the jurisdiction in which auditors practice. Clearly, limiting auditors' liability for acts of ordinary negligence to only primary beneficiaries is most advantageous to auditors and exposing them to liability for ordinary negligence to foreseeable parties is most disadvantageous to auditors. One study[11] classified various jurisdictions (as of 2000) as follows:

- *Privity or near-privity.* Arkansas, Idaho, Illinois, Kansas, Louisiana, Michigan, Montana, Nebraska, New Jersey, New York, Pennsylvania, Utah, Virginia, Wyoming.
- *Restatement of torts* (foreseen). Alabama, Alaska, Arizona, California, Colorado, Florida, Georgia, Hawaii, Iowa, Massachusetts, Missouri, New Hampshire, North Carolina, Ohio, South Carolina, Tennessee, Texas, Washington, West Virginia.
- *Reasonable foreseeability.* Mississippi, Wisconsin.

Auditors' legal liability to third parties as established by these and other cases under common law is summarized in Exhibit C.1.

Auditors' Defenses for Third-Party Claims

Auditors can defend a common law action by presenting arguments and evidence to mitigate third-party plaintiffs' claims and evidence. Assuming that the plaintiff has demonstrated an economic loss and materially misstated financial statements, defenses available to auditors against third parties include the following (note that these are similar to

EXHIBIT C.1 Summary of Auditors' Liability to Third Parties under Common Law

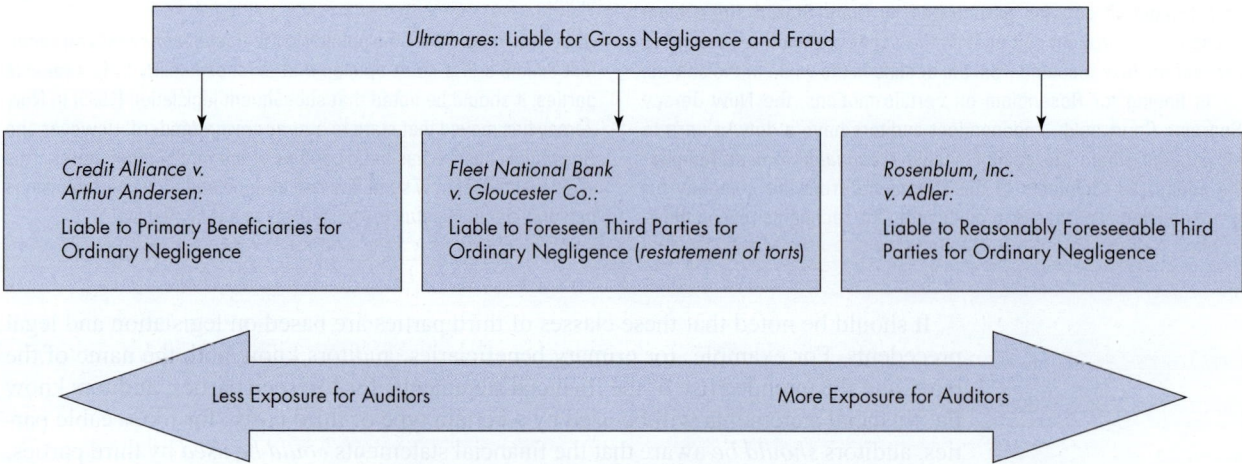

[11] C. Pacini, M. J. Martin, and L. Hamilton, "At the Interface of Law and Accounting: An Examination of a Trend toward a Reduction in the Scope of Auditor Liability to Third Parties in the Common Law Countries," *American Business Law Journal,* Winter 2000, pp. 171–225.

defenses available against clients, except for the unavailability of the contributory negligence defense in cases brought by third parties):

1. The third party did not have appropriate standing to sue in that jurisdiction (for example, bringing suit for ordinary negligence if the appropriate relationship between auditors and third party does not exist). Recall that auditors' liability to third parties for ordinary negligence differs significantly depending on the jurisdiction in which the action is brought.
2. The third party's loss was caused by events other than the financial statements and auditors' examination (causation defense). For example, the failure of an entity (and losses incurred by parties providing capital to that entity) may result from poor business practices and decisions, not misstated financial statements.
3. Auditors' work was performed in accordance with professional standards (e.g., GAAS for audits of financial statements), which is generally interpreted to mean that auditors were not negligent (ordinary negligence).

Liability for Compilation and Review Services

People find it easy to think about common law liability in connection with audited financial statements. Do not forget, however, that accountants also render compilation and review services and are associated with the resultant *unaudited* financial information. Users expect public accountants to perform these services in accordance with professional standards and courts can impose liability for accounting work found to be substandard. Accountants have been assessed damages for work on such statements, as shown in the *1136 Tenants' Corporation v. Max Rothenberg & Co.* case. In this case, the court concluded that accountants engaged to perform "write-up" (compilation) work had a duty to inform clients of indicators of fraud that were identified during the engagement.

One significant risk involved with compilation and review engagements is that the client may fail to understand the nature of the service being given. Accountants should use a conference and an engagement letter to explain clearly that a compilation engagement (write-up) does not involve gathering sufficient appropriate evidence and is lesser in scope than a review engagement. Similarly, a review service should be explained in terms of being less extensive than an audit engagement conducted in accordance with GAAS. Clear understandings at the outset (along with clearly worded engagement letters) can enable accountants and clients to avoid later disagreements. In *Iselin v. Landau* (1992), the court decided that the lack of an opinion on reviewed financial statements precluded the third party (**William Iselin & Company**) from bringing a lawsuit against the auditors (**Mann Judd Landau**) because of losses suffered from the bankruptcy of one of Iselin's customers. (Mann Judd Landau had performed a review engagement on the financial statements of Iselin's customer.)

↳ REVIEW CHECKPOINTS

C.3 For what type of actions can clients bring suit against auditors under common law? What must clients prove prior to bringing suit in each case?

C.4 In terms of tort liability, what level of responsibility do auditors owe clients under common law?

C.5 What must third parties prove in a common law action seeking recovery of damages from auditors?

C.6 What legal theory is derived from the *Ultramares* decision? Can auditors rely on the *Ultramares* decision today?

C.7 Define and explain *privity, primary beneficiary, foreseen party*, and *foreseeable party* in terms of the degree of failure to exercise the appropriate level of professional care on the part of auditors that would trigger the liability.

C.8 What defenses are available to auditors against suits brought by clients under common law? Against suits brought by third parties under common law?

C.9 What additional defenses can accountants use in lawsuits related to compilation and review engagements?

LIABILITY UNDER STATUTORY LAW

LEARNING OBJECTIVE C-3
Describe auditors' liability to third parties under statutory law.

Auditors can be liable to individuals when they violate a specific law or statute when performing professional services; this is referred to as *statutory liability*. Several federal statutes provide sources of potential liability for auditors, including the Federal False Statements Statute, the Federal Mail Fraud Statute, the Federal Conspiracy Statute, the Securities Act of 1933 (Securities Act), the Securities Exchange Act of 1934 (Securities Exchange Act), and the Sarbanes-Oxley Act. Federal securities regulation in the United States was enacted in the 1930s not only as a reaction to the events of the early years of the Great Depression but also as a culmination of attempts at "blue-sky" regulation by states.[12] The Securities Act and the Securities Exchange Act require registrants to disclose important financial and nonfinancial information required for informed investment decisions. The securities acts and the SEC operate for the protection of investors and for the facilitation of orderly capital markets. Even so, no federal government agency, including the SEC, rules on the *quality* of investments. The securities acts have been characterized as "truth-in-securities" law. Their spirit favors the otherwise uninformed investing public and caveat vendor—let the seller beware of violations—is applied to the issuer.

As the following graphic shows, auditors are exposed to liability under the Securities Act and the Securities Exchange Act when investors purchase or sell securities ([1] in the graphic). If an economic loss is suffered [2] and if the financial statements contain a material misstatement [3], auditors may be held liable for failure to detect the material misstatement.

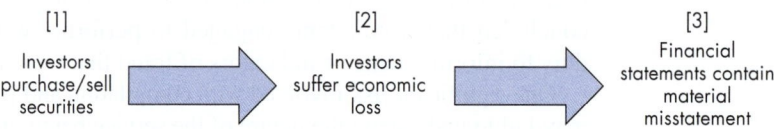

Although not involving an auditor, the following Auditing Insight demonstrates the need for shareholders to prove they suffered an economic loss to successfully bring suit.

AUDITING INSIGHT — Who Needs to Show a Loss?

In a federal judge's decision to overturn a jury award of $5.55 per share to shareholders of **Apollo Group, Inc.** (owner of the **University of Phoenix**), the judge did not dispute the contention that Apollo may have misled investors by withholding a negative report on student recruitment policies contained in a Department of Education Review. However, he indicated that "[the plaintiffs] failed to prove that Apollo's actions caused investors to suffer any harm."

Source: "Verdict Against Apollo Group Overturned," *The Wall Street Journal*, August 6, 2008, p. B5.

Because of the availability of class action litigation and the wide dissemination and use of financial information filed with the SEC, litigation against auditors under the Securities Act and Securities and Exchange Act is the highest growing area of concern for auditors. The following sections discuss auditors' liability under these acts in more detail.

↳ REVIEW CHECKPOINT

C.10 How does auditors' liability under statutory law arise?

---

[12] The term *blue sky* comes from a state judge's remark during a securities fraud case: "These securities have no more substance than a piece of blue sky."

THE SECURITIES ACT OF 1933 (SECURITIES ACT)

LEARNING OBJECTIVE C-4
Specify the civil and criminal liability provisions of the Securities Act of 1933.

The Securities Act of 1933 regulates the initial issuance of securities by registrants to the investing public through a market (including **initial public offerings**, or **IPOs**). The Securities Act provides that no person may lawfully buy, sell, offer to buy, or offer to sell any security by means of interstate commerce unless a **registration statement** is *effective* (a legal term essentially meaning *filed and accepted by the SEC*). A registration statement is a set of documents filed with the SEC prior to the offering of securities. An important component of the registration statement is a **prospectus**, which is a legal document offering securities for sale and includes significant information about the issuing entity, including its historical financial statements and other necessary disclosures. Certain exemptions exist for limited offerings, offerings by small investors, and offerings involving financially sophisticated investors; these exemptions can be found in section 3, section 4, and Regulation D of the Securities Act.

The general point concerning the Securities Act is that, with some minor exceptions, *all* issuances of securities to the public must be registered with the SEC. Importantly for the auditor, the Securities Act requires that the registration statement include financial statements and required disclosures that ". . . shall be certified by an independent public or certified accountant"; this language requires an audit examination. Auditors are required not only to audit the financial statements as of the most recent date of the financial statements but also to ensure that these statements are fairly stated up to the date the registration statement becomes effective, which could possibly be up to one year beyond the date of the financial statements. This audit requirement provides the basis for auditors' liability to investors under the Securities Act.

Section 11: Civil Liability

Section 11 of the Securities Act is of great interest to auditors because of the duties and responsibilities it establishes. This section discusses the principal criteria defining civil liabilities under the statute.

Section 11. Securities Act of 1933

The following excerpts from Section 11 are of particular importance in identifying the responsibilities of auditors under this Act.

Section 11(*a*): . . . any person acquiring such security [in a registered offering] . . . may sue:

- Every person who signed the registration statement.
- Every person who was a director of . . . or partner in, the issuer.
- Every accountant, engineer, or appraiser.
- Every underwriter with respect to such security.

Section 11(*b*): Notwithstanding the provisions of subsection (a), no person, other than the issuer, shall be liable as provided therein who shall sustain the burden of proof that . . . as regards any part of the registration statement purporting to be made upon his authority as an expert . . . he had, after reasonable investigation, reasonable grounds to believe . . . that the statements therein were true and that there was no omission to state a material fact. . . .

While section 11(*a*) notes that a number of parties involved in the registration and sale process might be liable to persons acquiring securities, section 11(*b*) generally limits the liability to the issuers of securities, with some exceptions. Because auditors are considered to be the "experts" regarding the fairness of the financial statements and must perform a "reasonable investigation" (an audit in accordance with GAAS), section 11(*b*) is of great importance to auditors. This requirement imposes liability for auditors for acts representing *ordinary negligence*.

Auditors commonly provide assurance to underwriters, who act as intermediaries between the offering entity and investing public by purchasing securities for investment or resale. Auditors provide **comfort letters** to underwriters that address, among other information, the independence of auditors and the fairness of the registrant's financial statements.

Section 11 includes two other very important implications for auditors. First, reviewing the first two words in section 11(*a*), "*any person*" (emphasis added) may bring suit against auditors. Essentially, the Securities Act treats *all* persons as being *reasonably foreseeable* and holds auditors liable to these persons. In addition, section 11 shifts the major burden of proof from the plaintiff (investor) to the auditors; essentially, plaintiffs must prove each of the following:

1. They suffered an economic loss.
2. The financial statements contained a material misstatement.

Recall that under common law liability, plaintiffs had to also allege and prove some level of failure to exercise the appropriate level of professional care and that the loss was caused by reliance on the misstated financial statements. Thus, under the Securities Act, the plaintiff is *not* required to demonstrate that the misstated financial statements caused the loss; the burden of proof regarding professional care rests with auditors. Section 11 has the following major implications for auditors:

- Auditors are liable for ordinary negligence.
- Auditors have potential liability to a large class of parties (investors in securities).
- Auditors (and not others) have the burden of proof, in this case, proving that a reasonable investigation under section 11(*b*) was conducted.

The final implication is particularly important because it presumes that auditors are "guilty until proven innocent" and has increased auditors' exposure to investors. However, section 11 was written with the protection of the investing public in mind, not the protection of the expert auditors. The first significant court case under section 11 was *Escott v. BarChris Construction Corporation.*

LEGAL PRECEDENT

ESCOTT V. BARCHRIS CONSTRUCTION CORP. (1968)

BarChris Construction Corporation built bowling alleys. In 1961, BarChris engaged in a public offering of convertible bonds that was subject to the provisions of the Securities Act. BarChris issued a registration statement that included financial statements audited by **Peat, Marwick, Mitchell & Co.** (now KPMG). The financial statements included material overstatements of revenues, current assets, gross profit, and backlog of sales orders and material understatements of contingent liabilities, loans to company officers, and potential liability for customer delinquencies. BarChris' worsening financial condition resulted in a default on interest payments (the economic loss) and BarChris eventually declared bankruptcy. **Barry Escott** and other investors sued BarChris's executive officers, directors, and auditor (Peat, Marwick, Mitchell & Co.) under the provisions of the Securities Act, citing lack of appropriate level of professional care during the conduct of the audit.

The judge ruled that the auditors had failed to perform a diligent and reasonable investigation [section 11(*b*)]. The judge found that the auditor had spent "only" 20.5 hours on the subsequent events review, had read no important documents, and "He asked questions, he got answers that he considered satisfactory, and he did nothing to verify them. . . . He was too easily satisfied with glib answers to his inquiries." The judge also said, "Accountants should not be held to a standard higher than that recognized in their profession. I do not do so here. The senior accountant's review [of subsequent events] did not come up to that standard. He did not take some of the steps which [the] written program prescribed. He did not spend an adequate amount of time on a task of this magnitude."

Case conclusion: The auditors' failure to perform a reasonable investigation of subsequent events did not satisfy section 11(*b*) and resulted in their liability to investors in BarChris' bonds.

Auditors' Defenses under the Securities Act

Section 11 provides two possible defenses to auditors, assuming that purchasers of securities are able to demonstrate they suffered a loss and the financial statements are materially misstated. Note that these defenses are similar to two defenses available to auditors for actions brought by clients and third parties under common law.

1. The *"due diligence" defense* provides that auditors who can prove they conducted a "reasonable investigation" will not be held liable under the Securities Act. A reasonable investigation can ordinarily be shown by conducting an audit in accordance with GAAS.
2. Under the *causation defense,* if auditors can prove that all or part of the plaintiffs' losses were caused by something other than the materially misstated financial statements included in the registration statement, they are not required to pay all or part of the damages. This defense may create some imaginative "other reasons." In the *BarChris* case, at least one plaintiff had purchased securities *after* the company had gone bankrupt. This claim was settled out of court.

Section 13: Statute of Limitations

Section 13 of the Securities Act requires any suits to be brought within one year after discovery of the materially misstated statement or omission or within three years after the public offering. These limitations restrict auditors' liability exposure to a determinable time span. In many cases, the statute of limitations is a viable defense available to auditors. Although Sarbanes-Oxley generally extended the statute of limitations to within two years of discovery and five years after the action for situations involving fraud, some questions exist as to whether these extended limitations apply to the Securities Act, particularly in cases not involving fraud.

Section 17: Antifraud

Section 17 of the Securities Act is the antifraud section. This section makes it unlawful to "use the mails or instruments of transportation in interstate commerce" in an effort to defraud others. As with section 11, plaintiffs are not required to demonstrate reliance on the fraudulent information or that the fraudulent information resulted in their loss. Therefore, the burden of proof still rests with auditors.

Section 24: Criminal Liability

Section 24 sets forth the criminal penalties imposed by the Securities Act. Criminal penalties are characterized by monetary fines, prison terms, or both. The key words in section 24 are "willful" violation and "willfully" causing materially misstated statements to be filed. Thus, while auditors have civil liability to third parties under section 11 in cases in which ordinary negligence can be demonstrated (failure to conduct a GAAS audit), criminal penalties are possible under the 1933 Securities Act only for instances in which auditors act with knowledge of the materially misstated financial statements (fraud and, perhaps, gross negligence). Section 24 establishes these penalties for fines at $10,000 and imprisonment for up to five years. The *United States v. Benjamin* case is an example of how auditors may be found criminally liable under the Securities Act.

LEGAL PRECEDENT

UNITED STATES V. BENJAMIN (1964)

The judgment in this case resulted in the conviction of auditors for willingly conspiring by use of interstate commerce to sell unregistered securities and to defraud investors in the sale of securities in violation of section 24 of the Securities Act. The auditors had prepared pro forma balance sheets and claimed that use of the words *pro forma* absolved them of responsibility. The auditors also claimed they did not know their reports would be used in connection with securities sales. The court found otherwise, showing that the auditors did in fact know about the use of their reports and that certain statements about asset values and acquisitions were materially misstated. The court made two significant findings: (1) the willfulness requirements of section 24 may be proved by showing that due diligence would have revealed the materially misstated statements and (2) use of limiting words such as *pro forma* does not justify showing false ownership of assets in any kind of financial statements.

> ### ⌕ REVIEW CHECKPOINTS
>
> C.11 What type of transactions are governed by the Securities Act?
>
> C.12 What is a *registration statement*? How does the registration statement introduce potential liability to auditors under the Securities Act?
>
> C.13 How is section 11 of the Securities Act different from the legal environment that exists under common law?
>
> C.14 What must the plaintiff prove in a suit under section 11 of the Securities Act seeking recovery of damages from auditors? What defenses are available to auditors in this situation?
>
> C.15 Describe the *due diligence* and *causation* defenses available to auditors under the Securities Act.
>
> C.16 What liability exposure for auditors is found in the Securities Act in (a) section 17 and (b) section 24?
>
> C.17 According to the *BarChris* decision, how did auditors violate generally accepted auditing standards ?

THE SECURITIES EXCHANGE ACT OF 1934 (SECURITIES EXCHANGE ACT)

LEARNING OBJECTIVE C-5
Specify the civil and criminal liability provisions of the Securities Exchange Act of 1934.

The Securities Exchange Act regulates daily trading of securities and requires most entities whose securities are traded in interstate commerce to register and file pertinent information with the SEC. Entities having total assets of $10 million or more and 500 or more stockholders are required to register under the Securities Exchange Act. The purpose of these size and share criteria is to define securities in which there is a significant public interest. (These criteria are subject to change by the SEC.) For auditors, the most significant aspect of the Securities Exchange Act is the requirement for registrants to file the following reports with the SEC:

- **Form 10-K**, also known as an *annual report,* that is filed annually within 60 days of the date of the entity's financial statements. These reports include financial statements that are audited by independent auditors.
- **Form 10-Q**, which is filed quarterly within 45 days of the end of the each of the first three fiscal quarters (the fourth quarter's results are filed within Form 10-K). These reports include financial statements that are reviewed by independent auditors.
- **Form 8-K**, also known as a *current events report,* that is filed periodically upon the occurrence of major events (e.g., earnings releases, major asset sales, acquisitions, and auditor changes). Independent auditors may review these reports or otherwise assist in their preparation.

The form and content of 10-K and 10-Q filings are governed by the SEC through **Regulation S-X** (which covers the annual and interim financial statements) and **Regulation S-K** (which covers other supplementary disclosures). In addition to these two regulations, auditors must be familiar with **Financial Reporting Releases (FRRs)**, which express new rules and policies about disclosure, and **Staff Accounting Bulletins (SABs)**, which provide unofficial, but important, interpretations of Regulations S-X and S-K. Taken together, these four pronouncements provide the authoritative literature for information that must be filed with the SEC.

Section 10 and Rule 10*b*-5: Antifraud

Section 10 of the Securities Exchange Act is used against auditors quite frequently. Like section 17 of the Securities Act, section 10 is a general antifraud section that makes it unlawful for persons to use "manipulative" or "deceptive" devices in connection with the purchase or sale of securities. Rule 10b-5, made by the SEC staff under their authority to create administrative rules related to the statute, is more explicit than section 10 in identifying auditors' specific responsibilities.

Rule 10b-5. Securities Exchange Act of 1934

Rule 10b-5. Employment of Manipulative and Deceptive Devices. It shall be unlawful for any person, directly or indirectly, by the use of any means or instrumentality of interstate commerce, or of the mails, or of any facility of any national securities exchange,

1. To employ any device, scheme, or artifice to defraud.
2. To make any untrue statement of material fact or to omit to state a material fact necessary in order to make the statements made, in the light of the circumstances under which they were made, not misleading.
3. To engage in any act, practice, or course of business which operates or would operate as a fraud or deceit upon any person in connection with the purchase or sale of any security.

An important point about Rule 10b-5 liability is that plaintiffs must prove **scienter** (a mental state embracing the intent to deceive, manipulate, or defraud) to impose liability under the rule. Mere failure to exercise the appropriate level of professional care is not enough cause for liability. Two cases (*Ernst & Ernst v. Hochfelder* and *Denise L. Nappier et al. v. PricewaterhouseCoopers*) illustrate the need for purchasers and sellers of securities to prove scienter on the part of auditors and confirm the inability for these parties to bring suit against auditors for ordinary negligence. The *Hochfelder* case was also significant in providing exposure for auditors in cases of gross negligence, even in the absence of scienter.

LEGAL PRECEDENT

ERNST & ERNST V. HOCHFELDER (U.S. SUPREME COURT, 1976)

In this case, **Hochfelder** represented investors in an escrow account with **First Securities of Chicago**; this account was maintained by Lester Nay (president of First Securities), who diverted funds for his own personal use through a fraudulent scheme that was revealed in a suicide note prepared by Nay. When the escrow accounts proved worthless (the economic loss), the investors (through Hochfelder) brought suit against the auditors (**Ernst & Ernst**), alleging that their negligence prevented them from uncovering the scheme and preventing their losses. Hochfelder specifically disclaimed any allegations of fraud or intentional misconduct on the part of Ernst & Ernst but wanted to see liability under section 10(b) imposed for ordinary negligence in the auditors' failure to uncover the fraudulent scheme.

The Court reasoned that section 10(b) in its reference to "employment of any manipulative and deceptive device" meant that intention to deceive, manipulate, or defraud is necessary to support a private cause of action under section 10(b) and failure to exercise the appropriate level of professional care is not sufficient. This decision is considered a landmark for auditors because it relieved them of liability for ordinary negligence under section 10(b) of the Securities Exchange Act and its companion SEC Rule 10(b)-5.

However, footnote 12 in this opinion noted that "[in] certain areas of the law recklessness is considered to be a form of intentional conduct for purposes of imposing liability for some act. We need not address here the question whether, in some circumstances, reckless behavior is sufficient for civil liability under 10(b) and Rule 10b-5."

Case conclusion: This case established precedent for the plaintiff's need to prove scienter to impose section 10(b) liability under the Securities Exchange Act. In addition, the reference to "recklessness" in the footnote to the opinion provides potential exposure to auditors for gross negligence under the Securities Exchange Act.

DENISE L. NAPPIER ET AL. V. PRICEWATERHOUSECOOPERS (2002)

Denise L. Nappier (treasurer of the state of Connecticut) successfully brought suit on behalf of shareholders (including Connecticut Retirement Plans and Trust Funds) against **Campbell Soup Company** and its directors for losses incurred upon declines in Campbell's stock price (the economic loss). In this suit, Nappier demonstrated that the purchase of these shares was influenced by audited financial statements that were shown to contain material misstatements. The shareholders then attempted to assert an additional claim against Campbell's auditors (**PricewaterhouseCoopers**), alleging that they violated the provisions of the Securities Exchange Act by being a party to the preparation and certification of fraudulent financial statements. The case was dismissed when the shareholders could not prove the allegation that PricewaterhouseCoopers operated with scienter in conducting their audits of Campbell's financial statements.

Section 18: Civil Liability

Section 18 sets forth the pertinent civil liability under the Securities Exchange Act. Under Rule 10*b*-5 and section 18, plaintiffs have the same burden of proof as under common law (that is, they must demonstrate that the loss was caused by reliance on the materially misstated financial statements and that the auditors failed to exercise the appropriate level of professional care). However, under the Securities Exchange Act, plaintiffs must demonstrate scienter on the part of auditors. Thus, plaintiffs must demonstrate all of the following:

1. They suffered an economic loss.
2. The financial statements contained a material misstatement.
3. The loss was caused by reliance on the materially misstated financial statements.
4. Auditors were aware that the financial statements contained a material misstatement (recall that, under *Hochfelder,* auditors may be held liable for gross negligence).

Of note, two key differences in liability under the Securities Exchange Act and Securities Act are that, under the former, (1) plaintiffs have the burden of proof and (2) auditors cannot be held liable for ordinary negligence. The importance of placing the burden of proof on the plaintiffs is illustrated by cases summarized in the accompanying Auditing Insight. Clearly, the shift of burden of proof from auditors (in the Securities Act) to plaintiffs (in the Securities Exchange Act) is an important distinction and determinant in plaintiffs' ability to successfully prevail in securities actions.

AUDITING INSIGHT — Prove It!

The importance of placing the burden of proof on plaintiffs is demonstrated by two decisions. The U.S. Court of Appeals for the Seventh Circuit (*Tricontinental Industries v. Pricewaterhouse Coopers, LLP*) and the U.S. Court of Appeals for the Second Circuit (*Lattanzio v. Deloitte & Touche, LLP*) dismissed charges against the accounting firms because plaintiffs failed to demonstrate that their losses were caused by materially misstated financial statements. The following excerpt from the Seventh Circuit Court in the former case is of particular note:

Although we agree with the district court that **Tricontinental's** scienter allegations are problematic, we believe that Tricontinental's claim for pre-closing fraud suffers from a more fundamental infirmity.... Tricontinental's claim falls short with respect to the last requirement: Tricontinental does not allege how PwC's fraud caused its losses.

Sources: *Tricontinental Industries v. PricewaterhouseCoopers LLP,* 2007, U.S. App. LEXIS 7247 (7th Cir., 2007); *Lattanzio v. Deloitte & Touche LLP,* 476 F.3d 147 (2d Cir. 2007).

Section 18 of the Securities Exchange Act establishes a statute of limitations of one year after discovery of the violation of the Act or within three years after the violation of the Act itself; for cases involving fraud, Sarbanes-Oxley extends these dates to two and five years, respectively.

Auditors' Defenses under the Securities Exchange Act

As a defense, auditors can attempt to demonstrate that they acted in "good faith" and had no knowledge of the material misstatement. (Causation is not a defense because it is presumed that the plaintiff has already demonstrated this in bringing suit). Although this would seem to imply that auditors are liable only for fraudulent actions under the Securities Exchange Act (by demonstrating they had no knowledge of the material misstatement), the *Hochfelder* decision has resulted in some uncertainty as to auditors' liability in the absence of scienter (specifically, for acts that may be considered to represent gross negligence). Importantly, in contrast to the Securities Act, auditors are not liable to shareholders for actions representing ordinary negligence under the Securities Exchange Act.

Section 32: Criminal Liability

Section 32 states the criminal penalties for violation of the Securities Exchange Act. Like that pertaining to section 24 of the Securities Act, the critical test is whether the violator acted "willfully and knowingly." Therefore, to be subject to criminal liability, auditors must be shown to be guilty of fraud. Sarbanes-Oxley markedly increased the criminal penalties for violating the Securities Exchange Act; currently, violators may be fined up to $5 million and imprisoned for up to 20 years. In addition, Sarbanes-Oxley provides that if the "person" was not a natural person (for example, an accounting firm), fines of up to $25 million can be assessed. The *United States v. Natelli* (better known as the "National Student Marketing" case) illustrates potential criminal liability for auditors charged with violations of section 32. (It is important to note that this case occurred prior to the increased liability imposed by Sarbanes-Oxley.)

LEGAL PRECEDENT

UNITED STATES V. NATELLI ("NATIONAL STUDENT MARKETING" CASE) (1975)

In this case, two auditors were convicted because of their involvement with materially misstated financial statements included in the proxy statement of **National Student Marketing Corporation**. These financial statements failed to reveal a $1 million write-off of "sales" (about 20 percent of the amount previously reported) and a corresponding large adjustment to National Student Marketing's operating income.

The court stated: It is hard to probe the intent of a defendant.... When we deal with a defendant who is a professional accountant, it is even harder at times to distinguish between simple errors of judgment and errors made with sufficient criminal intent to support a conviction, especially when there is no financial gain to the accountant other than his legitimate fee.

Both the audit partner in charge of the engagement (**Anthony Natelli**) and his supervisor were fined and received jail sentences of one year each. Although a federal appeals court reversed the supervisor's conviction, it upheld Natelli's conviction because of this apparent motive and action to conceal the effect of some accounting adjustments. Natelli's sentence was eventually reduced to 60 days.

Foreign Corrupt Practices Act (FCPA)

In 1977, Congress passed the FCPA, which:

- Made it illegal for corporations or their officers to knowingly bribe foreign officials or participate in bribery schemes involving foreign officials to obtain or retain business.
- Required entities to develop and maintain effective internal controls.

In 1988, the FCPA became codified as an amendment to the Securities Exchange Act. As a result, auditors may be liable for violations of this act if they should have identified these violations during their examination. In a recent settlement, German conglomerate **Siemens AG** agreed to pay $800 million to settle bribery investigations involving payment to foreign government officials; Siemens did not admit to the bribery allegations, but it did acknowledge having inadequate controls and maintaining improper accounting records. This was the largest fine ever imposed under the FCPA.[13] Recent investigations involving alleged payments made by **Hewlett-Packard** to secure a contract for the delivery and installation of an information network to Russia's prosecutor general, offers by **Goldman Sachs** and other financial institutions for payments to a Libyan investment authority, and **Oracle's** software sales to government agencies in Western and Central Africa indicate that increasing scrutiny is being placed on potential violations of FCPA, as noted in the accompanying Auditing Insight.[14]

---

[13] "Siemens to Pay Huge Fine in Bribery Inquiry," *The Wall Street Journal*, December 15, 2008, p. B1.

[14] "H-P Bribe Probe Widens," *The Wall Street Journal*, September 10, 2010, p. B1; "SEC Probes Goldman Over Libyan Dealings," *The Wall Street Journal*, August 10, 2011, p. C1; "U.S. Probes Oracle Dealings," *The Wall Street Journal*, August 31, 2011, p. B1, B2.

> ### AUDITING INSIGHT | Increased Focus on FCPA
>
> The U.S. Department of Justice is increasing its enforcement of potential FCPA violations, as evidenced by the following:
>
> - Nearly 80 percent of corporate acquisitions have either ended or been renegotiated because of anticorruption issues or potential violations of the FCPA. These decisions are likely driven by the experiences of companies such as **General Electric**, which was required to pay $23.4 million in fines to settle FCPA violations at **Ionics** and **Amersham** that occurred prior to General Electric's acquisition of these entities.
>
> - All off the 10 largest settlements for violations of FCPA have occurred since 2008; 8 occurred in 2010 alone.
> - In 2000, prosecutors brought no charges in FCPA criminal actions; in 2009, they pursued 34 actions with an additional 150 open investigations in process.
>
> **Sources:** "The Bribery Law Racket," *Forbes,* May 24, 2010, pp. 70–77; "Deal-Breaker: Fear of the FCPA," *CFO.com,* February 15, 2011.

SUMMARY OF AUDITORS' LIABILITY TO CLIENTS AND THIRD PARTIES

Thus far, we have discussed auditors' potential liability to clients and third parties under both common law and statutory law (Securities Act of 1933 and Securities Exchange Act of 1934, respectively). Exhibit C.2 summarizes various elements of this liability, including (1) the level of professional care (performance) owed to various parties by auditors, (2) the burden of proof, and (3) various defenses available to auditors. Most noteworthy in Exhibit C.2 is the fact that plaintiffs have the burden of proving that auditors' failure to exercise the appropriate level of professional care caused the loss ("burden of proof") under common law and the Securities Exchange Act of 1934; however, the burden of proof is with auditors under the Securities Act of 1933. See Exhibit C.3 for a summary of important cases that have either developed auditor liability (common law) or clarified various provisions of the Securities Acts.

It is important to note that auditors' liability will continue to evolve over time. In a 2007 case (*Tellabs, Inc. v. Makor Issues & Rights, Ltd.*), the U.S. Supreme Court held that trial courts must consider all plausible inferences of scienter and that cases should be permitted to proceed only if the possibility of scienter is "cogent and at least as compelling as any opposing inference."[15] Some cases have been dismissed using this standard, but other cases have taken the view that the burden of proof regarding scienter still remains with the defendant. Future cases and rulings will likely provide further clarification as to the relative burden of proof in cases involving accusations of scienter.

> ### ↳ REVIEW CHECKPOINTS
>
> C.18 Identify the contents of Form 10-K, Form 10-Q, and Form 8-K. How are auditors involved with the information in these filings?
>
> C.19 What are (a) Regulation S-X, (b) Regulation S-K, (c) Financial Reporting Releases, and (d) Staff Accounting Bulletins?
>
> C.20 Who may bring suit against auditors under the Securities Exchange Act? What must these parties demonstrate in order to bring suit?
>
> C.21 What defenses are available to auditors under the Securities Exchange Act?
>
> C.22 What are the criminal penalties associated with violations of the Securities Exchange Act?
>
> C.23 What is *scienter*? How do the findings in *Ernst & Ernst v. Hochfelder* and *Denise L. Nappier et al. v. PricewaterhouseCoopers* relate to scienter?
>
> C.24 What are the major differences in auditors' liability under the Securities Act of 1933 and the Securities Exchange Act of 1934?

---

[15] *Tellabs, Inc. v. Makor Issues & Rights, Ltd.*, 127 S. Ct. 2499 (2007).

EXHIBIT C.2   Summary of Auditors' Liability

Source of Liability	Party(ies) Involved	Plaintiff Proof	Type of Offense	Auditors' Defenses
Common law	Client	• Economic loss • Auditors' breach of contract or failure to exercise the appropriate level of professional care • Loss caused by breach of contract or failure to exercise appropriate level of professional care	• Breach of contract • Ordinary negligence • Gross negligence • Fraud	• No breach of contract or no failure to exercise the appropriate level of professional care • Economic loss caused by other factors (causation) • Clients partially responsible for loss (contributory negligence)
	Third parties	• Economic loss • Auditors' failure to exercise the appropriate level of professional care • Material misstatements in financial statements • Loss caused by reliance on materially misstated financial statements	• Ordinary negligence (depends on jurisdiction and standing of party) • Gross negligence • Fraud	• Lack of appropriate standing (relationship) between third party and auditors • Loss caused by factors other than financial statements and auditors' examination • Work performed in accordance with GAAS or other professional standards
Securities Act of 1933	Purchasers of securities in an initial registration	• Economic loss • Material misstatements in financial statements	• Ordinary negligence • Gross negligence • Fraud	• Due diligence (auditors conducted a GAAS audit) • Loss caused by factors other than financial statements and auditors' examination
Securities Exchange Act of 1934	Purchasers and sellers of securities through subsequent transactions	• Economic loss • Material misstatements in financial statements • Loss caused by reliance on materially misstated financial statements • Auditors were aware of material misstatements and acted with intent (scienter)	• Gross negligence • Fraud	• Auditors acted in good faith • Auditors had no knowledge of material misstatements

EXHIBIT C.3
Significant Cases Affecting Auditors' Liability

Case	Significance
Smith v. London Assurance Corp. (1905)	• Established auditors' liability to clients for breach of contract
Ultramares Corp. v. Touche (1931)	• Established rights of third parties not in privity with auditors to bring legal action • Concluded that auditors are generally not liable to third parties not in privity for ordinary negligence but could be liable for gross negligence
Credit Alliance v. Arthur Andersen (1985)	• Established auditors' liability to primary beneficiaries for ordinary negligence
Rusch Factors v. Levin (1968); Fleet National Bank v. Gloucester Co. (1994)	• Established auditors' liability to foreseen parties for ordinary negligence (*restatement of torts doctrine*)
Rosenblum, Inc. v. Adler (1983)	• Established auditors' liability to foreseeable parties for ordinary negligence
Escott v. BarChris Construction Corp. (1968)	• Confirmed auditor liability for ordinary negligence to investors under the Securities Act • Established importance of auditors' review of subsequent events
Ernst & Ernst v. Hochfelder (1976)	• Confirmed auditors' liability to shareholders under the Securities Exchange Act if scienter is demonstrated • Provided potential exposure to auditors for gross negligence even in absence of scienter

THE CHANGING LANDSCAPE OF AUDITORS' LIABILITY

LEARNING OBJECTIVE C-6
Understand recent developments that affect auditors' liability to clients and third parties.

The preceding discussion identifies the significant exposure of auditors to legal liability for their actions to various parties. Most people would argue that auditors performing substandard work *should* be held liable for that work, but a number of factors have increased auditors' exposure to litigation brought by plaintiffs:

- Increased pressure to hold auditors accountable in light of a number of highly publicized audit failures in the early 2000s (e.g., **Enron** and **WorldCom**) and the significant losses of billions of dollars to investors in those companies.
- Investors' and other individuals' awareness of litigation against auditors as an avenue to recover losses, regardless of the actual reason for and cause of those losses.
- The existence of highly complex accounting standards and difficulty in interpreting and evaluating financial statements prepared under those standards (for example, **General Electric,** a large multinational with talented accounting personnel has restated its financial results twice since 2005 because of complex standards related to accounting for derivative instruments).
- The doctrine of joint and several liability, which may expose auditors to extensive and unreasonable losses when they are only partially at fault.
- The availability of class action suits, which makes it attractive for a small number of individuals to bring suit on behalf of a larger number of others.
- The availability of joint and several liability, class action suits, and contingent fee arrangements make litigation against auditors an attractive opportunity for plaintiff attorneys.

> **AUDITING INSIGHT** | **Are CPAs a Target?**
>
> In addition to the number of factors listed here that have increased auditors' exposure to litigation brought by plaintiffs, a recent article identified the following additional factors that are providing auditors increased exposure for liability claims:
>
> - A reduced likelihood of judges dismissing charges against auditors.
> - The availability of insurance, which makes auditors a desirable target for attorneys for recovery.
> - Mergers of smaller firms and larger firms and difficulties during the transition period of these mergers because of the lack of effective risk management practices for smaller firms.
> - Reductions in staff by accounting firms in response to the economic downturn.
> - Clients' increased interest in pursuing professional liability claims to recoup losses during the economic downturn.
>
> **Source:** "Target CPAs," *Accounting Today*, July 1, 2011, pp. 1, 53.

The auditing profession considers the U.S. tort liability system a crisis of expanding liability exposure in need of reform. Some important reforms that have been implemented or are currently being discussed in response to these damages are summarized in the remainder of this section. Some of these reforms influence auditors' liability under common law and statutory law described in the preceding sections.

Sarbanes-Oxley

The corporate scandals of **Enron** and **WorldCom** were the impetus for the creation and passage of the *U.S. Public Company Reform and Investor Protection Act of 2002*, better known as the *Sarbanes-Oxley Act*. This act seeks to strengthen corporate accountability and governance of public entities. Although the more publicized aspects of Sarbanes-Oxley affect corporate officers and directors, some of its provisions affect auditors' statutory liability under the securities acts by increasing the penalties for auditors' involvement in financial statement fraud. Many of the aspects of Sarbanes-Oxley that affect auditors' planning, implementation, and reporting processes are discussed in other chapters in this book. Sarbanes-Oxley has impacted auditors' liability as follows:

- Extended the statute of limitations for bringing suit under the Securities Exchange Act to the earlier of (1) two years after the discovery of facts relating to violations of the act or (2) five years following the violation of the act. In addition, as noted earlier, the penalties for securities fraud have been increased to provide for fines of up to $5 million and imprisonment of up to 20 years for violations of the Securities Exchange Act.

- Increased penalties for mail fraud and wire fraud from 5 years of imprisonment to 20 years of imprisonment.

- Addressed the destruction, alteration, or falsification of records in federal investigations and bankruptcies. Although these issues are addressed in laws regarding obstruction of justice and were the means by which the Department of Justice successfully prosecuted **Arthur Andersen,** Sarbanes-Oxley adds another avenue to pursue actions against accounting firms that fail to cooperate with federal investigations.[16] Firms and individuals found to have altered or destroyed documents with the intent to impede an investigation may be subject to fines and imprisonment for up to 20 years. In addition, under *Auditing Standard No. 3*, accountants performing an audit or review must maintain all engagement documentation for a period of 7 years. Firms that do not comply with the record-retention provision are subject to fines and imprisonment of individual violators within the firm for up to 10 years. This provision of Sarbanes-Oxley has forced many firms to review and revise their record-retention policies.

---

[16] Arthur Andersen was indicted and convicted of obstruction of justice, which resulted in the firm's collapse. This conviction was subsequently reversed by the U.S. Supreme Court, but it was too late to save Andersen. See "KPMG Faces Indictment Risk on Tax Shelters: Justice Officials Debate Whether to Pursue Case; Fears of 'Andersen Scenario,'" *The Wall Street Journal*, June 16, 2005, p. A1.

In addition to the preceding items, Sarbanes-Oxley amended federal sentencing guidelines that increase financial and criminal penalties when securities fraud, obstruction of justice, and criminal fraud exist. This means not only that auditors face a higher liability risk but also that Sarbanes-Oxley may influence the courts in decisions regarding awards in civil cases. These provisions are considered a setback for the accounting profession's initiative to reduce auditors' liability.

> ### AUDITING INSIGHT — When Does the Auditors' Responsibility End?
>
> A recent case may expand liability under the Securities Exchange Act by requiring auditors to evaluate the appropriateness of previously issued opinions. In *Overton v. Todman & Co, CPAs PC*, plaintiffs alleged that **Todman & Co.** (auditors) became aware of misstatements in the financial statements of **Direct Brokerage** following the issuance of their unqualified opinion on Direct Brokerage financial statements in 2002 (these misstatements existed at the date of Todman & Co.'s opinion, but Todman & Co. was unaware of them at that time). **David Overton** subsequently used these financial statements to invest and loan more than $2 million to Direct Brokerage; Overton suffered an economic loss when Direct Brokerage ceased operations in 2004.
>
> The U.S. Court of Appeals for the Second District ruled that Todman & Co.'s failure to correct or withdraw its previously issued opinion resulted in liability under section 10(b) and Rule 10b-5. The court did note that its findings only required auditors to correct previous opinions for facts existing at the date of these opinions, not update these opinions based on subsequent developments.
>
> Source: *David Overton and Jerome Kransdorf v. Todman & Co., CPAs, PC, and Trien, Rosenberg, Rosenberg, Weinberg, Ciulo & Fazzari*, 478 F.3d 479 (2d Cir. 2007).

Racketeer Influenced and Corrupt Organizations Act

The Racketeer Influenced and Corrupt Organizations Act (RICO) was enacted to combat organized crime in businesses and other organizations by providing for extended criminal penalties and civil courses of action for various offenses. RICO targeted members of organized crime, but an unintended consequence of this legislation was exposure of its provisions to auditors, whom attorneys threatened to classify as "racketeers" and impose the threat of penalties for treble (triple) damages under the law. In 1988, **Laventhol & Horwath** (at the time, the seventh largest accounting firm) became the first firm to lose a jury trial under RICO statutes related to its role in a cattle-breeding venture in which almost 3,000 investors lost more than $20 million (Laventhol & Horwath subsequently filed for bankruptcy in 1990).[17]

In 1993, the U.S. Supreme Court (in *Reeves vs. Arthur Young*) ruled that auditors are not subject to RICO complaints unless they "actively participate" in the management or operation of a corrupt business. Thus, failure to exercise the appropriate level of professional care (i.e., ordinary negligence) is not sufficient to use the provisions of RICO in a lawsuit against auditors.

Aiding and Abetting

Under the legal doctrine of aiding and abetting, plaintiffs have the ability to include parties in legal actions who were indirectly involved with particular offenses. In the past, shareholders argued that auditors' failure to exercise the appropriate level of professional care exposed them to liability through this legal doctrine. In *Central Bank v. First Interstate Bank* (1994), the U.S. Supreme Court severely limited the extent to which the aiding and abetting doctrine could be used against auditors. More recently, in *StoneRidge Investment Partners v. Scientific-Atlanta,* the Supreme Court ruled that investors who suffer losses because of corporate fraud can typically recover losses only from the entity, its officers, and its directors, not from others who are engaged in business with the corporation. Although *StoneRidge* did not directly address involvement of auditors, the Court's

---

[17] "Laventhol to Pay $15 Million in Suit," http://articles.philly.com/1988-05-10/business/26262663_1_laventhol-horwath-rico-suits-rico-statute (accessed July 18, 2011).

decision has been viewed as making it more difficult for plaintiffs to recover damages in civil actions from bankers, attorneys, and accountants under the so-called legal theory of scheme liability.[18] However, pending legislation introduced by members of the Senate Banking Committee would allow civil actions to be brought against a participating party (such as an auditor) who "knowingly or recklessly provides substantial assistance" to anyone violating securities laws.[19]

Organization of Accounting Firms as Limited Liability Partnerships

Almost all of the major accounting firms have names that end with the designation LLP (limited liability partnership). Prior to 1990, accounting firms were organized as partnerships. One of the major disadvantages of the partnership form of organization is that the personal assets of all partners within the firm were at risk (i.e., were subject to loss via litigation) for the actions of all others within the firm. In the early 1990s, decisions in New York and Hawaii to permit and recognize limited liability partnerships to practice within their jurisdictions led to accounting firms reorganizing themselves as limited liability partnerships.

A **limited liability partnership** combines the advantages of the traditional partnership form of organization (taxation of partnership income to the partners, limited ownership of partnership interests) with the liability protection afforded to corporations. Specifically, in a limited liability partnership, any claims against the partnership are limited to partnership assets unless an individual partner directly participated in the action giving rise to the claim. After the Department of Justice indicted Arthur Andersen over the audits of Enron, some partners of the firm expressed concern about whether their limited liability partnership agreement would shield nonparticipating partners from claims (this was never strictly tested in the courts).[20] It is important to note that organization of a firm as a limited liability partnership does not affect the firm's legal liability but only the extent to which the individual partners' assets were subject to loss via litigation.

Proportionate Liability

One significant concern for auditors is the doctrine of **joint and several liability**, which allows a successful plaintiff to recover the full amount of a damage award from any defendant found to have failed to exercise the appropriate level of professional care regardless of the relative guilt of this defendant compared to other defendant(s). Stated another way, if both the auditors and the client are found to have been responsible for misstatements in the client's financial statements, plaintiffs can seek recovery from either or both parties. Often in cases of business failures, auditors are the only parties with "deep pockets" of financial resources to pay damages. Thus, when a group of defendants (auditors, management, and client) is found liable for damages, auditors may be required to pay the entire amount even though they may be only partially at fault. In contrast, under **proportionate liability**, a defendant is required to pay a proportionate share of the court's damage award depending on the degree of fault determined by a judge and jury (e.g., 20 percent, 30 percent, but not 100 percent).

Proportionate liability was largely accomplished at the federal level in 1995 with the passage of the *Private Securities Litigation Reform Act*. Civil lawsuits for damages now are governed by these proportionate liability terms:

- The total responsibility for loss is divided among all parties responsible for the loss.
- If other defendant(s) are insolvent, a solvent defendant's liability is extended to 50 percent more than the proportion found at trial. (For example, if an accounting firm is found 20 percent responsible for a loss and the client and its managers are insolvent, the accounting firm will have to pay 30 percent of the loss but not 100 percent as before.)

---

[18] "You Can't Sue the Bean Counters," *BusinessWeek,* January 28, 2008, p. 30; "Can Shareholders Sue Third Parties?" *The Wall Street Journal,* October 6–7, 2007, p. A19.

[19] Could New Regs Bring More Lawsuits? *CFO.com,* January 11, 2010.

[20] "Partners Forever? Within Andersen, Personal Liability May Bring Ruin," *The Wall Street Journal,* April 2, 2002, pp. C1, C16.

- Only the defendants who knowingly committed a violation of securities laws remain jointly and severally liable for all of the plaintiffs' damages. (This is the imposition of penalty for actively participating in an actual fraud.)

The Private Securities Litigation Reform Act includes an exception to these provisions to compensate smaller investors. If plaintiffs have a net worth of less than $200,000 and lost 10 percent or more of the net worth because of auditors' failure to exercise appropriate levels of professional care, auditors remain jointly and severally liable.

AUDITING INSIGHT — Joint and Several Liability

In July 2005, a federal jury found **Coopers & Lybrand** (which has since merged with **Price Waterhouse** to form Pricewaterhouse Coopers) and the president of the client (**Ambassador Insurance Company**) to be jointly liable for losses incurred by policyholders of Ambassador, which became insolvent in 1983. The jury assigned the liability as 60 percent against Arnold Chait (president of Ambassador) and 40 percent against Coopers & Lybrand, but Chait died during the 1990s with insufficient assets in his estate. As a result, PricewaterhouseCoopers was required to pay the entire $182.9 million settlement for an audit conducted more than 20 years ago! (This judgment was upheld at the appellate level in September 2008.)

Sources: "PwC to Pay $182.9M for Coopers Audit," *CFO.com*, October 3, 2005; "Pricewaterhouse Is Ordered to Pay $182.9 Million," *The Wall Street Journal*, October 5, 2005, p. B6.

Class Action Suits

It is not unusual for shareholders or investors who have suffered losses to band together and bring legal action against entities and/or auditors. In a **class action** suit, a relatively small number of aggrieved plaintiffs with small individual claims can bring suit for large damages in the name of an extended class. After a bankruptcy, for example, 50 bondholders who lost $40,000 might decide to sue and can do so on behalf of the entire class of bondholders for *all* of their alleged losses (say $40 million). Attorneys take these cases on a contingency fee basis (a percentage of the judgment, if any). The size of the claim and the zeal of the attorneys can make the class action suit a serious matter. For example, an appeals court's decision to "certify" a class action suit against **Wal-Mart Stores, Inc.** for sexual discrimination had the potential to expose the retailer to liability and potential damages to 1.6 million past and present female employees.[21] In what is being viewed as a significant victory for defendants, the U.S. Supreme Court (in a 5-4 vote) recently ruled that the plaintiffs in this case could not establish the "common injury" necessary for class action consideration.[22]

In the past, most class action lawsuits were adjudicated in state courts, and a great deal of "jurisdiction shopping" was performed to find a court that might be more sympathetic to the plaintiffs. Some of the large corporate failures (e.g., **Lincoln Savings and Loan, Enron, WorldCom**) have resulted in class action lawsuits that have proven costly for defendants to defend and difficult for them to win. In February 2005, the *Class Action Fairness Act* was signed into law. This act is designed to expand federal jurisdiction over class action lawsuits and is estimated to result in the movement of 40 percent of class action lawsuits from various state courts to federal court. Federal courts are preferable venues for defendants in class action lawsuits because:

- Class action lawsuits come under more scrutiny in federal court compared to state courts.
- Federal courts have more resources at their disposal in managing class action cases than state courts.

---

[21] "Wal-mart Wants to Skip This Class," *CFO.com*, October 15, 2004; "Wal-mart Ruling Has Wide Reach on Discrimination," *The Wall Street Journal*, March 23, 2009, p. A2.

[22] "Justices Curb Class Actions," *The Wall Street Journal*, June 21, 2011, pp. A1, A2.

- State courts have been alleged to unfairly discriminate against defendants from other jurisdictions.
- State court verdicts often affect plaintiffs in other jurisdictions (states). A verdict in federal court is regarded as more appropriate when it is applied to multiple jurisdictions.

It is important to note that not all class action lawsuits will come under federal jurisdiction, and the rules for determining whether a state or federal court has jurisdiction over a case are complex. It is too early to determine the exact effects of the Class Action Fairness Act on lawsuits against auditors, but initial perceptions are that it may reduce class action lawsuits and provide a more impartial venue for auditors in defending themselves against class action lawsuits.

In addition to the Class Action Fairness Act, Congress enacted the *Securities Litigation Uniform Standards Act* in 1998. The most significant provision of this legislation requires class action lawsuits with 50 or more parties to be filed in the federal courts. As noted earlier, federal courts are generally more favorable venues for class action lawsuits for the defendants (auditors).

AUDITING INSIGHT — How Big Is the Class?

In 2010, the number of class action settlements (86), total dollar amount of settlements ($3.1 billion), and average settlement ($36 million) were at their lowest levels since 2003 (the final year preceding major settlements in the **World Com, Enron**, and **Tyco** cases). Since 2000, the high levels of settlement activities are 119 cases (2005), $18.6 billion in settlements (2006, which includes approximately $8 billion related to Enron), and an average settlement of $207 million per case (2006). However, Cornerstone Research notes that damages from the liquidity crisis and subprime mortgage crisis in late 2008 may spur higher levels of class action activity (and related settlements) in future years.

Source: *Securities Class Action Settlements—2010 Review and Analysis* (Cornerstone Research, 2011).

Auditors' Liability Caps

A final development in the legal liability arena is related to various measures of limiting (or "capping") auditors' liability to both clients and third parties. In their engagement letters, auditors are attempting to limit their potential liability to clients through wording such as the following (excerpted from **United Rental's** 2006 proxy statement):

> In connection with the audit of the 2005 financial statements, the company entered into an engagement agreement with Ernst & Young LLP.... That agreement is subject to alternative dispute resolution procedures and an exclusion of punitive damages.

A strict reading of this language suggests that United Rental is barred from bringing suit against Ernst & Young and would need to seek redress through mediation and arbitration; furthermore, it suggests that Ernst & Young would be liable only for compensatory (not the often more costly punitive) damages. Although the effectiveness of this language in limiting auditors' liability has not been legally tested, some negative publicity over these agreements has resulted in Ernst & Young's deciding no longer to include language related to exclusion of punitive damages in its engagement letters (it continues to include the language related to alternative dispute resolution).[23]

In addition to liability to clients, some recent actions have been taken to potentially limit auditors' liability to third parties. In late 2006, the Committee on Capital Markets Regulation (a group of business, financial, investor, legal, and accounting leaders) was formed in response to evidence that the U.S. public markets were losing registrants to foreign and private equity markets. Among other areas, their report addressed liability issues facing public entities and other parties (including auditors). This group did not

[23] "More Companies Are Disclosing Pacts with Auditors on Liability Caps," *The Wall Street Journal*, June 22, 2006, p. C4.

provide a specific recommendation, but its report suggested dollar liability caps and safe harbors against certain types of auditing activities as a possible mechanism for protecting accounting firms against large monetary losses.[24] In addition, Conrad Hewitt (at the time, the SEC's chief accountant) called for limiting the exposure of accounting firms to lawsuits citing concerns if one of the remaining Big Four were to be forced out of business because of litigation.[25]

Other Recent Developments

Auditor liability continues to change along with changes in the landscape of the auditing profession. In 2009, a U.S. judge denied **Deloitte Touche Tohmatsu's** motion for a summary judgment that would relieve the firm of any liability for audits of **Parmalat** conducted by its Italian member firm (**Deloitte & Touche SpA**). This action clearly expands liability for international accounting firms in cases in which the firm itself provides little actual service to the client. Speaking on behalf of the plaintiffs, attorney Stuart Grant noted, "Judge Kaplan has finally made the law reflect reality. These accounting firms sell themselves as world-wide, seamless organizations. Now they are going to be held responsible in the same fashion. In essence, Judge Kaplan has said that the parent can't hide from the misdeeds of its children."[26]

AUDITING INSIGHT — What Affects Litigation?

Three recent studies have examined factors influencing litigation.

- Schmidt concluded that litigation against auditors related to financial statement misstatements is more likely when the misstatement is associated with (1) financial fraud, (2) a regulatory investigation, (3) a large decline in stock price, and (4) a higher number of errors in applying GAAP. In addition, the results of this study showed that litigation against an auditor/firm resulted in that office's demonstrating more conservative behavior with respect to other clients (such as lower levels of positive financial statement accruals and a longer time period for issuing the audit reports).
- Casterella et al. found that larger accounting firms, firms experiencing significant growth, firms with a higher number of claims outstanding against them, and firms that have been investigated or disciplined by a professional oversight body had higher levels of litigation risk.
- Boone et al. found that auditors involved with engagements having higher litigation risk were less likely to acquiesce to client earnings management behavior and that the Private Securities Litigation Reform Act reduced the risk of litigation against auditors.

Sources: J. Schmidt, "Financial Statement Misstatements, Auditor Litigation, and Subsequent Auditor Behavior," Unpublished working paper, 2011, University of Texas at Austin; J.R. Casterella, K.L. Jensen, and W.R. Knechel, "Litigation Risk and Audit Firm Characteristics," *Auditing: A Journal of Practice & Theory,* November 2010, pp. 71–82.; J.P. Boone, I.K. Khurana, and K.K. Raman, "Litigation Risk and Abnormal Accruals," *Auditing: A Journal of Practice & Theory,* May 2011, pp. 231–256.

↳ REVIEW CHECKPOINTS

C.25 List some of the major changes in auditors' liability provided by Sarbanes-Oxley.

C.26 What is the difference between *joint and several liability* and *proportionate liability*?

C.27 What major changes did the Private Securities Litigation Reform Act provide? What major changes did the Class Action Fairness Act provide?

C.28 What new requirement was enacted in the Securities Litigation Uniform Standards Act that affected class action lawsuits?

---

[24] "Panel Seeks Cap on Liability of Accounting Firms," *The Wall Street Journal,* November 30, 2006, p. C3. The report of the committee can be found at www.capmktsreg.org/pdfs/11.30Committee_Interim_ReportREV2.pdf (accessed July 18, 2011).

[25] "SEC's Hewitt: Indemnify the Big Four," *CFO.com,* January 29, 2007.

[26] "A Parmalat Ruling May Broaden Liability," *The Wall Street Journal,* January 29, 2009, p. C4; "Judge: OK to Sue Deloitte over Parmalat," *CFO.com,* January 30, 2009.

Summary

This module summarizes the potential liability auditors have to clients and third parties who rely on their work. Auditors can be liable under either common law (based on prior legal decisions and precedents) or statutory law (violating a written law). Auditors' liability to clients arises through an economic loss suffered because of failure to perform the engagement in accordance with the contract (breach of contract) or because of auditors' failure to exercise the appropriate level of professional care (tort liability). Because of the close relationship between auditors and clients, auditors owe their clients a very high degree of performance and are liable when they commit ordinary negligence (lack of reasonable care), gross negligence (lack of minimal care), or fraud (knowledge and intent to deceive).

Auditors' liability to third-party investors or creditors under common law arises because of economic decisions made by these parties using audited financial statements. Under common law, auditors are liable to all third-party users for levels of failure to exercise the appropriate level of professional care representing gross negligence or fraud. With respect to ordinary negligence, three separate approaches to liability are for third parties who are primary beneficiaries (*Credit Alliance v. Arthur Andersen*), foreseen third parties (restatement of torts, *Fleet National Bank v. Gloucester Co.*), or foreseeable third parties (*Rosenblum, Inc. v. Adler*). The legal precedent in the jurisdiction in which the action is brought determines auditors' liability to third parties for ordinary negligence.

Under statutory liability, the Securities Act of 1933 and the Securities Exchange Act of 1934 dictate liability to investors in securities. These acts differ based on both the burden of proof and the level of failure to exercise the appropriate level of professional care required to bring suit. Under the Securities Act, the burden of proof is on auditors; purchasers of securities may bring suit for ordinary negligence, gross negligence, or fraud. Under the Securities Exchange Act, the burden of proof is on purchasers or sellers of securities and suit can only be brought for gross negligence or fraud. Clearly, the Securities Act imposes the highest degree of care on auditors and the lowest barriers for plaintiffs to bring suits against auditors.

Although Sarbanes-Oxley has expanded the statute of limitations as well as the penalties to auditors under the Securities Exchange Act, other recent developments have reduced (or advocate a reduction in) auditors' exposure to legal liability. These developments include the Private Securities Litigation Reform Act, the Class Action Fairness Act, and various calls for liability limitations (or caps).

Key Terms

breach of contract: A claim that accounting or auditing services were not performed in the manner described in the contract, 637

causation defense: An argument available to auditors who can show that a plaintiff's economic loss was caused by a factor other than the auditors' failure to exercise the appropriate level of professional care or breach of contract, 638

class action: A situation in which a group of plaintiffs comes together in a legal action against another party, 658

comfort letter: A letter issued by auditors to underwriters of securities that provides an opinion on the fairness of the issuers' financial statements, 646

common law: The liability for injuries that is based on reasons other than violation of a written law or statute. Under common law, legal precedent is used in assessing the degree of responsibility or fault of the parties; auditors have common law liability to clients and non-shareholder third parties, 636

constructive fraud: A failure to provide any care in fulfilling a duty owed to another including a reckless disregard for the truth (similar to gross negligence), 639

contributory negligence: A legal defense theory in which the plaintiff's own failure to perform with the appropriate level of professional care bars recovery from auditors, 638

"deep pockets" theory: The concept that lawsuits may be brought against auditors not because they are necessarily at fault but because they are the only party with resources against which recovery can be made, 636

expectation gap: The difference between the actual work and assurance required by GAAS and the expectation of that work by the general public, 636

Financial Reporting Releases (FRRs): Reports prepared by SEC staff that express new rules and policies about disclosure, 648

foreseeable party: The individuals or organizations whose decisions normally rely on audited financial statements and opinions on those financial statements, 641

foreseen party: A limited class of individuals or organizations that could be reasonably expected to rely on auditors' work, 640

Form 8-K: The "current events" report filed periodically at the occurrence of major events, such as earnings releases, major asset sales, acquisitions, and auditor changes, 648

Form 10-K: Annual filing of financial statements and related disclosures by public companies with the SEC, 648

Form 10-Q: Quarterly filing of financial statements and related disclosures by public companies with the SEC, 648

fraud: The misrepresentation of facts that the individual knows to be false with the intention to deceive, 638

gross negligence: The breach of duty owed to another party because of a lack of minimal care (similar to constructive fraud), 638

initial public offering (IPO): The initial issuance of securities by a registrant entity to the investing public through a market that is subject to the provisions of the Securities Act of 1933, 645

joint and several liability: The legal doctrine that when multiple defendants are named, the full amount of a damage award may be collected from any of the defendants named in the lawsuit even though they may be only partially at fault, 657

limited liability partnership: A form of organization adopted by most large accounting firms that combines the advantages of a traditional partnership with the liability protection afforded to corporations, 657

ordinary negligence: The unintentional breaches of duty owed to another as a result of a lack of reasonable care, 638

plaintiff: The person or organization that initiates a lawsuit (client or third-party user of financial statements), 637

primary beneficiary: A person known by name to the auditor for whose primary benefit the audit or other accounting service is performed, 640

privity of contract: A situation in which parties have a contractual relationship, 637

proportionate liability: The legal doctrine that payment of a share of the court's damage award be based on the extent (or proportion) of fault exhibited by a convicted defendant, 657

prospectus: A legal document offering securities for sale and includes significant information about the issuing entity, including its historical financial statements and other necessary disclosures, 645

registration statement: A set of documents, including a prospectus, that a company files with the SEC prior to an initial public offering, 645

Regulation S-K (SEC): The requirements relating to all business, analytical, and supplementary financial disclosures other than financial statements themselves, 648

Regulation S-X (SEC): The accounting requirements for annual and interim financial statements filed under both the Securities Act and the Securities Exchange Act, 648

scienter: A mental state embracing the intent to deceive, manipulate, or defraud prior to committing those actions (for example, auditors' knowledge of a misstatement in the financial statements and the intentional failure to disclose this misstatement in their report), 649

Staff Accounting Bulletins (SABs): The unofficial but important interpretations of Regulation S-X and Regulation S-K by SEC staff, 648

statutory law: The legal rules affecting liability based on violations of written laws or statutes. Auditors have statutory liability to third party investors under the securities acts, 637

tort: A civil complaint charging that the action of one person caused injury (personal or financial) to another; such action against auditors is normally initiated by users of financial statements, 637

Multiple-Choice Questions for Practice and Review

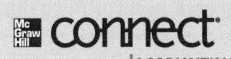 All applicable Exercises and Problems are available with McGraw-Hill's *Connect® Accounting*

LO C-2

C.29 A lack of reasonable care that may be characterized by the failure of auditors to follow GAAS in the conduct of the audit is known as
  a. Constructive fraud.
  b. Fraud.
  c. Gross negligence.
  d. Ordinary negligence.

LO C-6 C.30 From the auditors' point of view, which of the following is a preferable provision for imposition of civil liability in a lawsuit for financial damages?
   a. Joint and several liability.
   b. Reasonably foreseeable users' approach to privity.
   c. Foreseen third parties' approach to privity.
   d. Proportionate liability.

LO C-1 C.31 Users of financial statements have a different perception concerning the nature of auditors' services than the actual objectives of an audit. This difference is known as
   a. Diverse liability perception.
   b. Reasonable foreseeable third parties.
   c. Insurance hypothesis.
   d. Expectations gap.

LO C-2 C.32 Individuals who believe they relied on misstated financial statements to make a decision and have suffered losses as a result will issue an action known as a
   a. Breach of contract.
   b. Tort.
   c. Securities litigation.
   d. Constructive fraud.

LO C-6 C.33 Assume that auditors lost a civil lawsuit for damages and the court found total losses of $5 million. If the auditors were determined to be 30 percent at fault and were the only solvent defendant, what is the auditors' likely obligation under proportionate liability?
   a. $5,000,000.
   b. Zero.
   c. $2,250,000.
   d. $1,500,000.

LO C-6 C.34 Suppose that the auditors in the preceding question participated knowingly in commission of violations of securities laws (with managers and directors of the audit client). What is the auditors' likely obligation?
   a. $5,000,000.
   b. Zero.
   c. $2,250,000.
   d. $1,500,000.

LO C-2 C.35 When a client sues an accountant for failure to perform consulting work properly, the accountants' best defense is probably based on the doctrine of
   a. Lack of privity of contract.
   b. Contributory negligence on the part of the client.
   c. Lack of any measurable dollar amount of damages.
   d. No negligence on the part of the consultant.

LO C-2 C.36 When creditors who relied on an entity's audited financial statements suffer monetary losses after a customer (the auditors' client) goes bankrupt, what must the plaintiff creditors in a lawsuit for damages show in a court that follows the doctrine in *Credit Alliance?*
   a. The auditors knew and specifically acknowledged identification of the creditors.
   b. The auditors could reasonably foresee them as beneficiaries of the audit because entities such as this client use financial statements to obtain credit from vendors.
   c. The plaintiffs were foreseen users of the audited financial statements because they were vendors of long standing.
   d. All of the above.

LO C-2 C.37 When accountants agree to perform a compilation or review of unaudited financial statements, the best way to avoid client's misunderstanding the nature of the work is to describe it completely in
   a. An engagement letter.
   b. The auditors' opinion.
   c. A report to the clients' board of directors at the close of the engagement.
   d. A management letter to the board of directors' audit committee.

LO C-4

C.38 Entities desiring to issue equity or debt must provide a set of financial statements to any prospective purchaser. This set of financial statements and other information for prospective purchasers is known as a
   a. Prospectus.
   b. Review.
   c. Patron's acquisition statement.
   d. Projected audited financial information.

LO C-3

C.39 The Securities Act of 1933 and Securities Exchange Act of 1934 contain
   a. Civil liability provisions applicable to auditors.
   b. Criminal liability provisions applicable to auditors.
   c. Neither *a* nor *b*.
   d. Both *a* and *b*.

LO C-2

C.40 Which of the following third parties is known by name to auditors as the audit is conducted?
   a. Foreseeable third party.
   b. Foreseen third party.
   c. General third party.
   d. Primary beneficiary.

LO C-5

C.41 Which of the following would be the auditors' most likely defense in an action brought under the Securities Exchange Act of 1934?
   a. The investor did not have privity with auditors.
   b. The investor did not suffer a loss based on the materially misstated financial statements.
   c. The auditors acted in good faith and were not aware of the materially misstated financial statements.
   d. The financial statements were not filed with the Securities and Exchange Commission.

LO C-4

C.42 Which of the following statements regarding auditors' liability under the Securities Act of 1933 is *not* true?
   a. The act relates to the initial issuance of securities to the public, normally through an initial public offering.
   b. Auditors' liability arises because of audited financial information filed with the SEC.
   c. Third parties must demonstrate that they relied on misstated financial statements that were examined by auditors.
   d. Auditors may be liable if they are found to have engaged in ordinary negligence.

LO C-5

C.43 Under the Securities Exchange Act of 1934, entities are required to report to the public about changing auditors on
   a. Form 10-K.
   b. Form S-1.
   c. Form 10-Q.
   d. Form 8-K.

LO C-4

C.44 Section 11(*b*) of the Securities Act of 1933 provides that individuals can be sued and may be liable for investors' losses in connection with a public securities offering under which of these circumstances?
   a. The chairman of the board of directors performed a reasonable investigation of facts in connection with preparing the section in the registration statement concerning the specification of the use of the proceeds of the offering.
   b. A consulting engineer performed a reasonable investigation and reported in the registration statement on the feasibility of construction of a roadway to be financed with the offering proceeds.
   c. The president of the issuing entity had no reason to doubt the report of the consulting engineer, although the president did not perform a separate reasonable investigation of her own.
   d. The officers of the issuing entity were relieved that the independent auditors did not make an issue about the excessive valuation of inventory held to support construction in progress.

LO C-5

C.45 In comparison to the burden of proof required of plaintiffs in civil lawsuits against independent auditors under common law, section 10(*b*) of the Securities Exchange Act of 1934
 a. Is the same regarding plaintiffs' need to prove damages or losses.
 b. Is the same regarding plaintiffs' need to establish privity or a beneficiary relationship with auditors.
 c. Does not require that plaintiffs prove their reliance on materially misstated financial statements.
 d. Does not require that plaintiffs prove that relying on the materially misstated financial statements caused their losses.

LO C-2

C.46 Which of the following cases provides auditors the broadest exposure for liability to third parties for ordinary negligence under common law?
 a. *Credit Alliance v. Arthur Andersen.*
 b. *Fleet National Bank v. Gloucester Co.*
 c. *Rosenblum, Inc. v. Adler.*
 d. *Ultramares.*

LO C-4, C-5

C.47 Which of the following is a major difference in auditors' liability under the Securities Act of 1933 and the Securities Exchange Act of 1934?
 a. The burden of proving reliance on misstated financial statements and the relationship between these financial statements and the economic loss.
 b. The auditors' required degree of professional care.
 c. Both of the above.
 d. None of the above.

LO C-4

C.48 When an entity registers a security offering under the Securities Act of 1933, the law provides an investor
 a. An SEC guarantee that the information in the registration statement is true.
 b. Insurance against loss from the investment.
 c. Financial information examined by independent auditors.
 d. Inside information about the entity's trade secrets.

LO C-2

C.49 A group of investors sued Anderson, Olds, and Watershed, CPAs (AOW) for alleged damages suffered when the entity in which they held common stock went bankrupt. To avoid liability under the common law, AOW must prove which of the following?
 a. The investors actually suffered a loss.
 b. The investors relied on the financial statements audited by AOW.
 c. The investors' loss was a direct result of their reliance on the audited financial statements.
 d. The audit was conducted in accordance with generally accepted auditing standards and with due professional care.

LO C-5

C.50 The Securities and Exchange Commission document that governs accounting in financial statements filed with the SEC is
 a. Regulation D.
 b. Form 8-K.
 c. Form SB-l.
 d. Regulation S-X.

LO C-5

C.51 Which of the following cases upheld the requirement that plaintiffs demonstrate scienter when bringing action under the Securities Exchange Act of 1934?
 a. *Ernst & Ernst v. Hochfelder.*
 b. *Escott v. BarChris Construction Corp.*
 c. *Smith v. London Assurance Corp.*
 d. *Ultramares.*

LO C-5

C.52 A public entity subject to the periodic reporting requirements of the Securities Exchange Act of 1934 must file an annual report with the SEC known as the
 a. Form 10-K.
 b. Form 10-Q.
 c. Form 8-K.
 d. Regulation S-X.

LO C-4 C.53 When investors sue auditors for damages under section 11 of the Securities Act of 1933, they must allege and prove
  a. Scienter on the part of auditors.
  b. The audited financial statements contained a material misstatement.
  c. They relied on the materially misstated financial statements.
  d. Their reliance on the materially misstated financial statements was the direct cause of their loss.

LO C-6 C.54 Which of the following is not part of Sarbanes-Oxley?
  a. An increased duty on the part of auditors to identify financial statement fraud.
  b. A requirement that the CEO and CFO certify the financial statements.
  c. Increased penalties for destruction of records in federal investigations.
  d. Increased penalties for mail fraud and criminal violations of the Securities Exchange Act of 1934.

LO C-2 C.55 If a CPA firm is being sued for common law fraud by a third party based upon materially false financial statements, which of the following is the best defense the auditors could assert?
  a. Lack of privity.
  b. Lack of reliance.
  c. A disclaimer contained in the engagement letter.
  d. Contributory negligence on the part of the client.

(AICPA adapted)

LO C-2 C.56 Locke, CPA, was engaged by Hall, Inc. to audit Willow Company. Hall purchased Willow after receiving Willow's audited financial statements, which included Locke's unqualified auditors' opinion. Locke was negligent in the performance of the Willow audit engagement; this negligence was caused by failure to perform the engagement in accordance with terms of the engagement letter. As a result of Locke's negligence, Hall suffered damages of $75,000. Hall appears to have grounds to sue Locke for

	Breach of Contract	Negligence
a.	Yes	Yes
b.	Yes	No
c.	No	Yes
d.	No	No

(AICPA adapted)

LO C-4 C.57 An investor seeking to recover stock market losses from a CPA firm associated with an initial offering of securities based on an unqualified opinion on financial statements that accompanied a registration statement, must establish that
  a. The audited financial statements contain a false statement or omission of material fact.
  b. The investor relied on the financial statements.
  c. The CPA firm did not act in good faith.
  d. The CPA firm would have discovered the false statement or omission if it had exercised due care in its examination.

(AICPA adapted)

LO C-5 C.58 Donalds & Company, CPAs, audited the financial statements included in the annual report submitted by Markum Securities, Inc., to the Securities and Exchange Commission. The audit was improper in several respects. Markum is now insolvent and unable to satisfy the claims of its customers. Customers have instituted legal action against Donalds based on Section 10(b) and Rule 10(b)-5 of the Securities Exchange Act of 1934. Which of the following is likely to be Donalds' best defense?
  a. The firm did not intentionally certify the false financial statements.
  b. Section 10(b) does not apply to the case.
  c. The firm was not in privity of contract with the creditors.
  d. The engagement letter specifically disclaimed any liability to any party that resulted from Markum's fraudulent conduct.

(AICPA adapted)

C.59 and C.60 are based on the following information:

West & Co., CPAs, rendered an unqualified opinion on the financial statements of Pride Corp., which were included in Pride's registration statement filed with the SEC. Subsequently, Hex purchased 500 shares of Pride's preferred stock as part of a public offering subject to the Securities Act of 1933. Hex has commenced an action against West based on the Securities Act of 1933 for losses resulting from misstatements of facts in the financial statements included in the registration statement.

LO C-4

C.59 Which of the following elements must Hex prove to hold West liable?
   a. West rendered its opinion with knowledge of material misstatements.
   b. West performed the audit negligently.
   c. Hex relied on the financial statements included in the registration statement.
   d. The misstatements were material.

(AICPA adapted)

LO C-4

C.60 Which of the following defenses would be *least* helpful to West in avoiding liability to Hex?
   a. West was not in privity of contract with Hex.
   b. West conducted the audit in accordance with GAAS.
   c. Hex's losses were caused by factors other than the misstatements.
   d. Hex knew of the misstatements when Hex acquired the preferred stock.

(AICPA adapted)

Exercises and Problems

 All applicable Exercises and Problems are available with McGraw-Hill's *Connect® Accounting*

LO C-2

C.61 **Breach of Contract.** While large-dollar lawsuits brought by shareholders grab the headlines, auditors are most often sued by the client for breach of contract.

Required:
   a. How can auditors be in breach of contract with a client?
   b. How can a client be in breach of contract with auditors?
   c. What are the best defenses for auditors against breach of contract lawsuits brought by their clients?

LO C-2

C.62 **Liability to Clients.** Thomas, CPA is a regional firm that provides a variety of services to its clients. The following summarizes some issues that it has encountered with three of its audit clients during the most recent year:

• Thomas was engaged by Brown Company to conduct an audit of its financial statements. Brown is a nonpublic entity that is seeking financing and is having the audit conducted because of user demand for audited financial statements. Because this was an initial audit, it took Thomas longer to conduct the audit than anticipated. During this time, economic conditions resulted in a general increase in interest rates and Brown's costs of obtaining financing were higher than it had anticipated.

• Green Stores has been an audit client of Thomas for more than 10 years. Following the most recent audit (which resulted in an unqualified opinion on Green Stores' financial statements), Green Stores learned that its treasurer had been engaged in a significant embezzlement scheme, resulting in losses in excess of $2 million by Green Stores. Throughout Thomas' 10-year relationship with Green Stores, it had issued unqualified opinions on Green Stores' financial statements and had not identified any weaknesses in Green Stores' internal control or other evidence that suggested the existence of this defalcation scheme.

• Fuchsia, Inc. has been an audit client of Thomas for the past five years. During the most recent audit, Thomas identified misstatements that understated Fuchsia's liabilities; Thomas believed that these misstatements should be corrected in order to fairly present Fuchsia's financial condition, results of operations, and cash flows in conformity with GAAP. Fuchsia refused to make these misstatements, and Thomas resigned from the engagement. Fuchsia has engaged another auditor, but the delays associated with this change in auditors may result in accelerated payments to Fuchsia's lenders for failure to provide them audited financial statements on a timely basis.

Required:

a. Without specific reference to any of the preceding situations, on what basis/general areas of liability may clients bring suit against auditors?
b. Without specific reference to any of the preceding situations, what facts must clients demonstrate to bring suit against auditors?
c. Without specific reference to any of the preceding situations, what defenses might be available to auditors for suits brought against them by their clients?
d. For each of the preceding clients, identify the potential basis or bases for legal action that might be brought against Thomas.
e. In your opinion, is Thomas likely to be liable to these clients for its actions? What factors should be considered in assessing Thomas' potential liability in these situations?

LO C-2

C.63 Common Law Responsibility for Errors and Fraud. Huffman & Whitman (H&W), a large regional accounting firm, was engaged by Ritter Tire Wholesale Company to audit its financial statements for the year ended January 31. H&W had a busy audit engagement schedule from December 31 through April 1 and decided to audit Ritter's purchase vouchers and related cash disbursements on a sample basis. The firm instructed staff members to select a random sample of 130 purchase transactions and gave directions about important deviations, including missing receiving reports. Boyd, the assistant in charge, completed the audit documentation, properly documenting the fact that 13 of the purchases in the sample had been recorded and paid without including the receiving report (required by stated internal control procedures) in the file of supporting documents. Whitman, the partner in direct charge of the audit, showed the findings to Lock, Ritter's chief accountant. Lock appeared surprised but promised that the missing receiving reports would be inserted into the files before the audit was over. Whitman was satisfied, noted in the audit documentation that the problem had been solved, and did not say anything to Huffman about it.

Unfortunately, H&W did not discover the fact that Lock was involved in a fraudulent scheme in which he diverted shipments of tires to a warehouse leased in his name and sent the invoices to Ritter for payment. He then sold the tires for his own profit. Internal auditors discovered the scheme during a study of slow-moving inventory items. Ritter's inventory was overstated by about $500,000 (20 percent), the amount Lock had diverted.

Required:

a. Do you believe Huffman & Whitman has any further audit responsibility with respect to the missing receiving reports? Explain.
b. Do you believe Huffman & Whitman failed to exercise the appropriate level of professional care? Why or why not?

LO C-2

C.64 Common Law Responsibility for Errors and Fraud. Herbert McCoy is the president of McCoy Forging Corporation. For the past several years, Donovan & Company, CPAs, has performed the company's compilation and some other accounting and tax work. McCoy decided to have Donovan & Company conduct an audit. He had recently received a disturbing anonymous letter that stated, "Beware; you have a viper in your nest. The money is literally disappearing before your very eyes! Signed: A friend." He told no one about the letter.

McCoy Forging engaged Donovan & Company, CPAs, to render an opinion on the financial statements for the year ended June 30. McCoy told Donovan he wanted to verify that the financial statements were "accurate and proper." He did not mention the anonymous letter. The usual engagement letter providing for an audit in accordance with generally accepted auditing standards (GAAS) was drafted by Donovan & Company and signed by both parties.

The audit was performed in accordance with GAAS. The audit did not reveal a clever defalcation plan. Harper, the assistant treasurer, was siphoning off substantial amounts of McCoy Forging's funds. The defalcations occurred both before and after the audit. Harper's embezzlement was discovered by McCoy's new internal auditor in October after Donovan had delivered the auditors' opinion. Although the scheme was fairly sophisticated, it could have been detected if Donovan & Company had performed additional procedures. McCoy Forging demands reimbursement from Donovan for the entire amount of the embezzlement, some $40,000 of which occurred before the audit and $65,000 after. Donovan has denied any liability and refuses to pay.

Required:

Discuss Donovan's responsibility in this situation. Do you think McCoy Forging could prevail in whole or in part in a lawsuit against Donovan under common law? Explain your conclusions.

(AICPA adapted)

LO C-2

C.65 **Auditors' Liability for Fraud.** Auditors may be liable to third parties for fraud in several ways.

Required:
a. Identify auditors' liability for fraud to third parties.
b. Distinguish between fraud and constructive fraud.
c. What is auditors' liability for constructive fraud to third parties?
d. In your opinion, is auditors' liability to third parties for fraud and constructive fraud appropriate (or "fair")?

LO C-2

C.66 **Accusation of Fraud.** (This exercise is based on the actual case of **Health Management, Inc.**) During the audit of the Health Management's 1995 financial statements, $1.8 million of inventory in transit was included on the entity's balance sheet. The auditors never obtained evidence of the existence of this inventory even though several questions had been raised concerning the excessively large amount of inventory in transit at year-end. In 1996, Health Management announced that it had discovered a series of accounting irregularities.

Required:
a. Do legal grounds exist to claim that the auditors committed fraud?
b. What would be the auditors' defense if such grounds exist?

LO C-2

C.67 **Common Law Liability Exposure.** An accounting firm was engaged to examine the financial statements of Martin Manufacturing Corporation for the year ending December 31. Martin needed cash to continue its operations and agreed to sell its common stock investment in a subsidiary through a private placement. The buyers insisted that the proceeds be placed in escrow because of the possibility of a major contingent tax liability that could result from a pending government claim against Martin's subsidiary. The payment in escrow was completed in late November. Martin's president told the audit partner that the proceeds from the sale of the subsidiary's common stock, held in escrow, should be shown on the balance sheet as an unrestricted current account receivable. The president held the opinion that the government's claim was groundless and that Martin needed an "uncluttered" balance sheet and a "clean" auditors' opinion to obtain additional working capital from lenders. The audit partner agreed with the president and issued an unqualified opinion on Martin's financial statements, which did not refer to the contingent liability and did not properly describe the escrow arrangement.

The government's claim proved to be valid and, pursuant to the agreement with the buyers, the purchase price of the subsidiary was reduced by $450,000. This adverse development forced Martin into bankruptcy. The accounting firm is being sued for deceit (fraud) by several of Martin's unpaid creditors who extended credit in reliance on the accounting firm's unqualified opinion on Martin's financial statements.

Required:
a. What deceit (fraud) do you believe the creditors are claiming?
b. Is the lack of privity between the accounting firm and the creditors important in this case?
c. Do you believe the accounting firm is liable to the creditors? Explain.

(AICPA adapted)

LO C-2

C.68 **Common Law Liability Exposure.** Risk Capital Limited, a Delaware corporation, was considering the purchase of a substantial investment in Florida Sunshine Corporation, a closely held corporation. Initial discussions with the Florida Sunshine Corporation began late in 2012.

Wilson and Wyatt, Florida Sunshine's auditors, regularly prepared quarterly and annual unaudited financial statements. The most recently prepared financial statements were for the year ended September 30, 2012.

On November 15, 2012, after extensive negotiations, Risk Capital agreed to purchase 100,000 shares of no par, class A capital stock of Florida Sunshine at $12.50 per share.

However, Risk Capital insisted on audited statements for 2012. The contract that was made available to Wilson and Wyatt specifically provided that Risk Capital shall have the right to rescind the purchase of said stock if the audited financial statements of Florida Sunshine for the calendar year 2012 show a material adverse change in the financial condition of the corporation.

The audited financial statements furnished to Florida Sunshine by Wilson and Wyatt showed no such material adverse change. Risk Capital relied on the audited statements and purchased the investment in Florida Sunshine. It was subsequently discovered that, as of the date of the financial statements, the audited statements were misstated and that in fact there had been a material adverse change in the corporation's financial condition. Florida Sunshine is insolvent, and Risk Capital will lose virtually its entire investment.

Risk Capital seeks recovery against Wilson and Wyatt.

Required:
Assuming that only ordinary negligence is proved, will Risk Capital prevail
a. Under a privity of contract standard?
b. Under a primary beneficiary standard?
c. Under a foreseen parties standard?

LO C-2

C.69 **Common Law Liability Exposure.** Smith, CPA, is the auditor for Juniper Manufacturing Corporation, a nonpublic entity that has a June 30 fiscal year. Juniper arranged for a substantial bank loan, which depended on the bank receiving audited financial statements showing a debt-to-equity ratio of no more than 2 to 1. The bank's deadline for receiving these financial statements was September 30. On September 25, just before the auditors' opinion was to be issued, Smith received an anonymous letter on Juniper's letterhead indicating that Juniper's five-year lease of a factory building that was classified in the financial statements as an operating lease was in fact a capital lease. The letter stated that Juniper had a secret written agreement with the lessor modifying the lease and creating a capital lease.

Smith confronted the president of Juniper, who admitted that a secret agreement existed but said it was necessary to treat the lease as an operating lease to meet the debt-to-equity ratio requirement of the pending loan and that nobody would ever discover the secret agreement with the lessor. The president said that if Smith did not issue a report by September 30, Juniper would sue Smith for substantial damages that would result from not getting the loan. Under this pressure and because the audit documentation contained a copy of the five-year lease agreement supporting the operating lease treatment, Smith issued the report with an unqualified opinion on September 29. In spite of the fact that it received the loan, Juniper went bankrupt. The bank is suing Smith to recover its losses on the loan, and the lessor is suing Smith to recover uncollected rents.

Required:
Answer the following, setting forth reasons for any conclusions stated.
a. Is Smith liable to the bank?
b. Is Smith liable to the lessor?
c. Was Smith independent?

(AICPA adapted)

LO C-2

C.70 **Common Law Liability to Third Parties.** Flacco, CPA, conducted the audit of Raven Company. As part of the preaudit conference, Flacco was informed by Raven's management that its audited financial statements would be presented to Baltimore National Bank to secure financing for a significant expansion opportunity. At the conclusion of the audit, Flacco issued an unqualified opinion that concluded that Raven's financial statements presented its financial condition, results of operations, and cash flows according to GAAP.

Using these financial statements, as well as Flacco's opinion on those statements, Raven obtained financing from the following parties: (1) Baltimore National Bank, (2) Regional State Bank, and (3) Maryland Equity Partners (a private equity firm). Each of these parties specifically requested audited financial statements and relied on these statements in providing financing to Raven. Six months after obtaining financing, Raven's financial condition worsened, and it declared bankruptcy, forcing Raven to default on its payments to Baltimore National Bank and Regional State Bank. In addition, Maryland Equity Partners' investment in Raven became worthless.

After the bankruptcy, the parties that had provided financing to Raven determined that Raven had intentionally misstated its financial statements by recording fictitious revenues and accounts receivable. These parties decided to file suit against Flacco for failure to identify the fictitious revenues and accounts receivable.

Required:

a. Define the following type of third parties: (1) *primary beneficiary,* (2) *foreseen third parties,* and *(3) foreseeable third parties.*

b. Considering the three types of third parties identified in (a), how would you classify (1) Baltimore National Bank, (2) Regional State Bank, and (3) Maryland Equity Partners?

c. Assume that court proceedings concluded that Flacco's work failed to comply with generally accepted auditing standards, but that Flacco was not aware of the misstatements nor was he grossly negligent in his performance. Which of the parties would be likely to prevail in its claim against Flacco?

d. Assume that court proceedings concluded that Flacco failed to send confirmations to Raven's customers and simply mathematically verified the summary listing of accounts receivable provided to him by Raven. Which of the parties would be likely to prevail in its claim against Flacco?

LO C-2

C.71 **Common Law Liability to Third Parties.** Madeoff is a small, nonpublic retailer seeking capital for expansion. To obtain necessary capital, Madeoff engaged Allen, CPAs to audit is annual financial statements. In discussing the engagement, Madeoff explicitly informed Allen that the purpose of the audit was to obtain additional financing for expansion into new markets. Madeoff obtained $3 million from lenders. These lenders included the following:

- First Trust and Bank provided $2 million. When engaging Allen, Madeoff indicated that it would use the audited financial statements and Allen's opinion on these statements to seek financing from First Trust and Bank; also, First Trust and Bank was specifically named in the engagement letter. Prior to committing the capital, First Trust and Bank had reviewed Madeoff's financial statements and, based on the financial condition reflected in its balance sheet, deemed Madeoff to be a qualified loan candidate.

- MoonTrust Bank provided $800,000 of capital to Madeoff. While not named in the engagement letter nor identified to Allen, Madeoff had previous business dealings with MoonTrust and maintained several accounts at MoonTrust. Based primarily on its prior relationships with Madeoff, MoonTrust approved the additional financing to Madeoff prior to receiving the audited financial statements or Allen's report on those financial statements.

- Alice Lay, a local philanthropist, provided $200,000 of capital to Madeoff. While her decision was primarily motivated by Madeoff's role in the community and its corporate citizenship, she did request and review Madeoff's audited financial statements and Allen's report on those financial statements prior to providing funding. Alice had never entered into a loan agreement of this nature in the past but felt personal ties to Madeoff and was interested in its continued success.

Approximately six months following these loans, Madeoff declared bankruptcy.

Following the bankruptcy, lenders discovered that Allen's audit failed to disclose several material financial statement misstatements that, if corrected, would have presented a less favorable depiction of Madeoff's financial condition, results of operations, and cash flows. These lenders are exploring potential litigation against Allen to recover the funds they provided to Madeoff.

Required:

a. Would these third parties more likely pursue litigation against Madeoff under common law or statutory law?

b. How would each of the lenders likely be classified based on their relationship with Allen and the potential use of Madeoff's financial statements and Allen's report?

c. Assume that Allen's audit did not comply with generally accepted auditing standards but that it did not demonstrate a lack of minimum care or actual knowledge of the misstatements. Given the circumstances noted, how would you assess each of these parties' ability to prevail against Allen in a potential claim?

d. Repeat (c), assuming that the parties could prove that Allen was aware that Madeoff's financial statements contained a material misstatement.

LO C-2

C.72 Liability in a Review Engagement. Mason & Dilworth (M&D), CPAs, were auditors for Hotshot Company, a closely held corporation owned by 30 residents of the area. Hotshot had previously engaged M&D to perform some compilation and tax work. Bubba Crass, Hotshot's president and holder of 15 percent of the stock, said he needed something more than these services. He told Mason, the partner in charge, that he wanted financial statements for internal use, primarily for management purposes but also to obtain short-term loans from financial institutions. Mason recommended a "review" of the financial statements and did not prepare an engagement letter.

During the review work, Mason had some reservations about the financial statements. Mason told Dilworth at various times he was "uneasy about certain figures and conclusions," but he would "take Crass's word about the validity of certain entries since the review was primarily for internal use in any event and was not an audit."

M&D did not discover a material act of fraud committed by Crass. The fraud would have been detected had Mason not relied so much on the unsupported statements Crass made concerning the validity of the entries about which he had felt so uneasy.

Required:
a. What potential liability might M&D have to Hotshot Company and other stockholders?
b. What potential liability might M&D have to financial institutions that used the financial statements in connection with making loans to Hotshot Company?

(AICPA adapted)

LO C-4, C-5

C.73 Liability Under the Securities Acts. Orange is a public entity whose shares are traded on a national exchange. A Public Company Accounting Oversight Board inspection revealed a deficiency in audits conducted by Orange's auditor, LeGrow. LeGrow had failed to perform important auditing procedures; after performing these procedures in response to the inspection, LeGrow identified several material misstatements and requested that Orange restate its financial statements. These restatements had the effect of reducing Orange's reported income and cash flow from operations and increasing its liabilities.

Upon the disclosure of these restatements, Orange's stock price declined over 40 percent. Angered over this decline, investors are contemplating bringing legal action against LeGrow for failing to detect the misstatements.

Required:
a. Assume that investors are bringing suit under the Securities Act of 1933. What would investors need to demonstrate to bring suit against LeGrow under this act?
b. What is LeGrow's potential liability to investors if LeGrow's audit was characterized as demonstrating (1) ordinary negligence, (2) gross negligence, or (3) fraud?
c. Repeat (a) and (b), assuming that investors are bringing suit under the Securities Exchange Act of 1934.
d. What are the primary differences in LeGrow's liability to investors under the Securities Act of 1933 and the Securities Exchange Act of 1934?

LO C-4, C-5

C.74 Liability Under the Securities Acts. Jones, CPA, audits a number of public companies. During the past year, some deficiencies with respect to audits conducted for two of Jones's clients in the software industry (SoftWare and ExternalDrive) were identified. These deficiencies related to Jones's audit procedures used to evaluate the revenue recognized by these clients. Some pertinent facts in each of these audits are summarized as follows:

SoftWare. In 2012, SoftWare issued securities to investors in an initial public offering with an average offering price of $50 per share. Jones audited the financial statements, which were later determined to have overstated revenues through premature revenue recognition. The net effect on SoftWare's operations was an overstatement of revenue by 25 percent and an overstatement of net income by 63 percent. Following the issuance, the market value of SoftWare's shares declined to $15 per share.

ExternalDrive. ExternalDrive has been a client of Jones for five years and has been publicly traded throughout that entire period. In 2012, ExternalDrive's Form 10-K revealed revenues of $25 million, net income of $8.5 million, and earnings per share of $1.40, all of which exceeded prior years' results and analysts' estimates. ExternalDrive's financial statements were subsequently found to have overstated revenues by $2.25 million, which reduced reported revenues and earnings per share by 11 percent and 24 percent, respectively.

Following the revelation of these misstatements, ExternalDrive's stock price declined from $18 per share to $9 per share.

You have been asked to defend Jones in legal actions involving shareholders of both companies and have engaged an auditing expert to evaluate Jones's performance. After reviewing the audit documentation and related professional literature, she concluded that Jones's performance was likely in violation of generally accepted auditing standards; however, it did not rise to the level of being considered "reckless" and it does not appear that Jones was aware of the departures from GAAP. In addition, while unrelated to Jones's audit, she observed that the market price of software companies had declined in a similar manner to that of SoftWare and ExternalDrive because of overall economic conditions.

Required:
a. Which statute would govern Jones's liability to shareholders of SoftWare? ExternalDrive?
b. What would shareholders of SoftWare and ExternalDrive need to demonstrate prior to bringing suit against Jones?
c. Based on the case facts as described, what possible defense(s) would you recommend to Jones in each of these situations?
d. Assume that these two cases went to trial and Jones's performance was deemed to be "reckless" in nature and that Jones possessed scienter. How does this change the likelihood of a favorable outcome for Jones?

LO C-6

C.75 **Class Action Lawsuits.** In the United States, it has become common to seek recovery of financial losses from other parties, often even if that other party is not at fault. Frequently this occurs by means of a class action lawsuit.

Required:
a. What is a class action lawsuit?
b. What advantages does a class action lawsuit have for the plaintiffs?
c. What disadvantages does a class action lawsuit have for the defendant?
d. How has recent legislation affected class action lawsuits?
e. Perform an Internet search for information regarding class action lawsuits against auditors. What are the (1) particulars of the lawsuit and (2) auditors' defenses?

LO C-2, C-4

C.76 **Liability under Common Law and the Securities Act of 1933.** Butler Manufacturing Corporation raised capital for a plant expansion by borrowing from a bank and making a stock offering. Butler engaged Weaver, CPA, to audit its December 2012 financial statements. Butler told Weaver that the financial statements would be given to Union Bank and certain other named banks and included in a registration statement for the stock offering.

In performing the audit, Weaver did not confirm accounts receivable and therefore failed to discover a material overstatement. Weaver also was aware of a pending class action product liability lawsuit that was not disclosed in Butler's financial statements. Despite being advised by Butler's legal counsel that the entity's potential liability under the lawsuit would result in material losses, Weaver issued an unqualified opinion on Butler's financial statements.

In May 2013, Union Bank relied on the financial statements and Weaver's opinion to grant Butler a $500,000 loan.

Butler raised additional funds in November 2013 with a $14,000,000 unregistered offering of preferred stock. This offering was sold directly by the entity to 40 nonaccredited private investors during a one-year period.

Shortly after obtaining the Union Bank loan, Butler experienced financial problems but was able to stay in business because of the money raised by the stock offering. Butler lost the product liability suit, resulting in a judgment that the entity could not pay. Butler also defaulted on the Union Bank loan and was involuntarily petitioned into bankruptcy. This caused Union Bank to sustain a loss and Butler's stockholders' investments became worthless.

Union Bank sued Weaver for failure to provide the appropriate level of professional care and common law fraud. The stockholders who purchased Butler's stock through the offering sued Weaver, alleging fraud under section 17 of the Securities Act of 1933.

These transactions took place in a jurisdiction providing for auditors' liability for ordinary negligence to known and intended users of financial statements.

Required:

Answer the following questions and give the reasons for your conclusions.

a. Will Union Bank be successful in its suit against Weaver under common law for (1) ordinary negligence and (2) fraud?

b. Will the stockholders who purchased Butler's stock through the offering succeed against Weaver under the antifraud provisions of section 17 of the Securities Act of 1933?

(AICPA adapted)

LO C-4, C-5

C.77 **Liability under the Securities Acts.** One of your firm's clients, Fancy Fashions, Inc., is a highly successful, rapidly expanding entity. It is owned predominantly by the Munster family and key corporate officials. Although additional funds would be available on a short-term basis from its bankers, they would represent only a temporary solution of the entity's need for capital to finance its expansion plans. In addition, the interest rates being charged are not appealing. Therefore, Chris Munster, Fancy's chairman of the board, in consultation with the other shareholders, has decided to explore the possibility of raising additional equity capital of approximately $15 million to $16 million. This will be Fancy's first public offering.

At a meeting of Fancy's major shareholders, its attorneys and a member of your firm spoke about the advantages and disadvantages of "going public" and registering a stock offering. One of the shareholders suggested that Regulation D under the Securities Act of 1933 might be a preferable alternative.

Required:

a. Assume that Fancy makes a public offering for $16 million and, as a result, more than 1,000 persons own shares of the entity. Following the public offering, what are the implications with respect to the Securities Exchange Act of 1934? (*Hint:* You can identify the thresholds for being subject to the reporting requirements of the Securities Exchange Act of 1934 through reference to the SEC's website, www.sec.gov.)

b. What federal civil and criminal liabilities under the Securities Act of 1933 could apply in the event that Fancy sells the securities without registration and a registration exemption is not available?

c. Using the SEC's website (www.sec.gov) as a reference, define "accredited investor" and discuss the exemption applicable to offerings made under Regulation D for accredited investors.

(AICPA adapted)

LO C-4

C.78 **Section 11 of Securities Act of 1933: Liability Exposure.** Chriswell Corporation decided to raise additional long-term capital by issuing $20 million of 12 percent subordinated debentures to the public. May, Clark & Company, CPAs, the company's auditors, were engaged to examine the June 30, 2013, financial statements, which were included in the bond registration statement.

May, Clark & Company completed its examination and submitted an unqualified auditors' report dated July 15, 2013. The registration statement was filed and became effective on September 1, 2013. On August 15, one of the partners of May, Clark & Company called on Chriswell Corporation and had lunch with the financial vice president and the controller. He questioned both officials on the company's operations since June 30 and inquired whether there had been any material changes in the company's financial position since that date. Both officers assured him that everything had proceeded normally and that the financial condition of the company had not changed materially.

Unfortunately, the officers' representation was not true. On July 30, a substantial debtor of the company failed to pay the $400,000 due on its account receivable and indicated to Chriswell that it would probably be forced into bankruptcy. This receivable was shown as a collateralized loan on the June 30 financial statements. It was secured by stock of the debtor corporation, which had a value in excess of the loan at the time the financial statements were prepared but was virtually worthless at the effective date of the registration statement. This $400,000 account receivable was material to the financial condition of Chriswell Corporation and the market price of the subordinated debentures decreased by nearly 50 percent after the foregoing facts were disclosed.

The debenture holders of Chriswell are seeking recovery of their loss against all parties connected with the debenture registration.

Required:
Are May, Clark & Company liable to the Chriswell debenture holders under section 11 of the Securities Act of 1933? Explain. (*Hint:* Review the *BarChris* case in this chapter.)

(AICPA adapted)

LO C-5

C.79 **Rule 10b-5 Liability under the Securities Exchange Act of 1934.** Gordon & Groton (G&G), CPAs, were auditors of Bank & Company, a brokerage firm and member of a national stock exchange. G&G examined and reported on the financial statements of Bank, which were filed with the Securities and Exchange Commission.

Several of Bank's customers were swindled by a fraudulent scheme perpetrated by Bank's president, who owned 90 percent of the voting stock of the company. The facts establish that G&G failed to perform the audit with the appropriate level of professional care but neither participated in the fraudulent scheme nor knew of its existence.

The customers are suing G&G under the antifraud provisions of section 10(b) and Rule 10b-5 of the Securities Exchange Act of 1934 for aiding and abetting the fraudulent scheme of the president. The customers' suit for fraud is predicated exclusively on G&G's failure to conduct a proper audit, thereby failing to discover the fraudulent scheme.

Required:
Answer the following, setting forth reasons for any conclusions stated.
a. What is the probable outcome of the lawsuit?
b. What might be the result if plaintiffs had sued under common law for ordinary negligence? Explain.

(AICPA adapted)

LO C-5

C.80 **Independence and Securities Exchange Act of 1934.** Anderson, Olds, and Watershed (AOW) have been the independent auditors for Accord Corporation since 1990. Accord is a public entity obligated to file periodic reports under the Securities Exchange Act of 1934.

Beginning in January 2012, the AOW litigation support consulting division performed a special engagement for Accord. The work involved a lawsuit that Accord had filed against Civic Company for patent infringement on microchip manufacturing processes. AOW personnel compiled production statistics—costs and lost profits—under various volume assumptions and then testified in court about the losses to Accord that had resulted from Civic's improper use of patented processes. The amounts at issue were very large with claims of $50 million for lost profits and a plea for $150 million punitive damages. Accord won a court judgment for a total of $120 million, and Civic has appealed the damage award. The case remained pending throughout 2012 and into 2013. By March 1, 2013, AOW had billed Accord $265,000 for the litigation support work.

In November 2012, AOW started the audit work on Accord's financial statements for the fiscal year ending December 31, 2012. During this work, AOW auditors found that Accord's management and board of directors did not fully disclose the stage of the appeal of the Civic Company case, had improperly deferred a material loss on new product start-up costs as an element of its inventory, and had accrued sales revenue for promotional chip sales that carried an unconditional right of return. As partner in charge of the engagement, D. Ward agreed with the president that the accounting and disclosure were suitable to protect Accord's shareholders from adverse business developments and he issued a standard unqualified opinion that was included in the entity's 10-K annual report filed with the SEC and dated April 1, 2013.

AOW then billed Accord for the $200,000 audit fee and sent a reminder for payment of the $265,000 consulting fee; both billings were dated April 2, 2013.

Required:
a. Was AOW independent for the audit of Accord for the fiscal year ended December 31, 2012? Explain.
b. Did Ward and AOW follow generally accepted auditing standards in the audit? Cite any specific standards that might have been violated and explain your reasoning.
c. Did Ward and AOW violate any section(s) of the Securities Exchange Act of 1934? Explain.

LO C-5

C.81 **Auditors' Liability under Securities Exchange Act of 1934.** Adam, an Illinois resident, was interested in purchasing stock in Joshua Foods, Inc. Joshua Foods has corporate headquarters in Fond du Lac, Wisconsin, and is incorporated in Delaware. Adam e-mailed Joshua

Foods' Investor Relations Department and requested its 2012 annual report including the financial statements. Adam also reviewed several analysts' opinions on the Internet, including the opinions provided from his Internet broker, Matthew & Co. ExpressTrade. Adam received the annual report in the mail. Based on the increasing revenues, the $8 million net income indicated on the financial statements, and the other information received from the analysts, Adam purchased $350,000 worth of stock.

Three months later, Joshua Foods announced that over the last three years, the company had included $25 million of fictitious revenue and had capitalized more than $30 million of charges that should have been expensed. These irregularities will result in a restatement of the fiscal 2012 financial statements resulting in a $1,250,000 loss for fiscal 2012. The press release from the company says that it will likely declare bankruptcy in the next few weeks. In the following two weeks, the value of Adam's holdings in the stock declined to $50,000.

Required:

a. You are Adam's attorney. List the various legal issues and precedents that you will use in trying to recover the losses Adam sustained.

b. You are the attorney for Joshua Foods' auditors. It is apparent that Adam will try to recover losses from your firm. List the defenses you would prepare to protect the auditors from liability.

c. How does Sarbanes-Oxley affect the position of either Adam's attorney or the auditors' attorney? You may find www.sarbanes-oxley.com helpful.

LO C-5 C.82 **Mini-Case: Litigation.** Refer to the mini-case "Unhealthy Accounting at HealthSouth" on page C14 and respond to question 5.

LO C-1 C.83 **Mini-Case: Ethics.** Refer to the mini-case "Andersen: An Obstruction of Justice?" on page C1 and respond to questions 1, 2, 3, 4, 5, and 7.

Internal, Governmental, and Fraud Audits

You have a chance to really learn and improve the business. You build relationships with the board and the major business leaders. You can move internal audit to more value-added processes. And it builds your ability to manage people and work with cross-functional teams.

> Michael Fung, CFO, Walmart North American stores division, on his four years spent in internal audit[1]

Professional Standards References

Topic	AU/ISA	PCAOB Reference*
Consideration of Fraud in a Financial Statement Audit	240	AU 316
Consideration of Laws and Regulations	250	AU 317
Consideration of Internal Control in an Integrated Audit		AS 5
Consideration of the Internal Audit Function in a Financial Statement Audit	610	AU 341
Compliance Auditing Considerations in Audits of Governmental Entities and Recipients of Governmental Financial Assistance	AU 801	AU 801
		ET/AT Standard
Compliance Attestation		AT 601
Independence, Integrity, and Objectivity		ET[†] 101–191
		IIA Standard
Independence and Objectivity		IIA 1100
Organizational Objectivity		IIA 1110
Individual Objectivity		IIA 1120
Proficiency		IIA 1210
Managing the Internal Audit Activity		IIA 2000
Nature of Work		IIA 2100
Governance		IIA 2110

[1] *CFO.com,* June 10, 2008.

Risk Management	IIA 2120
Control	IIA 2130
Engagement Planning	IIA 2200
Planning Considerations	IIA 2201
Engagement Objectives	IIA 2210
Engagement Scope	IIA 2220
Performing the Engagement	IIA 2300
Communicating Results	IIA 2400
Criteria for Communicating	IIA 2410
Quality of Communications	IIA 2420
Resolution of Senior Management's Acceptance of Risks	IIA 2600

[†]AU references represent standards issued by the ASB prior to April 16, 2003, that have not been superseded by the PCAOB.
[*]ET indicates ethics standard.

LEARNING OBJECTIVES

This module introduces governmental, internal, and fraud auditing. These fields differ in important respects from financial statement auditing practiced by independent CPAs in public accounting. However, you will find that all fields of auditing share many elements. Fraud auditing can be very exciting. It has the aura of detective work—finding things people want to keep hidden. The explanations and examples in this module will help you understand the working environment, objectives, and procedures that characterize governmental, internal, and fraud auditing.

Your learning objectives are to be able to:

LO D-1 Define *internal auditing;* describe internal audit institutions (e.g., IIA); describe how internal auditors interact with independent auditors; explain internal auditors' independence problems; and list features of internal audit reports.

LO D-2 Define *governmental auditing;* describe governmental audit institutions (e.g., GAO); describe how governmental auditors interact with independent auditors; explain governmental auditors' independence problems; and list features of governmental audit reports.

LO D-3 Explain the function of standards and measurements in economy, efficiency, and program results audits.

LO D-4 Describe the Single Audit Act of 1984 in relation to audits of governmental fund recipients.

LO D-5 Define *fraud auditing* and describe various engagements performed by fraud auditors.

LO D-6 Describe the elements necessary for a successful fraud examination and explain the differences in the way fraud examiners and external auditors handle evidence.

LO D-7 Describe the ways CPAs can assist in prosecuting fraud perpetrators.

INTRODUCTION

In the summer of 2002, **WorldCom** announced that its financial statements were misstated by more than $7 billion. The misstatement was the result of capitalizing ordinary expenses. WorldCom's vice president of internal audit, Cynthia Cooper, discovered the accounting fraud. Despite opposition from WorldCom's chief financial officer, Cooper took her findings to the chairman of the audit committee of WorldCom's board of directors. The actions of WorldCom's internal auditors led to the disclosure of one of the largest financial statement frauds in history. Cooper was subsequently named one of *Time* magazine's three "2003 Persons of the Year."

"EXTERNAL," GOVERNMENTAL, AND INTERNAL AUDITS

In today's environment of Sarbanes-Oxley, the Public Company Accounting Oversight Board (PCAOB), and increased public scrutiny, organizations are asking public accounting firms for more assistance. Public accounting firms are no longer able to provide internal audit services to their publicly traded audit clients. However, organizations that need assistance with internal audit, investigation, and other related services can turn to public accounting firms that do not serve as their financial service auditor. One of the main segments in most large public accounting firms is outsourced and cosourced internal audit services, and this opportunity has led to several business ventures focused primarily on providing internal audit and other nonaudit services to clients (e.g., **Protiviti Inc.**).

Many of the tasks and processes that internal auditors and governmental auditors perform are similar to those that financial statement auditors perform. However, services performed by governmental and internal auditors do vary considerably. When internal and governmental auditors perform audits of financial information, the scope of the engagement typically is wider than the scope performed by an external auditor. Internal auditors and governmental auditors often have objectives that go beyond the fair presentation of the financial numbers such as the efficiency of the financial reporting process. Furthermore, government and internal auditors often will perform audits of monthly financial statements or other internal financial reports to ensure that information for management decisions is reliable. In this module, we will explore the services provided by internal auditors and governmental auditors and gain an understanding of the elements that help to define what is meant by a *quality audit*.

A discussion of internal auditing, governmental auditing, and financial statement auditing performed by public accounting firms is often confusing. Many governmental and internal auditors are CPAs and perform services similar to those performed by public accounting firms. Indeed, several state audit organizations are considered independent auditors and issue opinions on the financial statements of government agencies. At the same time, many public accounting firms are employed to audit the financial statements of government entities such as counties, cities, and school districts. To further complicate the discussion, many public accounting firms offer internal audit services to non-SEC clients and nonfinancial statement audit clients alike. It is important to note that while the PCAOB prohibits auditors of public companies from providing internal audit services to their public audit clients, auditors of privately held and not-for-profit (NFP) entities may still provide both internal and external audit services to their clients. For purposes of this module, therefore, *external* auditing refers to financial statement auditing performed by CPAs in public accounting firms and thereby distinguishes public practice from governmental and internal practice.

INTERNAL AUDITS

LEARNING OBJECTIVE D-1
Define *internal auditing;* describe internal audit institutions (e.g., IIA); describe how internal auditors interact with independent auditors; explain internal auditors' independence problems; and list features of internal audit reports.

In the past, *internal auditors* have been defined as auditors working for the organization that they were auditing. Internal auditors were employed by an organization such as a bank, hospital, city government, or industrial company. However, in recent years, many professional services firms are providing internal audit services to the business community. Therefore, internal auditors may now be employed by either the organization they are auditing or an independent professional services firm.[2] Many corporations believe that they gain expertise and improve control over audit costs when the internal audit function is "outsourced" to an external audit firm. Conversely, many companies believe that an "in-house" internal audit function is better aligned with the company's goals and objectives and auditors gain more experience and expertise with the company's organization

---
[2] Professional services firms include public accounting firms that offer a variety of auditing, accounting, and consulting services and some consulting firms that do not perform financial statement audit services but do provide other services including internal audit services (e.g., Protiviti).

and business. Currently, we are seeing more firms implementing a "cosourcing strategy" in which the company retains an "in-house" internal audit department augmented by auditors from an outside firm. This strategy allows the company to have a core audit group dedicated to the company with specialized "institutional knowledge" in company policy, procedure, and strategy, yet the company can obtain expertise and audit knowledge of a professional services firm directly for specific engagements or projects.

The Institute of Internal Auditors (IIA), the organization that sets standards and governs the internal audit profession, defines **internal auditing** and states its objective as follows:

> Internal auditing is an independent, objective, assurance and consulting activity designed to add value and improve an organization's operations. It helps an organization accomplish its objectives by bringing a systematic, disciplined approach to evaluate and improve effectiveness of risk management, control, and governance processes.

Several key elements in this definition warrant further evaluation.

Independence (IIA *Standards 1100* and *1110*)

You may be wondering how internal auditors employed by the company being audited can classify themselves as independent and objective. Although internal auditors employed by the entity under audit cannot be disassociated from their employers in the eyes of the public, they seek organizational and individual independence. Internal auditors achieve independence during the audit process when they are free from direction or constraint by the managers of the business unit under audit. To establish this organizational independence, many internal audit organizations report directly to the audit committees of the board of directors. Such reporting relationship reduces management's influence over the audit scope and reporting.

An element that greatly assists the internal audit department in establishing an independent and objective organization is the audit charter. While many departments and organizations have charters, it is particularly important for the internal audit department to have one. An internal audit charter approved by senior management and the board of directors provides:

- A commitment from management to the establishment of an independent and objective audit organization.
- A definition of the authority and responsibility of the audit department.
- A definition of the scope of the audit department's activities.
- The department's authorization to perform audits, request materials, and gather evidence.
- The performance and reporting requirements for the audit department.

These elements provide an essential foundation for building an independent department. The audit charter for the University of Tennessee System is provided in Exhibit D.1.

The other key aspect of independence and objectivity concerns the attitude of the individuals engaged in the audit. An internal auditor must have an impartial, unbiased attitude in performing the audit. In addition, individual auditors must not have any conflicts of interests. Such conflicts may result when the same company employs family members or outside business interests appear to affect audit judgments (see IIA *Standard 1120* and the IIA Code of Ethics).

As previously mentioned, many public accounting firms are performing internal audit work for clients. While this is strictly prohibited for public companies by Sarbanes-Oxley, the PCAOB, and the Securities and Exchange Commission, public accounting firms can provide internal audit services to clients that are not publicly traded and to publicly traded companies who are not audit clients. However, great care should be given concerning independence issues, both independence in fact and independence in appearance. Auditors should take great care to avoid even the appearance that they are auditing their own work or are biased in their audit judgments due to revenue and relations emanating from internal audit work.

EXHIBIT D.1 Internal Audit Charter of the University of Tennessee System

CHICAGO MERCANTILE EXCHANGE INC.

The University of Tennessee System
Internal Audit Charter

PURPOSE and SCOPE
Internal auditing at the University of Tennessee is an independent appraisal activity established to examine and evaluate the activities of the university as a service to management and the Board of Trustees. Internal Audit assists management in effectively carrying out their duties and responsibilities by examining financial and operational internal control systems, including administrative information systems, to evaluate the extent that:

- Financial, property, and information assets are safeguarded;
- Information is accurate and reliable;
- University policies and external laws and regulations are followed;
- Resources are employed efficiently and economically; and
- Operations and programs are being carried out as planned, and their results are consistent with university objectives.

AUTHORITY and RESPONSIBILITY
Internal auditors shall be authorized full and complete access to all university records (either manual or electronic), physical properties, and personnel relevant to a review. The corresponding responsibility of internal auditors is to handle documents and information obtained during a review in the same prudent manner as by those employees normally responsible for them.
In fulfilling their responsibilities, internal audit departments at each campus or unit will:

- Develop and implement audit plans and programs that respond to both risk and cost-effectiveness criteria;
- Suggest policies and procedures where appropriate;
- Provide audit reports that identify internal control issues (among others) and make cost-effective recommendations to strengthen controls;
- Facilitate the resolution of audit issues with administrators who have the most direct involvement and accountability;
- Maintain auditing standards, consistent with those established by the Institute of Internal Auditors, Inc., to ensure the effectiveness and quality of the internal audit effort; and
- Investigate allegations involving theft or misuse of university assets.

In their staff functions, internal auditors have no direct responsibility or authority over any of the operating activities examined, and their review shall not relieve others of their responsibilities. Furthermore, the independence of the internal auditors should not be compromised by their implementing procedures, preparing records, or engaging in activities that internal auditors would normally review.

REPORTING STRUCTURE
The internal audit function reports to the Audit Committee of the Board of Trustees with supporting responsibilities to the chief financial officer. Campus/institute internal auditors report to the Knoxville audit office with supporting responsibilities to the campus/institute chief executive and respective chief business officers. When requested, internal auditors may attend senior-level staff meetings and serve on various university committees. Their role at such meetings should be limited to rendering advice and staying abreast of strategic, governance, and risk issues.

At the conclusion of each audit, Internal Audit will issue timely reports to audited parties, senior management, the State of Tennessee Division of Internal Audit, and the Audit Committee.

Initially approved by the Audit Committee on March 3, 2004.
Revised November 30, 2005
Approved by the Audit Committee on November 4, 2010.

AUDITING INSIGHT   Does Everyone Know What They're Doing?

An auditor was reviewing the mortgage procedures at a large bank including a discussion with a clerk in charge of escrow accounts. The clerk knew about receiving funds and placing them in the escrow account. The clerk knew to pay for surveys, inspections, title investigations, and other fees from the escrow account. However, the clerk was not aware that once the property sale was completed, any remaining funds were to be taken by the bank as revenue. The auditor found $77,000 in unrecorded revenue.

Source: Personal experience of author.

Value-Added Audit

The objectives of an internal audit and an external audit are vastly different. Generally speaking, internal auditors perform little of their work on the financial statements. In-house internal auditors audit their companies all year, often months removed from both the previous or next issue of annual financial statements. Internal auditors are primarily concerned with affecting the company's bottom line; hence, the definition includes the phrase *to add value and improve an organization's operations.* Internal auditors add value to a company primarily by following four audit objectives:

1. Recognizing and analyzing industry, business, and operational risks.
2. Improving the economy and efficiency of the operations.
3. Ensuring compliance with management directives.
4. Serving as management's representative.

Recognizing and Analyzing Industry, Business, and Operational Risks

A major goal of an internal audit organization is to gain as much expertise as possible concerning the industry, business, and operational areas of the company. This expertise allows the internal auditors to recognize and evaluate changes in the economy, business environment, technology, regulatory environment, and management. These types of changes often result in additional risks faced by the organization. The internal audit department must take a proactive approach to reduce or eliminate these risks. By reducing or eliminating risks that might create potential losses, the internal audit organization adds value to the company.

Improving Economy and Efficiency of the Operations

Over a period of a few years, an internal auditor will have evaluated almost every department and almost every aspect of a company's business. This experience makes the auditor a valuable asset to the organization. Indeed, many organizations use internal audit as a training ground for management and entities highly value the experience gained as a member of the internal audit organization (note the quote from Michael Fung, CFO of **Wal-Mart Stores, Inc.,** at the beginning of this module). This experience also enables the internal auditor to evaluate many aspects regarding the performance of a particular department or process. For example, an internal auditor for Sears may visit five or six distribution centers in a given year. A particular distribution center may have developed a procedure that enables orders to be processed faster. The internal auditor may be able to recommend this "best practice" to other facilities.

An important ingredient in successfully recommending changes in a company's operations is for the auditor to have a complete business and technical perspective of the operation under evaluation. For example, auditors are not successful in implementing meaningful change in a marketing department without completely considering the marketing perspective on the processes and procedures used in that specialty. Many internal audit organizations enhance this critical element of internal audit by adding personnel with backgrounds in production, engineering, computer science, and other relevant disciplines to the internal audit staff (IIA *Standard 1210*).

Ensuring Compliance with Management Directives

Management provides all departments and operations with directives regarding the desired performance of the company's business. These directives are designed to ensure that the company complies with laws and regulations; that departments are operating efficiently and effectively; and that risks are minimized. Many of these directives are found in the policy and procedure manuals maintained by each functional area. Internal audit is charged with reporting on departments' compliance with these directives. Often these directives delineate the internal controls established by management to reduce or eliminate risk within a functional area.

It is important to recognize the distinction between the compliance issues of internal auditors and those of external auditors. External auditors review compliance with internal controls that are relevant to the financial reporting process. The internal auditors are concerned with any noncompliance that (1) increases the risk faced by the company or (2) diminishes the efficiency or effectiveness of the company's operations. Basically, internal auditors are concerned with any noncompliance that might adversely affect the company's likelihood of meeting its goals and objectives.

Serving as Management's Representative

The complexities of managing a large organization often prohibit senior management from visiting locations and departments critical to the success of the organization. For example, because of the number of distribution centers operated by **Sears,** it would not be feasible for the vice president of materials management to personally visit and review every individual operation at each distribution center. Therefore, the reports from the internal audit department may be the only critical objective evaluations received by that manager regarding certain distribution centers and other key operations.

It should be evident that the four audit objectives discussed here are not mutually exclusive. For example, the evaluation of compliance with company policies and procedures includes elements of reducing risk, evaluating economy and efficiency, and being management's representative.

Scope of Service

Internal auditors make recommendations that result in additional profits or cost savings for their companies. In this capacity, they function as management consultants. Within the IIA definition of "to evaluate and improve effectiveness of risk management, control, and governance processes," almost any type of assessment of any aspect of the organization is feasible. In fact, it is difficult to define the variety of audits that the modern internal audit department performs.

The stated objective of internal auditing is phrased in terms of "helping the organization accomplish its objectives." To achieve this goal, internal auditors provide services including (1) financial audits of financial reports and accounting control systems; (2) compliance audits that ensure conformity with company policies, plans, and procedures and with laws and regulations; (3) operational audits that evaluate the economy and efficiency of business process; and (4) audits of effectiveness in achieving program results in comparison to established objectives and goals (IIA *Standards 2100* and *2210*).

Financial Audits

Internal auditors usually do not audit quarterly or year-end financial statements in the same manner as external auditors. However, internal auditors may evaluate areas that management believes may be of concern to the external auditors such as areas that were found to have problems in the prior audit. Such a preliminary evaluation may allow for correction of errors prior to the arrival of the external auditors.

Internal auditors more likely perform audits of financial reports for internal use. This type of audit provides managers assurance that the information they are using in the decision-making process is relevant and reliable. Such an assurance function reduces management's risk in making daily operating decisions or in determining appropriate action to address a unique problem. This type of auditing is similar to the auditing described elsewhere in this textbook.

Compliance Audits

In many functional areas, management's primary concern is compliance with policies, procedures, laws, and regulations—thus, the definition of **compliance audits**. The degree of management's concern for such audits may vary by industry or by functional area. For example, compliance with laws will be of more concern in the banking, insurance, and health care industries as compared with a company in the retail industry. Also, in an audit of the human resources department, the main audit objective may be compliance with policies and procedures designed to ensure conformity with laws regarding fair hiring and proper dismissals of employees.

> **AUDITING INSIGHT**   Did I Take That Trip?

Toni McEwen, an internal auditor at **Deerfield College,** was auditing expense accounts. To her surprise, an expense report of Bruce Livingstone, a supervisor at the Deerfield College School of Dentistry's business office, listed her as a traveling partner on a recent business trip. Livingstone (who was married) took his girlfriend on a business trip at the college's expense but needed to list another college employee if the college was to pay for the expenses. Listing an auditor as his traveling partner was probably not the best way to cover this fraud!

Because fraudulent behavior in management often leads to additional fraudulent behavior (tone at the top), the auditors launched an investigation of the business office. The auditors uncovered $63,000 in fictitious vendor payments, perpetrated by Cheryl Brown, an administrative assistant working for Livingstone.

Source: "One Fraud Leads to Another," *Internal Auditor,* December 2008.

> **AUDITING INSIGHT**   How Hard Did You Study for Your Last Exam?

Internal auditors evaluate an organization's compliance with every aspect of policy and procedure. An internal audit at Auburn University found a grade for a scholarship athlete was changed without the professor's knowledge, raising the athlete's grade for the semester just over the 2.0 minimum for graduation.

Source: "An Audit Reveals More Academic Questions at Auburn," *The New York Times,* December 10, 2006.

Operational Audits

In the past, the terms *internal auditing* and *operational auditing* were used almost interchangeably because the vast majority of audits performed by internal auditors were operational audits. The internal auditing activity known as **operational auditing** refers to auditors' study of business operations for the purpose of making recommendations about economic and efficient use of resources, effective achievement of business objectives, and compliance with company policies. The goal of operational auditing is to help managers discharge their management responsibilities and improve profitability. Therefore, operational auditing is included in the definition of internal auditing given previously. In a similar context, an AICPA committee defined operational auditing performed by independent public accounting firms as a distinct type of consulting service having the goal of helping a client improve the use of its capabilities and resources to achieve its objectives. So, internal auditors consider operational auditing an integral part of internal auditing and external auditors define it as a type of consulting service offered by public accounting firms.

Governance Audits

The definition of internal auditing includes evaluating the *governance process.* According to **MetricStream**, a quality and risk management consulting organization,

> Internal Audit supports the [Board of Directors] and its committees by independently assessing the effectiveness of an organization's system of internal controls as well as compliance with statutory, legal and regulatory requirements. Given the importance the [Board of Directors] attaches to this role, organizations are making every effort to adopt internal audit across the enterprise for better management of risk and effective compliance with regulation. As internal audit adopts new roles—provide assurance and establish trust through assessment of design, implementation, and application of internal controls across all disciplines—organizations are looking for ways to make the internal audit function an integral part of governance and an instrument to improve business performance.[3]

---

[3] www.metricstream.com/insights/governance_internal_auditing.html.

In this role as an integral part of governance, the auditor reports on a wide variety of critical information. It is essential that management understand the risks that the business and industry are facing. It is also imperative that management receive objective, timely feedback concerning corporate strategies and initiatives in order to effectively guide the corporation and fulfill their fiduciary responsibilities. **Governance audits** ensure that senior management receives accurate and timely information concerning management and leadership throughout the organization as well as the proper implementation and execution of company strategy and plans. This function of internal audit is continuing to grow in both scope and importance.

AUDITING INSIGHT — Internal Auditors Produce Interest Income

During an audit of the cash management operations at branch offices, internal auditors found that bank deposits were not made until several days after cash and checks were received. Company policy was to complete the bookkeeping before making the deposit.

The auditors showed branch managers a cost-efficient way to capture the needed bookkeeping information that would permit the release of the cash and checks. Management agreed to implement the timely deposit of checks and transfers to headquarters through an electronic funds transfer system from local banks to the headquarters bank, performing the bookkeeping afterward.

The change resulted in additional interest income in the first year in the amount of $150,000.

Other Audits

Internal auditors may perform audits that are specific to the nature of the business they serve. For example, auditors who work with manufacturing companies may provide **quality control audits** designed specifically to determine whether the product meets the standards established by management. Customer service departments also may be subject to a quality audit to ensure that customers are being served in the manner prescribed by the company. The auditors are not a substitute for the quality control department, but they can review the work of quality control, quality control reports, and the responses of management to issues raised by quality control.

Another type of audit performed in some organizations is an **environmental audit**.[4] Many organizations deal with materials that must be handled in manners prescribed by law (e.g., what does Sears do with those old batteries, tires, and oil?). Auditors can review procedures, record keeping, liability issues, and compliance as they relate to the organization's environmental issues. In addition, auditors can make recommendations to reduce waste (e.g., reusable shipping containers) and make products that are more environmentally friendly (e.g., recyclable packaging materials).

Internal Audit Standards

The IIA is the international organization that governs the standards, continuing education, and general rules of conduct for internal auditors as a profession. The IIA also sponsors research and development of practices and procedures designed to enhance the work of internal auditors wherever they are employed.

The IIA issues *International Standards for the Professional Practice of Internal Auditing* (IIA *Standards*) (see the IIA website at www.theiia.org). The IIA standards are classified in three major categories:

1. Attribute standards
2. Performance standards
3. Implementation standards

---

[4] Many organizations are engaged in *sustainability accounting* that includes an environmental component. However, due to the highly technical nature of environmental laws and policy, most organizations that have significant exposure have an environmental audit function.

Aptly named, the attribute standards address the *characteristics of internal auditors* (e.g., independence, objectivity) *and organizations* performing internal audit activities. Performance standards relate to *conducting internal audit activities* and provide a *measure of quality* against which the performance of internal audit activities can be measured. The attribute and the performance standards apply to internal audit services in general. Implementation standards, on the other hand, are specific applications of the attribute and performance standards to specific types of engagements (e.g., assurance or consulting engagements).

Internal auditors are expected to comply with the IIA's standards of professional conduct. IIA audit standards are recommended and encouraged, but compliance with them depends on their acceptance, adoption, and implementation by practicing internal auditors. Many internal audit organizations include compliance with IIA standards in their department charters and in their audit reports (note the reference to the IIA standards in the audit charter of the University of Tennessee System in Exhibit D.1). The IIA standards require internal auditors to be skilled in dealing with people and in communicating effectively. Such a requirement may be considered implicit in GAAS related to training and proficiency, but little is said in GAAS about effective communication, perhaps because the audit report language is so standardized. External auditors tend to believe the public has the responsibility to learn how to understand their audit reports while internal auditors believe it is their responsibility to see that management and the audit committee understand the audit findings and recommendations.

The IIA also issues practice advisories. Because of the diversity of entities serviced by internal auditors, guidance from practice advisories is not mandatory. Practice advisories suggest "best practices" in internal audit, and internal audit organizations are encouraged to implement those practices that are applicable to the business and industry they serve.

Many of the IIA standards deal with the organization and management of the internal audit department. CPAs in public practice have similar standards, but their standards are included in the AICPA quality control standards rather than in GAAS. However, observance of quality control standards is considered essential for proper auditing practice in accordance with GAAS. The AICPA quality control standards are incorporated by reference in GAAS and enforced through the peer reviews and monitoring activities of accounting firms.

Although AICPA standards for financial statements are comprehensive, the related IIA standards are very brief. It would be extremely difficult to provide detailed specifications on internal audit reports because the reports vary by entity and audit objective. The best the IIA can provide is an outline of desirable audit report characteristics.

The IIA also controls the certified internal auditor (CIA) program. This certification is a mark of professional achievement that has gained international acceptance. To become a CIA, a candidate must hold a college degree and pass an examination on internal auditing and related subjects. The exam has four parts:

- Part 1—The internal audit activity's role in governance, risk, and control.
- Part 2—Conducting the internal audit engagement.
- Part 3—Business analysis and information technology.
- Part 4—Business management skills.

Candidates also must have two years of audit experience (internal audit or public accounting audit) obtained before or after passing the examination. Holders of masters' degrees need only one year of experience. You can sit for the CIA exam prior to completion of your bachelor's degree. For more details, consult the IIA's website (www.theiia.org).

Internal Audit Reports

Internal audit reports are not standardized as are external auditors' reports on financial statements. Each report is different because internal auditors need to communicate findings on a variety of assignments and audit objectives. The key criterion for an internal audit report is clear and concise communication of findings and recommendations.

The reporting stage is the internal auditors' opportunity to capture management's undivided attention. To be effective, a report cannot be unduly long, tedious, technical, or laden with minutiae. It must be accurate, concise, clear, and timely. It must speak directly to the risks the auditors evaluated. Most quality audit reports ensure that significant issues are described by five elements:

1. The *condition* the auditor identified.
2. The *criteria* that renders the condition inappropriate.
3. The *cause* of the condition.
4. The *effect* the condition may have on the company.
5. The *recommendation* that may eliminate or mitigate the condition.

For example, let's say that, during a compliance audit of the human resource area, you notice that a recent candidate for an accounting position was asked several inappropriate questions on the employment application. An inappropriate question might be "have you ever been arrested?" (Questions may ask only whether someone has ever been convicted because a person is considered innocent until proven guilty.) After further investigation, you discover that the human resource department ran out of current job applications and decided to use some old applications kept in storage. The auditor needs to report the following for this audit finding:

1. Condition—inappropriate questions asked of job candidates.
2. Criteria—fair hiring laws and company policies.
3. Cause—use of old job applications due to stock out of current applications.
4. Effect—possible lawsuits and adverse publicity.
5. Recommendation—destroy obsolete job applications to prevent further use and maintain a copy of the current form on the computer (to be printed if another "stock out" situation occurs).

Generally, internal auditors meet with the business unit's management team to review the audit report before it is distributed to senior management. This meeting is called the **exit conference**. Its purpose is to inform the business unit's management of the audit results, reach an agreement on the correctness of the findings, and learn of the corrective action management plans. Sometimes disagreements concerning audit findings occur. In the interest of fair and complete disclosure, many auditors include management's reasons for disagreement in the audit report.

Internal audit reports are sent to the highest level of management in the organization, often including the CEO and the audit committee. Usually the senior manager overseeing a business unit (e.g., the vice president of materials management for distribution centers and purchasing) would receive audit reports and respond to senior management and the audit committee regarding which recommendations will be implemented. The manager also must explain why certain recommendations will not be implemented. Top management and the audit committee may compel management to reconsider selected actions.

Once senior management agrees with acceptance or rejection of audit recommendations, the business unit is obligated to implement the accepted recommendations. The IIA standards include a requirement for a **follow-up** to ascertain that appropriate action is being taken on accepted recommendations. Only after the follow-up is completed is the audit considered "closed." External auditors do not have a similar follow-up requirement.

> ### ↳ REVIEW CHECKPOINTS
>
> D.1 How can internal auditors achieve practical independence?
> D.2 What auditing services do internal auditors provide?
> D.3 What special professional certification is available for internal auditors?
> D.4 Who is responsible for enforcing compliance with laws and regulations in the business?

GOVERNMENTAL AUDITS

LEARNING OBJECTIVE D-2
Define *governmental auditing;* describe governmental audit institutions (e.g., GAO); describe how governmental auditors interact with independent auditors; explain governmental auditors' independence problems; and list features of governmental audit reports.

Government officials and recipients of federal monies are responsible for carrying out public functions efficiently, economically, effectively, ethically, and equitably while achieving desired public objectives. High-quality auditing is essential for government accountability to the public and transparency regarding linking resources to related program results.[5]

Many federal agencies (e.g., Army, Navy, Department of Transportation) have governmental auditors who are charged with ensuring compliance with agency and department policies and procedures. The accounting, auditing, and investigative agency of the federal government is the Government Accountability Office (GAO). It audits the departments, agencies, and programs of the federal government (even if they are subject to audits by their own internal audit staffs) to determine whether the laws passed by the U.S. Congress are followed and to determine whether programs are being implemented with economy and efficiency and are achieving desired results. The U.S. Congress always receives copies of GAO reports.

Congress Relies on the GAO

- "Senator Richard (Dick) Blumenthal (D-CT) sent a letter to the Government Accountability Office (GAO) requesting an investigation of drug shortages. In his letter, Senator Blumenthal requests that the GAO investigation "examine the extent of hospital shortages of pharmaceutical products and the prevalence of these shortages in recent years, the impact of such shortages on patient care, possible explanations, and potential legislative or administrative approaches to addressing this problem." [a]
- "Sen. Susan Collins, R-Maine, has asked the Government Accountability Office to review the statutory framework for federal agency chief information officers and potential modifications that could further enhance CIOs' authorities."[b]
- Sen. Susan Collins (R-Maine) has asked the Government Accountability Office (GAO) to audit a program that helps federal employees who suffer on-the-job injuries. The ranking member of the Senate Homeland Security panel, Collins wrote in a letter to the GAO that she is concerned that the Federal Employees' Compensation Act program has "potential for waste, fraud, and abuse."[c]
- When approving the Katrina Housing Tax Relief Act of 2007, the U.S. House Ways and Means Committee included an amendment requiring the GAO to report on any waste, fraud, or abuse.[d]
- "Congress did not write a blank check for spending in Iraq. We need to know funds are being used appropriately, which is what the GAO will do," Senator Tom Harkins.[e]
- "Every time we open these GAO reports we find more outrageous spending," Senator Chuck Grassley.[f]
- Senator Diane Feinstein asked the GAO to conduct an investigation of e-voting machines—especially those that fail to produce paper receipts for the ballots cast.[g]
- "The 2007 GAO High Risk Update correctly highlights the need for policy makers to conduct a critical review of existing transportation funding mechanisms," Senator James Inhofe.[h]
- "We will continue our work to transform [Department of Homeland Security] into a first class department, with a special emphasis on information sharing and the other areas on the GAO's high-risk list," Senator Joe Lieberman.[i]
- Sen. Charles Grassley asked the GAO to review the Long Term Care Insurance industry, particularly its claims policies and practices, and whether state insurance regulators are adequately investigating claim denials.[j]
- Senate Budget Committee Chairman Kent Conrad and Senator Sheldon Whitehouse have asked the GAO to study the "best practices" used by state hospitals and other countries to reduce health care costs and improve quality.[k]

[a] "Senator Requests GAO Study of Drug Shortages," *American Society of Anesthesiologists*, March 14, 2011.
[b] "Senator Requests GAO Review of CIO Roles," *Washington Business Journal*, March 8, 2011.
[c] "Senator Asks for GAO Audit of Compensation Program," *The Hill*, January 11, 2011.
[d] "Katrina Relief Bill Contains Hulshof Provision," *States News Service*, March 29, 2007.
[e] "Harkin Calls on State Department to Allow GAO Auditors in Baghdad," *States News Service*, March 12, 2007.
[f] "Grassley: Time for Waste, Fraud and Abuse of Government," *Capitol Hill Press Releases*, March 7, 2007.
[g] "Feinstein Calls for Probe into E-voting Machines: Senator Asks GAO to Look at Potential for DRE Malfunctions, Election Fraud," *ComputerWorld*, February 23, 2007.
[h] "Inhofe Welcomes New GAO High-Risk Series Update," *States News Service*, February 1, 2007.
[i] "Sens. Lieberman, Collins Vow to Remove Department of Homeland Security from 'High-Risk' List," *US Fed News*, January 31, 2007
[j] "Grassley Probes LTC Insurers' Claim Handling Practices," *National Underwriters*, October 8, 2007.
[k] "Sens. Ask GAO to Study 'Best Practices,'" *AHA News*, December 8, 2008.

---

[5] *Government Auditing Standards*, January 2007, p. 1.

The U.S. Comptroller General heads the GAO. In one sense, GAO auditors are the highest level of internal auditors for the federal government. State and federal agencies and other local government units use the GAO's *generally accepted government auditing standards* (GAGAS) to guide their audits. These standards are published in a book with a yellow cover, referred to as the **Yellow Book**.

Many states also have audit agencies similar to the GAO. They answer to state legislatures and perform the same types of work described here as GAO auditing. In another sense, the GAO and many state agencies are really external auditors with respect to government agencies they audit because they are organizationally independent.

Many government agencies have their own internal auditors and inspectors general. Well-managed local governments also have internal audit departments. For example, most federal agencies (e.g., Department of Defense, Department of the Interior), state agencies (e.g., education, welfare, controller), and local governments (e.g., cities, counties, tax districts) have internal audit staffs. Governmental auditors are charged with looking for projects that do not spend the taxpayers' money wisely. If you were a governmental auditor looking at the project in the Auditing Insight, would you raise any issues?

AUDITING INSIGHT | Million Dollar Pen

During the heat of the space race in the 1960s, the U.S. National Aeronautics and Space Administration decided it needed a ballpoint pen to write in the zero gravity confines of its space capsules. After considerable research and development, the Astronaut Pen was developed at a cost of approximately $1 million. The pen worked and also enjoyed some modest success as a novelty item back here on Earth.

The Soviet Union, faced with the same problem, used a pencil.

Types of Audits

The GAO shares with internal auditors many of the same elements of expanded-scope services. The GAO, however, emphasizes the accountability of public officials for the efficient, economical, and effective use of public funds and other resources. The GAO defines and describes *expanded-scope governmental auditing* in terms of three types of governmental audits:

1. Financial statement audits.
2. Attestation engagements.
3. Performance audits.

Financial Statement Audits

Financial statement audits determine whether the financial statements of an audited entity present fairly the financial position, results of operations, and cash flows in conformity with generally accepted accounting principles. In addition, financial audits can have other objectives, including:

- Issuing special reports for specified elements, accounts, or items of a financial statement.
- Reviewing interim financial statements.
- Issuing letters for underwriters.
- Reporting on the processing of transactions by service organizations.
- Auditing compliance with regulations relating to federal award expenditures and other governmental financial assistance.

Attestation Engagements

Attestation engagements involve providing an opinion on subject matter or an assertion about the subject matter that is the responsibility of another party. The subject matter of an attestation engagement may take many forms, including historical or prospective performance or condition, physical characteristics, historical events, analyses, systems and processes, or behavior. Examples of such engagements include reporting on

- Internal control over financial reporting or compliance with specified requirements
- Compliance with requirements of specified laws, regulations, rules, contracts, or grants.
- Management's discussion and analysis presentation.
- Prospective or pro forma financial information.
- The reliability of performance measures.
- The reasonableness and allowability of proposed contract amounts.
- Performance of specified procedures on a subject matter.

Performance Audits

Performance audits provide objective analysis so that management and those charged with governance and oversight can rely on information to improve program performance and operations, reduce costs, facilitate decision making by corrective action, and contribute to public accountability.[6]

Performance audits may be requested by management or a legislative body or may be mandated by the law, grant, or contract under which an agency or company is operating or receiving money. Performance audits provide an objective and systematic examination of evidence of the performance and management of a program against objective criteria. Performance audits provide information to improve program operations and facilitate decision making by those with oversight responsibility. Examples of performance audits include assessing:

- The extent to which legislative, regulatory, or organizational goals and objectives are being achieved.
- The relative ability of alternative approaches to provide better program performance or eliminate factors that inhibit program effectiveness.
- The relative cost and benefits or cost effectiveness of program performance.
- The degree to which, if at all, a program produced the intended results.
- The degree to which, if at all, a program produced unintended effects.
- The extent to which programs duplicate, overlap, or conflict with other related programs.
- The degree to which, if at all, the audited entity is using sound procurement practices.
- The validity and reliability of performance measures and/or financial information related to the program.

The audit of a governmental organization, program, activity, or function may involve one or more of these audit types. The scope of the work is determined by the needs of the users of the audit results.

LEARNING OBJECTIVE D-3
Explain the function of standards and measurements in economy, efficiency, and program results audits.

Audit Procedures—Economy, Efficiency, and Program Results Audits

The general evidence-gathering procedures used during the audit of financial statements in governmental audits are basically the same as the ones used by external auditors. These procedures are explained in other chapters in this textbook. However, the audit problems are usually different in audits of *economy, efficiency,* and *program results.* Also, although internal auditors occasionally perform audits of this nature, the vast majority of these audits are performed in the governmental sector.

Governmental and internal auditors must be as objective as possible when developing conclusions about efficiency, economy, and program results. This objectivity is achieved by (1) finding standards for evaluation, (2) determining the actual results of the

---
[6] *Government Auditing Standard 1.25,* January 2007.

program, and (3) comparing the actual results to the standards. Finding standards and deciding on relevant measurements is often difficult.

Students are often surprised by the difficulty in establishing standards and measurement criteria because these issues are not prominent during a financial statement audit. In a financial statement audit, the standards (which are the objective criteria) have already been set in the establishment of GAAP.

AUDITING INSIGHT — Establishing Standards

In the mid-1990s, the Florida state legislature gave millions of dollars to school districts to improve education for the next millennium. The program was called "Blueprint 2000." The legislature asked the Office of the Auditor General to monitor the use and performance of these funds. It took a team of auditors almost a year to establish standards and measurement criteria so that successful audits could begin.

Source: Personal experience of author.

When dealing with standards, measurements, and comparisons, auditors must keep inputs and outputs in perspective. Evidence about inputs—personnel hours and cost, material quantities and costs, asset investment—are most important in connection with reaching financial audit conclusions. For economy, efficiency, and program results, output measurements are equally important. Management has the responsibility for devising information systems to measure output. Such measurements should correspond to program objectives set forth in laws, regulations, administrative policies, legislative reports, or other such sources. Auditors must realize that output measurements are usually not expressed in financial terms (for example, water quality improvement, educational progress, weapons effectiveness, materials-inspection time delays, and test program reporting accuracy).

Many economy and efficiency audits, and most program audits, are output oriented. Auditors need to be careful not to equate program activity with program success without measuring program results. These features are significantly different from auditors' roles with respect to financial statement audits for which the primary concern is with the reporting on the accounting for inputs.

An Example of Setting Performance Audit Criteria

Kinerville has instituted a new program in its school system. The program provides a healthy balanced breakfast for underprivileged students in grades K–12. You have been asked to audit the program's effectiveness. In planning this audit, the following issues must be resolved:

First, what is the goal of the program? If you said, "to feed hungry children," you would be only partially correct. The actual goal of school breakfast programs is based on the assumption that children do better in school when they have a good breakfast. Therefore, the main purpose of the program is to improve the educational experience for underprivileged children.

Second, by what standard would you measure success? A comparison to other students in the school who are not in the program? If these students are not "underprivileged," is this a fair measure? Should Kinerville's school district withhold breakfasts from some underprivileged children so there is a comparison group? Is there a moral issue with this type of evaluation? (This is an ethical question that the medical profession wrestles with on a regular basis because in studies of a new medicine, placebos are given to ill patients.) Would a comparison with other schools in other districts be appropriate? Maybe, but the comparison group would have to be carefully selected and matched on many demographic factors.

Third, what is the measure that will be used for comparison? Increased grades? Higher standardized test scores? What are the problems with these measures? Will teachers change their teaching methods and focus exclusively on test preparation? Can there be other reasons for an increase in test scores?

Lastly, how large an improvement is required for the program to be successful?

You may want answers to all of these questions, but real concrete answers do not exist. Most of these issues can be resolved with tests and measures that have some positive aspects and some negative aspects, and the audit team may need to have several measures and make many difficult judgments.

> ↳ **REVIEW CHECKPOINTS**
>
> D.5 What auditing services do governmental auditors provide?
>
> D.6 What difficulties do auditors find when conducting a performance audit?
>
> D.7 How can governmental and internal auditors try to achieve objectivity when developing conclusions about economy, efficiency, or program results?

GAO Government Auditing Standards

The GAO establishes GAGAS that guide all audits for federal government agencies and facilities and all audits of entities receiving federal funds. Note that these standards must be adhered to even if a CPA firm is engaged to perform one of these audits. (Rule 501 of the AICPA Code of Conduct makes the *failure to follow government standards during a government audit* an act discreditable; see Module B.) In addition, many state and local governments have adopted GAGAS as the audit standards for agencies, municipalities, and government districts (e.g., school districts).

In many areas, GAGAS are similar to the AICPA *Statements on Auditing Standards.* However, GAGAS go beyond the AICPA standards in several respects. Government auditing standards impose additional rules and regulations about handling government funds and accounts.[7] A sample of this literature includes the following:

- Single Audit Act of 1984. This is the federal law that established uniform requirements for audits of federal financial assistance provided to state and local governments (discussed later in the chapter).
- *OMB Circular A-133,* "Audits of States, Local Governments, and Non-profit Organizations." This Office of Management and Budget guidance helps auditors implement the Single Audit Act of 1984 for governmental units and a wide range of nonprofit organizations (e.g., colleges, universities, and voluntary health and welfare organizations, hospitals).
- *OMB Circular A-122,* "Cost Principles for Nonprofit Organizations."
- *OMB Circular A-110,* "Uniform Requirements for Grants to Universities, Hospitals, and Other Nonprofit Organizations."
- *OMB Circular A-102,* "Uniform Requirements for Grants to State and Local Governments."
- *OMB Circular A-87,* "Cost Principles for State and Local Governments."
- *OMB Circular A-21,* "Cost Principles for Educational Institutions."
- *AICPA Audit and Accounting Guide,* "Audits of State and Local Governments."

Because most governmental programs are created by grants and operate under laws and regulations, GAGAS explicitly require review and testing for compliance with applicable laws and regulations. Governmental auditors must be especially diligent when noncompliance with laws and regulations could result in errors or frauds that could be material to the financial statements. The Auditing Standards Board issued *SAS 74* (AU 801) to guide CPAs on governmental audits.

GAGAS have more elaborate specifications for audit documentation and reporting than GAAS requires. The GAO standards require the following written reports in financial statement audits:

1. An audit report on financial statements.

2. A report on the auditee's compliance with applicable laws and regulations, including a report of irregularities, frauds, illegal acts, material noncompliance, and internal control deficiencies.

3. A report on the auditee's internal control and the control risk assessment.

---

[7] Extensive government audit literature can be found at three important websites: (1) the OMB website (www.white-house.gov), (2) the AICPA website (www.AICPA.org/belt/a133.htm), and (3) the GAO website (www.GAO.gov).

EXHIBIT D.2 Significant Revisions to Government Auditing Standards

Area	Emphasis or Nature of Revision
Ethics	Heightened emphasis on ethics principles
Nonaudit services	Additional guidance on the acceptance of professional services other than audit services and the impact on audit work
Recent developments in auditing and internal control	Revised standards that increase transparency concerning restatements, uncertainties, and unusual events
Performance auditing	Additional guidance on the overall framework for high-quality performance auditing including reasonable assurance and its relationship to risk and level of evidence used to support findings and conclusions
Audit language	Standardized audit language throughout the standards
Auditor responsibilities	Reinforcement of the auditors' role in accountability and improvements for government operations

GAGAS also contain an elaborate set of guidelines for reports on performance audits. These audits cover such a wide range of subjects (from food programs to military contracts) that no "standard" report is possible. The details of these standards can be found on the GAO website (www.gao.gov). These GAO standards are good guides for internal audit reports and for operational audit reports (consulting services engagements) prepared by CPAs in public practice.

In January 2007, the GAO updated the government auditing standards. A review of these changes indicates six specific issues designed to increase the transparency and accountability of audits. A review of these changes (see Exhibit D.2) indicates that the GAO (1) believes these issues to be significant in increasing audit consistency and quality and (2) is moving in a manner consistent with the Public Company Accounting Oversight Board (PCAOB).

↳ REVIEW CHECKPOINTS

D.8 What scope of practice do GAGAS suggest or require?

D.9 Why do GAGAS require a review for compliance with laws and regulations in conjunction with financial audits?

Single Audit Act of 1984 and Amendments of 1986

LEARNING OBJECTIVE D-4
Describe the Single Audit Act of 1984 in relation to audits of governmental fund recipients.

The federal government requires audits of state and local governments that receive federal financial assistance through appropriations, grants, contracts, cooperative agreements, loans, loan guarantees, property, interest subsidies, and insurance. Prior to 1985, audit teams from several federal agencies often visited state and local governments. The Single Audit Act of 1984 (the Act) replaced the system of expensive and duplicative grant-by-grant audits with an organizationwide **single audit** encompassing all federal funds that a government unit receives. When a state or local government, university, or community organization receives federal financial assistance from several federal agencies, all of these agencies are supposed to rely on the single audit report instead of requiring other auditors to enter the same unit to audit various grants.

The Act established an annual audit requirement for all governments, agencies, and nonprofit organizations that expend $500,000 or more of federal funds. A single audit, conducted in accordance with GAGAS, covering financial statements, compliance with laws and regulations, and internal control is required. The act does not require expanded scope audits of economy, efficiency, or program results. However, federal agencies may require, and pay for, additional audits of economy, efficiency, and program results to monitor the benefits of federal fund expenditures.

The auditors can be from public accounting firms or from state and local agencies provided they meet the GAO independence and proficiency requirements. In a single audit, the auditors are supposed to determine and report whether:

1. The financial statements present fairly the financial position and results of operations in accordance with GAAP.
2. The organization has internal controls to provide reasonable assurance that it is managing federal financial assistance programs in compliance with applicable laws and regulations.
3. The organization has complied with laws and regulations that may have a material effect on its financial statements and on each major federal assistance program.

OMB *Circular A-133* imposes additional audit and reporting requirements. These reports are directed toward information about the accountability of agencies that receive federal funds:

- A supplementary schedule of federal financial assistance programs showing expenditures for each program.
- A report of the compliance audit procedures showing the extent of testing and the amount and explanation of questioned expenditures.
- A report on internal control, identifying significant controls designed to provide reasonable assurance that federal programs are being managed in compliance with laws and regulations and identifying material weaknesses.
- A report of fraud, abuse, or illegal acts that become known to the auditors.

Government audits under the Yellow Book and the Single Audit Act Amendments of 1996 (including OMB *Circular A-133*) are difficult and time consuming. The GAO requires auditors to have 24 hours of continuing education in governmental auditing to qualify for planning an audit, conducting fieldwork, and preparing reports. GAO also imposes requirements for continuing education and participation in a peer review program.[8]

Governmental audits require more work on compliance and reporting on internal control than external auditors normally perform in an audit of financial statements of a private business. The reason is the federal government's concern for laws, regulations, and control of expenditures. More than $450 billion of federal funds are used by state and local governments for various programs, so the stakes are high. See Exhibit D.3 for the Single Audit Report for the City of Palm Springs, California, for the fiscal year ended June 30, 2010.

GAO Audit Reports

GAGAS has three sets of reporting standards: one for financial audits, one for attestation engagements, and another for performance audits.

Financial audit reports start with an audit report like the external auditors' standard report except that the description of the audit in the scope paragraph must include a reference to GAGAS. The report on financial statements contains an opinion regarding conformity with GAAP, just as the reports independent auditors in public practice give on nongovernmental organizations. In addition, GAGAS include reports on internal control, fraud, illegal acts, violations of provisions of contracts, grant agreements, abuse of government assets, and tests of compliance with laws and regulations as part of the financial reporting requirements. The detailed financial reporting standards can be found on the GAO website (www.gao.gov).

Governmental auditors, like their public accounting firm counterparts, may be asked to perform attestation engagements. Attestation engagements provide an opinion or conclusion concerning a specific subject or an assertion about a subject. It is important when reporting on attestation engagements to clearly specify the subject matter or assertion, the conclusions, and any significant reservations concerning the subject matter or assertion addressed in the report.

---

[8] Most CPAs in public practice have similar continuing education and peer review requirements in connection with their state licenses and voluntary membership in the AICPA but not specific to governmental auditing. However, the GAO makes the requirements even for CPAs who do not have similar demands from their state boards or who choose not to belong to the AICPA. In this manner, the GAO exercises its own control over government audit quality.

EXHIBIT D.3 Single Audit Report for the City of Palm Springs, California, Fiscal Year Ended June 30, 2010

CERTIFIED PUBLIC ACCOUNTANTS

- Brandon W. Borrows, CPA
- Donald L. Parkar, CPA
- Michael K. Chu, CPA
- David E. Hale, CPA, CFP
  A Professional Corporation
- Donald G. Slatar, CPA
- Richard K. Kikuchi, CPA
- Susan F. Matz, CPA
- Sholly K. Jackiey, CPA

REPORT ON INTERNAL CONTROL OVER FINANCIAL REPORTING
AND ON COMPLIANCE AND OTHER MATTERS BASED ON AN AUDIT
OF FINANCIAL STATEMENTS PERFORMED IN ACCORDANCE
WITH <i>GOVERNMENT AUDITING STANDARDS</i>

To the Honorable Mayer and Members of City Council
City of Palm Springs, California

We have audited the financial statements of the governmental activities, the business-type activities, each major fund, and the aggregate remaining fund information of the City of Palm Springs, California, (the City) as of and for the year ended June 30, 2010, which collectively comprise the City's basic financial statements and have issued our report thereon dated November 15, 2010. We conducted our audit in accordance with auditing standards generally accepted in the United States of America and the standards applicable to financial audits contained in *Government Auditing Standards,* issued by the Comptroller General of the United States.

Internal Control Over Financial Reporting

In planning and performing our audit, we considered the City's internal control over financial reporting as a basis for designing our auditing procedures for the purpose of expressing our opinions on the financial statements, but not for the purpose of expressing an opinion on the effectiveness of the City's internal control over financial reporting. Accordingly, we do not express an opinion on the effectiveness of the City's internal control over financial reporting.

A *deficiency in internal controls* exists when the design or operation of a control does not allow management or employees, in the normal course of performing their assigned functions, to prevent or detect misstatements on a timely basis. A *material weakness* is a deficiency, or combination of deficiencies, in internal control such that there is a reasonable possibility that a material misstatement of the City's finacial statements will not be prevented, or detected and corrected on a timely basis.

Our consideration of internal control over financial reporting was for the limited purpose described in the first paragraph of this section and was not designed to identify all deficiencies in internal control over financial reporting that might be deficiencies, significant deficiencies or material weakness. We did not identify any deficiencies in internal control over financial reporting that we consider to be material weaknesses, as defined above.

Compliance and Other Matters

As part of obtaining reasonable assurance about whether the City's financial statements are free of material misstatement. we performed tests of its compliance with certain provisions of laws, regulations, contracts, and grant agreements, noncompliance with which could have a direct and material effect on the determination of financial statement amounts. However, providing an opinion on compliance with those provisions was not an objective of our audit, and accordingly, we do not express such an opinion. The results of our tests disclosed no instances of noncompliance or other matters that are required to be reported under *Government Auditing Standards.*

This report is intended solely for the information and use of management, the City Council, federal awarding agencies and pass-through entities, and is not intended to be and should not be used by anyone other than these specified parties.

Lance, Soll & Lunghard, LLP

November 15, 2010

Both attestation engagement reports and performance audit reports are completely different from financial audit reports. Like that for internal audit reports, the GAO objective is clear communication for the purpose of making recommendations and improving operations. Hence, the Yellow Book's performance audit reporting standards require timely, well-written communications of findings and recommendations for action. The managers of an audited entity are expected to respond to the report, and this response is usually included in the final version of the report. Unlike internal audit reports, most GAO reports are available to the public and can be requested from the Government Printing Office.

However, performance audits have another side. GAGAS requires the reports to tell about illegal acts, abuse of public money and property, noncompliance with laws and regulations, and internal control weaknesses. These matters reflect negatively on an organization's management. The details of performance audit reporting can be found on the Government Accountability Office website at www.gao.gov.

AUDITING INSIGHT — Which Side Is Supplying?

A report from the GAO states that U.S. military officials do not know what happened to 30 percent of the weapons the United States distributed to Iraqi forces from 2004 through early 2007 as part of the effort to train and equip Iraqi forces. The latest estimate is that more than 14,000 weapons are unaccounted for!

Source: "Weapons Given to Iraq are Missing," *The Washington Post*, August 6, 2007.

REVIEW CHECKPOINTS

D.10 What audit fieldwork requirements do GAGAS and the Single Audit Act of 1984 impose that AICPA generally accepted auditing standards do not?

D.11 What are the major differences between independent auditors' reports on financial statements and internal and governmental reports on efficiency, economy, and program results audits?

D.12 Why do you think GAGAS reporting standards permit performance audit reports to include the views of responsible officials concerning the auditors' findings, conclusions, and recommendations?

FRAUD AUDITS

LEARNING OBJECTIVE D-5
Define *fraud auditing* and describe various engagements performed by fraud auditors.

The responsibilities of external auditors, internal auditors, and governmental auditors often require the identification of suspected fraud. *SAS 99* and *SAS 110* require auditors to use information obtained during the planning and performance of the audit to identify risks that may result in a material misstatement due to fraud. In addition, auditors need to be aware of the various types of frauds, their signs (red flags), and the need to follow up to determine whether a suspicion is justified. If justified, auditors need to alert management and call in the experts.

A focused effort by internal auditors on the prevention, deterrence, and detection of financial statement misstatements arising from asset misappropriation is consistent with their broad mission of maximizing owners' wealth (which requires safeguarding the entity's assets). In carrying out their mission, internal auditors should be aware of the risks and warning signs of fraud.[9]

Most frauds are found through anonymous tips (40.2 percent) or management review (15.4 percent). Internal auditors uncover about 13.9 percent of discovered fraud, and

---

[9] W. Hillison, D. Sinason, and C. Pacini, "The Role of the Internal Auditor in Implementing *SAS 82*," *Corporate Controller*, July/August 1998, p. 21. Although *SAS 82* has been superseded by *SAS 99*, the content of the quote is still valid.

external auditors get credit for finding about 4.6 percent of the frauds.[10] Once a fraud is suspected, a fraud examiner may be called to investigate further.

For governmental auditors, the basic requirements are to know the applicable laws and regulations, to design the audit to detect abuse and illegal acts, and to report their findings to the proper level of authority. All governmental auditors are required to prepare a written report on their tests of compliance with applicable laws and regulations, including all material instances of noncompliance and all instances or indications of illegal acts that could result in criminal prosecution. Reports are directed to the top official of an organization and, in some cases, to an appropriate oversight body, including other government agencies and audit committees. Persons receiving the audit reports are responsible for reporting to law enforcement agencies.

Compliance auditing in governmental audits is a matter of considerable concern, and the AICPA has issued *SAS 74* (AU 801), "Compliance Auditing Applicable to Governmental Entities and Recipients of Governmental Financial Assistance." *SAS 74* tailors the discussion of responsibilities regarding errors, frauds, and illegal acts, GAO standards, and certain government bulletins to the special requirements of government entities and other recipients of government financial assistance.

The Art of Fraud Examinations

LEARNING OBJECTIVE D-6
Describe the elements necessary for a successful fraud examination and explain the differences in the way fraud examiners and external auditors handle evidence.

Auditors are required to provide reasonable assurance that financial statements are free of material misstatements due to fraud. During an audit, auditors may uncover facts or circumstances that indicate that fraud may exist. At this point, a fraud examination may commence and may require the assistance of a certified fraud examiner (CFE).[11]

Fraud examinations combine the expertise of auditors and criminal investigators. Fraud examiners are fond of saying that their successes are the result of accident, hunches, or luck. Nothing can be further from reality. Successes come from experience, logic, and the ability to see things that are not obvious (as for Sherlock Holmes, famous detective of literature, sometimes it is "the dog that did not bark" that is the clue). Fraud examinations, broadly speaking, involve familiarity with many elements: the human factor, organizational behavior, common fraud schemes, evidence and its sources, standards of proof, and red flags.

Independent auditors of financial statements and fraud examiners approach their work differently. Some of the most important differences are:

- Financial statement auditors follow a program/procedural approach designed to accomplish a fairly standard job; fraud examiners work in unique and unusual situations in which little is standard.
- Financial statement auditors note errors and omissions; fraud examiners also focus on exceptions, but they must be aware of peculiarities and patterns of conduct as well.
- Financial statement auditors assess control risk to design audit procedures; fraud examiners habitually "think like a crook" to imagine ways controls could be subverted for fraudulent purposes.
- Financial statement auditors use the concept of materiality (dollar size large enough to matter). Most fraud examiners believe that "immaterial fraud" is an oxymoron. Fraud is often larger than it appears, fraud left unchecked tends to grow, and fraud indicates a lack of integrity on the part of the person or persons involved. For these reasons, fraud examiners often pursue even small frauds.
- Financial statement audits are based on theories of financial accounting and auditing logic; fraud examination is grounded in a theory of behavioral motive, opportunity, and rationalization.

Financial statement auditors often use inductive reasoning—that is, they sample accounting data, derive audit findings, and project ("induct") the finding to a conclusion

---

[10] Association of Certified Fraud Examiners, *2010 Report to the Nation: Occupational Fraud and Abuse.*

[11] The CFE designation is offered by the Association of Certified Fraud Examiners. Information concerning the designation and requirements can be found on its website (www.cfenet.com).

about the population of data sampled. Fraud examiners often enjoy the expensive luxury of using deductive reasoning—that is, after being tipped off that a certain type of loss occurred or probably occurred, they can identify the suspects, make clinical observations (e.g., stakeouts), conduct interviews and interrogations, eliminate dead-end results, and establish a legal case against the alleged fraudster. They can conduct covert activities that usually are not used in the financial audit. The "expensive luxury" of the deductive approach involves surveying a wide array of information and information sources, eliminating the extraneous, and retaining the selection that proves the fraud.

Successfully identifying and catching fraud perpetrators often depend on the awareness of auditors. The identification of evidence that may indicate a fraud, the handling of that evidence, and the timely involvement of the fraud examiner may mean the difference between stopping a fraud and recovering stolen assets or continuing the expansion of fraud in the client's business.

AUDITING INSIGHT | What Car Are You Driving?

A government fraud auditor uncovered a fraud while driving into the parking lot of the city hall of a small town. The auditor always parked in the employee lot (saving the customer parking for residents conducting business with city hall). In the parking lot, along with the Fords and Chevrolets, was a candy-apple red Porsche. After parking his car, the auditor went over to the Porsche and began to look the car over. When someone from city hall came out, the auditor began a conversation.

Auditor: This is certainly a beautiful car!
City hall employee: Yes, it is.
Auditor: Do you know how many horsepower it has?

City hall employee: Not a clue. The car belongs to Bob. I'm certain he'd tell you.
Auditor: Great. I would love to find out more about this car. Where would I find Bob?
City hall employee: Oh. Bob's a city inspector. You'll find him in the inspector's office.
Auditor: Thanks!

Further investigation revealed that Bob had been taking kickbacks.

Source: Story told by a government fraud auditor at an Association of Certified Fraud Examiner seminar.

↳ REVIEW CHECKPOINT

D.13 Compare and contrast the type of work performed by external auditors (auditing financial statements to render an opinion) and fraud examiners.

Fraud Examiner Responsibilities

When a fraud examiner is called, fraud is strongly suspected or already recognized. The Association of Certified Fraud Examiners (ACFE) indicates that assignments are initiated only with **predication**, which means a reason to believe fraud may have occurred.[12]

Fraud examiners' attitudes and responsibilities differ from those of other auditors in two additional respects: internal control and materiality. Fraud examiners' interest in internal control policies and procedures involves less evaluation of strengths and more evaluation of weaknesses. Fraud examiners "think like crooks" to imagine fraud schemes that get around an organization's internal controls.

Fraud examiners have four main objectives in performing an investigation. First, fraud examiners must determine whether a fraud does exist. Second, once fraud examiners determine that a fraud does exist, the examiner must determine the scope of the fraud. For organizations that received an external audit, the median fraud, when discovered, had been in operation for over 18 months.[13] Therefore, fraud examiners must attempt

---

[12] The Professional Standards and Practices for Certified Fraud Examiners can be found on the association's website at www.acfenet.org.
[13] Association of Certified Fraud Examiners, *2010 Report to the Nation: Occupational Fraud and Abuse.*

to determine when the fraud started and what assets have been misappropriated. Third, fraud examiners must identify the perpetrators. The examiners must take great care not to falsely accuse employees and not to solicit help from management personnel who might be involved in the fraud. Finally, examiners must determine how the fraud occurred and whether changes in controls or policy can eliminate this type of fraud in the future.

Fraud examiners' attitude about *materiality* differs from that of auditors. Other auditors may have a large-dollar amount as a criterion for an error that is big enough to matter, but fraud examiners have a much lower threshold and many operate under the theory that there is no such thing as an immaterial fraud. In fact, fraud is sometimes compared to an iceberg in the sense that most of it is hidden and only a small part may be visible. A fraud loss of $20,000 this year may not be material to an external auditor, but $20,000 each year for a 15-year fraud career amounts to $300,000 in the fraud examiner's eyes—and it is big enough to matter!

> ## REVIEW CHECKPOINTS
>
> D.14 Internal auditors have one of the highest incidents of fraud detection (higher then external auditors). Why might this be true? To what extent would you think internal auditors include fraud detection responsibility in their normal audit assignments?
>
> D.15 In fraud examiners' terminology, what is *predication*?
>
> D.16 Why might fraud examiners' attitudes about control systems and materiality differ from that of other auditors?

A Fraud Audit Example

Alice, a fraud examiner, has been called into Bulldog Corporation because an accounts payable fraud is suspected. Several vendor invoices were paid to Longhorn Enterprises, a vendor not on the approved vendor list. Although this may indicate a fictitious vendor set up by someone in the company as a fraud, it also may be an indication of someone not following procedure. It is possible that the purchases from this vendor were valid, but the vendor was not put on the approved vendor list. The fraud examiner must determine whether this is a fraud or just a case of not following procedure. The fraud examiner may take several steps to identify whether Longhorn Enterprises exists.

DOES FRAUD EXIST?

Alice has called the secretary of state's office, checked the telephone book, asked directory assistance, and searched the Internet but has not found any indication of a company called Longhorn Enterprises. In addition, the invoices from Longhorn Enterprises have no telephone number and only a post office box as an address. Finally, there are no creases on the invoices in the file, indicating they were probably not mailed to the company.

HOW LARGE IS THE FRAUD?

Convinced that Longhorn Enterprises does not exist, Alice sets out to determine the extent of the fraud and searches the cash disbursements journal and accounts payable records looking for checks paid to Longhorn Enterprises. After finding 32 invoices paid over the last two years. Alice contacts Bulldog's bank and gets copies of the canceled checks, front and back. Alice makes copies of all of the invoices and places the originals in a plastic bag (they are evidence and may have fingerprints or other forensic information). All the originals are locked up for safekeeping. The total of the checks is $67,245.

WHO COMMITTED THE FRAUD?

Alice notices that the checks are endorsed by hand (most companies endorse checks with a stamp)and that the checks are deposited in Smalltime Regional Bank. Because Bulldog pays its employees through direct deposit, Alice can compare the banks used by employees with the bank used to deposit Longhorn Enterprises' checks. Alice compares that list with the list of employees who are involved in the purchasing and payables process and finds three purchasing and payable employees who use the Smalltime Regional Bank. Alice takes this information to an attorney, who assists in getting a subpoena for the bank records and postal information concerning the post office box. Alice finds that both the post office box and bank account are registered to Dallas Fry, an accounts payable clerk who uses Smalltime Regional Bank for payroll deposits. The bank records also show transfers of money from the bank account, listed as LE Inc., to Fry's personal bank account.

Next Alice talks with other employees in the accounts payable area and discovers that Fry has purchased a new car and took an expensive vacation last year. Alice is now ready to confront Fry with the evidence and obtain a confession.

HOW COULD THIS FRAUD HAPPEN?

Finally, from Fry's confession, Alice determines that the assistant treasurer routinely approves small payments without scrutinizing the supporting documentation. Fry inserted fictitious invoices in stacks of other invoices for the assistant treasurer to sign. Alice's final report included that the assistant treasurer's failure to follow procedure that allowed the fraud to occur.

LEARNING OBJECTIVE D-7
Describe the ways CPAs can assist in prosecuting fraud perpetrators.

Building a Fraud Case

Building a case against a fraudster is a task for trained investigators who know how to conduct interviews and interrogations, perform surveillance, use informants, and obtain usable confessions. In almost all cases, the postdiscovery activity proceeds with a special prosecutorial attitude and with management cooperation or leadership. The district attorney and police officials also may be involved. Prosecution of fraudsters is advisable because, if left unpunished, they often go on to steal again. In addition, failure to prosecute sends a negative message to other potential fraudsters in the organization.

Protecting the Evidence

While engaged in audit work, auditors should know how to preserve the *chain of custody* of evidence. The chain of custody is the crucial link of the evidence to the suspect, called the *relevance* of evidence by attorneys and judges. If documents are lost, mutilated, coffee soaked, or compromised (so a defense attorney can argue that they were altered to frame the suspect), they can lose their effectiveness for the prosecution. Auditors should learn to mark evidence, writing an identification of the location, condition, date, time, and circumstances as soon as it appears to be a signal of fraud. This marking may be on a separate tag or page, or the original may be marked in a manner that preserves the integrity of the document. The original document should be put in a protective envelope (plastic) for preservation and investigation work should proceed with copies of the documents instead of originals. A record should be made of the safekeeping and of all persons who used the original. Any eyewitness observations should be promptly recorded in a memorandum or on tape (audio or video) with corroboration of colleagues if possible. Other features of the chain of custody relate to interviews, interrogations, confessions, documents obtained by subpoena, and other matters, but auditors usually do not conduct these activities.

Obtaining Litigation Support

Independent CPAs often accept engagements for litigation support and expert witnessing. This work is often referred to as **forensic accounting**, which means the application of accounting and auditing evidence to legal problems, both civil and criminal. Litigation support can take several forms, but it usually amounts to consulting in the capacity of helping attorneys document cases and determine damages. Expert witness work involves testifying to findings determined during litigation support and testifying about accounting principles and auditing standards applications. The AICPA, ACFE, and IIA conduct continuing education courses for auditors who want to become experts in these fields.

> ↳ **REVIEW CHECKPOINTS**
>
> D.17 Why is prosecution of fraud perpetrators generally a good idea?
>
> D.18 Why do fraud examiners handle information in a different manner than auditors? Why is this important?

Summary

Governmental and internal auditing standards include the essence of the AICPA's generally accepted auditing standards (GAAS) but also include standards for audits of economy, efficiency, and program results. In addition, the internal auditing standards contain guidance for the management of an internal audit department within a company. The auditor's responsibilities, professional organizations, and standards are summarized in Exhibit D.4.

EXHIBIT D.4 Summary of Auditor Information

Auditor	Primary Functions	Professional Organization	Certification	Standards
Internal auditor	Evaluate departments and functions (1) to determine operational efficiency and effectiveness and compliance with laws, regulations, policies and procedures and (2) to provide consulting services to management.	Institute of Internal Auditors www.theiia.org	Certified Internal Auditor (CIA) Various specialty certifications such as certified financial services auditor (CFSA)	International Standards for the Professional Practice of Internal Auditing
Governmental auditors	Evaluate government entities to determine (1) compliance with laws, regulations and policies as well as efficiency and effectiveness in the performance of programs and (2) to investigate government operations as mandated or directed by government oversight bodies.	Association of Government Accountants www.agacgfm.org	The certified government financial manager (CGFM)* and certified government auditing professional (CGAP) (offered through the IIA)	Government auditing standards (The Yellow Book)
Fraud auditor	Provide investigative services to auditors and management when the predication of fraud exists.	Association of Certified Fraud Examiners www.acfe.com	Certified fraud examiner (CFE)	CFE Code of Professional Standards

All auditors hold independence as a primary goal, but internal auditors must establish an internal organizational independence from the managers and executives whose areas they audit. Governmental auditors must be concerned about factual independence with regard to social, political, and level-of-government influences.

Governmental auditing is complicated by the special context of audit assignments intended to accomplish accountability by agencies that handle federal funds—grants, subsidies, entitlement programs, and the like. The requirements of the GAO standards and the Single Audit Act of 1984 impose on the audit function the responsibility for compliance audit work designed to determine agencies' observance of laws and regulations, of which there are many. Auditors must report not only on financial statements but also on internal control, violations of laws and regulations, fraud, abuse, and illegal acts. These elements are all part of the federal oversight of federal spending facilitated by auditors.

Governmental and internal audit reports are not standardized as are the GAAS reports on audited financial statements. Auditors must be very careful that their reports communicate their conclusions and recommendations in a clear and concise manner. The variety of assignments and the challenge of reporting in such a free-form setting contribute to making governmental auditing, internal auditing, and consulting services exciting fields for career opportunities.

Fraud awareness auditing starts with knowledge of the types of errors, frauds, and illegal acts that can be perpetrated. External, internal, and governmental auditors all have standards for care, planning, detection, and reporting of errors, frauds, and illegal acts. Fraud examiners, on the other hand, have little in the way of standard programs or materiality guidelines because of the unlimited nature of frauds. However, auditors must exercise technical and personal care because accusations of fraud are always taken very seriously. For this reason, after preliminary findings indicate fraud possibilities, auditors should enlist the support of management and assist fraud examination professionals in bringing an investigation to a conclusion.

Key Terms

compliance audit: An examination designed to ensure that an organization is following applicable laws, regulations, and management directives; usually performed by internal auditors but may be performed by governmental or external auditors as well, 683

environmental audit: An examination designed to ensure that an organization is following environmental standards established by laws, regulations, and management directives; may recommend methods of reducing environmental problems by reducing or reusing waste or by-products of an organization's processes, 685

exit conference: A meeting that occurs at the end of an internal audit between the auditors and management of the organization being audited in many external audits and is a required part of an internal audit, 687

follow-up: A process required of internal auditors to ensure that significant audit findings have been addressed by the auditee in accordance with the agreement between the auditor and management, 687

forensic accounting: The application of accounting and auditing evidence to resolve legal issues in civil and criminal law, 700

governance audit: An examination designed to provide management the information required to make governance decisions or to ensure that high-quality information is provided for these decisions, 685

internal auditing: An examination service provided to a company to assist the company to meet its corporate goals and objectives by evaluating and recommending risk management, control, and governance processes, 680

operational auditing: An examination designed to evaluate the processes and procedures of an organization or an area within an organization to ensure the process or area is operating efficiently and effectively, 684

performance audit: An examination designed to ensure that the resources of an organization are being used appropriately and that its objectives are being met, 690

predication: A suspicion that a fraud may have occurred, 698

quality control audit: An examination designed to ensure that an organization is meeting its quality control standards; usually involves determining that personnel responsible for performing quality control are meeting the goals and objectives established and that quality information is being reported to appropriate members of management, 685

single audit: An governmental examination standard that allows an entity to receive one audit of its financial statements, compliance with laws and regulations, and internal control that will be utilized by multiple agencies granting money to the entity, 693

Yellow Book: The common name used to refer to the generally accepted government auditing standards (GAGAS), 689

Multiple-Choice Questions for Practice and Review

 All applicable Exercises and Problems are available with McGraw-Hill's *Connect® Accounting*

LO D-1

D.19 Which of the following would be considered in determining whether an internal audit department is independent?
 a. The organizational level of the chief audit officer and the objectivity of the audit staff.
 b. A requirement for the auditors to report to the audit committee and the composition of that committee.
 c. The organizational status of the audit committee and the individual independence of internal auditors in the department.
 d. The nature of the audit charter and the objectivity of the audit staff.

LO D-1

D.20 Which of the following would be considered the most significant problem for internal audit if the chief audit executive reports to the controller?
 a. The controller would amend the audit schedule so more audit time was spent on accounting issues.
 b. The controller may have no training as an internal auditor.
 c. During times when the budget needs to be cut, internal audit would likely be the first to lose funding.
 d. The controller can control the scope of audits and censor audit reports before being sent to management and the audit committee.

LO D-1   D.21 Which of the following is *not* an internal audit objective designed to add value to a purchasing department?
   a. A review of the bidding process indicates that a company may be operating under two different names and therefore purchasing is not getting the three independent bids required by policy.
   b. The purchasing process is causing unnecessary delays in ordering product.
   c. The purchasing department is not following a new human resource policy requiring a six-month performance review for new employees.
   d. The director of purchasing is new to the organization and has made several decisions regarding vendor approvals with which the auditor does not agree.

LO D-1   D.22 In an internal auditor's report, audit findings would include all of the following *except*
   a. The effect of audit finding on the auditee or the company.
   b. The cause of the audit finding.
   c. The relevance of the audit finding on the audit.
   d. The recommendation to correct the audit finding.

LO D-1   D.23 Governmental auditors' independence and objectivity are enhanced when they report the results of an audit assignment directly to
   a. Managers of the government agency under audit and in which the auditors are employed.
   b. The audit committee of directors of the agency under audit.
   c. Political action committees of which they are members.
   d. The congressional committee that ordered the audit.

LO D-2   D.24 In all audits of governmental units performed according to GAGAS, the most important work is
   a. Compliance auditing.
   b. Obtaining a sufficient understanding of internal control.
   c. Documentation of the audit.
   d. Exit interviews with managers in the governmental unit.

LO D-1   D.25 Which of the following is considered different and more limited in objectives than the others?
   a. Operational auditing.
   b. Performance auditing.
   c. Management auditing.
   d. Financial statement auditing.

LO D-3   D.26 A typical objective of an operational audit is for the auditor to
   a. Determine whether the financial statements fairly present the company's operations.
   b. Evaluate the feasibility of attaining the company's operational objectives.
   c. Make recommendations for achieving company objectives.
   d. Report on the company's relative success in attaining profit maximization.

LO D-2   D.27 A governmental auditor assigned to audit the financial statements of the state highway department would not be considered independent if the auditor
   a. Also held a position as a project manager in the highway department.
   b. Was the state audit official elected in a general statewide election with responsibility to report to the legislature.
   c. Normally works as a state auditor employed in the department of human services.
   d. Was appointed by the state governor with responsibility to report to the legislature.

LO D-2   D.28 Governmental auditing can extend beyond audits of financial statements to include audits of an agency's efficient and economical use of resources and
   a. Constitutionality of laws and regulations governing the agency.
   b. Evaluation of the personal managerial skills shown by the agency's leaders.
   c. Correspondence of the agency's performance with public opinion regarding the social worth of its mission.
   d. Evaluations concerning the agency's achievements of the goals set by the legislature for the agency's activities.

LO D-1   D.29 Which of the following best describes how the detailed audit plan of a financial statement auditor compares with the audit client's comprehensive internal audit program?

a. The comprehensive internal audit plan covers areas that an external auditor would normally not review.
b. The comprehensive internal audit plan is more detailed although it covers fewer areas than an external audit would normally cover.
c. The comprehensive internal audit plan is substantially identical to the audit program used by an external auditor because both review substantially identical areas.
d. The comprehensive internal audit plan is less detailed and covers fewer areas than an external auditor would normally review.

LO D-1   D.30 Which of the following is usually *not* part of an internal audit department's audit charter?

a. A commitment from management to ensure the independence of the internal audit department.
b. A definition of the scope of the audit department's activities.
c. The organizational structure of the internal audit department.
d. The reporting requirements of the internal audit department.

LO D-2   D.31 Which of the following would you *not* expect to see in an auditor's report(s) on the financial statements of an independent government agency?

a. A statement that the audit was conducted in accordance with generally accepted government audit standards.
b. A report on the agency's compliance with applicable laws and regulations.
c. Commentary by the agency's managers on the audit findings and recommendations.
d. A report on the agency's internal controls.

LO D-4   D.32 The federal Single Audit Act of 1984 requires auditors to determine and report several things about state and local governments that receive federal funds. Which of the following is *not* normally required to be reported?

a. An opinion on the fair presentation of the financial statements in accordance with generally accepted accounting principles.
b. A report on the government's internal control related to federal funds.
c. The government's performance in meeting goals set in enabling legislation.
d. A report on the government's compliance with applicable laws and regulations.

LO D-2   D.33 The Government Accountability Office (GAO) describes expanded-scope governmental auditing to include all of the following *except*

a. Financial statement audits.
b. Attestation engagements.
c. Compliance audits.
d. Performance audits.

LO D-1–D-3   D.34 In government and internal performance auditing, which of the following is the *least* important consideration when performing the fieldwork?

a. Determining the applicable generally accepted government accounting principles pronounced by the GASB.
b. Defining problem areas or opportunities for improvement and defining program goals.
c. Selecting and performing procedures designed to obtain evidence about operational problems and production output.
d. Evaluating evidence in terms of economy, efficiency, and achievement of program goals.

LO D-2   D.35 Which of the following is the *least* important consideration for a governmental auditor who needs to be objective when auditing and reporting on an agency's achievement of program goals?

a. Measure the actual output results of agency activities.
b. Compare the agency's actual output results to quantitative goal standards.
c. Perform a comprehensive review of management controls.
d. Determine quantitative standards that describe goals the agency was supposed to achieve.

LO D-4   D.36 Compliance auditing performed under the Single Audit Act of 1984 in accordance with GAGAS is necessary for an auditor's

a. Report on the auditee's internal control, including reportable conditions and material weaknesses.

b. Opinion on the auditee's observance, or lack thereof, of applicable laws and regulations.

c. Opinion on the auditee's financial statements.

d. Report of a supplementary schedule of federal assistance programs and amounts.

LO D-6 D.37 Which *two* of the following characterize the work of fraud examiners?

a. Analysis of control weaknesses for determination of acceptable fraud risk.

b. Analysis of control strengths as a basis for planning other audit procedures.

c. Determination of a materiality amount that represents a significant misstatement of the financial statements.

d. Thinking of a materiality amount in cumulative terms—that is, becoming large over a number of years.

LO D-6 D.38 When auditing with "fraud awareness," auditors should especially notice and review employee activities under which of these conditions?

a. The company always estimates the inventory but never takes a complete physical count.

b. The petty cash box is always locked in the desk of the custodian.

c. Management has published a company code of ethics and sends frequent communication newsletters about it.

d. The board of directors reviews and approves all investment transactions.

LO D-6 D.39 The best way to enact a broad fraud prevention program is to

a. Install airtight control systems of checks and supervision.

b. Name an "ethics officer" who is responsible for receiving and acting upon fraud tips.

c. Place dedicated "hotline" telephones on walls around the workplace with direct communication to the company ethics officer.

d. Establish a corporate culture conducive to ethical behavior in the workplace.

LO D-6 D.40 A reason to believe that a fraud has occurred is called

a. Deliberation.

b. Forensics.

c. Predication.

d. Restitution.

LO D-7 D.41 In a fraud audit, original documents must be protected from damage and tampering to

a. Establish motive.

b. Develop documentation for employee dismissal.

c. Protect the chain of custody.

d. Ensure that suspects are unaware of an investigation in progress.

LO D-1 D.42 An environmental audit might include all of following *except*

a. Determining that proper tracking of waste material is being maintained by the organization.

b. Reviewing the liability account established for pending environmental claims against the company.

c. Reviewing the environmental history of another company that the internal auditor's organization is interested in purchasing.

d. All of the above are appropriate issues for an environmental audit.

Exercises and Problems

All applicable Exercises and Problems are available with McGraw-Hill's *Connect® Accounting*

LO D-1, D-2, D-5 D.43 **Identification of Audits and Auditors.** Audits may be characterized as (a) financial statement audits, (b) compliance audits, (c) economy and efficiency audits, and (d) program audits. The work can be done by independent (external) auditors, internal auditors, or governmental auditors (including IRS auditors and federal bank examiners). Following is a list of the purpose or products of various audit engagements. [Students may need to refer to Chapter 1.]

a. Analyze proprietary schools' spending to train students for oversupplied occupations.

b. Determine the fair presentation in conformity with GAAP of an advertising agency's financial statements.
c. Study the Department of Defense's expendable launch vehicle program.
d. Determine costs of municipal garbage pickup services compared to comparable service subcontracted to a private business.
e. Audit tax shelter partnership financing terms.
f. Study a private aircraft manufacturer's test pilot performance in reporting on the results of test flights.
g. Periodically have U.S. comptroller of currency examine a national bank for solvency.
h. Evaluate the promptness of materials inspection in a manufacturer's receiving department.
i. Report on the need for the states to consider reporting requirements for chemical use data.
j. Render a public report on the assumptions and compilation of a revenue forecast by a sports stadium/racetrack complex.

Required:

Prepare a three-column schedule showing (1) each of the engagements listed, (2) the type of audit (a, b, c, or financial statement, compliance, economy and efficiency, or program)), and (3) the kind of auditors you would expect to be involved.

LO D-1   D.44 **Organizing a Risk Analysis.**   You are the director of internal auditing of a large municipal hospital. You receive monthly financial reports prepared by the accounting department, and your review of them has shown that total accounts receivable from patients has steadily and rapidly increased over the past eight months.

Other information in the reports shows the following conditions:

- The number of available hospital beds has not changed.
- The bed occupancy rate has not changed.
- Hospital billing rates have not changed significantly.
- The hospitalization insurance contracts have not changed since the last modification 12 months ago.

Your internal audit department audited the accounts receivable 10 months ago. The audit documentation file for that assignment contains financial information, a record of the risk analysis, documentation of the study and evaluation of management and internal risk mitigation controls, documentation of the evidence-gathering procedures used to produce evidence about the validity and collectability of the accounts, and a copy of your report, which commented favorably on the controls and collectability of the receivables. However, the current increase in receivables has alerted you to a need for another audit so any problem will not get out of hand. You remember news stories last year about the manager of the city water system who got into big trouble because his accounting department double-billed all residential customers for three months.

Required:

You plan to perform a risk analysis to understand the problem if indeed one exists. Write a memo to your senior auditor listing at least eight questions to use to guide and direct the risk analysis. (*Hint:* The questions used last year were organized under these headings: (1) Who does the accounts receivable accounting? (2) What data processing procedures and policies are in effect? and (3) How is the accounts receivable accounting done? This time, you will add a fourth category: (4) What financial or economic events have occurred in the last 10 months?)

(CIA adapted)

LO D-1   D.45 **Study and Evaluation of Management Control.**   The study and evaluation of management risk control in a governmental or internal audit is not easy. First, auditors must determine the risks and the controls subject to audit. Then they must find a standard by which performance of the control can be evaluated. Next they must specify procedures to obtain the evidence on which an evaluation can be based. Insofar as possible, the standards and related evidence must be quantified.

Students working on this case usually do not have the experience or theoretical background to determine control standards and audit procedures, so the following scenario gives certain information (in italics) that internal auditors would know about or be able to learn on their own. Fulfilling the requirement thus amounts to taking some information from the scenario and learning other things by using accountants' and auditors' common sense.

The Scenario

Ace Corporation ships building materials to more than a thousand wholesale and retail customers in a five-state region. The company's normal credit terms are net/30 days; it offers no cash discounts. Jerry Clark is the chief financial officer and is concerned about risks related to maintaining control over customer credit. In particular, Clark has stated two management control principles for this purpose.

1. Sales are to be billed to customers accurately and promptly. Clark knows that errors will occur but thinks company personnel should be able to hold quantity, unit price, and arithmetic errors down to 3 percent of the sales invoices. Clark considers an invoice error of $1 or less not to matter and believes that prompt billing is important because customers are expected to pay within 30 days. Clark is very strict in thinking that a bill should be sent to the customer one day after shipment and believes the billing department is staffed well enough to be able to handle this workload. *The relevant company records consist of an accounts receivable control account; a subsidiary ledger of customers' accounts in which charges are entered by billing (invoice) date and credits are entered by date of payment receipts; a sales journal that lists invoices in chronological order; and a file of shipping documents cross-referenced by the number on the related sales invoice copy kept on file in numerical order.*

2. Accounts receivable are to be aged and followed up to ensure prompt collection. Clark has told the accounts receivable department to classify all customer accounts in categories of (a) current, (b) 31–59 days overdue, (c) 60–90 days overdue, and (d) more than 90 days overdue. Clark wants this trial balance to be complete and to be transmitted to the credit department within five days after each month-end. In the credit department, prompt follow-up means sending a different (stronger) collection letter to each category, cutting off credit to customers that are more than 60 days past due (putting them on cash basis), and giving the over-90-days accounts to an outside collection agency. These actions are supposed to be taken within five days after receipt of the aged trial balance. *The relevant company records, in addition to the ones listed, consist of the aged trial balance, copies of the letters sent to customers, copies of notices of credit cutoff, copies of correspondence with the outside collection agent, and reports of results—statistics of subsequent collections.*

Required:

Take the role of a senior internal auditor. You are to write a memo to the internal audit staff to inform them about comparison standards for the study and evaluation of these two management control policies. You also need to specify two or three procedures for gathering evidence about performance of the controls. The body of your memo should be structured as follows:

1. Control: Sales are billed to customers accurately and promptly.
    a. Accuracy.
        (1) Policy standard . . .
        (2) Audit procedures . . .
    b. Promptness.
        (1) Policy standard . . .
        (2) Audit procedures . . .
2. Control: Accounts receivable are aged and followed up to ensure prompt collection.
    a. Accounts receivable aging.
        (1) Policy standard . . .
        (2) Audit procedures . . .
    b. Follow-up prompt collection.
        (1) Policy standard . . .
        (2) Audit procedures . . .

D.46 **Quality Control Audit of a University.** In a quality audit, defining the measurement criteria is often difficult and time consuming. You have been a student at a college or university for several years and should have a basic understanding of its academic operations. You have been engaged to perform a quality audit of your university.

Required:

a. How would you measure quality in a university environment? What departments are responsible for measuring quality?

b. What audit evidence would you look for in performing the quality audit?

LO D-1

D.47 **Internal Audit of Inventory.** External auditors usually calculate inventory turnover (cost of goods sold for the year divided by average inventory) and use the ratio as a broad indication of inventory age, obsolescence, or overstocking. External auditors are interested in evidence relating to the material accuracy of the financial statements taken as a whole. Internal auditors, on the other hand, calculate turnover by categories and classes of inventory to detect problem areas that might otherwise be overlooked. This kind of detailed analytical audit might point to conditions of buying errors, obsolescence, overstocking, and other matters that could be changed to save money.

The data shown in Exhibit D.47.1 are for turnover, cost of sales, and inventory investment for a series of four historical years and the current year. In each of the years, the external auditors did not recommend any adjustments to the inventory valuations.

Required:

Calculate the current-year inventory turnover ratios. Interpret the ratio trends and identify what conditions might exist. As an internal auditor, write a memo to the vice president for production explaining your findings, possible causes related to problems, and additional investigation that should be conducted.

LO D-1

D.48 **Internal Auditors in the Fast-Food Industry.** Internal auditors perform risk-based audits that go beyond the risks of the financial statements. Assume you are on the internal audit staff of **McDonald's.**

Required:

a. Identify the risks in the fast-food industry associated with
   1. Competition.
   2. Customer preference.
   3. The economy.

EXHIBIT D.47.1 Inventory Data

	\multicolumn{4}{c}{Inventory Turnover}	\multicolumn{2}{c}{Current-Year Inventory ($000)}
	2009	2010	2011	2012	Beginning	Ending
Total inventory	2.1	2.0	2.1	2.1	$3,000	$2,917
Materials and parts	4.0	4.1	4.3	4.5	1,365	620
Work-in-process	12.0	12.5	11.5	11.7	623	697
Finished products:						
Computer games	6.0	7.0	10.0	24.0	380	500
Flash drives	8.0	7.2	7.7	8.5	64	300
Semiconductor parts	4.0	3.5	4.5	7.0	80	400
Keyboards	3.0	2.5	2.0	1.9	488	400

Additional Information
Current Year ($000)

	Transfers	Sales	Cost of Goods Sold	Gross Profit	Compared to prior year
Materials and parts	$3,970*	NA	NA	NA	
Work-in-process	7,988[†]	NA	NA	NA	
Computer games	2,320[‡]	$2,000	$2,200	$<200>	Sales volume declined 60%[§]
Flash drives	2,236[‡]	3,000	2,000	1,000	Sales volume increased 35%
Semiconductor parts	2,720[‡]	4,000	2,400	1,600	Sales volume increased 40%
Keyboards	712[‡]	1,000	800	200	Sales volume declined 3%

NA means not applicable.
*Cost of materials transferred to Work-in-Process.
[†]Cost of materials, labor, and overhead transferred to Finished Goods.
[‡]Cost of goods transferred from Work-in-Process to Finished Product Inventories.
[§]Selling prices also were reduced and the gross margin declined.

4. Technology.
5. Regulation.
6. Other risks.

b. Explain how each of the risks you identified could affect McDonald's.

c. Explain how these risks might affect the internal audits performed by the internal audit staff for McDonald's.

LO D-2

D.49 **CPA Involvement in an Expanded-Scope Audit.** A public accounting firm has been engaged to audit a local food distribution program funded by the U.S. Department of Agriculture. The engagement is to encompass both financial and performance audits that constitute the expanded scope of a GAGAS audit and is to be conducted in accordance with the audit standards published by the Government Accountability Office (GAO).

Required:

a. The accountants should perform sufficient audit work to satisfy the financial and compliance element of GAGAS. What is the objective of such audit work? (*Hint:* Go to the Generally Accepted Government Auditing Standards at www.gao.gov.)

b. The accountants should be aware of general and specific kinds of uneconomical or inefficient practices in such a program. What are some examples?

c. What might be some standards and sources of standards for judging program results?

LO D-6

D.50 **Selection of Effective Extended Procedures.** The following lettered items are some "suspicions," and you have been requested to select some effective procedures designed to confirm or repudiate the suspicions.

a. The custodian of the petty cash fund may be removing cash on Friday afternoon to pay for weekend activities.

b. A manager noticed that eight new vendors had been added to the purchasing department approved list after the assistant purchasing agent was promoted to purchasing manager three weeks ago. The manager suspects all or some of them might be fictitious companies set up by the new purchasing manager.

c. The payroll supervisor may be stealing unclaimed paychecks of people who quit work and do not pick up the last check.

d. Although no customers have complained, cash collections on accounts receivable are down. The counter clerks may have stolen customers' payments.

e. The cashier may have "borrowed" money, covered it by holding each day's deposit until cash from the next day(s)'s collection is enough to make up the shortage from an earlier day, and then send the deposit to the bank.

Required:

Write the suggested procedures for each case in definite terms so another person can know what to do.

LO D-1

D.51 **Internet Exercise: Audit Charters.** Most universities have internal audit departments, and most of them have audit charters that are available on the university website (although you may need to hunt to find it). Go to the website of your college or university and find the internal audit department. Find and print the audit charter or its equivalent. If you are having trouble finding it, call or e-mail the internal audit department and ask whether someone can provide a copy of the audit charter. If your university does not have an internal audit department or does not make its charter available, check the website of one of the larger public universities in your state.

Required:

As described in the audit charter:

a. What are the responsibilities of the internal audit department?

b. What authority does the internal audit department have?

c. To whom does the internal audit department report?

d. When the internal audit department issues a report, who gets it?

e. Are there any items described in the audit charter that you find surprising or interesting?

LO D-1

D.52 **Internet Exercise: Governmental Audit Reports.** Go to the website of the town where you reside and find the Comprehensive Annual Financial Report (CAFR). Find and print the auditor's report. **Warning:** Be careful! CAFRs can be more than 100 pages, so make certain you're printing only the auditor's report.

Required:

a. Who audited the financial statements in the CAFR?
b. How does the auditor's report compare to the three-paragraph standard report used when auditing for-profit companies' financial statements?
c. What additional paragraphs were added to the report?

LO D-6

D.53 **Collecting Evidence in a Fraud Examination.** A fraud examiner was called into a business because of a suspicion of fraud. An assistant manager in a bookstore is taking books off the shelf, bringing them to the return book area, completing a customer return form, and pocketing the money. This is done late in the day when few other employees are in the store and they are involved in closing activities that occupy them in other areas.

Required:

a. What are the objectives of the fraud examiner in performing a fraud audit?
b. What evidence could the fraud examiner obtain that would help reach the objectives of the audit?
c. How should the fraud examiner handle the evidence obtained?

LO D-2

D.54 **Auditing the Effectiveness of a Loan Program.** The following problem is based on an actual program and situation.

The Office of Economic Opportunity (OEO) designed special impact programs to have a major impact on unemployment, dependency, and community tensions in urban areas with large concentrations of low-income residents or in rural areas having substantial migration to such urban areas. The purpose of these experimental programs—combining business, community, and personnel development—is to offer poor people an opportunity to become self-supporting through the free enterprise system. The programs are intended to create training and job opportunities, improve the living environment, and encourage development of local entrepreneurial skills.

Assume that the OEO has identified Mayville as a participant in the special impact program. The Mayville program received more than $50 million in federal funds and obtained another $10 million from private Foundations.

Problems

Mayville is a three-square-mile section of Mega City with a population of approximately 200,000. This area has serious problems of unemployment and underemployment and inadequate housing.

Mayville's problems are deeply seated and have resisted rapid solution. They stem primarily from the fact that local residents, to a considerable degree, lack the education and training required for the jobs available elsewhere in the city and from the lack of jobs in the area. Unemployment and underemployment, in turn, reduce buying power, which has a depressing effect on the area's economy.

The magnitude of the Mayville problems is indicated by the following data disclosed by the U.S. census:

1. Of the total civilian labor force, 8.9 percent was unemployed compared with unemployment rates of 7.1 percent for Mega City and 6.8 percent for the standard metropolitan statistical area (SMSA).
2. Per capita income was $14,106, compared with $22,720 for New York City and $29,909 for the SMSA.
3. Families below the poverty level made up 27.8 percent of the population, compared with 12.4 percent in New York and 9.2 percent in the SMSA.
4. Families receiving public assistance made up 25.4 percent of the population, compared with 9.6 percent in New York and 7.5 percent in the SMSA.

A number of factors aggravate the area's economic problems and make them more difficult to solve. Some of these are

- A reluctance of industry to move into Mega City.
- A net outflow of industry from Mega City.
- High city taxes and a high crime rate.
- A dearth of local residents possessing business managerial experience.

The area's housing problems resulted from the widespread deterioration of existing housing and are, in part, a by-product of below-average income levels resulting from unemployment and underemployment. These problems were aggravated by a shortage of mortgage capital for residential housing associated with a lack of confidence in the area on the part of financial institutions, which, as discussed later, seems to have been somewhat overcome.

Mayville was the target of several special impact programs. Included were programs designed to stimulate private business, to improve housing, to establish community facilities, and to train residents in marketable skills. There were two programs to stimulate private business: a program to loan funds to local businesses and a program to attract outside businesses to the area.

Under the business loan program begun five years ago, the sponsors proposed to create jobs and stimulate business ownership by local residents. At first, investments in local businesses were made only in the form of loans. Later, the sponsors adopted a policy of making equity investments in selected companies to obtain the sponsors' voice in management. Equity investments totaling about $159,000 were made in four companies.

Loans were to be repaid in installments over periods of up to 10 years, usually with a moratorium on repayment for six months or longer. Repayment was to be made in cash or by applying subsidies allowed by the sponsors for providing on-the-job training to unskilled workers. Loans made during the first two years of the program were interest free. Later, the sponsors revised the policy to one of charging below-market interest rates. Rates charged were from 2 to 5 percent. This policy change was made to (1) emphasize to borrowers their obligations to repay the loan and (2) help the sponsors monitor borrowers' progress toward profitability.

Prospective borrowers learned of the loan program through (1) information disseminated at neighborhood centers, (2) advertisements on radio and television and in a local newspaper, and (3) word of mouth. Those who wished to apply for loans were required to complete application forms providing information relating to their education, business and work experience, and personal financial statements and references. The sponsors set up a management assistance division, which employed consultants to supplement its internal marketing assistance efforts and to provide management, accounting, marketing, legal, and other assistance to borrowers.

The sponsors proposed to create at least 1,700 jobs during the first four years of the loan program by making loans to some 73 new and existing businesses.

Required:

Put yourself in the position of the GAO manager in charge of all audits pertaining to the Office of Economic Opportunity. The Mega City field office has been assigned to conduct a detailed review of the special impact program described here. Prepare a memo to the Mega City field office in which you indicate, in as much detail as is possible from the information provided, the specific steps the field office should perform in conducting an evaluation of the program effectiveness of the special impact loan program.

LO D-1

D.55 **Operational Audit: Customer Complaints.** Danny Deck, the director of internal auditing for Rice Department Stores, was working in his office one Thursday when Chris McMurray, president of the company, burst in to tell Deck about a problem. According to McMurray, "Customer complaints about delays in getting credit for merchandise returns are driving Sally Godwin up the wall! She doesn't know what to do because she has no control over the processing of credit memos."

Godwin is the manager in charge of customer relations and tries to keep everybody happy. Upon her recommendation, the company adopted an advertising motto: "Satisfaction Guaranteed and Prompt Credit When You Change Your Mind." The motto is featured in newspaper ads and on large banners in each store.

Deck performed a preliminary review and found the following:

1. Godwin believes customers will be satisfied if they receive a refund check or notice of credit on account within five working days.

2. The chief accountant described the credit memo processing procedure as follows: When a customer returns merchandise, the sales clerks give a smile, a "returned merchandise receipt," and a promise to send a check or a notice within five days. The store copy of the receipt and the merchandise are sent to the purchasing department, where buyers examine the merchandise for quality or damage to decide whether to put it back on the shelves, return it to the vendor, or hold it for the annual rummage sale. The buyers then prepare a brief report and send it with the returned merchandise receipt to the customer relations

department for approval. The buyer's report is filed for reference and the receipt, marked for approval in Godwin's department, is sent to the accounting department. The accounting department sorts the receipts in numerical order, checking the numerical sequence, and files them in preparation for the weekly batch processing of transactions other than sales and cash receipts, both of which are processed daily. When the customer has requested a cash refund, the checks and canceled returned merchandise receipts are approved by the treasurer, who signs and mails the check. When the credit is on a customer's charge account, it is shown on the next monthly statement sent to the customer.

3. The processing in each department takes two or three days.

Required:

a. Analyze the problem. How much time does it take the company to process the merchandise returns?

b. Formulate a recommendation to solve the problem. Write a brief report explaining your recommendation.

LO D-2

D.56 **GAO Auditor Independence.** The GAO reporting standards for performance audits state that each report should include "recommendations for action to correct the problem areas and to improve operations." For example, an audit of the Washington Metropolitan Area Transit Authority found management decision deficiencies affecting some $230 million in federal funds. The GAO auditors recommended that the transit authority could improve its management control over railcar procurement through better enforcement of contract requirements and development of a master plan to test cars.

Suppose the transit authority accepted and implemented specific recommendations made by the GAO auditors.

Required:

Do you believe these events would be enough to impair the independence of the GAO auditors in a subsequent audit of the transit authority? Explain and tell whether it makes any difference to you that the same or different person performs both the first and subsequent audits.

LO D-3

D.57 **Efficiency Standards.** The U.S. Postal Service (USPS) advertises prompt delivery schedules for express mail (overnight delivery) and priority mail (two-to–three-day delivery). The USPS knows various risks that may arise to thwart a timely (as advertised) delivery but believes that systems and controls are in place and operating to mitigate the risks. The USPS advertised that 94 percent of express mail and 87 percent of priority mail was delivered on time from the time the mail was postmarked to the time it reached the destination post office. However, a consulting firm studied the USPS operations and determined that the express mail arrived at the recipients' addresses on time 81 percent of the time (not 94 percent) and the priority mail arrived timely 75 percent of the time (not 87 percent).

Required:

What can account for the difference in these performance statistics between the USPS delivery rates and the consultant's rates? (*Hint:* Think in terms of orientation to customers and standards for measuring performance.)

LO D-6

D.58 **The Perfect Crime.** Embezzlers often try to cover up by removing canceled checks they made payable to themselves or endorsed on the back with their own names. Missing canceled checks are a signal (red flag). However, people who reconcile bank accounts may not notice missing checks if the bank reconciliation is performed using only the numerical listing printed in the bank statement. Now consider the case of truncated bank statements for which the bank does not even return the canceled checks to the payer. All of the checks are "missing," and the bank reconciler has no opportunity to notice anything about canceled checks. Consider the following story of a real embezzlement.

The embezzler hired a print shop to print a private stock of Ajax Company checks in the company's numerical sequence. In his job as an accounts payable clerk, he intercepted legitimate checks written by the accounts payable department and signed by the Ajax treasurer and then destroyed them. He substituted the same-numbered check from the private stock made it payable to himself in the same amount as the legitimate check, and "signed" it with a rubber stamp that looked enough like the Ajax Company treasurer's signature to fool the paying bank. He deposited the money in his own bank account.

The bank statement reconciler (a different person) was able to agree the check numbers and amounts listed in the cleared items in the bank statement to the recorded cash disbursement (check number and amount) and thus did not notice the trick. The embezzler was able to process the vendor's "past due" notice and next month statement with complete documentation, enabling the Ajax treasurer to sign another check the next month paying both the past due balance and current charges. The embezzler was careful to scatter the double-expense payments among numerous accounts (telephone, office supplies, inventory, etc.) so the double-paid expenses did not distort any accounts very much. As time passed, the embezzler was able to recommend budget figures that allowed a large enough budget so his double-paid expenses in various categories did not often pop up as large variances from the budget.

Required:

List and explain the ways and means you believe someone might detect this fraud scheme. Think first about the ordinary everyday control procedures. Then think about extensive detection efforts assuming a tip or indication of a possible fraud has been received. Is this a "perfect crime"?

LO D-1

D.59 **Impact of Changing Rules.** Many companies outsource their internal audit function to CPA firms.

Required:

a. What benefits might be gained from having a CPA firm provide its internal audit services?
b. What benefits might be gained from having an in-house internal audit department?
c. What concerns might arise from having a CPA firm provide its internal audit services?

LO D-1, D-6

D.60 **Looking for Evidence of Fraud.** Wen-Li is an internal auditor for Main Electrical Supply in Springfield, Illinois. During her audit, she came across the invoice shown in Exhibit D.60.1. The invoice is in almost pristine condition with few marks and no creases. The invoice was properly filed in a vendor folder marked Best Office Supply, which is on the approved vendor list, but the vendor review sheet, which is required to place a vendor on the approved vendor list, is missing from the file.

Three other invoices were in the file:

June 14, 2010	Invoice 0076	$238.99
July 17, 2010	Invoice 0082	324.55
August 16, 2010	Invoice 0085	386.82

Required:

a. Is this a legitimate invoice? What information might lead you to suspect that this invoice may indicate a fraud?
b. What type(s) of fraud might this indicate?.

EXHIBIT D.60.1 Vendor Invoice

September 15, 2012

Best Office Supply Company
P.O. Box 1934
Springfield, Illinois 62705

Invoice #0089

Bill to:
Main Electrical Supply
506 Commerce Avenue
Springfield, IL 62707
217-555-2230

Product	Quantity	Price per Unit	Total Cost
Pens	10 Boxes	$3.65	$36.50
Copy paper	15 cases	$15.76	$236.40
Toner cartridges	8 units	$22.56	$180.48
Total			$453.38

Payment is due immediately upon receipt

Overview of Sampling

There are three kinds of lies: lies, damned lies, and statistics.

Benjamin Disraeli, former British Prime Minister

Professional Standards References

Topic	AU/ISA Section	PCAOB Reference*
An Audit of Internal Control over Financial Reporting That Is Integrated with an Audit of Financial Statements		AS 5
Overall Objectives of the Independent Auditor and the Conduct of an Audit in Accordance with Generally Accepted Auditing Standards.	200	AS 8
Identifying and Assessing the Risks of Material Misstatement	315	AS 12
Materiality in Planning and Performing an Audit	320	AS 11
Performing Audit Procedures in Response to Assessed Risks and Evaluating the Audit Evidence Obtained	330	AS 13
Audit Evidence	500	AS 15
Audit Sampling	530	AU 350

*AU references represent standards issued by the ASB prior to April 16, 2003 that have not been superseded or amended by the PCAOB

LEARNING OBJECTIVES

Module E introduces the sampling process and illustrates how sampling can be used during an audit.

Your objectives are to be able to:

LO E-1 Understand the basic principles of sampling, including the differences between statistical and nonstatistical sampling and sampling and nonsampling risk.

LO E-2 Understand the basic steps and procedures used in implementing a sampling plan.

LO E-3 Identify the two situations in which sampling is used in an audit.

LO E-4 Understand how the basic steps and procedures used in a sampling plan apply to an audit.

INTRODUCTION

Phar-Mor, a national chain of drugstores, inflated its profits by creating fictitious increases in inventory. How did the auditors fail to detect these misstatements? The auditors visited and observed inventory counts in only four of Phar-Mor's 300 stores and performed price tests on 25 to 30 items at the four stores. Even worse, they informed Phar-Mor months in advance which stores they would visit. Phar-Mor made sure that these stores would be fully stocked and the fictitious inventory was "allocated" to the remaining 296 stores. None of the items examined by the auditors were fraudulent; however, the auditors' failure to obtain a representative *sample* of an adequate number of stores and inventory items (and do so on a surprise basis) led them to miss a $500 million fraud resulting in more than $300 million in judgments against the CPA firm.[1]

WHAT IS SAMPLING?

LEARNING OBJECTIVE E-1
Understand the basic principles of sampling, including the differences between statistical and nonstatistical sampling and sampling and nonsampling risk.

Consider the following information that we frequently hear and read in the media during an election year:

Based on a sample of 1,000 eligible voters, Candidate A has 45 percent of the vote, with a margin for error of plus or minus 4 percent.

This statement means the pollsters have a certain level of confidence that Candidate A's true (but unknown) share of the vote is between 41 percent (45 percent minus 4 percent) and 49 percent (45 percent plus 4 percent). This range is based on the sample of 1,000 eligible voters.

Why do we not know the actual percentage of the vote? Because it would not be cost effective for any pollster to survey each and every possible voter. (In fact, it would probably be impossible to do so!) Pollsters cannot with any certainty provide a single estimate of the candidate's share of the vote unless all voters in the *population* are surveyed and would actually vote as they say they would vote. Instead, pollsters provide a range of estimates that has a high (but unspecified) chance of including the true percentage of the vote.

This scenario is one example of the use of **sampling**, the objective of which is to make a statement about a **population** of interest (in this case, all eligible voters) by examining only a subset (or **sample**) of that population (in this case, the voters responding to the pollster's inquiries).

Just as surveying every eligible voter is not cost effective, it is not cost effective for an audit team to examine every occurrence of a control procedure, transaction in an account balance, or component of an account balance during an audit examination. Two major stages in the audit examination during which sampling is used are

1. The study and evaluation of a client's internal control to determine whether important control policies and procedures are functioning as intended to prevent and detect material financial statement misstatements.[2]
2. The conduct of substantive procedures to determine whether the client's account balances or classes of transactions are recorded and presented in conformity with generally accepted accounting principles.

The remainder of this module discusses sampling in a generic (nonaudit) context. In addition, we provide a broad overview of the use of sampling in these two audit contexts. The overview of sampling is followed by a brief introduction to audit sampling. Audit

---

[1] J. T. Wells, "Ghost Goods: How to Spot Phantom Inventory," *Journal Of Accountancy*, June 2001, pp. 33–36; D. M. Cottrell and S. M. Glover, "Finding Auditors Liable for Fraud," *The CPA Journal* July 1997.

[2] In this module, the focus on sampling with respect to internal control is the assessment of control risk to determine the nature, timing, and extent of substantive procedures. However, it is important to note that this discussion also applies to engagements subject to the provisions of PCAOB *Auditing Standard 5* with respect to the audit team's responsibility to evaluate a client's internal control under section 404 of the Sarbanes-Oxley Act.

sampling is somewhat different from the sampling you learned in basic statistics. First, auditors are more concerned about incorrectly accepting a hypothesis (i.e., that the account is correctly stated). These were called *type II* or *beta errors* in your statistics classes. Normal hypothesis testing is concerned more with incorrectly rejecting hypotheses (*type I* or *alpha errors*). These types of errors are discussed in more detail later. Second, accounting distributions are generally more *skewed* than distributions of other data. In other words, there are generally many more low-dollar items or items without errors than high-dollar items or items with errors. Because accounting statisticians have developed helpful, time-saving tables to analyze these distributions, your study of audit sampling will focus more on the appropriate understanding and application of the tables than performing complex calculations. The next two modules provide detailed illustration of the use of sampling tables in the audit team's study of internal control (Module F) and the audit team's substantive procedures (Module G).

When Should Sampling Be Used?

To illustrate the basic concepts associated with sampling, assume that **Wilson Sporting Goods** (Wilson) was interested in determining whether amateur golfers could hit its golf balls farther than competitors' golf balls.[3] Wilson has determined that if its golf balls increase the distance of an amateur's shots by five or more yards, it can reliably claim that its ball can improve distances (or is "longer") relative to the competition. (It is not important for you to know how the distance five yards was determined, but it incorporates a margin for error or randomness.)

One possible way to test Wilson's claim is to have every amateur golfer in the world (a number totaling in the millions) hit both a competitor's golf ball and Wilson's golf ball. The distance each ball is hit would be determined and the difference in distances would be calculated. Assuming that no computational errors were made in the calculations, Wilson would know the average increase in distances (if any) with certainty.

Would an engagement team consider using sampling to answer this question? Sampling is typically used when the question of interest has the following two characteristics:

1. *The need for exact information is not important.* Considering the preceding example, the engagement team would be more interested in testing all golfers if it wanted to know an exact increase in distance (for example, does Wilson's golf ball increase distances by *7.5 yards* as opposed to *5.0 yards or more?*).
2. *The number of items comprising the population is large.* If the number of amateur golfers were 100, the engagement team would be more likely to test all 100 golfers than if the number of amateur golfers were more than a million.

Essentially, sampling trades *effectiveness* for *efficiency*. That is, sampling allows an individual to obtain information about a population of interest in a fraction of the time it would take to examine the entire population. In other words, *sampling is more efficient*. However, because the individual is not examining all items in the population, there is a chance that sampling will not provide the correct answer to the question being examined (*sampling is less effective*). Sampling is used when the gains associated with efficiency exceed the losses associated with effectiveness. As discussed later, certain types of sampling plans allow the losses associated with reduced effectiveness to be quantified and limited to relatively low levels.

Sampling Risk versus Nonsampling Risk

As noted, sampling can result in the loss of effectiveness; that is, basing a conclusion about a population on a sample drawn from that population could fail to provide the correct conclusion. For example, assume that the engagement team tested 50 golfers, calculated the distances for the two golf balls, and concluded that Wilson's golf ball provided an average increase in distance of six yards. Recall that the engagement team is interested

[3] "After This, CPAs May Take over Instant-Replay Duties for Football," *The Wall Street Journal,* July 9, 1991, p. B1.

AUDITING INSIGHT ▽ Sampling's OK, Sampling's not OK

MBIA Inc. can use statistical sampling to pursue repurchase demands against **Bank of America Corp.**, a judge said in a lawsuit claiming MBIA was fraudulently induced to insure $21 billion in mortgage-backed securities,. MBIA asked New York State Supreme Court Judge Eileen Bransten to allow company lawyers to develop evidence using samples from 368,000 mortgages in 15 securitized pools to establish its fraud claims rather than go through each loan. Proceeding loan by loan might lead to "a delay of several years before trial," Philippe Z. Selendy, an attorney for Armonk, New York-based MBIA, said in an October 13 letter to the judge.

On December 22, 2010, Bransten ruled that "the court does not find any prejudice in deciding the motion before it and allowing the use of statistically significant samples of the securitizations at issue." She said the defendants could also choose to use their "own sampling chosen in a statistically valid manner" to rebut MBIA's arguments.

Source: J. Gittelsohn and M. C. Fisk, **"Bank of America Loses Evidence Ruling in MBIA Suit,"** *Bloomberg Businessweek* December 29, 2010, http://www.businessweek.com/news/2010-12-29/bank-of-america-loses-evidence-ruling-in-mbia-suit.html (accessed July 19, 2011).

President Barack Obama's nominee to head the Census Bureau ruled out using statistical sampling to adjust the results of the 2010 census, apparently easing Republican concerns and making his confirmation likely. Robert Groves, director of the University of Michigan's Survey Research Center and a former Census Bureau official, is an expert on statistical sampling. Proponents of sampling say it helps produce a more accurate count of the population, especially when it comes to traditionally undercounted groups, such as minorities living in urban areas. But many Republican lawmakers insist that sampling violates the Constitution.

Dr. Groves, during his confirmation hearing Friday, said he wouldn't use sampling to adjust the 2010 count. Asked whether he would consider using it in a future census, he said: "There are no plans to do that for 2020."

Source: "Census Pick Rules Out Using Sampling in 2010," Timothy J. Alberta, *The Wall Street Journal*, May 16, 2009, p. A2

---

in determining whether the increase in distance is more than five yards. If the true average increase in distance (which the engagement team would not know unless it tested all amateur golfers) is seven yards, the use of sampling has provided the engagement team the correct conclusion.

Now assume that the distances of the sample of 50 golfers provided an average increase in distance of four yards. In this case, the engagement team's conclusion that Wilson's golf ball did not increase the distances of shots of amateur golfers would be incorrect because the true average increase in distance (unknown to the engagement team) is seven yards.[4] This situation is an example of **sampling risk**, which is the likelihood that the decision made based on the sample (in this case, that the increase in distance was four yards and Wilson's ball does not provide an increase in distance) differs from the conclusion that would have been made if the entire population had been examined (in this case, that the increase was seven yards and Wilson's ball does provide an increase in distance).

Obviously, other samples of 50 different golfers drawn from the population would provide the engagement team different averages. Some of these samples provide results consistent with the population and others do not. The ones that do not provide results consistent with the population (all samples providing an average increase in distance of less than five yards) represent examples of sampling risk. This relationship is shown in Exhibit E.1.

When decisions made based on the sample differ from decisions that would be made if the entire population had been examined, sampling error has occurred. *Sampling error* is caused when the sample drawn from the population does not appropriately represent that population. *Sampling risk* is the likelihood of sampling error. In this instance, Wilson's golf ball did not provide the sample of golfers drawn from the population with as large an increase in distance as it would for the average amateur golfer. This case is referred to as selecting a **nonrepresentative sample**, which is a sample that differs substantially on one or more key characteristics of interest from the population from which the sample is drawn.

---

[4] Recall that the engagement team stipulated that the distance increase must equal or exceed five yards for it to reliably conclude that Wilson's ball will provide a distance increase. Therefore, even though Wilson's ball provided a distance increase of four yards in this sample, this difference is not large enough to provide the engagement team a reliable conclusion.

EXHIBIT E.1
The Effect of Various Sample Averages on Conclusions

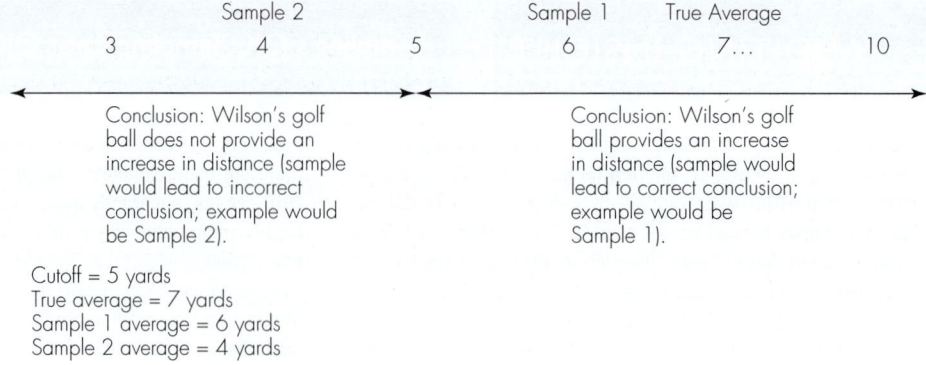

Cutoff = 5 yards
True average = 7 yards
Sample 1 average = 6 yards
Sample 2 average = 4 yards

Sampling risk can never be eliminated (unless, of course, the engagement team were to test all amateur golfers in the population), but it can be controlled to relatively low levels. Three major steps can control sampling risk in the sampling process:

1. *Determining an appropriate sample size.* As a higher percentage of items in the population is examined, sampling risk decreases.
2. *Ensuring that all items have an equal opportunity to be selected.* If all items have an equal opportunity to be selected, the likelihood of sampling risk decreases.
3. *Evaluating sample results to control sampling risk.* The results from a sample are "adjusted" to consider the likelihood that the sample being evaluated does not appropriately represent the population. We discuss this "adjustment" later.

In both the Wilson example and in an audit, sampling risk arises for the same reason: the use of a nonrepresentative sample. Auditors using statistical sampling take appropriate measures to increase the likelihood that they select a representative sample for examination.

Nonsampling risk represents the probability that an incorrect conclusion will be reached as a result of reasons unrelated to the nature of the sample. Even if the auditors examine all items, they are still subject to nonsampling risk. Nonsampling risk typically occurs because of errors in judgment or execution. For example, if the engagement team incorrectly measures the yardage, the sample average will be incorrect and can result in an inappropriate conclusion. Note that this error is not caused by a nonrepresentative sample but by an *evaluator error*. In an auditing context, *nonsampling error* arises when auditors use an inappropriate procedure or misinterpret evidence they have obtained.

AUDITING INSIGHT Polling Problems

In the month leading up to the 2008 California presidential primary, at least a dozen polling firms canvassed the state, phoning tens of thousands of households. Two main providers of polling data, Real Clear Politics and Pollster.com, didn't place a single call. Both consolidate surveys from various sources to produce composite numbers meant to smooth out results. Statisticians criticize their methods, but their numbers are used by news organizations eager for a way to make sense of conflicting polls.

Combining pollsters has its critics. Polls have different sample sizes, yet those with more respondents are weighted the same. They are taken at different times, some before respondents have absorbed the results from other states' primaries. They cover different populations, especially during primaries when turnout is traditionally lower. Some pollsters apply less stringent screens to identify likely voters. Also, pollsters apply different weights to adjust for voters they've missed. Wording of questions can differ, which makes it tricky to count undecided voters. Even identifying these differences isn't easy because some of the included polls aren't adequately footnoted.

Despite these weaknesses, John McIntyre, cofounder of Real Clear Politics, says that averaging polls is better than cherry-picking individual ones, which is what campaigns might do to highlight numbers favoring their candidate or journalists might do to create the impression of a close race. McIntyre requires at least three polls before producing an average. His site's numbers, he says, provide "a clearer picture of where things truly stand."

Source: "Election Handicappers Are Using Risky Tool: Mixed Poll Averages" Carl Bialik., *The Wall Street Journal* (Eastern Edition), Feb. 15, 2008, p. B1.

Statistical Sampling versus Nonstatistical Sampling

The preceding section on the possible exposure to sampling risk notes a significant limitation with the use of sampling. This risk cannot be eliminated, but certain sampling plans allow the risk to be measured and controlled at acceptable levels. These plans are referred to as *statistical sampling plans*.

Statistical sampling plans apply the laws of probability to selecting sample items for examination and evaluating sample results. Specifically, statistical sampling methods enable the audit team to make quantitative statements about the results and to measure the sufficiency of evidence gathered (i.e., determine a sufficient sample size) and evaluate the results in such a way to control sampling risk. **Nonstatistical sampling** plans do not meet either of these criteria. Thus, these two types of plans differ in terms of how sample size is determined and how the results are evaluated.

Although the phrase *nonstatistical sampling* sounds less professional and less favorable, nonstatistical sampling methods can be appropriate in some circumstances. In certain cases, it is not necessary (or desirable) to use the laws of probability to select sample items. For example, if a client's accounts receivable balance includes 1,000 individual customer accounts but a large percentage of the dollar amount is contained in only a few accounts, the audit team could reasonably decide to select only those few accounts for examination as long as the team believes there is a low risk that a combined total misstatement in the smaller accounts is material. In making this decision, the team violates one of the provisions of statistical sampling (random selection of items). However, it is both efficient and effective for the audit team to select the sample in this fashion!

Generally accepted auditing standards do *not* require the use of statistical sampling procedures. In fact, a survey of practicing auditors in public accounting, industry, and government revealed that 85 percent of all samples were *selected* using nonstatistical procedures and 64 percent of all samples were *evaluated* using nonstatistical evaluation methods.[5] The use of nonstatistical sampling methods is often justifiable when the costs of using statistical sampling methods exceed the benefits of doing so. However, nonstatistical sampling should not be used solely as a means to reduce sample sizes. AU 530 suggests that sample sizes developed for a nonstatistical sampling plan should be comparable to those "resulting from an efficient and effectively designed statistical sample, considering the same sampling parameters."

The terms *statistical and nonstatistical sampling* and *sampling and nonsampling risk* are sometimes used interchangeably. However, it is important to note that they are indeed quite different. To understand this, sampling risk exists in both a statistical and nonstatistical sample because either type of sampling plan can result in the selection of a sample that does not appropriately represent the population. However, statistical sampling plans allow sampling risk to be measured and controlled to acceptable levels. Similarly, nonsampling risk can exist in either type of sampling approach because an individual could make a mistake in evaluating sample results in either a statistical or nonstatistical sampling application.

⤷ REVIEW CHECKPOINTS

E.1 During what stages of the audit examination can sampling be used?

E.2 What is *sampling risk?* How does it occur?

E.3 What is *nonsampling risk?* How does it occur?

E.4 How is sampling risk controlled?

E.5 What is *statistical sampling?* How does it differ from nonstatistical sampling?

E.6 Is nonstatistical sampling permitted under generally accepted auditing standards?

---

[5] T. W. Hall, J. E. Hunton, and B. J. Pierce, "Sampling Practices of Auditors in Public Accounting, Industry, and Government," *Accounting Horizons*, June 2002, p. 129.

THE BASIC STEPS INVOLVED WITH SAMPLING

LEARNING OBJECTIVE E-2
Understand the basic steps and procedures used in implementing a sampling plan.

In general, sampling can be viewed as including the following major steps:

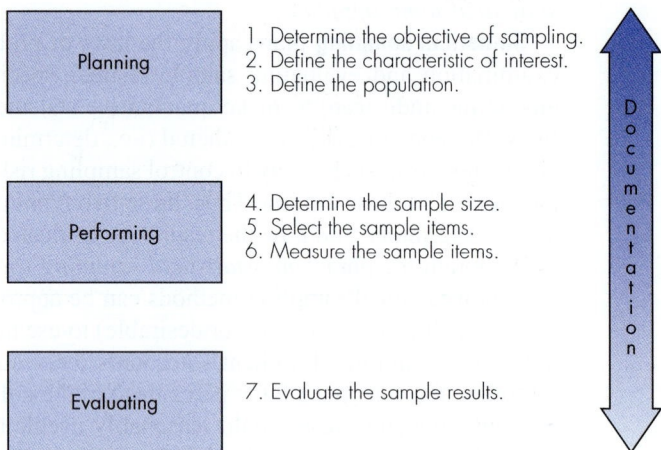

As an example of the process illustrated, consider our example of determining whether Wilson's golf ball provides an increase in distance for amateur golfers. In this module, we provide a very nontechnical example of this process that does not involve calculations to illustrate how the sampling process works. Modules F and G provide a more comprehensive example of this process and how it is employed in various stages of the audit team's examination.

Planning

Determine the Objective, Define the Characteristic of Interest, and Define the Population

The *objective of the sampling application* is directly related to the question of interest. In this example, the objective is to determine whether Wilson's golf ball increases distance; because the engagement team's conclusion with respect to this question is evidenced by whether the increase exceeds five yards, the increase in distance is the *characteristic of interest*. Clearly defining the characteristic of interest in a sampling application is critical because it is the measure that will be obtained from the sample items and eventually evaluated against some criterion (related to the objective of the sampling application).

Defining the population can sound straightforward, but it must be defined carefully to be able to meet the objective of the sampling application. In our example, the population should be defined as all amateur golfers in the world. If the population is defined as amateur golfers who belong to country clubs, subscribe to *Golf Magazine,* or attend a Professional Golf Association (PGA) tournament each year, the results will not appropriately represent the entire population.

Performing

Determine Sample Size

Although many factors are considered in determining the appropriate sample size, the acceptable level of sampling risk is one important factor. Recall that an advantage of *statistical* sampling plans is that they allow determining a sample size that measures and controls exposure to sampling risk. An individual who wishes to reduce sampling risk to lower levels needs to select more items for examination as shown.

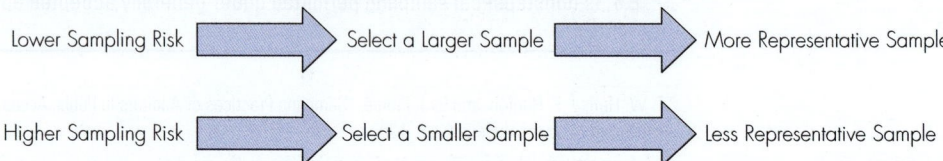

Assume that, based on an acceptable level of sampling risk of 10 percent (i.e., a 10 percent chance Wilson will claim its balls increase distance when, in fact, they *do not* or, conversely, that they do not increase distance when, in fact, *they do*), the engagement team determines that a sample size of 50 items is needed. At this point, do not be concerned with how the size of 50 was determined. Other factors also influence sample size; these factors will be discussed later in this module.

Select the Sample Items

Once the sample size has been determined, the sample needs to be selected from the population. Recall that *population* is defined in this example as all amateur golfers throughout the world. Also recall that the acceptable level of sampling risk is 10 percent and that the sample size necessary to control sampling risk at this level is 50 amateur golfers (we illustrate the determination of these two factors as well as how they relate to one another in subsequent modules). Four methods that can be used to select a sample are discussed next.

Unrestricted Random Selection When using **unrestricted random selection** (often referred to as **random selection**), the engagement team selects items from a population so that each item has an equal chance of being selected. This type of selection process can be used only when items in the population are numbered or can easily be assigned a number. The use of random selection consists of a two-step procedure:

1. A series of random numbers is identified by either a random number table or a computer program.
2. The random numbers from step 1 are matched to numbered items in the corresponding population.

To illustrate the use of random selection, the engagement team selected the following numbers from a random number table: 120, 268, and 341. Using an alphabetical listing of amateur golfers throughout the world, the engagement team would test the 120th, 268th, and 341st golfers. One key feature of random selection is that another individual is able to replicate the procedure and select exactly the same items. In addition, every item has an equal probability of being selected.

Systematic Random Selection When using **systematic random selection** (commonly referred to as **systematic selection**), the individual randomly selects a starting point from within the population and examines every *n*th item thereafter, where *n* is determined based on the number of items in the population and the necessary sample size. Systematic selection has the advantage of ensuring that all items have an equal probability of selection while providing a more efficient method of selecting items than unrestricted random selection.

The following basic steps are used in systematic selection.

1. Determine the necessary **sampling interval**. The sampling interval identifies the frequency with which items are selected within the population. It is determined by dividing the number of items in the population by the necessary sample size.
2. Select a random starting point from within the population (a number equal to or less than the sampling interval) and select the item in the population corresponding to this number.
3. Add the sampling interval to the random starting point. The item in the population corresponding to this number is the next item selected.
4. Add the sampling interval to the total from step 3. The item in the population corresponding to this number will be the next item selected.
5. Repeat step 4 until the number of items equal to the necessary sample size is selected.

To illustrate the use of systematic selection, recall that the population is all amateur golfers throughout the world and the necessary sample size is 50. For purposes of illustration, assume that the population of amateur golfers totaled 1,000 (it is surely much higher than this!).

A sampling interval of 20 is calculated (1,000 golfers ÷ 50 items = 20); thus, every 20th item would be selected for examination. If the random starting point is 15, the first three items selected would be as follows:

Item 1: 15 (random starting point)
Item 2: 35 (15 + 20)
Item 3: 55 (35 + 20)

In some cases, several random starting points are used to ensure a more random sample. For example, in the preceding situation, the engagement team could use one random start and select the additional 49 items as noted. Alternatively, they could use five random starts and select an additional nine items for each of these starting points. In either case, a total of 50 items (the necessary sample size) would ultimately be selected.

Like random selection, systematic selection is advantageous because another individual can replicate the selection of the sample if both the random starting point and sampling interval are known. In addition, like random selection, every item in the population has an equal chance of being selected, which provides a reasonable likelihood of selecting a representative sample.

One limitation of systematic selection is that the population must be randomly ordered. Because systematic selection essentially bypasses a number of items, a nonrandomly ordered population can result in bypassing a number of items having similar characteristics. For example, if the population of amateur golfers were arranged alphabetically, bypassing a number of golfers whose last name begins with B (or any other letter) would not appear to influence the representativeness of the sample. However, if the population were arranged by club membership and then by ability (or golf handicap index), and, for the sake of argument, each club had 20 members, then systematic selection could possible result in the best member from each club being selected. This is obviously an unlikely scenario, but it should be considered.

Haphazard Selection When using **haphazard selection**, items are selected in an unstructured manner but without any intentional bias. Although this can be done in any number of ways, one way is to identify items (golfers) as they arrived at the clubhouse or flipping through membership rosters from country clubs selecting items until a total of 50 were selected. Contrary to the connotation of the word *haphazard,* items chosen by haphazard selection are not taken in a careless manner, and the results are expected to be representative of the population.

One significant limitation of haphazard selection is that, unlike either random selection or systematic selection, the sampling method cannot be described in sufficient detail to permit another individual to replicate it. Some describe haphazard selection as a method of choosing items without any special reason for including or excluding items, thus obtaining a representative sample. However, haphazard selection methods do not permit individuals to measure the probability of selecting sample items. In addition, although items are selected in a nonsystematic manner, studies have found that bias in selecting items (either conscious or unconscious) often exists.[6]

Block Selection The use of **block selection** involves selecting a series of contiguous (or adjacent) items from the population. One example of block selection is the selection of the first 10 golfers from the membership roster at each of five different country clubs for a total of 50 sample items. In this case, the population unit is really a list of golfers. Block selection is less desirable because it is difficult to efficiently obtain a representative sample; ordinarily, a relatively large number of blocks need to be selected to be representative.

Which Selection Method Should Be Used? The use of statistical or nonstatistical sampling procedures has a significant impact on the method of sample selection. Random or systematic selection is used with statistical sampling because these methods (1) provide a reasonable likelihood of obtaining a representative sample, (2) allow the probability of

[6] T. W. Hall, T. L. Herron, and B. J. Pierce, "How Reliable Is Haphazard Sampling?" *The CPA Journal,* January 2006, p. 26.

obtaining sample items to be determined, and (3) allow the sample selection process to be replicated. As a result, these methods allow sampling risk to be measured and controlled to acceptable levels. In contrast, haphazard and block selection do not meet these criteria; they could result in a random sample, but quantitatively evaluating the randomness of the sample selected using them is difficult.

In practice, computer software has greatly increased the efficiency and effectiveness of selecting sample items, particularly when using systematic random selection or unrestricted random selection. Software applications use client data files and parameters designated by the individual to select the appropriate sample items.

AUDITING INSIGHT — Survey of Selection Methods

A survey of practicing auditors in public accounting, industry, and government accounting revealed that they used the following methods to select sample items (based on audits conducted by respondents during the most recent six months):

Statistical Selection		Nonstatistical Selection	
Random selection	3%	Haphazard selection	74%
Systematic selection (or variation)	12%	Block selection	3%
Total	15%	Other	8%
		Total	85%

In addition to illustrating the methods of sample selection used in practice, these results indicate the extent to which nonstatistical sampling methods are used in practice to select samples (as noted, these methods are used in 85 percent of all audits).

Source: T. W. Hall, J. E. Hunton, and B. J. Pierce, "Sampling Practices of Auditors in Public Accounting, Industry, and Government," *Accounting Horizons*, June 2002, p. 129.

Measure the Sample Items Once the sample size has been determined and the sample has been selected, the next step is to *measure the sample items*. In our example, measuring the sample items consists of having each golfer hit a series of shots with Wilson's golf ball and the competitors' golf balls and recording the distances.[7] It is at this point that nonsampling risk can occur. Examples of nonsampling risk include incorrectly transcribing a distance or making some other mathematical error during the measurement process. After selecting the 50 golfers and averaging the distances, assume that an average increase in distance of 6.7 yards for Wilson's golf ball is calculated.

Summary: Wilson Golf Ball Example

At this point, we have performed the following sampling procedures:

1. *Define the objective of sampling.* In this case, the sampling objective is to determine whether using Wilson's golf ball provides amateur golfers an increase in distance.
2. *Define the characteristic of interest.* This is the increase in distance gained by using Wilson's golf ball (specifically, whether this increase is at least five yards).
3. *Define the population.* The population is defined as all amateur golfers in the world.
4. *Determine the sample size.* Based on the acceptable exposure to sampling risk of 10 percent, a sample size of 50 has been determined.
5. *Select the sample items.* Items are selected using one of four selection methods (unrestricted random selection, systematic random selection, haphazard selection, or block selection).
6. *Measure the sample items.* Based on the distance using the golfers' existing golf ball and the Wilson golf ball, the average increase in distance is 6.7 yards.

[7] Of course, physical conditions such as type of club used, wind, and course altitude would have to be considered.

> ### ↳ REVIEW CHECKPOINTS
>
> E.7 What are the seven major steps involved with sampling?
>
> E.8 What is the importance of carefully defining the population of interest?
>
> E.9 How does sampling risk affect sample size?
>
> E.10 Briefly identify and explain the four methods used to select sample items.
>
> E.11 What methods of sample selection are appropriate to use with a statistical sampling plan? Why?

Evaluating the Sample Results

Based on the sample average increase in distance of 6.7 yards, can the engagement team conclude that amateur golfers could hit the Wilson golf ball longer than its competitors' golf balls? This average exceeds the five-yard criterion, but it is possible that the engagement team did not select a representative sample. (In addition, the engagement team could have made a computational error and introduced nonsampling risk, but we assume that no such errors were made.)

To evaluate the sample results, the sample average must be "adjusted" to control for the acceptable level of exposure to sampling risk. This is done by forming a range of estimates that have a certain probability of including the true (but unknown) population value. Although we illustrate the calculation of this range in a subsequent module, assume that we can conclude with 90 percent probability that the true population average increase in distance is between 5.2 yards and 8.2 yards (the sample estimate of 6.7 yards plus and minus a 1.5-yard point adjustment factor). This example introduces the following concepts:

- The **precision** (or **allowance for sampling risk**) is the numeric distance from the estimated population value in which the true (but unknown) population value may lie with a given probability. In this case, the precision is 1.5 yards.
- The **reliability** (or **confidence level**) is the likelihood of achieving a given level of precision. In the example, the reliability is 90 percent, which is equal to 100 percent minus the acceptable sampling risk of 10 percent.
- The **precision interval** is a range around the sample estimate that has a certain likelihood (equal to reliability) of including the true population value. In this example, the precision interval is 5.2 to 8.2 yards.

Note that, for any given level of reliability, a unique level of precision exists (in this case, 1.5 yards). If the engagement team desires a higher level of confidence regarding the closeness of a sample estimate to the true population value (say 95 percent), the precision interval is wider (say the sample estimate, ± 3 yards). That is, the wider the range, the more confident one can be that a number falls within a range. Stated another way, each level of precision is associated with a given level of confidence.

What is the overall conclusion? Because the likelihood is 90 percent that the true population's average increase in distance is between 5.2 and 8.2 yards, the engagement team can reliably conclude that the average increase in distance is more than five yards. Therefore, it appears that Wilson's golf ball can be hit a longer distance than its competitors' balls. What is the chance that this conclusion is incorrect? It is less than 10 percent. Because this is less than the acceptable level of sampling risk, it is safe to conclude that Wilson does have a longer distance golf ball as evidenced by an increase of five yards. See Exhibit E.2 for the relationship between this precision interval and the five-yard criterion.

On the other hand, would the engagement team's conclusion change if, for the same confidence level, the precision were determined to be three yards? In this case, the precision interval would be 3.7 yards to 9.7 yards (sample average of 6.7 yards ± 3 yards). As in Exhibit E.2, the results are a bit less certain because the lower level of the precision interval is below the criterion distance of five yards. In this case, statistical theory could be

EXHIBIT E.2
Precision Intervals for Two Hypothetical Sample Results

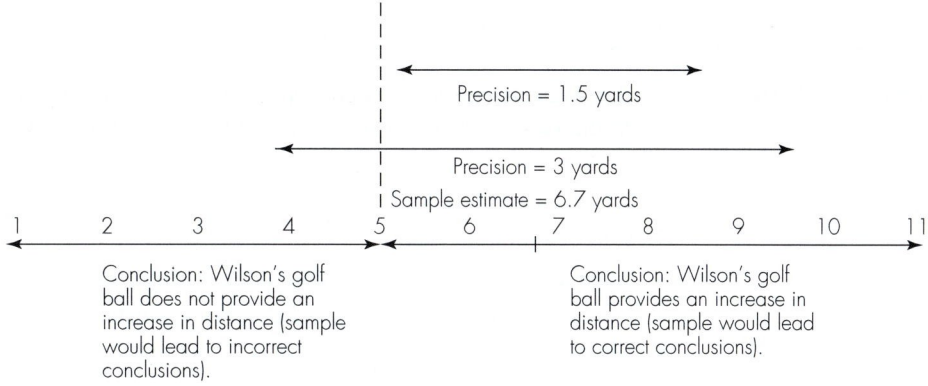

used to determine the precise probability that the true population's average was below five yards and compare that to the acceptable level of sampling risk of 10 percent. However, the evidence in this latter case is clearly less convincing than that for a precision of 1.5 yards.

In discussing the concept of precision, it is important to note that the terminology can be a bit misleading. Although the precision of 3.0 yards is higher than that of 1.5 yards, the latter is often referred to as being a *more precise* estimate because the precision interval is more closely centered on the sample estimate. In some instances, a more precise estimate is referred to as being characterized by *a higher level of precision*.

Documenting the Sampling Procedure

For each of the seven major steps in the sampling process, important judgments and conclusions must be properly documented. Proper documentation for audit samples could be a focal point of supervisory or quality reviews. Some important information that would be documented in the Wilson example follows:

- *The objective of the sampling application, characteristic of interest, and definition of the population* (steps 1–3).
- *The factors affecting sample size (along with the method or rationale for those factors) and determination of sample size;* in this case, the engagement team would document the acceptable level of sampling risk of 10 percent, the rationale for this level of sampling risk, and the determination of the sample size of 50 items (step 4).
- *The method of selecting the sample and description of items selected for examination.* If systematic selection is used, the engagement team would document the random starting point, the sampling interval of 20 items, and the list of the items selected (step 5).
- *The method of measuring sample items and summary of measurements.* In this case, the engagement team would document that golfers hit a series of shots with Wilson's golf ball and competitors' golf balls and the distances of each. In addition, the engagement team would document that the overall increase in distance using Wilson's golf ball is 6.7 yards (step 6).
- *The evaluation of sample results and overall conclusion with respect to the sample.* In this case, the engagement team would document the precision, reliability, and overall conclusions with respect to the sample (step 7).

↳ REVIEW CHECKPOINTS

E.12 Define the terms *precision* (allowance for sampling risk), *reliability* (confidence), and *precision interval*.

E.13 Describe the basic procedure used to evaluate sample results.

USE OF SAMPLING IN THE AUDIT

LEARNING OBJECTIVE E-3
Identify the two situations in which sampling is used in an audit.

We have discussed some key concepts related to sampling and provided an example of how sampling can be used in a nonaudit setting. Our discussion has focused on the following questions:

- What is sampling?
- Why is sampling used?
- What are the different risks associated with the use of sampling?
- How does statistical sampling differ from nonstatistical sampling?
- What are the major steps involved with sampling?

Now we consider the use of sampling in the audit examination. The AICPA Audit Guide defines **audit sampling** as the "application of an audit procedure to less than 100 percent of the items within an account balance or class of transactions for the purpose of evaluating some characteristic of the balance or class."[8] Sampling is recognized in the scope paragraph of a standard auditors' opinion that says, "An audit includes examining, on a *test basis*, evidence supporting amounts and disclosures in the financial statements" (emphasis added). As we have previously mentioned, auditors use sampling in one of two situations during their examination: (1) studying and evaluating the client's internal control and (2) performing substantive procedures on account balances and classes of transactions.

The following three conditions must be met for an application to be classified as *audit sampling*:

1. Less than 100 percent of the items composing the population must be examined.
2. The results of the sample must be projected to the population being examined.
3. The projected results must be compared to some existing criterion.

With respect to the study and evaluation of the client's internal control, the audit team's objective is to determine whether important control policies and procedures are functioning effectively to prevent or detect financial statement misstatements. In making this evaluation, the audit team is interested in determining whether the rate at which internal control activities are not functioning (referred to as the **rate of deviation**) exceeds some rate permissible by the audit team (referred to as the *tolerable rate of deviation*). The use of sampling in this context is referred to as *attributes sampling*.[9]

When used in substantive procedures, the audit team's objective is to determine whether an account balance or class of transactions is recorded and presented according to generally accepted accounting principles. In making this evaluation, the audit team is interested in determining whether the amount of dollar misstatement in the account balance or class of transactions exceeds some permissible amount (referred to as **tolerable misstatement**). The end result of the audit team's substantive procedures is the determination as to whether the client's account balances are fairly stated according to generally accepted accounting principles. The use of sampling in this context is referred to as *variables sampling*.

Refer to Exhibit E.3 for a summary of the objectives, sampling units, and evaluations made by the audit team in these two situations.

Attributes Sampling

Attributes sampling is used when the audit team examines a subset of items within a population to determine the extent to which a particular attribute exists within that population. To understand why the audit team uses attributes sampling, recall how the *audit risk model* is used in the audit examination. **Audit risk** is the likelihood that auditors will unknowingly fail to modify their opinion on financial statements that are materially

---

[8] "Audit Sampling," *AICPA Audit Guide,* May 1, 2008, p. 133.

[9] Attributes sampling may be used in rare occasions for tests not related to internal controls. For example, auditors of insurance companies might use attributes sampling to test whether contracts are prepared in a prescribed format.

EXHIBIT E.3 Use of Sampling during the Audit Examination

Audit Application	Objective	Sampling Unit	Evaluation
Study and evaluation of internal control (attributes sampling)	Determine whether internal control policies and procedures are functioning in preventing or detecting misstatements	Instances in which control policies or procedures should have been applied	Compare rate of deviation to tolerable rate of deviation
Substantive procedures (variables sampling)	Determine whether account balance or class of transactions is fairly recorded and presented	Transactions or components of account balances or classes of transactions	Compare misstatement to tolerable misstatement

misstated. That is, audit risk represents the likelihood that the audit team will issue an unqualified opinion on financial statements that are materially misstated.

The audit risk model that was introduced earlier in the text follows:[10]

$$AR = RMM \times DR$$

where

- AR = Audit risk (the likelihood that a material misstatement occurs, is not detected by the client's internal control, and is not detected by the audit team's substantive procedures)
- RMM = Risk of material misstatement (IR × CR)
- IR = Inherent risk (the likelihood that an account balance or class of transactions contains a material misstatement in the absence of internal control)
- CR = Control risk (the likelihood that the client's internal control policies and procedures fail to prevent or detect a material misstatement)
- DR = Detection risk (the likelihood that the audit team's substantive procedures fail to detect a material misstatement)

The audit team uses *attributes sampling* in assessing control risk. Recall that auditors study and evaluate the client's internal control to determine the extent to which they can rely on specific internal control policies and procedures to prevent and detect misstatements. Based on the design and operating effectiveness of these policies and procedures, auditors decide on the extent to which they can rely on the client's internal control. This degree of reliance, in turn, influences the nature, timing, and extent of the auditors' substantive procedures.

How do auditors decide whether they can rely on internal control policies and procedures? In the planning stages of the audit, auditors assess control risk at a planned level; they then perform tests of controls to determine whether the controls are functioning (that is, the controls have been implemented and are performed by client employees) consistent with the planned level of control risk. The general procedure used by the audit team to assess control risk is summarized here:

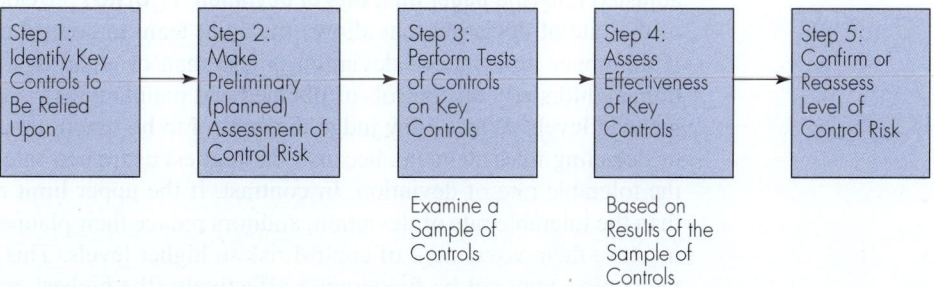

---

[10] AU 200 expresses the product of inherent risk and control risk as the *risk of material misstatement*. This standard notes that auditors may choose to make a combined assessment of the risk of material misstatement or separate assessments of inherent risk and control risk.

Attributes sampling is used in the third (perform tests of controls on key controls) and fourth (assess effectiveness of key controls) steps illustrated. Based on the results of these tests of controls, auditors evaluate their preliminary assessment of control risk and, ultimately, determine the *nature, timing,* and *extent* of substantive procedures. The following summarizes the audit team's study and evaluation of internal control (and possible decisions based on this study and evaluation):

- If the controls are operating at the planned level of effectiveness, auditors can support the reliance on internal control and maintain their assessment of control risk and detection risk at planned levels.
- If controls are not operating at the planned level of effectiveness, auditors should reduce the planned reliance on internal control and increase their assessment of control risk, which would result in performing substantive procedures for lower levels of detection risk (more effective substantive procedures).

Thus, attributes sampling provides the audit team an indication of the operating effectiveness of the client's internal control. This indication allows the audit team to determine the appropriate level of control risk that, with previous assessments of audit risk and inherent risk, allows the audit team to determine the necessary level of detection risk. The necessary level of detection risk determines the nature, timing, and extent of the audit team's substantive procedures.

Sampling Risks Associated with Attributes Sampling

Recall that *sampling risk* is the likelihood that the decision made based on the sample differs from the decision that would have been made if the entire population had been examined. Also recall that sampling risk is the result of the possibility of selecting a nonrepresentative sample (one that does not appropriately represent the population of interest).

In attributes sampling, the audit team's ultimate objective is to assess control risk. In so doing, the audit team attempts to determine the extent to which the client's controls are functioning effectively in preventing or detecting misstatements (i.e., operating effectiveness). For a variety of reasons, it is neither practical nor realistic for the audit team to require controls to be functioning 100 percent of the time in order to be able to rely on them. When evaluating the effectiveness of the client's controls, auditors typically think in terms of the *maximum rate of deviation* that could exist before they would reduce reliance on that control **(tolerable rate of deviation**, or **TRD**).

To illustrate, assume that the audit team decides that a control should function at least 96 percent of the time to be considered effective (we illustrate how this percentage is determined in a subsequent module). Stated another way, the audit team is willing to accept that the control does not function 4 percent of the time (100 percent–96 percent). This 4 percent represents the tolerable rate of deviation.

Although auditors never know the true population rate of deviation with any certainty, they can use sampling tables to "adjust" the *sample rate of deviation* to one that has a certain probability of equaling or exceeding the true rate of deviation. Simply stated, this adjusted rate (the **upper limit rate of deviation**, or **ULRD**) provides a conservative estimate of the rate of deviation that allows the audit team to control exposure to sampling risk. If the upper limit rate of deviation is less than or equal to the tolerable rate of deviation, auditors rely on controls as planned and maintain their assessment of control risk at planned levels. Why? They judge the control to be functioning effectively in preventing or detecting misstatements because the highest estimated rate of deviations is less than the tolerable rate of deviation. In contrast, if the upper limit rate of deviation is higher than the tolerable rate of deviation, auditors reduce their planned reliance on controls and increase their assessment of control risk to higher levels. This decision is made because the control may not be functioning effectively (the highest estimated rate of deviations exceeds the tolerable rate of deviation).

Once a tolerable rate of deviation has been established and upper limit rate of deviation has been computed, auditors compare the rates. The decision made by the audit team is as follows:

Because sampling is being used to evaluate the operating effectiveness of controls, the audit team is exposed to sampling risk. Consider the following matrix. The two columns represent the two possible outcomes if the entire population were examined; the two rows represent the two possible decisions that auditors could make based on their sample of controls (ARD = actual rate of deviation, TRD = tolerable rate of deviation, ULRD = upper limit rate of deviation). Auditors calculate upper limit rate of deviation by adjusting the rate of deviation in their sample for sampling error to determine the highest possible rate of deviation for a given confidence level.

	Decision Based on True State of the Population	
	ARD ≤ TRD (rely on internal control as planned)	ARD > TRD (reduce planned reliance on internal control)
Decision Based on Examining Sample — ULRD ≤ TRD (rely on internal control as planned)	A: Correct decision	B: Risk of overreliance (risk of assessing control risk too low)
ULRD > TRD (reduce planned reliance on internal control)	C: Risk of underreliance (risk of assessing control risk too high)	D: Correct decision

Cells A and D do not expose the audit team to sampling risk because the decision to rely on the client's controls as planned (cell A) or to reduce the planned reliance on the client's controls (cell D) is consistent with the decision the audit team would have made had the entire population been examined.

Examine the outcome of cell C. In this instance, the auditors' sample of controls indicates that the rate of deviation exceeds the tolerable rate of deviation; as a result, they would choose to reduce the reliance on internal control and assess control risk at higher levels. However, unknown to the auditors, the rate of deviation in the population is actually lower than the tolerable rate of deviation. This situation is referred to as the **risk of underreliance** (or the **risk of assessing control risk too high**). In this instance, the auditors' sample results in the decision to reduce their reliance on internal control (i.e., *under rely on internal control*), which results in higher assessments of control risk.

In contrast, cell B represents a situation in which the auditors choose to maintain their reliance on internal control because the upper limit rate of deviation is less than or equal to the tolerable rate of deviation. However, in the population, the actual rate of deviation exceeds the tolerable rate of deviation. As a result, the auditors inappropriately rely on internal control and maintain the assessment of control risk at lower levels. This is referred to as the **risk of overreliance** (or the **risk of assessing control risk too low**). In this instance, the sample results in the auditors' decision to rely on internal control as planned (i.e., *overrely on internal control*), which results in lower assessments of control risk.

Which of these risks is of more concern to the auditor? If control risk is assessed at unnecessarily high levels (the risk of underreliance), the resulting detection risk is lower than is necessary to reduce audit risk to acceptable levels. As a result, the nature, timing, and extent of the audit team's substantive procedures is more effective than necessary. Ultimately, the overall level of audit risk that the auditors achieve is lower than necessary. Thus, assessing control risk too high causes an *efficiency loss* for the audit team because more extensive substantive procedures are performed than necessary to reduce overall audit risk to acceptable levels.

If control risk is assessed too low, the resulting detection risk is higher than appropriate in the circumstances. When this occurs, the auditors' substantive procedures do not reduce the overall audit risk to an acceptable level. This happens because the auditors believe that internal control is more effective in preventing or detecting misstatements than is the case. The ultimate result of failing to reduce audit risk to an acceptable level is issuing an unqualified opinion on financial statements that are materially misstated, resulting in a reputation loss or litigation by shareholders and other third parties relying on the auditors' work. Therefore, assessing control risk too low exposes the auditors to an *effectiveness loss*.

Given a choice of the two sampling risks, the risk of overreliance clearly is of more concern to auditors than the risk of underreliance. As a result, auditors explicitly control their exposure to this risk to acceptable levels when (1) determining the necessary sample size and (2) evaluating sample results.

↳ REVIEW CHECKPOINTS

E.14 Define *attributes sampling.* When is it used in the audit examination?

E.15 What is the *tolerable rate of deviation?* How does the audit team use it when deciding whether to rely on internal control?

E.16 What are the two sampling risks associated with attributes sampling? What types of losses are associated with each of these risks?

E.17 Why is the audit team more concerned with the risk of overreliance than with the risk of underreliance?

Variables Sampling

Variables sampling is used to examine a population when auditors want to estimate the amount (or value) of some characteristic of that population. Auditors use variables sampling when performing substantive procedures to evaluate the fairness of an account balance or class of transactions. Following the assessment of control risk, auditors use the audit risk model to determine the necessary level of detection risk for assertions related to account balances or classes of transactions. **Detection risk** is the risk that the auditors' substantive procedures (both tests of details and analytical procedures) fail to detect a material misstatement that exists within an account balance or class of transactions.

The auditors' detection risk is embodied in the *nature, timing,* and *extent of substantive procedures.* Of these characteristics, the *extent* of substantive procedures (i.e., number of transactions or components examined) is most closely associated with the use of variables sampling. Auditors increase the sample size in response to lower planned levels of detection risk and decrease sample size in response to higher planned levels of detection risk.

When performing variables sampling, auditors select items for examination and evaluate the correct amount at which the item should be recorded, which is referred to as the **audited value** or **audited balance**. Depending on the method of variables sampling used, auditors use the evidence from the sample items to estimate either the (1) audited value of the account or (2) the amount of misstatement in the account (Audited value–Recorded amount).

Auditors can use one of two statistical sampling approaches with variables sampling. **Classical variables sampling** uses the laws of probability and the central limit theorem to estimate either the amount of misstatement in the account balance or class of transactions or the audited value. These procedures provide the auditors a range of estimates that has a specific probability of including the true amount of misstatement or the true account balance.

The second statistical sampling approach that auditors can use is **monetary unit sampling (MUS)**. MUS provides auditors an estimate of the amount of misstatement in the account balance or class of transactions. The distinguishing feature of MUS is that it tends to select larger transactions (or components) within an account balance for examination.

In addition to these statistical sampling approaches to variables sampling, auditors can and, in practice, frequently do use nonstatistical sampling methods. As noted earlier in this module, the advantage of nonstatistical sampling methods is that they are normally less complex and costly to use. A disadvantage of these methods is that they do not permit the audit team to control the exposure to sampling risk.

Because the purpose of this module is to introduce the basic concepts of sampling, a more detailed discussion of both classical variables sampling and monetary unit sampling is beyond the scope of this module. These sampling methods are discussed in more detail in Module G.

Sampling Risks Associated with Variables Sampling

When performing substantive procedures, auditors evaluate the fairness of the account balance or class of transactions by estimating the difference between the recorded account balance and the audited account balance; this difference is referred to as the **sample estimate of misstatement**, which is then adjusted to control for sampling risk and (much like the sample rate of deviation discussed in the preceding section) compared to an amount of misstatement that auditors are willing to allow in the account without concluding that it is materially misstated. This amount is based on *performance materiality* and other audit procedures and is known as tolerable misstatement. Auditors set the level of tolerable misstatement based on the magnitude of the account balance or class of transactions in relation to important financial statement subtotals such as total assets, total revenues, or net income.

If the **upper limit of misstatement (ULM)**, which adds *precision* to the sample estimate of misstatement, is less than or equal to the tolerable misstatement, auditors conclude that the account balance is fairly stated. Although auditors do not propose an adjustment to the account balance for these projected misstatements, the client should correct all misstatements discovered (unless clearly inconsequential). In contrast, if the ULM exceeds the tolerable misstatement, auditors conclude that the account balance is materially misstated and propose an adjustment to the account balance.

As they do in attributes sampling, auditors compare the adjusted sample estimate of the misstatement to the tolerable misstatement. The decision made by auditors is as follows:

Auditors may be exposed to sampling risk if the sample of components or transactions of the account balance is not representative of the population in terms of the extent to which they are misstated. Consider the following matrix. The two columns represent the

---

*Similar to attributes sampling, auditors cannot simply compare the sample estimate of misstatement to the tolerable misstatement. Instead, the sample estimate of misstatement must be adjusted in a conservative direction (upward) to reflect potential sampling risks. This upward adjustment is discussed and illustrated in more detail in Module G.

two possible outcomes if the entire population were examined; the two rows represent the two possible decisions auditors could make based on the sample of transactions or components of the account balance (AM = actual misstatement, TM = tolerable misstatement, ULM = upper limit on misstatement).

		Decision Based on True State of the Population	
		AM ≤ TM (conclude account is fairly stated)	AM > TM (conclude account is misstated)
Decision Based on Examining Sample	ULM ≤ TM (conclude account is fairly stated)	A: Correct decision	B: Risk of incorrect acceptance
	ULM > TM (conclude account is misstated)	C: Risk of incorrect rejection	D: Correct decision

Cells A and D do not represent sampling risk because the decision to conclude either that the account balance is fairly stated (cell A) or that the account balance is misstated (cell D) is consistent with the decision auditors would have made had the entire population been examined.

Examine the outcome of cell C. In this instance, the sample of transactions and components indicates that the misstatement might exceed the tolerable misstatement. As a result, auditors would conclude that the account is misstated. However, the amount of misstatement in the population is actually less than the tolerable misstatement, suggesting that the account balance is fairly stated. This is referred to as the **risk of incorrect rejection** because auditors' initial judgment is to *incorrectly reject* the account balance as fairly stated.

In contrast, cell B represents a situation in which auditors conclude that the account balance is fairly stated (because the upper limit on misstatement is less than or equal to the tolerable misstatement); however, in the population, the actual misstatement exceeds the tolerable misstatement. As a result, auditors inappropriately conclude that the account balance is fairly stated. This is referred to as the **risk of incorrect acceptance** because the auditors' judgment is to *incorrectly accept* the account balance.

Which of these risks is of more concern to auditors? If the auditors commit incorrect rejection and initially conclude that the account balance is misstated, the client typically requests that the auditors expand the sample size or gather additional evidence before making an adjustment to the financial statements. As this occurs and as the sample becomes more representative of the population, the auditors ultimately reach the correct conclusion. What is the cost to them? They were required to perform additional substantive procedures beyond those performed to control detection risk to acceptable levels. Thus, the incorrect rejection causes an *efficiency loss* for the auditors.

If the auditors commit the incorrect acceptance and conclude that the account is not misstated, they most likely do not perform additional procedures or examine additional items related to that account balance or class of transactions. As a result, the auditors conclude that the account balance is fairly stated when, in fact, it is materially misstated. This is the basic definition of *detection risk*. The ultimate result of failing to propose an adjustment to materially misstated financial statements is issuing an unqualified opinion on financial statements that are materially misstated, resulting in a reputation loss or litigation by shareholders and other third parties relying on the auditors' work. This results in an *effectiveness loss* for the auditors because they made an incorrect conclusion with respect to the client's account balance.

This discussion should make clear that the risk of incorrect acceptance is of more concern to auditors than the risk of incorrect rejection. As with the risk of overreliance in attributes

EXHIBIT E.4 Sampling Risks When Using Sampling in the Audit Examination

Type of Sampling	Risk	Type of Loss
Attribute	Risk of overreliance (assessing control risk too low)	Effectiveness (auditors could face litigation if misstatements are not detected)
	Risk of underreliance (assessing control risk too high)	Efficiency (auditors perform unnecessary procedures)
Variables	Risk of incorrect acceptance	Effectiveness (auditors could face litigation if misstatements are not detected)
	Risk of incorrect rejection	Efficiency (auditors perform unnecessary procedures)

sampling, auditors explicitly control their exposure to the risk of incorrect acceptance when determining the necessary sample size and when evaluating sample results.

Summary: Sampling Risks for Audit Sampling

Exhibit E.4 summarizes the sampling risks associated with attribute and variables sampling. Note that both types of sampling have risks that expose auditors to effectiveness and efficiency losses. Although any form of sampling risk is not desirable, auditors are particularly concerned with sampling risks that expose them to effectiveness losses.

> ### ↳ REVIEW CHECKPOINTS
>
> E.18 Define *variables sampling*. When is it used in the audit examination?
>
> E.19 What is *tolerable misstatement*? How do auditors use it when deciding whether account balances are fairly recorded?
>
> E.20 What are the two sampling risks associated with variables sampling? What types of losses are associated with these risks?
>
> E.21 Why are auditors more concerned with the risk of incorrect acceptance than the risk of incorrect rejection?

▽ AN OVERVIEW OF AUDIT SAMPLING

LEARNING OBJECTIVE E-4
Understand how the basic steps and procedures used in a sampling plan apply to an audit.

Earlier, we identified the following seven-step procedure used in any sampling application:

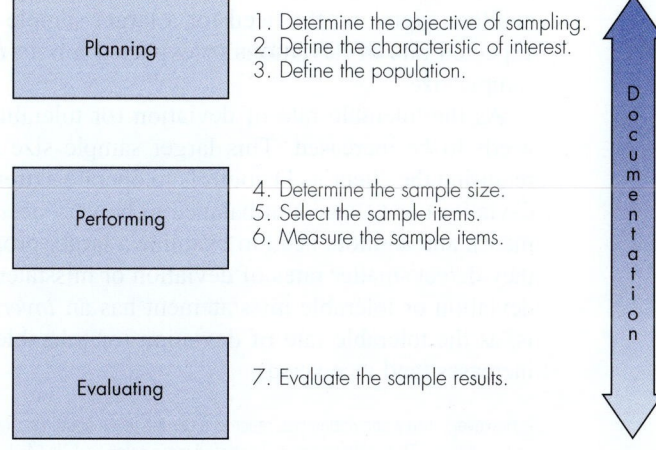

This subsection provides a brief overview of how this seven-step procedure is applied to sampling in an audit setting. Modules F and G apply this procedure using a comprehensive example for attributes and variables sampling, respectively.

Planning

In the planning stages, auditors determine the objective of the sampling application and define the characteristic of interest and the population. For attributes sampling, the objective is usually to assess the operating effectiveness of a key control, the characteristic of interest is the extent to which the control is functioning effectively, and the population includes all possible applications of the control by client personnel. In a variables sampling application, the objective is to determine an estimate of the extent of misstatement in an account balance or class of transactions, the characteristic of interest is the extent of misstatement in the account balance or class of transactions, and the population includes all components or transactions composing the account balance or class of transactions. Auditors often perform **dual-purpose tests** by examining documents for both attributes and monetary misstatements. For example, an invoice might be examined for the attribute of a credit authorization signature (control test) and the monetary misstatement of an incorrect price (substantive test).

Performing

Determine the Sample Size

In either type of sampling application, four key factors affect the auditors' determination of sample size: (1) the population size, (2) the expected rate of deviation (or expected misstatement), (3) the tolerable rate of deviation (or tolerable misstatement), and (4) the auditors' acceptable exposure to sampling risk. In addition, for certain types of variables sampling applications, the population variability also affects the sample size. The effect of these factors on sample size is summarized in Exhibit E.5. At this point, you should attempt to *conceptually* understand how these factors affect sample size and not become overly concerned with how the auditors assess them. The method of assessing these factors is discussed in more detail in Modules F and G.

As the size of the population increases, a larger sample is typically necessary to support conclusions based on that population. This relationship is fairly logical; a sample of 50 items drawn from a population of 100 items is more likely to be representative than the same sample of 50 drawn from a population of 100,000 items. Therefore, we can state that population size has a *direct relationship* with sample size. That is, as the population size increases, the sample size increases (and vice versa).[11]

As the expected rate of deviation or expected misstatement increases, the sample needs to be larger. Again, this relationship seems logical because higher rates of deviation (or higher levels of dollar misstatement) represent potential problems to the auditors, signaling the need for a larger sample size. As a result, like population size, expected rate of deviations or expected misstatements have a *direct relationship* with sample size.

As the tolerable rate of deviation (or tolerable misstatement) decreases, the sample needs to be increased. This larger sample size results from the fact that auditors are requiring the client's (1) controls to operate extremely effectively (small tolerable rate of deviation) or (2) account balance to be very accurately stated (small tolerable misstatement), and auditors need to examine a larger proportion of the population to ensure that they detect smaller rates of deviation or misstatements. In this case, the tolerable rate of deviation or tolerable misstatement has an *inverse relationship* with sample size. That is, as the tolerable rate of deviation (or tolerable misstatement) decreases, sample size increases (and vice versa).

---

[11] However, once a population size reaches a certain level, additional increases in population size do not have significant effects on sample size. This relationship is illustrated more completely in Module F.

EXHIBIT E.5
Factors Affecting Sample Size

Factor	Effect on Sample Size
Population size	*Direct* (as population size increases, sample size increases)
Expected rate of deviation (expected misstatement)	*Direct* (as expected rate of deviation or expected misstatement increases, sample size increases)
Tolerable rate of deviation (tolerable misstatement)	*Inverse* (as tolerable rate of deviation or tolerable misstatement decreases, sample size increases)
Sampling risk	*Inverse* (as acceptable sampling risk decreases, sample size increases)
Population variability	*Direct* (as variability increases, sample size increases)

Sampling risk represents the likelihood that the auditors' decision based on the sample differs from the decision that would be made based on the population. Recall that sampling risk results from a nonrepresentative sample. To increase the representativeness of the sample and reduce sampling risk, the audit team should increase the size of the sample (e.g., a sample of 100 percent would provide a zero sampling risk). Therefore, like the tolerable rate of deviation (or tolerable misstatement), sampling risk has an *inverse relationship* with sample size.

The variability of a population reflects differences between the value of individual items within the population and the mean of those items. Population variability is often measured as the **standard deviation** (or **standard error of the mean**). Clearly, as the components of a population differ more (i.e., have a higher level of variability), the audit team needs to examine a larger number of items to obtain a representative sample. As a result, population variability has a *direct relationship* with sample size. Because values in an attributes sampling application possess only one of two values (i.e., the control was present or it was not), population variability is considered by estimating the *expected rate of deviation* in the population.

Exhibit E.5 summarizes how the factors just discussed are related to sample size. The method of determining these factors, as well as calculations of sample size using these factors, are presented in subsequent modules.

Select Sample Items

Once the sample size has been determined, the auditors select the sample. The items selected are either potential applications of important controls (attributes sampling) or components or transactions of an account balance or class of transactions (variables sampling). If *unrestricted random selection* is used, auditors use a list of random numbers either drawn from a random number table or generated from a computer program and then select items in the population corresponding to those random numbers. With *systematic random selection*, auditors select one or more random starting points from within the population and select every *n*th item thereafter until the appropriate number of items has been selected. Both unrestricted random selection and systematic random selection are appropriate to use with statistical sampling because all items in the population have an equal probability of selection and these methods allow another individual to replicate the sample selection process.

In contrast, *block selection* and *haphazard selection* do not provide auditors a method of identifying the likelihood that a specific item will be selected for examination. In addition, these methods do not permit another individual to replicate the sample based on stated criteria. As a result, they are not used with statistical sampling.

Measure Sample Items

After the sample items have been selected, auditors perform the appropriate audit procedures and measure each item. For attributes sampling, auditors perform tests of controls to evaluate whether client personnel have performed the control policy of interest. For variables sampling, auditors perform substantive procedures to determine the correct amount (audited balance) of each component or transaction selected for examination.

Evaluating

The final step in either attributes or variables sampling is to evaluate the sample results that involves the following four-step procedure:

1. Identify either the rate of deviation (attributes sampling) or difference between audited values and recorded values (variables sampling) from the sample items.
2. Adjust the information in step 1 to control the auditors' exposure to sampling risk. This adjustment is referred to as the *allowance for sampling risk*.
3. Compare the adjusted estimate in step 2 to either the tolerable rate of deviation (attributes sampling) or the tolerable misstatement (variables sampling).
4. Based on the comparison in step 3, make the decision with regard to the effectiveness of the client's internal control (attributes sampling) or fairness of the account balance (variables sampling).

Documenting the Sampling Procedure

As they perform the procedures in each of these steps, auditors should document important judgments, assumptions, and conclusions because this documentation will provide evidence of conclusions with respect to the operating effectiveness of the client's internal control and the fairness of the client's account balances. Documentation should be sufficient to enable another audit team to replicate the tests and for a reviewer to evaluate the results.

↳ REVIEW CHECKPOINTS

E.22 What are the objectives of attributes and variables sampling?

E.23 What factors affect the sample size used in an attributes sampling application? How do these factors affect sample size?

E.24 What factors affect the sample size used in a variables sampling application? How do these factors affect sample size?

Summary

This module introduces the sampling process and discusses how sampling is used in an audit. One of the major disadvantages of sampling is that the decision made based on the sample could differ from the decision that would have been made after examining the entire population. This disadvantage (referred to as *sampling risk*) can be overcome to some extent through the use of statistical sampling methods. Statistical sampling methods control the individual's exposure to sampling risk by selecting a sufficient sample size and evaluating sample results in such a way to control sampling risk.

Using sampling in practice often presents auditors problems. The accompanying Auditing Insight presents some deficiencies noted by the PCAOB in its inspections of large auditing firms. In these excerpts, "the Firm" represents one of these firms.

Two major approaches to sampling used in an audit examination are *attributes sampling* (in the study and evaluation of internal control) and *variables sampling* (in the auditors' substantive procedures). This module discussed the risks associated with these sampling approaches and the various factors that influence the sample size. Attributes sampling and variables sampling are discussed in more detail in Modules F and G, respectively.

AUDITING INSIGHT | PCAOB Inspections and Sampling

- . . . many of the samples the Firm used in its substantive tests of the valuation of various types of Level 3 financial instruments were insufficient (sometimes a sample of only one item) in light of the significance and complexity of the instruments and the heightened risk the Firm identified with respect to their valuation.
- . . . the Firm's testing of the controls over the assignment and monitoring of loan grades was insufficient, as the Firm failed to assess the competence of the individuals performing the control on which it relied. Further, because it selected a sample of which a majority of the items had not been subject to the control, it tested only a relatively small number of items when testing the control.
- For accounts receivable, the Firm sent confirmation requests to customers for a sample of unpaid invoices; however, the Firm's sample size was insufficient to achieve the necessary level of assurance. Although the Firm assessed the control risk relating to the existence of accounts receivable as moderate, the Firm determined the sample size for confirmations of accounts receivable using a formula that assumed a lower level of risk. Additionally, the Firm's sample size was influenced by an expectation that analytical procedures would provide additional audit evidence, but those analytical procedures were inadequate as substantive tests because the Firm's expectations were not sufficiently precise to provide the necessary degree of assurance.
- . . . the Firm did not obtain supporting documentation for nearly half of the journal entries that it had selected for testing, primarily because the Firm understood that the issuer did not retain such documentation. The Firm performed no alternate procedures for these entries beyond making inquiries of management. Further, there was no evidence in the audit documentation, and no persuasive other evidence, that the Firm had tested the completeness and accuracy of the population of journal entries from which the sample was selected for testing. Also, there was no evidence in the audit documentation, and no persuasive other evidence, that the Firm had identified that a number of the journal entries that it had selected for testing contained individually significant
- In applying loan review procedures to a sample of the issuer's non-homogenous loans, the Firm failed to determine its sample size based on relevant risks, and the sample of loans selected was not representative of the population because the selection was made from only "higher balance" loans. As a result, the audit procedures were not effectively designed to achieve the objectives of evaluating whether the issuer had identified the loans that should be considered to be classified loans.

Sources: 2008 PCAOB Inspection of BDO Seidman (July 9, 2009); 2009 PCAOB Inspection of Ernst & Young (July 2, 2010); 2009 Inspection of KPMG LLP (October 5, 2010); and Inspection of McGladrey & Pullen, LLP (May 6, 2009). All reports can be found on the PCAOB website.

Key Terms

allowance for sampling risk (precision): The numeric distance from the estimated population value in which the true (but unknown) population value may lie with a given probability; used to adjust the sample estimate to control exposure to sampling risk, 724

attributes sampling: A form of selection used to determine the extent to which some characteristic (attribute) occurs within a population of interest; used by auditors during tests of controls, 726

audit risk: The likelihood that auditors will unknowingly fail to modify their opinion on financial statements that are materially misstated, 726

audit sampling: The application of an audit procedure to less than 100 percent of the items within an account balance or class of transactions for the purpose of evaluating some characteristic of the balance or class, 726

audited balance: See *audited value*, 730

audited value (audited balance): The amount at which an account balance or component should be recorded, assuming no departures from the appropriate reporting framework (i.e., GAAP or IFRS), 730

block selection: A method of choosing sample items in which a series of contiguous (or adjacent) items is chosen from the population, 722

classical variables sampling: An approach that uses the laws of probability and the central limit theorem to provide an estimate of either the amount of misstatement or the true balance of an account balance or class of transactions, 731

confidence level: See *reliability*, 724

detection risk: The likelihood that the auditors' substantive procedures will fail to detect a material misstatement that exists within an account balance or class of transactions, 730

dual-purpose test: An audit procedure used as both a test of controls and a substantive test, 734
haphazard selection: A method of selecting sample items in an unstructured manner but without any intentional bias, 722
monetary unit sampling (MUS): An approach that provides auditors an estimate of the amount of misstatement in the account balance or class of transactions; tends to select higher value transactions (or components) within an account balance for examination, 731
nonrepresentative sample: An example that differs substantially from the population on one or more key characteristics of interest from which it is drawn, 717
nonsampling risk: The likelihood that an incorrect conclusion will be reached because of reasons unrelated to sampling, 718
nonstatistical sampling: A plan that does not apply the laws of probability to choose representative items for examination and evaluate the results; does not allow an individual to control exposure to sampling risk, 719
population: The entire group of items about which a conclusion is desired in a sampling application, 715
precision: See *allowance for sampling risk,* 724
precision interval: A range around the sample estimate that has a certain likelihood (equal to reliability) of including the true population value, 724
random selection: Method of choosing sample items so that every combination of some number of items in the population has an equal probability of being chosen, 721
rate of deviation: The proportion at which internal control activities are not functioning as intended, 726
reliability (confidence level): The likelihood that the true population value lies within the precision interval, 724
risk of assessing control risk too high: See *risk of underreliance,* 729
risk of assessing control risk too low: See *risk of overreliance,* 729
risk of incorrect acceptance: The likelihood that auditors will conclude that the client's account balance is fairly stated when it is materially misstated, 732
risk of incorrect rejection: The likelihood that auditors will conclude that the client's account balance is materially misstated when it is fairly stated, 732
risk of overreliance (risk of assessing control risk too low): The likelihood that the auditors' sample will provide evidence that the client's controls are functioning effectively when they are not functioning effectively, 729
risk of underreliance (risk of assessing control risk too high): The likelihood that the auditors' sample will provide evidence that the client's controls are not functioning effectively when they are functioning effectively, 729
sample: A subset of items drawn from a population of interest, 715
sample estimate of misstatement: The difference between the recorded account balance and the audited account balance, 731
sampling: The process of making a statement about a population of interest based on examining only a subset (or sample) of that population, 715
sampling interval: In a sequential process, the frequency with which items are selected within the population; determined by dividing the number of items in the population by the necessary sample size, 721
sampling risk: The likelihood that the decision made based on the sample will differ from the decision that would have been made if the entire population had been examined, 717
standard deviation (standard error of the mean): A measure of the variability of the population, 735
standard error of the mean: See *standard deviation,* 735
statistical sampling: A plan that applies the laws of probability to select items for examination and evaluates the results; allows an individual to control the exposure to sampling risk, 719
systematic random selection (systematic selection): The method of choosing sample items in which a starting point is selected and a fixed number of items are bypassed between selections, 721
systematic selection: See *systematic random selection,* 721
tolerable misstatement: The maximum amount by which an account balance or class of transactions can be misstated and be accepted by the audit team as being fairly presented, 726
tolerable rate of deviation (TRD): The maximum proportion of variability the audit team allows without modifying the planned reliance on an internal control policy or procedure, 728
unrestricted random selection (random selection): A method of choosing items in which all items in the population are assigned a number and selected based on random numbers picked from a random number table or generated from a computer program, 721

upper limit on misstatement (ULM): The amount that has a (1–*Risk of incorrect acceptance*) probability of equaling or exceeding the true amount of misstatement in the population, 731

upper limit rate of deviation (ULRD): A measure that adjusts the chosen proportion of variability for the audit team's acceptable level of sampling risk; the proportion that has a (1–*Risk of overreliance*) probability of equaling or exceeding the true population rate of deviation, 728

variables sampling: A form of examination used to examine a population to estimate the amount or value of some characteristic of that population; used by auditors during their substantive procedures, 730

Multiple-Choice Questions for Practice and Review

 All applicable Exercises and Problems are available with McGraw-Hill's *Connect® Accounting*

LO E-4

E.25 In an audit sampling application, an auditor
 a. Performs procedures on all items in a balance and makes a conclusion about the entire balance.
 b. Performs procedures on less than 100 percent of the items in a balance and formulates a conclusion about the entire balance.
 c. Performs procedures on less than 100 percent of the items in a class of transactions to become familiar with the client's accounting system.
 d. Performs analytical procedures on the client's unaudited financial statements when planning the audit.

LO E-1

E.26 Auditors consider statistical sampling to be characterized by the following:
 a. Representative sample selection and nonmathematical consideration of the results.
 b. Carefully biased sample selection and mathematical calculation of the results.
 c. Representative sample selection and mathematical calculation of the results.
 d. Carefully biased sample selection and nonmathematical consideration of the results.

LO E-1

E.27 In which of the following scenarios would the use of sampling be most appropriate?
 a. The population consists of a relatively small number of items.
 b. The need for precise information about the population is not important.
 c. The decision to be made is relatively critical.
 d. The costs associated with an incorrect decision are extremely high.

LO E-1

E.28 The risk that the decision made based on the sample will differ from the decision made based on the entire population is referred to as
 a. Audit risk.
 b. Examination risk.
 c. Sampling risk.
 d. Nonsampling risk.

LO E-1

E.29 Which of the following is *not* a method that auditors use to control their exposure to sampling risk during the examination?
 a. Determining an appropriate sample size.
 b. Performing the appropriate audit procedure.
 c. Ensuring that all items have an equal opportunity to be selected.
 d. Evaluating sample results using a mathematical basis.

LO E-1

E.30 Which of the following is an advantage of nonstatistical sampling?
 a. It measures the audit team's exposure to sampling risk.
 b. It is required by generally accepted auditing standards.
 c. It ensures that samples are randomly selected.
 d. It is typically less complex than statistical sampling.

LO E-1

E.31 Selecting a sample using a series of random numbers to identify sample items is referred to as
 a. Block selection.
 b. Haphazard selection.
 c. Systematic random selection.
 d. Unrestricted random selection.

LO E-2 E.32 If systematic selection is used with a starting point of 10, a population size of 100, and a necessary sample size of 20, the first three items selected for examination would be
a. 10, 110, 210.
b. 110, 210, 310.
c. 10, 15, 20.
d. 15, 20, 25.

LO E-1 E.33 A limitation of systematic random selection is that this method
a. Has a relatively low likelihood of yielding a representative sample.
b. Results in a larger sample size than other selection methods.
c. Can result in bypassing a number of items having similar characteristics.
d. Cannot be used with statistical sampling plans.

LO E-1 E.34 Which of the following is appropriately used for statistical sampling applications?

	Unrestricted Random Selection	Block Selection
a.	Yes	Yes
b.	Yes	No
c.	No	Yes
d.	No	No

LO E-1 E.35 Which of the following pairs of selection methods could appropriately be used in statistical sampling applications?
a. Unrestricted random selection, block selection.
b. Block selection, haphazard selection.
c. Systematic random selection, haphazard selection.
d. Unrestricted random selection, systematic random selection.

LO E-1 E.36 The distance from the sample estimate that has a certain likelihood (equal to reliability) of including the true population value is known as the
a. Confidence.
b. Mean.
c. Precision.
d. Precision interval.

LO E-1 E.37 The likelihood that an identified precision interval contains the true (but unknown) population value is the
a. Confidence.
b. Mean.
c. Precision.
d. Sampling risk.

LO E-1 E.38 Which of the following statements is *not* true if the precision interval for a sampling risk of 10 percent ranges from 60 to 70?
a. A 10 percent probability exists that the true population value is less than 60 or more than 70.
b. A 90 percent probability exists that the true population value is less than 60 or more than 70.
c. The reliability is 90 percent.
d. The precision is 5.

LO E-2 E.39 In audit sampling applications, sampling risk is
a. A characteristic of statistical sampling applications but not of nonstatistical applications.
b. The probability that the audit team will fail to recognize erroneous accounting in the client's documentation.
c. The probability that accounting misstatements will arise in transactions and enter the accounting system.
d. The probability that an audit team's conclusion based on a sample might be different from the conclusion based on an audit of the entire population.

LO E-3   E.40 The risks of incorrect acceptance in variables sampling and of assessing control risk too low in attributes sampling both relate to
a. Effectiveness of an audit.
b. Efficiency of an audit.
c. Control risk assessment decisions.
d. Evidence about assertions in financial statements.

LO E-3   E.41 The type of sampling most frequently used by auditors during their study of internal control is referred to as
a. Attributes sampling.
b. Control sampling.
c. Monetary unit sampling.
d. Variables sampling.

LO E-3   E.42 Which of the following components of the audit risk model is most closely associated with attributes sampling?
a. Audit risk.
b. Control risk.
c. Detection risk.
d. Inherent risk.

LO E-3   E.43 The audit team will choose to reduce the reliance on controls if the _____ is greater than the _____
a. Tolerable rate of deviation; upper limit rate of deviation.
b. Upper limit rate of deviation; tolerable rate of deviation.
c. Expected rate of deviation; tolerable rate of deviation.
d. Tolerable rate of deviation; expected rate of deviation.

LO E-1   E.44 An advantage of statistical sampling over nonstatistical sampling methods is that statistical methods
a. Afford more assurance than a nonstatistical sample of equal size.
b. Provide an objective basis for quantitatively evaluating sampling risk.
c. Can more easily convert the sample into a dual-purpose test useful for substantive procedures.
d. Eliminate the need to use judgment in determining appropriate sample sizes.
(AICPA adapted)

LO E-3   E.45 When using sampling in the study of internal control, the audit team would compare a conservative estimate of the rate of deviation to the
a. Expected rate of deviation.
b. Sample rate of deviation.
c. Statistical rate of deviation.
d. Tolerable rate of deviation.

LO E-1   E.46 Which of the following would *not* result in exposure to nonsampling risk?
a. Measuring the characteristic of interest in an inappropriate manner.
b. Selecting items that are not representative of the population of interest.
c. Making an unintentional mistake in measuring the characteristic of interest.
d. All of the above would result in exposure to nonsampling risk.

LO E-1   E.47 Which of the following statements is *not* true with respect to nonstatistical sampling?
a. It cannot be used in an audit conducted in accordance with generally accepted auditing standards.
b. It considers a number of factors in determining the appropriate sample size.
c. When using it, an individual makes some estimate of the characteristic of interest.
d. It requires the use of judgment on the part of the individual performing the sampling application.

LO E-2   E.48 In a sampling application to determine the average weight of students enrolled in a fitness class, if the sample estimate is 120 pounds, the precision is 10 pounds, and the reliability is 90 percent, which of the following statements is true?
a. There is 10 percent likelihood that the average weight of a student in the class is more than 130 pounds.

b. There is 10 percent likelihood that the average weight of a student in the class is less than 110 pounds.

c. There is 90 percent likelihood that the average weight of a student in the class is less than 110 pounds or more than 130 pounds.

d. There is a 90 percent likelihood that the average weight of a student in the class is between 110 and 130 pounds.

E.49 Which of the following steps would normally be performed last in a sampling application?

a. Examine sample items and determine the sample estimate.

b. Determine the level of reliability for the sampling application.

c. Identify the objective of the sampling application.

d. Determine the appropriate sample size.

E.50 The risk of incorrect rejection and the risk of underreliance relate to the

a. Effectiveness of the audit.

b. Efficiency of the audit.

c. Preliminary estimates of performance materiality.

d. Tolerable misstatement.

(AICPA adapted)

Exercises and Problems

All applicable Exercises and Problems are available with McGraw-Hill's *Connect® Accounting*

LO E-1

E.51 **Sampling Risk.** You and a friend are deciding whether to pack heavy clothing for a trip to the northeastern United States. You have decided that you would need heavy clothing only if the temperature is expected to fall below 50 degrees during your trip. You have studied the past 50 years' seasonal temperatures in the northeast. You are considering the use of sampling to calculate an expected average temperature; you will base your decision to pack heavy clothing on the results of your sample.

Required:

a. What is *sampling risk?* What two types of sampling risks are present in this context?

b. Describe the "costs" associated with the sampling risks in (a).

c. How would your sampling plan differ if you used statistical sampling versus nonstatistical sampling?

d. What are the advantages and disadvantages of using statistical sampling methods in an attempt to answer your question?

LO E-1

E.52 **Sampling and Nonsampling Risk.** This module provided a detailed example of the use of sampling to determine whether individuals could increase their driving distance by using a Wilson golf ball.

Required:
Indicate whether each of the following situations reflects sampling risk (S), nonsampling risk (NS), both sampling risk and nonsampling risk (B), or neither sampling risk nor nonsampling risk (N).

a. Distance markers on the practice range are incorrectly placed.

b. At one course, you arrive on the day of the club championship.

c. Some of the golfers are using 3-woods, not drivers, for their shots.

d. At one course, you arrive on ladies' day, on which females have exclusive access to the course.

e. The Wilson golf balls are all new, but some of the comparison golf balls are not.

f. Your assistant makes an error in recording several driving distances.

LO E-1

E.53 **Sampling and Nonsampling Risk.** Read the following five independent sampling applications.

Required:

Indicate whether each situation is characteristic of sampling risk (S) or nonsampling risk (N). Provide a brief explanation for your answer.

a. You are estimating the average net income of passengers on a particular airline flight. You randomly select three rows of seats (a total of 18 passengers) and calculate the average income of those passengers.

b. When estimating the average time for swimmers in a 25-meter freestyle race, you inadvertently include the times of swimmers from other events (butterfly, breaststroke, and backstroke) in your sample.

c. When estimating the average time necessary to finish an examination, the class of students you randomly selected was an honors section of the course.

d. When estimating the percentage of sixth-grade students who plan to attend college, your sample includes a disproportionate number of students attending intermediate schools located in small college towns (many of the parents are affiliated with the local university).

e. When estimating the total amount of money held in savings accounts by people of various nationalities, you make some inadvertent mistakes in converting various currencies into U.S. dollars.

LO E-1

E.54 **Basic Sampling.** You are attempting to determine whether you are taller or shorter than the average of students currently enrolled in your university. You have just learned about sampling and have decided to sample students to determine the average height at your university.

Required:

a. Define *sampling*.

b. What are the advantages and disadvantages of using sampling to answer this question as opposed to examining the entire population?

c. In which situations would you be more likely to use sampling (applied to this particular example) as opposed to examining the entire population?

LO E-1, E-2

E.55 **Basic Sampling.** You are evaluating the feasibility of opening a new 10-screen movie theater in a town that has only one existing theater. To be viable, the proposed theater would need an average attendance of at least 15,000 patrons per month. The theater would show movies every day; each of the 10 screens would have a capacity of 120 patrons. An average month has the following characteristics with respect to potential patrons:

Weekdays: 21 days with a total of 20 shows per day (2 show times × 10 screens)

Weekends: 9 days with a total of 40 shows per day (4 show times × 10 screens)

Because the current theater maintains no records, you must physically visit the theater and count patrons.

Required:

a. What are some possible methods you can use to estimate the number of patrons on the evenings you visit?

b. What are some precautions that you should consider to ensure a representative sample?

c. What are two possible types of sampling risk that are present in this context? Which of these risks is of more concern to you?

d. Assume that your sampling procedure was employed to provide you 95 percent confidence. How would you react to the following independent outcomes (each sample estimate and precision represents an estimate of the number of patrons per day)?

1. Sample estimate of 600 patrons, precision of 30 patrons.
2. Sample estimate of 680 patrons, precision of 150 patrons.
3. Sample estimate of 490 patrons, precision of 35 patrons.

LO E-1

E.56 **Basic Sampling.** You are employed by Northeast Airlines and have been asked to determine the rate of on-time arrivals for competing airlines at a proposed hub location. Northeast is known for its outstanding customer service and constantly ranks in the top three among all airlines in on-time arrivals with an average rate of 82 percent of all flights. Because it would be a new entrant in this particular airport, Northeast does not believe it can compete unless its on-time arrival rate can surpass that of the airlines currently serving this hub.

Because each of the four major competitors has hundreds of flights arriving at the hub on a daily basis, you are considering the use of sampling to estimate an on-time arrival rate.

Required:

a. Define *sampling*. What are the primary advantages and primary disadvantages of using sampling in this application?

b. Briefly describe how you would identify the population of flights from which you intend to sample.

c. Define *sampling risk* and *nonsampling risk*. Provide an example of how each could be present in this situation.

d. List some characteristics of various flights that could give you increased exposure to sampling risk in this application.

e. Once you have estimated an on-time arrival rate for its competitors, what information can you provide to Northeast Airlines to assist it in its decision process?

LO E-2

E.57 **Sample Evaluation.** In the most recent local election between two candidates, you heard your local news anchor indicate that your preferred candidate had 48 percent of the vote with a margin for error (precision) of ± 6 percent. The news anchor also indicated a reliability of 99 percent for these results.

Required:

a. Define the terms *sample estimate, precision,* and *reliability.*

b. Based on the information given, what is the possible range of support that your preferred candidate could have when all votes are counted?

c. Provide a brief summary (one sentence) describing what you can determine from the anchor's report.

d. How do you feel about your candidate's chances of winning the election?

e. How would you feel about your candidate's chances of winning if the anchor's report was identical except that the margin for error was only ± 1 percent?

LO E-2

E.58 **Sample Evaluation.** For each of the following independent cases, identify the missing value(s).

	1	2	3
Precision	20	(C)	10
Sample estimate	56	80	(E)
Reliability	95%	(D)	98%
Precision interval	(A)	75 to 85	111 to 131
Sampling risk	(B)	10%	(F)

LO E-2

E.59 **Sample Evaluation.** The National Football League (NFL) is interested in determining whether the average age of its fan base is less than 35 years of age to identify this demographic for potential advertisers. Following are the results for three different stadiums for fans attending an NFL game on a given weekend. In all cases, assume a sampling risk of 5 percent.

	Sample 1	Sample 2	Sample 3
Precision	5	3	8
Sample estimate	26	34	40

Required:

a. Construct a precision interval for each of these samples.

b. Given the sampling risk of 5 percent, provide a single-sentence summary of the results to the NFL for each sample.

c. What is your basic conclusion regarding each sample?

d. If the NFL increased its acceptable level of sampling risk, how would that affect the precision interval and your conclusions? If they decreased the acceptable level of sampling risk, how would that affect the precision interval and your conclusions? Why?

LO E-2

E.60 **Sample Evaluation.** Gloria Bush has performed a sampling plan to estimate the number of children per household in her neighborhood. In doing so, she established a 10 percent acceptable level of sampling risk and found a sample estimate of 2.5 children per household. Based on the acceptable level of sampling risk, she calculated a precision of 0.7 children per household.

Required:
a. Define the terms *precision* and *reliability*. How are these terms related?
b. What is the precision interval in this example? What statement can Bush make based on her sample evidence?
c. Assume that she desires a lower sampling risk (5 percent). How will this affect the precision interval?
d. If she is interested in knowing whether the number of children per household exceeds 1.5 children, how would you advise her based on the following outcomes? In all cases, assume that the sample estimate is 2.5 children per household.
   1.) Reliability = 90 percent; precision = 0.7 child per household.
   2.) Reliability = 95 percent; precision = 1.4 children per household.
   3.) Reliability = 99 percent; precision = 1.8 children per household.
e. What causes the differences in the relationships noted in (d)?

LO E-2

E.61 **Sample Evaluation.** Your political consulting group, Electem, Inc., is assisting a local political candidate, Alice Evans, to determine the likelihood of her election to office during the upcoming campaign. She would like to have an extremely high level of confidence (95 percent) that she would receive more than a majority of the ballots cast.

After conducting an extensive survey, you have determined that 53 percent of voters would prefer Evans with a precision of 5 percent and a corresponding reliability of 95 percent. In determining this information, your notes of the sampling process revealed the following information:

1. The district that she would represent is composed of eight neighborhoods. You randomly chose four of these neighborhoods and, within each, had workers poll voters (using a door-to-door technique) from the first 25 households that responded.
2. Your workers canvassed the neighborhoods during the day from 12 P.M. to 3 P.M.
3. Your workers asked voters to respond to the following question: "Do you support Alice Evans during the upcoming election?"
4. In one neighborhood (a community with restricted access to nonresidents), your workers could not obtain a sample of 25 voters using a door-to-door polling technique. As a result, they used a telephone survey to obtain the 25 responses for this neighborhood.
5. Some of your workers observed that, at homes indicating they would support Evans for office, campaign signs for her chief rival were present. The workers were surprised that these same households indicated they would support Evans.
6. George Clinton, one of your workers, indicated that he misunderstood the survey instructions, which indicated that a voter could indicate "yes," "no," or "undecided." George thought that he was required to obtain a "yes" or "no" answer; when voters indicated they were undecided, he pressed them to make a decision (which they ultimately did).
7. Billy Bush, another worker, did not verify the names of the individuals to whom he was speaking.

Required:
a. Based on the sample results, without considering any of the information included in (1)–(7), what would you advise Evans about her electability?
b. How would your advice to her change if she established the following levels of reliability (assume that the sample estimate of 53 percent is unchanged)?
   1. Reliability = 99 percent, precision = 8 percent.
   2. Reliability = 90 percent, precision = 2 percent.
c. Summarize why your advice to Evans would change based on the reliability and precision noted in (b).
d. For each of the seven issues included in your sampling notes, indicate how that issue could affect the advice you provide to Evans and her ability to rely on the sample evidence.

LO E-2

E.62 Sample Evaluation. Marts, Inc., a local fund-raising organization, is considering the feasibility of a fund-raising campaign to assist a youth organization in building a new recreation center in College Bryan, Texas. Marts has been asked to determine whether this campaign would be successful in raising $1.5 million, the amount needed to construct and equip the center.

Because unsuccessful fund-raising efforts have a negative impact on Marts' ability to obtain future clients and engagements, it has established a reliability of 99 percent; that is, Marts wants to have a very high level of confidence that the $1.5 million can be successfully raised in the local community. Because a total of 50,000 citizens live in the College Bryan area, the average gift necessary to ensure a successful campaign is $30 per person ($1,500,000 ÷ 50,000). Based on the sampling risk associated with 99 percent reliability, Marts determined a sample size of 200 and surveyed each of these individuals with respect to their willingness to donate to the fund-raising campaign. The average level of support indicated by these 200 persons was $35 per person.

Required:

a. Based on Marts's sample, calculate the sample estimate for the total amount that could be raised under this fund-raising effort.

b. Based only on the sample estimate, how would you advise Marts as to the potential success of its fund-raising campaign?

c. What is the primary limitation to Marts in making its decision based only on the sample estimate?

d. What is sampling risk? What types of factors could influence Marts's exposure to sampling risk in this particular situation?

e. Using the sample estimate calculated in (a), determine the precision interval if the calculated precision were
   1. $100,000.
   2. $200,000.
   3. $300,000.

f. How would you advise Marts regarding the potential success of the fund-raising campaign based on the precision intervals calculated in (e)?

g. Assume that Marts believes that 99 percent reliability is too stringent and is considering lowering the reliability to 95 percent. How will this change affect the precision interval and the likelihood that Marts will conclude that the fund-raising campaign will ultimately be successful?

LO E-1, E-2

E.63 Basic Sampling: Comprehensive. Reagan Russell is considering opening a multipurpose hardware and lawn store in Anytown, USA. Based on his knowledge of the industry, he believes that if the average household income is more than $35,000, the store will ultimately be successful. He was planning to attempt a census of the income levels in Anytown but has heard about sampling and is now considering using sampling to obtain the necessary information to make his decision.

Required:

a. What would you tell Russell about the advantages and disadvantages of sampling?

b. Russell is interested in knowing the advantages and disadvantages of statistical sampling. What would you tell him?

c. Russell has heard about sampling and nonsampling risk and is concerned about them.
   1. Define *sampling risk* and *nonsampling risk*.
   2. How can Reagan control his exposure to sampling and nonsampling risk?
   3. What are some possible examples of sampling and nonsampling risk in this situation?

d. Assume that Russell decided to use an unrestricted random selection to obtain a sample of households for examination. If he determined a sample size of 100 households, describe how he could select the sample from the city's property tax rolls.

e. Instead of unrestricted random selection, Russell asked you whether he could just pick four or five streets and examine all of the households on those streets. What would you tell him?

f. Assume that Russell has set a sampling risk of 10 percent and found a sample estimate of $39,000 with a precision of $3,000. How would you explain the results to Russell? What advice would you give him?

g. Repeat (f) assuming that Russell found a sample estimate of $42,000 and a precision of $10,000.

LO E-2

E.64 **Sample Selection.** Arianna Casey is trying to select a sample of registered voters in Hoops County to see how they intend to vote on funding a stadium for the local professional basketball team. She has determined that a sample of 1,000 voters will be necessary to provide an acceptable minimum level of sampling risk (15 percent). The state has more than 3 million registered voters who are listed (sorted by ZIP code) in an electronic data file maintained in the state commissioner's office. The commissioner has agreed to allow Casey to have access to this data file for her project.

Required:
a. What is sampling risk? What steps can Casey take to control her exposure to sampling risk?
b. How would she define the population in this case?
c. What are some potential methods of selecting the sample (as specifically applied to this application)?
d. What precautions should Casey take to ensure that she selects a representative sample?

LO E-2

E.65 **Sample Selection Methods.** You are employed by FishWrap, Ltd., a local newspaper distribution company, and are attempting to determine the average level of customer satisfaction with the newspaper's delivery service. All customers are included in a comprehensive database that includes the following information: customer name, delivery address, telephone number, type of service (weekly only, weekend only, weekly/weekend), length of service (how long they have subscribed to the newspaper), and name of carrier.

Because the local area has 10,500 subscribers, FishWrap has decided to sample its customers instead of surveying the entire population. Based on a number of factors (including precision and reliability), FishWrap has determined that a sample of 150 customers is necessary.

Required:
a. In this application, what are some of the major characteristics of subscribers that should be considered to ensure that a representative sample is selected?
b. Identify and briefly define four major methods used to select a sample.
c. How could you select a sample from the population using each of these methods?
d. The information in each list is arranged in descending order based on length of service. Indicate how each of the following factors could impact your ability to use the four methods of selecting a sample from a population:
   1. The database is a typed list of information.
   2. The database is an electronic list of information and cannot be sorted on any other characteristic.
   3. The database is an electronic list of information and can be sorted on any characteristic.
e. How does each of the following factors impact your ability to evaluate whether you have selected a representative sample from the population?
   1. Delivery address does not include ZIP code or other reasonable way of identifying physical location within the subscription area.
   2. The length of service is classified as follows: less than six months, six months to one year, more than one year.
   3. If customers have relocated within the subscription area, their length of service has been reset to zero even when they continued their subscriptions.

LO E-1

E.66 **Sampling and Nonsampling Risk.** Arthur Castle is interested in identifying the average number of family members living in each household in his neighborhood. He has heard about sampling and thinks that it could help him identify this information. In considering the application of sampling to this particular situation, he considers the following characteristics of his neighborhood:
a. Many of his neighbors are dual-income career couples and are away from home in the mornings and afternoons.
b. His neighborhood has two distinct types of homes. The value of the homes in the more established section is in the $300,000 and above price range; most of the individuals have resided in this section for quite some time. The value of homes in the newer section is in the $150,000–$200,000 range, most of which have been built and occupied within the last two years.
c. A small park has been built in the neighborhood. Because of safety considerations, many families with small children have chosen to live near the park.

d. A wooded area backs up to one section of his neighborhood. Because of the privacy offered by the wooded area, as well as the relative lack of traffic, older residents have chosen to live in this part of the neighborhood.

e. Several families have frequent visitors to their homes, particularly on the weekends.

Required:

For each of these characteristics, indicate whether it has the potential to affect sampling risk, nonsampling risk, both sampling risk and nonsampling risk, or neither sampling risk nor nonsampling risk.

LO E-1

E.67 **Sampling and Nonsampling Risk.** You are conducting a research study to determine the effect of a two-week workout and diet regimen on the weight loss experienced by individuals between the ages of 30 and 35 years. Health Busters, a local fitness club, has allowed you access to some of its members for their voluntary participation. Your research study will use the following methodology:

1. Solicit participation from health club members.
2. Ask members who agree to participate to weigh themselves and self-report their weight to you at a specific time.
3. Provide members a scheduled set of workouts and dietary restrictions for the upcoming two weeks.
4. Via telephone survey, obtain the members' weights following the two-week period.
5. Based on the initial weight measurement and final weight measurement, calculate the net weight gain or loss.

Required:

a. How would each of the following characteristics of the methodology affect sampling risk and nonsampling risk?

1. You solicited member participation during the early morning hours when most of the members working out were doing so before going to work that day.
2. Males constituted 85 percent of your sample.
3. The health club is located near downtown where most residents are either single or married without children.
4. Because of traffic, expensive parking, and reasonable proximity of their homes to their offices, most of the patrons walk to their offices (or, in inclement weather, take taxicabs or public transportation).
5. Because of privacy concerns, you agreed to allow participants to self-report their initial and final weight measurements.
6. Because of time constraints, you were unable to monitor participants' workouts or diets during the two-week period.

b. Suggest some improvements to the methodology described to reduce potential exposure to sampling risk and nonsampling risk.

LO E-2

E.68 **Sample Selection Methods.** You are interested in selecting a sample of 100 students on your campus to participate in a survey of the effects of coffee on students' ability to comprehend material from a faculty member's lecture. You have decided to limit your selection to business majors and have obtained a comprehensive list (ranked in descending order based on grade point average) of all business majors. This list is 22 pages long and contains the names of 2,200 business majors.

Required:

a. When selecting your sample, what precautions should you take to ensure a representative sample?

b. Briefly describe how you might select the sample using each of the following methods: (1) unrestricted random selection, (2) systematic random selection, (3) haphazard selection, and (4) block selection.

c. What are some of the advantages and disadvantages of using the selection methods described in (b)?

LO E-4

E.69 **Factors Affecting Sample Size.** Indicate how each of the following factors influences the sample size in an attributes and variables sampling application by using I (inverse relationship), D (direct relationship), or U (unrelated).

	Attributes Sampling	Variables Sampling
Population size		
Expected rate of deviation (expected misstatement)		
Tolerable rate of deviation (tolerable misstatement)		
Sampling risk		
Population variability		

LO E-2

E.70 **General Sampling.** Alex Fishkin is trying to decide on a new location for an ice cream and candy shop. He has decided that if the average number of children per household within a one-mile radius of a proposed shop exceeds 1.3, it would be financially successful and would provide him an annual net income of $50,000 (the minimum acceptable amount). If not, he would stand to lose his initial investment of $150,000.

Required:
   a. What factors would influence Fishkin's decision to use sampling to answer this question?
   b. What are some of the advantages and disadvantages of using sampling to answer this question?
   c. Define *sampling risk*. Describe two different outcomes that may reflect Fishkin's exposure to sampling risk. Which of these outcomes would be of more concern to him?
   d. If the initial investment was $10,000 instead of $150,000, how do you think Fishkin would evaluate the potential outcomes of the two sampling risks noted in (c)?
   e. Define *nonsampling risk*. Describe some potential nonsampling risks that Fishkin could encounter in this application.

LO E-3

E.71 **Audit Sampling: Types of Audit Samples.** You have been assigned to the audit of Phillip's, Inc., a chain of convenience stores. As part of the audit planning, you decide to perform the following tests:
   1. Perform a walkthrough of purchase transactions by selecting one purchase and following it through all processing steps from the initial purchase order to recording in the general ledger.
   2. Select a sample of purchase vouchers and ensure they are supported by receiving documents.
   3. Select a sample of payroll checks and agree the time to the time cards and ensure they have supervisor approval. Using the sample, project the total payroll expense for the year.
   4. Select a sample of items from the inventory on hand and estimate the total inventory on hand at the balance sheet date.
   5. Vouch all long-term debt issued during the year to the loan agreement and the cash received.
   6. Select a sample of long-term debt agreements and ensure they have been approved in the board of directors minutes.
   7. Evaluate the control environment by inquiring of personnel as to the existence of a code of conduct.

Required:
   a. Define the terms *attributes sampling, variables sampling,* and *dual-purpose testing*.
   b. Indicate whether each of the items (1)–(7) suggests an attributes sample, a variables sample, a dual-purpose test, or if it is not an example of sampling.

LO E-4

E.72 **Various Sampling Concepts.** You overheard the following comments during a conversation between Roger Nadal and Rafael Federer about a specific sampling application.

Required:
Refer to appropriate professional standards and comment on the validity of each of these statements.
   a. "Using nonstatistical sampling is so much easier than using statistical sampling. Statistical sampling requires far too many judgments. Under nonstatistical sampling, I can just pick items, evaluate them, and make my decision."
   b. "I wish nonstatistical sampling were allowable in generally accepted auditing standards audits. In some cases, the additional time required by statistical sampling just isn't worth the benefits."

c. "Once we control the sampling risk, we're home free. Assuming we select a representative sample, there's nothing else that we need to worry about."

d. "Be careful if you try to set sampling risk at too low a level. You will need to select more items, which will increase the amount of audit time."

e. "Those transactions with Wimbledon are always so difficult to audit. Let's exclude them from our sampling frame. We can pick other items and have a sufficiently large sample to meet generally accepted auditing standards."

f. "I'm about to perform a walkthrough on Flushing's processing of sales transactions to understand their nature. What level of sampling risk should I consider in planning my sample of transactions?"

LO E-4

E.73 **General Sampling.** The accounting firm of Mason & Jarr performed the work described in each of the following separate cases. The two partners are worried about properly applying auditing standards regarding sampling. They have asked your advice.

Required:

Write a report addressed to Mason & Jarr stating whether they did or did not observe the essential elements of auditing standards in each case. When applicable, refer to the appropriate professional standards regarding audit sampling.

a. Mason selected three purchase orders for the purchase of raw materials from LIZ Corporation's files. He started at the beginning in the accounting process and traced each one through the accounting system. He saw the receiving reports, purchasing agent's approvals, receiving clerks' approvals, vendors' invoices (now stamped PAID), entry in the cash disbursement records, and canceled checks. This work gave him a first-hand familiarity with the cash disbursement system, and he felt confident about understanding related questions in the internal control questionnaire completed later.

b. Jarr observed the physical inventory at SER Corporation. She had a list of the different inventory descriptions with the quantities taken from the perpetual inventory records. She selected the 200 items with the largest quantities and counted them after the client's shop foreperson had completed his count. She decided not to verify the count accuracy of the other 800 items. The shop foreperson miscounted in 16 cases. Jarr concluded the rate of miscount was 8 percent and that as many as 80 of the 1,000 items might be counted incorrectly. As a result, she asked him to recount everything.

c. CSR Corporation issued seven separate commercial paper notes near the fiscal year-end to finance seasonal operations. Jarr confirmed the obligations under each series with the independent trustee for the holders, studied all seven indenture agreements, and traced the proceeds of each issue to the cash receipts records.

d. At the completion of the EH&R Corporation audit, Mason obtained management representations as required by generally accepted auditing standards from the president, the chief financial officer, and the controller. He did not ask the chief accountant at headquarters or the plant controllers in the three divisions for management representations.

e. Jarr audited the Repairs and Maintenance account of Kerr Corporation by vouching all entries of more than $5,000 (totaling $278,000) to supporting documents. She compared the sum of all remaining entries ($75,000, a material amount) in relation to the prior-year total of $56,000 and decided the amounts were reasonable and did not perform any additional procedures with respect to these entries.

LO E-4

CPA REVIEW

E.74 **Kaplan CPA Exam Simulation: Sample Sizes.**

Required:

Go to the Kaplan website link at www.mhhe.com/louwers5e, click on Abernathy, Inc. (Sample Size) AUD TBS, and complete your answer.

Attributes Sampling

> *There are five kinds of lies: lies, damned lies, statistics, politicians quoting statistics, and novelists quoting politicians on statistics.*
>
> *Stephen K. Tagg, marketing faculty member, University of Strathclyde*

Professional Standards References

Topic	AU/ISA Section	PCAOB Reference*
An Audit of Internal Control over Financial Reporting That Is Integrated with an Audit of Financial Statements	N/A	AS 5
Overall Objectives of the Independent Auditor and the Conduct of an Audit in Accordance with Generally Accepted Auditing Standards.	200	AS 8
Identifying and Assessing the Risks of Material Misstatement	315	AS 12
Materiality in Planning and Performing an Audit	320	AS 11
Performing Audit Procedures in Response to Assessed Risks and Evaluating the Audit Evidence Obtained	330	AS 13
Audit Evidence	500	AS 15
Audit Sampling	530	AU 350

*AU references represent standards issued by the ASB prior to April 16, 2003, that have not been superseded or amended by the PCAOB.

LEARNING OBJECTIVES

Module F provides a comprehensive example of the use of attributes sampling in the audit team's study of internal control.

Your objectives are to be able to:

LO F-1 Identify the objectives of attributes sampling, define *deviation conditions,* and define the population for an attributes sampling application.

LO F-2 Understand how various factors influence the size of an attributes sample.

LO F-3 Determine the sample size for an attributes sampling application.

LO F-4 Identify various methods of selecting an attributes sample.

LO F-5 Evaluate the results of an attributes sampling application by determining the *upper limit rate of deviation.*

LO F-6 Define *sequential sampling* and *discovery sampling* and identify when these types of sampling applications could be used.

LO F-7 Understand how to apply nonstatistical sampling to attributes testing.

INTRODUCTION

The following sampling deficiency was noted by PCAOB inspection teams when reviewing tests of controls by a large auditing firm:

> . . . the Firm's testing of the controls over the assignment and monitoring of loan grades was insufficient, as the Firm failed to assess the competence of the individuals performing the control on which it relied. Further, because it selected a sample of which a majority of the items had not been subject to the control, it tested only a relatively small number of items when testing the control.[1]

This deficiency illustrates how difficult it can be to achieve a proper sampling plan that results in a representative sample. In this case, the audit team did not limit their sample to transactions subject to the control they were interested in and selected a majority of loans that were irrelevant to the test. In addition, they apparently did not properly assess the likelihood of mistakes because they did not consider the competence of the employees performing the controls. As you will see, defining a population and estimating expected deficiencies are important steps in audit sampling.

Auditors apply sampling for tests of controls on almost every engagement. As you read in Chapter 5, the Sarbanes-Oxley Act requires auditors of public companies to test the effectiveness of internal controls. Moreover, auditors of all entities should test the operating effectiveness of controls where control risk is less than 100 percent and the audit team is relying on them to reduce substantive procedures. This module focuses on the use of attributes sampling in conducting tests of controls. **Attributes sampling** is used to determine the extent to which some attribute (or characteristic) exists within a population of interest. In tests of controls, that attribute is whether a specific control was applied by client personnel and is functioning to prevent or detect financial statement misstatements. Controls whose evaluation would not involve sampling include (1) controls that are tested once or only infrequently when effective information technology general controls are present, (2) segregation of duties or other controls that do not provide documentary evidence of performance, and (3) certain controls related to the control environment when the audit team is not interested in estimating a rate of deviation (such as management integrity or audit committee effectiveness). Similarly, not all audit procedures are suitable for sampling. Inquiry and observation and analytical procedures would be difficult to perform by sampling.

The following seven-step procedure serves as the basis for our illustration of attributes sampling.

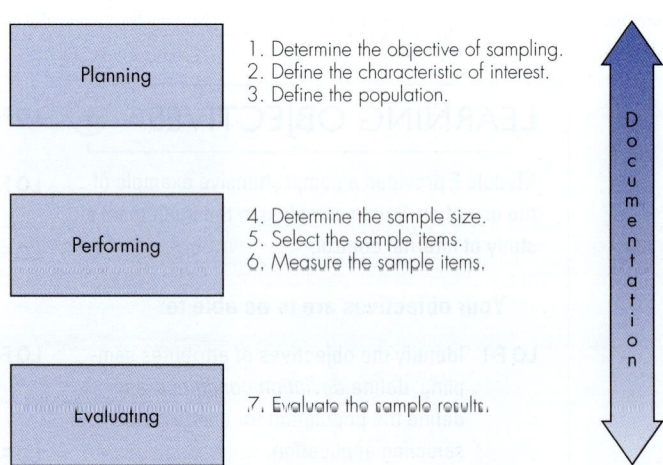

[1] PCAOB Inspection of Ernst & Young (July 2, 2010).

To illustrate the application of the process, we focus on the audit team's study and evaluation of important controls for the revenue cycle of AirCon Company, a manufacturer of high-technology products. In the revenue cycle, two important assertions about events or transactions are *occurrence* (that is, do recorded sales and accounts receivable represent bona fide sales?) and *accuracy* (are sales and accounts receivable recorded correctly?). The audit team uses the audit risk model to determine the necessary level of detection risk (nature, timing, and extent of substantive procedures) for these two assertions.

Attributes sampling is employed to verify the audit team's assessment of control risk. That is, the audit team obtains evidence as to the *operating effectiveness* of key controls. This is the focus of the AirCon Company example.

ATTRIBUTES SAMPLING: PLANNING

LEARNING OBJECTIVE F-1
Identify the objectives of attributes sampling, define *deviation conditions,* and define the population for an attributes sampling application.

Determining the Objective of Sampling

The objective of attributes sampling is related to the particular control policy or activity being examined. The audit team begins by identifying relevant assertions related to classes of transactions. Then key control objectives are matched to these assertions. The major categories of control objectives for the revenue cycle (which is the focus of the AirCon Company example we use in this module) are shown in Exhibit F.1.

The first step in the attributes sampling process is to identify the objective of attributes sampling, which is related to examining key controls corresponding to the management assertions of interest to the audit team. For the examination of AirCon's revenue cycle, the two major assertions of interest are *occurrence* and *accuracy*. Once the relevant assertions have been determined, the audit team then specifies one or more controls that, if functioning, allow the client to achieve these assertions. The following is a summary of the assertions and controls that will be tested for AirCon. In addition, for each of these two assertions, the audit team has identified one control that will be tested.[2]

Assertion	Control
Occurrence	Sales invoices are supported by a valid shipping document[3]
Accuracy	Sales invoices are initialed by client personnel as evidence of verification of mathematical accuracy

Defining the Deviation Conditions

Once the specific controls have been identified, the audit team must next define the deviation. The word **deviation** (commonly referred to as **error, occurrence,** or **exception**) refers to instances in which the client and/or its personnel do *not* follow prescribed controls; in other words, deviations are instances in which controls *are not functioning as*

EXHIBIT F.1
Some Control Assertions for the Revenue Cycle

Occurrence	Does the recorded sale represent an actual sale made to a customer?
Completeness	Have all valid sales been recorded?
Cutoff	Are sales at the beginning or end of a period included in the proper period?
Accuracy	Has the sale been recorded at the proper dollar amount?
Classification	Have sales to subsidiaries and affiliates been classified as intercompany sales and receivables?

---

[2] In practice, a higher number of controls would pertain to the occurrence and accuracy assertions. We limit the number of controls examined by the audit team to focus on the application of attributes sampling.

[3] Of course, the possibility exists that the shipping document was fraudulently prepared in an effort to boost sales. However, this possibility is beyond the scope of our discussion of attributes sampling.

intended. Defining the deviation conditions at the outset is important because deviation conditions provide the audit team evidence regarding the *operating effectiveness* of the client's internal control.

AirCon's control policies indicate that client personnel write their initials in a preprinted "verified by" space on the invoice after mathematically verifying the accuracy of each sales invoice. For the control activity that a sales invoice must be supported by a shipping document, a deviation would be a situation in which a shipping document does not exist to support a sales invoice. The deviation conditions defined by the audit team are as follows:

Control Activity	Example of Deviation
Sales invoices are mathematically verified by client personnel	Lack of employee initials on sales invoice or mathematically incorrect invoice
Sales invoices are supported by a valid shipping document	Instance in which a sales invoice is not accompanied by a shipping document

While defining deviation conditions seems to be relatively straightforward, it is important that the audit team consider the surrounding circumstances. For example, if AirCon makes sales to customers on its premises, it will have sales invoices that are not (and should not) be accompanied by a shipping document. Defining these occurrences as deviation conditions would understate the operating effectiveness of the client's internal control. This potential issue can be avoided by defining the population more specifically (i.e., sales invoices representing sales that were shipped to customers).

Note that a deviation does not necessarily indicate that an error in processing a transaction has occurred. For example, an employee could have mathematically verified a sales invoice but forgotten to record her or his initials on the sales invoice. In addition, the invoice could be correctly calculated regardless of whether the invoice was verified. However, the failure of client employees to document their performance of key controls represents a deviation from that control procedure and causes the audit team concern and should be investigated.

Notice that the nature of deviations is appropriate for the use of *attributes sampling,* which concerns determining the extent to which some attributes (in this case, deviation conditions) exist within the population. Attributes sampling is normally used to test controls that leave documentary evidence of performance. For example, if the audit team is looking for evidence of client employee initials or other evidence that a control procedure was performed, the answer can be only "yes" (the control procedure was performed) or "no" (the control procedure was not performed). With this definition, the audit team can count the number of deviations and use the count when evaluating the evidence.

Defining the Population

The *population* is the set of all items about which a conclusion is desired. In attributes sampling, the population represents all potential applications of the control policy or procedure of interest. Population definition is important because audit conclusions can be made only about the population from which the sample was selected. For example, consider the following relationships between the sales invoice and shipping document in the revenue cycle:

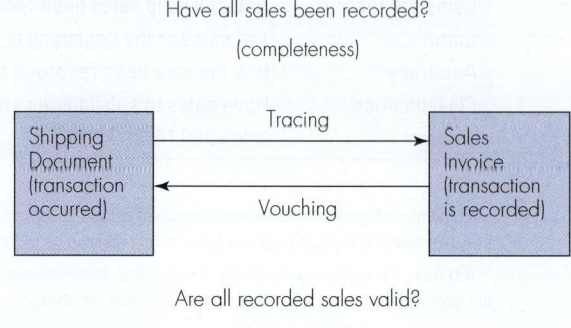

Notice that, by defining the population as sales invoices, the audit team is examining only transactions that have been recorded. As a result, this population cannot be used to provide evidence for the *completeness* assertion. However, this population is appropriate if the audit team is interested in verifying that all recorded sales invoices represent valid transactions (as evidenced by the presence of shipping documents), which corresponds to the *occurrence* assertion.

Conversely, if the population is defined as all shipping documents, the audit team is (presumably) examining only transactions that have occurred (*occurrence*), but tracing the shipping document to the corresponding sales invoices provides evidence with respect to *completeness*. In summary, the definition of the population is directly related to the very first step in the attributes sampling process (determining the objective of sampling).

Recall that the audit team is examining the following controls:

- Extensions and footings on sales invoices are mathematically verified.
- Sales invoices are supported by a shipping document.

As a result, the population should be defined as all sales invoices prepared by AirCon during the period under audit.

A complicating factor in defining the population is the timing of the audit work. Tests of controls ideally should be applied to transactions throughout the entire period under audit because the audit team wants to reach a conclusion about control risk during the entire period. However, audit teams often perform tests of controls at an interim date, which is any date prior to the date of the financial statements. One limitation of interim testing is that the entire population will not be available for examination on this date. If interim testing is done, the audit team must extend these tests to year-end transactions to ensure that the sample includes control policies and procedures applied throughout the entire year. If the tests are not extended, the audit team must obtain other evidence to conclude on the operating effectiveness of the controls during the period not covered.

A factor similar to interim testing is the need for the audit team to determine the **physical representation of the population**. The physical representation is the frame of reference that the audit team uses in selecting the sample, also referred to as the *source* of the sample. That is, the audit team will select the sample from the physical representation. Some possible physical representations for selecting a sample of sales invoices include these:

- A journal list of recorded sales invoices.
- Copies of sales invoices contained in a file.
- A computerized list of sales invoices.

The primary concerns about the physical representation are that it is complete and corresponds with the actual population. For example, if the journal list used by the audit team to select sales invoices does not include invoices for the month of December, the audit team will not be able to select a random sample from the year. The audit team should exhibit appropriate levels of professional skepticism and take specific steps to ensure that the physical representation provides the complete population. For example, a sales journal can be footed using a computer-assisted audit technique (CAAT) and agreed to the general ledger, or software controls can be examined to ensure that all sales in the general ledger came from the sales journal. If the test of controls is performed at an interim date and the audit teams plan to extend the test to the end of the period, they can project the population based on past experience. It is preferable to *overestimate* the projected population to ensure all possible future transactions are included.

AirCon Company has a computerized list of all sales invoices prepared during the year. It can be sorted by date, customer, or dollar amount. The audit team will use it to select the sample.

The first three steps in the sampling process for AirCon Company are summarized next.

Summary: Steps 1–3 in the Sampling Process for AirCon Company

1. The audit team's objective in sampling is to evaluate the operating effectiveness of controls related to the occurrence and accuracy assertions.
2. The audit team defined deviation conditions as (a) lack of employee initials on sales invoices or mathematical error on a sales invoice (accuracy) and (b) a sales invoice that is not accompanied by a shipping document (occurrence).
3. The audit team defined the population as a computerized list of all sales invoices prepared during the year.

↳ REVIEW CHECKPOINTS

F.1 Define *attributes sampling*. In what stage of the audit would it be used?

F.2 How do the management assertions relate to the objectives of attributes sampling?

F.3 Define *deviation condition*. Why are deviation conditions so important in an attributes sampling application?

F.4 Why is appropriately defining the population of interest so important in an attributes sampling application?

ATTRIBUTES SAMPLING: PERFORMING

LEARNING OBJECTIVE F-2
Understand how various factors influence the size of an attributes sample.

The next three steps in attributes sampling relate to performing critical procedures necessary to gather evidence. These steps include determining sample size, selecting the sample, and measuring sample items.

Determining Sample Size: Factors to Consider

The *sample size* represents the number of items that the audit team examines. Four main factors influence the sample size in an attributes sampling application:

- Sampling risk (risk of overreliance—risk of assessing control risk too low).
- Tolerable rate of deviation.
- Expected population deviation rate.
- Population size.

Sampling Risk

Sampling risk is the likelihood that the decision made based on the sample differs from the decision that would have been made had the entire population been examined. There are two types of sampling risks for attributes sampling applications: the **risk of underreliance** and the **risk of overreliance** (sometimes referred to as the *risk of assessing control risk too high* and the *risk of assessing control risk too low,* respectively). Exhibit F.2 summarizes some of the key characteristics of these risks.

As shown in Exhibit F.2, the risk of overreliance occurs when the audit team's sample evidence suggests that the control is functioning effectively (the adjusted sample rate of deviation is less than or equal to the tolerable rate of deviation) when the true (but unknown) state of the population is that the control is *not* functioning effectively (population rate of deviation is higher than the tolerable rate of deviation). Because the risk of overreliance results in the audit team's failure to reduce audit risk to acceptable levels (an effectiveness loss), controlling exposure to this risk is of primary importance. Although the risk of underreliance is also a form of sampling risk, this risk will actually result in the audit team's achieving a lower level of audit risk than planned. Therefore, in an attributes sampling plan, the audit team will control only the exposure to the risk of *overreliance* in determining the appropriate sample size.

EXHIBIT F. 2 Sampling Risks Associated with Attributes Sampling

Sampling Risk	Sample Results	Unknown State of the Population	Loss
Risk of underreliance (risk of assessing control risk too high)	Adjusted sample rate of deviation > Tolerable rate of deviation *Conclusion:* Control is not functioning	Population rate of deviation ≤ Tolerable rate of deviation *Conclusion:* Control is functioning	Efficiency loss because additional substantive procedures will be performed
Risk of overreliance (risk of assessing control risk too low)	Adjusted sample rate of deviation ≤ Tolerable rate of deviation *Conclusion:* Control is functioning	Population rate of deviation > Tolerable rate of deviation *Conclusion:* Control is not functioning	Effectiveness loss because an insufficient level of substantive procedures will be performed

How does the audit team assess the acceptable level of the risk of overreliance? Generally, this risk depends on the planned level of control risk (which reflects the degree of reliance that the audit team wishes to place on the client's internal control). Recall that *control risk* is the risk that the client's internal control fails to prevent or detect material misstatements in an assertion related to an account balance, class of transactions, or disclosure. As the planned level of control risk is lower, it becomes quite important for the audit team to reduce the exposure to the risk of overreliance.

Exhibit F.3 illustrates one possible method of relating the planned level of control risk to the risk of overreliance and tolerable rate of deviation (we discuss tolerable rate of deviation in the following subsection). Although the numerical relationships in Exhibit F.3 are not strictly observed in practice, they illustrate that lower planned levels of control risk are associated with lower levels of risk of overreliance.[4]

Assume that the audit team has decided to assess control risk at low levels (0.30) for the occurrence assertion and moderate levels (0.50) for the accuracy assertion. Based on the relationships in Exhibit F.3, assume that these assessments of control risk are translated into 5 percent and 10 percent risks of overreliance for the occurrence and accuracy assertions, respectively.[5]

Tolerable Rate of Deviation

The **tolerable rate of deviation** is the maximum rate of deviations permissible by the audit team without modifying the planned assessed level of control risk. In determining the tolerable rate of deviation, the audit team should consider (1) the planned assessed level of control risk and (2) the degree of assurance desired by the audit evidence in the sample. If the audit team wishes to assess control risk at low levels, it seems reasonable to hold the client's internal control to a higher standard (that is, use a lower tolerable rate of deviation). In contrast, if control risk is high, the audit team can use a higher tolerable rate of deviation before reducing the reliance on internal control. Also, if the audit team requires a high degree of assurance from

EXHIBIT F.3 Effect of Control Risk Assessments on Risk of Overreliance and Tolerable Rate of Deviation

Control Risk (Qualitative)	Control Risk (Quantitative)	Risk of Overreliance	Tolerable Rate of Deviation
Low	0.10–0.30	5%	3%–7%
Moderate	0.40–0.60	5%–10%	6%–12%
Slightly below maximum	0.70–0.90	10%	11%–20%
Maximum	1.00	Not applicable	Not applicable

[4] A white paper authored by nine large accounting firms (the Big Four plus BDO Seidman LLP, Crowe Chizek and Company LLC (Now Crowe Horwath LLP), Grant Thornton LLP, Harbinger PLC, and McGladrey & Pullen LLP) noted that to achieve a high level of assurance that controls are operating effectively (lower levels of control risk), audit teams should *not* assess the risk of overreliance or the tolerable rate of deviation at levels above 10 percent. See "A Framework for Evaluating Control Exceptions and Deficiencies," December 20, 2004.

[5] Exhibit F.3 reflects the common practice of selecting one of two levels of the risk of overreliance (5 percent and 10 percent).

the test because related accounts are highly material and/or because they are not performing additional tests of controls, it again makes sense to have a lower tolerable rate of deviation.

Exhibit F.3 illustrates how tolerable rate of deviation can be related to control risk assessments. Although control risk is not always assessed numerically in practice, note that lower levels of control risk are associated with lower tolerable rate of deviation (and vice versa). Using Exhibit F.3, if the audit team established a low acceptable control risk (between 0.10 and 0.30), the corresponding tolerable rate of deviation would range from 3 to 7 percent. Notice that the audit team could attempt to refine the tolerable rate of deviation even more by identifying a very low level of control risk (say 0.10) and assessing a specific tolerable rate of deviation associated with that level (say 3 percent). A direct assessment of this type may not always be done in practice, but Exhibit F.3 illustrates that the tolerable rate of deviation is a continuous measure and is directly related to the planned level of control risk. Note, however, that the tolerable rate of deviation is a judgment made by the audit team based on the level of control risk and may consider evidence from sources such as walkthroughs, inquiries, or evidence about related controls.

As noted in the preceding subsection, AirCon Company's control risk was assessed at a low level (0.30) for the occurrence assertion and a moderate level (0.50) for the accuracy assertion. Using the matrix in Exhibit F.3, assume that the audit team translated these assessments into tolerable rate of deviation of 6 percent and 10 percent for the occurrence and accuracy assertions, respectively.

Expected Population Deviation Rate

Audit teams usually know or suspect that some level of deviation occurs in the client's internal control policies or procedures; this rate is referred to as the **expected population deviation rate**. The concept of reasonable assurance suggests that the client's internal control policies and procedures will not function perfectly (i.e., a zero rate of deviation). Thus, some level of deviations is typically observed and is incorporated into the determination of sample size.

How is the expected population deviation rate determined? If the client represents a recurring engagement, the audit team has some knowledge of rate of deviations from prior engagements. These rates might need to be adjusted if changes in the client's controls have occurred since the prior audit, but previous-year rates serve as a reasonable starting point. For example, if the observed rate of deviation from prior audits was 4 percent but the audit team is aware of improvement in controls, the current-year rate of deviation could be estimated at a lower level (say 3 percent). If, on the other hand, the engagement is a first-year engagement, the audit team might use a small sample (referred to as a *pilot sample*) to estimate the rate of deviations.

In establishing the expected population deviation rate, the audit team should consider the relationship between this rate and the tolerable rate of deviation. Simply stated, for tests of controls (and attributes sampling) to be used, the expected population deviation rate must be less than the tolerable rate of deviation. For example, in the AirCon example, the audit team assessed the tolerable rate of deviation for the occurrence assertion at 6 percent; in this instance, it makes little sense to invest the time to perform tests of controls if the expected population deviation rate is higher than 6 percent. If so, the audit team would likely choose to reduce reliance on internal control, increase the level of control risk, and conduct more extensive substantive procedures.

The **allowance for sampling risk** (or **precision**) is the proximity of a sample estimate to the maximum rate of deviation at a given confidence level. For planning purposes, the difference between the tolerable rate of deviation and the expected population deviation rate can be viewed as a form of *planning precision*. Considering the joint effects of the tolerable rate of deviation and the expected population deviation rate as the difference between the two is lower (which could reflect either a higher expected population deviation rate, a lower tolerable rate of deviation, or both), the audit team's sample estimate therefore needs to be more precise, which requires a larger sample size. This is so because if the sample rate of deviation (the results of examining the sample, discussed later in this module) is anticipated to be very close to the tolerable rate of deviation, the audit team has very little room for error in making the decision.

Based on their previous experience in examining the operating effectiveness of these controls for AirCon Company, the audit team assessed the expected population deviation rate at 2 percent and 3.5 percent for the occurrence and accuracy assertions, respectively.

Population Size

Common sense probably tells you that samples should be larger for larger populations (a *direct relationship*). Strictly speaking, your common sense is accurate; clearly, the sample size for a population of 10 items would be smaller than for a population of 1,000 items. However, once a population reaches a certain size, any increase has a minimal effect on sample size. As a result, unless the population size is very small (which is not common for most attributes sampling applications), the audit team does not consider population size in determining sample size to a great extent.

To illustrate, the AICPA's *Audit Sampling Guide* provides the following sample sizes for different populations for the same level of the *risk of overreliance,* expected population deviation rate, and tolerable rate of deviation:

Population Size	Sample Size
100	33
200	35
500	37
1,000	37
1,000	38
2,000	38

The preceding illustrates that, once the population exceeds 500 items, the effect of population size on sample size is relatively limited. Because AirCon processes more than 20,000 sales invoices per year, the population is of sufficient size not to influence the audit team's sample size. What about extremely small samples sizes? Often controls such as bank reconciliations are only performed monthly or at some other interval; as such, this type of control has a population size of only 12 items in a given year. Exhibit F.4 suggests the sample sizes in such circumstances.

Summary of sample size factors

Exhibit F.5 summarizes the general relationships between the factors discussed in this section and sample size.

Determining Sample Size: Using AICPA Sampling Tables

LEARNING OBJECTIVE F-3
Determine the sample size for an attributes sampling application.

How does the audit team use the preceding factors in determining sample size? The AICPA has developed sampling tables that specifically incorporate the (1) risk of overreliance, (2) expected population deviation rate, and (3) tolerable rate of deviation. These tables also identify the number of deviations the audit team can find and still accept the control as operating effectively (number of expected deviations), which can give the audit team an idea of whether the sample size is realistic. These tables are also helpful in determining sample sizes for *discovery sampling* applications discussed later in this module. In practice, computer programs are frequently used to determine sample size; these programs

EXHIBIT F.4
Sample Sizes for Small Audit Populations

Control Frequency and Population Size	Sample Size
Quarterly (4)	2
Monthly (12)	2–4
Semimonthly (24)	3–8
Weekly (52)	5–9

Source: American Institute of Certified Public Accountants, "Audit Sampling," *Audit and Accounting Guide* (New York: AICPA, 2008).

EXHIBIT F.5 Factors Affecting Sample Size

Factor	Determination Based On	Effect on Sample Size
Sampling risk	The audit team's judgment concerning level of control risk (typically set at low levels)	*Inverse* (as acceptable sampling risk decreases, sample size increases)
Tolerable rate of deviation	The level of control risk (as level of control risk is lower, tolerable rate of deviation is lower) and degree of assurance required	*Inverse* (as acceptable tolerable rate of deviation decreases, sample size increases)
Expected population deviation rate	Prior audits (for recurring engagements) or a pilot sample of controls (for first-year engagements)	*Direct* (as expected population deviation rate increases, sample size increases)
Population size	The number of applications of control policy or procedure to transactions	*Direct* (as population size increases, sample size increases; however, recall that the effect is negligible once the population reaches a certain size)

follow the logic of the statistical formulas that are used to construct the AICPA sampling tables. The AICPA tables are used as follows:

1. Based on the risk of overreliance, the appropriate sample size table is selected. Tables for a 5 percent and 10 percent risk of overreliance are reproduced as Exhibits F.6 and F.7, respectively.
2. The row of the table corresponding to the expected population deviation rate for the control being examined is determined.

EXHIBIT F.6 Sample Size Table for 5 Percent Risk of Overreliance (Number of Expected Deviations)

Expected Population Deviation Rate	2%	3%	4%	5%	6%	7%	8%	9%	10%	15%	20%
0.00%	149 (0)	99 (0)	74 (0)	59 (0)	49 (0)	42 (0)	36 (0)	32 (0)	29 (0)	19 (0)	14 (0)
0.25	236 (1)	157 (1)	117 (1)	93 (1)	78 (1)	66 (1)	58 (1)	51 (1)	46 (1)	30 (1)	22 (1)
0.50	313 (2)	157 (1)	117 (1)	93 (1)	78 (1)	66 (1)	58 (1)	51 (1)	46 (1)	30 (1)	22 (1)
0.75	386 (3)	208 (2)	117 (1)	93 (1)	78 (1)	66 (1)	58 (1)	51 (1)	46 (1)	30 (1)	22 (1)
1.00	590 (6)	257 (3)	156 (2)	93 (1)	78 (1)	66 (1)	58 (1)	51 (1)	46 (1)	30 (1)	22 (1)
1.25	1,030 (13)	303 (4)	156 (2)	124 (2)	78 (1)	66 (1)	58 (1)	51 (1)	46 (1)	30 (1)	22 (1)
1.50		392 (6)	192 (3)	124 (2)	103 (2)	66 (1)	58 (1)	51 (1)	46 (1)	30 (1)	22 (1)
1.75		562 (10)	227 (4)	153 (3)	103 (2)	88 (2)	77 (2)	51 (1)	46 (1)	30 (1)	22 (1)
2.00		846 (17)	294 (6)	181 (4)	127 (3)	88 (2)	77 (2)	68 (2)	46 (1)	30 (1)	22 (1)
2.25		1,466 (33)	390 (9)	208 (5)	127 (3)	88 (2)	77 (2)	68 (2)	61 (2)	30 (1)	22 (1)
2.50			513 (13)	234 (6)	150 (4)	109 (3)	77 (2)	68 (2)	61 (2)	30 (1)	22 (1)
2.75			722 (20)	286 (8)	173 (5)	109 (3)	95 (3)	68 (2)	61 (2)	30 (1)	22 (1)
3.00			1,098 (33)	361 (11)	195 (6)	129 (4)	95 (3)	84 (3)	61 (2)	30 (1)	22 (1)
3.25			1,936 (63)	458 (15)	238 (8)	148 (5)	112 (4)	84 (3)	61 (2)	30 (1)	22 (1)
3.50				624 (22)	280 (10)	167 (6)	112 (4)	84 (3)	76 (3)	40 (2)	22 (1)
3.75				877 (33)	341 (13)	185 (7)	129 (5)	100 (4)	76 (3)	40 (2)	22 (1)
4.00				1,348 (54)	421 (17)	221 (9)	146 (6)	100 (4)	89 (4)	40 (2)	22 (1)
5.00					1,580 (79)	478 (24)	240 (12)	158 (8)	116 (6)	40 (2)	30 (2)
6.00						1,832 (110)	532 (32)	266 (16)	179 (11)	50 (3)	30 (2)
7.00								585 (41)	298 (21)	68 (5)	37 (3)
8.00									649 (52)	85 (7)	37 (3)
9.00										110 (10)	44 (4)
10.00										150 (15)	50 (5)
12.50										576 (72)	88 (11)
15.00											193 (29)
17.50											720 (126)

Note: This table assumes a large population. Sample sizes of more than 2,000 not shown.
Source: American Institute of Certified Public Accountants, "Audit Sampling," *Audit and Accounting Guide* (New York: AICPA, 2008).

EXHIBIT F.7 Sample Size Table for 10 Percent Risk of Overreliance (Number of Expected Deviations)

Expected Population Deviation Rate	\multicolumn{11}{c}{Tolerable Rate of Deviation}
	2%	3%	4%	5%	6%	7%	8%	9%	10%	15%	20%
0.00%	114 (0)	76 (0)	57 (0)	45 (0)	38 (0)	32 (0)	28 (0)	25 (0)	22 (0)	15 (0)	11 (0)
0.25	194 (1)	129 (1)	96 (1)	77 (1)	64 (1)	55 (1)	48 (1)	42 (1)	38 (1)	25 (1)	18 (1)
0.50	194 (1)	129 (1)	96 (1)	77 (1)	64 (1)	55 (1)	48 (1)	42 (1)	38 (1)	25 (1)	18 (1)
0.75	265 (2)	129 (1)	96 (1)	77 (1)	64 (1)	55 (1)	48 (1)	42 (1)	38 (1)	25 (1)	18 (1)
1.00	398 (4)	176 (2)	96 (1)	77 (1)	64 (1)	55 (1)	48 (1)	42 (1)	38 (1)	25 (1)	18 (1)
1.25	708 (9)	221 (3)	132 (2)	77 (1)	64 (1)	55 (1)	48 (1)	42 (1)	38 (1)	25 (1)	18 (1)
1.50	1,463 (22)	265 (4)	132 (2)	105 (2)	64 (1)	55 (1)	48 (1)	42 (1)	38 (1)	25 (1)	18 (1)
1.75		390 (7)	166 (3)	105 (2)	88 (2)	55 (1)	48 (1)	42 (1)	38 (1)	25 (1)	18 (1)
2.00		590 (12)	198 (4)	132 (3)	88 (2)	75 (2)	48 (1)	42 (1)	38 (1)	25 (1)	18 (1)
2.25		974 (22)	262 (6)	132 (3)	88 (2)	75 (2)	65 (2)	42 (1)	38 (1)	25 (1)	18 (1)
2.50			353 (9)	158 (4)	110 (3)	75 (2)	65 (2)	58 (2)	38 (1)	25 (1)	18 (1)
2.75			471 (13)	209 (6)	132 (4)	94 (3)	65 (2)	58 (2)	52 (2)	25 (1)	18 (1)
3.00			730 (22)	258 (8)	132 (4)	94 (3)	65 (2)	58 (2)	52 (2)	25 (1)	18 (1)
3.25			1,258 (41)	306 (10)	153 (5)	113 (4)	82 (3)	58 (2)	52 (2)	25 (1)	18 (1)
3.50				400 (14)	194 (7)	113 (4)	82 (3)	73 (3)	52 (2)	25 (1)	18 (1)
3.75				583 (22)	235 (9)	131 (5)	98 (4)	73 (3)	52 (2)	25 (1)	18 (1)
4.00				873 (35)	274 (11)	149 (6)	98 (4)	73 (3)	65 (3)	25 (1)	18 (1)
5.00					1,019 (51)	318 (16)	160 (8)	115 (6)	78 (4)	34 (2)	18 (1)
6.00						1,150 (69)	349 (21)	182 (11)	116 (7)	43 (3)	25 (2)
7.00							1,300 (91)	385 (27)	199 (14)	52 (4)	25 (2)
8.00								1,437 (115)	424 (34)	60 (5)	25 (2)
9.00									1,577 (142)	77 (7)	32 (3)
10.00										100 (10)	38 (4)
12.50										368 (46)	63 (8)
15.00											126 (19)
17.50											457 (80)

Note: This table assumes a large population. Sample sizes of more than 2,000 not shown.
Source: American Institute of Certified Public Accountants, "Audit Sampling," *Audit and Accounting Guide* (New York: AICPA, 2008).

3. The column of the table representing the assessed tolerable rate of deviation for the control being examined is identified.
4. The sample size is determined by identifying the junction of the row from step 2 and the column from step 3.

See Exhibit F.8 for a summary of important assessments made by the audit team for AirCon's two controls. These assessments relate to the risk of overreliance, tolerable rate of deviation, and expected population deviation rate. (Recall that the population size of 20,000 was sufficiently large so it did not influence the audit team's sample size.)

Referring to the sample size table in Exhibit F.6 (5 percent risk of overreliance) and reading the sample size at the intersection of the 2 percent expected population deviation rate row and the 6 percent tolerable rate of deviation column reveals a sample size related to the occurrence assertion of 127 items. Using the sample size table in Exhibit F.7 (10 percent risk of overreliance) and reading the sample size at the intersection of the 3.5 percent expected population deviation rate row and the 10 percent tolerable rate of deviation column reveals a sample size for the test of controls related to the accuracy assertion of 52 items.[6]

[6] Exhibit F.8 illustrates different risks of overreliance, tolerable rates of deviations, and expected population deviation rates for the two controls examined for AirCon Company. We do so primarily to show how these factors affect sample size. In practice, the cost of identifying and selecting sample items in attributes sampling is often far higher than the cost of measuring and evaluating these items. As a result, when selecting a single document to evaluate more than one control, the audit team may use the largest of the sample sizes and examine all controls related to the document selected.

EXHIBIT F.8
Assessments of Risk of Overreliance (ROO), Tolerable Rate of Deviation (TRD), and Expected Population Deviation Rate (EPDR) for AirCon Company

Control	ROO	TRD	EPDR
Occurrence: Sales invoices are prepared only for items shipped to customers	5.0%	6.0%	2.0%
Accuracy: Extensions and footings on sales invoices are mathematically verified	10.0	10.0	3.5

In reviewing Exhibit F.6, you can see how the various factors affect sample size. For example, reading across the 2 percent expected population deviation rate row, you see that if the tolerable rate of deviation for the occurrence control were reduced from 6 percent to 5 percent, the necessary sample size would increase from 127 items to 181 items. This increase is consistent with the *inverse relationship* between the tolerable rate of deviation and sample size noted in Exhibit F.4.

	Tolerable Rate of Deviation			
	5%	6%	7%	8%
2%	181	127	88	77

Decrease in tolerable deviation rate results in larger sample size

Examining the 6 percent tolerable rate of deviation column in Exhibit F.6, you can see how various levels of the expected population deviation rate affect sample sizes. Note that, if the expected population deviation rate were lowered from 2 percent to 1 percent, the sample size for the occurrence assertion would decrease from 127 items to 78 items, consistent with the *direct relationship* between the expected population deviation rate and sample size noted in Exhibit F.4.[7]

Expected Population Deviation Rate	Tolerable Rate of Deviation = 6%
0%	49
1%	78
2%	127
3%	195

Decrease in expected population deviation rate results in smaller sample size

Finally, comparing the cell entries in Exhibits F.6 and F.7 illustrates the *inverse relationship* between the risk of overreliance and sample size. For the occurrence control, the sample size for a risk of overreliance of 5 percent is 127. If the risk of overreliance were increased to 10 percent but the expected population deviation rate and tolerable rate of deviation were held constant at 2 percent and 6 percent, respectively, the sample size would decrease to 88 items (see Exhibit F.7).

Exhibit F.9 is an example of audit documentation prepared for the tests of controls performed for AirCon Company. At this point, you should focus on the first six columns of this exhibit, which summarize the control being examined (column 1), level of control risk (column 2), risk of overreliance (column 3), tolerable rate of deviation (column 4), expected population deviation rate (column 5), and sample size (column 6).

---

[7] Note that the sample size does not necessarily change with each incremental change in the expected deviation rate. For example, using a 6 percent tolerable rate of deviation and a 5 percent acceptable risk of overreliance, the sample size is 78 for expected deviation rates ranging from 0.25 percent to 1.25 percent. However, the sample size increases to 103 when the expected deviation rate increases to 1.50 percent.

EXHIBIT F.9 Sample Audit Documentation for AirCon Company Tests of Controls

Control Examined	Control Risk	ROO	TRD	EPDR	n (A)	Devs	ULRD	Conclusion
Occurrence: Sales invoices are prepared only for items shipped to customers	Low (0.30)	5.0%	6.0%	2.0%	127	2	5.0%	Can rely on internal control as planned because ULRD < TRD
Accuracy: Extensions and footings on sales invoices are mathematically verified	Moderate (0.50)	10.0	10.0	3.5	52	4	15.4	(B) Cannot rely on internal control as planned because ULRD > TRD

ROO = Risk of overreliance
TRD = Tolerable rate of deviation
EPDR = Expected population deviation rate
n = Sample size
Devs = Number of deviations observed
ULRD = Upper limit rate of deviation, using ROO, n, and Devs

(A) = Items selected from the firm's random number generator using a starting point of 667
(B) = Based on sample results, increased control risk to slightly less than maximum (0.80)

The fourth step in the sampling process (determining the sample size) for the AirCon Company example is summarized here.

Summary: Step 4 in the Sampling Process for AirCon Company

4. Based on the acceptable risk of overreliance, expected population deviation rate, and tolerable rate of deviation, the audit team determined sample sizes of 127 (for the occurrence control) and 52 (for the accuracy control).

> ### ⌕ REVIEW CHECKPOINTS
>
> F.5 Define the terms (a) *sampling risk,* (b) *tolerable rate of deviation,* and (c) *expected population deviation rate.* How does the audit team assess or determine these factors?
>
> F.6 What two types of sampling risks could an audit team encounter when performing attributes sampling?
>
> F.7 In attributes sampling, why is the risk of overreliance more important than the risk of underreliance?
>
> F.8 What is the relationship between sample size and (a) sampling risk, (b) tolerable rate of deviation, and (c) expected population deviation rate?
>
> F.9 Describe the general procedure used by the audit team to determine sample size using AICPA sampling tables.

Selecting the Sample

LEARNING OBJECTIVE F-4
Identify various methods of selecting an attributes sample.

The audit team's basic goal in selecting a sample is to increase the likelihood that it is representative of the population. For example, if the audit team is examining a sample of sales invoices, this sample should include sales invoices that

- Have been prepared throughout the year.
- Represent both large and small dollar amounts.
- Have been prepared by different individuals involved in the invoice preparation process.
- Represent different customers and/or geographic areas.

For example, considering the first item, if sales invoices for only the month of November are examined, differences in the persons, processes, or other factors involved in the preparation or processing of sales invoices in the month of November can result in a nonrepresentative sample.

The audit team then selects the sample from the population (see appendix F.A. for a discussion of selection methods). If the audit team wants to use statistical sampling, either random selection or systematic selection is appropriate so that there is a known probability of selecting a representative sample. Assume that the audit team uses random selection and selects the sample of invoices for examination. Tickmark (A) in Exhibit F.9 provides a starting point for selecting the sample of sales invoices. AirCon's audit team used a CAAT on the sales invoice file that totaled the invoices for agreement to the general ledger. It also scanned the file for gaps and duplicate numbers. Finally, the program printed a listing of 150 randomly selected invoices. (It is a good practice to select a few more items than needed to replace any cases in which an invoice was voided and therefore not processed by the client.) The audit team examined the first 52 invoices selected for both the *accuracy* and *occurrence* assertions and the next 75 for *occurrence* assertion only (recall that the necessary sample size for the occurrence assertion was 127, or 52 + 75).

AUDITING INSIGHT | Danger in Systematic Selection

Assume that a company has a constant payroll of 50 hourly employees paid weekly throughout the year (that is, no employees were hired or terminated during the year). With 52 pay periods, 2,600 payroll transactions are processed each year (52 pay periods × 50 employees). Based on the acceptable risk of overreliance, tolerable rate of deviation, and expected population deviation rate, the audit team determined a sample size of 104 payroll transactions and used a systematic selection method to select a sample of 104 paychecks for tests of controls.

Based on the population size and sample size, the sampling interval is 25 (2,600 ÷ 104). A random starting point was selected (Moe Howard's payroll transaction) and every 25th entry thereafter was selected. The audit team selected 52 payroll entries for Howard and 52 entries for Lucy Fine.

What made this sample nonrepresentative? A sample size of 104 results in auditing two transactions per week (104 ÷ 52 weeks). The fact that the population of employees (50) was evenly divisible by the sampling interval (25 items) coincidentally resulted in the same employees' records being repeatedly selected for examination.

Summary: Step 5 in the Sampling Process for AirCon Company

5. Using a CAAT to generate random numbers and a starting point of 667, the audit team selected 150 invoices and examined 127 of them. Of these, the audit team evaluated 52 for controls related to the accuracy and occurrence assertion and 75 for controls related only to the occurrence assertion.

Measuring Sample Items

Once the audit team has determined the sample size (step 4) and selected the sample items (step 5), they are ready to measure the sample items. When measuring the sample items in an attributes sampling application, the audit team determines whether the control has been appropriately performed. It is important that the audit team not perform the control but examine some form of evidence that client personnel performed it. If there is no evidence of the control being performed, the item will be classified as a deviation. The audit team examines evidence on the operating effectiveness of important controls by performing *tests of controls*.

Although measuring sample items is typically straightforward, one issue that could arise relates to missing items. For example, when evaluating a control related to a sales invoice that cannot be located, the audit team would classify this particular item as a deviation. The fact that the document is missing could indeed reflect the fact that a control was not applied in the intended manner and the related document has been intentionally destroyed or removed from the physical representation of the population.

Measuring sample items is the step in the sampling process when nonsampling risk can occur. *Nonsampling risk* is the risk that the audit team's sample provides an incorrect conclusion for reasons other than the representativeness of the sample. For example, the

EXHIBIT F.10 Tests of Controls for AirCon Company

Assertion	Control	Test of Control
Occurrence: Sales invoices are prepared only for items shipped to customers	Existence of shipping document for all sales invoices	Check for existence of shipping document accompanying sales invoices
Accuracy: Extensions and footings on sales invoices are mathematically accurate	Existence of initials of client employee indicating mathematical verification	Examine invoices for evidence of client employee initials or recalculation of a sample of invoices*

*Recalculation can be a dual-purpose procedure that tests the control and the account balance. Of course, proper recalculation does not mean the control occurred, but an error means that it was not effectively applied.

audit team could make an unintentional error in evaluating evidence (such as classifying a deviation as a nondeviation or *vice versa*).

See Exhibit F.10 for the tests of controls performed for AirCon Company by the audit team.

As shown in the seventh column of Exhibit F.9, a total of two deviations for the occurrence control and four deviations for the accuracy control were noted.

Summary: Step 6 in the Sampling Process for AirCon Company

6. The audit team's tests of controls identified two deviations for the occurrence control and four deviations for the accuracy control.

⤷ REVIEW CHECKPOINTS

F.10 What are some important considerations for the audit team when selecting sample items?

F.11 What are *tests of controls*? What is the audit team's goal in performing them in an attributes sampling application?

F.12 When performing tests of controls, how would the audit team classify a situation when encountering a missing item?

▽ ATTRIBUTES SAMPLING: EVALUATING

LEARNING OBJECTIVE F-5
Evaluate the results of an attributes sampling application by determining the *upper limit rate of deviation*.

Calculating the Upper Limit Rate of Deviation

At this point, the audit team has planned the sample (by identifying the objective of sampling, defining a deviation condition, and defining the population) and performed the basics of the sampling plan (by determining the sample size, selecting the sample, and measuring the sample items). As noted in the preceding section, the audit team's tests of controls revealed two deviations for the occurrence control and four deviations for the accuracy control.

Based on this information, the audit team can calculate a **sample rate of deviation**, which represents the rate of deviations from key controls noted by the audit team in their sample. The sample rate of deviation is calculated by dividing the number of deviations noted in the sample by the sample size. Thus, the sample rate of deviation for the occurrence and accuracy controls were 1.6 percent (2 deviations ÷ 127 invoices) and 7.7 percent (4 deviations ÷ 52 invoices), respectively. Because the tolerable rate of deviation for these controls are 6 and 10 percent, respectively, the audit team's initial conclusion might be to rely on the controls as planned because the sample rate of deviation is less than the tolerable rate of deviation.

What is the fallacy with this approach? The audit team's sample might not represent the population. This problem can occur, for example, if the audit team selected sales invoices for which controls were functioning more effectively than for the population as a whole. If the sample is not representative, the sample rate of deviation can significantly understate the true population rate of deviation. Although audit teams never know the true population rate of deviation with any certainty, they can use sampling tables to "adjust" the sample rate of deviation to one that has a certain probability of equaling or exceeding the true rate of deviation. Simply stated, this adjusted rate (the **upper limit rate of deviation**) provides a conservative estimate of the population rate of deviation that allows the audit team to control exposure to sampling risk to acceptable levels.

The upper limit rate of deviation provides the following information:

- There is a (1 − *Risk of overreliance*) probability that the true population rate of deviation is less than or equal to the upper limit rate of deviation.
- There is a (*risk of overreliance*) probability that the true population rate of deviation exceeds the upper limit rate of deviation.

Audit teams can use formulas or tables to determine the upper limit rate of deviation from the sample rate of deviation; in practice, computer programs that follow the logic of the formulas are used to determine upper limit rate of deviation. Exhibits F.11 and F.12 allow the upper limit rate of deviation to be determined for an acceptable risk of overreliance of 5 percent and 10 percent, respectively. Like the sample size tables shown in Exhibits F.5 and F.6, the values in these tables are determined by using the appropriate parameters in relatively complex statistical formulas. Using Exhibits F.11 and F.12, the audit team would calculate the upper limit rate of deviation as follows:

1. Based on the acceptable risk of overreliance, select the appropriate evaluation table.
2. Identify the row representing the appropriate sample size.
3. Identify the column corresponding to the number of deviations found by the audit team.
4. The upper limit rate of deviation is the value found at the intersection of the row in step 2 and the column in step 3.

EXHIBIT F.11 Sample Evaluation Table for 5 Percent Risk of Overreliance

| Sample Size | \multicolumn{11}{c}{Actual Number of Deviations Found} |
	0	1	2	3	4	5	6	7	8	9	10
20	14.0	21.7	28.3	34.4	40.2	45.6	50.8	55.9	60.7	65.4	69.9
25	11.3	17.7	23.2	28.2	33.0	37.6	42.0	46.3	50.4	54.4	58.4
30	9.6	14.9	19.6	23.9	28.0	31.9	35.8	39.4	43.0	46.6	50.0
35	8.3	12.9	17.0	20.7	24.3	27.8	31.1	34.4	37.5	40.6	43.7
40	7.3	11.4	15.0	18.3	21.5	24.6	27.5	30.4	33.3	36.0	38.8
45	6.5	10.2	13.4	18.4	19.2	22.0	24.7	27.3	29.8	32.4	34.8
50	5.9	9.2	12.1	14.8	17.4	19.9	22.4	24.7	27.1	29.4	31.6
55	5.4	8.4	11.1	13.5	15.9	18.2	20.5	22.6	24.8	26.9	28.9
60	4.9	7.7	10.2	12.5	14.7	16.8	18.8	20.8	22.8	24.8	26.7
65	4.6	7.1	9.4	11.5	13.6	15.5	17.5	19.3	21.2	23.0	24.7
70	4.2	6.6	8.8	10.8	12.7	14.5	16.3	18.0	19.7	21.4	28.1
75	4.0	6.2	8.2	10.1	11.8	13.6	15.2	16.9	18.5	20.1	21.6
80	3.7	5.8	7.7	9.5	11.1	12.7	14.3	15.9	17.4	18.9	20.3
90	3.3	5.2	6.9	8.4	9.9	11.4	12.8	14.2	15.5	16.9	18.2
100	3.0	4.7	6.2	7.6	9.0	10.3	11.5	12.8	14.0	15.2	16.4
125	2.4	3.8	5.0	6.1	7.2	8.3	9.3	10.3	11.3	12.3	13.2
150	2.0	3.2	4.2	5.1	6.0	6.9	7.8	8.6	9.5	10.3	11.1
200	1.5	2.4	3.2	3.9	4.6	5.2	5.8	6.5	7.2	7.8	8.4
300	1.0	1.6	2.1	2.6	3.1	3.5	4.0	4.4	4.8	5.2	5.6
400	0.8	1.2	1.6	2.0	2.3	2.7	3.0	3.3	3.6	3.9	4.3
500	0.6	1.0	1.3	1.6	1.9	2.1	2.4	2.7	2.9	3.2	3.4

Note: This table presents ULRDs as percentages and assumes a large population.
Source: American Institute of Certified Public Accountants, "Audit Sampling," *Audit and Accounting Guide* (New York: AICPA, 2008).

EXHIBIT F.12 Sample Evaluation Table for 10 Percent Risk of Overreliance

Sample Size	\multicolumn{11}{c}{Actual Number of Deviations Found}
	0	1	2	3	4	5	6	7	8	9	10
20	10.9	18.1	24.5	30.5	36.1	41.5	46.8	51.9	56.8	61.6	66.2
25	8.8	14.7	20.0	24.9	29.5	34.0	38.4	42.6	46.8	50.8	54.8
30	7.4	12.4	16.8	21.0	24.9	28.8	32.5	36.2	39.7	43.2	46.7
35	6.4	10.7	14.5	18.2	21.6	24.9	28.2	31.4	34.5	37.6	40.6
40	5.6	9.4	12.8	16.0	19.0	22.0	24.9	27.7	30.5	33.2	35.9
45	5.0	8.4	11.4	14.3	17.0	19.7	22.3	24.8	27.3	29.8	32.2
50	4.6	7.6	10.3	12.9	15.4	17.8	20.2	22.5	24.7	27.0	29.2
55	4.2	6.9	9.4	11.8	14.1	16.3	18.4	20.5	22.6	24.6	26.7
60	3.8	6.4	8.7	10.8	12.9	15.0	16.9	18.9	20.8	22.7	24.6
65	3.5	5.9	8.0	10.0	12.0	13.9	15.7	17.5	19.3	21.0	22.8
70	3.3	5.5	7.5	9.3	11.1	12.9	14.6	16.3	18.0	19.6	21.2
75	3.1	5.1	7.0	8.7	10.4	12.1	13.7	15.2	16.8	18.3	19.8
80	2.9	4.8	6.6	8.2	9.8	11.3	12.8	14.3	15.8	17.2	18.7
90	2.6	4.3	5.9	7.3	8.7	10.1	11.5	12.8	14.1	15.4	16.7
100	2.3	3.9	5.3	6.6	7.9	9.1	10.3	11.5	12.7	13.9	15.0
125	1.9	3.1	4.3	5.3	6.3	7.3	8.3	9.3	10.2	11.2	12.1
150	1.6	2.6	3.6	4.4	5.3	6.1	7.0	7.8	8.6	9.4	10.1
200	1.2	2.0	2.7	3.4	4.0	4.6	5.3	5.9	6.5	7.1	7.6
300	0.8	1.3	1.8	2.3	2.7	3.1	3.5	3.9	4.3	4.7	5.1
400	0.6	1.0	1.4	1.7	2.0	2.4	2.7	3.0	3.3	3.6	3.9
500	0.5	0.8	1.1	1.4	1.6	1.9	2.1	2.4	2.6	2.9	3.1

Note: This table presents ULRDs as percentages and assumes a large population.
Source: American Institute of Certified Public Accountants, "Audit Sampling," *Audit and Accounting Guide* (New York: AICPA, 2008).

To illustrate the use of sample evaluation tables, consider the findings for the occurrence control for AirCon Company. Recall that the audit team examined a sample of 127 sales invoices for the potential occurrence of this control, found two deviations, and calculated a sample rate of deviation of 1.6 percent. Using Exhibit F.11 (for a risk of overreliance of 5 percent), the audit team would locate the row corresponding to a sample size of 127 items and the column for two deviations. Note that Exhibit F.11 contains a row for sample sizes of 125 and 150 but not 127. When choosing between two samples to use in this table, it is more conservative to use the smaller number. In this instance, the audit team can do one of the following:

1. Select an additional 23 items for examination for a sample size of 150 (the next highest sample size in the sample evaluation table).
2. Evaluate the results of the sample using a smaller sample size of 125. This provides a conservative (higher) measure of the upper limit rate of deviation because the same number of deviations will be attributed to a smaller number of sample items.
3. Interpolate the values in Exhibit F.11 and estimate an upper limit rate of deviation for a sample of 127 items.

Because the original sample of 127 is very close to the sample size row of 125, assume that the audit team evaluates the two deviations using a sample size of 125. Reading the value in the table at the intersection of this row and column reveals an upper limit rate of deviation of 5.0 percent, as shown in the following excerpt from Exhibit F.11.

Sample Size	\multicolumn{4}{c}{Actual Number of Deviations Found}
	0	1	2	3
125	2.4	3.8	5.0	6.1

The upper limit rate of deviation is composed of the following components:

- A sample rate of deviation of 1.6 percent (2 deviations ÷ 127 items = 1.6 percent).[8]
- An *allowance for sampling risk* of 3.4 percent (Upper limit rate of deviation of 5.0 percent − Sample rate of deviation of 1.6 percent = 3.4 percent). The allowance for sampling risk represents the "adjustment" of the sample rate of deviation for the acceptable risk of overreliance.

Now let us consider the results for the accuracy control. Using a risk of overreliance of 10 percent (Exhibit F.12), note that a row for a sample of 52 items is not shown. Again, because this sample size is close to the row for a sample size of 50 and using 50 is more conservative than using 55, the four deviations would be evaluated using a sample size of 50. Reading the upper limit rate of deviation at the intersection of the row for a sample size of 50 and the column for 4 deviations yields an upper limit rate of deviation of 15.4 percent. This upper limit rate of deviation is comprised of a sample rate of deviation of 7.7 percent[9] and an allowance for sampling risk of 7.7 percent (15.4 percent − 7.7 percent = 7.7 percent). In this case, the upper limit rate of deviation of 15.4 percent exceeds the sample rate of deviation of 10 percent.

⌕ REVIEW CHECKPOINTS

F.13 What is the sample rate of deviation? How does the audit team calculate it?

F.14 What is the upper limit rate of deviation? What information does the upper limit rate of deviation provide to the audit team?

F.15 What factors influence the determination of the upper limit rate of deviation?

F.16 Describe the general process used to determine the upper limit rate of deviation using AICPA sampling tables.

F.17 What options are available to the audit team for determining the upper limit rate of deviation if the audit team's sample size is not included in the AICPA sampling tables?

F.18 If the audit team examines a sample of 100 items, finds six deviations, and calculates an upper limit rate of deviation of 10.3 percent, what is the allowance for sampling risk?

Making the Evaluation Decision

The previous subsection discussed the determination of the upper limit rate of deviation for the occurrence and accuracy controls. Comparing the upper limit rate of deviation (ULRD) for the two key controls to the tolerable rate of deviation (TRD) for these controls (also shown in the documentation example in Exhibit F.9) reveals the following:

Control Procedure	ULRD		TRD	Conclusion
Occurrence: All sales invoices are supported by shipping documents	5.0%	<	6%	Control is operating effectively
Accuracy: Sales invoices are mathematically verified	15.4%	>	10%	Control is not operating effectively

---

[8] The fact that the audit team uses a sample size of 125 items to determine the upper limit rate of deviation does not affect the calculation of the sample rate of deviation using the original sample size (127 items).

[9] The fact that the audit team uses a sample size of 50 items to determine the upper limit rate of deviation does not affect the calculation of the sample rate of deviation using the original sample size of 52 items (4 deviations ÷ 52 items = 7.7 percent sample rate of deviation).

The audit team's decision rule after calculating the upper limit rate of deviation can be summarized as follows:

1. If the upper limit rate of deviation ≤ the tolerable rate of deviation:
   a. Rely on internal control as planned and maintain control risk at planned levels.
2. If the upper limit rate of deviation > the tolerable rate of deviation:
   a. Reduce reliance on internal control and increase control risk *or*
   b. Expand the sample size to attempt and achieve an observed upper limit rate of deviation less than the tolerable rate of deviation.

How would the audit team proceed from this point? It appears that the control for the occurrence assertion is functioning effectively. As a result, the audit team could decide to rely on internal control as planned and maintain the planned level of control risk as well as the planned level of detection risk.

For the accuracy assertion, the audit team has one of two options. The first option is to reduce the planned degree of reliance on internal control, increase the planned level of control risk, and reduce the planned level of detection risk by performing more effective substantive procedures. Recall that the upper limit rate of deviation for the accuracy control is 15.4 percent; assume that a tolerable rate of deviation of 16 percent would correspond to a control risk assessment of 0.80 (slightly below maximum) (see Exhibit F.3). Thus, without gathering any further evidence, the audit team could increase the assessment of control risk from 0.50 (moderate) to 0.80 (slightly below maximum) and correspondingly decrease the necessary level of detection risk. This decrease in the necessary level of detection risk would require the audit team to perform more effective substantive procedures. This option is reflected by tickmark (B) in Exhibit F.9.

Alternatively, the audit team could attempt to reduce the upper limit rate of deviation to a level below the tolerable rate of deviation of 10 percent by examining an expanded sample of controls. In Exhibit F.12, read down the column for four deviations (the number found by the audit team) to find an upper limit rate of deviation that is less than 10 percent. Notice that if a total of 80 items is examined and a total of four deviations is noted, the upper limit rate of deviation is 9.8 percent. Therefore, one option available to the audit team is to examine an additional 28 items (80 items − Original sample of 52 items). Consider, however, that the most likely result of examining 28 additional items is to find two more deviations (7.7% sample rate of deviation × 28 items = 2.2 deviations). This would result in an upper limit rate of deviation of 12.8% (a total of six deviations over a sample of 80 items), which still exceeds the tolerable rate of deviation. (The upper limit rate of deviation is lower than the original upper limit rate of deviation of 15.4% because increasing the sample size reduces the allowance for sampling risk.) Therefore, examining additional items is generally not an effective solution unless the upper limit rate of deviation is very close to the tolerable rate of deviation.[10]

Which option would the audit team select? This decision depends on the relative costs of increasing the tests of controls versus the costs associated with performing more extensive substantive procedures. If the cost of examining additional items is relatively low and the likelihood of observing no additional deviations is high, the audit team would likely decide to extend the sample of controls. However, if the cost of selecting and evaluating additional items is relatively high and the audit team is likely to encounter additional deviations, it could be more cost effective to perform more effective substantive procedures. Either approach will maintain audit risk at an acceptable level.

---

[10] The AICPA Audit Sampling Guide recommends as a rule of thumb that if the audit team decides to test more items, then they increase the sample by at least the number of items in the original sample.

Summary: Step 7 in the Sampling Process for AirCon Company

7. The audit team determined an upper limit rate of deviation of 5.0 percent and 15.4 percent for the occurrence and accuracy controls, respectively. Based on a comparison of the upper limit deviation rate to the tolerable rate of deviation, the audit team would

- Conclude that the occurrence control is functioning effectively and rely on internal control as planned.

- Conclude that the accuracy control is not functioning effectively and either (1) reduce reliance on internal control or (2) expand the sample to examine a larger number of items.

See Exhibit F.13 for a summary of the total costs that the audit team could incur under some alternative scenarios for testing the accuracy control. This illustration assumes that the cost to perform a test of control is $6 per item and the cost to perform a substantive procedure is $10 per item. The following should be evident from Exhibit F.13:

1. To support lower levels of control risk, the audit team must set a lower tolerable rate of deviation and the sample results must support lower upper limit rates of deviation.
2. Lower levels of control risk and lower tolerable rates of deviation result in a larger sample for tests of controls.
3. Lower levels of control risk are associated with smaller samples for substantive procedures.

At this point, the audit team may choose to examine the additional 28 invoices and attempt to attain a moderate assessment of control risk. Doing so would result in an additional cost of performing tests of controls of $168 ($480 − $312) while providing a cost savings in the form of reduced substantive procedures of $190 ($1,360 = $1,170), assuming the audit team does not find additional errors.

One final issue in calculating the upper limit rate of deviation is the effect of the acceptable risk of overreliance on the upper limit rate of deviation. Conceptually, it would seem logical that lower levels of this risk would provide a more conservative (i.e., higher) upper limit rate of deviations. By examining Exhibit F.12, you should note that the upper limit rate of deviation for a sample size of 200 items, five deviations, and a 10 percent risk of overreliance is 4.6 percent. Compare this to the upper limit rate of deviation of 5.2 percent for a risk of overreliance of 5 percent (Exhibit F.11). Essentially, a higher acceptable risk of overreliance would increase the likelihood that the audit team can conclude to rely on internal control as planned.

Qualitative Evaluation of Deviations

The focus thus far has been on quantitative factors: sample sizes, numbers of deviations, tolerable rate of deviation, and upper limit rates of deviation. Regardless of the results of the attributes sampling application, the audit team should conduct a *qualitative evaluation* of deviations to determine their nature and cause. In some cases, deviations can truly represent an isolated incident on a specific transaction; in others, they can represent something far more serious.

EXHIBIT F.13
Alternative Audit Approaches for the Accuracy Control

Control Risk	TRD	Tests of Controls n	Tests of Controls Cost	Substantive Procedures n	Substantive Procedures Cost	Total Cost
Moderate (0.50)	10%	80	$480	117	$1,170	$1,650
Slightly below maximum (0.80)	16	52	312	136	1,360	1,672

TRD = Tolerable rate of deviation
n = Sample size

A qualitative evaluation of deviations attempts to answer questions such as these with regard to observed deviations:

- Do deviations represent a pervasive error made consistently on all transactions or an isolated mistake made on a specific transaction?
- Are deviations intentional or unintentional in nature?
- Do deviations represent a misunderstanding of instructions or careless attention to duties?
- Do deviations have implications with regard to the effectiveness of other controls (for example, information technology general controls or other Committee of Sponsoring Organizations of the Treadway Commission, or COSO, components)?

If any deviations appear to be pervasively occurring throughout the sample, to represent intentional actions on the part of client employees, to represent careless attention, or to have implications with respect to other controls, they have additional implications for the audit and should be discussed with the client and its audit committee. It is important that the audit team not accept client explanations too readily without corroboration or attempt to "explain away" serious deviations.

ATTRIBUTES SAMPLING: DOCUMENTING

As shown in the overview of the seven-step procedure for attributes sampling, the audit team is required to document various information related to the sampling procedure. Some of this information is shown in Exhibit F.9 and typically includes the following:

- Information on the objective of sampling, definition of deviation conditions, and definition of the population from which the sample was selected, including the physical representation (steps 1–3).
- The levels of the risk of overreliance, tolerable rate of deviation, and expected population deviation rate as well as the rationale for these assessments (step 4).
- The sample size determined based on the factors discussed (step 4).
- Information on the selection of sample items and a list of items selected and examined by the audit team (step 5).
- Results of the tests of controls performed on each item selected and sample rate of deviation (step 6).
- Information regarding the number of deviations and the upper limit rate of deviation (step 7).
- The audit team's conclusion with respect to the operating effectiveness of the control and the implications of this effectiveness on the audit team's reliance on internal control and substantive procedures (step 7).

REVIEW CHECKPOINTS

F.19 What is the audit team's decision rule with respect to the relationship between the upper limit rate of deviation and the tolerable rate of deviation?

F.20 What options are available to the audit team if the upper limit rate of deviation is less than or equal to the tolerable rate of deviation?

F.21 What options are available to the audit team if the upper limit rate of deviation is higher than the tolerable rate of deviation?

F.22 What information does the audit team typically document in an attributes sampling application?

SEQUENTIAL SAMPLING AND DISCOVERY SAMPLING

LEARNING OBJECTIVE F-6
Define *sequential sampling* and *discovery sampling* and identify when these types of sampling applications could be used.

The AirCon Company example in this module used a *fixed sampling plan* in which the audit team selected and evaluated a single sample. In some instances, audit teams may use a *sequential sampling plan* to provide flexibility and efficiency, particularly if they anticipate a relatively low rate of deviation. To illustrate, assume that the tolerable rate of deviation is 5 percent, the expected population deviation rate is 0.5 percent, and there is a 10 percent risk of overreliance. In this case, if the first 50 items selected by the audit team did not reveal any deviations, the facts that (1) the difference between the tolerable rate of deviation and expected population deviation rate is high and (2) the preliminary evidence regarding the operating effectiveness of the client's internal control appears to be favorable could allow the audit team to conclude that the control is functioning effectively. Alternatively, if one or more deviations are noted in the sample of 50 items, the evidence might not be sufficient and the audit team would need to gather additional evidence.

Sequential sampling methods provide the audit team the opportunity to draw conclusions using a smaller sample than a traditional fixed sampling plan. It is sometimes called "stop-or-go" sampling because the plan allows the audit team to *stop* after examining a relatively small sample and evaluate the results. If the results are clearly acceptable or clearly unacceptable, the audit team can draw its conclusion; if the results are inconclusive, the audit team can *go* forward and examine additional items. Sequential sampling plans generally operate as follows:

1. Based on the acceptable risk of overreliance, tolerable rate of deviation, and expected population deviation rate, determine an initial sample size and examine the items. This initial sample size is smaller than that determined using the AICPA sampling tables in a fixed sampling plan.

2. Based on the number of deviations noted, one of three courses of action may be taken:
    a. If the number of deviations is sufficiently low, conclude that the control is operating effectively; no additional items need be selected.
    b. If the number of deviations is sufficiently high, conclude that the control is not operating effectively and increase the level of control risk beyond the planned level.
    c. If the number of deviations does not permit a clear decision in (a) or (b), increase the sample size and repeat the preceding steps.

Exhibit F.14 is a sequential sampling table suggested by the AICPA *Audit Sampling Guide*. Using the parameters from above, the sample size from Exhibit F.7 would be 77 items. However, if you select a sample of 50 items and find zero deviations, the upper limit rate of deviation from Exhibit F.12 is 4.6, and your sample results allow you to conclude that the control is functioning effectively and to assess control risk at the planned level.

Alternatively, if your sample revealed one to three deviations, the level of sampling risk is not sufficient to support your assessment of control risk at the planned level. In this instance, you could consider increasing your sample size. (The *Sampling Guide* suggests equal additional increments, e.g. 0–50, 51–101) Note that this guidance assumes finding no deviations in the additional sampling increment. If a review of the Group 2 row

EXHIBIT F.14 Four Step Sequential Sampling Plan

			Accumulated Deviation		
Group	Number of Sampling Units	Accumulated Sampling Units	Accept Planned Assessed Level	Sample More	Increase Planned Assessed Level
1	50	50	0	1–3	4
2	51	101	1	2–3	4
3	51	152	2	3	4
4	51	203	3	N/A	4

of Exhibit F.14 discovers one deviation in the first increment and the audit team selects 51 additional items and finds one more deviation, they still cannot accept the control as operating effectively. If audit team finds one deviation in the first 50, then it is likely they will find one in the next 51, assuming that the samples are representative.

Sequential sampling is used when the expected population deviation rate is relatively low in relation to the tolerable rate of deviation. Because decisions to expand the sample are based on the results of items that have been selected, it is important that the audit team examine items in the order in which they were *selected*. A significant advantage of this approach is that it could allow the audit team to evaluate the operating effectiveness of controls more efficiently. One disadvantage of this method is that the allowable rate of deviations in the sample is lower than that in a fixed sampling plan (i.e., sequential sampling is more conservative). In addition, the audit team should be careful in continuing to extend the sample using a sequential sampling approach if the preliminary sample evidence does not support the planned level of control risk because an extremely high number of items could ultimately be examined.

Another variation of attributes sampling is **discovery sampling,** a form of attributes sampling that is used when deviations from controls are very critical yet are expected to occur at a relatively low rate. Discovery sampling should be used when a control is extremely important for the audit team's examination or when the audit team suspects the existence of fraud. In this situation, the audit team uses samples sizes from Exhibits F.6 and F.7 corresponding to number of expected deviations equaling zero. Then, if even one deviation is discovered, the audit team stops immediately and concludes that the control is not operating effectively.

↳ REVIEW CHECKPOINTS

F.23 What is *sequential sampling*? What are its advantages and disadvantages?

F.24 Define *discovery sampling*. When is it typically used?

NONSTATISTICAL ATTRIBUTES SAMPLING

LEARNING OBJECTIVE F-7
Understand how to apply nonstatistical sampling to attributes testing.

Nonstatistical sampling is acceptable for use in auditing, and it is commonly used in practice. The first three steps of the seven-step procedure introduced at the beginning of the Module "Attributes Sampling: Planning" are exactly the same whether the audit team uses statistical or nonstatistical sampling. The objectives, population, and the characteristics of interest would be identical. It is a common misperception that sample sizes will be smaller using nonstatistical sampling compared to using statistical sampling, but AU 530 is clear that the sample sizes under statistical and nonstatistical sampling methods should be comparable.

The fourth step in the sampling plan, selecting the sample, may be performed differently for nonstatistical sampling than for statistical sampling. As nonstatistical sampling does not make use of tables based on probabilities, the sample is not required to be selected randomly. Haphazard or block selection may be used as well as random or sequential selection. As described in Appendix F.A, when using **haphazard selection**, items are selected in an unstructured manner but without any intentional bias (e.g., picking vouchers out of the file drawer). The use of **block selection** involves selecting a series of contiguous (or adjacent) items from the population (e.g., all disbursements in August). Haphazard and block selection do not consist of selecting the sample in a careless manner. The audit team should expect the sample to be representative of the population. Still, audit teams must be aware that using methods in which the probabilities of selecting each item are unknown exposes them to a higher risk of bias in the sample that might lead to an unrepresentative sample (sampling risk).

The fifth step, determining the sample size, may also be quite different under nonstatistical sampling. The sample size is based on the audit team's judgment. The AICPA's *Audit Sampling Guide* (para. 3.37) is clear that the audit team is not required to quantify the parameters previously discussed (i.e., tolerable rate of deviation, risk of overreliance, expected population deviation rate) but may use general terms such as "none, few, or many." However, the audit team may use tables such as those at Exhibits F.6 and F.7 to guide their decision. At the end of the day, the sample sizes for statistical and nonstatistical sampling should be comparable.

Step 6, measuring the sample items, also is performed exactly the same way whether statistical or nonstatistical sampling is being used. The primary difference between the two methods occurs at step 7, evaluating sample results. Audit teams first calculate the sample rate of deviation. If the sample rate of deviation is higher than the tolerable rate of deviation, the audit team can conclude that the control is not working effectively and revise the planned detection risk. However, if the sample rate of deviation is less than or equal to the tolerable rate of deviation, audit teams cannot conclude that the control is operating effectively. They must use professional judgment to estimate the allowance for sampling risk to determine the likely rate of deviation in the population. They may examine tables such as the ones in Exhibits F.11 and F.12 to guide their judgment, knowing that the tables cannot be strictly relied upon in a nonstatistical setting. Generally, if the sample rate of deviation is higher than the expected population rate of deviations, the audit team will conclude that the controls are not working as well as they expected when assessing control risk.

For example, if the audit team of AirCon Company had decided to use nonstatistical sampling, they would still need to select a sample size comparable to the one they would select using the statistical sampling tables. Assume that they decided on 120 items for the occurrence assertion and selected the sales invoices by going through the sales invoice files and selecting 120 sales invoices using haphazard selection. If they found two deviations as in the previous example, the sample rate of deviation would be 1.7 percent (rounded). This is considerably lower than the tolerable rate of deviation of 6 percent and even lower than the expected population deviation rate of 2 percent. Thus, the audit teams might reasonably conclude that the control is operating effectively.

If, in testing the accuracy assertion, the audit team examined 50 of the invoices and found four deviations, their sample rate of deviation would be 8 percent. This is also below the tolerable rate of deviation of 10 percent, but it is above the expected population deviation rate of 3.5 percent. This situation is more problematic for the audit teams. Because the sample rate of deviation is higher than the expected population deviation rate, the audit team would likely reject the control, increase control risk, and increase their substantive testing.[11] On the other hand, they might decide to increase their sample size, hoping they would not find more deviations. (Again, the rule of thumb is to add at least as many items as the original sample).

As you can see, nonstatistical sampling is similar in nature to statistical sampling. The audit team performs the same tests of controls, and the objective of those tests is the same as that under statistical sampling. The primary difference is that a greater degree of audit team judgment is used in (1) determining the necessary sample size and (2) evaluating the sampling results by adjusting the sample rate of deviation for sampling risk.

↳ REVIEW CHECKPOINTS

F.25 In what steps of a sampling plan would the use of nonstatistical sampling differ from the use of statistical sampling?

F.26 How should an audit team using nonstatistical sampling for attributes testing evaluate the results of the test?

---

[11] Alternatively, they might refer to a table such as the one in Exhibit F.11, which also would lead them to reject the control.

Summary

This module discusses attributes sampling, which the audit team uses to evaluate operating effectiveness of internal control. When performing attributes sampling, the audit team's primary objective is to assess the extent to which the client's internal control policies and procedures are functioning effectively. As with any sampling application, the audit team is exposed to sampling risk (the risk that the decision made based on the sample differs from the decision that would have been made if the entire population had been examined). The audit team controls this sampling risk (referred to as the *risk of overreliance* or the *risk of assessing control risk too low*) in determining the appropriate sample size and evaluating the sample results.

After the sample is selected, the audit team performs tests of controls to determine whether the control is functioning as intended. A sample rate of deviation is determined by dividing the number of deviations by the sample size; this rate is adjusted to control for the acceptable exposure to the risk of overreliance to determine the upper limit rate of deviation. The upper limit rate of deviation is a measure that has a (1 − Risk of overreliance) probability of equaling or exceeding the true rate of deviation in the population.

Once calculated, the upper limit rate of deviation is compared to the tolerable rate of deviation. If the upper limit rate of deviation is less than the tolerable rate of deviation, the audit team can rely on internal control as planned and accept the planned level of control risk. If the upper limit rate of deviation is higher than the tolerable rate of deviation, the audit team can either increase the assessed level of control risk or expand the sample to attempt to provide an upper limit rate of deviation that is lower than the tolerable rate of deviation. Decisions regarding the assessed level of control risk should consider the costs of performing additional tests of controls versus the cost savings from reduced substantive procedures.

Audit teams may use nonstatistical sampling for attributes testing. Most of the steps of the sampling plan are performed exactly the same way as with statistical sampling. Sample sizes should be comparable to those determined for statistical sampling. The sample may be selected using nonprobabilistic techniques such as haphazard or block sampling. Evaluating the results of the sample is solely based on professional judgment because there is no method to mathematically estimate the allowance for sampling risk.

Key Terms

allowance for sampling risk (or precision): The difference between the upper limit rate of deviation and the sample rate of deviation; "adjusts" the sample rate of deviation to allow the audit team to control the exposure to the risk of overreliance, 758

attributes sampling: A form of selection used to determine the extent to which some characteristic (attribute) exists within a population of interest; used by the audit team during tests of controls, 752

block selection: A method of choosing sample items in which a series of contiguous (or adjacent) items is selected from the population, 773

deviation (error, occurrence, or exception): A condition that refers to instances in which client personnel do not follow prescribed controls, 753

discovery sampling: A form of attributes sampling that audit teams use when deviations from controls are very critical but are expected to occur at a relatively low rate, and the expected population deviation rate is set to zero, 773

expected population deviation rate: The rate of variations anticipated by the audit team in the client's internal control policies or procedures; based on prior experience or a pilot sample, 758

haphazard selection: The method of choosing sample items in an unstructured manner but without any intentional bias, 773

physical representation of the population: An audit team's frame of reference for selecting a sample, 755

risk of overreliance (*risk of assessing control risk too low*): The likelihood that the audit teams' sample will provide evidence that the client's controls are functioning effectively when examining the entire population would indicate they are not functioning effectively, 756

risk of underreliance (*risk of assessing control risk too high*): The likelihood that the audit teams' sample will provide evidence that the client's controls are not functioning effectively when examining the entire population would indicate that they are functioning effectively, 756

sample rate of deviation: The extent of variations found in the audit team's sample; determined by dividing the number of deviations by the sample size, 765

sampling interval: In a sequential process, the frequency with which items are selected within the population; determined by dividing the number of items in the population by the necessary sample size, 792

sequential sampling: A plan in which an initial sample is selected and the audit team (1) draws a final conclusion regarding the effectiveness of the control or (2) selects additional items before drawing a final conclusion regarding the effectiveness of the control; also referred to as *stop-or-go sampling,* 772

systematic random selection (systematic selection): The method of choosing sample items in which a starting point is selected and a fixed number of items are bypassed between selections, 792

systematic selection: See *systematic random selection,* 792

tolerable rate of deviation: The maximum rate of variation permissible by the audit team without modifying the planned assessed level of control risk, 757

unrestricted random selection (random selection): A method of choosing items in which all items in the population are assigned a number and selected based on random numbers picked from a random number table or generated from a computer program, 792

upper limit rate of deviation: A measure that adjusts the sample rate of variation for the audit team's acceptable level of sampling risk; the rate of deviation that has a (1 − *Risk of overreliance*) probability of equaling or exceeding the true population rate of deviation, 766

Multiple-Choice Questions for Practice and Review

All applicable Exercises and Problems are available with McGraw-Hill's Connect® Accounting

LO F-1

F.27 Which of the following major stages of the audit is most closely related to attributes sampling?
   a. Determining preliminary levels of materiality.
   b. Performing tests of controls.
   c. Performing substantive procedures.
   d. Searching for the possible occurrence of subsequent events.

LO F-1

F.28 Which of the following steps in attributes sampling is most closely related to identifying key controls corresponding to the relevant management assertions?
   a. Determine the objective of sampling.
   b. Define the deviation condition.
   c. Define the population.
   d. Determine the sample size.

LO F-2

F.29 Which of the following factors has a *direct* relationship with sample size in an attributes sampling application?

	Tolerable Rate of Deviation	Expected Population Deviation Rate
a.	Yes	Yes
b.	No	Yes
c.	Yes	No
d.	No	No

LO F-2

F.30 Which of the following sampling risks does the audit team control in an attributes sampling application (ROO = risk of overreliance, ROU = risk of underreliance)?

	ROO	ROU
a.	Yes	Yes
b.	No	Yes
c.	Yes	No
d.	No	No

LO F-2   F.31 Why is the audit team more concerned with controlling the exposure to the risk of overreliance than with the risk of underreliance?
   a. Only the risk of overreliance results in an incorrect audit decision.
   b. The risk of underreliance is not related to the audit team's study and evaluation of internal control.
   c. The risk of overreliance can ultimately result in the audit team's failing to reduce audit risk to acceptable levels.
   d. The risk of underreliance can be controlled by performing tests of controls during the interim period.

LO F-2   F.32 Which of the following would *not* result in the audit team's selecting a larger sample of controls for examination?
   a. A reduction in the risk of overreliance from 10 percent to 5 percent.
   b. An increase in the tolerable rate of deviation from 3 percent to 6 percent.
   c. An increase in the expected population deviation rate from 2 percent to 4 percent.
   d. All of the above would result in a larger sample of controls.

LO F-2   F.33 Baily Cox, an audit manager, judged that the test of controls of the company's 50,000 purchase transactions should be based on a tolerable rate of deviation of 6 percent, a risk of overreliance of 5 percent, and an expected population deviation rate of 3 percent. Using AICPA sample size tables, the appropriate sample size in this situation would be
   a. 49.
   b. 78.
   c. 132.
   d. 195.

LO F-2   F.34 Tony LaRussa, an audit manager, considered the control risk assessments listed in the left column of the following table in evaluating A. Cardinal's internal control over sales transactions. The sample sizes for the substantive procedures of the customer accounts receivable are shown to the right of each control risk. What risk of overreliance (ROO) could be assigned for tests of controls at each control risk level?

Control Risk	Accounts Receivable Sample	ROO
0.20	400	?
0.50	390	?
0.80	350	?
0.90	190	10%

   a. From top to bottom: 5%, 10%, 1%.
   b. From top to bottom: 10%, 1%, 5%.
   c. From top to bottom: 1%, 10%, 5%.
   d. From top to bottom: 1%, 5%, 10%.

LO F-5   F.35 Assume that Dylan Lee found two deviations in a sample of 90 transactions. Using AICPA sample evaluation tables, the upper limit rate of deviation at a 5 percent risk of overreliance is
   a. 2.0%.
   b. 2.2%.
   c. 5.9%.
   d. 6.9%.

LO F-5   F.36 The interpretation of the upper limit rate of deviation in an attributes sampling application is
   a. The estimated rate of deviation in the population with probability equal to the risk of overreliance that the population deviation rate is higher.
   b. The estimated rate of deviation in the population with probability equal to the risk of overreliance that the actual rate of deviation is lower.
   c. The estimated rate of deviation in the population with certainty that the actual rate of deviation is lower.
   d. The estimated rate of deviation in the population with certainty that the actual rate of deviation is higher.

LO F-5   F.37 If an audit team examined 100 transactions and found one deviation from an important control procedure, the audit conclusion could be that control risk can be assessed at the associated control risk level when

a. The tolerable rate of deviation is 2 percent.
b. The tolerable rate of deviation is 3 percent.
c. The tolerable rate of deviation is 4 percent.
d. More information about decision criteria is available.

LO F-5   F.38 If an audit team calculated an upper limit rate of deviation of 5 percent when the tolerable rate of deviation was 4 percent, both at the same risk of overreliance, control risk should be

a. Assessed at the level associated with the 4 percent tolerable rate of deviation.
b. Increased and substantive procedures should be adjusted accordingly.
c. Assessed at the maximum level (100 percent) because the company's performance failed the test.
d. Decreased and substantive procedures should be adjusted accordingly.

LO F-1   F.39 In which of the following circumstances would the audit team most likely use attributes sampling?

a. Selecting customer accounts receivable for confirmation.
b. Selecting inventory items for verification of physical quantities.
c. Selecting purchase orders for indication of proper authorization.
d. Selecting additions to property, plant, and equipment during the year.

LO F-5   F.40 Using AICPA sample evaluation tables, what is the conclusion from a statistical sample of internal controls when a sample of 125 documents indicates five deviations if the tolerable rate of deviation is 5 percent, the expected population deviation rate is 2 percent, and the allowance for sampling risk is 3 percent?

a. Accept the evidence as support for assessing a low control risk because the tolerable rate of deviation less the allowance for sampling risk is less than the expected population deviation rate.
b. Use the evidence to assess a higher control risk than planned because the sample rate of deviation plus the allowance for sampling risk exceeds the tolerable rate of deviation.
c. Use the evidence to assess a higher control risk than planned because tolerable rate of deviation plus the allowance for sampling risk exceeds the expected population deviation rate.
d. Accept the evidence as support for assessing a low control risk because the sample rate of deviation plus the allowance for sampling risk exceeds the tolerable rate of deviation.

LO F-5   F.41 An audit team designed a sample that would provide a 10 percent risk of overreliance that not more than 7 percent of sales invoices lacked credit approval. From previous audits, the audit team expected that 3 percent of the sample invoices lacked proper approval. From the sample of 90 invoices, 7 were found to lack credit approval. Using AICPA sample evaluation tables, the upper limit rate of deviation was

a. 3.3%.
b. 4.5%.
c. 7.8%.
d. 12.8%.

LO F-5   F.42 Based on the information in the preceding question, the allowance for sampling risk was

a. 2.2%,
b. 5.0%,
c. 7.8%,
d. 10.0%.

LO F-5   F.43 If the _____ exceeds the _____, the audit team would decide to rely on internal control as planned and maintain control risk at planned levels.

a. upper limit rate of deviation; tolerable rate of deviation.
b. tolerable rate of deviation; upper limit rate of deviation.
c. expected population deviation rate; tolerable rate of deviation.
d. tolerable rate of deviation; expected population deviation rate.

LO F-5 F.44 If the sample evidence does *not* support the planned level of control risk, the audit team could
  a. Increase the assessed level of control risk.
  b. Perform additional substantive procedures, reducing the necessary level of detection risk.
  c. Expand the sample to achieve an observed upper limit rate of deviation less than the tolerable rate of deviation.
  d. All of the above are acceptable.

LO F-5 F.45 Which of the following best describes the method of determining the upper limit rate of deviation?
  a. Expected population deviation rate + Allowance for sampling risk.
  b. Risk of underreliance + Allowance for sampling risk.
  c. Sample rate of deviation + Allowance for sampling risk.
  d. Tolerable rate of deviation + Allowance for sampling risk.

LO F-3 F.46 Which of the following factors used to determine sample size is normally based on the extent to which the audit team expects to rely on the internal control being examined?
  a. Allowance for sampling risk.
  b. Expected population deviation rate.
  c. Sample rate of deviation.
  d. Tolerable rate of deviation.

LO F-6 F.47 A type of sampling application in which a relatively small initial sample is examined and decisions regarding expanding that sample are based on the results of this initial sample is known as
  a. Attributes sampling.
  b. Discovery sampling.
  c. Sequential sampling.
  d. Statistical sampling.

LO F-6 F.48 Jerry Tim is examining an important internal control in the audit of Langly Company. In past audits, deviations from this control have been observed at a minimal rate (less than 0.1 percent); however, because the account balance affected by this control is highly susceptible to fraud, it is important that Jerry obtain a high level of assurance that deviations occur at no higher than a predetermined (low) rate. Which of the following sampling methods would Jerry most likely use to evaluate this control?
  a. Attributes sampling.
  b. Discovery sampling.
  c. Sequential sampling.
  d. Statistical sampling.

LO F-7 F.49 In which step of a sampling plan is nonstatistical sampling different from statistical sampling?
  a. Define the characteristic of interest.
  b. Define the population.
  c. Measure the sample items.
  d. Evaluate the sample results.

LO F-7 F.50 The primary benefit of using nonstatistical sampling is that
  a. It generally results in a smaller sample size.
  b. It removes the need to consider allowance for sampling risk.
  c. It is simpler to use.
  d. All of the above are true.

Exercises and Problems

All applicable Exercises and Problems are available with McGraw-Hill's *Connect®* Accounting

LO F-1 F.51 **Test of Controls Objectives and Deviations.**

Required:
Review each of the following controls. Identify (1) the objective of the audit team's test of controls and (2) one example of a deviation from the control.

a. The credit department supervisor reviews each customer's order and approves credit by making a notation on the order.

b. The billing department must receive written notice from the shipping department of actual shipment to a customer before a sale is recorded. The sales record date is supposed to be the shipment date.

c. Billing clerks carefully identify the correct catalog list prices for goods shipped and calculate and verify the amounts billed on invoices for the quantities of goods shipped.

d. Billing clerks review invoices for intercompany sales and mark each one with the code 9 so they will be posted to intercompany sales accounts.

LO F-2, F-3, F-5

F.52 **General Attributes Sampling.** Frazier Holyfield, a new staff accountant, is evaluating important controls over the revenue cycle and, more specifically, assessing the operating effectiveness of the control that all shipments made to customers by Top Rank, Inc., have been properly invoiced.

Required:

Comment on the following actions that Holyfield performed. You should evaluate each action independently of any other actions.

a. Holyfield decided to inspect documentary evidence that all shipments made by Top Rank have been invoiced by matching shipping documents with invoices. Accordingly, she has identified the population from which she intends to sample as all sales invoices. Top Rank has a computerized list of invoiced sales that she can use to select the appropriate sample.

b. Because Holyfield plans to place a high degree of reliance on this particular control, she assesses the risk of overreliance at 5 percent. In previous years, a 10 percent level was used, but consultation with the engagement manager (Mike Evander) and partner (Donna Arum) indicate that a higher degree of reliance is planned in the current audit.

c. Frazier assessed the expected population deviation rate at 1 percent. While the rate of deviation from prior audits has approximated 2 percent, Top Rank has made several improvements in its processing of sales invoices; as a result, she believes that a lower expected population deviation rate is appropriate.

d. Based on the risk of overreliance (5 percent), the expected population deviation rate (1 percent), and the tolerable rate of deviation (4 percent), Frazier uses sampling tables to calculate a sample size of 156. She then increases the sample size to 175 because the population of sales invoices is extremely large (more than 30,000 sales invoices are processed per year).

e. Based on her tests of controls, Holyfield determined a sample rate of deviation of 2 percent. Using this rate of deviation, along with the appropriate risk of overreliance, she determined an allowance for sampling risk of 2.5 percent. Because the sum of these two (4.5 percent) is less than the risk of overreliance, Holyfield concluded that the control is operating effectively and decided to rely on this control as planned to reduce the scope of her substantive procedures.

LO F-1

F.53 **Examples of Deviations.** Dana Beckham, CPA, is performing an attributes sampling application for Posh Company. In doing so, Beckham is interested in determining whether quantities on sales invoices are verified by client personnel and agreed with those on the corresponding shipping documents. Per Posh Company's instructions, client personnel are supposed to place checkmarks next to the quantities on the sales invoices to identify that these quantities have been verified.

During the tests of controls, Beckham selected a total of 100 invoices for examination. Of these invoices, 95 had checkmarks clearly indicated on them. Beckham's examination of the remaining five invoices revealed the following:

1. On one invoice, checkmarks were not placed next to the quantities; however, the designation "OK" was written next to them.

2. One of the invoices selected for examination could not be located. Posh Company indicated that invoices occasionally are discarded when customers return the merchandise for credit.

3. No marks or identification was noted next to the quantities on one of the invoices; however, this invoice was marked "VOID."

4. A checkmark was placed on an invoice; however, this checkmark was not adjacent to any of the quantities and could not easily be associated with specific quantities noted on the invoice.
5. One of the invoices contained 15 different types of items. However, only five checkmarks were placed on the invoice, all adjacent to items from the same location in the warehouse.

Required:
a. For each of the five invoices noted, indicate whether you believe the item represents a deviation. Please justify your treatment of the invoice.
b. What is one fallacy associated with assuming that the internal controls related to the 95 remaining invoices are functioning effectively?

LO F-1

F.54 **Examples of Deviations.** Madison Perry, CPA, is conducting an audit of Parker, Inc. In so doing, Perry is performing a study of Parker's internal control and has identified a number of important controls related to purchases on which to rely. These controls are as follows:

1. There is segregation of duties between the individual authorizing the purchase, the individual preparing the purchase order, and the individual receiving goods and services being purchased.
2. Verification of approval of purchases is evidenced by having the individuals performing the verification place their initials on the purchase order.
3. On receipt of goods or services, invoices from vendors should be matched to purchase orders. This matching is evidenced by a handwritten notation of the purchase order number on each invoice.
4. Mathematical verification of vendor invoices should be evidenced by having the individuals performing the verification place their initials on the invoice itself.
5. Payments should be made only for vendor invoices that have been matched to purchase orders and mathematically verified.

Required:
a. For each of the five controls, describe one test of control that Perry could perform to verify the operating effectiveness of the control.
b. For each of the five controls, provide an example of a deviation that Perry might identify.
c. Assume that Perry encountered the following situation(s) during the tests of controls. Discuss whether you believe these situations represent deviations from the controls.
  1. For a sample purchase, Perry could readily determine that different individuals authorized the purchase and prepared the purchase order. However, because receiving personnel were on vacation, the individual authorizing the purchase initially received the goods and services being purchased. This is a one-time occurrence and happened only on the day when all receiving personnel were on vacation or otherwise absent from work.
  2. For one purchase, the individual did not initial the purchase order to evidence verification but signed it at the bottom.
  3. One vendor invoice did not have handwritten notation of the purchase order number; however, the notation "OK, approved" was written.
  4. For one purchase, a vendor invoice could not be located. As a result, a substitute invoice was identified and this invoice was properly verified by Parker's personnel.
  5. Perry identified a single cash disbursement to a vendor that was related to five separate invoices; all five invoices were properly approved for payment. Parker commonly combines several invoices into a single check to save costs.
d. Once identified by Perry, how do deviations affect the conclusion made with respect to the operating effectiveness of Parker's internal control?

LO F-1

F.55 **Examples of Deviations.** Cameron Jones, CPA, is verifying that all sales made by Hicks Company to customers on account are properly approved by credit personnel. Hicks has established the following control related to this objective: On receipt of a purchase order, evaluate the customer's creditworthiness. If the customer's name is included on an approved customer list, issue a credit authorization and begin processing the sale.

Required:

a. Define the word *deviation*. Provide an example of a deviation from this control.

b. In what stages of an attributes sampling plan does the audit team consider deviations? How do deviations influence the attributes sampling process?

c. What test of control could Jones perform to detect deviations from this control?

d. In addition to their effect on Jones's ability to rely on this control, would the following matters raise additional concerns?

1. The deviations were inadvertent mistakes and omissions made over a period of time by a number of different employees.

2. The deviations were all related to the activities of a recently hired employee that occurred during the person's first month with Hicks Company and appeared to be inadvertent mistakes and omissions. Additional tests of controls revealed that no deviations were noted following this period.

3. The deviations were the result of intentional activity on the part of Hicks Company's employees to increase reported sales to meet targeted earnings levels.

LO F-4, F-5

F.56 **Timing of Test of Controls and Sample Selection.** Susan Hill was examining controls for the authorization of cash disbursements. She selected cash disbursement entries made throughout the year and vouched them to paid invoices and canceled checks bearing the initials and signatures of employees authorized to approve the disbursements. She performed the work on September 30 when the company had issued checks numbered 43921 to 52920. Because 9,000 checks had been issued in nine months, she reasoned that 3,000 more could be issued in the three months before the December 31 year-end. About 12,000 checks had been issued last year. She wanted to take one sample of 100 disbursements for the entire year, so she selected 100 random numbers in the sequence 43921 to 55920. She audited the 80 checks in the sample that were issued before September 30, and she held the other 20 randomly selected check numbers for later use. She found no deviations in the sample of 80, a finding that, in the circumstances, would cause her to assign a low (20 percent) control risk to the probability that the system would permit improper charges to be recorded in expense and purchase/inventory accounts.

Required:

Prepare a memorandum to the audit manager (dated October 1) describing the audit team's options with respect to evaluating control performance for the period from October through December.

LO F-4

F.57 **Sample Selection.**

Required:

Read each of the following cases. Explain for each case how you could select a sample having the best chance of being representative of the population using (1) unrestricted random selection and (2) systematic random selection (refer to Appendix F.A).

a. You need to select a sample of recorded cash disbursements. The client used two bank accounts for general disbursements. Account 1 was used during January–August and issued checks numbered 3633–6632. Account 2 was used during May–December and issued checks numbered 0001–6000.

b. You need to select a sample of purchase orders. The client issued prenumbered purchase orders in the sequence 9000–13999. You realize that if you select five-digit random numbers from a table and look for numbers in this sequence, 95 percent of the random numbers you scan will be discards because a table has 100,000 different five-digit random numbers. (The computer is down today!) How can you alter this sequence to reduce the number of instances in which the numbers in the table do not correspond to numbers in the population?

c. You need to select a sample of perpetual inventory records so you can count the quantities while the stock clerks take the physical inventory. The perpetual records have been printed in a control list showing location, item description, and quantity. You have a copy of the list. It is 75 pages long, with 50 lines to a page (40 lines on the last page). Find an efficient way to select 100 lines for your test of the client's counting procedure.

LO F-4

F.58 **Sample Selection.** Robert Janice, CPA, is verifying a sample of controls related to the approval of vouchers for payment. His client, Fave Company, uses a prenumbered voucher system in which a voucher is prepared and approved for all receiving reports and the corresponding vendor's invoice. Based on the prior audit, Janice has verified that the first receiving report number for the year is 12794 and the final receiving report prepared this year is 38121.

Required:

Indicate how Janice could use (1) unrestricted random selection and (2) systematic random selection to select the sample for sample sizes of 50, 100, and 500 (refer to Appendix F.A).

LO F-4

F.59 **Sample Selection.** Hunter McNeal is studying and evaluating Branyon's internal controls related to the mathematical verification of sales invoices. In this verification, Branyon's control policies require that employees perform the following procedures:

- Verify that sales invoices are prepared only for items actually shipped to customers. This policy is evidenced by requiring employees to place a checkmark next to quantities on the sales invoices.
- Verify that prices charged to customers are from approved price lists. This policy is evidenced by requiring employees to place a checkmark next to prices on the sales invoice.
- Verify that extensions and footings on invoices are mathematically accurate. This policy is evidenced by requiring employees to initial the bottom of the invoice in a section marked "Mathematically verified by."

To verify the operating effectiveness of these policies, McNeal established an expected population deviation rate of 3 percent, a tolerable rate of deviation of 6 percent, and a risk of overreliance of 10 percent. Using these parameters, McNeal determined a necessary sample size of 132 invoices, is now ready to select invoices for examination, and is considering the use of systematic selection.

Required:

a. McNeal wants to ensure that the selection of a representative sample of sales invoices. What are some of the characteristics that should be considered to ensure that the sample is representative of the population of sales invoices?

b. What issues do the use of systematic selection introduce with respect to McNeal's ability to select a representative sample of sales invoices from the population (refer to Appendix F.A)?

c. Identify any issues associated with the use of systematic selection in the following independent circumstances.

1. Branyon does not maintain invoices in a computerized format but files paper ones manually by date. McNeal has full access to the files containing the invoices.

2. Branyon does not maintain invoices in a computerized format but files paper ones manually according to customer classification ("A" represents high-volume customers; "B," middle-volume customers; and "C," low-volume customers). McNeal has full access to the files containing the invoices.

3. Branyon does not maintain invoices in a computerized format but files paper ones manually by date. Because they are maintained off-site, McNeal does not have full access to the files; however, Branyon has offered to pull invoices selected by McNeal and make them available for the tests of controls.

4. Branyon maintains invoices in a computerized format arranged alphabetically by customer name. This file can be sorted by date, amount of sale, customer number, customer classification, and ZIP code. McNeal has full access to the computerized files.

LO F-3

F.60 **Sample Size Determination.** Jule Phillips is examining the internal control of Cowboy Company and has identified the mathematical verification of sales invoices as an important control and decided to test this control. Based on a discussion with Cowboy's management, Phillips determined that Cowboy Company's employees were required to indicate their compliance with this control by writing their initials in an appropriate place on the invoice copy.

Assume that Phillips established an acceptable risk of overreliance of 5 percent, an expected population deviation rate of 3 percent, and a tolerable rate of deviation of 9 percent.

Required:

a. Using AICPA sample size tables, what is the appropriate sample size?

b. Indicate how Phillips would assess the three parameters that are used to determine sample size (risk of overreliance, expected population deviation rate, and tolerable rate of deviation).

c. Use the original parameters but now assume that Phillips is willing to increase the acceptable risk of overreliance to 10 percent. Using AICPA sample size tables, what is the new sample size to examine?

d. Provide an explanation for the change in sample size noted in (c).

LO F-3

F.61 Sample Size Determination. Review each of the following independent sets of conditions.

Required:
Use AICPA sample size tables to identify the appropriate sample size for use in a statistical sampling application (ROO = risk of overreliance, expected population deviation rate = expected population deviation rate, TRD = tolerable rate of deviation). Based on comparing the sample sizes across different combinations of these factors, what is your conclusion regarding the relationship of each of these factors to sample size?

a. ROO = 5%, EPDR = 0%, TRD = 7%.
b. ROO = 5%, EPDR = 3%, TRD = 7%.
c. ROO = 5%, EPDR = 3%, TRD = 6%.
d. ROO = 10%, EPDR = 0%, TRD = 7%.

LO F-3

F.62 Sample Size Determination. Review each of the following independent sets of conditions.

Required:
Use AICPA sample size tables to identify the appropriate sample size for use in a statistical sampling application (ROO = risk of overreliance, EPDR = expected population deviation rate, TRD = tolerable rate of deviation). Based on comparing the sample sizes across different combinations of these factors, what is your conclusion regarding the relationship of each of these factors to sample size?

a. ROO = 5%, EPDR = 1%, TRD = 4%.
b. ROO = 5%, EPDR = 1.5%, TRD = 4%.
c. ROO = 5%, EPDR = 1.5%, TRD = 6%.
d. ROO = 10%, EPDR = 1.5%, TRD = 4%.

LO F-3

F.63 Sample Size Determination. For each of the following independent cases, use AICPA sample size tables to identify the missing value(s).

	Control 1	Control 2	Control 3	Control 4
Risk of overreliance	5.0%	5.0%	10.0%	(d)
Expected population deviation rate	1.25%	2.5%	(c)	1.25%
Tolerable rate of deviation	7.0%	(b)	6.0%	6.0%
Sample size	(a)	68	153	78

LO F-3

F.64 Sample Size Determination. Grady Cambridge, CPA, is performing attributes sampling to determine whether all purchases on account are properly approved by the client. Because the client typically makes more than 2,000 purchases on account per year, Cambridge has decided to use sampling instead of examining the entire population of purchases. Based on past experience with this client, Cambridge anticipates a rate of deviation of 1 percent.

Required:
a. What factors should Cambridge consider in determining the necessary sample size? How would the level of these factors be determined?
b. Once the appropriate factors have been determined, describe the process that Cambridge would use in determining the necessary sample size.
c. Assume that Cambridge established a risk of overreliance of 10 percent and a tolerable rate of deviation of 6 percent. Using AICPA sample size tables, determine the appropriate sample size to use in evaluating the controls over approval of purchases on account.
d. How would the following changes impact (a) the factors used to determine sample size and (b) the sample size examined by Cambridge? (Do not determine an exact sample size but indicate whether the sample size would be larger, smaller, or unchanged. Treat each of these changes in factors independently in providing your answers.)
   1. Because of increased sales and new lines of business, the number of purchases made by the client on account increased markedly from more than 2,000 to nearly 5,000 during the current year.

2. The client remediated some control deficiencies related to the purchasing function noted in Cambridge's prior audits. One of these control deficiencies related specifically to the approval of purchases made by the client.
3. The client has had turnover in the purchasing function during the most recent year. This turnover resulted in a higher-than-normal number of deviations during the first few months of the new employees' tenure. The deviation rate since then has decreased to historical levels.
4. Cambridge has decided that it would be cost beneficial to seek a reduction in control risk from moderate to low.
5. Cambridge has decided that it is no longer efficient to test controls at current levels and accordingly increased control risk from moderate levels to high levels.
6. Because some of its previous suppliers are no longer in business or no longer competitive with respect to price, the client has added a number of new vendors to its approved vendor listing.

e. What are the trade-offs Cambridge must make between increasing the reliance on internal control and maintaining the current level of reliance on internal control?
f. What factors should Cambridge consider in deciding whether to increase the reliance on internal control?

LO F-5

F.65 Sample Results Evaluation. Jamie Plane is testing the effectiveness of an important control for Blackheart, Inc. Plane is placing a high level of reliance on this control and has assessed a relatively low risk of overreliance (5 percent) and tolerable rate of deviation (6 percent). Based on the acceptable risk of overreliance, expected population deviation rate, and tolerable rate of deviation, Plane determined a sample size of 60 items. The tests of controls revealed three deviations.

Required:
a. Calculate the sample rate of deviation.
b. Using AICPA sample evaluation tables, calculate the upper limit rate of deviation and allowance for sampling risk.
c. Why does the upper limit rate of deviation differ from the sample rate of deviation?
d. What would Plane's conclusion be with respect to the operating effectiveness of the control? What options are available at this time?
e. Ignoring the effects on sample size, how would Plane's decision to accept a higher risk of overreliance (10 percent) affect the conclusions made with respect to the operating effectiveness of the control?

LO F-5

F.66 Sample Results Evaluation.

Required:
Review each of the following independent sets of conditions. For each condition, calculate the (1) sample rate of deviation, and use AICPA sample evaluation tables to identify the (2) upper limit rate of deviation and (3) allowance for sampling risk (n = sample size, d = deviations, ROO = risk of overreliance). Based on comparing the upper limit rate of deviation across different combinations of these factors, what is your conclusion regarding the relationship of each of these factors to the upper limit rate of deviation?
a. $n = 60$, d = 4, ROO = 5%.
b. $n = 60$, d = 6, ROO = 5%.
c. $n = 60$, d = 6, ROO = 10%.

LO F-5

F.67 Sample Results Evaluation.

Required:
Review each of the following independent sets of conditions. For each condition, calculate the (1) sample rate of deviation, and use AICPA sample evaluation tables to identify the (2) upper limit rate of deviation, and (3) allowance for sampling risk (n = sample size, d = deviations, ROO = risk of overreliance). Based on comparing the upper limit rate of deviation across different combinations of these factors, what is your conclusion regarding the relationship of each of these factors to the upper limit rate of deviation?
a. $n = 100$, d = 8, ROO = 5%.
b. $n = 100$, d = 4, ROO = 5%.
c. $n = 100$, d = 8, ROO = 10%.

LO F-5 F.68 **Sample Results Evaluation.**

Required:

For each of the following independent cases, use AICPA sample size and sample evaluation tables to identify the missing value(s).

	Control			
	1	2	3	4
Sample size	30	(d)	200	50
Number of deviations	2	4	(g)	2
Sample rate of deviation	(a)	(e)	2.5%	(i)
Risk of overreliance	5.0%	5.0%	10.0%	(j)
Upper limit rate of deviation	(b)	12.6%	(h)	(k)
Allowance for sampling risk	(c)	(f)	2.1%	8.1%

LO F-5 F.69 **Sample Results Evaluation.** Assume that you are working on the audit of a small company and are examining purchase invoices for the presence of a "received" stamp. The omission of the stamp is thus a deviation. The population is composed of approximately 4,000 invoices processed by the company during the current year.

You decide that a rate of deviation in the population as high as 5 percent would not require any extended audit procedures. However, if the population rate of deviation is more than 5 percent, you would want to assess a higher control risk and conduct more extensive substantive tests.

In each case, write the letter of the sample (A or B) that, in your judgment, provides the best evidence that the rate of deviation in the population is 5 percent or lower (using a risk of overreliance of 5 percent). Assume that each sample is selected at random. Refer to AICPA sample evaluation tables if necessary.

	Case 1		Case 2		Case 3		Case 4		Case 5	
Sample	A	B	A	B	A	B	A	B	A	B
Number of invoices examined	75	200	150	25	200	100	100	125	200	150
Number of deviations	1	4	2	0	6	2	1	3	8	4
Sample rate of deviation	1.3	2.0	1.3	0.0	3.0	2.0	1.0	2.4	4.0	2.7

LO F-5 F.70 **Sample Results Evaluation.** Kendall Jackson, CPA, is examining the operating effectiveness of the internal control of Town Mo, a large conglomerate in the music industry. As part of the evaluation, Jackson determined a necessary sample size of 93 items (based on a tolerable rate of deviation of 5 percent, an expected population deviation rate of 0.5 percent, and a risk of overreliance of 5 percent). After properly selecting the 93 items, Jackson found no deviations from the prescribed control procedures.

Required:

a. Based on Jackson's sample, determine the sample rate of deviation and upper limit rate of deviation. (Because the AICPA sample evaluation tables do not contain a row for a sample size of 93, round down and use a sample size of 90.)

b. Explain the difference between the upper limit rate of deviation and the sample rate of deviation observed in (a). How does this difference relate to the use of statistical sampling?

c. What would Jackson conclude with respect to the operating effectiveness of Town Mo's internal control?

d. If Jackson found three deviations in the sample, calculate the sample rate of deviation and use AICPA sample evaluation tables to determine and upper limit rate of deviation. What would Jackson conclude with respect to the operating effectiveness of Town Mo's internal control in this case?

e. Using AICPA sample evaluation tables, what is the maximum number of deviations that Jackson could identify without reducing the reliance on Town Mo's internal control?

f. Repeat (e) using a 10 percent risk of overreliance. What is the explanation for any differences between this number of deviations and that in (e)?

LO F-1–F-5

F.71 **Evaluating a Sampling Application.** Tom Barton, an assistant accountant with a local CPA firm, was recently graduated from Other University. He studied statistical sampling for auditing in college and wants to impress his employers with his knowledge of modern auditing methods.

Barton decided to select a random sample of payroll checks for the test of controls using a tolerable rate of deviation of 5 percent and an acceptable risk of overreliance of 5 percent. The senior accountant told Barton that 2 percent of the checks audited last year had one or more errors in the calculation of net pay. He decided to audit 100 random checks. Because supervisory personnel had paychecks with higher amounts than production workers, he selected 60 of the supervisor checks and 40 checks of the others. He was very careful to see that the selections of 60 from the April payroll register and 40 from the August payroll register were random.

The audit of this sample yielded two deviations, exactly the 2 percent rate experienced last year. The first was the deduction of federal income taxes based on two exemptions for a supervisory employee whose W-4 form showed four exemptions. The other was payment to a production employee at a rate for a job classification one grade lower than it should have been. The worker had been promoted the week before, and Barton found that in the next payroll he was paid at the correct (higher) rate.

When he evaluated this evidence, Barton decided that these two findings were really not control deviations at all. The withholding of too much tax did not affect the expense accounts and the proper rate was paid the production worker as soon as the clerk caught up with the change orders. Barton decided that having found zero deviations in a sample of 100, the upper limit rate of deviation at 5 percent risk of overreliance was 3 percent, which easily satisfied his predetermined criterion.

The senior accountant was impressed. Last year he had audited 15 checks from each month and Barton's work represented a significant time savings. The reviewing partner on the audit also was impressed because she had never thought that statistical sampling could be so efficient, and that was the reason she had never studied the method.

Required:
Identify and explain the mistakes made by Tom and the others.

LO F-2, F-3

F.72 **Comprehensive Attributes Sampling.** Audra Dodge, CPA, is performing an attributes sampling plan for her audit of Truck Company. In her audit of cash disbursements, she has identified preparing a voucher and marking it as "paid" prior to preparing and mailing a check to the vendor as an important control. Dodge defined any voucher that was not marked as "paid" as being a deviation.

In performing her sampling application, she established the following parameters:

Risk of overreliance	5 percent
Expected population deviation rate	2.75 percent
Tolerable rate of deviation	7 percent

Required:

a. Identify what factors Dodge considered in establishing the risk of overreliance, expected population deviation rate, and tolerable rate of deviation.

b. Assume that Dodge wished to place additional reliance on this control. How would that affect the three parameters in (a)?

c. Based on the original parameters, use AICPA sample size tables to determine the appropriate sample size.

d. If Dodge selected the sample size in (c) and found four deviations, what is the sample rate of deviation?

e. Using AICPA sample evaluation tables, what is the upper limit rate of deviation? (*Note:* If the sample size cannot be directly located on the sample evaluation table, round down to the next highest sample size.)

f. What would Dodge's conclusion be with respect to the functioning of this control?

LO F-1, F-4, F-7   F.73 **Comprehensive Attributes Sampling.** Aubrey Marblehead is conducting tests of controls on the control that quantities on Rock's receiving reports are appropriately verified. In so doing, Marblehead has inquired of Rock's receiving personnel, who said that they place a mark near the quantities verified and sign the receiving report upon delivery. Marblehead has decided to use nonstatistical sampling for this engagement. Based on the importance of this control and the rate of deviation that has been observed in prior audits, Marblehead has established the following parameters.

Risk of overreliance	5 percent
Expected population deviation rate	1.5 percent
Tolerable rate of deviation	4 percent

Based on the parameters established, Marblehead decides to use a sample of 100 receiving reports.

Required:
a. How would Marblehead define a deviation condition?
b. How would Marblehead appropriately define the population? What steps should be taken to ensure that it is complete?
c. If Rock has a computerized list of all receiving reports, what are some options available to Marblehead in selecting specific items for examination? What precautions should be taken before undertaking the selection of items?
d. For each of the following deviations, determine the sample rate of deviation and indicate Marblehead's decision with respect to the functioning of the control.
   1. 2 deviations.
   2. 4 deviations.
   3. 10 deviations.

LO F-1, F-4, F-7   F.74 **Nonstatistical Attributes Sampling.** Monroe Curtis is auditing the revenue cycle of Kentucky Distilleries and has elected to perform a nonstatistical test of controls. Kentucky Distilleries sells Old Horse Bourbon to wholesale distributors around the country. Because the sale of bourbon is strictly controlled, Curtis does not expect deviations to be present in the system and has assessed control risk as low and selected a sample size of 50 sales. Curtis has defined a deviation as a recorded sale not being supported by a shipping document with a federal tax stamp.

Required:
a. How does nonstatistical sampling differ from statistical sampling?
b. Why would Curtis choose to perform nonstatistical sampling instead of statistical sampling?
c. How should Curtis select the sample (see Appendix F.A)?
d. What conclusion should Curtis make if one deviation is found?

LO F-1, F-2, F-3, F-5   F.75 **Comprehensive Attributes Sampling.** The firm of Buy and Best, CPAs, is engaged to conduct the audit of Radio Hut, a retailer of electronic and other high-technology products. Because of technological advances in Radio Hut's inventory products, an important risk that it faces is that prices charged by suppliers reflect current industry prices (which tend to fluctuate relatively significantly, particularly as new technologies are introduced and as older technologies are discontinued). The nature of Radio Hut's inventories is such that a small number of suppliers exist and each supplier has a similar pricing structure. This pricing structure is reflected in an electronic industry pricing guide, which is updated on a daily basis.

You are a staff accountant with Buy and Best and have been asked to identify a potential audit approach to address this risk. In the past, your firm has decided to place relatively limited reliance on internal control policies related to Radio Hut's purchasing function and has instead conducted relatively extensive substantive procedures related to its inventories. However, the new partner on the Radio Hut engagement has successfully reduced substantive procedures for the other clients in the retail industry by performing more extensive tests of controls. Because of previous experience in the industry as well as having used this audit approach successfully for other clients, the new partner asks you to evaluate the possibility of using more extensive tests of controls in the audit of Radio Hut.

The following controls are relevant to Radio Hut's processing of vendor invoices:

- Similar to most retailers in the industry, Radio Hut has a highly automated inventory monitoring and control system. Based on anticipated product life, current sales, and existing inventory levels, an automatic purchase order is generated when inventory levels reach predetermined thresholds.
- Once a purchase order has been generated, the store manager reviews it prior to transmitting it to the appropriate vendor. This review ensures that the vendor is from an approved list and that the proposed purchase is consistent with the store's objectives and near-term plans (for example, not purchasing a large number of laptop computers just prior to a major promotion for tablets).
- Upon receipt of the items, warehouse personnel prepare "blind" copies of a receiving report, noting the quantity of each item received.
- Purchasing personnel verify the vendors' invoices by (1) comparing the invoice to a purchase order by referencing the purchase order number on the vendor invoice, (2) comparing quantities on the vendor invoice to quantities from the receiving report prepared by warehouse personnel, (3) comparing prices on the invoice for reasonableness through reference to industry pricing data, and (4) mathematically verifying the accuracy of the invoice.

These controls have been in place for a number of years, and Radio Hut has experienced relatively little turnover in its purchasing and related functions. You did not observe any remediation or major changes with respect to these controls or to Radio Hut's control environment during the past year.

You reviewed the prior audit documentation, which was prepared by another staff accountant who has since left the firm. Based on your review, you prepared the following notes:

- The control policy tested by the staff accountant is the employee verification of the reasonableness of prices on the invoices by placing a checkmark or other notation adjacent to the price on the invoice.
- Using an expected population deviation rate of 1 percent, a tolerable rate of deviation of 7 percent, and a risk of overreliance of 10 percent, a sample of 55 invoices was selected.
- Tests of controls revealed three misstatements; based on the sample size of 55 and a risk of overreliance of 10 percent, the upper limit rate of deviation was 11.8 percent. Because this exceeded the tolerable rate of deviation 7 percent, the other staff accountant reduced reliance on the control policy and conducted more extensive substantive procedures.

Required:

a. Comment on the appropriateness of the work done in the prior audit with respect to testing this control policy.
b. Based on the results of tests of controls in the prior year, what are your initial thoughts regarding the viability of increasing your reliance on this control policy in the current audit?
c. How will your decision to increase the reliance on the control policy affect the sample size in the current audit? What specific factors will be affected by this decision?
d. Assume that you have established a risk of overreliance of 5 percent, a tolerable rate of deviation of 6 percent, and an expected population deviation rate of 1 percent. Using AICPA sample size tables, what is the necessary sample size in the current audit? Is this sample size consistent with your expectations compared to that examined in the prior year?
e. Using AICPA sample size tables, what factor(s) resulted in the increased sample size from the prior year? Can you determine the extent to which each factor contributed to this increase?

[Note: Requirements (f)–(h) are unrelated to (a)–(e).]

f. Refer to the AICPA sample evaluation tables. Assuming a sample size of 100 items, how many deviations would be permissible for you to rely on this control policy using a 5 percent risk of overreliance and a 6 percent tolerable rate of deviation?
g. Repeat (f), assuming that you decided to reduce your reliance on internal control and establish a risk of overreliance of 10 percent.
h. What does a comparison of your results in (f) and (g) tell you about the effect of the risk of overreliance on the upper limit rate of deviation?

LO F-1, F-2, F-5

F.76 **General Attributes Sampling.** You overheard the following dialogue between Joe Ashley (a staff assistant) and Monique Estrada (his supervisor).

Required:
Referring to appropriate professional standards, comment on each of these statements.
a. "It's unfortunate that generally accepted auditing standards don't allow us to use nonstatistical sampling for this control. I just don't feel that the extra time and effort to use statistical sampling are worth the benefits."
b. "I'm not sure what level of control risk we should plan to use. We need to determine the amount of substantive procedures that we will conduct and then assess control risk accordingly."
c. "We really need to be careful to limit our exposure to the risk of overreliance. This risk could result in our failure to perform enough substantive procedures."
d. "Separation of duties is such an important control that we should use statistical sampling to evaluate the extent to which the custody, recording, and approval functions for purchases are performed by different individuals."
e. "Because we're really relying heavily on this control, it's important that it be operating very effectively. That's why I set the tolerable rate of deviation at such a low level."
f. "We found six deviations of the 120 items we examined. That's a 5 percent rate of deviation. Because our tolerable rate of deviation is 8 percent, it looks like we can rely on internal control as planned."
g. "A deviation is a deviation. Some of these problems were honest mistakes, but others looked like client employees intentionally ignored the controls. However, they all have the same effect on the upper limit rate of deviation."
h. "Because our upper limit rate of deviation is lower than the tolerable rate of deviation, we don't have to do anything with the deviations we found."

LO F-1, F-2, F-7

F.77 **Comprehensive Nonstatistical Attributes Sampling.** Marty Alewine, a newly promoted senior at your firm, has been assigned as in charge of the audit of Doxey Electronics. Doxey has been a client of your firm for years. Controls are considered effective, and statistical attributes sampling to test sales transactions has been used for several years. Last year's audit documentation reveals the following: risk of overreliance, 5%; expected population deviation rate, 2%; tolerable rate of deviation, 5%; sample size, 181; deviations found, 3; and upper limit rate of deviation, 4.2%. Alewine's conclusion from the documentation is that the controls were accepted as operating effectively.

Deciding to use nonstatistical sampling this year to reduce audit hours, Alewine selected 100 invoices from the December invoice files, reasoning that tests closer to year-end are more effective, by selecting every 10th invoice until 100 invoices had been identified. Two invoices differed in amount from the shipping document, and one invoice could not be located. Alewine decided to accept the controls as effective again this year, reasoning the sample rate of deviation was only 2%, which is much less than the tolerable rate of deviation used last year.

Required:
As the manager of the Doxey Electronics audit, you have been reviewing the audit documentation. Prepare a list of reviewer comments to discuss with Alewine.

LO F-6

F.78 **Discovery and Sequential Attributes Sampling.** Sydney Siebenthaler, the audit manager for Jennifer's Running Shirts, Inc., has just returned from a continuing education class on audit sampling and now wants to use discovery sampling or sequential sampling on the Jennifer's audit because the class instructor said that the sample sizes would be significantly smaller. "Talk about a no-brainer!" Siebenthaler exulted.

Jennifer's has good controls, and the audit team has performed tests of controls over the payroll procedures in previous years to reduce substantive tests of payroll accounts to only analytical procedures. In the previous year, the audit team used the following parameters: risk of overreliance, 10%; expected population deviation rate, 2%; and tolerable rate of deviation, 10%, which resulted in a sample size of 38. The auditors increased (rounded) the sample size to 40 items, and one deviation was found. The resulting upper limit deviation rate was 9.4%, and the control was accepted as operating effectively.

Required:
a. Define *discovery sampling*.
b. Do you agree that discovery sampling should be used on the audit of Jennifer's?
c. How would discovery sampling be used?
d. Define *sequential sampling*.
e. Do you agree that sequential sampling should be used on the audit of Jennifer's?
f. How would sequential sampling be used?

LO F-4

F.79 **Kaplan CPA Exam Simulation: Sample Sizes. (Also Module E. 74)**

Required:
Go to the Kaplan website link at www.mhhe.com/louwers5e, click on Abernathy, Inc. (Sample Size) AUD TBS, and complete your answer.

LO F-3

F.80 **ACL Assignment.**

Required:
Go to the ACL website link at www.mhhe.com/louwers5e, click on ACL Assignments, and complete the assignment for Module F.

Appendix F.A

Sample Selection Methods

UNRESTRICTED RANDOM SELECTION

When using **unrestricted random selection** (often referred to as **random selection**), auditors select items from a population so that each item has an equal chance of being selected. This type of selection process can be used only when items in the population are numbered or can easily be assigned a number. The use of random selection consists of a two-step procedure:

1. Identify a series of random numbers by using either a random number table or a computer program.
2. Match the random numbers from step 1 to the corresponding numbered items in the population.

To illustrate the use of random selection, the engagement team selected the following numbers from a random number table: 120, 268, and 341. Using a computer list of sales invoices, the engagement team would test invoice numbers 120, 268, and 341. One key feature of random selection is that another individual is able to replicate the procedure and select exactly the same items. In addition, every item has an equal probability of being selected.

SYSTEMATIC RANDOM SELECTION

When using **systematic random selection** (commonly referred to as **systematic selection**), the individual randomly selects a starting point from within the population and examines every nth item thereafter, (n is determined based on the number of items in the population and the necessary sample size). Systematic selection has the advantage of ensuring that all items have an equal probability of selection while providing a more efficient method of selecting items than unrestricted random selection.

The following basic steps are used in systematic selection.

1. Determine the necessary **sampling interval**, which identifies the frequency with which items within the population are selected. The sampling interval is determined by dividing the number of items in the population by the necessary sample size.
2. Select a random starting point from within the population (a number equal to or less than the sampling interval) and select the item in the population corresponding to this number.
3. Add the sampling interval to the random starting point. The item in the population corresponding to this number is the next item selected.
4. Add the sampling interval to the total from step 3. The item in the population corresponding to this number will be the next item selected.
5. Repeat step 4 until the number of items equal to the necessary sample size is selected.

To illustrate the use of systematic selection, assume that the population is all sales for the period and the necessary sample size is 50. For purposes of illustration, assume that the population of sales totaled 1,000 invoices. A sampling interval of 20 is calculated (1,000 invoices ÷ 50 items = 20); thus, every 20th invoice would be selected for examination. If the random starting point is 15, the first three invoices selected would be as follows:

Item 1: 15 (random starting point)
Item 2: 35 (15 + 20)
Item 3: 55 (35 + 20)

In some cases, several random starting points are used to ensure a more random sample. For example, in the preceding situation, the engagement team could use one random start and select the additional 49 invoices as noted. Alternatively, they could use five random starts and select an additional nine invoices for each of these starting points. In either case, a total of 50 invoices (the necessary sample size) would ultimately be selected.

Like random selection, systematic selection is advantageous because another individual who knows both the random starting point and sampling interval can replicate the sample selection. In addition, like random selection, every item in the population has an equal chance of being selected, which provides a reasonable likelihood of selecting a representative sample.

One limitation of systematic selection is that the population must be randomly ordered. Because systematic selection essentially bypasses a number of items, a nonrandomly ordered population can result in bypassing a number of items having similar characteristics. For example, if a population of employees were arranged alphabetically, bypassing a number of employees whose last name begins with B (or any other letter) would not appear to influence the representativeness of the sample. However, if the population was arranged by department and then by seniority and, for the sake of argument, each department had 20 members, then systematic selection could possibly result in the highest paid employee from each department being selected. This is obviously an unlikely scenario, but it should be considered.

HAPHAZARD SELECTION

When using *haphazard selection*, items are selected in an unstructured manner but without any intentional bias. Although this can be done in any number of ways, one way is to identify invoices by flipping through the invoice files and selecting items until a total of 50 has been selected. Contrary to the connotation of the word *haphazard,* items are not selected in a careless manner under haphazard selection and results are expected to be representative of the population.

One significant limitation of haphazard selection is that, unlike either random selection or systematic selection, the sampling method cannot be described in sufficient detail to permit another individual to replicate it. Some describe haphazard selection as a method of choosing items without any special reason for including or excluding items, thus obtaining a representative sample. However, haphazard selection methods do not permit individuals to measure the probability of selecting sample items. In addition, although items are selected in a nonsystematic manner, studies have found that bias in selecting items (either conscious or unconscious) often exists.[12]

BLOCK SELECTION

The use of *block selection* involves selecting a series of contiguous (or adjacent) items from the population. One example of block selection is the selection of the first 10 sales at each of five different factories for a total of 50 sample invoices. Block selection is less desirable because it is difficult to efficiently obtain a representative sample; ordinarily, a relatively large number of blocks need to be selected to be representative.

WHICH SELECTION METHOD SHOULD BE USED?

The use of statistical or nonstatistical sampling procedures has a significant impact on the method of sample selection. Random or systematic selection is used with statistical sampling because these methods (1) provide a reasonable likelihood of obtaining a representative sample, (2) allow the probability of obtaining sample items to be determined, and (3) allow the sample selection process to be replicated. As a result, these methods allow sampling risk to be measured and controlled to acceptable levels. In contrast, haphazard and block selection do not meet these criteria; they could result in a random sample, but quantitatively evaluating the randomness of the sample selected by using them is difficult.

In practice, computer software has greatly increased the efficiency and effectiveness of selecting sample items, particularly when using systematic random selection or unrestricted random selection. Software applications use client data files and parameters designated by the audit team to select the appropriate sample items.

---

[12] T. W. Hall, T. L. Herron, and B. J. Pierce, "How Reliable Is Haphazard Sampling?" *The CPA Journal,* January 2006, p. 26.

Variables Sampling

> *USA Today has come out with a new survey—apparently, three out of every four people make up 75 percent of the population.*
>
> David Letterman, late night talk-show host

Professional Standards References

Topic	AU/ISA Section	PCAOB Reference*
An Audit of Internal Control over Financial Reporting That Is Integrated with an Audit of Financial Statements	N/A	AS 5
Overall Objectives of the Independent Auditor and the Conduct of an Audit in Accordance with Generally Accepted Auditing Standards.	200	AS 8
Identifying and Assessing the Risks of Material Misstatement	315	AS 12
Materiality in Planning and Performing an Audit	320	AS 11
Performing Audit Procedures in Response to Assessed Risks and Evaluating the Audit Evidence Obtained	330	AS 13
Evaluation of Misstatements Identified during the Audit	450	AS 14
Audit Evidence	500	AS 15
Audit Sampling	530	AU 350

*AU references represent standards issued by the ASB prior to April 16, 2003, that have not been superseded or amended by the PCAOB.

LEARNING OBJECTIVES

Module G provides a comprehensive example of the use of variables sampling in the audit team's substantive procedures.

Your objectives are to be able to:

LO G-1 Define *variables sampling* and understand when it is used in the audit.

LO G-2 Understand the basic process underlying *monetary unit sampling* (MUS) and when to use it.

LO G-3 Identify the factors affecting the size of an MUS sample and calculate the sample size for an MUS application.

LO G-4 Evaluate the sample results for an MUS by calculating the projected misstatement, incremental allowance for sampling risk, and basic allowance for sampling risk.

LO G-5 Understand the basic process underlying *classical variables sampling* and the use of classical variables sampling in an audit.

LO G-6 Understand the use of nonstatistical sampling for variables sampling.

INTRODUCTION

The following sampling deficiencies were noted by PCAOB inspection teams when reviewing substantive procedures by large auditing firms:[1]

- ... many of the samples the Firm used in its substantive tests of the valuation of various types of the Level 3 financial instruments were insufficient (sometimes a sample of only one item) in light of the significance and complexity of the instruments and the heightened risk the Firm identified with respect to their valuation.

- For accounts receivable, the Firm sent confirmation requests to customers for a sample of unpaid invoices; however, the Firm's sample size was insufficient to achieve the necessary level of assurance. Although the Firm assessed the control risk relating to the existence of accounts receivable as moderate, the Firm determined the sample size for confirmations of accounts receivable using a formula that assumed a lower level of risk. Additionally, the Firm's sample size was influenced by an expectation that analytical procedures would provide additional audit evidence, but those analytical procedures were inadequate as substantive tests because the Firm's expectations were not sufficiently precise to provide the necessary degree of assurance.

This deficiency illustrates the pitfalls that can arise in using professional judgment when applying sampling to substantive procedures. In the eyes of the PCAOB inspection teams, the firms referred to made poor judgments related to sample sizes, risk assessment, and reliance on analytical procedures. We will see that sound professional judgment is required throughout the application of statistical and nonstatistical sampling plans. That is why firms employ quality control standards to ensure that professional judgments are satisfactory.

DEFINITION OF VARIABLES SAMPLING

LEARNING OBJECTIVE G-1
Define *variables sampling* and understand when it is used in the audit.

Module F illustrated the use of sampling in the audit team's study and evaluation of the client's internal control, or *attributes sampling*. This module focuses on the use of *variables sampling*. Whereas attributes sampling looks at binary (yes/no) distributions, **variables sampling** examines continuous distributions of amounts or values. Thus, it is used to examine a population when the audit team wants to estimate "true" balance or the misstatement of a particular account or class of transactions. The **true balance** is the amount at which the account should be recorded if no misstatements exist. A *misstatement* is the difference between the true balance and the recorded balance of the account. Variables sampling is used during the substantive procedures stage of the audit.

The following seven-step procedure serves as the basis for our illustration of variables sampling:

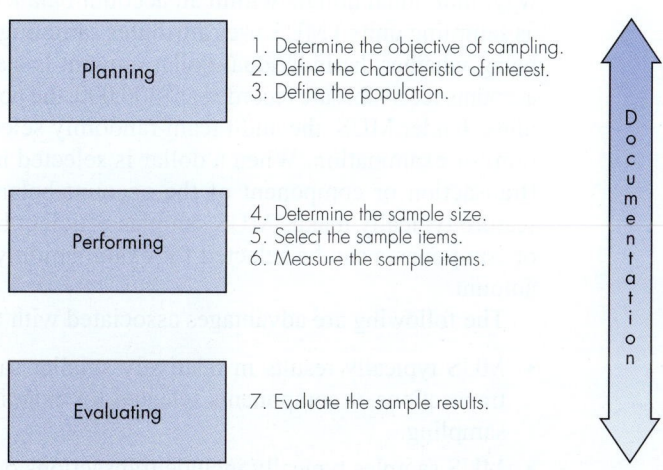

[1] 2009 Inspection of KPMG LLP (October 5, 2010); and 2008 Inspection of McGladrey & Pullen, LLP (May 6, 2009).

The audit team can use one of two statistical approaches for variables sampling. **Monetary unit sampling (MUS)** provides an estimate of the amount of misstatement in the account balance or class of transactions. The distinguishing feature of MUS is that it tends to select higher dollar transactions or components within an account balance for examination. **Classical variables sampling** uses the laws of probability and the central limit theorem to estimate either (1) the amount of misstatement in the account balance or class of transactions or (2) the "true" balance for an account balance or class of transactions. Classical variables sampling procedures provide a range of estimates with a specific probability of including the amount of misstatement or the "true" account balance. Nonstatistical sampling may also be used for variables sampling.

Auditors use both MUS and classical variables sampling to determine the fairness of the client's financial statements. When using either of these variables sampling methods, auditors examine transactions or components of clients' account balances or class of transactions. Based on this sample of transactions or components and analytical procedures, auditors then assess the overall fairness of the account balance or class of transactions.

> ↳ **REVIEW CHECKPOINTS**
>
> G.1 Define *variables sampling*. In what stage of the audit is variables sampling used?
>
> G.2 What are two statistical approaches available to the audit team for variables sampling?

SAMPLING IN SUBSTANTIVE PROCEDURES: MONETARY UNIT SAMPLING (MUS)

LEARNING OBJECTIVE G-2
Understand the basic process underlying *monetary unit sampling* (MUS) and when to use it.

MUS is one method of variables sampling the audit team uses in performing substantive procedures; it selects individual dollars from an account balance for verification. Under MUS, items in the sample are selected based on their size; that is, each item in the sample has a probability of being selected that is proportional to its size. Thus, this method of selection is often called **probability proportional to size (PPS) selection**. For example, a customer's account recorded at $30,000 is 10 times more likely to be selected than a customer's account recorded at $3,000. Other names frequently used for MUS include combined attributes-variables (CAV) sampling, cumulative monetary amount (CMA) sampling, and dollar-unit sampling (DUS).

The unique feature of MUS is its definition of the population as the number of dollars (euros, yuan, yen, etc.) in an account balance or class of transactions. (Viewed another way, individual dollars within an account balance or class of transactions are identified as sampling units.) MUS uses attributes sampling principles with the attribute of interest being whether the individual dollar amount is stated properly or not. Thus, if a client's accounts receivable are recorded at $300,000, the population is defined as 300,000 one-dollar units. Under MUS, the audit team randomly selects individual dollars from the population for examination. When a dollar is selected in this fashion, the entire "logical unit" (transaction or component of the account balance) is selected for examination. This feature typically makes MUS samples efficient because a small number of transactions or components can be selected for examination yet account for a relatively large dollar amount.

The following are advantages associated with the use of MUS:

- MUS typically results in relatively smaller sample sizes (in terms of the number of transactions or components selected for examination) compared to classical variables sampling.
- MUS samples typically include transactions or components reflecting relatively large dollar amounts.

- MUS is more effective in identifying misstatements in accounts when overstatement is the primary concern (such as revenues and assets).
- MUS is generally simpler to use than classical variables sampling, which often requires complex calculations.

In contrast, the following are disadvantages associated with the use of MUS:

- MUS provides a more conservative (higher) estimate of misstatement in the account balance or class of transactions compared to classical variables sampling. As a result, MUS is more likely to signal the need for an adjustment in the account balance or class of transactions, which will entail performance of additional procedures by the audit team.
- MUS is not effective in identifying misstatements in accounts when understatement is the primary concern (such as liabilities and expenses).
- The expansion of an MUS sample is difficult when preliminary results indicate that the account balance or class of transactions is materially misstated.
- MUS requires special considerations for logical units having a zero or negative balance. In some cases, logical units having these characteristics indicate employee fraud.

In summary, MUS is best used when the audit team expects to find few or no misstatements and when overstatement (existence assertion) is of greatest concern. In contrast, when a relatively large number of misstatements is expected or when understatement (completeness assertion) is of greatest concern, MUS is less effective.

To illustrate the use of MUS, consider the audit team's examination of accounts receivable for Rice, Inc. Rice's accounts receivable have a recorded value of $300,000 comprising 1,500 individual customer accounts. The audit team is examining the *existence* and *valuation and allocation* assertions and selects customer accounts for confirmation. This example illustrates how the audit team calculates sample size, selects sample items, and evaluates sample results through manual calculations. When the client maintains its records in computerized format, computer software is used to perform these tasks.

MUS: Planning

In the planning stages of MUS, the audit team determines the objective, defines the attribute of interest, and defines the population. The objective of any variables sampling application is to provide evidence regarding the fairness of the relevant assertions. These assertions determine the type of substantive procedures selected by the auditor, which ultimately determines the nature of items selected for examination. To verify the *existence* and *valuation and allocation* assertions, the audit team confirms accounts receivable and selects a sample of "items" for confirmation as shown:

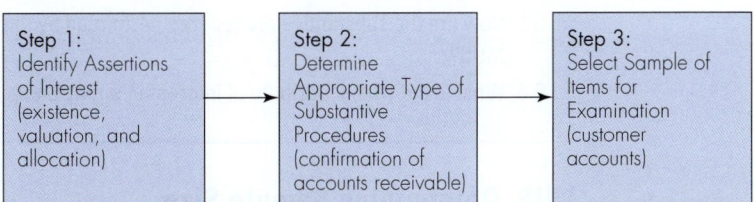

Once the objective of sampling has been determined, the audit team defines the attribute of interest. In a variables sampling application, the audit team is interested in determining the proper amount at which the items *should be* recorded; this amount is often referred to as the **audited value**, which is simply the dollar amount at which the item would be recorded assuming that no mistakes in judgment or mistakes in the application of generally accepted accounting principles were made. In an MUS application, the attribute of interest is the difference between the recorded value and the audited value, or the amount of *misstatement*.

The final step in the planning stage of MUS is to define the population of interest. As noted earlier, one of the most important distinctions of MUS is that the population is defined as all of the *individual dollars* (or euros, yuans, yen, etc.) within the account balance or class of transactions. Recall that Rice's accounts receivable comprise 1,500 individual customer accounts and are recorded at $300,000. As a result, MUS for Rice defines the population as 300,000 individual dollars of accounts receivable.

As with attributes sampling, the audit team's objective is critical in defining the population of interest. For example, consider the difference between the *existence assertion* and the *completeness assertion*. For existence, the audit team is interested in determining whether a *recorded* customer account is *bona fide* (that is, whether the account exists). In this case, the population of interest is defined as recorded account balances. In contrast, when examining the completeness assertion, the audit team is interested in ensuring that all transactions that actually occurred were included in the customer account balances. Thus, the population of interest in this case is composed of transactions representing bona fide sales. These relationships are summarized as follows:

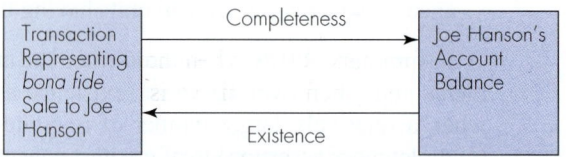

AUDITING INSIGHT — Are These Transactions Too Small?

One reason that **Ernst & Young** may have failed to detect a massive fraud at **HealthSouth** (the nation's largest provider of diagnostic imaging, outpatient surgery, and rehabilitation services) is its definition of the population from which its team selected transactions. HealthSouth executives knew that Ernst & Young would not examine items of less than $5,000; as a result, they decomposed large entries that reclassified expenses as assets into thousands of individual journal entries having amounts of less than $5,000.

Source: "Behind the Wave of Corporate Fraud: A Change in How Auditors Work," *The Wall Street Journal,* March 25, 2004, pp. A1, A14.

↳ REVIEW CHECKPOINTS

G.3 Define *monetary unit sampling (MUS)*. What is the unique feature of MUS?

G.4 What are the advantages and disadvantages of using MUS? Under what conditions is it best used?

G.5 How are the substantive procedures performed by the audit team related to the objective of MUS?

G.6 What is the typical attribute of interest in an MUS application?

MUS: Determining Sample Size

LEARNING OBJECTIVE G-3
Identify the factors affecting the size of an MUS sample and calculate the sample size for an MUS application.

The *sample size* represents the number of items that the audit team examines. In variables sampling, these items are transactions or components underlying the account balance or class of transactions being audited. Four main factors influence the sample size in an MUS application:

- Sampling risk (risk of incorrect acceptance).
- Tolerable misstatement.
- Expected misstatement.
- Population size.

EXHIBIT G.1 Sampling Risks Associated with Variables Sampling

Sampling Risk	Sample Results	Unknown State of the Population	Loss
Risk of incorrect acceptance	Upper limit on misstatements ≤ Tolerable misstatement *Conclusion:* Account is fairly stated	Actual misstatement > Tolerable misstatement *Conclusion:* Account is not fairly stated	Effectiveness loss because the audit team will make an incorrect conclusion and issue an inappropriate opinion on the financial statements
Risk of incorrect rejection	Upper limit on misstatements > Tolerable misstatement *Conclusion:* Account is not fairly stated	Actual misstatement ≤ Tolerable misstatement *Conclusion:* Account is fairly stated	Efficiency loss because additional transactions or components will be examined*

*If examining the additional transactions or components does *not* eventually result in the audit team making a correct decision, an effectiveness loss also would be incurred for the risk of incorrect rejection. This loss would occur because the audit team is proposing an adjustment to financial statements that are not materially misstated. However, because of the need to provide compelling evidence to the client prior to initiating a financial statement adjustment, these instances are relatively rare in practice.

Sampling Risk

Sampling risk occurs when the sample selected by the audit team is not representative of the population from which it is drawn. There are two types of sampling risks for variables sampling applications: the **risk of incorrect acceptance** and the **risk of incorrect rejection**. The risk of incorrect acceptance is sometimes referred to as *beta risk* or *type II error;* the risk of incorrect rejection is sometimes referred to as *alpha risk* or *type I error.* Refer to Exhibit G.1 for a summary of some of the key characteristics of these risks.

Because the risk of incorrect acceptance results in the audit team issuing an inappropriate opinion on financial statements that are materially misstated, controlling exposure to this risk is of primary importance. Therefore, under MUS, the audit team controls exposure to the risk of incorrect acceptance in determining the appropriate sample size. If the audit team wants to reduce sampling risk, the necessary sample size increases. As the sample size increases, the likelihood that the sample is representative of the population increases (i.e., sampling risk would be zero if 100 percent of the account were examined). Therefore, sample size varies inversely with sampling risk.

How is the level of the risk of incorrect acceptance established? Recall the audit risk model introduced earlier in the text.

$$\text{Audit risk (AR)} = \text{Risk of material misstatement (RMM)} \times \text{Detection risk (DR)}$$

This model can be slightly expanded to replace detection risk with the risks associated with the two major types of substantive procedures performed by the auditor: analytical procedures and tests of details. Because these two types of substantive procedures are considered independent, detection risk equals the joint probability of analytical procedures risk (AP) and tests of details risk (TD), resulting in the following expanded audit risk model:

$$AR = RMM \times AP \times TD$$

where

- AR = Audit risk (the risk that a material misstatement occurs, is not prevented or detected by the client's internal control, and is not detected by the audit team's substantive procedures)
- RMM = Risk of material misstatement[2] (IR × CR)
- AP = Analytical procedures risk (the risk that the audit team's analytical procedures fail to detect a material misstatement)
- TD = Tests of details risk (the risk that the audit team's test of details procedures fail to detect a material misstatement)

[2] AU 200 expresses the product of inherent risk and control risk as the *risk of material misstatement.* This standard notes that auditors may choose to make a combined assessment of the risk of material misstatement or separate assessments of inherent risk (IR) and control risk (CR).

Once the audit team has established AR, assessed IR based on the susceptibility of the account balance or class of transactions to misstatement, performed tests of controls to determine the appropriate level of CR, and assessed the effectiveness of analytical procedures to determine AP, the audit risk model can be algebraically manipulated to solve for TD:

$$TD = \frac{AR}{RMM \times AP}$$

TD represents the risk that the audit team's substantive tests of details fail to detect a material misstatement in an account balance or class of transactions. Were this to occur, the audit team would conclude that the account balance or class of transactions was fairly stated when, in fact, it was misstated. This risk is similar in both concept and effect to the *risk of incorrect acceptance*. Thus, the audit team establishes the level of the risk of incorrect acceptance *after* defining the remaining components of the audit risk model and "solving" the expanded audit risk model for TD. See Exhibit G.2 for a guideline that might be used for determining the appropriate risk of incorrect acceptance for tests of details (TD) given the audit team's assessment of risk of material misstatement (RMM) and analytical procedures risk (the risk that analytical procedures and other relevant substantive procedures might fail to detect aggregate misstatements greater than tolerable misstatement).

Exhibit G.3 illustrates the relationships between the various factors that affect sample size in variables sampling.

For the examination of Rice's accounts receivable, assume that the audit team sets audit risk (AR) to relatively low levels (0.05, or 5 percent). In addition, because of the susceptibility of accounts receivable to misstatement in the absence of internal control, assume that inherent risk (IR) is assessed at the maximum level (1.00, or 100 percent). Next, assume that the audit team's study and evaluation of internal control yielded a moderate assessment of control risk (0.50, or 50 percent). Finally, assume that the audit team decided not to employ extensive or highly effective analytical procedures; as a result, analytical procedures risk (AP) is assessed at the maximum level (1.00, or 100 percent). Using these assessments, the necessary level of the risk of incorrect acceptance is 10 percent, calculated as shown:

$$TD = \frac{AR}{RMM \times AP}$$

$$TD = \frac{0.05}{0.50 \times 1.00}$$

$$TD = 0.10 \text{ or } 10 \text{ percent}$$

Tolerable Misstatement

The level of **tolerable misstatement** is the maximum amount the account balance or class of transactions can be misstated without the audit team requiring an adjusting entry to prevent a qualified or adverse opinion (AU 530). In other words, the audit team determines, in

EXHIBIT G.2
Allowable Risk of Incorrect Acceptance (TD) for Various Assessments of RMM and AP; for AR = 0.05

		TD		
		AP		
RMM	10%	30%	50%	100%
10%	*	*	*	50%
30%	*	55%	33%	16%
50%	*	33%	20%	10%
100%	50%	16%	10%	5%

*The allowable level of AR of 5 percent exceeds the product of RMM and AP, and, thus, the planned test of details may not be necessary unless specified by regulation or other standards (e.g., confirmation or inventory observation procedures).

Note: The table entries for TD are computed from the illustrated model: TD equals AR/(RMM × AP). For example, for RMM = 0.50, AP = 0.30, TD = 0.05/(0.50 = 0.30) or 0.33 (equals 33%).

EXHIBIT G.3 Factors Influencing Sample Sizes for a Substantive Test of Details in Sample Planning

	Conditions Leading to:		
Factor	**Smaller Sample Size**	**Larger Sample Size**	**Related Factor for Substantive Sample Planning**
a. Assessment of inherent risk	Low assessed level of inherent risk	High assessed level of inherent risk	Allowable risk of incorrect acceptance
b. Assessment of control risk	Low assessed level of control risk	High assessed level of control risk	Allowable risk of incorrect acceptance
c. Assessment of risk related to other substantive procedures directed at the same assertion (including analytical procedures and other relevant substantive procedures)	Low assessment of risk associated with other relevant substantive procedures	High assessment of risk associated with other relevant substantive procedures	Allowable risk of incorrect acceptance
d. Measure of tolerable misstatement for a specific account	Larger measure of tolerable misstatement	Smaller measure of tolerable misstatement	Tolerable misstatement
e. Expected size and frequency of misstatements, or the estimated variance of the population	Smaller misstatements or lower frequency, or smaller population variance	Larger misstatements, higher frequency, or larger population variance	Expected Misstatement
f. Number of items in the population	Virtually no effect on sample size unless population is very small		

advance, the largest misstatement that they will allow (or tolerate) before they conclude that the account balance or class of transactions is materially misstated. Logically, as the amount of tolerable misstatement decreases, the necessary sample size increases because auditors need to examine more of the population to ensure that there are not numerous small misstatements that would accumulate to a material amount. Therefore, tolerable misstatement has an *inverse relationship* with sample size.

The audit team assesses tolerable misstatement judgmentally after considering the recorded balance as well as the relationship between the account balance or class of transactions with important financial statement subtotals (such as total assets, total revenue, and net income). Auditors normally estimate tolerable misstatement after calculating *performance materiality* for the various account balances and classes of transactions. Performance materiality is less than materiality and is determined in order to address the risk that the aggregate of individually immaterial misstatements may cause the financial statements to be materially misstated and to provide a margin for possible undetected misstatements. This is done so that, when the results of all audit procedures across various account balances and classes of transactions are aggregated and a cushion for undetected misstatements is added, the overall level of financial statement materiality is maintained. Tolerable misstatement is the application of performance materiality to a particular sampling procedure and may be the same amount or an amount lower than performance materiality (for example, when the population being sampled is only a subset of the entire account balance).

In the audit of Rice's accounts receivable, assume that the audit team assessed tolerable misstatement at $10,000 (or 3.33 percent of the recorded balance of $300,000). This is consistent with rules of thumb commonly used in practice such as assessing performance materiality at between 1 and 5 percent of asset balances.

Expected Misstatement

The **expected misstatement** is the amount of misstatement the audit team anticipates in the account balance or class of transactions. The audit team's estimate of expected misstatement is ordinarily based on prior experience with the client, that is, the amount by which misstatements have been identified in specific accounts in prior audits. Unless the client has changed its method of processing and recording transactions, the audit team's experience in prior audits is ordinarily a good indicator of what to expect in the current year. If the engagement is a first-year engagement, the audit team can estimate the expected misstatement based either on a small preliminary sample (referred to as a *pilot sample*) or on experience with other clients in the same industry.

Recall that MUS should be used when a small number of misstatements are expected. Therefore, if the expected misstatement is large relative to the tolerable misstatement, the audit team may consider another form of variables sampling such as classical variables sampling. For the audit of Rice's accounts receivable, the audit team estimates an expected misstatement of $4,000. This estimate is based on the percentage of misstatements that have been observed in prior audits of Rice.

How does expected misstatement affect sample size? It seems reasonable to surmise that, as the expected misstatement increases (particularly in relation to tolerable misstatement), the audit team increases the level of assurance provided by substantive procedures. To do so, the team would examine a larger number of components or transactions (i.e., the necessary sample size increases). Therefore, expected misstatement has a *direct relationship* with sample size.

The *precision* (or *allowance for sampling risk*) is the amount from the estimated population value in which the true (but unknown) population value may lie with a given probability. For planning purposes, the difference between the tolerable misstatement and the expected misstatement can be viewed as *planning precision*. When the difference between tolerable misstatement and expected misstatement is low, the audit team's sample estimate needs to be more precise, which requires a higher sample size. If expected misstatement equals or exceeds tolerable misstatement, there is no point in performing the test because the audit team expects to reject the population as misstated, so the audit team should save time and move directly to alternative or expanded procedures.

Population Size

One of the unique characteristics of MUS is that the sampling unit is defined as a dollar in an account balance or class of transactions. Thus, Rice's accounts receivable amount of $300,000 is characterized as a population size of 300,000 one-dollar items. Logically, as the population size increases, the necessary sample size increases. This represents a *direct relationship* between population size and sample size.

To determine the appropriate sample size, the audit team may use a table such as the one in Exhibit G.4, which is taken from the AICPA *Audit Sampling Guide*.

After determining the appropriate risk of incorrect acceptance, expected misstatement, tolerable misstatement, and population size, the audit team divides the expected misstatement by the tolerable misstatement and the tolerable misstatement by the population. They then find the appropriate risk of incorrect acceptance on the table and follow the line for the ratio of expected misstatement to tolerable misstatement across to the column for tolerable misstatement as a percentage of population to find the appropriate sample size. In the Rice example, the ratio of expected misstatement to tolerable misstatement is 0.40 ($4,000 ÷ $10,000). The tolerable misstatement as a percentage of the population is 3.33% ($10,000 ÷ $300,000). Because the table does not contain a value for 3.33%, the audit team can interpolate between 3% and 4% or use 3% to be conservative. Given a 10% risk of incorrect acceptance, the appropriate sample size is 191 items if 3% is used. Alternatively, the audit team could determine a sample size of 175 if interpolation is used as follows:

1. Determine the difference between sample size for 3% (191) and 4% (143), or 48 items (191 − 143 = 48).
2. Calculate the amount of the difference in (step 1) related to incremental percentage higher than 3% [(3.33% − 3%) × 48 items = 16 items].
3. Adjust the sample size for 3% downward for the difference in (step 2) (191 − 16 = 175). This reduced sample size results from an increased level of tolerable misstatement relative to the population size.

Based on the preceding calculation, the audit team decides to use a sample size of 175.

EXHIBIT G.4 MUS Sample Sizes

Risk of Incorrect Acceptance	Ratio of Expected to Tolerable Misstatement	50%	30%	10%	8%	6%	5%	4%	3%	2%	1%	0.50%	Expected Sum of Taints
5%	—	6	10	30	38	50	60	75	100	150	300	600	—
5	0.10	8	13	37	46	62	74	92	123	184	368	736	0.37
5	0.20	10	16	47	58	78	93	116	155	232	463	925	0.93
5	0.30	12	20	60	75	100	120	150	200	300	600	1,199	1.80
5	0.40	17	27	81	102	135	162	203	270	405	809	1,618	3.24
5	0.50	24	39	116	145	193	231	289	385	577	1,154	2,308	5.77
10	—	5	8	24	29	39	47	58	77	116	231	461	—
10	0.20	7	12	35	43	57	69	86	114	171	341	682	0.69
10	0.30	9	15	44	55	73	87	109	145	217	433	866	1.30
10	0.40	12	20	58	72	96	115	143	191	286	572	1,144	2.29
10	0.50	16	27	80	100	134	160	200	267	400	799	1,597	4.00
15	—	4	7	19	24	32	38	48	64	95	190	380	—
15	0.20	6	10	28	35	46	55	69	91	137	273	545	0.55
15	0.30	7	12	35	43	57	69	86	114	171	341	681	1.03
15	0.40	9	15	45	56	74	89	111	148	221	442	883	1.77
15	0.50	13	21	61	76	101	121	151	202	302	604	1,208	3.02
20	—	4	6	17	21	27	33	41	54	81	161	322	—
20	0.20	5	8	23	29	38	46	57	76	113	226	451	0.46
20	0.30	6	10	28	35	47	56	70	93	139	277	554	0.84
20	0.40	8	12	36	45	59	71	89	118	177	354	707	1.42
20	0.50	10	16	48	60	80	95	119	159	238	475	949	2.38
25	—	3	5	14	18	24	28	35	47	70	139	278	—
25	0.20	4	7	19	24	32	38	48	64	95	190	380	0.38
25	0.30	5	8	23	29	39	46	58	77	115	230	460	0.69
25	0.40	6	10	29	37	49	58	73	97	145	289	578	1.16
25	0.50	8	13	38	48	64	76	95	127	190	380	760	1.90
30	—	3	5	13	16	21	25	31	41	61	121	241	—
30	0.20	4	6	17	21	27	33	41	54	81	162	323	0.33
30	0.40	5	8	24	30	40	48	60	80	120	239	477	0.96
30	0.60	9	15	43	54	71	85	107	142	213	425	850	2.55
35	—	3	4	11	14	18	21	27	35	53	105	210	—
35	0.20	3	5	14	18	23	28	35	46	69	138	276	0.28
35	0.40	4	7	20	25	34	40	50	67	100	199	397	0.80
35	0.60	7	12	34	43	57	68	85	113	169	338	676	2.03
50	—	2	3	7	9	12	14	18	24	35	70	139	—
50	0.20	2	3	9	11	15	18	22	29	44	87	173	0.18
50	0.40	3	4	12	15	19	23	29	38	57	114	228	0.46
50	0.60	4	6	17	22	29	34	43	57	85	170	340	1.02

Column headings: Tolerable Misstatement as a Percentage of Population

REVIEW CHECKPOINTS

G.7 What are the two sampling risks associated with variables sampling? What types of losses are associated with each of these risks?

G.8 How does the audit team determine the acceptable level of the risk of incorrect acceptance? What is the relationship between this risk and sample size?

G.9 How does the audit team determine tolerable misstatement? What is the relationship between tolerable misstatement and sample size?

G.10 How does the audit team determine expected misstatement? What is the relationship between expected misstatement and sample size?

G.11 In an MUS application, how is the population size defined? What is the relationship between population size and sample size?

MUS: Selecting the Sample

When using MUS, the audit team normally selects the sample using a *systematic random selection* method. When a systematic method is used, the audit team determines a random starting point within the population, which represents the first item selected. The audit team then bypasses a fixed number of items in the population and selects the next item for examination. This process is continued until the number of sampling units equal to the necessary sample size has been selected.

One unique feature of using systematic random selection in MUS is that the sampling unit is defined as *an individual dollar within an account balance.* However, it is not reasonable for the audit team to examine only a dollar of a customer's account balance; the entire balance should be verified. Thus, the audit team examines the **logical unit** that contains the individual sampling unit that is selected for examination. In this case, the logical unit is the individual customer's account; however, it could be an item of inventory, an account payable to a specific vendor, or any other component of an account balance or class of transactions.

To select an MUS sample, the audit team calculates a **sampling interval** by dividing the recorded account balance by the necessary sample size. In the examination of Rice's accounts receivable, recall that its accounts receivable were recorded at $300,000 and that the audit team determined a necessary sample size of 175 items. The sampling interval (that should be rounded down to achieve the necessary sample size) is $1,714, as follows:

$$\text{Sampling interval} = \frac{\text{Population size (recorded balance)}}{\text{Sample size}}$$

$$= \frac{\$300,000}{175}$$

$$= \$1,714 \text{ (rounded)}$$

Thus, the audit team examines every 1,714th dollar of Rice's accounts receivable. Recall that the tolerable misstatement for Rice's accounts receivable was assessed at $10,000. As a result, the audit team examines every customer account that would be material to the financial statements taken as a whole. This is an explicit advantage of MUS because it results in higher dollar components of an account balance or class of transactions having a higher likelihood of selection. In contrast, if the audit team randomly selected 175 customer accounts (of the 1,500 individual accounts) for examination, no guarantee exists that the larger dollar accounts would be selected.

Exhibit G.5 illustrates the selection of the first few items from Rice's accounts receivable. (In practice, assuming that the client maintains its records in computerized form, the selection would be done using computer-assisted audit tools, or CAATs.)

Note the following in reviewing Exhibit G.5:

- The Account column refers to individual customer accounts. Note that Rice's accounts receivable are composed of 1,500 individual customer accounts.
- The balance in each account is listed in the Account Balance column. These are the logical units that the audit team will examine if a dollar within those balances is selected for examination.
- The Cumulative Balance column is simply a running total of the account balances. Note that Rice's total accounts receivable are recorded at $300,000.
- The Dollar Selected column reflects a random start of 600 and a sampling interval of 1,714. Each entry in this column is determined by adding the sampling interval to the preceding entry. These are the individual dollar units selected for examination.
- Any account with a balance of more than $1,714 has a 100 percent chance of being selected (i.e., if you come to a stream that is 15 feet wide and you can jump only 12 feet, your feet will get wet).

EXHIBIT G.5
MUS Sample Selection of Customer Accounts for Rice, Inc.

Account	Account Balance	Cumulative Balance	Dollar Selected
1	$ 126	$ 126	
2	819	945	600
3	1,411	2,356	2,314
4	75	2,431	
5	92	2,523	
6	204	2,727	
7	3,817	6,544	4,028
			5,742
8	315	6,859	
9	271	7,130	
10	1,000	8,130	7,456
11	448	8,578	
12	983	9,561	9,170
13	121	9,682	
14	406	10,088	
15	1,651	11,739	10,884
16	339	12,078	
*	*	*	
*	*	*	
1,500	$ 687	$300,000	

If a dollar within an account balance is selected, the logical unit (i.e., customer account balance) is selected for examination. For example, using a random start of 600, the audit team would examine the 600th dollar of the population. In Exhibit G.5, note that account 2 (recorded at $819) contains dollars 127 through 945. Because this account contains the 600th dollar, the audit team examines the entire account. As noted previously in this module, one of the limitations of MUS is that special considerations must be made to examine logical units with a zero or negative balance.

Two other important points can be observed in Exhibit G.5:

1. MUS tends to select higher dollar transactions or components for examination. Note that the use of MUS selected the six largest dollar account balances shown in Exhibit G.5 for examination. Although MUS will not always select the highest dollar transactions or components, it provides a relatively high probability that these components will be selected. (Any account balance that is higher than the sampling interval has a 100 percent chance of selection.)

2. Account 7, recorded at $3,817, was selected "twice." This phenomenon can occur in MUS when individual logical units (i.e., accounts) are larger than the sampling interval. In these cases, the audit team counts this account as two selections and continues. As a result, the actual number of logical units examined under MUS can be smaller than the determined sample size.

MUS: Measuring Sample Items

Once the sample items have been selected, the audit team performs the appropriate substantive procedure and measures the sample items. In the examination of Rice's accounts receivable, the audit team sends a confirmation to the customers whose accounts were selected for examination and performs any additional follow-up procedures to verify discrepancies noted by the customers or perform alternative procedures for confirmations not returned by customers. After all procedures were performed, the audit team noted three misstatements, which are summarized in Exhibit G.6.[3]

The *audited value* is the amount at which the logical unit should have been recorded, assuming no misstatements or misapplications of generally accepted accounting principles.

---

[3] The misstatements shown in Exhibit G.6 include only overstatements (i.e., situations in which the recorded balance exceeds the audited value). Although MUS is most useful in detecting overstatement errors, it can be extended to include understatement errors. We discuss treatment of understatements later in the module.

EXHIBIT G.6
Misstatements Noted in Examination of Rice, Inc.'s Accounts Receivable

Account	Recorded Balance	Audited Value	Difference	Tainting Percentage
10	$1,000	$ 900	$ 100	10%
598	3,840	1,920	1,920	50
1139	525	420	105	20
			$2,125	

The **tainting percentage** represents the percentage by which the account is misstated. It is determined by dividing the difference between the recorded balance and the audited value by the recorded balance.

Note that the actual misstatement detected in Rice's accounts receivable is $2,125. This amount is less than the tolerable misstatement of $10,000, but the audit team has not considered misstatements that could exist within the accounts that have not been examined. Projecting these misstatements across the population is the final step of MUS, which is evaluating sample results. Measuring sample items is the point at which *nonsampling risk* can be encountered. *Nonsampling risk* is the probability that an inappropriate conclusion is reached for reasons other than the representativeness of the sample. For example, the audit team could fail to note exceptions indicated by Rice's customers on their accounts receivable confirmations or could perform inappropriate substantive procedures that fail to detect misstatements that exist in the sample accounts.

> ### ↳ REVIEW CHECKPOINTS
>
> G.12 Describe the process used to select an MUS sample. Why does this process tend to select larger dollar components or transactions for examination?
>
> G.13 What is the *sampling interval?* How is it calculated?
>
> G.14 How does the audit team proceed if one logical unit contains two separate dollar selections?
>
> G.15 What is the *audited value* of a transaction or component of an account balance or class of transactions?
>
> G.16 What is the *tainting percentage?* How is it calculated?

MUS: Evaluating Sample Results

LEARNING OBJECTIVE G-4
Evaluate the sample results for an MUS sample by calculating the projected misstatement, incremental allowance for sampling risk, and basic allowance for sampling risk.

At this point, the audit team has performed the following major steps in the audit of Rice's accounts receivable:

1. Made the following preliminary assessments prior to beginning the sampling process:
   a. Determined that Rice's accounts receivable were recorded at $300,000 and were composed of 1,500 individual customer accounts.
   b. Set audit risk at 5 percent, assessed inherent risk at 100 percent, control risk at 50 percent, and analytical procedures risk at 100 percent.
   c. Assessed expected misstatement at $4,000 and tolerable misstatement at $10,000.
   d. Based on audit risk, inherent risk, control risk, and analytical procedures risk, determined a risk of incorrect acceptance of 10 percent.
2. Using assessments of expected misstatement, tolerable misstatement, population size, and the risk of incorrect acceptance, determined a sample size of 175 items.
3. Based on the sample size of 175 items and the population size of $300,000, calculated a sampling interval of $1,714 ($300,000 ÷ 175).

4. Using systematic random selection, identified 175 dollar units and examined the related logical unit (customer account balance) through accounts receivable confirmation and follow-up procedures.
5. Through the substantive procedures performed in step 4, identified three misstatements totaling $2,125 (see Exhibit G.6).

As with all statistical sampling applications, the audit team must now adjust the detected misstatements to control for exposure to the risk of incorrect acceptance. This process requires the audit team to calculate a conservative estimate of the total misstatement composed of three separate components: projected misstatement, incremental allowance for sampling risk, and basic allowance for sampling risk.

Projected Misstatement

The **projected misstatement** assumes that the entire sampling interval contains the same percentage of misstatement as the item examined by the auditor. Recall that when using MUS, the audit team selects individual dollars and examines the logical unit (in this case, the customer account balance) containing that unit. Note that, if the logical unit is less than the sampling interval, some portion of that interval remains unexamined by the auditor. Therefore, one reasonable approach is to assume that the remainder of the sampling interval contains the same percentage of misstatement as the item the audit team examined.

From Exhibit G.6, you can see that the audit team detected three misstatements. Exhibit G.7 illustrates how these misstatements are projected to the sampling interval from which they were drawn.

While the calculations in Exhibit G.7 are straightforward, note that the misstatement related to account 598 is not projected to the sampling interval in the same manner as the other two misstatements. Why? Recall from Exhibit G.6 that this account has a recorded balance of $3,840 and an audited value of $1,920. *Because the recorded balance is higher than the sampling interval, there is no need to project the misstatement to the sampling interval.* As a result, the projected misstatement for this particular account would equal the actual misstatement detected by the auditor.

Incremental Allowance for Sampling Risk

The calculation of the projected misstatement in Exhibit G.7 assumes that the remainder of the sampling interval is misstated to the same extent (based on the tainting percentage) as the item examined by the auditor. Of course, the remainder of the interval could be misstated to a higher, lower, or same extent as the item examined. To control exposure to sampling risk, the audit team calculates an adjustment to the projected misstatement that uses the confidence factors shown in Exhibit G.8. This adjustment is referred to as the **incremental allowance for sampling risk** and is calculated as follows:

1. For all projected misstatements whose recorded value is less than the sampling interval, rank the projected misstatements in descending order based on the dollar amount.
2. For each misstatement in step 1, determine the incremental confidence factor associated with the discovery of the misstatement. The confidence factor associated with zero overstatement errors and a 10 percent risk of incorrect acceptance from Exhibit G.8 is 2.31; for one overstatement error, the factor is 3.89. As a result, the *incremental confidence*

EXHIBIT G.7
Calculation of Projected Misstatement for Rice, Inc.'s Accounts Receivable

Account	Difference	Tainting Percentage		Sampling Interval		Projected Misstatement
10	$ 100	10%	×	$1,714	=	$ 171.40
598	1,920	50	×	N/A	=	1,920.00
1139	105	20	×	1,714	=	342.80
	$2,125				=	$2,434.20

EXHIBIT G.8 Monetary Unit Sampling—Confidence Factors for Sample Evaluation

Number of Overstatement Misstatements	\multicolumn{9}{c}{Risk of Incorrect Acceptance}
	5%	10%	15%	20%	25%	30%	35%	37%	50%
0	3.00	2.31	1.90	1.61	1.39	1.21	1.05	1.00	0.70
1	4.75	3.89	3.38	3.00	2.70	2.44	2.22	2.14	1.68
2	6.30	5.33	4.73	4.28	3.93	3.62	3.35	3.35	2.68
3	7.76	6.69	6.02	5.52	5.11	4.77	4.46	4.35	3.68
4	9.16	8.00	7.27	6.73	6.28	5.90	5.55	5.43	4.68
5	10.52	9.28	8.50	7.91	7.43	7.01	6.64	6.50	5.68
6	11.85	10.54	9.71	9.08	8.56	8.12	7.72	7.57	6.67
7	13.15	11.78	10.90	10.24	9.69	9.21	8.79	8.63	7.67
8	14.44	13.00	12.08	11.38	10.81	10.31	9.85	9.68	8.67
9	15.71	14.21	13.25	12.52	11.92	11.39	10.92	10.74	9.67
10	16.97	15.41	14.42	13.66	13.02	12.47	11.98	11.79	10.67
11	18.21	16.60	15.57	14.78	14.13	13.55	13.04	12.84	11.67
12	19.45	17.79	16.72	15.90	15.22	14.63	14.09	13.89	12.67
13	20.67	18.96	17.86	17.02	16.32	15.70	15.14	14.93	13.67
14	21.89	20.13	19.00	18.13	17.40	16.77	16.20	15.98	14.67
15	23.10	21.30	20.13	19.24	18.49	17.84	17.25	17.02	15.67
16	24.31	22.46	21.26	20.34	19.58	18.90	18.29	18.06	16.67
17	25.50	23.61	22.39	21.44	20.66	19.97	19.34	19.10	17.67
18	26.70	24.76	23.51	22.54	21.74	21.03	20.38	20.14	18.67
19	27.88	25.91	24.63	23.64	22.81	22.09	21.43	21.18	19.67
20	29.07	27.05	25.74	24.73	23.89	23.15	22.47	22.22	20.67

factor for the discovery of the first overstatement error is 1.58 (3.89 − 2.31). The incremental confidence factor for the second overstatement error is 1.44 (5.33 − 3.89).

3. For each misstatement in step (1), multiply the projected misstatement by the incremental confidence factor (determined in step [2]) minus 1.00 (subtracting 1.00 accounts for the fact that the misstatement has already been projected over the sampling interval when determining the projected misstatement).[4] For projected misstatements when the recorded value is higher than or equal to the sampling interval, no incremental allowance for sampling risk needs to be determined because the projected misstatement exceeds the sampling interval.

The calculation of the incremental allowance for sampling risk for Rice's accounts receivable is shown in Exhibit G.9. The incremental allowance for sampling risk attempts to control for the possibility that the misstatements detected in items examined by the audit team were not representative of the misstatements in the remainder of the sampling interval that was not examined by the auditor.

Basic Allowance for Sampling Risk

Both the projected misstatement and the incremental allowance for sampling risk apply to sampling intervals in which the audit team's substantive procedures revealed a misstatement. However, what about those sampling intervals in which no misstatement

EXHIBIT G.9 Calculation of Incremental Allowance for Sampling Risk for Rice, Inc.'s Accounts Receivable

Account	Projected Misstatement		Incremental Confidence Factor		Incremental Allowance for Sampling Risk
1139	$342.80	×	0.58 (1.58 − 1.00)	=	$198.82
10	171.40	×	0.44 (1.44 − 1.00)	=	75.42
Incremental allowance for sampling risk					$274.24

[4] Alternatively, the audit team could multiply the projected misstatement by the incremental confidence factor and subtract the projected misstatement from this same amount. This calculation yields the same result as that illustrated in Exhibit G.9.

was discovered? For example, assume that the audit team examined customer account 627 (recorded at $200) and found no misstatement. Is it reasonable to conclude that the entire sampling interval of $1,714 represented by account 627 contained no misstatements? To respond to this matter, the audit team calculates a **basic allowance for sampling risk** in an attempt to provide a statistical measure of the misstatement that could be included in sampling intervals in which the audit team did not detect a misstatement.

Although the philosophy behind the calculation of the basic allowance for sampling risk is somewhat technical, the calculation is relatively straightforward. To calculate the basic allowance for sampling risk, multiply the sampling interval by the confidence factor for the risk of incorrect acceptance. The confidence factor corresponding to zero overstatement errors is selected because these sampling intervals did not contain an overstatement error. The basic allowance for sampling risk for Rice's accounts receivable is calculated as follows:

$$\text{Basic allowance for sampling risk} = \text{Sampling interval} \times \text{Confidence factor}$$
$$= \$1{,}714 \times 2.31$$
$$= \$3{,}959.34$$

Note that the basic allowance for sampling risk would be calculated in all instances even when the audit team detected no misstatements.

Upper Limit on Misstatements

The **upper limit on misstatements** is the sum of the three components discussed in this subsection: the projected misstatement, the incremental allowance for sampling risk, and the basic allowance for sampling risk. The upper limit on misstatements is the amount that has a (1 − *Risk of incorrect acceptance*) probability of equaling or exceeding the true amount of misstatement in the population. Stated another way, there is a (*risk of incorrect acceptance*) probability that the true amount of misstatement in the population exceeds the upper limit on misstatements.

How do auditors use the upper limit on misstatements? They compare this measure to the amount of tolerable misstatement, as follows:

Upper Limit on Misstatements ≤ Tolerable Misstatements ⟶ Accept Account Balance as Fairly Recorded

Upper Limit on Misstatements > Tolerable Misstatements ⟶ Conclude That Account Balance Is not Fairly Recorded

The upper limit on misstatements comprises

- Actual misstatements detected totaling $2,125.
- An additional projection of those misstatements to the sampling interval of $309.20 (Projected misstatement of $2,434.20 − Actual misstatements of $2,125.00).
- A total allowance for sampling risk of $4,233.58 (Incremental allowance for sampling risk of $274.24 + Basic allowance for sampling risk of $3,959.34).
- Calculating the upper limit on misstatements for Rice, Inc.'s accounts receivable, we find

Projected misstatement	$2,434.20
Incremental allowance for sampling risk	274.24
Basic allowance for sampling risk	3,959.34
Upper limit on misstatements	$6,667.78

Based on the upper limit on misstatements, the audit team would conclude that the true misstatement in accounts receivable has a 90 percent chance (1 − Risk of incorrect acceptance of 10 percent) of being less than or equal to $6,667.78. Conversely, the true misstatement in accounts receivable has a 10 percent chance (risk of incorrect acceptance of 10 percent) of being more than $6,667.78.

Because the tolerable misstatement for accounts receivable is $10,000, the audit team would accept the account balance as being fairly stated. In so doing, they have controlled the risk of incorrect acceptance to a level of 10 percent. The audit team ordinarily accumulates the three misstatements actually identified (see Exhibit G.6) and recommends that the client adjust the financial statements to reflect these misstatements. If the client does not make the adjustment, the $2,125 will be included on the score sheet (discussed in Chapter 11) as a "known misstatement." The added allowances of $4,542.78 ($6,667.78 − $2,125.00) are included on the score sheet as a "likely misstatement." The audit team also investigates the causes of all misstatements to ensure they do not represent a lack of controls or a pattern of fraud. Despite the fact that the account balance is not materially misstated, generally accepted auditing standards require auditors to accumulate these misstatements and communicate them to those charged with governance and include them in the management representation letter.

What would have occurred if the upper limit on misstatements had exceeded $10,000? For example, assume that the upper limit on misstatements was calculated as $14,500. In this situation, the audit team would conclude that the true misstatement in the population had a 90 percent chance of being less than or equal to $14,500, which does not allow them to conclude that the account balance is fairly stated. In this instance, one of two options exists:

1. The audit team could increase the sample size and examine additional items. These additional items would effectively reduce the sampling interval used, reducing the projected misstatement, incremental allowance for sampling risk, and basic allowance for sampling risk. If enough additional items are examined and *no misstatements are detected,* the recalculated upper limit on misstatements could fall below the tolerable misstatement of $10,000. If so, the audit team could conclude that the financial statements were not materially misstated.

2. The audit team could recommend making an adjustment to the recorded balance of the client's accounts receivable. With an upper limit on misstatements of $14,500, an adjustment of $4,500 would result in a revised upper limit on misstatements of $10,000 ($14,500 − $4,500). This revised upper limit on misstatements allows the audit team to conclude that the account balance is fairly stated at a risk of incorrect acceptance of 10 percent.

In any event, the audit team would likely recommend that the client review all similar accounts to ensure that they did not contain the same type of misstatement as that found in the sampling procedures. Most clients voluntarily review their accounts in this manner if they suspect misstatements. The audit team also requests that the client correct the known misstatements ($2,125 in the Rice example; see Exhibit G.6).

Exhibit G.10 summarizes the important components of the upper limit on misstatements.

Understatements

As we stated before, MUS is used primarily to detect overstatements. However, in practice, instances in which an understatement would be detected along with the overstatements often occur. One common method for including understatements in the evaluation of results of an MUS sample is simply to subtract the projected understatement caused by the detected misstatement from the upper limit on misstatements calculated based on overstatements found and the basic allowance for sampling risk. Thus, if Rice, Inc.'s auditors found that, in addition to the misstatements discussed previously, account 573 also was understated by $500, the auditors would project the understatement error as shown in Exhibit G.11.

The net upper limit on misstatements would then be the upper limit on misstatements calculated previously ($6,667.78.) less the projected understatement of $857.00, or $5,810.78

EXHIBIT G.10
Summary of Components of Upper Limit on Misstatements

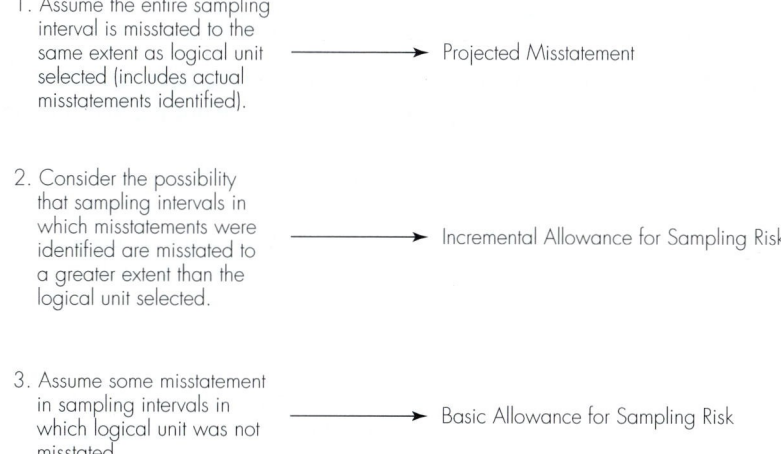

This is a conservative estimate of the upper limit on misstatements because it does not consider an allowance for sampling risk for the understatement.[5]

The extreme case of understatement is an account with a zero balance. Under MUS, such an account would never be selected. Auditors should search for accounts with zero balances in situations where a zero balance would be unusual. For example, the auditors could identify a major customer that maintained a sizeable account receivable balance throughout the year; however, the accounts receivable balance at year-end is stated at zero. This account should be examined to ensure that it is not misstated.

Qualitative Evaluation of Misstatements

The preceding discussion focuses on calculating the upper limit on misstatements and comparing this upper limit on misstatements to the tolerable misstatement. However, it is important that the audit team also consider the nature of the misstatements discovered during the MUS process. Very specifically, any misstatements that indicate fraudulent activity on the part of the client (for example, an intentional overstatement of a customer's account or the creation of a fictitious account) have additional implications for the audit and should be discussed with the client and those charged with governance.

↳ REVIEW CHECKPOINTS

G.17 Identify the three components of the upper limit on misstatements. How is each component calculated?

G.18 Why are misstatements in logical units that are higher than the sampling interval not projected over the sampling interval?

G.19 What is the *upper limit on misstatements*? What information does it provide the auditor?

G.20 What options are available to the audit team if the upper limit on misstatements exceeds the tolerable misstatement?

EXHIBIT G.11
Calculation of Projected Misstatement for Rice, Inc.'s Accounts Receivable Understatement

Account	Difference	Tainting Percentage		Sampling Interval		Projected Misstatement
573	$500	50%	×	$1,714	=	$857.00

[5] If the auditor added an allowance for sampling risk for the understatement, the risk of incorrect acceptance would be somewhat higher than 10 percent; see D.M. Roberts, *Statistical Auditing* (New York: AICPA, 1978).

CLASSICAL VARIABLES SAMPLING

LEARNING OBJECTIVE G-5
Understand the basic process underlying *classical variables sampling* and the use of classical variables sampling in an audit.

When performing substantive procedures, an alternative approach to MUS is classical variables sampling. Its methods use normal distribution theory and the central limit theorem to provide an estimated range of either the *recorded balance* of the account balance or class of transactions or the *misstatement* in the account balance or class of transactions. The central limit theorem indicates that, because larger sample sizes provide a sampling distribution that more closely reflects a normal distribution, larger sample sizes yield a lower level of sampling risk. The audit team then uses these estimates to determine whether the account balance or class of transactions is fairly stated.

Classical variables sampling methods are typically employed less frequently in practice than MUS methods. This section briefly illustrates one form of classical variables sampling, **mean-per-unit estimation**, which estimates the total amount of the account or class of transactions by determining an average for each item and multiplying the average times the number of items in the population. As with the MUS example in the preceding section, we illustrate the manual calculations necessary to determine sample size and evaluate sample results. However, if the client maintains its records in computerized form, the audit team typically uses computer software to perform these tasks.

Classical Variables Sampling: Planning

In the planning stages of classical variables sampling, the audit team determines the objective of sampling, defines the attribute of interest, and defines the population as in MUS. We continue to use the basic information from the examination of Rice, Inc.'s accounts receivable introduced in the previous section. Recall that Rice's accounts receivable are composed of 1,500 individual customer accounts and are recorded at $300,000. Also recall that the audit team is interested in evaluating the *existence* and *valuation and allocation* assertions and that the following assessments or judgments have been made prior to selecting individual customer accounts for confirmation:

- Overall audit risk = 5 percent.
- Inherent risk for the assertions = 100 percent.
- Control risk related to the assertions = 50 percent.
- Analytical procedures risk related to the assertions = 100 percent.
- Risk of incorrect acceptance = 10 percent (based on preceding risks).
- Expected misstatement = $4,000.
- Tolerable misstatement = $10,000.

One issue regarding classical variables sampling is whether certain items should be included in the population to be sampled. For example, suppose that Rice's five largest customer balances totaled $120,000 and that all of these balances were higher than the $10,000 tolerable misstatement. Also assume that no other customer had a balance higher than $2,000. What should the audit team do? Obviously, they would like to examine the five large balances separately because they constitute 40 percent ($120,000 ÷ $300,000) of the recorded balance of accounts receivable and each of these items is an *individually significant item* (that is, each item exceeds the tolerable misstatement). The audit team would then sample from among the remaining 1,495 accounts, none of which is individually significant.

When using classical variables sampling, the audit team can reduce the variability of the population and ensure the selection of individually significant items by subdividing the population into different (more homogenous) groups based on account size. This process of subdivision known as **stratification** is useful because it permits the audit team to reduce the necessary sample size in a classical variables sampling application by reducing the variability within each stratum. Stratification also allows auditors to give more attention to high-dollar items. In the preceding scenario, the audit team could subdivide the population into two subgroups, or **strata**: the five large-dollar accounts and the remaining 1,495 customer accounts.

Classical Variables Sampling: Determining Sample Size

The formula for calculating sample size using mean-per-unit estimation is

$$n = \left(\frac{N \times [R(IR) + R(IA)] \times SD}{TM - EM}\right)^2$$

where

n = Sample size
N = Population size (number of accounts)
$R(IR)$ = Confidence factor for the risk of incorrect rejection
$R(IA)$ = Confidence factor for the risk of incorrect acceptance
SD = Standard deviation
TM = Tolerable misstatement
EM = Expected misstatement

The remainder of this section focuses on the two new factors that are considered in classical variables sampling but not MUS: the risk of incorrect rejection and standard deviation. Discussion of the determination of the remaining factors and their effects on sample size can be found in the section on MUS in this module.

Risk of Incorrect Rejection

Unlike MUS (which considers only the risk of incorrect *acceptance*), classical variables sampling explicitly considers the risks of both incorrect acceptance and incorrect *rejection* in determining sample size. The *risk of incorrect rejection* is the probability that the audit team will conclude that the account balance is materially misstated when, in fact, it is fairly stated. As with any sampling risk, lower levels of the risk of incorrect rejection would result in an increase in the necessary sample size. That is, the risk of incorrect rejection has an *inverse relationship* with sample size.

Remember that the risk of incorrect rejection results in an efficiency loss to the audit team because prior to proposing an adjustment to the financial statements, the team ordinarily expands the sample to include additional components or transactions. The key question of interest to the audit team in assessing the level of exposure to the risk of incorrect rejection is related to the *efficiency loss* that this risk causes; that is, what is the cost to the audit team of expanding the sample? In some cases, the audit team can quickly and inexpensively select additional items; if so, it would be more cost efficient to examine a smaller initial sample and subsequently select additional items if necessary. This smaller initial sample would be achieved by assessing a higher level of the risk of incorrect rejection.

In contrast, if the cost of expanding the sample is relatively high, the audit team would be concerned about it and would ordinarily choose to assess a lower level of the risk of incorrect rejection. This lower risk would, in turn, result in an increased initial sample size.

How are sampling risks incorporated in the determination of sample size? Refer to Exhibit G.12 for a list of confidence factors for various levels of the risk of incorrect rejection and the risk of incorrect acceptance that can be used in classical variables sampling.

EXHIBIT G.12 Confidence Factors for Different Levels of Sampling Risk in Classical Variables Sampling

Level of Risk	Risk of Incorrect Rejection	Risk of Incorrect Acceptance
0.01	2.58	2.33
0.05	1.96	1.65
0.10	1.65	1.28
0.15	1.44	1.04
0.20	1.28	0.84

The determination of these factors is beyond the scope of the text, but they represent various areas of observations that fall within a certain number of standard deviations in a normally distributed population.

After considering the costs of selecting and confirming additional accounts receivable balances, assume that the audit team sets the risk of incorrect rejection for Rice at 15 percent. (Recall that the risk of incorrect acceptance has been established at 10 percent.)

Standard Deviation

The **standard deviation** represents the variability of the population being examined; it is the average of the squared differences between each item in the population and the population mean. When the population is more variable (i.e., the items composing the population differ more widely with respect to dollar amount), the standard deviation increases. When the standard deviation of dollar amounts is higher, it is more difficult for the audit team to select a representative sample. To do so, the team increases the necessary sample size. Thus, the standard deviation has a *direct relationship* with sample size. That is, as the standard deviation increases, the sample size increases.

How can the audit team estimate the standard deviation? In using mean-per-unit estimation, the audit team is interested in knowing the standard deviation of audited values of customer accounts. As with expected misstatement, the audit team can either rely on experience from prior audits or use a small subsample (pilot sample) in the current year. Assume that the sample standard deviation for Rice's accounts receivable is $31 (the standard deviation is easily calculated by using CAATs or programs such as Microsoft Excel; its calculation is beyond the scope of this text).

Recall that, if the population is highly variable, the audit team can use stratification to reduce the variability of the population. By examining individually significant items and selecting a sample from a stratum of the population with lower variability, the audit team can reduce the necessary sample size.

Calculating Sample Size

At this point, the sample size can be determined as follows (the sample size is rounded up to be conservative):

$$n = \left(\frac{N \times [R(IR) + R(IA)] \times SD}{TM - EM}\right)^2$$

$$= \left(\frac{1{,}500 \times (1.44 + 1.28) \times \$31}{\$10{,}000 - \$4{,}000}\right)^2$$

$$= 444.37, \text{ or } 445 \text{ accounts}$$

N (the number of accounts) can be readily determined from the client's records; in this case, Rice's accounts receivable include 1,500 customer accounts. The factors for R(IR) and R(IA) correspond to a risk of incorrect rejection of 15 percent and risk of incorrect acceptance of 10 percent and are drawn from Exhibit G.12. Based on previous audits, the standard deviation was estimated as $31. Tolerable misstatement determined based on the recorded account balance and overall financial statement materiality was established at $10,000. Finally, the audit team judgmentally established the expected misstatement of $4,000 based on previous audits. We use the sample size of 445 in the remainder of this example to illustrate classical variables sampling.

Earlier, we noted that stratified sampling can be useful in reducing sample sizes if a great deal of variability exists in the population. Using the preceding formula, if the audit team decided to examine the five individually significant customer account balances and reduce the variability of the remainder of the population from $31 to $26, the sample size for the nonsignificant items would be 311 accounts.[6] Including the five individually

---

[6] The sample size formula would be modified by replacing the 1,500 customer accounts with 1,495 and the $31 sample standard deviation with $26.

significant items, the total sample would be 316. This provides an example of how using stratification can result in a more efficient sample for the auditor.

> ### REVIEW CHECKPOINTS
>
> G.21 Define *classical variables sampling*. How does it provide the audit team evidence as to the fairness of an account balance or class of transactions?
>
> G.22 What is *stratification?* What are the benefits to the audit team of stratifying the sample?
>
> G.23 What is the *standard deviation?* How does it affect the necessary sample size?
>
> G.24 Identify differences between the determination of sample size under classical variables sampling and MUS.

Classical Variables Sampling: Selecting the Sample

One of the basic tenets of statistical sampling methods is that each sampling unit has an equal probability of selection. The sample of Rice's customer accounts could be selected in either of the following ways:

1. Identify 445 random numbers and select the corresponding customer accounts for confirmation (unrestricted random selection).
2. Randomly select a starting point (or a number of starting points) in the population and select every nth customer account thereafter for confirmation (systematic random selection).

One very important difference between sample selection under classical variables sampling and MUS is the definition of the sampling unit. Classical variables sampling defines the sampling unit as a logical unit or a customer account balance. As a result, the audit team will select 445 of Rice's 1,500 customer account balances for examination. In contrast, MUS defines the sampling unit as an individual dollar of accounts receivable and selects individual dollars for examination. Unlike MUS, classical variables sampling does not ensure that the highest dollar account balances are selected for examination. A one-dollar account has an equal probability of being selected as a one million-dollar account!

Classical Variables Sampling: Measuring Sample Items

Once the sample size has been determined and the sample has been selected, the audit team measures the sample items. In the audit of accounts receivable, measuring sample items requires the audit team to determine the audited value of the customers' accounts receivable. This will be done using standard accounts receivable confirmation procedures as well as additional procedures necessary to follow up on any discrepancies revealed by the confirmation procedures. The procedures performed in measuring sample items for Rice's accounts receivable under classical variables sampling are identical to those performed under MUS. In addition, as under MUS, this stage could expose the audit team to nonsampling risk if the substantive procedures fail to detect misstatements that exist in sample customer accounts.

Assume that the audit team's examination of the 445 customer accounts receivable revealed a total audited value of $86,775. Therefore, the mean audited value per unit is $195 ($86,775 ÷ 445). In addition, the standard deviation of the audited values is $25.

Classical Variables Sampling: Evaluating Sample Results

Evaluating sample results requires the audit team to determine an overall estimate of the audited balance (based on the mean audited value per unit) and construct an interval of sample estimates that controls the exposure to the risk of incorrect acceptance (10 percent) and risk of incorrect rejection (15 percent). This interval is referred to as the **precision interval**, and once it has been constructed, the audit team's decision rule is as follows:

- Accept the account balance as being fairly stated if the difference between the recorded balance and the farthest precision estimate is smaller than or equal to the tolerable misstatement.
- Reject the account balance as being fairly stated if the difference between the recorded balance and the farthest precision estimate is larger than the tolerable misstatement.

The first step in the construction of the precision interval is to determine the overall estimate of the audited balance. If the mean audited value of the sample of customer accounts is $195, the audit team's best estimate of the audited balance of the entire account is determined by multiplying $195 by the number of accounts in the population (1,500), or $292,500 ($195 x 1,500 = $292,500).

Next the audit team determines the appropriate level of precision. *Precision* is the numeric distance from the estimated population value in which the true (but unknown) population value may lie with a given probability. The determination of precision allows the audit team to construct a precision interval that controls exposure to sampling risk to acceptable levels. The audit team calculates precision using the following formula:

$$\text{Precision} = N \times R(IA) \times (SD \div \sqrt{n})$$

where

n = Sample size
N = Population size (number of accounts)
$R(IA)$ = Confidence factor for the risk of incorrect acceptance
SD = Standard deviation (for items selected for examination)

Recall from the calculation of sample size that the population size is 1,500 customer accounts, the confidence factor for the risk of incorrect acceptance is 1.28, and the sample size is 445. Also, after measuring the sample items, recall that the standard deviation of audited values is $25. The precision is calculated as $2,275:

$$\text{Precision} = N \times R(IA) \times (SD \div \sqrt{n})$$
$$= 1{,}500 \times 1.28 \times (\$25 \div \sqrt{445})$$
$$= \$2{,}275$$

Once the precision has been calculated, the precision interval can be determined by adding and subtracting it from the sample estimate. The relationship between the sample estimate, precision, and the recorded balance is shown as

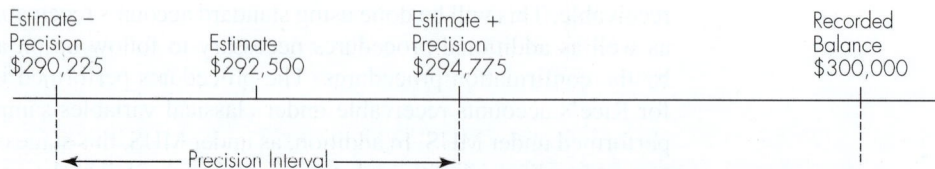

The significance of the precision interval is that it has a (1 − *Risk of incorrect acceptance*) probability of including the true balance; conversely, the true balance has a (*risk of incorrect acceptance*) probability of falling outside the precision interval. The difference between the recorded balance and the farthest end of the precision interval ($300,000 − $290,225 = $9,775) is compared to the tolerable misstatement ($10,000). In this case, the population can be accepted as being fairly stated. If the precision interval were $3,000, then the lower end of the interval would be $289,500 ($292,500 − $3,000 = $289,500), the distance from the recorded balance would be $10,500, and the population would be rejected based on the audit team's conclusion that the account balance is materially misstated.

As under MUS, the audit team can choose one of two courses of action when the sample evidence suggests that the account balance is materially misstated:

1. *The audit team could increase the sample size and examine additional items.* Referring to the formula for calculating precision, this would decrease the precision, resulting in the lower end for the precision interval being higher than $290,225. Thus, the audit team would be more likely to accept the balance as being fairly stated (i.e., the distance between the recorded balance and the end of the precision interval would be more likely to be less than or equal to the tolerable misstatement).

2. *The audit team could recommend adjustment of the client's accounts receivable.* In the rejected case above (i.e. precision interval = $3,000), the audit team would recommend an adjustment of at least $500 so that the difference between the new recorded balance ($299,500) and the farthest precision estimate would be the tolerable misstatement, $10,000. Often clients would likely investigate all the accounts to determine the exact amount of adjustment required.

Other Approaches to Classical Variables Sampling

This subsection illustrated one approach to classical variables sampling (mean-per-unit estimation). Two other approaches available to the auditor are discussed here. **Difference estimation** is used to calculate an average difference between audited values and book values; the audited balance is then estimated by adjusting the recorded account balance by this average difference. **Ratio estimation** determines the ratio (relationship) of audited values to recorded values and then estimates the audited balance by multiplying the recorded balance by this ratio.

Difference estimation and ratio estimation normally provide smaller sample sizes than mean-per-unit estimation because the standard deviations of differences or ratios are typically smaller than the standard deviations associated with mean values. However, these methods require reliable measures of the book value. As a result, mean-per-unit estimation is most frequently employed when a reliable measure of the book value is not available, such as following a fraud. These methods also require that a certain number of differences be expected to exist in the population in order to make a meaningful projection. The AICPA *Audit Sampling Guide* suggests that the audit team should expect a minimum of 20 differences in the sample to use either of these methods.

In either case, once the audited balance has been estimated, the audit team proceeds in a fashion similar to that of mean-per-unit estimation. The audit team constructs a precision interval around the estimate of the misstatement and identifies whether this precision interval falls within the tolerable misstatement. If so, the account balance is accepted as being fairly stated, and the audit team has limited the risk of incorrect acceptance to an acceptable level. If not, the audit team rejects the account balance as being fairly stated and either gathers additional evidence or proposes an adjustment to the account balance.

Because these methods are very similar to mean-per-unit estimation, further discussion of difference estimation and ratio estimation is beyond the scope of this text.

MUS VERSUS CLASSICAL VARIABLES SAMPLING

This module has discussed two major approaches to variables sampling: MUS and classical variables sampling. These methods differ primarily with respect to determining the necessary sample size, selecting sample items, and evaluating sample results.

When should each be used? Recall that the distinguishing feature of MUS is that it defines the sampling unit as an individual dollar within an account balance or class of transactions. As a result, this method has a tendency to identify large-dollar items for examination. This is a primary benefit associated with the use of MUS. In contrast, classical variables sampling defines the sampling unit as a logical unit (i.e., customer account balance) and will not necessarily select large-dollar items for examination.

Compared to classical variables sampling, MUS is most appropriate in these circumstances:

1. Overstatements are of more concern to the audit team (such as the audit of assets and revenues) because MUS automatically selects items with larger recorded balances for examination.
2. It is difficult or impractical to estimate the standard deviation. MUS does not use the standard deviation in determining a sample size or evaluating sample results.
3. Zero or few misstatements are anticipated.
4. The population is relatively heterogeneous with respect to the dollar amount of components and a number of relatively large-dollar items exist (i.e., a high level of variation exists).

MUS is advantageous in these situations, because this method automatically selects items that are larger than the sampling interval.

In contrast, classical variables sampling should be used when understatements are of concern, the standard deviation can be estimated, misstatements are anticipated, and the population is relatively homogenous with respect to the dollar amount of components.

↳ REVIEW CHECKPOINTS

G.25 How does sample selection under classical variables sampling differ from sample selection under MUS?

G.26 Define *precision* and the *precision interval*. What factors are used to determine the level of precision?

G.27 What is the audit team's decision rule when comparing the recorded balance to the precision interval?

G.28 When selecting a variables sampling approach, when should the audit team use MUS and classical variables sampling?

▽ NONSTATISTICAL SAMPLING

LEARNING OBJECTIVE G-6
Understand the use of nonstatistical sampling for variables sampling.

To this point, the discussion has focused on statistical sampling methods. The primary advantage of these methods is that they explicitly measure and control the audit team's exposure to sampling risk in determining the sample size and evaluating the sample results. However, it is important to note that generally accepted auditing standards do not require the use of statistical sampling methods. In many cases, it is easier and more efficient to use **nonstatistical sampling methods**.

To illustrate the use of nonstatistical sampling for Rice's accounts receivable, recall that its accounts receivable are composed of 1,500 individual customer accounts and are recorded at $300,000. Also recall that the audit team is interested in evaluating the *existence* and *valuation and allocation* assertions and that the following assessments or judgments have been made prior to selecting individual customer accounts for confirmation:

- Overall exposure to audit risk = 5 percent.
- Inherent risk for the assertions = 100 percent.
- Control risk related to the assertions = 50 percent.
- Risk of material misstatement = 50 percent (1.00 × 0.50).
- Analytical procedures risk related to the assertions = 100 percent.
- Risk of incorrect acceptance = 10 percent (based on preceding risks).
- Expected misstatement = $4,000.
- Tolerable misstatement = $10,000.
- Included in the population are five items of more than $10,000 totaling $120,000.

To determine the sample size under nonstatistical sampling, the AICPA's *Auditing Sampling Guide* suggests using the MUS table in Exhibit G.4. Such a sample would be selected using PPS selection and would likely result in selecting fewer accounts than the sample size because large accounts would be selected more than once. On the other hand, the audit team may believe PPS selection is not efficient for their situation (perhaps there is no computerized list available). Using nonstatistical sampling, they can use their *professional judgment* to determine the sample of accounts.

To illustrate, assume that the audit team decides that a sample of 75 items is sufficient based on their professional judgment and results of previous audits, but they want to be sure to examine all the large items in the population. As a result, they examine all five accounts greater than $10,000 and find no misstatements and then select a sample of 70 items (account balances) for examination. As noted previously, because the five large accounts totaled $120,000, the audit team has sampled from a total of $180,000 of accounts receivable ($300,000 − $120,000). Under nonstatistical sampling, the audit team can use a *nonprobabilistic selection technique* such as block selection or haphazard selection. When using **haphazard selection**, auditors select items in an unstructured manner but without any intentional bias (e.g., picking vouchers out of the file drawer). The use of **block selection** involves selecting a series of contiguous (or adjacent) items from the population (e.g., all cash disbursements in August). Statistical sampling requires the use of probabilistic selection techniques in which all items have an equal probability of being selected. However, the audit team should still make efforts to obtain a representative sample. Once the 70 items have been selected, they are measured. If the 70 items have a recorded balance of $10,000 and an audited balance of $9,900, the audit team could estimate the audited balance as follows:

$$\frac{\text{Audited value of sample}}{\text{Recorded balance of sample}} \times \text{Recorded balance of population} = \frac{\$9,900}{\$10,000} \times \$180,000 = \$178,200$$

The difference between the recorded balance ($180,000) and the audited balance ($178,200) is $1,800. Because the tolerable misstatement is $10,000 and the expected misstatement is $4,000, the audit team would conclude that the account balance is fairly stated. (Recall that no errors were identified in the five large accounts totaling $120,000). A limitation of the audit team's conclusion is that, in this particular case, the audit team did not statistically control and is unable to identify the risk of incorrect acceptance, but because the projected misstatement is less than both the tolerable misstatement and expected misstatement, the audit team can feel fairly confident that the total account balance is not materially misstated.

Alternatively, the audit team could choose to evaluate the results by projecting the misstatement to the population based on the number of items examined. For example, the 70 items had a total overstatement of $100, or $1.43 per item ($100 ÷ 70 items, rounded up for conservatism). Multiplying this $1.43 per item by the number of items in the population (1,495) yields a projected misstatement of $2,137.85, which again is less than the tolerable misstatement of $10,000 and the expected misstatement of $4,000. This approach is used when the audit team believes misstatements are related to the *number* of items instead of their *relative size*. For example, the client may have omitted a $1.43 shipping charge from each of its sales; if so, it would be logical to assume that each item was misstated by a similar dollar amount. If systematic sampling were used, these methods can be applied to each sampling interval, the same as with MUS.

In any case, the client should be requested to correct the $100 known misstatement, and the audit team should investigate the causes of the misstatements. If the projected misstatements exceed the expected misstatements, the audit team should consider other audit evidence and other misstatements to determine whether the financial statements are materially misstated. The audit team may decide to broaden the sample as discussed for the statistical sampling results (recall, the *Audit Sampling Guide* recommends doubling the sample size). Alternatively, the audit team can request management to examine the entire account or class of transactions to identify and correct any misstatements.

VARIABLES SAMPLING: DOCUMENTING

The audit team is required to document various information related to the sampling procedure. The information that would be documented depends on the type of sampling application (MUS, classical variables sampling, or nonstatistical sampling) but generally includes the following:

- Information on the objective of sampling and assertions evaluated, definition of the characteristic of interest, and definition of the population and the sampling unit, including how the audit team verified the completeness of the population (steps 1–3).[7]
- The sampling technique used and the definition of a misstatement.
- The method and parameters used to determine the sample size, which could include sampling risks, tolerable misstatement, expected misstatement, standard deviation of mean values, population size, assessment of inherent risk and control risk, and risk that other substantive procedures will fail to detect a misstatement. In addition to the levels of these factors, the audit team also should document the rationale for these assessments (step 4).
- The sample size determined based on the factors discussed (step 4).
- Information on the selection of sample items and a list of items selected and examined by the audit team (step 5).
- A description of the substantive procedures performed on each item selected, a list of misstatements (step 6), and the determination of the upper limit on misstatements (MUS), precision interval (classical variables sampling), or estimated audited balance (nonstatistical sampling) (step 7).
- The audit team's conclusion with respect to the fairness of the account balance, including qualitative factors considered, and the effect of this conclusion on the opinion on the financial statements.

> ↳ **REVIEW CHECKPOINTS**
>
> G.29 How does nonstatistical sampling differ from statistical sampling?
> G.30 What factors affect the size of a sample in a nonstatistical sampling application?
> G.31 What information related to variables sampling applications does the audit team typically document?

Summary

This module discusses variables sampling, which the audit team uses in performing substantive procedures. When performing variables sampling, the audit team has the primary objective of determining whether an account balance or class of transactions is fairly stated. As with any sampling application, the audit team is exposed to sampling risk (the risk that the decision made based on the sample differs from the decision that would have been made if the entire population were examined). Using statistical sampling allows the audit team to control this sampling risk (referred to as the *risk of incorrect acceptance*) in determining the appropriate sample size and evaluating the sample results. Two primary statistical types of variables sampling plans are monetary unit sampling (MUS) and classical variables sampling.

---

[7] Steps refer to the seven-step procedure discussed at the beginning of this module.

When using MUS, the audit team calculates an upper limit on misstatements, which has a (1 − *Risk of incorrect acceptance*) probability of equaling or exceeding the true amount of misstatement in the population. If the upper limit on misstatements is less than or equal to the tolerable misstatement, the audit team would conclude that the account balance is fairly stated; in contrast, if the upper limit on misstatements exceeds the tolerable misstatement, the audit team would either propose an adjustment to the account balance or class of transactions or expand the sample. MUS is unique in defining the sampling unit as an individual dollar in an account balance or class of transactions. As a result, MUS tends to select larger dollar components for examination.

Classical variables sampling uses normal distribution theory and the central limit theorem to provide a range of either the recorded balance of the account balance or class of transactions or the misstatement in the account balance or class of transactions. Under mean-per-unit estimation, the audit team identifies a precision interval that has a (1 − *Risk of incorrect acceptance*) probability of including the true account balance. If the difference between the recorded account balance and the furthest end of the precision interval falls within the tolerable misstatement, the audit team concludes that the account balance is fairly stated. Conversely, if the difference between the recorded account balance and the furthest range of the precision interval is higher than the tolerable misstatement, the audit team concludes that the account balance is materially misstated and would either propose an adjustment to the client or expand the sample.

Nonstatistical sampling is acceptable under GAAS. Instead of using statistical theory to determine sample size and allowance for sampling risk, auditors rely on their professional judgment. They can employ statistical tables and formulas for guidance, but they are not required to do so. Nonprobabilistic sampling methods such as haphazard or block selection can be used as long as the audit team believes the results are representative of the population. The audit team uses the sampling results to estimate the misstatement in the population and professional judgment to allow for sampling risk. As with all audit sampling, qualitative factors are considered when making the final assessment.

Key Terms

audited value: The amount at which an account balance or class of transactions should be recorded, assuming no departures from generally accepted accounting principles, 797

basic allowance for sampling risk: A component of the upper limit on misstatements determined by multiplying the sampling interval by the confidence factor corresponding to the appropriate risk of incorrect acceptance; its calculation acknowledges that sampling intervals can contain some level of misstatement despite the fact that the logical unit drawn from that sampling interval was not misstated, 809

block selection: A method of choosing sample items in which a series of contiguous (or adjacent) items is chosen from the population, 819

classical variables sampling: An approach that uses the laws of probability and the central limit theorem to provide an estimate of either the amount of misstatement or the true balance of an account balance or class of transactions, 796

difference estimation: A classical variables sampling method that bases its calculation of the estimated account balance on differences between audited values and recorded values of components of the account balance or class of transactions, 817

expected misstatement: The amount of misstatement the audit team anticipates in the account balance or class of transactions, 801

haphazard selection: The method of choosing sample items in an unstructured manner but without any intentional bias, 819

incremental allowance for sampling risk: A component of the upper limit on misstatements determined by adjusting the projected misstatement for the change in confidence factors resulting from detecting the misstatement; its calculation acknowledges that the sampling interval can be misstated to a greater extent than the logical unit drawn from that sampling interval, 807

logical unit: The component of an account balance or class of transactions containing an individual dollar selected under MUS; can include customer account balances, items of inventory, and accounts payable to specific vendors, 804

mean-per-unit estimation: A classical variables sampling method that bases its calculation of the estimated balance on the average audited values of components of the account balance or class of transactions, 812

monetary unit sampling (MUS): A variables sampling method in which the population is viewed as being composed of individual dollars (or euros, yuans, yen, etc.) within an account balance or class of transactions; effective in ensuring that large dollar components are selected for examination, 796

nonstatistical sampling methods: A sampling method that does not attempt to measure the audit team's exposure to sampling risk in determining sample size or evaluating sample results, 818

precision interval: Used in classical variables sampling, an interval of sample estimates that controls the audit team's exposure to the risk of incorrect acceptance and risk of incorrect rejection, 816

probability proportional to size (PPS) selection: A method of sample selection used for MUS sampling in which each dollar or monetary unit is the sample item, resulting in a sample that has a higher likelihood of including higher dollar components or transactions, 796

projected misstatement: A component of the upper limit on misstatements determined by multiplying the sampling interval by the tainting percentage; its calculation assumes that the entire sampling interval is misstated to the same extent as the logical unit drawn from that sampling interval, 807

ratio estimation: A classical variables sampling method that bases its calculation of the estimated balance on the ratio of audited values to recorded values of components of the account balance or class of transactions, 817

risk of incorrect acceptance: The likelihood that the auditors will conclude that the client's account balance is fairly stated when it is materially misstated, 799

risk of incorrect rejection: The likelihood that the auditors will conclude that the client's account balance is materially misstated when it is fairly stated, 799

sampling interval: A break used in MUS to represent the frequency with which sampling units are selected; determined by dividing the recorded amount of the population (account balance) by the sample size, 804

standard deviation: A measure of the variability of the population calculated by summing the squared differences between each item in the population and the population mean and dividing by the sample size minus 1, 814

strata: A subgroup into which a population is divided to reduce sample size; has a smaller standard deviation with respect to the characteristic of interest than the complete population, 812

stratification: The process of subdividing a population into more homogenous subgroups (or *strata*); reduces the necessary sample size in a classical variables sampling application, 812

tainting percentage: An amount that represents the proportion by which a logical unit is misstated; determined by dividing the amount of the misstatement by the recorded balance, 806

tolerable misstatement: The maximum amount by which the account balance or class of transactions can be misstated without the audit team concluding that the account balance or class of transactions is materially misstated; based on *performance materiality,* 800

true balance: The amount at which the client's account balance should be recorded if no misstatements or departures from GAAP existed, 795

upper limit on misstatements: The amount that has a (1 − *Risk of incorrect acceptance*) probability of equaling or exceeding the true amount of misstatement in the population, 809

variables sampling: A form of sampling used to examine a population to estimate the amount or value of some characteristic of that population; used by auditors during their substantive procedures 795

Multiple-Choice Questions for Practice and Review

 All applicable Exercises and Problems are available with McGraw-Hill's *Connect® Accounting*

LO G-1

G.32 Which of the following major stages of the audit is most closely related to variables sampling?
   a. Determining preliminary levels of performance materiality.
   b. Performing tests of controls procedures.
   c. Performing substantive procedures.
   d. Searching for the possible occurrence of subsequent events.

LO G-1 G.33 Which of the following types of variables sampling plans has a tendency to select higher-dollar items for examination?
  a. Difference estimation.
  b. Mean-per-unit estimation.
  c. Monetary unit sampling.
  d. Ratio estimation.

LO G-1 G.34 Variables sampling methods can be used to estimate

	Amount of Misstatement	True Account Balance
a.	Yes	Yes
b.	Yes	No
c.	No	Yes
d.	No	No

LO G-2 G.35 When the audit risk is 0.015, inherent risk is 0.50, control risk is 0.30 (i.e., RMM = 0.15), and analytical procedures risk is 0.50, the risk of incorrect acceptance is
  a. 0.02
  b. 0.20
  c. 0.50
  d. 2.00

LO G-2 G.36 When making a decision about the dollar amount in an account balance based on a sample, the audit team considers the risk of incorrect acceptance to be more serious than the risk of incorrect rejection because
  a. The incorrect rejection decision impairs the efficiency of the audit.
  b. The audit team will do additional work and discover the misstatement of the incorrect decision.
  c. The incorrect acceptance decision impairs the effectiveness of the audit.
  d. Sufficient appropriate audit evidence will not have been obtained.

LO G-2 G.37 The unique feature of monetary unit sampling is that
  a. Sampling units are not chosen at random.
  b. A dollar unit selected in a sample is not replaced before the sample selection is completed.
  c. Auditors need not worry about the risk of incorrect acceptance decision.
  d. The population is defined as the number of monetary units in an account balance or class of transactions.

LO G-3 G.38 When determining sample size under monetary unit sampling, an audit team does *not* need to make a judgment or estimate of
  a. Audit risk.
  b. Tolerable misstatement.
  c. Expected misstatement.
  d. Standard deviation.

LO G-2 G.39 Which of the following statements is correct about monetary unit sampling?
  a. The risk of incorrect acceptance must be specified.
  b. Smaller logical units have a higher probability of selection in the sample than larger units.
  c. Each logical unit in the population has an equally likely chance of being selected in the sample.
  d. The projected misstatement cannot be calculated when one or more misstatements are discovered.

LO G-2 G.40 One of the primary advantages of monetary unit sampling is the fact that
  a. It is an effective method of sampling for evidence of understatement in asset accounts.
  b. The sample selection automatically achieves high-dollar selection and stratification.
  c. The sample selection provides for including a representative number of small-value components.
  d. Expanding the sample for additional evidence is relatively simple.

LO G-3

G.41 Which of the following would *not* cause the audit team to select a larger sample of items under a monetary unit sampling application?
 a. A reduction in the risk of incorrect acceptance from 10 percent to 5 percent.
 b. An increase in the tolerable misstatement from $30,000 to $60,000.
 c. An increase in the expected misstatement from $20,000 to $40,000.
 d. All of these would result in selecting a larger sample.

LO G-4

G.42 Assume that an account with a recorded balance of $5,000 has an audited balance of $3,000. Using MUS, if the sampling interval is $1,500, the projected misstatement would be
 a. $600
 b. $900
 c. $2,000
 d. $3,000

LO G-4

G.43 If the _____ is less than the _____, the audit team would conclude that the account balance is fairly stated.
 a. Projected misstatement; tolerable misstatement.
 b. Tolerable misstatement; projected misstatement.
 c. Upper limit on misstatements; tolerable misstatement.
 d. Tolerable misstatement; upper limit on misstatements.

LO G-4

G.44 If the upper limit on misstatements is calculated at $17,800 and the tolerable misstatement is $15,000, what is the minimum amount of adjustment necessary for the audit team to issue an unqualified opinion on the client's financial statements?
 a. $0
 b. $2,800
 c. $4,800
 d. $14,800

LO G-5

G.45 Alice Rathermel audited LoHo Company's inventory using sampling. She examined 120 items from an inventory compilation list and discovered net overstatement of $480. The audited items had a book (recorded) value of $48,000. There were 1,200 inventory items listed, and the total recorded inventory amount was $490,000. What is the projected misstatement using mean-per-unit estimation?
 a. $480
 b. $576,000
 c. $10,000
 d. $480,000

LO G-5

G.46 To determine the sample size for a classical variables sampling application, an audit team should consider the tolerable misstatement, risk of incorrect acceptance, risk of incorrect rejection, population size, population variability, and
 a. Expected misstatement in the account.
 b. Overall materiality for the financial statements taken as a whole.
 c. Risk of assessing control risk too low.
 d. Risk of assessing control risk too high.

LO G-4

G.47 Which of the following components is *not* used in determining the upper limit on misstatements?
 a. Basic allowance for sampling risk.
 b. Incremental allowance for sampling risk.
 c. Projected misstatement.
 d. Tolerable misstatement.

LO G-4

G.48 The projected misstatement is determined by multiplying the sampling interval by the
 a. Expansion factor.
 b. Incremental confidence factor.
 c. Confidence factor.
 d. Tainting percentage.

Module G *Variables Sampling* **825**

LO G-4 G.49 Which of the following steps involved with determining the upper limit on misstatements is ordinarily performed *earliest?*
  a. Multiply the sampling interval by the tainting percentage.
  b. Determine the audited amount of the item and compare it to the recorded amount.
  c. Calculate the basic allowance for sampling risk.
  d. Calculate the incremental allowance for sampling risk.

LO G-3 G.50 A component of an account balance has a recorded balance of $10,000 and an audited balance of $8,000. Using MUS, if the sampling interval is $20,000, the projected misstatement would be
  a. $2,000
  b. $4,000
  c. $5,000
  d. $10,000

LO G4 G.51 Which of the following statements is *not* true with respect to the calculation of the upper limit on misstatements?
  a. The tainting percentage is determined based on the difference between the recorded balance and the audited balance.
  b. A separate incremental allowance for sampling risk is calculated for each misstatement discovered by the auditor.
  c. If no misstatements are detected, the basic allowance for sampling risk equals zero.
  d. The projected misstatement is determined by multiplying the sampling interval by the tainting percentage.

LO G-5 G.52 Which of the following courses of action would an audit team most likely follow in planning a sample of cash disbursements if the audit team is aware of several unusually large cash disbursements?
  a. Increase the sample size to reduce the effect of the unusually large disbursements.
  b. Continue to draw new samples until all unusually large disbursements appear in the sample.
  c. Set the tolerable deviation rate at a lower level than originally planned.
  d. Stratify the cash disbursements population so that the unusually large disbursements are selected.

(AICPA adapted)

Exercises and Problems 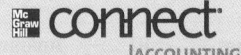 All applicable Exercises and Problems are available with McGraw-Hill's *Connect® Accounting*

LO G-1, G-5 G.53 **Monetary Unit Sampling and Classical Variables Sampling.**

Required:
For each of the following independent situations, indicate the advantages and disadvantages of MUS and classical variables sampling.
  a. You are selecting a sample of customer accounts receivable balances for confirmation. The sample is to be selected from a population of customer accounts receivable, the total of which exceeds $4,000,000. This list comprises 4,000 individual customer accounts that are relatively similar in dollar amount with balances ranging from $800 to $8,000. In past years, you have identified a moderate level of misstatement in the client's accounts receivable although the level of misstatement was always less than the tolerable misstatement.
  b. You are selecting a sample of accounts payable balances for confirmation with vendors. The population is a list of accounts payable to vendors; at year-end, the total (unaudited) accounts payable balance is $800,000. Amounts owed by the client to 200 separate vendors

are included in this balance. Because the client has two major suppliers, a disproportionate amount of this balance ($500,000) is concentrated in these two accounts.

c. You are selecting a sample of customer accounts receivable balances for confirmation. The population is a list of customer accounts receivable; at year-end, the accounts receivable total is $2,500,000. Compared to most of your clients, the number of customer accounts included in this balance is relatively small and the balances range from $1,000 to $525,000.

LO G-3

G.54 **Sample Selection: Monetary Unit Sampling.** Emerson Washburn is examining the accounts receivable of Anaheim Company and has decided to use MUS to select a sample of customer accounts for confirmation. Anaheim's accounts receivable totaled $3,500,000 and comprised 3,000 different customer accounts ranging in amount from $200 to $125,000. Based on the characteristics of the population and acceptable risk of incorrect acceptance, tolerable misstatement, and expected misstatement, Washburn determined a sample size of 20 accounts.

Required:

a. Without making any calculations, briefly describe how Washburn would select a sample of customer accounts from the population of accounts receivable.

b. If Washburn selected a random starting point of 172,600, what are the first four dollars that would be selected? How would Washburn proceed to evaluate these dollars?

c. What would Washburn do if two of the dollars selected are contained within the same customer account?

d. Anaheim maintains its accounts receivable balances in a computerized file that has the following information: (1) customer number, (2) customer name, (3) total account balance, and (4) account status (current versus past due). For each of these elements, comment on any procedures that Washburn should perform before selecting the sample if the population were arranged based on these elements (for example, arranged numerically by customer number, alphabetically by customer name).

LO G-3

G.55 **Sample Selection: Monetary Unit Sampling.** You have been assigned to select an MUS sample from Whitney Company's detailed inventory records as of September 30. Whitney's controller gave you a list of the 23 different inventory items and their recorded book amounts. The senior accountant told you to select a sample of 10 dollar units and the inventory items that contain them.

Required:

Prepare audit documentation showing a systematic selection of 10 dollar units and the related logical units. Arrange the items in their numerical identification number order and use a random starting point at the 1,210th dollar.

ID	Amount	ID	Amount	ID	Amount	ID	Amount
1	$1,750	7	$1,255	13	$ 937	19	$2,577
2	1,492	8	3,761	14	5,938	20	1,126
3	994	9	1,956	15	2,001	21	565
4	629	10	1,393	16	222	22	2,319
5	2,272	11	884	17	1,738	23	1,681
6	1,163	12	729	18	1,228		

LO G-3

G.56 **Sample Size Determination: Monetary Unit Sampling (MUS).** The recorded accounts receivable balance for Warner Company was $500,000.

Required:

For each of the following independent sets of conditions, determine the appropriate sample size for the examination of Warner's accounts receivable in MUS. Based on the differences in your calculations, identify the general relationship between different factors and sample size. (RIA = risk of incorrect acceptance, TM = tolerable misstatement, EM = expected misstatement).

a. RIA = 5 percent, TM = $50,000, EM = $10,000.

b. RIA = 5 percent, TM = $50,000, EM = $25,000.

c. RIA = 10 percent, TM = $50,000, EM = $10,000.
d. RIA = 10 percent, TM = $50,000, EM = $25,000.

LO G-3

G.57 **Sample Size and Sampling Interval Determination: Monetary Unit Sampling (MUS).** Reagan Simmons is conducting the audit of Ace, Inc., and is using MUS to select a sample of inventory items for examination. The recorded balance in Ace's inventory account was $1,200,000. In carrying out the sampling plan, Simmons established a risk of incorrect acceptance of 5 percent, a tolerable misstatement of $100,000, and an expected misstatement of $20,000.

Required:

a. What parameters would Simmons consider in determining the sample size for Ace's inventory?
b. How would Simmons identify or establish each of these parameters?
c. Determine the necessary sample size for the audit of Ace's inventory.
d. Based on the sample size determined in (c), what is the appropriate sampling interval?
e. Briefly describe how Simmons would select the sample from a computerized inventory list that Ace maintains.

LO G-3

G.58 **Sample Size and Sampling Interval Determination: Monetary Unit Sampling (MUS).** Casey Paul is considering the use of MUS in examining Stanley's accounts receivable, which were recorded at $300,000. Using the audit risk model, Paul has identified a necessary risk of incorrect acceptance of 10 percent and has established a tolerable misstatement of $25,000 and an expected misstatement of $10,000.

Required:

a. Determine the necessary sample size for the audit of Stanley's accounts receivable.
b. Based on the sample size determined in (a), what is the appropriate sampling interval?
c. Briefly describe how Paul would select the sample from a computerized customer list that Stanley maintains.
d. How would each of the following changes in Paul's sampling plan impact the sample size and sampling interval? For each change, use the original parameters noted in the problem background. (Verify your answer by calculating the sample size associated with each change.)
   1. A reduction in the necessary level of the risk of incorrect acceptance to 5 percent.
   2. An increase in the expected misstatement to $12,500.
   3. A decrease in the tolerable misstatement to $20,000.

LO G-3

G.59 **Sample Size and Sampling Interval Determination: Monetary Unit Sampling (MUS).** Blythe Drake is conducting an audit of Newman and is using MUS to select a sample of customer accounts receivable for confirmation. Newman's accounts receivable are recorded at $10,000,000 and comprise 2,000 customer accounts. Drake has established the following parameters for the investigation:

- Risk of incorrect acceptance = 5 percent.
- Tolerable misstatement = $250,000.
- Expected misstatement = $50,000.

Required:

a. Determine the sample size and sampling interval that Drake used in the audit of Newman's accounts receivable.
b. Based on the calculations in (a), briefly describe how Drake would select customer accounts from the population of accounts receivable balances for confirmation.
c. Holding all other factors constant, determine the sample size and sampling interval assuming each of the following independent changes in Drake's sampling parameters:
   1. Because of improvements in Newman's internal control policies related to accounts receivable processing from previous years, Drake believes that a risk of incorrect acceptance of 10 percent is now acceptable in the current engagement.
   2. Because of the closeness of certain ratios to key debt covenants (particularly the current and quick ratios, which are highly influenced by accounts receivable), Drake believes that the tolerable misstatement should be decreased from $250,000 to $125,000.

3. Because of unusual circumstances in the previous year, some misstatements occurred in sales transaction processing that resulted in misstatements in accounts receivable. These misstatements are not anticipated to occur during the upcoming year. As a result, Drake believes that expected misstatement can be decreased from $50,000 to $25,000.

d. How do the changes noted in (c) illustrate the relationship between sample size and various factors?

e. Describe the relationship between the sample size and sampling interval. Provide a brief explanation as to the nature of this relationship.

LO G-3

G.60 **Sample Size Relationships: Monetary Unit Sampling.** For each of the following cases, provide the missing information.

Recorded balance	$1,500,000	$190,000	(C)
Sample size	115	(B)	124
Sampling interval	(A)	4,222	18,000

LO G-3

G.61 **Sample Size Relationships: Monetary Unit Sampling.** Noel Frehley is examining the accounts receivable of Kiss Company and is considering the use of MUS. Kiss's accounts receivable are recorded at $400,000. Based on the necessary level of risk, Frehley has established a risk of incorrect acceptance of 5 percent. In addition, based on previous audits, Frehley estimates misstatements of $10,000. Finally, based on the overall level of performance materiality, Frehley has established tolerable misstatement at $20,000.

Required:

a. Determine the necessary sample size for Frehley's examination of Kiss Company's accounts receivable.

b. Assume that Frehley was interested in trying to reduce the necessary sample size. What are some options available in this regard?

c. Based on a discussion with the senior manager, Frehley knows that increasing the level of the risk of incorrect acceptance will reduce sample size. For the same level of expected misstatement, tolerable misstatement, and population size, determine the sample size for a risk of incorrect acceptance of 10 percent.

LO G-4

G.62 **Projected Misstatement Calculation: Monetary Unit Sampling.** For each of the following independent misstatements, identify the missing value:

	1	2	3	4
Recorded balance	$15,000	$30,000	(e)	$12,000
Audited balance	$12,000	(c)	$6,000	(g)
Tainting percentage	(a)	5%	25%	(h)
Sampling interval	$50,000	(d)	$25,000	$48,000
Projected misstatement	(b)	$5,000	(f)	$24,000

LO G-4

G.63 **Upper Limit on Misstatements Calculation: Monetary Unit Sampling (MUS).** Jordan Thomas is using MUS to examine a client's accounts receivable balance. Using a sample size of 100 items and a sampling interval of $12,300, Thomas identified the following misstatements:

Item	Recorded Balance	Audited Balance
1	$15,000	$12,500
2	10,000	4,000
3	3,000	2,000

Required:

a. Calculate the upper limit on misstatements assuming a risk of incorrect acceptance of (1) 5 percent and (2) 10 percent.

b. Based on your calculations in (a), comment on the relationship between the risk of incorrect acceptance and the upper limit on misstatements.

LO G-4

G.64 **Upper Limit on Misstatements Calculation: Monetary Unit Sampling (MUS).** Carson Allister is performing an MUS application in the audit of Bird Company's accounts receivable. Based on the acceptable level of the risk of incorrect acceptance of 5 percent and a tolerable misstatement of $120,000, Allister has calculated a sample size of 75 items and a sampling interval of $25,000. After examining the sample items, the following misstatements were identified:

Item	Recorded Balance	Audited Balance
1	$35,000	$28,000
2	10,000	8,000
3	6,000	3,000

Required:
a. Calculate the upper limit on misstatements for Bird Company's accounts receivable.
b. Provide a brief description of the meaning of the upper limit on misstatements calculated in (a).
c. What would Allister's conclusion be with respect to the fairness of Bird's accounts receivable balance?

LO G-4

G.65 **Upper Limit on Misstatements Calculation: Monetary Unit Sampling.** The auditors mailed positive confirmations on 60 customers' accounts receivable balances. The company's accounts receivable balance comprised 2,356 customer accounts with a total recorded balance of $19,600,000, and the sampling interval was $280,000. The auditors received four positive confirmation returns reporting exceptions. Upon follow-up, they found the following:

- *Account 2333.* Recorded amount $8,345. The account was overstated by $1,669 because the client made an arithmetic mistake recording a credit memo. The company issued only 86 credit memos during the year. The auditors examined all of them for the same arithmetic mistake and found no similar misstatements.
- *Account 363.* Recorded amount $7,460. The account was overstated by $1,865 because the company sold merchandise to a customer with payment due in six months plus 15 percent interest. The billing clerk made a mistake and recorded the sales price and the unearned interest as the sale and receivable amount. Inquiries revealed that the company always sold on "payment due immediately" terms but had made an exception for this customer. Numerous sales transactions had been audited in the sales control audit work and none had shown the extended terms allowed to Account 363.
- *Account 1216.* Recorded amount $19,450. The account was overstated by $1,945 because an accounting clerk had deliberately misadded several invoices to create extra charges to a business that competed with his brother's business unrelated to the company. The accounting clerk (who was a temporary employee) had forged the initials of the supervisor who normally reviewed invoices for accuracy. The auditors examined all invoices for this and other customers processed by this clerk and found no similar misstatements.
- *Account 2003.* Recorded amount $9,700. The account was overstated by $1,455 because of a fictitious sale submitted by a salesperson, apparently part of an effort to boost third-quarter sales and commissions. The auditors learned that the salesperson was employed from August 20 through October 30 before being dismissed as a result of customer complaints. They examined all other unpaid balances attributed to this salesperson and found no other fictitious sales.

Required:
a. Decide which, if any, of the account misstatements should be considered monetary misstatements and included in the calculation of the upper limit on misstatements using monetary unit sampling.
b. Calculate the upper limit on misstatements and decide whether the evidence from these misstatements indicates that the accounts receivable balance is or is not materially misstated. (The tolerable misstatement for the accounts receivable was $1,000,000, and the auditors had already decided on a risk of incorrect acceptance of 5 percent.)
c. Are any additional procedures required of the audit team regarding account 1216 or account 2003?

LO G-4

G.66 Upper Limit on Misstatements Calculations: Monetary Unit Sampling. Assume that Parker Fran has calculated a sampling interval for Tide, Inc.'s inventory of $10,000 and has conducted an examination of a sample of inventory balances. Fran has identified the following three misstatements:

Item No.	Recorded Balance	Audited Balance
X-21	$3,000	$1,200
Z-24	550	440
AA-02	6,000	1,500

Required:

Calculate the upper limit on misstatements for the following levels of the risk of incorrect acceptance. In general, what relationship do you observe between the risk of incorrect acceptance and the upper limit on misstatements?

a. 5 percent.
b. 10 percent.

LO G-4

G.67 Upper Limit on Misstatements Calculations: Monetary Unit Sampling. Clyde Billy is conducting the audit of Hoops, Inc., and is examining Hoops's inventory balances. Billy plans to select a sample of inventory items for examination and will verify quantities and perform price tests to ascertain that the items are properly recorded according to generally accepted accounting principles.

Billy determined a sampling interval of $100,000 and, using systematic random selection techniques, has identified the following misstatements:

Item No.	Recorded Balance	Audited Balance
10-865	$ 12,600	$ 8,400
20-954	110,000	95,000
30-781	55,000	44,000
40-269	80,000	60,000

Required:

a. Using a 5 percent risk of incorrect acceptance, calculate the upper limit on misstatements.
b. Provide a brief description of the meaning of the upper limit on misstatement using the information calculated in (a).
c. Reperform (a) using a risk of incorrect acceptance of 10 percent.
d. What relationship do you observe between the acceptable level of the risk of incorrect acceptance and the upper limit on misstatements? Provide a brief explanation about what causes this relationship.
e. Based on the levels of the upper limit on misstatements determined in this example, what are the advantages and disadvantages of establishing lower and higher acceptable levels of the risk of incorrect acceptance?

LO G-1, G-3, G-4

G.68 Comprehensive Problem: Monetary Unit Sampling (MUS). Zachary Mayo is a new staff accountant participating on his first audit engagement. He has been assigned to the Foley Company engagement and is examining Foley's accounts receivable. Foley maintains a computerized ledger of its accounts receivable balances, which are recorded at $5,000,000 and comprise 5,560 individual customer accounts.

Mayo established the following parameters for use in this year's audit. In so doing, he relied extensively on parameters established in prior audits:

- Expected misstatement is established at $100,000, which is the average amount of misstatement identified in the past five audits. During the past year, Foley has experienced a great deal of turnover among its sales processing personnel and has made some relatively large sales that present some unusual revenue recognition issues. In addition, accounts receivable have increased by almost 15 percent from the prior year.
- The tolerable misstatement is 10 percent of the ending accounts receivable balance, or $500,000 ($5,000,000 × 0.10). Compared to previous years, Foley's financial condition

has slightly deteriorated. Its current and quick ratios, while still above levels necessary to satisfy its debt covenants, have deteriorated.

- The risk of incorrect acceptance is 10 percent, which is the same as that used in the previous year. In evaluating the components of the audit risk model, some of the issues related to the turnover among sales processing personnel as well as the more limited use of analytical procedures during the current audit represent important differences from previous years.

Mayo sent positive confirmations. His work identified the following differences between audited balances and recorded balances.

Customer	Recorded Balance	Audited Balance
R. Gerer	$ 15,000	$10,000
D. Wings	25,000	20,000
L. Goss	60,000	30,000
K. David	120,000	90,000

Unfortunately, Mayo resigned from the firm shortly after identifying these differences. The only documentation you were able to locate was information related to (1) the levels of expected misstatement, tolerable misstatement, and risk of incorrect acceptance that were used in the Foley audit and (2) the four confirmations returned by customers indicating differences between their records and Foley's recorded balances.

Required:

a. Mayo decided to use MUS primarily because it had been used in previous audits of Foley. Based on the nature of this sampling application, was the use of MUS appropriate?

b. Based on the parameters established by Mayo, determine the sample size and sampling interval he used in the sampling application.

c. Describe the sample selection process used by Mayo. Are you able to replicate or otherwise determine which customer balances he confirmed?

d. Based on the four overstatements identified by Mayo, calculate the upper limit on misstatements. Based on this upper limit on misstatements, what general statement can be made with respect to the extent of misstatement in the account balance?

e. What is your initial decision with respect to the fairness of Foley's accounts receivable balance?

f. Review each of the parameters established by Mayo (expected misstatement, tolerable misstatement, and risk of incorrect acceptance). Do any differences in the current engagement raise questions with respect to the level of these parameters?

g. What are the potential effect(s) of the changes in parameters noted in (f) on the sampling application?

LO G-3, G-4

G.69 Comprehensive Problem: Monetary Unit Sampling. Clint Walker was examining the accounts receivable of Country Music, Inc. Its accounts receivable were recorded at $1,500,000. Based on past audits, Walker established tolerable misstatement at 10 percent of the recorded account balance and anticipated a very small level of misstatement in Country Music's accounts receivable ($50,000). In his previous assessments of audit risk, risk of material misstatement, and analytical procedures risk, Walker had established a necessary risk of incorrect acceptance of 10 percent.

Required:

a. Calculate the sampling interval and sample size that Walker would use in the audit of Country Music.

b. Reperform the calculations in (a) if Walker had established a risk of incorrect acceptance of (1) 5 percent and (2) 20 percent. Based on your calculations, describe the relationship between the necessary level of the risk of incorrect acceptance and the sample size and sampling interval.

c. [*Note: Requirement (c) is unrelated to requirements (a) and (b).*] If Walker had detected the following four overstatements, determine the projected misstatement.

Recorded Balance	Audited Balance	Sampling Interval
$ 3,500	$ 1,750	$8,000
1,000	200	8,000
12,000	10,000	8,000
5,000	4,000	8,000

d. Based on the results in (c) and using a 10 percent risk of incorrect acceptance, calculate the upper limit on misstatements.

e. Reperform the calculation in (d) using a risk of incorrect acceptance of (1) 5 percent and (2) 20 percent. Based on your calculation, describe the relationship between the necessary level of the risk of incorrect acceptance and the upper limit on misstatements.

f. Using a risk of incorrect acceptance of (1) 5 percent, (2) 10 percent, and (3) 20 percent, what would Walker's conclusion be with respect to Country Music's accounts receivable? How do different levels of the risk of incorrect acceptance influence the likelihood of concluding that the account balance is fairly stated?

LO G-3, G-4

G.70 **Monetary Unit Sampling with Understated Account.** Dylan Mays is auditing the accounts receivable of Channel Company. Channel's accounts receivable were recorded at $2,000,000 and comprised more than 1,500 customer accounts. However, Channel's 10 largest customers' balances comprised a high percentage of the recorded accounts receivable (over $500,000, or 25 percent). As a result, Mays is considering the use of MUS.

Based on prior audits and other judgments, Mays has established the following parameters:

Risk of incorrect acceptance	5%
Tolerable misstatement	$120,000
Expected misstatement	$24,000

Required:

a. Briefly identify what factors Mays should consider in determining sample size and how these factors would be assessed.

b. Calculate the necessary sample size and sampling interval used by Mays in the audit of Channel Company.

c. Given the information in (b), describe how Mays would select the sample from Channel's computerized accounts receivable ledger.

d. *[Note: Requirement (d) is unrelated to requirements (b) and (c).]* If Mays detected the following four misstatements, determine the projected misstatement.

Recorded Balance	Audited Balance	Sampling Interval
$45,000	$40,000	$13,000
8,000	6,000	13,000
12,000	9,000	13,000
10,000	12,000	13,000

e. Based on the results in (d) and a 5 percent risk of incorrect acceptance, calculate the upper limit on misstatements.

f. Based on the calculation in (e), what would Mays's conclusion be with respect to Channel Company's accounts receivable?

LO G-5

G.71 **Sample Size Determination: Classical Variables Sampling.** The recorded inventory balance for Faulk Company was $1,000,000 and comprised 2,500 customer accounts.

Required:

For each of the following independent sets of conditions, determine the appropriate sample size for the audit of Faulk's inventory using classical variables sampling (mean-per-unit estimation). Based on the differences in your calculations, identify the general relationship between different factors and sample size. (RIA = risk of incorrect acceptance, RIR = risk of incorrect rejection, TM = tolerable misstatement, EM = expected misstatement, SD = standard deviation)

a. RIA = 5 percent, RIR = 5 percent, TM = $50,000, EM = $20,000, SD = $40.
b. RIA = 10 percent, RIR = 5 percent, TM = $50,000, EM = $20,000, SD = $40.

c. RIA = 10 percent, RIR = 10 percent, TM = $50,000, EM = $20,000, SD = $40.
d. RIA = 5 percent, RIR = 5 percent, TM = $30,000, EM = $20,000, SD = $40.
e. RIA = 5 percent, RIR = 5 percent, TM = $50,000, EM = $10,000, SD = $40.
f. RIA = 5 percent, RIR = 5 percent, TM = $50,000, EM = $10,000, SD = $30.

LO G-5

G.72 **Sample Size Determination: Classical Variables Sampling.** Shannon Solomon, CPA, is auditing the accounts receivable of Warner Company and is using mean-per-unit estimation. Accounts receivable were recorded at $2,000,000 and comprised 1,250 individual customer accounts. Solomon established the following parameters for the audit of accounts receivable:

- Using firm policy, tolerable misstatement for accounts receivable is established at 6 percent of the recorded account balance.
- Based on prior audits of Warner's accounts receivable, the standard deviation of audited balances is estimated to be $100.
- Based on prior audits of Warner's accounts receivable, Solomon estimates that accounts receivable will be misstated by 4 percent of the recorded account balance.

Solomon is now establishing the acceptable levels of the risk of incorrect acceptance and the risk of incorrect rejection for the audit of Warner Company's accounts receivable.

Required:

a. What factors should Solomon consider in establishing acceptable levels of the risk of incorrect acceptance and the risk of incorrect rejection?

b. What are the advantages and disadvantages to Solomon of establishing lower levels of the risk of incorrect acceptance and the risk of incorrect rejection?

c. If Solomon establishes levels of the risk of incorrect acceptance and the risk of incorrect rejection of 5 percent, what is the resultant sample size?

d. Determine the sample size for each of the following combinations of risk of incorrect acceptance and risk of incorrect rejection:

1. Risk of incorrect acceptance of 5 percent, risk of incorrect rejection of 10 percent.
2. Risk of incorrect acceptance of 10 percent, risk of incorrect rejection of 5 percent.
3. Risk of incorrect acceptance of 10 percent, risk of incorrect rejection of 10 percent.

e. Based on the sample sizes you calculated in (c) and (d), how do the levels of sampling risks affect sample size?

LO G-5

G.73 **Evaluating Results: Classical Variables Sampling.** Kyle Berry is using mean-per-unit estimation in the audit of Leonard's inventory balances. Leonard's inventory is recorded at $240,000 and comprises 1,200 different items. Berry determined a sample size of 120 items and performed the appropriate substantive procedures and based on this sample, determined the following:

Average audited value (per item)	$204
Standard deviation of audited values	$22

A summary of some additional parameters estimated by Berry follow:

Tolerable misstatement	$17,500
Expected misstatement	$7,500
Risk of incorrect acceptance	5%
Risk of incorrect rejection	10%

Required:

a. What is Berry's estimate of the audited value of Leonard's inventory?

b. Calculate the precision and precision interval for Leonard's inventory. Provide a brief description of the meaning of the precision interval.

c. What is Berry's conclusion with respect to Leonard's inventory balance?

d. Using a risk of incorrect acceptance of (1) 1 percent and (2) 10 percent, calculate the precision and the precision interval for Leonard's inventory.

e. Based on your answers to (b) and (d), how does the risk of incorrect acceptance affect the precision interval and conclusions about the fairness of the account balance?

LO G-5

G.74 **Evaluating Sample Results: Classical Variables Sampling.** You are auditing Hernandez, Inc.'s accounts receivable balance using classical variables sampling. Hernandez's accounts receivable comprised 2,500 customer accounts and were recorded at $3,500,000.

Using a risk of incorrect acceptance and a risk of incorrect rejection of 5 percent, you selected a sample of 200 accounts for examination and confirmed the accounts with the customers. The total recorded balance of these 200 accounts was $1,000,000; based on your confirmations as well as an investigation of differences reported by customers, you determined an audited balance of $900,000.

Required:

a. What is the sample estimate of Hernandez's accounts receivable balance using mean-per-unit estimation?

b. If Hernandez used difference estimation or ratio estimation, how would you expect the sample size to be different?

c. In what circumstances should each of the different methods of classical variables estimation be used?

d. If you calculate a sample estimate of $3,000,000 and precision of $750,000, form a precision interval for Hernandez's accounts receivable using mean-per-unit estimation. Briefly describe the meaning of the precision interval as well as your conclusion with respect to Hernandez's accounts receivable balance (tolerable misstatement = $175,000).

LO G-5

G.75 **Comprehensive Problem: Classical Variables Sampling.** Jessie Howe is examining Met Company's accounts receivable balance and has decided to use mean-per-unit estimation. Met's accounts receivable were recorded at $650,000 and comprised 2,000 individual customer accounts. Howe established tolerable misstatement at 5 percent of the recorded balance. Based on prior experience with Met, Howe assessed expected misstatement at $22,500 and estimated a standard deviation of the mean audited value of $30.

Required:

a. Using the preceding parameters, identify the appropriate sample size for the following combinations of risk of incorrect acceptance (RIA) and risk of incorrect rejection (RIR):
  1. RIA = 1 percent, RIR = 5 percent.
  2. RIA = 1 percent, RIR = 10 percent.
  3. RIA = 5 percent, RIR = 10 percent.

b. What factors would Howe consider in establishing the risk of incorrect acceptance and the risk of incorrect rejection?

c. Based on the results in (a), how do the risk of incorrect acceptance and the risk of incorrect rejection influence the determination of sample size?

d. If Howe had determined an audited value of $330 per account and a standard deviation of audited values of $30, determine the precision interval for each of the following combinations of the risk of incorrect acceptance (RIA) and risk of incorrect rejection (RIR). In each of these cases, what is Howe's conclusion with respect to Met's accounts receivable?
  1. RIA = 1 percent, RIR = 5 percent.
  2. RIA = 1 percent, RIR = 10 percent.
  3. RIA = 5 percent, RIR = 10 percent.

e. Based on the results in (d), how do the risk of incorrect acceptance and risk of incorrect rejection influence the precision interval and evaluation of results?

LO G-5

G.76 **Comprehensive Problem: Classical Variables Sampling.** Wade Wallace designed a classical variables sampling application to examine the accounts receivable for Rasheed, Inc. After considering several possibilities, Wallace decided to use mean-per-unit estimation. The following parameters are noted through a review of Wallace's audit documentation:

Recorded balance of accounts receivable	$800,000
Number of customer accounts included in accounts receivable balance	2,000
Risk of incorrect acceptance	5 percent
Risk of incorrect rejection	20 percent
Tolerable misstatement	$50,000
Expected misstatement	$10,000
Standard deviation of audited value	$52

Required:

a. Describe how Wallace would establish each of these parameters.
b. What is the appropriate sample size for this application?
c. Assume that Wallace is considering an increase in the necessary level of the risk of incorrect acceptance to 10 percent. How would this increase affect the sample size?
d. Using a 5 percent risk of incorrect acceptance, assume that Wallace determined a $380 average audited value per item and a $50 standard deviation of audited values. Construct the precision interval for Rasheed's accounts receivable.
e. Based on the precision interval in (d), provide Wallace's conclusion with respect to Rasheed's accounts receivable.
f. Repeat (d) and (e) assuming that the average audited value per item is $405. Why does Wallace's conclusion differ from that reached in (e)?

LO G-6

G.77 Evaluating Sample Results: Nonstatistical Sampling. Finley Gunny is using nonstatistical sampling in the examination of Highway Company's accounts receivable, which were recorded at $350,000. Gunny determined a tolerable misstatement of $15,000 and a sample size of 49 items.

Required:

a. How does the audit team determine sample size using nonstatistical sampling?
b. If the items selected by Gunny had an aggregate recorded balance of $50,000 and an aggregate audited balance of $45,000, calculate the estimated audited balance.
c. What would Gunny conclude with respect to the fairness of Highway's accounts receivable?

LO G-6

G.78 Nonstatistical Sampling. Marley Brown is planning the substantive procedures for the audit of Longhorn Company's inventory, which had a recorded (unaudited) balance of $6,500,000. In prior audits, Brown used monetary unit sampling but is now considering the use of nonstatistical sampling. Brown has established a tolerable misstatement of $250,000 and a sample size of 71 items.

Required:

a. Compared to monetary unit sampling, what are the advantages and disadvantages to Brown of using nonstatistical sampling in this year's audit of Longhorn's inventory?
b. Compare the factors used by Brown in determining sample size under monetary unit sampling to those that would be used in nonstatistical sampling.
c. Brown is considering increasing the analytical procedures in order to reduce the tests of details of the inventory. What factors would Brown consider in deciding whether to perform more extensive analytical procedures?
d. If the items selected by Brown had an aggregate audited balance of $970,000 and an aggregate recorded balance of $1,000,000, what would be the conclusion with respect to the fairness of Longhorn's inventory?

LO G-2

G.79 Mistakes in a Monetary Unit Sampling (MUS) Application. Kelsey Mead, CPA, was engaged to audit Jiffy Company's financial statements for the year ended August 31.

Required:

Describe each incorrect assumption, statement, and inappropriate application of sampling in Mead's procedures in the following.

For the current year, Mead decided to use MUS to select accounts receivable for confirmation because MUS uses each account in the population as a separate sampling unit. Mead expected to discover many overstatements but presumed that the MUS sample size still would be smaller than the corresponding sample size for classical variables sampling.

Mead reasoned that the MUS sample would automatically result in a stratified sample because each account would have an equal chance of being selected for confirmation. Additionally, the selection of negative (credit) balances would be facilitated without special considerations.

Mead computed the sample size using the risk of incorrect acceptance, the total recorded book amount of the receivables, and the number of misstated accounts allowed. Mead divided the total recorded book amount of the receivables by the sample size to determine the sampling interval and then calculated the standard deviation of the dollar amounts of the accounts selected for evaluation of the receivables.

Mead's calculated sample size was 60 and the sampling interval was determined to be $10,000. However, only 58 different accounts were selected because two accounts were so large that the sampling interval caused each of them to be selected twice. Mead proceeded to send confirmation requests to 55 of the 58 customers. Each of the three accounts originally selected for the sample had insignificant recorded balances under $20. Mead ignored these three small accounts and substituted the three largest accounts that had not been selected by the random selection procedure. Each of these accounts had balances in excess of $7,000, so Mead sent confirmation requests to these customers.

The confirmation process revealed two differences. One account with an audited amount of $3,000 had been recorded at $4,000. Mead projected this to be a $1,000 misstatement. Another account with an audited amount of $2,000 had been recorded at $1,900. Mead did not count the $100 difference because the purpose of the procedure was to detect overstatements.

In evaluating the sample results, Mead decided that the accounts receivable balance was not overstated because the projected misstatement ($1,000) was less than the allowance for sampling risk.

(AICPA adapted)

LO G-2, G-3

G.80 **Sampling Application Evaluation: Variables Sampling.** The law firm of Spade & Associates hired Dylan Sayers to review the audit of the 2012 financial statements that Hammer & Wimsey, CPAs, had completed for Golden Sound and Records Company. Specifically, the attorneys engaged Sayers to determine whether the audit of Golden Sound's inventory of sound equipment and CDs conformed to generally accepted auditing standards. After Golden Sound declared bankruptcy three months ago (eight months after the 2012 audited financial statements were issued), stockholders sued Golden Sound, alleging distribution of misleading financial statements, and Hammer & Wimsey hired Spade & Associates to prepare a defense in the event that Hammer & Wimsey were included later in the lawsuit. The first time Golden Sound had been audited was 2012.

Golden Sound's business had grown rapidly. The company had 40 stores in 2010, opened 36 more in 2011, and added 23 more (for a total of 99) during 2012. The following accounting information showed the growth of the inventory:

	June 30		
	2010	2011	2012
Sound equipment	$5,800,000	$10,000,000	$12,200,000
CDs	2,200,000	6,800,000	9,000,000
Total inventory	$8,000,000	$16,800,000	$21,200,000
Number of stores	40	76	99

Sayers reviewed the Hammer & Wimsey audit documentation and prepared this summary:

In April 2012, Bobby Earl (Hammer & Wimsey audit manager on the Golden Sound engagement) met with Golden Sound's managers and discussed the procedures for taking the physical inventory as of June 30. Mikki LaTouche (Golden Sound's chief financial officer) suggested that the auditors' inventory observation be conducted at the stores located in large cities where Golden Sound had started business. According to LaTouche, "These stores are well stocked with a representative selection of all types of equipment and musical releases available across all the stores. The store managers are well acquainted with the inventory and can conduct an accurate counting with experienced store employees. The newer stores carry less stock, and the managers are relatively new to their jobs. You'll get a more accurate inventory-taking observation in the more established stores."

Earl agreed and noted in the audit documentation that the prospect of sending audit teams to distant stores in the Midwestern and Southeastern states (where Golden Sound had established new stores in the past year or so) would be very costly in terms of auditors' time and travel expenses. Together, LaTouche and Earl selected eight of the stores in the Western Region. Earl supervised experienced audit teams as they observed the inventory counts at these eight stores. The auditors observed that the Golden Sound store managers gave good instructions to the inventory takers and that the count records were in good order. Test counts showed only minor mistakes, which the managers promptly and conscientiously corrected.

Everyone was interested in making accurate counts because Golden Sound had no reliable perpetual inventory records, and the financial statement amounts for inventory were determined by this physical inventory. In fact, Earl wrote in the internal control communication to the board of directors and in the management letter addressed to the CFO the observation that Golden Sound needed to establish reliable inventory records for physical control and profit enhancement. The auditors determined the following inventory amounts in the eight stores. Using the total inventory of $1,712,700 in these stores, Earl divided by eight to find the average per store, then multiplied by 99, and projected the total inventory in the amount of $21,194,663. Because this amount was only $5,337 less than the book value of inventory in the general ledger, Earl and the reviewing partner did not perform further work and incorporated the recorded inventory amount of $21,200,000 in the 2012 financial statements along with a standard unqualified auditor's report.

Required:
Complete Sayers' engagement by evaluating the Hammer & Wimsey conduct of the inventory portion of the Golden Sound 2012 audit. Use auditor's responsibilities from Chapter 2 to guide your answer.

LO G-2, G-5

G.81 **Monetary Unit and Classical Variables Sampling.** Indicate whether each of the following characteristics applies to monetary unit sampling (MUS), classical variables sampling (CVS), both MUS and CVS (both), or neither MUS nor CVS (neither).

a. May be used in conjunction with substantive procedures.
b. Tends to select higher dollar items for examination.
c. Is more effective in identifying overstatements.
d. Incorporates assessments of tolerable misstatement in determining sample size.
e. Incorporates assessments of the population variability in determining sample size.
f. Controls the audit team's exposure to the risk of incorrect rejection and the risk of incorrect acceptance.
g. Requires the audit team to project discovered misstatements to the population.
h. Can expose the audit team to nonsampling risk.
i. May be used in conjunction with the study and evaluation of internal control.
j. Is more appropriate for use when a higher number of misstatements is anticipated.

LO G-4

G.82 **Monetary Unit Sampling (MUS).** Georgie Costanza, CPA, is auditing the accounts receivable of Vandalay Industries and is considering the use of MUS techniques. Costanza has a number of questions regarding the use of MUS and has asked you to provide answers to them.

Required:
a. Under generally accepted auditing standards, can Costanza use nonstatistical sampling in the examination of Vandalay accounts receivable?
b. What are the advantages to using statistical sampling in the audit?
c. What are the risks associated with sampling and to what type of losses do they expose Costanza?
d. How does Costanza establish the appropriate level of the risk of incorrect acceptance?
e. Is Costanza permitted to specify that certain items be examined, or do all items need to be randomly selected?
f. How can Costanza increase the likelihood that the items in the sample are representative of the population?
g. Other than the dollar amount of the misstatements, are any other factors important for Costanza to consider with respect to the misstatements?

LO G-1, G-2, G-6

G.83 **ACL Assignment.**

Required:
Go to the ACL website at www.mhhe.com/louwers5e, click on "ACL Assignments," and complete the assignment for Module G.

G.84 **Mini-Case: Sampling.**

Required:
Refer to the mini-case "Unhealthy Accounting at HealthSouth" on page C14 and respond to question 6.

Auditing in a Computerized Environment

To err is human, but to really foul things up you need a computer.

Paul Ehrlich, technology commentator

Professional Standards References

Topic	AU/ISA Section	PCAOB Reference*
Consideration of Internal Control in an Integrated Audit		AS 5
Identifying and Assessing the Risks of Material Misstatement	315	AS 12
Auditors' Responses to Risks of Material Misstatement	330	AS 13
Audit Considerations Relating to an Entity Using a Service Organization	AT 801	AU 324

*AU references represent standards issued by the ASB prior to April 16, 2003, that have not been superseded or amended by the PCAOB.

LEARNING OBJECTIVES

Given its extensive use by clients, audit teams must consider clients' computer technology during all stages of the audit engagement. A textbook cannot describe fully all complexities of computerized processing of business transactions, so this module assumes that you have had a course in computer concepts and general computerized processing. Chapter 3 provides a brief introduction of the effect of computerized processing on audit planning; the focus of this module is on the audit team's examination of the client's computerized processing system and its related computer controls. The module is subdivided into three parts. The first part reviews the basic elements of a computerized processing system and the related controls. The second part describes the procedures that audit teams perform to test the operating effectiveness of the client's computer controls. The module concludes with a discussion of computer fraud and the controls that can be used to prevent it.

Your objectives are to be able to:

LO H-1 Identify how the use of a computerized processing system impacts the audit examination.

LO H-2 Provide examples of general controls and understand how these controls relate to transaction processing in a computerized processing system.

LO H-3 Provide examples of automated application controls and understand how these controls relate to transaction processing in a computerized processing system.

LO H-4	Describe how the audit team assesses control risk in a computerized environment.	**LO H-6**	Describe the characteristics and control issues associated with end-user and other computing environments.
LO H-5	Identify how audit teams perform tests of controls in a computerized environment.	**LO H-7**	Define and describe computer fraud and the controls that can be used to prevent it.

INTRODUCTION

It has been a rough few years for the **Federal National Mortgage Association,** or **Fannie Mae,** as it is popularly known. Its takeover by the U.S. government in 2008 has been well documented, including the fact that Fannie Mae was experiencing problems prior to this landmark event. On December 6, 2006, the government-sponsored mortgage giant made its first periodic filing with the Securities and Exchange Commission since June 30, 2004. Why? Fannie Mae's audit committee and board of directors determined in December 2004 that previous financial statements had not been prepared in conformity with GAAP and needed to be restated. After almost two years, Fannie Mae reported the net impact of its restatement: a decrease in retained earnings as of June 30, 2004, of $6.3 *billion.* During this time, Fannie Mae dismissed its chief executive officer, chief financial officer, and public accounting firm (replacing **KPMG** with **Deloitte & Touche**). Its stock price fell from a high of $80.82 in the first quarter of 2004 to a low of $46.30 in the third quarter of 2006.

Why did these problems occur? An examination of Deloitte & Touche's report on Fannie Mae's internal control over financial reporting provides a clue. This report identified eight material weaknesses in internal control over financial reporting. Two of these relate to Fannie Mae's information technology applications:[1]

- Application of Accounting Principles Generally Accepted in the United States of America: [Fannie Mae] did not maintain effective internal control relating to its process and information technology applications for determining, monitoring, disseminating, implementing, and updating accounting policies that complied with accounting principles generally accepted in the United States of America.

- Information Technology Applications and Infrastructure: [Fannie Mae] did not maintain effective internal control related to information technology applications and infrastructure, including access controls, change management controls, and controls over end-user computing including spreadsheets.

Ultimately, this restatement was judged to be the result of a "flawed" system of accounting for the costs associated with loans and securities acquired by Fannie Mae from lenders. One particularly troubling problem was a $1.2 billion error in Fannie Mae's investment accounts that resulted from incorrect formulae in spreadsheet cells used to calculate the market value of these investments.[2]

As the Auditing Insight "PCAOB Inspections and Computer Controls for Big Four Audits" discusses, evaluating the operating effectiveness of controls in a computerized processing environment poses challenges to audit teams, many of whom simply rely on the work of information technology (IT) auditors without having an adequate understanding of the nature of this work. The PCAOB identified these matters in its annual inspections of audits conducted by the Big Four firms (**Deloitte & Touche** [now **Deloitte**], **Ernst & Young, KPMG,** and **PricewaterhouseCoopers [now PwC]**). Each of these findings relates to an unidentified audit conducted by one of these four firms.

---

[1] *Fannie Mae 2004 10-K* (filed with the Securities and Exchange Commission on December 6, 2006).
[2] "Fannie Mae Corrects Mistakes in Results," *The New York Times,* October 30, 2003, p. C1.

> ### AUDITING INSIGHT — Does Anybody Understand It?
>
> The importance and challenges of auditing in a computerized processing environment can be illustrated by early findings related to the assessment of internal control over financial reporting required by Sarbanes-Oxley. Almost all of the entities reporting material weaknesses or internal control deficiencies have found computerized processing to be a major source of the weaknesses. Additional conclusions of this survey of chief financial officers include
>
> - Accounting regulators have not done a sufficient job in detailing entities' responsibilities with respect to computer controls to satisfy section 404 requirements.
> - Audit teams do not have a sufficient understanding of computerized processing issues to render an appropriate opinion on computer controls.
> - Only 26 percent of respondents indicated that it would be "easy" to remediate computerized processing control issues noted in the section 404 audit.
>
> However, it appears that companies are improving their controls related to computerized processing. A recent study revealed that the percentage of companies reporting material weaknesses in internal control related to computer processing has declined from 3.6% in 2004 (the first year of implementation of Sarbanes-Oxley) to 0.9% in 2009.
>
> **Source:** "Sarbox Surprises," *CFO.com*, June 22, 2005; "IT-Control Weakness Wanes," *CFO.com*, September 16, 2010.

> ### AUDITING INSIGHT — PCAOB Inspections and Computer Controls for Big Four Audits
>
> - The firm chose not to test the operating effectiveness of information technology controls, despite the fact that the client's business is technology intensive and processes large volumes of customer data.
> - The firm's audit documentation indicated that the results of the test of general controls did not support a conclusion that the client's information processing was reliable. However, the firm did not perform additional procedures to address this finding nor modify its audit strategy in response to this finding.
> - The firm did not test the accuracy and completeness of data used to estimate allowance for loan losses because it did not test controls over the transfer of data between the client's information technology systems.
> - The firm's testing did not adequately address the risk that critical data in the issuer's computerized systems related to the pricing of services could have been inappropriately modified during the year.
>
> **Source:** 2005–2010 PCAOB Inspections of Deloitte & Touche, Ernst & Young, KPMG, and PricewaterhouseCoopers. All reports can be found on the PCAOB's website www.pcaob.org

COMPUTERIZED PROCESSING SYSTEMS

LEARNING OBJECTIVE H-1
Identify how the use of a computerized processing system impacts the audit examination.

In Chapter 3, we discussed the impact that client use of computerized processing has on the audit examination. It is important to reiterate that the client's use of computerized processing *does not* affect the objective of an audit, the need for audit teams to study and evaluate the client's internal control, or the need for audit teams to gather appropriate evidence on which to support their opinion. In Chapter 5, some important controls operating within a computerized processing system were briefly identified. In this module, we more thoroughly identify the elements of a computerized processing system and the controls operating within these systems.

To identify considerations that emerge when the client uses computerized processing, Exhibit H.1 illustrates the computerized processing of sales transactions. Audit teams would identify the sequence of activities, files, documents, and controls shown in Exhibit H.1 by performing a *walkthrough* of sales transactions during the study and evaluation of internal control. The process is as follows:

1. A *customer order* for products or services is received. If received via mail or telephone, client personnel enter the relevant information (customer name/number, items requested, and quantities requested) in a *customer order transaction file*. If the order

EXHIBIT H.1
Computerized Processing of Sales Transactions

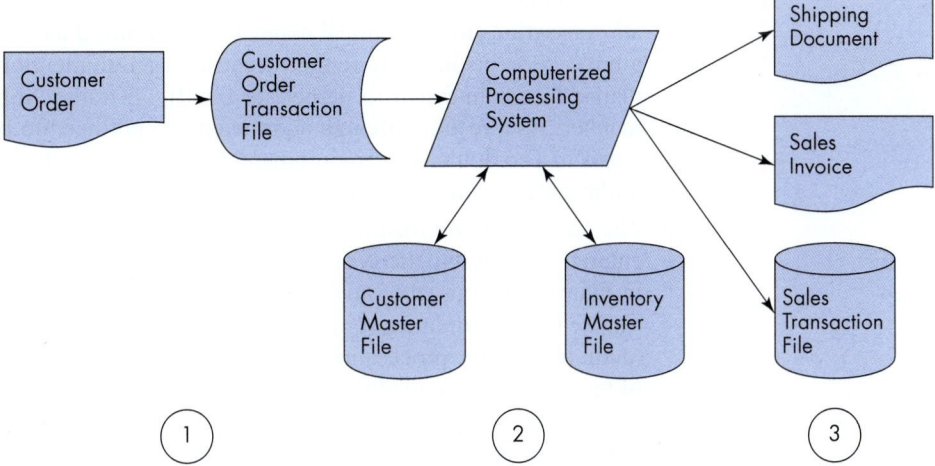

is received electronically, information is entered by the customer and automatically included in a *customer order transaction file* (this is similar to the process used when you make online purchases).

2. The customer order transaction file is then submitted for *computerized processing*. At this point, the system accesses the *customer master file* using the customer name/number to ensure that the sale is made to an approved customer and that his or her credit limit has not been exceeded. If the order is received from a new customer, the transaction would be identified as requiring a credit check prior to further processing. The program then accesses the *inventory master file* to verify that the desired item(s) are available and identifies the current inventory prices. The dual arrows from the two master files to the computerized processing symbol indicate that these files are accessed by the computerized system and are updated after processing to reflect the customer order.

3. The computerized system then processes the order and, using the price from the inventory master file and quantity from the customer order, prepares a *shipping document* and *sales invoice* and updates the *sales transaction file*.

The processing shown in Exhibit H.1 is similar to the sequence of events when you place an order for a product online. When accessing the vendor's website, you are requested to enter various types of information (name, address, and credit card information) into a file that is analogous to the customer order transaction file. If you have not previously ordered from that vendor, you are given an option to "save" your information in a customer profile (similar to the customer master file) for future use. If you are a continuing customer, you are usually given the option to bypass the entry of this information if it has been saved in your customer profile. (Because you are required to enter a valid credit card prior to making a purchase, there is no need for a credit check in this environment!)

The vendor's system then accesses an inventory master file and can instantaneously inform you whether the items you have ordered are in stock. In addition, the program determines the current price of the items and provides you with an electronic sales invoice that you are required to review prior to the final processing of the sale.

The following matters are introduced in computerized processing environments such as that shown in Exhibit H.1 and need to be considered by the audit team:

1. *The possibility of input errors.* The need for client personnel to convert (enter) information into electronic format introduces the possibility of errors. As discussed later in this module, clients implement various controls that are designed to prevent or detect input errors.

2. *The existence of systematic rather than random processing errors.* In a manual processing system, random errors occur because humans are processing transactions and

humans make random mistakes. In contrast, computerized processing systems handle all transactions in an identical manner. As a result, if a computerized system processes a transaction erroneously (either because of an unintentional programming error or a planned error intended to perpetrate fraud), all transactions are affected in the same manner. As a result, although audit teams do not need to be concerned about random errors in a computerized environment, they need to evaluate the accuracy of processing in these environments because of the systematic processing errors that can occur.

3. *The lack of an audit trail.* In a computerized processing environment, data are often entered directly into the system and processing is completed electronically. As a result, in many situations, the only "hard copy" is the final result of processing, or output. This leaves the audit team in the position of not having the ability to view a paper trail (audit trail) of the processing of transactions. As discussed later in this module, the use of techniques embedded in client computer programs allows audit teams to electronically view the various stages of transaction processing that would not otherwise be possible because of the lack of hard copy documentary evidence.

4. *The possibility of inappropriate access to computer files and programs.* The use of computerized processing introduces the possibility that inappropriate access to computer files and programs can occur, both on- and off-site. This possibility requires clients to implement strong password controls for access and periodically monitor what files and programs have been accessed and by whom.

5. *The reduced human involvement in the processing of transactions.* The use of computerized processing reduces human involvement in the processing of transactions. For example, a computerized program will perform the credit check that would have been performed by humans in a manual processing system. In addition, when using a manual system, humans would have accepted the customer order, prepared a sales invoice, and entered that invoice into a sales transaction file. Human involvement in the various aspects of the transaction would have allowed obvious processing errors to be identified (for example, the sale of a business class airline ticket for $40, which actually happened at **British Airways**).[3] To mitigate the reduced level of human involvement in computerized processing environments, clients implement controls to verify the accuracy of processing and the reasonableness of its output.

Recall from Chapter 5 that the major phases in the audit team's evaluation of internal control are understanding, assessment, and testing. Following is a brief overview of how the use of a computerized processing system affects the audit team's procedures performed in those phases. As you can see, the major difference in a computerized processing system is that the audit team must obtain an understanding of, consider, and test the operating effectiveness of additional controls related to the computerized processing of transactions

Phase 1: Understanding	• Obtain understanding of controls established by the client related to the computerized processing of transactions.
	• Document controls established by the client related to the computerized processing of transactions.
Phase 2: Assessment	• Consider controls established by the client related to computerized processing of transactions in the preliminary assessment of control risk.
Phase 3: Testing	• Identify controls related to the computerized processing of transactions to be tested and the degree of compliance required.
	• Perform tests of controls related to the computerized processing of transactions.
	• Evaluate degree of compliance and perform the planned (or revised) substantive procedures.

Once again, the major issue introduced in the computerized processing of transactions is the need for the audit team to understand, consider, and evaluate automated controls

[3] "When Airline Fares Are Too Good to Be True," *The Wall Street Journal,* March 25, 2010, pp. D1, D3.

that have been designed to mitigate the risk of material misstatement at the assertion level. Controls operating within a computerized processing system may be classified as follows:

- **General controls** apply to all applications of a computerized system (for example, the processing of transactions across various cycles).
- **Automated application controls** are controls that are applied to specific business activities within a computerized processing system to address management assertions regarding the financial statements. Thus, automated application controls relate to specific types of transactions and operating cycles (for example, processing of transactions within the revenue cycle).

Specific examples of general controls and automated application controls are discussed in more detail in the following section.

> ### REVIEW CHECKPOINTS
>
> H.1 Identify five major considerations that are introduced when the client uses computerized processing.
> H.2 What are the three major phases in the audit team's evaluation of internal control? How does the use of computerized processing affect the procedures performed in those phases?
> H.3 Identify and define the two major types of controls in a computerized processing system.

COMPUTER CONTROLS

LEARNING OBJECTIVE H-2
Provide examples of general controls and understand how these controls relate to transaction processing in a computerized processing system.

As noted earlier in this module, the first two phases of the audit team's evaluation of internal control are (1) obtaining an understanding of controls and (2) based on this understanding, forming an assessment of control risk. In a computerized environment, this understanding and assessment must consider both general controls and automated application controls, which are discussed in this section.

General Controls

Because general controls apply to all applications of a computerized processing system, the effectiveness of these controls has a pervasive effect on the entity's computerized processing of transactions. As a result, it is important that audit teams identify and test the effectiveness of these controls. The five categories of general controls are hardware controls, program development controls, program change controls, computer operations controls, and access to programs and data controls.

Hardware Controls

Hardware refers to the physical equipment or devices that constitute a computer. **Hardware controls** are "built in" to the processing equipment by the manufacturer and provide reasonable assurance that data are not altered or modified as they are transmitted within the system. The most important hardware control incorporated in all computers is a *parity check* that ensures that the coding of data internal to the computer does not change when data are moved from one internal storage location to another. An additional hardware control commonly found is an *echo check*, which involves a magnetic read after each writing to "echo" back to the sending location and compare results. Audit teams can evaluate the existence of these controls by reviewing information technology specifications and various forms of documentation.

Another important control related to computer hardware is *preventive maintenance* on the related equipment. Audit teams should determine whether regular maintenance is scheduled and whether the schedule is followed and documented. Maintenance frequently is under contract with the technology vendor. In such cases, audit teams should review the contract as well as the record of regular maintenance work. Other general evidence on hardware reliability may be obtained from a review of operating reports and downtime logs.

Program Development Controls

The objectives of **program development controls** are to provide reasonable assurance that (1) acquisition or development of computer programs and software is properly authorized, is conducted in accordance with entity policies, and supports the entity's financial reporting requirements; (2) appropriate users participate in the software acquisition or program development process; (3) programs and software are tested and validated prior to being placed into operation; and (4) all software and programs have appropriate documentation.

An important program development control is the entity's use of the **systems development life cycle** (SDLC) process to plan, develop, and implement new computerized processing systems (or databases). The SDLC begins with the identification of system requirements (basically, what does the entity need the system to do?); see Exhibit H.2. The feasibility analysis stage examines whether the entity should purchase the system "off the shelf" (i.e., from a commercial vendor), develop the system internally, or modify an off-the-shelf system for internal use. The answer depends on the entity's resources and expertise. Once a decision has been made that a new system is feasible, system specifications are developed. Programmers next write programs to accomplish those specifications and then design procedures. On conversion from the old system to the new one, training employees to use the new system is critical. Upon successful implementation, the system must continue to be monitored to ensure that problems do not arise. As they do occur (e.g., due to capacity constraints), the cycle begins anew: Is there a better system to meet the entity's needs?

Effective SDLC controls ensure that the entity:

- Follows established policies and procedures for acquiring or developing software or programs.
- Involves users in the design of programs, selection of prepackaged software and programs, and testing of programs.
- Tests and validates new programs and develops proper implementation and "back out" plans (plans to cancel the results of processing in the event of an error or program failure) prior to placing the programs into operation.
- Periodically reviews policies and procedures for acquiring and developing software or programs for continued appropriateness and modifying these policies and procedures as necessary.

In addition to the use of the SDLC, it is important that appropriate documentation exist for each of the entity's programs. *Documentation* describes the system and its controls and is the means of communicating the essential elements of the computerized processing system to both current and potential users. In evaluating controls over

EXHIBIT H.2
Systems Development Life Cycle

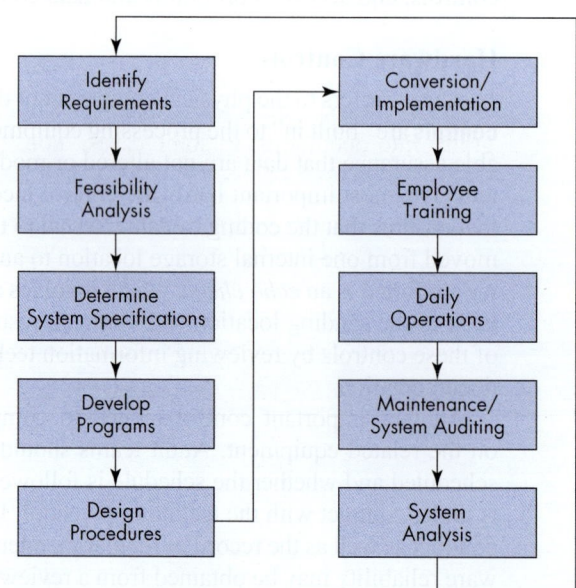

documentation, audit teams review the documentation to (1) gain an understanding of the system and determine whether the documentation is adequate to support the proper use of the programs and (2) determine whether client personnel follow standards. Of utmost importance is whether the client has established systems development and documentation standards. Unless written standards exist, determining whether the program development controls and the documentation are adequate is difficult.

The accompanying Auditing Insight illustrates common problems that have been observed related to the implementation of new systems and programs.

AUDITING INSIGHT | The Problems with New Systems

The following common control issues have been identified related to the implementation of new computerized processing systems. To the extent that these issues result in inaccurate processing of transactions or the inability to identify errors in processing, they will impact the integrity of the data generated by the systems and, ultimately, the fairness of the entity's financial statements.

- Imposing unrealistic deadlines, resulting in inadequate testing of the system.
- Failing to use controls that are packaged with the new systems.
- Failing to review reports generated by new systems.
- Providing inadequate training to employees on the use of new systems.
- Failing to ensure that system access capabilities reflect appropriate separation of duties.
- Allowing excessive customization of new systems, which compromises the integrity of these systems.

Source: "IT-Control Weakness Wanes," *CFO.com*, September 16, 2010.

Program Change Controls

The objectives of **program change controls** parallel those related to program development in the preceding subsection. These controls are implemented by the entity to provide reasonable assurance that requests for modifications to existing programs (1) are properly authorized, conducted in accordance with entity policies, and support the entity's financial reporting requirements, (2) involve appropriate users in the program modification process, (3) are tested and validated prior to being placed into operation, and (4) have been appropriately documented. Like program development controls, the use of an SDLC (and the analogous controls related to the use of an SDLC) is an important consideration when modifying existing programs. It is also important that the entity prepare appropriate documentation with respect to the program modifications. The accompanying Auditing Insight describes two recent examples in which the failure to properly implement system updates resulted in negative consequences for the companies involved.

In addition to the controls included within the SDLC, two other important controls for program changes relate to "emergency" change requests and the migration of new programs into operations. In some cases, modifications to existing programs need to occur outside of the SDLC process. If so, it is important that

1. Appropriate documentation exists to support the "emergency" nature of the program modifications.
2. These modifications should be subject to standard approval procedures after they have been made.
3. When programs have been modified, they should be migrated (or moved) into operation only by appropriate individuals.

Computer Operations Controls

In a computerized processing system, transactions can be processed using either *batch* or *real-time* (also known as *online* or *interactive*) processing methods. **Batch processing** is characterized by grouping similar transactions to be processed in a group (or batch) and processing these transactions at the same time using the same program. Simple batch processing

AUDITING INSIGHT | Be Careful of System Upgrades

Hershey's Harrowing Halloween

Like all organizations, immediately before the turn of this century, **Hershey Foods** faced a potential "Y2K" problem involving program coding that used only two-year digits (e.g., 99 for 1999) instead of four, therefore causing problems for date-related procedures. To address the problem and update their old systems, Hershey undertook an ambitious system upgrade. In September 1999, facing implementation delays due to software integration complexities and a December 31, 1999, implementation deadline, Hershey decided to switch from its old system to its new system with a flip of a switch ("the cold turkey approach") rather than the originally planned module-by-module approach. Unfortunately, the implementation "didn't take." Customer Halloween candy orders fell through the cracks. Candy inventory was "lost," remaining unaccounted for in warehouses. The consequence was an estimated $150 million in lost sales.

Source: "Trick or Treat: Hershey's Biggest Dud Has Turned Out to Be Its New Technology," *The Wall Street Journal,* October 29, 1999, p. A1.

Overstock and Underreport

Implementation of a system upgrade by **Overstock.com** (an Internet retailer that primarily sells surplus and returned merchandise) resulted in the failure to properly reduce its revenue for customer returns. In his letter to shareholders, CEO Patrick Bryne indicated that "when we upgraded our system, we didn't hook up some of the accounting wiring; however, we thought we had manual fixes in place. We've since found that these manual fixes missed a few of the unhooked wires." The result? Overstock restated its financial statements for the period 2003–2007, reducing revenues by $12.9 million and increasing net losses by $10.3 million.

Source: "Botched ERP Hookup Spurs Restatement," *CFO.com,* October 24, 2008.

---

systems deal with one component of an entity at a time such as payroll or billing. For example, all payroll records are run at one time immediately prior to the entity's normal pay period.

In contrast, **real-time processing** involves processing transactions as they occur without delay. For example, as you send a text message, read an email, or download a file using your phone, these transactions are entered automatically into your carrier's revenue and receivable accounts; therefore, accounting records are automatically updated as soon as the transactions occur. At the end of each billing period, your bill is produced from these transactions that have been processed individually as they occur.

Computer operations controls are concerned with providing reasonable assurance that (1) the processing of transactions through the computerized processing system is in accordance with the entity's objectives, (2) processing failures are resolved on a timely basis and do not affect or unnecessarily delay the processing of other transactions within the batch, and (3) actions are taken to facilitate the backup and recovery of important data when the need arises.

A summary of important roles performed in a computerized processing environment follows:

- *Systems analysts* examine requirements for information, evaluate the existing system, and design new or improved computerized processing systems (along with the program specifications and documentation).
- *Programmers* prepare flowcharts and code the logic of the computer programs required by the overall computerized processing system designed by the systems analyst. They also often prepare program documentation.
- *Computer operators* operate the computer for each accounting application system according to written operating procedures found in the computer operation instructions.
- *Data conversion operators* prepare data for machine processing by converting manual data into machine-readable form or directly entering transactions into the system using remote terminals.
- *Librarians* maintain control over (1) system and program documentation and (2) data files and programs used in processing transactions. The librarian function or librarian software should control access to systems documentation and access to program and

data files by using a checkout log (a record of entry and use) or a password to record the use by authorized persons.
- The *control group* ensures the integrity of data, accuracy of processing and output, and controls distribution of output to appropriate user groups.

Separation of the duties performed by *systems analysts, programmers, and computer operators* is an important general control. The typical idea is that anyone who designs a computerized processing system should not do the technical programming work, and anyone who performs either of these tasks should not be the computer operator when data are processed. Persons performing each function should not have access to each other's work, and only the computer operators should have access to the equipment. Separation of these duties reduces the likelihood that a program could be designed, written, and run to generate fictitious transactions that may serve as part of a defalcation scheme. Accordingly, the lack of separation of duties along the lines described should be considered a serious weakness in general control.

In addition to the separation of duties listed here, the entity's system should ensure that any processing failures are resolved on a timely basis and do not delay the processing of other transactions. Typically, this would identify and document (through an exception report or file) transactions for which processing failures occur with timely follow-up and resolution of processing of these transactions.

Finally, computer operations controls are implemented for files and data used in processing. The three major objectives of these operations controls are:

1. *The files used in computerized processing are appropriate.* This is accomplished through the use of *external labels* on portable files and the use of *header and trailer labels* on internal records.
2. *The files are appropriately secured and protected from loss.* This is accomplished by storing them in fireproof and waterproof locations and periodic backups that are maintained in remote (off-site) locations. Storage of backup files at an off-site location may be part of business continuity planning (often referred to as *disaster recovery planning*) that encompasses more than data recovery.
3. *Files can be reconstructed from earlier versions of information used in processing.* This is accomplished by creating and implementing policies for retaining prior versions of files for specified periods of time. In some cases, even when appropriate backup procedures exist, files may become damaged and the only alternative is to reconstruct them from previous versions.

One of the most popular methods of file reconstruction is the *grandfather-father-son process.* This involves retaining backup files such as the current transaction file and the prior master file from which the current master file can be reconstructed. Refer to Exhibit H.3 for an illustration of the grandfather-father-son process.

Access to Programs and Data Controls

Access to programs and data controls provide reasonable assurance that access to programs and data is granted only to authorized users. The proliferation of computer "hackers" has resulted in organizations paying increased attention to access controls. Many of the computer frauds mentioned later in this module were the result of individuals both within and outside an entity obtaining unauthorized access to that entity's data.

The most common form of control related to access is the use of *passwords*. You are required to enter passwords to access your university's computer network, your bank account from an automated teller machine, and many other information services. The entity should establish an information security policy and identify various levels of access for each employee, based on the requirements for their position and job responsibilities. Restricting access in this manner serves as an important component of separation of duties related to the authorization to execute transactions, recording of transactions, and custody of the related assets.

EXHIBIT H.3
Grandfather-Father-Son File Retention

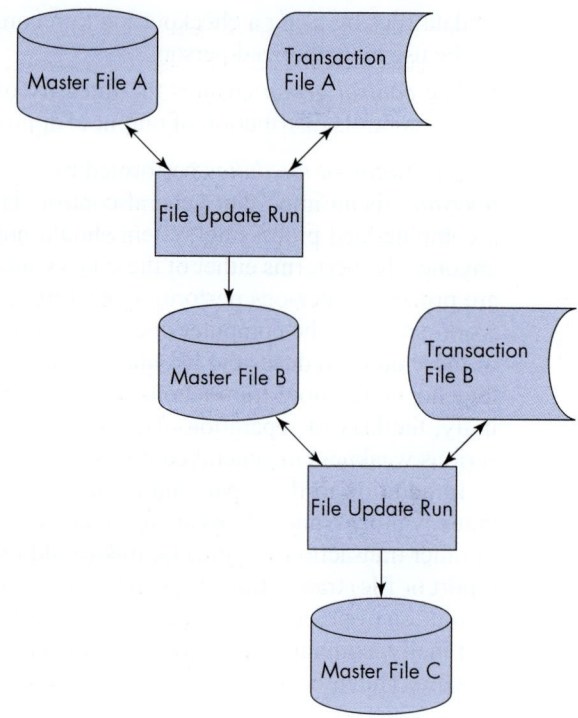

Once established, employee access should be restricted based on passwords. Important characteristics of passwords are that they should be of sufficient length (number of characters); include letters, numbers, and (in some instances) symbols; and be modified periodically (every six months is common). Establishing passwords in this manner reduces the likelihood of an employee's password being hacked (or "guessed") by others. A study showed that a password with six lowercase alphabetic characters could be hacked through computer-generated algorithms in 10 minutes, while a password with nine characters (including lowercase, uppercase, numbers, and symbols) would take 44,530 *years* to hack.[4]

In addition to passwords, physical security controls over terminals and input devices (such as locked doors and the use of badges or swipe cards to access certain locations) also are used. However, with the increasing ability of employees to access systems remotely (i.e., off-site), physical security controls are becoming less effective in restricting access to programs and data. The importance of physical access controls is illustrated in the accompanying Auditing Insight.

AUDITING INSIGHT   Logging On?

During 2007, **Société Générale** trader Jérôme Kerviel engaged in a €£4.9 billion ($7 billion) fraud by executing a series of elaborate (but fictitious) transactions to conceal significant losses from unauthorized trades. The report from Société Générale's internal investigation of this fraud reveled that Kerviel "used the Front Office computer system to post numerous fictitious or unwarranted entries but we have not detected the utilization of any other agent's ID without his or her knowledge."

Source: "Société Générale Releases Fraud Investigation Findings," *Computer Fraud & Security*, July 2008, pp. 2–3.

Other common controls to restrict access to programs and data include:

- Establishing time limits when user sessions automatically "time out" after a predetermined period of time (*automatic terminal logoff*).

[4] "Say Goodbye to All Those Passwords," *Bloomberg Businessweek*, January 31, 2011, p. 36.

- Periodically reviewing and confirming the access rights granted to employees.
- Ensuring that modifications in the level of access permitted to individual users have been properly authorized and are consistent with changes in these individuals' job responsibilities.
- Ensuring that access to programs and data is removed for recently terminated employees on a timely basis.
- Monitoring of user activity to ensure that only authorized users are accessing programs and data.
- Promptly reporting and communicating observed security breaches.

Summary

To evaluate internal control in a computerized processing system, audit teams determine the existence and effectiveness of these five categories of general controls. Always remember that effective general controls are pervasive and provide for a safe and secure computing environment that is necessary for the effectiveness of automated application controls. Simply stated, if general controls are not designed or operating effectively, audit teams are not likely to place a great degree of reliance on the client's internal control. In such cases, the assessment of control risk (and risk of material misstatement) is likely relatively high, requiring more effective substantive tests. In particular, *Auditing Standard (AS) 5* identifies the important impact of program change controls, computer operations controls, and access to programs and data controls on the effectiveness of automated application controls.

One final and very important consideration made by the audit team when evaluating the effectiveness of general controls relates to the use of information produced by the entity during the audit. Professional standards are clear that an audit team cannot merely rely on information produced by the entity's computerized processing system without testing general controls with a particular emphasis on the controls that have been designed to ensure that the information is complete and accurate. Without this type of testing, the auditor would have to test the completeness and accuracy of the information using substantive testing procedures, typically a far more time-consuming process.

Because the effectiveness of automated application controls depends on the effectiveness of general controls, these controls affect any assertions that are addressed by automated application controls. However, from a broad perspective, general controls primarily affect the accuracy and occurrence assertions, as shown here:

Assertion	Explanation	Examples
Accuracy	Ensuring the accuracy of data and testing computer programs prior to implementation increases the probability that transactions are processed properly	• Hardware controls • Program development controls • Program change controls • Computer operations controls
Occurrence	Restricting inappropriate access to programs and data reduces the probability that fictitious transactions are entered into the system and processed	• Computer operations controls (particularly separation of duties) • Access to programs and data controls

Exhibit H.4 summarizes the general controls in each of the areas of a client's computerized processing environment.

LEARNING OBJECTIVE H-3
Provide examples of automated application controls and understand how these controls relate to transaction processing in a computerized processing system.

Automated Application Controls

Automated application controls are those applied to specific business activities within a computerized processing system to achieve financial reporting objectives. Thus, automated application controls are specific to each cycle (e.g., revenue and collection, acquisition and expenditure) and refer to a client's activities designed to ensure the proper recording of transactions and to prevent or detect errors and frauds for transactions within

EXHIBIT H.4 General Controls: Category, Examples, and Objectives

Category	Examples	Objective(s)
Hardware controls	• Parity check • Echo check • Preventative maintenance	• Prevention or detection of erroneous transmission of data
Program development	• Use of systems development life cycle (SDLC) for authorization, user involvement, and testing and validation of new programs • Appropriate documentation for new programs	• Programs developed and software acquired by the entity are consistent with the entity's objectives
Program change	• Use of systems development life cycle (SDLC) for authorization, user involvement, and testing and validation of modifications to existing programs • Appropriate documentation to support "emergency" changes to existing programs • Implementation of program changes performed by appropriate personnel • Appropriate documentation for modifications to existing programs	• Modifications to existing programs are authorized and are consistent with the entity's objectives
Computer operations	• Separation of functions of systems analysts, systems programmers, and computer operators • Procedures for resolving transaction processing failures • Use of external and header and trailer labels to identify files and programs • Storage of files in fireproof and waterproof locations and periodic backup of files • Policies for file retention and the capability to reconstruct files from previous versions	• Transactions are processed in accordance with the entity's objectives • Appropriate files and records are used in processing transactions • Files are appropriately secured and protected from loss • Files can be reconstructed from previous versions
Access to programs and data	• Use of passwords and appropriate types of passwords • Physical security over terminals and input devices • Use of time limits and automatic "time out" of sessions • Periodic review of user access rights • Removal of access rights for terminated employees on a timely basis • Monitoring of activity and immediate communication of any security breaches	• Access to programs and data is restricted to authorized users

↳ REVIEW CHECKPOINTS

H.4 List the five major categories of general controls and identify the objectives of each.

H.5 Briefly identify and describe specific types of hardware controls. How can audit teams evaluate these controls?

H.6 What is the SDLC? What type of controls does the use of the SDLC include with respect to program development and changes?

H.7 Distinguish between batch and real-time processing. Provide an example of when each of these methods would be used.

H.8 Describe the duties of systems analysts, programmers, computer operators, data conversion operators, librarians, and the control group. Which duties should be separated within the computer department?

H.9 Identify and provide examples of controls related to the use of files and data.

H.10 Why are general controls so important in the audit team's evaluation of internal control and assessment of control risk and the risk of material misstatement?

these cycles. Because automated application controls are related to specific transactions, audit teams rely extensively on the effectiveness of these controls to mitigate the risk of material misstatement at the assertion level for account balances or classes of transactions. Automated application controls are organized under three categories: input controls, processing controls, and output controls.

Input Controls

Input controls are designed to provide reasonable assurance that data received for processing by the computer department have been properly authorized and accurately entered or converted for processing. These controls also provide the opportunity for entity personnel to correct and resubmit data initially rejected as erroneous. The following controls are particularly important:

- *Data entry and formatting controls.* These controls are related to the design of the data entry interface to provide a familiar and consistent format and reduce the frequency of input errors by personnel. Two such design features are the use of *pull-down menus* (which allow users to select from among a limited number of alternative choices rather than inputting data) and *standardized formats and screens* (which increase user familiarity with various fields and reduce the likelihood that data are inadvertently input in an incorrect field). For example, consider the likelihood of errors when data are input as a string of numeric and alphanumeric characters as opposed to a form in which users can use a tab key to move between fields. A third important design feature is the ability of personnel to review input prior to submitting it for processing within the system (known as *online editing and sight verification*).

- *Authorization and approval controls.* Only properly authorized and approved input should be accepted for processing. In a computerized environment, some authorizations (e.g., automatic creation of a purchase order when an inventory item reaches a predetermined reorder point) can be computer controlled or accomplished by utilizing a *digitized signature,* an approved encrypted password that releases a transaction by assigning a special code to it.

- *Check digits.* Numbers are often used in computerized processing systems in lieu of customer names, vendor names, and so forth. A *check digit* is an extra number tagged onto the end of a basic identification number such as an employee number or account number. When the identification number is entered (along with the check digit), the computer program calculates the correct check digit and compares it to the one on the input data. When the digits do not match, an error message is indicated on the device or printed out on an input error report. Check digits are used to detect coding errors or keying errors such as the transposition of digits (e.g., coding 387 as 837).

- *Record counts.* Tallies of the number of transactions submitted for data conversion. The known number of records entered can be compared to the count of records produced by the data-conversion device (e.g., the number of sales transactions or count of records). Differences between the manual counts of transactions and the number of transactions processed indicate that transactions may not have been inputted (if the manual count exceeds the processed count) or may have been inputted more than once (if the processed count exceeds the manual count).

- *Batch totals.* Used in the same way as record counts except that the batch total is the sum of some important and numerically meaningful quantity or amount (e.g., the total sales dollars in a batch of invoices). These totals allow input errors to be detected prior to submission for processing and ensure that all transactions are entered once and only once.

- *Hash totals.* These are similar to batch totals except that the hash total is not meaningful for accounting records (e.g., the sum of all the invoice numbers). Like batch totals, these totals allow input errors to be detected prior to submission for processing and ensure that all transactions are entered once and only once.

- *Valid character tests.* Used to check input data fields to determine whether they contain numbers when they are supposed to have numbers or alphabetic characters when they are supposed to have alphabetic characters.
- *Valid sign tests.* Signed data fields are checked for appropriate positive or negative signs.
- *Missing data tests.* Evaluate data fields to verify whether any are blank when they must contain data for the record entry to be correct.
- *Sequence tests.* Applied to evaluate the input data for numerical sequence of documents when sequence is important for processing, as in batch processing. This validation routine also can check for missing documents in a prenumbered series.
- *Limit and reasonableness tests.* Computerized checks used to determine whether data values exceed or fall below some predetermined limit. For example, a payroll application can have a limit test to flag or reject any weekly payroll time record of 50 or more hours.
- *Error correction and resubmission procedures.* Policies and procedures that ensure identification of input errors on a timely basis and correction and resubmission by appropriate personnel for processing.

In thinking about input controls, you experience many examples of these when placing orders for merchandise online. If you enter a credit card number in an incorrect format (with or without dashes), enter quantities exceeding some reasonable amount, or inadvertently omit a field, you will be prompted that an error exists and encouraged to correct that error and resubmit your order. After all, the retailer does not want to lose your sale!

Processing Controls

Processing controls are designed to provide reasonable assurance that data processing has been performed accurately without any omission or duplicate processing of transactions. Many processing controls are similar in nature to input controls, but they are used in the processing phases rather than at the time input is verified. The most fundamental (yet important) processing control a client can implement is periodically testing and evaluating the processing accuracy of its programs. Other important processing controls include the following:

- *File and operator controls.* To ensure that proper files are used in applications, external and internal labels can be used to identify files. In addition, the systems software should produce a log that records time and use statistics for specific computer applications; supervisory personnel should review this log on a periodic basis.
- *Run-to-run totals.* Movement of data from one department to another or one processing program to another should be controlled. One useful control is the *run-to-run* total that refers to sequential processing operations (or runs) on the same data. These totals can be record counts, batch totals, and/or hash totals obtained at the end of one processing run. The totals are distributed to the next run and compared to corresponding totals produced at the end of the second run.
- *Control total reports.* **Control totals** (record counts, batch totals, hash totals, and run-to-run totals) should be calculated during processing operations and summarized in a report. Entity personnel (normally, the control group) should have the responsibility for comparing and/or reconciling these totals to input totals or totals from earlier processing runs.
- *Limit and reasonableness tests.* These should be programmed to ensure that illogical conditions do not occur (for example, depreciating an asset below zero or calculating a negative inventory quantity). These conditions and others that are considered important should generate error reports for supervisor review.
- *Error correction and resubmission procedures.* Although previously mentioned as an input control, controls related to the identification of errors or unusual conditions encountered in processing transactions on a timely basis and correction and resubmission for processing should also be implemented by entities as transactions are processed.

Output Controls

Output controls represent the final check on the accuracy of the results of computerized processing. Output controls are concerned with detecting errors rather than preventing errors (as was the focus with input and processing controls). These controls also should be designed to provide reasonable assurance that only authorized persons receive output (or other type of reports generated by the computerized processing system) or have access to files produced by the system. Typical output controls are the following:

- *Review of output for reasonableness.* An individual knowledgeable about the nature of the transactions and processing should perform an overall review of the output for reasonableness. This allows systematic errors that might otherwise go undetected in more detailed testing to be identified (for example, an employee being paid 10 times his or her normal salary).
- *Control total reports.* Control totals produced as output should be compared and/or reconciled to input and run-to-run control totals produced during transaction processing. An independent data control group should be responsible for reviewing output control totals and investigating differences.
- *Master file changes.* During computerized processing, permanent information stored in master files is often updated or modified; these files should be viewed as "outputs" of the computerized processing. Any changes should be properly authorized by the entity and reported in detail to the user department from which the request for change originated because an error can be pervasive. For example, as noted in the Auditing Insight "Always Lower Prices," incorrectly changing prices can cause the sale of products and services to be billed at incorrect levels.
- *Output distribution.* Systems' output (whether electronic or hard copy) should be distributed only to persons authorized to receive the output. A distribution list should be maintained and used to deliver report copies. The number of copies produced should be restricted to the number needed to prevent unauthorized use.

AUDITING INSIGHT — Always Lower Prices

- Customers at **Meijer, Inc.** (a retailer of groceries and general merchandise in the Midwestern United States) received an unexpected windfall when all items the chain sold were mistakenly discounted by 50 percent in the company's master price file; the discount was supposed to have applied only to Oriental rugs.
- In October 2009, **British Airways PLC** mistakenly offered tickets from the United States to India for $40 (it had intended to *increase* its ticket prices by $40) and had to cancel 1,200 reservations for 2,200 passengers. In a similar type of mistake contained in a computerized file, **UAL** (United Airlines) inadvertently dropped a zero from its ticket prices and offered round-trip business class flights from Los Angeles and San Francisco to New Zealand for $1,062 (rather than $10,620). Unlike British Airways, UAL honored all tickets sold.

Source: "Meijer Glitch Led to Discount," *Chicago Tribune,* May 24, 2007; "When Airline Fares Are Too Good to Be True," *The Wall Street Journal,* March 25, 2010, p. D1, D3.

Exhibit H.5 is a summary of the automated application controls discussed in the preceding section. Note that some of these controls (record counts, batch totals, hash totals, and limit and reasonableness tests) may be used as both input controls and processing controls. Also note that the columns of Exhibit H.5 correspond to the following management assertions (notice that some of these controls affect multiple assertions):

- Input of individual transactions and data is accurate: Accuracy.
- All transactions are entered: Completeness.
- Transactions entered only once: Occurrence.
- Processing of transactions is accurate: Accuracy.

EXHIBIT H.5 Automated Application Controls

	Input of Individual Transactions and Data Is Accurate (Accuracy)	All Transactions Are Entered (Completeness)	Transactions Are Entered Only Once (Occurrence)	Processing of Transactions Is Accurate (Accuracy)	Other
Data entry and formatting	X				Ensures that input is approved and authorized
Check digits	X				
Record counts		X	X	X	
Batch totals	X	X	X	X	
Hash totals	X	X	X	X	
Valid character tests	X				
Valid sign tests	X				
Missing data tests	X				
Sequence tests		X			
Limit and reasonableness tests	X			X	
Error correction and resubmission	X			X	
Periodically testing and evaluating processing accuracy of programs				X	
File and operator controls				X	Ensures that appropriate files are used in applications
Run-to-run totals				X	
Control total reports				X	
Review of output for reasonableness				X	
Master file changes				X	Ensures that changes to master file data are authorized
Output distribution					Ensures output is distributed only to authorized users

> ### REVIEW CHECKPOINTS
>
> H.11 What is the objective of input controls?
>
> H.12 How can data entry and formatting controls minimize the likelihood of input errors?
>
> H.13 Briefly describe record counts, batch totals, and hash totals. What types of errors in input would each of these controls likely identify?
>
> H.14 How do input controls affect management's assertions with respect to the financial statements?
>
> H.15 What is the objective of processing controls? List and briefly describe different processing controls.
>
> H.16 What is the objective of output controls? List and briefly describe different output controls.

ASSESSING CONTROL RISK IN A COMPUTERIZED ENVIRONMENT

LEARNING OBJECTIVE H-4
Describe how the audit team assesses control risk in a computerized environment.

Recall from our earlier discussion the three major phases in the audit team's evaluation of internal control. The first phase is *obtaining an understanding of internal control*; during this phase, the audit team identifies the various controls (manual controls, general controls, and automated application controls) that the client has implemented. At this point, the audit team is aware of the types of controls that have been implemented but has not considered how these controls influence the risk of material misstatement or the operating effectiveness of these controls.

When the audit team has obtained an understanding of internal control, the audit team then *forms an assessment of control risk* (the second phase in the audit team's evaluation of internal control), which involves the following major steps:

1. Identify specific control objectives based on the types of misstatements that can occur in significant accounting applications.
2. Identify the points in the flow of transactions where specific types of misstatements could occur.
3. Identify specific control procedures (such as the general controls and automated application controls described in the preceding section) designed to prevent or detect these misstatements.
4. Evaluate the design of control procedures to determine whether the design suggests a low control risk and whether tests of controls might be cost effective.

These four steps parallel those in a manual processing environment. In addition to the type of controls that the audit team considers (general controls and automated application controls), one important difference in assessing control risk in a computerized environment is identifying the points in the flow of transactions where misstatements could occur (step 2) because many additional steps and sources of potential misstatement are introduced. These sources can be classified as in Exhibit H.6.

Once the audit team has identified the points where a misstatement could occur, they focus on specific control procedures implemented by the client to prevent or detect such misstatements. For example, one possible misstatement could involve preparing invoices (and billing customers) using incorrect prices because an inappropriate inventory price file is used in processing transactions. In this case, one control procedure might be as follows:

Source of Misstatement		Control Procedure
Use of inappropriate inventory price file to prepare invoices	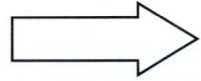	The billing program should identify the most current version of the inventory price file

EXHIBIT H.6
Points of Potential Misstatement in a Computerized Processing Environment

Potential Source of Misstatement	Control(s)
1. Preparing and converting data to machine-readable form	Various input controls
2. Accessing files and programs during computer processing	Computer operations controls related to file identification (external labels and header and trailer labels)
3. Transferring data between computer programs and applications	Processing controls (run-to-run totals, control totals)
4. Updating master file information following processing	Output controls (related to master file changes)
5. Processing transactions by computer programs	Processing controls and output controls
6. Correcting and resubmitting errors at input or during processing	Error correction and resubmission procedures

At this point, the audit team has

1. Obtained an understanding of internal control, including the general controls and automated application controls implemented by the client for the computerized processing of transactions (phase 1).
2. Formed a preliminary assessment of control risk based on considering the general controls and automated application controls implemented by the client for the computerized processing of transactions (phase 2).

The next step in the audit team's evaluation of internal control is to test the operating effectiveness of these controls (phase 3). The following illustrates three important controls that would mitigate the risk of material misstatement for the accuracy assertion for sales transactions along with how the audit team would test these controls in a manual processing environment and the implications for testing these controls in a computerized environment:

Control	Manual Tests of Controls	Implications for Testing in a Computerized Environment
Credit sales are approved by the credit department	Examine invoice for evidence of credit approval	If authorized customer file is updated and accurate, audit team can examine input controls to ensure that only authorized customer numbers are accepted for processing
Quantities shipped to customers are compared to quantities invoiced	Compare quantities shipped from shipping documents to quantities on sales invoices or examine evidence of client comparison of quantities	If sales invoice processing program uses input from computerized shipping document transaction file, audit teams can ensure that quantities are appropriately accepted from shipping document transaction file
Mathematical accuracy of invoices is checked by client personnel	Recalculate mathematical accuracy of invoices or examine evidence of client verification of mathematical accuracy	If calculations are made by the sales invoice processing program, audit teams can verify the (1) operating effectiveness of limits and reasonableness tests and (2) accuracy of the invoice processing program

The process of testing the operating effectiveness of controls in a computerized processing environment is discussed in the next section.

> ### ↳ REVIEW CHECKPOINTS
>
> H.17 What is the audit team's objective in obtaining an overall understanding of internal control in a computerized processing environment?
>
> H.18 What are the major steps in audit team's assessment of control risk in a computerized environment?
>
> H.19 List points at which misstatements may be introduced in a computerized environment.

TESTING CONTROLS IN A COMPUTERIZED ENVIRONMENT

LEARNING OBJECTIVE H-5
Identify how audit teams perform tests of controls in a computerized environment.

Audit teams can use one of two broad approaches in a computerized environment. Exhibit H.7 is an illustration of **auditing around the computer**. When auditing "around" the computer, audit teams select a sample of source documents and verify the correspondence of the input (100 units sold at $70 per unit) with the output (sales and receivables of $7,000) (see the top row of Exhibit H.7). The client's computerized processing system processes the transactions, but audit teams treat the system as a "black box" and are concerned only with the accurate processing of transactions. No attempt is made to evaluate the existence or effectiveness of computer controls. When significant computer controls have not been implemented and the client essentially uses the computer to calculate amounts, auditing around the computer may be appropriate. However, audit teams are still required to obtain an understanding of the controls and cannot ignore them; they will just not test the operating effectiveness of these controls. In addition, for audits of public entities, the requirements of *AS 5* would not permit audit teams to issue opinions on the operating effectiveness of internal control over financial reporting if this approach were used.

In contrast, audit teams can **audit through the computer**. When doing this, audit teams evaluate the client's hardware and programs to determine the reliability of operations and test the operating effectiveness of the related computer controls. *Auditing through the computer* is common in practice because many computerized processing systems have significant controls implemented within the related programs; indeed, it is normally cost effective for clients to implement these controls to ensure the accurate processing of transactions. In cases such as this, ignoring the computer controls results in audit teams' not evaluating important features of the client's internal control.

How would audit teams choose between these two approaches? Although it would be difficult to envision many circumstances when auditing around the computer would be a viable approach, auditing through the computer would be particularly advantageous in the following circumstances:

1. *Complexity of computer processing.* Audit teams ordinarily audit *through* the computer when the client's computer applications are more complex rather than when the client uses the computer for relatively straightforward calculations.
2. *Implementation of computer controls.* Audit teams would ordinarily audit *through* the computer when the client has implemented extensive computer controls rather than when the client has implemented less extensive computer controls.
3. *Existence of source documents and audit trail.* Audit teams would ordinarily audit *through* the computer when source documents exist only in electronic form and when the results of computerized processing are used as inputs in subsequent stages of processing.

EXHIBIT H.7
Example of Auditing around the Computer

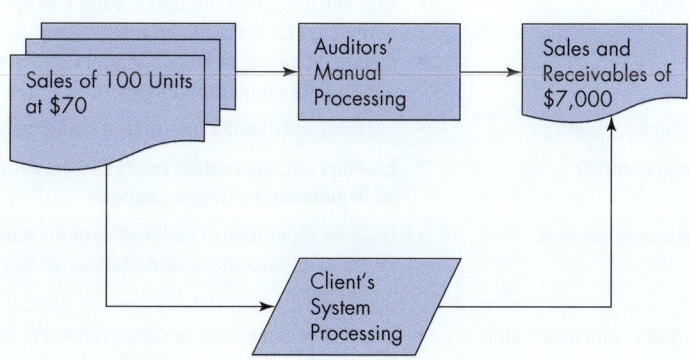

> ### ⤷ REVIEW CHECKPOINTS
>
> H.20 What is the difference between auditing "through the computer" and auditing "around the computer"?
>
> H.21 What factors do audit teams consider when deciding whether to audit around versus through the computer?

When auditing through the computer, it is necessary for audit teams to evaluate the operating effectiveness of controls involved in the computerized processing of transactions. Recall from Chapter 5 the four methods of testing the operating effectiveness of controls: (1) inquiry, (2) observation, (3) document examination, and (4) reperformance. Refer to Exhibits H.8 (for general controls) and H.9 (for automated application controls) for examples of how audit teams can use these methods to test the operating effectiveness of computerized controls.

These methods of testing general controls and automated application controls in Exhibit H.8 and H.9 are similar to tests of controls in a manual processing environment; these tests are necessary because of potential sources of misstatement that are introduced when computerized processing is undertaken. In addition to these tests, audit teams should evaluate the actual processing activity of the client's programs as part of their tests of controls. Because this processing occurs at the transaction level, the audit team uses a form of "reperformance" to evaluate transaction processing. These methods, which may use actual ("live") data or simulated ("dummy") data, are discussed in the remainder of this section. It is important to note that, although these methods evaluate the accuracy with which transactions are processed, they also provide the audit team the opportunity to evaluate various input controls (for example, the use of check digits, record counts, batch totals, hash totals, and others).

Techniques Using Actual Data

Program-Embedded Techniques

One option for testing the effectiveness of the client's computerized processing is through special audit modules designed for and coded into computer programs. These **program-embedded techniques** allow audit teams to select specific transactions of interest before or during processing and evaluate various stages of processing at a subsequent time. Program-embedded techniques also enable internal auditors to continuously monitor the client's information processing system. Some examples of program-embedded techniques include:

1. *Tagging transactions.* The audit team "tags" selected transactions with an indicator at input. A computer trail of all processing steps of these transactions in the application system can be printed or stored in computer files for subsequent evaluation by the audit team.

EXHIBIT H.8 Methods of Testing General Controls

Type of Control	Method of Testing
Hardware controls	• Examine computer documentation and specifications to determine the existence of parity checks and echo checks • Inquire, observe, or inspect documentary evidence of preventative maintenance on appropriate computer equipment
Program development controls	• Examine documentation related to the development of programs
Program change controls	• Examine documentation related to proper authorization for program changes and implementation of those changes
Computer operations controls	• Observe separation of duties of systems analysts, programmers, and computer operators • Examine documentary evidence regarding the use of backup and file reconstruction techniques
Access to programs and data controls	• Examine documentary evidence related to authorization for accessing programs and data • Observe the use of passwords required to access programs and data

EXHIBIT H.9 Methods of Testing Automated Application Controls

Type of Control	Method of Testing
Input controls	• Inquire, observe, or examine documentary evidence regarding the use of various input controls (check digits, batch totals, hash totals, etc.) • Examine documentary evidence related to the resolution of errors identified by input controls
Processing controls	• Inquire, observe, or examine documentary evidence that the client periodically tests programs for processing accuracy • Through reperformance, test the client's programs for processing accuracy • Inquire, observe, or examine documentary evidence regarding the use of various processing controls (file and operator controls, run-to-run totals, etc.) • Examine documentary evidence related to the resolution of errors or unusual conditions identified during processing
Output controls	• Inquire, observe, or examine documentary evidence that the client reviews output for reasonableness • Examine documentary evidence related to the use of control total reports and reconciliation of those reports to input and run-to-run totals • Examine documentary evidence related to authorization for changes in master file information • Observe, inquire, or inspect documentary evidence related to limited distribution of output to identified users

2. *Audit files (embedded audit modules).* Auditor-selected transactions are written to, or embedded in, a special file for later verification. This verification allows audit teams to create special limits, reasonableness, or other audit tests as well as evaluate the accurate processing of transactions

3. *Snapshot.* A "picture" of the main memory of transactions and database elements is taken before and after computerized processing operations have been performed. The picture is then retained for the audit team's evaluation. For example, audit teams can save the contents of an accounts receivable balance before and after a sales transaction is posted. Using these balances, along with the sales transaction, audit teams can verify whether the update processing was correct.

4. *Monitoring systems activity.* Elements of hardware and software are available to monitor the individuals who access the system, the various applications and operations accessed, and the time these applications and operations are accessed. For example, a record of passwords used to enter accounting transactions can be captured and compared to the list of persons authorized to enter these transactions. Access of programs at unusual times (e.g., other than during normal operating periods) suggests the possibility of hacking or other inappropriate use.

5. *Extended records.* Special programs provide an audit trail of an individual transaction by accumulating the results of all application programs that contributed to the processing of the transaction. The accumulated results are stored either as additional fields of the transaction record or as a separate audit file. For example, the snapshot example of accounts receivable balances before and after update processing could be added to the sales transaction, making an extended transaction record. Thus, audit teams can follow the flow of a transaction without reviewing several files at various times and stages of processing.

6. *Program analysis techniques.* **Program analysis techniques** are software packages that assist audit teams in understanding the logic of an application program following the flow of transactions and data through an application program and identifying the data files used in processing transactions though an application program. For example, some packages can access source code and translate this code into flowcharts or decision tables that can be used to understand the logic of an application program.

The accompanying Auditing Insight describes a situation in which an internal auditor worked "after hours" to ensure that his efforts would not be noticed as he investigated the possibility of fraud. (This example is related to monitoring systems activity).

AUDITING INSIGHT | After Hours Internal Auditing

Gene Morse (an internal auditor with **WorldCom**) used that company's computer systems to track individual journal entries that ultimately allowed him to unearth evidence of the former telecom giant's unprecedented fraud. Because downloading more than 350,000 transactions slowed WorldCom's servers, he began working at night when the demand on the servers was lower and his efforts were less likely to be noticed by WorldCom's information technology staff. He also purchased a compact disk burner with his personal funds and copied the data in the event that others might find and destroy his evidence.

Source: "How Three Unlikely Sleuths Exposed Fraud at WorldCom," *The Wall Street Journal,* October 30, 2002, p. A1.

Parallel Simulation

The methods discussed thus far allow the audit team to evaluate the processing of transactions as the processing occurs. However, in some situations, doing so may be either impossible or less desirable, and the audit team may need to evaluate computer controls following the processing of those transactions. This occurs if periods throughout the year are selected for evaluation; it is simply not feasible to request the client to "re-process" transactions through its formal system.

The primary technique used to test computer controls in this manner is called **parallel simulation** (also known as *controlled reprocessing* and *comparison program utilization*). When using parallel simulation, the audit team prepares a computer program designed to process client data properly. The result of the audit team's processing of actual client data is compared with the result of the actual data processed through the client's normal system. The concept of parallel simulation is illustrated in Exhibit H.10.

One disadvantage of using auditor-prepared programs to conduct parallel simulations is the time, effort, and expertise necessary to prepare these programs, but computer-assisted audit techniques (CAATs) make the parallel simulation option easier. CAATs (such as IDEA and ACL) were initially discussed in Chapter 3; these audit software programs consist of numerous prepackaged subroutines that can perform most tasks needed in auditing and business applications.

EXHIBIT H.10
Testing Controls with Parallel Simulation

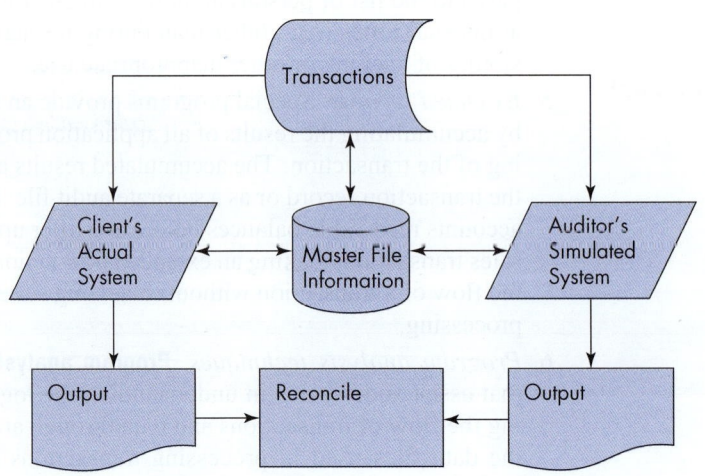

When using any form of parallel simulation, the audit team must take care to determine that the actual transactions selected for processing are representative of transactions ordinarily processed by the client. Thus, some exercise in random selection and identification of important transactions could be required in conjunction with parallel simulation.

Techniques Using Simulated Data

One limitation of using actual data is that these data are often very "clean" and seldom contain error conditions. As a result, the use of actual data may not permit the audit team to determine whether the system controls are operating as intended and would effectively prevent or detect error conditions if such conditions occurred. For example, a computerized payroll system may have a control that should identify and deny the preparation of payroll checks for employees with fictitious identification numbers. In most situations, it is unlikely that an actual data set would contain such conditions and the audit team would not be able to determine whether the control is functioning as intended. As a result, the use of simulated (or dummy data) is often preferred in testing such controls.

Audit teams often use two methods to test computer controls using simulated data: (1) the *test data* approach and (2) the *integrated test facility (ITF)* approach. When using these methods, audit teams create a series of simulated transactions that are processed through the client's computerized system. The use of simulated transactions under these approaches allows audit teams to:

1. Evaluate the accuracy of transaction processing by comparing the results obtained from manual processing of simulated data and transactions with the results obtained from processing these same data and transactions through the client's computerized system.
2. Evaluate the operating effectiveness of the client's input controls by creating transactions with known error conditions (for example, using invalid account numbers or using two transactions having the same document or control number).

Under both approaches, the series of simulated transactions should contain known errors to test the client's input controls and consist of transactions to test different processing alternatives (for example, calculations of pay for both hourly and salaried employees). Because all transactions are processed identically in a computerized environment, only one of each type of condition needs to be included. Prior to processing the transactions through the client's system, audit teams determine the expected results of processing and compare these results to the actual results. See Exhibit H.11 for the **test data** approach. Test data can be processed either separately or simultaneously with

EXHIBIT H.11
Testing Controls with Test Data

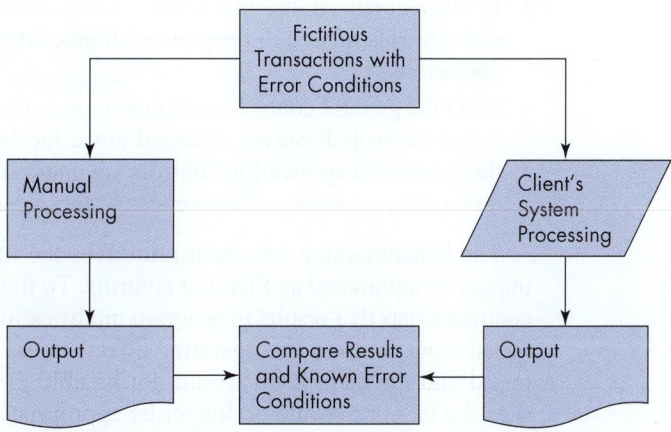

actual transactions; if processed with actual transactions, care must be taken to ensure that simulated data are not comingled with the actual transactions.

An **integrated test facility (ITF)** is a technique in which the audit team creates a dummy department or branch (sometimes referred to as a *minicompany*); this minicompany includes records of employees, customers, vendors, receivables, payables, and other accounts. The method overcomes one limitation of the test data approach (the fact that simulated data might accidentally be commingled with actual data). Like the test data approach, the simulated transactions used with an ITF should include an example of one of each type of error condition and evaluate different processing alternatives.

A great deal of care is required when using an ITF because the fictitious master file records, the transactions, and the account outputs are placed in the actual information processing system and in the client's records. The account amounts and other output data must be reversed or adjusted out of the financial statements. Also, care must be taken not to damage or misstate any of the client's master file records and account balances.

One important issue in processing data through the client's computerized processing system (whether using test data or an ITF) is that the system or program used by audit teams in these tests is the same as that actually used by the client in processing transactions (i.e., the client has not created an "alternative" program that differs from its actual program). Audit teams can make this determination by requesting the program from the librarian on a surprise basis or requesting access to the program immediately following processing by the client. One advantage of the ITF approach compared to the test data approach is that creating a separate minicompany facilitates the audit team's ability to process the simulated transactions along with the client's actual transactions, ensuring that the client's actual programs are being evaluated.

Benchmarking

Throughout this module, we have mentioned the pervasive effect of general controls and the way that the effectiveness of general controls influences the audit team's ability to rely on automated application controls. Because automated application controls are not subject to "human failure," audit teams do not need to be concerned with random deviations in these controls that may occur from one year to the next. *AS 5* permits audit teams to use a **benchmarking** approach to evaluating the operating effectiveness of automated application controls, as follows:

- The audit team tests the operating effectiveness of automated application controls on which they intend to rely; the level of operating effectiveness based on these tests is referred to as the *baseline*.
- In subsequent audits, the audit team evaluates and tests the effectiveness of general controls related to program changes, access to programs and data, and computer operations.
- If (1) the general controls continue to operate effectively and (2) the automated application controls have not changed since the baseline, audit teams may conclude that the automated application controls are operating effectively without repeating specific tests of the operating effectiveness of these controls.

The benchmarking approach reinforces the importance of general controls and their impact on automated application controls. To illustrate, if a weakness in program change controls exists that results in program modifications that either eliminate or modify established input controls, the operating effectiveness of the input controls would be compromised and the audit team would not be able to rely upon these controls as in the past (i.e., the baseline would no longer be appropriate). *AS 5* notes that, when using a benchmarking strategy, audit teams should periodically reestablish the baseline performance of automated application controls.

Summary

Refer to Exhibit H.12 for a summary of the computerized processing system audit tools and techniques discussed in this section. These tools and techniques are used to test the computerized processing of transactions as well as the operating effectiveness of computer controls.

> ### ⌕ REVIEW CHECKPOINTS
>
> H.22 List four methods used by audit teams to test the operating effectiveness of controls.
>
> H.23 What are program-embedded techniques?
>
> H.24 How does monitoring system activity identify potential unauthorized or inappropriate use of computer applications and operations?
>
> H.25 What is the difference between the test data technique and the integrated test facility technique?
>
> H.26 When using the test data or integrated test facility approach, what type of simulated transactions should the audit team create?
>
> H.27 What is the difference between the use of test data and of parallel simulation?
>
> H.28 Describe how audit teams may use a benchmarking approach when evaluating the operating effectiveness of automated application controls.

EXHIBIT H.12 Advanced Computerized processing System Audit Tools and Techniques

Technique	Description	Advantages	Disadvantages
Techniques Using Actual Data			
Program-embedded techniques	Audit modules that are designed and coded into the client's computerized programs	Allows audit teams to select transactions and evaluate processing steps and results	Requires special programming skills
Parallel simulation	Processes actual transactions through programs designed to replicate appropriate processing by the client's computerized processing system	Permits comparison with actual processing without entering simulated data into client systems	Can be expensive to develop programs if CAATs cannot be used
Techniques Using Simulated Data			
Test data	Processes simulated transactions through the client's computerized processing system and compares those results to predetermined results	Efficient because it requires only one of each type of condition to be tested	• Separate processing may not correspond to programs actually used by client • Test data have the potential to be commingled with actual data
Integrated test facility	Processes simulated transactions related to a fictitious department or branch created by audit teams	• Because simulated data are processed along with actual data, programs are more likely to be those actually used by client • Separate minicompany" isolates transactions tested by audit teams from other transactions processed by the client	Data entered and processed as part of the minicompany must be reversed or adjusted out of the financial statements

END-USER COMPUTING AND OTHER ENVIRONMENTS

LEARNING OBJECTIVE H-6
Describe the characteristics and control issues associated with end-user and other computing environments.

As the storage and computation capacities of personal computers, laptops, tablets, and other portable computing devices surpass those of older mainframe computers, more and more of the day-to-day program development activities have become the responsibility of those individuals ("end users") who use the programs in the entity's daily operations. Because of their proliferation, these environments should not be neglected in the assessment of control risk (and risk of material misstatement). These environments range from the use of commonly available software applications and spreadsheets (such as Microsoft Access and Excel) to sophisticated programs tailored to a specific company's needs.

End-user computing environments introduce the following control issues that audit teams must consider:

1. *Lack of separation of duties.* Within the accounting function, individuals may be in position to initiate and authorize source documents, enter data, operate the computer, and distribute output reports. Within the computer function, small entities may fail to separate the functions of programming and operations. This lack of separation of duties occurs because of a lack of resources, not the entity's indifference with respect to internal control.
2. *Lack of physical security.* Computers and files often are located in end-user departments, not in a separate, secured area. As a result, access to computer terminals as well as programs and data files (which may be stored on universal serial bus (USB) drives and other portable storage devices) may not be properly restricted.
3. *Lack of program documentation and testing.* Because users often modify or adapt existing programs for their own use, end-user computing environments are often characterized by a lack of appropriate program documentation and testing.
4. *Limited computer knowledge.* The extensive reliance on packaged software and utility programs in end-user environments may result in personnel having limited computer knowledge.

End-User Computing Control Considerations

Most of the control issues noted in the previous section result from the lack of separation of duties and computer controls. It follows that most of the audit team's control considerations and techniques are designed to overcome these deficiencies. Audit teams should consider the entire control system, including manual controls, and look for compensating control strengths that could offset apparent weaknesses. This section discusses four such types of controls: computer operations controls, data entry controls, processing controls, and systems development and modification controls.

Computer Operations Controls

An end-user computing environment is similar to the one-person bookkeeping department because a small number of individuals (in some cases, only one individual) perform the systems analysis, systems design, and programming operations. The main controls involve limiting the concentration of functions (to the extent possible) and establishing the proper supervision over individuals performing these functions.

With respect to separation of duties, important compensating controls that increase the likelihood of accurate processing include (1) comparison of manual control totals with totals from computer output and (2) careful inspection of output for accuracy. In addition, some of the following operations controls may be useful in this regard:

- Joint operation of computerized processing by two or more individuals.
- Rotation of assigned duties among individuals.
- Comparisons of computer use time to averages or norms and investigation of excess usage.
- Proper supervision of computer operations.
- Required vacations for all individuals.

Data Entry Controls

In end-user computing environments, the most important controls are those over online data entry (accounting transactions). Some of these controls include:

- *Restrictions on access to input devices.* Common controls used to restrict access to input devices include (1) locking terminals, (2) requiring the use of passwords to access files, initiate changes, and access programs, and (3) using *automatic terminal logoff that terminates* the link between the computer and the system after a specified period of time.
- *Standard screens and computer prompting.* Computers can be programmed to produce a standard screen format when a particular function is accessed. The operator must complete all blanks as prompted by the computer, thus ensuring that complete transactions are entered before they are submitted for processing.
- *Online editing and sight verification.* The input edit and validation controls discussed previously can be programmed to occur at the time of input. In some installations, the data on the screen are not released until they have been sight verified and the operator signals the computer to accept the entire screen. This control allows input errors to be detected prior to submission of the related data for processing.

AUDITING INSIGHT — Problems with Data

One important control consideration in an end-user computing environment is with the extensive use of laptop computers and other portable computing devices. Their use introduces issues because of the potential for theft and the loss of significant data if the machine itself is stolen or lost. Some recent examples of significant data losses include:

- **Boeing** lost the names, Social Security numbers, and salary data for 382,000 of its employees.
- **Ernst & Young** lost the credit information for 243,000 of **Hotels.com's** workers.
- **Starbucks** lost the Social Security numbers of 60,000 of their current and former employees.

Source: "The Biggest Lost-Laptop Incidents of 2006," *Fortune*, January 22, 2007, p. 36.

Processing Controls

Important controls to ensure the appropriate processing of data include the following:

- *Transaction logs.* Transaction entry through the terminal should be captured automatically in a computerized log. The transaction logs (for each terminal or each class of terminals) should be summarized into the equivalent of batch totals (record counts, batch totals, or hash totals).
- *Control totals.* Master files should contain records that accumulate the number of records and batch totals. The update processing should automatically change these control records.
- *Data comparisons.* The summary of daily transactions and the master file control totals from the computer should be compared to manual control totals maintained by the accounting department.
- *Audit trail.* The transaction logs and periodic dumps of master files should provide an audit trail and means for recovery. In addition, some computer installations have systems software that can provide a log of all files accessed and all jobs processed.

Systems Development and Modification Controls

In our discussion of general controls, we discussed the importance of program development and program change controls. In end-user computing environments, many application programs are purchased from computer manufacturers or software vendors not completely familiar with online control techniques. Purchased programs should be reviewed carefully and tested before implementation. It is particularly important that end users evaluate whether these programs meet their processing needs. The client should carefully test those programs developed internally within the client (as well as subsequent modifications to them). In addition, because end users may create these programs, it is important that adequate documentation exist to allow others to use the program and make subsequent modifications.

AUDITING INSIGHT | Spreadsheet and Data Controls

One important consideration in an end-user computing environment is the ability to protect access to data in spreadsheets and other financial databases, especially when multiple users share these spreadsheets. Enhanced password and data encryption features are becoming an important control when various individuals within the entity use the same spreadsheets. **Microsoft** has developed Excel Services to enable spreadsheet sharing among users; Tom Rizzo, director of **SharePoint Technology,** notes that "the functions offered in Excel Services, particularly being able to lock down and hide data for specific groups of users, are highly flexible and can be personalized for individual sets of users."

The importance of spreadsheets is perhaps best illustrated by a $1.2 billion error in **Fannie Mae's** investment accounts that resulted from incorrect formulae in cells that calculated the market value of these investments.

Sources: "How to Put Your Spreadsheet in Lockdown," *CFO.com,* November 14, 2006; "Fannie Mae Corrects Mistakes in Results," *The New York Times,* October 30, 2003.

Service Organizations

Because of a relative lack of expertise and a cost-benefit analysis, organizations (referred to as a *user entity*) may outsource specialized data processing to other organizations (referred to as *service organizations*). In such cases, specialized transactions (payroll is a common example) are processed in a computerized environment that is remotely located from the user entity's premises. The proliferation of "cloud computing" and growing use of these services is likely to increase the extent to which data and transactions are processed at locations other than the client's premises. As a result, the various computer controls discussed throughout this module are not easily accessible to audit teams.

In cases such as this, the user entity's auditors obtain a report from the service organization's auditors. It is important to note that the user entity's auditors must still evaluate controls that are related to the service organization's computerized processing of transactions. However, this evaluation considers the procedures performed and results obtained by the service organization's auditors.

The reports on controls over processing at service organizations are discussed in detail in Module A.

↳ REVIEW CHECKPOINTS

H.29 Which important duties are generally *not* separated in end-user computing environments?

H.30 What are the major control issues in end-user computing environments?

H.31 What control procedures can be used to achieve control over computer operations in an end-user computing environment?

H.32 What control procedures can be used to achieve control over computerized processing in an end-user computing environment?

COMPUTER ABUSE AND COMPUTER FRAUD

As technology has advanced, so has the ease and speed with which fraud can be perpetrated. Just as criminals use the Internet to commit "cybercrimes" in many forms (such as introducing computer viruses, hacking, committing cybertheft, spamming, phishing, creating evil twins, and performing credit scams and Ponzi schemes), corporate wrongdoers

LEARNING OBJECTIVE H-7
Define and describe computer fraud and the controls that can be used to prevent it.

use computers to perform their schemes. Computer experts generally agree that an ingenious programmer can commit theft or misappropriation of assets that is difficult, if not impossible, to detect. Even the use of technology as simple as a spreadsheet can provide aspiring fraudsters an avenue to commit fraud. Former vice president and CFO of the information and learning division of **ProQuest Company** concealed fictitious sales transactions by using "hidden rows" that would not be revealed when printed as hard copy and using a white-colored font that rendered the fraudulent information invisible.[5] The accompanying Auditing Insight provides information about characteristics of computer fraud.

AUDITING INSIGHT — How Are Computer Frauds Perpetrated?

A study by the **U.S. Secret Service** and **CERT Coordination Center** (a computer security response group) revealed that most frauds committed using computers were relatively easy to conduct and did not require extensive technical skill. Some key findings included:

- Simple user commands exploiting existing "loopholes" in the programs were used in 87 percent of the cases.
- Only 23 percent of the frauds were committed by information technology specialists or others with significant technical knowledge.

- Of the frauds discovered, 61 percent were performed by noninformation technology staff, including customers and supervisors.
- Although auditing and monitoring procedures identified 20 percent of the incidents, fraudsters could avoid detection by avoiding specific time periods. As one fraudster noted "the end of the month was hot, the end of the quarter was hotter, and the end of the year was really hot."

Source: "Insider Attacks—Easy to Do—Hard to Detect," *Computer Fraud & Security,* September 2004, p. 2.

Computer fraud is a matter of concern for entities, investors, and audit teams. Experts in the field have coined two definitions related to computer chicanery: *Computer abuse* is the broad definition, but *computer fraud* is probably the term used more often. Both terms involve the use of computer technology by a perpetrator to achieve a gain at the expense of a victim.

Computer abuse and fraud include such diverse acts as intentional damage or destruction of a computer and the use of the computer to assist in a fraud. Perpetrators of the financial fraud at the **Equity FundingCorporation of America** used a computer to print thousands of fictitious records and documents that otherwise would have occupied the time of hundreds of clerks. Some services (such as "computerized" dating services) have promoted business on the promise of using computers when they are not actually used. Recently, federal prosecutors charged 11 people with stealing more than 41 million credit and debit card numbers, which is the largest hacking and identity theft ring ever identified;[6] one of its primary targets was **TJX Cos.**, which is discussed in the accompanying Auditing Insight. Recent incidents involving **Citigroup, Inc., Google, Inc., Lockheed Martin, Michaels Stores, Inc.,** the **NASDAQ Stock Market**, **Public Broadcasting Services,** and **Sony Corp.** illustrate that, despite significant efforts that have been enacted to prevent cyber attacks, these incidents continue to be a significant threat to businesses and their customers' information.[7] In 2008, the retail industry (31 percent) and financial services industry (30 percent) accounted for more than 60 percent of all reported security breaches.[8]

---

[5] "SEC: Ex-CFO Used Spreadsheets for Fraud," *CFO.com,* July 22, 2008.

[6] "11 Charged in Theft of 41 Million Card Numbers," *CFO.com,* August 6, 2008.

[7] "Fallout from Cyber Attack Spreads," *The Wall Street Journal,* January 29, 2010, p. B1; "Hackers Penetrate Nasdaq Computers," *The Wall Street Journal,* February 5-6, 2011, pp. A1, A4; "Hacker Raids Sony Videogame Network," *The Wall Street Journal,* April 27, 2011, p. A1; "Thieves Swipe Debit Card Data," *The Wall Street Journal,* May 13, 2001, pp. B1, B2; "Hackers Broaden Their Attacks," *The Wall Street Journal,* May 31, 2001, pp. B1, B2; "Citigroup Says Hacking Affected 360,000 Cards," *The Wall Street Journal,* June 16, 2011, p. B2.

[8] "FBI Probes Hack at Citibank," The Wall Street Journal, December 22, 2009, pp. A1, A16.

> **AUDITING INSIGHT** | **Attention Shoppers**
>
> **TJX Cos.**, a retail giant that owns **T.J. Maxx** and **Marshall's**, experienced a security breach when customer information was stolen from a computer network from an "unauthorized intruder." Hackers are believed to have used a radio antenna and laptop computer to decode data streaming through the air between handheld price-checking devices, cash registers, and store computers. Subsequent evaluations concluded that TJX's network had less security than many home computer networks; one person familiar with the situation noted that "it was as easy as breaking into a house through a side door that was wide open."
>
> What are the total damages? As many as 200 million credit cards could have been compromised from four years of transactions. It could cost banks as much as $300 million to replace cards; although TJX recognized a $118 million charge in the second quarter of 2007, its ultimate costs may exceed $1 billion over five years for consultants, security upgrades, attorney fees, and marketing programs designed to reassure customers. The perpetrator, Albert Gonzalez, received a prison sentence of 20 years and one day—the stiffest sentence ever given in a hacking case.
>
> While unprecedented in potential magnitude, TJX is not unique in having its customers' information compromised. Other recent breaches of credit and debit-card data in recent years involved **B.J.'s Wholesale Club, Inc.** (40,000 cards), **DWS Retail Ventures, Inc.** (1.4 million cards), **CardSystems, Inc.** (40 million cards), and **Dollar Tree Stores, Inc.** (800 cards).
>
> Sources: "Giant Retailer Reveals Customer Data Breach," *The Wall Street Journal*, January 18, 2007, pp. D1, D6; "How Credit-Card Data Went out Wireless Door," *The Wall Street Journal*, May 4, 2007, pp. A1, A12; "TJX Profit Falls 57% on Costs Tied to Data Breach," *The Wall Street Journal*, August 15, 2007, p. B3; "Hacker Gets 20 Years in Data Theft," *The Wall Street Journal*, March 27, 2010, p. A3.

Computer financial frauds range from the crude to the complex, and they hit financial institutions with alarming frequency. Moreover, computer financial frauds are frustratingly difficult to detect in the ordinary course of business.

Preventive, Detective, and Damage-Limiting Controls

Entities can implement control procedures designed to prevent and detect computer frauds and to limit the extent of damage from them. Prevention controls keep errors and frauds from entering the system. Detection controls are designed to discover frauds should they get past the prevention controls. Damage-limiting controls are designed to limit the damage if a fraud does occur. For example, transaction limit amounts restrict the amount of an individual fraudulent transaction to a preset tolerable amount. Some example prevention, detection, and damage limitation controls are presented in Exhibit H.13.

As in Exhibit H.13, controls can be classified in three different levels: (1) administrative, (2) physical, and (3) technical. The *administrative level* refers to general controls that affect the management of an entity's computer resources. These controls are similar in nature to the entity's control environment and relate to the individuals employed by the entity and limitations or limits on the nature and scope of activities they perform.

The *physical controls* affect the computer equipment and related documents. The "inconspicuous location" control simply refers to placing computing devices out of the way of casual traffic. Of course, the equipment used daily must be available in employees' workplaces, but access must be controlled to prevent unauthorized persons from simply sitting down and invading the system and its data files.

Technical controls include some matters of electronic wizardry. Data encryption techniques convert information to scrambled form or code so that it looks like garbled nonsense when transmitted or retrieved from a file. In recent years, industrial spying has increased. Businesses should assume that public and private intelligence services intercept and analyze data submitted by wire and airwaves (e.g., satellite transmission) for the purpose of commercial advantage. Elaborate password software is necessary to thwart unscrupulous industrial spies who try to break into an entity's computerized processing system. (Hackers have been known to program telephones to call random numbers to find a computerized processing system and then try millions of random passwords to try to get in!) *Programmed range and reasonableness checks* refer to computer monitoring

EXHIBIT H.13 Protecting the Computer from Fraud (Selected Controls)

	Objective of Control		
	Prevention	**Detection**	**Damage Limiting**
Administrative Controls			
Security checks on personnel	X		
Separation of duties	X		
Access and execution log records (properly reviewed)		X	
Program testing after modification		X	
Rotation of computer duties		X	X
Transaction limit amounts			X
Physical Controls			
Inconspicuous location	X		
Controlled access	X		
Computer room guard (after hours)	X	X	
Computer room entry log record	X	X	
Preprinted limits on documents (e.g., checks)			X
Data backup storage			X
Technical Controls			
Data encryption	X		
Access control software and passwords	X		
Transaction logging reports		X	
Control totals (batch and hash totals)	X	X	
Program source comparisons (of versions of programs)		X	
Range checks on permitted transaction amounts			X
Reasonableness checks on permitted transaction amounts			X

of transaction processing to try to detect potentially erroneous or fraudulent transactions. These are the equivalent of the low-tech imprint you may have seen on some negotiable checks (for example, "Not negotiable if over $500").

Computer Forensics

Computer forensics is one of the fastest growing areas of fraud investigation. The Federal Bureau of Investigation (FBI) defines **computer forensics** as the science of acquiring, preserving, retrieving, and presenting data that have been processed electronically and stored on computer media. In other words, when computer hard drives are used as storage media, evidence can be retrieved even when the data have been deleted. Computer forensics has proven useful in tracking terrorists, prosecuting child pornographers, and even in impeaching a president. Compromising e-mails between President Bill Clinton and Monica Lewinsky and between Congressman Mark Foley and one of his pages, although deleted, were recovered by computer forensic specialists. More recently, computer forensic specialists recovered communications related to the **Bay Area Laboratory Co-operative (BALCO)** steroids scandal in baseball and an affair between then-Detroit mayor Kwame Kilpatrick and his chief of staff. The FBI has also used computer forensics to successfully identify the creators of several widespread computer viruses.

> **REVIEW CHECKPOINTS**
>
> H.33 Identify physical controls, technical controls, and administrative controls that protect computerized processing systems from fraud.
>
> H.34 What is computer forensics? How can it be used in fraud investigation?

Summary

When clients use computerized processing, the audit team's general responsibilities do not change. However, the use of computerized processing does require audit teams to consider computer controls implemented by the client in obtaining an understanding of internal control, assessing control risk, and testing the operating effectiveness of controls. These steps will result in the audit team's assessment of control risk and the risk of material misstatement; as in a manual processing environment, this risk will affect the nature, timing, and extent of the audit team's substantive procedures.

Two primary types of computer controls exist. General controls apply to all application systems and have a pervasive effect on the client's computerized processing. Major categories of these controls include hardware controls, program development controls, program change controls, computer operations controls, and access to programs and data controls. Automated application controls are implemented with respect to the computerized processing of specific types of transactions and include input controls, processing controls, and output controls.

The examination of client computer controls can take different forms. Audit teams can audit "around" the computer as if computerized processing did not exist except as a very fast and accurate manual accounting processor. Alternatively, with enough computer expertise, audit teams can audit "through" the computer to test the operating effectiveness of the computer controls. Tests of computer controls described in the module include techniques using actual client data and techniques using simulated data created by the audit team.

The ultimate goal of the tests of computer controls is to reach a conclusion about the operating effectiveness of control procedures in a computerized system. This conclusion allows audit teams to assess the control risk (and risk of material misstatement) and determine the nature, timing, and extent of other substantive procedures for auditing the related account balances. This control risk assessment decision is crucial, particularly in computerized processing systems, because subsequent work can be performed using data files that are produced by the computerized processing system.

Not all businesses use large-scale systems, so this module includes an end-user environment orientation to information processing systems. Audit teams must be aware of the typical control problems associated with such installations as well as concerns when end-users develop their own applications. This module concluded with a section on computer fraud and computer forensics. Although computer financial frauds range from the crude to the complex, computer financial frauds are frustratingly difficult to detect in the ordinary course of business. Computer forensics provides a tool to help audit teams in their efforts to detect computer fraud and abuse.

Key Terms

access to programs and data controls: A type of general control that provides reasonable assurance that access to programs and data is granted only to authorized users, 847

auditing around the computer: An approach to auditing in a computerized processing environment in which audit teams reconcile input to processing results without evaluating computer controls, 857

auditing through the computer: An approach to auditing in a computerized processing environment in which audit teams evaluate the client's hardware and programs to determine the reliability of operations and test the operating effectiveness of the related controls, 857

automated application controls: Controls applied to specific business activities within a computerized processing system to address management assertions regarding the financial statements; major categories are input controls, processing controls, and output controls, 843

batch processing: A method of processing transactions in which similar transactions are collected and periodically processed together through the same computer program, 845

benchmarking: An approach used to evaluate the operating effectiveness of automated application controls that relies on the baseline operating effectiveness of those controls from prior audits, the continued operating effectiveness of general controls, and the lack of changes in the automated application controls, 862

computer forensics: The science of acquiring, preserving, retrieving, and presenting data that have been processed electronically and stored on computer media, 869

computer operations control: A type of general control that provides reasonable assurance that (1) the processing of transactions through the computerized processing system is in accordance with the entity's objectives, (2) processing failures are resolved on a timely basis and do not affect or unnecessarily delay the processing of other transactions within the batch, and (3) actions are taken to facilitate the backup and recovery of important data when the need arises, 846

control total: Totals that are determined prior to data input and compared to totals that are generated following input; ensure that all entries were made, no entries were inadvertently made more than once, and that entries were accurately made, 852

general controls: Controls that apply to all application systems and help ensure their continued proper operations. Major categories of general controls are hardware controls, program development controls, program change controls, computer operations controls, and access to programs and data controls 843

hardware control: A type of general control that is "built in" to the computer equipment and provides reasonable assurance that data are not altered or modified as they are transmitted within the system, 843

input control: A type of automated application control designed to provide reasonable assurance that data received for processing by the computer department have been properly authorized and accurately entered or converted for processing, 851

integrated test facility (ITF): A technique used to evaluate computerized processing and test computer controls by creating and processing simulated transactions through a dummy department or branch, 862

output controls: A type of automated application control that is concerned with detecting errors following processing and providing reasonable assurance that only authorized persons receive output or have access to files produced by the system, 853

parallel simulation (or *controlled reprocessing* or *comparison program utilization*): Reprocessing actual client data through a program prepared by the audit team and comparing the results of those generated by the client's normal system to evaluate the accuracy of computerized processing and test computer controls, 860

processing control: A type of automated application control designed to provide reasonable assurance that data processing has been performed accurately without any omission or duplicate processing of transactions, 852

program analysis techniques: Software packages that assist audit teams in understanding the logic of an application program, 859

program change control: A type of general control implemented to provide reasonable assurance that requests for modifications to existing programs (1) are properly authorized, conducted in accordance with entity policies, and support the entity's financial reporting requirements, (2) involve appropriate users in the program modification process, (3) are tested and validated prior to being placed into operation, and (4) have been appropriately documented, 845

program development control: A type of general control implemented to provide reasonable assurance that (1) acquisition or development of computer programs and software is properly authorized, is conducted in accordance with entity policies, and supports the entity's financial reporting requirements, (2) appropriate users participate in the software acquisition or program development process, (3) programs and software are tested and validated prior to being placed into operation, and (4) all software and programs have appropriate documentation, 844

program-embedded technique: Special modules designed and coded into computer programs that allows audit teams to select specific transactions of interest before or during processing and evaluate various stages of processing at a subsequent time, 858

real-time processing: A method of processing transactions that does so on an individual basis as the transaction occurs, 846

systems development life cycle: Process used to plan, develop, and implement new computerized processing systems, 844

test data: Simulated transactions prepared by the audit team that are processed through the client's computer systems to evaluate computerized processing and assess computer controls, 861

Multiple-Choice Questions for Practice and Review

All applicable Exercises and Problems are available with McGraw-Hill's Connect® Accounting

LO H-2

H.35 In a computerized processing system, hardware controls are designed to
   a. Arrange data in a logical sequential manner for processing purposes.
   b. Correct errors in the computer programs.
   c. Monitor and detect errors in source documents.
   d. Detect and control errors arising from use of equipment.

LO H-3

H.36 An example of a program in which the audit team would be most interested in testing automated application controls is a(n)
   a. Payroll processing program.
   b. Operating system program.
   c. Data management system software.
   d. Utility program.

LO H-2

H.37 Which of the following would reduce the effectiveness of internal control in a computerized processing system?
   a. The computer librarian maintains custody of computer program instructions and detailed lists.
   b. Computer operators have access to operator instructions and detailed program lists.
   c. The control group is solely responsible for the distribution of all computer output.
   d. Computer programmers write and debug programs that perform routines designed by the systems analyst.

LO H-1

H.38 Which of the following is true with respect to fraud risk factors in a computerized environment?
   a. Employees in a computerized environment are highly skilled.
   b. Audit teams cannot evaluate the computerized processing system during the year.
   c. Higher dollar amounts are involved in a computerized environment.
   d. Employees have increased access to information systems and computer resources in a computerized environment.

LO H-2

H.39 Controls used in the management of a computer center to minimize the possibility of using an incorrect file or program are
   a. Control totals.
   b. Record counts.
   c. Limit checks.
   d. External labels.

LO H-5

H.40 Audit teams would most likely use computer-assisted audit techniques to
   a. Make copies of client data files for controlled reprocessing.
   b. Construct a parallel simulation to test the client's computer controls.
   c. Perform tests of a client's hardware controls.
   d. Test the operative effectiveness of a client's password access control.

LO H-5

H.41 Which of the following computerized processing systems generally can be audited without examining or directly testing the computer programs of the system?
   a. A system that performs relatively uncomplicated processes and produces detailed output.
   b. A system that affects a number of master files and produces limited output.
   c. A system that updates a few master files and produces no other printed output than final balances.
   d. A system that performs relatively complicated processing and produces very little detailed output.

LO H-1

H.42 The client's computerized exception reporting system helps audit teams conduct a more efficient audit because it
   a. Condenses data significantly.
   b. Highlights abnormal conditions.
   c. Decreases the necessary level of tests of computer controls.
   d. Is an efficient computer input control.

LO H-5   H.43 Audit teams use the test data method to gain certain assurances with respect to
   a. Input data.
   b. Machine capacity.
   c. Control procedures contained within the program.
   d. General controls.

LO H-5   H.44 When using test data, why are audit teams required to prepare only one transaction to test each computer processing alternative?
   a. The speed and efficiency of the computer results in reduced sample sizes.
   b. The risk of misstatement is typically lower in a computerized processing environment.
   c. Audit teams generally perform more extensive substantive testing in a computerized processing environment, resulting in less need to test processing controls.
   d. In a computerized processing environment, each transaction is handled in an identical manner.

LO H-5   H.45 When auditing a computerized processing system, which of the following is *not* true of the test data approach?
   a. The client's computer programs process test data under the audit team's control.
   b. The test data must consist of all possible valid and invalid conditions.
   c. The test data need consist only of those valid and invalid conditions in which audit teams are interested.
   d. Only one transaction of each type need be tested.

LO H-5   H.46 Audit teams cannot test the reliable operation of computer control procedures by
   a. Submitting test data at several different times for processing on the computer program the client uses for actual transaction processing.
   b. Manually comparing detailed transactions that the internal auditors used to test a program to the program's actual error messages.
   c. Programming a model transaction processing system and processing actual client transactions for comparison to the output produced by the client's program.
   d. Manually reperforming actual transaction processing with comparison of results to the actual system output.

LO H-5   H.47 Audit teams can obtain evidence of the proper functioning of password access control to a computerized processing system by
   a. Writing a computer program that simulates the logic of an effective password control system.
   b. Selecting a random sample of the client's completed transactions to check the existence of proper authorization.
   c. Attempting to sign on to the computerized processing system with a false password.
   d. Obtaining representations from the client's computer personnel that the password control prevents unauthorized entry.

LO H-5   H.48 When processing controls within the computerized processing system may not leave visible evidence that could be inspected by audit teams, the teams should
   a. Make corroborative inquiries.
   b. Observe the separation of duties of personnel.
   c. Review transactions submitted for processing and comparing them to related output.
   d. Review the run manual.

LO H-6   H.49 Which of the following statements most likely represents a control consideration for an entity that performs its accounting using portable computing devices?
   a. It is usually difficult to detect arithmetic errors.
   b. Unauthorized persons find it easy to access the computer and alter the data files.
   c. Transactions are coded for account classifications before they are processed on the computer.
   d. Random errors in report printing are rare in packaged software systems.

LO H-2   H.50 Computerized processing performed concurrently with a particular activity so that results are available to influence a decision being made is referred to as
   a. Batch processing.
   b. Real-time processing.
   c. Integrated data processing.
   d. Random access processing.

LO H-2

H.51 Which of the following is *not* a characteristic of a batch processing system?
  a. The collection of similar transactions that are sorted and processed sequentially against a master file.
  b. The input of transactions prior to processing.
  c. The production of numerous printouts.
  d. The posting of a transaction as it occurs to several files without intermediate printouts.

LO H-3

H.52 A customer intended to order 100 units of product Z96014 but incorrectly ordered product Z96015, which is not an actual product. Which of the following controls most likely would detect this error?
  a. Check digit verification.
  b. Record count.
  c. Hash total.
  d. Redundant data check.

LO H-3

H.53 Which of the following automated application controls would offer reasonable assurance that inventory data were completely and accurately entered?
  a. Sequence checking.
  b. Batch totals.
  c. Limit tests.
  d. Check digits.

LO H-2

H.54 Which of the following persons is responsible for controlling access to systems documentation and access to program and data files?
  a. Programmers.
  b. Data conversion operators.
  c. Librarians.
  d. Computer operators.

Exercises and Problems

 All applicable Exercises and Problems are available with McGraw-Hill's *Connect® Accounting*

LO H-5

H.55 **Auditing "around" versus Auditing "through" Computers.** Audit teams may audit around or through computers in the examination of financial statements of clients who use computerized processing systems.

Required:
  a. Describe the auditing approach referred to as *auditing around the computer*.
  b. Under what conditions do audit teams decide to *audit through the computer* instead of *around* the computer?
  c. In auditing "through" the computer, audit teams can use *test data*.
     1. What is the test data approach to testing computer controls?
     2. Why do audit teams use the test data approach?
  d. How can audit teams be satisfied that the client is actually using the computer program tested to process its accounting data?

(AICPA adapted)

LO H-5

H.56 **Auditing "around" versus Auditing "through" Computers.** You are auditing payroll for Alexander, Inc., which uses computerized processing for its payroll transactions; the various steps in Alexander's system follow:
  • As employees provide services, they enter hours worked on timesheets that their supervisor approves at the conclusion of the pay period. Timesheets have an identifying field that indicates whether the employee is an hourly (H) or a salaried (S) employee.
  • The following data are entered into the input file: (1) employee number, (2) number of hours worked, and (3) employee status (hourly versus salaried).

- For hourly employees, the number of hours worked is multiplied by the wage rate (obtained from the employee master file) to calculate gross pay. For salaried employees, the employee's salary rate is obtained from the employee master file.
- When gross pay has been determined, deductions are automatically calculated using information from the employee master file and standard deduction tables (for federal tax withholdings, FICA withholdings, and Medicare withholdings).
- Net pay is calculated by subtracting deductions from gross pay.

Required:
a. What are the primary sources of error that can occur in the computerized processing system just described?
b. How would you examine Alexander's payroll if auditing "through" the computer? What key controls would you evaluate?
c. How would you examine Alexander's payroll if auditing "around" the computer?
d. What factors would you consider in deciding whether to audit "through" versus "around" the computer?

LO H-2, H-5

H.57 **Tests of Controls: General Controls**. The audit team of Packer Company identified the following general controls in obtaining its overall understanding of Packer's internal control over the computerized processing of transactions:

1. Packer has routine maintenance on its computer equipment and related technology scheduled and performed every six months.
2. Packer has formal, written systems development and documentation standards for the implementation of new programs.
3. Prior to implementing modifications to its existing programs, Packer tests and validates the program changes to ensure accurate processing.
4. Packer has appropriately separated the responsibilities of systems analysts, programmers, and computer operators.
5. Packer's computer files are protected from loss through frequent backups and storage at an off-site location.
6. Access to computer files and programs is protected through the use of passwords.
7. On a monthly basis, Packer reviews any revisions in the access rights of its employees to ensure consistency between their new job responsibilities and files and programs they may access.

Required:
Consider the four methods of testing the operating effectiveness of controls (inquiry, observation, document examination, and reperformance). For each of the preceding controls, provide an example of how Packer's audit team might choose to test the operating effectiveness of the control using the four methods of test of controls (for example, how would the audit team use inquiry, observation, document examination, and reperformance to test control #1, routine maintenance on computer equipment and related technology?). [*NOTE:* Not all types of tests of controls are appropriate for testing all of the controls.]

LO H-3, H-5

H.58 **Tests of Controls: Input Controls**. Knight Company is a medium-size manufacturing entity that uses a computerized system to process its customer orders. Orders are collected and processed on a daily basis in batches. In its processing of customer orders, Knight requires input of the following information into a daily customer order file (# represents a numeric field; A represents an alphabetic field):

- Customer number (######).
- Item number (AA######).
- Quantities (####).

After this information has been entered, the computer program accesses the valid customer master file to ensure that the sale is to an authorized customer and does not exceed that customer's credit limit. The program then accesses the inventory master file, verifies that the appropriate quantities are on hand, and identifies the most current price. The program then prepares an invoice by multiplying the quantities the customer ordered by the appropriate price and generates a total amount for the sale.

To prevent and detect errors during the input process, Knight has established the following controls:

1. Data entry personnel must enter a valid password to access the data entry program.
2. A check digit is appended to the customer number as a seventh digit.
3. The following control totals are manually determined prior to input and then compared to a total generated by the computer program: (a) number of records entered, (b) sum of customer numbers, and (c) sum of quantities.
4. The program rejects a customer number or inventory quantity containing an alphabetic character and any entry for item numbers having an inappropriate character in the given field. Data entry personnel are prompted to reenter the information upon rejection of the original entry.
5. Any quantities ordered in excess of 9,999 are highly unusual and require special authorization by Knight's management. Any such entries are rejected and written to a rejected order file for follow-up and authorization.
6. If data entry is attempted for a customer whose number is not in the customer master file (either a new customer or an erroneous entry for an existing customer), the transaction is rejected and written to a rejected order file. Depending on the reason for the invalid customer number, a credit check is conducted (if an order from a new customer) or the entry is corrected (if an erroneous entry of the customer number).

Required:

Consider the four methods of testing the operating effectiveness of controls (inquiry, observation, document examination, and reperformance). For each of the preceding controls, provide an example of how Knight's audit team might choose to test the operating effectiveness of the control using the four methods of test of controls (for example, how would the audit team use inquiry, observation, document examination, and reperformance to test control #1, use of valid passwords?). [*NOTE:* Not all types of tests of controls are appropriate for testing all of the controls.]

LO H-3, H-5

H.59 Tests of Controls: Processing and Output Controls. Mark Company's audit team is evaluating the controls that Mark has implemented over the computerized processing of payroll transactions. During the understanding and assessment stages of the audit, the following processing and output controls have been identified as being important in this processing:

1. To detect unauthorized access to payroll programs and processing, a system log is generated and reviewed on a weekly basis. This log identifies the programs that have been accessed during the past week, the individual(s) that have accessed those programs, and the time(s) during which the programs have been accessed. This log is reviewed and any unexpected or unauthorized access is investigated immediately.
2. Control totals are determined prior to the input of data and compared to computer-generated totals following transaction processing.
3. Any gross pay calculations in excess of $25,000 per month are identified and written to a rejected transaction file for separate investigation because Mark's highest paid employee whose salary is processed through the system earns $300,000 per year.
4. The system generates a report of any errors or unusual situations identified during transaction processing. This report is reviewed and any items are resolved in a timely manner, and the resolution is documented by notations made on the report.
5. Any changes to employee master file information since the last payroll period are evaluated to ensure that they have been properly authorized by the appropriate personnel.
6. The output is reviewed for reasonableness prior to distribution to users.

Required:

Consider the four methods of testing the operating effectiveness of controls (inquiry, observation, document examination, and reperformance). For each of the preceding controls, provide an example of how Mark's audit team might choose to test the operating effectiveness of the control using the four methods of test of controls (for example, how would the audit team use inquiry, observation, document examination, and reperformance to test control #1, the generation and review of the system log?). [*NOTE:* Not all types of tests of controls will be appropriate for testing all of the controls.]

LO H-3

H.60 **Computer Internal Control Questionnaire Evaluation.** Assume that, when conducting procedures to obtain an understanding of Denton Seed Company's internal controls, you checked "No" to the following internal control questionnaire items:
- Does access to online files require specific passwords to be entered to identify and validate the terminal user?
- Does the user establish control totals prior to submitting data for processing? (Order entry application subsystem.)
- Are input control totals reconciled to output control totals? (Order entry application subsystem.)

Required:
Describe the errors and frauds that could occur because of the weaknesses indicated by the lack of computer controls.

LO H-2

H.61 **Batch versus Real-Time Processing.** In a computerized processing environment, transactions may be processed using either batch or real-time processing.

Required:
a. Distinguish between batch and real-time processing. When is an entity more likely to use each method?
b. Assume that input controls have been implemented to detect errors in entering numbers corresponding to customer accounts. How does the use of batch and real-time processing influence employees' ability to make corrections to these account numbers if input errors have been made?

LO H-2

H.62 **File Retention and Backup.** You have audited the financial statements of Solt Manufacturing Company for several years and are making preliminary plans for the audit for the year ended June 30. This year, however, Solt has installed and used a computerized processing system.

The following output computer files are produced in the daily processing runs:
- Cash disbursements sequenced by check number.
- Outstanding payable balances (alphabetized).
- Purchase journals arranged by (a) account charged and (b) vendor.

Solt's records as described are maintained in electronic format. All files are stored in a restricted area within the computer room. A grandfather-father-son policy is followed in retaining and safeguarding the files.

Vouchers (with supporting invoices, receiving reports, and purchase order copies) are filed by vendor code. Another purchase order copy and the checks are filed numerically.

Required:
a. Explain the grandfather-father-son policy. Describe how files could be reconstructed when this policy is used.
b. Discuss whether Solt's policies for retaining and safeguarding the files provide adequate protection against losses of data.

(AICPA adapted)

LO H-2

H.63 **Separation of Duties and General Control Procedures.** You are engaged to examine the financial statements of Horizon Incorporated, which has its own computer installation. During the preliminary understanding phase of your study of Horizon's internal control, you found that Horizon lacked proper separation of the programming and operating functions. As a result, you intensified the evaluation of the internal control surrounding the computer and concluded that the existing compensating general controls provided reasonable assurance that the objectives of internal control were being met.

Required:
a. In a properly functioning computerized environment, how is the separation of the programming and operating functions achieved?
b. What are the compensating general controls that you most likely found?

(AICPA adapted)

LO H-3, H-5

H.64 Test Data and Integrated Test Facility. You are conducting the audit of Warner Company and are focusing on its processing of invoices for sales made to its customers. Warner's control procedures specify the following with respect to the preparation of sales invoices:

- Customers must be included in an approved customer listing.
- Invoices are prepared only for sales that have been properly approved (through an approved sales order).
- Customers are invoiced for all quantities shipped (from the shipping document, which is prepared after goods have been retrieved and prepared for shipment).
- Inventory item numbers correspond to appropriate inventory items sold by Warner and all prices charged to customers are current.

Upon receipt of a customer request, Warner's computerized system requires entry of the (a) customer number, (b) item(s) requested, and (c) quantities requested. Upon entry, the customer number is verified against the approved customer listing and any existing credit limits or conditions are accessed. (For a first-time customer, a separate credit approval process is undertaken and the customer is added to the approved customer listing.) If approved, a prenumbered sales order is generated and the information is maintained in an electronic sales order file. A copy of the sales order is forwarded to inventory stores to authorize the release of the goods for shipment.

After goods have been retrieved and prepared for shipment, the sales order number and quantities shipped are entered in an electronic shipping document file. At this point, the program accesses the electronic sales order file and compares the quantities from the two files. If all goods ordered are in stock and will be shipped, the electronic inventory file is accessed (which includes current prices) and the invoice is prepared and mathematically totaled. The appropriate information is then written to an electronic completed invoice file. If all goods ordered are not in stock (i.e., a backorder situation), only the goods shipped are included on the invoice and a "backorder" notation (along with quantities of goods on backorder) appears on the invoice to inform the customer that the remaining goods will be shipped separately. For backorders, customers are billed (invoiced) only for items shipped, and shipping charges for the entire amount appear on the invoice related to the final shipment of goods filling a particular sales order. The appropriate information is then written to an electronic backorder invoice file for subsequent completion.

After being generated, the invoice is mailed to the customer for payment.

Required:

a. Identify the type of input controls that should exist in this environment.

b. Assume that you are developing test data to evaluate the operating effectiveness of Warner's computerized controls. What type of error conditions would you incorporate into the test data? How many different types of transactions or conditions would you need to create?

c. If you were using an integrated test facility to evaluate the operating effectiveness of Warner's computerized controls, how would your approach differ from that in (b)?

d. What other considerations might you evaluate with respect to data input to ensure that employees cannot modify information to reduce billings to customers who then provide a "kickback" to the employee?

LO H-2, H-3, H-7

H.65 Computer Frauds and Missing Control Procedures. The following are brief stories of actual employee thefts and embezzlements perpetrated in a computerized processing environment.

Required:

What type of control procedure that might have prevented or detected the fraud was missing or inoperative?

a. An accounts payable terminal operator at a subsidiary entity fabricated false invoices from a fictitious vendor and entered them in the parent entity's central accounts payable/cash disbursement system. Five checks totaling $155,000 were issued to the "vendor."

b. A bank provided custodial and record-keeping services for several mutual funds. A proof-and-control department employee substituted his own name and account number for those of the actual purchasers of some shares. He used the computerized processing system to conceal and shift balances from his name and account to names and accounts of the actual investors when he needed to avoid detection because of missing amounts in the investors' accounts.

c. The university's computerized processing system was illegally hacked. Vandals changed many students' first name to Susan, student telephone numbers were changed to the number of the university president, grade point averages were modified, and some academic files were completely deleted.

d. A computer operator at a state-run horse race betting agency set the computer clock back three minutes. After the race was completed, he quickly telephoned bets to his girlfriend, an input clerk at the agency, gave her the winning horse and the bet amount, and won every time!

LO H-2

H.66 **General Controls.**

Indicate the benefits of each of the following examples of general controls.

a. Echo checks are designed and built into the computer by the manufacturer.
b. The company schedules regular maintenance on its computer hardware.
c. The company involves users in its design of programs and selection of prepackaged software and programs.
d. New programs are tested and validated prior to being implemented.
e. Documentation is required prior to modifying existing programs using "emergency" change orders.
f. The duties of system analysts, programmers, and computer operators are appropriately separated.
g. Appropriate backup and data retention policies are implemented.
h. The access rights granted to employees are periodically reviewed and evaluated, giving consideration to known changes resulting from promotions and transfers within the company.

LO H-2

H.67 **General Controls.** For each of the following examples of general controls, classify the control based on appropriate category (hardware controls, program development controls, program change controls, computer operations controls, and access to programs and data controls). In addition, for each, provide the objective of the control and one example of how audit teams might test the operating effectiveness of the control.

a. The entity schedules periodic, preventative maintenance on computer equipment.
b. The entity requires the use of passwords and requires these passwords to be modified every three months.
c. Proper documentation exists for "emergency" change requests for programs.
d. Important files, programs, and documentation are backed up and stored in a safe, off-site location.
e. The entity involves users in the design of programs and selection of prepackaged software.
f. The entity resolves failures for transactions processed in a real-time environment on a timely basis.
g. All program development activities are consistent with the entity's needs and objectives.
h. All modifications to existing programs are properly documented.
i. The functions of systems analyst, computer programmer, and computer operator are performed by different individuals.
j. The entity monitors which individuals access various programs and cross-checks this use against an authorized user listing.
k. Echo checks and parity checks are incorporated ("built in") to the computer hardware by the manufacturer.

LO H-3

H.68 **Automated Application Controls: Input Controls.** In its computerized processing system over payroll transactions, Brady Company enters the following data from its employees' attendance records (# corresponds to a numeric field; A corresponds to an alphabetic field):

- Employee number (###-##-####, the employees' Social Security number).

- Entity division (AA##, an alphanumeric field containing two letters corresponding to the location of the employee and two numbers corresponding to that employees' supervisor).
- Hours worked (###.##, a weekly total of hours worked in 0.25-hour increments).

After data entry, these data are processed against the information maintained in that employee's master file record. The records are accessed based on employee number. If the employee is an hourly employee, the number of hours worked is multiplied by the pay rate; if a salaried employee, the hours worked are checked against a range of acceptable hours. After the gross pay is determined, information in the master file record is used to calculate income tax, FICA, and other withholdings from that employee's pay.

Required:

Provide an example of how Brady Company might incorporate each of the following input controls to verify the accuracy of input of employee attendance record information.

a. Data entry and formatting controls.
b. Check digit.
c. Record counts.
d. Batch totals.
e. Hash totals.
f. Valid character tests.
g. Valid sign tests.
h. Limit or reasonableness tests.
i. Error correction and resubmission procedures.

LO H-2, H-3

H.69 **Identify Computer Control Weaknesses.** Ajax, Inc., an audit client, recently installed a new computerized processing system to process its shipping, billing, and accounts receivable records more efficiently. During interim work, an assistant completed the review of the computerized processing system and the internal controls. The assistant determined the following information concerning the new computerized processing system and the processing and control of shipping notices and customer invoices.

Each major computerized function (i.e., shipping, billing, accounts receivable) is permanently assigned to a specific computer operator who is responsible for making program changes, running the program, and reconciling the computer log. Responsibility for custody and control over the various databases and system documentation is randomly rotated among the computer operators on a monthly basis to prevent any one person from access to the database and documentation. Each computer programmer and computer operator has access to the computer room via a magnetic card and a digital code that is different for each card. The systems analyst and the supervisor of computer operators do not have access to the computer room.

The computer system documentation consists of the following items: program lists, error lists, logs, and database dictionaries. To increase efficiency, control totals (both batch totals and hash totals) and processing controls are not used in the system.

Ajax ships its products directly from two warehouses that forward shipping notices to general accounting. There, the billing clerk enters the price of the item and accounts for the numerical sequence of the shipping notices. The billing clerk also prepares daily summaries of the units shipped and the sales amounts. Shipping notices and summaries that are forwarded to the computer department for processing the computer output consist of the following:

- A three-copy invoice that is forwarded to the billing clerk.
- A daily sales register showing the aggregate totals of units shipped and sales amounts that the computer operator compares to the summaries.

The billing clerk mails two copies of each invoice to the customer and retains the third copy in an open invoice file that serves as a detail accounts receivable record.

Required:

a. Prepare a list of weaknesses in internal control (manual and computerized) and describe one or more ways to address each.
b. Suggest how Ajax's computerized processing over shipping and billing could be improved through the use of remote terminals to enter shipping notices. Describe appropriate computer controls for such an online data entry system.

LO H-2, H-3

H.70 **Identify Control Weaknesses and Recommendations.** Georgia Beemster, CPA, is examining the financial statements of the Louisville Sales Corporation, which recently installed a computerized processing system. The following comments have been extracted from Beemster's notes on computer operations and the processing and control of shipping notices and customer invoices:

- To minimize inconvenience, Louisville made the conversion to the new computerized processing system without changing its existing system. The vendor supervised the conversion and trained all computer department employees in systems design, operations, and programming.
- Each computer run is assigned to a specific employee who is responsible for making program changes, running the program, and answering questions. This procedure has the advantage of eliminating the need for records of computer operations because each employee is responsible for her or his own computer runs.
- At least one computer department employee remains in the computer room during office hours and only computer department employees have keys to the computer room.
- The vendor provided Louisville with systems documentation consisting of a set of record formats and program lists. This documentation and the files are maintained in the computer department.
- Louisville considered the desirability of computer controls but decided to retain the manual controls from its existing system.
- Louisville's products are shipped directly from public warehouses, which forward shipping notices to general accounting. There, a billing clerk enters the price of the items and accounts for the numerical sequence of shipping notices from each warehouse. The billing clerk also prepares daily summaries of the units shipped and the unit prices.
- Shipping notices and daily summaries are forwarded to the computer department for input and processing. Extension calculations are made on the computer. Output consists of invoices (in six copies) and a daily sales register. The daily sales register shows the aggregate totals of units shipped and unit prices, which the computer operator compares to the daily summaries.
- All copies of the invoice are returned to the billing clerk. The clerk mails three copies to the customer, forwards one copy to the warehouse, maintains one copy in a numerical file, and retains one copy in an open invoice file that serves as a detailed accounts receivable record.

Required:
Describe the weaknesses in the internal control over information and data flows and the procedures for processing shipping notices and customer invoices. Recommend some improvements in these control policies and procedures. Organize your answer sheet with two columns, one headed Weaknesses and the other headed Recommended Improvements.

(AICPA adapted)

LO H-3

H.71 **Automated Application Controls.** The following provides a brief description of the computerized payroll system used by Merriman in its biweekly processing of payroll for its employees.

1. Employees automatically record their attendance (hours worked) as they log in at the beginning and end of the workday.
2. At the end of each payroll period (every two weeks), employees print and authorize their attendance records, submitting them to their supervisor. The computer prenumbers these attendance records and generates them in chronological order based on when the employee submits his or her final attendance for that payroll period.
3. Supervisors review the attendance records submitted by their employees and authorize these records, which the supervisors then forward to data entry conversion operators.
4. Data conversion operators input the attendance record number, employee number, and hours worked from the attendance records that have been approved by the employee supervisors into a file to be used for computerized processing.
5. Once the entire batch of records has been accepted for processing, the computer program accesses the payroll master file data. Gross salary is then calculated as follows:
    - Gross salary for hourly wage employees is determined by multiplying the number of hours worked from the transaction file by the wage rate contained in that employee's master file record.

- Gross salary for salaried employees is determined directly from the employee's master file record.
6. After the calculation of gross salary, information from the employee's payroll master file data as well as federal income tax and FICA withholding tables, is used to calculate deductions from that employee's pay.
7. A payroll register is generated, distributed, and reviewed for reasonableness and obvious processing errors.
8. Following the review of the payroll register, funds are transferred into the account designated by the employee (for those employees who have authorized electronic transfer of funds) or paychecks are prepared and held for employees (for employees who have not authorized electronic transfer of funds).

Required:
For each of the preceding steps in Merriman's payroll processing, identify appropriate controls that the company has either implemented or should implement to ensure the authorized and accurate processing of payroll transactions.

LO H-3

H.72 **Flowchart Control Points.** Each number of the flowchart in Exhibit H.72.1 identifies a control point in the computerized payroll processing system. List the control points and, for each point, describe the type of internal control procedure that should be implemented.

LO H-6

H.73 **Internal Control Considerations in End-User Computing Environments.** Because of the use of personal computers by many businesses, audit teams must know about the potential internal control weaknesses inherent in such an environment. This knowledge is crucial if audit teams are to make a proper assessment of the related control risk and to plan an effective and efficient audit approach.

EXHIBIT H.72.1
Flowchart Control Points

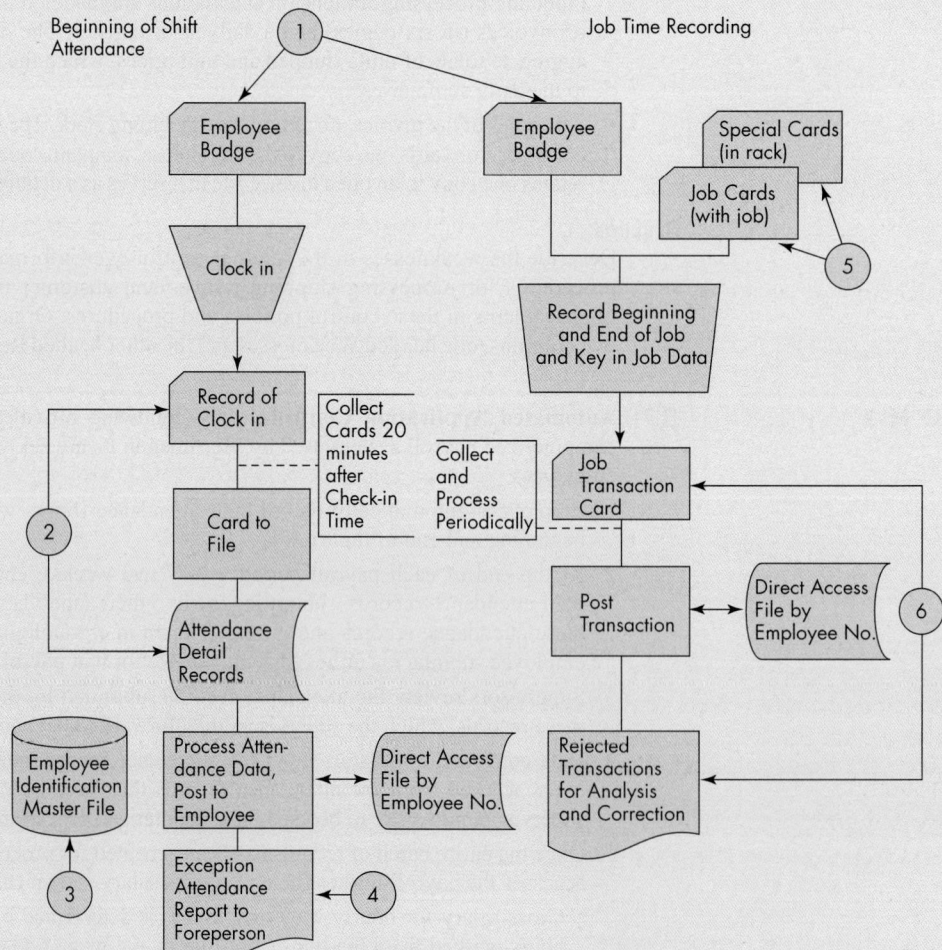

Required:

In the following case study, assume that you are participating in the audit of Chicago Appliance Company and that the background information was obtained during the planning phase of the engagement. You have been asked to (a) consider the potential internal control weaknesses that exist in this end-user application and (b) assess how those internal control weaknesses could alter the audit plan for the current year.

BACKGROUND INFORMATION

Chicago Appliance is a wholesale distributor of electric appliances. Its sales in each of the last two years have been approximately $40 million. All accounting applications are handled at Chicago's corporate office.

Computerized processing operations have historically centered on an onsite mainframe computer. The computer applications include accounts payable and cash disbursements, payroll, inventory, and general ledger. Accounts receivable and fixed asset records have been prepared manually in the past. Internal controls in all areas have been considered strong in the last few years.

During the past year, financial management decided to automate the processing of sales, accounts receivable, and fixed asset transactions and accounting. Management also concluded that purchasing personal computers (PCs) and related available software was more cost effective than increasing the mainframe computer capacity and hiring a second computer operator. The controller and accounting clerks have been encouraged to find additional uses for the PCs and to "experiment" with them when they are not too busy.

The accounts receivable clerk is enthusiastic about the PCs, but the fixed-asset clerk seems somewhat apprehensive about them because he has limited prior experience with computers. The accounts receivable clerk explained that the controller had purchased a "very easy-to-use" accounts receivable software application program for the PC, which enables her to input the daily information regarding billings and receipts quickly and easily. The controller has added some personally developed programs to the software to give it better report-writing features.

During a recent demonstration, the accounts receivable clerk explained that the program required her to input only the customer's name and invoice amount in the case of billings or the customer's name and check amount in the case of receipts. The computer then automatically updates the respective customer's account balance. At the end of every month, the clerk prints and reconciles the accounts receivable trial balance to the general ledger balance and the controller reviews the reconciliation.

The fixed asset program also was purchased from an outside vendor. The controller indicated that the software package had just recently been put on the market and that it was programmed to compute tax depreciation based on recent changes in the federal tax laws. The controller also stated that, because of the fixed asset clerk's reluctance to use the computer, information from the manual fixed asset records had been input. The controller indicated, however, that the fixed asset clerk would be responsible for the future processing related to the fixed asset files and for generating the month-end and year-end reports used to prepare the related accounting entries.

The various accounts receivable and fixed asset files are all adequately labeled as to the type of program or data file. They are arranged in an organized manner near the PC.

(Adapted from a case contributed by
PricewaterhouseCoopers to *The Auditor's Report*.)

LO H-3, H-5

H.74 Test Data Transactions in a Payroll Processing Program. Use the computer-based electronic audit documentation on the textbook website to perform a test of the computerized payroll processing program.

The electronic audit documentation contains a simple program that accepts payroll transaction input and calculates an individual's weekly gross and net pay. When you come to the proper place in the program, you will see places to input these data:

- Employee identification (Social Security number).
- Regular pay rate (round dollars, no cents).
- Regular time (hours, 40 or fewer).
- Overtime (hours over 40).
- Gross earnings to date (gross pay prior to this payroll entry).

According to the client's description of the computer controls in the system:

1. The program checks for valid employee identification.
2. The regular pay rate is tested for reasonableness.
3. The system will accept no more than 40 regular-time hours.
4. There is a limit on the number of overtime hours that will be paid (72 hours). Overtime hours are only paid if the employee works 40 regular-time hours.
5. Overtime is paid at the rate of 150 percent of the regular pay rate.
6. Social Security and Medicare taxes and federal income tax withholdings are calculated automatically according to applicable laws and regulations.

Applicable Laws and Regulations (assume the following for this case)
- The minimum wage is $7.25 per regular hour.
- Social Security tax is 6.2 percent on the first $106,800 of gross pay and Medicare tax is 1.45 percent of all pay.
- Federal income tax withholding is assumed to be 23 percent of gross pay.

Required:
The payroll calculation program contains control deficiencies. Your job is to identify and describe them. Follow the instructions in the electronic audit documentation. Devise and enter test transactions of your own making. Write a memo to the audit partner identifying and describing the control failures in the payroll calculation program.

Cases

▼ Andersen: An Obstruction of Justice?

PROBLEM

Most students are familiar with Andersen as a CPA firm that failed to detect fraudulent financial activities in the audits of several companies including Sunbeam, Waste Management, Enron, and WorldCom. Although much has been written about the quality of these audits and how increasing the firm's revenues from both audit and nonaudit services may have supplanted audit quality as the main objective of Andersen as a firm, we should not lose sight of the facts that led to Andersen's demise and the findings that have occurred since Andersen ostensibly closed its doors as an audit and accounting firm.

In effect, Andersen had already received the maximum penalty even before the trial began. Once Anderson had been indicted, most of its clients had decided that an audit by a firm under indictment would be of little value even if allowed by the Securities and Exchange Commission (SEC). During the shareholder proxy season in early 2002, company after company announced it would no longer retain Andersen as its auditor. Whether the firm was able to defend itself or not, the days of Andersen as a viable audit firm had come to an end.

ANDERSEN GOES TO TRIAL

In May 2002, Andersen LLP was tried for obstruction of justice in connection with the destruction of documents during a time period prior to a formal SEC investigation of Enron, one of Andersen's largest clients. The main witness for the prosecution was David Duncan, a former Andersen partner in charge of the Enron audit, who had already pled guilty to obstruction of justice. The guilt or innocence of Andersen hinged on the question of corporate direction. If Duncan had acted illegally on his own in an effort to save himself from consequences resulting from an SEC investigation of Enron, then Andersen as a firm would not likely be found guilty of obstructing justice. However, if Duncan had acted illegally on the direction of Andersen's management within the scope of his position in an attempt to save Andersen from the consequences of Enron, the firm as a whole would be held liable. Therefore, the issues to be determined were whether (1) illegal acts had been committed and (2) had they been committed on behalf of Duncan or on behalf of Andersen.

The Prosecution's Case

The chief prosecutor for the government was Samuel Bruell. The main points in Bruell's case follow:

- Top partners in Andersen's Chicago office had permitted Enron to use aggressive accounting practices that were very questionable given the nature of Enron's business.
- In late September through early October 2001, Andersen's legal department had begun creating a strategy designed to protect Andersen from regulators and litigants.
- A major part of the strategy was to invoke Andersen's document retention policy, which, according to prosecutors, was an obscure policy that its employees seldom read or followed on its audits. In addition, the policy had been revised in 2000 by an Andersen partner who had been disciplined by the SEC for his involvement in the Waste Management audits. According to Bruell, management had known that invoking the policy would lead to the

destruction of "tons of papers and tens of thousands of computer files" that would be of interest to investigators.[1]

- The prosecution presented notes from an October 9 conversation between Nancy Temple, Andersen's legal council, and attorneys in Andersen's legal department. This conversation indicated that Temple had believed an SEC investigation was imminent and that such an investigation could have devastating consequences for Andersen. Andersen was still operating under a court order signed in 2000 (due to a settlement of the Waste Management lawsuits) that could trigger a suspension of its license to audit publicly traded companies if it was found to have engaged in additional securities law violations.
- Duncan had admitted to destroying documents to keep them out of the investigation and that his actions were taken under direction and with the consent of Andersen management in Chicago.
- Finally, C. E. Andrews, an Andersen partner, in his testimony before Congress in January 2002, had said that Duncan had given every appearance of destroying documents in anticipation of requests for documents from federal investigators.[2]

Andersen's Defense

Andersen's attorneys, led by Rusty Hardin, defended Andersen against all charges brought by the government.

- The government's case had fallen short of proving Andersen's guilt or even proving that a crime had occurred.
- Duncan had shredded documents prior to any formal investigation (Andersen was not subpoenaed until November 8, 2001) and the elimination of unnecessary documents was a normal audit procedure.
- It was clearly sound business practice to consult with the corporate attorneys with regard to potential litigation and the firm's rights and obligations with regard to that investigation. In fact, Duncan, at Temple's request, had saved many documents that could have proved detrimental to Andersen.
- Hardin argued that Duncan was innocent and that the government had overstated its case against him in order to pressure him to cooperate with its investigation in exchange for a reduced sentence.
- While the prosecution focused on the part of the document retention policy that instructed auditors on the documents that could be destroyed, parts of the retention policy indicated which documentation was required to be retained in the audit files.

THE CASE GOES TO THE JURY

Although the prosecution and defense presentations were very contentious, possibly the most contentious part of the case focused on the instructions that Judge Melinda Harmon gave to the jury. The instructions hinged on the wording of the statute that makes it a crime to

> *knowingly* use intimidation or physical force, threaten, or *corruptly persuade* another person . . . with intent to . . . cause that person to withhold documents from or alter documents for use in an official proceeding [emphasis added].[3]

Although both sides believed that the jury needed instructions that clarified the meaning of the statute in question, two issues were paramount in the argument concerning the instructions:

1. The phrase *knowingly . . . corruptly persuade* had been discussed at length. The government had contended that the word *knowingly* was not meant as a modifier of the term *corruptly persuade*. The jury had been instructed that

   > Even if the petitioner honestly and sincerely believed that the conduct was lawful, you may find the petitioner guilty.[4]

---

[1] Alexi Barrionuevo and Jonathan Weil, "High Noon: Andersen's Criminal Case Goes to the Jury," *The Wall Street Journal*, June 6, 2002, pp. C1, C20.
[2] Ibid.
[3] 18 U.S.C. § 1512 (b)(2)(a) and (b).
[4] William Rehnquist, "Flawed Instruction Led to Andersen Verdict," *Chicago Daily Law Bulletin*, June 1, 2005.

2. The government had contended that the word *corruptly* needed to be defined for the jury. Prior rulings in the 5th district court (the same court district that was trying the Andersen case) had stated that *corruptly* was

   knowingly and *dishonestly,* with specific intent to *subvert or undermine* the integrity of the proceedings [emphasis added].[5]

   The government had insisted on excluding the word *dishonestly* and adding the word *impede* to the phrase "subvert and undermine." The instruction provided to the jury had not included the word *dishonestly* and included the phrase "subvert, undermine, or impede" government fact finding.

Having heard the testimony and been given these instructions, the jury convicted Andersen of obstruction of justice after deliberating for 10 days.

ROUND TWO

On May 31, 2005, in a unanimous decision, the U.S. Supreme Court overturned the Andersen conviction on the basis of flawed instructions to the jury. In writing the opinion, Chief Justice William Rehnquist cited the following arguments:

- Merely providing a person with information regarding a course of action cannot be construed as **persuading** another person . . . with **intent** to . . . *cause* that person to withhold documents.
- It is not necessarily **corrupt** in *persuading another person . . . with intent to . . . cause* that person to withhold documents. It may be proper for an attorney to persuade a client to withhold documents under attorney-client privilege from an investigation. In this circumstance, such persuasion would not be corrupt. Therefore, the withholding of documents from an investigation cannot by itself be presumed to be a *corrupt* action.
- Document retention polices are created to keep documents from being obtained by certain individuals and organizations, including the government. These policies are common in business and it is not wrongful for a manager to instruct employees to abide by such a policy.
- The term *knowingly* does modify the term *corrupt* both linguistically and per the intent of the statute. The jury instructions did not convey the requisite consciousness of wrongdoing that should be required for conviction.
- Substituting the term *impede* in place of *dishonestly* in the jury instructions removed the requirement that the action be with knowledge and forethought of wrongdoing. The term *impede* has a much broader concept. Anyone who innocently persuades another to withhold information might be considered to impede an investigation. Clearly, the term *corruptly* was included in the statute to exclude such innocent behavior from being consisted unlawful.
- A *knowingly corrupt persuader* cannot be someone who persuades others to shred documents under a document retention policy that was not enacted with regard to any particular proceeding in which those documents might be material. A series of events is not sufficient to indicate an intent to obstruct an investigation.

CONCLUSION

The headlines following the Supreme Court decision were telling:

"A Posthumous Victory," *USA Today,* June 1, 2005.
"Arthur Andersen's Hollow Victory," *The Economist,* June 4, 2005.
"Too Late for Andersen," *Legal Times,* June 6, 2005.
"A Bittersweet Court Victory for Andersen," *Legal Times,* June 6, 2005.

Although Andersen's verdict had been overturned because of faulty jury instructions, it was far from a vindication that what Andersen had done was correct. In addition, such a decision came much too late to provide anything but a moral victory to Andersen's former employees.

It is unlikely that the government will retry Andersen. First, there is little to gain in terms of either financial or other penalties. Andersen has already received the "death penalty" (and is no longer a viable entity), whether guilty or innocent. Second, should Andersen be retried and be

---

[5] Ibid.

found not guilty, the Department of Justice and the SEC would suffer severe blows to their reputation and receive a multitude of criticism from the business community. On the other hand, a retrial might be what the government needs to fend off criticism of being overzealous and overreaching in its prosecution of Andersen. But it does appear that the risks outweigh the rewards. Third, the government has received everything that it wanted with regard to Enron, WorldCom, and Andersen with the passage of the Sarbanes-Oxley Act. Most notably, a result of the Andersen case is a stricter document retention policy with more severe penalties for not following that policy.

It is interesting to note that many legal experts believe that the Department of Justice and the SEC took a vastly different attitude toward the 2005 tax-shelter problems of KPMG because of the lessons learned from the Andersen prosecution. Clearly, in the Andersen case, there had been no winners and the elimination of another international CPA firm would cause additional harm to innocent employees and create additional chaos in the business community.

Finally, in March 2007, a federal judge gave final approval to a $72.5 million settlement between Andersen and investors who sued the accounting firm over its role in Enron's collapse.[6] This finally put to rest the case of Andersen and Enron, but the repercussions may live on indefinitely.

DISCUSSION QUESTIONS

1. Look up the term *corrupt* in the dictionary. What is its definition? Was *corrupt* appropriately applied to the actions of Andersen?
2. The issues that overturned the Andersen verdict were based on faulty jury instructions, not on whether Andersen was in fact guilty or innocent. Based on the information in this case and other information you know, do you believe Andersen violated the law?
3. Do you believe that the Supreme Court's opinion overturning the lower court's decision was appropriate?
4. Should the SEC and the Department of Justice have tried Andersen as a firm or should they have targeted specific individuals who had engaged in acts the two bodies believed to be unlawful?
5. Although Andersen's conviction was overturned, do you believe that its employees acted in an ethical manner?
6. Comment on the actions of David Duncan and Nancy Temple. Which of these parties do you believe was more responsible for the Andersen saga?
7. The class action lawsuit against Andersen also named the Canadian Imperial Bank of Commerce, J.P. Morgan Chase, Citigroup, Merrill Lynch, and Credit Suisse Group as codefendants with Andersen. Why would the plaintiffs name so many entities in their lawsuit? Merrill Lynch and Credit Suisse asked a U.S. appeals court to rule that the complaint should not have been certified as a class action suit. Why would these entities make such a claim?

[6] Jeff Feely, "Settlement Approved for Enron Investors," *Washington Post*, March 10, 2007.

⏷ PTL Club—The Harbinger of Things to Come?

The PTL scandal is a picture-perfect, suitable-for-framing example of how auditors with a modicum of skepticism and alertness could have been heroes instead of goats. PTL was an accident waiting to happen even before Tammy got the notion that heading to the mall was the perfect cure for her blues. Auditors who were concerned with doing more than the absolute bare minimum required by GAAS and GAAP could have exposed this fraud much earlier, saving innocent and gullible viewers tens of millions of dollars.

Robert A. Prentice, "Anatomy of a Fraud: Inside the Finances of the PTL Ministries,"
American Business Law Journal, *November 1, 1993*

In January 1974, Jim and Tammy Bakker launched the PTL Club, which for more than a decade was one of the most successful television ministries. At its peak, the PTL Club broadcast from nearly 200 television stations to a national audience estimated at 12 million viewers. PTL stood for both "Praise the Lord" and "People That Love." The Bakkers combined a traditional talk show format with religious entertainment, emotional personal testimonies, and frequent campaigns for financial support. The Bakkers established a Christian theme park, Heritage USA, which attracted fundamentalist Christians for prayer and fun. They had the country's third most popular amusement park with biblically themed rides and attractions and a large shopping mall selling Christian tapes, records, books, and religious action figures. At its height in 1986, more than 5 million people visited Heritage USA annually, and the PTL Club was raising $10 million a month.

The Bakker's ministry was so popular that, in the final days of the 1980 presidential campaign, Jimmy Carter summoned Jim Bakker to pray with him aboard Air Force One. Ronald Reagan invited Jim and Tammy to his first inaugural, and three years later, Reagan told the National Association of Religious Broadcasters' convention that "The PTL TV network is carrying out a master plan for people that love."[1]

While millions of people tuned into the PTL Club for its entertainment and religious inspiration, it had many detractors. Many concluded that "PTL" stood for "Pass the Loot," a reference to the Bakkers' frequent, passionate fund-raising appeals and to Jim and Tammy's lavish lifestyle. The Bakkers' perceived excesses included

- A vacation retreat in the Great Smoky Mountains.
- A $449,000 Palm Springs home with a spectacular view of the Santa Rosa Mountains from the heated pool and hot tub (remember to think 1980s dollars).
- Vacations in $350-a-night hotel suites in Hawaii.
- A 1981 Christmas bash for PTL executives at Cafe Eugene in Charlotte that included $9,000 worth of truffles flown in from Brussels.
- An ocean-front condominium near Palm Beach, which PTL bought for the Bakkers and spent more than $200,000 to furnish. (The Bakker's had recently made a vow to be "good stewards of God's money.")
- A $340,000 five-level lakeside home with another $73,000 in renovations and, of course, a 43-foot houseboat tied to the dock.
- A heated and air-conditioned doghouse for Tammy's dogs.
- Tammy's minks and Gucci handbags.
- A new Mercedes, a 1953 Rolls-Royce, a Corvette, and several Cadillac limousines.
- A basement health spa and indoor pool in their home in Heritage USA. In his dressing room, Bakker installed gold-plated bathroom fixtures and an $11,000 sauna and Jacuzzi.

---

[1] Art Harris, "The Good Life at PTL: A Litany of Excess," *The Washington Post*, May 22, 1987, P. A1.

The crown jewel in the Bakkers' opulent lifestyle was the 4,000-square-foot suite at the PTL ministry's Heritage USA theme park and retreat. The "presidential suite" in the Heritage Grand Hotel was designed for use by the Bakkers, although they often preferred their nearby lakeside home. The suite included gold-plated swan bathroom fixtures, antique beds, and mirrored walls in the bedroom. The suite also included Tammy's 10-by-60-foot closet. While other celebrities also used the presidential suite, they had to be cleared through Bakker's office. One prosecutor noted the hypocritical conduct in the suite. "People sent their money in for an attractive place where there was no smoking, no alcohol—no alcohol except for Mr. Bakker in the Presidential Suite,"[2] referring to Bakker's secret taste for wine and vodka screwdrivers that former staffers detailed in interviews with *The Washington Post*.

Bakker's frequent explanation for his expenditures was that "God wants his people to go first class." At the same time, this lifestyle inspired Ray Stevens' country song, "Would Jesus Wear a Rolex on His Television Show?"

TROUBLE IN PARADISE

The world of PTL and Heritage USA began to collapse in 1987. Jim Bakker had a tryst with church secretary, Jessica Hahn. The PTL Club paid her $256,000 to drop her $12 million lawsuit (later to be characterized as a bribe or "hush money" in court). The Internal Revenue Service questioned $1.3 million of PTL expenditures for the Bakkers, threatening the PTL's tax-exempt status (which eventually was revoked and the organization eventually had to pay back taxes and penalties). The Pentecostal Assemblies of God, which had ordained Bakker, defrocked him.

A confidential payroll account was kept without the board's knowledge. When Laventhol & Horwath (L & H) became PTL's auditor in May 1985, William Spear, a senior L & H partner, "kept the books" for this secret account. After writing checks for each other, friends, or themselves, the Bakkers or other top executives would call Spears with the information so the check register would be accurate and additional funds could be transferred if the account balance dwindled. Prosecutors categorized this fund as "unrecorded payroll"; creditors who lost millions and defrauded donors called it a "slush fund."

The funds for all these activities were primarily generated from partnership interests sold in four different resort hotels built or planned at Heritage USA. These resort properties were to be financed solely by selling "lifetime partnerships" to persons "donating" $1,000. Similar to a timeshare, the donors received four days and three nights for their immediate family in one of the resort hotels, annually, for the rest of their lives. To induce donors to provide money, Bakker supposedly limited the number of partnerships in each project and often exaggerated the number of lifetime partnerships that had been sold. Although the money from selling partnership interests was to be used only for construction of the buildings, more than $100 million was diverted from just two of the projects to fund PTL day-to-day operations.

Eventually, many more than the limited number of lifetime memberships were sold, making it physically impossible for every member to exercise their hotel rights. Bakker sold more than 66,000 partnerships in his Heritage Grand Hotel, although he promised followers only 25,000 would be sold, and 74,000 partnerships in the never-finished Towers Hotel, even though he had said only 30,000 would be sold. The followers contributed $158 million between 1984 and 1987 for the partnerships. In addition, a lifetime partnership could be worth over a million dollars if a family of five came to PTL each year and used all facilities and other perks associated with their membership. In the criminal case against Bakker, the government characterized the financing of building operations through lifetime partnerships as a giant "Ponzi" scheme.

WHERE WAS THE OVERSIGHT?

Following PTL's bankruptcy, evidence surfaced indicating that the PTL's board of directors had functioned improperly. When Jim Bakker needed money, he simply told other key PTL officials to tell a board member to introduce a resolution recommending a bonus. The board met 23 times between July 5, 1983, and February 16, 1987, when it approved bonuses ranging from $10,000 to $390,000 for Jim Bakker 13 times. In 21 of those meetings, the board also approved bonuses of $2,000 to $170,000 for Tammy Bakker. From June 1986 to March 1987, Jim and Tammy Bakker received more than $1 million and $335,000 in bonuses, respectively. These bonuses were over and above salary and expenses the Bakkers used to maintain their lavish lifestyles. From 1984 to

---

[2] Art Harris, "Jim Bakker, Driven by Money or Miracles?" The Washington Post, August 29, 1989, p. C1.

1987, they received more than $4.8 million in salary, bonuses, and other payments. Each of two other PTL executives, David Taggart and Richard Dortch, received bonuses of almost half a million dollars. Despite receiving this exorbitant amount of money, Jim Bakker announced on TV that he was too poor to buy his $1,000 lifetime membership this month but would put it on his credit card (as viewers were urged to do) and pay for it the following month.

WHAT DID THE AUDITORS KNOW?

The mid-1980s had six very large international accountings firms (called the *Big-Six*) including Deloitte, Haskins & Sells (now a part of Deloitte and Touche), PTL's auditor until May 1985. Laventhol & Horwath (L & H) was then the seventh largest accounting firm. Jim Bakker used both of these highly regarded firms to reassure his viewers of the PTL Club's financial integrity. He often appeared on television to present audited financial statements as indicators of his personal honesty and the PTL Club's financial integrity. After all, PTL paid large fees to nationally reputable accounting firms to inspect its books. Would someone hiding financial misconduct do that? For example, on April 18, 1986, in the midst of allegations against Jim Bakker, he told his television audience:

> We don't mind letting you know that we print audits of this ministry. We have done it for, what, ten years now, and we go through an audit almost a hundred percent of the time. An outside auditing firm, one of the big audit firms of America, is in here at all times auditing this ministry at our own expense, thousands of dollars, tens of thousands of dollars, to be responsible. And we are going to go forward, but it's time God's people say enough is enough.[3]

However, as Jim Bakker repeatedly used the auditors' good reputation to assure his audiences of the PTL Club's honesty and integrity, the accounting firms should have known that Jim Bakker was misleading PTL members.

Deloitte admitted that it had known of the advertised limit on the sale of memberships but argued that no oversales occurred until shortly after May 31, 1984, the end of the fiscal year for which it had prepared its last PTL financial statements. However, it took considerable criticism for not knowing or reporting on the oversale occurring shortly after May 31, 1984, because its report was dual dated August 31, 1984, and October 24, 1984. (While auditing standards specify the auditors' responsibilities for subsequent events when the report is dual dated, the judicial system and the court of public opinion may not always see these responsibilities similarly.) Conversely, L & H admitted that it had known that more than 25,000 Grand Hotel lifetime partnerships had been sold but denied that it had any knowledge that a limit was placed on the number of partnerships even though this limit was widely publicized.

Both Deloitte and L & H wrote checks from the PTL secret account to the Bakkers and other key employees (but did not sign them to avoid an obvious conflict of interest with their audit roles). Both firms prepared the Bakkers' tax returns. Tax law prohibits tax-exempt organizations from providing excessive private enumeration. Both accounting firms claimed to have been unaware that the IRS was seriously considering revoking PTL's tax-exempt status due to the compensation being paid to the Bakkers. Furthermore, after one outside law firm resigned because of concerns over excessive compensation, PTL's new law firm argued that the compensation was not excessive because the auditors reviewed the amounts paid.

Many red flags should have been evident to both audit firms. Although legal issues were raised regarding the lifetime partner concept, neither audit firm had indicated that this concept presented audit issues. Deloitte had addressed its concerns about the excessive compensation; the dramatically increasing personal expenses of senior executives; and the selling of merchandise at astronomical markups (PTL purchased statues of David and Goliath for $10 and represented them on television as being worth $1,000). But these issues did not lead to a modified audit report opinion or other disclosures.

Financial documentation was often designed to hide items from the auditors. For example, bonuses were not recorded in the minutes of the board of directors meetings but in "addendums" to the minutes that were added at a later date. A year's worth of records regarding travel and other expenses were "lost" and were never provided to L & H. Auditors could not find documentation for other expenditures, including $27 million of $80 million spent on construction projects.

---

[3] Robert A. Prentice, "Anatomy of a Fraud: Inside the Finances of the PTL Ministries," *American Business Law Journal*, November 1, 1993.

In a 23-page memo, Deloitte spent 22 pages listing inadequacies in PTL's internal controls. Both accounting firms knew that PTL had an unreasonably high number of separate bank accounts and a tremendous problem with bounced checks. A draft of Deloitte's 1984 audit report expressed a concern over "whether PTL would be able to continue as 'a going concern' based on current assets of only $8.6 million against $28.5 million in current liabilities." A going concern issue was not included, however, in the issued audit report.

AFTER THE FALL

Jim Bakker relinquished his ministry after admitting to the extramarital tryst, and he and his wife, Tammy Faye, exiled themselves to Palm Springs, California. In March 1987, to help avoid bankruptcy and restore its reputation, the PTL Club's new boards appointed the Rev. Jerry Falwell, then a well-respected and well-known television minister, to take over the organization. He was to defend the PTL Club against legal threats from creditors, disgruntled contributors, and the IRS.

The IRS Examination Report contended that tax-exempt rules had been violated because of excessive payments to Bakker, his family, and other PTL officers. Revenue examiners asserted that Bakker's compensation of $968,000 in a three-year period was "unreasonable" and that his total compensation should not have exceeded $331,000. PTL Club lawyers argued that Bakker's compensation was reasonable "because he is the guiding light of the ministry and is the key to PTL's success in fund raising."[4]

The PTL Club hired Arthur Andersen to extensively audit PTL activities in an effort to gain a true picture of its financial position. Besides those problems already outlined, the new auditors found the following:

- $92 million in funds that could not be accounted for (later reduced to $12 million as PTL executives found documents).
- $71 million debt.
- Missing records documenting $27 million in construction expenditures. (Building contractors insisted that they submitted the records to PTL as they performed the work.)
- Operating losses of $27 million sustained by the organization in the nine months preceding Bakker's resignation.

Based on the new information, PTL officials were convinced that Bakker knew that the ministry's financial situation was out of control long before the scandal over the sexual encounter forced him to step down.

LAVENTHOL & HORWATH

Founded in 1915 in New York, Horwath & Horwath merged in 1967 with Laventhol Krekstein Griffith & Co. of Philadelphia. L & H experienced massive growth exemplified by a nearly quadrupling of revenues during the 1980s, fueled through acquisitions by developing expertise in unique areas of practice and by accepting risky clients. From 1984 to 1990, L & H acquired 64 small practices increasing its revenues to $345 million. At its peak, the firm had more than 50 offices and 460 partners. Merging so many practices and commensurate different cultures created a patchwork of ethics and values and a sense that increasing the revenue stream was the firm's paramount objective. The drive for growth led the firm to accept clients without appropriately screening them and to accept clients known to be risky.

L & H often sought expertise that pushed the envelope. One of its most notable and lucrative revenue streams was finding tax write-offs for investors in hotels. This practice waned when the IRS reformed the tax code. L & H also developed a specialty in services to the commercial real estate industry, an industry which, in the late 1980s, was mired in an economic recession that resulted in empty buildings and falling prices. One client was pushing a bogus tax shelter involving genetically engineered cows, resulting in L & H's being the first accounting firm to lose a jury trial under federal racketeering law. L & H often found itself in court fighting allegations of sloppy audit work. Following the filing of lawsuits associated with their PTL work, the firm had 115 legal actions against it, seeking a total of $362 million.

L & H tried to survive despite the legal and fiscal pressures. Before its collapse, employees had accepted a 10 percent pay cut, and the payments to retired partners were significantly cut. Still, the

[4] Gary Klott, "PTL's Ledgers: Missing Records and Rising Debt," The New York Times, June 6, 1987, sect. 1, p. 8.

firm found itself so short of cash that appeals from employees to borrow money occurred daily. Finally, the firm gathered its partners in Houston for a special meeting to address the critical situation. The vote was unanimous to dissolve Laventhol, resulting in what was then the largest collapse of an accounting firm. On November 21, 1990, Laventhol & Horwath declared bankruptcy and 3,273 employees were out of work.

GOING TO COURT

In a 28-page indictment, Jim Bakker was charged with 24 counts of fraud and conspiracy. The jury convicted Bakker, who was sentenced to 45 years in prison (the sentence was reduced on appeal and Bakker was in prison only from 1989 to 1994). In a civil case brought by disgruntled lifetime partners, Bakker was found liable for common law fraud and almost $130 million in damages (although no money was ever collected). The same jury exonerated Deloitte & Touche (successor to Deloitte, Haskins & Sells) from fraud because the intention (scienter) to aid in the fraud had not been proved.

Richard Dortch, PTL's former second in command, and Bakker aides David and James Taggart were also charged. Dortch, who was to have stood trial with Bakker, agreed to plead guilty to four counts of conspiracy and fraud and was sentenced to eight years (later reduced to two years) in prison and a $200,000 fine. His light sentence was in part due to his agreement to testify against Bakker. Taggart, former PTL executive vice president, received the maximum sentence of 18 years and 5 months on a conviction for income tax evasion. His brother, James Taggart, PTL's decorator, was sentenced to 17 years and 9 months.

L & H declared bankruptcy to shield itself from lawsuits, debt repayment (much of which was incurred to finance its acquisitions), and other liabilities. Once L & H declared bankruptcy, all lawsuits, including the PTL lawsuits, were suspended, and in 1992, the bankruptcy court combined the PTL claims and other lawsuits into the bankruptcy proceedings. PTL creditors and members joined a long list of creditors in bankruptcy court with total claims of nearly $2 billion. A federal bankruptcy court approved a plan to collect $47 million from 629 partners and other professional-level firm members, although L & H was not "conceding any allegations in the complaint."[5] The assessments, which were to be paid over 10 years, averaged between $75,000 and $400,000 per employee. Although PTL creditors received only a few cents on the dollar, members received nothing.

CONCLUSION

The AICPA has stated that the accounting profession must learn from past cases to prevent the reoccurrences of similar detrimental activities. Although the PTL engagement by itself did not destroy L & H, it contributed greatly at a time when the firm was already awash in debt and legal proceedings. PTL became the proverbial "straw that broke the camel's back." Furthermore, the PTL engagement is viewed as emblematic of the types of clients and quality of audit work that characterized Laventhol in the mid-1980s.

The L & H case changed the face of the accounting profession. Historically, the accounting profession had demanded that accountants practice as partnerships on the theory that professionals should stand by their work and not be shielded from the costs of their mistakes. It also made financial sense to adopt that structure because profits in a partnership are divided and taxed to the individual. Corporations, on the other hand are taxed twice; once as a company and then as individuals on their corporate dividends. After Laventhol, the accounting profession moved to organizing under limited liability partnerships (LLP) and companies (LLC). These structures provide legal protection to the partners and top executives in the firm.

DISCUSSION QUESTIONS

1. What similar factors led to the demise of both Laventhol & Horwath and Andersen?
2. The AICPA stated that the profession must learn from past cases to prevent reoccurrences of similar detrimental activities. Do you believe that Andersen's partners would have adopted a different management philosophy if they had recently studied the Laventhol & Horwath case?
3. Although audit reports should provide assurance to investors and creditors that financial information presented is free of material misstatements and in accordance with GAAP, should audit reports be used to solicit investments, credit, or sales in a manner similar to Jim Bakker's? How can a CPA firm prevent such behavior?

---

[5] "Laventhol Bankruptcy Plan," *The New York Times*, August 25, 1992.

4. During the trial, Mary K. Cline, senior auditor for Deloitte, Haskins and Sells stated:

   "Well, we made a lot of judgments during the audit, and we were auditing the balance sheet as of May 31, and there was no reason in my judgment to look at this number after May 31."[6]

   a. Should the oversale of lifetime partnerships be classified as a subsequent event?
   b. Should Deloitte have evaluated the sales occurring after the balance sheet date of May 31, 1984?
   c. Should L & H been aware of the sales limits on lifetime memberships? If so, what should they have done about it?

5. Why do you think audit firms are willing to accept high-risk clients?
6. What analytical and audit procedures could have led Deloitte and L & H to have more easily detected and reported PTL Club's financial problems?
7. Why would a staff auditor want to be "part of the client's team" and consent to questionable practices rather than being an "independent watchdog" and contest such practices?
8. How could the auditors have known and understood the PTL business better in order to audit more efficiently and effectively?
9. Is it the auditors' responsibility to verify that the client meets tax-exempt status?
10. Did the preparation of checks violate the auditors Code of Ethics?

ADDITIONAL SOURCES

Carol F. Venable, "Anatomy of a Fraud: Inside the Finances of the PTL Ministries," *American Business Law Journal,* November 1, 1993.

Gary L. Tidwell, *Anatomy of a Fraud: Inside the Finances of the PTL Ministries* (New York: John Wiley, 1993).

Alison Leigh Cowan, "Bankruptcy Filing by Laventhol," *The New York Times,* November 22, 1990, p. 1.

J. Weber and M. Galen, "Behind the Fall of Laventhol," *BusinessWeek,* December 24, 1990, pp. 54–55.

William E. Schmidt, "For Jim and Tammy Bakker, Excess Wiped Out a Rapid Climb to Success," *The New York Times,* May 16, 1987, p. 8.

"Former Leader of PTL Ministry Is Found Liable for $130 Million," *The New York Times,* December 15, 1990, p. 12.

Art Harris and Michael Isikoff, "The Good Life at PTL: A Litany of Excess," *The Washington Post,* May 22, 1987, p. A1.

Art Harris, "Jim Bakker, Driven by Money or Miracles?" *The Washington Post,* August 29, 1989, p. C1.

Richard N. Ostling and Joseph J. Kane, "Jim Bakker's Crumbling World," *Time,* December 19, 1988, p. 72.

"Laventhol Bankruptcy Plan," *The New York Times,* August 25, 1992, p. D2.

Gregory Richards, "The Other Big Accounting Firm Meltdown—Laventhol & Horwath's Final Days: a 'Sad Tragedy to Watch'," *Philadelphia Business Journal,* August 2, 2002.

Michael Isikoff, "PTL Contributors Sue Ministry's Accounting Firm," *The Washington Post,* November 19, 1987, p. C10.

Gary Klott, "PTL's Ledgers: Missing Records and Rising Debt," *The New York Times,* June 6, 1987, p. 8.

M. Galen and J. Weber, "Too Big, Too Fast," *BusinessWeek,* December 3, 1990, pp. 35–36.

---

[6] *Anatomy of a Fraud: Inside the Finances of the PTL Ministries, 1993* (New York: John Wiley), p. 215.

GM: Running on Empty?

Founded in 1908, General Motors Corp. (GM) is truly an iconic American corporation. From 1931 through 2008, GM was the world's largest automobile manufacturer, and in 1955, it became the first company in any industry to report more than $1 billion in revenues. GM's market share peaked at 51 percent in 1962. GM's domination in the market was such that many recommended the company be subject to scrutiny under antitrust laws. In 1971, former President Lyndon Johnson made the statement "now what's good for General Motors really is good for America."[1]

GM's net income reached an all-time high of $6.7 billion in 1997, and the automaker continued to generate positive net income through 2004. In 2005, things began to change. GM reported a net loss of more than $10 billion and has continued to post annual losses since that time with losses reaching almost $31 billion in 2008. (GM's cash flow from operations in 2008 was a negative $12 billion.) A summary of various measures of GM's financial condition for the six-year period from 2003 through 2008 is presented in GM Exhibit 1.[2]

Because of concerns with the ultimate impact of GM's financial struggles on the world economy, GM received $13.4 billion in government loans in December 2008 and has requested an additional $16.6 billion. President Barack Obama's administration pledged interim financing to allow GM to develop a restructuring plan, requested then-CEO Rick Wagoner to resign, and announced a plan to replace at least 6 of the 12 members of GM's board of directors. All of these events occurred in a market in which the economic conditions sharply decreased demand for automobile purchases. Not surprisingly, GM's stock reached a low (at that time) of $1.45 per share on March 6, 2009. (With one brief exception, GM's stock traded between $30 per share and $82 per share between 1983 and 2008.) GM's high, low, and closing stock prices for the period 2003–2008 are summarized in GM Exhibit 2.

In its March 4, 2009, report on GM's financial statements, GM's auditors (Deloitte & Touche) concluded that GM's financial statements were fairly presented in conformity with GAAP. However,

GM EXHIBIT 1
Summary of Financial Information: General Motors Corp. (amounts in millions)

	2003	2004	2005	2006	2007	2008
Total assets	$448,507	$479,603	$476,078	$186,192	$148,883	$91,047
Stockholders' equity	25,268	27,726	14,597	(5,441)	(37,094)	(86,154)
Revenues	182,543	193,571	192,605	207,349	181,112	148,979
Operating income	2,862	12,081	(16,931)	(7,668)	(4,390)	(21,284)
Net income	3,822	2,805	(10,567)	(1,978)	(38,732)	(30,860)
Cash flow from operations	7,600	13,061	(16,856)	(11,759)	7,731	(12,065)

Source: *General Motors Corp. 2003–2008 10-K reports.*

GM EXHIBIT 2
Annual High, Low, and Closing Stock Prices: General Motors Corp.

Source: *Wharton Research Data Services.*

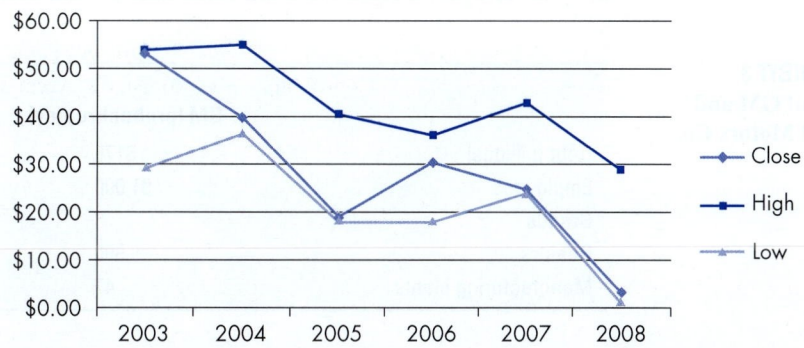

---

[1] "The Black on GM's Board," *Time*, September 6, 1976.
[2] Data for 2003 through 2005 include General Motors Acceptance Corporation (GMAC), which served as the financial services arm of General Motors Corp. GM sold a controlling interest in GMAC in November 2006; as a result, data for 2006 through 2008 do not include results related to GMAC.

Deloitte expanded its report to include the following paragraph to recognize uncertainties regarding GM's ability to continue as a going concern:

> The accompanying consolidated financial statements for the year ended December 31, 2008, have been prepared assuming that the Corporation [GM] will continue as a going concern. As discussed in Note 2 to the consolidated financial statements, the Corporation's recurring losses from operations, stockholders' deficit, and inability to generate sufficient cash flow to meet its obligations and sustain its operations raise substantial doubt about its ability to continue as a going concern. Management's plans concerning these matters are also discussed in Note 2 to the consolidated financial statements. The consolidated financial statements do not include any adjustments that might result from the outcome of this uncertainty.

GM'S REORGANIZATION

In April 2009, GM's Chief Executive Officer Frederick "Fritz" Henderson (who succeeded Rick Wagoner) created a restructuring plan to save GM. Under this plan, the debt owed to unsecured bondholders, the United Auto Workers, and the U.S. government (which totaled $74.4 billion across the three groups) would be reduced by $44.6 billion in exchange for a 99 percent interest in the emerging company. In addition, the terms of this plan called for the closure of 42 percent of GM's dealers.[3]

On June 1, 2009, the once unthinkable happened: GM filed for Chapter 11 bankruptcy. Under the terms of the bankruptcy plan, two entities were created: an "old GM" (subsequently named Motors Liquidation Company), a public company that owns four brands in the process of being phased out (Hummer, Saab, Pontiac, and Saturn), and a "new GM," a private company that is majority owned by the U.S. government (a 60% stake), with the Canadian government (11.7%), United Auto Workers (17.5%), and GM's unsecured bondholders (10%) owning large minority stakes. The new GM (known as **General Motors Co**.) received the Buick, Cadillac, Chevrolet, and GMC brands. General Motors Co. emerged from bankruptcy and began its operations on July 10, 2009, just 40 days after the filing. A brief profile of GM (the combined entity prebankruptcy) and General Motors Co. (the "new GM" that emerged postbankruptcy) is shown in GM Exhibit 3.[4]

A BOOST FOR THE AUTO INDUSTRY

On July 1, 2009, the U.S. government announced the Car Allowance Rebate Program (popularly known as the "Cash for Clunkers" program) to provide incentives for the automobile industry. Initially, $1 billion was appropriated for this program, but overwhelming demand from consumers resulted in an additional $2 billion allocation when the original funds were exhausted. More than 690,000 transactions were rebated under this program, 17.6 percent of which were for General Motors Co. automobiles.[5] Despite this program, GM's 2009 retail sales were down 17 percent from 2008. The company noted that its sale of more than 246,000 vehicles in August was "far and away the company's highest total and retail sales performance of 2009."[6]

GM EXHIBIT 3
Profile of GM and General Motors Co.

	GM (prebankruptcy)	General Motors Co. (postbankruptcy)
Debt (billions)	$176	$48
Employees	91,000	68,500
Brands	8	4
Dealers	5,900	3,600
Manufacturing plants	47	34

[3] "Plan Seeks a Smaller, Focused—and Profitable—GM," *The Wall Street Journal*, April 28, 2009, p. A8B.
[4] "GM Set to Exit Bankruptcy," *The Wall Street Journal*, July 10, 2009, p. A1.
[5] "Cash for Clunkers Wraps Up with Nearly 700,000 Car Sales and Increased Fuel Efficiency, U.S. Transportation Secretary Declares Program 'Wildly Successful,'" *U.S. Department of Transportation Press Release* 2009-08-26.
[6] "Car Makers Benefit from Cash for Clunkers," http://www.foxbusiness.com/story/markets/car-makers-benefit-cash-clunkers/ (accessed August 1, 2011).

EPILOGUE

In November 2010, GM returned to public company status with an initial public offering that raised $23.1 billion, one of the largest such offerings in the history of the United States[7]; GM's stock price closed at $34.19 that day. Deloitte & Touche's opinion on GM's 2010 financial statements (issued on March 1, 2011) concluded that GM's financial statements were presented in conformity with GAAP and made no reference to the going-concern uncertainties that GM had previously faced. In addition, 2010 was GM's most profitable year since 1999[8] with reported net income (before noncontrolling interests and dividends to preferred shareholders) of $6.3 billion.

DISCUSSION QUESTIONS

1. Reviewing GM's financial information in GM Exhibit 1 and its stock price in GM Exhibit 2, when do you first see signs of GM's impending financial distress?
2. In referencing professional standards, what factors auditors should consider in evaluating potential going-concern uncertainties?
3. Considering your response to questions 1 and 2, do you believe that the going-concern uncertainty is warranted? Do you believe that Deloitte & Touche should have issued a going-concern opinion prior to 2008?
4. What economic factors existing in the United States during 2008 might have accelerated Deloitte & Touche's decision to issue an audit opinion modified to disclose going-concern uncertainties?
5. Do you believe that the events immediately following GM's bankruptcy have alleviated the concerns that led to the issuance of the going-concern uncertainty? What issues would auditors need to consider in evaluating the ability of General Motors Co. (the "new GM") to continue as a going concern?
6. Many companies believe that a going-concern opinion is a *self-fulfilling prophecy* (that is, when a company receives a going-concern opinion, customers will not purchase products with warranties, suppliers will not provide short-term credit, and investors and creditors will not invest or loan). Would GM's going-concern opinion influence your decisions regarding either purchasing a car from GM or investing in GM's stock? Is a going-concern a self-fulfilling prophecy?

---

[7] "Total for GM Offering Rises to $23.1 Billion," *The Wall Street Journal*, November 27, 2010, p. B4.
[8] "GM Rebounds with Best Year Since 1999," *The Wall Street Journal*, February 25, 2011, p. B1.

Unhealthy Accounting at HealthSouth

PROBLEM

In 1996, key executives of HealthSouth, one of the nation's largest providers of health care services, began a massive fraud that eventually amounted to $2.7 billion.[1]

HealthSouth was founded in 1984 by Richard Scrushy and coworkers at Lifemark, a Houston-based company that owned and managed hospitals.[2] They took HealthSouth public in 1986, and by 1996 the company's market value had grown to $12 billion.[3] The massive fraud began in 1996.[4]

According to the government's complaint, Scrushy, the chief executive officer, insisted that the company meet or exceed earnings expectations established by Wall Street analysts. Senior officers would present actual accounting earnings to Scrushy, and if they did not meet the forecasts, he reportedly told them to "fix it." Unknown to Scrushy (according to his testimony at trial), a team of senior accounting personnel, known as "the family," held "family meetings" to determine ways to increase accounting earnings. They would look for "holes" in the balance sheet to be filled. The fictitious accounting entries they used to plug those holes were referred to as "dirt." Methods included overestimating insurance reimbursements, overstating fixed assets, improperly capitalizing expenses, and overbooking reserve accounts.[5]

The "family" members started by manipulating contractual allowances by consolidating entry adjustments after the end of each quarter. The allowances accounted for the differences between what HealthSouth charged patients and the amounts the company could collect from the patients' health insurers. By lowering the allowances improperly, HealthSouth improved its net revenue and bottom-line earnings. To offset the contractual allowances, the company increased inventory, intangible assets, fixed assets, and even cash. The fictitious fixed asset line item at each facility was listed as "AP summary."[6] The company's CFO, William Owens, a former Ernst & Young (E&Y) senior manager and one of five CFOs who pled guilty to the fraud, also used the acquisition of Horizon/CMS to book $400 million worth of goodwill as part of the cover-up. He pulled the trick off with the help of two HealthSouth colleagues and a finance executive from Horizon.[7]

On paper, HealthSouth maintained impeccable corporate policies. It established a confidential whistle-blower hotline in 1997; developed a nonretaliation policy, which gave the compliance director direct access to the board; and established a centralized finance function. This centralized function seemed to be a particular advantage because other health care companies were falling apart as a result of problems in field offices. Reviewing these policies, it is not difficult to see why a massive fraud did not seem likely.[8]

Despite its appearances, actual corporate governance was quite different. Many decisions were made at the executive level, which limited checks and balances along the way. The audit committee met only once a year. The accounting systems in the field did not interface with the corporate enterprise-resource-planning software, making it necessary for results to be consolidated at the corporate level, where it was easy to "cook" the numbers.[9]

Scrushy, a former gas station attendant, fit the profile of the overbearing CEO who sets the wrong tone at the top. He reportedly managed by fear and intimidation. Scrushy installed security cameras throughout headquarters to watch employees. He allowed rank-and-file employees into his executive suite only when he wanted to berate them.[10] According to the government's complaint, accounting personnel advised Scrushy in 1997 to abandon the fraud, but he refused, saying, "Not until I sell my stock."[11] The five CFOs realized the error of their ways, but most felt helpless

---

[1] "Keeping Secrets: How Five CFOs Cooked the Books at HealthSouth," *CFO.com*, June 1, 2005.

[2] www.richardmscrushy.com/biography.aspx.

[3] "HealthSouth Faked Profits, SEC Charges—A $1.4 Billion Overstatement Cited as CEO Is Accused of Ordering 'Massive Accounting Fraud,'" *The Wall Street Journal*, March 20, 2003, p. C1.

[4] *Securities and Exchange Commission v. HealthSouth Corp. and Richard M. Scrushy*, Civ. Action No. CV-03-J-0615-S (N.D. Ala. filed March 19, 2003), Complaint for Injunctive and Other Relief.

[5] Ibid.

[6] Ibid.

[7] "Keeping Secrets."

[8] Ibid.

[9] "Questioning the Books: Audit Committee Met Only Once during 2001," *The Wall Street Journal*, March 21, 2003, p. A2.

[10] "Keeping Secrets."

[11] *SEC v. HealthSouth Corp.*, Civ. Action No. CV-03-J-0615-S, Complaint for Injunctive and Other Relief.

to blow the whistle or even leave the company. One, Michael Martin, testified he tried to quit, but Scrushy reportedly said, "Martin, you can't quit. You'll be the fall guy."[12] Later, when Treasurer Leif Murphy decided to leave the company because of the fraud, Martin punched him twice at his going-away party and wrote on his farewell card, "Eat [expletive] and die."[13]

AUDIT APPROACH

HealthSouth was the largest client of the Birmingham office of E&Y. The 2001 audit fee was $1.2 million, and the firm billed an additional $2.5 million for other services. Many of HealthSouth's senior accounting staff had been E&Y employees.[14]

In hindsight, there had been red flags for the auditors to pursue. For example, from 1999 to 2001, net income rose nearly 500 percent while revenue grew only 5 percent.[15] The audit team also took no action when members learned that internal auditors were denied access to the corporate books. Finally, the team did not sufficiently investigate employee complaints.

The auditors were not oblivious to HealthSouth's risky profile. Jim Lamphron, a partner on the audit, said they focused on two risk factors: (1) "Company officials harboring a strong interest in seeing a rising stock price" and (2) "Management ranks dominated [by] those at the top. . . . Specifically, we were focusing on Richard Scrushy."[16] Despite E&Y's awareness of important fraud risks, the "family" was adept at the cover-up, making it difficult to detect certain aspects of the fraud. The SEC said that HealthSouth employees knew that E&Y questioned additions to fixed assets at any particular facility only if the additions exceeded a certain dollar threshold ($5,000), so the company avoided exceeding that dollar amount by spreading the adjustments below this materiality limit to various accounts and locations. When the auditors did question an accounting entry, HealthSouth officials created false documents to cover their tracks. When E&Y auditors asked for fixed assets ledgers for various facilities, accounting personnel would regenerate the ledgers, replacing the AP Summary line with the name of a specific fixed asset that did not exist at the facility.[17]

DISCOVERY

The fraud scheme was noticed by company whistle-blowers, who seemed to be disregarded. One anonymous e-mail was sent to the auditors saying the company "fleeced shareholders" and listed four suspicious accounting practices. E&Y's review determined that the issues raised by the author of the e-mail "did not affect the presentation of HealthSouth's financial statements." Another e-mail, from Michael Vines and forwarded to audit partner Jim Lamphron, was passed to CFO William Owens and George Strong, the audit committee chairman. Owens provided fake invoices for the questioned entries and dismissed the seriousness of this e-mail, indicating that Vines was just a disgruntled former employee.[18] (Vines had made frequent comments about the company's accounting on the employee electronic chat room and was regarded as something of a pest.)[19]

In October 1999, Diana Henze, assistant vice president of finance, noticed that earnings would jump with each iteration of quarter-end consolidations. She confronted Owens, who was controller at the time, and accused him of fraud. When she went to Kelly Cullison, corporate compliance officer, she was told the compliance officer "did not have access to the supporting documents" to determine whether or not the journal entries were legitimate. Henze brought the matter to her supervisor, cofounder Tony Tanner, who told her the entries were the result of reversing out a number of reserves and that the matter was closed.[20] Henze said that she was subsequently passed over for a promotion that would have given her more involvement with the books. When she asked

---

[12] "Keeping Secrets."
[13] "Former HealthSouth Executive Describes Deception and Abuse," Bloomberg News, February 18, 2005, p. E04.
[14] "Did Ernst Miss Key Fraud Risks at HealthSouth?" The Wall Street Journal, April 10, 2003, p. C1.
[15] "Missing the Red Flags," BusinessWeek, April 14, 2003, p. 72.
[16] "Scrushy Watch: The End Is Near: With Only a Handful of Witnesses Left, the Defense Needs a Lucky Break," www.birminghamweekly.com, December 1, 2005.
[17] SEC v. HealthSouth Corp.
[18] "Missed Signal: Accountant Tried in Vain to Expose HealthSouth Fraud—Ex-Employee Took His Case to Auditors, Then Web—But Convinced No One—What about the Others?" The Wall Street Journal, May 20, 2003, p. A1.
[19] "The Economy: Ernst & Young Got a Warning on HealthSouth," The Wall Street Journal, April 24, 2003, p. A2.
[20] "Executives on Trial: Witness Says HealthSouth Tried to Appease Street," The Wall Street Journal, February 23, 2005, p. C4.

why a less-qualified person got the job, Owens told her, "You have made it clear you won't do what we asked."[21]

William Owens finally went to the authorities when his wife threatened to divorce him because she thought (correctly) that he would end up in jail.[22] Owens agreed to wear a wire when meeting with Scrushy. Scrushy is on tape as saying, "You got accountants signing off on all this." In an impromptu meeting at a lake, Scrushy is recorded as telling Owens, "Just remember, I got eight kids. I got a bunch of babies at home. They need their daddy." Scrushy also told Owens, "If you want to go public with all this, get ready to get fired, and everyone goes down with you," according to the transcript of the recording Owens made of Scrushy.[23] Once Owens came forth, the investigation quickly uncovered the massive fraud as other employees cut deals with prosecutors.

Scrushy is a local hero in Birmingham with supporters in all corners. A lavish donor to local colleges, libraries, and medical centers, he was also a regular preacher at area churches. He even aired his own TV talk show each day before he appeared in court and hosted his own Web site (www.richardmscrushy.com/).[24] His defense attorneys sought to depict him as a detached leader and visionary rather than a micromanager with unchallenged influence. In the end, he was acquitted of all charges in what many see as a blow to enforcement of the Sarbanes-Oxley Act (Scrushy had certified statements on the 10-K dated August 14, 2002, under the Sarbanes-Oxley Act).[25] Jurors said key witnesses were not credible, and the prosecution failed to present substantial evidence linking the fraud to Scrushy. "The smoking gun wasn't pointing toward Mr. Scrushy[26]."

Scrushy subsequently settled claims from the SEC by paying $81,000,000.[27] However, in October 2006, he was convicted for paying $500,000 to a campaign of former Alabama Governor Don Siegelman in exchange for a seat on a hospital regulatory board. He was sentenced in June 2007 to nearly seven years in prison.[28] In July 2009, a jury awarded $2.88 billion in a civil suit brought by HealthSouth shareholders. It is believed to be the largest penalty ever levied against one executive. This case was brought before a lone judge, not a jury.[29] In April 2011, the Alabama Supreme Court denied Scrushy's appeal of the verdict.[30]

DISCUSSION QUESTIONS

1. What are several red flags that E&Y either was or should have been aware of in the audit of HealthSouth?
2. What procedures can auditors perform to detect fraudulent entries made during the consolidation process?
3. How can auditors determine a company's true "tone at the top"?
4. What is the appropriate response by auditors to information from "disgruntled" employees?
5. HealthSouth has sued E&Y, and E&Y is the target of a federal securities class action suit. What are E&Y's likely defenses against HealthSouth? Against the class action suit?
6. HealthSouth concealed the fraud by keeping the fraudulent transactions below $5,000. What recommendation would you have to E&Y to improve its sampling practices?

---

[21] "Witness Lost Promotion after Asking Questions," *USA Today*, February 22, 2005, www.usatoday.com/money/industries/health/2005-02-22-scrushy-usat_x.htm.
[22] "Keeping Secrets."
[23] Ibid.
[24] Ibid.
[25] *SEC v. HealthSouth Corp.*
[26] "Clean Sweep: HealthSouth's Scrushy Is Acquitted; Outcome Shows Challenges For Sarbanes-Oxley Act; SEC Suit Still Ahead; No Job Offer From Company" *Wall Street Journal* June, 29 2005: .p. 1.
[27] "Scrushy Case Comes to Muted Settlement," *The Wall Street Journal*, April 24, 2007, p. A3.
[28] "Business and Finance," *The Wall Street Journal*, June 29, 2007, p. A1.
[29] Valerie Bauerlein and Mike Esterl, "Judge Orders Scrushy to Pay $2.88 Billion in Civil Suit," *The Wall Street Journal*, June 19, 2009, p. B1.
[30] "Scrushy's Appeal Request Denied by Alabama High Court," *Modern Healthcare* 41 (16) April 18, 2011, p. 4-4.

KPMG: How Many Firms?

BACKGROUND

How many major accounting firms are needed to provide companies sufficient choice? Because of their scale, expertise, and international presence, the world's largest corporations have traditionally relied on the largest accounting firms to conduct their audits. As late as 1988, the "Big Eight" firms (Arthur Andersen & Co., Arthur Young & Company, Coopers & Lybrand, Deloitte Haskins & Sells, Ernst & Whinney, KPMG, Price Waterhouse & Co., and Touche Ross & Co.) dominated the market for audit services. In 1989, mergers between Ernst & Whinney and Arthur Young (to form Ernst & Young) and Deloitte Haskins & Sells and Touche Ross (to form Deloitte & Touche, now Deloitte) reduced choices to six providers. The merger of Price Waterhouse and Coopers & Lybrand in 1998 as PricewaterhouseCoopers (now PwC) limited them to five.

While a company's options with respect to the choice of an independent auditor were reduced by almost 50 percent, not until the Justice Department's dissolution of Arthur Andersen in 2002 were concerns raised about the lack of choices in the market for audit services and its impact on the competitiveness of the industry. (Arthur Andersen's verdict was overturned by the Supreme Court in 2005, but its partners and personnel had pursued other employment opportunities, and it is unlikely that the firm will reemerge as a major international accounting firm under either its former or an alternative name.)

The gulf between the Big Four and the next tier of accounting firms can be best illustrated by comparing KPMG (the smallest of the Big Four, in terms of revenues) with RSM/McGladrey & Pullen, the fifth largest accounting firm. In 2010, KPMG's revenues from audit and assurance services totaled $2.4 billion, compared to $651 million at RSM/ McGladrey & Pullen.[1] Viewed from a consumer's standpoint, in 2010, Big Four firms audited all Fortune 100 companies and all but 6 of the Fortune 500 companies.[2]

In addition to a smaller set of large accounting firms, public companies are constrained by provisions of the Sarbanes-Oxley Act. In an effort to enhance auditor independence, Sarbanes-Oxley prohibits auditors from providing various types of nonaudit services to their audit clients. This prohibition was in response to the large shift of accounting firm revenues from primarily audit revenues to revenues for other services.[3] For example, in 1975, the percentage of total revenues from the then-Big Eight firms derived from audit services ranged from 62 percent (Touche Ross & Co.) to 76 percent (Price Waterhouse & Co.); in 2000, this same percentage ranged from 31 percent (Deloitte & Touche) to 45 percent (KPMG).[4]

As a result of Sarbanes-Oxley, public companies have engaged other Big Four firms for nonaudit services. As just one example, at one time, the Big Four firms provided **Wabtec Corp.** auditing (Ernst & Young), internal control testing (Deloitte & Touche), acquisitions advising (KPMG), and tax services (PricewaterhouseCoopers). If Wabtec decided to change auditors yet retain a Big Four firm, it would need to consider the effect of these services on the independence of its new auditor. A survey by J.D. Powers & Associates of the 400 companies with more than $1 billion in revenue revealed that 55 percent of these companies are using more than one Big Four firm to provide various types of services (including audit services).[5]

The bottom line is that two independent developments (a smaller number of international accounting firms and Sarbanes-Oxley's limitations on the nonaudit services that can be provided by a company's auditors) have significantly impacted companies' choices of auditors. Perhaps this dilemma can be best reflected by the experiences of two large organizations.

First, in 2005, **Intel Corp.** considered proposals for its audit engagement from all four firms. It retained Ernst & Young, which has audited Intel's financial statements for more than 30 years.

---

[1] *Accounting Today Top 100 Firms*, 2010.

[2] Data on auditor identity was drawn from *Audit Analytics* database.

[3] One particularly striking example of this shift was Arthur Andersen's revenues derived from providing services to Enron. In the last year of the firm's audit of Enron, Andersen's audit revenues were $25 million while revenues from other services provided to Enron were $27 million. These other services included business process and risk management consulting, tax compliance and consulting, due diligence procedures related to acquisitions or other activities, work performed in connection with registration statements, and various statutory or other audits (information drawn from Enron's March 27, 2001, proxy statement filed with the Securities and Exchange Commission).

[4] Stephen A. Zeff, "How the U.S. Accounting Profession Got Where It Is Today: Part II," *Accounting Horizons*, December 2003, p. 270.

[5] "Firms' Auditor Choices Dwindle," *The Wall Street Journal*, June 21, 2005, p. C1.

This decision was largely driven by the nonaudit service provided to Intel by the other Big Four firms. Cary Klafter, Intel's corporate secretary, noted that "because there are only a limited number of large multinational audit firms that do the kind of work that we need, if we were to switch audit firms, all sorts of dominos would fall."[6]

Second, when **Fannie Mae** dismissed KPMG as its auditor in the wake of an accounting scandal, its choices for a successor were slim: Deloitte & Touche had been advising the federal government in its probe of Fannie Mae, Ernst & Young had been providing consulting services to Fannie Mae's audit committee responding to the probes related to the scandal, and PricewaterhouseCoopers audited **Freddie Mac**, a major competitor.[7]

Could something happen to limit companies' choices even further?

THE PROBLEM

From 1996 through 2002, KPMG received $124 million in tax consulting fees from promoting tax shelters that allowed individuals and corporations to improperly avoid more than $1.4 billion in federal taxes.[8] E-mail messages obtained and released by the Internal Revenue Service indicated that KPMG officials were aware that the tax shelters were questionable.

As one example, a shelter referred to as *bond-linked issue premium structures (BLIPS)* created $5 billion in tax losses for investors. Under this shelter, clients would purchase foreign currency from offshore banks with funds borrowed from those same banks only to sell the currency back to the same bank a few months later. These investments were presented to the Internal Revenue Service as seven-year investments.[9] Other shelters in question carried similar names such as *FLIP, OPIS,* and *SOS*.

THE OUTCOME

On August 26, 2005, KPMG admitted to criminal tax fraud and agreed to a payment of $456 million in penalties (an average of $300,000 per KPMG partner); the government agreed to deferred adjudication and, in January 2007, dismissed all criminal charges against the firm. Subsequently, Judge Lewis Kaplan of the U.S. District Court for the Southern District of New York dismissed indictments against 13 of 16 former KPMG partners and, on December 18, 2008, two of the remaining three partners were convicted on multiple counts of tax evasion (the remaining partner was acquitted).[10]

In the midst of this activity, federal prosecutors indicted four current and former partners of Ernst & Young on similar charges. The shelters designed and sold by these partners brought Ernst & Young $120 million in fees. Those familiar with the matter do not expect that the firm itself will face criminal charges in this matter;[11] however, on May 8, 2009, four current and former E&Y executives were convicted.

THE ISSUE

KPMG has avoided the fate of Arthur Andersen: dissolution. However, the KPMG case has raised numerous questions about the future of the accounting profession if the small number of international accounting firms should become even smaller. For example, the Securities and Exchange Commission discussed various actions to assist companies in changing auditors if KPMG was indicted, including allowing companies to seek waivers to the stricter independence rules on a case-by-case basis and allowing KPMG to continue to perform audits if it were indicted. An unidentified SEC official indicated that "we have scenarios in place for any eventuality that could come out of this."[12] In addition, prior to the settlement, Deloitte & Touche, Ernst & Young, and PricewaterhouseCoopers reportedly requested that their partners not solicit current KPMG clients.[13]

---

[6] Ibid.

[7] "Fannie Mae's Dismissal of KPMG Shows Dwindling Choices among Big Four," *The Wall Street Journal*, December 23, 2004, p. C1.

[8] "Grand July Investigating KPMG Tax Shelters," *CFO.com*, February 23, 2004.

[9] "Inside the KPMG Mess," *BusinessWeek*, September 12, 2005, pp. 46–47.

[10] "Former KPMG Executives Convicted of Tax Evasion," *The Wall Street Journal*, December 18, 2008, p. C4.

[11] "Tax-Shelter Indictments Leave a Cloud over Ernst," *The Wall Street Journal*, May 31, 2007, p. C1.

[12] "SEC Weighs a 'Big Three' World," *The Wall Street Journal*, June 22, 2005, p. C1.

[13] "No Poaching from KPMG, Say Audit Firms," *CFO.com*, August 24, 2005.

DISCUSSION QUESTIONS

1. Do professional standards allow a company's auditors also to provide tax services and retain their independence?
2. How have provisions of the Sarbanes-Oxley Act limited a public company's choice of auditors?
3. What are some of the advantages and disadvantages of permitting auditors to provide nonaudit services (such as tax services) to clients?
4. What is the impact of a smaller number of major international accounting firms on public companies?

Something Went Sour at Parmalat[1]

PROBLEM

There was much confusion when Italian dairy food giant Parmalat defaulted on a $187 million bond payment in mid-November 2002. Default on a bond payment seemed difficult to believe considering that a Parmalat subsidiary in the Cayman Islands had a $4.9 *billion* cash balance in a Bank of America account. The problem was that the cash account did not exist.

Subsequent investigation revealed that, over a 15-year period, Parmalat's management had falsified accounts and created assets to hide losses of $10 billion from Parmalat's Latin American operations. Other allegations charged that Parmalat's management had lied about repurchasing $3.6 billion in bonds, which they had never done. By hiding losses and increasing assets on its balance sheet, Parmalat was able to continue to borrow enough money from investors and creditors to conceal and perpetuate the massive fraud.

AUDIT APPROACH

From 1990 to 1999, the Italian branch of Grant Thornton audited Parmalat. Under Italian law, however, Parmalat was forced to change auditors periodically and chose the Italian branch of Deloitte Touche Tohmatsu (Deloitte & Touche SpA) to be the company's new auditor in 2000. Grant Thornton, however, continued to audit Parmalat's off-shore subsidiaries located in the Cayman Islands.

Auditors first inquired about the Cayman Islands account in December, 2002, and received a letter on Bank of America letterhead in March, 2003, confirming the existence of the account. The letter, however, was a forgery, created in Parmalat's headquarters. Nevertheless, the $4.9 billion was listed on the subsidiary's balance sheet as of December 31, 2002, and was consolidated into Parmalat's balance sheets dated December 31, 2002, and June 30, 2003.

The auditors missed several red flags. First, the size of the account, on its own, should have been a red flag. It is very unusual for a large company to have so much cash in a single bank account. In addition, between January 2000 and September 2003, Parmalat raised more than $5 billion in debt offerings. With so much cash available in the Cayman Islands, why was Parmalat continuing to borrow money?

Second, the communication received from the Bank of America was in the form of a facsimile (see Parmalat Exhibit 1), which raises two issues. First, a fax transmission is not subject to the same level of control as returning an original confirmation. Essentially, a fax can be sent from almost anywhere and the originating phone number can be falsified by simply changing the phone number in the transmitting fax machine. A mailed confirmation, however, passes through the federal mail system and is postmarked with the originating zip code. Also, this particular fax was smudged, raising more suspicions. Forgers routinely "age" their "originals" by repeatedly photocopying them to obscure any tell-tale photocopying lines. Given these circumstances, the auditors should have followed up directly with the bank.

Third, when such large balances represent a significant portion of a company's balance sheet (in this case, 38 percent of Parmalat's assets were in the subsidiary's bank account), auditors should take additional care to obtain additional corroboration. All told, the combination of a large bank account and a questionable form of confirmation should have provided Deloitte & Touche SpA sufficient warning to dig deeper.

DISCOVERY

Parmalat management also told Deloitte & Touche SpA that the company had a $617 million investment in an open-ended mutual fund that it could access at any time. The company, however, was unsuccessful in its attempts to retrieve the funds. Because no evidence was available to support management's claims, Deloitte & Touche SpA included a qualification in its audit review report highlighting the lack of evidence and alerted regulators of suspicions of a larger fraud.

Initial investigation revealed that massive amounts (estimates as high as $19 billion) of assets were missing or nonexistent. Parmalat and its subsidiaries filed for bankruptcy protection in Italy on December 27, 2003.

---

[1] G. Edmondson and L. Cohn, "How Parmalat Went Sour," *BusinessWeek Online*, January 12, 2004.

PARMALAT EXHIBIT 1

```
DEC 17 2003 16:01 FR BANK OF AMERICA    2019743939 TO 916467334872    P.01
```

Bank of America
New York Branch

Grant Thornton Spa
Largo Augusto, 7
20122 MILANO, ITALY

March 5, 2003

Re: Bonlat Financing Corporation
BANY Account No.: 6550-2-52252
BANY Securities Deposits No.: 6550-2-85419

Dear Sir/Madam

We have received your request for audit purposes dated December 20, 2002. We confine our response to certain information concerning account balances and securities deposits from our records at this office.

1. As of the close of business on December 31, 2002, our records indicate the following deposit balance(s):

Account Type	Account Name	Account Number	Account Balance
Demand Deposit	Bonlat Financing Corporation	6550-2-52252	USD $336,812,328.64 CR
AutoInvest Account	Bonlat Financing Corporation	N/A	N/A

2. As of the close of business on December 31, 2002, our records indicate the following Securities Deposit balance(s):

Account Type	Account Name	Account Number	Account Balance
Securities Deposit	Bonlat Financing Corporation	6550-2-85419	EUR €2,811,000,000.00
Securities Deposit	Bonlat Financing Corporation	6550-2-85419	USD $949,000,000.00

3. As of the close of business on December 31, 2002, our records indicate the following Letter of Credit balance.

Trade Finance	Customer Name	Reference Number	Outstanding
N/A	N/A	N/A	N/A

This information is for your CONFIDENTIAL use and is furnished in reply to your inquiry. No responsibility is assumed by Bank of America or its officers to the accuracy or completeness of this information. No representation is made as to any other relationship the subject may have with other Bank of America offices.

Sincerely,

Agnes Belgrave

Bank of America
100 West 33rd Street, New York, NY 10001

During the ongoing investigation, a Parmalat employee who had disobeyed orders to destroy company documents turned over a number of incriminating computer disks to investigators. With evidence mounting, Parmalat's founder and CEO Calisto Tanzi admitted to prosecutors that he was aware of the fraud. He also admitted to misappropriating Parmalat assets (more than $1 billion, prosecutors believe) to cover losses in other family-owned companies. It is unlikely that investigators will ever know for certain what happened to the missing funds (whether they were used to cover operating losses, pay creditors, or illegally enrich management). Twenty other Parmalat executives, including members of Tanzi's family, and the company's former CFO, former board members, and even lawyers, were indicted on charges including fraud, embezzlement, false accounting, and misleading investors. On June 28, 2005, a judge accepted plea bargains from 11 of those charged and sentenced them to prison ranging from 10 months to 2.5 years. In his January, 2008 trial, Calisto Tanzi was found guilty of securities laws violations and was sentenced to 10 years in prison for his role in the fraud. More than two years later, in December 2010, Tanzi was also found guilty of fraudulent bankruptcy and criminal association and sentenced to an additional 18 years in jail.

DISCUSSION QUESTIONS

1. What steps does an auditor ordinarily take when confirming cash balances held on deposits with financial institutions?
2. What additional steps should the auditors have taken when they received the smudged fax copy printed on Bank of America letterhead?
3. What *red flags* did the auditors miss?
4. What steps should Deloitte & Touche SpA have taken with respect to Grant Thornton's audit of the Cayman Island subsidiaries?

GE: How Much Are Auditors Paid?

> The financial report accompanying this letter is historic in that it is our first one covered by Section 404 of The Sarbanes-Oxley Act of 2002 (SOX). . . . But what does it mean to you? Is it a "check-the-box" bureaucracy based on an overreaction to the market scandals of yesterday? None of us likes more regulation, but I actually think SOX 404 is helpful. It takes the process control discipline we use in our factories and applies it to our financial statements. Implementing SOX 404 cost GE $33 million in 2004. But we think it is a good investment.
>
> *Jeffrey R. Immelt, Chairman of the Board and Chief Executive Officer,*
> *General Electric*
> *Letter to Shareholders from 2004 annual report*

BACKGROUND

Since its required implementation in 2004, section 404 of Sarbanes-Oxley has generated a great deal of controversy. Its requirement that auditors assess the operating effectiveness of their clients' internal controls over financial reporting and express opinions on the effectiveness of their clients' internal controls over financial reporting and on management's assessment of its internal control over financial reporting (this latter responsibility has since been rescinded) has imposed significant costs on accelerated filers.[1]

The costs of Sarbanes-Oxley have been cited as having significant impact on the U.S. capital markets. For example, a higher dollar amount of initial public offerings (IPOs) has been made on overseas exchanges since the implementation of section 404. Many companies cite the high costs of Sarbanes-Oxley compliance as a factor in their choice of stock market listing; in 2002 (prior to Sarbanes-Oxley), 9 of the top 20 IPOs were on U.S. stock exchanges compared with only 3 of the top 20 IPOs in 2006. In addition, during 2006, total IPO values on both the London/AIM and Hong Kong stock exchanges exceeded values on the New York Stock Exchange.[2]

Among other reasons, the high costs of compliance with section 404 resulted in the issuance of *Auditing Standard No. 5 (AS 5)*, which superseded *Auditing Standard No. 2*. Major changes under *AS 5* include (1) eliminating the requirement for auditors to evaluate and opine on management's assessment of internal control over financial reporting, (2) encouraging auditors to adopt a "top-down, risk-based" approach, resulting in more efficient audits, and (3) expanding the potential use of others' work in the assessment of internal control over financial reporting. Then-SEC Chairman Christopher Cox notes that, as a result of the passage of *AS 5*, "the unduly high costs of implementing section 404 of the [Sarbanes-Oxley] act will come down" because companies "will be able to focus on the greatest risk of material misstatements in the financials."[3] Some estimate that this reduction could be as much as 10 percent.[4]

In addition to the provisions of section 404 related to internal control over financial reporting, Sarbanes-Oxley reduced auditors' ability to provide nonaudit services to their clients. Section 201 prohibits two major types of services that had become significant revenue sources for accounting firms: (1) financial information systems design and implementation and (2) internal audit outsourcing. Not coincidentally, these were two areas in which Arthur Andersen provided extensive services to Enron prior to its failure. Furthermore, section 202 requires that the entity's audit committee approve all nonaudit services (with the exception of those less than 5 percent of the total revenues paid to the accounting firm).

---

[1] *Accelerated filers* are those public entities filing financial statements with the SEC that have market capitalizations of more than $75 million. Initially, public entities with market capitalizations of less than $75 million were to be subject to the provisions of section 404 in 2005 (one year following the effective date for accelerated filers). However, smaller entities have yet to implement section 404.

[2] "Business Wins Its Battle to Ease a Costly Sarbanes-Oxley Rule," *The Wall Street Journal*, November 10, 2006, p. A1.

[3] "Painful Memories: SEC Grilled on 404 Costs," *CFO.com*, June 12, 2007.

[4] "AS5 Could Trim Audit Bills by 10%," *CFO.com*, May 4, 2007.

HOW DID SARBANES-OXLEY AFFECT ACCOUNTING FIRM REVENUES?

The preceding suggests that Sarbanes-Oxley could have a significant (yet indeterminable) effect on accounting firm revenues. On one hand, the internal control requirements of section 404 would presumably increase total revenues; however, the prohibition against providing financial information systems design and implementation and internal audit outsourcing services would likely reduce revenues. In addition, the requirement that the entity's audit committee approve all nonaudit services would presumably heighten these individuals' awareness of potential conflicts related to these services and reduce the likelihood that such services will be approved (or reduce the dollar level at which they are approved).

GE Exhibit 1 summarizes fees paid by **General Electric** to its auditors (KPMG, LLP) for various years both preceding and following the issuance of Sarbanes-Oxley; GE Exhibit 2 provides similar information for the average of Fortune 100 companies during these same years.[5] "Audit fees" are identified based on SEC rules and include fees paid for the (1) audit of the annual financial statements, (2) review of quarterly financial statements, (3) audit of the effectiveness of internal control over financial reporting, (4) attestation of management's report on the effectiveness of internal control over financial reporting, and (5) other services provided in connection with statutory and regulatory filings and engagements. "Audit-related" fees include other fees that can be reasonably related to the preceding services as well as fees paid for due diligence and audit services on mergers and acquisitions and fees paid for audit services on employee benefit plans.

SEC-REQUIRED FEE DISCLOSURES

One additional phenomenon that may influence the fees reported by GE and the Fortune 100 companies in Exhibits GE 1 and 2 are the disclosure requirements implemented by the SEC. In November 2000, the SEC adopted requirements that registrants disclose the various types of fees paid to its financial statement auditors; under this initial guidance, audit fees included fees paid for the annual financial statement audit and those paid for the reviews of quarterly financial statements. Beginning in 2003, the SEC expanded the definition of *audit fees* to include services that

GE EXHIBIT 1 Fees Paid by General Electric to Auditors (in millions)

	2000	2002	2004	2006	2008	2010
Audit fees	$23.9	$38.7	$78.2	$85.8	$94.3	$89.9
Audit-related fees	15.5	23.3	15.5	20.6	31.5	9.7
Tax fees	13.8	21.2	8.9	9.0	7.2	9.3
Financial information systems fees	50.4	0.0	0.0	0.0	0.0	0.0
Other fees	0.0	6.1	0.0	0.0	0.0	0.0
Total fees	$103.6	$89.3	$102.6	$115.4	$133.0	$108.9

Source: Various General Electric proxy statements.

GE EXHIBIT 2 Average Fees Paid by Fortune 100 Companies to Auditors (in millions)

	2000	2002	2004	2006	2008	2010
Audit fees	$7.1	$8.1	$16.3	$17.3	$18.1	$20.7
Audit-related fees	0.9	2.8	2.8	2.6	3.2	3.3
Tax fees	1.1	4.5	4.0	2.6	2.3	2.8
Financial information systems fees	3.9	0.0	0.0	0.0	0.0	0.0
Other fees	16.2	4.1	0.5	0.2	0.0	0.3
Total fees	$29.2	$19.5	$23.6	$22.7	$23.6	$27.1

Source: Data extracted from Wharton Research Data Services.

[5] The fees shown in Exhibits GE 1 and GE 2 reflect only those amounts paid to the entity's financial statement auditors. It is likely that other accounting firms that are not involved with the financial statement audit also provide services to these entities. However, these latter data are not publicly available.

"generally only the independent accountant can reasonably provide, such as comfort letters, statutory audits, attest services, consents and assistance with and review of documents filed with the [SEC]."[6] Some argued that broadening the definition of audit fees would be misleading in terms of user perceptions of auditors' independence. Barbara Roper, director of investor protection for the Consumer Federation of America, noted that "it's absolutely industry's water that's being carried here. It makes it look like their audit fees are bigger, their nonaudit fees are smaller, and it masks the conflict of interest."[7] Clearly, any comparison of fee breakdowns prior to and following Sarbanes-Oxley must consider the SEC's revised definition of audit fees.

DISCUSSION QUESTIONS

1. From a conceptual standpoint, how do the requirements of Sarbanes-Oxley related to nonaudit services affect perceptions of the auditors' independence?
2. Assume that your firm was auditing General Electric in 2000 and was recommending an adjustment to its financial statements that reduced net income. Based on the fees paid to your firm in 2000, what incentive(s) might your firm consider in insisting upon this adjustment? How would your firm's incentive(s) differ after 2004?
3. Compare General Electric's fees prior to (2000 and 2002) and following (2004, 2006, 2008, and 2010) the implementation of Sarbanes-Oxley. Based on the trends in these fees and various components of these fees, comment on the effect of Sarbanes-Oxley on General Electric's fees.
4. Repeat question 3 for the Fortune 100 companies. Are the trends for these companies similar to those for General Electric?
5. For General Electric and the Fortune 100 companies, can you identify the increased costs of section 404 compliance cited in the press?
6. Comparing the fees in 2004 versus those in 2008 and 2010 for General Electric and Fortune 100 companies, does it appear that *AS 5* has reduced costs of section 404 compliance?

---

[6] Securities and Exchange Commission, "Strengthening the Commission's Requirements Regarding Auditor Independence," *Release No. 33-8183*, March 26, 2003.

[7] "Redefined by the SEC, 'Audit Fees' Get Murky," *The Wall Street Journal*, January 22, 2003.

Satyam Computer Services, Ltd.—India's Enron

Imagine that you are on the board of directors of a company and you receive a letter from the chairman of the board that starts, "With deep regret and tremendous burden that I am carrying on my conscience[1]" and goes on to say that the company's balance sheet carries inflated cash of more than $1 billion, $77 million (m) of accrued interest that is nonexistent, $253m of understated liability arranged by the chairman, and overstated receivables of $101m and that the income statement shows overstated profits for the last several years. Imagine that you were the audit partner, or if you had just awarded the company your global award for excellence in corporate governance (since rescinded)! This is what happened on January 7, 2009, to the board of directors of Satyam Computer Services, its auditor Price Waterhouse India (PWI, the Indian arm of PricewaterhouseCoopers International, PwC), and Dr. Ola Ulsten, former Swedish prime minister and chairman of the Golden Peacock Awards.[2] As for the shareholders, the value of shares dropped about $2 billion the next week.

HISTORY OF SATYAM

Satyam, which means "truth" in Sanskrit, was founded by B. Ramalinga Raju in 1987 and grew to be a leading outsourcing firm used by major international companies. India's fourth-largest software and services firm, it reported revenue of $555m (actual revenue of $434m) and had 53,000 employees in 2008 (or did it? Stay tuned).

Chairman of the board Raju's confession seemed to spring from the board of directors' denial of the purchase of Maytas (Satyam spelled backward), a Raju family-controlled company owning thousands of acres of property. Apparently, Raju planned to use Maytas assets to offset the fictitious assets at Satyam.

The press had noted the company's related-party dealings. Raju's family members were on the Satyam board and friends were in senior management. Even though it was a large company, no financial experts were on the audit committee.

INDIAN ACCOUNTING ENVIRONMENT

Indian accounting standards are broadly similar to international standards, and the Indian accounting profession is largely self-regulated. Traditionally, general standards of corporate ethics and accounting have been suspect in India. Many companies had been created during License Raj, a period of government intervention in which businesses had to work with politicians and pay bribes. In India "promoters,"[3] who include business families and other corporate insiders, held almost half of the shares on the National Stock Exchange. However, because of its listing on the NYSE, Satyam was subject to the Sarbanes-Oxley Act, which should have induced stricter governance.

Although the Big Four accounting firms have been eagerly touting the growth potential in India, development there has been hampered by heavy national restrictions on the size and number of audit clients a partner can serve. The relationship between PwC and PWI underlines what many see as the patchwork nature of the big accounting firms. Each is a collection of national partnerships under a global umbrella organization. The profession has tried to standardize practices and ethics across the firms, but senior partners privately admit that quality can still be patchy. Some say the Big Four firms in India rely on trainee chartered accountants and sometimes accountants simply copy the previous years' audits and the internal auditors' work because they have limited time to complete the current audit.

THE FRAUD

India's biggest corporate fraud apparently started in April 2002 when IT companies' American depository receipts (ADRs)[4] were popular among foreign investors. At that time, Raju decided to

---

[1] "In India, Crisis Pairs With Fraud'" JOE Nocera: January 9, 2009 http://www.nytimes.com/2009/01/10/business/10nocera.html?ref=ramalingaraju (accessed September 14, 2011).

[2] A set of prestigious national and global awards designed to improve productivity and quality in organizations given by the World Council for Corporate Governance.

[3] Persons who are in overall control of the company and who are instrumental in formulating a plan to offer securities to the public. A promoter group includes the promoter, an immediate relative, and if the promoter is a company, any subsidiary or other company in which the parent company holds more than 10 percent of equity. http://www.opendb.net/element/19071.php.

[4] Shares of overseas-based companies are traded as ADRs on U.S. stock markets in U.S. dollars.

maintain two subaccounts under a single company bank account. He and his cronies controlled the main bank account, and the statements of the subsidiary account were under the control of the company's finance and account reconciliation (FAR) team. The accounting team would receive two bank statements for the same account: a genuine set of statements from the bank and a second set of fictitious statements provided by Raju and his team. The FAR had to accept the fictitious bank statements (and related interest accruals). Allegedly, even the auditors relied on the documents supplied by Raju instead of obtaining third-party verification. The CFO, Srinivas Vadlamani, who was arrested, said he had not been directly involved but knew there had been something suspicious for more than five years. He had been specifically asked not to look at deposits. Vadlamani said the plan was carried out by creating a paper trail of fabricated invoices, forged balance sheets, and counterfeit bank statements in a scheme involving about10 junior staff.

Initial investigations have revealed that an in-house Satyam team developed software to generate altered invoices that included the genuine name of a client and of the client's project manager but with an overstated invoice amount. For example, a Satyam client, XYZ, pays 100 rupees to Satyam's bank account as fees. The original bank statement showed 100 rupees deposited by XYZ, but the statement provided by Raju overstated this figure. Year after year, altered invoices in the name of genuine clients and employees were created and went unnoticed by auditors.

The unrecorded liability of $253m was the amount that private companies owned by Raju lent to Satyam. To keep analysts and investors at bay, the loan amount wasn't shown in the books. Had it been shown, it would have raised eyebrows. After all, why would a company incur this liability when it had so much cash on its books? (Analysts already had been asking why the company kept so much cash in interest-free accounts.) As the chairman's letter mentioned, this amount had been arranged over the previous two years to fund Satyam/s operations.

In addition, the public prosecutor noted that the CFO (Vadlamani) had admitted during interrogation that Satyam had just 40,000 employees vs. the 53,000 officially claimed, and the fictitious wages were siphoned off. The prosecutor claims Raju used a fictitious name to divert $4m a month from the company's account for his personal wealth. India's Serious Fraud Investigation Office has found that $100m raised through the issuance of ADRs did not end up in the company's bank accounts and has still not been found.

Although the company's bank balance was fictitious, the employees had to be paid real salaries. To meet these expenses, Raju and his family started pledging their stake in the company. The shares were pledged by a holding company, SRSR Holdings, which in turn had approximately 300 subsidiaries. India's Central Bureau of Investigation (CBI) has found that some of the documents of the companies created by Raju contained land records and names of land mafia agents,[5] indicating that the case may be more than just an accounting fraud.

THE AUDITORS

Even though PWI had been Satyam's auditor since 2000, it resigned. Indian police have arrested two partners of PWI on charges of criminal conspiracy and cheating. PwC may also face class action suits in the United States.

PwC says, "The audits were conducted by PWI in accordance with applicable auditing standards[6]." Vadlamani, the former CFO, said the auditors had not been complicit in cooking the books and had been given forged documents. The auditors had relied on documents provided by management such as account balance statements and letters of confirmation of account balances.

Dennis Nally, global leader of PwC, said to *Business Today*:

> If our job was described as to provide a 100 per cent assurance that there have been no material mistakes and no frauds have been committed, that would require audit firms to significantly increase the amount of work we do today and have much more forensic and different types of auditing. As we all know, when there is a desire at the top of an organization to commit a massive fraud, individuals in the organization that have participated in the fraud can do a lot of different things to keep it away from individuals, including auditor firms, the Board of Directors and the analyst community.[7]

---

[5] These agents formed a network of mafia-style operators that obtained illegal permits and illegally developed low-priced subsidized land and apartments and sold them to the public for high prices.

[6] Jackie Range and Scott Patterson, "Price Waterhouse Defends Its Audit Procedures," *The Wall Street Journal*, eastern edition, January 9, 2009, p. B5.

[7] Puja Mehra, "Our Job Is Not to Certify That There's No Fraud': *Business Today* July 26, 2009.

FOLLOW-UP

Indian authorities arrested Raju and his brother Rama on complaints of cheating, forgery, breach of trust, and other charges. Police called in cyberforensic experts who can retrieve erased data from computers. In all, ten people have been arrested for the fraud. All of them, including Raju, are out on bail (as of this writing).

PWI suspended its chief relationship partner and engagement leader on the Satyam audit, set up an advisory board, conducted a review of work and processes, and appointed a new head of quality assurance and risk management. While screening through the minutes of some of the board meetings, investigators found that the total audit fees paid to PWI for its domestic and international accounts was around $1.4m, almost double the figure mentioned in the balance sheet.

The information concerning the probe initiated by the Crime Investigation Department (CID), the Serious Fraud Investigation Office (SFIO), and Institute of Chartered Accountants of India (ICAI) was handed to the CBI in February, 2009. The Securities and Exchange Board of India had its own investigation team go through the company's books.

A senior CBI official, who did not wish to be identified, confirmed to *Business Today* that Raju seems to have come clean in his confession letter except for his statement about not having benefited in financial terms as a result of inflated results. "We are yet to establish if there was any diversion of funds from Satyam to any of Raju's entities. This will take some time to investigate," added the CBI official[8]. Decoding the biometric laptops used by Raju and his team, screening the internal financial software of the company and minutes of the board meetings for the final six years, scanning papers of the approximately 300 companies created by Raju and his family, and scrutinizing the land records under these companies was expected to keep the CBI busy for months.

During an interrogation session, Raju is believed to have said that he never did anything wrong because everyone else in the industry does it.

On April 5, 2011, the PCAOB and the SEC announced a joint penalty of $7.5m against the five firms composing PW India, a member of PwC. It is the largest such penalty ever assessed against a registered foreign accounting firm. The firms were also given other sanctions, including a six-month ban on accepting new SEC clients and the imposition of quality controls.

In the release of its findings, the PCAOB said the auditors had relied on management to send confirmation requests to Satyam's bank and to return responses to the auditors even though the audit programs "explicitly acknowledged that the engagement team should maintain control of the process of sending confirmation requests and receiving confirmation responses relating to the confirmation of cash."[9] Moreover, a network firm partner reviewing the documentation "advised that the engagement team 'can only take credit for [cash] confirmations we send [to] and receive directly [from the banks].'"[10] The partner "noted that the Company had a significant balance of fixed deposits and advised the engagement team to 'document that confirmations have been received [from the banks] for such amounts.'" There had been similar shortcomings in the confirmation of accounts receivable, even though the firm had noted numerous internal control deficiencies. "These confirmation deficiencies contributed directly to the auditors' failure to uncover the Satyam fraud," said James R. Doty, PCAOB Chairman[11].

DISCUSSION QUESTIONS

1. Do you agree with Dennis Nally's comments?
2. How do you think Raju could have used Maytas assets to cover up the fraud?
3. Why are related-party frauds more difficult to detect than frauds with no related parties?
4. Should U.S. public accounting firms try to audit internationally in cultures they may not understand? If so, how can they maintain quality audits?
5. Can an international firm have one set of absolute ethics standards that must be followed at all times, or do ethics standards need to be flexible enough to account for variations in cultures?
6. How can auditors ensure they are receiving authentic documentation, not forgeries?
7. In your opinion, should PWI be subject to civil litigation? PwC?

---

[8] Rachna M. Koppikar and Puja Mehra, "Satyam: Unraveling the Fraud," *Business Today*, July 2009.

[9] PCAOB. "PCAOB Announces Settled Disciplinary Order Against PricewaterhouseCoopers International Firms in India for Audit Violations Related to Satyam. April 5, 2011.

[10] Ibid.

[11] Ibid.

ADDITIONAL SOURCES

Anand Adhikari, "The Problem Within; When the Bulk of the Auditing Work Involves Junior Auditors, Trouble Can't Be Too Far Behind," *Business Today,* February 22, 2009.

Geeta Anand and Romit Guha, "Corporate News: Satyam Bank Documents at Issue—Fraud Probe Sheds Light on How Outsourcing Company Inflated Its Balance Sheet," *The Wall Street Journal,* eastern edition, January 20, 2009, p. B3.

Anonymous, "Business: Offshore Inmate; the Satyam Scandal," *The Economist,* January 17, 2009, p. 64.

Eric Bellman and John Satish Kumar, "Founder Arrested, Board out at Satyam," *The Wall Street Journal,* eastern edition, January 10, 2009, p. B1.

Eric Bellman and Jackie Range, "Corporate News: Satyam Probe Scrutinizes CFO, Audit Committee," *The Wall Street Journal,* eastern edition, January 14, 2009, p. B3.

"Corporate News: Satyam Backs Removal of Auditors," *The Wall Street Journal,* eastern edition, February 23, 2009, p. B3.

Jennifer Hughes, "Accountants Go into Shock at 'India's Enron,'" *Financial Times,* January 9, 2009, p. 16.

Nandini Lakshman, "Nine Charged in Hyderabad in Satyam Fraud," *BusinessWeek,* April 7, 2009.

Joe Leahy, "Details of Alleged Satyam Fraud Emerge," *FT.com,* January 22, 2009.

Kenan Machado and Romit Guha, "Satyam Founder Raju Is Granted Bail," *The Wall Street Journal,* eastern edition, August 19, 2010, p. B.8

Lakshman, Nandini, and Kripalani, Manjeet "Is the Worst Over for Satyam?" *BusinessWeek Online,* 2/4/2009

PCAOB, Release No. 105-2011-002, April 5, 2011.

"PricewaterhouseCoopers Speaks to Puja Mehra on Improving Audit Practices," *Business Today,* July 2009.

Jackie Range and Joann S. Lublin, "The Satyam Scandal: Spotlight on India's Corporate Governance," *The Wall Street Journal,* eastern edition, January 8, 2009, p. A9.

Jackie Range, "Corporate News: Additional $100 Million Said to Be Missing from Satyam," *The Wall Street Journal,* eastern edition, May 1, 2009, p. B2.

Jackie Range and R. Jai Krishna, "Corporate News: More Staff Arrested at Satyam—Former Finance Chief at Indian Software Firm Defends Outside Auditors," *The Wall Street Journal,* eastern edition, April 7, 2009, p. B2.

Jackie Range, "Corporate News: Accountants for Satyam Arrested by Indian Police," *The Wall Street Journal,* eastern edition, January 26, 2009, p. B3.

Ahmed Rumman, "Satyam Auditor Seeks to Repair Image," *The Wall Street Journal,* eastern edition, March 6, 2009, p. B5.

Joshi Sonal, "India after Busting Land Mafia Organized Crime Involving Former Government Officials and Apartment Developers," http://www.indiadaily.com/editorial/3897.asp, August 1, 2005.

Salil Tripathi, "India Faces an 'Enron Moment,'" *The Wall Street Journal,* eastern edition, January 9, 2009, p. A11.

Craig Whitcher, Tyler Caskill, Andrew Reece, and Jake Denoncourt, "Satyam Case," Working Paper, George Mason University, 2009.

Index

Page numbers followed by n refer to notes.

A

Abbott, L. J., 60
Ability to continue as going concern, 465–466;
    see also Going-concern uncertainties
Absolute assurance, impossibility of, 46
Academy Awards, 18
Access to programs and data controls
    automatic terminal logoff, 848
    common controls, 848–849
    passwords, 847–848
    physical security controls, 848
    proliferation of hacking, 847
Accountability, 230
Accountants
    responsibilities in compilation, 560
    responsibilities in review, 559
Account balance
    acquisition and expenditure cycle, 325, 329
    analytical procedures for, 138–140
    assertions in production cycle, 381
    debt and equity accounts, 425
    management assertions about, 10
    materially misstated, 817
    production cycle, 375
    revenue and collection cycle, 279, 283
Accounting; *see also* Fraudulent financial
        accounting
    for accounts receivable, 276
    cash basis framework, 566
    complicated topics in, 415
    components, 10
    and control system flowchart, 188–190
    cover-up attempts, 229
    equity method, 431–432
    fraudulent, 123
    for investments, 428
    for leases, 412–143
    modified cash basis framework, 566
    other comprehensive bases of, 566
    outsourcing of, 100
    payroll, 358
    problems for inventory, 369
    skewed distributions, 716
    software for, 99
    special purpose frameworks, 566–568
    violations at General Electric, 430
Accounting and Review Services Committee,
        558, 609
Accounting cycles, 231–232
Accounting estimates, 422
    auditing, 135–136
    definition, 135
    finance and investment cycle
        examples of estimates, 422
        kinds of controls, 422
    review of, 458–459
    subjective, 133
Accounting principles
    AICPA rule, 609–610
    changes in, 512–513
    company selection of, 135–136
    in India, C26
Accounting Principles Board, 609
    Opinion No. 18, 431
Accounting Research Bulletins, 609–610

Accounting Services Executive Committee, Trust
        Services Data and Integrity, 573
Accounting Standards Board Codification 250, 512
Accounting Standards Codification
    No. 340, 331
    No. 350, 333
Accounting Standards No. 3 on audit documentation,
        107–108
Accounting Standards Update, 412
Accounts
    attention directing, 140
    cycles of, 92
    factors relating to misstatements, 133
    in finance and investment cycle, 415
    review for audit completion, 457–458
    selected for confirmation, 285
    significant, 185
    unusual entries, 458
Accounts payable
    confirms with vendors, 330
    finding fraud signs in, 335–336
    recording, 323, 325
Accounts payable trial balance, 324
Accounts receivable
    accounting for, 276
    collectability, 273
    computerized process, 277
    confirmation of, 285–289
    existence assertion, 283
    factoring, 290
Accounts receivable aging, 278
Accounts receivable testing, 278
Accruals, 422
Accrued income taxes, substantive procedures, 330–331
Accrued liabilities, substantive procedures, 330, 331
Accuracy assertion
    for payroll cycle, 195
    in purchasing and disbursement, 182
Accuracy in recording transactions, 13
ACL software, 102
Acquisition and expenditure activities, 232
Acquisition and expenditure cycle; *see also* Payroll
        cycle
    assertions about transactions and events, 327
    audit evidence
        accounts payable trial balance, 324
        fixed asset reports, 324
        open purchases, 323
        purchases journal, 324
        unmatched receiving reports, 323
        unmatched vendor invoices, 323
    audit issues, 335–341
    audit plans, 354–355
    audit risk model, 335
    control risk assessment
        account balances, 325
        control activities, 325
        custody, 325–326
        entity-level controls, 325
        periodic reconciliation, 326
        summary of, 326–328
        tests of controls, 326
    Financial Accounting Standards Board on, 318
    fraud cases: extended procedures, 336–339
        phony doctors, 338–339
        printing money, 337–338
        fraud signs in accounts payable, 335–336
    inherent risks
        company examples, 319
        misstated costs and expenses, 319

        noncancelable purchase agreements, 319
        relative assertion risks, 320
        unrecorded liabilities, 319
    internal control questionnaire, 351–353
    linked to production cycle, 369–370
    professional standards references, 317
    PCAOB inspections, 340
    substantive procedures
        auditing other accounts in, 330–334
        completeness assertion, 328–330
        other expenses, 334
        presentation and disclosure, 334
    typical activities
        basic activities, 320–321
        purchasing goods and services,
            321–322
        receiving goods and services, 322
        recording assets, expenses and
            liabilities, 323
    WorldCom fraud, 318
Acts discreditable, 612–613
Actual costs vs. standard costs, 372
Actual rate of deviation, 729
Act-utilitarianism, 593
Adelphia Communications, Inc., 124, 319, 634
Adhikari, Anand, C29
Adjusting entries
    for audit completion, 467–469
    research on, 469
    rollover method, 468
    uncorrected misstatements, 468
Administrative level controls, 868, 869
Adverse opinion, 201, 501
    definition, 54–55
    and departures from GAAP, 503, 504–505
    and departures from GAAS, 503
    effect on internal control, 204
    on internal control, 199
Advertising, AICPA rules, 613–614
Advisory Committee on the Auditing
        Profession, 635
Advisory services, 20–21
Aged trial balance, 278
Agreed-upon procedures
    attestation standards, 550, 551
    in compliance attestation, 553
    purpose, 549–550
    reports, 550, 551
Agreed-upon procedures engagement, 549
AICPA; *see* American Institute of Certified Public
        Accountants
AICPA Auditing Statements of Position, 39
Aiding and abetting, 656–657
AIG Credit Facility Trust, 518
Alberta, Timothy J., 717
Albrecht, W. S., 222n, 225n, 228n
Alexander Grant & Company, 593
Allen, C., 616
Allocation, 12
Allowance for sampling risk, 724–725, 758, 768
    basic, 808–809
    incremental, 807–808
    in MUS, 802
Allstate Trucking, 50
Alpha errors, 716
Alternative procedures, revenue and collection
        cycle, 289
Amazon.com, 183
Ambassador Eyewear Group, 290
Amerco, 521, 634

II

Index

American Accounting Association, 5, 6, 21, 119n, 170
    Committee on Basic Auditing Concepts, 4
American Bankers Association, 240
American Bar Association, 461
American depository receipts, C26–C27
American Institute of Certified Public Accountants, 21, 47, 119n, 170, 240, C9; *see also* Assurance Services Executive Committee; Code of Professional Conduct
    on assurance services, 8, 570
    Attest Engagements on Greenhouse Gas Emissions Information, 574
    Audit Sampling Guide, 130, 759, 772, 802, 816, 819
    Audit Standards Guide, 39
    Center for Public Company Audit Firms, 55
    on client confidentiality, 146
    and codes of conduct, 594
    on core competencies, 27
    definition of audit sampling, 726
    Division for Firms, 566–567
    on educational requirements, 24
    and generally accepted government auditing standards, 692
    Joint Ethics Enforcement Program, 617–618
    Joint Trial Board, 618
    on operational auditing, 684
    on operational audits, 22
    Private Companies Practice Section, 566–567
    Professional Ethics Executive Committee, 595, 596–597
    on purpose of audit, 5
    on purpose of audits, 497
    on review and compilation services, 558
    rules as moral clause, 612
    rules of conduct
        accounting principles, 609–610
        acts discreditable, 612–613
        advertising and solicitation, 613–614
        commissions and referral fees, 614–615
        compliance with standards, 609
        confidentiality, 610–611
        contingent fees, 612
        form and organization name, 615–616
        general standards, 608
        integrity and objectivity, 607–608
    sampling tables, 760–763
    on self-regulation, 36
    and state licensing process, 25
    WebTrust Service, 573–574
    and XBRL reporting, 9
American International Group (AIG), 411, 472, 518, 634
American Medical Association, 165
American Stock Exchange, 145
America Online, 273
Amersham, 652
Analytical procedures
    for audit completion, 457–458
    for audit planning stage, 136
    and audit stages, 458
    at beginning of audit, 142
    by computer, 103
    definition, 97, 136
    at end of audit, 142
    examples, 142
    information sources and form of, 97
    for obtaining evidence, 90–98
        Auditing Standards Board on, 91
        PCAOB on, 91
        types of procedures, 92
    production cycle, 380–381
    revenue and collection cycle, 284
    in risk assessment, 136–142
        asking what could be wrong, 140–141
        cash flow analysis, 141–142
        compare expectations with recorded amount, 139
        compare results with forecasts, 141
        define significant differences, 139
        develop expectations, 138
        documentation, 140
        horizontal analysis of statements, 139
        investigate significant differences, 139–140
        vertical analysis of statements, 139
    for sampling risk, 799–800
    and Sarbanes-Oxley Act, 142
Anand, Geeta, C29
Andrews, C. E., C2
Annual report; *see* Form 10-K
Antifraud section
    Securities Act, 647
    Securities Exchange Act, 648–649
AOL Time Warner, 608
Apollo Group, Inc., 644
Apple Inc., 521
Appropriate evidence, 50
    requirements for, 51
    and sufficient evidence, 52
Appropriate financial reporting framework, 549
    application of requirements, 568–570
        standards, 568
        written report/oral advice, 570
Approved vendor list, 321
Arm's length transactions, 413
Arredy, James T., 135
Arthur Andersen, 43, 135, 493, 657, C23
    dissolution of, 410, C17
    and Enron, 77, 117, 589, 598, 604
    prosecution of, 655
    and PTL Club, C8
    and WorldCom, 318, 458
Arthur Andersen, case
    aftermath, C3–C4
    codefendant in class action suit, C4
    failure to detect fraud, C1
    overturned by United States Supreme Court, C3
    trial for obstruction of justice, C1–C2
        conviction, C2–C3
        defense argument, C2
        prosecution case, C2
Arthur Young & Company, C17
Asare, S. K., 524
Asbury Automotive Group, 514
Ashtom, R. H., 98
Assertion risks for revenue and receivables, 270
Assertions
    about payroll cycle, 195
    debt and equity accounts, 425
    investment accounts, 428
    risk level of, 128
Assets, 12, 458
    custody of, 180
    misappropriation, 126
    missing or nonexistent, C20
    periodic reconciliation, 326
    writing of, 414
Associated with financial statements, 519–520
Association of Certified Fraud Examiners, 698
    and codes of conduct, 595
    on core competencies, 27
    study on revenue recognition, 272
Assurance, 3
    definition, 3
    reasonable vs. absolute, 46
Assurance services
    Academy Awards and, 18
    audit services, 18–19
    consulting services excluded, 9
    definition, 7, 571–572
    elements and boundaries of, 8
    enhanced business reporting, 572
    examples, 8–9
    eXtensible Business Reporting Language, 572
    and information technology, 9
    and megatrends and business risks, 571
    nonaudit attestation engagements, 19
    Professional Sports Authenticator, 7
    reasons for developing, 570–571
    relation to auditing and attestation, 7–9
    for sustainability, 574–575
    sustainability reporting, 574–575
    trust services, 572–574
Assurance Services Executive Committee (AICPA)
    on new business risks, 571
    XBRL Assurance Task Force, 572
Astronaut Pen, 689
Attention directing, 140
Attestation, 3, 48
Attestation engagement
    applying agreed-upon procedures, 549–550, 551
    assumptions on prospective/pro forma financial information, 442
    compared to audit, 549
    compliance attestation, 553–554
    definition, 6
    engagements related to, 549
    examination of entity's internal control, 552
    example, 548
    examples, 6
    financial forecasts and projections, 550–552
    governmental auditing, 689–690
    introduction to, 548–549
    professional standards, 549
    professional standards references, 546
    pro forma financial information, 550–552
    relation to assurance services, 7–9
    responsible party, 48
    review and compilation as subset of, 558
    review of management's discussion and analysis, 554
    and service organizations, 554–557
    subject matter, 48
    summary of reports, 557
    types of
        agreed-upon procedures, 549
        examination, 548
        review, 549
    for Wilson Sporting Goods, 7
Attestation engagement reports, 696
Attestation services, 48
Attestation standards, 549
    for assurance engagements, 74
    and attest function, 74
    in compliance attestation, 553
    definition, 74
    for field work, 75
    general, 75
    and performance principle, 74
    principles, 75
    for reporting, 75
    reporting under, 74
    standards vs. principles, 74
Attest Engagements on Greenhouse Gas Emissions Information, 574
Attest function, 74
Attorney letters
    American Bar Association guidelines, 461
    attorney's response, 460
    client's responsibility, 460
    contents, 460
    and contingent liabilities, 459–461
    pending litigation, claims and assessments, 459–461
    sample, 462
    unasserted claims, 461
Attorney's response, 460–461
Attributes sampling
    to assess control risk, 727–728
    and audit risk model, 726–727
    discovery sampling, 773

documentation, 771
evaluation
    calculating upper limit rate of deviation, 765–768
    evaluation decision, 768–770
    qualitative evaluation of deviations, 770–771
nonstatistical, 773–774
planning
    defining deviation conditions, 753–754
    defining population, 754–755
    determining objective, 753
professional standards references, 751
purpose, 752
revenue cycle assertions, 753
sample items measurement, 764–765
sample selection, 763–764
    block selection, 793
    deciding on method, 793
    haphazard selection, 793
    systematic random selection, 792–793
    unrestricted random selection, 792
sample size determination
    expected population deviation rate, 758–759
    population size, 759
    and sampling risk, 756–757
    tolerable rate of deviation, 757–758
    using AICPA tables, 760–763
sampling risks associated with
    effectiveness loss, 730
    efficiency loss, 730
    risk of overreliance, 729–730
    risk of underreliance, 729
    tolerable rate of deviation, 728–729
    upper limit rate of deviation, 728–729
sequential sampling, 772–773
seven step procedure, 752
substantive procedures, 728
tests of controls, 728
versus variables sampling, 795
Attribute standards, 685–686
Audit
analytical procedures in planning, 138
appropriate financial reporting framework, 549
compared to review of interim financial information, 564
of depreciation schedule, 332
differentiated from attestation engagement, 549
of elements, accounts or items in statements, 565–566
previous, 137–138
PCAOB requirements
    engagement planning, 197–198
    evaluating deficiencies, 198–199
    reporting on internal control, 199–200
    tests of controls, 198
    top-down approach, 198
    wrapping up, 199
purpose of, 497
quality audit, 679
sampling use in, 715
stages of, 42, 47, 49, 51, 53
types of work, 21
Audit Analytics database, 502
Audit committee
auditor's meeting with, 476
of board of directors, 145
inquiry in risk assessment, 143–144
for internal control, 177
Sarbanes-Oxley Act on, 475
skills and composition of, 177
Audit communications
of all misstatements, 468
attorney letters, 459–462
client acceptance, 79
engagement letter, 81, 82, 550
with individuals charged with governance, 475–476

internal control deficiencies, 198–199
management letter, 476
summary of, 475–476
termination letter, 81
written representations, 463–465
Audit completion
audit timeline, 456–457
and Dell Inc., 454–455
fieldwork procedures, 457–470
professional standards references, 453
responsibilities following audit report release date
    communications on governance, 475–476
    management letter, 476
    omitted procedures, 474
    summary of audit communications, 476–477
subsequent events, 470–472
subsequently discovered facts, 472–473
Audit completion date, 456
Audit documentation
arrangement and indexing, 106–108
audit standards for, 105
current files, 105–106
definition, 104
lead schedule, 106
permanent files, 104–105
purpose, 104
software for, 104
Audit documentation review, 469–470
Audited balance, 730–731
in nonstatistical sampling, 819
Audited financial statements
auditors' reports
    consistency of, 511, 512–513
    departures from GAAP, 504–506
    emphasis-of-a-matter paragraphs, 512, 518
    going-concern uncertainties, 511, 513–514
    group financial statements, 512, 516–517
    justified departures from GAAP, 511, 514–516
    lack of independence, 510–511
    other than standard report, 503
    purpose, 497–498
    scope limitations, 507–510
    standard report, 498–502
future of audit reporting, 523–524
General Motors problems, 495
information accompanying, 522–523
integrated with internal control on reporting, 552
professional standards references, 493
reporting topics
    association with financial statements, 518–520
    comparative statements, 520–521
    miscellaneous information, 522–523
    required supplementary information, 523
    summary statements, 521–522
review engagement, 496
SEC rule on filing, 454–455
Audited value, 730–731, 797
in MUS, 804
Auditee, 498
Audit efficiency, 191
Audit engagement
meaning of risk in, 77–78
staffing, 84
understanding internal control prior to, 185
Audit evidence; see also Evidence
acquisition and expenditure cycle
    about intangible assets, 332–333
    accounts payable trial balance, 324
    fixed asset reports, 324
    mergers and acquisitions transactions, 334
    open purchase orders, 323
    physical inspection, 332–333
    purchases journal, 324
    unmatched receiving reports, 323

unmatched vendor invoices, 323
vouching, 333
from client personnel, 463
in fraud cases, 700
on going-concern uncertainties, 465–466
payroll cycle
    clearing accounts, 360
    employee W2 reports, 361
    governmental and tax reports, 260
    labor cost analysis, 360
    payroll register, 359
    personnel files, 259
    year-to-date earnings records, 360–361
prior to and after date of the financial statement, 456
production cycle, 373–375
    inventory reports, 374
    production plans and reports, 374
    sales forecasts, 374
revenue and collection cycle
    accounts receivable listing and aging, 278
    cash receipts listing, 278
    credit check files, 277
    customer statements, 279
    pending order master file, 277
    price list master file, 278
    sales analysis reports, 278
    sales detail (journal) file, 278
in revenue and collection cycle, 270
to test cash
    bank reconciliation, 237
    bank statements, 239–240
    canceled checks, 237–239
    cash disbursements journal, 237
    cash receipts journal, 236–237
Audit failure, 637
potential for, 455
Audit fees
definition, C24–C25
paid by Fortune 100 companies, C24
paid by General Electric 2000–2010, C24
Audit files, 859
Auditing
attestation as, 3
definition and fundamental principles, 42
in early America, 6
failure at Madoff Investment Securities, 45
with fraud awareness, 230
and high-profile fraud, 2
issues in acquisition and expenditure cycle, 339–341
long-term liabilities, 425–426
overall approach for revenue and collection cycle, 269–271
overview, 5
as profession, 37
purpose of, 5
relation to assurance services, 7–9
systematic process
    criteria for evaluating evidence, 5
    obtaining evidence, 4–5
trouble spots in investments and intangibles, 430
types of, 5
use of specialists, 85
Auditing around the computer, 857
Auditing estimates on taxes, 331
Auditing standards; see also Generally accepted auditing standards
versus audit procedures, 39–40
compared to attestation standards, 549
compliance with, 609
convergence of, 40
definition, 39
direct-effect noncompliance, 146–147
and enterprise risk management, 121
fraud risk assessment, 144
and fundamental principles, 40–42

14 Index

Auditing standards; *see also* Generally accepted auditing standards—*Cont.*
   on independent audit, 145–146
   indirect-effect noncompliance, 147
   on materiality, 88
   multiple sets of, 40
   new, 77–78
   on risk of material misstatement, 126
   rule-making bodies, 40
   for special purpose frameworks, 567
Auditing Standards
   No. 3 on audit documentation, 104
   No. 5 on internal control, 50, 442
   No. 5 on public company audits, 199–200
   No. 5 on reporting requirements, 200–201
   source of, 38
Auditing Standards Board, 14, 40, 524, 609
   on audit evidence, 91
   development of standards, 38
   and fundamental principles, 40–42
   on management assertions, 11
   origin and functions, 11n
   reporting for nonpublic companies, 544
   Statement of Position 09-1, 572
Audit marks and explanations, 107
Audit of cash, 231–251
   accounting cycles, 231–232
   cash disbursements
      control activities, 235
      risk of material misstatement, 236
      tests of controls, 235
   cash receipts
      control activities, 232–234
      tests of controls, 234
   evidence to test cash
      bank reconciliation, 237
      bank statements, 239–240
      canceled checks, 237–239
      cash disbursements journal, 237
      cash receipts journal, 236–237
   extended procedures to detect fraud
      analyze mix of cash and checks, 249
      count and recount petty cash, 248
      covert surveillance, 249–250
      document examination, 249
      examine endorsements on checks, 248
      expenditure analysis, 250
      horizontal and vertical analysis, 250
      inquiry, 249
      marked coins and currency, 248
      measure deposit time lag, 249
      net worth analysis, 250
      reasonableness tests, 250
      retrieve customers' checks, 248
   procedures
      bank reconciliation, 240–244
      proof of cash, 245–246
      schedule of interbank transfers, 244–245
   professional standards references, 220
   ways to detect fraud
      case of missing petty cash, 246–247
      laundry money skim, 247
Auditor independence, 589; *see also* Independence
Auditors; *see also* Certified public accountants
   assurances to underwriters, 645–646
   basis for inherent risk assessment, 131
   causes of client losses, 636
   certification requirements, 26
   chartered accountants, 25
   companies free to change, 79–80
   confidentiality of client information, 146
   deceived on inventory, 387–388
   decision not to use confirmation, 285
   direct personal knowledge as evidence, 51
   education requirements, 24

effects of Sarbanes-Oxley Act on profession
   high costs of compliance, 807
   reduced revenue, C24
   restrictions on nonaudit services, 807
examination, 24
and expectation gap, 636
experience for certification, 25
failure at HealthSouth, 144
fees paid to, C24
focus on relevant assertions, 128
and Generally accepted auditing standards, 37–42
   performance, 46–53
   reporting, 53–60
   responsibilities, 42–45
for HealthSouth, C15
information technology, 85
insider trading, 611
from Internal Revenue Service, 23
kinds of certification, 23–24
knowledge of production process, 369
legal liability, 89
limited reporting engagement, 500
meeting with audit committee, 476
number of firms, C17–C18
professional skepticism, 15–18, 221
professional standards references, 1
for PTL Club, C7–C9
and registration statements, 645
response to significant risks
   communicate fraud risk, 145–146
   document risk assessment, 146
   evaluation of accumulated results of procedures, 144–145
responsibilities after date of the financial statement
   subsequent events, 470–472
   subsequently discovered facts, 472–473
responsibilities for noncompliance with laws and regulations, 146–148
responsibility for internal control, 172–174
responsibility to third-party users, 636
risk assessment
   audit team discussion, 143
   business risk, 121
   definitions of fraud, 126
   development of standards, 121
   fraud risk factors, 122–123
   information gathering, 137–138
   information risk, 121–122
   inquiry, 143–144
   and management plans to mitigate risk, 121
   preliminary analytical procedures, 138–142
   recent examples of fraud, 124
   red flags, 123
   risk factor assessment, 144
   risk factor identification, 137–144
   skills and knowledge needed for, 121
   types of fraud, 123–125
   understanding client's strategies, 121
risks faced by, 118
role in subprime crisis, 635
sanctioned by PCAOB, 60
for Satyam Computer Services, C27
SEC constraints, 16
skepticism in financial and investment cycle, 410
skill sets, 27
state certification and licensing, 25
tips on detecting inventory fraud, 388
understanding client's business
   client's accounting principles, 135–136
   company business risks, 135
   company objectives and strategies, 135
   company performance measures, 136
   economic factors, 133
   industry conditions, 133

   nature of company, 134–135
   regulatory factors, 133
understanding of information systems, 183
understanding of management process, 178
use of management assertions, 10–11
Auditors' defenses, 636
   for client claims, 638
   under Securities Act, 646–647
      causation, 647
      due diligence, 647
   under Securities Exchange act, 651
   in third-party claims, 642–643
Auditors' liability, 635; *see also* Legal liability
   changing landscape of
      aiding and abetting, 656–657
      class action suits, 658–659
      increased exposure to litigation, 654
      liability caps, 649–660
      and limited liability partnerships, 657
      proportionate liability, 657–658
      Racketeer Influenced and Corrupt Organizations Act, 656
      recent changes, 660
      Sarbanes-Oxley Act, 655–656
   under common law, 637–643
      to clients, 638
      to third parties, 638–643
   legal environment, 635–637
   significant bases affecting, 654
   under statutory law
      Foreign Corrupt Practices Act, 651–652
      legislation involved, 644
      Securities Act of 1933, 645–648
      Securities Exchange Act of 1934, 648–651
Auditor's liability caps, 659–660
Auditors' report on internal control over financial reporting
   components, 200–201
   definition, 200
   modifications
      effect of adverse opinion, 204
      effect of scope limitation, 204, 205
      material weakness, 201–203
      other situations, 204–206
   standard report, 202
Auditors' reports
   date of, 456
   dual date, 472
   on elements, accounts, or items in statements, 565–566
   on internal control over financial reporting, 496
   for special purpose frameworks, 567–568
Audit plan
   acquisition and expenditure cycle, 354–355
   audit strategy in., 148
   considering work of internal auditors, 84–85
   cycle of accounts, 92
   definition, 47, 82, 105
   engagement partner, 82–83
   finance and investment cycle, 451–452
   goals of, 83–84
   and management assertions, 14
   nature and extent of, 83
   production cycle, 407–408
      physical inventory observation, 407
      pricing and compilation, 407–408
   professional standards in, 82–83
   revenue and collection cycle, 315–316
   risk assessment, 83
   staffing the engagement, 84
   time budget, 86–87
   use of information technology auditors, 83
   use of specialists, 83
Audit plan sample
   audit approach, 167
   audit strategy, 167
   company overview, 165

customers, supplies, and competitors, 165–166
government influences, 165
product pricing, 165
revenue and collection cycle
    controls, 166
    risks, 166
Audit procedures
    in allowable detection risk, 129
    versus auditing standards, 39–40
    cautions on conduct of, 98
    dealing with management assertions, 14
    definition, 39
    and detection risk, 128
    evaluating accumulated results of, 145
    extended, 145
    on finding pending litigation, claims, and assessments, 460
    to gather evidence in acquisition and expenditure cycle, 332–334
    for governmental audits, 690–691
    integrated, 172
    under lack of independence, 510–511
    limited, 523
    to obtain evidence
        analytical procedures, 97–98
        confirmation, 96–97
        inquiry, 95–96
        inspection of documents, 93–95
        inspection of tangible assets, 95
        observation, 95
        recalculation, 97
        reperformance, 97
        scanning of documents, 95
    omitted, 474
    in Parmalat case, C20
    purpose of, 90
    related to financial reporting, 179
    reliance on internal control, 175
    substantive procedures, 49
    for understanding internal control, 185
Audit program, 47, 149
Audit reporting
    on consistency, 511, 512–513
    on departures from GAAP, 504–506
    elements of
        conformity with GAAS, 497
        matters affecting audit or client, 498
        unusual aspects of audit examination, 497–498
    on financial statements and related disclosures, 496
    future of, 523–524
    and General Motors problems, 494–495
    on going-concern uncertainties, 511, 513–514
    on internal control over financial reporting, 496
    justified departures from GAAP, 511, 514–515
    on lack of independence, 510–511
    miscellaneous information, 522–523
    nonpublic companies, 544–545
    other than standard report, 503
    purpose, 497–498
    reissued report, 520
    required supplementary information, 523
    Sarbanes-Oxley Act requirements, 496
    scope limitation report, 507–510
    standard report, 498–502
    summary of issues, 526
    types, 518
        association with financial statements, 519–520
        comparative statements, 520–521
        emphasis-of-a-matter paragraphs, 512
        group financial statements, 512, 516–517
        summary financial statements, 521–522
    updated report, 520
Audit report release date, responsibilities following
    communications on governance, 475–476
    management letter, 476

omitted procedures, 474
summary of communications, 476–477
Audit reports
    Government Accountability Office, 694–696
    use of materiality for, 90
Audit risk
    breakdown of, 127
    definition, 118, 127, 212, 726–727
    professional standards references, 116
    and sampling risk, 799–800
Audit risk model
    acquisition and expenditure cycle, 335
    assessing components of, 270
    and audit sampling, 726–727
    audit strategy in, 148
    control risk, 128
    definition, 269
    definition of audit risk, 127
    detection risk, 128
    in engagement planning, 269–270
    inherent risk, 127–128
    insights produced by, 130
    matrix approach to detection risk, 131
    multiplication of risks, 128–129
    planned detection risk, 129–130
    production cycle, 389
    qualitative measures of risk, 130
Audit sampling
    attributes sampling, 726–730
    compared to sampling, 716
    conditions for, 726
    definition, 726
    documenting procedures, 736
    dual-purpose tests, 734
    evaluating results, 736
    for internal control, 726
    overview, 733
    performing
        determining sample size, 734–735
        sample items measurement, 735
        sample items selection, 735
    planning stage, 734
    rate of deviation, 726
    in substantive procedures, 726
    summary of sampling risks, 733
    tolerable misstatement, 726
    variables sampling, 730–733
Audit Sampling Guide (AICPA), 130, 758, 772, 802, 816, 819
Audit services, 18–19
Audit strategy
    basis for preparing audit plan, 149
    definition, 148
    establishing, 148–149
    example, 167
Audit strategy memorandum, 148–149
Audit team, 27
    brainstorming by, 143
    collecting and evaluating evidence, 50–53
    computerized tests of controls
        auditing around the computer, 857
        audit through the computer, 857–858
        benchmarking, 862
        parallel simulation, 860–861
        program-embedded techniques, 858–860
        simulated data techniques, 861–862
    considerations in computerized processing
        existence of systematic vs. random errors, 841–842
        inappropriate access to files, 842
        lack of audit trail, 842
        output errors, 841
        reduced human involvement, 842
    disagreements in, 47
    effect on internal control of computerized systems, 842–843
    fraud only in financial statements, 125

identifying controls to test, 193
inspection of stockholders' equity, 427
internal control communication, 206–207
management letter, 206
managing identified risks, 178
need for specialized skills, 85
for new clients, 84
performing tests of control, 193–196
preliminary assessment of control risk, 191–193
problems with end-user computing, 864
reasons for evaluating internal control
    assess risk of material misstatement, 174
    effectiveness of control, 172–174
    identify fraud risk, 172
reassessment of control risk, 196
statistical approaches for variables sampling
    classical variables sampling, 796
    monetary unit sampling, 796
understanding client's internal controls
    decision on testing controls, 190–191
    documentation of controls, 190–191
    focus on significant accounts, 185
    identifying controls to test, 185–187
    identifying entity-level controls, 185–187
    identifying transaction-level controls, 186–187
    internal control questionnaire, 188–190
    prior to engagement, 185
understanding materiality, 48
understanding of control activities, 179–180
use of materiality, 90
walkthrough of computerized transactions, 840–841
work in production cycle, 379
work on bank reconciliation, 234–244
Audit through the computer
    advantages, 857
    evaluate effectiveness of controls, 858
    significant controls, 857
Audit timeline
    audit completion date, 457
    audit report release date, 46
    date of the auditors' report, 456
    date of the financial statements, 456
    interim testing, 456
    schematic for, 456
    subsequent events, 473
    subsequently discovered facts, 457, 473
Audit trail
    on computer, 102
    definition, 99
    in end-user computing, 865
    existence of, 857
    from information systems, 183
    lack of, 842
Audit work
    date of, 107
    interim, 86
    tests of controls and timing of, 755
    year-end, 86
Aurora Foods, Inc., 319
Authority for internal control, 176
Authorization
    of cash disbursements, 235
    of credit, 276
    to execute transactions, 180
    of expenditures, 325
    in finance and investment cycle, 423
    of investments, 419
    of securities offerings, 416
    of transactions, 230
Authorization and approval controls, 851
Automated application controls, 849–851; *see also* Computer controls
    definition, 843
    methods of testing, 859
Automatic terminal logoff, 848, 865

Automobile industry
    Car Allowance Rebate Plan, C12
    rise and fall of General Motors, C11–C13
Auto Parts & Repair, Inc., 334
Availability of trust services, 573
Available-for-sale securities, 431

B

Background checks, 230–231
Baddeloo, Marlene, 7
Bagger, Stein, 269
Bains, Jaswindes, 357
Baker Hughes Inc., 148
Bakker, Jim, C5–C9
Bakker, Tammy, C5–C8
Balance assertions for revenue and
        receivables, 270
Balance sheet, management assertions on, 12
Balance sheet ratios, 164
Banco Espirito Santo, 634
Bank Administration Institute, 240
Bank confirmation letter, 240–242
Bank examiners, 5, 23
Bank of America, 243, 414, 717
    in Parmalat case, C20
Bank of New England, 634
Bank reconciliation, 230, 233
    in audit evidence, 237
    in audit of cash, 240–244
    audit team work, 243–244
    cutoff bank statement, 23
    dangers of, 240
    electronic audit confirmation, 243
    procedures, 243
    proof of cash, 245–246
    vouching deposits in transit, 243
Bankruptcy
    General Motors, 495, C12
    and going-concern uncertainties, 514
    Laventhal & Horwath, C8–C9
    Lehman Brothers, 16
    Parmalat, C20
    PTL Club, C9
Banks
    Check Clearing for the 21st Century
            Act, 245
    loan covenants, 413
Bank statements, 238–239
Banner Corporation, 424
BarChris Construction Corporation, 646
Bar codes for inventory count, 384
Barrionuevo, Alexi, C2n
Barron's, 137
Baseball cards, 7
Baseline, 862
Basic allowance for sampling risk, 808–809
Batch processing, 845–846
Batch totals, 851
Bay Area Laboratory Cooperative, 869
BDO Consulting, 126
BDO Seidman LLP, 619, 633–634
Beazer Homes USA Inc., 122
Beckstead and Watts, LLP, 36–37, 60
Bell, Kristen, 375
Bellman, Eric, C29
Benchmark, for calculating materiality, 88–89
Benchmarking, 862
Bernard L. Madoff Investment Securities, 2, 45, 411
Berra, Yogi, 453
Berton, Lee, 7
Best Buy, 458, 520–521
Best practices for brainstorming, 143
Beta errors, 716
Big bath, 414
Big Eight accounting firms, C17

Big Four accounting firms, 6
    decrease on consulting services, 21
    in India, C26
    litigation involving, 634
    nonaudit services, C17–C18
    origin of, 18–19
    PCAOB inspections, 455
    PCAOB inspections on computer
            controls, 840
    report on deficiencies, 59–60
    revenues in 2010, 19
    on use of internal auditors, 85
Big GAAS/Little GAAS, 39
Bill and hold, 297
Billing, 176
Bill of lading, 276, 322
Bill of materials, 371
BJ's Wholesale Club, Inc., 868
Black, Conrad, 124
Blank form confirmation, 285
Blank purchase order, 325
Blind purchase order, 322
Block selection, 722
    in attributes sampling, 793
    in nonstatistical attributes sampling, 773
    in nonstatistical sampling, 819
Bloomberg Businessweek, 137
Bloomingdale's, 385
Blue sky regulations, 644
Blumenthal, Richard, 688
Board of directors
    and internal control, 176
    minutes of meetings, 137, 138
Bodner, Martin, 356
Boeing Company, 388
Bologna, G. J., 222n
Bond indenture, 425
Bond-linked issue premium structures, C18
Bond payment default, C20
Bonds, 416
    recording, 417
Boone, J. P., 660
Borders Group, Inc., 466
Boston Scientific Corporation, 424
Brainstorming, for risk assessment, 143
Bransten, Eileen, 717
Braswell, M., 143
Brazel, J. F., 143
Breach of contract, 637, 638
    cause of client losses, 636
    definition, 637
Bribery, 322, C26
    of employees, 125
Bridge workpaper, 191–192
Bristol-Myers, 273
British Airways, 842, 853
Brown, Cheryl, 684
Bruell, Samuel, C1
Bryant, Kobe, 375
Budget comparisons, 141
Budliov, Barry, 290
Buffett, Warren, 116
Burden of proof
    in common law liability, 638, 639
    recent changes, 654
    under Securities Act of 1933, 646
    under Securities Exchange act, 650
Bush, Loretta Fredy, 135
Business environment, 2
Business expansion, 136
Business magazines, 137
Business reporting, 572
Business risk, 2
    auditor assessment of, 121
    definition, 118
    in inherent risk assessment, 136
    kinds of, 178

    management plans to mitigate, 121
    types of, 118
Business risk analysis, 682
Business Today, C27, C29

C

CAAT; *see* Computer-assisted auditing techniques
Cablevision, 319
Calculated liabilities and credits, 417
Campbell Soup Company, 649
Canadian Institute of Chartered Accountants, 557
    Attest Engagements on Greenhouse Gas
            Emissions Information, 574
    WebTrust Service, 573–574
Canceled checks, 237–239
    examination of endorsements, 248
Capital, raising, 416–417
Capital budget, 416
Capitalizing, 319
Capital leases, 413, 414
Capital markets, effects of Sarbanes-Oxley
        Act on, C23
Capital stock, 427
Car Allowance Rebate Plan, C12
CardSystems, Inc., 868
Carpenter, T. D., 143
Cash
    checks and mix of, 249
    controls over, 231
    liquidity of, 231
    methods of receiving, 232–233
Cash basis framework, 566
Cash disbursements
    control activities, 235
    internal control questionnaire, 265–266
    tests of controls, 235
    vouching, 329
Cash disbursements journal, 237
Cash flow analysis, 141–142
Cash flow forecast, 415–416
Cash for Clunkers, C12
Cash management
    fidelity bonds, 233
    relevant assertions, 236
Cash receipts
    control activities, 232–234
    recording, 233
    tests of controls, 234
Cash receipts journal, 236–237
Cash receipts listing, 278
Cash receipts processing, 232
    internal control questionnaire, 265
Caskill, Tyler, C29
Castarella, J. R., 660
Castellena, J. F., 177
Categorical imperative, 592
Causation defense, 638, 647
Cayman Islands account, C20
Celestica Inc., 424
Cendant, 124, 634
Census Bureau, 572
Center for Audit Quality Alert 2009-55, 572
Center for Medicare and Medicaid Services, 166
Central Bank v. First Interstate Bank, 656
Central Bureau of Investigation, India, C27
Central limit theorem, 812
CEOs
    coercing CFOs into fraud, 125
    examples of fraud by, 124
    and strong control environment, 228
CERT Coordination Center, 867
Certification
    education requirements, 24
    examination for, 24–25
    experience required, 25

Index 17

global perspective, 25
by states, 25
summary of requirements, 26
types of, 23–24
Certified forensic accountant, 23
Certified fraud examiner, 23
Certified information systems auditor, 23
Certified information systems security professional, 23
Certified information technology professional, 23–24
Certified internal auditor, 23
Certified management accountant, 23
Certified public accountants, 21, 23
core competencies required, 27
education requirements, 24
independence, 8
services performed by, 8
state certification and licensing, 25
uniform mobility, 25
Certified public accountants exam, 121
Chain of custody, 230
Chain of custody of evidence, 700
Channel stuffing, 273
by Vitesse Semiconductor Corporation, 274
Characteristic of interest, 720
Chartered accountants, 25
Charter International, 514
Chazen, C., 611n
Check Clearing for the 21st Century Act, 245
Check digits, 851
Check forgery, 221, 237–238
Check kiting, 244–245
Checks, third-party, 360
Check 21, 245
Chief financial officers, coerced into fraud, 125
China Construction Bank, 619
Chiquita Brands International Inc., 148
Chisholm Bierwolf Nelson & Morrill LLC, 517
Chrysler Corporation, 495
Chung Mong-koo, 124
Church, B., 59
Circumstance-imposed scope limitations, 507–508
Citibank, 423
Citigroup, Inc., 414, 471, 867
CIT v. Glover, 640
Civil liability
Securities Act of 1933, 645–646
Securities Act vs. Securities Exchange act, 650
Securities Exchange Act of 1934, 650
Clancy & Company PLC, 517
Class Action Fairness Act of 2005, 658–659
Class action suit, 658–659
co-defendants with Arthur Andersen, C4
Classical variables sampling
definition, 731, 796
difference estimation, 817
evaluating sample results
if account balance misstated, 817
precision interval construction, 815–816
significance of precision interval, 815
mean-per-unit estimation, 812
methods
central limit theorem, 812
normal distribution theory, 812
versus monetary unit sampling, 817–818
planning stages
individually significant items, 812
stratification of population, 812
ratio estimation, 817
sample items measurement, 815
sample selection, 815
sample size determination
calculating, 814–815
formula, 812
risk of incorrect rejection, 813–814
standard deviation, 814
Classification, 13–14
Classification assertion, for payroll cycle, 195

Clearing account, 360, 458
Client acceptance or continuance
cases of rejection, 78
changes of auditors, 79–80
contact with predecessor auditor, 79–80
evaluation, 137–138
filings with SEC, 80
policies for, 79
and predecessor auditor, 78
retention reviews, 79
search for potential problems, 79
Client advocate, serving as, 608
Client-imposed scope limitations, 507, 508
Client losses
from breach of contract, 636
from fraud or misrepresentation, 636
Client relationships, 57
Client representation, 463
Clients
auditor liability to, 638
auditor search for problems with, 79
auditor understanding of
nature of business, 47
for risk assessment, 49, 133–136
confidentiality of information about, 146
documents prepared by, 94
engagement letters for, 82
financial involvement with, 601
going-concern uncertainties, 465–466
integrity of management, 78–79
inventory-taking instructions, 382–383
loans to or from, 601
opinion shopping, 568
rule on confidential information, 610–611
summary of auditors' liability, 652–654
termination letters, 82
whistle-blowing on, 610–611
Clinton, Bill, 869
Cloud computing, 99–100, 866
Clouse, Thomas, 377
Coalition to Advance the Protection of Sports Logos, 419
Code of Ethics for Professional Accountants, 24
Code of Professional Conduct (AICPA), 43, 80, 558
consequences of violating
public regulatory discipline, 618–619
self-regulatory discipline, 617–618
independence, 598–603
advocacy, 602–603
familiarity threat, 601
management participation, 602–603
on independence, 589
Rule 203, 514–515
Codes of conduct, 230
Codes of ethics, international convergence, 616
Codes of professional conduct, 590
Cohen, J., 476
Collectability
of accounts receivable, 173
review for, 289–290
Collins, Susan, 688
Collins & Aikman, 319
Collusion, among employees, 222
Colombian terrorist group, 148
Colonial BancGroup, 424
Comfort letters, 646
Commissions, 614
AICPA rules, 514–615
definition, 614
as impairment of independence, 615
permitted, 614
Committee of Sponsoring Organizations, 185, 501, 502, 552, 771
composition of, 119
definition of internal control, 170
integrated internal control framework, 175–184
Internal Control over Financial Reporting, 176

Committee on Accounting Procedures, 609–610
Committee on Capital Markets Regulation, 659–660
Common law, 636
Common law liability
audit failures, 637
auditors' defense in client claims, 638
to clients
breach of contract, 638
fraud, 638
gross negligence, 638
ordinary negligence, 638
legal precedents, 638–641
plaintiffs in, 637
summary of, 65
third-party liability, 638–643
tort actions, 637
Communication
in ERM, 120
in internal control, 183–184
Companies
auditor understanding of
management personnel, 134
operating characteristics, 134
organizational structure, 134
significance of investments, 134
sources of earnings, 134
sources of funding, 134
business risks, 136
employee hotlines, 228
ethics officers, 228
going-concern status, 142
identification of related parties, 134
indicators of noncompliance, 147
internal control and size of, 177–178
misstatements by, 273
objectives, 118, 136
overview of fraud types, 125
performance measures, 136
perils of related-party transactions, 135
risks faced by, 118
selection of accounting principles, 135–136
separation of duties in, 180–181
strategies, 118, 136
Comparative financial statements
reporting on, 520–521
review and compilation service, 561–562
Comparison program utilization, 860
Compensating control, 193, 421
Competence and capabilities
and due care, 44–45
from education, 43
of internal auditors, 84
Competitive bids, 321–322
Competitors, fraud pertaining to, 125
Compilation, 19
Compilation and pricing procedure, 380
Compilation and review services, liability for, 643
Compilation engagement
accountants' responsibilities, 560
plain-paper engagements, 561
purpose, 560
types of reports, 560–561
Compilation services, and fraud, 561
Completeness
definition, 12–13
of recorded sales, 277
risk level of, 128
Completeness assertion
acquisition and expenditure cycle, 328–330
about account balances, 329
search for unrecorded liabilities, 329–330
versus existence assertion, 798
for inventory count, 383
for long-term liabilities, 425
for payroll cycle, 195
production cycle tests of controls, 379, 380
in purchasing and disbursement, 182

Completeness assertion—Cont.
  revenue and collection cycle, 270
  for sales, 276
Completeness direction, 195
  dual-direction tests of controls, 288–289
Complexity, 2
Complex transactions, 414
Compliance
  with auditing standards, 609
  costs of Sarbanes-Oxley Act, 200
  with ethical requirements, 80–82
  with independence requirements, 80–82
  with management directives, 682–683
  in management objectives, 170
Compliance attestation
  conditions for, 553
  contractual obligations, 553
  federal and state regulatory requirements, 553
  major steps, 553
  risk considerations, 553
  types of reports, 553, 554
Compliance audits
  fraud in, 697
  by internal auditors, 684
Compliance controls, 170
Component auditors, 517
  function of, 516–517
Computer abuse; see Computer fraud
Computer-assisted auditing techniques, 97, 278
  for analytical procedures, 103
  for confirmation, 103
  for document examination, 103
  for fraud investigation, 103
  for recalculation, 102–103
  for scanning, 103
  software packages, 101–102
Computer Associates, 273
Computer Associates 28 International Inc., 124
Computer controls
  automated application controls, 854
    definition, 849–851
    input controls, 851–852
    processing controls, 852
  general controls
    access to programs and data control, 847–849
    computer operations controls, 845–847
    hardware controls, 843
    program change controls, 845
    program development controls, 844–845
    summary on, 849, 850
  implementation of, 857
  output controls
    control total reports, 853
    master file change, 853
    output distribution, 853
    review for reasonableness, 853
Computer forensics, 869
Computer fraud
  and computer forensics, 869
  cybercrimes, 866–867
  hackers, 868
  key findings on, 867
  preventive, detective, and damage-limiting controls, 868–869
  at ProQuest, 867
  recent incidents, 867
  types of activities, 867
Computer-generated purchase orders, 325
Computer-initiated transactions, 99
Computerized information processing, 181–182
Computerized payroll
  control functions, 362
  service organizations for, 362
Computerized processing environment, 181
  computer as audit trail, 102
  effect on audit plan
    computer-assisted techniques, 101–103
    data availability, 101

extent of use, 100
need for specialized skills, 101
organizational structure, 100
evaluation criteria
  cloud computing, 99–100
  initiation of transactions, 99
  potential for error or fraud, 99
  potential management supervision, 99
  temporary transaction trails, 99
  uniform processing, 99
Computerized processing systems
  and assessment of internal control, 840
  audit team walkthrough of transactions, 840–841
  automated application controls, 843
  cloud computing, 866
  computer operators, 847
  control group, 847
  control issues related to, 845
  control risk assessment, 855–856
  data conversion operators, 846
  effect on understanding of internal control, 842–843
  end-user computing, 864–866
  existence of systematic vs. random errors, 841–842
  general controls, 843
  inappropriate access to files, 842
  lack of audit trail, 842
  librarians, 846–847
  objectives of operations controls, 847
  outsourcing, 866
  points of potential misstatement, 856
  possibility of input errors, 841
  and processing failures, 847
  professional standard references, 838
  reduced human involvement, 842
  separation of duties, 847
  systems analysts, 847
  testing controls, 857–862
Computerized sales and accounts receivable, 277
Computer operations controls
  batch processing, 845–846
  end-user computing
    data entry controls, 865
    limiting concentration of functions, 864
    processing controls, 865
    separation of duties, 864
    systems development and modification, 865–866
  objectives, 846
  purpose, 846
  real-time processing, 846
Computer operators
  functions, 846
  separation of duties, 847
Computer processing complexity, 857
Concurring partner review, 470
Condensed financial statements, 521
Conference Board, 125
Confidence level, 724–725
Confidential client information, 146
  AICPA rule, 610–611
  breach of, 610
  privileged information, 610
  and whistle-blowing, 610–611
Confidentiality of trust services, 573
Confirmation
  of accounts/notes receivable
    auditor's decision not to use, 285
    blank form confirmation, 285
    controlling mailing of, 287–288
    dealing with misstatements, 288
    dual-purpose nature of, 292–293
    electronic process, 287–288
    evidence of existence, 285
    negative confirmation, 285–287
    performance date, 289
    positive confirmation, 285–287

  procedures for interim date, 289
  response to positive confirmation, 289
  of accounts payable, 330
  applications, 96
  of capital stock, 427
  cautions on, 98
  by computer, 103
  of evidence, 96–97
  for notes and bonds payable, 425–426
  revenue and collection cycle, 291
Confirmation letter, 96–97
Conflict of interest, 3
  at Ernst & Young, 16
  examples of, 607
  occasions for, 15–16
Congressional Joint Committee on Taxation, 14
ConocoPhilips, 424
Conrad, Kent, 688
Consequences of business decisions, 3
Consignment goods, 386
Consistency in auditors' report, 511, 512–513
Consolidata, Inc., 593
Consolidated Edison, Inc., 417, 418
Constructive fraud, 637, 639
Consultants, fraud pertaining to, 125
Consulting services, 9
  regulation of, 20–21
Consulting Services Executive Committee, 609
Consumer Federation of America, C25
Context, 8
Contingency, 459
Contingency fees, 615
Contingent fees
  AICAP rules, 612
  definition, 612
Contingent liabilities, 459–461
Continuing audit files, 104; see also Permanent files
Continuing professional education, 24, 43
Contra-assets, 458
Contract, engagement letter as, 82
Contract cost padding, 125
Contractual agreements, 553
Contra-liabilities, 458
Contributory negligence, 638
Control activities
  acquisition and expenditure cycle, 325
  audit team understanding, 179
  for cash disbursement, 235
  for cash receipts, 232–234
  compensating controls, 193
  definition, 178
  documentation of, 179
  at Enron, 179
  in ERM, 120
  finance and investment cycle
    compensating control, 421
    oversight or review, 421
    problems with separation of responsibilities, 421
  information processing activities, 181–182
  payroll cycle
    control checking procedures, 361
    internal control questionnaire, 362
    payroll report, 361
    separation of responsibilities, 361
  performance reviews, 180
  physical controls, 181
  to prevent and detect errors/fraud, 179–180
  preventive controls, 179–180
  principles related to, 179
  in production cycle
    detailed check of activities, 376
    separation of responsibilities, 376
  revenue and collection cycle, 280
  selection and development, 179–180
  separation of duties, 180–181
  spreadsheet goofs, 182
  standards for audit teams, 179

testing, 179
test of operating effectiveness, 191
Control-checking activities, 325
Control environment
    audit committee, 177
    function, 176
    and management team, 176–177
    principles, 176
    and quality of earnings, 176–177
    and size of companies, 177–178
    survey items for assessing, 177
Control group, 847
Controlled reprocessing, 860
Control risk, 118, 127
    attributes risk sampling for, 727–730
    definition, 49, 128
    to determine tests of controls, 198
    preliminary assessment, 191–193
        bridge workpaper, 191–192
        compensating controls, 192
    reassessment, 196
    in risk of material misstatement, 174
Control risk assessment, 727–728
    acquisition and expenditure cycle
        account balances, 325
        control activities, 325
        custody, 325–326
        entity-level controls, 325
        periodic reconciliation, 326
        summary of, 326
        tests of controls, 326
    in computerized environment
        audit team understanding, 855
        focus on control procedures, 855
        steps, 855
        test operating effectiveness, 855–856
    finance and investment cycle
        auditors' work on, 421
        authorization, 423
        control activities, 421
        control over accounting estimates, 422
        custody, 423
        record keeping, 423
        summary of, 424
    payroll cycle, 361
    production cycle
        account balances, 375
        control activities, 376
        custody, 376–377
        direction of tests of controls, 379
        effect on substantive procedures, 375
        entity-level controls, 376
        internal control questionnaire, 377, 405–406
        summary, 379
        tests of controls, 377–378
    revenue and collection cycle, 270
        account balances, 279
        control activities, 280
        control considerations, 279–280
        internal control questionnaire, 280
        summary of, 282
        tests of controls, 280–282
Controls
    compensating, 193
    in computerized processing systems, 845
    entity-level, 185–187
        acquisition and expenditure cycle, 325
        in production cycle, 376
        revenue and collection cycle, 275
    identified for testing, 193
    ongoing evaluation of, 184
    physical, 181
    tests performed on, 190–196
    transaction-level, 186–187
Control system flowchart
    constructing, 188–190
    definition, 188
    illustration of, 190

Control total reports, 852, 853
Control totals, 852, 865
Convergence of standards, 40
Cookie jar reserves, 122, 126
Cooper, Cynthia, 168, 318, 678
Coopers & Lybrand, 44, 368, C17
Copyrights
    auditor questions about, 333
    custody of, 419
Coram, P. J., 524
Core competencies, 27
Corporate charters and bylaws, 137
Corporate culture at Enron, 179
Corporate governance, new focus on, 571
Corporate social responsibility, 574
COSO; *see* Committee of Sponsoring Organizations
Cosourcing strategy, 680
Cost(s)
    comparisons in production cycle, 377
    of compliance with Sarbanes-Oxley Act, 200
    of inventory, 369
    misstated, 319
Cost accounting
    assumptions of, 134
    in production cycle
        overhead allocation, 373
        records needed for, 372
        standard vs. actual costs, 372
Cost accounting department, 360, 373
Cost-benefit analysis of internal control, 171
Coster, F. Donald, 37
Cost of goods sold, manipulation of, 369
Cost of goods sold ratio, 164
Cottrell, D. M., 390n, 715n
Countrywide Financial, 124, 634
Covered members, 598
Covert surveillance, 249–250
Cover-up attempts in accounting, 229
Cowan, Alison Leigh, C10
Cox, Christopher, C23
CPA Candidate Bulletin, 25
CPA examination, 24–25
CPA firms
    audit services, 18
    internal audit services, 22
    involved with PTL Club, C7–C8
    as limited liability partnerships, 657
    number of firms, C17–C18
    rules on form of organization and name, 615–616
CPA Mutual Insurance Company of America, 636
Crawford, Robert M., Jr., 362
Crazy Eddie's, 369
Credit Alliance v. Arthur Andersen, 640, 654
Credit card fraud, 868
Credit check files, 277
Credit granting, 275–276
Creditors, fraud pertaining to, 125
Credit sales, 276
Cressey, D. R., 225n
Crime Investigation Department, India, C28
Criminal liability
    under Securities Act of 1933, 647
    under Securities Exchange Act, 651
Cross-referencing, 106
Cullison, Kelly, C15
Cuomo, Andrew, 634
Current assets report; *see* Form 8-K
Current files
    and audit plan, 105
    composition of, 105
    evidence documentation, 105–106
    planning documentation, 105
Current ratio, 164
CUSIP number, 420
Custody, 230
    and access to blank forms, 326
    of assets, 180, 325–326

    of blank checks, 235
    of cash, 232
    in finance and investment cycle, 423
    fraud in, 377
    of investments, 419
    in payroll cycle, 358
    in production cycle, 376–377
    transfer of, 276
Customer master file, 841
Customer orders, 275–276
Customer order transaction file, 840–841
Customer returns and allowances, 273–274
Customers
    authorization of credit, 176
    billing, 176
    delivery of goods/services to, 176
    fraud pertaining to, 125
Customers' checks, retrieving, 248
Customer statements, 279
Cutoff
    definition, 12–13
    for payroll cycle, 195
Cutoff bank statement, 243
Cutoff date, 13
Cutoff errors, 12–13, 290
Cutting, R. T., 177
Cybercrimes, 866–867
Cycle counts, 385, 390
Cycles of accounts, 92

D

Daewoo, 124
Dangling debit theory, 123
Data
    availability of, 101
    computer operations controls, 847
Databases, 137
Data comparisons, 865
Data conversion operators, 847
Data encryption, 868
Data entry and formatting controls, 851
Data entry controls, end-user computing, 865
Data files, revenue and collection cycle, 277–279
Data mining, 101
Data warehousing, 101
Date of audit work, 107
Date of the auditors' report, 456, 499
    lag between date of financial statements and, 473
    and subsequently discovered facts, 472
Date of the financial statement, 47–48, 456
    lag until date of auditors' report, 473
    and subsequent events, 470–472
Daugherty, B., 59n
Davidson, Laurence Viele, 124
Days' sales in inventory ratio, 164
Days' sales in receivables ratio, 164
Debt and equity accounts, 425
Debt financing, 415
Debt-to-equity ratio, 164
Decision makers, assurance services for, 8
Decisions
    affecting business risk, 2–3
    and information risk, 3
Deep pockets theory, 636, 657
Deerfield College, 684
Defalcation, 126
Defective products, 125
Deferred items, 458
Deficiencies
    communication of, 206–207
    material weakness, 201
    reporting, 184
    significant vs. material weakness, 199
    types of, 198–199

Delivery, 276
Dell, Michael, 454
Dell Inc., 172, 473
    investigation by SEC, 174, 454
Deloitte, Heskins & Sells, C7–C8, C17
Deloitte & Touche, 60, 299, 455, 495, 512, 514, 619, 634, C9, C17
    client rejection, 79
    hired by Fannie Mae, 839
    rejection of client, 78
    revenues 2010, 19
Deloitte Touche SpA, 660
Deloitte Touche Tohmatsu, 660
    and Parmalat, C20
Denise L. Napier et al v. PricewaterhouseCoopers, 649
Denoncourt, Jake, C29
Department of Defense, 22
Department of Human Resources, 22
Department of Justice, 148
    in aftermath of Andersen trial, C4
    enforcement of Foreign Corrupt Practices Act, 652
Department of the Interior, 22
Department of the Treasury, 472
Departures from GAAP, 54–55, 503, 504–506
    auditors' reports on
        adverse opinion, 504–505
        materiality, 504
        qualified opinion, 504
    definition, 504
    justified, 511, 514–515
Departures from GAAS, 503
Deposits in transit, 243
Deposit slips, 233
Deposit time lag, 249
Depreciation schedule, 332
Derivative securities, 429
    for hedging, 120
Design deficiency, 198
Design effectiveness, 187
Destruction certificate, 423
Detection risk, 127, 799
    allowable, 129
    basic definition of, 732
    definition, 52, 128, 730
    matrix approach, 131
    planned, 129–130
    in revenue and collection cycle, 270–271
    for significant risks, 145
Detective controls, 180
Development of standards, 38
Deviation conditions, in attribute sampling, 753–754
Deviations, 753
    quantitative evaluation of, 770–771
Difference estimation, 817
Digitized signature, 851
Diligence Inc., 610
Direct Brokerage, 656
Direct-effect illegal acts, 222
Direct-effect noncompliance, 146–147
Direction of tests of controls
    completeness, 194
    dual-direction, 195
    occurrence, 194–196
    in production cycle, 379
Disclaimer of opinion, 501
    because of lack of independence, 510–511
    definition, 55
    and departures from GAAP, 503
    on internal control over financial reporting, 204
    on internal control, 199
    and scope limitation reports, 508, 510
    and unaudited financial statements, 519–520
Disclosure
    about fees, 605
    for investments, 429–430
    for special purpose frameworks, 568

Discount pricing, 368
Discovery sampling, 773
    using AICPA tables, 760
Discriminant Z-score, 164
Disraeli, Benjamin, 633, 714
Division of responsibilities, 516–517
Documentary evidence, 51
Documentation
    of analytical procedures, 140
    of attributes sampling, 771
    of audit sampling procedures, 736
    in computerized processing, 844–845
    of control activities, 179
    of internal control
        control system flowchart, 188–190
        decision on tests of controls, 190–191
        internal control questionnaire, 188, 189
        narrative description, 188
    long-term debt and interest expense, 426
    of risk assessment, 146
    of sampling procedures, 725
    of variables sampling, 820
Document examination
    by computer, 103
    to detect fraud, 249
    in tests of controls, 194
Documents
    formal authorization, 94
    inspection of
        prepared by client, 94
        prepared by outside parties, 93–94
        scanning, 95
        tracing, 94
        vouching, 94
    ordinary, 94
Dollar Tree Stores, Inc., 868
Dooley, James T., 387
Doran, John P., 414
Dortch, Richard, C7, C9
Doty, James R., 1, 587, 603, C28
Double billing, 125
Doubtful account ratio, 164
Dromm, Kenneth, 362
Drugstore.com, 381
Dual control, 419
Dual date, 472
Dual-direction tests of controls, 195
    of inventory count, 383
    revenue and collection cycle, 281–282
Dual-purpose procedures, 292–293
Dual-purpose tests, 734
    definition, 196
Due care, 43–45, 80
    and competencies and capabilities, 44–45
    definition, 44
    in principles of conduct, 596–597
Due diligence defense, 647
Dun & Bradstreet, 141
Duncan, David, C1, C2
Dupont Corporation, 471
DWS Retail Ventures, Inc., 868

E

E. S. Bankest, 633–634
Earnings
    channel stuffing, 273
    company sources of, 134
Earnings before interest and taxes/total assets ratio, 164
Earnings management, 458
eBay, 7, 183, 377
Ebbers, Bernie, 124, 168
Echo check, 843

E-commerce
    growth of, 572–573
    lack of security, 572–573
Economic factors, in inherent risk assessment, 134
Economic motivation, 225–226
EDGAR database, 80
Education
    for competence and capabilities, 43
    required for certified public accountants, 24
Effectiveness loss
    in attributes sampling, 730
    in variables sampling, 732
Efficiency loss
    in attributes sampling, 730
    from risk of incorrect rejection, 813
    in variables sampling, 732
Egocentric motivation, 225
Ehrlich, Paul, 838
Eining, M. M., 225n
Electronic audit confirmation, 243
Electronic confirmation process, 287–288
Electronic data interchange, 276, 321
Electronic product codes, 384
Electronic signatures, 101
Electro Scientific Industires, 387
1136 Tenants' Cooperative v. Max Rothenberg & Company, 643
Elliott, J., 122n
Elliott, R. K., 222n, 225n
El Paso, 411
Embedded audit modules, 859
Embezzlement, 125
    definition, 126, 222
Emmons, D. W., 165n
Emphasis-of-a-matter paragraphs, 523
    in auditors' report, 512, 518
Employee assistance programs, 228
Employee bribery, 125
Employee fraud, 125
    collecting evidence of, 230
    definition, 126, 222
    direct-effect illegal acts, 222
    in down economy, 221
    at Electro Scientific, 387
    embezzlement, 222
    and errors, 222
    examples, 221, 223, 224, 225, 226, 227, 231, 233
    financial scope of, 223
    fraudster characteristics, 223–224
    fraud triangle
        motivation, 225–226
        opportunity, 226
        rationalization, 227
    at Kraft Foods, 322
    prevention of
        difficulties, 227–228
        employee monitoring, 228–230
        enforcement, 230–231
        integrity by example, 230–231
        internal control activities, 228–230
        managing people pressures, 228
    professional standards references, 220
    red flags, 222–223
    sources of, 221–222
    white-collar criminals, 223–224
Employee hotlines, 228
Employees
    collusion among, 222
    monitoring to prevent fraud, 228–230
Employee W2 reports, 358, 361
Ending inventory, overstated, 369
End-of-period adjustments, 174
End-user computing
    audit team issues
        lack of documentation and resting, 864
        lack of physical security, 864

lack of separation of duties, 864
limited computer knowledge, 864
control considerations
computer operations controls, 864
data entry controls, 865
processing controls, 865
systems development and modification, 865–866
spreadsheet and data controls, 866
Engagement, unable to complete, 608
Engagement letter, 636
for agreed-upon procedures, 550
definition and purpose, 82
example, 81
internal control considerations, 82
and termination letters, 82
Engagement partner, 82–83
Engagement performance, in quality control, 57
Engagement planning, 76–107
audit documentation, 104–108
audit plan, 86–87
audit team disagreements, 47
in computerized environment, 99–103
computer as audit tool, 101–103
effect on planning, 100–103
considering work of internal auditors, 84–85
for Enron, 77
materiality, 87–90
pre-engagement activities, 77–82
procedures for obtaining evidence, 90–98
PCAOB requirements, 197–198
professional standards references, 76
staffing, 84
steps, 47
time budget, 86–87
time for, 47–48
understanding client's business, 47
use of information technology auditors, 85
use of specialists, 85
Engagement quality reviewer, 470
Engagement quality reviews, 470
Enhanced business reporting, 572
Enright, Guy, 610
Enron Corporation, 2, 3, 36, 38, 56, 58, 78, 124, 135, 169, 416, 493, 514, 521, 589, 594, 598, 604, 654, 655, 657, 658, 659, C1, C23
and Arthur Andersen, 43, 77, 117, C4
corporate culture, 179
financial statements, 14
special purpose entities, 410
Enterprise risk management
definition, 119
elements of, 119–120
manager use of, 178
paralleling auditing standards, 121
Enterprise risk management assessment, 8
Entity-level control
acquisition and expenditure cycle, 325
and assessment, 187
definition, 185
identifying, 185–187
in production cycle, 376
revenue and collection cycle, 275
Environmental audit, 685
Equity Funding Corporation of America, 867
Equity method of accounting, 431–432
ERM; see Enterprise risk management
Ernst & Ernst v. Hochfelder, 649, 654
Ernst & Whinney, C17
Ernst & Young, 52, 54, 60, 269, 272, 455, 466, 472, 520–521, 605, 611, 634–635, 659, 798, 839, C17
and HealthSouth, C14, C15
indictment on tax shelters, C18
litigation against, 16
rejection of client, 78
revenues 2010, 19
Error correction and resubmission procedures, 852

Errors, 753
definition, 126, 222
versus fraud, 123
potential for, 99
preventive controls for, 179–180
Escott v. BarChris Construction Corporation, 646, 654
Ethical behavior, 590
Milgram's experiment, 590
Ethical codes of conduct, 594–595
Ethical decision process, 590–591
Ethical problem, 590
Ethical requirements
compliance with, 80–82
for quality control, 56
Ethical values, 176
Ethics
definition and elements of, 589–590
enforcing agencies, 611
problem situation, 590
Ethics officers, 228
Evaluation decision in attributes sampling, 768–769
Event identification, in ERM, 120
Events
completeness and cutoff, 12–13
management assertions about, 10
production cycle, 379
valuation and allocation, 12
Evidence; *see also* Audit evidence
appropriate, 50, 51
audit procedures for obtaining
analytical procedures, 97–98
confirmation, 96–97
inquiry, 95–96
inspection of documents, 93–95
inspection of tangible assets, 95
observation, 95
recalculation, 97
reperformance, 97
types of, 92
audit trail, 99
chain of custody of, 230
composition of, 4
concerning fraud, 230
criteria for evaluating, 5
criteria for gathering, 51–52
definition, 50
and detection risk, 52
documentary, 51
external, 51
external-internal, 51
internal, 51–52
key characteristics, 53
management assertions, 51
from management assertions, 14
persuasive, 50–51
protection in fraud cases, 700
purpose of obtaining, 4–5
quality hierarchy, 51–52
questionable at Parmalat, C20
relevant and reliable, 51
and risk of material misstatement, 49
substantive procedures to evaluate, 50–51
sufficiency, 52
used by governmental auditors, 5
verbal, 52
verified by computer, 102–103
Examination, 548
in compliance attestation, 553
of management's discussion and analysis, 554
Exception, 753
Existence, 12
alternative procedures to ensure, 289
of investments, 428
provided by confirmation, 285
risk level of, 128
of subsequent events, 471

Existence assertion
accounts receivable, 283
for audit of accounts receivable, 270
in classical variables sampling, 812
versus completeness assertion, 798
for inventory count, 383
in nonstatistical sampling, 818
Exit conference, 687
Expanded-scope governmental auditing, 22, 689
Expectation gap, 636
Expectations, in analytical procedures
compared with recorded amount, 139
developing, 138
investigate significant differences, 139–140
Expected misstatement
definition, 801
in nonstatistical sampling, 819
in sample size determination, 801–802
Expected population deviation, 759
in attributes sampling, 758–759
in nonstatistical attributes sampling, 774
Expected rate of deviation, 734
Expenditure analysis, 250
Expenditures, capitalizing, 319
Expense accounts
padding, 125
testing, 334
Expenses
misstated, 319
prepaid, 330
recognizing, 318
Experience, 43
required for certification, 25
Explanation paragraphs, 512
Explanatory paragraph, 55
Extended audit procedures, 248; *see also* Fraud detection
definition, 145
finance and investment cycle fraud
off-balance sheet financing of inventory, 433–434
revenue forecasts, 435–436
shell corporation, 434–435
unregistered sale of securities, 432–433
for fraud in acquisition and expenditure cycle, 336–339
phony doctors, 338–339
printing money, 337–338
for fraud in production cycle, 389–391
revenue and collections cycle fraud, 292–298
Extended records, 859
eXtensible Business Reporting Language, 572; *see also* XBRL
Extent of tests performed, 129
External auditing, 679
External auditors, 21
consideration of work of internal auditors, 84–85
control risk assessment, 128
evaluation of control environment, 228
evidence provided to, 4
financial reporting objectives, 170
External evidence, 51, 243
External-internal evidence, 51
ExxonMobil, 369

F

Factor, accounts receivable, 290
Fair value measurement
auditing, 429–432
classification of marketable securities, 431
confirmation, 431
disclosure, 430
with equity method of accounting, 431–432
hierarchy of, 429

Fair value measurement—*Cont.*
   income accounts, 431
   nature of investments, 431
   vouching investment costs, 431
Fake credit checks, 125
Fakunle, Olaronke, 335
False advertising, 125
False benefit claims, 125
False invoices, 125
False loss claims, 125
False refunds, 125
Falwell, Jerry, C8
Familiarity threat
   cooperative relationship with client, 601
   definition, 599
   family members, 601
   financial relationship with client, 601
   loans to or from clients, 601
Family members, 601
Fannie Mae, 2, 182, 411, 512, 518, 866
   accounting problems, 839
   dismissal of KPMG, C18
Farrelly, Jim, 340
FASB; *see* Financial Accounting Standards Board
Fastow, Andrew, 135
FastTrak Corporation, 48
Federal Accounting Standards Advisory Board, 609
Federal Bureau of Investigation, 249
   on computer forensics, 869
Federal Conspiracy Statute, 644
Federal Deposit Insurance Corporation, 513
Federal Emergency Management Agency, 120
Federal False Statements Statute, 644
Federal Mail Fraud Statute, 644
Federal Mogul, 471
Federal Reserve System, 237–238
Federal Trade Commission, on contingent fees, 612
Fedewa, Mark, 167
Fees, disclosure about, 605
Feinstein, Diane, 688
Ferguson, Ronald E., 124
Fictitious wages, C27
Fidelity bonds, 233
Fieldwork
   procedures performed during
      adjusting entries, 467–468
      attorney letters, 459–462
      audit documentation review, 469–470
      completing substantive procedures, 457–459
      financial relationship disclosure, 467–469
      going-concern uncertainties, 465–466
      written representations, 463–465
   standards, 41, 42, 75
File and operator controls, 852
Files, computer operations controls, 847
Finance and investment cycle
   audit plan, 451–452
   control risk assessment
      auditors' work, 421
      authorization, 423
      control activities, 421
      control over accounting estimates, 422
      custody, 423
      record keeping, 423
      summary of, 424
   Enron's special purpose entities, 410
   example of accounting estimates, 422
   examples of shenanigans, 411
   fraud cases: extended procedures
      off-balance-sheet financing of inventory, 433–434
      revenue forecasts, 435–436
      shell corporation, 434–435
      unregistered sale of securities, 432–433
   inherent risks
      complex transactions, 414
      impairments, 414

      lease accounting, 412–413
      loan covenants, 413
      not disclosing information, 415
      presentation and disclosure, 414
      related-party transactions, 413
   internal control questionnaire, 448–450
   PCAOB inspections, 437
   professional standards references, 409
   recent financial restatements, 410–411
   substantive procedures
      financing activities, 425–427
      investing activities, 428–432
   typical activities
      debt and stockholders' equity, 415
      financial planning, 415–416
      investing transactions, 417–420
      major functions, 415
      number of accounts, 415
      periodic reconciliation, 417
      raising capital, 416–417
      record keeping for long-term liabilities, 417
Financial Accounting Standards Board, 515, 523, 609–610
   on disclosure for investments, 429
   on expense recognition, 318
Financial crisis, auditor's' role in, 635
Financial disclosure, 414
Financial distress ratios, 164
Financial Executives Institute, 170
Financial Executives magazine, 413
Financial forecasts, 550–552
Financial instruments, complicated, 428
Financial instruments, valuation of, 422
Financial literacy, 177
Financial planning, 415–416
Financial projections, 550–552
Financial ratios
   balance sheet ratios, 164
   financial distress ratios, 164
   operations ratios, 164
Financial relationships, 44
Financial reporting; *see also* Internal control
   appropriate framework, 549
   Auditing Standards Board requirements, 11
   auditors' report on internal control over, 200–206
   on completeness and cutoff, 12–13
   cover-up attempts, 229
   at Dell Inc., 174
   effects of Sarbanes-Oxley Act on, C23
   end-of-period adjustments, 174
   on existence and occurrence, 12
   fraudulent, 122–123
   function, 10
   by internal auditors, 21
   international standards, 54
   at Krispy Kreme, 172–173
   in management objectives, 170
   management's annual report on internal control over, 199
   organizations designed to improve, 170
   overview of requirements, 568
   PCAOB requirements, 11
   presentation and disclosure, 13–14
   in real world, 14
   reasons for evaluating internal control over, 172–174
   reports on internal control over, 496
   on rights and obligations, 12
   Sarbanes-Oxley Act on, 10
   with special purpose frameworks, 566–568
   summary on, 10–11
   understandability, 13–14
   unqualified opinion on internal control over, 201
   on valuation and allocation, 13
Financial reporting competencies, 176
Financial reporting framework, 9, 54
Financial Reporting Releases (SEC), 648

Financial reporting standards, 41, 42
Financial results, compared to forecasts, 141
Financial statement assertions, 83
Financial statement audits
   by internal auditors, 684
   overview, 5
Financial statement disclosures, 469
Financial statements; *see also* Audited financial statements
   audit teams and fraud in, 125
   comparative, 520–521
   date of, 47–48, 456
   disclosures
      contingent liabilities, 459–461
      litigation, claims and assessments, 460–461
   double set of, C27
   elements, accounts or items in, 565–566
   of Enron Corporation, 14
   errors vs. fraud in, 123
   forged, C27
   of General Motors, C11–C12
   governmental auditing, 689
   group, 516–517
   horizontal analysis, 139
   horizontal and vertical analysis, 250
   inaccuracy permitted, 87
   including footnote disclosures, 53
   interim, 496
   management assertions about, 10–14
   material information in, 87
   and materiality, 87–90
   misleading, due to GAAP, 515
   penalties for misleading, 171–172
   relation to management assertions, 15
   summary, 521–522
   transparent, 13–14
   vertical analysis, 139
   as window into operations, 118
Financing requirements, 136
First, Bill, 358
First-in, first-out method, 369, 386
First Securities of Chicago, 649
Fisk, M. C., 717
FitzPatrick, R. C., 641n
Fixed asset reports, 324
Fixed sampling plan, 772
Fleet National Bank v. Gloucester Company, 641
Flesher, D., 6
Flextronics, 424
Fogarty, J., 468n
Foley, Mark, 869
Follow-up, 687
Footnote disclosure, 10, 53
   long-term liabilities, 426
Forbes, 137
Forbes, Walter, 124
Ford, Henry, 367
Ford Motor Company, 495
Foreign Corrupt Practices Act
   as amendment to Securities Exchange Act, 651
   examples of infractions, 148
   increasing enforcement of, 652
   purpose, 651
   recent investigations, 651
Foreign currency options, 429
Forensic accountants, 174
Forensic auditing, 700
Foreseeable party, 637, 641
Foreseen party, 640
   definition, 637
Forgery
   on blank documents, 326
   of financial statements, C27
   of time cards, 363–364
Form 8-K (SEC), 80, 146, 648
Form 10-K (SEC), 496, 565, 648

Form 10-Q (SEC), 648
Fortress Re, 634
Fortune, 137
Fraud; *see also* Employee fraud
   in acquisition and expenditure cycle, 319
   Ambassador Eyewear Group, 290
   in auto sales, 375
   cause of client losses, 636
   check forgery, 237–238
   check kiting, 244–245
   coercion of CFOs into, 125
   compliance audit, 697
   cookie jar reserves, 122, 126
   in custody, 377
   at Deerfield College, 684
   definition, 122, 222, 637
   Global Crossing, 272
   inconsequential vs. consequential, 145–146
   insurance and tax fraud, 250
   with invoices, 324
   at Koss Corporation, 284
   management rationales for, 122
   in payroll cycle, 356
      Pay + Plus Payroll, 362
      time card forgery, 363–364
   percentage increase 2005–2011, 126
   potential for, 99
   preventive controls for, 179–180
   red flags, 123
   related parties used in, 413
   in revenue and collection cycle, 269
   in review and compilation, 561
   on rise, 126
   signs in accounts payable, 335–336
   Sirena Apparel Group, 290
   at Société Générale, 848
   types of
      defalcation, 126
      embezzlement, 126
      employee fraud, 126
      fraudulent financial reporting, 123
      larceny, 126
      management fraud, 123
      overview of, 125
      white-collar crime, 125
Fraud audit questioning, 249
Fraud audits
   art of examination, 697–698
   building a case, 700
   example, 699
   fraud examiner responsibilities, 698–699
   identification of fraud, 696–697
   knowledge of applicable laws, 697
   obtaining litigation support, 700
   performance standards references, 677–678
   protecting evidence, 700
Fraud cases
   in acquisition and expenditure cycle, 336–339
      phony doctors, 338–339
      printing money, 336–337
   finance and investment cycle
      off-balance-sheet financing of inventory, 433–434
      revenue forecasts, 435–436
      shell corporation, 434–435
      unregistered sale of securities, 432–433
   revenue collection cycle, 292–298
      canny cashier, 293–294
      dating of transactions, 297–298
      frequent billing, 296–297
      taxman, 294–296
Fraud detection, 696–697
   in audit of cash
      case of missing petty cash, 246–247
      laundry money skim, 247
   auditor responsibility, 125
   audit team responsibility, 125

extended procedures
   analyze mix of cash and checks, 249
   count and recount petty cash, 248
   covert surveillance, 249–250
   document examination, 249
   examine endorsements on checks, 248
   expenditure analysis, 250
   horizontal and vertical analysis, 250
   inquiry, 249
   marked coins or currency, 248
   measure deposit time lag, 249
   net worth analysis, 250
   reasonableness tests, 250
   retrieve customers' checks, 248
   during inventory inspection, 382
Fraud examinations, 697–698
Fraud examiners
   compared to other auditors, 698
   main objectives, 698–699
   and materiality, 699
Fraud investigation
   by computer, 103
Fraud prevention program
   difficulties in building, 227–228
   employee monitoring, 228–230
   enforcement, 230–231
   integrity by example, 230–231
   internal control activities, 228–230
   managing people pressures, 228
   strong control environment, 228
Fraud risk factors, 123
   relation to misstatement, 126
Fraud risks
   communication of, 145–146
   identified in planning stage, 172
   key questions for, 229
   in purchasing departments, 321
   significant risks, 144
Fraudsters
   building a case against, 700
   characteristics, 223–224
   generating false payments, 335
   personality red flags, 222–223
   prosecution of, 231
Fraud triangle
   motivation, 225–226
   opportunity, 226
   rationalization, 227
Fraudulent accounting, 123
Fraudulent financial accounting
   Arthur Andersen, 589
   Bernard L. Madoff Investment Securities, 3
   cases
      Arthur Andersen, C1–C4
      HealthSouth, C14–C16
      Parmalat, C20–C22
      PTL Club, C5–C10
      Satyam Computer Services, Ltd., C26–C28
   and consulting service regulation, 20–21
   effect on analytical procedures, 142
   Enron Corporation, 77, 117, 135, 410, 589
   examples, 2
   and failure of self-regulation, 36
   Gemstar-TV Guide, 465
   HealthSouth, 52, 89, 144, 244, 798
   McKesson & Robbins, 37–38
   at NutraCea, 280
   and passage of Sarbanes-Oxley Act, 169
   at Phar-Mor, 368–369, 390–391
   recent examples, 38, 124
   Satyam Computer Services, 240
   through year-end adjustments, 144
   WorldCom, 318, 589, 678
   Xinhua Finance Ltd., 135

Fraudulent financial reporting
   definition, 122
   examples, 122
   related party transactions, 413
Freddie Mac, 411, C18
Fred Stern & Company, 639
Free Enterprise Fund, 37
Free Enterprise Fund v. Public Company Accounting Oversight Board, 37
Friedman, Thomas L., 571n
Friehling, David, 45
Frieswick, K., 330n
Fundamental principles
   compared to standards, 41
   and definition of auditing, 42
   performance, 46–53
   purpose, 40–41
   reporting, 53–60
   responsibility, 42–45
Funding, company sources, 134
Fung, Michael, 677, 682
Futures contracts, 429

G

GAAP; *see* Generally accepted accounting standards
GAAS; *see* Generally accepted auditing standards
GAGAS; *see* Generally accepted government auditing standards
Galen, M., C10
Gap Inc., 411
Garcia, Michael, 356
Gay, G., 442
Geiger, M. A., 514
Geisler & Oppenheimer, 619
Gemstar, 273
Gemstar-TV Guide International, 124, 465
General attestation standards, 75
General authorization, 180
General controls; *see also* Computer controls
   definition, 843
   methods of testing, 858
General Electric, 411, 430, 636, 652, 654
General Electric, case
   effects of Sarbanes-Oxley Act on auditors, C23–C24
   fees paid to auditors, C24
   SEC disclosure requirements, C24–C25
Generalization argument, 592
Generally accepted accounting principles, 5, 549; *see also* Departures from GAAP
   on accounts receivable, 173
   based on going-concern principle, 513
   on cost accounting, 372
   on face value, 429
   Fannie Mae accounting not in compliance, 839
   interim financial information, 564
   on inventory, 369
   misleading financial statements due to, 515
   versus special purpose frameworks, 566–568
   and types of opinions, 501
   unqualified opinion in conformity with, 54–55
Generally accepted auditing standards, 9, 39, 74
   on audit documentation, 470
   and Auditing Standards Board, 38
   versus audit procedures, 39
   and audit report, 497, 498
   audits based on, 636
   basic vs. fundamental principles, 41
   big vs. little, 39
   categories of, 40–42
   components of, 38
   definition, 38
   departures from, 503
   for governmental entities, 39–40

Generally accepted auditing standards—*Cont.*
   implications of following, 500
   on internal control, 197
   kinds of requirements, 38–39
   milestones in history of, 37–38
   multiple sets of standards, 40
   and PCAOB, 38
   performance principle, 46–53
   purpose, 38
   reporting principle, 53–60
   requirement in inventory counting, 380
   requirement on modified reports, 512
   responsibility principle, 42–45
   and sampling methods, 719
   and SEC, 38
   on verbal evidence, 52
Generally accepted government auditing standards, 689
   and AICPA standards, 692
   audit documentation, 692
   literature on, 692
   on performance audits, 693
   significant reviews, 693
   single audit, 693–694
Generally Accepted Privacy Principles, 573
General Motors, 369, 514, 634
   case
      bankruptcy, C12
      Car Allowance Rebate Plan, C12
      financial information 2003–2008, C11
      going-concern uncertainties, C11–C12
      government bailout, C11
      profile of company, C12
      reorganization in 2009, C11–C12
      return as public company, C13
      stock price performance 2003–2009, C11
   losses and bailout, 494–495
General Re, 124
General standards, 41, 42
General standards of conduct, 608
General use of prospective financial information, 550
Ghost employees, 356
Giant Stores, 641
Gibbins, M., 469
Gill, John D., 229
Gittelsohn, J., 717
Global Crossing, 272
Globalization, 571
Glover, S. M., 40n, 390n, 715n
Going concern, 142
Going-concern principle, 513
Going-concern uncertainties
   ability to continue, 465–466
   in auditors' report, 511, 513–514
   Border Group failure, 466
   companies receiving opinions on, 514
   definition, 513
   General Motors, 495, C12
   mitigating factors, 513
   reports and bankruptcy, 514
   research and reports, 514
   self-fulfilling prophecy, 513
Going green, 8
Goldman Sachs, 651
Gold mining claims, 434–435
Gold Peacock Awards, C26
Golf Magazine, 720
Gonzalez, Albert, 868
Goods
   delivery of, 276
   purchasing, 321–322
   receiving, 322
Goodwill
   example of impairment, 424
   impairment of, 332, 414
   test of, 333

Goodyear Tire Company, 411
Google, Inc., 867
Gorbachev, Mikhail, 17
Governance audits, 684–685
Government, fraud pertaining to, 125
Government Accountability Office, 25, 40
   examples, 23
   functions, 22, 688
   membership, 689
   reliance of Congress on, 688
Governmental Accounting Standards Board, 515, 609
Governmental auditing
   attestation engagements, 689–690
   audit procedures, 690–691
   audit reports, 694–696
   compliance audit fraud, 697
   definition and functions, 22–23
   expanded scope, 689
   federal agencies, 688–689
   financial statements, 689
   and Government Accountability Office, 688–689
   performance audits, 22–23, 690, 691
   performance standards references, 677–678
   Single Audit Act of 1984 and Amendments, 693–694
   standards, 692–693
   state agencies, 689
   Yellow Book standards, 689
Governmental auditing standards, 39–40
Governmental auditors, 21
   evidence used by, 5
   tasks performed by, 679
Governmental reports, 360
Government Auditing Standards, 40
Grandfathered loans, 601
Grant Thornton, 284, 388, 660
   and Parmalat, C20
Grassley, Charles, 688
Gray, G. L., 524
Green, B. P., 561
Green, Raymond, 290
Greene, F. D., 641n
Grocer's Spotlight, 137
Gross margin percentage
   inflating, 381
   and inventory, 380–381
Gross margin ratio, 164
Gross negligence, 637
Gross revenue, 272
Gross revenue benchmark, 89
Group auditors, 516–517
Group engagement team, 516
Group financial statements, in auditors' report, 512, 516–517
Grover, Robert, 717
Guardado, J. R., 165n
Guha, Ramit, C29
Gullapali, D., 413n
Gunny, K., 60n

H

Hackers, 847, 868
Hahn, Jessica, C6
Hall, T. W., 722n, 723
Hamilton, L., 642n
Hamilton, Nick, 610
Haphazard selection, 722
   in attributes sampling, 793
   in nonstatistical attributes sampling, 773
   in nonstatistical sampling, 819
Hardin, Rusty, C2
Hardware, 843
Hardware controls
   definition, 843
   echo check, 843

   parity check, 843
   preventive maintenance, 843
Harkins, Tom, 688
Harmon, Melinda, C2
Harris, Art, C10
Harvard Business Review, 137
Hash totals, 851
Hatfield, T. C., 469
Hawley, Frederick Barnard, 116, 118
Headings, 106
Health Management, 369
HealthSouth, 2, 51, 52, 89, 124, 144, 244, 458, 634
   case
      auditors and risk factors, C15
      conviction of CEO, C16
      massive fraud at, C14–C15
      whistle-blowers, C15–C16
   fraud at, 798
Hedging investments, 429
Hedging with derivatives, 120
Henderson, Frederick, C12
Henze, Diana, C15
Heritage USA, C5, C6
Hermanson, D. R., 59n
Herron, T. L., 722n, 723, 793n
Hertz Global holdings, 500
Hewitt, Conrad, 660
Hewlett-Packard, 471, 472, 651
Higher level of precision, 725
High-quality evidence, 51
Hill, W. T., 793n
Hillison, W., 225, 696n
Hiring, background checks, 230–231
Historical cost accounting, 134
Hoitash, R., 176n
Holder of the privilege, 610
Hollinger International Inc., 124
Hong Kong stock exchange, C23
Horizon/CMS, C14
Horizontal analysis, 250
   definition, 139
Hospital Corporation of America, 358
Hot checks, 125
Houghton, C., 468n
Household International, 273
Houston, R. W., 59n, 469
Hughes, Jennifer, C29
Human relations department, 357–358
Human resources
   and internal control, 176
   and quality control, 57
Hunton, J., 176n
Hurricane Katrina, Walmart's response, 120
Hurtt, Kathy, 17
Hurtt skepticism scale, 17
Hylas, R. E., 98
Hyundai, 124

I

IBM, 369
IDEA software, 102
Ideological motivation, 225
IEC, 5
Imhofe, James, 688
Immelt, Jeffrey, C23
Impairments, 414
Imperative principle, 592
Implementation standards, 685
Imprest bank account, 359
Income, manipulation of, 172, 174
Income accounts, 431
Income statement, management assertions on, 12
Income taxes, accrued, 330–331
Income tax expense, 330–331
Incompatible responsibilities, 180–181

Index 115

Inconspicuous location control, 868
Incremental allowance for sampling risk, 807–808
Incremental confidence factor, 807–808
Indenture, 425
Independence, 43–45
  AICPA rules
    for all audits, 598
    covered members, 598
    familiarity threat, 601
    identified threats, 599
    independence in appearance, 598
    independence in fact, 598
    management participation and advocacy, 602–603
    questionable practices, 599
    and SEC definitions, 600
    summary, 599
  commissions as impairment of, 615
  compliance with requirements, 80–82
  definition, 598
  effects of Sarbanes-Oxley Act, 605
  failure at Arthur Andersen, 598
  Government Accountability Office rules, 606
  of internal auditors, 680
  and nonaudit services, 604–605
  PCAOB rules
    disclosure about fees, 605
    nonaudit services, 604–605
    nonindependent relationships, 603
  in principles of conduct, 596–597
  results of lack of, 80–82
  SEC rules
    disclosure about fees, 605
    nonaudit services, 604–605
    nonindependent relationships, 603
  versus service, 594
  threats to, 44
    adverse interest, 599
    advocacy threat, 599, 602–603
    familiarity threat, 599, 601
    financial self-interest, 599
    management participation, 599, 602–603
    self-review, 599
    undue influence, 599
  violations of, 44
Independence in appearance, 43, 80, 598, 603
Independence in fact, 43, 80, 598, 603
Independence in mental attitude, 43, 80, 589
Independent auditor, 21
Independent auditors, at start of audit, 4–5
Indexing of audit documentation, 106–108
India
  accounting environment, C26
  Central Bureau of Investigation, C27
Indirect-effect compliance, 147
Indirect-effect noncompliance, 147
Individuals charged with governance, 475–476
Industrial age, shift to knowledge age from, 571
Industrial spying, 868
Industry accounting and auditing guides, 137
Industry conditions
  fraud risk factors, 123
  in inherent risk assessment, 133
Industry developments, 136
Industry risk analysis, 682
Information
  control of, 8
  improving quality of, 8
  in internal control, 183–184
  materially false and misleading, 122
  reliable, 2–3
  sources for risk assessment, 137–138
Information and communication, in ERM, 120
Information assurors, 9
Information processing control activities, 181–182

Information risk, 2–3, 118
  auditor assessment of, 121–122
  definition, 121–122
Information risk assessment, 8
Information systems
  audit trail left by, 183
  definition, 183
  in small and medium-sized businesses, 184
Information Systems Audit and Control Association, 27
Information technology, 571
  in assurance services, 9
  in control activities, 179
Information technology auditors, 85
Inherent risk, 118
  acquisition and expenditure cycle
    company examples, 319
    misstated costs and expenses, 319
    noncancelable purchase agreements, 319
    relative assertion risks, 320
    unrecorded liabilities, 319
  assertions in revenue and collection cycle, 270
  definition, 49, 127–128, 131
  to determine tests of controls, 198
  evaluation of, 83
  finance and investment cycle, 411–415
    complex transactions, 414
    impairments, 414
    lease accounts, 412–413
    loan covenants, 413
    not disclosing information, 415
    presentation and disclosure, 414
    related-party transactions, 413
  payroll cycle, 356
  production cycle, 369, 370
    in inventory counts, 390
  in risk of material misstatement, 174
  significant accounts based on, 185
Inherent risk assessment
  categories of misstatement, 131–133
  company accounting principles, 135–136
  company business risks, 135
  company objectives and strategy, 135
  company performance measures, 135
  identification of risk factors, 134–135
  industry, regulatory, and economic factors, 133–134
  nature of the company, 134–135
  process, 132
  understanding client's business, 133
In-house internal audit function, 679–680
Initial public offerings, 645
  effect of Sarbanes-Oxley Act on, 200, C23
Input controls
  authorization and approval, 851
  batch totals, 851
  check digits, 851
  data entry and formatting, 851
  error correction and resubmission procedures, 852
  hash totals, 851
  limit and reasonableness tests, 852
  missing data tests, 852
  record counts, 851
  sequence tests, 852
  valid character tests, 852
  valid sign tests, 852
Input errors, 841
Inquiry
  by auditors in risk assessment, 143–144
  cautions on, 98
  to detect fraud, 249
  to obtain evidence, 95–96
  in tests of controls, 193–194
  verbal, 96
Insider trading, 125, 611
Inspection, 59

Inspection of documents
  cautions on, 98
  to obtain evidence, 93–95
Inspection of tangible assets
  cautions on, 98
  to obtain evidence, 95
Institute for Chartered Accountants of India, C28
Institute of Internal Auditors, 21, 119n, 170
  and codes of conduct, 594
  on core competencies, 27
  definition of internal auditing, 680
  independence standards, 680
  internal auditing standards, 685–696
  International Standards for the Professional Practice of Internal Auditing, 685
  scope of service, 683–685
Institute of Management Accountants, 27, 119n, 170
  and codes of conduct, 595
Insurers, fraud pertaining to, 125
Intangible assets
  assertions about, 331–333
  audit evidence about, 332–333
  custody of, 419
  record keeping, 420
Integrated audit procedures, 172
Integrated report, 501
Integrated test facility, 862
Integrity
  AICPA rules
    conflicts of interest, 607
    misrepresentation, 607
    serving as client advocate, 608
  in control environment, 176
  in principles of conduct, 596–597
Integrity by example, 230–231
Integrity of management, 78–79
Intel Corporation, C17–C18
Interactive date, 9
Interbank transfers, 244–245
Interest expense, 426
Interest rates, 422
Interest rate swaps, 429
Interim Auditing Standards, 38
Interim audit work, 86
Interim date, 47
  for performing confirmation, 289
Interim financial information
  definition, 563
  report on, 565
  responsibilities for reporting on, 563–564
  SEC on, 563
Interim financial statements, 496
Interim review of internal controls, 564
Interim testing, 456
  limitations, 755
Internal audit charter, 680
Internal auditing
  cosourcing strategy, 680
  definition, 21, 680
  independence, 680
  outsourced or in-house, 679–680
  performance standards references, 677–678
  and public accounting firms, 679
  scope of services
    compliance audits, 683
    environmental audits, 685
    financial audits, 683
    governance audits, 684–685
    operational audits, 684
    quality control audits, 685
  stated objectives, 683
  value-added elements, 682–683
Internal auditor certification program, 686
Internal auditors, 21
  changing nature of work, 679
  competence, 84

Internal auditors—*Cont.*
  evidence provided to, 4
  external auditor consideration of work of, 84–85
  functions, 21–22
  independence, 680
  objectivity, 84
  outsourcing or in-house, 679–680
  tasks performed by, 679
Internal audit reports
  elements of, 686–687
  exit conference, 687
  reported findings, 687
  senior management oversight, 687
Internal audit standards
  attribute standards, 685–686
  certified internal auditing certification, 686
  and GAAS, 686
  implementation standards, 685–686
  and internal audit department, 686
  performance standards, 685–686
  practice advisories, 686
Internal control
  to achieve management objectives, 170
  attributes risk sampling for, 727–730
  auditor responsibility, 172–174
  audit procedures and reliance on, 175
  audit sampling for, 726
  in computerized environment, 840
  and control risk, 128
  coping with fraud schemes, 222
  cost-benefit analysis, 171
  definition, 49, 170–171
  effect of computerized processing, 842–843
  in engagement letters, 82
  at Fannie Mae, 839
  features of effective system, 230
  importance in audit engagement, 50
  integrated framework, 175
    control activities, 178–182
    control environment, 176–178
    information and communication, 183–184
    monitoring, 184
    risk assessment, 178
  interim review, 564
  Krispy Kreme report, 172–173
  lapse at Allstate Trucking, 50
  limitations, 170–171
  management responsibilities, 171–174
  to prevent fraud, 228–230
  purpose of, 169–170
  reasonable vs. absolute assurance from, 170
  reporting on, 199–200
  Sarbanes-Oxley Act on, 169–170, 171
  strong, 228
  types of audit opinions, 199
Internal control communication, 206–207
Internal control deficiency
  definition, 198
  design deficiency, 198
  material weakness, 199
  operating deficiency, 198
  significant deficiency, 199
Internal control evaluation
  assess control risk, 191–193
  audit team understanding of, 185–191
  components as criteria for, 185
  design effectiveness, 187
  identify controls to test, 193
  ongoing evaluation, 184
  operating effectiveness, 187
  perform tests of controls
    direction of tests, 194–196
    methods, 193–194
    reassess control risk, 196
  phases of, 186
  professional standards references, 168
Internal control letter, 207

Internal Control over Financial Reporting: Guidance for Smaller Public Companies (COSO), 176
Internal control over financial reporting integrated with audited financial statements, 442
Internal control paragraph of standard report, 498, 499, 501–502
Internal control questionnaire
  in acquisition and expenditure cycle, 326, 351–353
  advantages, 188
  for cash activities, 234
  cash disbursements, 265–266
  definition and purpose, 188
  finance and investment cycle, 449–450
  illustration of, 189
  inventory, 406
  payroll cycle, 362
  production cycle, 377, 405–406
  revenue and collection cycle, 313–314
Internal control tests, 83
Internal environment, in ERM, 119
Internal evidence, 51–52
Internal Revenue Code, 23
Internal Revenue Service, 5, 20, 23, 25, 249, 360, 361, 362
  on contingent fees, 612
  Examination Report on PTL Club, C8
  and PTL Club fraud, C6
  on tax shelters, C18
International Auditing and Assurance Standards Board, 24, 40
International Ethics Standards Board for Accountants, 24
  Code, 616
International Federation of Accountants, 24
  and accounting standards, 596
  and codes of conduct, 594
International Financial Reporting Standards, 55
International financial reporting standards, 5, 54, 549
International Standards for the Professional Practice of Internal Auditing, 685
International standards on auditing, 24
International Standards on Auditing, 40
Interpretive publications, 39
Interpublic, 273
Interviews, 96
Inventory
  accounting problems, 369
  analytical procedures, 380–381
  auto sales fraud, 375
  Boeing company report, 388
  consignment goods, 386
  fraud at Electric Scientific, 387
  fraudulent manipulation of, 368–369
  internal control questionnaire, 406
  largest current asset, 369
  located away from client's premises, 386
  not on year-end date, 384–385
  off-balance-sheet financing, 433–434
  output of production cycle, 371
  physical observation of, 381–386
  potential for fraud, 387–388
  tips on detecting fraud, 388
Inventory accounts, 370
Inventory control
  just-in-time systems, 371
  materials requisition, 372
  production orders, 372
Inventory count
  auditors not present for, 386
  client's instructions, 382–383
  cycle counts, 385, 390
  under difficult circumstances, 384–385
  GAAS requirement, 380
  manual, 383
  measurement challenges, 383

  by professional inventory teams, 385–386
  radio frequency identification, 384–385
  statistical counting, 385
  using bar code scanners, 384
  when located away from premises, 386
Inventory count sheet, 382
Inventory master file, 841
Inventory reports, 374
Inventory roll-forward, 385
Inventory-taking instructions, 382–383
Investing transactions
  authorization, 419
  custody, 419
  forms of, 417–419
  periodic reconciliation, 420
  record keeping, 420
Investment accounting, 428
Investment costs, 431
Investments by companies, 134
Investors, need for reliable information, 2–3
Ionics, 652
IPOC International Growth Fund Ltd., 610
Iron curtain method, 468
Iselin v. Landau, 643
Isikoff, Michael, C10
Islanders Bank, 424
ITFactory, 269

J

J.D. Power & Associates, C17
J.M. Smucker Company, 429
Jenkins, J. G., 143
Jensen, K. L., 660
Jerris, S., 143
Joe, J., 468n, 514
Joint and several liability, 657–658
Joint custody, 419
Joint Ethics Enforcement Program (AICPA), 617–618
Jolly, Bobby L., 414
JPMorgan Chase, 243, 414
Justified departures from generally accepted accounting principles
  in auditors' report, 511, 514–515
  definition, 515
Just-in-time systems, 371

K

Kane, C. K., 165n
Kane, Joseph J., C10
Kant, Immanuel, 592
Kaplan, Lewis, C18
Kaplan CPA Review, 25
Katrina Housing Tax Relief Act, 688
Katz, David M., 126
Keeton, Morris, 591–592
Kellogg Company, 471
Kerviel, Jerome, 848
Keulian, Viken, 375
Khurana, I. K., 660
Kickbacks, 125, 321
Kieslowski, Krzysztof, 493
Kilpatrick, Kwame, 869
Kim Woo Choong, 124
Klafte, Cary, C18
Klott, Gary, C10
Kmart, 169
Knechel, W. R., 660
Knight, Frank, 119
Knowledge-based economy, 571
Knowledge needed for risk assessment, 121
Koppikor, Rachna, C28n

Koss, Michael, 284
Koss Corporation, 284
Kozlowski, Dennis, 124
KPMG, 332, 387, 455, 465, 521, 574, 610, 634, C4
    case
        admission of tax fraud, C18
        dismissed by Fannie Mae, C18
        nonaudit services, C17–C18
        and number of auditing firms, C17–C18
        revenues in 2010, C17
        tax consulting fees, C18
    dismissed by Fannie Mae, 839
    forensic accountants, 174
    and General Electric, C24
    revenues 2010, 19
Kraft Foods, 322
Krishna, R. Jai, C29
Krishnamurthy, G., 476
Krispy Kreme, 190–191, 205
    report on internal control, 172–173
Kroger, 411
Kumar, John Satish, C29
Kumar, Sanjay, 124

L

L.B. Smith, Inc., 640
Labor cost analysis, 360
Labor distribution, 360
Lack of independence report, 510–511
Lakshman, Nandini, C29
Lamborghini, 375
Lamphron, Jim, C15
Landis, M., 143
Lapping, 233, 282
Larceny, 126
La Spada, Anthony, 362
Last-in, first-out method, 369, 386
Laundry money skim, 247
Laventhal & Horwath, 656
    auditors for PTL Club, C6–C8
    bankruptcy of, C8–C9
Law enforcement agencies, 611
Laws; see Common law; Legal liability;
        Noncompliance with laws and
        regulations; Statutory law
Lawsuits, auditor questions about, 333
Lay, Kenneth, 124
Leadership
    by example, 56
    responsibility for quality, 56
Lead schedule, 106
Leahy, Joe, C29
Lear Corp., 514
Lease accounts, 412–143
Leases, 422
Legal environment, 634–635
Legal liability, 89; see also Common law liability;
        Statutory law liability
    Auditing Advisory Committee on, 635
    changing landscape for auditors, 654–660
    deep pockets theory, 636
    legal environment, 635–637
    legal terminology, 637
    professional standards references, 633
    recent settlements with accounting firms, 634
    Wells notice, 634–635
Legal terminology, 637
Lehman Brothers Holdings, Inc., 381, 458,
        634–635
    bankruptcy, 16
Lending of credibility, 3
Lennox, C., 58
Leslie Fay, 369
Letterman, David, 546, 794
Leung, Elsie, 465

Lewinsky, Monica, 869
Liabilities, 12, 458
    accrued, 330
    contingent, 459–461
    for known rights of return, 273–274
    long-run, 417
    recording, 323
    unrecorded, 243, 319, 324
Liability caps, 659–660
Librarians, 846–847
Library of Congress E-Resources Online
        Catalog, 137
License Raj, C26
Licensing
    of certified public accountants, 25
    substantial equivalency, 25
Lieberman, Joe, 688
Life Partners Holdings, Inc., 473
Ligand Pharmaceuticals, 60, 299, 619
Lightle, S. S., 177
Limit and reasonableness tests, 852
Limited computer knowledge, 864
Limited liability partnerships, 637, 657
Limited procedures, 523
Limited reporting engagement, 500
Limited use of prospective financial
        information, 550
Lincoln Savings and Loan, 658
Lindquist, R. J., 222n
Liptak, Adam, 124
Liquidity, and fraud, 133
Litan, Avvat, 276
Litigation
    class action suits, 658–659
    against Ernst & Young, 16
    factors influencing, 660
    increased exposure to, 654
    against PCAOB, 37
Litigation, claims, and assessments, pending,
        459–461
Litigation support, 700
Livingstone, Bruce, 684
Loan covenants, 413
Loans
    grandfathered, 601
    to or from clients, 601
    permitted, 601
Lockbox arrangement, 232
Lockheed Martin, 867
Loebbecke, J. K., 225n
Logical unit, 796
London/AIM stock exchange, C23
London Assurance Corporation, 639
Lone Moon Brewing, 323
Longo, Peter, 385
Long-term liabilities, 425–426
    record keeping for, 417
Lorenz, James E., 387
Lower-of-cost-or-market testing, 387
Lower-of-cost-or-market valuation, 369, 377
Lublin, Joann S., C29

M

Machado, Kenan, C29
Macy's, Inc., 385
Madoff, Bernard L., 3, 35, 36, 78, 124
Madoff Investment Securities, 124
Mahadeo, Saganno, 237
Mailroom fraud, 223
Maines, Natalie, 375
Management
    identifying business risks, 178
    inquiry in risk assessment, 143–144
    integrity of, 78–79
    internal auditors as representatives of, 683

    internal audit reports sent to, 687
    objective setting by, 120
    objectives in internal control
        compliance, 170
        financial reporting, 170
        operations, 170
    outsourcing noncore functions, 554
    of people pressures, 228
    plans to mitigate business risks, 121
    reports on internal control over financial
        reporting, 496
    responsibility for internal control, 171–174
    responsibility for risk management
        enterprise risk management, 119–120
        paradox of risk, 119
        sources and types of risk, 118
Management assertions
    for Auditing Standards Board, 11
    on completeness and cutoff, 12–13
    as evidence, 4, 51
    on existence and occurrence, 12
    in financial statements, 10–11
    importance of, 14
    Miniscribe fraud, 12
    presentation and disclosure, 13–14
    for PCAOB, 11
    relation to financial statements, 15
    on rights and obligations, 12
    Sarbanes-Oxley Act on, 10
    summary on, 10–11
    understandability, 13–14
    on valuation and allocation, 13
    WorldCom fraud, 13
    worthless at Enron, 14
Management directives, ensuring compliance with,
        682–683
Management fraud
    definition, 123
    at Enron Corporation, 117
    professional standards references, 116
    rationales for, 122
    risk factors, 123
Management letter, 206, 476
Management objectives, obstacles to achieving,
        170–171
Management personnel, 134
Management reports, revenue and collection cycle,
        277–279
Management representation, 463
    inquiry into, 95–96
Management's annual report on internal control over
        financial reporting, 199
Management's discussion and analysis, 19, 522
    examination and review, 554
Management's philosophy and operating style, 176
Management supervision, 99
Managerial relationships, threat to
        independence, 44
Managers, fraud pertaining to, 125
Mann Judd Landau, 643
Manual physical inventory count, 383
Marked coins or currency, 248
Marketable securities, 420
    classification of, 431
Market of inventory, 369
Market value
    of equity/total debt ratio, 164
    of securities, 431
Marshalls, 276, 868
Martin, M. J., 642n
Martin, Michael, C15
MasterCard, 273
Master file changes, 853
Matching, 318
    bill of lading to purchase order, 322
    problem in, 319
Material information, 87–88

Materiality
    in audit plan, 87–89
    calculating
        benchmark for, 88–89
        engagement circumstances, 89
        nature of item or issue, 89
        possible cumulative effects, 89–90
    establishing level of, 87–88
    for fraud examiners, 699
    inaccuracy permitted, 87
    material information, 87–88
    performance, 88–90
    professional judgment on, 90
    related to knowledge of fraud, 145
    of uncorrected misstatements, 468
    use by audit teams, 90
Materiality concept, 48
Material misstatements, 10–11, 48
    business risk leading to, 136
    detecting, 46
    errors vs. fraud, 123
    and relevant assertions, 185
Materials requisition, 372
Materials transfer ticket, 372
Material weakness, 197, 206–207
    effect on opinion, 204
    in internal control, 199
    in internal control over financial reporting, 201–203
    at Krispy Kreme, 205
Mathematical computations, 51
Matrix approach to detection risk, 130–131
Maximum rate of deviation, 728–729
MBIA Inc., 717
McCracken, S., 469
McDonald's Corporation, 54, 55
McEwen, Toni, 684
MCI, 319
McIntyre, John, 718
McKesson & Robbins, 37–38
McNeal, A., 233
Mean-per-unit estimation, 812
    formula for sample size determination, 812
Medeeros, Emanuel, 324
Medicare taxes, 361
Mehra, Puja, C27n, C28n
Meijer, Inc., 853
Members of an unlimited class, 641
Menon, K., 514
Mental attitude, 43, 80, 589
Merck & Company, 456
Mergers and acquisitions transactions, 334
MetricStream, 684
MGM Mirage, 514
Michaels Stores, Inc., 867
Microsoft Access, 864
Microsoft Corporation, 461
Microsoft Excel, 190, 864
Microsoft Excel Service, 866
Milgram, Stanley, 590, 594
Millennium Chemicals, 411
Miller, C. G., 561
Miller, R. L., 611n
Miniscribe, 12
Minutes of board meetings, 137, 138
Misappropriation of assets, 126
    definition, 222
Miscellaneous accounts, 458
Misrepresentation, cause of client losses, 636
Misrepresentation of facts, 607
Missing data tests, 852
Misstated costs and expenses, 319
Misstatements
    and confirmation process, 288
    detecting, 89
    general categories of, 131–132
    in inventory, 381–382
    investigating causes of, 819–820
    points of, in computerized environment, 856
    in revenue and collection cycle, 273
    susceptibility factors, 133
    uncorrected, 468
Mitigating factors, 513
Mix of cash and checks, 249
Mock, T. J., 524
Modified cash basis framework, 566
Modified opinions, 501
Monetary unit sampling
    advantages, 796–797
    versus classical variables sampling, 817–818
    definition, 731, 796
    definition of population, 796
    disadvantages, 797
    distinguishing feature, 796
    evaluating sample results, 806–811
        basic allowance for sampling risk, 808–809
        incremental allowance for sampling risk, 807–808
        projected misstatement, 807
        qualitative evaluation of misstatements, 811
        understatements, 810–811
        upper limit on misstatements, 809–810
    existence assertions, 797
    planning stages
        defining attribute of interest, 797
        defining population, 798
        determining objective, 797
    probability proportionate to size selection, 796
    sample items measurement, 805–806
    sample selection, 804–805
    sample size, 802
    sample size determination
        expected misstatement, 801–802
        factors influencing, 798
        population size, 802–803
        sampling risk, 799–800
        tolerable misstatement, 800–801
    value and allocation assertions, 797
Monitoring
    in ERM, 120
    of internal control
        common controls, 184
        fundamental principles, 184
        in small and medium-sized businesses, 184
    by PCAOB, 59
    for quality control
        examples, 57–58
        purpose, 57
Monitoring systems activity, 859
Monus, Mickey, 368–369, 390
Moral clause of AICPA rules, 612
Morgenson, Gretchen, 124
Morse, Gene, 860
Motivations
    for employee fraud
        economic, 225–226
        egocentric, 225
        ideological, 225
        psychotic, 225
    ideological, 225
Motive, 225
Motors Liquidation Company, C12
Mozilo, Angelo R., 124
Murphy, Leif, C15
MUS; see Monetary unit sampling

N

Nally, Dennis, C27n
Napier, Denise L., 649
Narrative description, 188

NASDAQ, 145, 867
Natelli, Anthony, 651
National Aeronautics and Space Administration, 689
National Association of State Boards of Accountancy, 25
National Commission on Fraudulent Financial Reporting, 170; see also Treadway Commission
National Stock Exchange, India, C26
National Student Marketing Association, 651
National Student Marketing case, 651
Nay, Lester, 649
Near privity, 640
Negative assurance, AICPA rule, 609–610
Negative confirmation, 285–286
Nelson, M., 122n
Net realizable value, 369
Net revenue, 272
Net sales/total assets ratio, 164
Network, The, 126
Net worth analysis, horizontal and vertical analysis, 250
New products and services, 136
New social structures, 571
New York Stock Exchange, 145, C23
    Satyam listing on, C26
Nikko Cordial, 411
Nonaudit attestation engagement, 19
Nonaudit services, C17–C18
    effects of Sarbanes-Oxley Act on, C23
    independence rule, 604–605
Noncancelable purchase agreements, 319
Noncompliance with laws and regulations
    auditor response to, 147
    companies involved in, 148
    direct-effect noncompliance, 146–147
    indicators of, 147
    indirect-effect noncompliance, 147
    Private Securities Litigation Reform Act, 147–148
Nonprobabilistic selection techniques, 819
Nonpublic companies, Auditing Standards Board report, 544
Nonrepresentative sample, 717
Nonsampling error, 718
Nonsampling risk, 764–765, 805
    definition, 618
    versus sampling risk, 716–718
Nonstatistical attributes sampling
    difference from statistical method, 774
    sample items measurement, 774
    sample rate of deviation, 774
    sample selection
        block selection, 773
        haphazard selection, 773
    sample size determination, 774
    steps in., 773–774
    testing accuracy assertions, 774
    tolerable rate of deviation, 774
Nonstatistical sampling
    definition, 719
    versus statistical sampling, 719
    for variables sampling, 731
Nonstatistical sampling methods
    audited balance estimate, 819
    causes of misstatements, 819–820
    example, 818
    expected misstatement, 819
    projected misstatement, 819
    sample selection
        block selection, 819
        haphazard selection, 819
        nonprobabilistic techniques, 819
    sample size determination, 819
    tolerable misstatement, 819
    for variables sampling, 796

Normal distribution theory, 812
Nortel, 273
Northrup Grumman, 333
Notes payable, recording, 417
Notes receivable, confirmation of, 285–289

O

OAO Yukos, 474
Obama, Barack, 495, 717, C11
Objective
    auditor awareness of, 121
    definition, 118
    in inherent risk assessment, 136
    of management on internal control, 170
    of MUS, 797
    of sampling, 720
Objective setting, in ERM, 120
Objectivity
    AICPA rules
        conflicts of interest, 607
        misrepresentation, 607
        serving as client advocate, 608
    of internal auditors, 84
    in principles of conduct, 596–597
Obligations on liabilities, 12
O'Bryan, Emily, 167
Observation, 95
    cautions on, 98
    in tests of controls, 194
Occurrence, 12, 141, 753
    for sales, 270
Occurrence assertion
    for payroll cycle, 195
    production cycle tests of controls, 379, 380
    in purchasing and disbursement, 182
Occurrence direction, dual-direction tests of controls, 288–289
Occurrence test, 191–196
Ocean World Seafood, 249
Off-balance-sheet assets, 414
Off-balance-sheet financing of inventory, 433–434
Off-balance-sheet information, 426, 427
Off-balance-sheet leases, 414
Off-balance-sheet transactions, 416–417
Omitted procedures, 474
Online editing and sight verification, 851, 865
Open purchase file, 329
Open purchase orders, 323
Operating deficiency, 198
Operating effectiveness
    of control activities, 191
    definition, 187
    tests of, 198
    tests of controls, 764
Operating leases, 413, 414
Operational auditors, 21
Operational audits, 21, 684
    definition and goal, 21
    definition of AICPA, 22
    by internal auditors, 684
Operational efficiency, 682
Operational risk analysis, 682
Operations
    company characteristics, 134
    fraud risk factors, 123
    indirect-effect compliance, 147
    in management objectives, 170
Operations controls, 170
Operations ratios, 164
Opinion
    AICPA rule, 609–610
    on comparative financial statements, 521
    types of, 501
Opinion paragraph of standard report, 498, 501
Opinion shopping, 568

Opportunity for employee fraud, 226
Options, 429
Oracle Corporation, 651
Orange County Register, 375
Orbital Sciences Corporation, 319
Ordinary negligence
    definition, 637
    in Securities Act of 1933, 645
Organizational structure, 134
    of computerized processing, 100
    and internal control, 176
Ostling, Richard N., C10
Other accounts, 458
Other comprehensive bases of accounting, 566
Other-matter paragraphs, 512
Output controls; *see* Computer controls
Output distribution, 853
Outsourcing
    accounting applications, 100
    of computer services, 866
    internal audit function, 679–680
    of noncore functions, 554
Overhead allocation, 373
Overstatement, in MUS, 797
Overton, David, 656
Overton v. Todman Company CPAs, 656
Owens, William, C14, C15–C16, C16
Owners, fraud pertaining to, 125
Ownership, 12

P

Pacini, C., 225, 642n, 696n
Packing slip, 276
Padded payroll, 125
Paine, Thomas, 268
Pajazetovic, Amela, 167
Palbaum, Brian, 465
Paradox of risk, 119
Parallel simulation, 860–861
Parity check, 843
Parmalat, 2, 98, 124, 634, 660
    case
        audit approach, C20
        bankruptcy, C20
        bond payment default, C20
        Cayman Islands account, C20
        CEO awareness of fraud, C21
        discovery, C20–C21
        hidden losses, C20
        indictments and convictions, C21–C22
        missing assets, C20
        red flags missed, C20
Paseo Hernando Early Learning Coalition, 340
Passwords, 847–848
Password software, 868
Patents
    auditor questions about, 333
    custody of, 419
Patterson, Scott, C27n
Payables, relative assertion risks, 320
Pay + Plus Payroll Administrators, 362
Payroll accounting, 358
Payroll cycle
    audit evidence
        clearing accounts, 360
        employee W2 reports, 361
        governmental and tax reports, 360
        labor cost analysis, 360
        payroll register, 259
        personnel files, 259
        year-to-date earnings records, 360–361
    computerized system, 362
    control activities, 361–362
    custody, 358
    falsified work hour records, 357

    forms of, 356
    fraud in, 356
    inherent risks, 356
    preparation by service organizations, 362
    self-policing aspect, 356
    tests of controls, 195–197
    time card forgeries, 363–364
    typical activities
        personnel, 357–358
        record keeping, 358
        supervision, 358
        timekeeping, 358
Payroll distribution, 361
Payroll expense testing, 334
Payroll register, 359
Payroll report, 361–362
Payroll taxes, 360
PCAOB; *see* Public Company Accounting Oversight Board
Peachtree software, 99
Peat, Marwick, Mitchell & Company, 646
Peer review
    conduct of, 59
    criticisms of, 58–59
    definition, 58
Pelino, Dennis S., 135
Pending order master file, 277
Pensions, underfunding, 415
People pressures, management of, 228
PeopleSoft, 605
Performance audit reports, 696
Performance audits, 22–23
    criteria, 691
    definition, 690
    examples, 690
    and GAAS, 693
    governmental audit, 690
Performance materiality, 801
    definition, 88
    use of materiality for, 90
Performance measures, for companies, 136
Performance principle, 41, 42
    and attestation standards, 74
    audit evidence, 50–53
    components for quality control, 57
    definition and elements, 46
    materiality, 48
    planning and supervision, 47–48
    reasonable assurance, 46
    risk assessment, 49–50
Performance review
    committee at Enron, 179
    in internal control, 180
Performance standards, 685–686
Perini Corporation, 226
Period-end journal entries, 172, 174
Periodic reconciliation, 326
    of assets and recorded amounts, 180
    of investments, 420
    of share outstanding, 417
Permanent files
    definition, 104
    kinds of, 104–105
Permitted loans, 601
Perry, Luke, 375
Personal financial planning, 562
Personality red flags, 222–223
Personnel, 357–358
Personnel files, 359
Persuasive evidence, 50–51
Petrocine, A. R., 641n
Petty cash
    count and recount, 248
    missing, 246–247
Petty theft, 221
Phar-Mor fraud, 368–369, 390–391
Phelps, Martin, 390

Philosophical principles of ethics, 591–594
　categorical imperative, 592–593
　function of, 592
　generalization argument, 593
　utilitarianism, 593
　weight of opinion, 591–592
Phony profits, 368–369
Physical controls, 275, 868, 869
　in internal control, 181
Physical inspection to gather audit evidence, 332–333
Physical inventory count, 382
Physical inventory inspection, 381–386
Physical inventory observation
　audit plan, 407
　client's instructions, 382–383
　definition, 382
　difficult circumstances
　　auditors not present, 386
　　cycle counts, 385
　　located away from premises, 386
　　not on year-end date, 384–385
　　professional inventory teams, 385–386
　manual inspection, 383
　physical count, 382
　radio frequency identification, 384
　using bar codes, 384
Physical observation, 51
Physical representation of population, 755
Physical security, 864
Physical security controls, 848
Pierce, B. J., 722n, 723, 793n
Pilgrim's Pride Corporation, 514
Pittman, J., 58
Plain-paper engagements, 561
Plaintiffs, 637
Planning
　audit sampling
　　attributes sampling, 734
　　dual-purpose tests, 734
　　variables sampling, 734
　　classical variables sampling, 812
　　for MUS, 797–798
Planning memorandum, 105
Planning precision, 802
Planning precision, in MUS, 802
Plant and equipment depreciation, 422
Policies related to financial reporting, 179
Pollster.com, 718
Ponzi scheme, 3
Population
　and audit sample size, 734
　defined for attributes sampling, 754–755
　defining, 720
　definition, 715
　definition in MUS, 796, 798
　physical representation of, 755
　sample item selection, 721
　size in attributes sampling, 758
　size in sample size determination, *802*
Population deviation rate, 758–759
　advantage, 773
　disadvantage, 773
　in sequential sampling, 773
Positive confirmation
　definition, 285–286
　response to, 289
Potomac Company, 6
Power buying, 368
PowerPoint, 189
Practitioner, 6
Precision, 758–759, 816
　higher level of, 725
　in MUS, 802
　in sampling, 724–725
Precision interval, 724–725
　construction of, 816
　significance of, 816

Predecessor auditors
　communication with, 78–79, 562
　definition, 78
　reporting disagreements with, 80
Predication, 698
Pre-engagement activities
　changes in auditors, 79–80
　client acceptance of continuance policies, 79
　compliance with independence and ethical requirements, 80–82
　dumping clients, 78
　engagement letters, 81, 82
　and integrity of management, 78–79
　new standards for, 77–78
　and predecessor auditors, 79–80
　as risk assessment, 77–78
　search for potential problems, 79
Preliminary audit procedures, 136–142
Prentice, Robert A., C5
Prepaid expenses, 330, 331
Prescribed forms, 562
Presentation and disclosure, 10, 13–14
　acquisition and expenditure cycle, 334
　finance and investment cycle, 414
　production cycle, 388
　revenue and collection cycle, 291
　for revenue and receivables, 270
　WorldCom fraud, 13
Presumptively mandatory requirements, 38–39
Preventive, detective, and damage-limiting controls
　administrative controls, 868
　physical controls, 868
　programmed range and reasonableness checks, 868–869
　technical controls, 868–869
Preventive controls, 180
Preventive maintenance, 843
Previts, G., 6
Prewitt, D. F., 40n
Price fixing, 125
Priceline.com, 272
Price list master file, 277
Price Waterhouse Company, C17
PricewaterhouseCoopers, 37–38, 454–455, 474, 495, 500, 521, 611, 634, 649, 839, C17, C18
　Academy Awards and, 18
　disclaimer of opinion, 205
　failure at Satyam, 240
　independence violations, 44
　rejection of client, 78
　revenues 2010, 19
　and Satyam Computer Services fraud, C26–C28
Price Waterhouse India, 474
Pricing and compilation tests, 386–387
　audit plan, 407–408
Primary beneficiaries, 637, 640
Principle of utilitarianism, 593
Principles of attestation, 75
Privacy of trust services, 573
Private Securities Litigation Reform Act of 1995, 147–148, 611, 657–658
Privileged information, 610
Privity of contract, 637, 638
Probabilistic selection techniques, 819
Probability proportionate to size selection, 796
Problem situation, 590
Processing controls
　audit trail, 865
　control total reports, 852
　control totals, 865
　data comparisons, 865
　error correction and resubmission procedures, 852
　file and operator controls, 852
　function of, 852
　limit and reasonableness test, 852

　run-to-run totals, 852
　transaction logs, 865
Processing errors, 841–842
Processing integrity of trust services, 573
Procurement, relative assertion risks, 320
Production cycle
　account balance assertions, 381
　assertion risks for inventory accounts, 372
　assertions about transactions/events, 379
　audit evidence, 373–375
　　inventory reports, 374
　　production plans and reports, 374
　　sales forecast, 374
　audit plan, 407–408
　audit risk model, 389
　control risk assessment
　　account balances, 375
　　control activities, 376
　　custody, 376–377
　　direction of tests of control, 379
　　entity-level controls, 376
　　internal control questionnaire, 377, 405–406
　　summary of, 380
　　tests of controls, 377–378
　fraud at Phar-Mor, 368–369
　fraud case: extended procedures, 389–391
　inherent risks, 369, 370
　inventory as output of, 371
　nature of transactions in, 371
　PCAOB inspections, 392
　professional standards references, 367
　substantive procedures
　　analytical procedures, 380–381
　　fraud potential in inventory, 387–388
　　GAAS requirements, 380
　　physical inventory observation, 381–386
　　presentation and disclosure, 388
　　pricing and compilation tests, 386–387
　typical activities
　　cost accounting, 372–373
　　inventory control, 372
　　link to acquisition and expenditure cycle, 369–370
　　production planning, 370–372
　　production sign-off, 372
　　sales forecast, 370
Production order, 372
Production plan, 370–371
　as audit evidence, 374
　results of errors in, 372
　shared with other departments, 372
Production planning
　costs associated with, 370–371
　critical to manufacturing, 371–372
　just-in-time management, 371
Production reports, as audit evidence, 374
Production sign-off, 372
Products, with radio frequency identification tags chips, 384, 385
Professional ethics
　AICPA rules of conduct, 607–616
　auditor independence, 599
　codes of conduct, 594–597
　　International Federation of Accountants, 596–597
　　Professional Ethics Executive Committee, 596–597
　　Public Company Accounting Oversight Board, 595–596
　　Securities and Exchange Commission, 595
　consequences of violating, 617–619
　decision process, 590–591
　definition of ethics, 589–590
　emphasis on independence
　　AICPA rules, 598–603
　　effect of Sarbanes-Oxley Act, 605–606
　　Government Accountability Office, 606

PCAOB, 603–605
SEC rules, 600, 603
Enron collapse, 589
International Ethics Standards Board for Accountants, 616
philosophical principles
act-utilitarianism, 593
generalization argument, 593–594
imperative principle, 592–593
reliance on weight of opinion, 591–592
rule-utilitarianism, 593
utilitarianism, 593
problem situations, 590
professional standards references, 587–588
Professional Ethics Executive Committee (AIPCA), 595
rules of conduct, 596–597
Professional Golfers Association, 720
Professional inventory teams, 385–386
Professional judgment, 52
definition, 45
on materiality, 90
Professional service firms, 18
Professional services, 8
Professional skepticism, 410
and conflicts of interest, 15–16
definition, 15
and employee fraud, 221
evidence gathering, 16
and former colleagues, 16
Hurtt skepticism scale, 17
and objectivity, 16
requirement for auditors, 45
time pressure, 16
Professional Sports Authenticator, 7
Professional sports logos, 419
Professional standards
auditor performance, 46–63
basic GAAS, 37–42
evaluation of CPA firms, 55–60
and PCAOB controversy, 36–37
recent audit failures, 36
reporting, 53–55
responsibilities, 42–45
self-regulation, 36
topics and references, 35
Professions, characteristics of, 37
Profit, phony, 368–369
Profit before taxes benchmark, 88–89
Pro forma financial information, 550–552
Program analysis techniques, 859
Program change controls
emergency change requests, 845
function, 845
program modifications, 845
and systems development life cycle, 845
Program development controls
documentation, 845
objectives, 844
systems development life cycle, 844–845
Program documentation and testing, 864
Program-embedded techniques
audit files, 859
extended records, 859
monitoring systems activity, 859
program analysis techniques, 859
snapshot, 859
tagging transactions, 858
Programmed range and reasonableness checks, 868–869
Programmers
functions, 846
separation of duties, 847
Projected misstatement, 807
in nonstatistical sampling, 819
Proof of cash, 245–246
Proper period, 12–13

Property, plant, and equipment
assertions about, 331–332
audit evidence about, 332, 333
Proportionate liability, 657, 658
ProQuest Company, 867
Prospective financial information, 550–552
general use, 550
limited use, 550
Prospectus, 645
Protiviti Inc., 679
Provident Financial Group, 411
Psychotic motivation, 225
PTL Club, case
auditors' knowledge of fraud, C7–C8
background, C5
collapse, C6
demise of Laventhal & Horwath, C8–C9
effect on accounting profession, C9
finding new auditors, C8
lack of oversight, C6–C7
perceived excesses, C5–C6
scale of corruption, C6–C7
trial, C9
Public accounting
assurance services
audit services, 18–19
nonaudit attestation engagements, 19
consulting and advisory services, 20–21
CPA firms, 18
and failure of self-regulation, 36
number of businesses in, 18
professional service firms, 18
revenues of Big Four firms, 19
tax services, 20
Public accounting firms; see also Big Four accounting firms; CPA firms
communication with predecessor auditors, 79–80
deficiencies found, 59–60
evaluation of
peer review, 58–59
PCAOB inspections, 59–60
regulatory bodies, 44–45
system of quality control, 56–58
and internal audits, 679
reporting disagreements with firm's auditors, 80
time budget, 86–87
tips on detecting inventory fraud, 388
Public Broadcasting Services, 867
Public Company Accounting Oversight Board, 9, 14, 39, 40, 55, 272, 499, 679; see also Auditing standards
and accounting standards, 595–596
and acquisition and expenditure cycle, 340
and audit completion, 455
on audit evidence, 91
changes to auditors' report, 524
and codes of conduct, 594
on contingent fees, 612
on controls in computerized environment, 839
controversy over, 36–37
creation of, 36
description, 11n
disciplinary actions, 618–619
on engagement letters, 82
on engagement planning, 77
and finance and investment cycle, 437
functions, 36
on identifying controls, 185–186
implications of following, 500
inspections, 474
on computer controls, 840
of firms, 59–60
in production cycle, 392
on internal auditing, 680
on internal audit services, 22
on justified departures from GAAP, 515
on management assertions, 11

on materiality, 87–88
peer review by, 59
penalties for Satyam case, C28
reason for, 38
reporting for nonpublic companies, 544
and revenue collection cycle, 300
review of tests for controls, 752
on sampling deficiencies, 795
sanctioning of auditors, 60
on tax services, 20
on uncorrected misstatements, 468
Public company audits, PCAOB requirements, 197–200
Public entity, 36
Public interest, in principles of conduct, 596–597
Public offerings, 645
Public Oversight Board, 58
Public regulatory discipline, 618–619
Pull-down menus, 851
Pulliam, S, 318n
Purchase cutoff, 330
Purchase lead time, 372
Purchase order, 321
blank, 325
blind, 322
computer-generated, 325
open, 323
Purchase requisition, 321
Purchases journal, 324
Purchases of goods and services, 321–322
Purchasing and disbursement cycle, 181–182
Purchasing departments, fraud in, 321

Q

Qualified opinion, 501
definition, 55
and departures from GAAP, 503, 504
and departures from GAAS, 503
and scope limitation reports, 508, 510
Qualitative evaluation of misstatements, 811
Qualitative materiality, 48
Quality assurance partner, 84
Quality audit, 679
Quality control audits, 685
Quarterly Corporate Fraud Index Network, 126
Qwest Communications, 273

R

Racketeer Influenced and Corrupt Organizations Act, 656
Radio frequency identification, 384, 385
Raghunandan, K., 514
Raising capital, 416–417
Raju, Ramalinga, C26–C28
Rama, D. V., 514
Ramon, K. K., 660
Random selection, 792–793
definition, 721
systematic, 721–722
unrestricted, 721
Range, Jackie, C27n, C29
Ratio estimation, 817
Rationalization of employee fraud, 227
Raw material inventory status report, 371–372
Reagan, Ronald W., 17, C5
Real Clear Politics, 718
Real-time processing, 846
Reasonable assurance
versus absolute assurance, 170
concept, 171
definition, 46
on detecting errors and fraud, 122
on financial controls, 279

122 Index

Reasonable assurance—*Cont.*
    in fraud detection, 125
    SEC on, 197
Reasonableness
    of accounting estimates, 459
    of sales forecast, 374
Reasonableness tests, 138, 250
Reasonably foreseeable persons, 646
Recalculation
    of audit, 97
    cautions on, 98
    by computer, 102–103
Receivables, assertion risks for, 270
Receivables turnover ratio, 164
Receiving report, 322
    unmatched, 323
Reconciliation, 233; *see also* Bank reconciliation
    of disbursements, 235
    periodic, 326
Record counts, 851
Recording
    accounts payable, 323
    of accounts payable, 325
    of cash disbursements, 235
    liabilities, 323
    of transactions, 180
Record keeping, 230
    in finance and investment cycle, 423
    of investments, 420
    for long-term liabilities, 417
    payroll cycle, 358
Records; *see* Documents
Red flags, 123
    for employee fraud, 222–223
    for fraud in revenue and collection cycle, 269
    at HealthSouth, C15
    missed at Parmalat, C20
    white collar criminals, 224
Reece, Andrew, C29
Reeves v. Arthur Young, 656
Referral fees, 615
    AICPA rules, 614–615
    definition, 615
Reflective choice, 590
Registrars, 416, 417
Registration statement, 645
Regulations; *see* Noncompliance with laws and regulations
Regulation S-K (SEC), 648
Regulation S-X (SEC), 511, 648
Regulatory auditors, 23
Regulatory bodies, 9
    for public accounting firms, 55–56
Regulatory factors, in inherent risk assessment, 133
Rehnquist, William, C2n, C3
Reinstein, A., 561
Reissued report, 520
Related party, 134, 413
Related-party transactions, 125, 413
    perils of, 135
    valuation of, 134
Relevance of evidence, 230
Relevant assertions
    auditor focus on, 128
    in cash management, 236
    definition, 127
    and material misstatement, 185
Relevant evidence, 51
Reliability, in sampling, 724–725
Reliable evidence, 51
Reliable information
    conditions calling for
        complexity, 2
        consequences of decisions, 3
        remoteness, 3
        time-sensitivity, 3
        investor need for, 2–3

Remoteness, 3
Reorganization, at General Motors, C12
Reperformance, 97
    in tests of controls, 194
Replacement costs, 369
Report
    on compiled financial statements, 560–561
    on financial statements and related disclosures, 496
    on internal control over financial reporting, 496
Reporting, under attestation standards, 74
Reporting principles, 41, 42, 55
    adverse opinion, 54–55
    definition, 53
    departures from GAAP, 54–55
    financial reporting framework, 54
    materiality concept, 55
    qualified principle, 55
    requirements, 54
    unqualified opinion example, 54
Reporting standards, 75
Research and development, vouching, 333
Responsibilities
    incompatible, 180–181
    for internal control, 176
    in principles of conduct, 596–597
Responsibility principle, 41, 42
    competence and capabilities, 43
    independence and due care, 43–45, 80
    kinds of auditor responsibilities, 42
    and Madoff scandal, 45
    professional judgment, 45
    professional skepticism, 45
Responsible party, 548
Restatement
    examples of, 411
    of financial results, 203
    of financial statements, 454
    reasons for, 319
Restatement of torts doctrine, 640
Retained earnings/total assets ratio, 164
Retention reviews, 79
Return on beginning equity ratio, 164
Revenue
    assertion risks for, 270
    of Big Four firms in 2010, 19
    effect of Sarbanes-Oxley Act on, C24
    net vs. gross, 272
Revenue and collection cycle, 231–232
    audit approach
        assessing assertions, 270
        calculating detection risk, 270
        consideration of inherent risk, 270
        determining evidence collection, 270
        identifying control activities, 270
        tests of controls, 270–271
        using audit risks model, 270
        walkthrough, 271
    audit plan, 315–316
    control risk assessment
        account balances, 279
        control activities, 279–280
        summary of, 282
        tests of controls, 280–282
    fraud at IT factory, 269–270
    fraud cases: extended procedures
        canny cashier, 293–294
        closing accounts, 297–298
        dual-purpose procedures, 292
        frequent billing, 296–297
        taxman, 294–296
    inherent risks
        collectabilty, 273
        customer returns and allowances, 273–274
        revenue recognition, 271–273
    internal control questionnaire, 313–314
    professional standards references, 268
    PCAOB inspections, 300

    substantive procedures
        alternative procedures, 289
        analytical procedures, 284
        assertions on account balances, 283
        confirmation of accounts/notes receivable, 285–289
        cutoff and sales returns, 290
        discerning population of assets to audit, 283
        dual-purpose procedure, 292
        presentation and disclosure, 291
        review for collectability, 289–290
        rights and obligations, 290
    typical activities
        accounting for accounts receivable, 276–277
        audit evidence, 277–279
        basic activities, 274
        billing customers, 276–277
        delivery of goods or services, 276
        entity-level controls, 275
        receiving and processing orders, 275–276
Revenue cycle assertions, 753
Revenue forecasts, 435–436
Revenue recognition
    and channel stuffing, 273, 274
    criteria, 271–272
    examples of company misstatements, 273
    improper, 272
    net vs. gross revenue, 272
    reasons for importance of, 272
    requirements, 271
Reverse mergers, and component auditors, 517
Review, 558
    of accounting estimates for audit completion, 458–459
    of audit documentation, 469–470
    for collectability, 289–290
    definition, 19
    of management's discussion and analysis, 554
Review and compilation
    appropriate accounting framework, 558
    Code of Conduct, 558
    compilation services, 560–561
    interim financial information
        report on, 565
        responsibilities for reporting on, 563–564
    professional standards references, 546
    review services, 558–559
    standards, 558
    summary, 562–563
    topics under
        additional paragraphs, 562
        communication with predecessor auditors, 562
        comparative financial statements, 561–562
        fraud, 561
        personal financial planning, 562
        prescribed forms, 562
Review engagement, 496, 549
Review evidence, obtaining, 558–559
Review notes, 469
Review of accounts, 457–458
Review of output for reasonableness, 853
Review services
    and fraud, 561
    negative assurance, 559
    obtaining evidence, 558–559
    professional standards, 559
    purpose, 558
RFIDJournal, 385
Rice, J. C., 59n
Richards, Gregory, C10
Rigas, John, 124
Rights and obligations, 290
Rights to assets, 12
Risk
    in audit engagement, 77–78
    qualitative measures of, 130

Risk assessment
    by auditors, 121–127
    in audit plan
        inherent risk, 83
        timing of internal control tests, 83
        timing of substantive tests, 83
        understand client's business, 83
    audit team action, 179
    communicate fraud risks, 145–146
    documentation of, 146
    in ERM, 120
    evaluate results of audit procedures, 145
    and internal control, 50
    in internal control, 178
    and management assertions, 10–11
    necessary relationships, 49–50
    preparation for
        assessing risk factors, 144
        audit team brainstorming, 143
        information sources, 137–138
        inquiry of audit committee and management, 143–144
        preliminary analytical procedures, 137–142
    primary purpose, 49
    professional standards references, 116
    reasonable assurance from, 46
    requirements for, 49
    respond to significant risks, 144–145
    and substantive procedures, 49
Risk assessment procedures, 90
Risk assessment process, 132
Risk factors
    assessing, 144
    identifying, 138–144
Risk management activities, 77–78
Risk of assessing control risk too high, 729–730, 756–757
Risk of assessing control risk too low, 729–730, 756–757
Risk of incorrect acceptance, 732–733, 809, 816
Risk of incorrect rejection, 732–733, 809–810
    in classical variables sampling, 813–814
Risk of material misstatement, 799
    assessment, 174
    auditing standards on, 126
    control activities, 179
    and control risk, 196
    definition, 49, 127
    and impairments, 414
    primary purpose of assessing, 49
    at relevant assertions level, 236
    revenue and collection cycle, 270
    tests of controls, 179
Risk of overreliance, 719–730, 759
    in attributes sampling, 756–757
    evaluation table, 766–767
Risk of underreliance, 729
    in attributes sampling, 756–757
Risk response, in ERM, 120
Risks
    faced by companies and auditors, 118
    of improper revenue recognition, 272
    multiplication of, 128–129
    unavoidability of, 118
Rizzo, Tom, 866
RMM; see Risk of material misstatement
Roberti, Mark, 385
Roberts, D. M., 811n
Roberts, Eric, 375
Roll-forward procedures, 457
Rollover method, 468
Roosevelt, Theodore, 587
Roper, Barbara, C25
Rosenblum, Inc. v. Adler, 641, 654
Rosen Canada Ltd., 335
Royal Ahold, 273
RSM/McGladrey & Pullen, C17

Ruff, Kevi Lee, 377
Rule-making bodies, 40
Rules for ethical behavior, 593
Rule-utilitarianism, 593
Rumman, Ahmed, C29
Run-to-run totals, 852
Rusch Factors, 640
Rusch Factors v. Levin, 654

S

Sachdiva, Sujata, 284
Sacred Heart Medical Center, 377
Safan, Ronald, 469
Safety-Kleen Corporation, 273, 634
Sales
    channel stuffing, 273
    computerized process, 277
    recorded in proper period, 290
Sales cutoff tests, 290
Sales detail (journal) file, 278
Sales forecast, 370
    as audit evidence, 374
    basis for production, 374
Sales invoice, 276, 841
Sales orders, 275–276
Sales returns, 290
Sales transaction file, 841
Sales transactions, pending order master file, 277
Salterio, S., 469
SALY (same as last year) forecast, 374
Sample estimate of misstatement, 731
Sample evaluation tables, 766–767
Sample items
    measurement
        for attributes sampling, 764
        for audit sampling, 735
        for classical variables sampling, 815
        in MUS
            audited value, 805
            and nonsampling risk, 806
            tainting percentage, 806
        in nonstatistical attributes sampling, 774
    measurement of, 723
    sampling risk and number of, 720–721
    selection
        block selection, 722
        computer software for, 723
        haphazard selection, 722
        systematic random selection, 721–722
    selection decision on method, 722–723
    selection for audit sampling
        block selection, 735
        haphazard selection, 735
        systematic random selection, 735
        unrestricted random selection, 735
    survey of selection methods, 723
    unrestricted random selection, 721
Sample rate of deviation, 728–729
    in attributes sampling, 765–766
    in nonstatistical attributes sampling, 774
Sample results evaluation
    in classical variables sampling
        actions when account balance misstated, 817
        audited balance estimate, 815–816
        precision interval construction, 816
        significance of precision interval, 816
    confidence level, 724–725
    in MUS
        basic allowance for sampling risk, 808–809
        incremental allowance for sampling risk, 807–808
        projected misstatement, 807
        qualitative evaluation of misstatements, 811

    steps performed, 806–807
    understatements, 810–811
    upper limit on misstatements, 809–810
    precision, 724–725
    precision interval, 724–725
    reliability, 724–725
    source of, 724
Sample selection
    for attributes sampling, 763–764
    in classical variables sampling, 815
    danger in systematic selection, 764
    in MUS
        example, 804–805
        sampling interval, 804
        systematic random selection, 804
    in nonstatistical sampling
        block selection, 819
        haphazard selection, 819
        nonprobabilistic techniques, 819
Sample size determination, 720–721
    in attributes sampling, 760–763
        expected rate of deviation, 758–759
        population size, 759
        and sampling risk, 756–757
        summary of size factors, 759
        tolerable rate of deviation, 757–758
    for audit sampling
        expected rate of deviation, 734
        key factors in, 734
        sampling risk, 735
        size of population, 734
        standard deviation, 735
        tolerable rate of deviation, 734
    in classical variables sampling
        calculating, 814–815
        formula, 812
        risk of incorrect rejection, 813–814
        standard deviation, 814
    for MUS, 802
        expected misstatement, 801–802
        factors influencing, 798
        population size, 802–803
        sampling risk, 799–800
        tolerable misstatement, 800–801
    in nonstatistical attributes sampling, 774
    in nonstatistical sampling, 819
Sampling; *see also* Attributes sampling; Audit sampling; Variables sampling
    in audit examination, 715
    audit use
        attributes sampling, 726–730
        variables sampling, 730–738
    basic stages
        define characteristic of interest, 720
        define population, 720
        determine objective, 720
        documenting procedures, 725
        evaluation of results, 724–725
        sample items selection, 721–723
        sample size determination, 720–721
    compared to audit sampling, 716
    definition, 715
    examples, 717
    nonrepresentative sample, 717
    nonstatistical, 773–774
    objective in attributes sampling, 753
    performing, 720–723
    planning, 720
    polling problems, 618
    population for, 715
    professional standards references, 714
    statistical vs. nonstatistical, 719
    for tests of controls, 752
    when to use
        exact information not important, 716
        large number of items in population, 716
Sampling error vs. sampling risk, 717

124 Index

Sampling interval, 721, 792
  in MUS, 804
Sampling plans, 719
Sampling risk
  allowance for, 724–725, 758, 768
  associated with attributes sampling
    efficiency loss, 730
    exposure to effectiveness loss, 730
    risk of overreliance, 729–730
    risk of underreliance, 729
    tolerable rate of deviation, 728–729
    upper limit rate of deviation, 728–729
  associated with variables sampling
    risk of incorrect acceptance, 732–733
    risk of incorrect rejection, 732–733
    sample estimate of misstatement, 731
    upper limit of misstatement, 731–732
  in attributes sampling
    risk of overreliance, 756–757
    risk of underreliance, 756–757
    summary of, 757
  basic allowance for, 808–809
  controlling, 718
  definition, 717
  incremental allowance for, 807–808
  versus nonsampling risk, 716–718
  and number of sample items, 720–721
  in sample size determination, 735
  versus sampling error, 717
  summary for audit sampling, 733
  for variables sampling
    risk of incorrect acceptance, 799–800
    risk of incorrect rejection, 799–800
    substantive procedures for, 799–800
Sampling unit, MUS vs. classical variables sampling, 815
Sam's Club, 384
Samson, W., 6
San Diego city officials, 415
SAP software, 99
Sarbanes-Oxley Act, 126, 203, 644, 679, 840, C16
  and analytical procedures, 142
  on audit committees, 475
  on audit communications, 475
  on audit of internal control system, 197
  and auditors' liability, 655–656
  on changes in internal control, 564
  constraints on accounting firms, C17
  on consulting services, 20–21, 589
  controversy over, C23
  costs of compliance with, 200
  creation of PCAOB, 36
  definition of internal control, 171
  effect on accounting for revenues, C24
  and employee hotlines, 228
  extension of statute of limitations, 647
  high costs of compliance, C23
  impact on capital markets, 807
  on independence, 605
  independence requirement, 43
  on inspection of firms, 59
  on internal auditing, 680
  on internal control, 169–170
  on management's financial reporting, 10
  nonaudit service restrictions, C23
  occasion for passage of, C4
  on peer review, 58–59
  penalties for misleading financial statements, 171–172
  on PCAOB inspections, 474
  quality control standards, 56
  reason for, 38
  reasons for passage of, 169
  on reports for SEC registrants, 496
  on responsibilities for internal control, 172
  result of corporate scandals, 589

Satyam subject to, C26
  on service organizations reporting, 555
  Supreme Court ruling, 37
  on tax accounting weakness, 330
  on 10-K filings, 463
  on 10-Q filings, 463
  on tests of controls, 752
Satyam Computer Services, Ltd., 2, 240, 474
Satyam Computer Services, Ltd., case
  arrests and convictions, C28
  auditors, C27
  company history, C26
  fictitious wages, C27
  fraud committed, C26–C27
  India accounting standards, C26
  inflated balance sheet, C26
  overstated receivables, C26
  penalties, C28
  two sets of statements, C26–C27
  understated liabilities, C26
  unrecorded liabilities, C27
Scanning, 94
  cautions on, 98
  by computer, 103
Schedule of interbank transfers, 244–245
Schelluch, P., 442
Schmidt, J., 660
Schmidt, Mike, 7
Schmidt, Susan, 167
Schnitzer Steel Industries, 148
Scientific-Atlanta, Inc., 273, 465
Scope and nature of services, 596–597
Scope limitation
  circumstance-imposed, 507, 508
  client-imposed, 507, 508
  definition, 55
  effect on auditor's report, 204, 205
Scope limitation reports
  disclaimer of opinion, 508, 510
  qualified opinion, 508, 510
  standard report, 508
  types of limitations, 507
  unqualified opinion, 508
Scope paragraph of standard report, 498, 500
Scrushy, Richard, 124, C14–C16
Search for unrecorded liabilities, 324
  definition, 329
  procedures, 329–330
Sears, 682, 683, 685
SeaView Video Technology, 273
Second-partner review, 470
Securities
  destruction certificate, 423
  market valuation, 431
  unregistered sale of, 432–433
Securities Act of 1933, 637, 644, 652
  antifraud section, 647
  auditors' defenses, 646–467
  civil liability, 645–646
  criminal liability, 647
  legal precedents, 646, 647
  provisions, 645
  statute of limitations, 647
  summary of auditors' liability, 654
Securities and Exchange Commission, 9, 43, 125, 135, 839, C1
  and accounting standards, 595
  in aftermath of Andersen trial, C4
  and Ambassador Eyewear Group, 290
  approval of Auditing Standards, 38
  on changing auditors, C18
  charges against Beazer Homes USA Inc., 122
  and codes of conduct, 594
  on comparative financial statements, 520
  constraints on auditors, 16
  on consulting services, 20
  disciplinary actions, 618–619

EDGAR database, 80
  filings on change of auditors, 80
  Financial Reporting Releases, 648
  Form 8-K, 146
  Forms, 648
  Form 10-K, 496
  on interim financial information, 563
  on internal auditing, 680
  on internal audit services, 22
  investigation of Dell Inc., 174, 454
  investigation of General Electric, 430
  investigation of McKesson & Robbins, 37–38
  investigation of Satyam, 240
  on lease accounting, 414
  and NutraCea, 280
  penalties for Satyam case, C28
  and Private Securities Litigation Reform Act of 1995, 147–148
  and PCAOB, 11n
  on reasonable assurance, 197
  registration requirement, 645
  Regulation S-K, 648
  Regulation S-X, 511, 648
  reporting requirements, 496
  required disclosures, C24–C25
  on revenue recognition, 271–272
  rules on filing audited financial statements, 454–455
  and San Diego city officials, 415
  and Sirena Apparel Group, Inc., 290
  Staff Accounting Bulletin
    No. 99, 468
    No. 108, 468
  Staff Accounting Bulletins, 648
  suit against KPMG, 469
  10-K filings (SEC), 463
  10-K reports, 37
  10-Q filings (SEC), 463
  on XBRL, 572
Securities and Exchange Commission Practice Section, 58
Securities Exchange Act of 1934, 637, 644, 652
  antifraud section, 648–649
  auditors' defenses, 650
  civil liability, 650
  criminal liability, 651
  on employment of manipulative and deceptive devices, 649
  and Foreign Corrupt Practices Act, 651–652
  legal precedents, 649, 651
  purpose, 648
  registration requirement, 648
  summary of auditors' liability, 654
Securities fraud, 125
Securities issuance, 645
Securities Litigation Reform Act, 660
Securities Litigation Uniform Standards Act of 1998, 659
Securities offerings, 416–417
Security
  of computers, 181
  of trust services, 573
Self-regulation, 617
  failure of, 36
Self-regulatory discipline, 617–618
Separation of duties
  in cash disbursements, 230, 235
  in computerized processing systems, 847
  in internal control, 180–181
  lacking in end-user computing, 864
  in production cycle, 376
Sequence tests, 852
Sequential sampling
  definition, 772
  operation of, 772–773
  population deviation rate, 772
Service organization control reports, 555, 557

Service organizations
  attestation engagements for
    reports, 555–556
      service organization control reports, 555, 557
  for computer processing, 866
  definition and examples, 554
  for payroll preparation, 362
Services
  delivery of, 276
  purchasing, 321–322
  receiving, 322
Services Fraud Investigation Office, India, C28
Settlement offer procedure, 617–618
SharePoint Technology, 866
Shefchik, L., 59
Shell company, 321
Shipping document, 841
Shockey, L. Jackson, 595
Shoplifting, 125
Short shipment, 125
Siegelman, Don, C16
Siemens AG, 148, 651
Signatures and initials, 107
Significant accounts, 185
Significant accounts disclosure, 127
Significant deficiency
  communication of, 206–207
  definition, 199
Significant risks
  definition, 144
  performing extended procedures, 145
  responding to, 144–145
Simulated data, techniques using
  integrated test facility, 862
  purpose, 861
  test data, 861–862
Sinason, D., 225, 696n
Singer, Marcus G., 593n
Single audit, 693, 694
Single Audit Act of 1984 and Amendments, 693–694
Sirena Apparel Group, Inc., 290
Skewed accounting distributions, 716
SK Foods, 322
Skilling, Jeffrey, 124, 179
Skills needed for risk assessment, 121
Small and medium-sized businesses
  information systems in, 184
  internal control environment, 177–178
  monitoring activities, 184
Smith v. London Assurance Corporation, 638, 654
Snapshot, 859
Snyder, Steve, 182
Social Security Administration, 361
Social Security taxes, 361
Société Générale, 848
Socioeconomic structures, 571
Software
  for audit documentation, 104
  for computer-assisted audit techniques, 101–102
Software services firm, C26–C28
Solicitation, AICPA rules, 613–614
Solomon, D., 318n
Solomon, K. I., 611n
Sonal, Joshi, C29
Sonic Automotive, Inc., 514
Sony Corporation, 867
Sophocles, 220
Source documents, 183
Special and restricted-use reports
  reports on application of requirements of appropriate framework, 568–570
  special-purpose frameworks, 566–568
  specified elements, accounts, or items, 565–566
  types of reports, 565

Specialists
  in audit planning, 85
  in computers, 101
  definition, 85
  information technology auditors, 85
Special purpose entities, 410, 521
Special purpose frameworks
  definition, 566
  disclosures, 568
  versus GAAP, 567
  modifications of auditors' reports, 567–568
  reasons for, 566–567
  standards for auditors, 567
  types of, 566
Special report, 547
Specific authorization, 180
Spreadsheet and data controls, 866
Spreadsheet goofs, 182
SRSR Holdings, C27
Staff Accounting Bulletins; see Securities and Exchange Commission
Standard and Poor's, 141
Standard and Poor's 500 companies, 135
Standard costs, 372
Standard deviation, 735
  definition, 814
  relation to sample size, 814
Standard error of the mean, 735
Standardized formats and screens, 851
Standard report
  basic components, 498
  features, 498–499
  internal control paragraph, 501–502
  introductory paragraph, 500
  opinion paragraph, 501
  reasons for issuing, 498
  scope paragraph, 500
  as unqualified opinion, 501
Star Air Ambulance Service, 335
Starbucks Corporation, 411, 575
Statement on Quality Control Standards No. 8, 56, 57
Statements of Auditing Procedures, 38
Statements of Financial Concepts
  No. 5, on expense recognition, 318
  No. 2 on understandability, 13
Statements of Financial Standards No. 149, 182
Statements on Auditing Standards, 38, 40, 549
  definition, 5n
Statements on Quality Control Standards (AICPA), 558
Statements on Responsibilities in Tax Practices, 20
Statements on Standards for Accounting Review Services, 549, 558, 561
Statements on Standards for Attestation Engagements, 5n, 598
State of mind, 43
States
  audit agencies, 22, 689
  boards of accountancy, 618
  certification and licensing by, 25
  insurance board auditors, 5
State Street Trust v. Ernst, 640
State Supreme Court of China, 619
Statistical sampling
  definition, 719
  to determine sufficiency, 52
  versus nonstatistical sampling, 719
  probabilistic selection techniques, 819
Statute of limitations
  extended by Sarbanes-Oxley Act, 647, 655
  in Securities Act, 647
Statutory law
  definition, 637
  summary of auditors' liability, 654
Statutory liability
  Foreign Corrupt Practices Act, 651–652
  legislation involved, 644

Securities Act of 1933, 645–646
Securities Exchange Act of 1934, 648–649
Stefaniak, C. M., 469
Stevens, Ray, C6
Stevenson, Robert Louis, 435
Stock certificate books, 423
Stockholders, fraud pertaining to, 125
Stockholders' equity, 415, 427
Stock price performance, of Fannie Mae, 839
Stocks, 416
Stolper, Andrew, 375
Stone Ridge Investment Partners v. Scientific Atlanta, 656–657
Stop-or-go sampling, 772
Strata, 812
Strategies
  auditor awareness of, 121
  definition, 118
  effects of implementing, 136
  in inherent risk assessment, 136
Stratification of population, 812
Strong, George, C15
Subjective estimates of accounts, 133
Subprime crisis, 635
Subsequent events, 470–472, 518
Subsequently discovered facts, 472–473
Substantial equivalency, 25
Substantive procedures, 90
  acquisition and expenditure cycle, 328–334
    accrued income taxes, 330–331
    accrued liabilities, 330
    analytical procedures, 330
    assertions about account balances, 329
    completeness assertion, 328–329
    gathering evidence, 332–334
    intangible assets, 331–332
    other expenses, 334
    prepaid expenses, 330
    presentation and disclosure, 334
    property, plant, and equipment, 331–332
    purchase cutoff, 330
    search for unrecorded liabilities, 329–330
  assessment of control risk, 196
  in attributes sampling, 728
  in audit completion
    analytical procedures, 457–458
    review of accounting estimates, 458–459
    review of accounts, 457–458
    roll-forward procedures, 457
  audit sampling, 726
  categories of, 128
  deficiencies noted by PCAOB, 795
  definition, 49, 292
  detection risk, 730
  dual-purpose procedures, 292–293
  to evaluate evidence, 50
  evidence gathered by, 270
  for financing activities
    long-term liabilities/related accounts, 425–426
    stockholders' equity, 427
  for investment activities
    auditing fair value measurement, 429–432
    control deficiencies, 428
    derivative instruments, 429
    investments with affiliates, 428
    nature of work, 428–429
  monetary unit sampling, 796–811
  nature, timing, and extent of, 174
  prior to year-end spread, 456
  production cycle
    analytical procedures, 379–380
    fraud potential in inventory, 387–388
    GAAS requirement, 380
    physical inventory inspection, 381–386
    presentation and disclosure, 388
    pricing and compilation tests, 386–387
    tips for detecting fraud, 388

Substantive procedures—*Cont.*
 revenue and collection cycle
  alternative procedures, 289
  analytical procedures, 284
  assertions about account balances, 283
  confirmation of accounts/notes receivable, 285–289
  cutoff and sales returns, 290
  extended procedures for fraud cases, 292–298
  notes about confirmations, 291
  presentation and disclosure, 291
  review for collectability, 289–290
  rights and obligations, 290
 for sampling risk
  analytical procedures, 799–800
  tests of details, 799–800
 versus tests of controls, 292
 use of materiality for, 90
Substantive tests
 determining nature and timing of, 83
 of transactions, 334
Successor accountants, 562
Sufficiency, 52
Sufficient evidence, 52
Summary financial statements, 521–522
Sunbeam Corporation, 458, C1
Supervision, in payroll cycle, 358
Supplementary information, 523
Suppliers, fraud pertaining to, 125
Sureparts Manufacturing Company, 285
Sustainability, 8, 574
Sustainability reporting, 574–575
Systematic random selection, 721–722
 in attributes sampling
  limitation, 793
  selection interval, 792
 in MUS, 804
Systematic selection, 721–722
System of quality control
 continuance of client relationship, 57
 deficiencies, 58
 definition, 56
 ethical requirements, 56
 human resources, 57
 leadership responsibility, 56
 monitoring, 57–58
 PCAOB inspections, 59
 purpose, 56
Systems analysts
 functions, 846
 separation of duties, 847
Systems development and modification controls, 865–866
Systems development life cycle, 844–845
SysTrust Service, 573

T

T. J. Maxx, 276, 868
Tagg, Stephen K., 751
Taggart, David, C7, C93
Taggart, James, C93
Tagging transactions, 858
Tainting percentage, 805
Tangible assets
 caution on inspection of, 98
 inspection of, 95
Tanner, Tony, C15
Tanzi, Calisto, 124, C21–C22
Tarpley, R., 122n
Tax accounting weaknesses, 330
Tax actions, in third-party liability, 639
Tax consulting, 20
Tax consulting fees, C18
Tax evasion, 125
Tax Executive Committee, 609

Tax fraud, C18
Tax laws, 20
Tax reports, 360
Tax services, scope and role of, 19
Tax shelters, C18
Taylor, M. H., 40n
Technical controls, 868–869
Tellabs, Inc. v. Makor Issues and Rights, Ltd., 652
Temple, Nancy, C2
Temporary transaction trails, 99
10-K reports (SEC), 37
 Sarbanes-Oxley Act on, 463
10-Q filings (SEC), Sarbanes-Oxley Act on, 463
Termination letters, 82
Terrorists, illegal payments to, 148
Tervo, W., 59n
Test data approach, 861–862
Tests of controls, 90; *see also* Attributes sampling
 accounting estimates, 422
 in acquisition and expenditure cycle, 326
  direction of tests, 328
  revealing weaknesses, 328
 attributes sampling, 728, 752, 753
 for audit plan, 351
 and audit team, 190–191
 bridge workpaper, 191–192
 for cash disbursement, 235
 for cash receipts, 234
 for computerized environment
  benchmarking, 862
  parallel simulation, 860–861
  program-embedded techniques, 858–860
  simulated data techniques, 861–862
 in computerized environment
  auditing around the computer, 857
  audit through the computer, 857–858
 direction of
  completeness, 194
  dual-direction, 195
  occurrence, 194–196
 dual-purpose, 196
 for entire audit period, 755
 for operating effectiveness, 764
 performance methods
  audit team choice, 194
  document examination, 194
  inquiry, 193–194
  observation, 194
  reperformance, 194
 prior to year-end spread, 456
 production cycle
  assertions about transactions, 379
  direction of, 379
  internal documentation, 378
  personnel, 377
 PCAOB requirements, 198
 PCAOB review, 752
 revenue and collection cycle, 281–282
  assertions about classes of transactions, 281
  dual-direction, 281–282
 in revenue and collection cycle, 271
 throughout period of audit, 193
Tests of details, for sampling risk, 799–800, 801
Theft of assets, 222
Theft of cash or property, 125
Thibodeau, J., 176n
Third-party checks, 360
Third-party liability
 auditor's defenses, 642–643
 classification as third party, 642
 classification of jurisdictions, 642
 Credit Alliance case, 640
 failure to exercise professional care, 638–639
 Fleet National Bank case, 640–641
 foreseeable parties, 641
 foreseen parties, 641

 near privity, 640
 primary beneficiaries, 640
 privity or near-privity jurisdictions, 642
 reasonable foreseeability jurisdictions, 641
 restatement of torts doctrine, 640
 restatement of torts jurisdictions, 642
 Rosenblum, Inc. case, 641–642
 Rusch Factors, 640
 summary of auditors' liability, 652–654
 third-party complaints, 639
 Ultramares case, 639–640
Third-party reimbursement maximization, 8
Third-party users
 auditor responsibility, 636
 losses, 636
Thompson, Bill, 636
Tick marks, 107
Tidwell, Gary L., C10
Time budget
 in first-time audit, 86
 illustration of, 86
 interim work, 86
 purpose, 86
 recording time reports, 87
 year-end work, 86
Time card forgery, 363–364
Timekeeping, 358
Time-sensitivity, 3
Time to plan audit, 47–48
Time Warner, 273
Timing
 of internal control tests, 83
 of substantive tests, 83
Titanic, 178
Titus, Harold H., 591–592
TJX Corporation, 276, 867, 868
Todman Company, 656
Tolerable misstatement, 726
 calculating, 801
 definition, 800
 in nonstatistical sampling, 819
 in sample size determination, 800–801
Tolerable rate of deviation, 728–729, 759
 in attributes sampling, 757–758
 and audit sample size, 734
 compared to upper limit rate of deviation, 768–769
 definition, 757
 in nonstatistical attributes sampling, 774
Tommy Hilfiger, 356
Top-down approach, 198
Topps baseball cards, 7
Tort action
 definition, 637
 fraud, 638
 gross negligence, 638
 ordinary negligence, 638
Total revenue benchmark, 88–89
Touche, Niven & Company, 639
Touche Ross & Company, C17
Tracing, 94
 for payroll cycle, 195
Trade magazines, 137
Trademarks, custody of, 419
Trade secrets, theft of, 125
Trading securities, 431
Transaction assertion
 in acquisition and expenditure cycle, 327
 production cycle, 379
 for revenue and receivables, 270
Transaction-level controls
 definition, 186
 identifying, 186–187
Transaction logs, 865
Transactions
 arm's length, 413
 authorization of, 230
 authorization to execute, 180
 automated, 181

classification, 13–14
completeness and cutoff, 12–13
complex, 414
complexity of, 133
computer-initiated, 99
custody of assets involved in, 180
existence and occurrence, 12
in finance and investment cycle, 410
fraud and volume of, 133
management assertions about, 10
occurrence and completeness, 183
in production cycle, 371
record counts, 851
recording, 180
related-party, 413
in sales
  authorization of credit, 276
  billing, 276
  delivery of goods/services, 276
  initiating, 275–276
stockholders' equity, 427
uniform processing, 99
valuation and allocation, 12
walkthrough, 187
Transaction trails, 99
TransAlta Corporation, 182
Transfer agent, 416, 417
Transparency, 13–14
  demand for, 571
Treadway, James, 170
Treadway Commission, 119n, 170, 501, 502, 771
Treasury Department, 20
Trial balance
  accounts payable, 324
  aged, 278
  for confirmation of accounts, 278
Tricontinental Industries v. PricewaterhouseCoopers, 651
Tripathi, Salil, C29
Triple-bottom line, 574
Trompeter, G., 142n
True balance, 795
Trustee, 417
Trust services
  definition, 573
  and growth of e-commerce, 572–573
  principles for engagements, 573
  SysTrust Service, 573
  WebTrust Service, 573–574
Trust Services Data and Integrity, 573
Trust Services Principles and Criteria, 573
Truth-in-securities law, 644
TRW Automotive Holdings Corporation, 514
Turner, Lynn E., 44, 635
TV Guide, 273
Twain, Mark, 587
Tyco International, 2, 124, 411, 634
Type I errors, 716
Type II errors, 716
Type 1 service organization report, 555
Type 2 service organization report, 555, 556
Tyson Foods, 369

U

UBS, 470
U-Haul International, 521
Ulsten, Ola, C26
Ultramares Corporation v. Touche, 639, 654
Unasserted claims, 461
Unaudited financial information, 643
Unconditional obligation, 592
Unconditional requirements, 38
Uncorrected misstatements, 469
  iron curtain method, 468
  rollover method, 468

Underfunded pension obligations, 415
Understandability, lacking in Enron statements, 14
Understatements, in MUS, 810–811
Underwriters, auditor assurances to, 645–646
Uniform CPA Examination, 24–25
Uniform mobility, 25
Uniform processing of transactions, 99
United Airlines, 853
United Auto Workers, C12
United Parcel Service, 571
United Rental, 659
United States Comptroller General, 689
United States Public Company Reform and Investor Protection Act of 2002, 655
United States Secret Service, 867
United States Senate Banking Committee, 657
United States Supreme Court, 410
  on materiality, 87–88
  overturns Arthur Andersen verdict, C3, C17
  ruling on Sarbanes-Oxley Act, 37
  on solicitation, 614
United States v. Benjamin, 647
United States v. Natelli, 651
Univer, Scott, 633–634
University of Phoenix, 644
University of Tennessee internal audit charter, 680, 681, 686
University of Texas, 419
Unmatched invoice file, 323
Unmatched receiving report file, 323
Unmatched receiving reports, 323, 329
Unmatched vendor invoice, 323–324, 329
Unqualified auditors' report on internal control over financial reporting, 201
Unqualified opinion, 501
  definition, 54
  and departures from GAAP, 503, 504
  and departures from GAAS, 503
  example, 54
  going-concern uncertainties, 513–514
  on internal control, 199
  justified departures from GAAP, 514–515
  and scope limitation reports, 508
Unrecorded liabilities, 243, 319
  search for, 324
Unrestricted random sampling, 792
Unrestricted random selection, 721
Updated report, 520
Update report, 561–562
Upper limit of misstatement, 731–732
Upper limit on misstatement
  definition, 809
  in MUS, 810–811
Upper limit rate of deviation
  in attributes sampling
    calculating, 766–767
    compared to tolerable rate of deviation, 768–769
    components, 768
    information provided by, 766
  definition, 728–729
U.S Airways, 424
User demand
  and financial accounting frauds, 2–3
  for reliable information, 2–3
User entity, 866
Usrey, S., 469
Utilitarianism, 593

V

Vadlamani, Srinivas, C27
Valero Energy Corporation, 424
Valid character tests, 852
Valid sign tests, 852

Valuation, 12, 141
  of inventory, 386
  of investments, 428
  lower-of-cost-or market, 369
  by lower-of-cost-or-market testing, 387
  provided by confirmation, 285
  risk level of, 128
Valuation assertion and collectability, 289–290
Value-added audit
  ensuring compliance, 682–683
  improving efficiency, 682
  recognizing risks, 682
  serving as management representation, 683
Value and allocation assertions
  in classical variables sampling, 812
  in nonstatistical sampling, 818
Variables sampling; *see also* Classical variables sampling; Monetary unit sampling
  versus attributes sampling, 795
  audited value/balance, 730–731
  classical, 731
  definition, 730, 795
  for detection risk, 730
  documentation, 820
  and misstatements, 795
  monetary unit sampling, 731
  MUS vs. classical, 817–818
  nonstatistical, 818–820
  nonstatistical methods, 731
  professional standards references, 794
  sampling risks, 799
  sampling risks associated with
    effectiveness loss, 732
    efficiency loss, 732
    risk of incorrect acceptance, 732–733
    risk of incorrect rejection, 732
    sample estimate of misstatement, 731
    tolerable misstatement, 731
    and upper limit of misstatement, 731–732
  seven-step procedure, 795
  substantive procedures, 730
  and true balance, 795
Venable, Carol T., C10
Vendor invoices, 323
  unmatched, 323
Vendors
  approved list of, 321–322
  confirm accounts payable with, 330
  fraud pertaining to, 125
Ventimiglia, Milo, 375
Verbal evidence, 52
Verbal inquiry, 96
Vertical analysis, 139, 250
Vines, Michael, 144, C15
Visa, 273
Vitesse Semiconductor Corporation, 274
Volkswagen Credit Inc., 375
Von Borstal, Octavo Garcia, 322
Voucher, 323
Voucher package, 323
Voucher system, in purchase of investments, 420
Vouching, 94
  cash disbursements, 329
  cautions on, 98
  deposits in transit, 243
  to gather audit evidence, 333
  investment costs, 431
  for payroll cycle, 195

W

Wabtec Corporation, C17
Wagoner, Rick, 495, C11, C12
Walking D Ranch Adventures, 414

Walkthrough
    for cash activities, 234
    of computerized transactions
        customer master file, 841
        customer order transaction file, 840–841
        inventory master file, 841
        sales invoice, 841
        sales transaction file, 841
        shipping document, 841
    definition, 187
    revenue and collection cycle, 280
    of transactions, 187
Wall Street Journal, 137, 200, 318
Walmart, 48, 120, 170, 183, 384, 682
Walt Disney Company, 435–436
War Fighting Center, 414
Washington, George, 6
Waste Management, Inc., 78, 319, C1, C2
Watson, Robert, 322
Webb, A., 469
Weber, J., C10
Webster, Daniel, 409, 587
WebTrust Service, 573–574
Weidbaum, Jack, 634
Weil, Jonathan, C2n
Wells, Joseph T., 229, 249n, 369n, 715n
Wells Fargo, 243, 414
Wells notice, 634–635
Wheelwright Philip, 589n
Whistle-blowing
    on clients, 610–611
    at HealthSouth, C15–C16
Whitcher, Craig, C29
White-collar crime, 125

White-collar criminals, 223–224
Whitehouse, Sheldon, 688
Whitehouse, Tammy, 125, 319n, 430
White Star Line, 178
Wilkie Farr & Gallagher, 635
William Iselin and Company, 643
Williams, D. D., 514
Willingham, J. J., 222n, 225n
Wilson Sporting Goods Company, 7, 716
Winchester Crown Court, England, 357
Winkler, Stephan, 233
Woodruff, Wardlow, Nelson, and Cash, 340
Working capital/total assets ratio, 164
Work-in-process, 377
Workpapers, 104; *see also* Audit documentation
Workplace, managing people pressures, 228
World Basketball League, 368
WorldCom, 2, 3, 13, 36, 38, 56, 58, 78, 124, 144,
    168, 169, 172, 317, 318, 458, 514, 589,
    594, 598, 654, 655, 658, 659, 678, 860,
    C1, C4
World Council for Corporate Governance, C26n
World Electronics, 390
World Poker Tour, 79
Worthington Industries, 387
WPT Enterprises, Inc., 79
Wright, A., 142n, 468n, 476, 524
Wright, S., 468n
Written representations
    contents, 463
    definition, 52
    form and purpose, 463
    sample, 464
    Sarbanes-Oxley Act on, 463

to support auditor opinion, 465
trustworthiness, 465
W2; *see* Employee W2 reports

X

XBRL, 8, 9, 572
XBRL Assurance Task Force, 572
Xerox Corporation, 169, 273, 411, 469, 634
Xinhua Finance Ltd., 135

Y

Yahoo!, 141
Yates, Buddy, 317
Year-end adjustments, 144
Year-end audit work, 86
Year-end date, 456
    inventory not on, 384–385
    roll-forward procedures, 457
Year-to-date earnings records, 360–361
Yellow Book, 689, 694, 696
Young, Michael, 634, 635
YRC Worldwide, 514
Yuen, Henry, 124, 465

Z

Zhang, T., 60n
Zhou Limin, 619
ZZZ Best, 98

Audit Standards (PCAOB)

AS No.	Date Issued	Title
1	2004	References in Auditors' Reports to the Standards of the Public Company Accounting Oversight Board
3	2004	Audit Documentation
4	2005	Reporting on Whether a Previously Reported Material Weakness Continues to Exist
5	2007	An Audit of Internal Control over Financial Reporting That is Integrated with an Audit of Financial Statements
6	2008	Evaluating Consistency of Financial Statements
7	2009	Engagement Quality Review
8	2010	Audit Risk
9	2010	Audit Planning
10	2010	Supervision of the Audit Engagement
11	2010	Consideration of Materiality in Planning and Performing an Audit
12	2010	Identifying and Assessing Risks of Material Misstatement
13	2010	The Auditor's Responses to the Risks of Material Misstatement
14	2010	Evaluating Audit Results
15	2010	Audit Evidence

Code of Professional Conduct (AICPA)

Article I—Responsibilities
Article II—The Public Interest
Article III—Integrity
Article IV—Objectivity and Independence
Article V—Due Care
Article VI—Scope and Nature of Services

Rule No.		Rule No.	
101	Independence	302	Contingent Fees
102	Integrity and Objectivity	501	Acts Discreditable
201	General Standards	502	Advertising and Other Forms of Solicitation
202	Compliance with Standards	503	Commissions and Referral Fees
203	Accounting Principles	505	Form of Practice and Name
301	Confidential Client Information		

Government Auditing Standards (U.S. General Accounting Office)

2011 Internet Version of Governmental Auditing Standards (the "Yellow Book") www.gao.gov/yellowbook

International Standards for the Professional Practice of Internal Auditing (IIA)

Title	Number
Attribute Standards	
Purpose, Authority, and Responsibility	1000
Independence and Objectivity	1100
Proficiency and Due Professional Care	1200
Quality Assurance and Improvement Program	1300
Performance Standards	
Managing the Internal Audit Activity	2000
Nature of Work	2100
Engagement Planning	2200
Performing the Engagement	2300
Communicating Results	2400
Monitoring Progress	2500
Resolution of Senior Management's Acceptance of Risks	2600

Auditing Standards Board Clarity Project—Previous AU Sections Mapped to Clarity Standards

Previous AU Section		New AU Section	New AU/ISA
	Statements on Auditing Standards—Introduction		
110	Responsibilities and Functions of the Independent Auditor	Overall Objectives of the Independent Auditor and the Conduct of an Audit in Accordance With Generally Accepted Auditing Standards	200
120	Defining Professional Requirements in Statements on Auditing Standards		
150	Generally Accepted Auditing Standards		
161	The Relationship of Generally Accepted Auditing Standards to Quality Control Standards	Quality Control for an Engagement Conducted in Accordance With Generally Accepted Auditing Standards	220
	The General Standards		
201	Nature of the General Standards	Overall Objectives of the Independent Auditor and the Conduct of an Audit in Accordance With Generally Accepted Auditing Standards	200
210	Training and Proficiency of the Independent Auditor		
220	Independence		
230	Due Professional Care in the Performance of Work		
	The Standards of Field Work		
311	Planning and Supervision	Planning an Audit	300
		Terms of Engagement	210
312	Audit Risk and Materiality in Conducting an Audit	Materiality in Planning and Performing the Audit	320
		Evaluation of Misstatements Identified During an Audit	450
314	Understanding the Entity and Its Environment and Assessing the Risks of Material Misstatement	Understanding the Entity and Its Environment and Assessing the Risks of Material Misstatement (Redrafted)	315
315	Communications Between Predecessor and Successor Auditors	Opening Balances—Initial Audit Engagements, Including Reaudit Engagements	510
		Terms of Engagement	210
316	Consideration of Fraud in a Financial Statement Audit	Consideration of Fraud in a Financial Statement Audit (Redrafted)	240
317	Illegal Acts by Clients	Consideration of Laws and Regulations in an Audit of Financial Statements	250
318	Performing Audit Procedures in Response to Assessed Risks and Evaluating the Audit Evidence Obtained	Performing Audit Procedures in Response to Assessed Risks and Evaluating the Audit Evidence Obtained (Redrafted)	330
322	The Auditor's Consideration of the Internal Audit Function in an Audit of Financial Statements	Using the Work of Internal Auditors (working title)	610
324	Service Organizations	Audit Considerations Relating to an Entity Using a Service Organization	402
325	Communicating Internal Control Related Matters Identified in an Audit	Communicating Internal Control Related Matters Identified in an Audit (Redrafted)	265
326	Audit Evidence	Audit Evidence (Redrafted)	500
328	Auditing Fair Value Measurements and Disclosures	Auditing Accounting Estimates, Including Fair Value Accounting Estimates and Related Disclosures (Redrafted)	540
329	Analytical Procedures	Analytical Procedures (Redrafted)	520
330	The Confirmation Process	External Confirmations	505
331	Inventories	Audit Evidence—Specific Considerations for Selected Items	501
332	Auditing Derivative Instruments, Hedging Activities, and Investments in Securities	Audit Evidence—Specific Considerations for Selected Items	501
333	Management Representations	Written Representations	580
334	Related Parties	Related Parties (Redrafted)	550
336	Using the Work of a Specialist	Using the Work of an Auditor's Specialist	620
337	Inquiry of a Client's Lawyer Concerning Litigation, Claims, and Assessments	Audit Evidence—Specific Considerations for Selected Items	501
339	Audit Documentation	Audit Documentation (Redrafted)	230
341	The Auditor's Consideration of an Entity's Ability to Continue as a Going Concern	Going Concern (working title)	570
342	Auditing Accounting Estimates	Auditing Accounting Estimates, Including Fair Value Accounting Estimates and Related Disclosures	540
350	Audit Sampling	Audit Sampling (Redrafted)	530
380	The Auditor's Communication With Those Charged With Governance	The Auditor's Communication With Those Charged With Governance (Redrafted)	260
390	Consideration of Omitted Procedures After the Report Date	Consideration of Omitted Procedures After the Report Release Date	585